ENCYCLOPEDIA OF AFRICAN AMERICAN HISTORY
1619–1895

FROM THE COLONIAL PERIOD TO
THE AGE OF FREDERICK DOUGLASS

About the Encyclopedia

The editorial board and Oxford University Press have developed two encyclopedias of African American history and culture. The purpose of the two sets is to provide a comprehensive view of the wealth of information about and scholarship on African Americans from 1619 to the present in what began as a collection of European colonies, but which became the United States of America.

Encyclopedia of African American History, 1619–1895:
From the Colonial Period to the Age of Frederick Douglass

Encyclopedia of African American History, 1896 to the Present:
From the Age of Segregation to the Twenty-first Century
(forthcoming)

ENCYCLOPEDIA OF AFRICAN AMERICAN HISTORY 1619–1895

FROM THE COLONIAL PERIOD TO THE AGE OF FREDERICK DOUGLASS

Editor in Chief

Paul Finkelman

VOLUME 1

A–E

OXFORD
UNIVERSITY PRESS
2006

OXFORD
UNIVERSITY PRESS

Oxford University Press, Inc., publishes works that further
Oxford University's objective of excellence
in research, scholarship, and education.

Oxford   New York
Auckland   Cape Town   Dar es Salaam   Hong Kong   Karachi
Kuala Lumpur   Madrid   Melbourne   Mexico City   Nairobi
New Delhi   Shanghai   Taipei   Toronto

With offices in
Argentina   Austria   Brazil   Chile   Czech Republic   France   Greece
Guatemala   Hungary   Italy   Japan   Poland   Portugal   Singapore
South Korea   Switzerland   Thailand   Turkey   Ukraine   Vietnam

Published by Oxford University Press, Inc.
198 Madison Avenue, New York, New York, 10016
http://www.oup.com

Oxford is a registered trademark of Oxford University Press.

Library of Congress Cataloging-in-Publication Data

Encyclopedia of African American history, 1619–1895 : from the colonial period to the age of Frederick Douglass /
Paul Finkelman, editor in chief.
p. cm.
Includes bibliographical references and index.
ISBN-13: 978-0-19-516777-1 (alk. paper)
ISBN-10: 0-19-516777-5 (alk. paper)
1. African Americans—History—Encyclopedias. 2. African Americans—History—To 1863—Encyclopedias.
3. African Americans—History—1863–1877—Encyclopedias. I. Finkelman, Paul, 1949–
E185.E545 2006
973'.0496073003—dc22
2005033701

Printing number: 9 8 7 6 5 4 3 2 1

Printed in the United States of America on acid-free paper

EDITORIAL AND PRODUCTION STAFF

ACQUIRING EDITOR
Ralph Carlson

DEVELOPMENT EDITOR
Anthony Aiello

ASSISTANT EDITORS
Timothy Sachs, Abigail P. Powers

CONSULTING EDITOR
Sarah Feehan

COPY EDITORS
Schlager Group, Inc.; Jason Miller; Arlt Creative Enterprises

PROOFREADERS
Carol Holmes, Mary Hawkins Sachs

ART RESEARCH
Amy Pastan and Vincent Virga

PERMISSIONS RESEARCHER
Susan Gamer

INDEXER
Coughlin Indexing Services, Inc.

COMPOSITOR
Matrix Publishing Services

MANUFACTURING CONTROLLER
Christine Critelli

COVER DESIGN
Nora Wertz

DIRECTOR OF EDITORIAL DEVELOPMENT AND PRODUCTION
Timothy J. DeWerff

PUBLISHER
Casper Grathwohl

For John Hope Franklin

A mentor, a role model, and a friend

Contents

Introduction

In 1903 the great African American scholar W. E. B. Du Bois predicted that the great problem of the twentieth century would be the "color line." Unfortunately, he was right. The twentieth century was one in which disputes over and discussions about race, ethnicity, and diversity often took center stage in the United States and abroad. As the volumes here show, however, the observation of Du Bois cannot be limited to the twentieth century. From the earliest settlement of America to the present, relations between Africans and Europeans—and then later African Americans and white Americans—have been central to U.S. history.

In many ways there are two African American histories: an internal history that charts how black communities developed over time, and an external history that shows how the interaction of blacks and whites has shaped the larger national history as well as the internal history of African Americans. In order to offer a comprehensive window into both of these histories Oxford University Press has developed a series of two encyclopedias: the *Encyclopedia of African American History, 1619–1895: From the Colonial Period to the Age of Frederick Douglass* and the *Encyclopedia of African American History, 1896 to the Present: From the Age of Segregation to the Twenty-first Century* (forthcoming).

The encyclopedias have been developed at the same time by the same group of editors. This first three-volume set covers the period from the earliest settlement of what became the United States until the death of Frederick Douglass in 1895. The second set begins with the rise of Jim Crow in the 1890s and ends with the present day. The editors and press have chosen to end the first set with the death of Douglass because he was the most important African American of his age, and perhaps the most significant figure in all of African American history. For nearly half a century Fred Douglass, as he was often called, was the de facto leader of black America. He was a towering figure in the antislavery movement, an adviser to President Lincoln, and a key player in postwar politics. In many ways he was the symbol of his age: a former slave who became a writer and a public speaker with an international reputation; a fugitive slave whose escape from bondage made him subject to seizure under federal law, yet who became the Marshal of the District of Columbia; an African American who as a citizen became a diplomat and thus an official representative of his nation. His death marked the end of an era for African Americans—an era that began with most blacks being held as slaves and ended with all African Americans as free citizens.

Ironically, Douglass's death also marks the beginning of a new era overshadowed by attacks on black freedom and black rights—an era of pervasive segregation, poverty, and second-class citizenship. The year that Douglass died, Booker T. Washington gave his famous "Atlanta Compromise" speech, in which he conceded that blacks would no longer, at least for the foreseeable future, be able to participate in politics in a meaningful way. Perceptions of Washington's role as a black leader have undergone a significant transformation since the early 1970s. Though he was once called an "Uncle Tom," most scholars today understand that he was politically shrewd, and politically powerful, despite his "compromise" speech. Even as he proclaimed to southern whites that he was uninterested in politics, he was working behind the scenes to enhance black political and economic power. But however we view Washington's political maneuvering, by the time Douglass died it is clear that the mantle of black leadership had shifted to Washington and that black life in America had clearly changed as most white politicians, with the support of most white Americans, maneuvered to put new limits on the everyday circumstances and lifelong aspirations of African Americans. A year after Douglass's death the U.S. Supreme Court upheld the concept of separate but equal in *Plessy v. Ferguson* (1896).

*

Because Douglass's death coincides with the advent of the age of segregation, we have chosen to end the first set with the year 1895. Doing so responds to divisions natural to the chronology of black history in the United States. We think this makes more sense than imposing a more typical and arbitrary end point, such as 1900, the beginning of the twentieth century, or even 1898, the year America entered the international political arena with its victory in the Spanish-American War. Some entries carry on their discussion for a few years beyond Douglass's death because history never falls neatly into compartmentalized events made up of precise developments. For example, though discussion of topics in this encyclopedia cuts off at 1895, many entries in this volume use census figures from 1900 as well as 1890 to explain developments in African American history.

The chronological organization of these two sets will allow readers to see and compare both the evolution of African American history and continuity within that history from one era to another. In fact, more than eighty topics can be found as entries in both sets—for example, entries on the military, literature, the performing and fine arts, on health and medicine, on science and technology, entrepreneurship and racial uplift, politics and political participation, childhood, the family, marriage, women, gender, and sexuality. Moreover, in the present set, many topics are treated as composite entries in order to accommodate the vast changes from 1619, when the first blacks arrived in Virginia, to 1895 when African Americans began a new fight for freedom from segregation, poverty, and political powerlessness—one that would shape American history throughout the twentieth century, and which affects all Americans to this day. By organizing large topics as composite entries we provide a way for the reader to focus on particular time periods, such as the colonial period, the antebellum era, or the post–Civil War and Reconstruction era. At the same time, this treatment allows the reader to look at these issues across the nearly three centuries covered in the encyclopedia.

There are nearly seven hundred entries and subentries in the *Encyclopedia of African American History, 1619–1895,* arranged in alphabetical order. Composite entries gather together discussions of similar or related topics under one headword. For example, under the entry "Slave Narratives" the reader will find three subentries: "The Slave Narrative in America from the Colonial Period to the Civil War," "Interpreting Slave Narratives," and "African British Slave Narratives." A headnote detailing the various subentries introduces each composite entry.

The contributors have sought to write in clear language with a minimum of technical writing or scholarly jargon. A selective bibliography at the end of each article directs the reader who wishes to pursue a topic in greater detail to primary sources, the most useful works on the topic, and the most important scholarly works in field. To guide readers from one article to related discussions elsewhere in the encyclopedia, cross-references appear at the end of all articles. Blind entries direct the user from an alternate form of an entry term to the entry itself. For example the blind entry for "Slave Codes" tells the reader to look under "Black Codes and Slave Codes, Colonial." The encyclopedia includes approximately three hundred images.

Volume 3 contains a chronology of African American history from the first arrival of blacks with Spanish explorers to 1895, a topical outline of articles, the directory of contributors, and the index. Readers interested in finding all the articles on a particular subject (e.g., resistance to slavery) can consult the topical outline, which shows how articles relate to one another and to the overall design of the encyclopedia. The comprehensive index lists all the topics covered in the encyclopedia, including those that are not headwords themselves.

The three volumes that make up the first set and the four volumes that make up the second set have substantial biographies of key figures in African American history, such as Douglass, Harriet Tubman, Booker T. Washington, W. E. B. Du Bois, Mary McLeod Bethune, Ida B. Wells-Barnett, Martin Luther King, and Malcolm X. The lengthy entries are not to be viewed as history based on the "great man" or "great woman," but rather as an acknowledgment that throughout American history these and other individuals have been central to the African American experience. However, the bulk of coverage in both sets is dedicated not to individual biographies, but to the wide range of events, activities, and issues that have shaped African American history. We hope these volumes will not only answer specific questions that users have, but also surprise anyone who might delve into them. We note facts and aspects of African American history that may surprise even some specialists. For example, most Americans believe that blacks did not hold public office until after the Civil War. Scholars may know of the few blacks like John Mercer Langston who held local office in the 1850s. But readers of these books will discover African Americans who were elected to public office in the colonial period and at least one black man who served in a state legislature in the 1830s. Most Americans have heard the phrase "the real McCoy," but few know that it refers to the authenticity of machines built by Elijah McCoy, one of the most successful black inventors and businessmen of the nineteenth century.

African American history did not develop in a vacuum, nor did it happen in isolation from the rest of American history. Thus, this encyclopedia includes entries on Americans who were not black, but who nonetheless had an impact on the development of African American history. Some were white activists, like William Lloyd Garrison and John Brown, who dedicated their lives to black freedom. Others were slaveholders and opponents of black liberty, who nevertheless were significant figures in the history of African Americans.

While these volumes are about "black history," in the end they tell the story of "American" history. Every February in schools across America teachers and students focus on black history month. My hope is that these two encyclopedias will help persuade all Americans that black history cannot be taught in a month, or segregated to one month. Rather, the history African Americans is part of the history of all Americans. Wherever our ancestors came from, whatever our ethnicity or race, all Americans have been affected by slavery, segregation, and integration, by black culture and by African and African American influences on American culture. My goal is not only to educate and teach people about black history, but more importantly, to show users of these volumes how the history of America *is*, to a great extent, the history of race and race relations. All Americans are in a sense "African Americans" because our culture and history has been deeply affected by the experience of Africans and their descendants in what is now the United States.

At another level, the history of African Americans provides the best measure for what the American people have tried to achieve through nationhood and the rule of law. The United States began with the assertions that all Americans were "created equal" and entitled to the same rights. Much of the history of our nation has been about implementing these ideas and applying them to all Americans. As these volumes show, for most of our history we failed to live up to these ideals. Enslaved

African Americans before the Civil War and segregated blacks later on were clearly not treated as equals—neither legally nor socially. They did not have the same rights as other Americans. The struggle to end slavery and to provide equal rights for all Americans has been, in many ways, the central and most enduring problem of American history. These volumes help us better understand the ongoing struggle for life, liberty, and the pursuit of happiness for all Americans.

*

The creation of this encyclopedia has been a group effort. My coeditors—Diane Barnes, Graham Hodges, Gerald Horne, and Cary Wintz—worked tirelessly on this project, as did my editors at Oxford, Tony Aiello and Tim Sachs. This project began under the general direction of Karen Day, the reference publisher, and Timothy DeWerff, the director of editorial development and production, both of whom enthusiastically supported it. When Karen moved on to other opportunities, Casper Grathwohl provided creative leadership and his own enthusiastic support for the project.

We have dedicated these volumes to the "dean" of African American history, John Hope Franklin. For me, John Hope has been a friend, a mentor, and a role model. At age ninety he continues to write and speak out on the importance of understanding our history so we can make our future better. We hope this work will aid all Americans in achieving that goal. We also hope these volumes will enable Americans to have a better understanding of the history of race in our nation, and thus learn how to overcome our past in the future.

Paul Finkelman
Tulsa, Oklahoma
December 2005

ENCYCLOPEDIA OF AFRICAN AMERICAN HISTORY 1619–1895

FROM THE COLONIAL PERIOD TO
THE AGE OF FREDERICK DOUGLASS

A

ABLEMAN V. BOOTH (SHERMAN BOOTH CASE).
The court case of *Ableman v. Booth* stemmed from the capture of a fugitive slave named Joshua Glover just outside of Racine, Wisconsin, on 10 March 1854. Federal marshals accompanying Glover's owner, a Missourian named Bennami Garland, broke into the shack Glover was occupying and forcibly detained him after a spirited resistance. Glover was taken overnight by wagon to the county jail in Milwaukee, thirty miles north. Garland and the federal marshals intended to take Glover before the U.S. district court judge the next morning to authorize his return to Missouri.

Sherman Booth, Milwaukee's most prominent abolitionist and the publisher of the Milwaukee *Free Democrat*, was alerted to Glover's incarceration by early morning and spread the news quickly throughout the abolitionist community. While lawyers obtained a writ of habeas corpus from a county court on Glover's behalf to protect him against illegal imprisonment, Booth and others decided to call a general meeting. By two thirty in the afternoon several thousand Milwaukeeans had gathered in the courthouse square to listen to speeches by Booth and others; the crowd resolved to stand by Glover. At about five o'clock Booth informed the crowd that federal officers would not honor the writ of habeas corpus for Glover, and consequently the crowd rushed the jail and freed Glover. Glover was escorted to Racine and shortly thereafter to Canada and freedom.

After a hearing the U.S. commissioner for Wisconsin determined that Sherman Booth should be held on bail until a federal grand jury was convened, and U.S. Marshal Stephen Ableman took Booth into custody. On 27 May, Booth applied to Justice Abram Smith of the Wisconsin Supreme Court for a writ of habeas corpus. Booth's lawyer, Byron Paine, argued during the hearing that the Fugitive Slave Law of 1850 was unconstitutional. Smith agreed, ordered Booth released, and publicly declared the law unconstitutional.

The U.S. district attorney appealed the case to the Wisconsin Supreme Court, which on 19 July also ruled the Fugitive Slave Law of 1850 unconstitutional. The court, however, made it clear that it would not disturb proceedings already under way in the U.S. district court. Be-

cause a grand jury had already indicted Sherman Booth under the Fugitive Slave Law, the court reasoned, jurisdiction in the matter belonged properly to the U.S. district court. The district attorney proceeded with trial, and on 13 January 1855 a jury found Booth guilty of aiding and abetting in the rescue of Joshua Glover, contrary to the provisions of the Fugitive Slave Law of 1850. Booth again petitioned the Wisconsin Supreme Court for a writ of habeas corpus, and on 3 February 1855 the court granted his petition, ordered Booth released, and affirmed its earlier ruling that the Fugitive Slave Law of 1850 was unconstitutional.

The Wisconsin court found the 1850 law contrary to the Constitution in three ways: it suspended the writ of habeas corpus for alleged fugitives, denied alleged fugitives the right to trial by jury, and delegated judicial functions to nonjudicial officers. The last point addressed the office of court commissioner, as the law had authorized U.S. district court judges to appoint commissioners to preside over hearings that would determine whether alleged fugitives could be removed to their home states. Article III, Section 1, of the U.S. Constitution prohibits Congress from investing judicial power in any department except the judiciary, and the Wisconsin court ruled that the commissioners—who lacked the lifetime tenure of "during good behavior" and the fixed salaries of federal judges—were not judicial officers and thus exercised a pretended power.

It was, however, the usurpation of Wisconsin residents' rights that most concerned the Wisconsin Supreme Court. The Fugitive Slave Law violated the due process of alleged fugitives, impinging on the rights of free black residents of Wisconsin. More important, the law usurped the right of Wisconsin's state courts to protect its citizens. The doctrine of states' rights, on which the Wisconsin Supreme Court based its opinion, held that states were the last defenders of civil liberties. This doctrine also posited that the states could be coequal interpreters of the Constitution alongside the various branches of the national government. The Wisconsin court's decision was a stunning one—and was made all the more so by the court's refusal to acknowledge the order by Chief Justice Roger B. Taney to send up the record of the case for review by the U.S.

Supreme Court. In effect, the Wisconsin court both nullified the Fugitive Slave Law of 1850 and denied the U.S. Supreme Court's appellate authority.

Organized in the wake of the Kansas-Nebraska Act and the rescue of Joshua Glover, Wisconsin's Republican Party publicly exalted the bold stand taken by the Wisconsin Supreme Court and made the protection of individual liberties one of its core issues. Republicans quickly captured both houses of the legislature in the elections of 1856. In January 1857 the Republican caucus in the Wisconsin legislature required that prospective candidates for the office of U.S. senator publicly declare their support of the Wisconsin Supreme Court's decision in Booth's habeas corpus cases. The antislavery party won another victory in 1859 when Byron Paine won the office of associate justice of the supreme court on a states' rights platform. In short, the issues at stake in *Ableman v. Booth* had radicalized Wisconsin politics and further polarized the country in the years leading up to the Civil War.

The U.S. Supreme Court, meanwhile, jointly decided the cases of *U.S. v. Booth* and *Ableman v. Booth* on 7 March 1859, despite the fact that the Wisconsin court still had not sent the official record of the case to Washington. Chief Justice Roger B. Taney wrote the opinion of the court: He affirmed the appellate power of the U.S. Supreme Court over the highest state courts and the jurisdiction of U.S. courts over the return of fugitive slaves to their home states. He also made clear that federal officers were not bound to obey writs of habeas corpus issued from state courts if they held prisoners by virtue of U.S. law. Taney affirmed the right of judicial tribunals to scrutinize legislation for its constitutionality and declared the Fugitive Slave Law of 1850 constitutional, albeit without scrutinizing it in any way.

The Wisconsin legislature responded by passing resolutions denouncing Taney's decision and reaffirming the Wisconsin court's position that it was the states' solemn duty to protect the liberties of their citizens. Declaring Taney's decision "in direct conflict" with the Constitution, the legislature pronounced it null and void. This standoff between Wisconsin and the U.S. Supreme Court would remain unresolved until the outbreak of the Civil War, when the Wisconsin Republican Party quietly dissociated itself from the states' rights doctrines that Southern states used to justify their secession from the Union.

[*See also* Abolitionism; Antislavery Movement; Canada; Civil Rights; Constitution, U.S.; Free African Americans before the Civil War (North); Fugitive Slave Law of 1850; Kansas-Nebraska Act; Laws and Legislation; Republican Party; Supreme Court; *and* U.S. Constitution, Slavery and.]

BIBLIOGRAPHY

Current, Richard E. *The Civil War Era, 1848–1873.* The History of Wisconsin, vol. 2. Madison: State Historical Society of Wisconsin, 1976. This excellent survey situates the rescue of Joshua Glover and the Booth trials in the context of the economic, political, and social history of Wisconsin.

Foner, Eric. *Free Soil, Free Labor, Free Men: The Ideology of the Republican Party before the Civil War.* New York: Oxford University Press, 1970. Chapters 3 and 4 discuss the moderate and radical antislavery jurisprudence that informed many of the participants in the Booth arguments.

McManus, Michael J. *Political Abolitionism in Wisconsin: 1840–1861.* Kent, OH: Kent State University Press, 1998. A sophisticated analysis of political rhetoric and voter behavior demonstrating how important the issues of abolitionism and civil liberties were to Wisconsin's Republican Party.

Swisher, Carl B. *The Taney Period, 1836–64.* History of the Supreme Court of the United States, vol. 5. New York: Macmillan, 1974. Swisher contextualizes the *Booth* cases in terms of federal constitutional relations, Taney's jurisprudence, and the worsening political and legal crises of the 1850s.

—H. ROBERT BAKER

ABOLITIONISM. [*This entry contains three subentries dealing with abolitionism from the late seventeenth century through the ratification of the Thirteenth Amendment in 1865. The first article discusses the definition of abolitionism as differentiated from antislavery activism, and its forms including Garrisonian and non-Garrisonian abolition. The second article describes abolitionism from the onset of slavery and colonization of North America through 1830. The final article discusses the emergence of Immediatism among black and white Americans and its influence on the debate over slavery.*]

Abolitionism as a Concept

The terms *abolition* and *antislavery* are often used interchangeably in the modern era, but in the eighteenth and nineteenth centuries they had different, and changing, meanings. These meanings were tied to organizational strategies and philosophies.

Before the American Revolution the term *abolition* referred to the movement in Great Britain to abolish the African slave trade. In Britain this term continued to apply to the international slave trade until 1808, when both Britain and the United States banned the trade. During and after the Revolution various "abolition" societies emerged in the United States. In 1775 opponents of slavery in Pennsylvania organized the nation's first abolition society; that society collapsed during the Revolution but in 1787 was reorganized as the Pennsylvania Society for Promoting the Abolition of Slavery, the Relief of Freed Negroes Unlawfully Held in Bondage, and for Improving

"The Abolition of the Slave Trade. Or the Inhumanity of Dealers in Human Flesh Exemplified in Captn. Kimber's Treatment of a Young Negro Girl of 15 for Her Virjen Modesty," a cartoon published in London on 10 April 1792. The sailor holding the rope is saying, "Dam me if I like it. I have a good mind to let go." One of the onlookers at the right says, "My Eyes Jack our Girles at Wapping are never flogged for their modesty." The other says, "By Gales, that's too bad if he had taken her to Blackwall all would be well enough. Split me I'm allmost sick of this Black Business." (Library of Congress.)

the Condition of the African Race. This organization became known as the Pennsylvania Abolition Society (PAS). After the war like-minded New Yorkers, led by John Jay and Alexander Hamilton, organized the New York Manumission Society. In the aftermath of the Revolution opponents of slavery organized similar societies in all of the other northern states as well as in Virginia, Maryland, and Delaware. The goal of these societies was to end slavery in their particular states and to end the African slave trade. These organizations became moribund, or simply disappeared, by the 1820s. They had served their purpose in the North, as all northern states either ended slavery outright or passed gradual emancipation acts to end slavery over the course of a number of years. By this time the federal government had also prohibited the importation of new slaves from Africa and American participation in the African slave trade.

In the 1820s the term *abolition* came to refer to people opposed to slavery, but it had no strong or clear meaning. There were no organizations agitating for the end of slavery and only a few Americans, most of whom were black, doing so. This changed dramatically in 1831 when William Lloyd Garrison began publishing the *Liberator*; he then organized the American Anti-Slavery Society in

1833. Earlier abolition societies had worked for gradual emancipation in the North, which involved freeing the children of slaves and allowing the institution to literally die out as existing slaves passed on. Garrison, however, was not content with gradual emancipation; he pushed for immediate abolition, arguing that slavery was deeply sinful and wrong. This was the beginning of the abolition movement, and followers of Garrison called themselves "abolitionists," sometimes referring to themselves as "immediatists"; they are known to historians as Garrisonians or Garrisonian abolitionists. The call for immediate abolition was strongly tied to the belief that slaveholding was a sin. The chief tactic of these first abolitionists was moral suasion—that is, they sought to persuade masters to give up slaveholding to avoid the sin of owning other human beings.

The Garrisonians soon faced challenges to their demand for the immediate abolition of slavery from allies within the movement, as well as from opponents of abolition, about the practicality of that demand. How, people wondered, could the nation immediately emancipate millions of illiterate, propertyless blacks? Even radicals like Garrison realized the enormity of the problem; they responded by arguing for "immediate abolition, gradually attained." By this they meant that opponents of slavery should immediately commit to the goal of full abolition of slavery, even if it could not be done overnight. Their model was Great Britain, which abolished slavery in its remaining American colonies over a five-year period in the 1830s.

In the early 1830s the Garrisonians flooded the postal system with pamphlets and papers urging an end to slavery. They sent publications to prominent southern politicians and churchmen and to lesser-known members of southern churches. Yet this moral suasion campaign, which consisted of denouncing the sin of slaveholding, led not to massive abolition but to mobs attacking post offices to destroy mail coming from the North. The Garrisonians also began what they called the "great petition campaign," sending thousands of petitions to Congress with hundreds of thousands of signatures to protest federal support for slavery. Rather than persuade Congress, however, the petitions led to a "gag rule," under which Congress refused to even read antislavery petitions. At the same time Garrisonians sent speakers throughout the North to gather support for their movement. While many joined the movement in this period, antislavery speakers, too, were often mobbed; most famously, the abolitionist publisher Elijah Lovejoy was killed while defending his press from a proslavery mob.

In addition to antislavery, the Garrisonians supported a variety of other causes, most notably women's equality. This led to women speaking before mixed—that is, male and female—audiences, which was considered shocking by most Americans, including many opponents of slavery. By the late 1830s the Garrisonians began to denounce established churches for their failure to take a stronger stand, or any stand at all, on slavery. At the same time, Garrison and his followers began to withdraw from all political activity, including voting, while denouncing the Constitution as a "Covenant with Death and an Agreement with Hell." The Garrisonians were perfectionists, unwilling to compromise or to ally with anyone who might compromise on the issue of slavery. The stubborn position of the Garrisonians, controversy regarding feminism and the churches, and the pressure of mob violence eventually led to factionalism within the abolitionist movement. In 1840 dissidents formed a new organization, the American and Foreign Anti-Slavery Society. Later that year some of the same men formed the Liberty Party, which ran the nation's first antislavery candidate for president in 1840.

The American and Foreign Anti-Slavery Society and the Liberty Party were more antislavery than abolitionist. Members believed in political action and in chipping away at slavery; they voted and participated in other political activities. The Liberty Party never won an election, but in 1844 it may have taken enough votes away from the Whig

slaveholder Henry Clay to throw the election to another slave owner, James K. Polk. This illustrated the power of antislavery ballots, even though it did not, in the short run, gain anything for the institution's opponents. Indeed, since Polk was an expansionist, it may be that the Liberty Party actually hurt the antislavery cause. However, in the next sixteen years the power of antislavery voting would become more significant.

In 1848 antislavery Democrats supported Martin Van Buren, who ran for president on the Free-Soil ticket. Not all Free-Soilers were fully antislavery—some just opposed the spread of slavery into the new territories—but the party was the movement's most successful political organization up to that time. The Free-Soil Party took enough votes away from the dough-faced proslavery Democratic candidate, Lewis Cass, to give the election to the Whig, Zachary Taylor. While Taylor was a slave owner, he opposed the spread of slavery into the territories recently acquired from Mexico, whereas Cass would have been willing to allow new slave territories. Van Buren, meanwhile, won over 290,000 popular votes—more than 10 percent of the total—demonstrating the growing power of antislavery sentiment.

In the next decade antislavery sentiment became more widespread. The Republican Party, formed in 1854, attracted almost all opponents of slavery except the small minority who remained loyal to the Garrisonian notion of withdrawing from political activity. Abraham Lincoln himself was no abolitionist; he advocated neither an immediate end to slavery nor even interference with the institution in the states where it existed. Yet he was firmly opposed to the creation of new slave states and just as committed to putting slavery, as he said, on "the course of ultimate extinction." Other Republicans, like Salmon Portland Chase of Ohio, came out of a more aggressive antislavery background, arguing that the federal government should do everything in its power to contain and restrict slavery. By 1860 a majority of northerners were antislavery, at the same time opposing abolitionists, whom they saw as radical and dangerous to the stability of the nation.

The evolution of the thought of Frederick Douglass illustrates the differences between the abolition and antislavery positions and how, by 1862, they had merged. After escaping from slavery, Douglass was hired as a lecturer by the Massachusetts Anti-Slavery Society, which was the state branch of Garrison's American Anti-Slavery Society. He endured mobbing and harassment as he traveled throughout the North, telling his story and lecturing on the need for abolition. At the time, he was a loyal Garrisonian, eschewing politics and demanding an immediate end to slavery. Upon his return from a trip to England, however, Douglass moved from the rigid abolitionism of the Garrisonians to a more practical antislavery stance. By 1851 he was advocating political activity as he merged his first newspaper, the *North Star*, with a Liberty Party paper to create *Frederick Douglass' Paper*, which then became the leading organ of political antislavery.

Douglass then participated in politics and voted for antislavery candidates. In 1860 the Garrisonians still rejected politics and refused to support Lincoln. Wendell Phillips, the most articulate Garrisonian speaker, referred to Lincoln as "the slave hound of Illinois" because as a lawyer he had once represented a master in a fugitive slave case. Douglass, on the other hand, was antislavery and far from perfectionist; he voted for Lincoln, as he understood that the Republicans, including their standard-bearer, were also truly antislavery, however tepidly. When the Civil War began, Douglass pushed Lincoln to take a firmer stand against slavery. By then a more practical antislavery agitator, Douglass did not attack the Republicans for not moving more quickly against slavery. Indeed, by late 1862 the antislavery Republicans had become the true party of abolition. The Emancipation Proclamation, issued on 1 January 1863, made abolition a Union war policy.

At long last, the Thirteenth Amendment, passed by Congress two years later and ratified in December 1865, turned even mainstream politicians into abolitionists. As a testament to the wisdom of Douglass's practical stance, when slavery's end did come, it was accomplished by the very politicians that the Garrisonian abolitionists had scorned. Ironically, abolition indeed came suddenly, without preparation and without any gradual process—just as those same abolitionists had been demanding for three and one-half decades.

[*See also* American and Foreign Anti-Slavery Society; American Anti-Slavery Society; Antislavery Movement; Antislavery Press; Black Abolitionists; Chase, Salmon Portland; Civil War; Clay, Henry; Democratic Party; Douglass, Frederick; Emancipation Proclamation; *Frederick Douglass' Paper*; Free-Soil Party; Garrison, William Lloyd; Garrisonian Abolitionists; Liberty Party; Lincoln, Abraham; Massachusetts Anti-Slavery Society; Moral Suasion; *North Star*; Perfectionism; Phillips, Wendell; Polk, James K.; Reform; Religion; Religion and Slavery; Republican Party; Slavery; Slave Trade; Slavery and the U.S. Constitution; Thirteenth Amendment; Whig Party; *and* Women.]

BIBLIOGRAPHY

Barnes, Gilbert Hobbs. *The Antislavery Impulse, 1830-1844.* New York: D. Appleton-Century, 1933.

Blight, David. *Frederick Douglass' Civil War: Keeping Faith in Jubilee.* Baton Rouge: Louisiana State University Press, 1989.

Steward, James Brewer. *Holy Warriors: The Abolitionists and American Slavery.* New York: Hill and Wang, 1996.

—PAUL FINKELMAN

Early Abolitionism: The Onset of Slavery through 1830

Only with the onset of the American Revolution did a true abolitionist movement finally get under way. Fortunately, the moral imperatives universally generated by the Revolution, and in turn the general progress of human rights and individual liberties accompanying that upheaval, would come to have a significant impact on the lives of African American slaves. Earlier abolitionist efforts, while minimal, at least prefigured the more substantial ideological shifts concomitant with the birth of the United States.

The simplest truth about seventeenth-century slavery was that the legal structure created to deal with the practice lagged far behind its ubiquitous growth, as did efforts to either contain or eliminate it. Abolitionist organization was virtually nonexistent; only symbolic efforts pointed the way to the abolitionist future. In 1630 in Massachusetts Bay, for example, the infant legislature enacted a law protecting captured runaway slaves from abuse by angry owners. In 1652 Rhode Island limited the maximum period of enslavement to ten years, and slaves could not be held beyond the age of twenty-four. In 1688 Germantown Quakers in the new colony of Pennsylvania passed an antislavery resolution notable only for its rarity. Such token efforts to contain or delimit slavery, not spearheaded by actual abolitionist organizations, were made in all North American colonies by the end of the century. By 1700, in a general population of about a quarter million, there were nearly thirty thousand African Americans, by far the greater portion of them slaves, living in the colonies; slavery had already become institutionalized in American life. Laws limiting slave movement and prescribing dire punishments for runaways and those inciting insurrection were on the books in all colonies. The slave trade was in full flower, and antislavery organization failed to blossom until the Revolution.

In the 1750s and 1760s two significant Philadelphia Quakers signaled the moderate activism that would bear fruit in the 1780s: John Woolman and Anthony Benezet both published widely read antislavery tracts that helped trigger some Revolutionary-era response and helped form a sound ideological abolitionist base. Their works crystallized and popularized the moral wrongness of slavery and influenced some of the founding fathers who came to prominence as "young men" of the Revolution.

Woolman's popular 1754 pamphlet *Some Considerations on the Keeping of Negroes* concentrated on the argument that slavery was at its roots unchristian. "Where slavekeeping prevails, pure religion and [religious] sobriety declines," Woolman wrote, adding that the institution "tends to harden the heart, and render the soul less susceptible . . . of the character of a true Christian." The Philadelphian's tract piqued a growing public awareness—at least in the colonies as far south as Maryland—that human slavery not only deprived slaves of all basic natural rights and individual liberties but corrupted the owning class as well. Woolman also indirectly indicted all those who did nothing to end human enslavement.

In 1766, as popular American Revolutionary activity heated up, Benezet, another Philadelphia Quaker, began to publish antislavery tracts that assaulted the continuing slave trade, publicizing "the Calamitous State of the Enslaved Negroes" and generally tying the rising sentiments favoring human rights and natural law in the colonies to the poisonous paradox that slavery increasingly constituted. He also linked the American problem to one that English abolitionists were already addressing abroad, far in advance of their American brethren. Eventually, in the nineteenth century, that connection bore organizational fruit; in the short run, however, increasingly well-known pre-Revolutionary antislavery ideology generated only scant organizational results. A notable exception was the 1775 formation of the Pennsylvania Society for the Abolition of Slavery. It was the first such society in the new nation—and as was indicative of how little it mattered, the organization did not meet regularly until 1784.

By that time Thomas Paine and Benjamin Rush, both major American Revolutionaries, had weighed in with influential pamphlets linking the need for the abolition of slavery to the larger cause of American independence and the achievement of republican-oriented natural rights. Other founding fathers, influenced by Enlightenment principles and the growing stream of antislavery propaganda from both the American continent and abroad, became convinced of the need to end slavery by means of gradual emancipation; these historical figures included Benjamin Franklin, Alexander Hamilton, John Jay, and George Mason, among others. In truth, their efforts were coming too late. By 1760 there were almost 1,600,000 people in the thirteen colonies. About one-fifth of that population, over 325,000, were African American, at least a quarter million of them slaves.

Manumission in the northern states for the most part followed the end of the war. An exception was a weak 1781 gradual emancipation law in Pennsylvania, which freed the offspring of slaves at age twenty-eight. The Massachusetts Supreme Court ended slavery at the close of the Revolutionary War—far ahead of its time—declaring that "the idea of slavery is inconsistent with . . . our Constitution, and there can be no such thing as perpetual servitude of a rational creature." Connecticut and Rhode Island followed with gradual emancipation legislation in 1784. Although in 1785 New York became the first state to officially sanction an abolitionist organization—its So-

ciety for Promoting the Manumission of Slaves—mainly as influenced by Hamilton and Jay, the state did not enact gradual emancipation until 1799. By shortly after the turn of the nineteenth century manumission laws were on the books in all northern states. The startlingly forward-looking Northwest Ordinance of 1787 excluded slavery in the territories west of the Appalachians and north of the Ohio River. This combination of circumstances effectively rendered the North "free" and the South "slave" as the new century dawned.

Still, aggressive abolitionist efforts lagged. In 1802 free blacks notably petitioned Congress to end the slave trade, proscribe fugitive slave laws, and fully put an end to slavery as an institution. But at the same time regression was the order of the day in Indiana; the new state legislated slavery as legal in contradiction to the Northwest Ordinance, and Congress failed to excise the state's law. For the most part, as the slave trade continued legally until 1808 and sub rosa thereafter, slavery was further institutionalized and flourished in the South. There was little adamant antislavery effort in response in the North and new West, even as the border state of Delaware and the western state of Illinois barred free blacks within their borders.

Negative progress was all too evident in 1816, when the American Colonization Society (ACS) was founded, not to free slaves for their own benefit but to buy them out of captivity and "resettle" them in Africa so as to eliminate their presence in the United States. That such an organization could be widely seen as credible was a damning commentary on the weakness of abolitionism. among whites. Earlier, notable blacks, including Paul Cuffe and Peter Williams, Jr., supported a return to Africa, but that support evaporated with the founding of the ACS. Blacks objected to the ACS founders' remarks that African Americans had no place in the United States and to descriptions that disparaged their economic and social contributions.

Again, black activists protested, and the center of that protest was once more Philadelphia. In 1817 Richard Allen and James Forten told a largely African American audience of three thousand that the ACS was an "outrage"; Forten denounced the society's offer to make him ruler of Liberia. The audience resolved that "whereas our ancestors (not of choice) were the first successful cultivators of the wilds of America . . . , to banish us from [America's] bosum would not only be cruel, but in direct violation of those principles, which have been the boast of the republic." Meager protests followed in Boston, New York City, and Hartford; these ineffective responses were occurring in the midst of the deepening institutionalization of southern slavery. Indeed, in 1821 the ACS, with federal support, succeeded in establishing the Republic of Liberia, with about twenty thousand free American blacks as its first citizens.

Some major radical white abolitionists emerged in the 1820s as effective propagandists, providing at least an ideological bridge to the Garrisonian abolitionism of the 1830s, even if organizational efforts remained stunted. In 1821 Benjamin Lundy, a Quaker from Ohio, published the *Genius of Universal Emancipation*, a journal that failed but led to the American Convention for the Abolition of Slavery, which was also ultimately aborted. These failures nevertheless kept both propaganda and organizational aspirations with regard to a burgeoning antislavery movement alive and in the public eye. In 1824 James Duncan of Indiana published his *Treatise on Slavery*, a widely circulated tract that reminded Americans that slavery not only was unconstitutional but also "violated fundamental moral law."

But it was left to the African American abolitionist David Walker, who became known at the end of the 1820s, to provide the most important propagandist bridge to the militant abolitionism that waited in the wings. Walker was a free black born in North Carolina who, by 1829, was a used-clothing dealer in Boston; he also headed the Colored Association of Boston. His radical antislavery pamphlet, widely read first in New England and later throughout the nation, was entitled *An Appeal to the Coloured Citizens of the World*. Both anticipating and energizing the radical white abolitionist William Lloyd Garrison, it called on African Americans in the South to seek their freedom—even through violent means if necessary. By the end of the year it had already gone through three editions, each one more militant than the last. The state of Georgia played into his hands by outlawing circulation of the tract and putting a price on Walker's head. Such extreme reactions only enhanced the document's impact; it galvanized abolitionist sentiment in white New England in general and Massachusetts in particular and certainly helped set the table for the radical organizational efforts that began a few years later. The first issue of Garrison's antislavery newspaper, the *Liberator*, was published on 1 January 1831, marking the opening of a new era of militancy and organizational success for the abolitionist movement.

[*See also* Allen, Richard; American Revolution; Benezet, Anthony; Cuffe, Paul; David Walker's *Appeal*; Emancipation; Forten, James; Franklin, Benjamin, and African Americans; Free African Americans to 1828; Fugitive Slaves; *Genius of Universal Emancipation*; Hamilton, Alexander, and African Americans; Jay, John, and Slavery; Laws and Legislation; Manumission Societies; Petitions; Religion; Riots and Rebellions; Slavery: Northeast; Slave Insurrections and Rebellions; Society of Friends (Quakers) and African Americans; Walker, David; Williams, Peter, Jr.; *and* Woolman, John.]

BIBLIOGRAPHY

Davis, David Brion. *The Problem of Slavery in the Age of Revolution, 1770–1823*. New York: Oxford University Press, 1975.

Hodges, Graham Russell. *Root and Branch: African Americans in New York and East Jersey, 1613–1863*. Chapel Hill: University of North Carolina Press, 1999.

Quarles, Benjamin. *Black Abolitionists*. New York: Oxford University Press, 1969.

Zilversmit, Arthur. *The First Emancipation: The Abolition of Slavery in the North*. Chicago: University of Chicago Press, 1967.

—CARL E. PRINCE

Immediate Abolitionism and the Civil War

The doctrine of immediate abolitionism became the antislavery movement's rallying standard in the three decades leading up to the Civil War. In the inaugural editorial of the *Liberator* (1 January 1831), the first newspaper in the United States dedicated primarily to the cause of immediate emancipation, the Massachusetts abolitionist William Lloyd Garrison proclaimed, "I will not equivocate—I will not excuse—I will not retreat a single inch—AND I WILL BE HEARD."

Garrison and other immediatists built their movement on years of black activism, revivalism, and transatlantic reform. According to the distinguished historian James Brewer Stewart, whose book *Holy Warriors* remains the standard treatment of the American abolition movement, immediatism was akin to a crusade against slavery and racial injustice. The doctrine of immediate emancipation compelled antebellum abolitionists to embrace and debate a range of strategies and tactics during the 1830s, 1840s, and 1850s, from the efficacy of slave violence to the formation of abolitionist political parties. In this sense, it is useful to conceive of the immediate abolition movement as a precursor to the modern civil rights movement. It had a long and varied history that cannot be reduced to a single leader, action, or incident.

The first generation of American abolitionists advocated gradual, not immediate, abolition. The Pennsylvania Abolition Society, founded in 1775 and the nation's leading antislavery group before 1830, aimed for slavery's gradual elimination. Pennsylvania passed the world's first gradual abolition act in 1780, requiring masters to register slaves with local officials and providing that all slaves would be liberated at the age of twenty-eight. Many liberal statesman and reformers favored Pennsylvania's gradualist model. Even prominent African American reformers like the Maryland activist Daniel T. Coker and the Pennsylvania preacher Absalom Jones publicly embraced gradualism; while privately advocating more radical measures, Jones and Coker realized that white leaders would consider only gradualist appeals. Between 1780 and 1804 every northern state in the new nation followed Pennsylvania's lead by passing gradual abolition laws. Only Massachusetts, in 1783, ended slavery by judicial decree.

While gradualist antislavery societies persisted through the 1820s, new generations of reformers embraced immediatist strategies during the next decade. In 1832 the New England Anti-Slavery Society was founded in Boston as the first regional abolition society dedicated to achieving the immediate end of bondage. In 1833 in Philadelphia, immediate abolitionists formed the American Anti-Slavery Society. Both groups became models for others in New York, Ohio, Michigan, and elsewhere; by 1836 there were roughly three hundred antislavery societies, located primarily in the North and Midwest. Immediatists harshly criticized gradual abolitionists, recalcitrant slaveholders, and colonizationists north and south who advocated sending free blacks to West African settlements. Immediatists also believed that racial equality was both desirable and possible in nonslaveholding states.

Gradual abolition groups in New York and Pennsylvania did not admit black members before 1830, but black activists did serve as cofounders of immediate abolition societies; African Americans constituted 25 percent of the New England Anti-Slavery Society's inaugural membership. In addition, immediatism bore the imprint of decades of black protest. From the Philadelphia preacher Richard Allen's 1794 *Address to Those Who Keep Slaves and Approve the Practice*, a moral condemnation of slave owning, to the Boston activist David Walker's militant 1829 pamphlet, *Appeal to the Coloured Citizens of the World*, African American reformers had developed a public protest movement that was immediatist in everything but name. Walker had previously worked as a correspondent for *Freedom's Journal*, the nation's first black newspaper (published in New York City between 1827 and 1829), which called for more aggressive antislavery stands. His *Appeal* went further, predicting a massive uprising unless white officials ended slavery at once. With serious debates occurring between black and white reformers over leadership, tactics, and racial discourse, the advent of immediatist societies in the 1830s instilled hope among black activists that they had entered a new age of race relations, where immediate abolitionists served as an interracial model for American society at large.

Religious revivalism and transatlantic reform were the other pillars of immediate abolitionism. The great revivalist surge known as the Second Great Awakening peaked during the 1820s and 1830s. Revivalism's emphasis on perfecting the world and eradicating sin funneled activists into the immediate abolitionist movement. Immediatists were also inspired by English reform movements. The British abolitionist Elizabeth Heyrich was one of the first transatlantic writers to publicly advocate immediatism; her essays were republished in American circles during the 1820s and 1830s, prompting American abolitionists to question the efficacy of gradualism. The British parliament's decision to pass a total emancipation act, which took effect 1 August 1833 and freed 780,000 slaves in the British Caribbean, solidified transatlantic influences.

Immediatists embraced a range of aggressive tactics between the 1830s and the Civil War. Under the banner of "moral suasion" they attempted to raise consciousness about the evil of slavery, sending abolitionist appeals directly to southern masters, blanketing local communities with abolitionist pamphlets and speakers, and publishing abolitionist newspapers. Female activists played a vital role in moral suasion campaigns. Women served as editors and orators, organizers of antislavery fairs and fundraisers, and directors of petition drives. By the Civil War abolitionist women had helped accumulate two million signatures on antislavery petitions.

Abolitionists predicted in the 1830s that moral suasion would compel guilty southern masters to liberate slaves and nonslaveholding whites to press for emancipation laws. When no revolution in American public sentiment occurred and the slave population doubled between the 1830s and early 1860s, the immediate abolition movement fragmented. Some activists advocated direct and even violent action. In 1843 the black activist Henry Highland Garnet called for an uprising among southern slaves. Other abolitionists resorted to political action. The Liberty Party, founded in 1840 as the first abolitionist political organization, tallied over sixty thousand votes in the presidential election of 1844. By the 1850s, while many moral suasionists disavowed politics, other immediate abolitionists supported the newly formed Republican Party.

What impact did immediate abolitionism ultimately have on American culture? Immediatists did not cause the Civil War, but they did shape Americans' view of slavery as a problematic and even evil institution—one intimately tied to sectional divisions. Furthermore, once Emancipation finally occurred during the Civil War, American politicians utilized the rhetoric and ideals of the antislavery movement to rationalize what Abraham Lincoln is known to have called a "new birth freedom." Finally, the movement served as a model for other reform groups, from the civil rights movement to the women's rights movement.

[*See also* Allen, Richard; American Colonization Society; Black Press; Civil Rights; Coker, Daniel T.; David Walker's *Appeal*; Emancipation; Great Awakening; Jones, Absalom; Newspapers; Petitions; Slavery: Northeast; Walker, David; *and* Women.]

BIBLIOGRAPHY

Kraditor, Aileen. *Means and Ends in American Abolitionism: Garrison and His Critics on Strategy and Tactics, 1834–1850*. New York: Pantheon Books, 1969.

Newman, Richard S. *The Transformation of American Abolitionism: Fighting Slavery in the Early Republic*. Chapel Hill: University of North Carolina Press, 2002.

Newman, Richard, Patrick Rael, and Philip Lapsansky, eds. *Pamphlets of Protest: An Anthology of Early African-American Protest Literature, 1790–1860*. New York: Routledge, 2001.

Stewart, James Brewer. *Holy Warriors: The Abolitionists and American Slavery*. Rev. ed. New York: Hill and Wang, 1996.

—RICHARD NEWMAN

ACCOMMODATIONISM. As African Americans fought racial prejudice in the United States following the Civil War, some black leaders proposed a strategy of accommodation. The idea of accommodation called for African Americans to work with whites and accept some discrimination in an effort to achieve economic success and physical security. The idea proved controversial: many black leaders opposed accommodation as counterproductive.

Booker T. Washington served as the champion of accommodation. Born a slave in 1856, Washington received a degree from the Hampton Institute before being invited to head up the Tuskegee Institute in Alabama. At Tuskegee, Washington used industrial education to promote accommodation by African Americans. Because of his background, Washington recognized the difficulties faced by southern blacks in their quest for civil rights. He knew firsthand that during the 1860s and 1870s whites in the South found it hard to accept African Americans as free. No one argued against the end of slavery, but most whites in the former Confederacy actively opposed black civil rights. Southern whites wanted to keep African Americans as a laboring force and as second-class citizens, and they passed laws, known as the black codes, designed to reinforce racial subjugation.

Washington understood the strong racial prejudice that still existed in the South. His approach to accommodation was designed to appease the white establishment while steadily promoting African American rights. By deferring to whites and playing the role of a second-class citizen in the company of southern whites, Washington was able to promote himself and his ideas. He also allied with southern white planters and businessmen against the poorer classes. Blacks tended to be used as strikebreakers, since they were denied membership in most labor unions. These actions helped win over many industrialists to support opportunities for African Americans. At the same time, however, Washington's accommodation approach isolated black workers in relation to white workers, who saw the African Americans as strikebreakers.

Washington's views on accommodation were common among black southerners during the last half of the nineteenth century. Every day, African American laborers and sharecroppers deferred to the system of racial segregation in the South in order to work and provide for their families. Even the black politicians who were elected to state and national political offices during Reconstruction, including Hiram Revels and Blanche Bruce, the first two African Americans elected to the U.S. Senate, found themselves taking up an accommodation role. While Revels and Bruce worked to introduce legislation to protect African American rights, the two senators usually voted with the leaders of the Republican Party.

Because of his position as president of Tuskegee, Washington was asked to give an address at the Atlanta Exposition in 1895. The speech, which became known as the "Atlanta Compromise," outlined the idea of African American accommodation. In his autobiography Washington recounted that he promoted friendship and cooperation between the races as a means of acquiring civil rights. He urged whites to give blacks opportunities in agriculture, mechanics, and commerce. He downplayed the necessity of social equality, instead claiming that African Americans sought economic unity. Washington finished by stating that through their work blacks proved themselves vital to the South and its economy, earning respect from whites and thus achieving equal rights. He told his audience, "In all things that are purely social we can be as separate as the fingers, yet one as the hand in all things essential to mutual progress."

Washington's ideas received some support among African Americans. In his autobiography, Frederick Douglass urged African Americans to stay in the South, which was dependent on black labor. Like Washington, Douglass felt that this dependence provided an advantage for African Americans. Black labor touched the South economically and thus was a more powerful force than any protest, fight, or political action.

Not every African American leader agreed with the practice of accommodation. The civil rights leader W. E. B. Du Bois, who had a PhD from Harvard, was the most prominent critic. Du Bois openly challenged Washington in his book *The Souls of Black Folk*, in which he argued that accommodation failed to support African American civil rights and higher education. He believed that blacks should pursue social and political equality as well as a classical education. As citizens, Du Bois argued, African Americans deserved immediate equality and he stated that they should help themselves, not rely on assistance from whites. According to Du Bois, Washington and other supporters of accommodation hurt efforts for equal rights by accepting second-class status.

By the twentieth century the practice of accommodation had fallen out of vogue. More African Americans supported the ideas of leaders like Du Bois. While Washington's views no longer remained popular, they held merit. Through accommodation, freed slaves established themselves in a hostile world. Washington and the policy of accommodation received support from white Americans; this, in turn, allowed African Americans to achieve some recognition of civil rights, which might not have occurred during the late 1800s. The idea also influenced later generations of black leaders, including Martin Luther King Jr. and his practice of nonviolent protest. Accommodation, though, remains a controversial topic, praised by some leaders and condemned by others.

[*See also* Bruce, Blanche Kelso; Civil Rights; Discrimination; Douglass, Frederick; Economic Life; Education; Reconstruction; Republican Party; Washington, Booker T; *and* Work.]

BIBLIOGRAPHY

Douglass, Frederick. *The Life and Times of Frederick Douglass* (1881). London: Wordsworth, 1996.

Du Bois, W. E. B. *The Souls of Black Folk*. Greenwich, CT: Fawcett, 1963.

Washington, Booker T. *Up from Slavery*. New York: Penguin, 1986.

—ROB FINK

ACCULTURATION. The acculturation of newly arrived enslaved Africans to the New World involved the interaction between Europeans and Africans. In this complex process Africans were often able to fuse their native culture with that of the Europeans who were their new masters. Indeed, elements of African traditions survived in many forms, including religion, dance, music, folklore, language, decorative arts, and architecture. With the closing of the slave trade and a decreasing number of native-born Africans, intense acculturation abated. Over time both cultures, European and African, were transformed by their coexistence and sharing of traditions. The richness and variety of American culture owes much to traditions brought by Africans to the New World.

Religious practices and beliefs were central to both the Africans and the Europeans. Early in slavery's history in North America, many whites actually opposed converting slaves to Christianity. They believed that baptizing African slaves might give them ideas about some day achieving freedom. By not converting slaves, Christian slaveholders also assuaged their consciences because it was more acceptable to hold heathens in chains than it was other Christians. Over time opposition to Christianizing slaves diminished, as religion came to be seen as a means of control. Some organizations, like the Anglican Church's Society for the Propagation of the Gospel, believed it was their mission to evangelize among blacks. Indeed, many whites believed that biblical exhortations such as "slaves, obey your masters" were useful for keeping the increasing numbers of Africans and African Americans in their place.

The historian John W. Blassingame notes that traditional African religious forms adapted easily to Christianity, with God taking the place of the Creator and Christ and the Holy Spirit replacing the lesser deities of African religions. Dances, music, amulets, funeral ceremonies, and other rituals from Africa found expression in European Christian religions. As Africans became Americans, the names of the gods and the origins of religious practices were lost to subsequent generations. However, African traditions such as call-and-response are even today identified with African American congregations. The passion and emotion blacks infused in their Christian religious services are also remnants of African ritual. White writers like Frederick Law Olmsted noted that slaves expressed themselves "with an intensity and vehemence almost terrible to witness."

African spirituality included a belief in spirits and charms, much like other folk religions. In *My Bondage and My Freedom* Frederick Douglass relates the story of his encounter with Sandy, "a genuine African," who "had inherited some of the so-called magical powers, said to be possessed by African and eastern nations." Sandy told Douglass about an herb that could be found in the woods that would help him by making it impossible for a white to ever whip him. At first Douglass rejected the idea, calling it "very absurd and ridiculous, if not positively sinful." Sandy pointed out to him that for all his intelligence and learning, Douglass was still being whipped by his master. Douglass agreed to take the root because "Sandy was so earnest, and so confident of the good qualities of this weed, that, to please him, rather than from any conviction of its excellence, I was induced to take it."

Folk tales and legends from Africa also survived the Americanization process. Stories centering on the trickster figure—the weak or slow animal that outwits the faster or more sophisticated creature—abound as part of the oral tradition. Besides the folklore itself, African languages also survived the Middle Passage to the New World as late as the 1830s and in many areas evolved into a local patois. One of the best known of the Creole dialects is the Gullah of the South Carolina Sea Islands. Creole dialects had discernible African-language patterns and were often unintelligible to others. Douglass talked about the Creole dialect spoken on Captain Edward Lloyd's plantation; he referred to it as "a mixture of Guinea and everything else you please." He added, "I could scarcely understand them [Captain Lloyd's slaves] when I first went among them, so broken was their speech; and I am persuaded that I could not have been dropped anywhere on the globe, where I could reap less, in the way of knowledge, from my immediate associates, than on this plantation."

Music played a central role in African culture and is distinguished by its complex rhythms. African rhythms combined with European music and the trials of slave life to produce a distinctive African American musical tradition. Blacks even adapted their musical instruments to the New World; for example, the African mbanza became the banjo. The spiritual was a powerful expression of the slaves' hatred of enslavement and was a covert way to communicate their desire for freedom. There were songs for nearly every occasion. Songs sung during work helped to break the monotony of toil. Other songs sung during religious services expressed the faith and spirituality of African Americans. Many songs were filled with the desire to end their bondage and become free people. The songs made a great impression on Douglass, who attributed his first stirrings of desire for freedom to them: "To those songs I trace my first glimmering conception of the dehumanizing character of slavery. I can never get rid of that conception. Those songs still follow me, to deepen my hatred of slavery, and quicken my sympathies for my brethren in bonds." By the 1890s the musical heritage preserved in African American culture would give birth to ragtime, jazz, and, later on, rhythm and blues and rock and roll.

North American architecture displays elements of the building traditions of West Africa and the West Indies. Architectural historians attribute the shotgun house to the arrival of immigrants in New Orleans from Toussaint Louverture's rebellion in Haiti at the end of the eighteenth century and into the early nineteenth century. Shotgun houses are one story tall, one room wide, and two or three rooms deep and have a front-gabled roof, a window and door on the facade, and usually a full-width front porch. Supposedly, the shotgun house acquired its name because the front and back doors are aligned and one could shoot a gun through the front door directly through the back and never touch a wall. Architectural historians believe the name may actually be a corruption of *togun*, which is a Yoruban word meaning "house." From New Orleans shotgun houses spread throughout the South and later to the North as a result of migration. Because they were narrow, shotgun houses were well suited to city lots and could be found in urban areas as well as on farms and plantations. Usually of wood frame construction, shotgun houses were relatively easy to erect; thus, they were often built for workers in company towns in the Ohio River and Mississippi River valleys. Variants of the shotgun house include the camelback house, which has a two-story rear addition, and the double shotgun house, which consists of two adjacent shotgun houses under one roof. While essentially of simple construction, a shotgun house could have elaborate decorations, such as gingerbread on the eaves of the roof or intricate scrollwork on the front porch.

Acculturation is a complex process, and it is often difficult to prove what survived from Africa and became a part of African American culture. Comparing African American and African traditions has been useful in determining the connections between the old and new worlds. Holding onto African culture and traditions was one way enslaved men and women could retain a sense of their own identity. Even in the later antebellum period, when there were fewer newcomers from Africa, slaves and free blacks maintained some of the cultural constructs of their ancestry. Over time African American traditions influenced and added to the diversity of American culture.

[*See also* Africa, Idea of; African Diaspora; Black Church; Black Family; Caribbean; Dance; Demographics; Douglass, Frederick; Ethnology; Haiti; Haitian Revolutions; Identity; Language; Literature; Lloyd Family; Lloyd, Edward, V; Music; *My Bondage and My Freedom* (1855); Race, Theories of; Religion; Religion and Slavery; Slave Trade; Slave Trade, Domestic; Slavery; *and* Toussaint Louverture.]

BIBLIOGRAPHY

Blassingame, John W. *The Slave Community: Plantation Life in the Antebellum South*. Rev. and enl. ed. New York: Oxford University Press, 1979. Still one of the classic works on slave life, Blassingame gives excellent examples of acculturation.

Stampp, Kenneth M. *The Peculiar Institution: Slavery in the Antebellum South*. New York: Knopf, 1956. One of the earliest accounts to take seriously the connections between African and African American culture.

Upton, Dell. *Architecture in the United States*. New York: Oxford University Press, 1998.

Vlach, John Michael. "The Shotgun House: An African-American Architectural Legacy." In *Common Places: Readings in American Vernacular Architecture*, edited by Dell Upton and John Michael Vlach. Athens: University of Georgia Press, 1986. Vlach's work on shotgun houses is critical to understanding their origin and diffusion.

—DONNA M. DEBLASIO

ADAMS, JOHN, ON AFRICAN AMERICANS. John Adams was born in Massachusetts in 1735 and grew up in relatively humble circumstances. After graduating from Harvard, he passed the bar and began his legal career. Adams's law practice was steady but unspectacular at a time of growing tension with England. He was a reluctant Revolutionary, even defending the British troops who fired on the crowd for unclear reasons in the Boston Massacre, but served faithfully in the First and Second Continental Congresses. Adams is well known for his insistence on a formal declaration of independence.

He remained in public service as a wartime diplomat to France and Holland and was instrumental in negotiating the treaty that ended the American Revolution. Adams continued his work overseas as ambassador to the English court before returning to the United States, where

John Adams, second president of the United States, in an engraving of c. 1828 by Pendleton's Lithography from the original series by Gilbert Stuart for Messrs. Doggett of Boston. (Library of Congress.)

he was chosen as George Washington's vice president. Adams then succeeded Washington as president and faced a host of problems with England and France. He returned to Massachusetts after his defeat in the 1800 election and stayed out of the public spotlight until his death in 1826. Adams was known for his blunt style and had opinions on most matters of his day. He was relatively silent, however, about his opinions on African Americans and made little mention of slavery or blacks in his diary. While Adams eventually became a dedicated opponent of slavery, his opinions of African Americans are difficult to discern and probably shifted during his lifetime.

Adams saw few blacks in his early years, as there were only about five thousand slaves in Massachusetts during the colonial era. He probably shared many of the prevailing white prejudices against blacks. Adams wrote a note to the Massachusetts governor Thomas Hutchinson in 1773 and signed it "Crispus Attucks," perhaps as a tribute to the African American man slain at the Boston Massacre; it was more probable, however, that Adams was comparing the situation of colonists to that of blacks, implying that both were being discriminated against in the

British Empire. As a congressman, he voted against black enlistment in the Continental army, arguing that African Americans could not be trained to be effective soldiers. His reaction to Thomas Jefferson's *Notes on the State of Virginia* also implied that Adams believed in racial inferiority. Jefferson described African Americans as inferior to whites even as he worried about the negative effects of slavery; Adams made no distinction between the two ideas, simply comparing Jefferson's words to diamonds.

In the course of his public career Adams came in contact with more African Americans and his opinions seemed to moderate somewhat. While in Paris in 1787 Sally Hemings, the slave and future mother of four children of Thomas Jefferson, lived with John and Abigail; she is the only slave known to have lived with the Adams family. John did not comment on the then fourteen-year-old Hemings, but Abigail thought her too immature to care for the children in the house. A free black woman served the Adams family as a cook while John was vice president, and she was the only servant who kept her employment when the family was forced to reduce expenses. The Adams family moved to Washington in the final months of John's presidency; the capital was home to many African Americans, something that did not escape Abigail's attention. She commented that she hated to see slaves working in the city and that the peculiar institution destroyed their initiative to work. In her opinion, two free men could do the work of a dozen slaves.

Even if Adams thought poorly of blacks, he hated slavery and spent much of his life trying to destroy it. He eventually gained the necessary financial resources, but Adams never purchased a slave; the thought repulsed him. In fact, neither he nor his family ever owned a slave, although Abigail's family owned two at one point. Massachusetts was one of the first states to emancipate its slaves in the Revolutionary era, and Adams shared this general opposition to the institution. He was good friends with Benjamin Rush, a man well known for his early and vigorous opposition to slavery. Adams wrote in 1765 that God had never intended the American colonies for slaves and wondered a decade later if Americans who held slaves had the right to complain about their lack of liberty. Adams, though, did not openly oppose slavery during the American Revolution; his goal was to simply win the war and sort out side issues later. Once the colonies won their independence on the battlefield, Adams assumed slavery would slowly die out.

In the end, despite his deep opposition to slavery, Adams took no action to bring about its demise. He thought the federal government should stay clear of the matter. He was confident that the states would see the best course—emancipation—and that freedom would slowly move south. Adams expected Virginia to be the first major southern state to emancipate its slaves, with Thomas Jefferson leading the way; he was wrong. Emancipation stalled at the Mason-Dixon Line, and Jefferson as well made almost no effort to combat slavery.

Adams remained silent with regard to slavery while serving as vice president and then as president. He gave several reasons for his lack of effort: He thought he might incite slave insurrections in the South if he spoke out, writing that he was terrified of armies of slaves marching across the country. Adams also noted that he had not been farther south than Washington and did not understand the southern plantation system. Thus he was in no position to judge the merits of slavery and would leave decisions with regard to the institution up to those who knew about it firsthand. Adams said little during his retirement as well, probably to protect his son's political career from controversy.

In private, Adams's doubts about slavery grew constantly. He described it as a crime against humanity that created catastrophic problems. One problem for Adams was miscegenation. He remarked that interracial sexual relations were unavoidable wherever slaves were present; he presumably believed that the power and exploitation inherent in slavery created opportunities for sexual exploitation. In the wake of the charges about Jefferson's relationship with Sally Hemings, Adams wrote that he believed one southern woman who said that every Virginia planter had fathered children with his slaves.

Adams never directly challenged Jefferson about the accusations but did tell his old friend that slavery was a growing problem, which future generations would have more difficulty confronting. He added that he believed abolition to be the only way to preserve the country, as it could not endure half slaveholding and half free. The Missouri Compromise of 1820 fueled Adams's fears. He endorsed the legislation that would have freed slaves in the state of Missouri, since it would have set a precedent for the federal government to abolish slavery in other states. A victory in the Missouri debates would have squarely positioned the federal government against the expansion of slavery and might have increased antislavery belief and action in the South. Adams thought further expansion of slavery would be harmful to the United States. The extension of the plantation system, with what Adams called great hordes of black serfs, would discourage immigration by white farmers.

Adams believed the danger to be so great at the time that he made his longest public statement to date on slavery. He said that the Revolutionary generation never intended for slavery to expand; slavery needed to be stopped so that whites could migrate to the West and not be con- cerned with the institution's detrimental effects. He described slavery as a gangrene infection that could kill its patient, even warning that if slavery was not terminated it would tear the nation in two. Adams was also scared that slaves would rebel against whites if forced to move to Missouri and that whites would respond by annihilating all African Americans.

A significant legacy of John Adams's fight against slavery was his son, John Quincy Adams. The elder Adams helped shape the staunchly antislavery opinions of the younger. John Quincy Adams battled against the southerners in the House of Representatives who prevented the discussion of antislavery petitions and was the primary attorney for the *Amistad* captives.

[*See also* Abolitionism; American Revolution; Attucks, Crispus; Hemings, Sally; Jefferson, Thomas, on African Americans and Slavery; Massachusetts; Missouri Compromise; Race, Theories of; *and* Stereotypes of African Americans.]

BIBLIOGRAPHY

Brown, Ralph A. *The Presidency of John Adams*. Lawrence: University Press of Kansas, 1975.

Capon, Lester J., ed. *The Adams-Jefferson Letters: The Complete Correspondence between Thomas Jefferson and Abigail and John Adams*. Chapel Hill: University of North Carolina Press, 1959.

McCullough, David G. *John Adams*. New York: Simon and Schuster, 2001.

Shaw, Peter. *The Character of John Adams*. Chapel Hill: University of North Carolina Press, 1976.

—ROBERT GUDMESTAD

ADAMS, JOHN QUINCY, ON AFRICAN AMERICANS.

Toward the end of his long life, the congressman John Quincy Adams (1767–1848), son of John and Abigail Adams, was notorious for his militant stands against slavery and its expansion in the Republic that his parents had helped found. It is possible to argue that he absorbed many of his views from his mother, who told her husband that she had doubts about southerners and their commitment to liberty. On 31 March 1776 Abigail Adams wrote in a letter to her husband,

> I have sometimes been ready to think that passion for liberty cannot be equally strong in the breasts of those who have been accustomed to deprive their fellow creatures of theirs. Of this I am certain, that it is not founded upon that generous and Christian principle of doing unto others as we would that others do unto us. (Withey, p. 81)

In fact, Abigail Adams's son's earlier career shows distinct caution on matters having to do with slavery and race. In time, however, he moved from casual indifference to intense passion.

The young Adams demonstrated his ambivalence during his years in the U.S. Senate, where he represented Massachusetts from 1803 to 1808. In 1805 he supported a group of Quakers who had introduced a petition calling for restrictions on slavery's growth, although two years earlier he had opposed any attempt to limit the importation of slaves into the newly acquired Louisiana Territory. "Slavery in a moral sense is an evil," he declared; nevertheless, he went on to state that "as connected with commerce, it has its uses." Also in 1805 when some senators moved to implement three years in advance the outlawing of slave importation as provided for in the U.S. Constitution, Adams joined those who argued that the measure was premature.

Whatever antislavery instincts Adams may have had at this point in his career, they were outweighed by his nationalism and expansionism. His nationalism was enhanced by his service in Europe from 1809 to 1817 as the American minister first to Russia and then to Great Britain. In London, Adams had no reservations whatsoever in arguing for the legal rights of southern slaveholders whose slave "property" had either escaped or been kidnapped during the War of 1812 and who, Adams maintained, were entitled to restitution under the recently negotiated Treaty of Ghent.

Not until after his return to the United States in 1817 to become secretary of state does any evidence of antislavery thinking appear in Adams's famous diary. In the midst of the congressional debates over slavery in the proposed state of Missouri, Adams had an extended conversation with the young proslavery secretary of war, John C. Calhoun. Adams later asked himself, "What can be more false and heartless than this doctrine that makes the first and holiest rights of humanity to depend upon the color of the skin?" In his diary he reflected upon the possible wisdom of northerners insisting that slavery expand no further than its present borders. If that resulted in the breakup of the Union, he considered, so be it; if it led to civil war, "as God shall judge me, I dare not say that it is not to be desired." However, as the secretary of state and as a man with presidential ambitions, he kept these views to himself. Later, as president, Adams attempted to acquire Texas, then a slaveholding province of Mexico, revealing that his expansionism was still competing with his antislavery instincts.

His ambivalence carried over into ideas on race. Although at no time does he seem to have indulged in any extensive reflections on the subject, like nearly all white males of the early nineteenth century Adams was a product of the stereotypical ideas about race that pervaded the era. In a published interview in 1833 he told the British actress Fanny Kemble that Shakespeare's *Othello* was flawed as drama because the white heroine Desdemona's love for her African husband was repugnant and "contrary to the laws of nature." (Adams may have had in mind the accusations aimed at the late president Thomas Jefferson regarding his fathering of children by one of his slaves, Sally Hemings—about which as a young man in 1803 Adams had published some racy lines of poetry.)

Yet years earlier, while in London, Adams's family had made the acquaintance of an African American schoolteacher from Boston named Sanders, who often accompanied Adams's three children on excursions in and around town. Sanders traveled to Haiti in the hope of establishing a school system there, and Adams advised him on the project while procuring the necessary passports. Throughout his life Adams corresponded with a number of blacks, including Thomas Gaillard, the mulatto son of a man whose cousin had been a colleague of Adams's in the Senate. Sympathizing with and encouraging Gaillard's arguments in favor of equal rights, Adams sought further information about the man's slave mother. Adams also took an interest in the case of Dorcas Allen, a black woman who had killed her two children in order to prevent them from being sold into slavery. She had in fact been free for many years but, lacking the proper papers, was being forced back into slavery. The case attracted the attention of not only Adams but also Francis Scott Key and others opposed to slavery. After several visits from the woman's husband, Adams donated fifty dollars to a fund raised to buy Allen's freedom.

In the 1830s, following the enactment of the congressional gag rule that prevented Congress from reading petitions dealing with slavery, Adams became slavery's most vociferous opponent in Congress. At the beginning of each session he could be counted on to tie up the proceedings of the House in defense of the right of petition. However, he disappointed the growing abolitionist movement in the North by refusing to enlist in their ranks and appearing to accept slavery where it already existed. To hard-liners like William Lloyd Garrison and James Gillespie Birney, Adams was a weak-kneed compromiser. Birney declared, "There is no man who is doing so much . . . to deaden the awakening sensibilities of our countrymen against the private iniquity and public disgrace of slavery, as Mr. Adams." Adams not only failed to join the abolitionist movement but also refused to support some of their more moderate proposals. In rebuttal to arguments for banning slavery in the District of Columbia, Adams pointed out that the passage of such a ban would merely result in slaveholders' removing their "property" to Virginia and thus would not free anyone. Moreover, unlike Birney or Garrison, Congressman Adams had taken an oath to support the U.S. Constitution, which, whether he liked it or not, had embraced slavery; he could not violate that oath and remain a member of the House of Representatives.

In 1841, however, his standing as a champion of both racial justice and antislavery was markedly enhanced when he appeared before the U.S. Supreme Court as senior counsel in the *Amistad* case. Two years earlier, in violation of the ban on the international slave trade, a group of free Africans had been kidnapped from their homes and taken to Cuba in the Spanish schooner *Amistad*. While in transport from one part of Cuba to another, the Africans rebelled and took over the vessel and demanded that its crew return them to their West African homeland. Through trickery the Spanish captain sailed the ship not to Africa but to Long Island, New York. Since landing in the United States the Africans had languished in jail. Northern abolitionists recruited Adams to add prestige to their side, which was working against attempts by Spain and the proslavery administration of President Martin Van Buren to condemn the Africans and return them to Cuba—to certain slavery and possible execution.

Adams did not disappoint the abolitionists. To the charge by the Spanish authorities that the Africans were robbers and pirates, Adams directed his notorious sarcasm. "Who were the merchandise, and who were the robbers?" he asked. "According to the Spanish Minister, the merchandise were the robbers and the robbers were the merchandise. The merchandise was rescued out of its own hands, and the robbers were rescued out of the hands of the robbers." Later, pointing dramatically to a copy of the Declaration of Independence hanging on the wall of the courtroom, he declared, "The moment you come to the Declaration of Independence, that every man has a right to life and liberty, as an inalienable right, this case is decided." It was clearly the high point in Adams's career as an antislavery crusader. "Some of us may have at times done thee injustice," wrote the abolitionist poet John Greenleaf Whittier, "but, I believe we now appreciate thy motives."

Adams died in 1848 after suffering a stroke on the floor of the House of Representatives. In the chamber at the time was a young congressman from Illinois, Abraham Lincoln. There is no record of their ever having met, but Adams's views on race and slavery reflected those of a growing majority of northerners as well as those of Lincoln himself. African Americans may not have been brothers and sisters, but they were men and women and were included in the scope of the Declaration of Independence. Both Adams and Lincoln were ambivalent about race, and neither man was an abolitionist, but both recognized that slavery's end would occur in a matter of time and that the least painful way to hasten that end would be to stop its growth. That events would turn out differently was a product of decisions made by others.

[*See also* Abolitionism; Adams, John, on African Americans; Constitution, U.S.; Declaration of Independence; Europe; Foreign Policy; Hemings, Sally; Jefferson, Thomas, on African Americans and Slavery; Kidnapping; Laws and Legislation; Louisiana; Massachusetts; New Spain and Mexico; Petitions; Race, Theories of; Slave Trade; Slavery: Mid-Atlantic; Slavery: Upper South; Society of Friends (Quakers) and African Americans; Supreme Court; *and* War of 1812.]

BIBLIOGRAPHY

Bemis, Samuel Flagg. *John Quincy Adams and the Union*. New York: Knopf, 1956.
Hecht, Marie. *John Quincy Adams: A Personal History of an Independent Man*. New York: Macmillan, 1972.
Jones, Howard. *Mutiny on the "Amistad."* New York: Oxford University Press, 1987.
Maclean, William Jerry. "Othello Scorned: The Racial Thought of John Quincy Adams." *Journal of the Early Republic* 4 (Summer 1984): 143–160.
Parsons, Lynn Hudson. *John Quincy Adams*. Madison, WI: Madison House, 1998.
Richards, Leonard L. *The Life and Times of Congressman John Quincy Adams*. New York: Oxford University Press, 1986.
Withey, Lynne. *Dearest Friend: A Life of Abigail Adams*. New York: Free Press, 1981.

—Lynn Hudson Parsons

AFRICA, IDEA OF.

AFRICA, IDEA OF. The idea of Africa changed dramatically from antiquity to the era of European exploration and colonization; European and African views of each other continually transformed as a result of the evolving nature of their interaction. The Atlantic slave trade, perhaps the most significant event in the history of Africa, forever changed the manner in which Africans and Europeans intermingled. Perceptions of Africa were fluid, shifting according to geographic, economic, political, racial, and religious factors stemming from within as well as outside the continent. By 1830 the most broadly held notion of Africa had transformed from one of reverence, by the peoples of antiquity, to one of contempt and apprehension, by early modern Europeans. For Africans in the diaspora, the land of their ancestors' birth remained a symbol of guidance, hope, and spirituality.

Antiquity. The history of Africa resembles that of other continents, with African peoples experiencing their own Iron Age and other stages of development well charted by scholars. The Greek philosopher and historian Herodotus thought highly of African civilization, although he divided Africa and Africans into two distinct peoples: Egyptians and Ethiopians. Herodotus praised the technological and civic advancements of the Egyptians and also noted their cultural ties to Ethiopians; he believed that the Egyptian practice of circumcision derived from intercultural contact with sub-Saharan Africans. Herodotus attributed Greek skill with the chariot to encounters with the master horsemen of the Berbers in North Africa. Within the

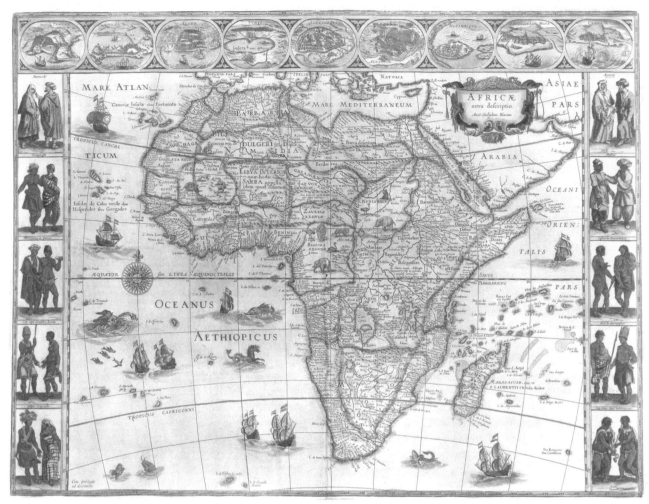

Africa, a map by William J. Blaeu from the *Atlas Major* of 1662. It is embellished with scenes of Tangiers, Ceuta, Algeria, Tunis, Alexandria, etc. across the top, and peoples of Africa at the two sides. (Bildarchiv Preussicher Kulturbesitz/Art Resource, N.Y.)

ancient Greek texts emerges the concept of two Africas: one of lighter-skinned North Africans, who were integral to the Mediterranean world and the other of darker-skinned Africans who lived south of the Sahara. Some historians suggest that the Greek accounts were among the first to racially differentiate Africans from Europeans and Asians.

Rome occupied much of North Africa after the fall of Carthage because it offered economic opportunities, territorial expansion, and a source of slaves. Roman, Jewish, and Greek converts to Christianity traveled extensively within the network of outposts held by the Roman Empire in North Africa, likewise converting Africans to this new religion. North Africa soon played a central role in the development of Christian theology, and during the first five centuries after the advent of Christianity the idea of Africa for missionaries carried with it visions of a vast

population open to conversion from their primitive tribal existence. This sense of Africa as a land awaiting Christian rescue would continue to develop among Europeans for centuries to come. Meanwhile, the spread of Islam throughout Africa, which was especially rapid in North Africa from the eleventh through thirteenth centuries by the Berbers and other Muslim powers, provoked African colonization of southern Europe. Spain fell to the Berbers during the twelfth century, worrying Europeans to the extent that they launched the Crusades to both retake the Holy Land and combat the growing Islamic presence in Europe.

Medieval to Early Modern Periods. For much of antiquity and the early Middle Ages, Africa's relationship with the rest of the world centered on the competition of empires, kingdoms, and religious ideals. Economics also played an important role in the way Africa was perceived by the outside world as well as by itself. Indeed, the Mediterranean world of this era saw an integrated system of trade in which North African powers were essential participants, as can be seen in the various European maps of the world from that period. These maps place the Mediterranean Sea, also known as the lake of the ancient world, at the center—thus leaving North Africa well within the boundaries of the page.

By 1400 Europe's conception of Africa was about to change; Europeans began to explore sub-Saharan Africa and encounter people who did not resemble the Africans of the north. Sailing beyond the Mediterranean Sea, the Portuguese led such exploration efforts. Equipped with technological advancements such as gunpowder, the compass, and the caravel that were often derived from Arab knowledge, Europeans sought new routes to the riches of Asia. The quest for wealth and empire dramatically transformed European worldviews.

With the fifteenth- and sixteenth-century voyages of exploration, two new worlds—the Americas and sub-Saharan Africa—opened up for the Old World, ending its isolation. Crucial to this exploration was the use and expansion of waterways throughout the Atlantic Ocean. Whether sailing along the coast of Africa or venturing to the Americas, the Spanish and Portuguese helped introduce new societies and new ideas of "the other" to Europe. Traditional ideas of Africa began to focus less on the many achievements of North African societies; instead, the views of the Continent belonging to scholars, adventurers, and others became rooted in notions of race, identity, and religion wherein Africans were perceived as tribal and uncivilized.

Questions remain among historians regarding the origins of racist ideology toward Africans. A general evolution of the European idea of Africa can nevertheless be traced; its foundation is firmly rooted in Christian ideology and the Bible. Perhaps the idea most influential to the European conception of Africa was the Hamitic hypothesis, or the "curse of Ham." Popular literature and theology from the sixteenth through nineteenth centuries suggested that black Africans gained their color when Ham was cursed by his father, Noah, to forever be his brothers' slave—while also being given black skin. Although it is not clear how strictly Europeans believed in the curse of Ham, such religiously rooted ideas shaped racial beliefs and helped to justify the enslavement of Africans.

Conceiving Black Africa. Travel writing, made famous as a genre by such authors as Richard Hakluyt and Samuel Purchas, also influenced Europeans' ideas of Africa. The images of the continent that emerged in the minds of many Europeans from these writings and accounts by noblemen, merchants, and missionaries consisted mainly of tropical, heavily forested lands inhabited by primitive people, plants, and animals. This "exotic" image of Africa was reinforced by playwrights and literary figures such as William Shakespeare and Samuel Johnson as well as by an ever-growing collection of topographical maps and recorded details of geography, plants, animals, and indigenous populations. Europeans based many of their opinions on information provided by Portuguese geographers who detailed landmasses and the political, social, and economic structures of the coastal peoples they encountered. Given that such accounts were meant not just to inform but also to sell, authors often emphasized the odd and unusual aspects of the peoples they encountered—sometimes leading to the dissemination of misleading information about social or political customs.

Europeans' conceptions of Africans and Africa were not limited, however, to the sometimes outlandish accounts of a handful of adventurers; Europeans encountered Africans with increasing frequency on their own turf. In 1551 at least 10 percent of the 100,000 inhabitants of Lisbon, Portugal, were African slaves. Just forty years later the increase in the slave population and the number of black festivals dotting the calendar led many Portuguese to consider Lisbon as much a black city as a white one. Moreover, by the end of the sixteenth century it was clear to most Portuguese that being black meant being unfree. Such notions spread beyond the slave-trading states of Portugal, Spain, and the Netherlands, as families of nobility throughout Europe owned domestic slaves.

As slavery became more deeply embedded in European culture, partly because of economic benefits, racial attitudes toward Africans hardened. Slave laws in Barbados, colonial Virginia, and other colonies codified the notion that being black meant being a slave, bonded in the service of a master for life. By the eighteenth century tremendous wealth was being generated through the sale of sugar, tobacco, indigo, and other slave-produced crops, which called for further importation of slaves from West Africa. Jesuit and other Christian missionaries soon infiltrated the region, sending back their own descriptions of barbaric peoples who were well outside the realm of Christian civility. Such reports proved influential to the European mind; Africa and Africans were considered far removed from European concepts of civilization.

Georg Wilhelm Friedrich Hegel (1770–1831) introduced early ideas of scientific racism to the European mind. Hegel's theory of universal history suggested that "civilization" emanated from select powers who diffused their superior ways to lesser people—particularly to "degenerate" Africans. Hegel's work drew on the Hamitic hypothesis, further entrenching the idea that even the sundry civilized aspects of black African culture could only have been derived from outside sources, such as Europe, the Middle East, or Asia. By 1830 the image of Africa in the European mind was centered on notions of incivility and barbarism—a far cry from the high esteem once held by the Greeks and Romans for North African empires such as Egypt.

Africa to Africans and African Americans. Africans in the diaspora conceived of Africa in a variety of ways. Olaudah Equiano's account of his capture, enslavement, and subsequent emancipation provides critical insight into how Africans and African Americans conceived of their ancestral homelands. In his work, *The Interesting Narrative of the Life of Olaudah Equiano, or Gustavus Vassa, the African* (1789), Equiano describes Africa as a "charming fruitful vale" in which children played freely, with few adults around to restrict them. His vision of the continent is almost wholly positive, illustrating how some enslaved Africans idealized the land to which most were never to return. Africa for them was a paradise—an Eden from which they were snatched.

Africans in the diaspora also considered their continent to be a bottomless resource by the use of which to deal with the horrors of slavery; Africans drew upon traditional cultural practices for strength. Folklore, circle dancing, and naming patterns illustrated how slaves remained linked to their cultural past despite the many efforts by whites to eradicate such practices. Africans in the diaspora incorporated traditional cultural practices throughout their new lives, creating languages, for example, that were part English and part African. Invented languages empowered enslaved Africans in a way that little else could, keeping them inextricably linked to a continent that represented freedom.

For many Africans in the diaspora, Equiano's work was a unifying story of emancipation and financial success by a freed black man in the Atlantic world. Equiano's vision of an Eden-like Africa was quickly challenged, however, by whites in the Americas and Europe. They argued that Africa was known as the "dark continent" because of its lack of civilization; cannibals were believed to be widespread. By 1830 the patriarchs of the tightly controlled slave societies of the American South were so intent on concretely impressing such ideas on American slaves that many suggested blacks were better off living as slaves in America than being exposed to African cannibals.

Other freed black men emerged as leaders in the struggle against slavery and the marginalization of Africans and African Americans in the United States. In 1816–1817 Paul Cuffe, a wealthy mulatto merchant from New England, sailed for West Africa to establish coastal trade and to drop off some fifty-eight African American passengers who planned to resettle in the area near Sierra Leone, Great Britain's African colony. At the same time several powerful whites organized the American Colonization Society to promote the further colonization of West Africa by African Americans. For whites—especially southern planters and politicians—Africa had become a potential repository of sorts, where they could ship unruly, rebellious, or newly freed slaves; Africa represented a solution to the threat of slave insurrection. On the other hand, for black leaders such as Cuffe and James Forten, a prominent black businessman from Philadelphia, the colonization of West Africa offered a way for African Americans to repatriate their cultural and ancestral homeland. Cuffe remained interested in Africa as a source of trade as well, hoping to increase his business opportunities along the

Moorish woman in the Levant, from an engraving by Le Hay of 1713 that appeared in Charles de Ferriol's *Collection of Prints Representing the Costumes of Various Asian Nations*. Ferriol, the marquis of Argental, was the French ambassador to Constantinople from 1699 to 1709; he commissioned a Dutch artist, Jean Baptiste Vanmour, to create a hundred such pictures of people there, and the resulting collection was an influential source for artists of the "exotic." (© Historical Picture Archive/Corbis.)

West African coast. Suspicions of the various motivations behind the colonization movement quickly arose, causing many blacks and abolitionist leaders to speak out against it, arguing that it was another ploy to limit the opportunities and control the population of African Americans.

Slavery and racist ideologies shaped both white and black concepts of Africa. The commonly held concept of Africa was, at one time, filled with stories of technological, social, and political triumphs; the continent was the home of some of the most powerful empires and trading states in the ancient world. By the Middle Ages and the onset of the age of exploration in the fifteenth and sixteenth centuries, Europeans had inverted several centuries of admiration for the continent, instead focusing on its seemingly uncivilized non-Christian populations and elements. At the same time Europeans encountered sub-Saharan Africa on a level previously unknown; the region's dark-skinned, tribal peoples became the key commodity of the Atlantic slave trade. Elaborate religious and scientific justifications of slavery ensued, creating a portrait of a continent some believed to be mired in a primitive age. For enslaved Africans in the diaspora, Africa often represented the opposite: an oasis of culture that they were desperately trying not to lose.

Slavery had become so firmly entrenched in American life and politics by 1830 that for many it seemed unlikely the institution would ever end. Images of Africa were prevalent throughout the United States, injecting energy into the activities of African Americans and whites alike. From the antislavery movement, to mounting tensions on the floor of Congress over the expansion of slavery, to the increasing profiles of freedpeople, ideas of Africa were as complex and varied as the people who wrote, spoke, and sung about the land. Frederick Douglass, the best-known black critic of slavery, worked to free slaves and helped to shape the minds of millions of African Americans and their ideas of Africa. Many other freedpeople advanced ideas of Africa that in some cases resembled Douglass's and in others directly conflicted with the popular leader's vision. By 1895 Africa represented a homeland full of images and cultural traditions that fueled black America's quest for freedom as well as the era's burgeoning civil rights movement.

Africa or America? African Americans in the early Republic presented mixed conceptions of Africa. Debate raged between advocates of colonization in Africa and those African Americans who wished to remain in America to fight for their freedom. The American Colonization Society, founded in 1816 to promote resettlement along Africa's western coast, and Paul Cuffe, a wealthy mulatto merchant from New England, argued emphatically for colonization on the premise that African Americans could

find freedom on the continent of their ancestors. While Africa held the promise of freedom for blacks, for whites, especially prominent politicians such as Henry Clay and Andrew Jackson as well as southern planters, colonization resolved the question of what to do with the growing abundance of freed slaves. Newly freed black men and women not only began to compete with working-class whites for jobs but also raised concerns about the prospect of violence and revolt against the white population.

Colonization became a symbol of racist American society for many black leaders. Douglass, among others, believed that American blacks should stay in the country to fight for their freedom and rights rather than simply flee the degrading system. He spoke out against the various back-to-Africa movements that arose throughout the nineteenth century as well as against the Exoduster Movement, when large numbers of African Americans migrated from the South to Kansas in the 1880s. Douglass argued that African Americans should not be refugees in their own country; Africa was an ancestral homeland, not their current home. Other opponents of colonization who surfaced in the African American community also argued for black strength and unity. Peter Williams, one of the cofounders of the first black newspaper in the United States, *Freedom's Journal*, emerged as an activist adamantly against the movement, although he assisted the *Freedom's Journal* editor John Brown Russwurm's emigration to Liberia in 1829. Such leaders proved their mettle by organizing conferences, abolition societies, and other activities aimed at ending slavery. To them Africa represented a distant past that all blacks in the diaspora should be proud of, but not one that should hinder their efforts to free themselves and their brethren and to shape their own future in a liberal society.

Africa represented misguided and fruitless spirituality for Douglass, a man of strong Christian conviction. As evidenced in his first autobiography, *Narrative of the Life of Frederick Douglass*, he considered remnants of African spirituality in the African American community a nuisance that contributed to whites' perceptions of blacks as backward and something other than civilized. The Christianity of Christ, the true religion in his mind—as opposed to the Christianity of Land, the form practiced by slaveholders—offered slaves freedom through its "pure, peaceful and impartial" tenets. Douglass further advocated the notion that African Americans, once emancipated, had to participate in government and become full members of society to set out on a path to suffrage and equality. Nevertheless, many African Americans bought into the idea of Africa as their homeland. By 1847 repatriated African Americans lived in the country established on their behalf, Liberia, which was governed by blacks and supported, and funded, by the United States.

Africa on the Plantation. African Americans who lived on plantations held very different views of Africa and African culture than black leaders such as Douglass. For them, Africa remained a memory often passed down orally from other slaves. So-called tribalism and African spirituality, as derived from the variety of ethnicities that composed slave populations, combined to create multifaceted cultural traditions that anchored many African Americans to the continent. In Africa, ethnic rivalries were often divisive, sometimes sparking conflict and affecting the groups that participated in the Atlantic slave trade as both captors and captives. In America, on the other hand, ethnic divisions yielded to the horrific common experience of blacks under slavery. Common traditions, such as dance and folklore, were utilized by African Americans to combat slavery's harshness. In combining specific African cultural traditions and transforming them into the common expressions of spirituality that many historians argue formed the foundation of modern African American culture, slaves invoked ideas of their homeland to cope with their marginalized positions.

To whites, however, cultural expressions such as the circle dance were often viewed as examples of blacks' heathen, uncivilized past. Representative of the "Dark Continent," an increasingly popular characterization of Africa in the minds of whites, cultural practices derived from Africa were shunned—though often tolerated—by plantation owners. Indeed, slave owners embarked on campaigns to convince slaves that Africa was a land of cannibals and barbarism, not the land of hope and freedom of black folklore. Interviews conducted after Emancipation and the Civil War illustrate the effectiveness of such attempts; many former slaves related notions of Africa as "dark" and uncivilized. Widespread belief in Christianity among African Americans further strengthened slave owners' arguments, as they could contend that Africa lacked the "civilizing" force of Christianity. The interviews reveal that many former slaves were convinced of Africa's backwardness and imagined they were better off under slavery in America than in non-Christian Africa. Belief in the mystique of the "Dark Continent" persisted until the last of the former slaves died in the twentieth century.

Africa factored heavily into the literature of African Americans, with poets and essayists recalling the continent in romantic tones. Ethiopia appeared regularly as a symbol in popular nineteenth-century writing and art. In Eliza Harris's "Ethiopia" the place name appears as a metaphor for Africans throughout the diaspora, soon to be saved by Christian conversion and its civilizing influence, which would deliver the continent's "human tigers" from their hunting lifestyle. Harris draws on common notions of Africa as a land rife with barbarous peoples. In "Ode to Ethiopia" Paul Laurence Dunbar writes of a day when, through the hard work of Africans and blacks throughout the world, Africa will rise to power once again. Dunbar invokes Christianity and industrialization as Africa's saviors, also suggesting the common notion among whites and blacks of an uncivilized, non-Christian nineteenth-century Africa. In African American literature and art, Africa simultaneously reflected strength, hope, and unity and called out for help in becoming enlightened.

Ethiopianism aided African Americans trying to reconnect with their ancestral homeland and reconcile the meaning in being a marginalized population; Ethiopia stood as an uncolonized Christian state in Africa, reminding African Americans of the possibility of freedom. Moreover, Ethiopia reminded black Americans of the historical accomplishments of Africans through its connections to ancient Egypt. Thus, Ethiopia stood as a positive example of black liberation. The wider continent, however, was weakened by the Atlantic slave trade, largely ignored by Christian missionaries until the mid-nineteenth century, and left undeveloped by American and European powers—while nevertheless serving as a home to repatriated blacks in Sierra Leone and Liberia. All these competing ideas of Africa gained popularity while the European scramble for Africa occurred. In the late nineteenth- and early twentieth-century division of Africa among colonial powers, Christianity, industrialization, and literacy were finally impressed on Africa's population. Dunbar's vision of how to save Africa seemed to be coming to fruition, though not necessarily with the outcome the poet had envisioned.

Finding Freedom. After the Civil War, freed blacks pursued education and jobs in efforts to make the most of freedom. It became clear, however, that Jim Crow laws would prohibit African Americans from attaining full membership in society by restricting suffrage and other rights and activities. As part of a growing resistance movement, leading black activists invoked Africa as a symbol of freedom, characterizing the continent as a place to start anew. Many believed that the United States offered little hope for justice and that the only option was to return to Africa, the home of their ancestors. The costs and logistical problems associated with going back prohibited widespread adoption of the idea; however, some twelve to fifteen thousand African Americans did return.

By the 1860s and 1880s American expansionists urged the country to refocus efforts on Africa. Unlike westward expansion across North America, which featured the gaining of new territory while "civilizing" Native Americans, the United States sent missionaries to Africa to spread the Gospel to natives without attempting to capture the land. To white America, Africa was still a land of barbarous, murderous tribes who could only benefit from introduction to a superior Anglo-American culture. Moreover, in reshaping Africa, Americans believed they could prosper economically from new relationships while also extending the ideology of liberty. Such notions would later fuel American colonization in the Philippines.

The colonization movement provides insight into the consciousnesses of African Americans and their unique ideas of Africa. For those who migrated to Liberia, Africa represented hope, with a sense of wonder radiating from the shoreline as their eyes saw the coast for the first time, sending waves of giddiness over them as they thought about their prospective freedom; Africa appeared in black art, literature, and social movements as a highly stylized metaphor for freedom. Still, for most African Americans, Africa evoked powerful emotions beyond any real encounters with the continent.

One example of the complexity of African American ideas of Africa can be found in the writings of Martin Robeson Delany. Born in Virginia, he worked alongside the most prominent antebellum abolitionists, including Douglass and William Lloyd Garrison. Delany was active in promoting colonization as a way to rediscover the fatherland, arguing that it was African Americans' duty to enlighten the continent with respect to Christian ideals. Delany believed that only African Americans could deliver Africans from the "darkness" of superstition and ignorance—and only in returning to Africa could they find freedom. Later in the nineteenth and twentieth centuries, freeing Africa from Euro-American economic and political shackles became a key symbol of freedom for all blacks throughout the diaspora, under the guidance of leaders such as Marcus Garvey and Malcolm X.

As the nineteenth century neared its end, science and scientific thought weighed in on the nature of Africa and Africans. Africa surfaced in scholarly investigation as a once-civilized continent, rivaling the best of the ancient Mediterranean world. Racial classifications of the nineteenth century typically placed Africans on the lower rungs of the social and anthropological hierarchy. Yet, as Europeans and Americans infiltrated the continent and met resistance, these formidable foes in a supposedly inferior land raised questions regarding the sources of such skills and strength. Some intellectuals argued in favor of the Hamitic hypothesis, which traced all remnants of sophistication in African societies to previous contact with white cultures. Others countered such ideas by exploring the history of African kingdoms that were comparable to the great powers of European history.

In the 1880s and 1890s W. E. B. Du Bois pioneered the recovery of Africa's history by utilizing ethnographic methods to reveal what has since become a prominent theme in the study of the diaspora: that despite the many sophisticated and powerful societies of Africa's past, contemporary degradation of blacks resulted directly—and solely—from the Atlantic slave trade, which commenced after centuries of highly complex and politically powerful kingdoms rose and fell on the continent. To Du Bois, Africa remained stagnant once slaving began to "rape" the continent in 1600. As such, Africa represented a glorious past that had to be recovered in order for members of the diaspora to attain freedom.

The idea of Africa grew increasingly complex between 1830 and 1895. For many black Americans, the continent was a source of inspiration, hope, and cultural remembrance. For others, Africa represented the one shot at freedom they believed they had. Fueled by colonization schemes, several thousand African Americans returned to their ancestral homeland (though with some eventually returning to the United States), helping to establish the free state of Liberia. African Americans also viewed Africa as a symbol of freedom. Whether through images of past powerful African kingdoms or of biblical descriptions of Ethiopia, returning Africa to its former glory represented the path to freedom for many in the diaspora. On the other hand, in creating empowering notions of Africa in their minds, many African Americans were provided with the motivation to fight for freedom in the United States. Black leaders from Douglass to Du Bois spoke out against colonization and in favor of staying home—in America—to liberate the sons and daughters of over two hundred years of bondage.

[*See also* African Diaspora; Africanisms; American Colonization Society; Civil Rights; Clay, Henry; Colonialism; Colonization; Cuffe, Paul; Dance; Delany, Martin Robeson; Douglass, Frederick; Dunbar, Paul Laurence; Emancipation; Emigration to Africa; Equiano, Olaudah; Ethnology; Europe; Evolution; Exoduster Movement; Festivals; Folklore; Forten, James; Garrison, William Lloyd; Identity; Liberia; Missionary Movements; Muslims; Race, Theories of; Russwurm, John Brown; Skin Color; Slavery; Slave Trade; Stereotypes of African Americans *and* Visual Arts.]

BIBLIOGRAPHY

Ater, Renee. "Making History: Meta Warrick Fuller's 'Ethiopia.'" *American Art* 17.3 (Autumn 2003): 12–31. An interesting discussion of one prominent African American artist's vision of Africa. This article contains many useful insights into the nature and meaning of the term "Ethiopia."

Davidson, Basil. *Africa in History: Themes and Outlines*. New York: Collier, 1991. One of the most readable and concise works of African history; also valuable for insightful critiques of African historiography and a discussion of popular ideas of Africa.

Douglass, Frederick. *Narrative of the Life of Frederick Douglass, an American Slave*. New York: Anchor Books, 1989. A seminal work recounting the black abolitionist's experiences under slavery.

Du Bois, W. E. B. *Dusk of Dawn*. New York: Schocken Books, 1968. An early work by Du Bois demonstrating his profound intellectual abilities and his willingness to counter popular scholarly trends of the day.

Fage, J. D., and Roland Oliver, eds. *Cambridge History of Africa*. Vol. 4: *From c. 1600 to c. 1790*, edited by Richard Gray. New York: Cambridge University Press, 1975. Although in need of some updating, this volume employs top scholars in African history to present a thorough portrait of the continent.

Gates, Henry Louis, Jr., and Nellie Y. McKay, eds. *The Norton Anthology of African American Literature*. New York: Norton, 1996. A thorough, massive compilation.

Gilroy, Paul. *The Black Atlantic: Modernity and Double Consciousness*. Cambridge, MA: Harvard University Press, 1993. Explores identity in the transatlantic African diaspora.

Gomez, Michael A. *Exchanging Our Country Marks: The Transformation of African Identities in the Colonial and Antebellum South*. Chapel Hill: University of North Carolina Press, 1998. An innovative work that suggests the importance of shared experience in overcoming the trauma of slavery.

Litwack, Leon, and August Meier, eds. *Black Leaders of the Nineteenth Century*. Urbana: University of Illinois Press, 1988. An edited collection examining prominent African American social, intellectual, and political leaders of the nineteenth century.

Miller, Joseph C. "History and Africa/Africa and History." *American Historical Review* 104.1 (February 1999): 1–32. A thorough discussion of the development of Africa in the minds of whites, beginning with the nineteenth century.

Miller, Joseph C. *Way of Death: Merchant Capitalism and the Angolan Slave Trade, 1730–1830*. Madison: University of Wisconsin Press, 1988. A massive analytical and quantitative study of the Atlantic slave trade that focuses primarily on slaves from the Congo region of Africa.

Mudimbe, V. Y. *The Idea of Africa*. Bloomington: Indiana University Press, 1995. An innovative and provocative study of knowledge and meaning in Africa and among Africans.

Thompson, Vincent Bakpetu. *The Making of the African Diaspora in the Americas, 1441–1900*. White Plains, NY: Longman, 1987. A comprehensive examination of the creation of diaspora.

Thornton, John. *Africa and Africans in the Making of the Atlantic World, 1400–1800*. New York: Cambridge University Press, 1998. A controversial though informative examination of the transference of African culture to the Americas.

—JEFFREY A. FORTIN

AFRICAN AMERICANS AND THE WEST.

The black businessmen William Alexander Leidesdorff and Andres Pico were both born in 1810 with something the abolitionist Frederick Douglass and millions of other Africans in the Western Hemisphere could not claim: their fathers' names. Leidesdorff took that birthright from the Virgin Islands to the far ends of what was to be the United States: Hawaii and California. Pico was able to rise to the highest political and military offices in Alta California because members of his family had already served as military commanders and established their own ranches along the Pacific coast.

West was the direction of freedom for thousands of African Americans who labored long and hard in the abolition movement with Douglass or who simply sought to avoid the segregation prevalent within the boundaries of the United States. They found vast areas where blacks were not only welcomed but also were in command of physical, political, military, maritime, and economic resources. Allen Allensworth, George Washington Bush, Allen B. Light, Clara Brown, James P. Beckwourth, Mary Fields, Bridget "Biddy" Mason, Mary Ellen Pleasant, and Benjamin "Pap" Singleton all took various routes in seeking the freedom that the western frontier offered.

Hard on their trails was the advance of slavery, which closed the sanctuary of the Seminoles to the south by the 1830s. From 1840 to 1865 slavery also flowed into the former Mexican province of Texas. Indeed, slaveholders sought to push slavery into all parts of the West, but the head start that abolitionists and their allies established allowed them to make the West one of the deciding factors in the Civil War. Once it was discovered in California, gold, the metal that had fueled slavery for the previous 350 years, turned out to be the financial muscle behind the Union victory.

Western Sanctuary. Since 1528 Africans had roamed freely throughout the lands west of the Mississippi, beginning with the expeditions of Álvar Núñez Cabeza de Vaca into Texas, Arizona, and New Mexico and the sea journey of Juan Antonio Cabrillo to the San Diego and San Francisco bays in 1542. Hernán de Cortés's party of seven hundred conquistadors, which conquered the Aztecs in 1518, included three hundred Africans, most notably Juan Garrido, described as "the Black Conquistador." Cortés was seeking the "island nation" of California, as described in the 1510 epic by Garcia Rodríguez de Montalvo, *Las Serges de Esplandian*. In Montalvo's paradise the land was populated solely by black women, albeit the world's fiercest warriors.

Much of the demand for African slaves in the 1500s and 1600s came from the sharp decline in the Aztec population. The cleric Bartolomé de Las Casas called for Africans to be brought to work the *encomiendas*, or grants of land and people, helping to launch the notion of race with his arguments about "rational man." By the mid-1600s the slave rebellions led by Gaspar Yanga and others had converted the Mexican system into mission serfdom. By the time Leidesdorff landed in California, blacks constituted 40 percent of the *pobladores*, or settlers, in the missions along the coast and held the largest land grants in the province.

In 1831 Pio Pico, a descendant of one of the twenty-six blacks who made up the majority of the founders of Los

Angeles, succeeded the province's first black governor, Manuel Victoria, and opened up the territory to foreign visitors. Pico was an advocate of secularization and the removal of control of the land from the Catholic Church. With his brother Andres, Pico eventually gained 532,000 acres in Southern California, and other Picos held land as far north as the Napa Valley. Other large black landowners included Maria Rita Valdez, whose Rancho Rodeo de Aguas is now called Beverly Hills; Tiburcio Tapia, whose holdings included Malibu and Venice; and Manuel Nieto, who owned the area now known as Orange County.

Many seaborne blacks discovered that the West was a place where they could flourish. Allen B. Light left his ship in San Diego in the 1820s and there became the commissary general in charge of the otter trade. Most English-speaking black migrants came from the whaling ports of New England, such as New Bedford, Massachusetts—meaning that many of Douglass's closest allies became safely ensconced in the western frontier.

William Leidesdorff's Danish father left him a substantial inheritance and a network of wealthy contacts, including a New Orleans businessman who welcomed William at the age of eighteen into the cotton-brokering business. The stay in New Orleans ended abruptly with an engagement to the daughter of a prominent business leader; the night before the wedding, however, Leidesdorff confided that he was black, causing the woman to immediately cancel the wedding. Heartsick, he took the captaincy of a ship that sailed off to Hawaii. Once there, he traded sugar for hides from California. By 1841 he had recognized the commercial potential of the San Francisco harbor and built the first shipping warehouse, shipyard, hotel, and general store in what was then known as Yerba Buena. Michel Micheltorena, the governor of Alta California, took a liking to the Caribbean captain and gave him a land grant in the delta called Rancho Rio de Americano (modern Folsom). Leidesdorff also acquired forty-one lots in the Yerba Buena and East Bay properties (modern Oakland, Danville, and Lafayette).

Although America had treated him harshly, Leidesdorff thought his business would be enhanced if California became part of the United States; as such he entered politics, becoming vice consul under Thomas Larkin. Leidesdorff wrote the report for the State Department on the Bear Flag Revolt, took out loans to buy provisions for U.S. troops in the Mexican-American War, and welcomed the commodore Robert Field Stockton into his home, the largest in Yerba Buena, to mark the end of the war. Andres Pico, the last Mexican governor of Alta California, and Larkin signed the Treaty of Cahuenga, an armistice declaring the end of the war in California and preserving the land rights of the Californians. Two years later, on 25 March 1848, the business partner John Sutter wrote Leidesdorff: "We intend to form a company for working the Gold mines, which prove to be rich. Would you not take a share in it? So soon as if it would not pay well, we could stop it at any time."

Ten days later Leidesdorff opened the first public school in California as chairman of the school committee. Soon thereafter he died, reportedly of an infection. He would have undoubtedly been in the catbird seat for capitalizing on the gold rush and such future developments as the transcontinental railroad. Regardless, the Leidesdorff estate was assessed at $1.4 million in 1854, but the captain John Folsom, a quartermaster in the U.S. Army, was able to buy it from Leidesdorff's mother for an unjust $50,000.

Before 1830 only the truly intrepid had taken the land trek across the continent. A slave named York led the explorers Meriwether Lewis and William Clark to Oregon in 1804. The frontiersmen Peter Ranne and James P. Beckwourth were part of the Ashley-Smith expedition from 1822 to 1824, which sought a central route to the Pacific.

By the 1840s miners, minstrels, and merchants were beginning to spread across the West. Gold and silver were the lures that sparked major migrations. In the annals of practically every state are the names of early African American pioneers who lived in the most remote locales, as certain occupations were reserved exclusively for blacks, such as serving as barbers or Pullman car porter. The evidence of their everyday status is the presence of seminal African American churches dating back to the 1850s in locales as far-flung as Sacramento, California; Great Falls, North Dakota; and Butte, Montana.

After the Civil War black military men, such as buffalo soldiers, and black cowboys cleared the way for the large-scale settlement of the West. Increasing numbers of whites then led to harsher discrimination against blacks and reduced the power of their traditional Native American allies and the extant Spanish-speaking mixed-race communities throughout the region.

Western Fights for Justice. After 1820 every state that joined the Union encountered the question of whether it would be a slave or free state. Kansas, Nebraska, and Missouri offered previews of the Civil War, as violent clashes between proslavery and abolitionist forces put settlers in danger. Furthermore, the territories of Missouri, Utah, Arizona, Oregon, Montana, and Idaho all considered anti-immigration laws banning blacks from becoming residents; Oregon passed such a law in 1857.

The five thousand blacks in California put up an especially vigorous fight against the anti-immigration proposal of the governor Peter Burnett after losing battles over three other types of discriminatory laws; suffrage and the right to testify against whites had already been taken away from African Americans, Native Americans, and Asians by the first California legislature. On 22 March 1857 the California legislature reported receiving petitions from black residents in the counties of Amador, Butte, Sacramento, Shasta, Siskiyou, Yolo, El Dorado, Mariposa, Nevada, Placer, San Francisco, and Sierra requesting the end of the law usurping blacks' right of testimony. The law had driven hundreds of black merchants from the San Francisco waterfront after a vicious attack on Peter Lester by a white shoplifting suspect, which drew no prosecution because Lester, a prosperous boot-shop owner, could not testify. In 1854 that same law had been used to prevent Leidesdorff's mother from testifying against John Folsom in the probate case that passed Leidesdorff's fortune into Folsom's hands. By 1863 the law restricting the right of testimony had been reversed in California.

Behind the scenes in the 1850s, Mary Ellen Pleasant, a former Underground Railroad conductor, provided some of the financial muscle behind the freedom struggle. Having grown wealthy from operating boardinghouses for miners in San Francisco, she hired escaped slaves to work in her properties and underwrote the legal defense of Archy Lee, a fugitive who asserted his freedom once he arrived in California. Pleasant also raised thirty thousand dollars from San Francisco blacks to help pay for the raid by John Brown at Harpers Ferry, Virginia. She also won a lawsuit in 1868 outlawing segregation on streetcars.

George Washington Bush told a fellow traveler in Idaho that he was going to Oregon to experience freedom. When he arrived there in 1845, he found that the state had passed an antiblack immigration law. Bush then settled near Olympia in a place called Platte, becoming one of the first settlers in what is now the state of Washington. As more settlers followed Bush, American claims to the area caused Great Britain to recognize the forty-ninth parallel as the international border between the United States and Canada and to withdraw claims to the Oregon Territory. Once the Washington Territory was organized, Bush's farm flourished, yet he was ruled ineligible to keep it because the Donation Land Act, which codified the distribution of land to settlers, only applied to whites and "half-breeds." The territorial governor unsuccessfully petitioned Congress to let Bush keep the farm and to receive full citizenship and the right to vote.

Mining, Merchants, Ministry, Military, and Minstrelsy. Gold was an important symbol of wealth and majesty to Africans because of its widespread use on the West African coast; the pilgrimage of the Songhay Empire ruler Mansa Musa to Mecca in 1332 was one of the events that led Europeans to explore the coast of Africa and was perhaps a catalyst for Montalvo's story of the island of California.

Khalifa, or "wise ruler," was the title that Musa was given by Muslim scholars in Mecca. African Americans were just as excited as other Americans when news came of gold discoveries in the West—first in California in 1848, then in British Columbia in 1857, Colorado in 1858, Idaho in 1860, Montana in 1862, and South Dakota in 1874.

Geographic features with names such as Negro Gulch and Negro Bar in the Sacramento River delta pointed out the presence of black miners. Moses Rodgers was the superintendent of a mine in Hornitos from 1869 to 1882 and was regarded as the finest metallurgist in the state. A. E. Coleman is credited with discovering gold in Julian, near San Diego; Henry Parker is credited with discovering gold in Idaho Springs, Colorado. Articles of incorporation for black-owned mining companies include Nil Desperandum Mining Company in San Francisco in 1863; Rare Ripe Gold and Silver Mining Company in Marysville, California, in 1864; and Elevator Silver Mining Company in 1869, which wished to "engage in mining in White Pine Camp, Nevada." Junius Lewis, born a slave in Mississippi in 1842, owned claims in Boulder, Colorado, through the 1920s in his Golden Chest Mining, Milling, and Tunnel Company.

The changes in fortune brought about by gold mining could be stunning. In 1860 thirty black miners in Virginia City, Nevada, reportedly sent money back to their former slave masters, who were poverty stricken because of the Civil War. The black miners did not stop at the Pacific coast. When the call of the gold rush came from Australia and Alaska, they set off for those shores as well.

Although some were able to hold on to gold diggings, it was more frequent that blacks in the West provided service businesses in or near mining communities. During San Francisco's gold rush more than one hundred black merchants worked on the waterfront as operators of express package-shipping outlets, lumberyards, printing shops, retail stores, hotels, laundries, newspapers, and barber shops. In 1855 the initial Colored Convention in California noted that blacks had accumulated $2 million.

Mary Ellen Pleasant accumulated a fortune estimated at $30 million by the 1880s and assisted many other black entrepreneurs while making large donations to black colleges back in the South. Stephen Bickford owned the water system in Virginia City, Montana. The Workingmen's Joint Stock Association of Portland, Oregon, organized mostly by African Americans, established a real estate business in 1869. Bridget "Biddy" Mason was brought west from Utah by Mormon slaveholders but gained her freedom by saving money earned doing odd jobs. She received her manumission papers in 1856 and moved to Los Angeles, where she cannily acquired $250,000 in property along Broadway. Clara Brown walked six hundred miles from Missouri to the goldfields at Central City, Colorado, in 1859 to look for her husband and three children, who had been sold by her second slave owner. She started a laundry business, began the first Sunday school and church in the area, and raised ten thousand dollars by the end of the Civil War. With those funds she was able to return to Kentucky and find thirty-two family members. She found her last remaining daughter in Council Bluffs, Iowa, in 1882. The stagecoach operator Mary Fields was a six-foot gunslinger who "broke more noses than any other person in central Montana; so claims the *Great Falls Examiner*, the only newspaper available in Cascade at the time." She also became an entrepreneur running a mail-delivery service.

With increased black populations came the rise of black churches. Barney Fletcher is credited with founding the first black church on the Pacific Coast; he established Saint Andrews African Methodist Episcopal (AME) Church in Sacramento in November 1850. Another AME congregation was established in St. Louis that same year. San Francisco became the home of three black churches: Third (First Colored) Baptist Church, the oldest black Baptist church on the West Coast; Bethel AME Church; and First (Saint Cyprian) AME Zion Church. These churches were the heart of the cultural and political activity of their communities, sponsoring classical music performances, plays, and parades and raising money for the abolitionist movement. By the time the California conference of the AME Church convened in September 1863, AME churches existed in Nevada, Idaho, Oregon, Washington, California, and British Columbia. The Colorado conference included churches in Montana and the Dakotas. The link between entrepreneurship and church formation is unmistakable. One of Bridget Mason's first priorities in Los Angeles was to assist in the formation of First AME Church in 1872.

Many African Americans who found their way West were part of the military. Ignacio Miramonte was commandant of the Presidio at Yerba Buena from 1838 to 1844, when Leidesdorff first sailed into San Francisco Bay. It was not uncommon for blacks to command military posts in Alta California. José Maria Pico, the father of Pio and Andres Pico, was the majordomo of San Luis Obispo in the 1790s. Emanuel Victoria, the first black governor of Alta California in 1830, had the rank of lieutenant colonel in the Mexican army. Andres Pico took the rank of general during the Mexican-American War and was third in command of all Mexican forces.

Once the U.S. Congress allowed blacks to enlist in the Union army in 1862, western blacks rushed to join. Nine regiments of the U.S. Colored Troops were raised from Missouri, Kansas, Iowa, and Arkansas. The Eighty-seventh Regiment, raised from Louisiana, served in Texas. In the Union navy eighteen black sailors served from

Texas, seven from California—including two thirteen-year-olds from San Francisco—and one each from North Dakota, Utah, and Iowa.

One of the most critical decisions in American history was the refusal to allow the 180,000 black soldiers who fought for the Union to serve in the South after the end of the Civil War—a decision that essentially left southern African Americans defenseless. Almost all of the colored troops were hastily demobilized, and to assuage southern whites, the six remaining regiments—out of nearly 150—were assigned to the West.

On 28 July 1866 Congress passed bills to form the all-black Ninth and Tenth Cavalry Regiments, and Thirty-eighth, Thirty-ninth, Fortieth, and Forty-first Infantry Regiments. In 1869 the infantry regiments were consolidated into the Twenty-fourth and Twenty-fifth Infantry Regiments. The ten thousand black soldiers were mainly stationed in the West, where they took on the duty of protecting settlers from Native Americans and robbers, building roads, laying cable, and protecting national forests. The forts in which they resided were as far-flung as Wyoming and the Presidio in San Francisco. Allen Allensworth, who served in the navy during the Civil War, reenlisted and was sworn in as a chaplain to serve the "Buffalo Soldiers," as the Native Americans christened the black military men of the West. Allensworth, one of the few black officers, rose to the rank of lieutenant colonel, the highest rank attained by an African American in the nineteenth century. Because many of his soldiers were illiterate, he undertook the task of teaching them to read; the strategies he devised still shape the army's educational philosophy today. Allensworth presented a paper on the army's educational system to the National Education Association in 1882.

Fifteen buffalo soldiers earned the Medal of Honor for their service in the Indian campaigns, for battles in New Mexico, Texas, Arizona, and Colorado. The first black West Point graduate, Lieutenant Henry O. Flipper, was assigned to the Ninth Cavalry. When Alaska became part of the United States, Captain Michael Healy, the highest-ranking black sailor in the Revenue Cutter Service, which sailed out of Oakland, became the military governor of Alaska. When he retired in 1903, he was the third-ranking officer in the service, which was the forerunner to the U.S. Coast Guard. Also sailing from Oakland was the whaling captain William Shorey, described as "Black Ahab." He was to be the last whaling captain to operate from the Pacific Coast.

One other factor that spread African Americans widely throughout the western frontier was music. An 1849 writer noted that "Ethiopian airs" were the most popular form of music in the mining camps of California. A monument to the 1880s-era California Theater on Bush Street in downtown San Francisco shows minstrel performers with distinctively black hair and features. Many such performers were initially whites performing in blackface, but toward the end of the nineteenth century an increasing number of blacks played those roles. Many minstrel-show performers then transitioned into the ragtime and jazz music that evolved in the next century. Opera and symphonies were also popular among black communities throughout the West. The Sacramento prodigies Anna Madah Hyers and Emma Louise Hyers had the opera *Urlina, the African Princess* written for their debut in San Francisco in 1872.

All-Black Towns and Western Reconstruction. John Horse, a Seminole leader, created one of the first all-black towns, Wewoka, in the 1840s in Indian Territory (present-day Oklahoma) before leading his band of mixed-race African Americans and Native Americans into Mexico to escape slavers. Edwin P. McCabe, a former state auditor of Kansas, sought to turn Indian Territory into a haven for blacks and encouraged migration from Kansas to Oklahoma. One of his legacies was the town of Langston, where Langston University was formed. Benjamin "Pap" Singleton was part of a movement to form all-black towns such as Nicodemus in Kansas in the 1870s. Mifflin Wistar Gibbs returned from British Columbia to join the movement and was sworn in as the first federal judge in Oklahoma. By 1891, 137,000 blacks were living in such all-black towns in the West. At least fifty such towns were organized in Oklahoma and Kansas between 1865 and 1920. Deerfield, Colorado, was an all-black town in that mining district that eventually became a ghost town.

In 1831 Pio Pico was the *jefe politico*, or "political chief," of Alta California. By the 1880s he was barely holding on to the vast reserves of land granted him during Mexican rule. His hotel, the Pico House, built in 1868, was considered the finest in the Southwest. It was the first three-story building in Los Angeles and the first with a steel frame. He had also taken an interest in Los Angeles's first oil well. But in failing health, with declining eyesight, he signed what he thought was a mortgage; the document was later interpreted as a deed to all of his land holdings, and Pico was unceremoniously evicted from his properties. Like Pico, Mary Ellen Pleasant was beset with legal battles, in her case with the senator William Sharon. Many of her extensive holdings were taken away by persons with whom she had stashed titles in order to avoid property restrictions for women.

By the 1880s in California, which had had four black governors under Mexican rule, a janitor's post at the state capitol in Sacramento was considered a high-status position for blacks. Pearly Munroe, who held that position, bought the land where Sutter's Mill stood in a tax sale.

He held on to that historic site for nearly sixty years, until the state bought it from him to convert it into a state historic park.

Captain Harry Dean, a descendant of the New England sailmaker Paul Cuffe, left California in 1870 on a voyage to Africa to create a colony of expatriated African Americans; Dean and a number of other African American pioneers of the West decided to tell their own stories. In 1907 the desperado Nat "Deadwood Dick" Love published his autobiography, *The Life and Adventures of Nat Love*, which covered his exploits in Texas, Arizona, Kansas, Nebraska, South Dakota, and Colorado. In *Shadow and Light*, Mifflin Wistar Gibbs, Peter Lester's partner in the boot store from the San Francisco gold rush era, tells of travels to British Columbia and his return to the United States to become the first black federal judge in Oklahoma and later a diplomat. In *The Long Old Road*, the Seattle resident Ho-

Nat Love, an African American cowboy. He claimed that his skill at roping earned him the nickname Deadwood Dick in South Dakota in 1876. This photograph is from his privately published autobiography of 1907. (© Bettmann/Corbis.)

race R. Cayton describes his role in the development of the Northwest. The black newspapers of the period are valuable resources regarding the normalcy of black life throughout the West. *Mirror of the Times*, *Pacific Appeal*, and *San Francisco Elevator* carried dispatches from throughout the area from their San Francisco bases.

William Leidesdorff and Andres Pico had competing visions of how to advance freedom in the West; both refused to accept the limitations of race. The history of the West is replete with examples of African Americans who equated the wide-open spaces with the freedom to excel. Just as the civil rights pioneers of the 1850s preceded the Reconstruction-era amendments, the western backlash against African Americans presaged the return of Jim Crow laws across the South. Black explorers, soldiers, sailors, miners, entrepreneurs, and laborers helped win the West for America, but they entered the twentieth century without having completely won their own freedom.

[*See also* African Methodist Episcopal Church; Black Church; Black Press; Brown, John; Buffalo Soldiers; Civil War; Civil War, Participation and Recruitment of Black Troops in; Douglass, Frederick; Harpers Ferry Raid; Jim Crow Car Laws; Mexican-American War; Minstrel Shows; Music; Native Americans and African Americans; Slavery; Underground Railroad; *and* Union Army, African Americans in.]

BIBLIOGRAPHY

Abajian, James de T., ed. *Blacks and Their Contributions to the American West: A Bibliography and Union List of Library Holdings through 1970*. Boston: G. K. Hall, 1974.

Aguirre Beltrán, Gonzalo. *La población negro de México, 1519–1810: Estudio, etno-histórico* [The Black Population of Mexico, 1519–1810: An Ethnohistoric Study]. Edited by Juan Alberto Barragan. Mexico City: D. F. Ediciones Fuente cultural, 1946.

Beckwourth, James P. *The Life and Adventures of James P. Beckwourth: Mountaineer, Scout, and Pioneer, and Chief of the Crow Nation of Indians*. New York: Harper and Brothers, 1856.

Beller, Jack. "Negro Slaves in Utah." *Utah Historical Society Quarterly* 4.2 (October 1929): 122–126.

Cayton, Horace R. *The Long Old Road*. New York: Trident Press, 1964.

Dean, Harry. *The Pedro Gorino: The Adventures of a Negro Sea-Captain in Africa and the Seven Seas in His Attempts to Find an Ethiopian Empire*. Boston: Houghton Mifflin, 1929.

Gibbs, Mifflin Wistar. *Shadow and Light: An Autobiography*. New York: Arno Press, 1968.

Harvey, June Rose. "Negroes in Colorado." *Colorado Magazine* 5.26 (April 1949): 165–175.

Hill, David G., Jr. "The Negro in Oregon: A Survey." Master's thesis, University of Oregon, 1932.

Love, Nat. *The Life and Adventures of Nat Love, Better Known in the Cattle Country as "Deadwood Dick."* Los Angeles, 1907.

Nakayama, Antonio. "California Pioneers from Sinaloa, Mexico." *Pacific Historian* 5.13 (Spring 1969): 66–69.

Templeton, John William, ed. *Our Roots Run Deep: The Black Experience in California*. 4 vols. N.p.: ASPIRE Books, 1991.

U.S. Department of Defense. *Black Americans in Defense of Our Nation: A Pictorial Documentary of the Black American Male and Female Participation and Involvement in the Military Affairs of the United States of America*. Washington, DC: U.S. Government Printing Office, 1991.

U.S. War Department. *The Negro in the Military Service of the United States, 1639–1886*. Washington, DC: National Archives, n.d.

—JOHN WILLIAM TEMPLETON

AFRICAN DIASPORA. [*This entry contains two subentries dealing with the African diaspora, from the origins of slave trade through nineteenth-century America. The first article focuses on the evolution and criticism of the diaspora, while the second article focuses on the cultural effects of this forced transatlantic migration.*]

The Origins of the African Diaspora through the Nineteenth Century

The concept of the African diaspora is a late-twentieth-century construct that historians and other scholars use to describe the flood of people out of Africa starting in the mid-fifteenth century and extending through the four hundred years that followed. During those long centuries the slave trade drained the African continent of millions of its inhabitants and transported them to every corner of the globe. The definition of the term *diaspora* is the scattering or dispersal of a people or culture to other lands or across the globe as a consequence of migration or exile. The forced emigration of millions of Africans, representing scores of peoples, certainly constitutes one of the most striking examples of this phenomenon. From the fifteenth through the nineteenth centuries, slave traders transported unprecedented numbers of captives to be sold into slavery and servitude throughout the known world. By the time most countries outlawed the international slave trade in the nineteenth century, forced emigrants had reached all the continents except Antarctica. This transportation, which began as a trickle in the second quarter of the fifteenth century, reached floodlike proportions by the mid-1700s.

Origins of Enslavement and the Slave Trade. There is no doubt that trade of Africans as slaves occurred prior to the initiation of the Atlantic slave trade in the sixteenth century. The focuses of these older systems of dispersal and trade were generally trans-Saharan, and the networks spread with the expansion of Islamic empires during the medieval period. The consequence of this trade was the transport of enslaved Africans across North Africa, down the east coast of the continent, into the Levant and other parts of southwestern Asia as well as the Balkans and parts of eastern and central Europe, and around the Mediterranean rim. Trade caravans moving across the Sahara contained West African slaves, prized since the ninth century for their metalworking and agricultural skills. By the advent of the fifteenth century African slaves were not uncommon in the Near East and Middle East, eastern Europe, and the trading states bordering the Mediterranean and Black seas. Along the Indian Ocean the dispersal of African slaves tended to follow the sea routes employed by Arab merchants.

Before the expansion of the Atlantic slave trade, the processes of African enslavement mirrored those of Europe and Asia. People of all three continents recognized three traditional methods by which people enslaved others. The majority of those enslaved lost their freedom as a consequence of war. Prisoners of war captured during a conflict frequently were sold into slavery. Raiding and kidnapping swelled the numbers of such captives and had the added benefits of a relatively low mortality rate among the raiding faction and the demoralization of the enemy. Some weaker tribes and states, preferring to sidestep the brutalities of open warfare and such raids, opted to simply pay tribute, in the form of slaves, to stronger neighbors.

Enslavement was also an outcome of legal or judicial action. In many regions crimes that could be punished by death were commuted to sale into permanent servitude. Slavery as a punishment frequently resulted from crimes involving adultery and the supernatural. Such infractions often culminated in the levying of a fine, generally equal to the cost of a slave, and those unable to pay were seized and sold. A case involving the wrongful death of another required compensation in the form of a slave. Debt was also a violation carrying the sentence of slavery. "Panyarring" was an extralegal practice in which a creditor could detain or kidnap and then sell a person responsible for an unredeemed debt. In some cases an entire family could be held responsible for the wrongs of one member and suffer the same punishment. The third method of enslavement was voluntary. In times of great political, economic, and social dislocation the number of such volunteers increased. Parents sold children they could not feed, whether the shortages resulted from abject poverty or famine. Others submitted to enslavement to escape personal threats, political or religious persecutions, or impending punishments for alleged crimes.

With the advent of the Atlantic trade, pressure to increase the number of slaves for purchase by European and American traders rocketed. Slavers in West Africa met some of the demand by refocusing the trade on port cities rather than the trans-Saharan markets. They compensated for the rest by increasing their exploitation of the traditional sources. Rigorous debate exists among scholars concerning the role of warfare in this process. Some contend that the Atlantic slave trade distorted the causes of wars, making their sole purpose the accumulation of slaves for the Atlantic markets, while other scholars argue that the trade only refocused the consequences of traditional warfare.

Origins of Enslaved Peoples. Any discussion of the African diaspora must include mention of where its subjects originated. The majority of slaves forced to leave Africa from the mid-1400s through the mid-1800s came from the continent's west coast. Starting just above Cape Verde in the north and west of the continent and running in a curve that extended southwest, then due west around the Gulf of Guinea, then south through Angola, cities sprang up primarily to facilitate a growing trade with Europe and later the Americas. Although this trading area had many resources, including gold, slaves were one of its major commodities. Trade ports along the west coast acted as conduits for slaves gathered from the hinterlands to be shipped out of Africa.

Most of the captives destined for the slave markets originated in areas not directly on the coast but rarely more than several hundred miles into the interior. The populations of cities such as Benin and Elmira and their leaders profited greatly from the proceeds of the trade and from control of European-style goods such as guns and alcohol. Although slaves gathered for the Atlantic trade represented virtually every region in Africa, more than 95 percent traced their origins to this area. For example, in the sixteenth century the exceptions hailing from the east coast of the continent were represented by a relative few from East Africa, Melin (assumed to be Malindi), Mozambique (the island capital, not the later Portuguese colony of the same name), and the region occupied by the Xhosa in the southeast. About 30 percent of the enslaved passed through ports on the Windward Coast, approximately 43 percent originated in the territories along the gulf of Guinea's Gold and Slave coasts, and the remaining 25 percent were funneled through Angola. In 1982 the historian Paul Lovejoy estimated that European and American slave ships carried approximately 11,698,000 Africans across the Atlantic into territories unknown to them. Basing his figures on research done earlier by the historian Philip Curtin, Lovejoy suggested that nearly 9,778,500 of those transported Africans were sold into slavery in the Americas and Caribbean.

Colonization and Slave Labor. The first break with the traditional slave-trading patterns in Africa occurred in the 1440s and coincided with the growth of European exploration and colonization. In 1441 a Portuguese vessel captained by Antam Goncalvez ventured along the Guinea coast of West Africa. When he returned to Portugal, Goncalvez brought with him ten African captives as a curiosity for his king. Three years later another Portuguese trading ship returned to its homeport carrying an additional 235 slaves to be sold in Europe. The change from oddity to cheap labor source took place when Europeans, bent on territorial exploration, conquest, and colonization, discovered the value of cultivating cash crops like sugarcane, coffee, rice, and indigo. African slaves—used first on Portuguese island holdings in the Atlantic, including the Madeira, Canary, and Azore islands—provided the intensive labor needed to cultivate those crops. Europeans rarely volunteered for transport to these locations except in supervisory positions.

The true increase in demand occurred as the Spanish, Portuguese, English, French, Dutch, and Danish carved out colonies in the Caribbean and America. The need for a captive labor force continued to accelerate throughout the nineteenth century. Although the European settlers first attempted to use Native Americans as laborers on their rapidly expanding plantations, the indigenous inhabitants had unfortunate habits that made their prolonged use difficult, if not impossible: they tended to escape or to succumb to European-borne infectious diseases. African slaves replaced native labor.

Spanish monarchs granted the first official license for the trade in slaves in 1518. Called the *Asiento*, the license granted to the holder the exclusive right to trade in slaves within Spanish domains. Charles I authorized the first license to Lorenzo de Gomenot, who guaranteed to transport four thousand African slaves per year to Spanish holdings in the Caribbean. At one time or another, representatives of Genoa, Portugal, the Netherlands, and Venice, among others, held *Asientos*.

Other European nations approached the slave trade in less restrictive ways and obtained slaves by all necessary means, up to and including piracy. The result of the tremendous demand was the forced immigration of 293,400 Africans to the Americas between 1451 and 1600. Between 1601 and 1700, as the participation in European imperialism expanded, another 1,494,600 individuals were transported. The waves of humanity drained out of Africa reached their peaks during the period between 1701 and 1810, when 5,737,600 persons were involuntarily enslaved and bound for the Americas. This had a direct correlation to the expansion of cash-crop agriculture and the movement of Creole populations into territories previously held by indigenous peoples. The distribution of Africans across the Americas was uneven. Brazil netted by far the greatest number of African slaves, importing 3,464,800. The slaveholders in Spanish, French, and English Caribbean holdings acquired 1,552,100, 1,600,200, and 1,665,000 Africans, respectively. The Dutch and Danish plantation economies in the Caribbean consumed another 500,000 and 28,000 in imports, respectively. Slavers

also shipped 339,000 slaves to ports on the North American mainland and 175,000 to the Old World.

Nineteenth-Century Diaspora. Although most nations in the Americas, beginning with the newly independent Haiti in 1804, banned the transatlantic trade in slaves during the opening decades of the nineteenth century, the African diaspora continued. Spanish and Portuguese colonies, such as Cuba and Brazil, found ways to avoid the bar and continued to import slave laborers from Africa until well past the middle of the nineteenth century. The diaspora continued in other ways as well. For example, in the United States the domestic slave trade flourished as cashcrop agriculture extended westward. The spread of cotton plantations across the Appalachians and into the Old South, the West, and Texas is representative of this phenomenon. On the mainlands of North America and South America, slaves ventured into the continents' interiors along with their masters. Many Africans and their American-born descendants who found or seized their freedom fled to the margins of civilization to carve out new lives for themselves and their offspring. Maroon settlements in the Caribbean and free black communities in the Ohio territories are indicative of this phenomenon.

Perhaps the most unusual manifestations of the continuing African diaspora were the colonization movements of the late eighteenth and nineteenth centuries. In 1787 the English resettled in Sierra Leone former slaves from North America and the West Indies who had sought refuge in England after the American Revolution. A few years later black immigrants from Nova Scotia and Maroons exiled from Jamaica joined the settlement in Sierra Leone. In the 1820s agents of the American Colonization Society sponsored freed slaves from the American South and established the state of Liberia, which became the first independent republic in Africa in 1847. Former slaves, or *emancipados*, and free persons of color from South America also joined in this repatriation movement during the nineteenth century, settling largely in Yorubaland (Nigeria).

Although nineteenth-century Americans would not have used the term *diaspora*, they were familiar with the concept. Southern slaveholders and their sympathizers used a variety of arguments to justify the initial enslavement of Africans and their right to exploit the American-born descendants of those first slaves. Since the incursions of the Portuguese in the fifteenth century, Christian Europeans rationalized the enslavement and transportation of Africans to foreign lands on the ground of faith. Simply put, slavery was God's work because it provided the opportunity to Christianize the heathens and infidels of Africa. By the 1800s slavery also allowed white masters to oversee the moral conduct of their charges. Nineteenth-century apologists also employed scientific arguments to justify the diaspora. They claimed that the white race was physically, economically, politically, and culturally superior to persons of color. Economic concerns also played a significant role in the defense of slaveholding. Slave owners perceived attempts to discredit the trade and possession of African slaves as a direct attack on what they claimed as private and personal property.

American Critics of Diaspora. The critics of slavery found little of value in the justifications of slaveholders and employed a range of moral and ethical arguments against the slave trade, the enslavement of Africans, and the continued holding of their descendants in states of permanent bondage. Abolitionists, black and white, found the trade repugnant and voiced their concerns about the "morality" of African enslavement, the continuation of the transatlantic trade, and the growth of the domestic slave trade. Frederick Douglass took a particularly strong stand.

On 20 July 1849, in an article entitled "The Slave Trade," Douglass's newspaper the *North Star* reprinted the "Tenth Annual Report of the B. & F. A. S. [British and Foreign Anti-Slavery Society]," which suggested that the horrors of the international slave trade far exceeded those of the domestic trade. The report quoted the late Sir T. F. Buxton:

> "For every slave embarked one is sacrificed"—in the wars connected with their capture—in their march from the interior to the coast, and during their detention at the barracoons—we have a picture presented to us of human guilt and human suffering, which has scarcely its parallel in the most savage period of the history of our race.

On 26 October 1851 *Frederick Douglass' Paper* ran an excerpt from a *London Daily Times* article that clearly illustrated the evils of the slave trade in particular and slavery in general. The article, which cited "a few brief extracts from a very able speech made by Lord Palmerston at Tiverton," stated, "It was indisputable that the crimes committed in regard to African slavery and the African slave trade had been greater in amount than all the crimes ever committed by the whole human race from the beginning of the world until now." Nineteenth-century Americans clearly contemplated the morality of the process of enslavement and the institution of slavery with the aid of Douglass and other like-minded advocates.

During the 1840s and 1850s abolitionist papers, particularly those affiliated with or sponsored by Douglass, also ran an avid campaign against the illegal, but prospering transatlantic slave trade between West Africa and Spanish Cuba and Portuguese Brazil. On 3 April 1851 the *North Star* provided information from a report written by the American minister in Rio de Janeiro, a Mr. Tod, which confirmed that more than forty-five thousand Africans had been transported to Brazil by slavers during the past

year. Tod stated in the report, "More or less of every cargo are murdered on the voyage, and the survivors are too often used as mere beasts of burden." The report implied that much of the trade employed American-built ships and flew under the United States flag. On 8 September 1854 an editorial in *Frederick Douglass' Paper* accused New York merchants of regularly engaging in the trade in slaves between West Africa and Cuba in spite of legal prohibitions against it and pointed to the U.S. government's awareness of such commerce. "The imbecility of the federal officials on this subject is absolutely incredible," the editorial stated.

Abolitionists reserved their harshest criticism, however, for the continuing African diaspora in America and those that permitted or participated in it. For example, abolitionists condemned as hypocritical legislation that banned the international trade in slaves but permitted the same commerce within the nation's borders. As early as 7 November 1828, critics voiced concerns over the domestic trade in *Freedom's Journal*, the first black-owned and operated newspaper in the United States. The paper, edited by Samuel E. Cornish and John B. Russwurm, reported that a vessel had sailed from New York City bound for New Orleans carrying an estimated two hundred slaves meant for sale, and it called on readers to do their duty as "Christians and Republicans" to oppose it. The author, identified simply as G. U. E., stated, "It wants nothing but a little concert to render this traffic as odious as that pursued by those on the coast of Africa, for in the eyes of justice they are one and the same." Frederick Douglass and as other antislavery advocates also voiced strong criticism of federal legislation they felt encouraged the propagation of slavery in the West. On 18 July 1850—on the advent of the Compromise of 1850, which allowed the spread of slavery south of 36°30′ in the newly acquired Mexican territories—the *North Star*, in an article called "The Divine and Republican Institution," reprinted an advertisement from a Richmond paper that Douglass felt characterized all that was wrong with the current system:

> Negroes! Negroes!—One Hundred Virginia Negroes will be in our mart about the 25th February next. Our partner, Thomas Dickens, started from Richmond on the 1st inst. We say to our friends and customers, if they will have patience and not buy until the drove arrives, they shall have the best negroes, to work their next crop of cotton, that have ever been purchased in this market. Among the lot there is a few choice house servants and cooks for the city trade. Our motto is, quick sales and short profits. We also will pay the highest market price for Negroes brought to our mart for sale. Persons visiting our city with Negroes will do well to see us before selling.

The article criticized the "slaveites, with Webster, Cass and Clay at their head" (referring to the three senators who led the campaign for passage of the Compromise:

Daniel Webster, Whig, of Massachusetts; Lewis Cass, Democrat, of Michigan; and Henry Clay, Whig, of Kentucky) for permitting the interstate trade to prosper for seventy-odd years. The Kansas-Nebraska Act in 1854 and the *Dred Scott* decision in 1857 also quickly became lightning rods for debate. The Kansa-Nebraska Act reversed federal policies concerning the extension of slavery and issues of states' rights and confirmed policies of popular sovereignty in the territories. The *Dred Scott* decision put to rest the contention that "free soil made a free man" and established that taking a slave into a free state did not alter his or her status. General public discontent with both actions clearly illustrated the divisive nature of slavery in the United States during the 1850s. Douglass, speaking of the U.S. Supreme Court's action in the *Dred Scott* case stated, "The very attempts to blot out forever the hopes of an enslaved people may be one necessary link in the chain of events preparatory to the complete overthrow of the whole slave system."

Only in the late twentieth century was the full scope and impact of the African diaspora realized. Scholars and other interested parties can appreciate the magnitude of this phenomenon only in retrospect. The diaspora changed the course of the development of four continents: North and South America, Europe, and Africa. It represents the scattering of peoples and the origins of new ones. It signaled the disruption and near extinction of some societies and marked the creation of syncretic and blended communities. The African diaspora resulted in the untold misery of millions of Africans entrapped in slavery for generations. It also gave birth to vibrant new cultures wherever Africans were taken.

[*See also* Abolitionism; Africa, Idea of; African Americans and the West; American Colonization Society; American Revolution; Antislavery Movement; Antislavery Press; Black Abolitionists; Black Press; Caribbean; Clay, Henry; Colonialism; Colonization; Compromise of 1850; Cornish, Samuel; Demographics; Douglass, Frederick; *Dred Scott Case*; *Frederick Douglass' Paper*; Haiti; Haitian Revolutions; Kansas-Nebraska Act; Liberia; Native Americans and African Americans; Newspapers; *North Star*; Proslavery Thought; Race, Theories of; Religion and Slavery; Russwurm, John Brown; Slave Trade; Slave Trade, Domestic; Slavery; Stereotypes of African Americans; *and* Supreme Court.]

BIBLIOGRAPHY

Berlin, Ira. *Many Thousands Gone: The First Centuries of Slavery in North America*. Cambridge, MA: Harvard University Press, 1998.

Blackburn, Robin. *The Making of New World Slavery: From the Baroque to the Modern, 1492–1800*. London: Verso, 1997.

Curtin, Philip D. *The Atlantic Slave Trade: A Census*. Madison: University of Wisconsin Press, 1969.

Davidson, Basil. *The African Slave Trade*. Rev. ed. Boston: Little, Brown, 1980.

Hine, Darlene Clark, William C. Hine, and Stanley Harrold. *The African American Odyssey*. Upper Saddle River, NJ: Prentice-Hall, 2000.

Jordon, Winthrop D. *White over Black: American Attitudes toward the Negro, 1550–1812*. Chapel Hill: University of North Carolina Press, 1968.

Klein, Herbert S. *Slavery in the Americas: A Comparative Study of Virginia and Cuba*. Chicago: University of Chicago Press, 1967.

Kolchin, Peter. *American Slavery, 1619–1877*. New York: Hill and Wang, 1993.

Lovejoy, Paul E. "Volume of the Africa Slave Trade: A Synthesis." *Journal of African Studies* 22 (1982): 473–501.

Reynolds, Edward. *Stand the Storm: A History of the Atlantic Slave Trade*. Chicago: I. R. Dee, 1993.

Thornton, John Kelly. *Africa and Africans in the Making of the Atlantic World, 1400–1680*. New York: Cambridge University Press, 1992.

—MARTHA PALLANTE

Cultural Effects of the Diaspora

In the past, scholarly interpretations of the cultural impact of transatlantic contacts posited a unidirectional movement of people from Africa to other regions of the globe. However, new research reveals this movement to be a series of interactions back and forth across seas, lands, and cultures, from earliest times up to the present. This new point of view elucidates the existence of a dynamic and continuous movement of peoples that forged the many different reinventions and reinterpretations of a combination of cultures of Africans and peoples of African descent. Consequently, the idea of an African diaspora is here approached from three major perspectives: the worldwide movement of Africans throughout history, the spreading of a cultural identity based on African origins and social conditions, and the spiritual or material return to Africa.

In terms of time, one can speak of at least three diaspora phases. The first was characterized by the voluntary or bonded dispersion of Africans throughout ancient and medieval times in the direction of Europe, some parts of Asia, and the Islamic world. In the second phase, from the end of the fifteenth to the nineteenth century, millions of Africans were transported as slaves within Africa and to the Americas, Europe, and Asia. Finally, after the abolition of the Atlantic slave trade and slavery in the New World, Africans and their descendents freely cross-linked popular cultures on both sides of the ocean. There is no doubt that from a demographic perspective, slavery during the modern era was responsible for the deepest interchanges and the most durable cultural creations and interactions.

Previous to the European expansion, Africans traveled abroad as free persons and often settled among their host peoples. From antiquity to medieval times, Africans moved around the world as merchants, soldiers, sailors, and missionaries. Some of them became residents of Europe, the Middle East, and Asia. Free Africans were also present in the exploration and development of several regions in the Americas. However, it was in the course of the slave trade that the African presence acquired a world dimension. Arab traders conducted a slave trade across the Sahara, the Mediterranean, the Red Sea, and the Indian Ocean, and they took Africans to Arabia, India, and the Far East.

From the fifteenth century on, Europeans accomplished the greatest dispersion of Africans in history. In 1444 Portugal established a company in Lagos to trade in slaves. In that first year alone the state, the church, and some merchants seized 240 bonded Africans. Along with the regular trade in goods between Arguin and Portugal, slave communities were established in Lisbon, Barcelona, Cádiz, Seville, Valencia, and some parts of the Spanish possessions in the Netherlands. By the end of the nineteenth century there were about fifteen thousand Africans in England. Slavery also emerged in France, and thousands of slaves and free Africans lived in France's major cities. The African presence was also felt along the coast of the northern Mediterranean, the southern Adriatic, as far north as Russia, and east to Turkey.

Atlantic Slave Trade. After they conquered regions of the Indian Ocean and Red Sea, Europeans seized from Muslims the maritime routes taking off from the eastern coast of Africa, which linked the region to Asia. By the end of the sixteenth century most of the world's regional markets were connected by a worldwide commercial network dominated by European traders. The exact number of Africans who were enslaved and transported abroad is unknown. The best estimates are those for slaves sent to the Americas: 12 million to 25 million Africans were transported predominantly to Brazil, followed by the British Caribbean, the French Caribbean, Spanish-American areas, and North America.

The nature of enslavement and its impact upon slaves are complex, but the process of becoming a slave has always been marked by resistance and sometimes by open rebellion. Slave defiance was evident from the very moment Africans were dragged from battlefields, abducted from farms and villages, or condemned by traditional laws. At the initial point of the journey, many tried to escape and return to their homelands. Only a few succeeded. Some were kept by local host societies for domestic and productive purposes or carried to the north for the trans-Saharan trade. The vast majority were bound with rope in groups of two, three, or more and taken to the slave ports on the African coast under the supervision of armed traders and guardians. The distances covered by these caravans varied over time and region, from sixty miles or so at the beginning of the Atlantic slave trade to between 375 and 435 miles at the end, in regions such as Senegambia, the Bight of Biafra, Sierra Leone, and West Central Africa. Many slaves died during the journey.

While waiting for embarkation, Africans chosen for the transatlantic voyage shared the experience of the barracoon, the area of their confinement. That was the first phase of their cultural transformation. The type and size of barracoons differed greatly, from exposed enclosures along the coast to weather-protected compounds in nearby communities or European-style castles and fortresses. Depending on local facilities and commercial practices, captives from different ethnic backgrounds may have found themselves hitched in the same barracoon. The waiting period to be exported depended on such conditions as the health of the captives and the availability of slavers. Their initial captivity could last for months.

For African slaves, the moment of embarkation constituted another important step toward the construction of new identities. Their shared misfortune operated as a cohesive force among enslaved Africans, fomenting opposition to European holders. Despite frequent cases of negligence, Portuguese laws required that captives be baptized before they left Africa. It was a painful experience. In Luanda, to demonstrate to authorities that a slave had undergone this Catholic ritual, a small cross was branded on each slave's chest, along with a royal coat of arms on the right breast and a mark of ownership on the left breast or arm. In many cases, these new inscriptions were added to already existent African ethnic marks, making visible the process of identity transformation.

Once embarked, slaves could either travel directly to the Americas or remain in slave ships offshore until cargoes were loaded. The Middle Passage, or transatlantic crossing, of three or four months' duration was only one of the many possible ways for slaves to reach the New World. It was common for a slaver not to take on its full complement of captives at one port of call; instead, the ship sailed from factory to factory until its quota was met. Sometimes slaves were sent to Atlantic islands such as Cape Verde, Madeira, São Tomé, and Príncipe, where a process of "seasoning" took place. Over the course of months or even years, slaves were taught the cultural practices and language of their masters, as well as their position in society and the skills required for the work they were supposed to do in the Americas. Seasoned slaves rendered a higher price in New World markets.

Middle Passage, Shipmates, and Seasoning. Rites of passage were common in many African societies, and the Middle Passage could be placed in the same category. It was a crucial and formative phase in the slaves' cultural redefinition. The survivors, from different backgrounds, became familiar with one another through the intensity of their common suffering. Strength of mind also helped enslaved Africans survive the Atlantic odyssey. Despite the great variety of languages, familial structures, religious beliefs, and political thoughts among Africans, similarities in some basic concepts among many cultures allowed those who found themselves captives to communicate with one another, to adopt new patterns of kinship, and to reshape their worldviews in order to explain and deal with their enslavement.

Entering abreast into the European vessels, men were chained at the wrists and ankles in groups of two, to prevent mutiny and escape. Women and girls were separated from male slaves and usually kept untied during the voyage, which was important to the creation and development of new relations among the captives. During the oceanic crossing new bonds of kinship were shaped. In the English Caribbean and North America the term *shipmates* designated people who had come over on the same ship. In Brazil and almost everywhere else in the Americas, shipmates had the same kinship status as those related by blood, and such ties survived for generations.

For years it was widely believed that the Africans brought to the Americas were so diverse and divided into small cultural and linguistic factions that very few of them could communicate with one another or with the slaves who were already settled. From this point of view, there was little basis for the idea of cultural transmission between specific African peoples to specific communities in the Americas. Slave traders and masters deliberately fragmented slaves, it was thought, as a way to prevent the formation of cohesive groups and thus the organization of rebellions and revolts. New research, however, points to the conclusion that, depending on when they arrived in the Americas, captives might be sent to plantations, mines, urban centers, or farms in the company of their shipmates, some of them from their own ethnic or linguistic group. Each Atlantic slave-trade ship characteristically collected Africans from the same coast and brought them largely to the same American port or region. It is clear that the points of departure in Africa and arrival in the Americas varied over time, but it is conceivable that Africans from the same geographical or cultural regions arrived in waves at the same places in the New World.

Once slaves were disembarked and sold in North America, they were immersed in a process of seasoning that could last from one to three years. To be productive, they had to adapt to the local weather, food, clothing, and land. On a more profound level, they had to understand the terms and conditions of being a slave. They were categorized as "new" or "outlandish," meaning they were aliens to the English language and had yet to be taught their new functions. The methods and specific nature of the seasoning process varied by region, time period, and the peculiarities of local activities. In some places, such as Virginia, outlandish Africans were not seasoned at all; rather, they were immediately sent to the fields. On the South Carolina coast during the early colonial period, gangs of newly arrived Africans were allotted to drivers, reliable slaves who instructed them. In Louisiana old slaves acted as tutors for small groups of newcomers, who were only gradually introduced to work.

In all the various situations, reliable slaves had to be able to communicate with the outlandish in some variation of the master's language. It is worth emphasizing here the direct impact of language upon identity. Once the training period was finished, the owner or the overseer would supervise the African-born slaves that joined the others, who had already learned to obey orders and work properly. Hence, a "political" education in inferiority was embedded into the words that accompanied the new slaves' preparation for work. Through the years, power relations of control and subordination and moral attributes of good and evil became associated with the colors of white and black. Notwithstanding, the imposition of the new language was not a triumph of masters over slaves. In the end, the process was transformative for both sides. The colonial language served as a lingua franca to fulfill the need of the diverse African-based communities for dialogue among themselves and as a mechanism to interface with the new world that surrounded them.

African American Cultures. No matter where they landed, enslaved Africans had to adjust to their new environment. Throughout the Americas, each arriving African was identified according to his or her "nation" by European owners, seasoned African slaves, and their Creole descendants. Africans often joined slave communities where members of their ethnic group or slaves with their same regional background predominated. These African "nations" did not necessarily conform to any existing nation-state in Africa.

In the New World, nation identities varied from place to place. For example, Islamized Africans from the Slave Coast and the Bight of Benin who were identified as Yarribas, Foulahs, and Hausas in the English-speaking Americas were designated as Lucumis in Cuba and as Ouidás, Ardas, Jêjes, Malês, Guinés, and Nagôs in Brazil. The nation identity was so important in some areas that membership in one or another could improve or diminish a slave's status. As a result, it was common for slaves to enter into a nation that had dominance, even if it was entirely different from their former cultural group in Africa.

For those who had been born in Africa, the solidarity that came with membership in a nation became a starting point for their political aspirations. Indeed, several resistance movements against American slave regimes were organized and led by African-born slaves affiliated with specific nations. From the early 1600s to 1694, Angolan fugitive slaves organized and defended a Maroon settlement in northeastern Brazil against Portuguese and Dutch authorities and slave owners. The Congo nation provided the major leaders of the Stono Rebellion of 1739 in South Carolina. In 1791 the Congo nation also organized guerrilla groups during the Haitian Revolution. Nations frequently formed alliances. Hausa and Yoruba groups, called Malês and Nagôs, respectively, used their Islamic beliefs to lead the multiethnic Malê revolt in Bahia, Brazil, in 1835. Besides providing a political instrument in the slaves' struggle for freedom, the nations formed a friendly milieu in which Africans could preserve their religious beliefs and cultural practices.

Both enslaved and free Creoles adopted many African values. This African heritage blended with European customs to constitute dynamic African American cultures. The religious legacy included rituals connected to burial practices, patterns of worship, and professions of faith. Among the various religious innovations created by Africans and their Creole descendants in the Americas were the African Christian religions of Santeria, Candomblé, Shango, Spiritual Baptist, Vodun, and Umbanda and the African Baptist faiths of North America.

The material culture of many communities settled by African-born slaves also retained African elements. Artifacts associated with food preparation, musical instruments, religious objects, woodcarvings, and even architectural styles were heavily influenced by African patterns. African populations had a powerful impact upon the musical forms, dance, and folk knowledge expressed by their descendants in the Americas. Ultimately, capture, the Middle Passage, and the overall work experience under slavery shaped the will to overcome adversity in many communities peopled by African descendants.

Return to Africa. Study of the African diaspora not only traces the introduction and transformation of specific African cultural influences in the Americas but also indicates reciprocal effects of the Americas on Africa. The return to Africa was a basic driving force for African American communities, functioning as a milestone in the slave resistance. According to some spiritual beliefs spread throughout the Americas, when an African slave died, his or her soul would fly back to the homeland to join the ancestors in liberty.

Dozens of Africans who had achieved their freedom returned to Africa. Some of them used their knowledge of European languages and commercial practices to successfully engage in the Atlantic slave trade. Many others established themselves on the West African coast as traders, craftsmen, farmers, and civil and commercial clerks. In Nigeria and Benin former Brazilian slaves, locally called *agudás* or *amarôs*, influenced architectural development by introducing new styles, techniques, and materials. Their influence can be seen in the organization of neighborhoods and in the construction of houses and temples. Returnees also introduced professions such as house builder, contractor, carpenter, tailor, jeweler, barber, and surgeon.

The abolition of the Atlantic slave trade and of slavery strengthened African and African American hopes of being able to return spiritually or physically to the African continent, just as it stimulated efforts by Europeans and other Americans to send them to Africa. Hundreds of freed slaves from Brazil, Cuba, the West Indies, and the United States went back to Africa, where they strengthened and diversified American influences. Ghana, Liberia, and Sierra Leone became important destinations for those who were returning. Numerous missions of African Christian churches from North America were sent to convert Africans, create schools and technical workshops where Africans could acquire new skills, and promote the exchange of ideas between African American communities and African peoples. The African diaspora of the modern era was a multidimensional phenomenon characterized by the circulation of peoples, goods, and ideas back and forth across the Atlantic and within specific areas of Africa, Europe, and the Americas over the course of four centuries.

[*See also* Africa, Idea of; Africanisms; Baptism; Baptists and African Americans; Black English Vernacular; Black Migration; Brazil; Caribbean; Demographics; Free African Americans to 1828; Haitian Revolution; Identity; Maroons; Occupations; Religion; Resistance; Riots and Rebellions; Slave Trade; *and* Stono Rebellion.]

BIBLIOGRAPHY

Harris, Joseph E., ed. *Global Dimensions of the African Diaspora*. 2nd ed. Washington, DC: Howard University Press, 1993.

Harris, Joseph E. *The African Diaspora*, edited by Alusine Jalloh and Stephen E. Maizlish. College Station: Texas A&M University Press, 1996.

Mann, Kristin, and Edna G. Bay, eds., *Rethinking the African Diaspora*. Portland, OR: Frank Cass, 2001.

Mariners' Museum. *Captive Passage: The Transatlantic Slave Trade and the Making of the Americas*. Washington, DC: Smithsonian Institution Press, 2002.

Thornton, John. *Africa and Africans in the Making of the Atlantic World, 1400–1800*. 2nd ed. New York: Cambridge University Press, 1998.

—CARLOS FRANCO LIBERATO

AFRICAN GROVE THEATER. The African Grove Theater, also known as the American Theater and the African Theater, entertained black and white New Yorkers from 1821 to 1823. The theater, founded by the former ship steward William Brown, was the first theater in the United States owned and operated by African Americans. The theater company performed a wide array of material in a series of Manhattan locations, attracting an interracial audience while drawing ire from contemporary white commentators and competitors. The theater gave scope to the ambitions of New York's emerging free African American community, while the hostility it attracted was indicative of the refusal of many whites to accept free blacks as social or political equals. The theater also provided a stage for two pioneering African American performers, James Hewlett, who was one of the first American one-man show artists, and Ira Aldridge, who went on to fame in British and European Shakespeare productions.

The African Grove Theater emerged from the volatile urban environment of early-nineteenth-century New York City. By the 1820s the gradual abolition of slavery in New York State was well on its way to completion. The city, already undergoing dramatic demographic and economic growth, was a magnet to newly freed African Americans as well as to runaway slaves. African American New Yorkers wished to see and be seen during the era and to enjoy the heady blend of freedom and excitement that the city afforded. Black street performers attracted crowds on market days; meanwhile, African Americans took their place in public life, promenading in their finest clothes, holding balls, founding churches, assembling for political addresses, and forming mutual aid societies. Although blacks and whites sometimes mingled in unregulated grog shops, free blacks were segregated in the city's respectable theaters and were excluded from its pleasure gardens. Tapping into the desire for entertainment and places to gather, as well as the expressive talents of the black community, Brown opened his pleasure garden in 1816, serving food and alcohol while entertaining customers with song-and-dance performances. Responding to neighborhood complaints about his outdoor facility, Brown soon debuted an indoor theater at the same address with a production of Shakespeare's *Richard III*.

The theater's repertoire reflected the wide scope of the company's talents, ambitions, and social concerns and the New York audience's varied taste. The company performed popular British imports, which included, besides Shakespeare, lighter musical fare such as the *Poor Soldier* and *Tom and Jerry*. Brown also staged his own *Shotaway; or, The Insurrection of the Caribs of St. Domingue*, believed to be the first drama ever written and produced by an African American. This play, based on a historic confrontation between British authorities and the leader of a West Indian tribe, who was a descendant of Native Americans and African slaves, placed black actors in roles of black resistance, leading some scholars to suggest that the drama had an antislavery agenda. The themes of slavery and resis-

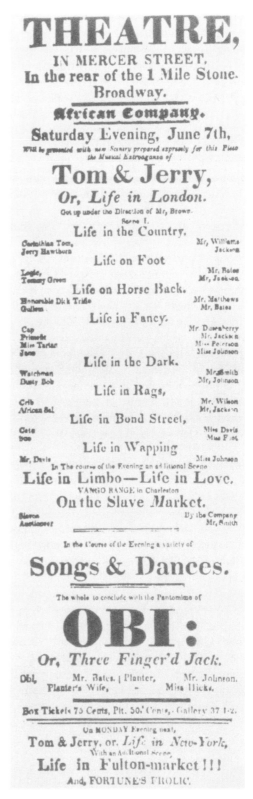

Announcement for the African Grove, c. 1821. This program featured both *Tom and Jerry* and *Obi*. (Billy Rose Theatre Collection, New York Public Library for the Performing Arts; Astor, Lenox, and Tilden Foundations.)

tance were perhaps more clear in Brown's insertion of a South Carolina slave market scene in *Tom and Jerry*, a play that Brown later further adapted, so that the main action of the play took place in New York rather than London, and in his production of John Fawcett's *Obi; or, Three Finger'd Jack*. *Obi* was based on the life of a Jamaican former slave's Robin Hood–like exploits. Besides drama, the African company continued to feature music and ballet.

Brown's company, which he preferred to call the "American Theater" but his detractors labeled the "African Theater," inspired a mix of curiosity, scorn, and hostility among whites. After moving to Greenwich Village and raising ticket prices, Brown's theater began to attract an increasing number of white customers. The theater experimented with both racially mixed and segregated seating. For one interested visitor, Mordecai Noah, a Democratic politician, editor, and playwright, the theater inspired an odd combination of interest, displeasure, and political opportunism. Noah's newspaper the *National Advertiser* mocked the dress, the speech, and the alleged cultural pretensions of the theater's black patrons as well as the performances onstage, even though the African Grove performed plays written by Noah himself. Noah also connected the public activities of free blacks to the political question of black citizenship. As delegates to New York's Constitutional Convention prepared to meet in Albany in 1821, Noah heaped scorn on free black New Yorkers and on the notion of black political participation. Noah insisted on referring to the company as the "African Theater," a title Brown only adopted with some reluctance.

The African Theater's mainstream white rival, the Park Theater, did not take kindly to the competition from the upstart African American troupe. Police harassment plagued Brown and his theater as they moved about the city, with Brown and his actors even being arrested as part of a crackdown on the allegedly unruly environment fostered in their playhouse. White harassment of the African Grove came to a crescendo on 10 August 1822, when a crowd of what one newspaper described as "ruffians" thoroughly trashed the theater at its Greenwich Village location. Although this incident did not permanently shut down Brown's operation, his company temporarily relocated to Albany. The theater opened again in Manhattan the following year but found survival difficult. Hewlett continued to perform in New York City and elsewhere, but harassment and the shifting popular white tastes toward white actors imitating blacks undermined the long-term viability of African American theater in New York and elsewhere.

The legacy of the theater is a mixed one. The theater expressed the cultural optimism of the nation's largest free black community and can claim impressive firsts in American history. Still, there is a bitter side of the theater's legacy.

The African Theater's demise was of a piece with the segregationist sentiment that swept across the antebellum North, even as slavery was legally dismantled. Moreover, New York City spawned a theatrical genre that perverted the notion of African American performance: through the blackface minstrel show, white entertainers created a set of stock African American characters that helped distort the black image in the white mind for generations.

[*See also* Aldridge, Ira; Dance; Discrimination; Free African Americans to 1828; Literature; Music; New York City; *and* Segregation.]

BIBLIOGRAPHY

Hay, Samuel A. *African American Theatre: An Historical and Critical Analysis*. New York: Cambridge University Press, 1994.

Marshall, Herbert, and Mildred Stork. *Ira Aldridge: The Negro Tragedian* (1958). Washington, DC: Howard University Press, 1993. This biography has an early chapter profiling the theater where Ira Aldridge got his start.

McAllister, Marvin Edward. "'White People Do Not Know How to Behave at Entertainments Designed for Ladies and Gentlemen of Colour': A History of New York's African Grove/African Theatre." Ph.D. diss., Northwestern University, 1997.

White, Shane. *Stories of Freedom in Black New York*. Cambridge, MA: Harvard University Press, 2002. Offers a provocative, searching interpretation of the African Grove Theater and the career of James Hewlett, setting these stories in the context of the racially charged, dynamic social environment of New York City as slavery drew to a close and free African Americans asserted their equality on the streets of a rapidly expanding urban landscape.

—DAVID N. GELLMAN

AFRICANISMS. Africanisms refer to African cultural and linguistic practices that survived the passage across the Atlantic Ocean, including language, music, dance, medicine, folk culture, food preparation, and many others. The extent to which enslaved Africans retained their culture was the subject of much debate in the twentieth century.

A sociologist rather than a historian first raised the question: in the early twentieth century E. Franklin Frazier doubted the persistence of African cultural forms in America. The anthropologist Melville Herskovits disagreed, arguing that significant numbers and types of Africanisms survived the Middle Passage. Sidney Mintz and Richard Price, who both examined black activity in the Caribbean, provided a more nuanced interpretation: they believed that no single African American culture was transported intact to the Americas but rather that the Middle Passage was crucial to a reinvention of slave self-identity. Modern historians commonly believe that once slaves arrived in the Americas, they began to think less about tribal African networks and more about their commonalties. Even though they were unable to re-create legal, governmental, and military practices, Africans in America influenced traditions with regard to agriculture, dance, religion, music, medicine, and folk culture. It is clear that slaves shaped their enslavement and enslavers in significant ways. American culture, then, can be seen as a story less of the survival of Africanisms and more of the blending of diverse cultures from Africa, North America, and Europe.

Since Africans came from diverse tribes and spoke a variety of languages, they lacked unity prior to contact with Europeans. Once transported to the Western Hemisphere, however, they forged an African identity, as there were striking differences between Africans and Americans. Africans shared a worldview that merged the secular and the sacred, a belief in living in close connection with ancestors, an acceptance of polygynous marriage, and an unfamiliarity with private ownership of land. As they unified into a slave community, Africans made the transition from self-definition by ethnicity to self-definition by race.

The recognition of a common culture was one important factor in the persistence of Africanisms; another was the plantation culture in North America. Slaves lived in communities, often beyond the reach of white authority, where they could use their preferred language, cooking styles, or weaving practices, for example. White colonists also aided in the retention of African culture: Masters often preferred one type of African ethnicity—such as Yoruba, Mande, Fulani, Wolof, or Coromantee—based on their skills or perceived dispositions. The Yoruba were considered less rebellious, while the Mande could aptly cultivate rice or indigo. Tribal clustering on plantations enabled slaves to readily communicate with one another and retain cultural practices.

African American cultural development had different paces and proportions in mainland North America. In the northern colonies few Africanisms survived because of the small number of slaves, their tendency not to live in large plantation communities, and a lower rate of importation of new Africans. In the Chesapeake region, Africans had more opportunities to retain their culture because of the plantation system as well as the heavy importation of Africans, especially between 1680 and 1740. The lower Mississippi valley, especially near New Orleans, produced a different pattern. A lack of administrative control and distance from large population centers fostered a strong blending of cultures. The unique cooking patterns of Louisiana and the persistence of voodoo are examples of a pattern where African influences survived and were blended with European and North American beliefs and behaviors.

Slaves in the Lowcountry of South Carolina and Georgia retained even more African culture than other bond servants. A strong Atlantic slave trade constantly refreshed African ideas and cultural practices, enabling slaves to preserve an African identity; the isolation of the slave communities on large plantations further nourished Africanisms. Indeed, African speech patterns, religious practices, and social customs in South Carolina and Georgia persisted much longer than did those in the Chesapeake. The extreme example was the Gullah community of the Sea Islands of Georgia and South Carolina. There, slaves spoke a language that was a fusion of English and West African dialects, using unique cadence, accents, intonations, and words. Gullah slaves fashioned buildings that were reminiscent of West African shelters, with mud walls and thatched roofs. They used a cement-like mixture called tabby, made of lime, crushed oyster shells, sand, and water, to create strong, permanent buildings.

Plantation slaves relied on folk treatments for medical care, thereby preserving both their health and their African past. In 1716 Onesimus, a slave belonging to the Puritan intellectual Cotton Mather, showed his master the live-virus principle of inoculation against smallpox. Mather received the credit, and Onesimus is largely forgotten. Slaves also used West African knowledge to treat snakebites and were more effective in doing so than most trained doctors of the period. Plantations often had conjurers who created medicines from roots and leaves and charms that served various purposes; large numbers of clay charms were unearthed on early plantations, indicating a strong African cultural presence. Female midwives retained African obstetric practices and also created poultices or potions for slaves. This reliance on folk medicine was part preference, part necessity. Slaves trusted one another more than they might trust a white doctor, and many owners simply neglected the health care of their bond servants. These African medical practices survived into the twentieth century and were important factors in supplementing African American health care.

Slaves contributed significantly to musical practices, and contemporary music still shows the influence of Africa. African slaves popularized the banjo, drums, washtub bass, jugs, gongs, and other instruments unfamiliar to Europeans. Slaves took instruments like the fiddle and put them to different musical uses than were found in white society. Not only were the instruments different but the genre of music heard in the slave quarters was also distinct from what a slaveholder normally heard. Antiphonal music predominated. Also known as "call and response," antiphonal music stresses chants or the alternation of singers; it places less emphasis on melody and more on syncopation. Historians see significant African cultural influences in music that is uniquely American, especially spirituals, jazz, blues, doo-wop, and rock and roll. Slaves effectively used music not only to retain African culture but also to send messages to one another. Call-and-response songs were used to warn slaves that a white overseer was approaching or to coordinate runaway attempts.

African traditions were crucial to profitable agricultural production in the colonies. In South Carolina and Georgia rice could be grown thanks mainly to slaves' knowledge and experience. Not only did the first rice seeds come from Madagascar but Africans also trained Europeans to grow it; cultivation practices in West Africa and South Carolina were virtually identical. Other crops brought directly from Africa included coffee, peanuts, millet, okra, sorghum, watermelon, and yams. Slaves creatively combined these and other foods into dishes that are now staples in the United States. Gumbo, jambalaya, cornbread, hoecakes (which became pancakes), grits, and other dishes all have African origins.

Just as slaves grew crops, they also tended livestock. Fulani slaves from West Africa were expert herdsmen who changed the way white colonists raised cattle. Europeans usually raised small herds confined in pastures; Fulani slaves introduced patterns of open grazing that made efficient use of abundant land and scarce labor. The historian Peter Wood argues that the word "cowboy" originated from the close association of slaves and cattle, just as "houseboy" sprang from the common practice of having slaves as servants.

The African influence on language and slave folklore was strong. Stories of Brer Rabbit, Brer Wolf, and others were strongly tied to the Wolof folktales of the Hausa, Fulani, and Mandinka. Trickster tales, hare stories, tortoise tales, and the Anansi (spider) fables all have African origins, and these characters remain popular in Nigeria, Angola, and other parts of West Africa. Many Mande and Wolof slaves were imported into South Carolina and were able to retain much of their language. Because owners preferred to use Wolofs as house servants and artisans, these slaves had extended contact with whites and were able to influence speech patterns. Whites incorporated African words and phrases into their vocabulary: "okay," "bogus," "boogie-woogie," "bug," "honky," "fuzz," "guy," "mumbo jumbo," "phony," and "yam" all have Wolof origins. The Gullah dialect as well became an important part of slave culture in the South Carolina rice plantations.

The religious practices of slaves likewise combined African ideas with European practices. West Africans and Europeans shared religious beliefs in spirits, magic, taboos, and the like. Slaves, however, also tended to believe that spirits inhabited inanimate objects such as rocks or trees and that such forces influenced everyday life. Magic and taboo were important ways to influence these spirits, and so West Africans prized the work of diviners,

healers, and conjurers. As they moved to North America, slaves retained these African beliefs and practices and mixed them with Christian ideas. This syncretism explains why slaves might have identified themselves as Christians while still believing in multiple gods. Slaves, for example, tended to identify African divinities with specific saints, retain conjuring practices, use mounded grave decorations, and prefer total immersion in baptism, a practice strongly associated with West African river cults. Bond servants in colonial America commonly believed that a funeral merely marked the transition from one world to the next and often buried food with the corpse for the journey.

Africanisms in religious belief and practice survived, in part, because slaves did not receive extensive religious training for several generations. Many owners were reluctant to proselytize to their slaves for fear that conversion to Christianity might entitle a slave to freedom. There were also lingering fears that the egalitarian nature of Christianity might inspire resistance or rebellion among slaves. These doubts wore away over time, especially since six southern colonies had passed laws by 1706 stipulating that baptism did not necessitate the emancipation of a slave. The number of slaves who professed to practice Christianity also increased during the revivals constituting the First Great Awakening. New denominations, particularly Baptists and Methodists, were more egalitarian and attracted large numbers of slave converts. This steady acculturation into Christianity meant that the presence of Africanisms in black religious life slowly faded.

Exceptions to the decline of African cultural influence in religion are the practices known as voodoo and hoodoo. Voodoo (or Vodun), which is subject to many contemporary stereotypes, is a belief system closely associated with Haiti and New Orleans. Traditional voodoo draws from West African beliefs in loyalty to land, family, and voodoo spirits. Although voodoo may involve magic, it places more stress on inner spirituality. A more widespread Africanism was hoodoo, which served as a type of supplement to Christianity. As practiced in the colonial South, hoodoo addressed issues such as spiritual protection, romantic success, and luck. It was typically used to solve concrete problems or situations. Slaves might use hoodoo charms, spells, or potions to win the affection of a mate, gain protection from punishment, or win a contest.

Africanisms should not be thought of merely as a catalog of individual practices or ideas that survived the jarring transition of the Middle Passage and the brutal oppression of slavery. Instead, Africanisms may be deemed just one of many cultural influences that have contributed to the rich diversity of American society.

[*See also* Africa, Idea of; African Diaspora; Artisans; Arts and Crafts; Baptism; Baptists and African Americans;

Black Church; Black English Vernacular; Cemeteries and Burials; Dance; Festivals; Folklore; Food; Great Awakening; Gullahs; Health; Identity; Language; Mather, Cotton, and African Americans; Methodist Church and African Americans; Midwifery; Painting and Sculpture; Religion; Resistance; Spirituality; Stereotypes of African Americans; *and* Trickster.]

BIBLIOGRAPHY

Frazier, E. Franklin. *The Negro Family in the United States.* Chicago: University of Chicago Press, 1939.

Gomez, Michael A. *Exchanging Our Country Marks: The Transformation of African Identities in the Colonial and Antebellum South.* Chapel Hill: University of North Carolina Press, 1998.

Herskovits, Melville J. *The Myth of the Negro Past.* Boston: Beacon Press, 1958.

Holloway, Joseph E., ed. *Africanisms in American Culture.* Bloomington: Indiana University Press, 1990.

Levine, Lawrence. *Black Culture and Black Consciousness: Afro-American Folk Thought from Slavery to Freedom.* New York: Oxford University Press, 1977.

Mintz, Sidney W., and Richard Price. *The Birth of African-American Culture: An Anthropological Perspective.* Boston: Beacon Press, 1992.

Morgan, Philip D. *Slave Counterpoint: Black Culture in the Eighteenth-Century Chesapeake and Lowcountry.* Chapel Hill: University of North Carolina Press, 1998.

Sobel, Mechal. *The World They Made Together: Black and White Values in Eighteenth-Century Virginia.* Princeton, NJ: Princeton University Press, 1988.

Thornton, John. *Africa and Africans in the Making of the Atlantic World, 1400–1680.* New York: Cambridge University Press, 1992.

Wood, Peter. *Black Majority: Negroes in Colonial South Carolina from 1670 through the Stono Rebellion.* New York: Knopf, 1974.

—ROBERT GUDMESTAD

AFRICAN METHODIST EPISCOPAL CHURCH.

[*This entry contains two subentries dealing with the African Methodist Episcopal Church, from its founding in the mid-eighteenth century through 1895. The first article provides a discussion of its relationship with its parent church and reasons for its breakaway, while the second article also includes discussion of the African Methodist Episcopal Zion Church and the role of both these institutions in African American society.*]

The Origins of the African Methodist Episcopal Church through 1830

Methodism arose in England as part of a movement within the established Anglican Church. It was carried to North America by the great English evangelists John Wesley in 1735 and George Whitefield in 1738. Systematic Methodist preaching began in the mid-Atlantic colonies in the 1760s; following the development of the system of circuits and itinerant preaching, membership spread rapidly. Among the most fervent converts were African Americans, who were drawn to the weak and struggling movement by the evangelical message of the priesthood of all believers and the dynamic of conversion.

Although Methodists were not immune to racial prejudice, the biracial character of early revivals, the public opposition of many of the English itinerant preachers to slavery, and the controversial ministry of some of the American-born preachers to the enslaved added to the denomination's appeal to African Americans. There was no official church policy, but Methodists' identification with the antislavery movement as well as their pacifism during the Revolutionary era led to wartime persecution and a powerful backlash against the denomination. The war and slavery forced most of the English itinerant preachers to flee the country, and sharpened the sense of distance between American and English Methodism. At the Christmas conference of 1784 American Wesleyans organized as the Methodist Episcopal Church.

By that time a core of able and articulate black church leaders had emerged. Respectful of their deep spirituality and the power and authority they commanded among their own people, Methodist leaders readily sent black men on itinerant missions but were reluctant to admit them to the church establishment. A shortage of white preachers and persistent pressure from black men eventually forced church leaders to yield. In 1799 Richard Allen, a former slave, was ordained a deacon by Francis Asbury, and in 1800 the General Conference of the Methodist Episcopal Church agreed to ordain local deacons. Black women, who made up a substantial part of all Methodist congregations—and formed a clear majority in many—also claimed the right to exercise religious authority by virtue of the priesthood of all believers. Though denied admission to the religious establishment on biblical and doctrinal grounds, black women such as Zilpha Elaw and Jarena Lee claimed spiritual ordination and functioned as "self-ordained" preachers. But it was primarily as visionaries and as exhorters, offering prayer and testimony to prepare the congregation for the conversion experience, that most women exercised religious influence. The visionary mode was believed to be a form of enthusiasm especially well suited to the female temperament.

The proselytizing efforts of black men and women resulted in the rapid rise of societies with predominantly or exclusively black membership, although black Methodists were members of many biracial churches. White Methodism gave black religious life its basic shape and substance, but traditional African beliefs and practices more definitively influenced black religious life; thus African American Methodists developed a spiritual identity that was

Bethel AME Church in Philadelphia, drawn in 1829 by William L. Breton. The church was founded by Richard Allen in 1794 and rebuilt in 1805. (Library Company of Philadelphia.)

both similar to and different from their African spiritual roots as well as white religious culture.

In general, black churches adhered to the same organizational forms, doctrine, and polity and used the same liturgical forms, prayers, and music as white churches. Yet black churches also developed their own distinctive ethos and character. Black Methodists interpreted the rhetoric of conversion, with its powerful themes of deliverance and divine justice, literally—stirring up vigorous activism among black converts. The hymns of Isaac Watts were standard in all Methodist worship, but music took on a primary role in black churches: songs were the source of sermon material and religious instruction alike for the largely illiterate enslaved population. The blending of prose sermon and music and the affective nature of black worship sharply distinguished it from that of whites— especially after 1815, when white Methodist worship became far more circumspect.

In the quarter century after the American Revolution, Methodism grew at a phenomenal rate, reaching a quarter million congregants by 1820 and a half million by 1830. Between 1800 and 1815 the number of black Methodists doubled from twenty thousand to over forty thousand, representing nearly one-third of the American Methodist population at the time. The growth and geo-

graphical expansion of black Methodism coincided with a rise in demand by blacks for full integration into the Christian community and the right to exercise authority within their own congregations. Until the Denmark Vesey conspiracy of 1822 put a stop to it, there was a distinct movement among large black urban churches toward the creation of separate churches. The first such secession was precipitated by racial discrimination: Jacob Fortie led the black members of the Lovely Lane and Strawberry Hill meetinghouses of Baltimore to withdraw after the white membership forbade black members to take communion with whites. Although Asbury denied their request to form a distinctly "African yet Methodist church" that "in temporals, shall be altogether under their own direction," the black secessionists were eventually able to establish two black churches in Baltimore: Sharp Street and Bethel.

Richard Allen, the first black Methodist to be ordained a deacon, and Absalom Jones, a religious leader of Philadelphia's free black community seemed to be moving in the same direction. In September 1790 they established the Free African Society, perhaps the first black mutual aid society in the United States. Frustrated with the arrogance and discrimination they experienced in Saint George's Methodist Church of Philadelphia, the two left to establish two African churches: Saint Thomas's African Episcopal Church and Bethel Methodist Church. The precipitating incident for their departure from Saint George's occurred one Sunday during prayers, when the Reverend Jones was rudely pulled from his knees by white elders and told to retire to segregated seating in the gallery. When the prayer was over "we all went out of the church in a body, and they were no longer plagued by us in the church," as Richard Allen remembered it. By the turn of the century an estimated 40 percent of Philadelphia's fifteen hundred black Methodists had joined one of the two African churches.

Until 1816, however, Bethel remained part of the Methodist Episcopal Church. Through skillful negotiation, Allen was able to assume a degree of autonomy for Bethel by limiting membership to "descendants of the African race." The struggle for independence intensified over control of property and the right to name preachers to lead Bethel's thirteen-hundred-member congregation. At one point the congregation blocked the aisles to prevent white preachers from mounting the pulpit. The controversy was ultimately resolved by a court decision ruling in favor of Allen's church. In 1816 Bethel joined with black congregations from Baltimore, Maryland; Salem, New Jersey; and Attleborough, Pennsylvania to form the African Methodist Episcopal Church, with Allen serving as its first bishop.

The development of a separate institutional life coincided with gradual emancipation in the northern states and the 1800 Gabriel conspiracy in Virginia to produce a powerful backlash that took different regional forms. In the slaveholding states efforts were renewed to reinforce the structure of slavery through comprehensive laws aimed at controlling the enslaved population and regulating relationships between the races. In the northern states the black-removal movement was formulated. A crucial step in effecting removal was the development of pictorial and literary representations that caricatured black Americans as evil or stupid and ridiculed their manners, dress, and dialect, creating a differentiated social identity that became the justification for literal removal. Throughout New England persons of color were "warned out" of towns and cities, were excluded from public schools and jury and militia service, had their mere presence taxed, and were denied or given restricted rights of suffrage. The culmination of these developments was the organization in 1817 of the American Colonization Society, the ultimate goal of which was the transportation of free persons of color to Liberia.

While the American Colonization Society represented the first institutional effort at removal, the colonization movement began in the 1780s when Thomas Jefferson, among others, argued for the "resettlement" of free people of color in Africa. Alarmed or inspired by the growing assertiveness of persons of color, slaveholders, northern reformers, Federalists, and evangelical Protestant clergy threw their support behind the colonization movement. A complex of motivations stirred evangelicals, some of whom viewed colonization as a strategy to end slavery and others as a means for black Americans to escape oppression. Some saw persons of color as agents of moral disorder or, alternatively, as mediators of African conversion or even as instruments for the transmission of "republican" values and practices to Africa.

Although some black nationalists later supported emigration, black Americans were almost universally opposed to colonization, which David Walker characterized as

> a plan got up, by a gang of slaveholders to select the free people of colour from among the slaves, that our most miserable brethren may be the better secured in ignorance and wretchedness, to work their farms and dig their mines, and thus go on enriching the Christians with their blood and groans. (Hinks, p. 58)

A combination of factors, including the vigorous opposition of the New England Anti-Slavery Society, the wide circulation of William Lloyd Garrison's influential *Thoughts on African Colonization* after 1832, and the impracticability of the project, contributed to an abatement of support for the strategy of colonization.

[*See also* African Union Methodism; Allen, Richard; American Colonization Society; Black Church; David Walker's *Appeal*; Denmark Vesey Conspiracy; Discrimination; Emancipation, Gradual; Fraternal Organizations and Mutual Aid Societies; Elaw, Zilpha; Free African Society; Gabriel Conspiracy; Jones, Absalom; Lee, Jarena; Methodist Church and African Americans; Missionary Movements; Religion; Spirituality; Spirituals; Stereotypes of African Americans; Vesey, Denmark; *and* Walker, David.]

BIBLIOGRAPHY

Frederickson, George. *The Black Image in the White Mind: The Debate on Afro-American Character and Destiny, 1817–1914.* New York: Harper and Row, 1971.

Frey, Sylvia R. " 'The Year of Jubilee Is Come': Black Christianity in the Plantation South in Post-Revolutionary America." In *Religion in a Revolutionary Age*, edited by Ronald Hoffman and Peter J. Albert. Charlottesville: University Press of Virginia, 1994.

Frey, Sylvia R., and Betty Wood. *Come Shouting to Zion: African American Protestantism in the American South and British Caribbean to 1830.* Chapel Hill: University of North Carolina Press, 1998.

Friedman, Lawrence J. *Inventors of the Promised Land.* New York: Knopf, 1975.

George, Carol V. R. *Segregated Sabbaths: Richard Allen and the Emergence of Independent Black Churches, 1760–1840.* New York: Oxford University Press, 1973.

Hinks, Peter P., ed. *David Walker's "Appeal to the Coloured Citizens of the World."* University Park: Pennsylvania State University Press, 2000.

Melish, Joanne Pope. *Disowning Slavery: Gradual Emancipation and "Race" in New England, 1780–1860.* Ithaca, NY: Cornell University Press, 1998.

—SYLVIA FREY

The AME Church and AME Zion Church through 1895

The origin of the African Methodist Episcopal (AME) Church is tied to the beginnings of the American Methodist movement in 1760; blacks had been present in the denomination since those beginnings. In the Revolutionary period this black presence was the result of Wesleyan Methodism's vigorous antislavery sentiments, drawing many slaves and free blacks alike. Such sentiments declined after 1784, however, giving way to increased segregation in Methodist congregations; such segregation spawned the AME Church. In 1787 a Sunday liturgy at Saint George's Methodist Church in Philadelphia was interrupted when an overly zealous white parishioner attempted to remove several black parishioners, including Richard Allen and Absalom Jones, to the area of the church designated for blacks. Thereupon many black members of the congregation followed Allen and Jones as they walked out of the church. The group of walkouts would split: some black dissenters followed Jones into the Episcopal Church, while others followed Allen and remained committed to Methodism.

Richard Allen was a slave who purchased his freedom and converted to Methodism in 1777. In 1783 and 1784 he served as an itinerant Methodist preacher in Delaware and New Jersey before settling in Philadelphia. By 1788 some of the dissenters who had originally followed Absalom Jones returned to Allen's group; Allen then used his own money to construct a church called Bethel, a name that would become synonymous with the AME Church. By 1794 the growing segregationist practices of the American Methodist churches from Baltimore to New Jersey had driven out many black members. Allen traveled extensively among these black Methodists, preaching and reaffirming the Methodist faith. On 9 April 1816 representatives from these dissident black Methodist congregations, including Richard Allen, met in Philadelphia. This group, representing over one thousand black Methodists, resolved to establish the African Methodist Episcopal Church and to elect Allen as its first bishop. In the following years the AME Church grew quickly; by 1822 its membership had risen to over nine thousand members, and its congregations ranged across the North, from Washington, D.C., to Pittsburgh, Pennsylvania.

The AME Church and its members were dedicated to education. This commitment first came to institutional

Bishops of the AME Church. Lithograph by J. H. Daniels of Boston, c. 1876. The portraits are of Richard Allen (center) and (clockwise from twelve o'clock) Morris Brown, William Paul Quinn, Daniel A. Payne, Jabez P. Campbell, Thomas Ward, John M. Brown, Jason A. Shorter, Alexander W. Wayman, Willis Nazrey, and Edward Waters. Surrounding them are scenes that include Wilberforce University, Payne Institute, missionaries in Hawaii, and the church's book depository in Philadelphia (Library of Congress.).

fruition in 1842, when various congregations took action to provide educational programs for their children. This emphasis on education was the keystone of the work of the AME Church's sixth bishop, Daniel Payne. Payne was born a free black in Charleston, South Carolina. In 1829 he opened a school for both free and enslaved black children, but in 1835 a South Carolina law made the teaching of those demographic groups illegal, forcing Payne to flee to New York. In the North he was associated with the Lutheran and Presbyterian churches before Morris Brown, Bishop Allen's successor, invited him to join the AME Church. Payne became an early advocate for an educated clergy. At the general conference of the AME Church in 1841 he wrote resolutions establishing a course of studies for the education of the clergy.

The segregationist practices of the Methodist Church in the late eighteenth century eventually spawned a second black church as well; the establishment of the African Methodist Episcopal Zion Church was an evolutionary process that occurred between 1780 and the 1820s. The process began with the recognition by the New York Conference of the Methodist Church of blacks' right to have their own church meetings. In 1796 the blacks of the Jones Street Church in New York established their own "African Chapel," which led to construction of the AME Zion Church in 1800.

The separation went into its final stage in 1820, when white dissent arose in the New York conference regarding the authority of the clergy and the lack of lay representation in church government. The Reverend William Stilwell, the white elder in charge of the black AME Zion Church, broke with the conference over the issue of control over church property. The lay members of the conference had prevailed in their attempt to divest the ministers of property control and transfer that control to the laity. Lacking a minister, the members of the AME Zion Church looked to the New York and Philadelphia conferences to ordain black ministers and establish a black conference. When the local conferences refused to ordain blacks and the General Conference of the American Methodist Church in 1824 refused to authorize a black conference, four black congregations—Zion, Long Island, Wesleyan, and Easton—moved to establish the AME Zion Church. This second black Methodist church did not grow as quickly as the AME Church; by 1831 the AME Zion Church had only 1,689 members.

Despite its smaller membership, the AME Zion Church was extremely active in antislavery activities, and many of its members were personally involved. Its mission churches in upstate New York, from Rochester to Buffalo, were important links on the Underground Railroad. The AME Zion Church in New Bedford, Massachusetts, was critical in assisting Frederick Douglass after his escape from slavery in 1838. Douglass and other prominent black abolitionists, such as Sojourner Truth (originally Isabella Baumfree) and Harriet Tubman, were members of the AME Zion Church. These individuals and their actions led many during the antebellum period to refer to the AME Zion Church as the "freedom church."

The AME Church also vigorously opposed slavery. Richard Allen's own home was a haven for fugitive slaves. Bishop Morris Brown served as an adviser to Denmark Vesey; when Vesey's 1822 attempt at a slave revolt in South Carolina failed, Brown barely escaped to the North. In the 1830s the church opposed the American Colonization Society's efforts to resettle free blacks in Africa, arguing that blacks were Americans and that the United States was their country as much as it was white Americans' country. In 1850, 1854, and 1856, the AME Church's general conference passed a series of formal resolutions calling for the end of slavery.

Prior to the Civil War, the missionary efforts of the AME and AME Zion churches were limited to the North, as such efforts in the South were seen as inflammatory and a threat to the slave system. The end of the Civil War opened up the entire South to the two black churches, and by 1880 their organizations had spread throughout the Old South. The two often found themselves in direct competition, resulting in bitter confrontations and occasionally in legal action over the ownership of church property. Bishop Daniel Payne, who had been forced to abandon his earlier efforts to educate blacks in South Carolina, returned in 1865 to assist in the establishment of the South Carolina conference, which included the Carolinas and Georgia. The AME Zion Church's representatives were close behind, establishing that church's North Carolina conference for the same region.

The bishop Henry M. Turner's efforts were the epitome of the efforts of the AME Church as a whole in the post–Civil War South. Turner began as a Methodist Episcopal preacher in 1860; soon after accepting a pastorate in Baltimore, he began recruiting blacks for the U.S. Army. He served as a chaplain for black troops and after the war accepted an appointment as a Freedmen's Bureau agent. He divided his time between religion and politics: he became the AME Church's major organizer in Georgia and was also elected a delegate to the Georgia Constitutional Convention in 1868 and 1870 and later to the Georgia State senate. In 1880 he was elected bishop at the AME Church's general conference. In the 1890s he left the United States and led the establishment of the AME Church in West Africa and South Africa.

During the post–Civil War period, the AME Church intensified its focus on education. In 1865 the church purchased Wilberforce University from the Methodist Church. Bishop Payne presided over the school for more

Juliann Jane Tillman, lithograph printed by Peter S. Duval from a portrait by A. Hoffy. It has the caption "Preacher of the A.M.E. Church" and is dated Philadelphia 1844. Women were not allowed to become leaders of the AME church in its early years, but they were permitted to teach and preach. (Library of Congress.)

BIBLIOGRAPHY

George, Carol V. R. *Segregated Sabbaths: Richard Allen and the Emergence of Independent Black Churches, 1760–1840.* New York: Oxford University Press, 1973. An excellent study of the role of Richard Allen and the development of the AME and AME Zion churches.

Payne, Daniel A. *History of the African Methodist Episcopal Church.* New York: Arno Press, 1969. The original authorized history of the church as prepared by the official historian.

Richardson, Harry V. *Dark Salvation: The Story of Methodism as It Developed among the Blacks in America.* Garden City, NY: Anchor Press/Doubleday, 1976. A comparative study that interrelates the development of American Methodism, AME, AME Zion, and other black Methodist churches.

—THOMAS E. CARNEY

AFRICAN UNION METHODISM. African Union Methodism originated in 1813 in Wilmington, Delaware, as one of several independent black Protestant denominations established in the early Republic in reaction to the racism of white-dominated churches. The pioneers of African Union Methodism first met as members of Wilmington's Asbury Methodist Episcopal Church, established in 1789. Its namesake was Francis Asbury, a leader in the spread of Methodism in late-eighteenth-century America. Asbury, an Englishman, opposed slavery and sought out African American converts. Half of Asbury's congregation would eventually comprise blacks; they were encouraged by both Asbury himself, who occasionally preached in Wilmington, and by Harry Hosier, a popular African American preacher who also ministered to Delaware Methodists.

Despite the church's gracious admission of African American members, white Methodists at Asbury Church still discriminated against blacks in church affairs. By the 1790s white Methodists in general had backed away from their earlier support for emancipation and racial egalitarianism. At Asbury Church blacks were required to worship in a balcony separated from the whites on the church floor, and they had to wait for communion until all whites had received it.

In 1805 approximately forty African American congregants left Asbury Church in protest of these and other indignities. They built a new church called Ezion, which remained within the larger Methodist Episcopal structure, and continued to suffer discrimination at the hands of white clergymen. The Philadelphia Methodist Conference, the governing body with jurisdiction over Wilmington, denied input from Ezion's black congregants in critical aspects of church-level governance, like pastor selection and the management of business affairs. Whites rather than blacks were assigned to preach at Ezion, and church leaders sometimes expelled blacks who demanded equal treatment. The battle for control came to a climax late in

than a decade, establishing it as a preeminent black university. Thereafter the church moved quickly to establish institutions of higher learning for blacks throughout the South. These would include Allen University in Columbia, South Carolina (1870); Morris Brown College in Atlanta, Georgia (1881); Daniel Payne College in Birmingham, Alabama (1880); Shorter College in North Little Rock, Arkansas (1886); and several others.

As the nineteenth century came to an end, the AME Church had grown from an obscure black denomination with a thousand members into the leading black church in the world, with over 400,000 members and with congregations in the North and South of the United States as well as in Africa and the Caribbean.

[*See also* American Colonization Society; Black Abolitionists; Black Church; Civil War, Participation and Recruitment of Black Troops in; Douglass, Frederick; Education; Freedmen's Bureau; Methodist Episcopal Church; Religion and Slavery; Riots and Rebellions; Segregation; Slave Insurrections and Rebellions; Truth, Sojourner; Tubman, Harriet; *and* Underground Railroad.]

1812 when Ezion's members called for the removal of James Bateman, the white elder from Philadelphia who had been assigned to preach to them; Bateman refused to leave. Bateman's intransigence forced his detractors to either quit Ezion or wage a costly court battle.

Under the guidance of Peter Spencer and William Anderson, two African American class leaders who had taken part in the original walkout from Asbury Church, the majority of Ezion's members founded a congregation that was entirely independent of white Methodism. The new Union Church of Africans—also called the African Union Church and African Union Methodism—signified its autonomy by dropping the word *Methodist* from its official title. Incorporated by the state of Delaware on 13 September 1813, the church was America's first independent black Methodist denomination.

African Union Methodism retained some features of white Methodism, such as the system of classes and class leaders—a form of laity-led communal worship supplementing minister-led Sunday services. However, African Union Methodists rejected the white Methodist Episcopal practices that they regarded as obstacles to all Christians' sharing equally in God's blessings. The new church abolished the episcopacy and the presiding eldership—offices that white Methodists had exploited to prevent black involvement in church governance. To promote democratic self-government, African Union Methodists allowed for equal participation by laity and clergy: primary authority for religious affairs was placed in the hands of local congregations, which controlled their church property and chose their own ministers. Borrowing from the yearly gatherings of both Methodists and Quakers, the African Union Church sponsored the Big Quarterly—an annual meeting held in Wilmington on the last Sunday of August, combining festivities, worship, and church business. The Big Quarterly spread the influence of African Union Methodism by attracting slaves and free blacks from surrounding states who had no formal connection with the church.

Unlike the itinerant ministry of the Methodist Episcopal Church, African Union ministers devoted themselves to a single congregation. A rooted ministry fit into the African Union's efforts to empower local congregations and enabled black ministers to find work and acquire property without financial aid from the church bureaucracy.

Perhaps the African Union Church's most striking break with white Methodism was its acceptance of women preachers. Black women were influential in most evangelical denominations but rarely had the opportunity to serve as licensed ministers. Indicative of the importance of women to the creation of African Union Methodism was the fact that three women from the original group that walked out of the Asbury Church went on to become African Union ministers. Although only men could hold the highest governing positions in the church, female preaching epitomized African Union Methodism's commitment to equality.

Like other free black institutions, the African Union Church fought against slavery and racism. African Union congregations criticized colonization, and at least one church—Hosanna Church in Oxford Township, Pennsylvania—was a station on the Underground Railroad. Conductors on the Underground Railroad also used the Big Quarterly to coordinate slave escapes.

In 1816 Richard Allen, who since the 1780s had fought for African American dignity among Philadelphia Methodists, tried to persuade leaders of other independent black Methodist congregations to join his newly founded African Methodist Episcopal (AME) Church. On behalf of African Union Methodists, Peter Spencer refused to merge with the AME Church because Allen's denomination used a different book of discipline and retained bureaucratic aspects of white Methodism, like clerical itinerancy and the episcopacy, that the African Union Church rejected. Some scholars speculated that another motive for Spencer's refusal was personal animosity between him and the strong-willed Allen.

Perhaps because of its decentralized character, the African Union Church grew slowly. In 1837 the church had 1,263 members distributed among twenty-one churches and three missions. African Union Methodists were concentrated within one hundred miles of Wilmington and were most numerous in northern Delaware and southeastern Pennsylvania, with a smaller presence in Maryland, New Jersey, and New York. By the 1840s a few African Union congregations were operating in New England. In 1843 Spencer and Anderson died, further weakening the ability of the African Union Church to grow. In the 1850s the church split into different denominations: the African Union Methodist Protestant Church and the Union American Methodist Episcopal Church. These churches survived into the twenty-first century.

[*See also* African Methodist Episcopal Church; Allen, Richard; Black Church; Discrimination; Hosier, Harry "Black Harry"; Integration; Methodist Church and African Americans; Religion; Segregation; Society of Friends (Quakers) and African Americans; Spencer, Peter; *and* Spirituality.]

BIBLIOGRAPHY

Baldwin, Lewis V. *"Invisible" Strands in African Methodism: A History of the African Union Methodist Protestant and Union American Methodist Episcopal Churches, 1805–1980*. Metuchen, NJ: Scarecrow Press, 1983.

Baldwin, Lewis V. *The Mark of a Man: Peter Spencer and the African Union Methodist Tradition; The Man, the Movement, the Message, and the Legacy*. Lanham, MD: University Press of America, 1987.

Russell, Daniel James. *History of the African Union Methodist Protestant Church.* Philadelphia: Union Star Book and Job Printing, 1920.

Williams, William H. *Slavery and Freedom in Delaware, 1639–1865.* Wilmington, DE: Scholarly Resources, 1996. Includes material on African American religion in the mid-Atlantic.

—FRANK TOWERS

ALDRIDGE, IRA (b. 24 July 1807; d. 10 August 1867), actor. Ira Frederick Aldridge was the son of Daniel Aldridge, a minister, and Lurona (maiden name unknown). Born in New York City, Aldridge was educated at the African Free School. Although his father wanted him to become a minister, Aldridge turned to the stage when he became fascinated by the fledgling African Grove Theater, run by William Brown and starring the pioneering black actor James Hewlett. The theater closed in 1823 after the New York City government, under pressure from racist mobs, refused to grant it a license. Recognizing that his career as a serious actor was limited in the United States because of prevalent prejudice against blacks, Aldridge immigrated to England in 1824 and became an attendant to the famed thespian Henry Wallack, whom he met through Wallack's brother, James. Aldridge and Henry Wallack would clash when the latter identified the young black man as his servant.

On arriving in London, Aldridge proceeded to act in minor roles in both the capital and smaller cities. He made his debut on October 1825 at the Royal Coburg Theatre, playing the royal slave Oroonoko in *The Revolt of Surinam*. That performance was followed by successes in *The Ethiopian* and *The Libertine Deflated*. The following spring he performed the leading role in Shakespeare's *Othello*. Aldridge used the stage name Mr. Keene and was also known as "the African Roscius" until he reverted to his family name in 1832. Despite racist ridicule of his speech, Aldridge proved popular with British audiences in London and around Great Britain. Over the next quarter century he expanded his repertoire to include *The Slave* and *The Padlock*—indicating that he was consciously valorizing his race in his performances. Nonetheless, in 1830 Aldridge assumed his first "white" role, playing Captain Hatteraick in *Guy Mannering*, and went on to become well known in the roles of Shylock in *The Merchant of Venice* and Rob MacGregor in *Rob Roy*. He also performed as King Lear and worked extensively with the famed British Shakespearean actor Edmund Kean.

Because London critics remained prejudiced against Aldridge, his venues were found largely in the provinces and on the Continent, where he toured in Belgium, Hungary, Germany, Austria, and Poland to much acclaim. He returned frequently to Europe, receiving the Gold Medal of the First Class for Art and Sciences from the king of Prussia and the Medal of Ferdinand from the emperor of Vienna along with honorary memberships in several acting groups. Hurt by racist caricatures in London and in America, Aldridge in fact preferred performing before appreciative European audiences. In 1858 Aldridge finally had a successful engagement in London and also became a British citizen.

Aldridge is known to have married twice. His first wife, an Englishwoman named Margaret Gill, whom he married in 1832, died in 1864. The following year Aldridge married a Swedish countess, Amanda Paulina von Brandt, with whom he had five children, one of which died in infancy. Aldridge died while on tour in Poland in 1867.

Aldridge was the first major African American actor with a lengthy career. He dominated the stage through his performances of Shakespeare's tragic characters in the nineteenth century, with his extraordinary physical pres-

Ira Aldridge as Aaron in Shakespeare's *Titus Andronicus,* c. 1850–1870, engraving from a daguerreotype by Paine of Islington, near London. The caption quoted Act 4, scene 2: "He dies upon my scimitar's sharp point, that touches this my firstborn son and heir!" (Library of Congress.)

ence, powerful, clear voice, and realistic style. He was known for interpreting his many roles in ways that non-English speakers could quickly grasp.

[*See also* African Grove Theater; Discrimination; *and* New York African Free Schools.]

BIBLIOGRAPHY

Aldridge, Ira. *Memoir and Theatrical Career of Ira Aldridge, the African Roscius*. London: J. Onwhyn, 1849.

Marshall, Herbert, and Mildred Stock. *Ira Aldridge: The Negro Tragedian*. Carbondale: Southern Illinois University Press, 1968.

—GRAHAM RUSSELL GAO HODGES

ALLEN, RICHARD (b. 14 February 1760; d. 26 March 1831), African American religious leader, founder of the African Methodist Episcopal Church, and abolitionist. Richard Allen was born a slave into Philadelphia's noted Chew family, whose patriarch Benjamin Chew was a prominent lawyer and served as Pennsylvania's chief justice from 1774 to 1777. In 1767 the family sold Richard

Richard Allen, shown in a lithograph by Peter S. Duval c. 1840, from a portrait by an unknown artist. Allen was not only a religious leader but also a prominent secular leader and social activist in the northern free-black community. (National Portrait Gallery, Smithsonian Institution/Art Resource, N.Y.)

to Stokeley Sturgis, a farmer in Kent County, Delaware. There Richard met a Methodist circuit rider, an encounter that transformed his life.

Unlike all other Protestant groups at the time, the Methodists made no distinctions based on color; moreover, they opposed slavery. Sometime around 1780, after attending a revival held by an itinerant Methodist preacher, Richard had a profound religious conversion. He began to attend Methodist prayer meetings, learned to read and write, and eventually presided over the local meetings. Soon after, inspired by a sermon given at his home by the charismatic Methodist preacher Freeborn Garrettson, Sturgis became convinced that slaveholding was wrong. He drafted a gradual manumission contract with Richard that permitted him to work for hire at farms and towns in the county. By 1786 Richard had purchased his freedom, having in the end earned most of the money by working for American forces during the Revolutionary War.

Taking the surname "Allen" to signify his new free status, Richard began to travel the Methodist circuit along the Eastern Seaboard from South Carolina to New York, preaching to blacks as well as whites. To support himself on his travels, he worked as a sawyer and wagon driver. In 1787 a Methodist elder of Philadelphia's Saint George's Methodist Church heard Allen preaching in a nearby town and asked him to preach to Saint George's black congregants. Although he was required to hold his services at 5:00 A.M. so as not to interfere with those of the whites, Allen agreed.

For the next five to six years, along with his fellow black preacher Absalom Jones, Allen ministered to the free black community at Saint George's and throughout Philadelphia. Together they founded the Free African Society, a nondenominational black mutual aid society, in 1787. Allen and Jones also nursed the idea of a separate Methodist church for black Philadelphians. Although Allen ultimately broke with the Free African Society over religious questions, he maintained his desire for a separate black Methodist church. That desire only increased as racial hostility mounted at Saint George's.

One Sunday morning in either 1792 or 1793, depending on accounts, white trustees at the church ordered black parishioners to the back of the church. At that moment Allen and Jones led black congregants in a dramatic walkout. Their group consequently organized into a semi-autonomous black Protestant congregation. When the issue of denominational affiliation arose, Allen and Jones insisted that the group retain its connection with Methodism. Others—including the prominent black businessman and social leader James Forten—disagreed and decided to affiliate with the Episcopal Church. They formed the new Saint Thomas African Episcopal Church and offered Allen the pastorate. When he refused, they persuaded

Jones to become their minister. Despite their differences, Allen, Jones, and Forten remained friends and committed fellow activists throughout their lives.

Undaunted in his quest for an independent black Methodist church, Allen and eleven like-minded Methodists purchased an old blacksmith shop in 1794, moved it to the corner of Sixth and Lombard streets in Philadelphia, and established Bethel Church, also known as Mother Bethel. The church installed Allen as preacher. In 1799 he became a deacon and, later, a church elder. In 1816 he led Bethel, along with five other black Methodist congregations in the North, in the establishment of a truly independent black Christian church, the African Methodist Episcopal (AME) Church. That same year, Jones and other ministers ordained Allen as the first presiding bishop of the AME Church. Over the next fifteen years the church flourished in the North, attracting thousands of free blacks disillusioned with the racism of white Protestant churches.

Allen's conviction that Methodism was the denomination best suited to the spiritual needs of blacks in the United States animated his single-minded pursuit of a separate black Methodist church. Although disappointed that Methodism eventually retreated from its earlier message of racial egalitarianism, he found in Methodism's purest and plainest form a means for spiritual healing and social uplift for blacks. Allen believed that Methodism's extemporaneous, heartfelt style of preaching could better reach African Americans than the more lofty, erudite, composed sermons of other Protestant faiths. He also valued Methodism's emphasis on personal discipline, which he felt provided the tools for individual uplift. In this, the community played a central role: Methodist communities furnished the crucial values—simplicity, honesty, modesty, and sobriety—by which all members were judged. Individuals were likewise expected to sustain and support the community of which they were a part. Allen's African Methodist Episcopal Church reflected this understanding of Methodism, and this understanding guided all of his other activities.

Besides being an important African American religious leader, Allen was a prominent secular leader and social activist in the northern free black community. In Philadelphia in the late eighteenth century he helped found the Bethel Benevolent Society, a moral-reform organization, and the African Society for the Education of Youth, a black day school. In 1793 Allen and Jones responded to the noted physician Benjamin Rush's call to mobilize the black community to serve during Philadelphia's yellow fever epidemic. Allen, Jones, and other members of the Free African Society cared for hundreds of victims, regardless of race. When reports circulated that blacks had profited from the epidemic, the two ministers published *A Narrative of the Proceedings of the Black People, during the Late Awful Calamity in Philadelphia in the Year 1793*

and a Refutation of Some Censures Thrown upon Them in Some Late Publications, defending the black community and documenting their heroic efforts. Jones and Allen also founded the Society for the Suppression of Vice and Immorality in 1809, and during the War of 1812 the two ministers, together with Forten, mobilized over two thousand free black men in defense of the city.

Allen's activism centered most on the abolition of slavery and the establishment of racial equality in the United States. In 1794 he published *An Address to Those Who Keep Slaves and Approve the Practice*, which attacked the institution of slavery. From 1797 to his death in 1831, Allen operated a station on the Underground Railroad for escaping slaves at Bethel Church. Beginning in 1799 he and Jones gathered the signatures of hundreds of blacks and petitioned the Pennsylvania legislature to abolish slavery. A year later they petitioned Congress. Allen also supported local antislavery societies in the North and contributed money and articles to the Presbyterian minister Samuel Cornish's antislavery paper, *Freedom's Journal*.

Allen vociferously opposed the American Colonization Society (ACS). Initially, he and other black leaders, such as Jones, Forten, and the black Presbyterian minister John Gloucester, had supported the migration of blacks to Canada as well as the black sea captain Paul Cuffe's plans for a black colony in Africa. After hosting a mass meeting on the issue in Philadelphia at Bethel Church in 1816, the activists were convinced by members of their community that colonization, and specifically the efforts of the ACS, represented an attempt to maintain existing social inequality between blacks and whites in the United States. A year later Allen, Jones, Forten, and Gloucester held another meeting at Bethel, protesting the deportation policies of the ACS.

Allen also joined Forten in organizing the national black convention of 1830 that established the American Society of Free Persons of Color. In the society's founding address, *An Address to the Free People of Color of These United States*, Allen called "for the speedy elevation of ourselves and brethren to the scale and standing of men." He endorsed a comprehensive program of racial equality, self-help, and agricultural and mechanical education that anticipated the ideas of Booker T. Washington in the twentieth century.

Allen's historical legacy can scarcely be overestimated. Upon his death, the black abolitionist David Walker proclaimed him one of "the greatest divines who has lived since the apostolic age." Indeed, like the apostles of the New Testament, Allen not only built churches, communities, and societies but also fashioned a distinctive social message. By the early twenty-first century, his AME Church claimed some eight thousand congregations and 3.5 million members throughout the world. It also supported a number of historically black colleges, such as Allen University in South Carolina and Wilberforce University in Ohio. Bethel AME, rebuilt in 1859, still stands on its original site in Philadelphia. Allen is interred in the basement, and the church holds a museum honoring his life and accomplishments. Allen's commitment to racial equality, though, is his greatest contribution. Blending religious devotion with a passion for social justice, he paved the way for future activists such as Martin Luther King Jr., who came closer to realizing his vision of a racially united United States.

[*See also* African Methodist Episcopal Church; American Colonization Society; Forten, James; Fraternal Organizations and Mutual Aid Societies; Free African Americans to 1828; Free African Society; *Freedom's Journal*; Gloucester, John; Jones, Absalom; Methodist Church and African Americans; Petitions; Presbyterians and African Americans; Religion; Temperance; Walker, David; *and* War of 1812.]

BIBLIOGRAPHY

Bell, Howard Holman. *Minutes of the Proceedings of the National Negro Conventions, 1830–1864.* New York: Arno, 1969.

George, Carol V. R. *Segregated Sabbaths: Richard Allen and the Emergence of Independent Black Churches, 1760–1840.* New York: Oxford University Press, 1973. Seminal work on the independent black church movement in the United States; focuses on Allen but also discusses Absalom Jones and John Gloucester.

Murphy, Larry, J. Gordon Melton, and Gary L. Ward. *Encyclopedia of African American Religions.* New York: Garland, 1993. Comprehensive encyclopedia of the African American religious experience through American history, with solid individual bibliographies.

Raboteau, Albert J. "Richard Allen and the African Church Movement." In *Black Leaders of the Nineteenth Century*, edited by Leon F. Litwack and August Meier, 1–21. Urbana: University of Illinois Press, 1988. An excellent analysis of Allen, his beliefs, and his role in the independent church movement; also discusses Absalom Jones.

Ripley, C. Peter, ed. *The Black Abolitionist Papers.* Vol. 3: *The United States, 1830–1846.* Chapel Hill: University of North Carolina Press, 1991. Vital introduction to the writings of black abolitionists in the United States, Canada, and Great Britain; excellent biographical footnotes.

Walker, David. *Walker's Appeal, in Four Articles: Together with a Preamble to the Coloured Citizens of the World, but in Particular, and Very Expressly, to Those of the United States of America.* Boston: David Walker, 1830.

Winch, Julie. *A Gentleman of Color: The Life of James Forten.* New York: Oxford University Press, 2002. Makes use of previously unexamined sources and extensively discusses black Philadelphia and its leaders.

—SCOTT A. MILTENBERGER

ALLEN, WILLIAM G. (b. 1820; d. ?), an abolitionist. William G. Allen was born in Virginia. In his autobiographical pamphlet *The American Prejudice against Color: An Authentic Narrative, Showing How Easily the Nation Got into an Uproar*, he described himself as "a quadroon, that is, I am of one-fourth African, and three-fourths Anglo-Saxon." Both his parents were free, his mother a mulatto, his father white. In 1838 Allen was accepted to the newly opened Oneida Institute in Whitesboro, New York, where he began to make connections with many leaders of the abolitionist movement. Following his graduation, Allen studied law in Boston, Massachusetts, under the abolitionist lawyer Ellis Gray Loring and then edited the *National Watchman*, based in Troy, New York, from 1842 until it ceased publication in 1847. Many of the antislavery ideas he developed during this period were later published in a series of letters he wrote to *Frederick Douglass' Paper* between 1852 and 1853.

While studying under Loring, Allen was offered and accepted an appointment as a professor of "Greek and German languages, and of Rhetoric and Belles-Lettres" at New York Central College in upstate New York, which had been founded by the American Baptist Free Mission Society in 1849. In his *American Prejudice* pamphlet Allen described the coeducational school as "the only College in America that has ever called a colored man to a Professorship, and one of the very few that receive colored and white students on terms of perfect equality."

At this time Allen was becoming well known as a lecturer and writer on the subjects of abolition, equality, and what was termed "amalgamation"—that is, integration—as well as for his involvement in the temperance movement. During a course of lectures delivered in Fulton, New York, he spent several days at the home of the white abolitionist the Reverend Lyndon King. There he met King's daughter, Mary, who was to begin her studies the following term at New York Central College. According to Allen, in less than two years the couple "had developed a relation to each other much more significant than that of teacher and pupil." They became engaged. Although Mary's sister and father initially approved of the interracial union, her brothers and stepmother were bitterly opposed. In fact, Mary and William would be pursued by a mob that "rescued" Mary and returned her to her home while forcing Allen to flee for his life. After a prolonged separation, the two were married on 30 March 1853, and on 9 April they sailed for Liverpool, England.

Like Allen, Frederick Douglass also became romantically involved with white women, allegedly including Ottilie Assing and Julia Griffiths. In 1884 he took as his second wife a white feminist, Helen Pitts. Although confronted with public prejudice, Douglass managed to escape the degree of persecution that had forced Allen and his wife to flee the country. Unlike Allen, Douglass bore a reputation that had been established long before his interracial marriage, which, more important, took place almost twenty years after the Civil War rather than before it.

Once settled in England, Allen continued to lecture on the subjects of abolition and African history and corresponded frequently with the likes of Douglass, Horace Mann, and William Lloyd Garrison. In 1853 he published

American Prejudice, the first of two autobiographical pamphlets he wrote. After a brief introduction describing his early life, *American Prejudice* details Allen's relationship with Mary, from the time they first met until their escape to England. The book sold well, and he and Mary toured the reformist circuit relating their experiences in America.

However, unlike other African Americans who visited and lived in England, including Douglass and William Wells Brown, Allen was never popular or able to earn much money. In 1856 he and Mary moved to Dublin, Ireland, where they had three children. Four years later he published the second of his autobiographical pamphlets, *A Short Personal Narrative, by William G. Allen (Colored American), Formerly Professor of the Greek Language and Literature in New York Central College, Resident for the Last Four Years in Dublin*, which ends with the Allens' arrival in England.

Allen and his family returned to England in 1860. By 1878 they were living in a boardinghouse in West London, where, according to letters from Allen held in the British and Foreign Anti-Slavery Society Papers, they existed on contributions from their friends. No records have been found concerning the death of William G. Allen; there appears to be no evidence that he ever returned to America.

[*See also* Abolitionism; Black Abolitionists; Brown, William Wells; Crofts, Julia Griffiths; Discrimination; Douglass, Frederick; Education; *Frederick Douglass' Paper*; Free African Americans before the Civil War (North); Garrison, William Lloyd; Integration; Mann, Horace; Marriage, Mixed; Mulattoes; Reform; Temperance; *and* Violence against African Americans.]

BIBLIOGRAPHY

Blackett, R. J. M. "William G. Allen: The Forgotten Professor." *Civil War History: A Journal of the Middle Period* 26.1 (March 1980): 39–52. Considered the most detailed account of the life of William G. Allen, this article was written, according to the author, "to restore Allen to his rightful place among his contemporaries."

Elbert, Sarah, ed. *The American Prejudice against Color: William G. Allen, Mary King, Louisa May Alcott*. Boston: Northeastern University Press, 2002. Included in this book are reprints of Allen's *American Prejudice against Color* and *Short Personal Narrative* as well as Louisa May Alcott's short novel *M.L.*, published in 1863 and purported to be the story of William and Mary Allen—but with a happier ending.

Quarles, Benjamin. *Black Abolitionists*. New York: Oxford University Press, 1969. An excellent study of the many African American men and women who played major roles in the abolitionist movement.

—PENNY ANNE WELBOURNE

AMERICAN ABOLITION SOCIETY. The American Abolition Society (AAS) was organized in 1855. It stemmed from the New York City Abolition Society, which had been founded in the 1830s by William Goodell to build support for his claim that slavery was unconstitutional. The AAS took the position that the Constitution was an antislavery document, which was consistent with Frederick Douglass's position after his split from his fellow abolitionist William Lloyd Garrison. Leading anti-Garrisonian abolitionists, some from the recently disbanded American and Foreign Anti-Slavery Society (AFASS), joined the AAS. Gerrit Smith, a wealthy, prominent abolitionist, served as the organization's president. Members of the executive committee included the evangelical reformers Arthur and Lewis Tappan, the physician and abolitionist James McCune Smith, the prominent Boston lawyer William Whiting, and Frederick Douglass. The membership of this committee indicates that the formation of the AAS represented the joining of two abolition forces: the political Smith-Goodell abolitionists, including Frederick Douglass, and the religious New York Christian abolitionists, led by Lewis Tappan.

Unlike earlier antislavery societies, such as the American Anti-Slavery Society and the AFASS, the AAS actively pursued a political agenda. The AAS took a radical and comprehensive position on slavery, arguing for immediate, universal abolition and equal treatment for newly freed slaves. In pursuit of these goals the AAS lobbied members of Congress, mounted a lecture campaign to challenge the constitutionality of slavery, and published a monthly journal called *Radical Abolitionist*. In 1856 the political arm of the AAS, the Radical Abolitionist Party, nominated Gerrit Smith for the U.S. presidency. Few in the AAS expected Smith to win, but many hoped that his candidacy would force the Republican Party to address the status and treatment of African Americans more explicitly. Indeed, three months before the national election, Frederick Douglass endorsed John C. Frémont, the Republican candidate; Lewis Tappan would vote for Frémont as well.

Like many antislavery societies in the 1850s, the AAS suffered from internal conflict. Some leaders in the AAS, particularly those who had been previously associated with the AFASS, including the Tappans, emphasized the importance of allegiance to orthodox Christian theology. This group went so far as to threaten to withhold support for Smith's presidential candidacy because of suspicions of unorthodox behavior. These leaders exhorted others in the AAS to refuse to worship or socialize with slaveholders. Others in the party advocated the use of violent means to accomplish abolitionist goals. Notably, from the founding of the AAS, Frederick Douglass, Gerrit Smith, and others considered violence a viable means to provoke the federal government to act decisively on the issue of slavery. But Lewis Tappan and others opposed both threats and acts of violence.

In the end, the AAS failed to attract popular support for its challenge to the constitutionality of slavery because in the 1850s most Americans were uncomfortable with the idea of immediate, uncompensated abolition. Instead, most Americans who opposed slavery threw their support behind the Republican Party. Following the landslide Republican victories in the 1858 elections, many officers, including Lewis Tappan, resigned from the AAS executive committee; the *Radical Abolitionist* produced its last issue around the same time. Finally, in early 1859 officers of the AAS met to disband the organization.

[*See also* Abolitionism; American and Foreign Anti-Slavery Society; American Anti-Slavery Society; Antislavery Movement; Antislavery Press; Douglass, Frederick; Garrison, William Lloyd; Goodell, William; Radical Abolitionist Party; Reform; Republican Party; Smith, Gerrit; Smith, James McCune; *and* Tappan, Lewis.]

BIBLIOGRAPHY

McKivigan, John R. *The War against Proslavery Religion: Abolitionism and the Northern Churches, 1830–1865*. Ithaca, NY: Cornell University Press, 1984. Focuses particularly on the religious issues within the AAS.

Perkal, M. Leon. "American Abolition Society: A Viable Alternative to the Republican Party." *The Journal of Negro History* 65.1 (Winter 1980): 57–71. A good overview of the political campaigns of the AAS.

Wyatt-Brown, Bertram. *Lewis Tappan and the Evangelical War against Slavery*. Cleveland, OH: Press of Case Western Reserve University, 1969. Provides information on Lewis Tappan's role in the AAS.

—Elizabeth Vander Lei

—Kristine Johnson

AMERICAN AND FOREIGN ANTI-SLAVERY SOCIETY. The American and Foreign Anti-Slavery Society (AFASS) resulted from a schism in the American Anti-Slavery Society (AASS). The conflict pitted those loyal to the radical Boston abolitionist William Lloyd Garrison against a faction led by the brothers Lewis and Arthur Tappan, prominent abolitionists who built and lost fortunes in the textile trade in New York City and were more conventionally religious than Garrison. The roots of the schism reached back to "clerical appeals" in 1837 that sanctioned the Garrisonians for using un-Christian language, for denouncing the moral authority of the Christian church and its leaders, for engaging in unorthodox activities, and for encouraging women to address public audiences at abolitionist gatherings.

Garrison continued to challenge mainstream churches for their complicity with slavery and pressed for more prominent roles for women in the abolitionist movement. Lewis Tappan and his associates continued to assert the primacy of traditional churchly Christianity and to oppose equal rights for women. After a tense standoff during the 1839 annual meeting, the Garrisonians succeeded in electing women to leadership roles at the 1840 meeting. At this, the Tappans and a minority of the AASS membership left the organization to form the American and Foreign Anti-Slavery Society (AFASS). Neither the AFASS nor the remaining AASS ever wielded the same power and authority as the original American Anti-Slavery Society.

At the outset the AFASS was hampered by the poor state of the national economy in general and of Lewis Tappan's bank account in particular. Nevertheless, the organization's leaders mounted a spirited campaign aimed squarely at orthodox Christian churches. At first their goal was limited and straightforward: they claimed that the northern churches' toleration of slavery amounted to support of it. The AFASS vigorously challenged churches to adopt antislavery policies. Through impassioned lectures and tracts, the AFASS attempted to warm the hearts of mainstream churchgoers to the plight of the slaves. The society published the *American and Foreign Anti-Slavery Reporter*, edited by Lewis Tappan, and later the *Liberty Almanac*, edited by Joshua Leavitt, and many pamphlets, including one by William Jay, the son of Chief Justice John Jay (1745–1829): *An Address to the Non-Slaveholders of the South*. The AFASS recruited prominent church members to critique the conservative nature of churches' opposition to the practice of slavery and to write articles for local newspapers.

Because of the poor state of its finances, the AFASS could fund only a few lecture agents. It did, however, fill large auditoriums for speeches by prominent abolitionists such as Frederick Douglass. (Douglass, for his part, maintained only nominal ties to the AFASS and never shared the passion of its leaders for church-focused abolitionist work.)

The leaders of the AFASS were well positioned to speak to traditional Christians. Most AFASS officers were active members of mainline Christian churches; in fact, most were clergy. Furthermore, many of the society's leaders brought years of experience and extensive social connections from their previous work for abolitionist causes. At least eight AFASS officers were African Americans, a presence unmatched in Garrison's AASS or most other abolitionist societies.

Because its finances were chronically tight, the AFASS traded heavily on the experience and contacts of its officers to build a base of support. But the organization was unable to lure significant numbers of local chapters away from the AASS and consequently never operated effectively at the local level. In addition to its work with churches in the United States and abroad, the AFASS focused attention on "come-outers," those who had left Christian churches either to protest the churches' tepid response to slavery or to avoid Christian fellowship with slaveholders (or, in extreme cases, even with those who did not actively oppose the practice of slavery).

Primarily through Lewis Tappan's longstanding connections with leaders of international antislavery groups, the AFASS enjoyed fraternal relationships with Christian antislavery organizations in both Canada and Britain. Orchestrating the international response to slavery in the United States was an early goal of the AFASS, but it proved difficult to generate enthusiasm or raise funds for such an intangible objective.

Initially, the AFASS took the stance of many antebellum Christians regarding politics: it rejected political activity as a sordid business that threatened the morality of all who engaged in it. Gradually, however, William Jay, Amos Phelps, and other members persuaded Lewis Tappan, and eventually the AFASS, that politics offered an additional line of attack on the institution of slavery. In 1841 the *Reporter* began informing readers of the activities of the Liberty Party. In 1845 the AFASS denounced the Whig and Democratic parties and endorsed the Liberty Party as the best political choice for abolitionists. While the battle for the heart of orthodox Christianity remained the primary focus of the AFASS, this support for the Liberty Party continued until the party's demise in the late 1840s.

Throughout its existence financial difficulties, weak support, and an overproliferation of objectives hampered the AFASS. Over time its members and even its leaders turned their attention to other antislavery work. In 1854 Lewis Tappan suggested to a friend that money would be better donated to the American Missionary Association than to the AFASS. In 1855 Frederick Douglass rebuked the AFASS for failing to have a single lecture agent in the field, and the AFASS faded from sight. Many of its prominent members subsequently joined the American Abolition Society.

[*See also* American Abolition Society; American Anti-Slavery Society; American Missionary Association; Comeouterism; Garrison, William Lloyd; Garrisonian Abolitionists; Jay, William; Liberty Party; *and* Tappan, Lewis.]

BIBLIOGRAPHY

McKivigan, John R. *The War against Proslavery Religion: Abolitionism and the Northern Churches, 1830–1865.* Ithaca, NY: Cornell University Press, 1984. Extensive coverage of the work of the AFASS with northern churches.

Wyatt-Brown, Bertram. *Lewis Tappan and the Evangelical War against Slavery.* Cleveland, OH: Press of Case Western Reserve University, 1969. Provides information on Lewis Tappan's role in the AFASS.

—ELIZABETH VANDER LEI
—KRISTINE JOHNSON

AMERICAN ANTI-SLAVERY SOCIETY. In the 1830s some Americans took a bold and uncompromising stand on the issue of slavery, demanding its immediate abolition without either colonization or compensation to slave owners. Sixty-two such like-minded opponents of slavery from nine states gathered in Philadelphia in December 1833 to form the American Anti-Slavery Society (AASS). William Lloyd Garrison, who two years earlier had begun publication of the *Liberator*, which took as its motto "No Union with Slaveholders," was one of the guiding lights behind the formation of the AASS and authored its Declaration of Sentiments. Others present at the convention included the wealthy New Yorkers Lewis and Arthur Tappan and the radical New Englander Samuel J. May. Four Quaker women and three African Americans also attended the meeting. The newly formed organization's goal was "the entire abolition of slavery in the United States." To accomplish this goal, members declared that they would work to convince slave owners that slavery was "a heinous crime in the eyes of God" as well as petition Congress to end slavery "in all portions of our common country, which come under its control." The Declaration of Sentiments also called for the elevation of the "character and condition of the people of color" and the removal of "public prejudice," such that African Americans might "share an equality with whites of civil and religious privileges."

The religious revivalism sweeping America during the Second Great Awakening in the 1820s and 1830s had a great impact on abolitionists, who held the deep conviction that slavery was a sin and that slaveholders were sinners. They translated the emphasis on individual conversion inherent in evangelicalism to the drive to bring slavery to an end by convincing slave owners that the "peculiar institution" was a crime against God and humanity. Abolitionists held the belief that slavery could be ended not through violence but through "moral suasion"; as they stated in the Declaration of Sentiments, they sought "the destruction of error by the potency of truth—the overthrow of prejudice by the power of love and the abolition of slavery by the spirit of repentance."

Abolitionists not only hoped for individual conversions on the part of slave owners but also intended to convince the clergy that they needed to condemn slavery from the pulpit. Many abolitionists, especially Garrison, believed that churches were immorally proslavery and were wrong in not supporting abolition. As the AASS's founding document stated, abolitionists promised to "aim at a purification of the churches from all participation in the guilt of slavery." Yet, despite their pleas and agitation, no major Protestant denomination advocated abolition outright. By the 1840s Garrison and some of the more radical abolitionists espoused increasingly anticlerical stands, thus serving to fracture the national antislavery movement.

The AASS not only relied on moral suasion—at least at the outset—but also promoted a policy of nonviolence. This stance, which rejected "the uses of all carnal weapons," was severely tested as abolitionists found themselves the victims of mob violence and the immediate end of slavery proved to be nowhere in sight. Additionally, some antislavery advocates concluded that rebellion of slaves against their oppressors was a justifiable, if violent, response to an unjust and evil institution. The abolitionist Abby Kelley Foster agreed that slavery itself was inherently violent and, in fact, constituted a form of warfare.

The 1850s severely tested the pacifist beliefs of many abolitionists. The violence rampant in Kansas Territory over the issue of slavery tested any nonresistant impulses harbored by abolitionists. Even the staunchly nonresistant Henry C. Wright eventually advocated violence in the form of slave rebellions. John Brown's raid on the federal arsenal in Harpers Ferry, Virginia, on 16 October 1859 caused further turmoil within abolitionist ranks. Many abolitionists capitulated to an extent, praising Brown for his motives but decrying his methods. Frederick Douglass, who broke with Garrison on the issue of violence, was one of Brown's financial supporters—along with other abolitionists like Gerrit Smith and Thomas Wentworth Higginson. As early as 1849 Douglass told an audience at Boston's Faneuil Hall that he would "welcome the intelligence tomorrow should it come, that the slaves had risen in the South, and that the sable arms which had engaged in beautifying and adorning the South were engaged in spreading death and devastation there."

To accomplish its lofty mission—that of bringing about the utter abolition of slavery—the AASS began to organize local and state antislavery societies. Within five years there were 1,350 societies affiliated with the AASS, with a total membership of 250,000. New York led the way with 274 societies, followed by Ohio's 213 and Massachusetts's 145. While the AASS was successful in recruiting members, there was still much public hostility toward abolitionists. Many Americans saw them as either small annoyances or, at worst, flaming fanatics. Indeed, this hostility sometimes manifested itself in the form of violence, where unsympathetic crowds mobbed abolitionist speakers. Sarah and Angelina Grimké, two southern-born sisters who were early lecturers against slavery, met even more abuse for not only publicly speaking out on a highly contentious issue but also daring to defy social norms defining the role of women. In 1837 the violence escalated when an angry mob in Alton, Illinois, killed the antislavery newspaper publisher Elijah Lovejoy as he tried to prevent the destruction of his printing press.

The AASS's lecturers, despite the abuse they often faced, were effective in persuading people that slavery had to be abolished; among the most influential speakers were for-

mer slaves like Frederick Douglass. In the 1840s Douglass began speaking publicly about his experiences as a slave and the evils of the institution. His eloquence and dignified appearance often surprised people who expected African Americans to be ill spoken and untidy. Indeed, some AASS members were uncomfortable with Douglass's polished demeanor and feared that people would not believe he had been a slave. Once Douglass began publication of the *North Star* in 1847—further exacerbating differences between himself and Garrison, who was still publishing the *Liberator*—the AASS dismissed him as a lecturer.

The AASS eventually employed a petition campaign designed to deluge Congress with thousands of signatures and force legislators to confront slavery. Women were especially active in the petition campaign, which proved so successful that the House of Representatives passed a "gag rule" in 1836 to automatically table all antislavery petitions. Despite the gag rule, antislavery petitions continued to pour in to Congress; in 1838 alone over 415,000 petitions arrived in Washington, D.C. Besides the petition campaign, abolitionists sent antislavery literature to the South to convince slave owners of the evils of slavery. Southern states actively fought to prevent the dissemination of abolitionist literature, taking steps such as burning the mailings.

AASS members faced not only opposition from outside but also dissension within the organization. Not all abolitionists agreed on every issue; by 1838 the differences had proved to be obstructively divisive, and two years later the more conservative faction was driven out of the AASS. Although it was not the only reason for the split, the role of women in the antislavery movement was one of the most contentious issues. Generally, the more conservative abolitionists did not want to muddle the antislavery cause with perceived secondary concerns like women's rights. Although they welcomed women as helpmates in the cause, conservatives believed that women should remain in auxiliary antislavery societies. The more radical abolitionists, known as Garrisonians, believed that the movement needed to have a "broad platform"—anyone opposed to slavery should be able to participate fully, including both African Americans and women.

Abolitionists also disagreed over political action. Many radical AASS members were hostile toward politics, with some even advocating not voting at all, seeing the whole political system as corrupt. They also asserted that the mere act of voting implied support for the proslavery Constitution. The radicals' antigovernment stance disturbed many conservatives, some of whom wanted to form a third political party dedicated to the abolition of slavery. There were also discussions and disagreements over the nature of the U.S. Constitution. The Garrisonians held that the

Constitution was a proslavery document that provided the means for slavery to continue to exist. Other abolitionists, mostly those outside the AASS, disagreed; they noted that the Constitution, while not perfect, was antislavery at least in spirit and allowed, if not encouraged, some steps toward the ending of slavery, such as the banning of the slave trade in the District of Columbia. A few abolitionists felt that the Constitution was an antislavery document and could be drawn upon to abolish slavery once and for all.

The abolitionists who supported political action threw in their lot with the Liberty Party. Organized in 1840 under the leadership of the New York abolitionist Gerrit Smith, the Liberty Party started with only one platform issue: the abolition of slavery. To broaden the party's appeal, Liberty men tried to appeal to other northerners by focusing on slavery's negative impact on northern agriculture, commerce, and nonfarm workers' wages. The Liberty Party nominated James Gillespie Birney for president in 1840 and again in 1844. By 1848, however, the limited appeal of the Liberty Party proved to be its death knell, and many of its adherents joined the newly formed Free-Soil Party.

Between 1838 and 1840 the dissension within abolitionist ranks over strategy and tactics dominated not only national AASS meetings but local meetings in the East as well, until the inevitable split occurred. At the 1840 AASS meeting in New York City, following the election of Abby Kelley to the executive committee by a vote of 557 to 451, the conservatives left the convention and formed a new organization, the American and Foreign Anti-Slavery Society. This left the AASS in the hands of Garrison and his followers. The division in the national AASS trickled down to the state level; in Ohio, for example, the Ohio Anti-Slavery Society split in a similar fashion. There, conservatives retained control of the Ohio Anti-Slavery Society, while the Garrisonians formed a new organization, which was first known as the Ohio American Anti-Slavery Society and later as the Western Anti-Slavery Society.

Frederick Douglass did not always toe the Garrisonian line; he angered AASS members when he agreed to speak at a meeting of the American and Foreign Anti-Slavery Society. Douglass also disagreed with the hard-line Garrisonian stand on politics, such as with regard to the Constitution; Douglass believed that the document "construed in the light of well established rules of legal interpretation, might be made consistent" with the preamble, and might "be wielded in behalf of emancipation." Unlike Garrison, Douglass saw that the political process might be one means by which slavery could be abolished.

Throughout the antebellum era the AASS continued agitating for an end to slavery. It published pamphlets and tracts, issued annual reports, and sent lecturers into the field. Once the Civil War broke out, however, the AASS primarily existed in name only and ceased most of its principal activities. The passage of the Thirteenth Amendment to the U.S. Constitution in December 1865 signaled an end to organized abolitionist activity—at least for William Lloyd Garrison. Wendell Phillips, one of Garrison's longtime associates and friends, broke with him first after Abraham Lincoln's second nomination as the Republican nominee for president in 1864 and then over the future of organized abolitionism. On 29 December 1865 Garrison ceased publication of the *Liberator* over the loud objections of Phillips. The following year the two men fought over the disposition of a cash bequest from a deceased abolitionist. The American Anti-Slavery Society continued to exist, trying to take on human rights issues, but finally dissolved in 1870.

[*See also* Abolitionism; American and Foreign Anti-Slavery Society; Antislavery Movement; Birney, James Gillespie; Brown, John; Constitution, U.S.; Douglass, Frederick; Faneuil Hall (Boston); Feminist Movement; Foster, Abby Kelley; Free-Soil Party; Garrison, William Lloyd; Garrisonian Abolitionists; Grimké, Angelina; Grimké, Sarah; Harpers Ferry Raid; Higginson, Thomas Wentworth; Liberty Party; Lincoln, Abraham; Lynching and Mob Violence; Massachusetts Anti-Slavery Society; May, Samuel J.; Moral Suasion; Nonresistance; *North Star*; Phillips, Wendell; Proslavery Thought; Reform; Religion; Religion and Slavery; Republican Party; Slavery and the U.S. Constitution; Smith, Gerrit; Society of Friends (Quakers); Tappan, Lewis; Thirteenth Amendment; Western Anti-Slavery Society; Women; *and* Wright, Henry C.]

BIBLIOGRAPHY

Kraditor, Aileen S. *Means and Ends in American Abolitionism: Garrison and His Critics on Strategy and Tactics, 1834–1850.* Chicago: Ivan R. Dee, 1989. Focuses on issues such as religion, women, and politics and their relationship to the various strands of abolitionist thought.

McFeely, William S. *Frederick Douglass.* New York: Norton, 1991. Discusses Douglass's relationship with the American Anti-Slavery Society.

Stewart, James Brewer. *Holy Warriors: The Abolitionists and American Slavery.* New York: Hill and Wang, 1976. Provides extensive discussion on the American Anti-Slavery Society.

—DONNA M. DEBLASIO

AMERICAN BOARD OF COMMISSIONERS FOR FOREIGN MISSIONS. Founded in 1810 by Congregational ministers from Massachusetts during the Second Great Awakening to send missionaries both abroad and to the southern and western United States—to convert Native Americans—the American Board of Commissioners for Foreign Missions (ABCFM) became mired in controversy over slavery at some of its missions. Within a few years of its founding, the ABCFM was the predominant missionary organization for northern Congregational and Presbyterian churches. It aimed to spread the Gospel and the values of a New England form of Christian lifestyle, with emphases on frugality, order, and faith. Beginning in 1816 the ABCFM established active missions among the Cherokees and the Choctaws, some of whom were slave owners. The ABCFM's representatives themselves also depended on local slave labor to create and maintain their Native American missions. Further, southern slaveholders soon became important financial contributors to the group's work.

Through the 1830s the ABCFM's association with slavery attracted little attention. With increased abolitionist agitation in the following decades, however, the ABCFM came under fire. In 1841 a group of New Hampshire ministers petitioned the ABCFM to clarify its slavery position. The group responded with a carefully worded statement specifying that the ABCFM could sustain no relation to slavery, which it described as evil, but emphasizing its overriding interest in the propagation of Christian teachings and further explaining that it would be improper for the group to question the motivations of its financial contributors or to adopt specifically abolitionist measures. In 1842, after receiving dozens more petitions on the subject, the ABCFM resolved to abstain from soliciting funds from slaveholders and to end the practice of employing slave-owning ministers at its Native American missions.

By 1844 the ABCFM was under sustained attack from northern abolitionists for admitting slave-owning Cherokees and Choctaws to membership in its churches and for the missionaries' own continued use of slave labor. Threatened with the withdrawal of financial support, the ABCFM promised to investigate these practices. By 1848 the organization was sending out its own workers to alleviate reliance on slave labor, but, citing the importance of the missionaries' independence, the ABCFM refused to interfere with their conversion of slave-owning Native Americans. Struggling to keep its critics at bay, the ABCFM promised that abolition would eventually result—once slave owners were brought into the mission churches and taught Christian values.

While the ABCFM was facing criticism from antislavery forces, southerners viewed some of the missionaries in their midst as abolitionists and sought their removal. Under increased pressure from abolitionists, and faced with the withdrawal of substantial financial contributions from critics in the North and the Midwest, the ABCFM removed its support for the Choctaw missions in 1859 and for the Cherokee missions the following year. Although some of the existing missionaries initially resolved to remain in place as independent agents, the withdrawal of the ABCFM's backing forced them to abandon all of the Native American missions by 1861. The ABCFM never recovered from its confrontation with abolitionism; supporters shifted their allegiance to the rival American Missionary Association, which had begun in 1846 as an outspoken critic of the ABCFM, combining evangelical teachings and missionary activities with an unwavering commitment to abolition.

Frederick Douglass disapproved of the actions of the ABCFM, particularly deploring the organization's refusal to take a stand in opposition to slavery. In an 1855 editorial appearing in *Frederick Douglass' Paper*, he argued that the group continued "showing its pro-slavery character." In a separate statement appearing the same year, Douglass warned, "There is no hope for the slave until slavery is earnestly reprobated by the religious organizations of the country."

[*See also* African Americans and the West; American Missionary Association; Antislavery Movement; Douglass, Frederick; *Frederick Douglass' Paper*; Native Americans and African Americans; *and* Religion and Slavery.]

BIBLIOGRAPHY

Kerber, Linda K. "The Abolitionist Perception of the Indian." *Journal of American History* 62.2 (September 1975): 271–295.

Perdue, Theda. *Slavery and the Evolution of Cherokee Society, 1540–1866*. Knoxville: University of Tennessee Press, 1979.

Strong, William Ellsworth. *The Story of the American Board: An Account of the First Hundred Years of the American Board of Commissioners for Foreign Missions*. Boston: American Board of Commissioners for Foreign Missions, 1910.

Whipple, Charles K. *Relation of the American Board of Commissioners for Foreign Missions to Slavery* (1861). New York: Negro Universities Press, 1969.

—JASON MAZZONE

AMERICAN COLONIZATION SOCIETY. [*This entry contains two subentries dealing with the American Colonization Society from its establishment in 1817 through 1895. The first article discusses reactions and controversy related to the society until 1830, while the second article includes discussion of debates within the free black community and attacks on the organization made by African American leaders such as Frederick Douglass.*]

The American Colonization Society to 1830

Founded by a group of former Federalists, evangelicals, and border South cosmopolitans in December 1816, the American Colonization Society (ACS) was, for a brief time, a politically powerful organization that promoted the removal of free blacks to western Africa as an answer to America's race problems. The Supreme Court Justice

Bushrod Washington served as its figurehead first president, while House Speaker Henry Clay of Kentucky and (society founder) Congressman Charles Fenton Mercer of Virginia ran the board of managers, the governing body of the society. In January 1819, at the request of the organization, Congress allocated $100,000 to facilitate removal and pay the salary of a colonial agent in Africa. Eli Ayers later purchased most of Liberia at gunpoint for less than three hundred dollars. To the extent that the society continued to receive federal funding throughout the administrations of James Monroe and John Quincy Adams, the ACS was the only antislavery organization that could rightly regard itself as virtually a branch of the federal government.

Because many northern black leaders for several decades had considered the notion of a mass return to Africa as a way of escaping American racism, several influential freemen, including Paul Cuffe, a successful merchant with commercial interests in Africa, initially made overtures to northern philanthropists connected with the society. In the border South, particularly in Baltimore, Maryland, and Richmond, Virginia, former slaves who concluded that they would never be allowed to prosper in a country that guaranteed equality only to whites often proved willing to accept the society's assistance in starting anew in a foreign land. Even the abolitionist Denmark Vesey briefly considered emigration to Africa in 1818 in response to the temporary closure of the African Methodist Episcopal Church in Charleston, South Carolina, by city authorities.

Once it became clear that no African Americans would be allowed to hold leadership posts in the society, the free black community began to separate themselves from the organization. Most of the society's leaders were petty slaveholders who resorted to crudely racist arguments to justify the removal of free blacks, and because the group hoped that all freed persons could be prodded into leaving the United States, society spokespersons declined to condemn the segregation emerging in northern cities. Most damaging to the society's attempts to recruit blacks was the refusal to state that its goal was the abolition of slavery. Hoping to win over southern planters with their moderation and talk of a white republic, society members not only believed that it was necessary to keep the focus of their endeavors on the removal of already freed blacks but also consistently denied, as Mercer insisted, that the "Society has nothing whatever to do with domestic slavery."

Philadelphia's emerging free black community took the lead in denouncing the idea of mass emigration on 15 January 1817, just days after the society was founded. The Reverend Richard Allen organized a meeting of more than one thousand blacks at his Bethel African Methodist Episcopal Church, to condemn the society and proclaim their intention of remaining in the land of their birth. *Freedom's Journal*, the young republic's first national black newspaper, was founded as an anticolonizationist publication; the *Journal* lost most of its subscribers shortly after the editor John Brown Russwurm altered his stance and began to write editorials in support of the society. But most subsequent black newspapers and pamphlets, including the abolitionist David Walker's incendiary 1829 *Appeal to the Colored Citizens of the World*, were consistently hostile to any plan for emigration directed by a white-run organization.

Despite the widespread opposition to the ACS in northern cities, the group was never the planter-controlled organization that Walker and its abolitionist critics claimed it to be, and assertions by modern scholars that proslavery activists endorsed the society in the hope of removing dangerous free blacks like Vesey are largely without foundation. Admittedly, in the border South, proslavery politicians such as President John Tyler and Secretary of State Abel P. Upshur hoped to use the organization to rid their state of free blacks, whom they believed inspired perilous dreams of liberty in those yet enslaved. But despite the racist tone of their public rhetoric, many white colonizationists privately harbored progressive views regarding black capabilities. Society spokespersons insisted that southern poverty was not the result of alleged African American incompetence, but rather that an economic institution based on unwaged labor deprived blacks of both the incentives and the education that made northern free wage workers so productive. Because many border state colonizationists boldly advocated the complete elimination of the African American labor force, slave and free alike, in the name of greater regional prosperity, Lower South planter politicians like Robert Turnbull of South Carolina bitterly castigated the organization as an "abolition society."

Modern historians also tend to regard any scheme of mass removal as an impossible one. But the society estimated the cost of sending one black settler to Liberia to be only twenty-five dollars. Since the black population during the early antebellum period grew by roughly six thousand people per year, it would cost Congress only $120,000 annually to remove every newborn or recently emancipated slave. Over the course of two to three decades, the white population would continue to grow, while the proportion of blacks in the national population would plummet, marginalizing unfree labor in the process. ACS defenders observed that a government that could force Native Americans to move west into Oklahoma was perfectly capable of compelling free blacks to sail east toward West Africa. Some politicians even noted that Washington could have conveyed 1.2 million black

Americans to Liberia for the same sum that it spent crushing native resistance in the Second Seminole War.

Virtually without support from either the northern black community or Deep South planters, the ACS effectively lost any influence in Washington after the administration of John Quincy Adams. In response to southern demands, President Andrew Jackson terminated all federal aid to the society in 1830, after which the organization ceased to be a viable part of the broad antislavery movement. In 1832 Maryland's legislature seceded from the parent body and incorporated its own state society. The following year, the jurist and reformer William Jay and the abolitionist James G. Birney publicly abandoned the organization; the abolitionist William Lloyd Garrison had ended his brief flirtation with the movement several years before, in 1829. In the hope of regaining its dwindling northern support, the ACS unsuccessfully tried to appease the American Anti-Slavery Society by firing five southern board members, including Mercer. The society continued to exist formally until 1899, but over the course of the nineteenth century, only 15,386 free blacks and former slaves immigrated to Liberia.

[*See also* Abolitionism; Allen, Richard; Cuffe, Paul; David Walker's *Appeal*; Free African Americans to 1828; *Freedom's Journal*; Jackson, Andrew, and African Americans; Monroe, James, and African Americans; Race, Theories of; Russwurm, John Brown; Vesey, Denmark, *and* Walker, David.]

BIBLIOGRAPHY

Egerton, Douglas R. "Averting a Crisis: The Proslavery Critique of the American Colonization Society." *Civil War History* 43 (September 1997): 141–156.

Egerton, Douglas R. *Charles Fenton Mercer and the Trial of National Conservatism*. Jackson: University Press of Mississippi, 1989.

Staudenrause, Philip J. *The African Colonization Movement, 1816–1865*. New York: Columbia University Press, 1961.

Tyler-McGraw, Marie. "Richmond Free Blacks and African Colonization, 1816–1832." *Journal of American Studies* 21.1 (1987): 210–217.

—DOUGLAS R. EGERTON

The American Colonization Society through 1895

The American Colonization Society (ACS) was founded on 28 December 1816 for the purpose of colonizing free blacks from the United States in areas of western Africa. The organization's principal founder was the Reverend Robert Finley, a Presbyterian minister from New Jersey who believed slavery to be a national sin. At the same time, Finley maintained a Jeffersonian-based conviction that because of a deeply rooted white prejudice against blacks and white fear of miscegenation, free blacks would never be able to achieve equal standing as citizens in the United States. In his 1816 pamphlet, *Thoughts on the Col-*

onization of Free Blacks, Finley emphasized the benefits of colonization, particularly the potential for black emigrants to establish self-governance abroad and to civilize and Christianize Africa.

Finley's rhetoric of nation building drew largely from the findings of Captain Paul Cuffe, a successful black Massachusetts merchant and ship owner. Discouraged by the lack of basic rights and representation for blacks in post-Revolutionary America, Cuffe successfully obtained British endorsement for a plan to colonize free U.S. blacks in the British colony of Sierra Leone. Cuffe returned to the United States to solicit free, skilled laborers from New York, Philadelphia, and Baltimore, and early in 1816 he transported thirty-eight black emigrants to the new colony. The success of this passage encouraged Finley, who appealed to Cuffe for support of his fledgling colonization plan. Cuffe volunteered his services and helped lay developmental plans for the proposed colonization society. However, owing to serious illness, Cuffe did not live past 1817 to witness the American Colonization Society fully taking root.

In 1816 Finley traveled to Washington, D.C., where he rapidly elicited support for his colonization plan from many members of the Supreme Court. The ACS was formed in the hall of the House of Representatives. Among its founding members were such notable figures as Francis Scott Key, Henry Clay, Daniel Webster, John Randolph, and James Monroe. The Supreme Court justice and Virginia slave owner Bushrod Washington, a nephew of George Washington's, was named the first president of the society. Prominent within the newly incorporated ACS was the presence of Virginia charter members. In Virginia several proposals for forcing free black populations out of the state had been made by the Virginia General Assembly prior to the founding of the ACS. The slave Gabriel's 1800 uprising, in which his followers had planned to seize Richmond and take over Virginia, was met by a wave of state legislation against free blacks, believed to have been coconspirators. Proposed removal laws could not be enforced, however, because there was no clear place to receive such refugees. On the other hand, the ACS could lend agency to such plans for black deportation.

While Finley's own motives were generally religious and molded on nineteenth-century reformist values of "relief for the wretched," a belief embraced by many popular nineteenth-century Christian reformers, his colonization plan would take its actual impetus from a sector of the population that clearly did not share his antislavery aims. Frederick Douglass, an outspoken opponent of the ACS, claimed in 1873 that among the founders were a few honest friends of the colored man who believed slavery was worse than emigration. But Finley died in 1818, leaving his legacy and the practical affairs of the ACS to be dominated by slaveholders and representatives of slave states.

Making of Liberia. In 1820 a society of Virginia slaveholders was the first to finance a voyage to Sierra Leone for the American Colonization Society. Eighty-six voluntary colonists and three missionaries, led by the Episcopal clergyman Samuel Bacon, arrived in Sierra Leone at a temporary settlement arranged by Paul Kizell, a partner of the late Paul Cuffe. It was an inauspicious start. The land was marshy and could not sustain crops, and there was no adequate supply of drinking water. Attempts to purchase a new permanent tract of land proved futile, despite negotiations. Conditions worsened, and many colonists died, among them, the voyage leader Bacon. An additional expedition in 1821 finally resulted in a land purchase from the local African chief King Peter, at the gunpoint of Lieutenant Robert Stockton of the American navy. The colony, which was finally established at Cape Montserado, some 225 miles south of Sierra Leone, was

Joseph Jenkins Roberts, in a copy daguerrotype by Rufus Anson, c. 1851, from an original attributed to Augustus Washington. Roberts arrived in Liberia in 1829, became its governor in 1841, and served as its first and seventh president. (Library of Congress.)

named Liberia. Its capital was called Monrovia as a tribute to its most powerful supporter.

The ACS could locate its strongest ally in the president of the United States, James Monroe, former governor of Virginia and staunch advocate of black emigration. As early as 1819 Monroe authorized Congress to appropriate funds in the amount of $100,000 to secure an African colony. He ordered U.S. warships to take supplies to the colony and commissioned navy sea vessels to convoy colonists from the United States to Sierra Leone and from African colonial outposts to the mainland. Despite Monroe's efforts and federal funding, recruiting black populations for settlement in Liberia proved difficult. Many free African Americans opposed the activities of the ACS and its efforts to rid the nation of all blacks who were not slaves.

Free Black Debate on Colonization. The first public opinion expressed by black leaders concerning the American Colonization Society came in January 1817, when a large congregation of free blacks from Richmond, Virginia, announced that although they would consider homeland colonization along the Missouri River, the Liberian colonization plan seemed tantamount to exile in a foreign country. The most publicized outcry against colonization was heard later that month from black Philadelphians. In a meeting in the city's Bethel Church, convened by colonization advocates James Forten, Absalom Jones, and Richard Allen, all among the best known of Philadelphia's African American emigration supporters, community blacks expressed their suspicions of an organization that dubbed them an alien and dangerous part of society. Some three thousand free black men of Philadelphia, nearly the entire black adult male population, denounced the work of the ACS. Forten, Jones, and Allen purportedly changed opinions at the conference, adopting the resolution that Philadelphians would not go to Africa and would fight against slavery in the United States. Black Philadelphians came together en masse to oppose colonization on four major occasions through the mid-1820s.

In keeping with such resolutions, African Americans who spoke against colonization generally resented being deprived of free U.S. citizenship and the rewards of their own toil in their homeland. At an 1851 Liberty Party meeting, Frederick Douglass pointed out the work that blacks had done in building the nation's economy, leveling trees, raising crops, and bringing food to the table of white Americans. For Douglass, emigration meant forfeiting a stake in the prosperity of the nation and undoing future efforts at African American cultivation and progress as a race. Like many other contemporaries, Douglass was suspicious of the rhetoric used to describe free blacks by such colonization advocates as Henry Clay, the ACS president from 1836 to 1849. The Whig politician Clay believed that colonization would rid the country of a useless and pernicious portion of its population. In "Henry Clay and Colonization Cant, Sophistry and Falsehood" (1851), Douglass addressed the racism endemic to the enterprises of the American Colonization Society and its leaders.

Closing Down Colonization. After Nat Turner's 1831 slave revolt in Southampton, Virginia, the largest in U.S. history, fears of collaboration between free blacks and slaves were galvanized throughout the South. In many cases, former bondpeople were subjected to a backlash of abuse and oppressive legislation, in some cases crushing their hopes of achieving any measure of liberty within the United States. Simultaneously, Virginia, Kentucky, and Maryland all contributed funding to the American Colonization Society. In 1832 more than one thousand blacks were taken to Liberia, nearly doubling its size. The ACS continued to issue a quarterly publication, the *African Repository and Colonial Journal* (initiated in 1825) to recruit settlers and investments. Colonization of Liberia was a slow process, however, and the ACS was unable to sponsor frequent voyages owing to the expense of transatlantic travel. In 1841 Joseph Jenkins Roberts, a successful merchant and Virginia émigré, became the first black ACS governor of Liberia. Liberia was becoming an increasing financial burden on the ACS and federal sources for expatriation projects could not be sustained. Liberia declared its independence from the United States in 1847, going on to become the first democratic republic in Africa.

During the Civil War era, emigration from the United States to Liberia cooled. After Emancipation, the organization affiliated itself with societies like Henry Highland Garnet's African Civilization, a society Douglass sharply challenged in his newspaper. After the Civil War, when increasing numbers of African Americans became interested in emigrating to Liberia, there remained little funding for travel. A longstanding opponent of the ACS, Douglass continued speaking out against the diminished organization, arguing that the very efforts to arrange such a thing as Liberian colonization stemmed from the belief that the black American had no right to be in the United States as a free being. By 1867 the ACS could report that it had conveyed some twelve thousand African Americans to Liberia. The society existed until 1912, but no longer as a colonization society. Instead, it focused its fundraising efforts on educational and missionary work within Liberia itself.

[*See also* Clay, Henry; Colonization; Douglass, Frederick; Emigration to Africa; Forten, James; Free African Americans before the Civil War (North); Free African Americans before the Civil War (South); Garnet, Henry Highland; Laws and Legislation; Liberia; Liberty Party; Racism; Slave Insurrections and Rebellions; *and* Turner, Nat.]

BIBLIOGRAPHY

American Colonization Society. *Third Annual Report of the American Colonization Society for Colonizing the Free People of Colour of the United States.* http://memory.loc.gov/cgi-bin/query/r?ammem/murray:@field(DOCID+@lit(lcrbmrpt1506)):@@@REF.

American Colonization Society. *Fourth Annual Report of the American Colonization Society for Colonizing the Free People of Colour of the United States.* http://memory.loc.gov/cgi-bin/query/r?ammem/murray:@field(DOCID+@lit(lcrbmrpt2513)):@@@REF.

Beyan, Amos J. *The American Colonization Society and the Creation of the Liberian State: A Historical Perspective, 1822–1900.* Lanham, MD: University Press of America, 1991.

Bruce, Dickson D., Jr. *The Origins of African-American Literature, 1680–1865.* Charlottesville: University Press of Virginia, 2001. In particular, see chapter 4, "The Era of Colonization, 1816–1828."

Douglass, Frederick. "African Colonization." In *The Life and Writings of Frederick Douglass,* edited by Philip S. Foner. Vol. 4. New York: International Publishers, 1950: 302.

Foner, Phillip S. *History of Black Americans: From Africa to the Emergence of the Cotton Kingdom.* Westport, CT: Greenwood, 1975. Details the role of Paul Cuffe in African colonization, the birth of the American Colonization Society, and the reaction of free blacks to the society.

Staudenraus, P. J. *The African Colonization Movement, 1816–1865.* New York: Columbia University Press, 1961. One of the best general studies of the American Colonization Society, but with less emphasis on the proslavery constituency of the ACS than other accounts.

—JUDITH MULCAHY

AMERICAN MISSIONARY ASSOCIATION. The American Missionary Association formed in 1846 in Albany, New York, as an alliance of Christian abolitionists who chose not to associate with the existing missionary agencies operated by various Protestant denominations. The spark for the formation of the association dates to the plight of the *Amistad* captives in 1839. This group of Africans enslaved in violation of international law successfully revolted against their captors aboard a Spanish slave ship—but ended up on trial in the United States when the ship drifted into a harbor on Long Island, New York. The well-publicized trial led many northern abolitionists to push mainstream missionary organizations, including the American Board of Commissioners for Foreign Missions, to assist the *Amistad* voyagers in their return to Africa, but the organizations refused. The frustrations of these Christian abolitionists led to the formation of three groups: the Union Missionary Society, the Western Evangelical Mission Society, and the Western Indian Missionary Committee. In 1846 all three groups combined to form the American Missionary Association.

The American Missionary Association initiated the publication of its monthly organ, *The American Missionary*, and set about establishing foreign missions in Africa, the Sandwich Islands (Hawaii), and the Far East. Early officers of the organization included William Jackson of Massachusetts, George Whipple of Ohio, and Lewis Tappan of New York. Funding came from small donations from established denominations, especially the Congregationalists. Shortly after its founding, the association expanded its activities to include missions among fugitive slave communities in Canada and organized a Home Department to direct expansion into western territories and southern states. Missions in the slave states were pioneered by the Kentucky planter-turned-abolitionist John G. Fee, who later founded Berea College with the association's support.

Frederick Douglass had little interaction with the American Missionary Association. As an advocate first of Garrisonian and later of political abolition, Douglass supported nonreligious means of bringing an end to slavery. Nevertheless, the association was an important element in the antebellum antislavery movement. The association's agitation led to reform in major denominational missionary groups, including the American Board of Commissioners for Foreign Missions and the American Home Missionary Society. In its refusal to affiliate with slaveholders, the organization set an important example for other groups working in the South. As the association and other established missionary organizations competed for contributions, those organizations came to adopt stronger antislavery positions to mollify contributors. The association also acted as a vehicle through which Christian abolitionists could lobby for antislavery action within mainstream Protestant denominations.

During the Civil War the American Missionary Association followed the Union army south, funding and supporting schools for freed men and women. In the period immediately surrounding the war, the association founded as many as five hundred schools for African Americans; during Reconstruction it focused efforts on funding institutions of higher education, including Fisk University in Nashville, Tennessee. Although the association expanded its western operations to include missions among Native Americans in the last quarter of the nineteenth century, its legacy remains tied to the abolition of slavery and the assistance and education of the freed African Americans of the South.

[*See also* American Board of Commissioners for Foreign Missions; *Amistad*; Antislavery Movement; Civil War; Douglass, Frederick; Education; Garrison, William Lloyd; Native Americans and African Americans; Reconstruction; Slave Insurrections and Rebellions; *and* Tappan, Lewis.]

BIBLIOGRAPHY

Beard, Augustus Field. *A Crusade of Brotherhood: A History of the American Missionary Association* (1909). New York: AMS Press, 1972.

McKivigan, John R. *The War against Proslavery Religion: Abolitionism and the Northern Churches, 1830–1865.* Ithaca, NY: Cornell University Press, 1984.

—L. DIANE BARNES

AMERICAN REVOLUTION. The historiographical debate over how radical the American Revolution was is an old one, but the belief that the war with Britain marked a social revolution in black life was first advanced not by an apologist for the founding fathers but by Benjamin Quarles, in his magisterial *Negro in the American Revolution*. First published in 1961, Quarles's pioneering study has never been out of print; in 1996 a second edition was released to celebrate its thirty-fifth year. Written at a time when many white Americans, not all of them in the southern states, were determined to deny black Americans their basic rights, Quarles was anxious to demonstrate the black contribution to American victory in 1781. The contribution of African Americans, his argument implicitly suggests, established their right to American citizenship, both in 1776 and in 1961. Far from being absent during the struggle with Britain, black Americans "welcomed the resort to arms," Quarles argues, and "quickly caught the spirit of '76." Slaves were natural revolutionaries, he wrote, with little to lose, no farms or shops to return home to, and no emotional or familial ties to England. Nearly five thousand black Patriots fought for independence, Quarles observes—"a respectable figure particularly since so many were not free to act."

Although Quarles reluctantly concedes that three times as many black Americans found liberty in the armies of King George than with Patriot forces, he concludes that for all of its failings the Revolution marked a new beginning for black liberty in all sections of the nation. The egalitarian spirit that informed the new political order, he suggests, doomed antiquated hierarchical assumptions that allowed one man to own another. "Despite its omissions and evasions," Quarles insists, "the Declaration of Independence held a great appeal for those who considered themselves oppressed." If it did not result in the immediate end of slavery, the conflict nonetheless "accelerated movement to better the lot" of black Americans in the young Republic.

Quarles, who died at the age of ninety-two shortly after the appearance of the second edition of his seminal work, never qualified his optimistic view that "the colored people of America benefited from the irreversible commitment of the new nation to the principles of liberty and equality." Quarles's seminal work has many admirers, but few wholeheartedly endorse its optimistic view of sweeping social change. Curiously, precisely those scholars who have been the most influenced by Quarles's pioneering study are the least inclined to endorse his sanguine assumptions about the foundations of radical change. Far from dramatically reorganizing the American social structure, they argue, or even laying the groundwork for the later abolitionist crusade, the failure of thc Revolutionary generation to move decisively against unfree labor made inevitable the carnage of civil war. Certainly, most modern students of the black experience in the age of the Revolution, all of them inspired in one way or another by the voluminous scholarship of Quarles, share a tendency to regard dramatic social change as a phenomenon that simply did not happen.

Most scholars concede that the early moments of the war created a climate of social insubordination and violence that American slaves used to their advantage. Even in staid Philadelphia the very real possibility of servile insurrection, combined with the incessant white rhetoric of liberty and equality, emboldened Pennsylvania slaves and gave them new hope; a Philadelphia gentlewoman discovered as much when a black man "insulted" her by refusing to yield the sidewalk and forcing her to step into the grimy street. Upon being reprimanded, the slave spat out, "Stay you d[amne]d white bitch, 'till Lord Dunmore and his black regiment come, and then we will see who is to take the wall." Across the Delaware River, Titus, a twenty-one-year-old New Jersey slave, threw down his hoe and headed south for Virginia. Three years later Titus returned to his home bearing the name Colonel Tye, a "warrior" in the British army.

Quarles briefly mentions the short, turbulent life of Colonel Tye in reviving the forgotten history of black Loyalists like him. But studies of southern blacks in the Revolutionary decades carry us far beyond the traditional bipolarity of white Patriots and black Loyalists. Especially on the southern seaboard the war was a complex triangular process. Africans and their descendants did not join either side as much as they exploited the conflict between two sets of white belligerents so as to forge their own freedom. Quarles may hint at British duplicity toward their black allies, but the war was shaped not only by Parliament's directives but also by African American resistance. Even in Lord Dunmore's 1775 proclamation, in which the last royal governor of Virginia offered to liberate slaves who joined "His Majesty's Troops," one finds evidence of British indifference to human bondage. Dunmore's intention was neither to overthrow the system nor to make war on it; rather, the proclamation was designed to encourage the defection of useful blacks, disrupting the psy-

Black privateer, in an oil painting of c. 1780; the subject has also been described as a Revolutionary War sailor. According to one estimate, some 5,000 black Americans took part in the fight for independence. (Newport Historical Society.)

chological security of whites without provoking a general rebellion.

Indeed, the British disinclination to offer the promise of unqualified black freedom and equality receives ample attention in the most recent scholarship on the war. Many Philadelphia slaves simply took advantage of the white flight brought on by British occupation to alter their condition; few readily picked up a musket to fight for that distant Parliament. It did not take politically astute bondmen long to discover that too many British officers regarded them as little more than useful tools—or potential laborers—in the military struggle. The British employed their once enthusiastic recruits to cook and wash and forage for food, often regarding them simply as another form of contraband property that they gave to enlisted men in return for meritorious service. As the war dragged on, the British openly abandoned their pose as liberators and sold their black recruits to raise much-needed funds to buy supplies for soldiers.

Because Parliament acted the part of a most reluctant liberator, unfree labor survived the chaos of war. British commanders labored mightily to calm the fears of Tory planters, who were frequently driven into Patriot ranks by every tentative step toward emancipation. Nor did the British wish to encourage a destructive racial war that would devastate the economic stability of a colonial society they hoped to reconquer. No better story illustrates the heartless nature of British racism than the tragic moment when the beleaguered British garrison at Yorktown ran short of supplies. To prevent his regulars from starving, Lord Cornwallis ordered the black Virginians who had taken refuge with his troops driven from their battered earthworks. The redcoats had "set them free," recorded a disgusted Hessian officer, "and now, with fear and trembling, they had to face the reward of their cruel masters."

Of course, one does not have to depict the redcoats as zealous liberators to understand how the chaos and dislocation of war had a pronounced effect upon slavery. Britain's refusal to move decisively against unfree labor, however, is of little moment to most historians of the Revolutionary age. It was once a given that the disorder of war, together with republican ideology and economic necessity, served to set slavery on the road to extinction in every northern state by 1804. Yet even this once-safe assumption is now under assault.

Gradual Emancipation in the States. Whereas historians previously emphasized the fact that gradual emancipation took place at all, many came to underscore the halting and conservative nature of northern manumission. Even in New England, where the minuscule number of transplanted Africans and a Calvinist critique of idle white hands seemed to indicate that the blot of slavery would be quickly erased, the death of unfree labor was surprisingly hard-won. Supporters of liberty labored to include freedom clauses in every new northern constitution, but only in Vermont was slavery dislodged through organic law. Even in Rhode Island (like Massachusetts, home to a good number of Atlantic slave traders), the state constitutional convention promised only to abolish slavery when "some favourable Occasion may offer." In no state was emancipation an effortless matter.

Specialists who have examined slavery's end in Pennsylvania challenge even the conventional interpretation that bondage quickly died in the Quaker stronghold from an overabundance of evangelical reform and natural rights theory. Far from being unique, Pennsylvania's experience mirrored that of other northern states: a small but determined band of reformers—white abolitionists, petty slaveholders with little use for a fundamentally precapitalist form of labor organization, and most of all, resolute bondpeople—forced the state to disengage itself from the institution. Although slavery was hardly an antiquated system with no future in the farming regions around Philadelphia, obstinate slaves played a leading role in dismantling the system by cajoling or even tormenting their masters and mistresses to release them.

Whereas earlier historians placed the Pennsylvania Religious Society of Friends at the heart of the struggle to eliminate slavery, Quakers came to appear as at best problematic reformers. They undeniably took an early position against slavery but were often more interested in simply purging the evil of slavery from their midst than in relieving the oppression of black Pennsylvanians. Quakers like John Woolman and Anthony Benezet worked tirelessly to convince others of their belief that owning human property was inconsistent with God's teachings, but in other ways Friends harbored reactionary views toward black abilities and occupational advancement. Moreover, once the freedom of African Americans had been obtained, Quakers expressed little interest in further assisting them.

Even Pennsylvania's Abolition Act of 1780, the first of its kind in the Americas, has come under new scrutiny. Historians once hailed this act, penned even before the British defeat at Yorktown, as the epitome of Enlightenment reform, but it was in fact the most restrictive of the five gradual abolition laws enacted by northern states between 1780 and 1804. Because it consigned to twenty-eight years of labor every child born to a slave woman after 1 March 1780, the law appealed more to the pocketbooks of Pennsylvania masters than to their consciences. And by condemning to lifelong servitude all bondpeople unlucky enough to be born before that date, the act immediately freed not a single slave. Since it was possible for slaves born as late as February 1780 to live out their lives as human property, it was not surprising that Pennsylvania, the first state to pass a gradual emancipation law, still housed a small number of slaves as late as 1847, midway through the Mexican-American War.

Colonial legislators were notorious for resorting to creative borrowing when it came to drafting legislation, and Pennsylvania's pioneering emancipation act unfortunately became the model for much of the North. In Connecticut bondpeople born after 1 March 1784 would become free—but not before they provided twenty-five years of uncompensated labor to their mother's owner. Worse yet, such term requirements signified an entirely new form of servitude. Unlike traditional indentures or apprenticeships, this peculiar transition into full freedom was noncontractual and placed binding legal requirements only on black laborers. Indentured servitude for whites in the late colonial period could be onerous enough, but the decades of uncompensated service imposed by states like Pennsylvania and Connecticut required no ongoing or terminal obligation whatsoever on the part of the proprietor.

The state of New York approached manumission in even more restrictive terms. Whereas slaveholding in Pennsylvania was predominantly an urban phenomenon, east of the Hudson the farmers of the hinterland were roughly twice as likely to own slaves as their city counterparts. Not until 1799 did the state pass an act for gradual emancipation, and not until 1827—just three decades before the outbreak of the Civil War—were those bondpersons born before the end of the eighteenth century finally liberated.

The New York emancipation act had one feature peculiar to that state: Although the law, like most passed in the North in the two decades after the Peace of Paris, held slaves in servitude until the ages of twenty-eight and twenty-five—for males and females, respectively—it also allowed masters to abandon black children a year after their birth. These children were regarded as paupers and bound out to service by the overseers of the poor. But because the state of New York paid a maintenance fee of $3.50 per month for each pauper, even if the caretaker was the former master, this law allowed white liberators to obtain a sizable return for their acts of conscience. The abandonment clause, in effect, was a hidden form of compensated abolition, and the state became the only place in the United States where masters were essentially paid to free their bondpeople. The clause, however, grew costly. Within only five years the state had paid over $20,000 for the program, and in 1804 the state assembly revoked it.

In short, if the founding fathers took a series of steps designed to bring about slavery's gradual demise, as was once widely argued, New York City, the Republic's largest slaveholding city next to Charleston, stood as a notable exception. The fact that the New York Manumission Society even allowed slave owners to become members suggests that many associates secretly wished to accomplish little more than the criticism of southern bondage. Politicians like John Jay organized a society ostensibly bent on the destruction of slavery, but typical of the group was Alexander Hamilton, who was born and raised in a Caribbean slave society and bought and sold slaves until the day of his death.

The theory that northern abolition was but a grudging and restrained process is best exemplified by New Jersey, the final state to pass a law for gradual emancipation. As in New York, abolitionists at length succeeded in passing a bill providing for gradual emancipation, but slaveholders won numerous concessions that influenced the pace and nature of its implementation. Throughout the 1790s proslavery legislators easily fought back numerous bills providing for piecemeal abolition. In fact, New Jersey lawmakers passed a 1794 bill rendering freedom lawsuits all but impossible. Even after passage of the 1804 gradual emancipation act—the last of its kind in the Revolutionary era—the future demise of bonded labor was almost imperceptible. Even then, few masters in their wills let notions of liberty decide issues of freedom for slaves born prior to 1804. Loyal service and economic change tended to weigh more heavily in New Jersey manumissions. As late as 1850, as Congress fought over the question of slavery in the territories, southern statesmen could point to the seventy-five slaves in Jersey's Monmouth County as evidence of northern hypocrisy.

Even this sluggish, propertied approach to implementing Revolutionary ideals ground to a halt at the southern border of Pennsylvania. In Delaware the state assembly actively encouraged and supported voluntary manumissions, but supporters of liberty lacked the votes to force passage of a gradual emancipation act. The best that the progressive faction could muster was a 1787 bill banning the exportation of bondpeople for sale in the Lower South. Caught between the two determined factions of abolitionists and small masters, the legislature concurrently supported two conflicting philosophies. The result was the private liberation of a majority of Delaware blacks by the end of the eighteenth century, even while some rural masters continued to hold slaves throughout the Civil War.

Revolution and Slavery: The Reality. Private manumissions and individual freedom suits were but small steps against a massive institution, and those who would depict the Revolution as a radical event must ultimately abandon political and economic theory in favor of actual numbers. The Revolution freed relatively few slaves. If egalitarian ideology and economic change served to dislodge bonded labor ever so slowly from much of the nation, it did so only in those parts of the Republic where few slaves resided. If anything, white independence from Britain only fastened slavery more securely upon the South by placing control of the plantation regime in the hands of an indigenous slaveholding elite. As the conflict with England dragged to a close, the question that troubled Georgia's Patriots was not how chattel slavery might be eradicated but how they might most expeditiously rebuild their war-torn plantation economy.

The reform spirit occasionally affecting the northern states did not hold much attraction for the slave-heavy Lower South. Lockean theory cut both ways and strengthened the chains of servitude almost as much as it severed them: John Locke argued that humans possessed a property both in themselves and in their physical possessions, which in the southern context included slaves. If the new American political order was based upon notions of mutual contract and the consent of the governed, both of which argued against the idea that one man could own another, it was equally true that gradual emancipation acts like those passed in the North could be regarded as violations of the natural property rights of masters. Because Thomas Jefferson's Declaration of Independence at once denounced slavery as immoral and sanctioned slave property as legitimate, a political revolution advanced in the name of property rights proved a formidable impediment to compulsory emancipation.

Clearly, English theories of social contracts fit none too neatly into a slaveholding society, and white southerners struggled mightily to qualify Revolutionary thought and reserve it for themselves. The concept of race proved especially useful in explaining why some people were not endowed with such routinely enumerated rights as liberty and equality. Consequently, the age of democratic revolutions ironically marked an inauspicious turning point in American race relations. In colonial society, a world based upon hierarchy and class, servitude was a racial institution, but it had never been explained or defended as such. The idea that blackness was itself prima facie proof of inferiority, if not of slave status, reached its apotheosis in the quarter century after independence. Although the process of legal classification based on race had been under way in the South since the interracial working-class revolt led by Nathaniel Bacon in 1676, until the rise of a universalist natural-rights ideology there had been little need to constitutionally deny the rights of citizenship to blacks.

For all the thick tomes designed to prove that the Revolutionary era witnessed both the first substantial challenge to bonded labor and an expansion of free black rights across the North, the hard evidence for radical social change is slim indeed, and modern scholars may be excused for suggesting the opposite. The separation from Great Britain may have been an opportunity for American slaveholders to begin anew; but if so, it was an opportunity lost. In 1776, the year in which Thomas Jefferson pronounced it a self-evident truth that all men were endowed with the inalienable right to liberty, fewer than 500,000 slaves lived on the English colonial mainland. By the 1790 census, despite the dislocation of war, the rise of private manumissions in Virginia and Maryland, and the passage of three gradual emancipation laws in the North, 698,000 slaves resided in the United States. If the Patriot elite honestly intended to slowly eradicate the blot of slavery, they had precious little to show for their efforts. If the promise of liberty was going to be extended to black Americans, it would be up to those in the slave quarters to seize it for themselves.

Seizing Their Liberty. Emboldened by Revolutionary theory and, in many parts of the South, by the near collapse of planter authority, black revolutionaries arose in unprecedented numbers in the two decades succeeding the conclusion of the conflict with Britain. Following the chaos of war, autonomous black regiments, countless minor slave plots, and several massive, politicized insurrections revealed a heightened black consciousness. Slave insurgents organized uprisings in Boston; in Perth Amboy, New Jersey; in Saint Andrews Parish, South Carolina; in Ulster County, New York; and in the Tar River Valley of North Carolina. But where slave rebels in Saint Domingue turned the plantation world upside down, those on the mainland only turned their wives into widows. Outside of South Carolina, which boasted a black majority, heavily armed white majorities and the inhospitable demography of the mainland militated against large-scale revolts.

Yet if Revolutionary slaves like Colonel Tye ultimately failed to force their Patriot masters to live up to the radical pretensions of the Revolution, bondpeople in other parts of the South nonetheless achieved a measure of autonomy previously unavailable to them. In the Georgia and South Carolina Lowcountry, the task system of labor organization had arisen in the decades before the Revolution. Various hypotheses have been advanced as to why planters turned from slave gangs to a task orientation, but little logic supports a single causal factor. Rather, a number of factors, especially the similarity of the system to West African cropping practices together with the African familiarity with rice cultivation, contributed to the development of the task system by the eve of the war. Because the task system provided bondpeople with a small measure of time to devote to their own gardens and handicraft industries, it allowed for a thriving informal, even underground slave economy. If the war for white independence did not evolve into a revolutionary movement for universal liberty, it did prompt a profoundly important redefinition and restructuring of slaves' concepts of freedom and economic rights.

The task system provided the catalyst for the burgeoning of the internal economies of the Lowcountry. The South Carolina planters who had flooded across the border at midcentury brought along their rice-planting operations and the task system of organizing unwaged labor. Most field hands, by working feverishly from dawn onward, managed to complete their tasks by midafternoon. Slaves were then at liberty to use their labor power to their own advantage. Men hunted, trapped, or engaged in handicraft industries such as the production of pottery; bondwomen, as they had done in West Africa, sold or traded vegetables and poultry in the nearest marketplace. Although many planters worried about the impact of this internal economy on their level of patriarchal control, they realized that such autonomous economic activities would hardly bring about the overthrow of unfree labor. Indeed, many penurious planters encouraged this informal economy, as they could then spend less on clothing for their human property. Most white businessmen also welcomed black entrepreneurship, as the enslaved vendors who dealt in fresh foodstuffs did

"Destruction of the Royal Statue in New York." This etching, from Chez Basset in Paris, late 1770s, was meant to depict the dismantling of an equestrian statue of George III in New York City on 9 July 1776; but the artist has actually shown a sculpture of a man standing and holding a scroll or baton. The men pulling it down seem to be mostly slaves. (Library of Congress.)

not compete with white retailers but rather purchased the fabrics and utensils that were the preserve of white importers. Urban bondpeople who sought fresh food did so in a public market dominated by both enslaved and free African American vendors. The rural bondpeople who supplied much of that food had no need to buy it.

The wartime disruption of the Lowcountry economy together with the military obligations of the master class and the rise in runaways to the British lines accelerated black economic autonomy in the Lower South. White absenteeism and the concomitant rise of slave drivers encouraged the growing independence of bondpeople and augmented the bargaining process between masters and drivers over work rhythms and routines. As impoverished planters sought to rebuild their war-torn plantation economies, they willingly accepted the re-creation of both the formal and informal slave economies that had been severely disordered by the Revolutionary War, precisely because they realized that they could strengthen slavery even while allowing blacks greater autonomy within it.

And while planter legislators struggled in vain to limit the economic independence of slaves, other forces worked to restore their spirits. Just as the war with Great Britain diminished patriarchal control, planter authority quickly

came under fire from another quarter: the black pulpit. If the Revolution failed to end unwaged labor in most parts of the Republic, a growing number of independent black churches nonetheless challenged the rising tide of white racism in the immediate aftermath of the war.

The high-water mark of black religiosity was reached in one of the most dramatic confrontations in early American church history. For a time, black Philadelphians worshipped with the aged patriot elite at Saint George's Methodist Episcopal Church. But in 1792, after freed congregants contributed money and muscle to the expansion of their church, Richard Allen and Absalom Jones were rudely yanked to their feet during prayers when they neglected to sit in a segregated section of the newly built gallery. Faced with the grim realization that a truly harmonious society was impossible even in a house of worship, blacks resolved to form a separate black church. Within two years Allen had founded what would become the African Methodist Episcopal (AME) Church. No better evidence exists that the Revolution had failed to bring about a more equitable society than the black exodus from white churches.

Like the Revolutionary ideology that fueled sporadic black rebellions at the war's end, African American churches helped create a new climate of black insubordination. Even in rural New Jersey, slaves and freedpersons continued to find collective expression through religion despite the fact that white-controlled churches refused to promote potential and qualified black ministers. Because the rise of Richard Allen's AME Church provided the black community with a foundation upon which to build, the independent black church movement took hold throughout northern New Jersey just as the first generation born after the emancipation act of 1804 came of age.

Independent churches began to bloom, in spite of periodic repression, even across the South—especially in urban areas, where free blacks enjoyed the relative freedom to construct new bastions of cultural sovereignty. Even as masters in the Lower South sought to purchase new Africans and restore order in the countryside, slaves and freedpeople, inspired by Richard Allen, moved to erect religious defenses against the dehumanizing effects of servitude. Their efforts to respond with integrity within the narrowly delimited options open to them led to the creation of Afro-Christianity, a black version of Christian theology whose vision was far from identical with the Christian goals of white Americans. These black-run institutions provided both slaves and freedpeople with the psychological and moral wherewithal necessary to withstand slavery. In short, independent black churches offered the most eloquent response to the conservative failures of the American Revolution.

Such examples of increasing black confidence and cultural autonomy were a genuine cause for white alarm. Yet most black ministers were pragmatists who believed that their primary responsibility was to protect the fragile black community and preserve a sense of hope for the future. North and South, white authorities routinely harassed black congregants and even closed black churches; such concerns often forced black ministers to surrender the principle of political leadership by negotiating with white protectors in hopes of keeping their churches open.

In an attempt to placate white society, black preachers urged their congregations to observe white standards of respectability and "one's proper place in society." Black leaders were painfully aware that flamboyant dress, unseemly gaiety, and raucous behavior might be used by malevolent whites to support the fiction that blacks were undeserving of freedom and equal rights. Their pleas often went unheeded. Indeed, northern blacks turned to African culture to forge weapons of survival that were almost as significant as black churches. The language and clothing of freedpeople both reinforced continuities with an African past and reflected a disdain for the dominant white society. Rejecting demands for acculturation, many urban blacks spurned wholesale assimilation in favor of creative adaptation to an often hostile world.

Perhaps the last words on the alleged radicalism of the American Revolution should go to an unnamed black rebel who in 1800 told a Virginia court that risking his life in the name of liberty was justified by the precedent established by the founding fathers. "I have nothing more to offer than what General Washington would have had to offer, had he been taken by the British and put to trial," the young bondman patiently explained. "I have adventured my life in endeavouring to obtain the liberty of my countrymen, and am a willing sacrifice in their cause." Upon hearing this declaration, white Americans promptly sentenced him to swing.

[*See also* African Methodist Episcopal Church; Allen, Richard; Benezet, Anthony; Black Church; Black Loyalists; Civil Rights; Clothing; Colonel Tye; Declaration of Independence; Gradual Emancipation; Hamilton, Alexander, and African Americans; Historiography of Early Black Life; Jay, John, on African Americans; Jones, Absalom; Language; Laws and Legislation; Manumission Societies; Massachusetts; Military; Murray, John (Lord Dunmore); New Jersey; New York Manumission Society; Race, Theories of; Resistance; Riots and Rebellions; *and* Society of Friends (Quakers) and African Americans.]

BIBLIOGRAPHY

Frey, Sylvia R. *Water from the Rock: Black Resistance in a Revolutionary Age*. Princeton, NJ: Princeton University Press, 1991.

Hodges, Graham R. *Root and Branch: African Americans in New York and East Jersey, 1613–1863*. Chapel Hill: University of North Carolina Press, 1999.

Holton, Woody. *Forced Founders: Indians, Debtors, Slaves, and the Making of the American Revolution in Virginia*. Chapel Hill: University of North Carolina Press, 1999.

Melish, Joanne Pope. *Disowning Slavery: Gradual Emancipation and "Race" in New England, 1780–1860*. Ithaca, NY: Cornell University Press, 1998.

Nash, Gary B., and Jean R. Soderlund. *Freedom by Degrees: Emancipation in Pennsylvania and Its Aftermath*. New York: Oxford University Press, 1991.

Quarles, Benjamin. *The Negro in the American Revolution*. Chapel Hill: University of North Carolina Press, 1961.

White, Shane. *Somewhat More Independent: The End of Slavery in New York City, 1770–1810*. Athens: University of Georgia Press, 1991.

—DOUGLAS R. EGERTON

AMERICAN REVOLUTION, MEMORY OF. The American Revolution, at its core, was a marked contradiction. On the one hand, American Revolutionaries claimed inalienable rights to liberty and freedom. On the other hand, they enforced the slavery of hundreds of thousands of African Americans. That incongruity was not always so clear to contemporaries, who often believed that blacks were inferior to whites, from whom they were thought to differ physically, mentally, and morally. Thomas Jefferson's opposition to slavery in *Notes on the State of Virginia* (1785) was undermined by, among other factors, his perception of black inferiority. Still, many in the eighteenth century did see a contradiction between slavery and the ideology of the American Revolution. Samuel Johnson, the famed British lexicographer, remarked in his 1775 political tract *Taxation no Tyranny*, "How is it that we hear the loudest *yelps* for liberty among the drivers of Negroes?" Prominent Americans (such as Samuel Hopkins, James Otis, Thomas Paine, and Benjamin Rush) also recognized this contradiction. Luther Martin, a lawyer and politician, even wrote that slavery was "inconsistent with the genius of republicanism and has a tendency to destroy those principles on which it is supported, as it lessens the sense of the equal rights of mankind, and habituates us to tyranny and oppression." African Americans who saw this paradox increasingly came to identify the ideology of the American Revolution as a foundation for their demands for freedom from slavery, as evidenced by events not only in the North but also in the middle states, and even in the South.

There was a time when historians did not think to measure the American Revolution against the enslavement of African Americans. However, in current scholarship the topic is debated frequently and fervently. Some portray the American Revolution as a significant step toward ending American slavery. For others, it is an initial, but limited step toward that end. And still others argue that the founders of the Revolutionary era prolonged slavery in America, in part by entrenching it in the U.S. Constitution. Balanced approaches have aimed to see the topic in a historical context and in a long time frame.

During the Revolutionary War and in its immediate aftermath, American slaves in some instances demonstrably benefited from Revolutionary ideology and actions. For instance, the spirit of the times led increasing numbers of slaves to petition, successfully, for freedom. The upheavals of war led to a faltering in the power of slaveholders, allowing slaves temporary relief in chaos or as runaways. In other cases, slaves were enlisted, as soldiers and seamen, in the Continental and British armies. Famously, Lord Dunmore in Virginia actively recruited blacks, forming the so-called Ethiopian Regiment, with promises of freedom. During the American Revolution the number of free blacks increased exponentially, principally as a result of gradual emancipation laws and manumission. A larger community of free blacks was one of the significant and lasting legacies of the American Revolution.

The memory of the Revolution played out in other ways long after the war had ended. Not least of all, it provided a concrete impetus to slaves involved in their own "revolutions" in the late eighteenth and early nineteenth centuries. Nor were the seemingly inherent paradoxes of the American Revolution lost on the blacks of Frederick Douglass's world. These paradoxes lived on in the memory of many African Americans, such as the Bostonian David Walker. David Walker's *Appeal to the Coloured Citizens of the World*, first published in 1829, circulated widely in the United States, where it spread a message of black resistance well after Walker's death in 1830. Walker (particularly concerned to challenge Jefferson's assessment of black inferiority) celebrated American freedom as enshrined in the Declaration of Independence but lamented and challenged the fact that blacks were excluded:

See your Declaration Americans!!! Do you understand your own language? Hear your language, proclaimed to the world . . . We hold these truths to be self evident—that ALL MEN ARE CREATED EQUAL!! that they *are endowed by their Creator with certain unalienable rights*; that among these are life, *liberty*, and the pursuit of happiness!! (Hinks, p. 78)

In *Colored Patriots of the American Revolution* (1855), William Cooper Nell fought slavery in nineteenth-century America by remembering African American contributions to the American Revolution. Drawing similar lessons to those of Walker and Nell, with whom he was acquainted, Douglass pointed out that for African Americans the American Revolution witnessed "the advent of a nation based upon human brotherhood and the self-evident truths of liberty and equality."

[*See also* Class; Constitution, U.S.; Douglass, Frederick; Emancipation; Jefferson, Thomas; Nell, William Cooper; Race, Theories of; *and* Walker, David.]

BIBLIOGRAPHY

Berlin, Ira. *Generations of Captivity: A History of African-American Slaves*. Cambridge, MA: Harvard University Press, 2003.
Davis, David Brion. *The Problem of Slavery in the Age of Revolution, 1770–1823*. Ithaca, NY: Cornell University Press, 1975.
Finkelman, Paul. *Slavery and the Founders: Race and Liberty in the Age of Jefferson*. 2nd ed. Armonk, NY: M. E. Sharpe, 2001.
Finkelman, Paul, ed. *Slavery, Revolutionary America, and the New Nation*. New York: Garland, 1989.
Frey, Sylvia R. *Water from the Rock: Black Resistance in a Revolutionary Age*. Princeton, NJ: Princeton University Press, 1991.
Hinks, Peter P. ed. *David Walker's "Appeal to the Coloured Citizens of the World"* (1829). University Park: Pennsylvania State University Press, 2000.
Nell, William Cooper. *Colored Patriots of the American Revolution* (1855). New York: Arno, 1968.
Quarles, Benjamin. *The Negro in the American Revolution*. Chapel Hill: University of North Carolina Press, 1961.

—MARK G. SPENCER

AMISTAD. On 28 June 1839 the schooner *La Amistad* sailed from Havana, Cuba, en route to Puerto Príncipe, carrying fifty-three Africans, including four children. These so-called slaves were in fact free Africans who had been stolen from their homes in West Africa and brought to Cuba. Two Spanish planters, José Ruiz and Pedro

"Death of Capt. Ferrer, the Captain of the Amistad, July, 1839," lithograph by John Warner Barber from his compilation *A History of the Amistad Captives*, 1840. (New York Public Library, Manuscripts, Archives, and Rare Books Division, Schomburg Center for Research in Black Culture; Astor, Lenox, and Tilden Foundations.)

Montes, purchased them, gave them Spanish names, and falsely labeled them as native Cubans. After the schooner's cook jokingly told them that they were to be "killed, salted, and cooked," the Africans decided to revolt. Three days after setting sail, the captives Joseph Cinqué and Grabeau led the Africans in using wood and knives to overpower the crew. During the battle three Africans as well as the schooner's captain and cook were killed.

After the revolt the Africans ordered the *Amistad* crew to return them to Africa. However, the Spaniards secretly turned the ship around each night and headed for America, where they were sure the Africans would be classified as property and returned to Cuba. After a journey of more than sixty days, in which several additional African lives were lost due to malnutrition and disease, the *Amistad* was discovered on 26 August 1839 off Culloden Point in Long Island Sound.

On boarding the *Amistad*, crew members of the Coast Guard brig *U.S. Washington* found that the schooner was under the control of forty-three surviving Africans. After being set free Ruiz and Montes informed the Americans that all the Africans were slaves. The schooner was then towed to New London, Connecticut, where the Africans were arrested and held for trial. Antonio, the cabin boy, was also held as a material witness. Unable to speak English, the Africans initially could not explain what had happened. After Josiah Willard Gibbs, a language professor at Yale, located an interpreter, James Covey, by shouting out African words on the docks, the full horror of the kidnappings became public knowledge. Covey, assisted by Grabeau, who spoke four languages, discovered that the Africans were Mende rather than Cuban.

The contents of the *Amistad*, including the Africans, became a hotly debated topic with international complications. Under a 1795 treaty that required that all property seized on the high seas be returned to its rightful owner, Spain demanded return of the schooner and all its contents or reimbursements for the total worth of the lost property, estimated at approximately seventy thousand dollars. President Martin Van Buren supported the Spanish position and insisted that the Africans be tried for murder and piracy or that they be returned to Cuba as slaves. The crew of the *Washington* also filed a successful claim under American salvage laws that allotted them a portion of any profits made from the seized vessel.

Sensing that the publicity was bound to sway public opinion in favor of their movement, abolitionists immediately adopted the cause of the Africans and formed the *Amistad* Committee. Leading the effort to get the story out and use it to highlight the evils of slavery were Lewis Tappan, an affluent New York merchant and abolitionist; Simon Jocelyn, a draftsman who had opened the first black church in New Haven, Connecticut; and Joshua Leavitt, a lawyer, minister, and editor of the abolitionist journal the *Emancipator*. The three men worked with the attorney Roger Sherman Baldwin to prepare the defense. The *Amistad* Committee also guided fund-raising efforts to defray legal costs. Tappan and Leavitt visited the jail and reported that the prisoners were generally healthy and comfortable. Abolitionists unsuccessfully pushed for Ruiz and Montes to be arrested and tried.

By this time Cinqué had become the hero of the *Amistad* drama, arousing the interest and admiration of a number of prominent Americans, including Frederick Douglass. In the speech "The Significance of Emancipation," Douglass told an audience in Canandaigua, New York, that Cinqué had endeared himself to American slaves by leading the slave revolt on the *Amistad*. Douglass's continued admiration for Cinqué was demonstrated by the fact that he hung an engraving of the African on the wall of his home library.

Representing the Africans, Baldwin argued that the United States had no authority to return the Africans to Spain, where the African slave trade was illegal. In September 1839 a federal district court agreed, determining that the Africans were not slaves and that the revolt had been undertaken in self-defense. A circuit court later agreed. The Africans were incarcerated for eighteen months while the case wound its way through the U.S. court system. Abolitionists and locals used this time to teach the Africans English and to convert them to Christianity.

John Quincy Adams, popularly known as "Old Man Eloquent," was an abolitionist by nature and had spearheaded opposition to the congressional rule in the mid-1830s. However, he was somewhat skeptical of the abolitionist movement because of what he saw as the radicalism of its members. As a former president of the United States and a member of the House of Representatives, he took a lively interest in the Amistad case from the beginning, although he initially refused to take an active role. After conceding that someone with experience and impeccable credentials should argue the case before the Supreme Court, Adams took the case and shaped his arguments around both natural and constitutional law and the premises set forth in the Declaration of Independence. He reminded the Court that many of the founding fathers, including George Washington and Thomas Jefferson, believed that slavery should be abolished because it violated the laws of God and nature. Adams declared that states had no power to declare slavery within their sovereign rights because it violated the concept of government by contract since slaves had no voice in government. While Adams gave the longest and most emotional argument, Baldwin was more persuasive and had more influence over the Court.

On 9 March 1841, in a 7 to 1 decision, the Supreme Court announced that the Africans were not slaves but free Africans and agreed that they had a right to defend themselves from their kidnappers. Therefore, Spain had no right to compensation for their lost "slaves." The Court did not declare slavery illegal in the United States, but it did rule that the U.S. government had no legal obligation to spend money to return the "Amistads," as they were called, to Africa.

Thus, abolitionists were forced to fund the trip privately. While the Africans waited to be returned home, they planted and harvested their own crops, sold handcrafts, drew pictures, wrote about their stories, and went on speaking tours to help earn money for their passage. After months of fund-raising efforts the thirty-five surviving Africans set sail for home on 27 November 1841.

Five members of the Union Missionary Society went with them to establish missions and schools in Sierra Leone. Cinqué, like a number of others, disappeared from the historical record after returning to Africa. Sarah Magru, one of the children enslaved on the Amistad, later attended Oberlin College and returned to work at the Mende mission.

The Amistad is seen as a turning point in the antislavery movement because the case educated millions of Americans about the barbarity of slavery. The story of the Amistad received renewed attention after the 1997 release of Steven Spielberg's movie Amistad.

[See also Adams, John Quincy; Africa, Idea of; Antislavery Movement; Douglass, Frederick; Film and Filmmakers; Foreign Policy; Jefferson, Thomas; Slave Trade; Slavery; Slavery and the U.S. Constitution; Supreme Court; and Tappan, Lewis.]

BIBLIOGRAPHY

Blasingame, John W., ed. The Frederick Douglass Papers. Series 1, Speeches, Debates, and Interviews. 5 vols. New Haven, CT: Yale University Press, 1979–1992. Douglass's mention of Joseph Cinqué in a speech given in Canandaigua, New York, on 3 August 1857 appears on page 206 of volume 2. On page 500 of volume 3, mention is made of an engraving of Cinqué in Douglass's library.

Brecher, Jeremy. "The Amistad Incident." Amistad America. http://www.amistadamerica.org. This is the most comprehensive Amistad site on the Internet. Besides the historical facts, the site contains information on efforts to keep the Amistad a part of living history.

Jones, Howard. Mutiny on the Amistad: The Saga of a Slave Revolt and Its Impact on American Abolition, Law, and Diplomacy. New York: Oxford University Press, 1987. Jones concentrates on the implications of the actions that led to the Amistad revolt.

Osagie, Iyunolu Folayan. The Amistad Revolt: Memory, Slavery, and the Politics of Identity in the United States and Sierra Leone. Athens: University of Georgia Press, 2000. Osagie places the revolt within the overall context of the antislavery movement.

U.S. Supreme Court. The Amistad, 40 U.S. 518 (1841). http://caselaw.lp.findlaw.com/amistad_case.html. The case includes a summary of events as well as details of the justices' decision.

The Voyage of "La Amistad": A Quest for Freedom. VHS. MPI Home Video, 1998. Excellent documentary that brings the events surrounding the Amistad revolt to life. It also includes personal glimpses into the lives of the kidnapped Africans.

—ELIZABETH R. PURDY

ANDREW, JOHN ALBION

ANDREW, JOHN ALBION (b. 31 May 1818; d. 30 October 1867), abolitionist, Massachusetts governor, and organizer of black military units for Civil War service. The son of Jonathan Andrew, a farmer and storeowner, and Nancy Green Pierce, a schoolteacher, John Andrew was born in Windham, Massachusetts (in the part of the state that became Maine in 1820). He attended Bowdoin College and graduated in 1837. He moved to Boston, where he entered the law and became active in politics. An idealistic lawyer, devoting much of his early career to pro bono work for prisoners and blacks, he made a name for himself fighting fugitive slave laws. He considered the abolitionist John Brown a hero and arranged for his defense counsel after Brown was caught at Harpers Ferry in 1859. In politics he was active with the "Young Whigs," an antislavery splinter group that became the Free-Soil Party. He served a term in the Massachusetts legislature (1857).

During the 1860 elections Andrew was the head of the Massachusetts delegation to the Republican National Convention and threw the state's support behind Abraham Lincoln. In return, the party supported Andrew in his election as governor. After taking office, Andrew put Massachusetts on a war footing, believing that war was imminent. From the start of the war he said that the goal was to free the slaves, and he pushed the Republicans to make abolition a priority. He was also an early proponent of arming blacks for the conflict.

On 17 July 1862 Congress approved the recruitment of blacks into armed service. After intense lobbying, Secretary of War Edwin Stanton authorized Andrew to organize a black regiment, the Fifty-fourth Massachusetts Infantry. One stipulation that Stanton placed on the regiment was that officers were to be white. Andrew formed the Massachusetts-Kansas Committee to recruit blacks and enlisted the help of the former slave and renowned abolitionist Frederick Douglass. Douglass raised more than six hundred men, including his sons Charles and Lewis, and brought them to Boston on 27 March 1863. On 18 May, Andrew presented the unit colors in a formal ceremony, calling the regiment an opportunity for black men to strike a blow for freedom. Douglass felt that the creation of the unit was a historic event for blacks, providing an opportunity to shape the fight for liberty. Andrew hoped the Fifty-fourth would serve as a model for a "Negro army." By the end of the war Massachusetts had raised three black regiments, two infantry and one cavalry.

Creating and administering the regiment became difficult for Andrew. He assured Douglass and the black recruits that they would receive pay equal to that of white volunteers, but Congress and the War Department authorized a lesser payment—as laborers, not soldiers. The Fifty-fourth (and Fifty-fifth, another black regiment) refused their pay, even when Andrew secured state funds to make up the difference. Congress finally passed a law forcing equal recognition. Andrew's recruiting efforts covered the entire Union and all Union-occupied southern states.

Andrew was reelected in 1864 but resigned in January 1866, considering his governorship "wartime services." Af-

John Andrew Albion, abolitionist and governor of Massachusetts. This unidentifed and undated lithograph may be a drawing after a photograph taken c. 1860. (Library of Congress.)

ter the war he disagreed with President Andrew Johnson's Reconstruction policies. Andrew believed that Reconstruction should be economic, not political, and that the nation should therefore be working cooperatively with southern leaders. He formed the American Land Company in October 1865 and within a few months had over 3 million acres of southern land for sale to encourage northerners to migrate. His death in 1867 followed a long illness that had plagued him since his last year as governor.

[*See also* Abolitionism; Brown, John; Civil War; Civil War, Participation and Recruitment of Black Troops in; Douglass, Frederick; Fifty-fourth Massachusetts Infantry Regiment; Fifty-fifth Massachusetts Infantry Regiment; Free-Soil Party; Harpers Ferry Raid; Johnson, Andrew; Military; Reconstruction; Republican Party; *and* Union Army, African Americans in.]

BIBLIOGRAPHY

Abbott, Richard H. *Cotton and Capital: Boston Businessmen and Antislavery Reform, 1854–1868.* Amherst: University of Massachusetts Press, 1991. Provides much detail about Andrew's antislavery activities.

Pearson, Henry Greenleaf. *The Life of John Andrew, Governor of Massachusetts, 1861–1865.* Boston: Houghton, Mifflin, 1904. Though dated, this is the only full-length biography of Andrew.

—MICHAEL C. MILLER

ANGLO-AFRICAN NEWSPAPER. A major forum for black authors and an important source of knowledge about African American culture, the *Anglo-African Newspaper* was published by Thomas and Robert Hamilton, the sons of the black leader William T. Hamilton. Thomas Hamilton had long been involved in African American journalism in New York, starting as a carrier for the *Colored American* in 1837 and later serving as a mail clerk for the *National Anti-Slavery Standard*. He began his own publishing career in 1841 by founding the weekly *People's Press*, which was intended as a replacement for the defunct *Colored American*. When this effort failed, Hamilton returned to the *National Anti-Slavery Standard* and also worked for the *New York Independent*.

The weekly *Anglo-African Newspaper* was started in 1859, with the 23 July issue stating that it was intended to be "a press of our own." Its motto, emblazoned on the masthead, was "Man must be free, if not through the law, then above the law." An accompanying magazine, the first issue of which appeared in January 1859, was devoted to the arts and culture. Writers for the *Anglo-African Newspaper* included Francis Ellen Watkins Harper, James W. C. Pennington, James Theodore Holly, and Martin Robison Delany. Important articles included James McCune Smith's feature on Thomas Jefferson, Pennington's history of the slave trade, and William Cooper Nell's discussion of black Revolutionary War veterans. The magazine first serialized Delany's novel *Blake; or, The Huts of America*. In 1859 the newspaper was a valuable source for news about John Brown's raid on Harpers Ferry, Virginia, and subsequent trial. The paper printed statistics on black demographics beginning in 1790; it also reprinted the transcript of the trial of Nat Turner, openly comparing the cases of Brown and Turner. The *Anglo-African* championed race pride, opening its columns to commentary on Yoruba culture. The paper published works by Frederick Douglass, John Mercer Langston, and Mary Ann Shadd, among many other notables of the day.

The newspaper was part of a trend—inspired, no doubt, by the harsh legal and social racism of the 1850s—to reconsider and endorse African American immigration to Africa. One the eve of the Civil War one writer argued, "My duty and my destiny are in Africa." Another complained of the despicable meanness displayed by the United States government toward Liberia. Still another article proclaimed Haiti to be the best refuge for oppressed American blacks. An author named only as "Volunteer" proclaimed the island nation to be the "nucleus of power to the black" and trumpeted the contention that slave dealers and slaveholders found there would be hanged "as surely as they are caught."

In 1860 financial setbacks for the Hamiltons forced the closing of the magazine and the sale of the newspaper to George Lawrence Jr., an agent for James Redpath, the famed abolitionist and journalist who advocated migration to Haiti. Within a few months, Thomas Hamilton had regained the newspaper, and Robert Hamilton taken charge of its finances. The *Anglo-American Newspaper* became indispensable for coverage of black participation in and views on the Civil War. Henry Highland Garnet, for example, wrote extensively on affairs in Washington, D.C., and letters from black soldiers appeared regularly in the newspaper. Though Hamilton and his writers criticized prejudice and discrimination in the North, they more constructively entered the political arena as avid supporters of Abraham Lincoln and the Republican Party. Hamilton and Garnet lobbied Lincoln for black citizenship and expanded civil rights. Just before the newspaper folded in December 1865, it applauded the efforts of northern teachers heading south to instruct the freed people. During their six-year run publishing the *Anglo-African Newspaper*, the Hamilton brothers greatly enhanced and distinguished black journalism.

[*See also* Black Press; Brown, John; Civil Rights; Civil War; Civil War, Participation and Recruitment of Black Troops in; Delany, Martin Robison; Demographics; Douglass, Frederick; Emigration to Africa; Garnet, Henry Highland; Haiti; Harpers Ferry Raid; Jefferson, Thomas; Langston, John Mercer; Liberia; Lincoln, Abraham; Nell, William Cooper; Pennington, James W. C.; Redpath, James; Republican Party; Smith, James McCune; *and* Turner, Nat.]

BIBLIOGRAPHY

Bullock, Penelope L. *The Afro-American Periodical Press, 1838–1909*. Baton Rouge: Louisiana State University Press, 1981.

Hodges, Graham Russell. *Root and Branch: African Americans in New York and East Jersey, 1613–1863*. Chapel Hill: University of North Carolina Press, 1999.

—GRAHAM RUSSELL GAO HODGES

ANTHONY, SUSAN B. (b. 15 February 1820; d. 13 March 1906), reformer and leader of the women's suffrage movement. Susan Brownell Anthony was born in Adams, Massachusetts, to an unusual family. Her father was a Quaker; at the religious meetings she attended as a child, women were allowed to speak and were on an equal footing with men. The family was prosperous, and her parents encouraged freethinking and activism in their children. Anthony became an abolitionist and participant in the Underground Railroad. She is best remembered as one of the leaders and organizers of the women's suffrage movement.

Anthony's family moved from Massachusetts to Rochester, New York, in 1845. Over the next few years, the abolitionist and former slave Frederick Douglass, also a resident of Rochester, became a frequent visitor and speaker at Sunday meetings at the Anthony farm, where abolition was discussed. Like many reform-minded people of the day, Anthony also joined the local temperance society. After being denied the chance to speak at temperance meetings because of her sex, Anthony founded the Daughters of Temperance. Although other members of her family were involved early in the fight for women's rights, it was not until after her 1851 meeting with the suffragist Elizabeth Cady Stanton that Anthony began to devote her time and efforts to achieve suffrage and property rights for women.

Anthony's activism often brought her into contact with Douglass, who became a good friend. Her growing interest in women's rights did not curtail Anthony's work in the abolition movement, and other causes appealed to both her and Douglass. In 1858, for example, in an early effort to ban capital punishment, Anthony, Douglass, and others worked to stop the execution of Marion Ira Stout in Rochester. Stout had been convicted of murdering his brother-in-law, Charles W. Littles, who had been abusive and unfaithful to Stout's sister. Implications of incest added spice to the April 1858 trial coverage. (Stout was hung for his crime on 22 October 1858.) Douglass wrote up a handbill announcing a town meeting, and Anthony circulated it. Douglass chaired the meeting and spoke eloquently but was subjected to racist insults from the crowd and was forced to adjourn the group without achieving its aims.

Anthony's diary indicates that she worked with the abolitionist Harriet Tubman on the Underground Railroad even after the Civil War had begun. Her more public efforts on behalf of ending slavery met with ugly protests at times. In Syracuse, New York, she was burned in effigy, and the charred dummy was dragged through the streets. In other cities rotten eggs were thrown at her, lights were doused, and pepper was thrown on heating stoves: all unsuccessful attempts to drive her from the podium.

When Anthony's father, Daniel, died in 1862, Frederick Douglass delivered a eulogy. After the Civil War, however, the friendship of Anthony and Douglass was interrupted. Anthony felt betrayed by Douglass's new focus on voting rights and citizenship for black men. Douglass ignored women's suffrage—black and white—during this period, arguing that this was "the Negro's Hour."

After the Civil War, Anthony and Stanton founded the National Woman Suffrage Association but were without the support of many of their abolitionist friends. Nevertheless, Anthony was a tireless organizer, traveling widely and speaking frequently for women's rights. She gathered signatures for petitions and put together conventions. In 1872 she was even arrested for voting in the presidential

Susan B. Anthony in 1900. The photographer, Frances Benjamin Johnson (1864–1952), was prominent in photojournalism—then a newly emerging field. Many famous people sat for Johnson. At the Paris Exposition of 1900 her images capturing the lives of African Americans were displayed in the "Negro Exhibit" arranged by W. E. B. Du Bois and Thomas Calloway. (Library of Congress.)

election. Anthony was not allowed to testify at her trial and was ordered to pay a fine. She refused, and the court took no further action against her.

The post–Civil War rift with Frederick Douglass lasted for decades. Anthony refrained from publicly supporting Douglass's second marriage, to a white woman, arguing that the equality of the sexes should be the only issue of her organization. Private comments to Stanton about the issue reveal that Anthony still smarted from Douglass's "betrayal" of women's rights. At the International Council of Women in 1888, however, several factionalized suffrage organizations came together in a show of unity. Anthony invited Frederick Douglass onto the stage along with the abolitionist Robert Purvis. In 1895, when Douglass was honored in Washington, D.C., by the National Council of Women, it was Anthony who escorted him to the platform. A few days later she was asked to give a eulogy at Douglass's funeral.

Anthony retired from her leadership positions in 1900, although she continued to speak publicly on occasion. Her last public words, often quoted, were proclaimed at her eighty-sixth birthday celebration: "Failure is impossible!" She died a few weeks later, but her work and influence continued. Several states granted women the right to vote before Anthony's death in 1906, but it was not until 1920 that the Nineteenth Amendment, passed by Congress and thirty-six states, became a reality. In an election that happened to fall on the hundredth anniversary of Anthony's birth, woman of the United States were able to vote in a national election for the first time.

[*See also* Antislavery Movement; Douglass, Frederick; Stanton, Elizabeth Cady; Suffrage, Women's; Temperance; Tubman, Harriet; Underground Railroad; *and* Voting Rights.]

BIBLIOGRAPHY
Barry, Kathleen. *Susan B. Anthony: A Biography of a Singular Feminist*. New York: New York University Press, 1988.
Sherr, Lynn. *Failure Is Impossible: Susan B. Anthony in Her Own Words*. New York: Times Books, 1995.
Ward, Geoffrey C., et al. *Not for Ourselves Alone: The Story of Elizabeth Cady Stanton and Susan B. Anthony—An Illustrated History*. New York: Knopf, 1999.

—VICKEY KALAMBAKAL

ANTIQUITY. Africa is the second-largest continent on earth and home to the longest continuous human occupations. It is the site of both hominid and human origins and the location of perhaps the earliest known Neolithic civilizational social complexes as well. Although most modern historical accounts have downplayed Africa and Africans, a wide range of research and evidence from across the social and physical sciences has overturned such omissions and begun to restore Africa to its proper place in the annals of human history. Many long-entrenched theories have been called into question or become the subject of vociferous debate as the result of new evidence.

Origins of the Name *Africa*. The use of the word *Africa* to describe the whole of the continent needs some clarification. Applied to any time from the earliest human origins until the rise of the Roman Empire, the word is an anachronism, a modern designation transplanted to eras when other terminology was in use. The conventional usage will be followed here, however, largely because the other, older names originating both inside and outside the continent have changed too many times to fully recount in such a short space and would prove confusing to most readers.

There is robust debate about the etymological origins of the term *Africa*, but it is widely accepted that at one early stage it referred to the North African coast in the region that in the modern era includes Tunisia and some of neighboring Libya. The Romans referred to this area as *Africa terra*, "land of the Afri" (plural of "Afer") and, after much rivalry with the polity there, centered in the great capital of Carthage, eventually annexed it as the Roman province of Africa.

Some believe that the name *Africa* derived from the Greek word *aphrike*, meaning "land without cold or horror," but linguistic evidence about the shift in Greek usage of *ph* for *f* has cast doubt on this explanation. Other possible origins include the Phoenician *afar*, or "dust"; the Latin *aprica*, or "sunny"; and, perhaps most convincingly, the names of Afridi or Berber tribes of the region, for whom plausible etymological connections can be maintained.

Hominid and Human Origins. Scientific discoveries in several fields provide strong evidence that not only the first hominids but also the first human beings lived in Africa and that all people alive are descended from a relatively small group of ancestors living on the African continent. It has long been thought that Africa witnessed the earliest steps in human evolution, but excavations at the end of the twentieth century and the beginning of the twenty-first pushed the dates back almost twice as far as was thought possible only a few years earlier. New techniques, new finds, and especially digs in areas insufficiently or never before explored revolutionized the field—though they perhaps sparked more new debates rather than fully solving previously unanswered mysteries.

For decades hominid development was thought to have diverged from that of other African primates with the emergence of *Australopithecus*, a bipedal human precursor with enlarged apelike brain casings that were still only one-third of modern human averages, roughly 4 million years ago (mya). Genetics, comparative morphological analyses, and related disciplines then converged on the hypothesis that hominids probably diverged from African apes about 6 to 7 mya. The intervening years, nearly half of the time hominids have existed, were largely shrouded in mystery until a series of exciting discoveries in Kenya, Ethiopia, and Chad shed light on this period. In the Awash region of Ethiopia, *Ardipithecus ramidus* was uncovered, dating to 4.5 to 5.5 mya. Then, *Orrorin tugenensis* was discovered in Kenya, dating to 6 mya (although debate exists as to whether this was a terrestrial biped or simply another species of arboreal ape). Most spectacularly, in 2001 and 2002 fossils later designated *Sahelanthropus tchadensis* were uncovered in northern Chad, dating to 6 to 7 mya and bearing mixed ape-human characteristics of clear hominid style. Another possible predecessor, *Samburupithecus*, was dated to more than 8 mya, although specialists debate whether it represents a direct human ancestor or a separate line of parallel evolutionary development and whether it was a hominid as opposed to an ape. Indeed, similar questions apply, to a greater or lesser extent, to all these new discoveries. However, there are strong reasons, such as skull morphological characteristics, to believe that *Ardipithecus* and *Sahelanthropus* were both hominids, potentially extending the human line back in time almost twice as far as *Australopithecus*.

Starting about 2.4 mya, the human genus *Homo* emerges in the African fossil record with *Homo habilis*, marked by a pronounced increase in brain size. *H. habilis* lived in Africa for about 1 million years. *Homo erectus*, ranging from 1.8 to 0.3 mya, exhibited an almost modern brain size and migrated across the world, from Africa to Asia, Europe, and the Indonesian archipelago. Hominids continued to become more gracile, with larger average brain capacities, until *Homo sapiens* emerged in the last 500,000 years. Fully modern humans, *Homo sapiens sapiens*, arose in Africa and then parts of Asia about 150,000 years ago and probably less than 50,000 years ago in Europe.

As with the origins of hominids, ideas about human origins underwent important revision in the late 1990s and early 2000s. Until 2003 the oldest specimens, from Africa and Israel, dated to 100,000 years ago, but in that year Tim White unearthed several skulls in Ethiopia that dated to between 154,000 and 160,000 years ago. Many scientists regarded this historic find as strong evidence for the "out of Africa" hypothesis, which postulates that modern humans migrated from Africa across the world and displaced existing archaic human species between 200,000 and 100,000 years ago. White himself went on to designate his find as an intermediate species, *H. sapiens idaltu*, and research in coming years is sure to expand this debate. At any rate, this second great African diaspora (the first being that of *H. erectus*) would indicate that human populations diverged only recently into distinct regions and into the semidistinct phenotypes associated in modernity with the social construction of "race."

A different hypothesis, however, generally referred to as "multiregionalism," suggests that *H. sapiens* might have evolved over a period of more than 2 million years, with some interbreeding between populations on the three Old World continents. New forms of evidence collection, such as mitochondrial DNA testing, has shown Neanderthals—long known to European archaeology and often postulated as human precursors, fixing human origins in Europe rather than Africa—to be unrelated to modern humans. This finding has bolstered the "out of Africa" theory, but advocates of multiregional theory continue to pose important questions. The debate is far from resolved, even or perhaps particularly in the explosive new area of genetics.

Modern Humans and the Rise of Agriculture in Africa. From at least 90,000 years before the present (ybp), *Homo sapiens sapiens* began to produce art—cave and rock paintings, beadwork, and other decorative material remains. By 30,000 ybp humans were extensively using carved bone tools, living in wood and fossilized-bone frame houses, hunting many medium-size and a few large animal species, fishing extensively with spears and eventually basket traps, using carrying bags, and creating jewelry. People had definitively shifted from being the hunted to becoming the hunters. Art increased in prevalence and included small carved animal statues and items that were probably calendars.

The Sahara, also referred to in part or in whole as the Sudan or Sahel, is the world's largest desert and was a well-watered region from 12,000 to 7,500 years ago, with the full complement of African flora and fauna seen today primarily south of the equator. Exploiting its rich fertility and numerous rivers and lakes, a highly advanced and specialized fishing culture developed throughout this region as early as 20,000 years ago and often traded with peoples living in adjacent but differentiated climatic regions, such as the Ethiopian highlands. It was in this society, and in its burgeoning trade and social contacts, that some of the first steps anywhere in the world were taken toward the development of the Neolithic cultural complexes known generally as civilization: domesticated agriculture and animals, substantial settled centers, social hierarchies, specialized religious leaders, technological advances, and the development of writing and record keeping.

Much debate remains, but the widely held notion that civilization began in the Mesopotamian river valleys of Southwest Asia and spread out from there has come into question. Some of this debate turns on what is recognized as civilization and what counts as domestication, but many scholars believe that either the world was witness to simultaneous and parallel development of these forms of advanced social organization or the Sudan-Ethiopia nexus was indeed the earliest in the world.

Excavations in the late twentieth and early twenty-first centuries increasingly supported the latter view, and a new perspective emerged that might explain the apparently sudden and decisive development of civilizational culture in the Mesopotamian region that eventually became Iraq. It was suggested that these cultural forms and technologies arrived as a package in the Persian Gulf from East African settlers traveling by boat. This hypothesis would take the old notion of a Fertile Crescent—stretching along the biblical route supposedly taken by Abraham from southern Iraq through the Kurdish highlands and finally down into the fertile Levant of modern Lebanon and Palestine-Israel—and turn it into more of a Fertile Circle, starting near the sources of the Nile River, spreading to the Persian Gulf, then along the Fertile Crescent route, and finally down into Egypt and the other end of the Nile. Excavations and adjunct research in formerly archaeologically unexplored regions of Africa promise to further the understanding of these processes and their chronological order.

Knowledge of this earliest civilizational period comes largely through a combination of linguistics and burgeoning archaeological excavation. Afro-Asiatic speakers, including the Cushitic speakers from whom Middle Eastern populations descended, developed what is termed the Erythraean agripastoral tradition in the Red Sea hills of eastern Africa. It included domestication of the earliest cattle in the world and grain-seed collection to produce flour. This cultural complex spread north toward Egypt and west across much of northern Africa. Nilo-Saharan speakers along the middle Nile developed the Sudanese agripastoral tradition, hunting large antelope, fishing in lakes and rivers, and copying the seed collection of their neighbors, leading to the collection (by 10,000 BCE) and the early domestication (by 8000 BCE) of sorghum. Sophisticated pottery and the domestication of cattle had equally early dates here, and finger millet, beans, gourds, black-eyed peas, groundnuts, cotton, and melons soon followed. Goats and sheep, domesticated in Southeast Asia, were also added, attesting to early interregional contacts.

In West Africa, dates of domestication have also moved back in time, and it now appears that Niger-Kongo speakers domesticated yams by 8000 BCE and thereafter added peas, groundnuts, guinea fowls, oil palms, raffia, and kola nuts. Later Bantu migrations, starting at least 2,500 ybp, spread these technologies, together with ironworking, throughout most of the southern continent. Khoisan speakers of southern and eastern Africa preceded the Bantu expansion; their sophisticated stone tool technologies for hunting were so successful that agriculture was simply not needed. Eventually, these people were absorbed as specialists into expanding Bantu societies and remain in isolation only in southwestern Africa, where desert conditions precluded agriculture.

Egypt, Nubia, and Early African Kingdoms. About 5,500 ybp a drying regional climate, coupled with increasing cultural complexity, led to the concentration of agricultural communities along the Nile floodplains and the development of large and highly sophisticated social entities, perhaps the first state and empire systems in the world. Earlier Nubian social systems moved north toward the central and upper Nile regions, and a long, illustrious succession of Egyptian

dynasties took shape. About 3100 BCE, King Narmer united Egypt into what is known as the dynasties of Ancient Egypt. From ca. 2575 to 2134 BCE the Old Kingdom dynasties ruled over Egypt, during which period the Great Pyramid of Giza was built as a tomb for the ruler Khufu. It is the only one of the so-called Seven Wonders of the ancient world that still exists. Scholars assumed it was built using slave labor until postcolonial Egyptian archaeologists began their own excavations in the area and learned that the opposite was in fact true: the pyramids probably were built by free people who contributed their labor out of a sense of civic duty to the state and their pharaoh king. Agricultural complexity, based on irrigation, increased greatly during these early dynasties, as did animal husbandry. Government tax collectors and scribes developed hieroglyphics, probably the first written language in the world.

The rise of the Middle Kingdom, from ca. 2040 to 1640 BCE, reunited Egypt after a period of famine and decentralization. Trade was now in the hands of merchants rather than the state, reaching the Red Sea coasts of the fabled land called Punt, as well as the interior of Central Africa, beyond Nubia. South Asian Hyksos invasions then briefly disrupted Egyptian rule, until Ahmose I reunited Egypt, founding the first in a series of dynasties known as the New Kingdom, which lasted from 1550 to 1070 BCE Giant statues and temples, such as the massive Temple of Luxor and the many structures found in the Valley of the Kings, marked this era, even more so than the pyramids of earlier eras. Centralized standing armies came into fashion, and the empire expanded to the south and the northeast. Eventually, Palestine and Nubia asserted their independence, and the period of great dynasties terminated.

Nubian societies along the upper Nile had preceded and persisted throughout the Egyptian dynasties. They now flourished around a vibrant global trade and intensive agricultural production, first in the state of Kush, with Napata as its capital. In the last centuries BCE, Meroe became the Nubian capital, centered on massive industrial iron production and exports. This iron technology had entered North Africa with the Southwest Asian invasions of the Hyksos, but farther south, in East and Central Africa, independent iron technology emerged at the same time as that of the Middle East, if not earlier. Once again, notions of technological diffusions into Africa from neighboring peoples have been overturned by scientific discoveries, as in the work of the Kenyan archaeologist Chapurukha Kusimba on the origins of iron technology in Africa.

The yam-planting traditions of West Africa, meanwhile, continued to develop in complexity, adding specialized rice production (later transported to the Carolinas by slaves in the modern era), cotton, and dried fish to their culture, as well as sophisticated woodworking and ironworking. In the middle of the last millennium BCE, the ironworking culture known as Nok was producing its famed terracotta clay heads. By at least 4,000 ybp the Bantu migrations into the forests of Central Africa had begun; the Bantu probably traveled the many rivers and lakes by dugout canoe, spreading the unique complex of West African traditions throughout the continent before the turn of the first millennium CE. Fusions were achieved with Cushitic, Sudanic, and Khoisan speakers whom the Bantu encountered as they went, and the ancestors of modern African Bantu-speaking societies came to occupy their modern-era locations mostly by the middle of the first millennium CE.

African Global Trade and Classical Civilizations. In the Ethiopian highlands and at the coast of the Red Sea, a complex civilization flourished from before 500 BCE to the dawn of the second millennium, with a capital eventually located in the city of Aksum. The region developed its own language and continued to perfect its unique agricultural complex, including coffee, which originated here, competing with and then eclipsing Meroe as the central trade hub of much of Africa, southern Asia, and the Indian Ocean. The trans-Saharan trade routes had more regularly linked successive West African kingdoms with North Africa and Iberia, and also West Africa with the Nile and East Africa. Trade was also well established by this time throughout the Mediterranean, with the Phoenicians, among Egypt, Nubia, and the Red Sea coasts, and along the length of the East African coast and the Indian Ocean and its islands.

Greece conquered Egypt in 332 BCE, and debate continues about the degree to which Egypt was drawn into the Mediterranean or Greece was drawn into Africa, though both are certainly true. Alexandria thrived as a great trade and cultural center, and Greece instituted the Ptolemaic dynasty, which ruled until the Roman conquest three hundred years later. North Africa then became a series of Roman provinces providing grain and other produce. The ancient city of Carthage, founded before 800 BCE, had rivaled Rome in significance for centuries but finally fell to it in 146 BCE. In the first centuries CE, Christianity spread to Egypt, Nubia, the Ethiopian kingdom of Axum, and Berber North Africa before being officially adopted by Rome. Like Judaism several millennia earlier and Islam six centuries later, this monotheistic religion was, from its inception, rooted in African as much as in Eurasian culture and geography.

In *The Periplus of the Erythrean Sea*, written in the first century CE, Greek travelers recorded the existence of highly developed trade at the East African port city of Rhapta, the location of which is in dispute. The region was already the site of iron production, trade with other regions of Africa and the Indian Ocean, and settlements

Lucius Septimius Severus was born in Africa and reigned as emperor from 193 to 211 AD. He is shown here in a Roman bust in the Capitoline Museum. The triumphal Arch of Septimius Severus, which still stands in the Roman forum, was built during his lifetime to commemorate his military victories. (Nimatallah/Art Resource, N.Y.)

diffusing in from the Indonesian archipelago with boat technology, modern chickens, and the xylophone, which became the African thumb piano. A vast Swahili civilization flourished in a series of towns and cities from Mogadishu and Lamu in the north to latter-day South Africa, Mozambique, and Madagascar in the south. Towns traded with one another and funneled East African products, such as the gold of Zimbabwe, to Mediterranean and Asian outlets, receiving porcelain and other goods in return. It is believed that the early cities, which developed complex multistoried stone architecture before the eighth century, brought together in various combinations Bantu-speaking farmers, Cushitic- and Nilotic-speaking pastoralists, Indonesian immigrants in the south, and sporadic Asian and North African traders and visitors. The impressive stone ruins of Great Zimbabwe reflect an example of an interior cattle-keeping African people oriented in part toward this coastal society and its trade, focused in this case on gold and, to a lesser extent, animal products, such as ivory and skins. The Bantu-based language of Swahili, still one of Africa's widest-used vernaculars into the twenty-first century, fused Arabic and other loan words in a culture often oriented around intensive dhow-based fishing, export trade, and other boat-centered activities.

The spread of sorghum to India by 2000 BCE attests to the validity of the apprehension held by W. E. B. Du Bois and other Pan-African scholars that ancient contacts and influences from Africa to Asia were ubiquitous. Further, Pan-Africanist scholars spoke of ancient articulations of West and East Ethiopia, referring to Ethiopia or Africa generally on the one hand, and the Middle East and South Asia on the other. It is only in the modern era that strict boundaries for the African continent have been drawn, attempting to exclude Greece, Rome, Palestine, Israel, the Levant, the Iberian Peninsula, Oman, Yemen, Saudi Arabia, Baghdad, the Persian Gulf, and even India, Indonesia, and beyond from consideration as part of the African world or its cultural diasporas. Exciting new discoveries, reflecting the emerging perspectives of postcolonial African scholars and their colleagues, are largely vindicating the views of the early Pan-Africanists.

[*See also* Africa, Idea of; African Diaspora; Language; *and* Race, Theories of.]

BIBLIOGRAPHY

Brain, C. K. *The Hunters or the Hunted? An Introduction to African Cave Taphonomy*. Chicago: University of Chicago Press, 1981. Classic archaeological text, with copious illustrations, that debunked the "man the hunter" theory and showed early humans to have actually been the hunted.

Connah, Graham. *African Civilizations: Precolonial Cities and States in Tropical Africa, an Archaeological Perspective*. New York: Cambridge University Press, 1987. An important synthesis, in readable but detailed format.

Diop, Cheikh Anta. *Precolonial Black Africa: A Comparative Study of the Political and Social Systems of Europe and Black Africa, from Antiquity to the Formation of Modern States*. Translated by Harold J. Salemson. Westport, CT: Lawrence Hill, 1987. One of Diop's many important works that challenge colonial dismissals of Africa by analyzing the continent as a whole and through a variety of early periods.

Du Bois, W. E. B. *The World and Africa: An Inquiry into the Part Which Africa Has Played in World History*. Enl. ed., with new writings on Africa, 1955–1961. New York: International, 1965. A great general text, written during the colonial era, collecting global African history into a synthesis that remains accurate and provocative.

Ehret, Christopher. *An African Classical Age: Eastern and Southern Africa in World History, 1000 B.C. to A.D. 400*. Charlottesville: University Press of Virginia, 1988. Major fusion, the first of its kind for the African continent, combining linguistic and archaeological evidence.

Gillon, Werner. *A Short History of African Art*. London: Penguin, 1984. Good overview from earliest cave and rock art to the modern era, with maps and copious illustrations.

Harris, Joseph E., ed. *Africa and Africans As Seen by Classical Writers*. William Leo Hansberry African History Notebook Series, vol. 2. Washington, DC: Howard University Press, 1977. Presents Hansberry's prescient perspectives on Ethiopia and "sub-Saharan" history generally. Hansberry was one of the first scholars of Africa to move beyond ancient Egypt as a focus.

Iliffe, John. *Africans: The History of a Continent*. New York: Cambridge University Press, 1995. Acclaimed synthesis of African history from earliest origins to the South African elections of 1994.

Keita, Maghan. *Race and the Writing of History: Riddling the Sphinx*. New York: Oxford University Press, 2000. Reviews the epistemological and racial basis of the construction of knowledge about Africa and some of the great African American scholars who transformed modern approaches to this history.

Kusimba, Chapurukha M. *The Rise and Fall of Swahili States*. Walnut Creek, CA: AltaMira Press, 1999. A detailed account of East African coastal history, with important explanations of iron-technology, urban origins, and coast-interior relations.

Kusimba, Sibel Barut. *African Foragers: Environment, Technology, Interactions*. Walnut Creek, CA: AltaMira Press, 2003. Groundbreaking synthesis and reappraisal of African gatherer-hunters from ancient to modern times.

Shaw, Thurstan, et al., eds. *The Archaeology of Africa: Food, Metals, and Towns*. New York: Routledge, 1993. One of the largest and most important collections of essays by leading scholars in the archaeology of African history.

—JESSE BENJAMIN

ANTISABBATARIANISM. During the early decades of the nineteenth century many American Christians advocated the virtues of Sabbath observance. These Sabbatarians opposed the desecration of the first day—that is, Sunday—and sought to make this religious observance a federal law. Antisabbatarianism emerged in response to this movement, objecting primarily to the invasion of theological opinion into democratic politics.

Throughout the seventeenth century the Sabbath had been enforced by the theocracies formed by Anglo-American colonialism. For strict Sabbatarians the Sabbath provided time for contemplation and the ritual celebration of American divine election. During the eighteenth century the legality of Sabbath enforcement was put into doubt by the constitutional separation of church and state; increased diversity in the colonies necessitated federal acquiescence and theocratic dissimilation. By the close of the Revolutionary War few Sabbath laws remained intact. However, as the colonies slowly melded into the United States, Christian leaders were increasingly concerned that the power of the federal government superseded the moral authority of religion.

When Congress passed a law in 1810 demanding that postmasters deliver mail every day of the week, the Sabbatarian movement was born. Supported by the evangelical culture that spread through the Second Great Awakening, ministers like Lyman Beecher argued that increasing profanation of the Sabbath signaled a collapsing society. In his 1827 sermon "The Memory of Our Fathers," Beecher argued that without the maintenance of the Sabbath "irreligion will prevail, and the immorality and dissoluteness, to an extent utterly inconsistent with the permanence of republican institutions." In this vein Beecher formed the General Union for Promoting the Observance of the Christian Sabbath in 1828 with the goal of protecting the fourth commandment and, axiomatically, the Christian structure of American social life.

Whereas Sabbatarians argued that Sabbath breaking signaled the corrosive cultural impact of the market, Antisabbatarians believed Sabbath laws replicated monarchic religious authority and prohibited economic advancement. Those hardest hit by Sabbath maintenance were not established entrepreneurs or religious leaders but nascent merchants and farmers on the commercial periphery who needed daily delivery and shipment of supplies and products. For these Americans, Sabbath maintenance meant the interruption of market processes and the slowed delivery of raw goods.

In addition to these economic considerations, many Antisabbatarians portrayed Sabbatarian advocates as members of an evangelical cabal. In Poughkeepsie, New York, the judge James Emott warned that the Sabbatarians were an "entering wedge" of a "grand system" that, if left unchecked, would establish an "ecclesiastical hierarchy" as "oppressive and dangerous" as any that existed in papal Rome. Antisabbatarian advocates, including the transcendentalist Orestes Brownson, the labor organizer Eli Moore, the utopian socialist Robert Dale Owen, and the radical abolitionists William Lloyd Garrison and Frederick Douglass, believed that laws protecting the Sabbath were attempts to legislate morality within a plural nation. Garrison and Douglass went even further, suggesting that religion ought to encourage the daily worship and enactment of God's will, not the selective honor of a single day. Garrison warned that if men made religious belief the practice of a single day, then the necessary social revolutions could never occur. By the late nineteenth century Antisabbatarian arguments had prevailed, and it was not until the mid-twentieth century that the United States would see the return of sacred Sundays.

[See also Douglass, Frederick and Garrison, William Lloyd.]

BIBLIOGRAPHY

Abzug, Robert H. Cosmos Crumbling: American Reform and the Religious Imagination. New York: Oxford University Press, 1994. Contains an excellent description of the Sabbatarian and Antisabbatarian movements on pages 105–124.

Beecher, Lyman. "The Memory of Our Fathers: A Sermon Delivered at Plymouth, on the Twenty-Second of December, 1827." In Sermons Delivered on Various Occasions. Boston: T. R. Marvin, 1828.

John, Richard R. "Taking Sabbatarianism Seriously: The Postal System, the Sabbath, and the Transformation of American Political Culture." Journal of the Early Republic 10 (Winter 1990): 517–567.

—KATHRYN LOFTON

ANTISLAVERY MOVEMENT. Frederick Douglass was perhaps the perfect embodiment of the American antislavery movement. As a young slave on a large Maryland plantation, he rebelled both physically and psychologically against bondage. When he escaped in 1838 Douglass used the Underground Railroad to make his way north. As a fugitive slave in New Bedford, Massachusetts, Douglass formally joined the abolitionist movement, quickly becoming one of the best-known speakers at antislavery meetings. With his two antebellum autobiographies, Douglass helped pioneer the genre of the slave narrative. His final postwar autobiography, Life and Times of Frederick Douglass, epitomized the successful reminiscences of abolitionists. He also edited three important abolitionist newspapers through antebellum society's most tumultuous years.

During the Civil War, which resulted in the emancipation of nearly four million slaves, Douglass advocated abolition as strenuously as ever and recruited black soldiers for the famous Fifty-fourth Massachusetts Infantry Regiment, the Union's first African American unit. Finally, long after the Civil War ended, an aging but still dedicated Douglass fought to preserve the memory of the antislavery struggle. "Whatsoever else I may forget," he declared at a Decoration Day (now Memorial Day) event in Rochester, New York, in 1883, as related by the historian David Blight, "I shall never forget the difference between those who fought for liberty and those who fought for slavery; between those who fought to save the Republic and those who fought to destroy it." Blight himself notes, "He viewed Emancipation as the central reference point of black history." One might add that the antislavery struggle was the central reference point of Douglass's long career as an abolitionist, orator, writer, editor, and ultimately the conscience of the American nation. In short, one cannot find a better guide to the evolving meaning and impact of the American antislavery movement than the life of Frederick Augustus Washington Bailey Douglass.

Antislavery before Douglass. While Douglass shaped the formal antislavery struggle virtually from the moment he entered it, even he realized that abolitionism had a long and distinguished—if not entirely successful—history in early America. The antislavery movement encompassed a truly broad array of people, movements, and ideas in eighteenth- and nineteenth-century America. Indeed, antislavery action dated to the beginning of bondage on the North American continent. About twelve million slaves were imported to the New World between the fifteenth and nineteenth centuries, but about one-half million came to North America. As recent scholarship has suggested, colonial slaves fought their bondage by resisting work, running away, and plotting rebellions.

A coherent body of antislavery thought matured only slowly and haltingly in both North American and transatlantic culture. Prior to the American Revolution, every British colony sanctioned bondage, and slavery was an integral part of the Anglo-American economy. Every major religious group contained slaveholders and sanctioned bondage. Several colonies prohibited even private manumission.

Quakers established the first formal antislavery movement in America during the 1750s. Defining slavery as a violation of religious principles, the Society of Friends in Pennsylvania insisted that slaveholders either relinquish their bondsmen or leave the denomination. Quakers thus became a vanguard of abolitionism during the Revolutionary era, staffing many of the leading antislavery groups and setting a precedent for other religious groups to follow. During the 1770s, 1780s, and 1790s Methodists, Baptists, and Anglicans all began debating slavery. While no group instituted Quaker-style prohibitions on slaveholding, religiously inspired acts of manumission occurred with greater frequency than ever in the twenty years following the American Revolution.

Revolutionary rhetoric had also undermined slavery's normative status by the end of the eighteenth century. American statesmen began identifying slavery not only as a moral wrong but also as an anomaly in a democratic republic. Thomas Jefferson famously wrote, "I tremble for my country when I recall that God is just." Enslaved people influenced emancipation efforts by using the disruptions of the Revolutionary War years either to run away—several thousand slaves fled with British troops in New York, Virginia, and elsewhere—or to bargain with masters for freedom. Thus for both religious and philosophical reasons, antislavery trends accelerated in the late 1700s. In Virginia, which had the new nation's largest slave population, guilty masters petitioned the legislature in such impressive numbers that the General Assembly of Virginia altered its emancipation policy in 1783: masters no longer needed to petition the assembly for permission to liberate enslaved people. Perhaps as many as six thousand slaves were liberated in the Old Dominion by the early 1800s.

To bolster abolition as a national movement—one not limited to religious groups or private emancipation acts—northern Quakers and their allies established the world's first abolition societies during the 1770s and 1780s. The Pennsylvania Abolition Society (PAS), inaugurated in 1775 and then reorganized in 1784, and the New York Manumission Society, formed in 1784, were the two largest and most important early abolition groups, with membership in each organization reaching several hundred at their peak. These first-generation abolitionists hoped to gradually end slavery at the state level, stop the overseas slave trade at the federal level, and encourage political leaders to make full emancipation a national goal. They worked strategically, lobbying political and legal leaders using skillful argumentation and deferential discourse; early abolitionists conceded that the slavery debate, if too heated, could divide the Union. Still, through local and state organizations as well as the American Convention of Abolition Societies (which met first in 1794 and then biennially until 1836), these groups petitioned governments to adopt gradual abolition laws. Pennsylvania created the world's first gradual emancipation act in 1780, requiring all masters to register bondpeople born after the law's passage with a state official; these slaves would then be freed at the age of 28. Between 1780 and 1804 every northern state would adopt similar laws or abolish slavery in their constitutions. Massachusetts ended slavery by judicial decree in 1783 after an enslaved person, Quok Walker, sued for his freedom.

Although they never advocated immediate emancipation at the national level, early abolitionists engaged in many other antislavery activities. Abolitionists took great pride in pushing the federal government to end the slave trade after 1807, as the Constitution had outlined but not mandated. They worked to ban slavery and the domestic slave trade in the federally controlled District of Columbia during the 1820s. Perhaps most impressively, both the Pennsylvania Abolition Society and the New York Manumission Society distinguished themselves by aiding kidnapped free blacks and, on occasion, fugitive slaves in courts of law. Early reformers' legal efforts helped liberate hundreds of slaves between the 1780s and 1830s.

As a formal movement, then, antislavery garnered early successes at the state level. However, it had stalled nationally by the early 1800s. The Continental Congress had adopted a few key antislavery provisions: in 1784 it considered, but did not adopt, an ordinance prohibiting slavery's expansion into future southwestern territories. In 1787 the Continental Congress did pass the Northwest Ordinance, prohibiting bondage from spreading into future midwestern states. But the new Constitution of 1787 solidified slavery's place in the Union with the three-fifths clause (which counted three-fifths of the enslaved population in the apportionment of congressional representatives and electoral votes), a promise of federal military aid to suppress slave insurrections, a guarantee of fugitive slave recovery (with the first Fugitive Slave Law in 1793), and a delay on the consideration of any slave trade ban until at least 1807. This last point is often overlooked. In the early 1800s South Carolina and Georgia alone imported nearly one hundred thousand slaves before the ban took effect.

In short, while slavery was slowly eradicated from northern states, it nevertheless grew demographically as well as geographically. At the time of the first federal census in 1790, about seven hundred thousand slaves and only sixty-three thousand free blacks lived in America. By 1830 the number of slaves had nearly tripled to 2 million, with free blacks then numbering 250,000.

Despite antislavery's gradualist beginnings and partial successes, Frederick Douglass acknowledged his debts to abolitionists of the colonial, Revolutionary, and early national periods. In speeches and newspaper articles during the 1850s he praised Quakers for their early dedication to emancipation. Douglass also saluted first-generation abolitionists' concerns for the education and advancement of free blacks.

Douglass also paid homage to African American reformers who fought for racial justice in the nation's earliest years. Although denied formal membership in early abolition societies, an inaugural generation of black activists emerged from both free and enslaved backgrounds to establish a vibrant protest tradition based on public reform tactics like pamphleteering and public oration. Long before Douglass published his first narrative, black pamphleteers like Richard Allen, Absalom Jones, James Forten, Lemuel Haynes, Peter Williams, and Prince Hall took aim at slavery and racial injustice through printed essays, sermons, and speeches. Allen and Jones—both former slaves—published the first copyrighted black pamphlet in Philadelphia in January 1794 titled *A Narrative of the Proceedings of the Black People during the Late Awful Calamity in Philadelphia*. The pamphlet took white Philadelphians to task for stereotyping black relief workers as harmful and shiftless—despite their heroic work during the city's famous yellow fever epidemic of 1793. Remove the stain of slavery, the pamphlet argued, and African Americans would become valuable citizens in their own right. Allen and Jones also attacked slavery as a religious sin.

Douglass duly recognized his debts to Allen, Jones, Forten, Williams, and other first-generation black leaders. These men not only had pushed for slavery's end but also had challenged racial discrimination in northern locales where bondage had been gradually eradicated. Their literary appeals—pamphlets and reprinted speeches—helped open new tactical avenues to abolitionism and pointed the way to moral suasion, as advocated by William Lloyd Garrison. From early black reformers Douglass also gleaned a broader philosophical outlook on black activism itself. His philosophy became grounded in a belief that the nation's racial problems were not intractable—that by following America's founding words and deeds, advocating liberty and justice for all, slavery could be eradicated and racial justice achieved.

While early antislavery activism formed one important part of Douglass's abolitionist heritage, enslaved people's protests formed another. In his speeches and autobiographies alike, Douglass alluded to the daily struggle of enslaved people as an inspiration for his activism. He often referred to slaves as "my brethren in bonds" and lauded their struggle to survive in the face of masters' incessant collective will to dominate their bond servants mentally as well as physically. Douglass understood most slaves' inability to physically stand up to slaveholders and knew that enslaved people longed for freedom. As he told a New York City audience on 6 May 1845, as he recorded in his first autobiography, *Narrative of the Life of Frederick Douglass*, "To you I bring a thankful heart . . . in the name of three millions of slaves, [and] I offer you their gratitude for your faithful advocacy in behalf of the slave."

Douglass also knew that the fight of enslaved people would not be recorded properly for many years to come. Thus he offered a steady stream of references and allusions to grassroots black protest in his speeches and publications. Several major rebellions occurred before Douglass entered the abolition movement: Gabriel's conspiracy (outside Richmond, Virginia, in 1800) and Denmark Vesey's revolt (in Charleston, South Carolina, in 1822) were elaborately planned but foiled before they started; Nat Turner's rebellion (in Southampton County, Virginia, in 1831) resulted in the deaths of more than fifty white citizens before being put down. Douglass paid particular attention to the slave revolutions in Haiti (1791–1804), which resulted in the creation of the Western Hemisphere's first black republic. The events in Haiti scared southern masters but inspired both black activists and southern slaves. In the 1850s *Frederick Douglass' Paper* included nearly two dozen references to the Haitian slave rebel Toussaint Louverture. On 2 March 1855 Douglass approvingly republished a lecture by C. W. Elliott praising the revolutionary leader as an icon who merely sought to bring liberty to black men everywhere. If Douglass did not believe that a massive slave rebellion was possible in America, he nevertheless believed that the words and ideas of rebels like Toussaint Louverture provided crucial insight into slaves' collective will to freedom.

Douglass and the Antislavery Renaissance. The antislavery movement changed drastically during the 1820s and 1830s—years when a young Douglass grew to hate bondage, escaped from Maryland slavery, and became a member of the American abolitionist community. Abolitionism changed still more as Douglass began to shape that community during the 1840s. Unlike first-generation activists who espoused gradualism, post-1830s reformers began to advocate immediate abolition. Organizationally, second-generation abolitionists initiated interracial antislavery societies (the Pennsylvania Abolition Society did not admit its first black member, Robert Purvis, until the 1830s). Second-wave activists also mobilized women as key reformers. Tactically, these so-called modern abolitionists attempted to rout bondage not by skillfully and deferentially lobbying elite political figures but by mobilizing public opinion through the press, oratory, and grassroots organization in both rural and urban areas. Older abolitionists still active in the 1830s worried that immediatists would ruin the Republic; post-1830s abolitionists engaged in tactics that early reformers had rejected, such as the forming of abolitionist political parties. In short, the American antislavery movement grew more militant and more diverse in the three decades leading up to the Civil War.

Like other abolitionists coming into the movement after 1830, Douglass found this modern brand of antislavery activism to be akin to a crusade—and he loved it. No sooner had Douglass read one of the leading organs of radical abolitionism—Garrison's newspaper the *Liberator* (first published on 1 January 1831)—on arriving in Massachusetts than he became a convert. In his 1845 *Narrative* Douglass noted, "I got a pretty correct idea of the principles, measures and spirit of antislavery reform, [and] my soul was set on fire." Antiabolitionists in the North and South, on the other hand, frowned on the movement as reckless and fanatical. Although it underwent a series of changes before the Civil War, the immediatist abolition movement would not disappear until its objective had been achieved.

While for years scholars focused on the 1831 publication of the *Liberator* as a signal event, later scholarship notes that Garrison's paper reflected but did not create the changes that occurred in the antislavery struggle. A new wave of religious revivalism had spread across American culture in the 1820s, demanding that Americans eradicate sin from society. Some reformers channeled revivalism into support for immediate abolitionism. Economic changes in northern culture led to slavery's becoming a southern institution—though one with important markets and financial backers in the North. Still, by the 1820s every northern state—as well as new northwestern states like Ohio and Illinois—forbade bondage. Black public protest became more aggressive and ramifying during the 1820s, influencing younger white reformers like Garrison, who had formerly been a moderate abolitionist.

Black public protest became particularly important during early debates over the founding of the American Col-

onization Society (ACS) in 1816. The ACS purportedly sought to send free blacks to African settlements as an inducement to slaveholders, who might then liberate their own bondpeople on the condition that they be exported overseas. Yet while some members of the ACS claimed to be antislavery advocates—indeed, some slaveholders feared the organization to be a Trojan Horse of antislavery itself—the group was dominated by slaveholders and northern antiabolitionists; the ACS assembled northerners and southerners alike who agreed that free blacks were nearly as problematic as slavery. Nevertheless, early abolition groups like the PAS refused to publicly condemn the ACS because it contained prominent members like Henry Clay and James Madison.

On the other hand, free black activists did not hesitate to attack the group; in fact, black reformers became the vanguard of the anticolonization movement before 1830 and therefore a key part of the transformation of American abolitionism. Anticolonization documents produced by free blacks would become a cornerstone not only of black protest but also of future antislavery activists; in 1832 Garrison published a collection of such documents, *Thoughts on African Colonization.* Black activists used *Freedom's Journal,* the first black-edited newspaper (published in New York City between 1827 and 1829) as a vehicle for anticolonizationist thought. The paper also established a national dialogue among black reformers over antislavery tactics in the colonization era. David Walker, a *Freedom's Journal* correspondent, emerged as a key spokesman during this period. His 1829 *Appeal to the Coloured Citizens of the World,* published in Boston and sent as far as Virginia and Georgia, aggressively challenged the notion that America was a white republic—and that blacks had to defer to white fears regarding abolition. Walker incredulously asked white Americans if they needed to have the Declaration of Independence reread to them and challenged black readers to mobilize nationally and demand abolitionism. Walker died mysteriously in 1830, but his pamphlet illuminated a more fiery pathway toward abolition.

The New England Anti-Slavery Society, the first immediatist group in America, founded in Boston in 1832, and the American Anti-Slavery Society (AASS), the first such national group, founded in Philadelphia in 1833, embraced a broad strategy of moral suasion. By convincing Americans of slavery's sinfulness, abolitionists hoped that the population at large would demand abolition from national leaders and that southern slaveholders would independently liberate slaves. Thus immediate abolitionists spent the majority of their funds on the publication and dissemination of antislavery petitions, pamphlets, newspapers, and eventually slave narratives; during the first quarter century of the antislavery movement, no organization had funded the publication of an explicit antislavery newspaper or had sought to capitalize on the literary output of former slaves.

The first abolitionist journals appeared in the late 1810s and early 1820s. Benjamin Lundy's *Genius of Universal Emancipation* (1821–1838) was one of the earliest such papers. After 1831 abolitionists supported not only the *Liberator* but a host of other antislavery papers as well, including the *Emancipator* (started by the AASS in New York City in 1836), the *Philanthropist* (published in Cincinnati at the same time), and the *National Anti-Slavery Standard* (1840–1870). Abolitionists also sponsored grassroots lecturing campaigns in northeastern and midwestern states. As James Brewer Stewart writes in his book *Holy Warriors*, by the early 1830s abolitionists were already embracing mass communication as a key tactic in the fight against slavery. Early mass media provided gripping accounts of slavery's evil and allowed women to become key figures in the movement. Indeed, both black and white female abolitionists engaged in a variety of activities to bolster the movement. They served as editors of newspapers, held local antislavery fairs throughout the North, and secured hundreds of thousands of signatures on state and federal antislavery petitions.

While the moral suasion approach emphasized appeals to morality over practical politicking, during the 1830s some immediate abolitionists pushed for attempts to alter public policy, too. Amos Phelps, a Massachusetts minister turned immediate abolitionist, argued that numerical majorities produced by moral suasion tactics could push for a constitutional amendment banning slavery. Garrison was supportive of Phelps's ideas.

Douglass's twin roles as orator and editor wonderfully illuminate moral suasion strategies. As related by Blight, his first speech before an interracial audience came on 11 August 1841. "I spoke but a few moments," he later recalled, "when I felt a degree of freedom, and said what I'd desired with considerable ease. From that time . . . I have been engaged in pleading the cause of my brethren." Douglass's words on that day electrified even immediate abolitionists who had been publishing, speaking, and protesting for over a decade. "I shall never forget his first speech," Garrison proclaimed. "I never hated slavery so intensely as at that moment; certainly, my perception of the enormous outrage which is inflicted by it, on the godlike nature of its victims, was rendered far more clear the never." Douglass became one of the featured speakers on the abolitionist circuit over the next decade, traveling throughout America and to Canada and Britain. One of Douglass's early epic tours saw him and Charles Lenox Remond visiting more than thirty midwestern locales in just three months during the fall of 1843. When Douglass

turned his lectures on his experiences into a personal narrative in 1845, *Narrative of the Life of Frederick Douglass*, it quickly became a best-seller.

Of course, Douglass's role as editor and author is well known. He published three newspapers from his new home in Rochester between 1847 and 1864: the *North Star* (1847–1851), *Frederick Douglass' Paper* (1851–1859), and *Douglass' Monthly* (1859–1863). In this endeavor Douglass expanded on one of the most important abolitionist tactics of the 1820s and 1830s—the creation of newspapers dedicated solely to the antislavery cause. He also published three autobiographies during his long life, illuminating one of the most important tools African Americans used to influence abolitionism after 1830: slave narratives. Some two hundred narratives flowed from the abolitionist press in the antebellum period; Americans became familiar with the tales of former slaves such as Frederick Douglass, Sojourner Truth, Solomon Northup, Henry "Box" Brown, and Harriet Jacobs. Addressing an increasingly literate white middle-class northern audience, slave narratives uncovered the realities of bondage and underscored the emotional toll of slavery on black Americans. Often framed by white interlocutors, slave narratives helped make antislavery a broader concern in American culture. Harriet Beecher Stowe's 1852 novel *Uncle Tom's Cabin*, which sold more than 1 million copies in the 1850s, helped ignite sectional debates over slavery in both political and cultural venues. After the novel's publication and success, Stowe published *A Key to Uncle Tom's Cabin*, listing the sources for her book, which included many slave narratives. Literary journals of the North proclaimed that slave narratives had become a whole new genre of American literature.

Although only a fraction of the northern white population ever joined the new interracial and immediatist antislavery societies after 1830 (perhaps 2 percent to 5 percent in some locales), abolitionist tactics and activities put disproportionate pressure on society in the thirty years leading up to the Civil War. Immediatists like Douglass believed that their moralizing strategies would halt slavery's growth and persuade masters to eradicate slavery in the South. There were indeed hopeful signs during the 1830s. Abolitionists' moral suasion tactics—massively bombarding the American public with discussions of the evil of slavery—produced a brief surge in antislavery growth. By the mid-1830s abolitionist organizations appeared in every northern state, signatures to abolitionist petitions numbered in the hundreds of thousands, and public debate over slavery occurred more regularly than ever before, from large eastern cities like Boston to new market towns like Buffalo in western New York. Yet slavery did not die even under such intense public scrutiny.

"New Method of Assorting the Mail, as Practiced by Southern Slave-Holders; or Attack on the Post Office, Charleston. S.C." Lithograph of 1835 showing a raid in July of that year by a mob that ransacked the mail and destroyed bundles of abolitionist periodicals, including *The Liberator.* The sign on the wall offers a bounty from New Orleans for the capture of Arthur Tappan, founder and president of the American Anti-Slavery Society. (Library of Congress.)

Between 1830 and 1860 the institution almost doubled in size, with the number of enslaved persons increasing from 2 million to 3.9 million. Moreover, slavery had spread into a host of new southern states, from Kentucky, Tennessee, Alabama, Mississippi, Florida, and Louisiana in the early national period to Missouri, Arkansas, and Texas in the 1820s and 1830s. Also, northern textile production—particularly of products either made from southern cotton or destined for southern plantations—depended heavily on the southern cotton industry.

Radical abolitionism faced increasing hostility by the 1840s, from not only southern slaveholders but also many northerners as well. Even in immediate abolition's stronghold, the Massachusetts governor Edward Everett tried to prevent abolitionist lecturers from speaking in the state. At the federal level Congress passed a gag rule preventing discussion of abolitionist petitions between 1836 and 1844. The idealism and hope of immediate abolitionists had hit a wall, and many reformers were ready to employ new tactics to slay bondage.

Douglass and the Coming of the Civil War. With antiabolitionism strengthening and slavery growing stronger, the antislavery movement began fragmenting into quarrelsome and even competing factions by the 1840s. Divisive issues abounded, including the degree of prominence of female activists within abolitionism; the

justifiability of violent tactics, even for free black northerners attempting to hold off kidnapping attempts; the use of the Constitution to battle slavery; and the possible formation of an abolitionist political party.

Douglass was a unique figure within the fragmenting antislavery movement as one of the few activists who could move among the various factions and still earn the respect of most of his abolitionist brethren. As such Douglass became one of the most thoughtful and introspective immediatists: he questioned the meaning of his activism at regular intervals and was not afraid of switching positions. His stand on the Constitution offers perhaps the best example. Although initially he aligned himself with the Garrisonian position of the 1840s and 1850s—that the Constitution sanctioned bondage and was therefore, in Garrison's words, "an agreement with Hell, a covenant with Death"—Douglass had changed his tune by the 1850s, arguing that the Constitution was in fact an antislavery document through and through. Starting his own newspaper in Rochester at this time, as Douglass confided in his last autobiography, *Life and Times of Frederick Douglass,* "compelled me to rethink the whole subject." The Constitution, he wrote, "could not well have been designed . . . to maintain and perpetuate" so evil an institution as slavery. Douglass's new views brought him into opposition with former friends; although "painful" to disagree with his cohorts, it was, he thought, the right position to take.

While antislavery debate touched on myriad issues in the two decades leading up to the Civil War, a few stand out because of their impact on both Douglass's antislavery activism and the movement as a whole. One issue concerned the movement's staffing and leadership. A year prior to Douglass's first public speech in 1841, the national antislavery movement had divided into organizations that disagreed over the question of women's roles. A faction that believed in the minimization of women's roles broke away from the American Anti-Slavery Society in 1840, forming the American and Foreign Anti-Slavery Society. Another faction, of which Douglass was a part, believed that women's activism should be central to the abolitionist struggle. Douglass, for one, was not afraid to share the stage with female reformers such as Abby Kelley Foster, who became the first female lecturing agent hired by the AASS in 1839. As Waldo Martin writes in his book *The Mind of Frederick Douglass*, beyond "black liberation," Douglass remained a lifelong advocate of women's equality. Though first and foremost committed to abolitionism, Douglass viewed "women's liberation" as a vital part of his reform vision. Indeed, for Douglass both abolitionism and women's rights reform stemmed from what Martin refers to as his "egalitarian humanism." He attended the first women's rights convention at Seneca Falls in 1848, favored women's suffrage, and worked together with a variety of female activists on the abolition circuit. In this sense Douglass's support of the women's rights movement exemplifies antislavery's capacious growth in antebellum society.

Regarding abolitionism itself, female activists formed a critical foundation of the movement after 1830. Although Quaker women in particular had spoken out against slavery in colonial and early national society, no female reformer had been asked—or even allowed—to join the leading antislavery groups of the new Republic. Thus, during the 1820s and 1830s women in Philadelphia, Boston, Baltimore, and other locales began mobilizing their own antislavery groups; they soon became members of the national antislavery movement as well. Inspired by women's activism in Great Britain—in the 1820s England's Elizabeth Heyrick became one of the first transatlantic white reformers to publicly advocate immediatism—as well as a new wave of revivalism, abolitionist women served as fund-raisers, publicists, editors, petition canvassers, and organizers of local abolition groups. Abolitionist women were responsible for gathering perhaps as many as 2 million signatures to antislavery petitions after 1830.

A related and equally contentious issue also roiled the abolitionist movement: the roles and tactics of black activists. Tensions between black and white reformers stretched back to the movement's very beginnings. In the early 1830s, when the first interracial abolitionist organizations were founded, many African American activists were instilled with the hope that they would be able to share power with whites. By the mid-1830s, however, black activists were expressing concerns about their relationships to condescending whites; some began to wonder why so few African Americans occupied leadership positions in the American Anti-Slavery Society. As the former slave and black abolitionist Henry Highland Garnet would proclaim of white reformers in the 1840s, "they are our allies—ours is the battle!" Douglass's ally James McCune Smith wrote in *Frederick Douglass' Paper* on 26 January 1855, "Blacks almost began the present movement. . . . They certainly ante-dated many of its principles." Indeed, the black convention movement remained an important part of the broader antislavery struggle between 1830 and 1864, during which time black activists held twelve national conventions—every year between 1830 and 1835, then in 1843, 1847, 1848, 1853, 1855, and 1864. These meetings witnessed debates over violent tactics, political strategies, relationships to white reformers and a host of economic issues. Douglass attended several of these national conventions and hosted the one in Rochester in 1853.

Tensions between black and white reformers translated into often-fierce tactical debates, particularly over the matters of violent revolt among southern slaves and self-defense among free blacks. While Garrisonian reformers embraced nonresistance, or opposition to violent struggle, many black reformers advocated a more practical position. In 1835, for instance, the New Yorker David Ruggles formed a vigilance society to protect free blacks and fugitive slaves from devious slave catchers; the society proclaimed physical confrontation acceptable if need be. Ruggles's organization would aid several hundred fugitive slaves and kidnapped free blacks—including Douglass himself when he fled from bondage. Similar groups would form in Boston and Philadelphia over the next twenty-five years. By the 1850s, following the passage of the new Fugitive Slave Law, confrontational fugitive slave rescues in Philadelphia, Boston, Detroit, Buffalo, Syracuse, and elsewhere became major news events and increased southern sensitivities over slavery's security in a union that comprised black as well as white abolitionists.

Douglass initially adhered to Garrison's moral suasion strategies, opposing Garnet's call for a slave uprising at the 1843 black convention in Buffalo, but shifted positions in the decade before the Civil War. Douglass joined the Radical Abolitionist Party in 1855, which sought to battle slavery in the southern states themselves. Douglass held secret discussions with John Brown before his raid on Harpers Ferry in October 1859; although convinced that the raid itself was ill advised and would fail, he refused to condemn the man's violent tactics. "Let every man work for the abolition of slavery in his own way," he wrote on 31 October 1859 in an attempt to clarify his role in the raid and his support of Brown. He added, "I would help all and hinder none"—including rebels like Brown.

Perhaps the most significant debate to occur within the antislavery movement was that over political tactics. Political party activity was initiated between the 1840s and the onset of the Civil War, causing vigorous debate. Garrisonian abolitionists came to view political parties as corrupt because they diluted reformers' moral imperative. Other activists saw political parties as a legitimate means to propagate antislavery principles. The Liberty Party, the inaugural abolitionist political organization, sought to end slavery in federally controlled areas such as the District of the Columbia and to limit slavery's expansion in western territories. The former-master-turned-abolitionist James Gillespie Birney received only seven thousand votes as the Liberty Party's first presidential candidate in 1840. In 1844 the Liberty Party still garnered only sixty thousand votes but may have helped determine the outcome of the election by winning roughly fifteen thousand votes in New York, where the slaveholding Whig and presidential hopeful Henry Clay lost to the Democrat James Polk by fewer than seven thousand votes. While it is impossible to know how many Liberty Party votes might have supported the moderately proslavery Clay over the more rabidly proslavery Polk, the close vote in New York certainly sent the message to politicians that the slavery vote mattered. For the first time antislavery politics had influenced the nation's governance.

The advent of the Free-Soil Party in 1848 intensified debate over antislavery politics. Free-Soilers embraced a policy of nonextension—but not of abolition in federally controlled areas. Their slogan of "free soil, free labor, free men" also spoke little of African American rights. The party's decision to nominate Andrew Jackson's former vice president Martin Van Buren, a Democrat who did not favor interference with southern slavery, created fierce opposition among many stalwart abolitionists. While Free-Soilers attracted more support than the Liberty Party, many abolitionists then renounced party politics altogether. Nevertheless, the Free-Soil Party made the strategy of nonextension of slavery in the West a viable one and provided a pivot point for the creation of the Republican Party. The Free-Soil Party also further underscored the power of antislavery political action, as significant numbers of votes were taken from the Democratic candidate, setting the stage for the election of the Whig candidate, Zachary Taylor.

The majority of black activists remained advocates of political tactics and strategies; by the 1850s, as John Stauffer notes in his book *The Black Hearts of Men*, African Americans overwhelmingly favored political action. Douglass supported a variety of political parties that not only opposed slavery in theory but also acted against the institution in deed. He supported the new Republican Party, the successor to the Free-Soil Party, as early as 1855 for its pledge to stop slavery's expansion in the western territories. Although he worried about Republicans' refusal to embrace racial equality and to make abolition in the South a goal, Douglass supported Abraham Lincoln in 1860.

While conceding property rights to southern masters, the Republican Party publicly condemned slavery as an evil institution and vowed to stop its expansion in the territories. The party included well-known statesmen, including the Massachusetts senator Charles Sumner, the Ohio governor Salmon Portland Chase, and the New York senator William Henry Seward, as well as new voices—most notably, Lincoln. If many die-hard abolitionists saw the Republican Party as little better than the Free-Soil Party—for its refusal to advocate immediate abolition—other reformers celebrated the Republicans' infusion of broad antislavery principles into mainstream politics. Indeed, the Republican Party's strong nonextension platform helped intensify sectional politics. Abraham Lincoln professed to hating slavery but admitted that the national government had no constitutional power to do anything about it in the South. Slavery's expansion, however, was another matter. Lincoln told Republicans to remain steadfast opponents of the spread of slavery into federally controlled territories. Republicans' antislavery—though not abolitionist—pledge, combined with southern secessionists' desire to cleave the Union, resulted in the bloodiest civil war of the nineteenth century. By 1865 secessionists' actions would also lead, ironically, to the emancipation of 3.9 million enslaved people in the South.

Douglass's Civil War. The Civil War (1861–1865) brought the antislavery movement its final victory over bondage. It represented for Douglass a period of turmoil and triumph—the turmoil of having to struggle to convince even northerners, from Lincolnite Republicans to average citizens, to declare war on slavery and the triumph of living to see slavery demolished by a Union Army that comprised black troops. While he became "the most famous black man in America," as John Stauffer declares in *The Black Hearts of Men*, and even an "insider" in Republican politics, Douglass also came to realize that his own "vision of perfection and heaven on earth" was "a sentimental illusion." Lincoln's initial refusal to embrace antislavery as a war aim was particularly frustrating to Douglass. But the Thirteenth Amendment, ending slavery nationally, was no small feat, and in witnessing its passage in 1865 Douglass recognized that he had lived to see a revolution in race relations.

Indeed, for all abolitionists the Civil War was both a challenging period and a celebratory one. Many Garrisonians refused to endorse Abraham Lincoln's presidency while nevertheless supporting his strong stand against slavery's expansion. Lincoln's refusal to embrace abolitionism prior to the preliminary Emancipation Proclamation of September 1862 frustrated abolitionists. Yet it was their vision of universal liberty that Lincoln eventually appealed to when he stated that the Civil War was engineering "a new birth freedom" for the Republic. In *The Struggle for Equality*, the historian James McPherson notes that abolitionists became more respected spokesmen for liberty in the 1860s, as men and women, black and white, envisioned a broad program of government-backed initiatives for black education and employment. Abolition's influence could also be seen in the passage of two other Civil War amendments: the Fourteenth Amendment, providing equality to American citizens regardless of race, which Congress sent to the states for ratification in 1866; and the Fifteenth Amendment, granting black men the right to vote, which passed in 1869 and was ratified in 1870.

Douglass's multifaceted role during the Civil War has been well documented: he not only continued to speak, publish, and mobilize public opinion in the North against slavery but also became a recruiter of black troops for the famous Fifth-fourth Massachusetts Infantry Regiment. "Nobody brought more authority to the antislavery lecture platform than Douglass," Donald Yacovone observes in *Freedom's Journey: African American Voices of the Civil War*, and "when the War began . . . he sought to ensure that the North correctly understood the causes of the conflict that had engulfed the nation": most pointedly, in Douglass's own words, "the foul slave system." Douglass's activism was aimed at a truly national audience. As thousands of slaves fled southern plantations, he made clear the notion that slavery was doomed and that blacks would be a part of the regeneration of the Union Army. He fought to maintain antislavery organizations until racial justice had been secured. When Garrison told fellow reformers in December 1864 that the day of jubilee was near, Douglass argued that the American Anti-Slavery Society should not disband prematurely—in fact, it would remain operative until 1870. Douglass convinced abolitionists they had to remain vigilant until African Americans had full political equality.

Douglass dedicated his later years to memorializing the antislavery struggle as a redefining event not merely for African Americans but for the American nation as a whole. "During the last third of his life," notes David Blight, "one of the most distinguishing features of [Douglass's] leadership was his quest to preserve the memory of the Civil War." At the center of that memory, as Douglass told black and white audiences at rallies in Rochester, Washington, New York City, and Chicago, was the notion that the Civil War was not about battles, tactics, and generals but about ideals of "freedom, citizenship, suffrage and dignity." Douglass's work to preserve those ideals coincided with a white backlash that would eventually overturn many of the gains of the Civil War. However, his vision of universal liberty as the birthright of every American—a vision that became synonymous with the antislavery struggle from the late 1830s until his death in 1895—made Douglass a hero of the nineteenth century and the antislavery movement a precursor to later civil rights struggles.

[*See also* Abolitionism; American and Foreign Anti-Slavery Society; American Anti-Slavery Society; American Colonization Society; American Revolution; Antislavery Press; Baltimore, Maryland, Slavery in; Birney, James Gillespie; Black Abolitionists; Black Press; Brown, Henry "Box"; Brown, John; Chase, Salmon Portland; Civil Rights; Civil War; Civil War, Participation and Recruitment of Black Troops in; Clay, Henry; Colonization; Constitution, U.S.; Democratic Party; Demographics; Detroit; *Douglass' Monthly*; Douglass, Frederick; Education; Emancipation; Emancipation Proclamation; Emigration to Africa; Feminist Movement; Fifteenth Amendment; Fifty-fourth Massachusetts Infantry Regiment; Forten, James; Foster, Abby Kelley; Fourteenth Amendment; *Frederick Douglass' Paper*; Free African Americans before the Civil War (North); Free African Americans before the Civil War (South); Free-Soil Party; Freedmen; Fugitive Slave Law of 1793; Fugitive Slave Law of 1850; Garnet, Henry Highland; Garrison, William Lloyd; Garrisonian Abolitionists; Haiti; Haitian Revolutions; Harpers Ferry Raid; Jacobs, Harriet; Jefferson, Thomas; Laws and Legislation; Liberty Party; *Life and Times of Frederick Douglass*; Lincoln, Abraham; Lundy, Benjamin; Moral Suasion; *My Bondage and My Freedom*; *Narrative of the Life of Frederick Douglass*; National Conventions of Colored Men; New York City; Nonresistance; *North Star*; Oratory and Verbal Arts; Polk, James; Proslavery Thought; Purvis, Robert; Radical Abolitionist Party; Reform; Religion and Slavery; Remond, Charles Lenox; Republican Party; Resistance; Riots and Rebellions; Ruggles, David; Seneca Falls Convention; Seward, William Henry; Slave Narratives; Slave Trade; Slave Trade, Domestic; Slavery; Slavery and the U.S. Constitution; Smith, James McCune; Society of Friends (Quakers); Stereotypes of African Americans; Stowe, Harriet Beecher; Suffrage, Women's; Sumner, Charles; Thirteenth Amendment; Toussaint Louverture; Truth, Sojourner; Turner, Nat; *Uncle Tom's Cabin*; Underground Railroad; Union Army, African Americans in; Voting Rights; Walker, David; Whig Party; *and* Women.]

BIBLIOGRAPHY

Blight, David. *Frederick Douglass's Civil War: Keeping Faith in Jubilee*. Baton Rouge: Louisiana State University Press, 1989.

Blue, Frederick J. *No Taint of Compromise: Crusaders in Antislavery Politics*. Baton Rouge: Louisiana State University Press, 2004.

Davis, David Brion. *The Problem of Slavery in the Age of Revolution, 1770–1823*. Ithaca, NY: Cornell University Press, 1975.

Douglass, Frederick. *Life and Times of Frederick Douglass: His Early Life as a Slave, His Escape from Bondage, and His Complete History*. New York: Gramercy Books, 1993.

Douglass, Frederick. *My Bondage and My Freedom*. Edited by John Stauffer. New York: Modern Library, 2003.

Douglass, Frederick. *Narrative of the Life of Frederick Douglass, an American Slave*. Edited by David W. Blight. Boston: Bedford Books, 1993.

Harrold, Stanley. *The Rise of Aggressive Abolitionism: Addresses to the Slaves*. Lexington: University Press of Kentucky, 2004.

Martin, Waldo E. *The Mind of Frederick Douglass*. Chapel Hill: University of North Carolina Press, 1984.

McPherson, James M. *The Struggle for Equality: Abolitionists and the Negro in the Civil War and Reconstruction*. Princeton, NJ: Princeton University Press, 1964.

Newman, Richard S. *The Transformation of American Abolitionism: Fighting Slavery in the Early Republic*. Chapel Hill: University of North Carolina Press, 2002.

Stauffer, John. *The Black Hearts of Men: Radical Abolitionists and the Transformation of Race*. Cambridge, MA: Harvard University Press, 2002.

Stewart, James Brewer. *Holy Warriors: The Abolitionists and American Slavery*. New York: Hill and Wang, 1996.

Trodd, Zoe, and John Stauffer, eds. *Meteor of War: The John Brown Story*. Naugatuck, CT: Brandywine Press, 2004.

Yacovone, Donald, ed. *Freedom's Journey: African American Voices of the Civil War*. Chicago: Lawrence Hill Books, 2004.

—RICHARD NEWMAN

ANTISLAVERY PRESS. On 1 January 1831, in Boston, Massachusetts, William Lloyd Garrison launched his weekly antislavery newspaper, the *Liberator*, and a new phase in the history of the antislavery press was under way. In his first editorial, Garrison brazenly declared,

> I *will* be as harsh as truth, and as uncompromising as justice. On this subject, I do not wish to think, to speak, or write, with moderation. . . . I am in earnest—I will not equivocate—I will not excuse—I will not retreat a single inch—AND I WILL BE HEARD. (Cain, p. 72)

The unforgiving tone of the *Liberator* was thenceforth established, reflecting the firmness of what was to be its purpose for the next thirty-five years. From the day of its inauguration to 29 December 1865, the *Liberator* loudly proclaimed Garrison's truths and his criticisms of proslavery advocates—as well as of those antislavery advocates whose views opposed his. The *Liberator* was the voice and soul of Garrison's abolitionist crusade.

By the time the *Liberator* appeared, it had become common practice for abolitionist reformers to disseminate their arguments in newspapers as well as through public lectures; Garrison proved no different in his approach. Such major publications as the *Liberator* and the American Anti-Slavery Society's organ, the *National Anti-Slavery Standard*, edited for two years by Lydia Maria Child, formed the backbone of antislavery activism in the antebellum era and through the close of the Civil War.

Antislavery Press before 1830. Prior to the radical fervor of the abolitionist crusade, antislavery sentiments had existed to a lesser degree almost as long as had slavery itself. Primarily a cause taken up by Quakers and Methodists, antislavery action was too moderate to sway the public away from the institution, in large part owing to the economic prosperity it brought to the country. At the heart of early antislavery protests were biblical passages that supported the condemnation of the enslavement of Africans in America as sacrilege against God. Early proponents of abolition also focused on America's founding democratic principles, identifying the hypocrisy inherent in slavery's existing in a country that purportedly promised liberty and equal rights to all its citizens. Early antislavery advocates called for the proscription of slavery in territorial expansion and of the slave smuggling that occurred well after the African slave trade had been closed in America. Some supported plans of gradual emancipation and the deportation of free blacks.

Colonization schemes, however, proved only as successful as their short reach across the color line, as organizations like the American Colonization Society were eventually exposed as fronts for racists who believed that whites were superior to blacks and that free African Americans were incapable of being self-sufficient and contributing to the growth and development of the nation. From unheeded calls for the immediate emancipation of slaves to more moderate ones for the simple social uplift of the free "sable sons of Africa," the beginnings of the antislavery movement witnessed the development of what would become the major focuses of the abolitionist crusade and its press from 1830 onward.

One of the earliest antislavery newspapers—one which reflected abolitionist principles that Garrison would later adopt—was the *Philanthropist*, of Mount Pleasant, Ohio, first edited and published by Charles Osborn. After seven months Benjamin Lundy became the paper's associate editor and most frequent contributor. Osborn, "an eminent minister in the Society of Friends," founded the paper on 29 August 1817 and remained its editor and publisher until October 1818, when Elisha Bates took over to run the newspaper under the same name for the next four years. A study of Osborn's involvement in abolition credits him as being Garrison's most noteworthy precursor. Indeed, as George W. Julian wrote in 1882, he managed to

COLORED SCHOOLS BROKEN UP, IN THE FREE STATES.

When schools have been established for colored scholars, the law-makers and the mob have combined to destroy them;—as at Canterbury, Ct., at Canaan, N. H., Aug. 10, 1835, at Zanesville and Brown Co., Ohio, in 1836.

IMMEDIATE EMANCIPATION.

Aug. 1, 1834, 30,000 slaves were emancipated in Antigua. Without any apprenticeship, or system of preparation, preceding the act, the chains were broken at a stroke, and they all went out FREE! It is now four years since these 30,000 slaves were "turned loose" among 2,000 whites, their former masters. These masters fought against the emancipation bill with all their force and fury. They remonstrated with the British Government—conjured and threatened,—protested that emancipation would ruin the island, that the emancipated slaves would never work—would turn vagabonds, butcher the whites and flood the island with beggary and crime. Their strong beseechings availed as little as their threats, and croakings about ruin. The Emancipation Act, unintimidated by the bluster, traversed quietly through its successive stages up to the royal sanction, and became the law of the land. When the slaveholders of Antigua saw that abolition was *inevitable*, they at once resolved to substitute immediate, unconditional, and entire emancipation for the gradual process contemplated by the Act. Well, what has been the result? Read the following testimony of the very men who, but little more than four years ago, denounced and laughed to scorn the idea of abolishing slavery, and called it folly, fanaticism, and insanity. We quote from the work of Messrs. Thome and Kimball, lately published, the written testimony of many of the first men in Antigua,—some of whom were among the largest slaveholders before August, 1834. It proves, among other points, that

EMANCIPATED SLAVES ARE PEACEABLE.

TESTIMONY. "*There is no feeling of insecurity.* A stronger proof of this cannot be given than *the dispensing, within five months after emancipation, with the Christmas guards, which had been uninterruptedly kept up for nearly one hundred years*—during the whole time of slavery.

"I have *never head of any instance of revenge* for former injuries." *James Scotland, Sen. Esq.*

"Insurrection or revenge *is in no case dreaded.* My family go to sleep every night with the doors unlocked. There is not the *slightest* feeling of insecurity —quite the contrary. Property is more secure, *for all idea of insurrection is abolished forever.*" *Hon. N. Nugent, Speaker of the House of Assembly.*

"There has been no instance of personal violence since freedom. I have not heard of a single case of even *meditated* revenge." *Dr.Daniell, member of the Council, and Attorney for six estates.*

"Emancipation has banished the *fear* of insurrections, incendiarism, &c." *Mr. Favey, Manager of Lavicount's.*

"I have never heard of an instance of violence or revenge on the part of the negroes." *Rev. Mr. Morrish, Moravian Missionary.*

A page from the *Anti-Slavery Almanac* of 1839. The almanac, distributed annually by the American Anti-Slavery Society, included poems, drawings, essays, reporting, and other abolitionist material. (Library of Congress.)

proclaim the doctrine of immediate and unconditional emancipation when William Lloyd Garrison was only nine years old and nearly a dozen years before that doctrine was announced by Elizabeth Heyrick, in England; and . . . edit and publish the first anti-slavery newspaper in the United States, and is thus entitled to take rank as the real pioneer of American abolitionism. (Blassingame, p. 3)

For Osborn, colonization meant gradual emancipation, which "placed conditions in its way," thus postponing freedom. Unwavering in his stance against slavery, Osborn boycotted goods produced by slave labor.

The *Philanthropist* was followed by the *Emancipator*, which was published between April and October 1820 and was edited and produced by Elihu Embree of Jonesborough, Tennessee. In his 31 August 1820 editorial, Embree confessed his past ownership of slaves and admitted his shame for not adhering to true Christian principles. In using his antislavery newspaper as a medium for redemptive protest against slavery, Embree called to those men "with clean hands" to "eradicate the stain upon our national escutcheon." During its six-month existence, the *Emancipator* served to advocate the abolition of slavery, report the movement's progress, biographically sketch its advocates, and mediate correspondence between antislavery societies.

Next, the popular antislavery newspaper *Genius of Universal Emancipation*, edited and published by Benjamin Lundy, in Mount Pleasant, Ohio, launched its first issue in 1821. Lundy, who had already regularly submitted articles to other antislavery newspapers and was actively involved in the antislavery movement to the extent that he organized the Union Humane Society, played an essential role in the antislavery movement. His main stance favored gradual emancipation, although he reported on various positions, including the dissenting ones of his coeditor, Garrison.

The *Genius of Universal Emancipation* was followed by John Finley Crow's *Abolition Intelligencer and Missionary Magazine*, first published in Shelbyville, Kentucky, on 7 May 1822, and Enoch Lewis's *African Observer, a Monthly Journal, Containing Essays and Documents Illustrative of the General Character, and Moral and Political Effects, of Negro Slavery*, first published in Philadelphia, Pennsylvania, in April 1827. The life span of each of these publications was just eleven months. Crow's *Abolition Intelligencer* editorial policy supported both the biblical monogenetic perspective of the creation of the human species and gradual emancipation, which he felt could be instituted through the revision of the Constitution. Crow's paper, therefore, aimed to

Meliorate . . . the situation of free people of colour, by giving them proper aid and encouragement in the discharge of the great duties of morality and religion—to defend the rights of those who are legally free . . . , and to prepare the public mind for taking the necessary preparatory measures for the future introduction of a system of laws, for the gradual abolition of slavery, as those degraded people may be prepared for the enjoyment of civil liberty. (Blassingame, p. 97)

Lewis's *African Observer* attempted to quell animosity between the North and South, dispel party disaffection, "trace the moral influence of slavery on those who breathe its atmosphere—and to point out the best means for its peaceful extinction."

The aforementioned papers were all produced by white men; black abolitionists, meanwhile, were championing their own cause alongside that of mainstream abolitionism. Black newspapers focused on the issues of slavery, abolition, racism, and the inclusion of free blacks in America's institutions. In opposing colonization, for instance, their stance was generally resolute, their protests fiery and straightforward. The first black newspaper, *Freedom's Journal*, formed by John Brown Russwurm and Samuel Cornish in New York in 1827, set the standard for black presses to follow; *Freedom's Journal* aimed to present the voice of a self-sufficient and determined free black community. On the other hand, black newspapers sometimes suffered shortcomings owing to the poor literacy rates of the black community. Addressing this later would be *Frederick Douglass' Paper*, which sought to "afford the most extensive opportunity for a free and full expression of sentiments by the illiterate as well as the learned."

David Walker gained stature in and improved the literacy of the black community through his assistance of fugitive slaves, his writings in *Freedom's Journal*, and his famously controversial pamphlet, *An Appeal to the Coloured Citizens of the World*. In his incendiary *Appeal*, published in 1829, Walker called with eloquence and passion for black people to unite, rise up against their oppressors, and fight for their freedom. The fear he stirred among the slavocracy evidenced the masterfully persuasive tone of his writing. Walker's *Appeal* certainly had an influence on Garrison, who published portions of it in his newspaper. Garrison even formed rhetorical and stylistic alliances with Walker; both often referred to the Declaration of Independence. Together, Walker and Garrison, soon fanning the flames lit by Nat Turner's 1831 revolt, ushered in a radical new age of abolitionist reform.

William Lloyd Garrison and the *Liberator*. Garrison joined the cause of antislavery more than a decade before the inaugural issue of his *Liberator* was printed on 1 January 1831; by and large, political journalism was his method. In October 1818, at the age of thirteen, Garrison became apprenticed to the printer of the *Newburyport Herald*. At age seventeen he began writing impressive political treatises for the *Herald* as well as other newspapers, namely, the *Haverhill Gazette*, the *Salem Gazette*, and the *Boston Commercial Gazette*. At the age of twenty-one Garrison purchased and edited a newspaper in Newburyport called the *Free Press*. The paper proved unsuccessful, but Garrison's career would not. In 1828 he copublished the *Journal of the Times* in Vermont, which supported the antislavery cause, and in 1829 Benjamin Lundy, impressed by his talents and zeal, requested his coeditorship on the Baltimore-based *Genius of Universal Emancipation*. For that publication, Garrison submitted his radical abolitionist position in opposition to Lundy. Their coeditorship later ended because of a shared libel suit—and Garrison's forty-nine days' incarceration for denouncing a ship merchant for transporting a cargo of slaves from Baltimore to Louisiana.

Upon his release from prison, Garrison submitted a prospectus for an antislavery journal to be published in Washington, D.C. Additionally, he prepared antislavery lectures, which he delivered along the northeastern coast from Boston to Philadelphia. Because his lectures particularly excited the crowds in Boston, he decided that that city would be a better place to run a newspaper.

Within the pages of the *Liberator*, Garrison waged war against slavery and racial inequality. His aims for abolitionist reform as presented in his paper were firm:

> Assenting to the "self-evident truth" maintained in the American Declaration of Independence, "that all men are created equal, and endowed by their Creator with certain inalienable rights—among which are life, liberty and the pursuit of happiness," I shall strenuously contend for the immediate enfranchisement of our slave population. (Cain, p. 71)

Garrison espoused the "immediate, unconditional emancipation of slaves without compensation to slave owners." Every stance he took in contending for the immediate liberation of slaves was expressed in the *Liberator*, which thus charted the development of his perspectives as well as the course of the abolitionist crusade. In an 1832 editorial entitled "Guilt of New England," Garrison held the North responsible for the continuation of slavery because of its peripheral involvement in the institution. This position, first presented in his famous 1829 speech "An Address to the American Colonization Society," was accompanied by a disunionist call for the dissolution of the United States: "So long as we continue one body—a union—a nation—the compact involves us in the guilt and danger of slavery." In a 29 December 1832 editorial entitled "On the Constitution and the Union," Garrison accused the nation's founding fathers of being hypocritical in the charter document; he charged that in striking the "infamous bargain which they made between themselves, they virtually dethroned the Most High God, and trampled beneath their feet their own solemn and heaven-attested Declaration."

As Garrison and fellow abolitionists organized antislavery societies across the country, their manifestos and progress were reported in the *Liberator*. The 14 December 1833 editorial, "Declaration of the National Anti-Slavery Convention," presented the aims of the new Philadelphia branch of the American Anti-Slavery Society. On 23 January 1836 Garrison offered "The Progress of Antislavery," a reprinted letter to a fellow abolitionist. The *Liberator* followed the format of religious reform newspapers in including such writings as well as in appending other movements to abolitionist reform. The following editorial titles reflect Garrison's various interests: "Rights of Woman" (1838), "Women's Rights" (1853), and "The Bible and Women's Rights" (1855).

The *Liberator* also chronicled the activities of black abolitionists. In support of Frederick Douglass—the fugitive slave who became the foremost black abolitionist and orator as well as the editor of his own antislavery newspapers, beginning with the *North Star*—the *Liberator* charted his activities in America and abroad and reprinted his speeches and letters. In a 1 July 1842 editorial, Garrison reported his impressions of Douglass from an antislavery meeting:

> After I had spoken at some length, I was followed by two witnesses on the side of non-resistance. . . . The first was Frederick Douglass. He stood there as a slave—a runaway from the southern house of bondage—not safe, for one hour, even on the soil of Massachusetts—with his back all horribly scarred by the lash . . . with every thing in his past history, his present condition, his future prospects, to make him a fierce outlaw, and a stern avenger of outraged humanity! He stood there, not to counsel retaliation, not to advocate the right of the oppressed to wade through blood to liberty . . . O no!—but with the spirit of Christian forgiveness in his heart, with the melting accents of charity on his lips, with the gentleness of love beaming in his eyes! His testimony was clear and emphatic. (Cain, p. 108)

Unfortunately, their friendship later became strained as a result of Douglass's production of the *North Star* and was finally severed when Garrison perceived Douglass's "new anti-slavery interpretation of the Constitution" as ambitiously self-serving. In his second autobiography, *My Bondage and My Freedom* (1855), Douglass discusses Garrison's disapproval of his ability to learn and think independently—and apart from the views of Garrison and other white abolitionists.

During its thirty-four-year run the *Liberator* targeted a northern audience, as there Garrison "found contempt more bitter, opposition more active, detraction more relentless, prejudice more stubborn, and apathy more frozen, than among slave owners themselves." The *Liberator* particularly attracted free black northerners; subscriptions were filled in New York, Philadelphia, and Boston, "where significant numbers of free black[s] resided." Indeed, black subscribers kept the newspaper running from its inception: "The receipt of $50 from James Forten, a wealthy colored citizen of Philadelphia, with the names of twenty-five subscribers, was the first cheering incentive to perseverance, and the journal was issued without interruption from that day." Garrison's often brash tone and his passion for emancipation led some readers to mistake him for an African American, and regardless of his identity his forceful attacks on racism maintained his appeal to black readers. White subscribers never exceeded 400, with the total number of subscribers ranging between 2,500 and 3,000.

The *Liberator*'s uncompromising tone and the "severity" of Garrison's language incited hostility in both the North and South, to the extent that Garrison's life was often threatened—even by democratic institutions: "In December, 1831, the Legislature of Georgia passed an act, offering a reward of $5,000 to any person who should arrest, bring to trial, and prosecute to conviction, under the laws of that State, the editor or the publisher" of the *Liberator*. Garrison's contemporary biographer, William Cain, reports: "On October 21, 1835, Garrison was accosted by twelve Boston men, roughed up, his clothes torn, and he was hauled by a rope along Wilson's Lane toward State Street."

On the whole, radical abolitionist reform met with hostility from the masses. Frantic public officials, perceiving such reform attempts as insurrectional, worked to suppress abolitionist mailings and newspapers. Violent adversaries went as far as to burn several abolitionist newspapers. Elijah P. Lovejoy, the editor of the *Alton Observer*, received the ultimate retribution for allotting space in his paper to the subject of abolition: aside from his paper's offices being set on fire four times, he lost his life to mob rule. Mainstream newspapers, meanwhile, hardly spared space on their sheets for the subject of abolition, perceiving antislavery reform as a public nuisance.

Despite mob violence and other opposition, abolitionist reform progressed. In 1832 Garrison and other abolitionists formed the New England Anti-Slavery Society, later renamed the Massachusetts Anti-Slavery Society; in 1833 they founded a national organization called the American Anti-Slavery Society. The American Anti-Slavery Society produced its own journal, the *National Anti-Slavery Standard*, following the model of the *Liberator*. While undergoing several name changes, the *National Anti-Slavery Standard* remained the weekly organ of the American Anti-Slavery Society from 1840 to 1870. It was published out of both New York and Philadelphia, and letters, editorials, poetry, advertisements, and illustrations filled its pages. In the manner of the mainstream press, the *Standard* also included local, national, and foreign news.

Like the *Liberator*, the *Standard* espoused immediate emancipation and racial equality. Immersed in American Enlightenment principles, the *Standard* set forth its objectives:

> It is manifestly the will of the Society that this paper should be conducted on the broad principle of the universal fraternity of the human race, irrespective of sect, party, sex, color or country. All who love freedom and abhor slavery, all who believe in the doctrine of immediate emancipation will receive from the conductors of this paper that equal consideration which the society itself accords, and be welcomed as co-laborers whenever they present themselves in that character. (Blassingame, p. 9)

The *National Anti-Slavery Standard* also had one purpose outside those of the *Liberator*: to expand the membership of the American Anti-Slavery Society and, as such, to formally initiate more followers into abolitionist reform. Presenting before its public an open argument in favor of abolition, the *Standard* professed a "freedom of expression [that] respect[s] the grand object of the society and the means for its accomplishment." To this end, the organ differed from the *Liberator* in that it avoided functioning as one man's paper. The *Liberator*, on the other hand, was thoroughly Garrison's: "Through crisis after crisis personal editorial control of the paper . . . was his in the sense that few influential organs of public opinion have ever belonged to one man."

While the *National Anti-Slavery Standard* was the American Anti-Slavery Society's weekly journal, the society also published four other journals, namely, the *Anti-Slavery Record*, *Human Rights*, the *Emancipator*, and the *Slave's Friend*. These journals were published on monthly bases, alternating weeks. The *Anti-Slavery Record* was issued out of New York City from January 1835 to December 1837; the abolitionists William Goodell, the Reverend Joshua Leavitt, and Amos Augustus Phelps all edited the journal, each serving for one year. *Human Rights* was issued out of New York from July 1835 to February 1839.

Lovejoy, eventually known as the martyr of abolition for losing his life to mob violence, edited several papers for the American Anti-Slavery Society. The first was the *St. Louis Observer*, which he served from November 1833 to July 1836; he was charged with inciting free black people in his position at the *Observer*, to which his opponents responded by destroying his office and the paper. He then moved his press to Alton, Illinois, where he established the *Alton Observer* on 1 October 1836. On 21 August 1837 the paper was destroyed, and on 7 November 1837 Lovejoy was murdered. Elisha Chester took over editorship of the *Alton Observer* in December 1837, but the paper ceased publication in 1838.

The war that abolitionist reformers waged against slavery was both moral and religious, and the movement's newspapers were its weapons. The antislavery press after 1830 furthered the reformist objectives and stances set forth by earlier abolitionist publications. They "put faces and voices to the crusade," introducing the public to prominent abolitionists such as Wendell Phillips, the poet John Greenleaf Whittier, the Englishman George Thompson, and Lydia Maria Child. The role of the antislavery press was to agitate as well as to disseminate beliefs regarding not only slavery but also the social climate that fostered the abominable institution. Abolitionists severely criticized the church and attacked America's government and its charter document for being hypocritical. In recording the historical course and progress of abolitionist reform, the antislavery press between 1830 and 1870 propagated social views that excited the spirit of freedom and justice in America's soul. Antislavery newspapers aroused the nation's ability to overcome all threats to the democratic life that it wished to provide for all its citizens.

[*See also* Abolitionism; American Anti-Slavery Society; American Colonization Society; Antislavery Movement; Bible; Black Abolitionists; Black Press; Black Uplift; Child, Lydia Maria; Colonization; Cornish, Samuel; Disunionism; *Douglass' Monthly*; Douglass, Frederick; Evolution; Feminist Movement; Forten, James; *Frederick Douglass' Paper*; Garrison, William Lloyd; Garrisonian Abolitionists; Goodell, William; Literature; Lundy, Benjamin; Massachusetts Anti-Slavery Society; Methodist Episcopal Church; *My Bondage and My Freedom*; *North Star*; Oratory and Verbal Arts; Phillips, Wendell; Racism; Reform; Religion; Religion and Slavery; Russwurm, John Brown; Slavery; Society of Friends (Quakers); Suffrage, Women's; Thompson, George; Turner, Nat; Violence against African Americans; Walker, David; Whittier, John Greenleaf; *and* Women.]

BIBLIOGRAPHY

Blassingame, John W., and Mae G. Henderson, eds. *Antislavery Newspapers and Periodicals*. 5 vols. Boston: G. K. Hall, 1980–1984.

Brown, William Wells. *The Travels of William Wells Brown* (1847). Edited by Paul Jefferson. New York: Markus Wiener, 1991.

Cain, William E., Ed. *William Lloyd Garrison and the Fight against Slavery: Selections from the "Liberator."* Boston: Bedford/St. Martin's, 1995.

Douglass, Frederick. *Life and Times of Frederick Douglass* (1881). Grand Rapids, MI: Candace Press, 1996.

Douglass, Frederick. *My Bondage and My Freedom* (1855). Edited by William L. Andrews. Urbana: University of Illinois Press, 1987.

Douglass, Frederick. *Narrative of the Life of Frederick Douglass, an American Slave* (1845). New York: Signet Classic, 1997.

Franklin, John Hope, and Alfred A. Moss Jr. *From Slavery to Freedom: A History of Negro Americans*. 6th ed. New York: Knopf, 1988.

Jacobs, Harriet. *Incidents in the Life of a Slave Girl* (1861). Edited by Lydia Maria Child. New York: Washington Square, 2003.

Lowance, Mason, ed. *Against Slavery: An Abolitionist Reader*. New York: Penguin, 2000.

Mott, Frank Luther. *American Journalism: A History, 1690–1960*. 3rd ed. New York: Macmillan, 1962.

Quarles, Benjamin. *Black Abolitionists*. New York: Da Capo, 1991.

Walker, David. *Appeal to the Coloured Citizens of the World, but in Particular and Very Expressly, to Those of the United States of America* (1829). Edited by Charles M. Wiltse. New York: Hill and Wang, 1965.

—CHERRON A. BARNWELL

ARCHITECTURE. There are two distinct topics in African American architecture: the places in which African Americans lived and the places built or designed by African Americans. The two might or might not be one and the same. Depending on their status, African Americans often inhabited places that were designed by whites, who were building in their own (mostly) European traditions. This was especially true of slaves. On large plantations, house slaves lived with the family in the "big house," while the rest lived in slave quarters that were typically designed by whites. On small farms and in urban areas slaves frequently shared the same living space as their masters. The design of the structures may have been European in origin, but often African American masons and carpenters constructed the buildings. Thus, in discussing African American architecture in early America, it is difficult to separate their building traditions from the dominant white culture.

Even African Americans who did design and construct their own buildings often built them in whatever was the popular style of the day. The Wilson Bruce Evans house, built in 1856 in Oberlin, Ohio, provides an extant example of a home designed and constructed by African Americans. Wilson Bruce and his brother, Henry, were free-born African Americans who lived in North Carolina. In 1854 they moved to Ohio and settled in Oberlin. The two brothers together built Wilson Bruce's house, an Italianate-style, side-hallway building. Italianate architecture was popular at the time. The side-hallway house type is sometimes referred to as a "three-quarters" Georgian, with an asymmetrical three-bay facade, door in either the left or right bay, and windows in the other two bays. Inside, a hallway comes off the entrance door, with a set of stairs to the second floor to either the right or left of the hall. The side hallway is also a part of the European vernacular tradition. The Evans brothers were literate and may have used one of the widely available pattern books as a guide for the new residence; they might also have seen the side-hallway house type in their native North Carolina.

The only type of housing that is definitely attributed to African American culture is the shotgun house. Long the topic of discussion among general historians and architectural historians alike, the shotgun house is believed to have originated in Haiti and been brought to the North American mainland by émigrés during the rebellion of the Haitian liberator Toussaint Louverture in the 1790s; the style continued to be popular into the first decade of the nineteenth century. The great majority of these Haitian men and women settled in New Orleans and built vernacular housing that was familiar to them. The shotgun, according to architectural historians, is a blend of West Indian and West African vernacular architectural

"African" house at Melrose plantation, Natchitoches Parish, Louisiana, photographed in June 1940 by Marion Post Walcott. It was built by mulattoes c. 1800 of brick and cypress slabs and probably was originally used as a storeroom, smokehouse, or jail. The walls of the upper story are now covered with art by the twentieth-century black painter Clementine Hunter. (Library of Congress.)

types. From New Orleans, shotgun houses spread throughout the South and into other states as a result of internal migration.

Shotgun houses are usually one-story buildings with a front gable roof, consisting of two inclined planes that meet in the middle and face front. Some variants may have hipped roofs, which form a pyramid shape. There are typically two bays on the facade, with the door in either the right or the left bay and a window in the opposite bay. The shotgun house, which may be two or three rooms deep and one room wide, often has a full-width front porch. The front and rear doors are lined up, thus giving rise to the name *shotgun*—it was said that a person could aim a gun through the front door and shoot directly through the back door without touching a wall. There is some evidence that the term *shotgun* may be an alteration of *togun*, a Yoruban (Niger-Congo) word for "house." The camelback shotgun is a variant on the traditional shotgun house. The camelback has a two-story rear addition attached to the one-story

front building. Another variant is the "double shotgun," which is essentially two side-by-side shotguns under one roof, allowing for two-family occupancy. The double shotgun can also have a camelback.

The historian John Michael Vlach, the authority on shotgun houses, was one of the first to document the connection between this vernacular housing type and African American folk culture. Vlach notes that on the North American mainland, New Orleans should be seen as the center of the development of the shotgun house. From New Orleans, the shotgun type disseminated into rural areas as well as to other cities. There are examples of rural shotguns, especially in the South, but this house type was normally found in urban areas. The long, narrow footprint made the shotgun particularly suited to city lots, which are usually longer than they are wide.

As African Americans migrated throughout the United States, they took the shotgun house with them. A number of notable examples of shotguns can be found in Ohio, especially in central and southern cities, such as Marietta and Gallipolis. In the later nineteenth and early twentieth centuries, companies in the Ohio and Mississippi river valleys often built housing for their workers that were essentially shotgun houses, because they were relatively inexpensive and easy to erect, especially with the advent of balloon framing in the 1830s. Balloon framing consisted of standardized and mass-produced lightweight planks that did not require the skills of a carpenter to nail together. While these houses were simple in form, a number of extant examples show design elements of popular styles. For example, one shotgun from about the 1860s in Gallipolis in southeastern Ohio has carpenter gothic decoration, a style of decoration popularly known as "gingerbread," on its full-width front porch. Thus, while shotguns were normally utilitarian structures, some had decorative elements reflecting the contemporary ornate architectural styles.

The shotgun house is the only building type that has been proved to have connections with African American folk traditions, but this does not mean that blacks were not active as builders. Their names may be lost to the historical record, but there is no doubt that both free and enslaved blacks were masons and carpenters, building houses and other structures for themselves, their employers, or their masters. Indeed, masters of large plantations, such as Thomas Jefferson, often used their slave labor not only to build structures on the master's property but even to construct public buildings. Both free and enslaved African Americans worked for contractors (many of whom were undertakers) on construction projects throughout the colonies and the new American nation. In eighteenth-century South Carolina, enslaved blacks monopolized nearly all of the trades, including carpentry and masonry, thus performing much of the construction work in the colony.

There is little doubt that African Americans played an important role in constructing the built environment, but many remain anonymous, especially in the colonial era and early Republic. The work of one notable African American craftsman is remarkable. In Youngstown, in northeastern Ohio, the African American master mason and bricklayer P. Ross Berry was the main contractor on a number of important public buildings and residences in the second half of the nineteenth century. Berry, who had settled in Youngstown by the beginning of the Civil War, built the Rayen High School (1866), the Youngstown Opera House (1874), the Mahoning County Courthouse (1876), and other significant buildings. There were no doubt many more skilled African American building craftsmen in the seventeenth, eighteenth, and early nineteenth centuries like Berry. Future research may uncover those names and their contributions to the American built environment.

[*See also* Artisans *and* Arts and Crafts.]

BIBLIOGRAPHY

Berlin, Ira. *Many Thousands Gone: The First Two Centuries of Slavery in North America*. Cambridge, MA: Belknap Press, 1998.

Gordon, Stephen C. *How to Complete the Ohio Historic Inventory*. Columbus: Ohio Historical Society, 1992.

Upton, Dell. *Architecture in the United States*. New York: Oxford University Press, 1998.

Vlach, John Michael. "The Shotgun House: An African-American Architectural Legacy." In *Common Places: Readings in American Vernacular Architecture*, edited by Dell Upton and John Michael Vlach, 58–78. Athens: University of Georgia Press, 1986.

—DONNA M. DEBLASIO

ARTISANS. While most African American workers in the colonial and early national periods were agricultural or maritime laborers, free and enslaved artisans were a small but significant portion of black populations in the Americas. In locations as diverse as Portuguese Brazil, French Louisiana, Dutch New York, and English Virginia and South Carolina, slaves translated skills that they had learned in Africa and in the New World into finished products for their owners. African American artisans became more numerous as eighteenth-century plantations in the English colonies grew in size, enabling planters to diversify their workforce. Physical size and strength as well as evidence of interest and ability marked slaves as candidates to learn a trade. Like others bound out to craftsmen, slaves served apprenticeships to white artisans, though later in the eighteenth century many of them learned their skills from fellow slaves. Unlike white apprentices or journeymen, however, most black artisans would remain slaves and could not set up their own independent workshops.

A shortage of white craftsmen and an increased demand for building skills and finished consumer goods presented black artisans with negotiating leverage unknown to other African Americans. As a result, these men resided in a middle space between white slave masters and the majority of bondpeople. Black artisans knew that their skills would permit them to achieve a competency or basic level of economic independence if they could successfully escape slavery. Slave owners did not always have work for their artisans to do, and yet they did not wish to lose access to these laborers. Instead, they made concessions to these men, often hiring them out to other rural white planters, tradesmen, or urban dwellers.

The contract between owner and hirer stipulated the length of the hiring term (varying between a few days and, more typically, an entire year) and the wages to be paid to the slave, who would deliver a set amount to his master. While this system provided income for the slave owner, it also offered the slave artisan limited freedom of movement and earning power, as he might strike a deal with the hirer to work additional hours or on Sundays for extra pay. Artisans sometimes were able to buy their freedom after saving their earnings. Free black artisans could occasionally parley their skills into remarkable independence. One black South Carolina cotton gin maker named William Ellison constructed important machines for nearby white planters, who generally praised his work. While his success was based upon white support and thus was tenuous, Ellison plowed his rare economic power into a plantation of his own, staffed by slaves.

More often, however, black artisans enjoyed liberty on a more restricted scale. The hiring-out system evolved in some quarters into a process by which artisans hired themselves to whites wanting skilled workers. This allowed slave craftsmen to choose their masters carefully and bargain with them for wages and prerogatives like geographical mobility and pace of work. In the course of a day's labor, black artisans might interact with white craftsmen both as hated inferiors and as accepted equals. Some historians have contended that a working-class culture across racial lines began to develop in some cities in the early national era, spurred in the North by emancipation and in the South by the dearth of white artisans and the presence of skilled blacks. White and black artisans (free and slave) in some cases forged social bonds in the workplace and the tavern that at least temporarily transcended racial animosity and fostered working-class hostility against planters and merchants.

Certainly, there remained hostility between whites and blacks, and artisans were often at the forefront of such struggles. For enslaved artisans, proximity to freedom through the hiring system did not conceal the fact that they were still in chains, and contact with free black communities in cities spurred efforts to obtain that freedom by any means possible. An enslaved blacksmith known only as Gabriel, who hired out his time in Richmond, Virginia, and Denmark Vesey, a free carpenter in Charleston, South Carolina, led slave revolts in 1800 and 1822, respectively. While artisans such as Ellison sought to distance themselves socially from enslaved blacks, Gabriel and Vesey tried to unite with other blacks in attempts to improve life for all African Americans, skilled and unskilled.

Artisans also enrolled in antislavery movements in the northern United States. James Forten, a free person of color who was apprenticed in 1785 to a white Philadelphia sailmaker, earned the artisan's trust and succeeded him as master craftsman in 1798. While journeymen at first doubted whether Forten could maintain accounts with white shipbuilders, he soon earned their trust and administered a successful, interracial workshop into the nineteenth century. Economic success and social standing on the wharves led to increased political activity for Forten. He joined other free blacks, such as the ministers Absalom Jones and Richard Allen, in the leadership of the antislavery movement in Philadelphia, writing pamphlets against the institution and enjoining white politicians to act on petitions for the abolition of slavery.

The decades after the American Revolution were the apex of black artisans' economic, social, and political leadership, at which time African Americans were able to enter a greater variety of trades in more substantial numbers than ever before. Industrialization, the process by which manufacturers and merchants succeeded in dividing labor tasks to enhance production and lower costs, closed avenues to economic independence for skilled men, black and white. White artisans, joining other whites who criticized abolitionist tactics and anxious about what industrialization portended, hoped that their own work would not be associated with slavery or with slaves. Skilled whites tried to distinguish white work from black work, forging agreements with artisans and manufacturers not to hire blacks. White journeymen were successful in expelling African Americans (such as the Baltimore ship caulker Frederick Douglass) from many of the trades, forcing them to accept lower-paying unskilled work on urban docks. Increasingly in the 1820s and 1830s, skill was to be associated solely with white workers, thus obscuring two hundred years of black participation in artisanal trades.

Artisans After 1830. The end of slavery in the north did not translate into improved opportunities for blacks in the artisan trades. While there were always a number of blacks in urban communities who performed skilled labor for their fellows, rarely if ever did those numbers grow into an entire class. Those who did work as artisans or, more commonly, as small shopkeepers were the elite in their respective black communities. Blacks who studied at church-supported schools in the north often learned artisan skills, but often could not find work in their field and so could not apply their skills. The few who did find work joined older former slaves who had worked for white masters and thus gained practical skills. Other black artisans came from the ranks of free blacks who chose to move north. The carpenter Michael Milliken moved from Virginia to Boston in the mid-1840s after short residencies in other northern cities. Frederick Douglass was an enslaved skilled caulker in Baltimore. His master hired him out until Douglass decided to escape to the north in 1838. After disguising himself as a sailor, Douglass arrived safely in New York City. There he came under the protection of David Ruggles, a bookseller and printer, who had connections with the caulkers and maritime workers in New Bedford, Massachusetts. Douglass went to New Bedford, but initially was unable to find work because of discrimination. Ruggles exemplifies the skilled black artisans of New York in that he had to supplement his work as a printer with bookselling and abolitionist activism. Even so, his lived at subsistence level at best and in poverty at other times.

Poverty was a frequent companion of skilled African Americans. Their elite status was highly fragile and even though skilled workers constituted 25 percent of black workers in Boston in 1850 and 1860, their struggle for survival was constant and often futile. They could be proud of their high literacy rates and traditions of defying discrimination and slavery, but opportunities were rare in skilled trades.

In the southern states, skilled workers were far more common. In the slave societies of the region, white workers generally lost place to enslaved artisans and the occasional free black worker. As in the north after 1830, black artisans tended to be the elite of their community. Over time, however, they too fell victim to racism and discrimination. By the onset of the Civil War, white employers became unwilling to hire black artisans because they wished to encourage them to leave the country via the American Colonization Society.

Discrimination in hiring and, later, in northern labor unions, kept large numbers of African Americans out of the industrial trades. These negative factors were important in the north and in the south. While skilled black artisans emerged from slavery in the south well prepared for freedom, they encountered a new source of opposition. While few northern white artisans were eager to come south and replace African Americans who were paid less than they were, immigrants quickly heeded the call and supplanted black labor. Southern contractors advertised in eastern and northern Europe and offered good terms to immigrant artisans. Upon arrival, however, immigrants often soon became disenchanted and left. Their places in turn were filled by rural whites eager to leave exhausted farmlands. As a result, African Americans artisans generally lost ground after freedom. Virtually the only places where blacks could achieve equal opportunities during the Civil War and post–Civil War periods were black towns settled in the Midwestern states. Sadly, in the last quarter of the nineteenth century, the industrial revolution had progressed so far that artisan skills seldom had much value. Still, these skills were often the principal ones taught at segregated schools and such colleges as Hampton Institute, founded in 1868. In the northern states, black populations dipped so far that black artisans were even rarer in the post–Civil War period than in preceding eras.

[See also Architecture; Arts and Crafts; Forten, James; Gabriel; Occupations; Vesey, Denmark; and Work.]

BIBLIOGRAPHY

Berlin, Ira. Generations of Captivity: A History of African-American Slaves. Cambridge, MA: Harvard University Press, 2003.

Egerton, Douglas R. Gabriel's Rebellion: The Virginia Slave Conspiracies of 1800 and 1802. Chapel Hill: University of North Carolina Press, 1993. Compelling analysis of a skilled artisan's role as participant in an interracial working-class culture in Richmond, Virginia, and as leader of an important slave revolt.

Foner, Eric. Reconstruction. New York: Harper and Rowe, 1987.

Harris, Leslie M. In the Shadow of Slavery: African Americans in New York City, 1626–1863. Chicago: University of Chicago Press, 2003. Thoroughly examines the class divisions and conflicts between northern blacks under Dutch and English colonial rule and during the extended period of Emancipation in early-nineteenth-century New York.

Hodges, Graham Russell. Root & Branch: African Americans in New York and East Jersey, 1613–1863. Chapel Hill: University of North Carolina Press, 1999.

Horton, James Oliver, and Lois E. Horton. Black Bostonians: Family Life and Community Struggle in the Antebellum North. New York: Holmes and Meier, 1979.

Johnson, Michael P., and James L. Roark. Black Masters: A Free Family of Color in the Old South. New York: Norton, 1984. A beautifully rendered portrait of the free black cotton gin maker and plantation owner William Ellison.

Morgan, Philip D. Slave Counterpoint: Black Culture in the Eighteenth-Century Chesapeake and Lowcountry. Chapel Hill: University of North Carolina Press, 1998. A comprehensive examination of African American life in colonial Virginia and South Carolina, focusing on important differences in the work culture of both places.

Winch, Julie. A Gentleman of Color: The Life of James Forten. New York: Oxford University Press, 2002. A sterling biography of a black artisan who became a leader in the early-nineteenth-century abolition movement.

—BRIAN P. LUSKEY
—GRAHAM RUSSELL GAO HODGES

ARTS AND CRAFTS. The colonial period in America was not noted for its fine arts; there was little in the way of sculpture, and most of the paintings that were made were stiff portraits in the manner of European, mostly British, art. The puritanical spirit that dominated America at the time was not one that nurtured the arts in general. Very little, if any, experimentation went on in any of the arts, as most art was regarded as frivolous and a distraction from what was held to be the serious and important business of religion and work. Within this context there is evidence that fine art in the form of portraits was made by Africans in colonial America. However, most of the known artifacts from both slave and free blacks are the work of artisans. Some of this work is of exceptionally high quality, and it includes just about every imaginable practical and decorative artwork—from the ornate iron railings adorning the balconies of New Orleans to fine clothing, silverware, pottery, and woodcarvings. The area in which black Americans were probably most accomplished was furniture making.

While it is unlikely that the early slaveholders bought slaves with the notion of employing them as artisans, it is clear that the talents of the Africans were quickly identified. Not long after the appearance of the first slaves on American shores, blacks were employed as cobblers, tailors, silversmiths, and carpenters, among other creative professions. There were, of course, economic reasons for training blacks in such skills. Artisans who arrived from Europe often either renounced their crafts to make more money as land and slave owners or charged very high prices for their crafts. Some white artisans, of course, trained slaves to do the work in order to make more products and thus more money. Even the paid work of free blacks was a desirable commodity, because it was much cheaper than that of whites.

It is clear that people of African descent distinguished themselves in nearly all art forms—from music to the making of every imaginable type of art and craft—from their first appearance in America. The record regarding early contributions by blacks in the fine arts, such as painting and sculpture, is less well documented. In part, this was because making fine art was often a secret activity for blacks.

Artisanry was one thing; after all, everyone needed tables and chairs, dressers and staircases, and it could be overlooked if they were a bit more beautiful or ornate than was absolutely necessary. The puritanical spirit could accept that working with wood and other materials was "real" work, not an obvious statement of self-expression such as that made by a painter, a sculptor, or a poet. And while whites had always allowed themselves to be entertained by the accomplished musicians in the African American population, giving a black person a canvas and a brush or a piece of marble to sculpt was another matter, a matter generally looked down upon for much the same reasons that reading was forbidden to slaves. Making visual artwork in colonial times was kept secret because of the danger involved if whites saw the work. Unfortunately, very little remains of the earliest works, as most were condemned as products of pagans or heretics and destroyed if discovered. Even beyond this kind of risk, black—and particularly slave—visual artists were hampered by the difficulty blacks faced in obtaining materials.

Artisans. The few remaining early artworks made by Africans in America are, as might be expected, based on recollections of life in Africa. Drums akin to African drums date from as early as about 1645. Other seventeenth-century artifacts include iron statues. The statues, as well as eighteenth-century works, such as walking canes and baskets, resemble similar pieces found in Africa. A wrought-

iron figure of a man, made by a Virginia slave, looks very much like wooden sculptures from the Sudan. The sculpture was found buried in the slave quarters of a Richmond blacksmith shop, indicating that the artist did not dare make this work in the open. The fact that it survived can almost certainly be attributed to the durability of iron. An early-nineteenth-century pair of carved wood chickens (a rooster and a hen) is reminiscent of a bronze rooster sculpture from Benin. These pieces are attributed to a slave of the pirate Jean Lafitte, who perhaps appreciated their beauty. Even in later works, such as carved mantelpieces, touches of African influence show up in the form of a mask worked into the pattern or possibly an abstract design that can be traced to West Africa.

In the area of ceramics, a group of so-called grotesque jugs have faces with oversized features that resemble those found on some African masks. By the early 1800s "Dave the Potter," a slave who had been taught to write, was signing and dating his pots, which are noted for their height and wide, ridged mouths. Dave the Potter is unusual in that his name is known. The vast majority of African American artisans were unknown, both be-

Silver footed cup by Peter Bentzon, the first black silversmith in the United States to mark his works with his name. Bentzon was born free c. 1783 in Saint Thomas, Virgin Islands; was apprenticed in Philadelphia; and was active mainly from 1817 to 1849. This cup—about 7 inches high and 4 inches in diameter—dates from 1841. (Philadelphia Museum of Art. Purchased with the Thomas Skelton Harrison Fund and with the partial gift of Wynard Wilkinson, 1994.)

Armoire by Celestin Glapion, c. 1790. Glapion was a free man of color and furniture-maker in colonial New Orleans. (Collection of Louisiana State Museum.)

cause it was not the practice to sign most art and artisan work in colonial times and because, with some exceptions, blacks were generally not given credit for their work, no matter how accomplished. And while the work of colonial blacks was often excellent, early African Americans did not change the realm of the visual arts in the same way that they did music, for example. It was possible to make innovations in music using just the voice or a simple instrument, but when it came to making things from expensive materials such as mahogany or silver, blacks were rarely allowed to deviate from the European norm.

All the same, blacks were entrusted with these materials and some slaves were sold as artisans, including silversmiths, even before the Revolutionary War. Blacks were so much a part of the colonial crafts world that some whites felt the need to hold them back. As early as 1755 the Provincial Legislature of South Carolina was petitioned to pass a law restraining blacks from entering trades where they already outnumbered whites. (The pro-

posed law would also have banned blacks from being left in charge of shops, from which one can conclude that many blacks, free and slave, were indeed entrusted with keeping shops.) Although very few works of any sort were signed, many black artisans followed local tradition and advertised their work widely, often including the information that the craftsman was a person of color.

As might be expected, some of the more enduring works by black artisans include furniture. Among the best-known black colonial furniture makers was Thomas Day, whose work was highly sought after in the early to middle 1800s. Day used many types of wood and was known for his graceful carvings on furniture and staircases. His work is often viewed as a synthesis between European and African design. One of his pieces often pointed to in this regard is a stair newel post in the Paschal House in Caswell County, North Carolina; the carving can easily be seen as an African statuette. Day was educated in Boston and Washington, D.C., and worked in North Carolina as a free black. By 1820 his work was widely advertised and well regarded. He became very wealthy, so wealthy that he owned slaves who helped run his business.

In Petersburg, Virginia, the freed-black craftsmen John Raymond and John Ventus paid taxes on their cabinet-making business and advertised it. Many slaves were also makers of fine furniture. John Hemings, the brother of Thomas Jefferson's companion Sally Hemings, made some of the most elegant woodwork and furniture at Jefferson's house, Monticello, in Virginia.

Slaves were also involved in the making of both textiles and fine clothes. Plantation owners began growing cotton and flax, as well as producing wool, in the 1770s, partly to clothe their slaves. The slaves were put in charge of weaving the cloth and making their own clothes. Many black women were also responsible for making elegant clothing to be worn by both white and black women, including another of Sally Hemings's siblings, Nance Hemings, who was a weaver trained on the Jefferson estate during the Revolutionary War. While the names of most black seamstresses are lost, some of their work is of the highest quality, the equivalent of couture.

Artists. There appear to have been few African Americans who made fine art in colonial America, but among those who did was the slave Scipio Moorhead, who created the engraving that served as frontispiece to Phillis Wheatley's 1773 book *Poems on Various Subjects*. It seems that Moorhead was a painter as well as an engraver; a hand-written note from Wheatley refers to him as "a young African painter." Wheatley herself, it should be noted, was repeatedly called on to prove that she, a black woman, could really produce the quality of work found in her book—a question that no doubt followed all African American artists of the colonial period.

Many observers have come to believe that the gifted Baltimore portrait artist Joshua Johnston, who was active in the late 1700s and early 1800s, was almost certainly black, but although Johnston's identity has been widely researched, there is no conclusive proof of his race. The idea that he might have been black started with various family stories, possibly family myths, about a free black man who painted portraits and with a will written by a Baltimore widow that named the artist of a portrait of her as "J Johnson." (As was the norm for the time, none of Johnston's portraits was signed.) A Joshua Johnston appears in the 1817 Baltimore directory as a "Free Householder of Colour." Johnston (or Johnson—there seems to be no continuity in the spelling) solicited customers for his portrait business. However, his advertisements do not mention the artist's race.

Other artists advertised their skills as portrait painters and named themselves as Negroes. A portrait painter who predated Johnston by a quarter century placed a wholly immodest advertisement in the *Massachusetts Gazette* in 1773, referring to himself as "a Negro Man whose extraordinary Genius has been assisted by one of the best Masters in London; he takes Faces at the lowest Rates [*sic*]." In Johnston's 1798 advertisement in the *Baltimore Intelligencer*, he also claims to be a genius, "a self-taught genius," and he refers to "many insuperable obstacles in the pursuit of his studies." These "insuperable obstacles" are often interpreted as a not-too-veiled reference to the painter's race.

Those who are skeptical that Johnston was black, including the artist and scholar Romare Bearden, think it unlikely that an African American of such achievement would have gone unnoted in Baltimore. At the time, the city contained a large and active abolitionist community that touted the achievements of notable blacks, such as Johnston's contemporary, the mathematician and astronomer Benjamin Banneker. However, most of Johnston's subjects were slave owners, and it might have been bad for business if he were to involve himself in the abolitionist movement. One more contradiction: some portraits of black leaders of the African Methodist Episcopal Church are believed to be in the style of Johnston and thus may point to his being black.

Middle and Late Nineteenth-Century Artists. By the Civil War, African Americans had more fully entered the world of fine art, and before the end of the nineteenth century, the painters Robert S. Duncanson, Edward M. Bannister, and Henry Ossawa Tanner, and the sculptor Edmonia Lewis had gained national and international reputations. Each of these artists achieved recognition in an environ-

Joshua Johnson's "Portrait of a Gentleman," who has been identified as the Reverend Daniel T. Coker. The portrait dates from c. 1805–1810. (American Museum in Britain.)

ment still hostile to the possibility that African American artists could excel. The feelings of many, possibly most, white Americans were summarized by an 1867 *New York Herald* article that declared, "the Negro seems to have an appreciation for art while being manifestly unable to produce it." In addition to having to endure this general environment of hostility, these acclaimed artists shared at least two other characteristics; all were born free in nonslave states (or Canada), and all were affiliated in some way with white abolitionists who, in some cases, helped the artist further his or her career.

Robert Scott Duncanson was the first African American to gain widespread acclaim as a fine art painter. Duncanson became established in the 1850s while still a self-taught artist and was widely known for his exquisitely detailed still-lifes, one of which would later hang in the Detroit Institute of Art. Duncanson was born around 1817 in upstate New York to a black American mother and a Canadian father of Scottish descent. He was given an important commission around 1850 when Nicholas Longworth hired Duncanson to paint eight murals in the foyer of Longworth's Cincinnati mansion. Subsequent owners of the house covered the paintings with wallpaper, but they were later restored for what would become the Taft Museum.

Duncanson, like several other nineteenth-century black artists, made and sold portraits of abolitionist leaders. In fact the Anti-Slavery League paid to send him to Glasgow, Scotland, to receive formal training. Duncanson returned to America around 1854 and much of his later work was affiliated with the Hudson River School of landscape painting. The Hudson River School artists began work around 1825 and followed William Cullen Bryant's demand that American artists needed to celebrate the natural beauty of their own country and not merely imitate the art of Europe. Duncanson traveled widely and painted landscapes in North Carolina, Pennsylvania, England, Ohio, Canada, and Scotland, among other places.

It is widely believed that Duncanson was the first African American professional fine art painter; on 30 May 1861 the *Cincinnati Gazette* declared him "the best landscape painter in the west." Despite his success, Duncanson felt compelled to leave the country because of racial tensions and so lived in Europe during the Civil War.

After returning to the United States, Duncanson once again flourished, especially in the Detroit and Cincinnati areas. In addition to landscapes, Duncanson was interested in popular literature and illustrated various texts, including *Uncle Tom's Cabin*.

The first African American sculptor of wide repute was Edmonia Lewis, who was born around 1843 to an African American father and a mother of Ojibwa Indian descent. The details surrounding Lewis's life are sketchy, but it appears that she was born in either New Jersey or New York and that she was orphaned at an early age and raised largely by her mother's tribe. Lewis was born with the name Wildfire, which she changed to Edmonia when she was a student at Oberlin College in Ohio. Her studies are said to have been financed by her brother, a successful prospector in California.

Though Lewis was a talented and popular student at Oberlin, she appears to have been embroiled in a bizarre episode in 1862 in which she was accused of poisoning two housemates with a drug known for its aphrodisiac qualities. It seems that Lewis was tried and acquitted of the charges against her, but then brutally beaten by a local mob. She left Oberlin before graduating and went to Boston.

In Boston, Lewis made and sold portraits of heroic figures, including abolitionists, and she won the John Brown medallion for her bust of Robert Gould Shaw, who led an all-black battalion during the Civil War. The money from the sale of these works allowed Edmonia Lewis to go to Rome in 1865, at which time she received formal training as a sculptor.

While in Rome, Lewis became accomplished as a sculptor in marble. Among the works she completed in the 1860s and 1870s were statues of Biblical figures such as Moses and Hagar and a bust of the Roman emperor Octavian. Lewis is best known, however, for her 1876 sculpture "The Death of Cleopatra," which stands more than five feet tall and was exhibited in Boston, Chicago, Rome, and San Francisco and received much critical acclaim.

Lewis worked in the naturalistic style that was popular in her time. Her Cleopatra, which depicts the Egyptian queen after being bitten by the asp that supposedly killed her, is a pastiche of styles and incorporates details from Greek, Roman, and Egyptian art. The hieroglyphic symbols on the sculpture are nonsense. The Cleopatra sculpture took a circuitous route to its eventual home at the Smithsonian National Museum of American Art. Lost for many years, it seems to have gone from place to place, including a bar, a graveyard (as a marker for a horse), and a storage yard.

Lewis made at least two works celebrating her ethnic heritage: "Old Arrow Maker" (1866–1872) depicts two Native Americans, and "Forever Free" (1867) two freed black slaves. Nonetheless by 1880 Lewis had expatriated and visited the United States only to show and sell her work. Lewis was last known to be living in Rome in 1911, and the time and place of her death remain unknown.

Edward Mitchell Bannister did not have the formal training that Duncanson and Lewis had, and yet he was the first African American to win a national prize for his art. The painting, later lost, was titled "Under the Oaks," and it won the first place Bronze Medal at the 1876 Philadelphia Centennial Exposition. It is said that the contest judges, upon learning Bannister's ethnicity, wanted to reconsider their judgment. However, the white competitors stood by the initial decision.

Bannister was born in 1828 in Canada to a West Indian father and mother of unknown heritage. His parents died when the artist was very young, and Bannister was raised by a white Canadian family. Bannister moved to Boston in 1848, where he started to paint in the realist style but then was inspired by the Barbizon School of landscape painting. This school, which had its roots in the work of such French artists as Theodore Rousseau and Camille Corot, rejected academic tradition in an effort to create what the artists considered a truer representation of nature.

Bannister was a prolific artist, and the Smithsonian National Museum of American Art would later acquire some 120 of his works. Bannister worked largely in an impasto style, using thick layers of paint with few details. When human subjects are included in his work, they appear to be of white people. Also recognized as a knowledgeable critic of art, Bannister was among the founding members of the famed Rhode Island School of Design. He died in Rhode Island in 1901.

The nineteenth and twentieth centuries were spanned by Henry Ossawa Tanner, whom many critics consider to be the greatest African American painter to date. Tanner's reputation was international and his work widely exhibited in France as well as America. Tanner was the founder of "religious genre" painting, in which Biblical subjects are depicted as ordinary people. Although considered by many to be old fashioned by the time of his death in 1937, Tanner's work, as well as his reputation, opened the way for the artists of the Harlem Renaissance and beyond.

[*See also* Architecture; Artisans; Banneker, Benjamin; Clothing; Free African Americans to 1828; Hemings, Sally; Music; Painting and Sculpture; Visual Arts; *and* Wheatley, Phillis.]

BIBLIOGRAPHY

Bearden, Romare, and Harry Henderson. *A History of African-American Artists: From 1792 to the Present*. New York: Pantheon Books, 1993.

Britton, Crystal A. *African American Art: The Long Struggle*. New York: Smithmark, 1996.

Driskell, David C. *Two Centuries of Black American Art*. Los Angeles: Los Angeles County Museum of Art, 1976.

Prown, Jonathan. "A Cultural Analysis of Furniture-making in Petersburg, Virginia, 1760–1820." *Journal of Early Southern Decorative Arts* 18.1 (May 1992): 1–173.

—REBEKAH PRESSON MOSBY

ASIANS. The first Asians to arrive in the United States in significant numbers were Chinese laborers attracted to the country after the discovery of gold in California. By the early 1870s nearly sixty-five thousand Chinese immigrants had entered the United States and had settled principally in California. The Chinese presence in the United States was facilitated by the Burlingame Treaty, negotiated in 1868, which established a mechanism for free and unfettered immigration to the United States.

Although the Burlingame Treaty was negotiated, in part, to secure the steady flow of Chinese to supply laborers for the American West, many Americans were suspicious of the new arrivals and more than willing to accept European immigrants. The "mysterious" appearance, clothing, food, and customs of Chinese immigrants made them unwelcome in the United States, particularly in areas with large concentrations of Chinese workers. In California, for instance, anti-Chinese opinions and actions were commonplace, and the state's congressmen expressed their opposition to the naturalization of Chinese immigrants. The majority of Congress endorsed these sentiments and passed legislation preventing Chinese immigrants from becoming U.S. citizens and denying them the privileges granted by the Fourteenth Amendment.

Working on railroads and farms and in mines and service industries, the Chinese soon became an important factor in the economy of California. Whites' attitudes toward Asians were ambivalent and were often the by-product of economic conditions. When the economy was bad, the white majority clamored for discriminatory provisions against the Chinese. When times were good, such prejudices subsided. By the late 1870s the Workingman's Party, led by Denis Kearney, was a primary voice urging discriminatory actions against the Chinese in California. Anti-Chinese rhetoric often translated into action, and the Chinese were routinely subjected to mass expulsions, economic boycotts, and physical violence.

Opposition to Asian immigrants was especially virulent in San Francisco, where in 1879 the Reverend Isaac Kalloch was elected mayor on the Workingmen's Party anti-Chinese platform. During his campaign for office, Kalloch was shot by a local newspaper publisher, Charles De Young, and thus gained the sympathy of voters. In mid-1880 the mayor's office published a sixteen-page pamphlet titled *Chinatown Declared a Nuisance!*, calling for the abatement of the Chinese neighborhood because it was a menace to public health.

In 1882 Congress responded to the public clamor against Chinese immigrants by passing the Exclusion Act, appeasing West Coast bigots and many labor leaders. The temporary provision of the act prohibited the immigration of Chinese workers into the United States. It was made permanent in 1902 and would stay in effect until Congress repealed it in 1943. While appeasing racial prejudice on the part of white Californians, the measure was a shortsighted one in that it quickly took away an abundant labor supply for California's growing agricultural industries. When Japanese immigrants began entering the country in the late nineteenth century, they too were unwelcome and, like the Chinese, were subject to discriminatory rhetoric and actions.

Frederick Douglass tracked the actions and prejudices Chinese immigrants faced during the 1850s. A San Francisco resident, writing under the pseudonym Nubia, acted as a regular correspondent for *Frederick Douglass' Paper*. In his letters Nubia compared the treatment of the Chinese in California with that of African Americans in the South, noting the similarities in racial discrimination and mistreatment. In March 1855 he railed about a proposed California law requiring ship captains to secure a five-hundred-dollar bond "for the good behavior of every person not eligible to citizenship they bring here." Nubia was convinced that the true purpose of such a law was to "prevent Chinese and Negro emigration."

[*See also* African Americans and the West; Civil Rights; Discrimination; Douglass, Frederick; Fourteenth Amendment; *Frederick Douglass' Paper*; Immigrants; *and* Racism.]

BIBLIOGRAPHY

Chan, Sucheng. *The Bittersweet Soil: The Chinese in California Agriculture, 1860–1910*. Berkeley: University of California Press, 1986.

Chang. Iris. *The Chinese in America: A Narrative History*. New York: Penguin, 2003.

Cohn, Warren I. *America's Response to China: An Interpretative History of Sino-American Relations*. 2nd ed. New York: Wiley, 1980.

Saxton, Alexander. *The Indispensable Enemy: Labor and the Anti-Chinese Movement in California*. Berkeley: University of California Press, 1971.

—BRUCE TAP

ATTUCKS, CRISPUS (b. c. 1723; d. 5 March 1770), often celebrated as the first martyr in the American bid for independence. The death of Crispus Attucks is shrouded in myth. John Adams, the future second president of the United States and the defense attorney for the British troops charged with Attucks's murder, accused him of being a rabble-rouser and the instigator of the confrontation that resulted in the now famously known "Boston Massacre" of 1770. John Hancock, a Boston merchant and, like Adams, a member of the Sons of Liberty, celebrated Attucks as a defiant patriot. Attucks's true role remains unclear—much like his life prior to 1770.

Attucks was most probably born a slave in Framingham, Massachusetts, in 1723. He was likely of mixed African and Native American parentage (*attuck* is the Natick Indian word for "deer"). In 1750, at about age twenty-seven, Attucks ran away from his master, most likely a William Brown. For the next twenty years he worked as a sailor and longshoreman in and around the port of Boston. In that city on the night of 5 March 1770, while purportedly awaiting a ship bound for North Carolina, Attucks found himself embroiled in a controversy that ultimately contributed to a revolution.

Following the Seven Years' War (1754–1763), Boston had become a hotbed for colonial discontent with British imperial policies. To recover the costs of defending the American colonies from French and Native American forces, British authorities had enacted various revenue-collecting measures—among them tariffs on sugar (via the Sugar Act of 1764), paper (via the Stamp Act of 1765), and various imported goods (via the Townshend duties of 1767). Believing that such taxes ought to have come not from the British Parliament but from their colonial assembly, Bostonians intimidated collectors and refused to pay outright. In response, the British Crown began quartering troops in the city both to protect tax collectors and to enforce smuggling laws. Clashes between Bostonians

and the soldiers were inevitable, but the resulting confrontations were rarely violent. The altercation that broke out on the evening of 5 March 1770, however, quickly escalated into bloodshed.

That night a barber's apprentice confronted a soldier for not having paid his master for services rendered. The two came to blows, the soldier striking the apprentice with his musket butt. The youth fled through the streets, screaming as he went. Rumors of the fight quickly began to circulate: the soldier was unprovoked, the apprentice had been stabbed, and the apprentice was dead. Bostonians congregated outside the barracks and customhouse on King Street; Attucks was at a tavern on that street when a British sentry's alarm bell rang. Perhaps having heard the rumors about the barber's apprentice, Attucks reportedly led a group of men armed with sticks to the barracks. There they found young boys pelting the soldiers with stone-bearing snowballs. Attucks's group immediately sided with the boys and began striking the soldiers. According to eyewitnesses, Attucks was at the lead and dared the soldiers to fire. Accounts vary, but nearly all concur that at some point someone shouted, "Fire!" The besieged soldiers promptly shot into the crowd, which quickly dispersed as eleven Bostonians fell. Five, including Attucks, were fatally wounded and perished in the street.

In the wake of the King Street altercation, Attucks and the others achieved the status of popular and, later, national heroes. A public funeral held three days later shut down the city. Shops were closed, and the bells of the Boston city churches as well as those of surrounding towns tolled in remembrance of the deaths. For several days Attucks and the others lay in state at Boston's Faneuil Hall. Ever eager to advance their political agenda, the Sons of Liberty seized the opportunity to attack British imperials. On 12 March the *Massachusetts Gazette*, published by the silversmith and Son of Liberty Paul Revere, depicted Attucks and three of the other victims in a pool of blood beneath the headline "Bloody Massacre." The ensuing public outcry forced a trial, in which nine soldiers were charged with murder. Only two were convicted, but all the British forces were forced to withdraw to an island in Boston Bay.

The Sons of Liberty kept Attucks's memory alive for years; until the adoption of the Declaration of Independence, they celebrated 5 March as a national holiday. Adams himself later identified that particular night as the birth of American independence. In 1888 Boston erected a monument to Attucks and the others on Boston Common. A poem written by John Boyle O'Reilly for the occasion declared that Attucks "was leader and voice that day: / The first to defy, and the first to die." For decades after, black and white scholars alike continued to honor Attucks in histories and textbooks as the first martyr in the American War of Independence.

The Boston Massacre. This engraving by Paul Revere accompanied an account of the massacre dated 12 March 1770. The caption included a poem beginning "Unhappy Boston! See thy sons deplore/The hallowed walks besmeared with guiltless gore . . . " and a list of the "unhappy sufferers," one of whom was Crispus Attucks. (New-York Historical Society.)

Historians later questioned Attucks's role in the so-called Boston Massacre. Some have suggested that he was far more a victim of historical circumstance, drunk on rum and spoiling for a fight, than a heroic champion against arbitrary authority. Others have objected to the uses of Attucks's memory, pointing out the contradiction in celebrating the death of a runaway slave in the cause of liberty for a nation that ultimately sanctioned the enslavement of just such men.

These issues aside, Attucks remains a crucial figure in African American history as well as the history of the United States. While scholars will never be sure of his precise intentions and actions on that fateful night, Attucks nevertheless offers an entry point into the experience of African Americans in colonial and Revolutionary America. The essential irony of his situation—as a runaway slave caught up in a fight for an independence he wouldn't share—is one of the most essential ironies of American history, which scholars and the public alike ought to recognize.

[*See also* Adams, John, on African Americans; American Revolution; Black Seafarers; Fugitive Slaves; Monuments, Museums, Public Markers; Native Americans and African Americans; Resistance; Riots and Rebellions; *and* Seven Years' War.]

BIBLIOGRAPHY

Bennett, Lerone, Jr. *Pioneers in Protest*. Chicago: Johnson, 1968. Collection of individual stories about well-known African Americans; approachable, yet lacking in analysis and citation.

Bolden, Tonya. *Strong Men Keep Coming: The Book of African American Men*. New York: Wiley, 1999. Solid but celebratory series of vignettes about noted African American men; lacks citation but nicely addresses the debates over Attucks's legacy.

Buckley, Gail Lumet. *American Patriots: The Story of Blacks in the Military from the Revolution to Desert Storm*. New York: Random House, 2001. Broad, accessible survey of African American involvement in America's wars; makes extensive use of scholarly works.

Nell, William C. *The Colored Patriots of the American Revolution, with Sketches of Several Distinguished Colored Persons*. With an introduction by Harriet Beecher Stowe. Boston: R. F. Wallcut, 1855. First history of African Americans in the American Revolution and the first to document Attucks.

Quarles, Benjamin. *The Negro in the American Revolution* (1961). Chapel Hill: University of North Carolina Press, 1996. Classic work on African American participation in the American Revolution; remains among the most comprehensive of studies.

—SCOTT A. MILTENBERGER

AULD FAMILY. Frederick Douglass first encountered the Auld family as a young child; he was transferred to their household when his first owner, Aaron Anthony, fell ill. Thomas Auld was married to Anthony's daughter, and Douglass would become Auld's legal property following Anthony's death. After escaping from slavery, Douglass raged against the Auld family in some of his published writings, using them as the model of cruel slave owners, but he reconciled with Thomas Auld more than a decade after the Civil War ended.

Information about the personalities and dispositions of Auld family members is discerned almost entirely from Douglass's writings; little independent confirmation of his descriptions exists. Records suggest that the Auld family immigrated to America before the Revolutionary War, when Hugh Auld Sr. fought with Maryland's Talbot County Militia. His son, Hugh Auld Jr., served in the War of 1812 as a lieutenant colonel with the Twenty-sixth Maryland Militia. Hugh Jr. married Zepporah Wilson, who gave birth to Thomas Auld on 10 September 1795.

On 16 January 1823 Thomas Auld, then a ship captain who would later become a merchant, married Lucretia T. Anthony in Talbot County. Lucretia had been born around 1807 to Aaron and Ann Catherine (Skinner) Anthony. As a young girl, Lucretia had treated her father's young slave, Douglass, comparatively well, patronizingly offering him bread for singing outside her window.

When Douglass was about eight years old, having earlier moved in with the Aulds, Thomas and Lucretia sent him to the Fells Point section of Baltimore, where he lived with Thomas's shipbuilder brother, Hugh; Hugh's wife, Sophia (Keitley); and their two-year-old son, Tommy. Douglass was to serve as a companion to young Tommy. Sophia Auld initially treated Douglass with kindness; in Douglass's first autobiography, *Narrative of the Life of Frederick Douglass* (1845), he described her as a "woman of the kindest heart and finest feelings" and said that "her face was made of heavenly smiles, and her voice of tranquil music." A churchgoing Methodist, Sophia Auld read the Bible aloud and chanted hymns while she worked, especially if she thought she was alone.

In 1826 Aaron Anthony and his daughter Lucretia died in rapid succession, and Thomas Auld became Douglass's owner. Douglass returned for only a brief time to his legal master's house before Thomas Auld sent him back to the home of Hugh. There Sophia Auld resumed reading aloud to the young slave, inspiring Douglass to ask her to instruct him. She taught him the rudiments and was proud of her deeds, but when she told her husband, Hugh commanded her to stop, explaining that literacy made slaves discontented. In later years Douglass proclaimed that it was Hugh Auld's forbidding pronouncements nearly as much as Sophia Auld's encouragement that gave him the determination to learn how to read.

Nevertheless, following her husband's admonishment to stop reading to Douglass, Sophia Auld became vigilant about blocking the young slave's efforts to become literate, snatching newspapers from his hands and forcing him to account for idle moments. Douglass blamed the changes in Sophia Auld on the institution of slavery itself, or, as he put it, the "fatal poison of irresponsible power." Her formerly sweet voice became harsh, he claimed, and her "angelic face gave place to that of a demon."

After Douglass was banned from reading, he began trading his food with white neighborhood boys—who were comparatively well educated but not necessarily well fed—in exchange for instruction. Around the age of twelve, using funds he raised by polishing boots, Douglass bought Caleb Bingham's popular schoolbook, *The Columbian Orator*, which fed his thirst for learning and oratory and led to his understanding that not everyone believed in the institution of slavery.

In March 1833 a quarrel between Hugh and Thomas Auld ended with Thomas insisting that he take Douglass back to his home on Maryland's Eastern Shore, where Thomas then lived with his second wife, Rowena, the daughter of a prosperous merchant. Rowena Auld, who was born on 22 July 1811 to William and Lydia (Rolle) Hambleton, married Thomas Auld on 19 May 1828. She was as bitter as Lucretia Auld had been even tempered, and Douglass suffered from the contrast. He records that Thomas and Rowena never gave their slaves enough to eat and were quite cruel.

When Douglass first returned to Thomas's household, Amanda, the daughter of Thomas and Lucretia, greeted him enthusiastically, but Rowena chastised Douglass for responding in kind. Both Douglass and Amanda suffered when the couple had two children of their own, Sarah Louisa (1833) and Roseanna (1836).

In August 1833 Thomas attended a Methodist revival, became a convert, and began hosting traveling preachers. However, much to Douglass's disappointment, his master's spiritual revelations did not correlate with an improvement in his treatment of slaves. Douglass was particularly outraged when Auld savagely beat a lame slave named Henny while feverishly quoting Bible verses. Douglass was not permitted to attend Sunday services while living in Thomas's home; when Douglass attempted to lead a religious class in secret, Auld and his colleagues viciously broke up the gathering.

In January 1834 Auld, concerned about Douglass's insubordination, farmed him out to Edward Covey, who was known as a "slave breaker" because of his ability to beat unwanted behaviors out of slaves considered unruly. After Covey indeed savagely beat him in August of that year,

Douglass fled back to Auld's home, begging for help; Auld denied the request. Douglass's stay with Covey lasted less than a year, and he was living with the Aulds again by Christmas.

Farmed out to a less cruel master in 1835, Douglass eventually attempted to escape slavery on 2 April 1836. Douglass was jailed for his actions, and Auld could have punished him much more severely in addition; instead, Thomas sent Douglass back to his brother Hugh's household in Baltimore, where the slave was to learn a trade. Hugh promised Douglass manumission when he reached the age of twenty-five; he briefly allowed Douglass to live outside the Auld home and hire out his own time, so long as he turned over most of his weekly wages. At length Hugh rescinded those privileges, however, giving Douglass the impetus to successfully escape slavery on 3 September 1838.

In December 1846 the Auld family allowed Douglass's freedom to be purchased through an intermediary. The capricious Rowena Auld, who might have fought the transaction, had died four years earlier, on 24 November 1842. Sometime thereafter, Thomas married a woman named Anna.

Although Douglass and Thomas Auld did not meet again for many years, Douglass published a letter in September 1848 openly berating Thomas and asking him in graphic detail how he would have felt if Douglass had enslaved Thomas's own daughter, Amanda. In the late 1850s Douglass received a written request for a meeting from Amanda Auld, who had married the Philadelphia coal merchant John Sears; Douglass eventually met her at her husband's place of business. Sears was initially resistant because of the way his father-in-law had been portrayed by Douglass in his books, but he eventually acquiesced. Douglass and Amanda Auld Sears chatted about their mutual admiration for Lucretia Auld, while she deftly deflected Douglass's criticisms of her father. Thomas Auld subsequently told his daughter that she had done well in reaching out to Douglass.

When Douglass spoke at a civil rights convention in 1866, Amanda Auld Sears and two of her children cheered, assuring him of their support. In 1877 Douglass visited the dying Thomas Auld, and the two made amends; Douglass was publicly criticized for this action, but it seemed to bring peace to both men.

In January 1878 John Sears contacted Douglass to inform him that Amanda Auld Sears was dying, and Douglass visited her. On 10 February Amanda Auld Sears' son Thomas sent news of her death.

[See also Anthony, Aaron; Baltimore, Maryland, Slavery in; Caulker's Trade; *Columbian Orator, The*; Covey, Edward; Douglass, Frederick; *and Narrative of the Life of Frederick Douglass*.]

BIBLIOGRAPHY

Douglass, Frederick. *Narrative of the Life of Frederick Douglass*. New York: Penguin, 1997.

Lampe, Gregory P. *Frederick Douglass: Freedom's Voice, 1818–1845*. East Lansing: Michigan State University Press, 1998.

Martin, Waldo E. *The Mind of Frederick Douglass*. Chapel Hill: University of North Carolina Press, 1994.

McFeely, William S. *Frederick Douglass*. New York: Norton, 1991.

—KELLY BOYER SAGERT

AUTOBIOGRAPHY. Autobiography has been a significant genre throughout the history of African American literature. In documenting the lives of African Americans, autobiographical writing has challenged racist beliefs and racially oppressive institutions—especially slavery—and provided examples of perseverance and resistance. Although they were primarily concerned with their individual thoughts and experiences, African American autobiographers have also helped define the character of African American people as a whole. As a literary form, African American autobiography evolved from its somewhat derivative beginnings into a distinctly African American literary movement.

Authenticity is a central issue in early African American autobiography. Although some autobiographers relied on amanuenses, the publication of narratives written by African Americans provided concrete evidence against racist claims that people of African descent were incapable of artistic and intellectually sophisticated writing. Writing provided a degree of independence that has often been denied black people in racist societies, and African American authors gained representation in the public sphere. Their works often met with resistance, however, and autobiographical narratives that depicted the horrors of slavery were the most likely to be challenged. Consequently, African American autobiographies were often prefaced by whites—typically abolitionists—who would attest to the veracity of the narrative. Although designed to strengthen credibility, such introductions implicitly undermined the autobiographers' authority.

Literary Characteristics. The evolution of African American autobiography as a literary form is closely related to matters of authenticity and independence. As African American authors adapted standard forms to fit specific contexts, new autobiographical subgenres emerged. Spiritual autobiographies mirror the black church tradition of testimony, and slave narratives replaced generic captivity narratives. Testimony, in which individuals give accounts of their faith and hope before the community, is a central feature of African American Christianity. Unlike traditional spiritual autobiographies, testimony speaks to and from a particular context instead of universalizing religious experience. Authors of spiritual autobiographies sometimes assume a prophetic role by addressing those who uphold oppression or remain neutral in the face of injustice, warning them that God will avenge the wrongs committed against people of African descent.

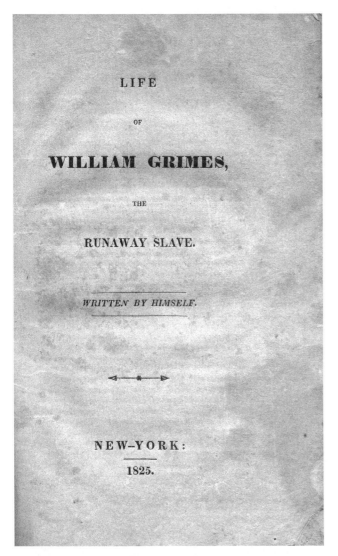

William Grimes's *Life*, title page. At the end of the first edition, Grimes dramatically offered his own skin to his country: "If it were not for the stripes on my back which were made while I was a slave, I would in my will leave my skin as a legacy to the government, desiring that it might be taken off and made into parchment, and then bind the constitution of glorious, happy, and free America. Let the skin of an American slave bind the charter of American liberty!" (University of North Carolina, Wilson Library.)

Narratives by former slaves dominated the first century of African American autobiography; many of these narratives also contain elements of spiritual autobiography. As the two subgenres are not mutually exclusive, the classification of individual works can be problematic. Many autobiographies by enslaved African Americans have strong spiritual components, and in some cases the spiritual significance overshadows the struggle for freedom. At the same time, not every depiction of slave life can be classified as a slave narrative. The slave narrative, which is a unique form of black diasporic writing, focuses on the lives of enslaved Africans and the individual narrator's struggle to be free of the yoke of slavery. The plot follows the narrator on the road to freedom and tends to be episodic, concentrating on critical incidents such as escape attempts. As slave narratives developed, autobiographers increasingly concerned themselves with portraying the psychological aspects of enslavement. The male subjects of early African American autobiographies presented themselves as independent—at least strong willed, if not physically strong—and as the embodiment of perseverance and dignity. As they became models for their race, these literary figures and their heroic images replaced degrading racial stereotypes and helped characterize African Americans as a great people.

Major Works. The oldest known African American autobiography, *A Narrative of the Uncommon Sufferings, and Surprizing Deliverance of Briton Hammon, a Negro Man*, dates from 1760. Like other early African American autobiographies, Hammon's narrative reflects the literary conventions of the time. Eighteenth-century African American autobiographies were primarily influenced by two popular literary forms, captivity narratives and spiritual autobiographies, and Hammon's *Uncommon Sufferings* contains elements of both. He also uses the narrative strategies of picaresque fiction. Hammon focuses on his experiences of captivity—from which he excludes slavery—and attributes his survival to Providence. The narrative gives an account of Hammon's adventures after his master allows him to join the crew of a ship bound for Jamaica. He endures a series of violent encounters and imprisonments before finally being reunited with his master thirteen years later. Hammon, who describes himself as a servant rather than as a slave, does not represent his ongoing servitude as captivity and considers himself free once he returns to his master. Throughout the narrative, he interprets events as indicative of God's providential care. Hammon alone survives the initial voyage, and his narrative suggests that despite his low social status, God had favored him.

A Narrative of the Most Remarkable Particulars in the Life of James Albert Ukawsaw Gronniosaw, an African Prince, which was published in 1770, contains a far more developed religious argument. Also emphasizing the workings of Providence, Gronniosaw traces his life from his boyhood in Africa through enslavement in the United States to his later years as a free man. His literary models, which he mentions in the narrative, are the spiritual autobiographies of John Bunyan and Richard Baxter. Gronniosaw offers limited descriptions of slave life, focusing instead on his spiritual pilgrimage and conversion to Christianity. In Gronniosaw's narrative, spiritual slavery eclipses physical bondage in importance; his perceived slavery to sin pushes him to the brink of suicide, but his bodily enslavement seems to have caused him little grief after his initial separation from his family. Gronniosaw describes how he related his experiences to a group of Dutch Calvinist ministers, who then examined him and were satisfied with his testimony. This incident not only enhances the credibility of the narrative but also indicates that the ministers accepted Gronniosaw as a brother in Christ. Although the narrative is traditional in many respects, it implicitly challenges racist notions of the spiritual inferiority of people of African descent.

A Narrative of the Lord's Wonderful Dealings with John Marrant, a Black (1785), which is primarily a spiritual autobiography, includes a self-contained captivity narrative. Like Gronniosaw, Marrant did not write his narrative. On the other hand, Marrant is unusual among early African American autobiographers because he was never a slave. After converting to Christianity as a youth, he became deeply religious and was ostracized by his family and friends. Leaving his home and venturing into unsettled territory, Marrant claims to have been taken captive by Cherokees. His narrative recounts how, after being repeatedly threatened with death, he not only wins his freedom but also converts his captors to Christianity. The 1785 version, which Marrant authorized, depicts the physical abuse of slaves, but later editions omitted this material. The title was also changed to *A Narrative of the Life of John Marrant*, shifting the emphasis away from the apparent favor shown by God to an African American. In 1790 Marrant supplemented his autobiography with a journal of his experiences as an ordained minister in Nova Scotia. David George and Boston King, who preached in Nova Scotia but eventually settled in Sierra Leone, also published autobiographies in the 1790s.

The first African American writer to use autobiography to its full extent in the fight against slavery was Olaudah Equiano, whose *Interesting Narrative of the Life of Olaudah Equiano, or Gustavus Vassa, the African*, was published in 1789. Longer than any previous African American autobiography, Equiano's narrative attacks slavery from multiple perspectives. He not only exposes slavery as inhumane and contrary to Christianity but also identifies and discusses the economic failings of slaveholding.

In addition to Equiano's explicit antislavery arguments, the quality of his writing served as evidence against the racist ideology that fueled the enslavement of people of African descent. Equiano wrote the narrative himself, and his prose is equally effective in appealing to both the emotions and the intellect. He portrays himself as exceptional but truly human; readers can sympathize with him, identify with him, and admire him.

Equiano's narrative also contains an account of his conversion, and he sees the hand of God guiding him throughout his life. Even if his enslavement is understood to result providentially in his conversion, such an interpretation does not diminish the narrative's condemnations of slavery. Equiano's attitude toward slavery evolves throughout the narrative, and it is possible that he is attempting to lead the reader to a stronger antislavery position than any of those explicitly stated in the text. In the end he clearly expects his readers to embrace the abolitionist cause. Equiano's autobiography, which became a model for nineteenth-century slave narratives, proved that such works could be powerful weapons in the fight against slavery.

Equiano composed and circulated his autobiography with the clear intention of strengthening his credibility, and subsequent autobiographers would continue to devise ways to enhance the authority of their narratives. Equiano sold his autobiography by subscription and published the subscribers' names in each volume. The list of subscribers, which included a number of prominent people, served to advertise and authenticate the narrative. Moreover, he directly addressed accusations of falsehood in his introduction to the work. Regardless, current scholarship has raised questions about the veracity of Equiano's autobiography. Such arguments have not been widely accepted, partly because of the long history of racially motivated challenges to the authority of African American writers.

A distinctly African American form of spiritual autobiography emerged early in the nineteenth century with *A Brief Account of the Life, Experience, Travels and Gospel Labours of George White, an African*, published in 1810, and *The Life, History, and Unparalleled Sufferings of John Jea, the African Preacher*, which appeared in 1811. White and Jea, both former slaves, departed from earlier models of spiritual autobiography and began the written tradition of African American testimony. Although there are important differences in the two narratives, both reflect the struggles of African American Christians to influence existing churches and establish autonomous worshiping communities. The heart of White's narrative focuses on his struggle to be granted a recognized ministry within the Methodist Society. He is repeatedly denied a preaching license before the Methodist quarterly meeting finally relents. Although one can surmise that White is rejected at least partly on account of racial prejudice, he leaves this conclusion to the reader; similarly, his condemnation of slavery lacks force. White's standing in the church may have led him to compromise his position.

John Jea, on the other hand, who remained independent, strongly attacks slavery. He also exhibits racial consciousness and pride in refusing allegiance to any country outside of Africa, even to the point of choosing imprisonment over military service. Despite the progressive nature of his political beliefs, however, Jea fails to comprehend the circumstances that resulted in his wife's madness. His narrative tragically illustrates the gap in early African American literature created by the absence of autobiographies by women.

In subsequent decades, narratives by African American women would articulate the particular problems faced by black women in a society dominated by males as well as whites. Jea's narrative indicates two other important trends. First, a significant change occurred when Wesleyan and other traditions displaced Calvinism among African Americans. Traditions that emphasized Providence, such as Calvinism, had led some people to view the transatlantic slave trade as the salvation of Africa. African American evangelicals, no longer bound by providential interpretations of the slave trade, condemned slavery without qualification or ambiguity. Second, Jea's racial pride foreshadows developments in both spiritual and secular autobiographies by African Americans, including those with black nationalist orientations.

By the nineteenth century the emerging tradition of African American autobiography was well under way. Writers could look to a distinctly African American literary tradition, and, in general, black autobiographical narratives became increasingly identifiable in form and content. Arising specifically from African American contexts and giving voice to the strivings of people of African descent, autobiography proved to be a powerful political and artistic force in the struggle for individual freedom and racial justice.

[*See also* African Diaspora; Black Church; Black Nationalism; Discrimination; Equiano, Olaudah; George, David; Gronniosaw, James Albert Ukawsaw; Hammon, Briton; Identity; Jamaica; Jea, John; King, Boston; Literacy in the Colonial Period; Literature; Marrant, John; Race, Theories of; Racism; Religion; Slave Narratives; Spirituality; Stereotypes of African Americans; White, George; *and* Women.]

BIBLIOGRAPHY

Andrews, William. *To Tell a Free Story: The First Century of Afro-American Autobiography, 1760–1865.* Urbana: University of Illinois Press, 1986.

Brooks, Joanna, and John Saillant, eds. *"Face Zion Forward": First Writers of the Black Atlantic, 1785–1798.* Boston: Northeastern University Press, 2002. Includes authoritative texts of John Marrant's narrative and journal and the autobiographies of David George and Boston King.

Costanzo, Angelo. *Surprizing Narrative: Olaudah Equiano and the Beginnings of Black Autobiography.* New York: Greenwood, 1987.

Davis, Charles T., and Henry Louis Gates Jr., eds. *The Slave's Narrative.* Oxford, U.K.: Oxford University Press, 1985.

Equiano, Olaudah. *The Interesting Narrative and Other Writings.* Edited by Vincent Caretta. New York: Penguin Books, 1995.

Foster, Frances Smith. *Witnessing Slavery: The Development of Antebellum Slave Narratives.* Westport, CT: Greenwood, 1979.

Hodges, Graham Russell, ed. *Black Itinerants of the Gospel: The Narratives of John Jea and George White.* Madison, WI: Madison House Publishers. New York: Palgrave, 2002. Hodges's substantial introduction places the narratives in the context of African American autobiography and religious history.

Saillant, John. "Traveling in Old and New Worlds with John Jea, the African Preacher, 1773–1816." *Journal of American Studies* 33.3 (1999): 473–490.

—SUSAN J. HUBERT

B

BAILEY, GAMALIEL (b. 3 December 1807; d. 5 June 1859), white antislavery journalist and political organizer. Gamaliel Bailey was born in Mount Holly, New Jersey. His father, Gamaliel Bailey Sr., was a silversmith and itinerant Methodist minister. His mother, Sarah Page Bailey, was a member of a locally prominent family that included several physicians. In 1816 the Baileys moved to Philadelphia, where young Gamaliel attended school and developed a lifelong interest in literature. Practical considerations, as well as family tradition, however, led him to attend the city's Jefferson Medical College, from which he graduated in 1828.

Bailey, who suffered from poor health, traveled to China as a seaman aboard a trading ship in 1829, under the assumption that a sea voyage would be therapeutic. When he returned to the United States in 1830, the religious, social, and sectional controversies of the time drew him into reform. His father had become a leader in the new Methodist Protestant Church, which had its headquarters in Baltimore. Consequently, family influence and Bailey's literary inclinations led to his appointment in 1831 as editor of the *Methodist Protestant*, a monthly journal published in that slaveholding city. There Bailey learned journalism, became moderately opposed to slavery, and began his long residence on the border between the free-labor and slave states.

In 1832 Bailey moved to Cincinnati, where, a year later, he married Margaret Lucy Shands, who shared his interests. The couple had twelve children, six of whom survived infancy. In Cincinnati, Bailey concentrated on medicine until 1834, when, while lecturing on physiology at Lane Theological Seminary, he joined in the slavery debate organized by the evangelical abolitionist Theodore Dwight Weld. Soon Bailey became an Ohio Anti-Slavery Society leader and assistant editor of the *Philanthropist*, an abolitionist weekly newspaper that James G. Birney brought to Cincinnati in 1836. That same year Bailey stood with Birney against an antiabolitionist mob.

In 1837 Birney left Cincinnati for an abolitionist leadership position in New York City, and Bailey became editor of the *Philanthropist*. Bailey also became the leading western abolitionist and an advocate of a brand of antislavery politics that could appeal to voters beyond abolitionist ranks. As the founder of the Ohio Liberty Party in 1840, he contended that its efforts must be restricted to abolishing slavery within the exclusive jurisdiction of Congress, rather than in the southern states. It was on this platform that Bailey and the antislavery activist Salmon P. Chase led most Liberty abolitionists into the Free-Soil Party in 1848.

Two years earlier a variety of political and church-oriented abolitionists had chosen Bailey to edit what became the *National Era*, a new national antislavery newspaper published in Washington, D.C. As editor of the *National Era* from 1847 until his death, Bailey helped shape national politics. Mixing antislavery articles with popular literature, he made the *National Era* one of the more influential American weekly papers. He encouraged women to contribute fiction to his newspaper, in which Harriet Beecher Stowe's *Uncle Tom's Cabin* originally appeared as a serial.

Bailey had been courageous in weathering a second mob attack on the *Philanthropist* in 1841, and in 1848 he endured a three-day riot following the *Pearl* slave escape attempt, when seventy-seven slaves failed in their attempt to flee Washington, D.C., aboard the schooner *Pearl*. But beyond his journalism, Bailey's suave manners and political skill had the biggest impact. He made his Washington home the center of antislavery social life, and he became an antislavery lobbyist in Congress. In 1854, during the struggle over the Kansas-Nebraska Act, he persuaded Whig and Democratic opponents of the bill to form a common caucus, which contributed to the formation of the Republican Party. Thereafter Bailey labored, despite persistent illness, to keep the new party centered on the slavery issue. Once again hopeful that a sea voyage might restore his health, he set out by steamer for Europe in June 1859, only to die at sea.

Bailey's career demonstrates the abolitionist influence in the border region and on antislavery politics. But his brand of abolitionism and his willingness to cooperate with politicians who did not support either immediate abolition or black rights alienated Frederick Douglass and other radical abolitionists. In 1848 Douglass criticized Bailey for contending that it was counterproductive to help slaves escape. Bailey's position seemed heartless to

Douglass, who in 1851 described the *National Era* as "attractive and fair seeming to the eye, but . . . as cold and lifeless as marble." Bailey, in turn, regarded Douglass as too extreme. In 1856 Bailey rejected a suggestion that he make Douglass coeditor of the *National Era*. Yet in 1870, long after Bailey's death, Douglass implicitly acknowledged his respect for Bailey's efforts by becoming coeditor of the *New National Era*.

[*See also* Antislavery Movement; Antislavery Press; Birney, James Gillespie; Chase, Salmon Portland; Douglass, Frederick; Free-Soil Party; Kansas-Nebraska Act; Liberty Party; *New National Era*; *Pearl* Incident; Republican Party; Stowe, Harriet Beecher; *Uncle Tom's Cabin*; *and* Weld, Theodore Dwight.]

BIBLIOGRAPHY

Gienapp, William E. *The Origins of the Republican Party, 1852–1856.* New York: Oxford University Press, 1987. Gienapp emphasizes Bailey's role in the formation of the Republican Party.

Harrold, Stanley. *Gamaliel Bailey and Antislavery Union.* Kent, OH: Kent State University Press, 1986. This is the only published biography of Bailey; it emphasizes his public role.

Harrold, Stanley. *Subversives: Antislavery Community in Washington, D.C., 1828–1856.* Baton Rouge: Louisiana State University Press, 2003. The book places Bailey within Washington's antislavery community and emphasizes his informal antislavery efforts.

—STANLEY HARROLD

BAILEY, HARRIET (b. c. 1820; d. 22 April 1900), a fugitive slave. Ruth Cox Adams, a fugitive slave from Maryland, adopted the name Harriet Bailey and lived with Frederick Douglass and his family from 1844 to 1847. Ruth Cox was born in Easton, Maryland, sometime between 1818 and 1822. Her father was an unknown free black man who disappeared after he went to Baltimore in search of better wages during Ruth's childhood. Her mother, Ebby Cox, was a slave in the Easton household of John Leeds Kerr, a lawyer who represented Maryland first in the House of Representatives (1825–1829 and 1831–1833) and then in the Senate (1841–1843).

When Kerr died in February 1844 he left instructions for all his property to be sold, including the slaves, and for the proceeds to be used to pay his debts. This turn of events probably prompted Ruth to flee north. By August 1844 she was living among Quakers in West Chester, Pennsylvania, where Frederick Douglass first met her on one of his speaking tours. Douglass offered Cox refuge in his home in Lynn, Massachusetts, and suggested the alias to protect her from slave catchers. She stayed there as an accepted member of the Douglass family, assisting Douglass's wife, Anna Murray, in housekeeping and piecework and acting as Anna's scribe when Douglass traveled to England in from 1845 to 1847.

In November 1847 Ruth, now known as Harriet, married Perry Frank Adams, a free black man from Talbot County, Maryland. The couple moved to Springfield, Massachusetts, where Perry eventually found work in a gold-chain factory. They lived in a boardinghouse and had three children: Matilda Ann (born in 1850), Ebby B. (1852), and Perry Frank Jr. (1854). They also adopted Samuel Hall (born in 1854) after his mother, Eliza Hall, one of their fellow boarders, died in 1859.

Harriet had been involved in an antislavery organization in Lynn, and her family continued to oppose slavery in Springfield. Perry Adams was supposed to have been a member of the League of Gileadites, an African American group organized in Springfield for self-defense in the wake of the Fugitive Slave Law of 1850 and endorsed by John Brown. Adams also attended the Massachusetts State Council, part of the national black convention movement, where the participants elected him as one of two vice presidents. The family boarded with Eli Baptiste, a black minister and abolitionist. Until approximately 1861 Harriet also maintained contact with the Douglass family, particularly with Anna and the Douglasses' daughter, Rosetta.

In 1861 the Adams and Baptiste families immigrated to Port-au-Prince, Haiti, under the sponsorship of the American-based Haitian Bureau of Emigration. Frederick Douglass, Rosetta Douglass, and Ottilie Assing, a German journalist who had befriended Douglass, also planned to sail on the same ship, the *Brig Maria*, out of New Haven, Connecticut, to visit. However, the shelling of Fort Sumter, which began the Civil War, caused the Douglasses and Assing to cancel their trip. The Adams family continued with the journey and remained in Haiti for approximately five years. As with many of the emigrants sponsored by the bureau, the Adams family returned to Springfield; Perry Adams Sr. died in 1868 of typhoid fever contracted in the tropics.

Harriet and her daughter, Matilda, moved to Providence, Rhode Island, in the 1870s, where Matilda married the African Methodist Episcopal minister William Vanderzee. Harriet, who had readopted the name Ruth, migrated west with the couple to Norfolk, Nebraska, in 1884. In 1894 Frederick Douglass reestablished his friendship with her after the Vanderzees sent him a *Norfolk Weekly News* article detailing her life. The two maintained a brief correspondence until Douglass's death in 1895. Adams lived five years longer; she died on 22 April 1900 and was buried in Wyuka Cemetery, Lincoln, Nebraska.

[*See also* African Methodist Episcopal Church; Bailey Family; Brown, John; Douglass, Anna Murray; Douglass, Frederick; Fugitive Slave Law of 1850; Haiti; *and* Lynn, Massachusetts.]

BIBLIOGRAPHY

"Adams' Escape." *Norfolk (NE) Weekly News*, 7 March 1894.

Carvalho, Joseph, III. *Black Families in Hampden County, Massachusetts, 1650–1855.* Boston: New England Historic Genealogical Society, 1984.

Coffee, Alice V. "Lest We Forget." Unpublished family history. Alyce McWilliams Hall Collection, Nebraska State Historical Society, Lincoln.

Douglass Papers. Library of Congress, Washington, DC.

Migliorino, Ellen Ginzburg, and Giorgio G. Campanaro. "Frederick Douglass's More Intimate Nature as Revealed in Some of His Unpublished Letters." *Southern Studies* 18 (Winter 1979): 480–487.

Ship's manifest. *Pine and Palm (Boston)*, 18 May 1861.

"Trip to Haiti." *Douglass' Monthly*, 1 May 1861.

—LEIGH FOUGHT

BAILEY FAMILY. Frederick Douglass was given the name of Frederick Augustus Washington Bailey at birth. His mother, Harriet Bailey, was a slave; his father was an unidentified white man—possibly Aaron Anthony—who was sometimes referred to as his master. As a young child Douglass was raised by his grandmother, Betsey Bailey. Although Betsey was legally a slave, she earned her own money and was married to a free black man named Isaac.

Bailey roots ran deep on the Eastern Shore of Maryland, with slaves of that name appearing in plantation ledgers as far back as June 1746. At that time Douglass's great-grandmother Jenny (or Jeney) was only six months old; Jenny's mother was either Sue or Selah, and her father was named Baly (born around 1701). It seems likely that Baly either was a descendant of slaves who had inhabited Talbot County since the 1660s or was brought to the United States from Barbados or another English colony in the West Indies. It is highly unlikely that the Bailey clan came directly from Africa.

Jenny gave birth to Betsey—Douglass's grandmother—in May 1774. When Betsey was twenty-three, she and her two young daughters, Milly and Harriet, were moved fifteen miles from the Skinner plantation, where the Bailey family had lived for generations, to Holme Hill Farm along Tuckahoe Creek. There Betsey, Isaac, Milly, and Harriet lived in a cabin in the woods near the creek. The cabin had a floor of packed clay and no windows. The downstairs consisted of one room; a ladder led to a tiny attic that served as straw-bed sleeping quarters. Although the dwelling was modest, it was significantly better than the communal quarters that housed many slaves.

Although Betsey was technically a bond servant, she did not live the traditional life of one. Her husband was a free man who made money by cutting firewood and crafting timbers from pine, oak, maple, and walnut trees; he was such a successful sawyer that on at least two occasions he leased a slave to assist in his endeavors. It is uncertain whether or not Isaac was Douglass's biological grandfather; although Isaac and Betsey were openly living as husband and wife in their cabin, Douglass's mother was already five years old at the time of the move to Holme Hill. It is also uncertain when and how Isaac obtained his freedom. A significant number of manumissions occurred in the region after the Revolutionary War, and some of those emancipated had names that were similar to Isaac's; none, however, can be conclusively connected to the man who married Betsey.

Betsey made and sold fishing nets and was known throughout the region as an expert in net making; she was allowed to keep the financial proceeds from her sales. She was also highly esteemed for her fishing and gardening skills, and people claimed that she had a "magic touch" for keeping sweet potato seedlings alive through the winter. As a further sign of her unusual status, she was apparently not leased out as many other slaves were; in fact, her master—and possibly Douglass's father—Anthony actually paid her for midwife services. Betsey Bailey gave birth to twelve children, at least ten of whom are assumed to be Isaac's: Milly, born before 1792; Harriet, born on 28 February 1792; Jenny, born in 1799; Betty, 1801; Sarah, 1804; Maryann, 1806; Stephen, 1808; Esther (or Hester), 1810; Augustus, 1812; Cate, 1815; Priscilla, 1816; and Henry, 1820. Besides raising her own children, Betsey subsequently took care of most of her twenty-five grandchildren while her daughters worked in the fields.

For practical reasons Betsey could not house all her grandchildren until full maturity; she raised Frederick, the son of Harriet, until he was six years old. By that time Harriet was working on the Anthony farm, twelve miles away from Betsey's cabin; remarkably, for a slave who worked in the fields, Harriet was literate. After Harriet began working at the Anthony farm, Frederick barely saw her, except on rare occasions when she showed up late at night after completing her work. On those days she would lay down next to her son until he fell asleep; she would be gone by morning. Douglass later recalled one occasion when, after he was mistreated and underfed by the plantation's cook, Katy, his mother scolded the cook and presented him with a heart-shaped ginger cake.

Douglass recalled his mother as having a dark and glossy complexion; many years later, when he saw an Egyptian drawing, he pointed out similarities between the facial features of the pharaoh and those of his mother, leading some to suggest that Douglass had Asian if not North African blood. Others have pointed out that Douglass's features had a Native American cast; a family letter points out that Betsey was of "Indian descent," and Anthony called him his "little Indian boy."

Although his precise ethnic heritage cannot be ascertained, it is known that Douglass had three older siblings: his brother, Perry (born in January 1813), and two sisters, Sarah (August 1814) and Eliza (March 1816). Douglass was born in February 1818 and given the middle name of Augustus in memory of Betsey's son, who had died two years earlier. Two younger sisters were also born: Kitty (March 1820) and Arianna (October 1822).

The young Frederick Bailey lived with his grandmother until 1824. Around August of that year the two went for a walk; Betsey, who declined to tell Frederick where they were going—or why—wore a freshly ironed turban and carried cornbread in her pocket. The day was hot and humid, and Betsey carried him part of the way. When they arrived at their destination—the Lloyd plantation on the Wye River—Frederick encountered his three older siblings, none of whom he remembered.

What Betsey knew, but Frederick did not, was that he was now to live on this plantation. Betsey most likely did not want to create a scene; thus, as soon as she had an opportunity, she slipped away without saying a word to her grandson. When the child realized what had happened, he was inconsolable. His older brother, Perry, offered ripe peaches and pears to comfort him, but Frederick hurled the fruit to the ground.

Although Frederick did see his grandmother again, the last time that he saw his mother was in 1825; she died in 1826, which he would not learn until much later. Also in 1826, Frederick was once again sent to a new home, this time in Baltimore. Although he was somewhat apprehensive of this move, his cousin Tom—the fourth son of Harriet's sister Milly, born on 21 September 1814—reassured him that he would find Baltimore a splendid place to live, far more interesting than Talbot County. Douglass did have a positive impression of the Baltimore waterfront, but in 1827, after the death of Aaron Anthony, he had to return to Talbot County to find out who his new owner would be. Although the news would be good for Douglass—he was awarded to Anthony's son-in-law, Thomas Auld, who promptly returned him to Baltimore—during the trip Douglass witnessed Andrew Anthony brutally beat Perry about the head until blood gushed forth.

Douglass, who fled from slavery in 1838, spent the next twenty-five years without significant connection to his birth family. He did eventually learn the fate of his family members. In 1832 his sister Sarah—who had become the property of Andrew Anthony, a man with a weakness for alcohol—was sold to Perry Cohee, a planter in Mississippi. Cohee also purchased Douglass's aunt Betty and several of Douglass's cousins.

His sister Eliza was manumitted in 1844. In fact, sometime before 1836 Thomas Auld sold Eliza and her two children to Eliza's husband, Peter Mitchell, for one hundred dollars. Because the law at the time required all freed slaves to leave the state in which they had lived, Mitchell did not set her free; he legally remained the owner, then, of his wife and children. In July 1844 the law in question was changed, and Eliza was officially freed. She and Mitchell eventually raised nine children: Jane, Louisa, Edward Napoleon, Peter II, John Emory, Susan, Ella, Mary Douglass, and Richard.

On 25 October 1845 Thomas Auld granted freedom to Tom Bailey, Douglass's cousin. That same day Auld also sold Douglass to Hugh Auld, Thomas's brother. Since Douglass had already escaped, Hugh Auld accepted funds from friends of Douglass to grant him manumission, and Frederick Douglass finally achieved the status of a free black American.

In 1849 Douglass's grandmother Betsey died. When Douglass published a rhetorical letter in 1848 to his former master, Thomas Auld, he shared his bitter feelings over the treatment of Betsey in her later years, accusing Auld of turning her "out like an old horse to die in the woods." In reality, though, Betsey had continued to live in her cabin until her mid-seventies; widowed and nearly blind, she was cared for by Auld until her death in November 1849.

Eliza reunited with her brother Frederick in November 1864, when he returned to Maryland for the first time in twenty-six years and delivered six lectures. Douglass noted how Eliza's straight and proud posture reminded him of their grandmother, and he learned that local residents affectionately knew his sister as Mammy Liza.

On 9 June 1865, while returning home after fighting in the Civil War, Douglass's son Lewis was traveling along Maryland's Eastern Shore and asked a man for directions. Lewis did not realize that the man he had spoken to was his cousin John, the son of Aunt Eliza. Eliza, who was expecting him, noticed the family resemblance and invited him to visit their home. At that time Tom Bailey, Douglass's cousin, was visiting Eliza as well. Lewis showed Tom photographs of Douglass, and Tom, who stuttered severely, remarked that he remembered the scar on the former slave's nose. Another visitor was the daughter of Douglass's brother, Perry.

In February 1867 Douglass received a letter from "Perry Downs . . . a brother of yours." He learned that Perry's wife, Maria, had been sold into slavery in Texas and that Perry had followed her there; he was working as a field hand for decent wages. By July, Perry, Maria, and their four children reached Rochester, New York, where they met up with Douglass; the brothers had not seen one another for nearly forty years. Although Douglass's children were not enthusiastic, Douglass built a home for Perry and his family on his property. The arrangement lasted until 1869, when Perry and his wife returned to Maryland.

On 26 September 1883 Douglass heard from Sarah, his sister, who had been sold south in 1832. Calling herself Sarah O. Pettit, she had written an affectionate letter to him.

Douglass did not use the family name of Bailey as an adult in order to disguise his identity during his fugitive years, not because he wanted to distance himself from his kin. His relationship with his birth family appears to have been warm or, at a minimum, congenial.

[*See also* Auld Family; Bailey, Harriet; Baltimore, Maryland, Slavery in; Black Family; Caribbean; Douglass, Frederick; Douglass, Lewis Henry; Downs, Perry; Identity; Lloyd Family; Lloyd, Edward, V; Rochester, New York; *and* Slavery.]

BIBLIOGRAPHY
Douglass, Frederick. *Narrative of the Life of Frederick Douglass, an American Slave* (1845). New York: Laurel, 1997.
McFeely, William S. *Frederick Douglass*. New York: Norton, 1991.
Preston, Dickson J. *Young Frederick Douglass: The Maryland Years*. Baltimore, MD: Johns Hopkins University Press, 1985.

—KELLY BOYER SAGERT

BALTIMORE, MARYLAND, SLAVERY IN. Although it was by and large a slave city, Baltimore boasted a large free black population, which included Frederick Douglass's wife, Anna Murray, who worked for a postman on the same street where Douglass lived with the Auld family. In the first half of the nineteenth century the free black population of Baltimore increased 3,000 percent, as African Americans were moving to many urban locations for better opportunities and more freedom.

Indeed, while Baltimore served as a bastion of freedom for many African Americans in the antebellum period, it was a city surrounded by slavery. To the south of Baltimore, in Prince George's County, where tobacco was a chief crop, the population in 1790 consisted of 11,176 slaves, or 52 percent of the county's population; the proportion changed little before 1850. Meanwhile, north and west of Baltimore the numbers of both free and enslaved African Americans steadily increased over the same period, as slavery gradually declined. To the east of Baltimore, on Maryland's Eastern Shore, the number of slaves in Caroline County between 1790 and 1850 decreased from 2,057 to 808. Along with the decrease in numbers of slaves came an increase in free blacks—from 421 to 2,788 in the same period of time.

In Baltimore between 1790 and 1810 the number of slaves grew to outstrip the number of whites in the city. This demographic shift occurred largely because planters moved to the city and brought their slaves with them. Between 1810 and 1830 the number of slaves in Baltimore declined from 4,700 to around 4,100, while the overall population in the city rose from 46,000 to 80,000. Of this 80,000, some 15,000 were free blacks, up from 5,600 in 1810. The free black population swelled during this time largely because of manumission or "term slavery," the process by which an enslaved person could work for a stipulated period of time to gain his or her freedom. On the whole, Baltimore was a city of complex labor relations, where free and enslaved African Americans worked in close proximity.

Above all, Baltimore was a city of opportunity for black Americans. Black men and women could work for wages or even establish their own businesses. In 1836 Anna Murray and her mother, Mary, ran a restaurant on Buxton Street. Frederick Douglass, new to the city from plantation life, was struck by the degree of opportunity to be found there. Baltimore was home to a class of slaves called "city slaves," whose work was not as brutal as concentrated plantation labor, and for whom extreme physical punishment did not occur as often. In his first autobiography, *Narrative of the Life*, Douglass comments:

> A city slave is almost a freeman, compared with a slave on the plantation. He is much better fed and clothed, and enjoys privileges altogether unknown to the slave on the plantation. There is a vestige of decency, a sense of shame, that does much to curb and check those outbreaks of atrocious cruelty so commonly enacted upon the plantation. (p. 38)

Douglass's notions of economic self-reliance most likely began in Baltimore, where he experienced glimmers of economic dignity; he lauded this sense of freedom in the *Narrative*:

> There I was immediately set to calking, and very soon learned the art of using my mallet and irons. In the course of one year from the time I left Mr. Gardner's, I was able to command the highest wages given to the most experienced calkers. I was now of some importance to my master. I was bringing him from six to seven dollars per week. I sometimes brought him nine dollars per week: my wages were a dollar and a half a day. After learning how to calk, I sought my own employment, made my own contracts, and collected the money which I earned. (p. 83)

An industrial port city, Baltimore offered free and manumitted African Americans work in shipyards not only as caulkers but also as brick makers, rope makers, shipbuilders, ironworkers, carpenters, and shoemakers—all trades that gave them and their families decent footing in the antebellum South. While life in Baltimore presented African Americans with economic opportunity, it remained a city of struggle, as racial tensions with regard to employment were heightened. Douglass recalled:

> Many of the black carpenters were freemen. Things seemed to be going on very well. All at once, the white carpenters knocked

off, and said they would not work with free colored workmen. Their reason for this, as alleged, was, that if free colored carpenters were encouraged, they would soon take the trade into their own hands, and poor white men would be thrown out of employment. (p. 81)

In the riot that ensued in this instance, Douglass's "left eye was nearly knocked out."

Douglass lived with Sophia and Hugh Auld in Baltimore on three occasions, and with each stay he acquired more of the skills he needed to live the life of a free man. Douglass first came to Baltimore in 1826 from the Eastern Shore. He found the Auld household comforting; there he was treated not as a pig but as a child, being fed not out of a trough but on a plate, at a table. For a while he received instruction in reading and writing from Sophia Auld, but the lessons ceased once Hugh learned about them. In October 1827 Douglass returned to Aaron Anthony's plantation because Anthony had died and all his property, including Douglass, had to be collected and redistributed. This valuation was heartbreaking to Douglass: "Men and women, old and young, married and single, were ranked with horses, sheep, and swine. There were horses and men, cattle and women, pigs and children, all holding the same rank in the scale of being, and were all subjected to the same narrow examination." After valuation, in November 1827, Douglass returned to Baltimore again to live with the Aulds. They moved to Philpot Street the following year, after Hugh Auld opened his own shipyard, where Douglass apprenticed as a ship's caulker. Douglass would remain with the Aulds until March 1833.

During this second stay in Baltimore, Sophia Auld's reading of the Bible, along with Hugh Auld's apprenticing of Douglass in Baltimore's shipyards, provided him with the stirrings of literacy that he would need to become one of the greatest orators and writers of his day. At the age of twelve Douglass entered Knight's Bookstore and bought *The Columbian Orator* for fifty cents. Reading and memorizing passages from the *Orator*, Douglass began to learn the cadences of some of the greatest rhetoricians in Western letters. In 1831, after converting to Christianity, Douglass joined the Bethel African Methodist Episcopal Church; he became familiar with William Lloyd Garrison and associated abolitionists through reading the local papers. Upon his return to the Eastern Shore in March 1833, Douglass could not settle down to plantation life. He opened a Sunday school and taught his fellow slaves how to read the Bible—while also forging passes to help him and four of his friends escape from slavery. When the plan was discovered, Douglass was jailed in Easton, Maryland; after enduring the threat of being sold south into more severe slavery, Douglass was returned to Baltimore in April 1836 with the promise, made by Hugh Auld, that if Douglass mastered the caulk-

ing trade, he would be granted his freedom on his twenty-fifth birthday.

During this, his third visit to Baltimore, Douglass lived on Fells Street with the Aulds; he attempted to obtain room and board outside the Auld household, a common practice in the city, but was denied on two occasions. Douglass had developed a sense of himself as a free man, and living with the Aulds clouded that vision. However, his living under the open sky of Baltimore, with its free black population, and even carrying money in his pocket, was not exclusively positive; twice, while working in the shipyards, Douglass was openly attacked. In 1837 he joined the East Baltimore Mental Improvement Society, a debating club for free black men, and met Anna Murray, to whom he eventually became engaged. When they met, Anna encouraged Douglass, a fledgling violinist, to continue his musical pursuits. She sold two featherbeds to help Douglass secure safe passage to New York City, where they were married on 15 September 1838, twelve days after Douglass's escape from slavery. They would remain married for forty-four years.

By 1850, twelve years after Douglass and Anna Murray left Baltimore, slavery in that city was in steady decline, with fewer than 7,000 slaves living alongside 30,000 free blacks and 175,000 whites. The city remained at odds concerning slavery and race. In April 1861 pro-Confederate civilians in Baltimore stoned Union troops. After the Civil War free blacks were forced out of Baltimore's caulking trade, which they had helped establish, and an attempt to open a black-run caulking shop in 1865 resulted in severe beatings. Nevertheless, Douglass, visiting Baltimore in 1866, had faith that the city would mature into a peaceable home for all races. Baltimore served as both a liberating and a confining place for African Americans; as such it was a microcosm of the South between 1820 and 1865—a place of political unrest, transformation, and contradiction.

[See also African Methodist Episcopal Church; Auld Family; Bible; Caulker's Trade; *Columbian Orator, The*; Demographics; Discrimination; Douglass, Anna Murray; Douglass, Frederick; East Baltimore Mental Improvement Society; Free African Americans before the Civil War (South); Garrison, William Lloyd; Oratory and Verbal Arts; Urbanization; Violence against African Americans; *and* Work.]

BIBLIOGRAPHY

Douglass, Frederick. *Narrative of the Life of Frederick Douglass, an American Slave.* In *Autobiographies*, edited by Henry Louis Gates Jr. New York: Library of America, 1994.

McFeely, William S. *Frederick Douglass.* New York: Norton, 1991.

Phillips, Christopher. *Freedom's Port: The African American Community of Baltimore, 1790–1860.* Urbana: University of Illinois Press, 1997.

Whitman, Stephen. "Diverse Good Causes: Manumission and the Transformation of Urban Slavery." *Social Science History* 19.3 (Fall 1995): 333–370.

—DELANO GREENIDGE-COPPRUE

BANNEKER, BENJAMIN (b. 9 November 1731; d. 9 October 1806), African American scientist and advocate for racial equality. Benjamin Banneker was born on a farm near Elkridge Landing, Maryland, on the Patapsco River, ten miles southwest of Baltimore. His mother, Mary Banneky, was a freeborn African American. Her parents were Molly Welsh, an English indentured servant, and Bannaka, a Dogon nobleman captured in the slave trade and bought by Molly Welsh. In 1700 Welsh freed Bannaka, and they married. Benjamin's father, was born in Africa and transported to America as a slave, where he was known as Robert. In Maryland, Robert purchased his freedom and married Bannaka and Molly's daughter, Mary Banneky, whose surname he adopted and later changed to Banneker. Robert's success in tobacco farming enabled him to buy enough land (seventy-two acres) to support his son and three younger daughters.

Benjamin Banneker was intellectually curious, especially about mathematics and science, but he had little formal education. (Scholars disagree about claims that he attended school for two years.) He learned to read with help from his parents and his grandmother. As a child, he studied the Bible and books given to him by a Quaker teacher. White Quakers befriended Banneker several times in his life. In 1753 William Qualls, a Quaker merchant from Baltimore, introduced Banneker to a European trader, who, after discussing the science of time with him, loaned Banneker his pocket watch. Banneker disassembled the watch, learned its inner workings, and then built a clock, entirely from wood parts, that kept precise time.

Although he was gifted in science, Banneker farmed for a living. His father taught Benjamin that farming and land ownership were keys to self-sufficiency. In 1759 Robert Banneker died, leaving Benjamin in charge of the family land. Childhood encounters with racist violence, including witnessing slave catchers kidnap a friend, reinforced Banneker's decision to stick close to his land, where he was known as a free person of good character. Nonetheless, he found ways to pursue his intellectual interests. The Ellicotts, a family of antislavery Quaker manufacturers from Philadelphia, aided him in this effort. In 1772 a branch of the Ellicott family built a flour mill near Banneker's land. The Ellicotts treated African Americans with respect and shared Banneker's interests in science. Banneker forged a close friendship with George Ellicott,

nephew of Andrew Ellicott III, one of the mill's founders. The Ellicotts' mill served as a community gathering place where Banneker could learn the news and study mill machinery. Banneker also sold some of his farm produce to the Ellicotts.

In 1791 this friendship created the opportunity for Banneker to participate in the survey of the Federal District (later known as the District of Columbia). President George Washington named Andrew Ellicott III to a commission that would survey land for the new capital. Ellicott persuaded the president to appoint Banneker as his chief scientific adviser. Banneker had studied surveying and could apply the geometrical projections of the city planner Pierre Charles L'Enfant to the Potomac River swamplands where Washington, D.C., was to be built. Banneker acquitted himself well and earned high praise from his associates on the survey, although racial prejudice subtly affected his experience. He dined separately from his white colleagues, and President Washington, who often visited the surveyors, avoided contact with Banneker.

In his spare time Banneker studied the stars with astronomical tools and treatises that George Ellicott had given him. Banneker wrote commentaries on the treatises

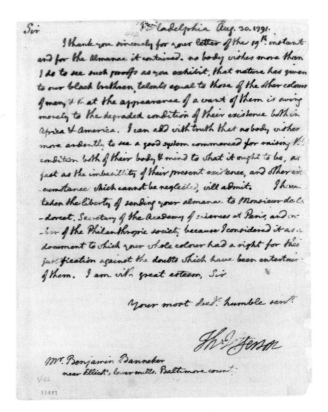

Thomas Jefferson's letter to Benjamin Banneker, 30 August 1791. This is the response—polite but noncommittal—to Banneker's appeal of 19 August. (Library of Congress.)

and crafted his own ephemeris, a chart of astrological movements during the year. Farmers used ephemerides, which were published in almanacs, as guides to seasonal weather variations. In 1789 Banneker demonstrated the accuracy of his calculations by predicting a solar eclipse. If published as an almanac, Banneker's ephemeris would earn him money and document the abolitionist argument that African Americans were capable of more than slave labor. Aware of this potential, abolition societies in Maryland and Pennsylvania helped Banneker publish his first almanac in 1792. Banneker continued publishing almanacs through 1797. The almanacs were popular with practical farmers and with opponents of slavery, one of whom presented a copy to the British Parliament.

While his first almanac was in press, Banneker broke with his reluctance to antagonize proslavery whites. On 19 August 1791 he sent Secretary of State Thomas Jefferson a copy of his almanac along with a letter that criticized Jefferson for owning slaves and asked him to advance the cause of racial equality and abolition. Impressed by the almanac, Jefferson forwarded it to the Academy of Science in Paris. Jefferson also sent Banneker a courteous reply, but he did not forthrightly endorse racial equality.

Banneker's challenge to Jefferson underscored the significance of his career for black freedom in the early Republic. His scientific achievements disproved claims made by whites like Jefferson who wanted to colonize free blacks in Africa. Colonizationists argued that free blacks must emigrate or be enslaved, because their alleged inferiority doomed them to failure in competition with whites. Banneker showed that free African Americans could match white accomplishments and live successfully in the United States. To publicize this point, Banneker included his correspondence with Jefferson in his 1793 almanac.

In 1792 Banneker sold his farm to the Ellicotts. In old age he supported full-time study with income from sales of almanacs and his land. An avid naturalist and beekeeper, Banneker determined in 1800 that locusts appeared in seventeen-year cycles. Although he was not a member of an organized church, Banneker was influenced by Quakerism. That influence manifested itself in an appeal for peace published in his 1793 almanac. Shy and retiring, Banneker never married. Some scholars speculate that he suffered from depression and alcohol abuse. He died in his family home, where he had lived after selling his land. During Banneker's funeral a fire burned his house and most of his scientific papers. Banneker had received anonymous threats from white racists after he became well known, and some scholars conjecture that racists set the fire. If so, they failed to destroy the legacy of African American achievement that Banneker left to the world.

[See also Discrimination; Free African Americans to 1828; Jefferson, Thomas, on African Americans and Slavery; Science; Society of Friends (Quakers) and African Americans; and Washington, George, and African Americans.]

BIBLIOGRAPHY

Bedini, Silvio A. *The Life of Benjamin Banneker: The First African-American Man of Science*. 2nd ed. Baltimore: Maryland Historical Society, 1999.

Cerami, Charles. *Benjamin Banneker: Surveyor, Astronomer, Publisher, Patriot*. New York: Wiley, 2002.

Conley, Kevin. *Benjamin Banneker*. New York: Chelsea House, 1989.

Du Bois, Shirley Graham. *Your Most Humble Servant*. New York: Messner, 1949.

—FRANK TOWERS

BAPTISM. Baptism, or ritual washing with water, has from ancient times signified regeneration or rebirth. Early purifications prescribed by Mosaic law symbolized the external washing away of internal uncleanness. It is unclear when baptism became institutionalized as a sacrament, but biblical scholars cite Jesus Christ's declaration to Nicodemus as the probable origin: "Unless a man be born again of water and the Holy Ghost, he can not enter into the Kingdom of God." As recorded in John 3:4 and Matthew 28, Christ commissioned his apostles to baptize. By the time of Augustine the idea that salvation was the unmerited grace of God and was achieved through the sacrament of baptism was part of Christian orthodoxy. The moment when God forgave original sin, baptism had immediate effects, including the remission of all sins and the infusion of sanctifying grace. It signaled as well the entry of the recipient into the church in full communion.

The Protestant Reformation did away with most of the sacraments, but both Luther and Calvin accepted the merit of baptism and retained most of the elements from the traditional liturgy. Calvin taught that baptism was necessary for adults but that infants of parents who were baptized were sanctified in the womb and were therefore free from sin without baptism. Although theologians accepted baptism as a Christian initiatory rite, in the eighteenth century many ordinary men and women still regarded it as a quasi-magical rite, and there was persistent anxiety within slave societies over the emancipating effects of Christian baptism on enslaved people.

In slavery's earliest years there was a widely held belief inherited from English social thought that credited Christianity, especially Protestantism, with the decline of the servitude of villenage, a vestige of the manorial system. The Elizabethan author William Harrison explained it this way:

As for slaves and bondmen we have none, naie such is the privilege of our countrie by the especiall grace of God, and bountie of our princes, that if anie come hither from other realms, so soone as they set foot on land they become so free of condition as their masters, whereby all note of servile bondage is utterlie removed from them. (p. 27)

The association with Christian baptism was made more explicit by Sir Thomas Smith. It is, he wrote, "the perswasion . . . of Christians not to make nor keepe his brother in Christ, servile, bond and underling for ever unto him, as a beast rather than as a man." Although Elizabethan intellectuals maintained that the mitigation of bond slavery was also supported by the common law, in fact, villenage survived in English law books and legal dictionaries well into the seventeenth century, by which time African slavery on an international scale had clearly emerged. By the end of the seventeenth century the English had made a thorough commitment to slavery, justified by English jurists on the grounds that slavery was brought into the world as punishment for sin and as a consequence of captivity in warfare between Christians and non-Christians.

The controversy over the Christianization of Africans was an outgrowth of previous developments in West and West Central Africa, where Catholic missionaries had been proselytizing since the fifteenth century; Protestant missionaries joined the competition for souls early in the eighteenth century. By the time the organized European slave trade began in the seventeenth century, a small minority of Africans professed to be Christians. Some of those who were forced into the brutal Middle Passage were already baptized Christians. The vast majority, however, clung to traditional African religious beliefs and practices. Appalled by the "heathen rites" brought out of Africa to the New World, Anglican churchmen, beginning with Morgan Godwyn, lobbied the Anglican hierarchy in London to begin organized missionary activity among enslaved Africans. Efforts to convert the "heathen" starting in the last two decades of the seventeenth century won few converts, both because Anglican doctrines and ritual had little appeal to enslaved Africans and because of powerful planter opposition.

Like their counterparts in other plantation colonies, planters feared that baptism would "infuse [slaves] with thoughts of freedom" and foster rebellion. The Anglican clergyman Francis LeJau tried to reassure white South Carolinians by requiring black catechumens to swear before their owners that they were not seeking baptism in order to claim freedom. Despite the repeated assurances of clergymen like LeJau, until well into the eighteenth century slaveholders continued to complain that baptism would empower slaves by making them "proud" and assertive. The obvious implication that it would ultimately abolish slavery rested on the old English equation of baptism and personal liberty and its attendant idea that no Christian could lawfully hold another in bondage. In an effort to reassure planters, colonial assemblies enacted laws declaring that the baptism of slaves did not imply their freedom. By the end of the seventeenth century Maryland, Virginia, New York, New Jersey, and North and South Carolina had all passed laws assuring slave owners that baptism did not necessitate manumission. Even so, planter opposition to Christianization did not end until the 1830s, and only then after southern evangelical Protestant church leaders had articulated a fully developed defense of slavery on biblical grounds.

In the meantime enslaved men and women were taking an increasingly active role in their own spiritual and religious transformation, in part as a means to come to terms with their shattered lives and in part to express defiance of the master and opposition to slavery. The appearance in the 1730s of Methodists and in the 1740s of the New Light Presbyterians and Separate Baptists dramatically changed the religious landscape, bringing into the Christian fold thousands of African converts. The strength of the evangelical appeal was in its acceptance of men and women, black and white, as spiritual equals. The new rites added by evangelicals to the traditional Protestant sacraments of the Lord's Supper and baptism—including love feasts, washing feet, anointing the sick, the right hand of fellowship, the kiss of charity, and "dry-christening" (as the ritual of laying hands on a newborn infant was derisively called)—envisaged a moral community that transcended race, class, and gender. But it was the core idea of salvation or rebirth in Christ that resonated most powerfully with enslaved men and women.

Traditional West and West Central African religions shared to a considerable degree certain overlapping ideas and practices, which made the transition to Protestant Christianity possible. The born-again message shared by Methodists, Congregationalists, and Presbyterians was enacted through a ritual cycle of total immersion symbolizing death. The laying on of hands that followed signaled the rebirth and entry into the Christian community. Africans' initiation experiences were also associated with the symbolic death and rebirth of initiates, while naming ceremonies symbolically represented the acceptance of the infant into the family and the community. Visionary experiences, which frequently accompanied the conversion ritual, also had African counterparts in possession experiences during which a divinity speaks through a medium rather than directly to God. In the half century following the American Revolution, the number of African Americans claiming a Christian identity increased steadily. Although they were part of the evangelical community, black Christian churches developed their own distinctive ethos and character.

[*See also* Baptists and African Americans; Black Church; Congregationalism and African Americans; Episcopalians

(Anglicans) and African Americans; Methodist Church and African Americans; Missionary Movements; Presbyterians and African Americans; Religion; *and* Spirituality.]

BIBLIOGRAPHY

Butler, Jon. *Awash in a Sea of Faith: Christianizing the American People*. Cambridge, MA: Harvard University Press, 1990.

Frey, Sylvia R., and Betty Wood. *Come Shouting to Zion: African American Protestantism in the American South and British Caribbean to 1830*. Chapel Hill: University of North Carolina Press, 1998.

Harrison, William. "The Description of England." In *Chronicles of England, Scotland, and Ireland*, edited by Raphael Holinshed. 6 vols. London: printed for J. Johnson, et al., 1807.

Smith, Sir Thomas. *The Common-Wealth of England, and Manner of Government Thereof*. London: printed by John Windet for Gregorie Seton, 1589.

Sobel, Mechal. *The World They Made Together: Black and White Values in Eighteenth-Century Virginia*. Princeton, NJ: Princeton University Press, 1987.

—SYLVIA FREY

BAPTISTS AND AFRICAN AMERICANS.

No faith has been more closely associated with the African American community historically than the Baptist Church. In the colonial period sectarian Baptists were some of the first Christians to attract a significant African American following. Black Baptist adherence expanded so dramatically over time that by the end of the twentieth century Baptist churches could claim twice as many African American members as any other religious group.

In the colonial and early national periods, Baptists were defined primarily by their practice of administering the rite of baptism only to professed believers, by full immersion in water. They were also distinguished by their literal interpretation of the Bible, rejection of civil authority over religious matters, and distaste for church governmental hierarchy. African Americans first became Baptists in significant numbers on the eve of the American Revolution, but North American Baptists can trace their origins more generally to Britain in the early seventeenth century, when a few Dissenters, heavily influenced by Puritan separatists in Holland, gathered in London and practiced believer baptism. The first North American Baptist congregation formed in Rhode Island in the 1630s, and handfuls of European Baptist immigrants joined with new converts in North America to found several churches in a number of colonies thereafter. Religious quickening in the mid-eighteenth century produced a dramatic period of church building in the 1760s and 1770s that is particularly notable for spreading the Baptist faith southward to Virginia, the Carolinas, and Georgia. The religious upheavals of the American Revolution then opened the way for the Baptists to move from the margins to the heart of the religious mainstream, particularly in the American South.

While a small number of African Americans had become members of Baptist churches in Rhode Island and Massachusetts by 1770, a sustained African American Baptist tradition developed with the rise of the Baptists in the southern colonies. That tradition originated in a biracial context. Many predominantly white southern churches included African American members during the Revolutionary era, and biracial worship continued to be common until the conclusion of the Civil War.

The meaning of biracial worship for African Americans is a matter of debate. Slaves and free blacks could find in Baptist worship not only the spiritual gratification and community connection that was important to all Baptists but also an egalitarian message in Baptist beliefs and worship practices that could attract and sustain an oppressed people. At the same time, biracial churches were firmly under the control of white congregants who discriminated against African American members and sometimes used the church to advance proslavery messages. Probably both to escape racism and to fully express their religious sensibilities, some African Americans developed separate, all-black Baptist churches, a process that dates to the colonial period.

In the Lower South a handful of African American religious leaders drove a rapid expansion of black Baptist institutions. George Liele, a slave from Georgia, is particularly notable in this regard. Converted in a biracial congregation, Liele preached extensively on plantations in his neighborhood, and his converts made up the core of a black congregation across the Savannah River in South Carolina, formally founded as Silver Bluff Church by a white preacher in 1775. Liele gained his freedom in the 1770s and traveled to Savannah, where his preaching produced enough African American converts to form a small congregation.

In the meantime, the disruptions of the American Revolution drove some congregants from Silver Bluff Church into Savannah. In 1788 one of Liele's followers, Andrew Bryan, organized Savannah Baptists into the First African Baptist Church. This church quickly expanded to include hundreds of members, joined the Georgia Baptist Association, and produced at least two other all-black congregations in Savannah by 1803—the Second Colored Baptist Church and the Great Ogeechee Baptist Church. Another of Liele's converts, Jesse Peters (also known as Jesse Galphin), relocated from Silver Bluff to Augusta during the war, took up the pulpit, and organized Springfield Baptist Church in 1787. David George, a Silver Bluff Church member, carried Liele's mission beyond the southern colonies. He departed with the British to Nova Scotia, where he founded a black Baptist church and ultimately traveled to the British colony of Sierra Leone, spreading the Baptist faith on the African continent.

George Liele himself relocated to Jamaica during the British evacuation and spent the remainder of his life spreading the Baptist faith to blacks in the Caribbean. Black Baptist practice thus might be described as a developing Atlantic world phenomenon by the early nineteenth century.

The first known black Baptist congregation in the Upper South, Bluestone Church, was formed on the plantation of William Byrd in 1758, in present-day Mecklenburg County, Virginia. Similar plantation Baptist churches came together in King and Queen County and Nottaway County in Virginia during and just after the American Revolution. The Virginia towns of Williamsburg, Portsmouth, and Petersburg all had black Baptist congregations by the early nineteenth century, which were followed shortly by the founding of churches in Richmond and Norfolk. The Upper South is probably most notable, however, for its prominent African American preachers—both Josiah Bishop and James Lemon ministered to predominantly white congregations for a time in the postwar years.

While the Baptist faith spread among African Americans most fully in the South, the early Republic witnessed the founding of black Baptist churches in the urban North as well. Thomas Paul stands out as a leader in this movement. He was the founding minister of Joy Street Baptist Church in Boston in 1805, and when blacks in New York City's Gold Street Baptist Church sought to withdraw to form their own congregation, Paul negotiated the process with resistant white congregants, producing the Abyssinian Baptist Church in 1808. Philadelphia's First African Baptist Church was founded the same year. Black Baptist churches in America's seaport cities were particularly noteworthy for their secondary functions as schools and self-help organizations for African Americans.

By 1830 about forty-five black churches had been founded, some under African American leadership and some under the authority of white preachers; a significant number of African Americans continued to join biracial churches as well. Free blacks were central to the founding of black churches, particularly in urban areas,

"The First Colored Baptist Church in North America," frontispiece from a book of the same title by Reverend James M. Simms, Philadelphia, 1888. The church had been established in Savannah, Georgia, a century earlier, on 20 January 1788. (New York Public Library; Manuscripts, Archives, and Rare Books Division, Schomburg Center for Research in Black Culture; Astor, Lenox, and Tilden Foundations.)

but slaves were also very actively involved in the process. As the borders of the United States extended westward, so, too, did separate black Baptist worship. Churches were founded in Kentucky, Alabama, Mississippi, Louisiana, and Missouri. Black Baptist congregations about which we have information were generally recognized as legitimate churches by the white Baptist community, but they were undoubtedly only part of the story of separate African American Baptist practice. Historians have widely acknowledged that independent African American worship, perceived as a threat to social control and to slavery, was subject to active suppression. The so-called invisible church—congregations that met informally and practiced clandestinely—sustained untold numbers of African Americans in the years before Emancipation.

Historians have debated the extent to which African Americans practiced a distinctive form of Baptist Christianity, tied to their African heritage. Some have argued that the Middle Passage—the journey of slaves from Africa to America—was so culturally damaging that few or no ties to any African beliefs or practices survived to be employed by Baptist converts. Others point to heightened emotionalism, emphasis upon bodily movement in worship, and active congregational participation in worship among African Americans as translated expressions of an African sacred cosmos. Most historians do agree, however, that conditions of enslavement and discrimination led African Americans to place special emphasis upon elements of Christianity that underscored spiritual equality, divine justice, and deliverance.

[See also American Revolution; Baptism; Black Church; Discrimination; Free African Americans to 1828; George, David; Liele, George; Missionary Movements; Paul, Thomas; Religion; and Spirituality.]

BIBLIOGRAPHY

Fitts, Leroy. A History of Black Baptists. Nashville, TN: Broadman Press, 1985.

Lincoln, C. Eric, and Lawrence H. Mamiya. The Black Church in the African American Experience. Durham, NC: Duke University Press, 1990.

Raboteau, Albert J. Canaan Land: A Religious History of African Americans. New York: Oxford University Press, 2001.

Sobel, Mechal. Trabelin' On: The Slave Journey to an Afro-Baptist Faith. Westport, CT: Greenwood Press, 1979.

Washington, James Melvin. Frustrated Fellowship: The Black Baptist Quest for Social Power. Macon, GA: Mercer University Press, 1986.

—JEWEL L. SPANGLER

BARBADOS. See Caribbean.

BASSETT, EBENEZER D. (b. 16 October 1833; d. 1908), the first African American diplomat. Ebenezer Don Carlos Bassett was born in Litchfield, Connecticut, the son of Tobias Bassett, a mulatto, and Susan Bassett of the Shagticoke branch of the Pequot tribe. He graduated with honors from the Connecticut State Normal School in 1853. Two years later he married Eliza Park, with whom he had three sons and two daughters. While he was the principal of a high school in New Haven, Connecticut, Bassett studied for a short time at Yale College. From 1857 to 1869 he was the principal of the Institute for Colored Youth, a Quaker school in Philadelphia that prepared students to become educators. He received high praise from the city's mayor for his work at the institute. During the Civil War, Bassett wrote many appeals to young black men to enlist in the Union Army.

Basset left the Institute for Colored Youth after the Civil War to become the first African American to officially represent the U.S. government abroad. When the Republican President Ulysses S. Grant took office in 1869, African Americans earnestly sought presidential appointments. Letters urging Bassett's selection came from many prominent black and white citizens, including twelve of his Yale professors. Bassett was appointed by Grant as the first African American minister resident and consul general to Haiti and chargé d'affaires to the Dominican Republic. The position in Haiti was especially significant, because people of African descent throughout the world held a particular admiration for Haiti, where a rebellion begun by Toussaint Louverture had succeeded in throwing off both slavery and colonialism in 1804. After Bassett's appointment was confirmed, Frederick Douglass sent him friendly congratulations.

Bassett arrived in Haiti during the presidency of Sylvain Salnave, who was soon overthrown and executed. During Bassett's eight-year diplomatic duty, Haiti had four different presidents and was wracked with political instability. Bassett had to deal frequently with Haitians seeking political asylum in the American minister's house, which had been the summer palace of Faustin-Élie Soulouque, the former emperor of Haiti. As damage to property often accompanied political skirmishes, Bassett also had to manage the recurring property claims by U.S. citizens against the Haitian government.

As an American minister to the island of Hispaniola, Bassett resided in the Haitian capital of Port-au-Prince. During this time the Grant administration tried unsuccessfully to annex the neighboring Dominican Republic. In 1871 the U.S. government sent Douglass on his first diplomatic assignment. He served as secretary of the presidential commission dispatched to the Dominican Republic to explore the possibility of annexation, or at least acquisition of a naval base. Opposition in the U.S. Congress thwarted the project. Bassett reported back to his superior, Secretary of State Hamilton Fish, that Grant's overtures in the Dominican Republic escalated anti-American sentiment in Haiti. In his *Life and Times of Fredrick Douglass*, Douglass writes that Fish spoke highly of America's first African American diplomat. Yet Fish thought the Haitians unjustified in their suspicions of the extension of American power and influence in the Caribbean, because the United States was no longer a slaveholding nation. The United States had made African Americans citizens and had even sent the African American Bassett abroad to represent the new postbellum American society.

Following custom, Bassett resigned and returned to the United States after a new U.S. president took office. From 1879 to 1888 he worked as the Haitian consul general in New York City. When Douglass was appointed minister resident and consul general to Haiti and chargé d'affaires to the Dominican Republic in 1889, Bassett offered to serve as secretary to his old friend. In a lowly position with a much-reduced salary, Basset returned to Port-au-Prince. His ability to speak both French and Haitian Creole served him well as Douglass's interpreter during the Môle Saint-Nicolas negotiations, whereby the United States sought unsuccessfully to obtain a naval base in Haiti. In 1891 Douglass resigned amid accusations that he was too enamored of the existence of a black republic to negotiate sternly with Haitians who carefully guarded their nation's autonomy. Such claims by U.S. merchants and overseas expansionists were championed in the white American press.

Unemployed after Douglass's resignation, Bassett returned to the United States and engaged in literary pursuits. He published *A Handbook on Haiti* in four languages for the Bureau of American Republics. In the early 1900s he was again briefly employed by Haiti as the consul general in New York City. Bassett spent his final years in Philadelphia, where he died and was buried in 1908.

[*See also* Civil War; Civil War, Participation and Recruitment of Black Troops in; Dominican Republic, Annexation of; Douglass, Frederick; Foreign Policy; Grant, Ulysses S.; Haiti; Haitian Revolutions; Marriage, Mixed; Môle Saint-Nicolas (Haiti) Annexation; *and* Toussaint Louverture.]

BIBLIOGRAPHY

Douglass, Frederick. *Autobiographies: "Narrative of the Life of Frederick Douglass, an American Slave"/"My Bondage and My Freedom"/"Life and Times of Frederick Douglass."* Edited by Henry Louis Gates Jr. New York: Library of America, 1994. Chapters 11–13 of *Life and Times of Frederick Douglass* contain Douglass's version of his diplomatic work in Haiti.
Heinl, Robert Debs, Jr., and Nancy Gordon Heinl. *Written in Blood: The Story of the Haitian People, 1492–1995.* 2nd ed., revised and expanded by Michael Heinl. Lanham, MD: University Press of America, 1996. One of the best general histories of Haiti in English.
McFeely, William S. *Frederick Douglass*. New York: Norton, 1991. A treatment of Bassett's role as Douglass's secretary in Haiti can be found in chapters 25 and 26.

—DAVID M. CARLETTA

BAYLEY, SOLOMON (b. c. 1771; d. 1839), a former slave and writer. Born into slavery in Delaware, Solomon Bayley toiled in bondage until 1799, when he successfully used the law to change his condition. His original owner illegally transported him and other family members to Virginia and sold them to a new master, who sought to take him to one of the new states in the West (probably Kentucky). He escaped back to Delaware, where he was pursued by his master. Using Delaware law, which prohibited the export of slaves out of state and declared any slave sold out of state to be free, Bayley threatened to use the courts to obtain his legal freedom. Faced with this prospect, his master relented and agreed to let him purchase his freedom. Bayley then worked to purchase the freedom of his wife and children over the next few years.

Settling in Kent County, Delaware, Bayley worked for nearly three decades as a tenant farmer. He also became a Methodist exhorter and was active in antislavery circles in nearby Wilmington, Delaware. In 1820 he came to the attention of the British abolitionist Robert Hurnard, who was visiting the area. Although Bayley had recounted his slave experiences orally for years, Hurnard recorded these accounts and published them, along with several of Bayley's own biographical letters, as the *Narrative of Some Remarkable Incidents in the Life of Solomon Bayley, Formerly a Slave, in the State of Delaware, North America* in 1825. Printed in London, the *Narrative* was circulated by British abolitionists as part of their campaign to end slavery in the British West Indies. It was thought that Bayley's story, which highlighted his deep Christian faith and fine moral character, would help deflect charges that slaves lacked the behavioral and moral qualities to function in freedom.

In 1828 Bayley and his wife, frustrated by the prejudice held against free blacks in Delaware, immigrated to Liberia with the assistance of the Union Colonization Society of Wilmington. Hoping to encourage further immigration, he penned a procolonization tract entitled *A Brief Account of the Colony of Liberia* in 1829. He apparently remained in Liberia until his death.

[*See also* Abolitionism; Autobiography; Black Migration; Free African Americans to 1828; Methodist Church and African Americans; *and* Slave Narratives.]

BIBLIOGRAPHY

Bayley, Solomon. *A Narrative of Some Remarkable Incidents in the Life of Solomon Bayley, Formerly a Slave, in the State of Delaware, North America.* London: Harvey and Darton, 1825.

Shick, Tom W. *Emigrants to Liberia, 1820–1843: An Alphabetical Listing.* Newark: Department of Anthropology, University of Delaware, 1971. http://dpls.dacc.wisc.edu/Liberia/.

—Roy E. Finkenbine

BEECHER, HENRY WARD (b. 24 June 1813; d. 8 March 1887), Congregationalist minister, reformer, abolitionist. Born to Lyman and Roxana Foote Beecher in Litchfield, Connecticut, Henry Ward Beecher was a member of one of the nation's most visible reform-minded families, and he would come to be acknowledged as one of nineteenth-century America's finest orators.

The ninth of ten children, who included the author Harriet Beecher Stowe and the educator Catherine Beecher, Henry grew up questioning the faith his father passionately espoused. Hoping to inspire his son, Lyman Beecher sent him to the Mount Pleasant Classical Academy in Amherst, Massachusetts, in 1827. There Henry committed to becoming a minister. He attended Amherst College (1830–1834) and Lane Theological Seminary in Ohio (1834–1837). After serving as a the pastor for two Congregational churches in Indiana, at Lawrenceburg and Indianapolis, he was called to the pulpit of the Plymouth Church in Brooklyn, New York, in 1847.

By the time Beecher returned to the East Coast, he already had a reputation as a fine speaker and a promoter of various reform causes. Eventually, he advocated temperance, abolition, theories of evolution, and women's suffrage. He frequently drew large audiences; the public rooms of his church, which held twenty-five hundred seats, often had standing-room-only crowds. Additionally, Beecher traveled the reform lecture circuit along the East Coast and in the trans-Appalachian West.

Beecher's antislavery work began relatively early in his career. While he was in the West, he participated in a number of revivals that featured abolitionist causes. It was during this period that he first encountered Frederick Douglass. After one such event in 1843, Beecher witnessed a group of abolitionists exhorting a crowd at Pendleton, Indiana, where a riot followed Douglass's appearance at the podium with a white companion. Beecher sharply criticized local officials for releasing the leaders because of popular pressure after their arrests. On the issue of slavery, however, he remained reticent. The next October, Beecher and his father were present when the Indiana Synod voted support for an open letter favoring abolition. Beecher was, however, conflicted on the issue of professing antislavery measures to his congregation. In a note to his brother Charles on the occasion of Charles's ordination in 1844, Beecher advised, "Preach little doctrine, except what is of moldy orthodoxy. . . . Take hold of the most practical subjects; popularize your sermons. . . . For a time, while captious critics are lurking, adapt your mode so as to insure that you shall be rightly understood."

As Beecher matured and grew more confident of himself and his audiences' sympathies, he became a more vocal advocate of abolition. By the 1850s he had acquired a martial tone in his oral and written exhortations. In 1856, as the constitutional crisis in Kansas rolled to a boil, Beecher referred to the antislavery violence there as "moral agency" and worked to raise money for Sharp's rifles, known thereafter as "Beecher's Bibles," for abolitionist settlers in the territory.

Beecher and Douglass rarely appeared in the same venues at the same time, but they spoke and wrote in the same places and to the same audiences. Although Beecher's stand on abolitionist issues was always moderate, Douglass found great value in his efforts. For example, after hearing Beecher speak on 16 May 1850 on the occasion of the anniversary of the founding of the American and Foreign Anti-Slavery Society, Douglass wrote in his newspaper the *North Star* that "Beecher poured forth one continuous strain of eloquence for more than an hour . . . riveting the attention of the vast assemblage despite attempts at interruption made by a few of the baser sort." In the *Frederick Douglass' Paper,* on 3 November 1854, Douglass referred to Beecher as "one the boldest thinkers and bravest speakers in America." Similarly, both men perceived the Civil War and its escalating violence as a "cleansing tragedy," necessary to rid the nation of slavery. The most serious breach between the two occurred in the aftermath of the war, when Beecher sided with Unionists such as Horace Greeley against the Radical Republicans and advocated policies that would facilitate reunion rather than punishing the South.

During the post–Civil War period Beecher continued to advocate reform. In effect, he became the spokesperson for the emerging values of the American middle class. He supported the theories of Charles Darwin and progressive notions concerning the evolution of American society. For a brief while, in 1876, scandal overshadowed his career when a longtime acquaintance, Theodore Tilton, accused Beecher of adultery with Tilton's wife. Beecher was eventually vindicated and received a vote of confidence from a national Congregational council. Right up to his death of a cerebral hemorrhage at age seventy-three, he was still seen as a vigorous and productive member of the ministry.

[*See also* Abolitionism; Antislavery Movement; Evolution; Greeley, Horace; Lane Theological Seminary; Oratory and Verbal Arts; Pendleton, Indiana; Reform; Stowe, Harriet Beecher; Suffrage, Women's; Temperance; *and* Tilton, Theodore.]

BIBLIOGRAPHY
Beecher, Henry Ward. *Autobiographical Reminiscences of Henry Ward Beecher.* Edited by T. J. Ellinwood. New York: F. A. Stokes, 1898.
Clark, Clifford E., Jr. *Henry Ward Beecher: Spokesman for a Middle-Class America.* Urbana: University of Illinois Press, 1978. A comprehensive biography that places Beecher firmly in his nineteenth-century context.
Ryan, Halford R. *Henry Ward Beecher: Peripatetic Preacher.* New York: Greenwood Press, 1990. This work narrates the course of Beecher's life through his sermons and orations.

—MARTHA I. PALLANTE

BELINDA (b. c. 1712; d. ?), a former slave who gained notoriety by petitioning for a portion of her former master's estate. Some scholars have labeled this the first African American call for reparations for slavery. Born in a village near the Volta River in the region of West Africa known as the Gold Coast (modern-day Ghana), Belinda spent her first years living a bucolic existence. That peace was broken at age eleven, when she was captured, sold into slavery, and transported to North America via the Middle Passage. For more than fifty years, she labored in bondage for her master, Isaac Royall, first in Antigua and then, after 1732, in Medford, Massachusetts. Royall, the largest slaveholder in the state, became an outspoken Loyalist and fled the colonies for Britain at the beginning of the American Revolution. After that, Belinda lived in an unofficial state of freedom until the Massachusetts courts ruled slavery unconstitutional in 1783 in the case of *Commonwealth v. Jennison.*

In February 1783 Belinda—then living in Boston with her invalid daughter—petitioned the Massachusetts legislature for a pension from the earnings of Royall's estate, probably with the authorial assistance of the black abolitionist Prince Hall. The petition argued that she had been "denied the enjoyment of that immense wealth, a part whereof hath been accumulated by her own industry, and the whole augmented by her servitude." This capitalist and reparationist argument moved the legislature to grant her an annual fifteen-pound pension. In 1787, payment of the pension having stopped, Belinda again petitioned the Massachusetts legislature, which ordered it resumed. The original petition received wide circulation at this time as a result of its being reprinted in the *American Museum,* a leading magazine. Nothing is known about Belinda's life after this date.

Belinda's original petition has been remembered and reinterpreted over more than two centuries by writers as diverse as the early black historian William Cooper Nell and the contemporary poet Rita Dove. Most, however, have misinterpreted it as a freedom suit. As a reading of the petition makes clear, it was an early call for reparations for slavery.

[*See also* American Revolution; Hall, Prince; *and* Petitions.]

BIBLIOGRAPHY
Carretta, Vincent, ed. *Unchained Voices: An Anthology of Black Authors in the English-Speaking World of the Eighteenth Century.* Lexington: University Press of Kentucky, 1996.

—ROY E. FINKENBINE

BELL, PHILIP ALEXANDER (b. 1808; d. 24 April 1889), African American abolitionist, editor, and journalist. Bell was born in New York City and educated at the African Free Schools in New York. He rose to national prominence on 25 January 1831, as secretary for a group of black New Yorkers protesting colonization.

Bell's reform work took place on the local and national levels, with an emphasis on black enfranchisement. As a member of the American Anti-Slavery Society, he served as subscription agent for William Lloyd Garrison's abolitionist newspaper, the *Liberator.* In addition, Bell advocated the organization of African American self-help programs and opposed segregation in churches and schools. He helped promote the National Negro Conventions of the 1830s and served as the New York delegate at three conventions. As director of the Phoenix Society, he promoted education for African Americans, and as a leader of the New York Political Association, Bell agitated for black suffrage and political rights.

Newspapers helped Bell spread his vision of an equal America. In January 1837, along with Charles B. Ray, Bell cofounded and edited the *Weekly Advocate,* the second African American newspaper in the United States. Samuel E. Cornish, with the help of Bell and Ray, edited the *Weekly Advocate,* and when its name changed to the *Colored American,* Bell remained involved in its weekly publication. With Cornish's retirement, Bell took over as editor of the *Colored American.* The *Colored American* distinguished itself from other antislavery serials of the time through its assertiveness and racial independence.

With the dissolution of the *Colored American* in 1839, Bell set up in New York City what he called an "intelligence office," an employment agency for African Americans. With no newspaper of his own, Bell continued to write for antislavery and reform newspapers, often under the pseudonym "Cosmopolite." During the 1850s Bell advanced the cause of black enfranchisement through his work with the New York State Suffrage Association and his involvement with the black state conventions. He proved to be an organizer on a national level as well. In the early 1850s Bell formed the Committee of Thirteen, a national organization that repudiated the Fugitive Slave Law of 1850. In 1853 Bell helped establish the National Council of Colored People, the first national black organization, which disbanded in Philadelphia in 1855.

In 1857 Bell moved to San Francisco, where he was briefly involved in real estate before becoming an associate editor of the *Pacific Appeal*, a weekly journal that dealt with events on both coasts affecting African American life. He remained associate editor until 1862. On 18 April 1865 he began publishing and editing his own newspaper, the *San Francisco Elevator*, which gained a wide audience of black readers throughout the United States. By the 1880s the *Elevator* had become the longest-running black newspaper in the nineteenth century, and Bell continued to edit the *Elevator* until his death. Although he died destitute, Bell was a pioneering black journalist who set the standard for black newspapers that Frederick Douglass's *North Star* and others would follow.

[*See also* Abolitionism; American Anti-Slavery Society; Antislavery Movement; Antislavery Press; Black Abolitionists; Black Politics; Black Press; Colonization; Cornish, Samuel; Douglass, Frederick; Fugitive Slave Law of 1850; Garrison, William Lloyd; Garrisonian Abolitionists; National Conventions of Colored Men; *North Star*; Political Participation; Ray, Charles B.; *and* Voting Rights.]

BIBLIOGRAPHY
Blassingame, John W., ed. *The Frederick Douglass Papers*. Vol. 1. New Haven, CT: Yale University Press, 1979.

Filler, Louis. "Bell, Philip Alexander." In *Dictionary of American Negro Biography*, edited by Rayford W. Logan and Michael R. Winston. New York: Norton, 1982.

Hembree, Michael F. "Bell, Philip Alexander." In *American National Biography*, edited by John A. Garraty and Mark C. Carnes, vol. 2. New York: Oxford University Press, 1999: 516–517.

—DELANO GREENIDGE-COPPRUE

BENEZET, ANTHONY (b. 31 January 1713; d. 13 May 1784), Quaker educator and abolitionist. Anthony Benezet was born to Huguenot parents in Saint-Quentin, Picardy, France. His father, Jean-Etienne Benezet, and his mother, Judith, had at least thirteen children, but more than half died at birth. The Protestant Huguenots had experienced a period of relative religious freedom lasting from the promulgation of the Edict of Nantes under Henry IV in 1598 until the revocation of the edict by Louis XIV in 1685, which led to renewed persecution by Catholics. Jean-Etienne Benezet belonged to a Protestant group known as the Inspirés de la Vaunage, which descended from the Camisards, who had violently resisted religious persecution in the Cévennes Mountains of southern France. The Benezet family fled France for the Netherlands in 1715, then went to England, and finally settled in Philadelphia in 1731.

In 1735 Anthony Benezet was naturalized as a British subject, and on 13 May 1736 he married Joyce Marriott, whose grandfather was the prominent physician Griffith Owen, a Quaker minister. The year of Benezet's admittance to the Society of Friends is not known, but he was well recommended by members of the society. Rejecting his father's desire that he join the family trading business, Benezet became a schoolteacher. In 1742 he took charge of the Friends' English School of Philadelphia (later renamed the William Penn Charter School); he also became one of the first educators to found a school for Quaker girls. In 1750 he began to teach young black children, primarily in his home, and soon founded the School for Black People, also known as the African School for Blacks or the Free African School. In *The Philadelphia Negro* (1899), the historian and civil rights pioneer W. E. B. Du Bois wrote "that on motion of one, probably Benezet, it was decided that the instruction ought to be provided for Negro children."

Benezet's students included Absalom Jones, the first minister of African descent in the Protestant Episcopal Church, and the sailmaker and entrepreneur James Forten. Richard Allen, the founder of the African Methodist Episcopal Church, also greatly appreciated Benezet's work as a teacher and abolitionist. Unlike many of his contemporaries who opposed the slave trade but went little further, Benezet actively fought to end slavery and proclaimed the complete equality of enslaved Africans. According to the historian Carter G. Woodson, Benezet "obtained many of his facts about the sufferings of slaves from the Negroes themselves, moving among them in their homes, at their places where they worked or on the wharves where they stopped when traveling." In *A Short Account of the People Called Quakers* (1780), Benezet wrote, "Having observed the many disadvantages these afflicted people labor under in point of education and otherwise, a tender care has taken place to promote their instruction in school learning, and also their religious and temporal welfare, in order to qualify them for becoming reputable members of society."

Religion and Writings. Benezet applied Quaker principles to his work with enslaved Africans, including the belief that all people are born equal in God's sight, the policy of nonviolence, and the disapproval of excessive material acquisitions and consumption. His observations led him to link Europeans, especially the British, with "the love of wealth" that he believed was brought on by the burgeoning Atlantic slave trade. Benezet argued that wealth drove men and nations to war, and he contrasted the constant desire for wealth in his own society with the image of

African societies that he derived from travel narratives by and discussions with enslaved and free Africans. He believed that, prior to the slave trade, Africans lived in relative freedom, with an abundance of the necessities of life. He asserted that the trade morally corrupted Europeans as well as some Africans, who became accomplices in the buying and selling of their fellows. His most important works on Africa were *A Short Account of That Part of Africa, Inhabited by the Negroes . . . and the Manner by Which the Slave-Trade Is Carried On* (1762) and *Some Historical Account of Guinea, Its Situation, Produce, and General Disposition of Its Inhabitants, with an Inquiry into the Rise and Progress of the Slave Trade, Its Nature and Lamentable Effects* (1771). Seven of his pamphlets also dealt exclusively with slavery.

The gentle Quaker's work greatly influenced the famed African-born abolitionists Quobna Ottobah Cugoano and Olaudah Equiano. Both men were kidnapped as children from Africa and relied on Benezet's writings to enhance their knowledge of their homelands. In his *Thoughts and Sentiments on the Evil and Wicked Traffic of Slavery and Commerce of the Human Species* (1787), Cugoano referred his readers to "the worthy and judicious Benezet" as giving "some striking estimations of the exceeding evil occasioned by that wicked diabolical traffic of the African slave trade." Equiano, in *The Interesting Narrative of the Life of Olaudah Equiano* (1789), advised readers to "see Anthony Benezet throughout" to bolster their understanding of the Africa of Equiano's youth, before the "arrival of the Europeans." In depicting his Ibo culture and homeland in what later became Nigeria, Equiano closely followed Benezet's geographical and physical accounts.

In preparing *An Essay on the Slavery and Commerce of the Human Species, Particularly the African* (1786), the British abolitionist Thomas Clarkson wrote of Benezet's *Some Historical Account of Guinea*, "In this precious book, I found almost all I wanted. I obtained by means of it knowledge of and gained access to the great authorities of Adanson, Moore, Barbot, Smith, Bosman and others." *Some Historical Account* became the first school textbook on Africa. Benezet analyzed the early travelers' accounts of Africa (such as those of Richard Jobson in 1623; André Brue, 1685; Jacques Barbot, 1678; and Wilhelm Bosman, 1709) to create his own description of Africa and to refute the proslavery descriptions of Africa and Africans.

Like many writers of the time—particularly Dissenters in the English-speaking world—Benezet relied heavily on biblical citations to buttress his arguments. He also drew upon Enlightenment philosophy and lessons learned from practical life. He followed the French political philosopher Baron de Montesquieu's argument in *The Spirit of Laws* (1748) that slavery had a destructive effect on both

the state and free men therein; Benezet noted that slavery destroyed both the white soul and the black body. He was also deeply influenced by the Scottish moral philosophers. He agreed with the legal theorist George Wallace, who wrote in his *System of the Principles of the Law of Scotland* (1760), "Men in their liberty are not *in comercia*, they are not either saleable or purchasable." Benezet quoted from the Scottish philosopher Francis Hutcheson, who in his *System of Moral Philosophy* (1755) declared that "no endowments natural or acquired, can give a perfect right to assume power over others, without their consent." Like Adam Smith he argued that slavery diminished the productive capacity and corrupted the morals of both races.

Benezet closely collaborated with the Quaker leader John Woolman. In 1754 they together wrote an antislavery Quaker tract, *Epistle of Caution and Advice, Concerning the Buying and Keeping of Slaves.* In the same year Woolman followed with *Some Considerations on the Keeping of Negroes*, which Benezet is believed to have edited. Benezet also had a tremendous influence on Benjamin Franklin, who credited his pamphlets and antislavery petition efforts with the decision of the Virginia House of Burgesses to petition the King for an end to the slave trade in 1772. Benezet also brought the Philadelphia physician Benjamin Rush, who later wrote anonymous tracts condemning slavery, into the struggle for black freedom

Benezet wrote many hundreds of letters, corresponding with religious leaders such as George Whitefield, John Wesley, and Moses Brown and secular leaders such as Franklin and Rush about his views on slavery and the slave trade. Upon receiving one of his pamphlets, the future Patriot firebrand Patrick Henry wrote on 18 January 1773, "I take this Opportunity to acknowledge ye receipt of Anthony Benezet's book against the slave trade. I thank ye for it." Henry added ruefully, "Would anyone believe that I am a Master of Slaves of my own purchase? I am drawn along by ye general Inconvenience of living without them; I will not, I cannot justify it." John Wesley's *Thoughts upon Slavery* (1774) is based almost entirely on Benezet's *Some Historical Account of Guinea*; the Quaker Benezet thanked the founder of Methodism for using his work. In 1783 Benezet addressed a letter to Britain's Queen Charlotte, urging her to help end the British slave trade. He wrote to Queen Sophia of Spain with a similar request.

International Influence. The correspondence between Benezet and the pioneer British abolitionist Granville Sharp proved to be one of the first links in the transnational fight against slavery and the slave trade. The two men collaborated in the famous *Somerset* case, and copies of Benezet's pamphlets were delivered to Lord Chief Justice Mansfield and his fellow jurists in 1771 before their ruling. Mansfield decided that James Somerset, a black who had been brought to England, could not be forcibly removed from the country by his master; Somerset was declared free. On 14 May 1772 Benezet wrote Sharp that "six hundred Copies had been delivered" of his pamphlet *A Caution and a Warning to Great Britain and Her Colonies* (1767) "to so many Members of both Houses of Parliament." It was Benezet who, through his correspondence, introduced Sharp and Franklin, writing on 4 April 1773, "I am glad to understand from my friend Benjamin Franklin, that you have commenced an acquaintance, and that he expects in the future to act in concert with thee in the affair of slavery." Together Sharp and Benezet developed new methods of collecting thousands of signatures on antislavery petitions and delivering them to their respective assemblies.

Benezet's descriptions of Africa proved to be so central that the British abolitionist leader William Wilberforce quoted him at length in the great 1792 parliamentary debates on ending the slave trade. At that time a motion was forwarded in favor of abolishing that trade—the first such action taken in any parliamentary body in the world. Although it did not win passage, it is credited with having brought about the beginning of the end of the international slave trade. Thousands of Benezet's pamphlets were distributed to abolition societies and members of the British parliament. He corresponded with the founders of the Société des Amis des Noirs (Society of Friends of the Blacks) in Paris, who initially authorized the translation of his works on Africa. Among these men were Jean-Pierre Brissot, a member of the Girondist movement during the French Revolution; Marie Jean Antoine Nicolas Caritat, marquis de Condorcet, a politician and defender of human rights, especially for women and blacks; Etienne Claviere, a peer of Brissot's in the Girondist movement; Honoré Gabriel Victor Riqueti, comte de Mirabeau, who was imprisoned because of his revolutionary activities; Abbé Guillaume-Thomas Raynal, a Jesuit priest who left the order to devote his life to politics; and Bishop Henri Grégoire, the leading antislavery figure during the French Revolution.

American Activism. When kidnapped blacks were transported through Philadelphia on their way south, Benezet intervened to obtain their freedom; in 1775 he became the first president of the Society for the Relief of Free Negroes Unlawfully Held in Bondage. In 1784, a few months before his death, this organization was refounded as the Pennsylvania Society for the Abolition of Slavery, for the Relief of Negroes Unlawfully Held in Bondage, and for Improving the Conditions of the African Race. In 1787 Benezet's old friend Benjamin Franklin took the helm of this society.

In early 1787 a number of free blacks, including Richard Allen and Absalom Jones, met to discuss the formation of a religious society for blacks. Feeling that their numbers were too small and their religious sensibilities too varied, they instead formed the Free African Society in April 1787. Its articles of incorporation were written under the aura of Benezet and indeed specified that a Quaker was always "to be chosen to act as Clerk and Treasurer of this useful institution." In January 1789 the society began to hold its meetings at the Quakers' African School House, which had been founded by Benezet. The society circulated petitions that were modeled in part on Benezet's earlier ones, and James Forten's opposition to African colonization schemes was similar to Benezet's. In voicing his own opposition to colonization, Benezet was an early advocate of giving land to free blacks.

There were many facets to the life of Anthony Benezet. As an educator he developed new ways to teach students to read, publishing *An Essay on Grammar* (1778) and *The Pennsylvania Spelling Book* (1778). Near the end of his life he began a study of the plight of the Native Americans and in 1784 published *Observations on the Situation, Disposition, and Character of the Indian Natives of This Continent*. He wrote several pamphlets on the Quaker religion and others such as *Thoughts on the Nature of War* (1759). He wrote *Remarks on the Nature and Bad Effects of Spirituous Liquors* (1788) and several other pamphlets on what he considered the harm done to society through liquor consumption.

On his deathbed Benezet uttered the words, "I am dying and feel shamed to meet the face of my maker, I have done so little in his cause." The blacks who followed his funeral processions felt different. Summing up the general feeling about the passing of Friend Anthony Benezet, the French writer and revolutionary Jean-Pierre Brissot wrote:

> What author, what great man, will ever be followed to his grave by four hundred Negroes, snatched by his own assiduity, his own generosity, from ignorance, wretchedness, and slavery? Who then has a right to speak haughtily of this benefactor of men? . . . Where is the man of all of Europe, of whatever rank or birth, who is equal to Benezet? Who is not obliged to respect him? How long will authors suffer themselves to be shackled by the prejudice of society? Will they never perceive that nature has created all men equal, that wisdom and virtue are the only criteria of superiority? Who was more virtuous than Benezet? Who was more useful to mankind? (Brookes, p. 460)

[*See also* Abolitionism; Africa, Idea of; African Methodist Episcopal Church; Allen, Richard; American Colonization Society; Cugoano, Quobna Ottobah; Education; Equiano, Olaudah; Forten, James; Franklin, Benjamin, and African Americans; Free African Society; Grégoire, Bishop Henri; Jones, Absalom; Petitions; Religion;

Slave Narratives; Society of Friends (Quakers) and African Americans; Temperance; *and* Woolman, John.]

BIBLIOGRAPHY

Benezet, Anthony. *A Short Account of the People Called Quakers: Their Rise, Religious Principles and Settlement in America*. Philadelphia: Joseph Crukshank, 1780.

Brissot, Jacques-Pierre. *Extracts from a Critical Examination of the Marquis de Chastellux's Travels in North America in a Letter Addressed to the Marquis*. July 1, 1786. Trinity College, Watkinson Library, Hartford, Connecticut.

Brookes, George S. *Friend Anthony Benezet*. Philadelphia: University of Pennsylvania Press, 1937.

Bruns, Roger, ed. *Am I Not a Man and a Brother: The Antislavery Crusade of Revolutionary America, 1688–1788*. New York: Chelsea House, 1977.

Clarkson, Thomas. *An Essay on the Slavery and Commerce of the Human Species, Particularly the African* (1786). New York: AMS Press, 1972.

Cugoano, Quobna Ottobah. *Thoughts and Sentiments on the Evil and Wicked Traffic of the Slavery and Commerce of the Human Species* (1787). London: Dawsons, 1969.

Drake, Thomas E. *Quakers and Slavery*. Gloucester, MA: Peter Smith, 1965.

Equiano, Olaudah. *The Interesting Narrative of the Life of Olaudah Equiano* (1789). Boston: Bedford Books, 1995.

Frost, J. William, ed. *The Quaker Origins of Antislavery*. Norwood, PA: Norwood Editions, 1980.

Hornick, Nancy Slocum. "Anthony Benezet and the Africans' School: Toward a Theory of Full Equality." *Pennsylvania Magazine of History and Biography* 99.4 (1975): 399–421.

Hutcheson, Francis. *A System of Moral Philosophy* (1755). New York: A. M. Kelley, 1968.

Jackson, Maurice. "Anthony Benezet: America's Finest Eighteenth-Century Antislavery Advocate." In *The Human Tradition in the American Revolution*, edited by Nancy L. Rhoden and Ian K. Steele, 1–17. Wilmington, DE: Scholarly Resources, 2000.

Jackson, Maurice. "'Ethiopia Shall Soon Stretch Her Hands unto God': Anthony Benezet and the Atlantic Antislavery Revolution." PhD diss., Georgetown University, 2001.

Jackson, Maurice. "The Social and Intellectual Origins of Anthony Benezet's Antislavery Radicalism." *Pennsylvania History* 6 (1999): 86–112.

Nash, Gary B., and Jean R. Soderlund. *Freedom by Degrees: Emancipation in Pennsylvania and Its Aftermath*. New York: Oxford University Press, 1991.

Soderlund, Jean R. *Quakers and Slavery: A Divided Spirit*. Princeton, NJ: Princeton University Press, 1985.

Straub, Jean S. "Anthony Benezet: Teacher and Abolitionist of the Eighteenth Century." *Quaker History* 57.1 (Spring 1968): 3–16.

Vaux, Roberts. *Memoirs of the Life of Anthony Benezet* (1817). New York: Burt Franklin, 1969.

Wallace, George. *A System of the Principles of the Law of Scotland*. Edinburgh: privately printed, 1760.

Woodson, Carter G. "Anthony Benezet." *Journal of Negro History* 2 (1917): 37–50.

—MAURICE JACKSON

BIBB, HENRY W. (b. 10 May 1815; d. 1 August 1854), an antislavery lecturer, author, and editor. Henry Walter Bibb was born a slave on the plantation of David White in Shelby County, Kentucky. His father, James Bibb, was a slaveholding planter and state senator; his mother, Mildred Jackson, was a slave. By 1825 Bibb began what he referred to as his "maroonage," or scheming of short-term escape. Excessively cruel treatment by several different masters engendered this habit. Bibb's life lacked stability; the slave's owner began hiring him out at a young age, and between 1832 and 1840 he would be sold more than six times and would relocate to at least seven southern states.

In 1833 Bibb met and fell in love with Malinda, a slave who lived four miles away in Oldham County, Kentucky. After determining that they had similar values regarding religion and possible flight, the two pledged honor to one another and considered themselves married in December 1834. Approximately one year later Malinda gave birth to Mary Frances, the only child to survive infancy of at least two the couple conceived.

Although Bibb had a family he did not lose sight of his ultimate goal of freedom. In December 1837 he made his first escape to the North, only to return to Kentucky a year later in an attempt to rescue his family. During one of several attempts to free them, Bibb was betrayed by other slaves and reenslaved. William Gatewood, the family's owner, sold the couple and their child to men who would then send the family to slave auctions in Louisiana. During the interim Bibb spent time in a labor prison; though appalled at the living conditions, the resourceful Bibb learned the basics of reading and writing from some of the white inmates there.

At the slave auctions in the fall of 1839, Deacon Whitfield, an owner of a plantation in the Red River area of Louisiana, bought the entire Bibb family. Whitfield's treatment of the slaves could be considered horrific. He failed to feed, clothe, and shelter them adequately; additionally, the merciless owner overworked and beat his slaves to the point of near death. Bibb, first alone and then with his family, attempted but failed to escape. Whitfield sold Bibb to gamblers who in turn sold him to a Native American man. It was during this time, in December 1840, that Henry Bibb saw his wife and child for the last time. Bibb considered the Native American to be the only humane owner he had ever had; he delayed his last escape for nearly a year, until the owner died. Indeed, the very night of the Native American's death, in the spring of 1841, Bibb made his final escape from slavery, managing to cross the Ohio River into freedom.

Bibb then worked in Perrysburgh, Ohio, for J. W. Smith, who had employed him in 1838 during one of his other escapes. After working for Smith through the summer of 1841, Bibb traveled to Detroit and attended the school of the Reverend W. C. Monroe, for just two weeks; this was the only formal education Bibb ever received. Not long after his escape, Bibb began orating his narrative for the antislavery cause, soon becoming an avid lecturer, particularly in Michigan. In 1843 Bibb attended a free black convention in Detroit, and throughout 1844 and 1845 he campaigned in Michigan and Ohio for the Liberty Party. Because of questions about the authenticity of Bibb's life story, the Liberty Party conducted an investigation of his credibility. By April 1845 the examination had proved Bibb's integrity, and he became employed full time as an antislavery lecturer.

Regretting the separation from his family, Bibb continued to try to retrieve them from the bonds of slavery. During the winter of 1845 he learned that Malinda had been sold by Deacon Whitfield and was her new master's concubine. With this information Bibb resolved that he would never be able to rescue his family and that his marriage was officially over. Two years later, in May 1847, Bibb met Mary E. Miles, a Bostonian known for her devotion to the antislavery cause and sympathy toward reform. The following June, Miles and Bibb married. That same month, Bibb attended the founding of the Free-Soil Party alongside his fellow escaped slave Frederick Douglass.

The fugitive published his story, *Narrative of the Life and Adventures of Henry Bibb, an American Slave*, in 1849. The narrative became a quick success and already had a third edition by the following year. After the passage of the Fugitive Slave Law of 1850, Bibb and his wife settled in Chatham, Canada West (now Ontario), for fear of their safety in the United States. While in Chatham, Bibb advocated not only abolition but also emigration and agricultural enterprise for fugitive slaves in Canada. To help voice his opinions, Bibb published and edited the bimonthly paper *Voice of the Fugitive*, with its first edition appearing on 1 January 1851. *Voice of the Fugitive* was the first black newspaper in Canada and had eleven hundred subscribers by the end of its first year. In addition to publishing the newspaper, Bibb and his wife took active roles in the community: they founded a day school, assisted in the building of a Methodist church, and assisted in the creation of temperance, educational, and antislavery societies. Additionally, Bibb devoted himself to a society that aided newly arrived fugitives and advocated that a black emigration convention be held in Toronto. As one of fifty delegates to attend the North American Colored Convention on 9 September 1851, Bibb presided over the gathering and advocated independence and separatism based on agriculture. To promote these goals, Bibb helped form the Refugee Home Society, a joint-stock company that attempted to acquire and sell Canadian farmland to black immigrants.

Despite Bibb's good intentions, he encountered opposition and hardship. By March 1853 the *Voice of the Fugitive* faced competition from the second black Canadian newspaper, the *Provincial Freeman*. In October of the

Henry Bibb, in an engraving by P. H. Reason that appeared as the frontispiece to *Narrative of the Life and Adventures of Henry Bibb, an American Slave*, 1849. Bibb ended his narrative with these words: "I trust that this little volume will bear some humble part in lighting up the path of freedom and revolutionizing public opinion. . . . And I here pledge myself, God being my helper, ever to contend for the natural equality of the human family." (Library of Congess.)

same year, a fire that Bibb suspected to be arson destroyed his office; the publisher never fully recovered from the setback. In fact, some of Bibb's peers considered his views controversial. He and Frederick Douglass, one of the most influential African Americans at the time, clashed on several issues. Bibb advocated sending Bibles to slaves as a means of promoting abolition; Douglass believed such thoughts absurd and considered Bibb "weak, insipid, and powerless." Stronger dissonance existed between the two men regarding their overall views of free blacks. While Bibb encouraged immigration to Canada and separatism, Douglass advocated assimilation. Bibb died in Canada on 1 August 1854 at the age of thirty-nine, without having attained his goals of ending slavery and establishing an African American colony in Canada.

[*See also* Antislavery Movement; Bible; Black Abolitionists; Black Family; Black Press; Black Separatism; Black Uplift; Canada; Colonization; Douglass, Frederick;

Education; Free-Soil Party; Fugitive Slave Law of 1850; Liberty Party; National Conventions of Colored Men; Native Americans and African Americans; Oratory and Verbal Arts; Reform; Slave Narratives; Slave Resistance; Slavery; Temperance; Violence against African Americans.]

BIBLIOGRAPHY

Andrews, William L. *To Tell a Free Story: The First Century of Afro-American Autobiography, 1760–1865.* Urbana: University of Illinois Press, 1986.

Bibb, Henry. *Narrative of the Life and Adventures of Henry Bibb, an American Slave* (1849). Mineola, NY: Dover, 2005.

Douglass, Frederick. "Frederick Douglass vs. Henry Bibb." *North Star*, 22 June 1849.

Hite, Roger W. "Voice of a Fugitive: Henry Bibb and Ante-bellum Black Separatism." *Journal of Black Studies* 4.3 (March 1974): 269–284.

Silverman, Jason H. *Unwelcome Guests: Canada West's Response to American Fugitive Slaves, 1800–1865.* Millwood, NY: Associated Faculty Press, 1985.

—HEIDI L. SCOTT GIUSTO

BIBLE. The abolitionist Fredrick Douglass was born into a culture saturated with biblical discourse. As a child he listened to preachers whose sermons were packed with biblical references. When the eight-year-old Douglass was sent to work for Hugh Auld in Baltimore, Maryland, his desire for literacy was stirred by hearing Sophia Auld read the Bible. Later he taught himself to write by copying passages from the Bible and the Methodist hymnal. Douglass's religious conversion heightened his longing to know the Bible, an ambition encouraged by the black preacher Charles Lawson, young Douglass's spiritual mentor. While living as a free man in New Bedford, Massachusetts, Douglass became a class leader and a local preacher at the African Methodist Episcopal Zion Church.

It is not surprising then that Douglass used biblical language in his speeches and writings when he began his work with the Massachusetts Anti-Slavery Society. Beginning with his first recorded speech in October 1841, Douglass exposed the religious hypocrisy of slave owners—including his own master, Thomas Auld—and pious Christians and church leaders, who justified slavery and its abuses with biblical texts such as Luke 12:47: "And that servant, which knew his lord's will, and prepared not himself, neither did according to his will, shall be beaten with many stripes." Douglass repeatedly called attention to this verse, a favorite text perverted by slave owners. Early in his first autobiography, *Narrative of the Life of Frederick Douglass* (1845), Douglass refutes another favorite verse of the proslavery Christians, the so-called Ham's Curse. Slavery advocates fallaciously argued that in Genesis 9:25–27, God cursed Ham, Noah's son, with slavery, and that Ham's descendants were slaves by divine decree. Doug-

lass, with a touch of irony, points to the mixed-blood slaves, many fathered by white masters, to drive home the error. In January 1851 Douglass likened slave owners to the false prophets of Matthew 7:15, "wolves in sheep's clothing" who "torture the pages of the Holy Bible" to justify their sins.

Douglass also cites scripture in the appendix to the *Narrative*; his indictment of Christianity in slaveholding America makes extensive use of Matthew 23. Although careful to distinguish between the "Christianity of Christ" and the Christianity of America, Douglass thunders in a prophetic refrain, "Woe to you, scribes and Pharisees, hypocrites." Like the ancient legalists, Douglass argues, Americans who profess to be Christians "strain at a gnat and swallow a camel" (Matthew 23:24). Douglass ends his jeremiad with yet another biblical reference, identifying another fallacy and labeling the Christianity of nineteenth-century America a lie: "If a man say, I love God, and hateth his brother, he is a liar: for he that loveth not his brother whom he hath seen, how can he love God whom he hath not seen?" (1 John 4:20)

Despite such frequent attacks, Douglass was well aware that much of the support for the abolitionist cause came from religious circles. While biblical discourse came naturally to Douglass, it also served him well as a tool to move an audience predisposed to attend to such language. In "To My Old Master, Thomas Auld," first published in the *North Star* on 3 September 1848, Douglass labels slavery "an outrage upon the soul," an offense that God himself would judge. Douglass repeatedly uses similar pronouncements of guilt and judgment to stir the hearts of his audience.

In his famous Fourth of July address, delivered in Rochester, New York, on 5 July 1852, Douglass used the words of the psalmist to compare slaves to the lamenting Israelites and to warn of divine judgment on a sinful nation (Psalm 137:1–6). The theme of the guilty nation recurred throughout Douglass's speeches. "No peace for the wicked," a phrase from Isaiah 48:22, resounded throughout Douglass's orations of the 1850s. A guilty nation, a guilty soul can know no peace, Douglass reiterated. On two occasions, 11 May 1853 and 30 October 1854, he rendered this assertion more dramatic by adding to it the voice of Joseph's brothers admitting their transgression against him (Genesis 42:21). Yet Douglass moved beyond condemnation of the slaveholding South to sound a warning against any compromise. In "An Antislavery Tocsin," delivered on 8 December 1850 in Rochester, he invokes patriotism and essentially redefines it as "righteousness" that "exalts a nation, while sin is a reproach to any people" (Proverbs 14:34).

To insist that slavery is evil and that those who condone it are sinners is, of course, to frame an argument in the most fundamental religious terms. In "Decision of the Hour," another Rochester lecture delivered on 16 June 1861, Douglass, emphasizing human choice, compares the earthly battle against slavery to war in heaven. The clear choice, Douglass insists, is between "right and wrong, good and evil, liberty and slavery." Compromise is impossible. On 12 February 1846, in Arbroath, Scotland, he blended verses to prove that true religion and slavery were mutually exclusive. From an Old Testament prophet he took a rhetorical question and reformed it as a direct assertion, "Two cannot walk together except they be agreed" (Amos 3:3). From Jesus's words, he took a single sentence, "No man can serve two masters" (Matthew 6:24). Such clear division between light and darkness lies at the heart of Douglass's moral argument.

Douglass's most frequent biblical reference was Matthew 7:12, the Golden Rule, which he cited in lectures between 1842 and 1893. In 1845 he identified it as "that broad, that world-embracing principle." On 15 October 1883 he evoked it in response to the Supreme Court's decision that the Civil Rights Act of 1875 was unconstitutional. For Douglass the Golden Rule condensed the basic principle of morality, the equality of all peoples. The perversion of the Christian gospel that allowed Christians to dehumanize their brothers and sisters was, in Douglass's mind, a failure to abide by Christ's command to "do unto others." The righteousness of the abolitionist movement was based on adherence to the Golden Rule. Douglass used it as the demarcation between the righteous and the damned.

Lawson had believed that God had a great purpose for the young slave who became Frederick Douglass, and that idea remained with Douglass. The adolescent who had helped Lawson read the Bible became one of the most eloquent users of biblical discourse of his time, perhaps of any time. In a speech delivered on 3 August 1846 at Newcastle upon Tyne, England, Douglass echoed Isaiah 61:1, "I glory in being called an infidel, if to be such, is to open the prison door and preach deliverance to the captive." Even in affirming his own identity, Douglass chose his language from the Bible.

[See also Abolitionism; African Methodist Episcopal Church; Auld Family; Baltimore, Maryland, Slavery in; Black Church; Civil Rights Act of 1875; Douglass, Frederick; Education; Free African Americans before the Civil War (North); Language; Literature; Massachusetts Anti-Slavery Society; Narrative of the Life of Frederick Douglass (1845); North Star; Oratory and Verbal Arts; Proslavery Thought; Religion; Religion and Slavery; Rochester, New York; Slave Narratives; and Supreme Court.]

BIBLIOGRAPHY

John W. Blassingame, ed. *The Frederick Douglass Papers.* Series 1, *Speeches, Debates, and Interviews.* 5 vols. New Haven, CT: Yale University Press, 1979–1992. This multivolume work includes Douglass's major speeches and interviews, including variants, from 1841 to 1895.

Douglass, Frederick. *Life and Times of Frederick Douglass: His Early Life as a Slave, His Escape from Bondage, and His Complete History, Written by Himself* (1881, 1892). Introduction by Rayford W. Logan. New York: Collier, 1962. This is the final revised, expanded edition of Douglass's autobiography.

Douglass, Frederick. *My Bondage and My Freedom* (1855). Edited by William L. Andrews. Urbana: University of Illinois Press, 1987. This is the second of Douglass's autobiographies, covering his life through his time in England. The appendix includes excerpts from several of his best-known speeches.

Douglass, Frederick. *Narrative of the Life of Frederick Douglass, An American Slave, Written by Himself* (1845). Edited by Benjamin Quarles. Cambridge, MA: Belknap Press, 1960. Douglass's first autobiography remains his most widely read work and the best known of all slave narratives.

Lampe, Gregory P. *Frederick Douglass: Freedom's Voice, 1818–1845.* East Lansing: Michigan State University Press, 1998. This is a thoroughly researched and revealing examination of Douglass's rhetoric and the forces that shaped it. Chapter 1, which focuses on the earliest influences, is particularly informative.

Mieder, Wolfgang. *"No Struggle, No Progress": Frederick Douglass and His Proverbial Rhetoric for Civil Rights.* New York: Peter Lang, 2001. Authored by a world-renowned expert on proverbs, this is a detailed examination of Douglass's use of biblical and folk proverbs.

—WYLENE RHOLETTER

BIRNEY, JAMES GILLESPIE (b. 4 February 1792; d. 25 November 1857), abolitionist and two-time presidential candidate for the Liberty Party. James Gillespie Birney was born in Danville, Kentucky, to a slaveholding family. He attended Transylvania University in nearby Lexington, Kentucky, and eventually graduated from Princeton University in 1810. After admittance to the bar, Birney returned to Danville to practice law and soon married into an influential Kentucky family. By the time he moved to Madison County, Alabama, in 1818, he already owned several slaves.

Following a brief stint in Alabama's General Assembly and some financial difficulties, Birney relocated to Huntsville, Alabama, to begin a law practice. After selling many of his slaves, he became involved with the colonization movement and supported the idea of restricting the internal slave trade. By 1832 Birney was an active agent for the American Colonization Society and made a lecture circuit around the South supporting the idea of emancipating slaves and transporting them to the new African colony of Liberia. He returned to Danville and rose to the level of vice president in the Kentucky Colonization Society.

In 1834 Birney's relationship to the antislavery movement took a different personal and professional direction. In that year he freed his remaining slaves and resigned his vice presidency with the Kentucky Colonization Society. Instead of the gradualist philosophy employed by colonizationists, Birney gravitated toward the immediatist position held by William Lloyd Garrison and the American Anti-Slavery Society. He helped form the Kentucky Anti-Slavery Society and began to travel across the nation in support of immediate abolitionism.

This was not a popular position to take in antebellum Kentucky, so in 1836 Birney moved to New Richmond, Ohio, to edit a new journal entitled the *Philanthropist*. Although the journal lasted only through 1837, Birney used the *Philanthropist* as a way to support a new approach to the struggle against slavery. He denounced both major parties, the Democrats and Whigs, for suppressing antislavery issues to achieve national followings. But Birney also criticized abolitionists for avoiding political action. In 1837 he became the executive secretary of the American Anti-Slavery Society and con-

James G. Birney, lithograph published by N. Currier, after a daguerreotype by Chilton, in 1844. Shortly before this, Birney had written the pamphlet "American Churches, the Bulwarks of American Slavery." It was accusatory, though in a final postscript he assured the reader that "there are considerable portions of the Methodist, Baptist, and Presbyterian churches, as well as the entire of some of the smaller religious bodies in America, that maintain a commendable testimony against slavery and its abominations." (Library of Congress.)

tinued to push for political action by attending state legislative sessions and corresponding with southern politicians.

Birney's push for political abolitionism reached its pinnacle in the spring of 1840 in Albany, New York, when an antislavery convention comprising delegates from six states nominated him for the office of president of the United States. The newly founded Liberty Party's campaign in 1840 generated just 7,069 votes for Birney; all of them were from northern states. Nonetheless, an antislavery political party was born, and Birney served as its presidential candidate in the next election. He received 62,300 popular votes for president in 1844 but failed to capture a single electoral vote. The Liberty Party enjoyed some notoriety in the 1844 election, however, because in New York, Birney's vote total was greater than the difference between that for the Whig candidate, Henry Clay, a slaveholder from Kentucky, and that for James K. Polk, the Democratic nominee and a slaveholder from Tennessee. Many people at the time believed that Birney's votes would have gone to the more moderate Clay, had he not been in the race.

At the same time that Birney's reputation soared among political antislavery circles with his high-profile presidential campaigns, his relationship with Frederick Douglass was not a strong one. Birney's personal ties to the South and his position that political action could undermine slavery set him on a different course from that of Douglass. In 1845 Douglass lauded Birney as an example of a person "who emancipated his slaves, and a hundred of others" but saw him as the exception rather than the rule for slaveholders. Douglass believed, as did many abolitionists at the time of the Liberty Party's formation, that a third party would ultimately fail to push antislavery to the forefront of the political agenda in the United States.

Birney's political career was cut short by a horse-riding accident that left him disabled for the rest of his life. Although he followed political and legal events closely, he could no longer actively participate in them. At the same time that Birney withdrew from public life, however, Douglass began to reconsider his own stand on political participation. Douglass's close friendship with Gerrit Smith, a supporter of the Liberty Party and a wealthy philanthropist, persuaded him to see political action as a positive force for antislavery. Thus, even though Birney and Douglass were never personally close, the former's vision of a strong abolitionist political party influenced the latter's transformation from a Garrisonian radical abolitionist into a respected public figure by the 1850s.

[*See also* Abolitionism; American Anti-Slavery Society; American Colonization Society; Antislavery Movement; Clay, Henry; Colonization; Democratic Party; Douglass,

Frederick; Emancipation; Garrison, William Lloyd; Liberia; Liberty Party; Polk, James K.; Slave Trade, Domestic; Smith, Gerrit; *and* Whig Party.]

BIBLIOGRAPHY

Fladeland, Betty. *James Gillespie Birney: Slaveholder to Abolitionist.* Ithaca, NY: Cornell University Press, 1955.

Kraut, Alan M. "Partisanship and Principles: The Liberty Party in Antebellum Political Culture." In *Crusaders and Compromisers: Essays on the Relationship of the Antislavery Struggle to the Antebellum Party System*, edited by Alan M. Kraut. Westport, CT: Greenwood, 1983.

Sewell, Richard H. *Ballots for Freedom: Antislavery Politics in the United States, 1837–1860.* New York: Oxford University Press, 1976.

—SEAN PATRICK ADAMS

BLACK ABOLITIONISTS. Historians acknowledge the existence of "two abolitionisms" in the antebellum United States—one black, one white. Although black and white abolitionists shared similar views about the moral evil of slavery, they held very different understandings of the relationship between slavery and race, which shaped their involvement in the antislavery struggle. Slavery and racism were distinct and separate evils for most whites. Few had firsthand experience with the "peculiar institution" and tended to regard it in abstract moral terms. Far too many white abolitionists paid little or no attention to the question of racial equality and, in fact, exhibited a great deal of prejudice and paternalism toward their darker-hued colleagues within the movement.

Most blacks, on the other hand, looked at slavery and racial discrimination through the lens of personal experience and saw them as two points on the same continuum. They believed that racism and bondage were merely different manifestations of the same problem. That understanding prompted black abolitionists to see the antislavery cause in more pragmatic terms. It also led them to conceive of abolitionism as an all-encompassing movement for racial equality—of equal importance was fighting for economic opportunity, social mobility, civil and political rights, equal education, and fair representation in the press and popular culture, on the one hand, and fighting against the institution of slavery, on the other. This stark conceptual division "separated black from white and generated a distinct black abolitionism." Because of the tendency of antebellum African American activists to view emancipation and equality as closely related goals and to fight for both at the same time, some historians have thought of their struggle as America's first civil rights movement.

Varieties of Involvement. "Every colored man is an abolitionist," bragged the Reverend Richard Robinson before a national gathering of the African Methodist Episcopal denomination in 1856, "and slaveholders know it." Robinson's remark underscored the broad commitment of antebellum African Americans to the struggle for emancipation and equality. That commitment, however, took a variety of forms. Geography, class, occupation, family background, church affiliation, legal status, gender, generation, and economic and legal constraints helped determine how individual blacks responded to American slavery and racism. But respond they did, employing tactics as varied as the situations in which they found themselves.

Fighting slavery and racism was especially difficult below the Mason-Dixon Line. Southern slaves usually fought against their slavery through covert means or by running away, although a few openly rebelled against the system. Legal constraints usually forced free blacks in the South to limit their resistance to covert means as well. Many quietly aided those escaping from bondage by hiding them in homes or churches, offering instructions and directions, forging passes or free papers, and providing transportation to assist slaves in their flight. Others raised monies to buy the freedom of family members and friends. Few could go beyond those measures. Prior to 1830, free blacks in some cities in the Upper South, particularly Baltimore, spoke out against colonization and slavery and cooperated with black abolitionists in the free states. But after Nat Turner's 1831 revolt, their right to assemble was increasingly restricted and their voices muffled.

Northern free blacks faced fewer formal constraints on their abolitionist involvement. But the degree to which individual blacks participated varied; blacks engaged in abolitionism ranged from community activists and professional abolitionists who lectured, wrote, and organized for the cause to those who instinctively opposed slavery and racism but could do little to further the cause directly. Between these two poles was the bulk of the African American community, mostly working-class folk, who offered irregular and less obvious assistance. A few working-class blacks attended occasional antislavery meetings, subscribed to abolitionist journals, signed petitions, donated what money they could afford, and even refrained—where possible—from buying slave-produced goods.

The role of the black masses increased dramatically, however, after the Fugitive Slave Law of 1850 was passed. As the need for protecting runaway slaves grew more urgent and the presence of slave catchers increased, so did the efforts of working-class blacks. What the times demanded, claimed the Bostonian Robert Johnson, himself a fugitive slave, "were men of overalls—men of the wharf—those who could do the heavy work in the hour of difficulty." Working-class men responded by hiding and transporting fugitives and participating in attempts to rescue those who had been recaptured. Working-class women often served as the eyes and ears of local vigilance committees, watching for slave catchers in northern communities and in the hotels and boardinghouses in which they worked. In addition to providing food, shelter, and medical attention to fugitives, they participated in a few slave rescues. During the decade leading up to the Civil War, black abolitionism became a community venture.

Only a few of the most active black abolitionists, however, came from the working class. The latter group simply lacked the time and resources for such extensive involvement. Most active abolitionists were drawn from the so-called black elite. These were the community leaders who chaired local gatherings, attended state and national black conventions, spoke and wrote on antislavery and civil rights questions, raised funds and enlisted workers, filled offices, circulated petitions, organized public protests, challenged inequalities through the courts, and joined with white abolitionists to sustain the broader movement. A core group of some three hundred African American leaders—some free blacks, some former slaves—became actively involved in black abolitionism on a day-to-day basis. A select few became professional abolitionists. These were the lecturers like William Wells Brown and Charles Lenox Remond, the editors like Frederick Douglass, and the antislavery office clerks like William C. Nell and William Still, who devoted all their time to the cause.

At first only men worked as professional abolitionists. By the 1850s, however, African American women had earned a more prominent place in the struggle. Mary Ann Shadd Cary edited the *Provincial Freeman*. Ellen Craft, Sojourner Truth, Frances Ellen Watkins Harper, Sarah Parker Remond, and Barbara Steward became sought-after antislavery speakers. Harriet Tubman gained lasting prominence for her work with the Underground Railroad. Freeborn blacks numerically dominated this core group, largely because of their preponderance within the black elite. Less than one-third of the most active black abolitionists had experienced bondage, but as the number of abolitionists who were former slaves increased in the 1840s, they gained an importance much greater than their numbers in the movement might suggest. They were especially effective as speakers and writers because their firsthand experience with slavery made them particularly attractive to readers and audiences. The number of former slaves within the ranks of the antislavery activists continued to grow in the decade before the Civil War, owing primarily to the growing importance of the work of the Underground Railroad and vigilance committees.

The most active black abolitionists performed essential roles in the antislavery movement. In the battle for public opinion over slavery, nothing moved audiences like a "true narrative fallen from the lips of a veritable fugitive." Black speakers, especially former slaves, gave the movement credibility as they effectively refuted proslavery myths that slaves were contented, well treated, and fit only for bondage. The American Anti-Slavery Society (AASS) hired Charles Lenox Remond, a freeborn black from Massachusetts, as its first African American lecturing agent in 1838. His eloquence and intelligence impressed white audiences and established a place at the podium for black abolitionists. Antislavery societies soon rushed other black speakers into the field, "preferring one who has felt in his own person the evils of slavery, and with the strong voice of experience can tell of its horrors." By the mid-1840s, a number of former slaves, including Frederick Douglass, William Wells Brown, Henry Bibb, and Samuel Ringgold Ward, regularly lectured for the movement.

At first, white abolitionists usually organized and sponsored these lecture tours, often subjecting the lecturers to close supervision and paternalistic treatment. Eventually, many black abolitionists chose instead to organize their own independent lecture tours. Whatever the case, they took the antislavery message to a wide variety of audiences—from local gatherings to national reform conventions—speaking in churches, schoolhouses, and town halls across the North. More than one hundred black lecturers even carried the antislavery message abroad to Great Britain, seeking to enlist audiences there in an effort to draw a "moral cordon" around slavery in the American South. These lecturers educated the public about the realities of bondage and won many converts to the cause. They also spoke about a range of other topics, from racism to temperance to politics, and raised funds to purchase family and friends out of bondage, to support antislavery newspapers, to aid and protect fugitive slaves, and to build various institutions in black communities. Some adopted innovative means of enlivening their presentations, displaying artifacts from the plantation or accompanying their lectures with moving scenes of slave life. Others used their lectures to sell antislavery literature, including their own autobiographical narratives.

Black abolitionists also moved readers through the printed word. Many former slaves published slave narratives—autobiographical accounts of their life in bondage. These works took the black abolitionist message beyond the lecture halls and into the parlors of white Americans. Innovations in print technology in the 1830s allowed for the cheap reproduction of such works, making them inexpensive and effective witnesses against slavery. The narratives recounted the horrors of slavery: brutal whippings, separation of families, the sexual vulnerability of slave women, and exciting escapes. Nearly four dozen book-length narratives were published between 1836 and the beginning of the Civil War; some, like those of Frederick Douglass and Solomon Northup, sold tens of thousands of copies in America and abroad. By the early 1840s, antislavery activists believed that these books were an "infallible means of abolitionizing the free states." Black abolitionists also published other types of antislavery works, including such critiques of American racial prejudice as Hosea Easton's *Treatise on the Intellectual Character and Civil and Political Condition of the Colored People* (1838) and such early works of African American history as William C. Nell's *Colored Patriots of the American Revolution* (1855). All sought to present blacks and the black experience in a more positive light.

After 1852, with the dramatic success of *Uncle Tom's Cabin* by Harriet Beecher Stowe, some black abolitionist authors sought to use fiction to advance the cause. They penned several novels and novellas about slavery in the South and racial prejudice in the North over the next decade, beginning with William Wells Brown's *Clotel* (1853) and Frederick Douglass's "The Heroic Slave" (1853). Stowe's novel also prompted additional slave narratives, including Harriet Jacobs's *Incidents in the Life of a Slave Girl* (1861), the only full-length account of slavery by a female runaway.

Efforts to aid fugitives from southern slavery also depended on the leadership and skills of black abolitionists. Although Quakers and other white activists were important to the loose network of individuals and groups known as the Underground Railroad, abolitionists recognized, as James G. Birney reported in 1837, that "such matters are almost uniformly managed by the colored people." William Still in Philadelphia, Lewis Hayden in Boston, David Ruggles in New York, Stephen Myers in Albany, Frederick Douglass in Rochester, and Jermain W. Loguen in Syracuse played key roles in urban vigilance committees, which dispensed food, clothing, money, and medicine to fugitives; provided them with legal services and temporary shelter; and transported them farther north, even to Canada.

Often, a black abolitionist's vocation proved to be a valuable resource to his vigilance committee work. In Boston, for example, the clothing dealers Hayden and Jonas W. Clarke could be counted on to outfit fugitives, the printer Benjamin F. Roberts published placards to warn against slave catchers and the Boston police, the attorney Robert Morris defended captured fugitives, and the physician John S. Rock attended to the ill and injured. Less well-known black activists performed similar roles in the small towns dotting the northern side of the Ohio River and Pennsylvania's border with slaveholding Maryland. A few individuals, like Harriet Tubman and John P. Parker of Ripley, Ohio, went into the slave states to safely lead individuals and groups away from the plantation. Even more subversive were such activists as Jacob R. Gibbs in Baltimore and Thomas Smallwood in Washington, D.C., who headed secret networks that helped slaves escape from southern cities. To a black abolitionist, "few things could be so satisfying as helping a runaway."

Beginnings. The beginnings of black abolitionism date back to the emergence of urban communities of freeborn blacks in the North and Upper South after the American Revolution. Because African Americans were not allowed to join organizations established during that era by white reformers to work for the gradual end of slavery, black activists fought for emancipation and equality through black community institutions—churches, lodges, and benevolent societies. In fact, the earliest black abolitionists were such community activists as Prince Hall in Boston and Richard Allen and Absalom Jones in Philadelphia. Denied other forms of access to the political arena, these leaders depended upon moral appeals and the power of the printed word. In the late eighteenth century they sent dozens of petitions to state legislatures and even to Congress, calling for an end to slavery, abolition of the Atlantic slave trade, protection against kidnappers, access to public education, voting rights, and land of their own in the new territories of the Old Northwest.

In the early nineteenth century black activists began to publish a substantial number of protest pamphlets aimed at influencing legislatures, sympathetic whites, and literate free blacks. A leading example was *Letters by a Man of Colour* (1813), by James Forten of Philadelphia, an articulate attack on slavery and racism in the early Republic. The most widely circulated of these pamphlets was David Walker's *Appeal to the Coloured Citizens of the World*, which went through three editions in 1829 and 1830. Walker, a black Bostonian with roots in slaveholding North Carolina, challenged literate blacks to stand up to racial injustice, while pointing out the hypocrisy of American slavery and prejudice. The *Appeal* attributed the ills of antebellum African Americans to bondage, enforced black ignorance, religious hypocrisy, and the movement for African colonization. Walker even hinted at the need to use violence. Smuggled into the South by free black sailors and white allies, his *Appeal* provoked considerable fear among slaveholders.

Black abolitionism developed a separate organizational presence by the late 1820s, in large part as a response to the rise of the African colonization movement. Founded in 1816, the American Colonization Society called for repatriating African Americans to the African continent; by 1822 it was recruiting black settlers for its newly created colony of Liberia on the West African coast. Most white abolitionists and antislavery organizations of the decade supported colonization as well as a gradual approach to emancipation. Most black abolitionists, however, rejected colonization, seeing it as an unjust threat to the future of African Americans on the North American continent. They organized mass meetings, wrote letters to antislavery journals, and privately persuaded white allies in an effort to diminish public support for a mass return to Africa. They reminded whites that they had helped build the new nation and thought of it as their "only *true and appropriate home*." An organized black abolitionist movement grew out of this struggle and showed what could be accomplished with greater coordination and persistent protest. Local groups dedicated to fighting for emancipation and equality emerged in Baltimore, Boston, New Haven, Philadelphia, and other free black communities. The Massachusetts General Colored Association, established by Walker and others in about 1826, started a continuing correspondence among these groups. Similarly, the first African American newspaper, the New York–based *Freedom's Journal*, which was published from 1827 to 1829, linked black abolitionists across the North and Upper South through its columns and a network of unpaid subscription agents.

The context of black abolitionism changed dramatically about 1830. After working closely with William Watkins and other black abolitionists in Baltimore during 1829 and 1830, William Lloyd Garrison emerged as the most prominent antislavery voice in the United States while helping to publish the *Genius of Universal Emancipation* in that city. He had adopted many of the beliefs of the black abolitionists, particularly their opposition to colonization and gradual emancipation. Likewise, they quickly embraced Garrison and, believing that he would help carry the call for immediate emancipation to other whites, largely subsidized his *Liberator*, the most strident and widely circulated antislavery journal in the 1830s. The movement soon found converts across the North; hundreds of new antislavery organizations were formed, beginning with the New England Anti-Slavery Society, which was created in 1832 at Boston's African Meetinghouse. One year later, abolitionists from several states gathered in Philadelphia to organize the AASS, which dominated the movement through the end of the decade. By 1836 more than five hundred AASS auxiliaries had been established across the North. Unlike earlier antislavery organizations, the AASS was interracial in nature; such previously all-black groups as the Massachusetts General Colored Association soon became part of the new organization.

Grateful for their new allies, black abolitionists muted their earlier militancy and shifted their approach during the 1830s. Abandoning Walker's tone and message, they emphasized the tactic of moral suasion and the strategy of moral reform. Moral suasion sought to convince people of the sinfulness of slavery through printed or spoken appeals to their conscience. Even such independent racial efforts as the black national conventions of the decade consistently posited that improvements must come "by moral suasion alone." The strategy of moral reform tried to persuade whites that African Americans were worthy of emancipation and equality through bringing about a change of behavior in the race. Because of the restraints imposed by inadequate schooling and lack of economic opportunity, went the argument, most African Americans fell short of white standards of education and conduct. Moral reformers believed that by demonstrating that blacks were capable of self-improvement, they could smash white stereotypes about blacks. Black abolitionists endorsed the social values of thrift, self-help, education, the work ethic, sobriety, and gentility as sure routes to racial advancement. William Whipper, a conservative activist in Philadelphia, spoke for many black abolitionists of the decade when he argued that "the prejudice which exists against [blacks] arises not from the color of their skin, but from their condition." Such a change in condition, they claimed, must precede any meaningful changes in race relations in the United States. Independent and aggressive black abolitionism lay dormant for nearly a decade.

Greater Independence. By about 1840, however, black abolitionists had begun to question the value of such singular dependence upon moral suasion, moral reform, and interracial activism. Instead of visible improvement, conditions seemed to be getting worse. Slavery was spreading farther westward, stereotyping in the press and popular culture was becoming cruder, the voting rights of free blacks had been rescinded in three states, Irish and German immigrants were displacing black workers in northern cities, and racial violence was escalating. Several dozen mob attacks on northern black communities in the 1830s and 1840s "mocked moral reform and underscored its failure." In these riots, white mobs had targeted the symbols of free black success—churches, businesses, the houses of the black elite, and the meeting places of moral reform organizations. Most black abolitionists were convinced that moral reform efforts had failed. Even Whipper had concluded that it was "not the lack of elevation, but complexion that deprived the man of color of equal treatment." They also abandoned a reliance on moral suasion, coming to understand that more assertive methods were needed. Many shared the view of Peter Paul Simons of Brooklyn that "physical and political efforts are the only methods left for us to adopt."

Black abolitionists were also disillusioned by the shortcomings of their white allies. They increasingly recognized that many white abolitionists were tainted by racism and lacked substantial commitment to racial equality. Theodore S. Wright of New York complained that his white colleagues "overlooked the giant sin of prejudice . . . at once the parent and the offspring of slavery." They criticized white allies for their paternalism and prejudice, sensing that they "presumed to *think* for, dictate to, and *know* better what suited colored people, than they know for themselves." They bristled at their secondary position in the movement—the AASS leadership was almost exclusively white, black agents were usually paid less than whites in similar positions, black lecturers were sometimes told what to say, and black clerks in antislavery offices remained mired in subservient positions.

Black abolitionists were also concerned about the factional feuding within the movement that diverted white abolitionists from the central task of freeing the slaves. The AASS splintered in 1840 over matters of tactics and goals. Garrisonians and more conservative abolitionists differed on questions of gender equality, criticism of the churches for supporting slavery, and the question of whether moral suasion should continue to be the sole means for ending bondage. By 1840 the two groups had moved beyond compromise. The dissidents walked out of the annual AASS convention and soon formed the American and Foreign Anti-Slavery Society as a rival to the AASS and the Liberty Party, in order to run antislavery candidates for office. Black abolitionists hoped to avoid these internecine squabbles and sought a return to more unified action. They saw all questions except slavery and racism as relatively unimportant, but their white allies pressured them to choose sides. Some sided with the Garrisonians or were attracted to the religious orthodoxy of the American and Foreign Anti-Slavery Society or the political abolitionism of the Liberty Party. Others decided to work alone, remaining independent of the white organizations. They sought greater autonomy, working with white allies when it suited their purposes or independently when that best served the cause. Many remembered that they had worked without white collaboration before 1830.

More than the relationship between black and white abolitionists changed after 1840. A new generation of African American activists emerged, filling a void left by the death or declining involvement of such prominent figures as William Hamilton and Peter Williams of New York, Nathaniel Paul of Albany, James Forten of Philadelphia, Samuel Cornish of New Jersey, and William Watkins of Baltimore. Whereas most of the key black abolitionists before 1840 had been free blacks, a high percentage of these new activists were former slaves—such individuals as Frederick Douglass, William Wells Brown, Samuel Ringgold Ward, Henry Highland Garnet, Jermain W. Loguen, James W. C. Pennington, Henry Bibb, and

Lewis and Milton Clarke came to dominate the movement. And the center of black abolitionism shifted westward. Black abolitionists from such western towns as Buffalo, Syracuse, Rochester, Pittsburgh, Cleveland, Cincinnati, Chicago, and Detroit assumed prominent roles in the fight against slavery.

These new leaders frequently worked independently of their white allies through such community institutions as the black church, the black convention movement, and the black press. Black churches often doubled as meeting places and centers for organized abolitionist activity. They became sites for protest gatherings, antislavery lectures, and planning sessions, and often housed black presses. Many were regular stops on the Underground Railroad and provided sanctuary for fleeing fugitives. The black convention movement took on new life at both the national and state level during the 1840s, creating statewide networks for challenging a variety of black laws and other racial inequalities.

The black press was also rejuvenated during the decade. The *Colored American*, which had been founded in 1837 by Samuel Cornish, soon illustrated how an independent print voice could stimulate independent action by black abolitionists. It openly challenged slavery and racism and urged black leaders to "speak out in THUNDER TONES." Establishing the pattern that black papers had followed prior to the Civil War, it functioned as an antislavery journal and a mouthpiece for the particular concerns of black communities. Abandoning their reliance on the *Liberator* and other white journals, black abolitionists established and supported a number and variety of black newspapers in the 1840s and 1850s, including the *North Star*, *Frederick Douglass' Paper*, the *Impartial Freeman*, the *Voice of the Fugitive*, the *Provincial Freeman*, the *Aliened American*, and several others. By the end of the 1850s, the *Weekly Anglo-African* sought to be an independent national voice for the entire African American population.

Black abolitionists also adopted new measures to combat slavery and racism in the 1840s and 1850s. These included petition campaigns, lawsuits, legislative appeals, and economic pressure. When these tactics failed, even more confrontational methods were used. A great deal of energy was invested in political action, in the belief that politics could be "a mighty Anti-Slavery engine." The push for suffrage became a focus of state black conventions in the 1840s and 1850s, at which statewide campaigns for black suffrage were organized in Michigan, Iowa, Indiana, Ohio, Connecticut, Pennsylvania, and New York. To gain the ballot, they petitioned, lobbied legislators, distributed printed appeals, and rallied the black community through the press. Black abolitionists in New York developed an extensive statewide network of suffrage organizations at the local, county, and state levels. In 1860 there were sixty-six black suffrage clubs in New York City and Brooklyn alone. Where voting was possible, these leaders used political action to advance civil rights, challenge black laws, and fight slavery, working at different times and in different places through the Whig, Liberty, Free-Soil, and Republican parties. A few black abolitionists even ran for local or statewide office on the Liberty and Free-Soil tickets.

More militant tactics were also explored. When moral suasion and political action failed to overturn discriminatory laws and practices, black abolitionists increasingly turned to more forceful means after 1840. They deliberately challenged Jim Crow seating practices on railroads and in streetcars in nearly every northern state, sitting in cars reserved for whites and forcing whites to eject or arrest them. A massive 1843 campaign against Massachusetts's three railroads ended segregated seating practices on common carriers in that state. Segregated school systems were also targeted. Robert Purvis refused to pay his school tax until the schools of Byberry, Pennsylvania, were integrated. African Americans in New York and Massachusetts boycotted and petitioned against Jim Crow schools for the same purpose. Under the leadership of William C. Nell, blacks in Boston mounted a decade-long protest against segregated schools, employing mass meetings, editorials, picketing, boycotts, petition campaigns, and legal action (the unsuccessful Roberts v. City of Boston case in 1849). School segregation was finally ended in 1855 by action of the state legislature.

More and more, black abolitionists debated the value of violence. During the 1830s they had generally suppressed talk about force and the shedding of blood at the prompting of their white allies, but some black leaders moved toward open advocacy of violent means in the 1840s and 1850s. Garrison's calls for nonviolent resistance seemed increasingly irrelevant as federal efforts to enforce fugitive slave laws threatened black communities and left few alternatives to using violence in self-defense. Black abolitionists also endorsed slave violence, openly celebrating such rebels such Denmark Vesey, Nat Turner, Joseph Cinque of the Amistad, and Madison Washington of the Creole as cultural heroes, often comparing them favorably to America's Revolutionary fathers. Henry Highland Garnet openly called for slave violence at the 1843 black national convention; the delegates defeated a measure to endorse this recommendation by only a single vote. At first, many black abolitionists distanced themselves from Garnet's call. But by the 1850s most had become convinced that slavery was too deeply rooted in American soil to be eliminated by peaceful means.

Crisis of Union. Political events of the 1850s—the Fugitive Slave Law of 1850; the Kansas-Nebraska Act, which reopened all of the western territories to slavery; the campaign to reopen the Atlantic slave trade; and the Dred Scott decision—disheartened many black abolitionists and led them to again question the progress of the antislavery cause. Southern slaveholders seemed to control the federal government, and antislavery progress seemed to be stalled, if not reversed. Particularly troubling was the Fugitive Slave Law and the Dred Scott decision. The former put the federal government in the business of catching and returning runaway slaves and threatened fugitives and free blacks alike. The latter, the Supreme Court case of Dred Scott v. Sandford (1857), affirmed the constitutionality of slavery in the western territories and denied black claims to American citizenship. Faced with these events during the decade of the 1850s, black abolitionists were forced to rethink their fundamental assumptions about slavery and race and to ponder their future as American citizens. Neither condition nor complexion seemed to adequately account for the depth and complexity of American racism. Neither moral suasion nor political action, or even violence, seemed to offer an adequate solution. Surveying twenty-five years of antislavery efforts, Charles Lenox Remond cynically labeled them "complete failures."

By the end of the decade the crises of the 1850s had stirred black abolitionists' interest in leaving the United States for a more welcoming place. Many looked to Canada as a temporary haven. Thousands of runaway slaves threatened with the Fugitive Slave Law sought new lives there. Others, such as Martin Robison Delany and James T. Holly, looked abroad to Haiti or West Africa. The black republics in the Caribbean as well as such African locations as Liberia and the Niger Valley were relatively enticing. Delany and Holly saw these as prime locations in which to develop a black nationhood that might work against slavery from a distance. Most black abolitionists, however, agreed with William T. Still, who believed that "the duty to *stay here and fight it out* seems paramount." Nevertheless, few African Americans were hopeful about their future in the United States. By 1860, even such confirmed opponents of emigration as Whipper and Douglass toyed with the idea of leaving the country.

The coming of the Civil War in 1861 restored African American hopes for Emancipation and equality. Black abolitionists saw in the conflict a real opportunity to end slavery and advance the fortunes of the race. They pressed the administration of Abraham Lincoln to enlist black troops in the Union army and to adopt Emancipation as a war goal. After these gains had both been achieved by 1863, blacks fulfilled many roles in the war effort. Some, like Martin Robison Delany and H. Ford Douglas, enlisted in black regiments. Others recruited for the Union cause, helping to fill the rosters of such regiments as the Fifty-

Fourth and Fifty-Fifth Massachusetts Infantry Regiments and other all-black units. They traveled thousands of miles addressing rallies across the North and signing up individual enlistees. Many, particularly black women activists, raised funds for black soldiers and the freedmen. They were at the center of relief efforts for the contrabands, collecting food, supplies, clothing, money, and medicine. Dozens of black abolitionists streamed southward to open schools and establish churches in the areas of the Confederacy occupied by Union forces. Like John Oliver of Boston, the first black teacher sent south by the American Missionary Association, they believed that "the work of Anti-Slavery men is not yet compleat [sic]" until the former slaves were ready to assume their full role and rights as American citizens. They continued to push for an end to slavery until that became a reality a few months after the cannons were stilled.

Black abolitionists emerged from the war mindful of the need for continued activism. They recognized that the Thirteenth Amendment offered "nothing but freedom" to the race; racial equality still eluded African Americans throughout the nation. The failure of the federal government to grant blacks full civil and political rights and to parcel out confiscated Confederate land to the freedmen left them disillusioned. So, too, did the readiness of their white allies to abandon the fight. The guns had barely fallen silent at Appomattox before Garrison and other white abolitionists called for dismantling antislavery organizations and shutting down antislavery journals, arguing that the work of abolition was done. Black abolitionists harbored no such illusions. Garnet argued in 1865 that "the battle has just begun in which the fate of the black race in this country is to be decided." Douglass contended that "the work does not end with the abolition of slavery but only begins." With such questions as racial equality, civil rights, the vote, and a fair Reconstruction unanswered, they understood that a great deal of work still lay ahead. In 1873 white abolitionists gathered in Chicago for a reunion to celebrate their roles in ending slavery and to consider their legacy. Black abolitionists, however, observing the piecemeal dismantling of Reconstruction in the South at that time, continued to battle for the equality that America had promised in its founding document.

[See also Abolitionism; Africa, Idea of; African Americans and the West; African Methodist Episcopal Church; American Anti-Slavery Society; American and Foreign Anti-Slavery Society; American Colonization Society; American Missionary Association; American Revolution; Amistad; Antislavery Movement; Antislavery Press; Baltimore, Maryland, Slavery in; Bibb, Henry W.; Birney, James Gillespie; Black Church; Black Nationalism; Black Press; Black Uplift; Canada; Civil Rights; Civil War; Civil War, Participation and Recruitment of Black Troops in; Class; Colonization; Constitution, U.S.; Cornish, Samuel; Delany, Martin Robison; Detroit; Discrimination; Douglass, Frederick; Dred Scott Case; Education; Emancipation; Emancipation Proclamation; Emigration to Africa; Entrepreneurs; Fifty-Fifth Massachusetts Infantry Regiment; Fifty-Fourth Massachusetts Infantry Regiment; Forten, James; Frederick Douglass' Paper; Free African Americans before the Civil War (North); Free African Americans before the Civil War (South); Free-Soil Party; Freedmen; Fugitive Slave Law of 1850; Garnet, Henry Highland; Garrison, William Lloyd; Garrisonian Abolitionists; Gender; Haiti; Immigrants; Integration; Jacobs, Harriet; Jim Crow Car Laws; Kansas-Nebraska Act; Laws and Legislation, Liberia; Liberty Party; Lincoln, Abraham; Literature; Loguen, Jermain Wesley; Lynching and Mob Violence; Massachusetts Anti-Slavery Society; Military; Moral Suasion; Myers, Stephen A.; National Conventions of Colored Men; Nell, William Cooper; North Star; Oratory and Verbal Arts; Pennington, James W. C.; Political Participation; Poverty; Progress; Purvis, Robert; Racism; Radical Abolitionist Party; Reconstruction; Reform; Religion; Religion and Slavery; Remond, Charles Lenox; Republican Party; Resistance; Riots and Rebellions; Roberts v. City of Boston; Ruggles, David; Segregation; Slave Narratives; Slave Resistance; Slavery; Slavery and the U.S. Constitution; Society of Friends (Quakers); Stereotypes of African Americans; Still, William; Stowe, Harriet Beecher; Supreme Court; Thirteenth Amendment; Truth, Sojourner; Tubman, Harriet; Turner, Nat; Uncle Tom's Cabin; Underground Railroad; Union Army, African Americans in; Urbanization; Violence against African Americans; Voting Rights; Walker, David; Ward, Samuel Ringgold; Whig Party; Whipper, William; Women; and Work.]

BIBLIOGRAPHY

Andrews, William L. To Tell a Free Story: The First Century of Afro-American Autobiography, 1760–1865. Urbana: University of Illinois Press, 1986. An overview of the slave narratives.

Blackett, R. J. M. Building an Antislavery Wall: Black Americans in the Atlantic Abolitionist Movement, 1830–1860. Baton Rouge: Louisiana State University Press, 1983. A study of the black abolitionists who visited the British Isles.

Bruce, Dickson D., Jr. The Origins of African American Literature, 1680–1865. Charlottesville: University Press of Virginia, 2001. Includes several good chapters on the slave narratives as well as fiction and nonfiction by black abolitionists.

Finkenbine, Roy E. "Boston's Black Churches: Institutional Centers of the Antislavery Movement." In Courage and Conscience: Black and White Abolitionists in Boston, edited by Donald M. Jacobs, 169–189. Bloomington: Indiana University Press, 1993.

Gara, Larry. "The Professional Fugitive in the Abolition Movement." Wisconsin Magazine of History 26 (1965): 196–204.

Griffler, Keith P. Frontline of Freedom: African Americans and the Forging of the Underground Railroad in the Ohio Valley. Lexington: University Press of Kentucky, 2004.

Hinks, Peter P. *To Awaken My Afflicted Brethren: David Walker and the Problem of Antebellum Slave Resistance*. University Park: Pennsylvania State University Press, 1997.

Horton, James Oliver, and Lois E. Horton. *Black Bostonians: Family Life and Community Struggle in the Antebellum North*. New York: Holmes and Meier, 1979. A study of a key community of northern activists.

Hutton, Frankie. *The Early Black Press in America, 1827 to 1860*. Westport, CT: Greenwood, 1993. Discusses the major black abolitionist journals.

McFeely, William S. *Frederick Douglass*. New York: Norton, 1991. The best biography of the leading black abolitionist.

Newman, Richard S. *The Transformation of American Abolitionism: Fighting Slavery in the Early Republic*. Chapel Hill: University of North Carolina Press, 2002. Includes a chapter on the use of petitions and protest pamphlets by early black abolitionists.

Pease, Jane H., and William H. Pease. *They Who Would Be Free: Blacks' Search for Freedom, 1830–1861*. New York: Athenaeum, 1974.

Quarles, Benjamin. *Black Abolitionists*. New York: Oxford University Press, 1969.

Rael, Patrick. *Black Identity and Black Protest in the Antebellum North*. Chapel Hill: University of North Carolina Press, 2002.

Ripley, C. Peter, ed. *The Black Abolitionist Papers, 1830–1865*. 5 vols. Chapel Hill: University of North Carolina Press, 1985–1992. Reprints most of the key documents by black abolitionists except for those of Frederick Douglass.

Ripley, C. Peter, Roy E. Finkenbine, Michael F. Hembree, and Donald Yacovone, eds. *Witness for Freedom: African American Voices on Race, Slavery, and Emancipation*. Chapel Hill: University of North Carolina Press, 1993. A good collection of documents by black abolitionists.

Swift, David Everett. *Black Prophets of Justice: Activist Clergy before the Civil War*. Baton Rouge: Louisiana State University Press, 1989.

Switala, William J. *Underground Railroad in Pennsylvania*. Mechanicsburg, PA: Stackpole Books, 2001. Includes information on black Underground Railroad agents in the eastern part of the network.

Winch, Julie. *Philadelphia's Black Elite: Activism, Accommodation, and the Struggle for Autonomy, 1787–1848*. Philadelphia: Temple University Press, 1988. Another useful study of a key community of black activists.

Yee, Shirley J. *Black Women Abolitionists: A Study in Activism, 1828–1860*. Knoxville: University of Tennessee Press, 1992.

—ROY E. FINKENBINE

BLACK BRIGADE. The Black Brigade was a military unit of at least eighty-two black men, women, and children who made up the last group of black Loyalists to leave New York City on 23 November 1783, known as Evacuation Day. Their final departure did not actually occur until a week later, when their ship, HMS *L'Abondance*, commanded by a Lieutenant Philips, finally cleared New York Harbor bound for Halifax, Nova Scotia, and freedom.

Assembled in New York City in the early 1780s and composed of black Loyalists from many of the former colonies, the Black Brigade was an elite fighting unit. Their status in the wake of the Revolutionary War, however, was a point of contention between the United States and England. The Black Brigade was listed in the "Book of Negroes," an agreement between General George Washington and Sir Guy Carleton, the commander in chief of British forces in North America. This agreement was created under article 7 of the peace treaty ending the American Revolution, which required both sides to return enemy property. At least three thousand black Loyalists left New York on English ships in 1783. As Washington and other Americans regarded black Loyalists as "property" while the British perceived them as soldiers freed by several proclamations made by English generals and governors during the war, the Book of Negroes was a list used for negotiations. In fact, such negotiations turned acrimonious and would affect Anglo-American relations for nearly thirty years.

The Black Brigade comprised at least two types of informal but valuable black military units that contributed to British war efforts. The first were "Black Shot" units composed wholly of armed slaves. The British first used Black Shot groups in Jamaica in the 1740s and 1750s and then again during the American Revolution. The second were "Black Corps" groups, which were special units of freed slaves, free blacks, and mulattoes. Both groups were auxiliaries to regular militia units or worked as rangers who could transfer between war zones to meet special crises.

New York was an incessant trouble zone in the early 1780s. After the defeat of the British general Charles Lord Cornwallis in 1781, peace became standard in other regions, yet the area around New York, known as the "Neutral Zone," continually erupted into civil war over the following two years. The Black Brigade specialized in quick probes into American-controlled territory in Upstate New York and eastern New Jersey. Along with the legendary guerrilla leader Colonel Tye and other freelancers, the Black Brigade raided Patriot homes and set up log-house forts along the Hudson River and on Sandy Hook, from which they regulated traffic and protected British forces in New York City. The Black Brigade propped up the fading hopes of white Loyalists in the region by assisting them in attacks on Patriot positions along the New Jersey coast in 1782.

The Black Brigade, along with other African Americans who supported the Crown in the American Revolution, received coveted passports known as General Birch Certificates, named after Samuel Birch, the British officer who granted them. These passes allowed bearers to board British ships bound for Nova Scotia. The certificates listed the bearers' names, ages, brief descriptions, and the dates upon which they had left their masters. The British commander Carleton had decided that any black who had joined the British before 1782 was entitled to protection and passage. The information included in the General Birch Certificates revealed the ability of members of the

Black Brigade to survive during wartime: For example, the Jones family left their masters in Monmouth County, New Jersey, in 1778. Thomas Cairnes, a twenty-two-year-old member, ran away from his master in South Carolina in 1775. Peter and Kate Harding left their masters in Virginia in 1776; their son Ebenezar was born free "within the British lines" and so was also entitled to passage.

The Black Brigade helped police the streets of New York City during the evacuation and prevented former masters from retaking self-emancipated slaves. When the British turned over the city to the Americans in November 1783, members of the Black Brigade were the last to depart. They left one last message: As General Washington and his troops marched down Bowery Road to Broadway to the tip of Manhattan Island, they found a British flag still flying atop a high pole. The Black Brigade had greased the pole, making it very difficult to climb. At length, one Patriot covered himself with dirt in order to ascend the pole and take down the flag. The members of the Black Brigade watched from the harbor until their ship sailed away to freedom.

[*See also* American Revolution; Black Loyalists; Blucke, Stephen; Colonel Tye; Free African Americans to 1828; *and* Military.]

BIBLIOGRAPHY

Hodges, Graham Russell, ed. *The Black Loyalist Directory: African Americans in Exile after the American Revolution.* New York: Garland, 1995.

—GRAHAM RUSSELL GAO HODGES

BLACK CHURCH. Any discussion of the early black church rightfully begins with an examination of the nature of the church. A debate began in the mid-twentieth century over this question, which centered on the presence or absence in the African American church of Africanisms—that is, indigenous African religious practices. In his seminal work *The Myth of the Negro Past*, Melville J. Herskovits argues vehemently for the strong presence of African traditions and practices in the early black Christian experience in North America. His argument is an attempt to refute the myth that black Americans' roots in Africa were of no consequence and were inferior to European-based culture. Herskovits's position, however, has had many critics, including E. Franklin Frazier, a noted black sociologist of the late twentieth century. Frazier and others have argued that the enslavement process (capture, sale, the Middle Passage, and "seasoning") almost completely stripped Africans of their native cultures; therefore, the African American culture that developed in the American colonies and later in the United States was a black adaptation of the dominant white culture.

Heskovits and Frazier represent the extreme ends of this issue. Albert J. Raboteau, in *Slave Religion*, offers a thesis that blends the two views. Like Frazier, he denies the existence of freestanding Africanisms that pulled black churches together, but he is unwilling to reject all of Herskovits's examples as meaningless. Rather, Raboteau argues that early African Americans reinterpreted their African traditions in light of their new experience with European Christianity. In support of this thesis, Raboteau cites practices in early black congregations such as ring dancing and singing, antiphonal participation, and hand clapping, which had their roots in the African experience but took on new significance in the black Christian churches.

The process of reinterpretation did not occur overnight, nor did it occur early in the colonial period, because of several interrelated factors. Practically speaking, seventeenth- and early-eighteenth-century churches were not open to blacks. Although there is evidence of black members of traditional white Christian churches prior to the 1740s, their numbers were not significant. It was not that the leadership of white churches did not want to convert blacks, free and slave, to their respective churches. They were, in fact, motivated to seek the conversion of the blacks. First, they were motivated by politics. Protestants, especially the English, were concerned that through their efforts to convert blacks, Spanish and French Catholics might gain the allegiance of the slaves and thus threaten the security of the Protestant colonies. More importantly, religion became a means to justify the institution of slavery for both Catholics and Protestants. Many clergy and nonclergy argued that slavery was proper and necessary to effect the conversion of Africans and thereby save their souls. Thus, many religious and secular leaders and groups, such as England's Charles II and the Anglican Church's Society for the Propagation of the Gospel in Foreign Parts (SPG), pressed their representatives in the colonies to convert both slaves and free blacks.

Despite this official policy favoring the conversion of blacks, there were many obstacles to making the policy a reality. The scarcity of ministers and resources caused local churches to focus on their existing white congregations, leaving few ministers for missionary work. The SPG, which provided Anglican ministers to the American colonies, and the Amsterdam classis, which provided ministers and oversight to the Dutch Reformed churches in New York, were besieged with more requests for ministers to care for their followers in the American colonies than they were capable of filling. This problem was further complicated by the environment in which ministers in the colonies had to work. Because parishes or churches were likely to encompass several hundred square miles, ministers required several weeks or even months to visit believers within their assigned territories. Given such requirements, little time or attention could or would be given to the conversion of blacks.

Possibly the greatest impediment to the conversion of slaves was the slave owners themselves. Initially, many slave owners refused to allow ministers of any denomination to have contact with their slaves for fear that conversion would lead to emancipation. This fear was not unfounded because there was legal precedent saying that one Christian could not hold another Christian in a state of slavery. In an attempt to address this concern and further the official policy favoring conversion, by the early eighteenth century the legislatures in at least six colonies enacted laws that stated that conversion to Christianity had no effect on the status of a slave.

Slave owners, however, had other reasons for opposing the conversion of their slaves. Before being baptized, a slave had to undergo a lengthy period of instruction. Slave owners viewed this process as economically damaging because it interfered with the productivity of slaves. Why should the owner forgo profits for the sake of the slave's soul? This question makes the underlying issue very apparent: owners believed that slaves were incapable of being instructed in Christianity or anything else beyond their menial tasks. In the eyes of the owners, slaves were "brutes," no different from farmyard beasts of burden. Finally, owners feared that if their slaves were converted to Christianity, the slaves would see themselves as equal to their owners. This would make them "saucy," or proud. Such feelings would make them ungovernable and eventually lead to rebellion.

The final barrier to the conversion of African Americans in the early colonial period would become a catalyst for the conversion of many blacks during the Great Awakening, the revivalist movement that swept over the American colonies about the middle of the eighteenth century. The formal environment of the American Protestant churches of the early colonial period was not inviting to blacks, free or slave. The conversion process in these churches was largely based on a formal process of instruction; on the other hand, African Americans viewed religion as an experience. When some white ministers began to emphasize the religious experience of conversion during the Great Awakening, a connection arose between white churches and African American traditions.

Early Black Presence in American Churches. Blacks began to appear in colonial Christian congregations soon after their arrival in Jamestown, Virginia, in 1619. Nevertheless, the number who came into the Christian churches during this early period was relatively small. One of the earliest references to the admission of a slave into the Puritan Congregational Church in Massachusetts was in 1641. Fifty years later, Cotton Mather established the Society of Negroes in Boston to provide Christian instruction to free blacks and slaves. In 1701 the Anglican Church formed the SPG to proselytize blacks and Native Americans. Both groups emphasized the intellectual experience of "knowing" one's religion. Neither effort gained real success.

Other denominations can also point to an early black presence. Emanuel, possibly a free black, was baptized into the Lutheran Church in New York in 1699. He was followed by Are Van Guinea and his wife, Jora. The Guineas, both of whom were free, later moved to the Raritan Valley in New Jersey and played a significant role in founding the Mountain congregation.

Blacks were also present in the colonial Roman Catholic Church because of their status as slaves who were owned by Catholic clergy and religious orders. The Jesuits in Maryland owned slaves as early as 1717, and the Ursulines, a French order of nuns who came to New Orleans in 1727, also became slave owners. Under the teachings of the Catholic Church during this period, it was the responsibility of slave owners to provide religious instruction for their slaves.

The most distinct anomaly during the colonial period was the Society of Friends, or the Quakers. As the first religious denomination to condemn slavery, without reservation, in 1688, the Quakers began to continually and vehemently voice their opposition to slavery. They also established schools for slaves and free blacks but did little or nothing to attract blacks into their congregations.

By the 1730s there were few blacks in any Christian church, and those who did belong were in predominantly white congregations. However, this period marked the origin of the black church in the Great Awakening. The historian Gary B. Nash writes in *Urban Crucible* that the first Great Awakening was "a profound cultural crisis involving the convergence of political, social, economic, and ideological forces that had been building for several generations." Beginning by at least the 1730s, the Great Awakening was an eruption of egalitarianism that challenged the established ecclesiastical authorities and opened the door for greater involvement in religion by everyone. The followers of George Whitefield, an Anglican missionary who helped initiate the Great Awakening, spread throughout the colonies, preaching extemporaneously to great crowds outside the physical and theological confines of the established churches. Despite these early origins, the Great Awakening only reached its peak in the South as the eighteenth century came to a close.

During this period the growth in church membership, particularly in the South, occurred primarily in the Baptist and Methodist congregations. According to estimates by Christine Heyrman in *Southern Cross*, although whites remained the clear majority in both denominations, black membership grew at greater percentage rates from 1790 to 1813. The increases that these churches saw in black membership in both the North and South resulted, at least in part, from the religious enthusiasm that was an integral part of the revivals sponsored by Baptists and Methodists. During the Great Awakening, most of the converts, black and white, were illiterate and did not approach life on an intellectual basis. Therefore, the majority of converts viewed their conversions as emotional, not intellectual, experiences. Typically, the convert's experience was the result of an individual response to the emotional pleadings and condemnations of a preacher, sometimes an African American, who focused on the experiential nature of the conversion process. The acceptance of religious enthusiasm by white Christian churches opened the door for blacks to engage in their African practices of enthusiasm, clapping, and antiphonal responses in the context of a Christian church. This positive experience brought many blacks into Christian churches. Unfortunately, racial prejudice and the practice of segregation later forced them to establish their own churches.

Rise of Independent Black Churches. The rise of independent black churches was a phenomenon of the late eighteenth and early nineteenth centuries that was accomplished over time and varied for each group. It occurred primarily in the Baptist and Methodist traditions. Other denominations, notably the Catholic Church, had sizable numbers of African Americans in some congregations, but blacks remained part of the white-dominated congregations, even when whites were the minority. Furthermore, the rise of independent black Baptist or Methodist churches did not mean that a majority of blacks left their white-dominated congregations. Nevertheless, the black churches represent an important part of the American religious experience.

The Baptist Church in North America dates from Roger Williams's founding efforts in Providence, Rhode Island, in the mid-1600s. The first known black Baptist, Quassey, appeared as a member of the Baptist Church in Newton, Rhode Island, in 1743. Thereafter, nineteen black members joined the Providence Baptist Church in 1762, and blacks came into the First Baptist Church of Boston in 1772. These examples, however, represent a small number of blacks in white-dominated congregations. The first black congregations developed in the South. Reputedly, the first black Baptist congregation, the African Baptist or Bluestone Church, was established by slaves in 1758 on William Byrd's plantation near the Bluestone River in Mecklenburg, Virginia. Sometime between 1773 and 1775

George Liele, a slave who converted during a revival, established the Silver Bluff Baptist Church in South Carolina on the Savannah River near Augusta, Georgia. Liele became a Baptist preacher, was freed by his owner, and immigrated to Jamaica sometime between 1782 and 1783, leaving a number of disciples behind him, including Andrew Bryan and Jesse Peters (also known as Jesse Galphin). These men became responsible for building the early black Baptist congregations. In 1788 Bryan, with the assistance of Peters, organized the Ethiopian Church of Jesus Christ, which was renamed the First African Baptist Church of Savannah a couple of years later. Peters became pastor of the Springfield Baptist Church of Augusta, Georgia, in the late 1780s. Numerous other black congregations followed in the Virginia cities of Williamsburg, Richmond, and Petersburg. By 1800 there were over twenty-five thousand black Baptists.

The development of black Baptist congregations was in large part the result of the organizational rules of the Baptist Church. Compared with other Protestant denominations, such as the Methodists and Presbyterians, the Baptist Church was much less centralized and had no requirement that each congregation be part of some central authority or association. After 1800 the growth of these independent black Baptist congregations decreased as Revolutionary fervor subsided and unrest within the slave community expanded. Notable examples of this development were the Gabriel conspiracy in 1800, the Denmark Vesey conspiracy in 1822, and Nat Turner's revolt in 1831. Plantation owners and other slaveholders viewed black congregations as allowing slaves to come together to hatch their rebellious plans. They responded by imposing rules that restricted slaves' ability to travel and limited the number of slaves that could gather in one place at one time. The rules seriously limited the growth of black Baptist congregations in the South.

In the North most new black churches were Methodist. After the 1730s Methodist societies developed in the American colonies, although the church was not formally established until later. Blacks were among the charter members of the first society founded in Frederick County, Maryland, in 1764, and a black servant, Betty, was among the charter members of the Joy Street Society in New York in 1776. Blacks were attracted by the enthusiastic spirit of Methodism and its opposition to slavery that John Wesley announced in 1743 in his "General Rules."

The American Methodist Church was formally organized at the General Conference of 1784, now known as the Christmas Conference. The leadership during this early period fell to Bishop Francis Asbury, who traveled extensively throughout the new states, often in the company of Harry "Black Harry" Hosier, an early black Methodist preacher. The Christmas Conference adopted

African Episcopal Church of St. Thomas in Philadelphia, "a Sunday morning view taken in June 1829." The artist was William L. Breton. (Historical Society of Pennsylvania.)

Wesley's condemnation of slavery, but within a few years the American Methodist Church began to reverse itself, declaring that slavery was a matter of individual conscience. Many Methodist churches in the North then began to segregate their congregations. Some historians have argued that the practice of segregation in churches in the colonial period originated with the Anglicans. That may be true, but the practice in the other denominations resulted independently from the internal policy of each church, not from any Anglican influence. Moreover, the practice of segregation in the Methodist Church was the primary impetus for the rise of independent black Methodist churches.

Although some historians dispute the assertion, the first independent black Methodist church was probably the lit-

tle known and relatively small African Union Church, which was founded by Peter Spencer (1782–1843), referred to as Father Spencer. Spencer was born a slave in Kent County, Maryland, and as a young man he moved to Wilmington, Delaware, where he soon became a fervent member of the Asbury Methodist Episcopal Church. He also quickly became disenchanted by the racial prejudice and resulting segregation practiced in the church. In 1805 he secured separate premises for the black members of the congregation. Named Ezion, the black church continued to operate within the Methodist Episcopal governing structure. Spencer and the Ezion congregation soon found that physically separating the races did not resolve their problems. The white leadership of the Asbury congregation refused to allow the blacks to participate in the business of running their church or even in selecting their pastor.

Although Spencer did not establish Ezion with the intention of forming a separate, independent church, after several years of litigation, in which the blacks lost their building, he and other members of his church recorded formal legal documents announcing their independence in 1813. The church was formally known as the Union Church of Africans and was later referred to simply as the African Union Church. Spencer continued to lead the church until his death.

Another independent black Methodist church and a black Episcopal congregation arose somewhat simultaneously in Philadelphia. These developments were the result of the segregation that led Richard Allen, Absalom Jones, and other black members to walk out of Saint George's Methodist Church in Philadelphia in 1787. Richard Allen (1760–1831) was a former slave who had converted to Methodism and served as an itinerant preacher in Delaware, Maryland, New Jersey, and Pennsylvania. He and Harry Hosier were the only blacks to attend the Christmas Conference of 1784. He then served as the preacher for the black members of Saint George's congregation. Absalom Jones (1746–1818) was the son of a house slave in Sussex, Delaware. He taught himself to read using the New Testament. At the age of sixteen he was sold to a store owner in Philadelphia and attended a night school for blacks operated by the Quakers.

The two men founded the Free African Society and built a church that was dedicated in 1794. Jones and many of his followers were accepted into the Protestant Episcopal Church of the United States of America. Their Philadelphia congregation became known as the African Protestant Episcopal Church of Saint Thomas. Jones was ordained a deacon in the Episcopal Church in 1795 and a priest in 1801. He remained the rector of Saint Thomas's until his death. Other African American congregations were established in the Protestant Episcopal Church and remained self-determining.

Richard Allen, however, was a devout Methodist, and along with a number of his followers, he separated from Jones and his Episcopalian congregation. He then began a nearly twenty-year period of constructing the African Methodist Episcopal (AME) Church. He brought together representatives of black Methodist congregations from Baltimore to New Jersey who had also been discriminated against by their parent white congregations. The AME Church was formally established on 9 April 1816 in Philadelphia with about one thousand members, but under the leadership of Allen, who became its first bishop, the membership grew to more than nine thousand by 1822, with congregations stretching from Washington, D.C., to Pittsburgh, Pennsylvania.

The AME Church was not the only black Methodist church that arose in this period. By the early 1790s blacks composed approximately 40 percent of the John Street Methodist Episcopal Church congregation in New York City. As in Philadelphia, however, the black members of the congregation were not permitted full participation in their church and were relegated to the rear and gallery of the church for services. The congregation also refused to ordain a black as a full preacher. Reacting to this treatment, in 1796 many black members established their own African chapel. By 1801 they had constructed a new church, Zion, and their own congregation, the African Methodist Church of the City of New York, under the leadership of Peter Williams Jr. and Francis Jacobs. The group was formally incorporated and the church property placed under the control of a board of trustees, whose members were required to be black members of the church.

In 1820 Zion Church and the Asbury African Methodist Episcopal Church of New York refused to affiliate with the AME Church, and they formed their own independent African denomination. Nearly three decades later, to clarify their independent status, *Zion* became part of the official name of the congregation, the African Methodist Episcopal Zion (AME Zion) Church. Although 1820 is generally given as the date of origin for the AME Zion Church, the process of separating from the Methodist Episcopal Church took more than eight years. Much of the credit for the break has been given to the Reverend James Varick (1750–1827). Varick was born in Newburgh, New York, the son of a slave mother. When the Varick family moved to New York City, James received training as a shoemaker and joined the John Street Methodist Church in the late 1760s. It appears that he was licensed to preach to the black members of the John Street congregation.

At the first general meeting of the AME Zion Church in August 1820, the members decided that they would not be affiliated with the AME Church and they would not remain under white control. Varick was selected as the interim supervisor for the denomination in June 1821 and was formally ordained by the white Methodist leaders. In July 1822 he became supervisor of the church; this title was later changed to bishop. During this period Varick was a major advocate for the rights of African Americans. He appeared before the 1821 New York Constitutional Convention and argued for the right of blacks to vote. He also ran a school for black children in his home.

Throughout this early period the major independent black churches had been limited to the North, but in the aftermath of the Civil War the dynamics of the black church in America would change greatly. During the colonial and early national periods (from the 1620s to the 1820s) African Americans came to an understanding of the "church" in their own terms, but the word did not have a single definition. Some developed black congregations within white churches, while others left the white-dominated denominations and established independent black churches. The ensuing antebellum, Civil War, and Reconstruction periods were much more turbulent times, in which many churches, black and white, were forced to redefine themselves—sometimes more than once. During the antebellum period black churches expanded in the North and the South while facing different and severe limitations. During the Civil War northern black churches often attached missionaries to the Union Army and "invaded" the South, looking to extend their respective influence and membership. Finally, from the late 1860s to 1900 black churches in both the North and the South exploded in terms of denominations and membership.

Antebellum Period. Throughout the United States the several independent black churches that had arisen in the early national period of American history continued to exist, but their individual experience varied considerably. In the North the African Union Church continued under the leadership of its founder, the Reverend Peter Spencer, until his death in 1843. The church maintained its independence, but its growth was minimal, adding only a few congregations and continuing today to be relatively unknown. The African Protestant Episcopal Church of Saint Thomas in Philadelphia also faced serious challenges in its leadership. The church's founder and first rector, the Reverend Absalom Jones, died in 1818. The congregation was not an independent church; it had remained a member of the Protestant Episcopal Church, the successor to the Anglican Church in the United States. Although Saint Thomas Church continued to be a black congregation after the Reverend Jones's death, for a number of years it was presided over by a series of white priests because of the lack of black Episcopalian clergy. Finally, in 1834 the Reverend William Douglass was appointed to the church.

"The First African Church, Richmond, Virginia," interior view from the western wing. This wood engraving of a drawing by William Ludwell Sheppard appeared in *Harper's Weekly* on 27 June 1874. Sheppard (1833–1912), a veteran of the Confederacy, was known for his genre painting, his images of Confederate soldiers, and his numerous statues. (Library of Congress.)

Douglass (unrelated to Frederick Douglass) was an African American originally from Baltimore. He served for a time as a Methodist itinerant preacher but then joined the Episcopal Church. He was ordained a deacon in 1834 and elevated to the priesthood in 1836. He then accepted the rectorship of Saint Thomas Church and continued to care for his congregation until his death in 1861.

The African Methodist Episcopal (AME) Church was the fastest growing of the independent black churches in the North. It was led by its founder, the bishop Richard Allen, until his death in 1831. He was succeeded by the bishop Morris Brown, who was a dedicated opponent of slavery. He had earlier headed the AME Church in South Carolina and was allegedly an adviser to Denmark Vesey, a free black who conspired to lead a slave revolt that was exposed before it began in 1822. As a result of the foiled Denmark Vesey conspiracy, Brown was forced to flee north, the AME Church was suppressed in South Carolina, and the church's activities were limited to the North. Nevertheless, the church continued to grow. By the late 1830s its membership exceeded eight thousand, and its congregations approached one hundred, extending from Washington, D.C., on the East Coast to Pittsburgh, Pennsylvania, on the Ohio River.

The AME Church during this period began to focus on the importance of education for both its clergy and its children. The bishop Daniel Payne became the major advocate of this activity. Payne was born in Charleston, South Carolina, and opened a school for African American children in that city in 1829. In 1835 the state legislature made the teaching of free black and slave children illegal. Fleeing north, Payne for a time became associated with the Lutheran and Presbyterian churches before joining the AME Church at the invitation of Bishop Brown. He soon became the advocate for education in the AME Church. At the AME General Conference in 1841 he authored resolutions that established the educational requirements for its clergy and also developed the clergy's course of studies. He helped establish and served as the first president of the AME Church's first institution of higher learning, Wilberforce University, in southwestern Ohio in 1856. In the years after 1842 many individual AME congregations took up Payne's calls and established educational programs for their children.

The African Methodist Episcopal Zion Church did not grow as quickly as its older sister, but the church took on an important role in the battle against slavery. The organized movement against slavery came into being in 1832 with the establishment of the New England Anti-Slavery Society by William Lloyd Garrison, Lewis and Arthur Tappan, and other abolitionists. The AME Zion Church was intimately tied to the movement, which in 1834 shifted deeper into the religious sphere with the revolt at Lane Theological Seminary in Cincinnati, when white students left the school because authorities acted to limit antislavery activities there. The AME Zion Church took a militant position on the issue of slavery. A number of AME Zion churches between Pennsylvania and Canada became stations for the Underground Railroad, and several members of the AME Zion Church became important leaders in that movement. Harriet Tubman, for instance, was a "conductor" on the railroad to freedom. Frederick Douglass, a lay minister and class leader in the AME Zion Church in New Bedford, Massachusetts, became one the most vocal critics of slavery. Because of its association with the Underground Railroad, many people referred to the AME Zion Church as the "freedom church."

Structurally, it was easier for African Americans to establish independent congregations in the Baptist Church than in the Methodist Church. Every Methodist congregation had to be recognized by the hierarchy, but each Baptist congregation was independent, pursuant to Baptist teaching. Very early on, however, it became the practice of Baptist congregations to come together to form local associations and larger conventions. The earliest all-black Baptist association developed in the emerging American West. The Providence Association in Ohio was first in 1834, followed by the Union Association of Ohio in 1836, and the Wood River Association in Illinois in 1839. As the number of black Baptist churches in the North grew, the congregations and associations established the Colored Baptist Home Missionary Society in 1844, which led to the Western Colored Baptist Convention. The pattern of growth seen in independent black Baptist churches in the North would be repeated in the South after the Civil War.

The experience of black Presbyterians was similar to and yet quite different from those of the Methodists and Baptists. Like the Methodist Church, the Presbyterian Church was very centralized. However, unlike black Methodists, who had to leave the Methodist Church to establish independent congregations, black Presbyterians wishing to establish their own congregations could remain within the white-dominated church. In 1807 the General Assembly of the Presbyterian Church approved the licensing of John Gloucester, a former slave. Shortly thereafter Gloucester and a small group of his followers established the First African Presbyterian Church of Philadelphia. Then, throughout the North black Presbyterian congregations were established, several by Gloucester's sons. In 1822 Samuel Cornish, a freeborn African American from Delaware, founded the First Colored Presbyterian Church of New York, which congregation he served until 1828. His successor was Theodore Wright, who had graduated from Princeton Theological Seminary in 1820. Despite the best efforts of these men and others like them, black Presbyterian churches did not enjoy the growth experienced by black Methodist and Baptist churches. In the South, although white Presbyterian missionaries were sent to plantations to work with slaves, few independent black Presbyterian churches were established.

Black churches in the South faced unique challenges. For slave owners the practice of slavery necessarily carried with it the fear of slave revolts. During the first three decades of the nineteenth century that fear became a reality. In 1800 Gabriel, a slave owned by Thomas H. Prosser in Henrico County, Virginia, organized a failed slave revolt that culminated in the execution of twenty-six slaves. In 1811 Charles Deslondes, a free mulatto from Saint Domingue, led a rebellion in the vicinity of New Orleans that resulted in the death of two whites and destroyed a few plantations. Denmark Vesey, to draw recruits for a planned 1822 slave rebellion in Charleston, South Carolina, used biblical references and analogies comparing slaves to the Israelites held in slavery by the Egyptians to attract and encourage the support of slaves. Several of Vesey's supporters were members of Charleston's AME Church, including the future bishop Morris Brown. The thwarted Vesey conspiracy resulted in the execution of thirty-seven slaves and free blacks. Perhaps the bloodiest rebellion of the antebellum period was organized in 1831 by Nat Turner, a slave in Southampton County, Virginia, who was an unaffiliated slave preacher. As many as fifty-nine whites were killed in the event. When questioned by white authorities after his capture, Turner said that God had directed him to lead the revolt.

These events had a profound, negative effect on black churches in the South. Many slave owners had previously refused to allow their slaves to have any contact with religion. They had argued that to allow slaves to practice any religion would foster the belief that freedom was possible, and that such an impression could only lead to unrest. Unsuccessful slave revolts, especially those with religious overtones like the Vesey and Turner revolts, seemed to confirm the beliefs of many slave owners that religion was contrary to and disruptive of the practice of slavery. Thus white authorities, both secular and religious, initiated actions throughout the South that restricted the religious practices of free blacks and slaves.

In some instances southern black churches were closed. This happened in 1822 when the African (Methodist) Church of Charleston, South Carolina, was shut down after Vesey's failed conspiracy. The Williamsburg Baptist Church in Virginia, which was founded in the 1780s, was dissolved in 1831 as a result of the Nat Turner revolt. When suppression of black churches was not possible, other means of control were found. Such was the case in New Orleans when the mayor Charles Waterman's failed attempt to close the black churches in New Orleans led

to three black Methodist churches being placed under the control of white supervisors, who carefully scrutinized the sermons of African American preachers. Another example of white control of black churches in this period occurred in Virginia, soon after Vesey's failed revolt: white pastors were assigned to the pulpits of Richmond's four African Baptist churches and held those positions until after the Civil War.

Not all such efforts to eliminate or assume control of black churches in the South were successful. For example, to circumvent efforts to suppress their churches, the member congregations of Georgia's Sunbury Baptist Association entered into an agreement in 1832 that reconstituted them as branches of white churches; the agreement carefully provided that the black Baptist churches were to continue to be responsible for their own operations, free from interference by the white churches. Despite repressive efforts by the state governments and slave owners, free blacks and slaves continued to swell the numbers of blacks in both the Methodist and Baptist churches in the South, albeit not always in independent black churches.

Post–Civil War Period. The end of the Civil War had profound repercussions, both positive and negative, on black churches. Southern black churches experienced great growth, and the independent black churches of the North, which for decades had been barred from conducting missionary work in the South among slaves and free blacks, had the opportunity to bring the newly freed men and women within their respective folds. On the other hand, such growth was challenged by preachers who had ministered to plantation slaves and wished to maintain and expand their congregations free from the intrusion of established northern churches.

One of the first AME Zion missionaries, James Walker Hood, was raised in Pennsylvania. When he moved to New York he joined the African Union Church and was licensed as a preacher. After a subsequent move to New Haven, Connecticut, a city with no African Union congregation, he joined the AME Zion Church, which recognized his license to preach. In 1864 he went to New Berne (later called New Bern), North Carolina, as a missionary for the AME Zion Church and eight years later became a bishop. By 1874 his diocese had grown to 366 churches and had more than twenty thousand believers. A strong advocate of the black church, Hood believed that the church and its ministers should be role models for the development of strong black communities. His success was shared by many other AME Zion missionaries throughout the South.

In 1865 the AME bishop Daniel Payne, who had fled South Carolina in the 1830s, returned to establish the South Carolina Conference, which included South Car-

Charles O. Campbell in the pulpit, probably at a church in Richmond, Virginia, 1879. (Library of Congress.)

olina, North Carolina, and Georgia. Assisting Payne was the bishop Henry M. Turner, who was a major organizer for the AME Church in Georgia and later served in the Georgia constitutional conventions of 1868 and 1870 as well as in the state senate. In the 1890s Turner took his missionary efforts on behalf of the AME Church to West Africa and South America.

In some instances the efforts of the AME and AME Zion churches were challenged and, indeed, thwarted by "slave preachers" who had established ministries on plantations. As freedmen themselves, these preachers sought to continue in their roles and resisted what they viewed as northern intrusion. What ensued was a religious war fought among the black preachers of various churches.

In *Souls of Black Folks*, W. E. B. Du Bois opines that "the preacher is the most unique personality developed by the Negro on American soil." Indeed, the preacher in the black community wielded great influence on all levels: he directed religious affairs and was the controlling factor in the formation of social and political relationships within the community. Many black preachers were both religious

and political leaders of their communities. Often overlooked, the slave preachers on plantations held similar positions. Unlike their northern counterparts, they could not base their status on wealth, influence, or even education because they had none of these. Nevertheless, plantation slaves viewed their preachers as holding pivotal positions in a system of spiritual power that was highly respected within their communities. Therefore, it was not surprising that some slave preachers became spiritual and civic leaders in post–Civil War black communities in the South.

One such slave preacher was John Jasper. Born a slave in Virginia, Jasper converted to the Baptist Church, saying that he had been called by God to preach. He became a member of the First African Baptist Church of Richmond, which was led by a white pastor. He soon gained a reputation among his fellow slaves as a preacher, but his ministry was limited to slaves' funerals. Immediately after the war he drew a small group of freedpeople around him and founded his own church, the Sixth Mount Zion Baptist Church. Under his guidance the church's congregation eventually grew to more than two thousand members. In the years after the war he made no effort to change his preaching style, which relied heavily on the stories from the Old Testament to bring both fear and hope into the hearts of his congregants. The northern missionaries criticized his kindhearted and accommodative attitude toward whites, his down-to-earth sermons, and his lack of education. What his critics failed to appreciate was that the freedpeople to whom he preached were less concerned with their preacher's education than with his knowledge of the Bible and his personal moral uprightness.

Another former slave preacher was Morris Henderson, who had preached before the Civil War under the close supervision of white pastors. After 1865 he and his supporters left the white-controlled Baptist congregation in Memphis, Tennessee, and founded the Beale Street Baptist Church, which like Jasper's church soon counted more than two thousand members. Henderson sought to care for both the spiritual and physical needs of his congregation. He organized programs to feed and educate the freedpeople of Memphis and became a leader in the black community. After 1872, however, he refused all efforts to use the church for political purposes, causing some consternation among the northern black missionaries but not among the members of his church.

Postwar Divisions. The post–Civil War period was a time of instability for black churches. Divisions and the ensuing establishment of new denominations were not new phenomena in nineteenth-century America. In the antebellum period, slavery, sometimes under the guise of other issues, had divided all the major Protestant denominations. The Presbyterian Church divided into four churches; the southern congregations of the Methodist Church formed their own church; many of the southern associations of the Baptist Church established a southern convention; and the Lutheran Church, which had split into northern and southern churches when the Civil War broke out, remained divided in the aftermath of the war, and the black churches became part of that division.

The earliest example of postwar divisions affecting black churches occurred in the Colored Cumberland Presbyterian Church, or, as it was sometimes known, the Second Cumberland Church. The first Cumberland Presbyterian churches, primarily located in the Upper South, had separated from the Presbyterian Church in 1810 over issues related to revivals and camp meetings. The Cumberland Church took positions on slavery and race that would be expected from any institution in the antebellum South. It segregated its worship ceremonies, with some churches holding Sunday afternoon ceremonies strictly for blacks. The church supported slavery but was not as radical on this issue as the southern Presbyterians. Blacks played a significant role in the Cumberland Church. By 1820 the church had some twenty thousand members. The church also ordained a small number of black ministers, usually slaves, who were permitted to preside over services for blacks under the close supervision of white ministers.

At the close of the Civil War a discussion developed over the continued presence of blacks in the Cumberland Church. Church historians and others have debated whether the black members left the church or were pushed out. Regardless, in 1869 the Cumberland Presbyterian General Assembly voted in favor of a resolution authorizing its black members to establish their own church. In 1874 the black members of the Cumberland Church met in their first General Assembly and established the Colored (or Second) Cumberland Presbyterian Church. At its inception the new black church had forty-six ministers and more than three thousand members. The black church certainly hoped for the support of its white mother church, but that support proved minimal and slow in coming. As a result, the Colored Cumberland Church grew slowly, if at all. Membership actually fell at the opening of the twentieth century, as some members followed the majority of their white brothers and sisters in rejoining the northern Presbyterian assembly.

The final division by African Americans in the Presbyterian Church occurred in the last decade of the nineteenth century. After the Civil War a great amount of racial tension developed in southern Presbyterian churches as a result of the patriarchal attitude held by southern Presbyterians toward black members of the church. That attitude also contributed to the success of northern Presbyterian missionaries in winning converts among southern black Presbyterians. In 1893 the Reverend A. L. Philips, the field secretary of colored evangelistic work in the southern Presbyterian Church, initiated a call to organize the African American members of that church into a separate black Presbyterian church. This movement reached a successful conclusion in 1898, when most of the black southern Presbyterians came together to form the Afro-American Presbyterian Synod. By the opening of the twentieth century the synod was composed of twenty-one ministers and more than thirteen hundred members. Its growth, however, was stymied by the efforts of other black churches, and in 1917 the synod was readmitted to the southern Presbyterian Church.

Unlike the Presbyterian Church, the Methodist Church experienced two divisions prior to the Civil War that resulted in independent black churches: the AME Church in 1816 and the AME Zion Church in 1824. Further divisions in the Methodist church occurred in the postwar period. In 1844 southern congregations separated from the Methodist Church over the issue of slavery and formed the Methodist Episcopal Church, South. In the aftermath of the Civil War tensions developed between white and black members of the southern offshoot. At a general conference held in New Orleans in April 1866 the Methodist Episcopal Church, South, authorized its bishops to begin to organize annual conferences for its African American ministers. By May 1870 five annual black conferences had been established, and reportedly the African American participants of these conferences unanimously petitioned for permission to establish their own independent black church. Some historians have recorded that both the black and white ministers of the southern church felt that two separate churches could better reach the two unique audiences. Thus, in December 1870 the Colored Methodist Episcopal (CME) Church met in its first general conference in Jackson, Tennessee. The conference elected its first bishops, the Reverend W. H. Miles and the Reverend R. H. Vanderhorst, who were ordained by bishops of the Methodist Episcopal Church, South. The membership of the new CME Church was roughly twenty-six thousand—which represented a substantial loss of members for the white southern church. The growth of the CME Church was primarily centered in the states of Alabama, Georgia, Mississippi, and Tennessee. By 1890 its membership grew to 103,000, and by 1896 it had 130,000 members. In 1956 the church adopted a new name: the Christian Methodist Episcopal Church.

A similar process of division and realignment occurred among the Baptist churches. Unlike the Presbyterian and Methodist churches, the Baptist churches aligned themselves in what were called conventions. Unlike presbyteries or general conferences, which are religious bodies, conventions are congregational bodies with no hierarchical structure—loose associations of churches sharing common beliefs and structures. In 1845 the Baptist conventions had also split over the question of slavery. Many southern Baptist churches met in Augusta, Georgia, in 1845 to form the Southern Baptist Convention, which continued into the twenty-first century. After the Civil War black Baptist churches established three conventions: the Foreign Baptist Convention in 1880, the American National Baptist Convention in 1886, and the Baptist National Education Convention in 1893. In 1895 in Atlanta, Georgia, these three conventions merged to form the National Baptist Convention, U.S.A. That convention, however, did not prove any more stable than its predecessors, for a schism in 1915 produced a second convention, the National Baptist Convention of America.

[See also African Methodist Episcopal Church; African Union Methodism; Africanisms; Allen, Richard; Antislavery Movement; Baptism; Baptists and African Americans; Bible; Black Abolitionists; Black Family; Catholic Church and African Americans; Civil War; Cornish, Samuel; Crime and Punishment; Denmark Vesey Conspiracy; Dutch Reformed Church and African Americans; Emancipation; Episcopalians (Anglicans) and African Americans; Free African Society; Gabriel; Gabriel Conspiracy; Garrison, William Lloyd; Garrisonian Abolitionists; Great Awakening; Hosier, Harry "Black Harry"; Identity; Jones, Absalom; Lane Theological Seminary; Liele, George; Mather, Cotton, and African Americans; Methodist Church and African Americans; Methodist Episcopal Church; Missionary Movements; Payne, Daniel A.; Political Participation; Presbyterians and African Americans; Reform; Religion; Religion and Slavery; Resistance; Riots and Rebellions; Slave Insurrections and Rebellions; Slavery; Society for the Propagation of the Gospel in Foreign Parts; Society of Friends (Quakers) and African Americans; Spencer, Peter; Spirituality; Tappan, Lewis; Tubman, Harriet; Turner, Nat; Underground Railroad; Vesey, Denmark; Violence against African Americans; and Williams, Peter, Jr.]

BIBLIOGRAPHY

Frazier, E. Franklin. *The Negro Church in America*. In *The Black Church since Frazier*, by C. Eric Lincoln. New York: Schocken Books, 1974. In this updated republication of Frazier's important work, Lincoln provides insightful commentary.

Genovese, Eugene D. *Roll, Jordan, Roll: The World the Slaves Made*. New York: Vintage, 1976. An extensive study of the proactive involvement of slaves in pre–Civil War society.

Herskovits, Melville J. *The Myth of the Negro Past*. New York: Harper and Brothers, 1941.

Heyrman, Christine Leigh. *Southern Cross: The Beginnings of the Bible Belt*. Chapel Hill: University of North Carolina Press, 1997. A classic study of the early period of the Bible Belt, in which the author gives significant attention to the role of blacks.

Lincoln, C. Eric, and Lawrence H. Mamiya. *The Black Church in the African American Experience*. Durham, NC: Duke University Press, 1990. A complete one-volume study of the black church, including developments in the eighteenth and early nineteenth centuries.

Murray, Andrew E. *Presbyterians and the Negro: A History*. Philadelphia: Presbyterian Historical Society, 1966. A fair and accurate treatment of African Americans in the Presbyterian Church.

Nash, Gary B. *The Urban Crucible: Social Change, Political Consciousness, and the Origins of the American Revolution*. Cambridge, MA: Harvard University Press, 1979

Raboteau, Albert J. *Slave Religion: The "Invisible Institution" in the Antebellum South*. New York: Oxford University Press, 1978. The classic study that covers all issues relating to religion and American slavery.

Wilmore, Gayrand S. *Black and Presbyterian: The Heritage and the Hope*. Philadelphia: Geneva Press, 1983. Emphasizes the theological rather than the historical aspects of the black experience in the Presbyterian Church.

—THOMAS E. CARNEY

BLACK CODES AND SLAVE CODES, COLONIAL.

In the colonial and early national periods most slave jurisdictions developed elaborate systems of law for the regulation of blacks. These were generally known as slave codes, although they usually applied to free blacks as well. After independence a new genre of law, known as "black codes," developed in a number of free states. These laws were designed to limit the growth of the state's free black population and to control the black population in those states. Ohio, which became a state in 1803, was the first to develop these laws. Indiana (1816) and Illinois (1819) adopted similar statutes.

Southern Slave Codes. In the seventeenth century the colonies regulated slaves in a rather haphazard and piecemeal way. The British settlers in North America had little or no experience with slavery in their home country, and thus slavery as an institution developed gradually. The legal system supported this development, but laws generally were passed to deal with one or two specific problems rather than to develop comprehensive regulations affecting slaves or free blacks. Thus, in the seventeenth century Virginia passed numerous individual laws to regulate the status of the blacks and to control slaves.

A 1661 statute provided that if whites and slaves ran away together, the whites, if captured, would serve extra time to make up for the lost time of the slaves, since no extra time could be added to a slave's term of service. A 1662 act held that the children of black women would serve according to the status of the mother. A 1667 act made clear that baptism would not lead to freedom. An act of 1669 declared that no one could be prosecuted for the "casuall killing of slaves" if slaves died during punishment. The law reasoned that no master would purposefully kill his slave "since it cannot be presumed that prepense malice . . . should induce any man to destroy his own estate." The Virginia legislature passed various acts to facilitate the capture of runaway slaves and to prevent slave insurrections. Starting in the 1690s the legislature passed a number of laws to prevent interracial marriage. An act of 1705 prohibited slaves or free blacks from testifying against whites.

Later in 1705 Virginia passed its first slave code, "An Act Concerning Servants and Slaves." The act dealt with indentured servants and slaves, although most of the provisions in the law were directed at indentured servants, who were mostly white. Nevertheless, the sections dealing with slavery were significant for the development of the institution. The law defined who a slave was and prohibited blacks from owning white servants. It did not prohibit interracial marriage, probably because the colonial legislature felt that it did not have the authority to regulate a religious sacrament, but the law provided fines and jail terms for those performing such marriages and for whites and blacks who married each other.

The law required servants—slave and free, black and white—to have passes if they left their masters' land. While punishing all servant women who had children out of wedlock, the law had greater penalties for white women who had children with blacks. It codified earlier statutes on the killing of slaves, the status of the children of black women, and the effect of baptism on slaves. The law prohibited slaves from owning weapons in most circumstances and set out the rules for when a slave might lawfully be killed by public authorities. While it was riddled with references to race, the law dealt primarily with status and did not, in general, seem to be concerned with race per se, but rather with people who held the status of "slave." It presumed that some blacks would be free and that many whites would be servants. One key provision focused on race: the law prohibited blacks, slave or free, from testifying against whites in court cases. This legal disability would be a hallmark of racial codes for the next 160 years. The law also made it a crime, punishable by thirty lashes, for a free black to "lift his or her hand, in opposition against any christian, not being negro, mulatto, or Indian."

In 1723 Virginia adopted its first law to be directed only at slaves and blacks. The law was designed to suppress insurrections and "for the better government of Negros, Mulattoes, and Indians, bond or free." It provided savage punishments for slaves, including dismemberment, cutting off of ears, and severe whippings. The law prohibited slaves and free blacks from meeting or gathering together except with the permission of a master and then only for certain purposes, such as attending church. Slaves found off a plantation without a pass were to be whipped. The law prohibited slaves from owning weapons, except as part of the defense of the frontier, but did allow some free blacks to own them, provided they were registered with local authorities. The law prohibited private manumission except for "meritorious service," and it prohibited free blacks from voting.

South Carolina's slave code of 1712 was barbaric and inhumane, even by the standards of the early eighteenth century. Punishments for running away included whipping, cutting off of ears, castration, branding on the cheek, and hamstringing. This and subsequent codes were designed to keep a dangerous population under control. The fear of slaves was doubtless enhanced by their race and African origin, and the slaves of South Carolina were dangerous. The state's inhuman system of bondage, oppression, and punishment made slaves especially rebellious and helped lead to the bloody Stono Rebellion of 1739.

In 1740 South Carolina passed a similar law, "An Act for the Better Ordering [of] Negroes and other Slaves in this Province," which was designed to provide comprehensive regulation of slaves and free blacks. Fearful of slave rebellions, in the wake of the Stono Rebellion, the new law banned slaves from the "using and keeping of drums, horns, or other loud instruments, which may call together or give sine [sic] or notice to one another of their wicked designs and purposes." Fearful that overly cruel punishment could also lead to rebellions, the law prohibited the willful murder and manslaughter of a slave, although the only punishments were relatively minor fines. Even smaller fines were to be meted out for any person who "shall wilfully cut out the tongue, put out the eye, castrate or cruelly scald, burn, or deprive any slave of any limb or member." This list of punishments reveals the barbaric nature of punishment at the time as much as it suggests the legislature's desire to change behavior. The law allowed punishments by "whipping or beating with a horsewhip, cow-skin, switch or small stick, or by putting irons on, or confining or imprisoning" a slave. The law also prohibited teaching any slave to read or write or allowing those already literate "to be employed in writing."

Other colonies regulated slaves and blacks in similar ways. Maryland's comprehensive slave code of 1715 noted that "many People have neglected to Baptize their Negroes, or suffer them to be Baptized, on a vain apprehension that Negroes by receiving the Sacrament of Baptism are manumitted and set Free." To address this concern, the code assured masters that "No Negroe or Negroes by receiving the Holy Sacrament of Baptism is hereby manumitted or set free, nor hath any Right or Title to Freedom or Manumission, more than he or they had before, any Law, Usage or Custom to the Contrary notwithstanding." The law provided penalties for both parents of a mixed-race child and fined anyone performing a mixed-race marriage. In 1717 the colony made it a felony to perform such marriages. That same year the Maryland legislature determined that "it may be of very Dangerous Consequences to admit and allow as Evidences" the testimony of any black, slave or free.

After the American Revolution southern states continued to remove some of the harsher aspects of punishment from their codes. In 1791, for example, North Carolina made murder of a slave a crime. At the same time, the southern states increasingly tied slaves and free blacks together in their regulations. In 1782 Virginia liberalized its manumission laws, but in 1806 the state began to require that recently emancipated blacks leave the state. The Virginia slave code, like that of other states, reflected an increasing hostility toward free blacks. In the 1820s South Carolina prohibited free blacks from entering the state, and other southern states did the same thing in the 1830s. Southern states also increasingly limited the rights of free blacks, especially in the wake of two failed slave rebellions, the Gabriel conspiracy in Virginia in 1800 and the Denmark Vesey conspiracy, discovered in 1822 in South Carolina. The latter was particularly frightening to whites because Vesey was a free black.

Northern Regulation of Blacks. The northern colonies also regulated free blacks along with slaves. In 1703–1704 Rhode Island prohibited free blacks and slaves from being out after 9 P.M. without a lawful excuse. Offenders were to be whipped "at ye Publick whipping post in s[ai]d. Town not Exceeding fifteen stripes upon their Naked back." Although known for its humane statutes, in 1697 Pennsylvania passed legislation to create special penalties regarding rape; blacks could be sentenced to death for raping whites and face castration for attempted rape. Whites who committed similar offenses would be fined, whipped, or imprisoned for a year for a first offense and for life for a second offense.

In 1700 and again in 1706 Pennsylvania adopted similar statutes to regulate the trial and punishment of blacks. Both laws dealt with the "manner of trial and punishment of negroes committing murder, manslaughter, buggery, burglary, rapes, attempts of rapes, and other high and heinous enormities and capital offenses." Both laws also provided a death sentence for any black convicted of "rape or ravishment" of a white woman and for murder, buggery, or burglary. Rape, buggery, and burglary were not capital offenses for whites in Pennsylvania. Indeed, the disparity of punishment is striking. While a black man would be executed for raping a white woman, a white man would be whipped with thirty-one lashes and sentenced to seven years at hard labor. A second offense resulted in castration and branding with the letter *R*. For the lesser offenses blacks were punished by castration, whipping, branding, and deportation. All of these punishments were more severe for blacks, slave or free, than for whites who committed the same crimes. Both the 1700 and 1706 acts also prohibited blacks from carrying guns and other weapons and from congregating in groups larger than four.

Colonial Massachusetts also presumed that blacks were a dangerous class and tried to regulate them accordingly. In 1693 the colony provided special penalties for people who purchased goods or provisions that "appear . . . to have been stol'n" from "any Indian servant, or negro or mulatto servant, or slave." Indians and blacks caught selling such goods were to be "whipped openly, not exceeding twenty lashes." No similar laws or penalties seem to have been used to control white servants.

In 1703 the fear of black crime continued to haunt Massachusetts. A law directed at "Disorders in the Night" began with this telling preamble: "Whereas great disorders, insolencies and burglaries are oftimes raised and committed in the night time by Indian, negro and molattos servants and slaves." Clearly, colonial government saw race, not status, as the danger. There were far more white servants than nonwhite servants in Massachusetts at this time, but they were not singled out for special legislation. The act placed a 9 P.M. curfew on all nonwhite servants and slaves and allowed for the summary arrest and committal of any found off the premises of their masters who were unable to "give a good and satisfactory account of their business." Because authorities in Massachusetts assumed that all blacks were either slaves or servants, this law created a presumption of illegal behavior for any black found on the streets after 9 P.M.

Other northern colonies adopted similar laws. New York prohibited black testimony, while New Jersey and Pennsylvania lumped free blacks together with slaves in regulating "runaways." Connecticut had a curfew for free blacks. Rhode Island allowed free blacks to be bound out as indentured servants "for keeping disorderly taverns," while Pennsylvania and Delaware bound out the children of poor blacks. In Pennsylvania and Delaware, which was more northern than southern at this time, a free black adult could be bound into servitude for "loiter[ing] or mispend[ind] his or her Time." The crime of loitering did not carry such a stiff penalty if the perpetrator was white.

During and after the Revolution the northern states either ended slavery outright, as did Massachusetts in its 1780 constitution, or took steps to end the institution through gradual abolition acts, as in Pennsylvania (1780) and New York (1799). In these states the need to regulate blacks gradually diminished. Some states, including Massachusetts, New York, and Pennsylvania, gave free blacks equal political rights. Pennsylvania's gradual abolition act eliminated all distinctions in criminal law between whites and blacks, including slaves, but did not allow slaves to testify against free people. The statute stated:

> That the offences and crimes of Negroes and Mulattoes, as well slaves and servants as freemen, shall be enquired of, adjudged, corrected and punished, in like manner as the offences and crimes of the other inhabitants of this state are and shall be enquired of, adjudged, corrected and punished, and not otherwise, except that a slave shall not be admitted to bear witness against a freeman.

Most of the other northern states gave free blacks full legal protections as well, including allowing them to testify against whites.

At the time of the Revolution free blacks could vote on the same terms as whites in all of the northern states except Connecticut and Rhode Island. However, the rise of Jeffersonian and Jacksonian democracy undermined these rights. By the time of the War of 1812, New Jersey had stripped blacks of the franchise. In 1821 the New York Constitutional Convention gave universal suffrage to white men by eliminating property requirements for voting. The leaders of the convention, who would soon emerge as the core of the state's Jacksonian movement, wanted to take the vote away from all blacks. Federalists in the state, especially the famed jurist James Kent, resisted this move, and in a compromise the state agreed to allow blacks to vote only if they owned property, as in the past. In the 1830s the Jacksonians in Pennsylvania granted full suffrage to whites while completely disenfranchising blacks. By the 1830s blacks in New England and the mid-Atlantic states were almost entirely free from bondage and from most formal racial regulations, but they lacked equal political rights, except in Maine, Massachusetts, Vermont, and New Hampshire.

Midwestern Black Codes. The most significant innovation in racial regulation came in the Midwest in the first two decades of the nineteenth century. The territories and states of the lower Midwest began with a presumptive ban on slavery stemming from the Northwest Ordinance of 1787, article 6 of which declared:

> There shall be neither slavery nor involuntary servitude in the said territory, otherwise than in the punishment of crimes, whereof the party shall have been duly convicted: provided always, that any person escaping into the same, from whom labour or service is lawfully claimed in any one of the original states, such fugitive may be lawfully reclaimed, and conveyed to the person claiming his or her labour or service as aforesaid.

The ordinance did not contain any direction on how it was to be implemented. At the time of its passage there were hundreds of slaves in what later became the states of Indiana and Illinois. Furthermore, many migrants from Virginia and Kentucky, some of them slave owners, were anxious to move into the region.

When it became a state in 1803, Ohio had few blacks and virtually no slaves. The state's constitution prohibited slavery and denied free blacks the right to vote. In 1804 and again in 1807 the legislature passed the first of a number of statutes known as "black laws," which provided an elaborate registration system for blacks entering the state. Blacks coming into Ohio had to provide proof of their freedom, register with local officials, and find two sureties who would sign bonds for five hundred dollars to guarantee that they would not become a burden on the state. These laws banned blacks from testifying in court against whites and denied them access to any sort of public assistance. When the legislature began to create a statewide system of public education in the 1830s, blacks found themselves excluded from these tax-supported schools.

Despite the registration laws, the black population of Ohio grew dramatically in this period. There were 337 blacks in Ohio in 1800, 1,899 in 1810, 4,723 in 1820, and 9,568 in 1830. Most blacks entering the state did not actually register under these laws, and there is no record of any court's ever forcing a black to leave the state for failing to register. While they were denied access to public schools, Ohio blacks were able to create their own schools and other institutions. Unlike the situation under the slave codes and black codes of the South, African Americans in Ohio were free to own property, enter a profession, and travel and move about without a pass system. By the 1850s there was at least one black attorney in Ohio, John Mercer Langston, and although his fellow African Americans were denied the franchise, his white neighbors would elect him to public office. The greatest threat to blacks from the state came from their inability to testify against whites and the fear that the registration laws might be enforced against them. Ohio repealed most of its black laws in 1849, although blacks were denied suffrage and the right to serve on juries until after the Civil War.

Indiana and Illinois developed laws similar to those in Ohio, and they allowed for long-term indenture of blacks brought into those territories. This created a system of quasi slavery in both places. Indiana effectively eliminated this system after statehood, in 1816, and by 1830 there were no blacks held in bondage in the state. Illinois, on the other hand, maintained bondage until the 1840s. As in Ohio, the registration laws in Indiana and Illinois were not very effective at slowing the growth of the black population. Both as territories and states, Indiana and Illinois remained beacons for free blacks and fugitive slaves. The Indiana black population grew from about 400 in 1800 (including over 250 slaves) to 1,230 by 1820 and 3,329 by 1830. Illinois had similar laws and regulations, and they were equally ineffective. In 1820 Illinois had 457 free blacks; by 1830 this population exceeded 1,600. These states maintained their black codes until the Civil War, strengthening them in the 1850s and during the war.

Despite the black codes, free blacks and fugitive slaves came to the lower Midwest in the first three decades of the nineteenth century because the region provided greater freedom and opportunity than did the Slave South. The upper Midwest never adopted such restrictions.

[*See also* Baptism; Crime and Punishment; Denmark Vesey Conspiracy; Discrimination; Emancipation, Gradual; Free African Americans to 1828; Fugitive Slaves; Gabriel Conspiracy; Indentured Servitude; Jackson, Andrew, and African Americans; Jefferson, Thomas, on African Americans and Slavery; Laws and Legislation; Literacy; Marriage, Mixed; Political Participation; Resistance; Riots and Rebellions; Slavery: Lower South; Slavery: Mid-Atlantic; Slavery: Northeast; Slavery: Upper South; Stono Rebellion; Violence against African Americans; *and* Voting Rights.]

BIBLIOGRAPHY

Benedict, Michael Les, and John F. Winkler, eds. *The History of Ohio Law*. Athens: Ohio University Press, 2004.

Finkelman, Paul. *Slavery and the Founders: Race and Liberty in the Age of Jefferson*. 2nd ed. Armonk, NY: M. E. Sharpe, 2001.

Higginbotham, A. Leon. *In the Matter of Color: The Colonial Period*. New York: Oxford University Press, 1978.

Middleton, Stephen. *The Black Laws in the Old Northwest: A Documentary History*. Westport, CT: Greenwood Press, 1993.

Morris, Thomas D. *Southern Slavery and the Law, 1619–1860*. Chapel Hill: University of North Carolina Press, 1996.

—PAUL FINKELMAN

BLACK ENGLISH VERNACULAR.

In modern times, Black English vernacular is alternately referred to as African American vernacular English, Black English, inner-city English, Ebonics, or African American English, although the last term is sometimes used to indicate a broader category comprising closely related dialects. The precise origins of Black English vernacular remain unsettled and controversial.

The theory regarding the beginnings of Black English vernacular that dominated the first half of the twentieth century is sometimes referred to as the Anglicist hypothesis, so named because it identifies the origins of Black English with the origins of other American English dialects, namely British English. According to this theory, from the early seventeenth century on, slaves (the first of whom, technically indentured servants, were brought to Jamestown in 1619) arrived in the southern United States speaking a variety of West African languages, including Hausa, Ibo, and Yoruba. Slaves learned English, though imperfectly, from plantation overseers and slave masters.

Slave children also learned from their white counterparts, with whom they were often allowed to play. In many cases, a white child would have a favorite slave of the same age who would be retained into adulthood as a personal servant. In addition, older female slaves were often charged with caring for the plantation owner's children and may have learned language skills from them. It is also likely, but generally not acknowledged within the Anglicist theory, that white children imitated the speech patterns of the female slaves who cared for them. The Anglicist hypothesis suggests that these interracial associations permitted slaves to learn a version of English similar to but less correct than the English spoken by southern whites. At the same time, slaves steadily lost their African language heritage; within two or three generations little or nothing remained of it.

Given the social, economic, and educational isolation of slaves from mainstream white society, slaves had limited opportunities to engage in extended conversations with the white elite. The Anglicist theory thus typically postulates a continuing divergence of Black English vernacular from Standard American English, or slave-language deficiency, with the divergence accelerating as later generations of slaves during the eighteenth and early nineteenth centuries learned English more exclusively within the slave community.

A different version of the Anglicist theory arose at the end of the twentieth century. In this understanding, it is thought that the English spoken by slaves was originally almost identical to the English spoken by southern whites but later in history diverged from it, as the black community became more cohesive. Linguists see this divergence continuing in the modern era among young urban African Americans who are economically and socially isolated from mainstream America.

By the 1960s an alternate explanation for the emergence of Black English vernacular had arisen. This account, known as the creole hypothesis, reflects the growing respect for African American culture as embedded in the civil rights movement and argues the continued importance of native African languages in the development of slaves' plantation English.

According to the creole theory, slaves speaking the same West African languages were deliberately separated in order to reduce the risk of cohesive attempts at rebellion. This enforced linguistic segregation occurred on both slave ships and American plantations. The common language for slaves brought to the United States thus became a pidgin of English and their various native African languages; this made communication possible with both blacks and whites. Children born to pidgin-speaking slaves in fact grew up speaking an English-African pidgin as their native language. At this point, the pidgin became a creole: a language derived from the mixture of two or more languages that becomes the speakers' first language. As new slaves arrived from Africa—a process that continued long after the slave trade was outlawed in 1808—they learned the creole from slaves who had grown up on the plantation.

Adherents of the creole theory often claim that the evolution of the language continued into a period of decreolization. As slaves moved further away from their African origins, their English converged more closely with Standard American English. Black English vernacular changed from a creole into a legitimate English dialect gradually approaching that spoken by whites, a process enhanced by African Americans' moving into the educational and economic mainstream of the country.

Linguists support their commitment to the creole theory with evidence of the continued existence of West African language elements in Black English vernacular, including such vocabulary as *goober* (peanut), *tote* (carry), *chigger* (mite), *yam* (sweet potato), *gumbo* (a type of thick soup), and *jazz*. Word usages also carried over from African language origins, such as the use of the word *man* in direct address.

A variety of phonological and syntactic elements, some of which may also originate in West African languages, further define Black English vernacular. Such elements are not uniformly present in the language of every speaker of Black English and are marked by individual, regional, and class variations. Examples include omission of the /r/ sound, except before vowels (*guard* becomes *god*); omission of the /l/ sound (*help* becomes *hep*); reduction of diphthongs to simple vowels (*toil* becomes *toy*); identical pronunciation of the /i/ and /e/ sounds of such words as *pin* and *pen*; and simplification of consonant clusters through the dropping of consonants at the ends of words. This last characteristic often leads to a dropped /d/, /t/, or /s/, including the /s/ ending for the third-person singular present, as in "she sing." Other characteristics of Black English vernacular include the use of double negatives, the repetition of the noun subject with a pronoun ("my father he go"), the omission of forms of the verb *to be* where in Standard English the verb can be contracted ("she sad"), and the use of *be* to indicate a habitual characteristic ("she be sad," meaning "she is usually sad").

Linguists have generally come to see Black English vernacular not as the result of bad speech habits or as the product of illogical thought but as a legitimate English dialect. It is as much a rule-driven language as any other form of English—including the dialect known as Standard American English. Linguists have also come to acknowledge the real possibility that language exchange was mutual, with southern whites adopting certain speech characteristics of blacks—especially the dropping of the /r/ sound. Such insights derive from deeper understandings of the nature of language, more familiarity with West African languages, and greater liberation from the limiting effects of racism on linguistic study.

[*See also* Africa, Idea of; African Diaspora; Africanisms; Black Family; Demographics; Education; Language; *and* Stereotypes of African Americans.]

BIBLIOGRAPHY

Dillard, J. L. *Black English: Its History and Usage in the United States*. New York: Random House, 1972. An early and important exposition of the creole hypothesis.

Poplack, Shana, and Sali Tagliamonte. *African American English in the Diaspora*. Malden, MA: Blackwell, 2001. Examines the language change during the period of slave transportation to the New World and proposes that slave speech first came to imitate and later diverged from southern white English.

Smitherman, Geneva. *Talkin and Testifyin: The Language of Black America*. Detroit, MI: Wayne State University Press, 1986. Argues that the language used by slaves retained the basic structure of West African languages while substituting English words.

Wolfram, Walt, and Erik R. Thomas. *The Development of African American English*. Malden, MA: Blackwell, 2002. Examines an isolated biracial community in North Carolina to explore the origins and development of African American vernacular English.

—EDWARD J. RIELLY

BLACK FAMILY. The television adaptation of Alex Haley's *Roots* (1976), which traced the history of a black family beginning with its African progenitor, Kunta Kinte, aired to wide public acclaim in the 1970s. The family saga generated considerable attention, as evidenced by a rise in popular interest about the black family and genealogical organizations across the United States. The following decade Dorothy Spruill Redford organized a reunion of more than two thousand descendants of enslaved Africans—including herself—and their masters, then wrote *Somerset Homecoming* (1988). From the end of the twentieth century, Edward Ball's *Slaves in the Family* (1998) tells the story of the intertwined lives of slaves and their masters in antebellum South Carolina.

Firsthand slave narratives, while limited in number, are excellent primary sources. Narratives that give accounts of enslaved Africans' introduction to the Americas, such as the two-volume *Interesting Narrative of the Life of Olaudah Equiano, or Gustavus Vassa* (1789), are rare. Harriet Jacobs, who wrote her autobiography, *Incidents in the Life of a Slave Girl* (1861), under the pseudonym Linda Brent, rendered a powerful female voice to the retelling of the slave experience. The companion text *Harriet Jacobs: A Life* (2004), by Jean Fagan Yellin, brought to bear a wealth of historical documentation pertaining to Jacobs's life story.

Several theories on the nature of the slave family have been proposed without producing a consensus. For the first half of the twentieth century a theory of paternalistic benevolence on the part of masters coupled with accommodation, promulgated by Ulrich Bonnell Phillips, went unchallenged; "paternalistic benevolence" inferred that kind masters treated slaves as part of their extended family, while "accommodation" held that contented slaves acquiesced to the master's will. Kenneth M. Stampp, author of *The Peculiar Institution* (1956), challenged prevailing thought in emphasizing the role of economic interest and highlighting the adversity of slavery. In 1965 Daniel Patrick Moynihan, a public-policy maker, drafted a controversial report that made reference to the black family and social ills—in particular to successive generations of female-headed households being a byproduct of slavery. To the contrary, Herbert Gutman, the author of *The Black Family in Slavery and Freedom, 1750–1925* (1976), proposed that two-parent households were more the norm during slavery. Eugene Genovese, in *Roll, Jordan, Roll* (1974), revealed both the resilience of the black family and the strains placed upon it by slavery.

African Presence. Olaudah Equiano, also known as Gustavus Vassa, a late-eighteenth-century African from Benin who was kidnapped and sold, chided the United States for its policy of racial slavery. While a version of slavery did exist in Africa, therein slaves were integrated into society. The first generation of Africans in the British American colonies, on the other hand, found the odds against stable-family formation insurmountable; strenuous work schedules, poor diets, and inadequate housing all proved to be limitations. Other barriers included language, same-sex living arrangements, and a shortage of black females. Black males—in demand for their physical strength, which was highly prized in a labor-intensive agricultural society—outnumbered females by a ratio of almost two to one in some regions. With respect to networks of extended families, both African and African American societies maintained strict taboos on marriage to cousins and derided promiscuity.

It is generally agreed the African slave trade between the late fifteenth and mid-nineteenth centuries disrupted some ethnic groups in particular. The fifteenth-century Portuguese chronicler Gomes Eanes de Zurara left stark eyewitness accounts of the horrific separation of families following arrival in Portugal. Expressions of emotion with regard to the calamity of separation ranged from guttural moaning and sobbing to the repetitive striking of one's own face and the throwing of one's body to the ground, which actions typified respective customs of mourning. Attempts by mothers to shield children with their bodies met with blows. African male resistance, which would be

difficult to squelch several centuries later, was countered with brute strength. Similar scenes were most likely repeated as enslaved Africans disembarked in seventeenth-century Barbados and the eighteenth-century British American colonies.

African Retentions. The debate over the degree to which African cultural patterns survived in the United States is not settled. Scholars have argued in favor of African retentions in a broad number of areas, including family structure, storytelling, music, dance, folk belief, and social norms. Some have made the case for the retention of cultural patterns especially in situations where voids existed and need prevailed. Others have claimed that the remnants of Africanisms were evident only in small segments of the black population in parts of Louisiana and coastal Georgia and South Carolina. In New Orleans, the presence of African-derived percussion instruments was witnessed. The tar-baby and tortoise-and-hare folktales as well as spirituals are generally agreed to have been transported from Africa. American diets that included rice, yams, okra, watermelon, peanuts, and sorghum resembled those in Africa.

The transformation away from African-based cultures typically occurred earlier in the Upper South than in the Lower South. The timing of state bans on imports of Africans was an important factor; the later the importation was prohibited, the more likely it was that Africanisms persisted. Delaware and Virginia had banned importations of Africans by 1778, at which time a few African-derived string instruments still survived in Virginia. Five years later Maryland prohibited the entry of Africans; North Carolina did likewise in 1794, Georgia in 1798. Both Georgia and South Carolina, however, unofficially permitted the importation of Africans well into the nineteenth century. The U.S. government abolished the African slave trade in 1808, by which time 600,000 Africans had been brought to the United States, according to conservative estimates.

South Carolina, with its large black majority, proved fertile ground for African cultural patterns to survive. By 1720 blacks had held a majority over whites for more than a decade. In 1803 South Carolina aggressively resumed the importation of Africans after a lapse of more than a decade; the state imported an estimated forty thousand additional Africans by 1808. Following the publication of Lorenzo Turner's groundbreaking work *Africanisms in the Gullah Dialect* in 1949, it was generally accepted that the language spoken by inhabitants of coastal South Carolina and Georgia was a blend of English and West African languages. South Carolina rice planters specifically sought to import Africans with applicable skills from the Grain Coast, now known as Sierra Leone; in 1685 enslaved

Africans who held knowledge of rice production and basketry showed English settlers how to cultivate rice in the Lowcountry. Clandestine shipments of enslaved Africans continued to arrive as late as the 1850s off secluded parts of the Georgia and South Carolina coasts. Such imports were relatively small but ended up concentrated in certain Lowcountry regions; conservative estimates placed the import numbers at one thousand annually over several decades.

Emergence of the Slave Family. Even remedial development of the slave family in the British American colonies was somewhat remarkable; the slave populations in Brazil and the Caribbean were maintained by importations of slaves rather than by births. Scholars have agreed that up until 1720 the slave population was not self-sustaining in the British American colonies; they have debated the factors that eventually contributed to increases in slave births as well as the development of the slave family. Some conjectured a strong contribution by paternalism, wherein masters practiced benevolence toward slaves, who they viewed as "their people." For example, masters typically gave personal gifts, such as clothing or increased food allotments, to families as incentives for high birthrates. Others have speculated that the overarching factor was the economic interests of masters: each slave birth was estimated to increase a master's worth by about two hundred dollars. It was likely a combination of economic interests and paternalism, along with more even sex distributions and improvements in nutrition and housing, that ultimately contributed to natural increases in the slave population.

Several factors had major influences on the development of slave families. The slave owner's demeanor, again, played a primary role, as evidenced by accounts of plantation life in slave narratives. The development of the slave family typically paralleled the stages of plantation growth. The early plantation stage was a time of unrest, when new masters typically gave strenuous work to groups of single, young adult slaves. In later stages males and females partnered, and the development of nuclear families typically became evident. The last plantation stage was initiated by financial trouble or the master's death, which led to the separation of possibly several generations of a slave family. Mothers and younger children were usually sold together—the father absent—on the auction block. A few scholars have suggested that males had a marginal role in the slave family; separations of mates in particular may have marginalized the role of the father, but this has remained unclear.

From the master's viewpoint slave marriages offered both pros and cons. Some scholars have argued that the existence of slave families perhaps provided an effective counterweight to potential participation in insurrections and other forms of resistance; slave narratives support the notion that fear of potential reprisals against family members kept slaves from engaging in any direct confrontation with masters. The presence of slave families on plantations was associated with a greater degree of economic stability. Slave family members provided a support group for task work and a strong social network. On the other hand, the family was the center of more passive resistance, as evidenced in acknowledgments by slave masters that families and underground black churches were typically outside their sphere of influence. Marriages between slaves, meanwhile, lacked any legal status and existed only at the behest of the master. Regardless of the reasons for and consequences of the existence of slave families, slaves derived consolation for the indignity of human bondage in compassionate networks of kin.

Quality of Family Life. Studies of postings for colonial Maryland runaways showed that one out of two were headed to see family members in distant places; a similar study in colonial Virginia indicated that one out of three left for such purposes. Several existing letters by literate slaves from the seventeenth and early eighteenth centuries contain references to the condition of family members. Taboos against marriage to cousins reinforced blacks' desires to keep track of kin. Female slaves possessed strong maternal instincts for all their children in spite of numerous external pressures. Sojourner Truth recalled that her mother, Mau-Mau Bett, who was a slave in New Netherland (later New York), grieved for the remainder of her life over children taken from her during slavery. It was not rare for older slaves, both male and female, to request to live around their children.

The slave family led a sometimes precarious existence within the framework of these influences. The autobiographer Harriet Jacobs, pursued by a lecherous, married master in North Carolina, entered into a relationship with a single attorney, with whom she bore two children. Her grandmother, who provided a strong moral influence, disapproved of the first pregnancy but counseled that a mother was to remain with her children no matter what the situation.

There was typically little, if any, lasting social stigma toward an unmarried female who bore one child out of wedlock. Some have argued that a woman of childbearing age who produced a live birth, even if out of wedlock, decreased her risk of separation; slave masters maintained economic interests in slave families and sold slave women entering childbearing age who were presumed infertile. Others have argued that the behavior of bearing one child out of wedlock represented more of a cultural pattern from Africa. In any case, following their first births, slave women then settled down and practiced fidelity. Slaves preferred to select marriage partners without the interference of masters and sometimes looked to other plantations for eligible candidates; however, slaves could typically only marry in such situations when both owners granted permission. Marriage ceremonies ranged from jumping over a broom to more formal celebrations officiated by preachers. While neither was legally binding, there is a remarkable record of long-standing slave marriages.

Transition to Freedom. Slaves showed their dissatisfaction with their slave status as well as their desire for freedom through various means. They practiced day-to-day resistance in initiating work slowdowns, breaking equipment, stealing supplies, committing arson, poisoning masters, and pretending to be sick, among other acts. Both free blacks and slaves sometimes participated in protests; several Massachusetts slaves circulated a protest document that sought increased freedom in 1773. Lawsuits were not uncommon in the Upper South and the North. New England slavery, which Puritans modeled after Mosaic traditions, recognized some legal rights for slaves. A string of favorable legal decisions in Massachusetts over a span of two decades culminated in the Quok Walker case of 1781, which led to the end of slavery there in 1783. Sojourner Truth, an eighteenth-century abolitionist, successfully sued for her son to be sent from slavery in Alabama to freedom in New York.

Slavery appeared to be on the decline by the time of the American Revolution, when egalitarian ideals expanded the dialogue about slave status. Military service in the Revolutionary War opened the door to a steady flow of manumissions. Among northeastern states, Pennsylvania led the way with passage of legislation for gradual emancipation in 1780, where manumission took effect at the age of twenty-eight; the average life expectancy was around forty. The free black population in Pennsylvania increased from almost 6,500 in 1790 to 38,000 in 1830. The invention of the cotton gin and heightened cotton production, however, further entrenched slavery throughout the Deep South. Maryland, North Carolina, and Virginia, where the soil was becoming depleted, sent slaves to the Cotton Belt. Virginia alone exported almost 300,000 slaves beginning in 1830.

In freedom there existed the potential for educational advancement, a greater role as protector for husbands, less limited legal recourse, and more opportunities to shape the household. One elderly slave who was offered manumission in colonial Virginia petitioned the legislature to remain in the area rather than migrate to another state, as the law demanded of recently freed persons of color. He desired to live near his family, which remained in slavery. Freed families faced limited job opportunities, coercive apprenticeships of children, restrictions on travel, and racial discrimination in the early and mid-eighteenth century.

Strong family ties figured prominently in the lives of nineteenth-century African Americans. In both slavery and freedom the family formed the core institution in the black community and was a vital element in the emergence of a distinct African American culture. Strong attachments to both nuclear and extended family offered love and companionship; gave support in times of distress; helped temper discrimination; educated, nurtured, and

"The Parting: Buy Us Too," lithograph, 1863. The artist, Henry Louis Stephens (1824–1882), a prolific illustrator of books and magazines who worked for Frank Leslie and Harper Brothers among others, was a noted caricaturist. However, this moving image of a slave being separated from his wife and child—which was part of a group called "From the Plantation to the Battlefield"—is entirely serious. (Library of Congress.)

socialized children; and provided for care for orphans, the elderly, and the disabled. The strength of black families in slavery and freedom demonstrates the capacity of a people to grow and thrive despite the presence of great obstacles.

Family and Plantation Slavery. The existence and encouragement of monogamous slave families was unique to slavery in the United States and, according to the historian John Blassingame, existed largely because of the unique near-equal sex ratio among American slaves. While sex ratios remained unbalanced among slave societies in Latin America owing to the continued importation of male slaves, after the American slave trade ended in 1808, slaves formed families, allowing the U.S. slave population to grow by natural increase. By 1830 there were 98.3 enslaved women for every 100 enslaved men, making it likely that members of either sex would be able to find mates among the slave population. While slave marriages were not legally recognized in most southern states, the family nevertheless served as an important survival mechanism, as therein adults found love, companionship, and empathy and children were socialized to learn the best means of thriving under the conditions of enslavement. Some masters were eager for their slaves to form matches and build strong family ties on their own plantations; it was reasoned that a married man with children was less likely to escape or rebel than his single counterpart. While some slaveholders expressed the genuine desire to promote moral behavior in their slave quarters, most encouraged the formation of families because family ties fostered discipline.

Marriage ceremonies could be formal or informal. In most cases the rite simply entailed asking the master's permission before moving in together. Other times more formal ceremonies were performed, especially for slaves in positions of prestige, such as house servants. Many Protestant denominations, including the Presbyterian and Episcopal churches, required that ministers perform slave weddings, even though the unions were not legally binding. On rare occasions slave weddings included big feasts at the plantation houses, but usually such celebrations took place after work hours in the slave quarters.

Relationships and marriage often linked slaves from different owners. "Abroad" marriage occurred when slaves from different plantations formed a union. This practice required the permission of both slaveholders and was sometimes denied because, according to law, any children produced in the relationship were the property of the female slave's owner. Some masters purchased their slave's mate, keeping the family intact and hoping to instill loyalty in both partners. Others simply discouraged their female slaves from looking beyond their home plantation for a mate. A limited number of enslaved men and women married members of the free black community. These relationships were sometimes complicated, depending on which partner was enslaved. Frederick Douglass's grandmother Betsey married Isaac Bailey, a free black sawyer, and the nine daughters and three sons she had with him were the property of her owner, Aaron Anthony. Whenever possible, free blacks purchased their enslaved family members and then manumitted them.

As might be expected, given the law making the children of an enslaved woman the property of her master, female-headed families were not unusual in the slave community. Some female-headed families resulted from relationships between white masters and enslaved women. The unequal power relationship between slaves and masters allowed for sexual exploitation of the enslaved. Although white women were known to have had assignations with enslaved men, more evidence exists to support widespread sexual relations between male slaveholders and female slaves. Douglass's father was a white man, and it has long been suspected that this man was his first owner, Aaron Anthony. Black men had little recourse for protecting their wives or children from such sexual exploitation.

The nature of plantation work meant that extended family members often assumed responsibility for child rearing. Especially on large plantations, family members could experience long periods of separation brought about by the work process, and elderly female slaves were often put to work minding boys and girls too young for the fields—as Douglass well remembered. Douglass's mother, Harriet Bailey, was hired to a plantation owner some distance from the plantation where he spent his early years. Raised by his elderly grandmother, he remembered seeing his mother only four or five times before her death in 1825. Despite enduring the grueling work of a field laborer, Bailey's maternal instincts were strong. Douglass recalled her walking the twelve miles from Perry Stewart's farm at night, after putting in a full day's labor, to visit with her children. She would lay with Douglass until he fell asleep, but she would be long gone by the time he awoke in the morning. He never saw his mother by the light of day.

The threat of having their families broken apart kept many slaves in line. While most slaveholders avoided family separations in order to maintain discipline, the nonlegality of slave families meant that slaveholders could tear them apart at will. Slave owners faced with debts often resorted to selling slaves in order to fend off creditors, often separating wives from husbands and parents from children in the process. The separation of family members through sale or trade was among the most brutal aspects of slavery.

Separation of husbands and wives usually meant the end of slave marriages, which had had no basis under law in the first place. The rending of black families increased with the shift of slavery to the cotton-producing states of the Deep South after 1820. As Upper South states shifted the production on their exhausted soil from tobacco to corn, wheat, and other less labor-intensive staples, slaveholders sought to profit from the sale of excess bond servants. Maryland, North Carolina, and especially Virginia became the prime sources for the slaves who would labor on the cotton plantations that were rapidly developing in the Deep South. The invention of the cotton gin and consequentially heightened production spread slavery throughout Georgia, Alabama, Mississippi, Louisiana, and finally Texas. Virginia alone exported about 300,000 slaves beginning in 1830. Between 1810 and 1820 the enslaved population of Georgia increased from 100,000 to 150,000, growing much more, to 462,000, by 1860. Douglass recalled that during his youth on a Maryland plantation, "scarcely a month passed without the sale of one or more lots [of slaves] to the Georgia traders." As slavery

Family record, "designed for the colored people of America by W. H. Cowell, Martin, Tennessee," 1880, with scenes contrasting slavery and freedom. The lithographer was Krebs of Cincinnati. (Library of Congress.)

moved both south and west, slave families suffered tremendously. John Blassingame estimates that slaveholders dissolved 66 percent of slave marriages in Mississippi, 50 percent in Louisiana, and 43 percent in Tennessee.

Urban South. Life for black families in southern cities was generally more fluid and less circumscribed than on rural plantations. For both free and enslaved African Americans southern cities provided ample opportunities for meeting potential partners, and it was not uncommon for marriages between slaves and free men and women to occur. In Deep South cities such as New Orleans and Charleston a "brown elite" of light-skinned African Americans intermarried frequently to create a free black aristocracy of sorts. In cities with active free black communities, families attended church, formed schools for their children (although sometimes clandestinely because of legal proscription), belonged to benevolent societies, and attended community events. In many southern states it was illegal to educate either slaves or free blacks, so the children of black families often received home schooling, if they learned to read and write at all. In Virginia, if free blacks sent their children out of the state for education, they were not permitted to return.

Urban blacks had often been separated from rural-dwelling relatives, as the majority of slaves lived on farms or plantations. As such, the urban setting distanced residents from family members who remained on plantations—although the brutality of slavery sometimes muted the pain of separation. When sent to live with a new master in Baltimore, the youthful Douglass had little regret in leaving the plantation because his mother was dead and his grandmother had been moved to a small cabin in a remote location. He later noted, "I had two sisters and one brother, that lived in the same house with me; but the early separation of us from our mother had well nigh blotted the fact of our relationship from our memories." Nevertheless, Douglass saw the value in family: as a young man in the city he met and courted Anna Murray, a free black woman, who aided his escape from slavery and became his wife of forty-five years.

Black Families in the North. With slavery all but extinct in northern states by 1830, black families faced less overall restriction. Most northern free blacks lived in urban areas, with large populations concentrated in New York and Philadelphia. Freedom allowed greater choice in marriage matches, although the historians James and Lois Horton have shown that color remained an important factor. In cities with large numbers of southern-born blacks, light-skinned men and women tended to marry others of light complexion. Most black families organized in nuclear or two-parent households, although extended families and expanded black households were not uncommon, especially in the years surrounding the demise of slavery. Universal public education made it possible for black children to attend school, although in northern communities with sizable black populations, most schools were segregated.

As in the South, many black families were headed by single women. In Cincinnati, Ohio, the number of female-headed households doubled between 1830 and 1850, accounting for about 22 percent of all families. The strain of maintaining the nuclear family in the late antebellum era may have caused a further decline in the number of households led by couples. In Boston the proportion of couple-headed families was less than two-thirds in 1850, and ten years later it had dropped to 60 percent. Similar drops occurred in Cincinnati and Philadelphia between 1850 and 1860. Interestingly, across the North households with children of fourteen years or younger were more likely to include two parents, suggesting that low life expectancies may have been an important factor in the rise of single-parent households. Research shows that most black women heading families tended to be in their late thirties or forties, so it is possible that the deaths of their husbands, not divorce or desertion, forced them to manage their families on their own.

Family in Freedom. Following Emancipation, the first activity for many former slaves was to seek out family. During the Reconstruction era newly freed blacks in the South set out with determination to restore their families. Accounts of blacks who traveled across the country in search of wives, children, and other family members from whom they had been separated during slavery were common. Although the Civil War brought many disruptions to all Southerners, the black family emerged from the conflict as a strong and vital institution. The threat to the stability of family relations posed by slavery was removed, allowing family ties to be solidified and marriages to become legally sanctified for the first time.

In families with able-bodied men, the women's labor was withdrawn from the paid labor force—at least temporarily—as wives made their children and their households priorities. The gendered division of labor in nuclear families became more clearly defined, with domestic chores falling to the women. In many cases, however, black families drawn into the sharecropping system realized that women's labor was essential to the family economy, and women gradually returned to perform field work in addition to their domestic responsibilities. In female-headed households, women's choices were more circumscribed, as they sought any work that would support their kin. Children also found their role in the post-Emancipation black family, as defined by their parents' situation. In the best cases, children were able to attend one of the newly established schools for freedpeople. In most black families, on the other hand, the labor of children was central to the family economy, and many youths labored in the fields alongside other family members.

The case study of Archie and Harriet Stevenson (formerly known as the Brewsters), who had fourteen children together during slavery, provides insight into the black family during times of both slavery and freedom. The couple began their marriage as the slaves of Moor Stephenson in Coweta County, Georgia. Slaves were handled as movable, valuable property and were included as parts of estates; upon Moor Stephenson's death, twenty-nine slaves from his estate, including the family of Archie and Harriet, were divided into lots of three or fewer. Each lot was then assigned a number and distributed by lottery—resulting in the separation of Archie and Harriet and their children. While some family members were merely hired out or rented, others were sold, mortgaged, attached to satisfy debts, or transferred to Texas with the expansion of the Cotton Kingdom.

Since the Stevensons were separated during slavery, the first full-scale picture of their post-Emancipation family life appears in the 1870 census. In that year Archie, Harriet, four of their children, and Noah Allen, who was presumably a brother or nephew, resided beside their son Dennis and his family in Coweta County; they had apparently managed to reunite at the end of the Civil War. As was typical for black families during the late nineteenth century, the Stevensons demonstrated a preference for male-headed households.

Indeed, the Stevenson kin grouped into arrangements with male household heads, reflecting a pattern outlined by the historian Herbert Gutman, author of *The Black Family in Slavery and Freedom, 1750–1925*. In the post-Emancipation era, second-generation Stevenson females married in their teens, while the Stevenson males married near age twenty or older: Nancy Stevenson married at age fifteen in 1875, Laura at age seventeen. Cass Stevenson married at age twenty-six in 1875, Aaron at age nineteen in 1877. Between 1870 and 1880 three of every five Stevenson households were nuclear. Some scholars speculate that the emerging trend of postponement of marriage, which was to become more pronounced later in the nineteenth century, was an economic decision. By the late nineteenth century men typically married between the ages of twenty-five and thirty-five, while women married between twenty and thirty.

During the Reconstruction era Archie and Harriet urged their adult children to use Stevenson as their surname; the free parents likely sought a common name to bind the family together. The majority of the second generation complied. Between 1867 and 1877 there occurred six marriages among the second generation of Stevensons in Coweta County, four being among the children of Archie and Harriet—who were listed under the surname Brewster in the 1870 census but changed their surname to Stevenson.

In freedom, the Stevenson family was drawn into sharecropping or tenant-farming arrangements along with the majority of African Americans who remained in the agricultural South. Georgia had a concentration of black farmers and the largest black population in the Deep South in the last two decades of the nineteenth century. The rise of the Ku Klux Klan and the surrounding political turmoil, which culminated in the conservative Redemption in Georgia around 1871, when white southern Democrats reclaimed political power after Reconstruction, initially stymied the material gains of thrifty black farmers. In 1879 the sixty-something Archie Stevenson rented twenty-seven acres in Coweta County, working fifteen acres in the cash crop of cotton, two in wheat, five in sorghum, and five in corn, while his son Sam paid cash rent. Many black tenant farmers, who were ensnared by the unscrupulous business practices of white landowners as well as by the volatility of the cotton economy, were relegated to landless existences. The black family offered a buffer that sometimes kept kin from complete dependency.

Family networks were vital to success within the rural black economy. As a family, the Stevensons pooled resources, provided child care for working parents, and supplemented the aged farmer's financial reserves. In 1880 Archie and Harriet shared their household with their twenty-something daughter Laura; her husband, Richard Morris; and the couple's children. The second generation of Stevensons, all born in slavery, interacted with an extensive network of kith and kin based in Coweta County between 1865 and 1895. Samuel Stevenson benefited from his wife, Ellen Bohannon Stevenson, who celebrated her haggling exploits in the market—one place in the segregated South where whites and blacks were on a par—and her family network. In 1891 Ellen's father, Lewis, sold Samuel an additional hundred acres in Coweta County. From the sprawling branches of five trees in the front yard dangled swings secured by thick grass ropes. The home was the favorite spot of the grandchildren of Wilson and Rillis Stevenson in Douglas County, Georgia, whose children sought economic opportunity in Atlanta and the mining centers of Birmingham, Alabama, in the 1890s.

The withdrawal of women from the workforce signified a renewal of commitment to the family. In freedom Harriet Stevenson was enumerated as keeping house in the 1870 and 1880 federal censuses. Harriet, who was believed to be seventy-five years old at the time of her death on December 12, 1894, was buried in the segregated Eastview Cemetery in Newnan, Georgia. At a time when burial sites typically were marked with broken dishware or rock piles, her children purchased Harriet's pinnacle-shape white granite memorial and inscribed on its pedestal "OUR MOTHER" in large capital letters. The Stevenson children apparently pooled their resources for the ostentatious memorial, which today stands as the second-oldest tombstone in Eastview Cemetery.

The renewed focus upon the family contributed to the strong influence of the mother in the black family, as evidenced by the memorial to Harriet, who bore all her children during slavery. When the second generation of Stevenson women worked, they chose jobs like those of laundress and farm laborer that kept them closer to home and family. Some scholars contend that the withdrawal of wives from the workforce was likely precipitated by husbands who valued expanded roles as providers and heads of household. Other scholars argue that women chose arduous occupations such as laundress, the requirements of which could be fulfilled without leaving home, as a means to increase their influence over the family. Whoever initiated the shift, it became a common choice for black women to stay home, allowing them more time to meet household needs.

Emergence of the Black Middle Class. The Stevensons valued the family and church as vital institutions in the black community and were committed to educational attainment and the realization of the dream of "forty acres and a mule." The black landowner represented one of the most stable components of black rural communities in the late nineteenth century. W. E. B. Du Bois wrote that landownership was one of the most significant indicators of black family progress. In 1885 the thirty-five-year-old Samuel Stevenson purchased forty acres in Coweta County for two hundred dollars, followed by twenty-five acres five years later. During the last two decades of the nineteenth century thrifty black families made considerable strides toward property ownership and formed an emerging black middle class.

While the Stevensons' desires to become independent landowners typified the aspirations of rural black families in the late nineteenth century, the scope of their success may have been atypical. The second generation of Stevenson males tended to practice farming, the exceptions being the brothers Washington Kellogg and Cass Stevenson, who were carpenter and drayman, respectively, in Newnan, Georgia. In 1879 Wilson Stevenson worked as a farmhand, logger, and huckster in Coweta County. He regularly walked over twenty miles from Salt Springs into Atlanta to save the twenty cents for the train ride. Sam Stevenson increased his material gains through the operation of stud services and the production and distribution of charcoal, ribbon cane, and sorghum syrup. He invested his profits into the purchase of guano, a superior fertilizer, which he distributed on credit to local black farmers. Southern farmers who managed their operations with an eye to self-sufficiency were somewhat atypical and had the potential to make strides. In the 1890s, however, proscriptive laws coupled with the collapse of the cotton economy signaled the wane of black material gains. Independent black landowner status was a significant achievement, as the black masses typically lived in sparsely furnished one- or two-room cabins.

In the mid-1880s Wilson Stevenson and his wife, Rillis, migrated forty-five miles from Coweta County to Salt Springs and joined the wave of black farming families who moved from rural districts to towns or cities in search of economic opportunity. The couple returned to rural life in 1887, when they purchased an eighty-acre farm conveniently situated on the Georgia Pacific railway for six hundred dollars. The property included a two-story house and six three- or four-room cabins, made of solid lumber, to be used as rental units. Members of the third generation of Stevensons benefited from living in Wilson's rental facilities when they were not fully occupied by tenant farmers. The spacious grounds of Wilson Stevenson's farm reflected a high standard of living with respect to the black family of the late nineteenth century.

Education was a critical element in the uplift of the black family following Emancipation. The second generation of Stevensons risked verbal abuse, economic sanctions, and bodily assaults to send their children to school in Newnan, Georgia, during the Reconstruction era. The teenage Lu Stevenson taught former slaves to read in Coweta County during the late 1860s, when unabated opposition to schools for blacks resulted in school closures. While many free blacks desired education, the goal typically remained unfulfilled in the antebellum era.

The third generation of Stevensons, born during the Civil War and Reconstruction, expanded their aspirations for educational attainment. Stevenson females attended schools and became teachers, while less attention was given to higher education for sons, who were expected to attain semiskilled work. Three educators came from the household of Wilson Stevenson. In 1890 his daughter Odelia was attending the teaching department at Spelman College in Atlanta. In black colleges in the South, an amazing 143,000 were trained in various educational and technical departments and five hundred graduated with degrees between 1875 and 1900. The desire of later generations of Stevensons for education was typical of the black masses, although its manifestation for them may have been atypical, as was the progress of earlier generations of Stevensons during the Reconstruction era. In spite of the harassment experienced by a generation of former slaves, they persisted in reaching their goals of building strong black families, founding schools for their children, and attaining the sometimes elusive dream of landownership.

[*See also* Africanisms; Autobiography; Bailey, Harriet; Black Church; Black Uplift; Civil War; Class; Demographics; Economic Life; Emancipation; Gender; Marriage, Mixed; Masculinity; Sexuality; Sharecropping; Slave Narratives; Slavery; Slave Trade; Urbanization; Women; *and* Work.]

BIBLIOGRAPHY

Blassingame, John W. *The Slave Community: Plantation Life in the Antebellum South*. Rev. ed. New York: Oxford University Press, 1979.

Davis, David Brion. *Slavery in the Colonial Chesapeake*. Williamsburg, VA: Colonial Williamsburg Foundation, 1986.

Douglass, Frederick. *My Bondage and My Freedom*. New Haven, CT: Yale University Press, 2003.

Douglass, Frederick. *Narrative of the Life of Frederick Douglass, an American Slave*. New Haven, CT: Yale University Press, 2001.

Du Bois, W. E. B. *The Souls of Black Folk*. New York: New American Library, 1969.

Genovese, Eugene D. *Roll, Jordan, Roll: The World the Slaves Made*. New York: Pantheon, 1974.

Gutman, Herbert G. *The Black Family in Slavery and Freedom, 1750–1925*. New York: Pantheon, 1976.

Yellin, Jean Fagan. *Harriet Jacobs: A Life*. New York: Basic Civitas, 2004.

Horton, James Oliver, and Lois E. Horton. *In Hope of Liberty: Culture, Community, and Protest among Northern Free Blacks, 1700–1860*. New York: Oxford University Press, 1997.

Jones, Jacqueline. *Labor of Love, Labor of Sorrow: Black Women, Work, and the Family from Slavery to the Present*. New York: Basic Books, 1985.

—ROLAND BARKSDALE-HALL
—L. DIANE BARNES

BLACK LOYALISTS. *Black Loyalists*, a term invented during the American Revolution, was used by the British to distinguish black, or African, from white, or European, Americans who remained loyal to Great Britain. Like most conflicts, the Revolution was waged on numerous fronts, and the term was deployed in a discursive arena in which the meanings of such slogans as "independence," "freedom," and "rights of man" were challenged and contested. The British seized upon the idea of declarations and drafted a series of proclamations (beginning with Lord Dunmore, the last royal governor of Virginia, and continuing with General Thomas Gage, Sir William Howe, and Sir Henry Clinton) in which they offered to emancipate the slaves of rebels in return for rendering services to "King and Crown." These were some of the most subversive documents drafted during the conflict.

In addition to exposing a contradiction between the theory and practice of freedom, British proclamations drove a wedge between the Patriots and their African and enslaved counterparts. They were not, however, part of some altruistic agenda concerning emancipation: freedom was not offered to the slaves of white Loyalists, although a good many ran away, nor were such proclamations extended to the British West Indies. Along with subverting republican ideologies, linking freedom to service withdrew the labor of Africans from the cause of the Patriots. Black labor had been instrumental to the colonial economy, and such was the case during the Revolution as well. The conflict drained half a million pounds per month for goods and services from the military chest, and the labor of blacks was essential in that, along with releasing British units for combat, it helped defray direct costs (for provisions, fuel, and rations) to the Exchequer.

Lured by British proclamations, black Americans (some free, but most enslaved) joined the British and were organized into units such as the Black Brigade, the Ethiopian Regiment, and the Black Pioneers, which assisted and supported British regiments. In addition to military formations, blacks served as "followers of army and flag" and performed informal but necessary tasks acting as teamsters, pilots, vendors, and spies, as well as aides-de-camp and personal servants. Blacks were by no means passive recipients. If service constituted agency, then African Americans precipitated one of the largest slave revolts in the Americas. Initial estimates in the range of 80,000 to 100,000 have been substantiated, suggesting that the number of black Loyalists may have exceeded their white counterparts.

Voting with their feet, Africans abandoned their former abodes and migrated to British-controlled New York, Savannah, and Charleston, where they formed communities. The New York community expanded from less than two hundred in 1776 to almost four thousand in 1783, transforming the city into one of the largest free-black communities in the New World. Blacks were billeted in "Negro quarters" the British leased from white Loyalists and in housing they confiscated from the rebels. These were not transient communities, and some indication of their vitality can be ascertained by accounts of "Ethiopian balls" and other festivities in which whites as well as blacks participated. Along with festivities, observers noted that African Americans formed or reconstituted families with both intergenerational and extra-kinship relations in communities that resembled the Maroon societies that coalesced in the West Indies.

Despite proclamations assuring their liberty, the plight of the black Loyalists was by no means secure, and negotiations concerning their disposition assumed top priority as the Revolution drew to a close. In an effort to honor British proclamations, Sir Guy Carleton, the British general who negotiated the peace with George Washington, interpreted article 7 of the Treaty of Versailles to mean that blacks who were within British-controlled areas were free. Best efforts aside, the Carleton (or British Headquarters) Papers are permeated with accounts of Patriots who entered British-controlled areas seeking to reclaim their "movable property."

The term "movable property" was used in the "intelligence" (military) correspondence for the common but nonetheless illicit practice of seizing slaves as contraband. Both sides confiscated slaves, and the British engaged in an illicit trade to the West Indies. Philip Morgan and Sylvia Frey estimated that the population of South Carolina dropped by twenty-five thousand, and Benjamin Quarles has suggested that, in addition to the official tallies, as many as ten thousand blacks were illicitly removed during the evacuation of Savannah and Charleston. Along with routine intelligence there is correspondence noting that Tortola in the British Virgin Islands and Saint Lucia in the Leeward Islands had become entrepôts for the sale of blacks "carried from the Southern Provinces."

Absolutes are difficult to verify, but some appreciation of scale and magnitude can be ascertained by looking at records maintained by the Jamaican planter-historian Edward Long. According to Long, the slave population of Jamaica increased from 160,000 in 1768 to 240,000 in 1788, with some 65,000 arriving between 1775 and 1785 despite cessation of the Africa trade and the loss of 15,000 during the conflict. It seems more likely than not that many of the 65,000 slaves originated in the Southern Provinces (Virginia, North Carolina, South Carolina, and Georgia) and were acquired from Tortola.

The transport and relocation of these communities constituted one of the largest evacuations in the Atlantic world. Between July 1782 and November 1783 Carleton evacuated Savannah, Charleston, and New York. Four convoys left Savannah in July, and three left Charleston in December and January. New York was the last and largest, and the evacuation began in June and was completed in November. Evacuation was one issue and relocation another. Canada was a destination for white and black Loyalists, and blacks established separate communities in Nova Scotia and New Brunswick. Dissatisfied with Canada, a substantial number departed for England; finding life little better there, they were induced to settle Sierra Leone.

A small but influential number opted for Jamaica. Among the more notable were Moses Baker and George Liele, who as folk, or itinerant, preachers laid the foundation for the practice of African Christianity. The history of the black Loyalists remains one of the untold stories in the making of the Atlantic world. While scholarly inroads into their diaspora have been undertaken, much remains to be studied concerning their plight and future in the New World and the Old.

[*See also* African Diaspora; American Revolution; Black Brigade; Black Family; Caribbean; Free African Americans to 1828; Liele, George; Riots and Rebellions; *and* Slave Trade.]

BIBLIOGRAPHY

Frey, Sylvia. *Water from the Rock: Black Resistance in a Revolutionary Age.* Princeton, NJ: Princeton University Press, 1991.

Hodges, Graham R. *The Black Loyalist Directory: African Americans in Exile after the American Revolution.* New York: Garland, 1996.

Morgan, Philip D. *Slave Counterpoint: Black Culture in the Eighteenth-Century Chesapeake and Lowcountry.* Chapel Hill: University of North Carolina Press, 1998.

Pulis, John W. "Bridging Troubled Waters: Moses Baker, George Liele, and the African-American Diaspora to Jamaica." In *Moving On: Black Loyalists in the Afro-Atlantic World*, edited by John W. Pulis. New York: Garland, 1999.

Quarles, Benjamin. *The Negro in the American Revolution.* Chapel Hill: University of North Carolina Press, 1961.

—JOHN W. PULIS

BLACK MIGRATION. Black migration within colonial America was a result of the demand for labor and the dynamics of white migration in the region. As the American economy grew and settlers pushed into new territory, black migration increased and became a regular feature of life.

Early Migration. Most of the African Americans brought to the colonies in the seventeenth century remained near the coast. As white settlement filtered into the backcountry, land needed to be cleared, houses built, and crops grown; white migrants turned to slave labor. Some masters brought slaves along to their new settlements while others purchased bondpeople after becoming established on their land. Before the American Revolution, however, this type of black migration remained insubstantial.

A notable number of slaves escaped bondage through flight. Although their numbers were small, such fugitives proved a threat to the plantation system. Their cause was aided by the Spanish government, which promised freedom and protection to all slaves who fled to Florida, then a Spanish possession. Other runaways escaped to the mountains and swamps to form Maroon communities. Traveling in large bands that included women and children, these slaves moved constantly in an effort to stay out of the reach of white authorities. They were successful only for a short time, especially after colonial society penetrated farther inland.

The American Revolution disrupted this migration and created opportunities for slaves to seize their freedom.

Even before the Declaration of Independence, Virginia's governor John Murray (1732–1809), the fourth earl of Dunmore, issued a proclamation offering freedom to slaves who fought for the Crown. Dunmore's proclamation caused panic among southern whites, especially when a significant number of slaves shouldered arms to put down the Revolution and an even greater number fled their plantations. At the war's end the British took thousands of slaves to Canada or the Caribbean. At least twenty thousand slaves (or about 5 percent of the southern black population) fled to the British or escaped to freedom during the war.

Black migration grew noticeably in the two decades after independence. Whites poured across the Appalachian Mountains, often bringing slaves with them. The present-day states of Georgia, Alabama, Tennessee, and Kentucky received most of these migrants. Perhaps 115,000 slaves moved from the Atlantic seaboard to the nation's interior between 1790 and 1810. Just like their forebears, most of these bondpeople did the heavy labor of carving farms out of the wilderness. A fairly consistent international slave trade stunted further black migration within the United States.

The tempo of black migration increased substantially after 1815 for a number of reasons. The ban on the Atlantic slave trade, though enacted in 1807, was finally being enforced. White settlers and the state and federal governments forced Native Americans off vast tracts of land in portions of Georgia, Tennessee, Alabama, Mississippi, and Louisiana. The lack of an immediate British or Spanish threat on the frontiers encouraged whites to migrate. As white migrants' demand for labor increased, planters and farmers back in the Chesapeake region experienced a decline in agricultural production; slave owners in Virginia, Maryland, and Delaware found themselves saddled with debt and less need for bond servants. Between 1810 and 1830 at least 278,000 slaves were forced to leave their homes and live in the area that would become the Cotton Kingdom.

Types of Forced Migration. Forced migration took various forms. Many owners brought slaves with them as they moved to the frontier. Such forced marches normally took about two months and wore slaves down with fatigue. Because the trip was so physically demanding and the process of creating a farm so difficult, planters typically left behind older slaves and purchased younger ones who might better withstand the grueling process. They later sent for the older slaves once the farm was established.

A second type of forced migration was the result of the purchase of slaves from the Upper South by slave owners in the Cotton Kingdom. Once slave owners established themselves in the Old Southwest, their need for labor only increased. They expanded landholdings so as to grow more cotton or sugar. Felling trees, digging out stumps, plowing the earth, and draining the swamps stretched slaves to the limit and often destroyed their capacity to work; others died in accidents or of disease. As mortality rates rose, fertility rates fell, forcing planters to buy more bondpeople. In 1822 the slave owner James Byers left his Louisiana cotton plantation to buy more slaves in Richmond, Virginia; he purchased thirty-seven bond servants and then arranged for their transportation to his home.

Such planters tried to avoid dealing with slave traders (also called speculators), who were responsible for the third type of forced migration to the Mississippi River valley. The interstate slave trade grew in strength and resulted in the transportation of between 40 and 70 percent of the slaves who would come to reside in the Cotton Kingdom. Slave traders purchased slaves at farms, auctions, and sheriff's sales, typically confining their purchases in taverns, county jails, or slave pens. Pens or slave jails quickly became fixtures in most large cities along the Atlantic seaboard. These facilities, usually outside the city limits or in bad neighborhoods, consisted merely of cramped cells where slaves might be chained to the wall. In later decades pens became more elaborate and had better sanitation, since abolitionists and curious foreign tourists made a point of visiting them.

Once a speculator had acquired enough slaves for a westward trip—typically forty or more—he might march them overland. Such groups of slaves, known as coffles, became a common sight on southern roads. The male slaves were often chained together in pairs, with a rope or chain being passed between each set of slaves. Women and children walked in small groups or rode in supply wagons if they were unable to withstand the grueling journey. Slave traders rode on horseback, spurring on their purchases with whips and guns if necessary.

Speculators also marched their slaves to the western edge of Virginia and loaded them on flatboats or steamboats for river voyages. They sometimes stopped in Kentucky or Tennessee to buy more slaves before arriving in the Deep South. Such groups usually numbered less than seventy-five and could roam the deck during the day but slept in chains at night while anchored. This mode of travel was more expensive but enabled slaves to arrive in better physical condition.

A third way to move slaves was via the coast trade, in which slaves were placed on seagoing vessels and then shipped along the Atlantic coast. Although this method was also expensive, it was the most efficient and did not require speculators to accompany their slaves; in addition, large numbers of slaves could be easily shipped at once. The country's largest slave-trading firm, Franklin and Armfield, was based in Alexandria, Virginia, and pos-sessed four ships that it used for the coast trade. On one of these ships, 180 slaves were crammed onto two raised platforms, each about five or six feet deep.

Interstate Slave Trade. Most of the slaves trapped in the coils of the interstate slave trade were bound for Natchez or New Orleans, Louisiana, the two largest slave marts of the Deep South. Slaves in New Orleans were sold at auction in the city's hotels or in the slave jails dotting the landscape. When put up for sale, bond servants were subject to the shattering indignity of inspection. Buyers were most concerned with finding whip marks, which might indicate that a slave was rebellious or difficult to control. They ran their hands over the bodies of slaves, squeezing muscles, testing joints, counting teeth, and looking for physical deformities. The slave Charles Ball remembered having to work his hands and fingers in quick motions to prove his ability to pick cotton. Women usually underwent some type of rude gynecological exam to determine whether they were capable of bearing children.

Slaves hardly consented to the demeaning nature of the interstate slave trade. Bond servants available for sale shaped transactions by concealing information or exaggerating accomplishments, literally trying to avoid certain buyers and pursue others. Some bond servants tried to escape the interstate slave trade altogether. In 1826 seventy-five slaves on a flatboat rose in rebellion, murdering the speculator who had purchased them and fleeing to Indiana. That same year slaves on the *Decatur*, a vessel in the coast trade, threw the captain and mate overboard and steered the vessel toward Haiti. Though both attempts failed in the end, they evidenced the fact that slaves were willing to risk their lives to escape a fate seen as worse than death. Other slaves took action to avoid the slave trade altogether. It was not uncommon for slaves to chop off hands or maim themselves in some other way, thus rendering themselves incapable of work. Slaves were not merely passive victims of the interstate slave trade but actively worked to undermine it. In the process, they shaped southern white perceptions of slavery.

[*See also* American Revolution; Black Loyalists; Caribbean; Declaration of Independence; Demographics; Maroons; Murray, John (Lord Dunmore); Resistance; Slave Trade; Slavery: Mississippi Valley; Slavery: West; *and* Urbanization.

BIBLIOGRAPHY

Bancroft, Frederic. *Slave Trading in the Old South* (1931). Columbia: University of South Carolina Press, 1996.

Berlin, Ira. *Many Thousands Gone: The First Two Centuries of Slavery in North America.* Cambridge, MA: Belknap Press, 1998.

Deyle, Steven. "The Irony of Liberty: Origins of the Domestic Slave Trade." *Journal of the Early Republic* 12 (Spring 1992): 37–62.

Gudmestad, Robert H. *A Troublesome Commerce: The Transformation of the Interstate Slave Trade*. Baton Rouge: Louisiana State University Press, 2003.

Kulikoff, Allan. "Uprooted Peoples: Black Migrants in the Age of the American Revolution, 1790–1820." In *Slavery and Freedom in the Age of the American Revolution*, edited by Ira Berlin and Ronald Hoffman. Charlottesville: University Press of Virginia, 1983.

Tadman, Michael. *Speculators and Slaves: Masters, Traders, and Slaves in the Old South*. Madison: University of Wisconsin Press, 1996.

Terry, Gail S. "Sustaining the Bonds of Kinship in a Trans-Appalachian Migration, 1790–1811: The Cabell-Breckinridge Slaves Move West." *Virginia Magazine of History and Biography* 102 (October 1994): 455–476.

—ROBERT H. GUDMESTAD

BLACK MILITIAS. A not fully acknowledged facet of Reconstruction, so-called black militias and the controversies their activities engendered fueled much of the anti-Republican backlash in the South. Black militias were not, as the name implies, composed exclusively of African Americans. In fact, even black-dominated militias were rare, except for the case of South Carolina, where that state's black majority and the willingness of the state's governors Robert K. Scott and Daniel H. Chamberlain to arm them resulted in mainly black militia regiments in some locales. Overall, the derogatory moniker "black militia" referred to any racially integrated unit, no matter how small or large its African American component.

After the war the South's provisional governors, many of whom harbored Confederate sympathies, reorganized their state's all-white militias to provide "law and order" in the rural areas where no reliable law enforcement existed. In reality, however, they were most concerned about the presence of black Union soldiers in the army's occupying forces, which they feared gave local freed people "extravagant expectations" of freedom. Although they were defeated, white southerners were unwilling to surrender to justice administered at the hands of African Americans. The postwar militias, whose ranks often included returned rebel veterans, sought to pacify black soldiers and local freed people by disarming them and, if necessary, assaulting or killing them.

Thus, in March 1867, Congress passed a new militia law that banned any military organization in the South that was not part of the regular army. But as gun violence against freed people continued to be a dire problem, Republicans soon realized that a prohibition on the militia handicapped their state governments, because it forbade the arming of their allies. Federal troop numbers in the South fell to just over five thousand by the end of 1867, and most of them were stationed near New Orleans, Louisiana; Mobile, Alabama; or other points of military convenience. The southern backcountry, where violence was rampant and policing was needed, had little federal protection. Without adequate federal military support, Republicans decided that their own best interests necessitated a state militia, and barely a year later Congress revoked the militia ban.

The participation of blacks in these militias varied from state to state. As previously mentioned, South Carolina experienced the most activity, along with Arkansas, where an all-out guerrilla war between Governor Powell Clayton's forces and the Ku Klux Klan dominated much of that state's Reconstruction period. Likewise, Texas actively employed an integrated militia and state police force, but they were short-lived. After its early "redemption" by Democrats in 1872, the Texas state legislature disbanded those units. Also notable is the case of the New Orleans Metropolitan Police. When the Republican governor Henry Clay Warmoth stripped the city's Democratic mayor of his control over the city police and made them a unit of the state militia, Warmoth forced the Metropolitans to integrate—something the mayor had refused to do despite federal orders requiring him to do so.

However, many state officials feared that arming black militias might incite further violence, and they hesitated to use them. Without exception, the presence of armed African Americans fanned the fires of southern indignation and often resulted in a violent outbreak between the militiamen and armed whites. Unfortunately, the militias were sometimes outnumbered and found themselves on the losing end of such confrontations. This was the case in Grant Parish, Louisiana, where fifty-nine black militiamen were gunned down in the town of Colfax. Jim Williams, a black militia captain in rural York County, South Carolina, was found murdered with a placard hung around his neck that read, "Gone to his last militia muster." Black militias received much of the aggression that southern whites felt against Emancipation and Reconstruction, and this made their organization a considerable risk.

Just as service in the army had given African American men a sense of personal and collective pride, militia service also provided them with a means to achieve their postwar political goals. Militia service and membership in the Union League often overlapped, as did the leadership of the two organizations. Militia drills and parades often accompanied political campaigns and rallies, a fact that brought charges of illegality and corruption against Republican governments. But African Americans looked to militia service as a way to secure both their political independence and their physical protection. Their uniforms, often homemade and brightly colored with heavy ornamentation, symbolized their collective aspiration to be counted as active members of their state governments. In the end, black militias and their efforts to secure

African American political inclusion gave white supremacists the means to label Reconstruction "the tragic era."

[*See also* Civil War; Colfax Massacre; Emancipation; Political Participation; Racism; Reconstruction; Republican Party; Union Army, African Americans in; *and* Violence against African Americans.]

BIBLIOGRAPHY

Hahn, Steven. "Extravagant Expectations of Freedom: Rumour, Political Struggle, and the Christmas Insurrection Scare of 1865 in the American South." *Past and Present* 157 (November 1997): 122–177.

Hahn, Steven. *A Nation under Our Feet: Black Political Struggles in the Rural South from Slavery to the Great Migration*. Cambridge, MA: Harvard University Press, 2003.

Singletary, Otis A. *Negro Militia and Reconstruction*. Austin: University of Texas Press, 1957.

—CAROLE T. EMBERTON

BLACK NATIONALISM. [*This entry contains two subentries dealing with black nationalism from the seventeenth-century slave trade through the late nineteenth century. The first article discusses the first formations of African national identities and the influence of various revolutions on black nationalism, while the second focuses on the most significant figures of the movement.*]

The Evolution of Black Nationalism

During the colonial period, the terms *nations* and *nationalism* were defined more by language or other cultural practices than by the political connotations of today. West African society in the seventeenth century, for example, was a network of over fifty sociolinguistic cultures. Linguistic boundaries could be flexible, as could aesthetics. Certain West African nationalities were ethnically and linguistically closer to some than they were to others, factors recognized by such acculturating characters as the Jesuits, who sought common languages, ones understood by as many as possible, to more easily catechize Africans into Christianity. West Africa also had some commercial interactions or trade that promoted cultural relationships. Politics tended to be diverse, at least before the era of the Atlantic slave trade, during which West African societies tended to be somewhat more homogeneous.

In the slave trade, sociolinguistic qualities and economic identity became intertwined. Nationalism formed or reappeared in slave barracks along the coast. Such slave factories as Cormantine (in present day Nigeria) created an identity for those enslaved people who emerged from them. After the New York Slave Revolt of 1712, for example, John Sharpe, the secretary of the Society for the Propagation of the Gospel in Foreign Parts (SPG), chronicled how "Some Negroes here of the Nations of the Carmantines and Pappa, conspired to destroy all the whites." One Antiguan planter noted of bondmen from Cormantine that, "Noe Man deserved a Cormantine that would not treat him as a Friend rather than a slave." Slave nationalism appeared through such statements and by the methods of swearing oaths that were derived from African customs. Two decades later in New York, a satirist critiquing the Pinkster holiday described how enslaved people gathered "according to their nations." African names and nationalities were also prominent in the Stono Revolt in South Carolina in 1739.

Scholars argue about the degree of multi-stop purchasing of slaves, with one side contending that "coasting" meant bringing together enslaved peoples from many ports, while others argue that slave traders, for reasons of economic management, tried to buy as many slaves from one factory as possible. John Thornton has reasoned that such a method ensured a considerable degree of homogeneity in the origins of slaves even as masters tried to blend in slaves from different ports to curb the potential for rebellion. Whichever pattern was used, enslaved people often overcame language differences in the lengthy voyage across the Atlantic and created dyadic relationships that fostered a new sense of nationalism—this time, African American. These new loyalties could be found as well on larger plantations or in cities. In the West Indies and on the North American continent, travelers recorded cultural activities such as funerals and celebrations as examples of nationhood. Marriage, when permitted, could also foster nationality. Some marriages might have predated enslavement and the trade itself. Such unions linked people of the same origins or nationality, allowing them to communicate in words, religion, and aesthetic concepts, and to transmit a national concept into the next generation.

The formation of such nationalities in blocks on plantations could have hazardous results for masters, as was the case with the Angolans and Senegambians, who rose up in Guadeloupe in 1656. Nationality may be seen in later revolts, as noted, and among groups of runaways who sometimes formed Maroon nations known to be in the interior of the West Indies, in South America, and, as has been more recently perceived, in North America. The power of the transfer of African relationships and culture into the New World meant that enslaved people arrived in America capable of finding help to resist the forced, barbaric homogenization of slavery and the mellower but no less potent acculturation of western religions.

Whether at the slave ports, on ships, or during enslavement in North America, African slaves did sometimes experience personal change. One such transformation took place as African languages melded into a patois composed of other African tongues and European and North American argot to create an Atlantic Creole lingua franca. Verbal methods such as singing helped facilitate the retention of these newer languages. Another avenue to preserving culture was aesthetics, as could be seen in the "Afro-Portuguese Ivories," which were African objects produced for the Portuguese market. Though consciously created to please European eyes, these retained distinctive African aesthetic characteristics. Musicians, too, were conveyors of African culture. Banjo players in New York City in 1738, for example, used an African "plucked" style, which approximated the percussive methods used throughout West Africa.

Influence and Resistance. Perhaps the deepest challenge to African nationality in the early colonial years was the influence of European traditions. While it may be an exaggeration to claim, as some historians do, that European faiths caused a holocaust of African theologies, the pervasiveness of Christianity at the very least served to obscure or distort these imported African religions. Beginning in Africa and continuing in the New World, state and dissenting European religions vied to replace African "paganism," with mixed results. Small groups of African Americans became closely associated with the Church of England and its tradition of dissent—welcoming denominations such as the Moravian, for example—but in the main, enslaved peoples in the North American colonies remained unchurched. By the 1750s even Church of England missionaries had begun to doubt whether Africans were capable of understanding Christian theology and had developed racist concepts of the soul. Even as African Americans learned English or Dutch, lived among European Americans, took European names, and experienced the Great Awakening, their degree of acculturation remained fairly small. Resisting religious instruction, they maintained a powerfully nationalist sense of their own religiosity. This is especially apparent in the slave culture, which filled the gap left by organized religion. In gatherings and frolics, a hardscrabble slave culture emerged, one that became evident during the New York Slave Conspiracy of 1741.

Celebrations were means by which African Americans could revive their African heritage. First appearing in the seventeenth century and continuing into the nineteenth, such holidays were more than a pressure valve. They represented a time when Africans could gather and revel in ways unthreatening to whites. However, appearances could be deceiving. During the New York Conspiracy of 1741, for example, blacks gathered on Pinkster Day to plot the overthrow of the government.

It is debatable whether or not such appearances of nationality derived from a single origin. Ira Berlin, for example, has argued that the slave trade made origins largely irrelevant for "freshwater" Africans coming in the mid-eighteenth century. However, Berlin contends that newcomers, unlike the Creole Africans who arrived in earlier periods, found most entry points to European culture closed to them. As a result plantations big and small became places of revival as enslaved blacks turned inward to create African burial grounds and churches. Certainly all of these elements—African retentions and nationality, acculturation and Christianity, and a slave culture—were present at the dawning of the American Revolution, an event that allowed African Americans to fully engage in nationalistic behavior and activities.

Revolution and Disillusionment. The American Revolution was the greatest impetus for African nationalism since the arrival of enslaved people from their home continent. However, while African Americans did fight on the side of the Patriots in the Revolutionary War, the vast majority who joined the battle did so on the side of the English. British officials and generals offered freedom to any slave willing to serve the King to suppress the rebellion. Americans had few answers except to deny that blacks could ably serve their cause. As a result upward of a hundred thousand enslaved blacks left their masters to fight for the Crown as soldiers, wagon men, servants, spies, and scouts, among other roles. Many blacks, though, did heed the revolutionary demands of their white counterparts, took part in riots against the British tax policies, offered their own petitions to the legislature in Massachusetts, and publicized their opinions about freedom in newspapers. Some traded military services for promises of freedom from their masters once the conflict was over. On the battlefields, thousands showed their mettle and impressed American and British officers alike. Blacks served in their own units, and while white officers nominally commanded them, a black leadership emerged from military service.

The proof of the influence of the American Revolution upon African Americans comes from evidence provided by those who lost. During 1782 and 1783 at least three thousand black men, women, and children departed from New York for Nova Scotia while another eight thousand left Savannah, Georgia, for the West Indies. The Nova Scotia group left in military units that they maintained while settling in their new homes. They asked for the same things Patriots did in the United States: land, pensions, and freedom. A clear leadership, including Stephen Blucke, Boston King, John Marrant, and others, emerged from the black Loyalist experience and from the ministry that appeared immediately after the Revolution. After a few years of disappointments in Nova Scotia, many black Loyalists demanded a chance to join others in Sierra Leone, where an initial group had gone from London in 1787. These one thousand and more departed from Nova Scotia and arrived in Sierra Leone to help create a nation with a constitution more radical than the one white Americans built in 1787. If African Americans had to go to Africa to live out their newfound republicanism, they would do it.

The example of the black Loyalists in Sierra Leone had a profound impact on African Americans left behind in the United States. After the American Revolution many northern states quickly put the system of servitude on the road to gradual emancipation, with New York and New Jersey being the last to do so in 1799 and 1804. The Chesapeake states toyed with the idea of abolition briefly, then turned back to slavery as their primary social and economic method. The idea of abolition went nowhere in the Carolinas or Georgia, and soon slavery became the road to prosperity in the new territories and states of the southeast. The Northwest Ordinance of 1787 forbade slavery in new states north of the Ohio River, but soon anti-black codes became intertwined with white civilization. Similarly, in the northern states, blacks generally became free by the early nineteenth century but found the doors to economic and social success nailed shut. A rising virulent racism had to give African Americans pause about whether they had any future in the United States. The period between 1790 and 1830 saw African Americans exploring that question in nationalist terms.

Perhaps reflecting their interest in black nation building in Sierra Leone and at the same time acknowledging a racial difference with white America, the organizers of black churches and benefit societies identified themselves as Africans. Thus arose the African Methodist Episcopal Church, the African Society, and the New York African mutual aid societies. The autobiographers John Jea and George White referred to themselves as Africans even though most of their lives had been spent in America. The wealthiest black in the United States, Paul Cuffe, backed the colonization of free blacks to Africa and found support from other leading blacks including Richard Allen and Peter Williams Jr. Cuffe did so years before the founding of the African Colonization Society. It was as if African Americans believed that Africa was their true destiny, even as they demanded the end of slavery and improved civil rights in the United States. One compelling force was the rising tide of racism, which insisted that blacks had no place in the American democratic experiment. Racism was apparent everywhere. In Congress, the future president James Madison rose to denounce a petition from Absalom Jones protesting the Fugitive Slave Act of 1793. Madison claimed that free blacks had "no claim" on the attention of Congress. Racist mobs threatened free blacks in major northern cities. Small wonder that Africa seemed so appealing.

The French Revolution and its aftermath in Haiti inspired African Americans. In Gabriel's Rebellion of 1800 in Virginia, black conspirators drawing from a spectrum of influences combined black nationalism, artisan republicanism, and the encouragement of a mysterious Frenchman who extolled the lessons of the French Revolution in local taverns.

The revolution in Haiti was a clear influence upon African Americans. Toussaint Louverture's triumph thrilled blacks just as it terrified whites. Black leaders such as Prince Hall of Boston found Haiti to be a confirmation of African American faith and moral perception. Even as events in Haiti turned from the initial optimism to the hardships imposed by Toussaint's successors, Haiti remained a beacon for African Americans. Prince Saunders, the remarkable African American who became a key player in Haitian relations with the United States and Europe, invited black Americans to consider his new country a place of refuge.

That idea initially did not go far. In the second decade of the nineteenth century, black Americans created their own nationalism and began to distrust migration as an answer. An important means of combating American racism was to produce example after example of talented, accomplished blacks. Borrowing from the work of Bishop Henri Grégoire, African Americans in pamphlets, poetry, and public talks invoked a lengthy list of great black people. In the beginning of the nineteenth century, then, black nationalism was composed of pride of accomplishment, a belief that African Americans should share in American freedoms, and a countervailing sense that perhaps Africa might be the better place for them. The most important issues before the movement were the battles against racism and slavery, and the drive for better civil rights.

After the abolition of American participation in the Atlantic slave trade in 1898, black nationalist ideas began to change. While over one hundred thousand enslaved Africans came into the United States through Charleston between 1800 and 1808, they remained enslaved and apart from the bubbling intellectual world of northern free blacks. After 1808 the number of African immigrants, forced or free, dropped to a trickle and would remain low until the late twentieth century.

Reforming America. Believing that a major victory had been won with the end of the Atlantic slave trade and further spurred by black community participation on the side of the Americans in the War of 1812 (in Virginia, however, enslaved blacks welcomed the English), black intellectuals in the North moved away from a pan-Africanism to demanding a place for blacks in a free United States.

Though Prince Saunders continued to invite African Americans and though Canada seemed a good place for freedom, another force turned African Americans away from Africa as a source of nationalism. Recent reports from Sierra Leone and its American counterpart, Liberia, had not been encouraging. Black Americans who went back in vessels sponsored by Cuffe lacked immunity from African diseases and died in droves. The new colony of Liberia lacked organization and funding. Worse, combining older environmental ideas and newer forms of pseudoscientific racism (much of it stemming from Thomas Jefferson), white Americans had hit upon a plan to rid the United States of free blacks. Organized in 1817, the American Colonization Society stated that its mission was to encourage and support free blacks that were willing to "return" to Africa and never come back. Part of the Society's message was that free blacks had no place in the United States and were incapable of working and living in equality with whites. Understandably, nationalist blacks were outraged. Richard Allen was but one of the many forceful critics of the American Colonization Society. Angry denunciations of the Society appeared in the nascent black press throughout the 1820s and 1830s. Allen's and other black voices soon made the term "African" less palatable to black Americans who increasingly preferred to call themselves "people of color" or "colored." One casualty was the collapse of interest in immigration to Haiti. Black Americans were now interested almost exclusively in reforming America by ending slavery and by forcing the country to live up to its promise and accepting them as equal citizens. David Walker's *Appeal* (1829), considered radical at the time, was perhaps the most profound statement of these beliefs.

Abandoning plans to migrate to Africa did not mean that black Americans forgot their origins or felt less pride in their ancestry. Articles appearing in *Freedom's Journal* between 1827 and 1829 on Haiti and Africa recognized black achievement. These articles and others, which refuted ideas of black degeneration, may have been part of the reason why John Russwurm, the talented editor of *Freedom's Journal*, suddenly resigned and left the United States for Liberia.

By 1830 black nationalism had become a nexus of ideas that sometimes competed with and other times supported each other. Black Americans now identified with the dream, if not the reality, of the United States. If they did not wish to migrate to Africa, they recognized themselves as a nationality distinct from white Americans and justly proud of their African heritage. Already there were signs of the popular ideas of uplift and self-help that would become commonplace in the antebellum years. The image and memory of Africa remained strong among black nationalists of 1830 even as they demanded freedom at home.

[*See also* African Methodist Episcopal Church; Allen, Richard; American Colonization Society; American Revolution; Blucke, Stephen; Cuffe, Paul; David Walker's *Appeal;* Festivals; *Freedom's Journal;* Fugitive Slave Act of 1793; Grégoire, Bishop Henri; Haitian Revolution; Hall, Prince; Jones, Absalom; King, Boston; Marrant, John; Music; New York Conspiracy of 1741; Religion; Riots and Rebellions; Saunders, Prince; Slave Rebellions and Insurrections; *and* Williams, Peter, Jr.]

BIBLIOGRAPHY

Berlin, Ira. *Many Thousands Gone: The First Two Centuries of Slavery in North America.* Cambridge, MA: Harvard University Press, 1998.

Dain, Bruce. *A Hideous Monster of the Mind: American Race Theory in the Early Republic.* Cambridge, MA: Harvard University Press, 2002.

Hodges, Graham Russell. *Root & Branch: African Americans in New York and East Jersey, 1613–1863.* Chapel Hill: University of North Carolina Press, 1999.

Stuckey, Sterling. *Slave Culture: Nationalist Theory and the Foundations of Black America.* New York: Oxford University Press, 1987.

Thornton, John K. *Africa and Africans in the Making of the Atlantic World, 1400–1680.* New York: Cambridge University Press, 1992.

GRAHAM RUSSELL GAO HODGES

The Key Leaders of Black Nationalism

Aimed at giving African Americans political empowerment, fostering economic self-reliance and cultural self-determination, and instilling pride in the black race, black nationalism in the age of Frederick Douglass was, as it has since remained, a complex ideology that defies any simple definition. Although the term did not exist at the time, the black-nationalist philosophy certainly did. It was manifest in the various back-to-Africa and other emigration movements, in violent slave rebellions, and in the many ways African Americans sought to prove their capacity for functioning independently in a white-dominated world. Essentially, it entailed all efforts by blacks to gain political and social equality that did not require integration or assimilation, or white help or charity. In that sense, black nationalism should be considered a counterconservative ideology, a recoiling from the racist oppression to which white America subjected the black race, and a stark contrast to the liberal integrationism of Frederick Douglass.

Historians have called the period from the birth of the United States to the demise of Garveyism—the Afrocentric philosophy espoused by Marcus Garvey—from 1776 to 1925, the age of "classical" black nationalism. Throughout this time racial integration in the white-dominated polity seemed little more than a pipe dream, despite the efforts of integrationists like Douglass, who consistently opposed black nationalism throughout his life. Black nationalists instinctively realized that there was no hope for fair treatment in America in their lifetime and thus explored other options, the primary one being emigration from the United States for some new nation of their own making. Indeed, the term "black nationalism" implies that the ultimate goal of the black race in America was to establish their own independent and sovereign nation. The British government's experiment in creating Sierra Leone in 1787 and repatriating free blacks there showed that modern black nationhood was possible. The success of black Haitians in achieving independence and nationhood in 1804 proved that blacks were capable of determining their own destiny without the help of a white government. Visionary blacks in the United States sought to replicate either or both of these examples throughout the nineteenth century.

Early Emigration and Back-to-Africa Movements. The first major development in North American black nationalism came with the creation of the American Colonization Society (ACS) in 1817. A white-run organization of politicians, philanthropists, and clergymen, the ACS worked in conjunction with the federal government to purchase a three-hundred-mile-long piece of territory on the coast of West Africa in 1819 on which to settle freed slaves. In 1822 the ACS–U.S. government consortium established the colony of Liberia and began moving settlers there. Over the next six decades about thirteen thousand souls were colonized there—hardly a great success considering the millions-strong black population in the United States.

Some black nationalists—such as Richard Allen, the founder of the African Methodist Episcopal (AME) Church; David Walker, the author of *An Appeal to the Coloured Citizens of the World*; and Henry Highland Garnet and Martin Robison Delany, the most renowned black nationalist abolitionists—criticized the Liberian experiment because it did not allow blacks the independence they sought. The situation began to change in 1841 when Liberia got its first black governor, J. J. Roberts. In 1847 the United States relinquished control of the colony; Liberia became a free nation, and Roberts became its first president. Despite such developments, most abolitionists, including Frederick Douglass, consistently opposed not only the Liberian experiment but all colonization schemes, believing they played into the hands of whites who merely wanted to rid the country of its black population.

Douglass was, as usual, mostly correct in his assessment of politicized Afrocentrism. Not only did early ACS leaders, including Henry Clay and James Monroe, want to excise the black population from the United States, but later white leaders such as Abraham Lincoln, the abolitionist Hinton Rowan Helper, the Minnesota senator William

Windom, the Alabama senator John Tyler Morgan, the South Carolina senator Matthew Butler, the North Carolina governor and senator Zebulon Vance, and many others did as well. Even so, black interest in emigration continued, mainly because the situation for slaves and free blacks alike deteriorated rapidly in the 1820s and 1830s, the result of several economic and political factors. By the 1820s the onset of the industrial revolution in Europe spurred the need for increased cotton production in the American South; the invention of the cotton gin and better strains of cotton, the opening of the southwestern territory around the Mississippi River, and the rise of the domestic slave-breeding industry all helped satisfy that need. The 1821 Missouri Compromise revealed the federal government's intention to continue propping up the institution of slavery and allowing it to spread.

The deterioration of the African American situation was hastened by Denmark Vesey's 1822 slave rebellion in South Carolina and Nat Turner's 1831 Virginia uprising, as well as by David Walker's advocacy of such violence in his 1829 *Appeal*, and the evolving abolition movement. The southern states responded to this series of attacks on their "peculiar institution" by passing increasingly oppressive slave codes in the 1830s. White scrutiny of the region's free blacks concomitantly intensified, forcing the small free black population to seek alternatives to staying in the South. Nor did the situation improve in the 1840s, as the abolition movement, which had begun fairly homogeneously, began to fragment. The reinvigoration of the Fugitive Slave Law as part of the Compromise of 1850 became the final impetus in convincing some blacks of the wisdom of leaving the United States. The almost incessant wrangling over the slavery issue in the 1850s—through the Kansas-Nebraska Act, the Bleeding Sumner and Bleeding Kansas episodes, the *Dred Scott* ruling, and John Brown's failed raid on Harpers Ferry and consequent execution—seemed to confirm black nationalists' suspicions that the problem was getting worse instead of better, such that emigration might be the only solution. Since the North was by and large equally racist and discriminating, migration northward was not as attractive an option as leaving the United States altogether.

The emigration schemes of the period were not confined merely to those making Africa the destination of choice. Black leaders such as Henry W. Bibb and Mary Ann Shadd moved to Canada in the 1840s and 1850s and published much literature encouraging others to do the same. Some, including Shadd, Garnet, and James T. Holly, did not stay long, however, deciding that white Canadians were not much of an improvement over their U.S. counterparts. Garnet began advocating emigration to Jamaica after visiting there in 1852, while Holly soon began espousing emigration to Haiti. At the same time, Delany published the first book to explore in depth the various possibilities for emigration—*The Condition, Elevation, Emigration, and Destiny of the Colored People of the United States, Politically Considered*—in which he argued that Central or South America would make the most suitable habitation for emigrants. Meanwhile, from the 1850s to the 1870s Liberia still held the golden door wide open for other black leaders, such as Edward Blyden and Alexander Crummell.

Despite the emergence of the Negro Convention Movement in the 1840s and 1850s, which sought to unify blacks into a common cause, the major themes of black nationalism throughout these pivotal decades were the absence of coordination by black leaders and the lack of uniformity in destinations for emigrants; those who were consistent in their advocacy of one strategy to uplift the race or one location for repatriation were exceptional. Edward Blyden remained fairly consistent in urging emigration to Liberia from 1850 to 1890, but he moved frequently around Africa, as well as to England, before ending his days in Sierra Leone. Alexander Crummell was likewise a dependable advocate of Liberia for about four decades but spent the last twenty-five years of his life in the United States. James T. Holly, who first flirted with Canadian and African emigration, became a permanent resident of Haiti in 1861 but only managed to move 111 recruits there over the course of the rest of his life.

Other black nationalists were even less consistent. Henry Highland Garnet and Martin Delany both vacillated between emigration to Africa or other destinations, as well as occasionally capitulating to the opportunity for personal advancement within the white-dominated United States. Garnet spent his last two decades moving from one place to another, and one job to another, in the United States, before dying while holding the post of U.S. minister to Liberia. Delany spent most of his last years in the United States as well, serving in various positions in the government, the military, and private enterprise. He made one final back-to-Africa effort in the late 1870s by leading the Liberian Exodus Joint Stock Steamship Company. After purchasing one ship and taking one load of emigrants to Africa, the venture folded, and Delany died in the United States.

Post-Civil War Emigration and Pan-African Movements. In the years after the American Civil War, a new generation of black nationalists emerged, led by Benjamin "Pap" Singleton and Henry M. Turner. The lack of coordination and destination never changed, however. Singleton, another disillusioned former Canadian emigrant, became the leader of what came to be known as the Exoduster Movement, organizing the Tennessee Emigration Society and other similar associations to drum up support for his

scheme. From 1875 to 1883 he led several thousand blacks to migrate from the South to Kansas and the surrounding territory with the thought that they could establish independent black towns and homesteads there, free from white control and discrimination. In 1879, at the height of the movement, about 40,000 blacks had trekked westward in search of new homes. Afraid that the South would be emptied of its valuable labor force, some whites attempted, with some success, to stop the exodus. In 1880 the U.S. Senate conducted hearings to investigate the causes of the Exoduster movement. These highly politicized hearings resulted in no substantial answers, as Democrats accused Republicans of encouraging blacks to leave the South for northern and western states to increase their voting strength there, while Republicans accused Democrats of driving blacks out of the South through discriminatory laws and practices implemented since the end of Reconstruction. Meanwhile the "Kansas Fever" died down, as many Exodusters realized that life in Kansas was no panacea. Nevertheless, some of the towns established by Exodusters and subsequent black imitators, such as Nicodemus, Kansas, and Langston, Oklahoma, still exist.

By 1883 Singleton had decided that conditions in Kansas—topographical and meteorological as well as racial—were not conducive to black settlement, and he began advocating emigration to Cyprus, an island in the Mediterranean Sea; it was a futile gesture. Meanwhile, Henry M. Turner, an AME clergyman promoted to bishop in 1880, began espousing the back-to-Africa idea and ultimately became its most prominent spokesman. In 1876 he became vice president of the ACS, the first black to hold such a high position in the organization. He did not, however, actually make a trip to Africa to see what he was sponsoring for another fifteen years, and he never took up residence there. His support of the ACS and the Butler Emigration Bill of 1890, both of which were generally considered racist in nature, drew the ire of many black leaders, while his unwillingness to partake of the life in Africa that he offered to fellow black Americans made him appear hypocritical to many observers.

Turner was the last of the contemporaries of Frederick Douglass to be widely known as a black nationalist, although many others would follow in the twentieth century. The time when Turner came on the scene marked a noticeable shift in rationale behind emigration. Turner, Crummell, and Blyden all began espousing "Pan-Africanism" in the years after the Civil War. Pan-Africanism, like black nationalism, arose as an ideology before the terminology was coined. Also like black nationalism, it was and still is a nebulous concept that defies any simple definition, but which mainly means a unification of people of African descent for the purpose of reclaiming "Africa for Africans," to quote Marcus Garvey. As these pre-Garvey

Pan-Africanists applied the ideology, it meant mainly African Americans moving to their ancestral motherland not so much because the Pan-Africanists wanted to help their fellows escape the racism of the United States as to promote the uplift of the dark continent in terms of civilization—specifically through education, Christian proselytization, industrialization, and technological development. While a noble intention to be sure, this Pan-African reason for emigration held no more appeal to integrationists like Douglass or accommodationists like Booker T. Washington than the earlier escapism did. To Douglass, Washington, and other leading blacks, the most important mission field for civilizing the black race lay in the United States.

Indeed, the timing of Turner's Pan-Africanism was unfortunate. It pitted his idea of elevating the black race to a higher plane of civilization, starting in Africa, against that of Washington, whose Tuskegee Institute and vocational education plan garnered the nation's attention and most humanitarians' affection—as well as the money of rich white philanthropists—in the 1880s and 1890s. It also pitted Turner against the forces of European imperialism, as England, France, Belgium, Italy, and others began to stake their colonial claims to Africa. It was thus possible that American blacks might have moved to Africa only to be swallowed up by another white nation.

Psychological Separatism. Although the major focus of classical black nationalists was always emigration, other manifestations of black nationalism can also be seen in the nineteenth century. The psychological separation of blacks from whites domestically was an acceptable alternative to physical/geographic separation. The goal of such separation was to prove black intelligence and resourcefulness to skeptical whites, as well as to give fellow blacks role models and racial pride. Examples of separatist efforts include blacks publishing their own newspapers, pamphlets, and books; leading their own abolitionist societies, organizing their own conventions, and starting their own businesses, banks, and life-insurance companies; recruiting black soldiers to fight for the Union in the Civil War; and staking a claim to the ivory tower by way of black colleges and universities founded during and after Reconstruction, such as Howard University in Washington, D.C.

After Samuel Cornish and John Brown Russworm published the first black weekly in 1827, *Freedom's Journal*, black abolition literature rolled off the presses almost continuously, despite the quick commercial failure of most. Most important of all such publications was David Walker's *Appeal to the Coloured Citizens of the World*, which addressed four interrelated topics: the deleterious effects of slavery upon black Americans, the woeful con-

sequences of the lack of education among the black population, the miseducation of blacks by Christian preachers, and the deceptive promise of a better life through the ACS's Liberian experiment. Essentially a militant, fundamentalist Christian polemic against slavery, the *Appeal* still reads today like it did then—as the work of a man with passion burning like fire in his veins.

In 1853 Martin Delany published the first serious black nationalist novel, *Blake; or, The Huts of America: A Tale of the Mississippi Valley, the Southern United States, and Cuba*, in response to Harriet Beecher Stowe's much celebrated *Uncle Tom's Cabin*. Unlike Stowe's humble and obedient slave character Uncle Tom, Delany's lead character was a Maroon determined to start a slave rebellion in Cuba, in imitation of Toussaint Louverture's actual rebellion in Haiti some sixty years before. Although *Blake* was not a great commercial success, it has both literary and historical merit as something of a black nationalist manifesto.

Delany would write two more books, for a total of four, in his lifetime. In between writing books he became the first black commissioned officer in U.S. military history. Several other black leaders, including Shadd and Garnet, would join him in recruiting soldiers for the Union army, while still others would join him in pursuit of literary achievement, including Crummell and Blyden. Crummell made his greatest contribution to black nationalism in founding the American Negro Academy in 1897, after the Frederick Douglass era had passed and just one year before Crummell himself died. This academy served as an outlet for black intellectuals/academicians in an age when few other outlets were available. It put black scholars in touch with one another, helped chart a course for the future of black nationalism, and paved the way for other black scholarly organizations to come.

In the end, none of the nineteenth century black nationalists came anywhere close to earning the fame of Frederick Douglass. Because of their radicalness, heterogeneity, and lack of clear direction and purpose, they were always a minority within the minority. Whites generally loathed them rather than respected them for their accomplishments, fearing that any one of them could be the next Nat Turner. Douglass, by contrast, seemed peace-loving and therefore safe to whites, diplomatically but consistently calling for integration and opportunity within the United States, never wavering from his original purpose and methods. Douglass's liberal dream of integration was realized posthumously, of course—and even eventually embraced by most of the white majority. Black nationalism in all its various forms has meanwhile remained a peripheral, minority, counterconservative worldview, still disturbing and unsettling to most whites and blacks alike.

[*See also* Africa, Idea of; African Methodist Episcopal Church; American Colonization Society; Bibb, Henry W.; Black Abolitionists; Black Press; Black Separatism; Black Theology; Black Uplift; Brown, John; Canada; Civil Rights; Civil War, Participation and Recruitment of Black Troops in; Clay, Henry; Colonization; Compromise of 1850; Cornish, Samuel; Crummell, Alexander; Delany, Martin Robison; Discrimination; Douglass, Frederick; *Dred Scott* Case; Economic Life; Education; Emigration to Africa; Entrepreneurs; Exoduster Movement; Fugitive Slave Law of 1850; Garnet, Henry Highland; Haiti; Harpers Ferry Raid; Howard University; Integration; Kansas-Nebraska Act; Liberia; Lincoln, Abraham; Literature; National Conventions of Colored Men; Racism; Religion and Slavery; Riots and Rebellions; Russwurm, John Brown; Segregation; Stowe, Harriet Beecher; Toussaint Louverture; Turner, Nat; *Uncle Tom's Cabin*; Walker, David; *and* Washington, Booker T.]

BIBLIOGRAPHY

Carr, Robert. *Black Nationalism in the New World: Reading the African-American and West Indian Experience.* Durham, NC: Duke University Press, 2002.

Essien-Udom, Essien Udosen. *Black Nationalism: A Search for an Identity in America.* Chicago: University of Chicago Press, 1962.

Jenkins, Robert L., Mfanya Tryman, Curtis Austin, and Thomas Adams Upchurch. *The Greenwood Encyclopedia of Black Nationalism.* Westport, CT: Greenwood Press, forthcoming.

Moses, Wilson J. *Classical Black Nationalism: From the American Revolution to Marcus Garvey.* New York: New York University Press, 1996.

Moses, Wilson J. *The Golden Age of Black Nationalism, 1850–1925.* Hamden, CT: Archon Books, 1978.

Stuckey, Sterling. *Slave Culture: Nationalist Theory and the Foundations of Black America.* New York: Oxford University Press, 1987.

Stuckey, Sterling. *The Ideological Origins of Black Nationalism.* Boston: Beacon Press, 1972.

Upchurch, Thomas Adams. *Legislating Racism: The Billion Dollar Congress and the Birth of Jim Crow.* Lexington: University Press of Kentucky, 2004.

—THOMAS ADAMS UPCHURCH

BLACK POLITICS. Broadly defined, black politics can include almost any group endeavor undertaken by Negroes, free or slave, male or female. Scholars have found political significance in social activities ranging from slave worship services to the creation of African American families to the formation of clubs and fraternal organizations. Defined more narrowly, as the exercise of citizenship, black politics underwent a revolutionary transformation from the early through the end of the nineteenth century.

Slaves were not considered citizens; they experienced a form of "social death" which denied them most civil and political rights. But free Negroes exercised the rights of citizenship in some parts of the Union. In Massachusetts, New York, Pennsylvania, Vermont, and New Hampshire blacks could vote. Even the slave states of Tennessee and North Carolina allowed free Negroes the privileges of the ballot box, though non-slave blacks had been disfranchised in 1810 in Maryland and in other southern states.

"Jacksonian" Restrictions. These rights were sharply restricted during the next quarter century, as "Jacksonian democracy" removed most barriers to voting and office holding by white men but denied, as much as possible, the political rights of free men of African descent. New York, for example, revised its state constitution in 1821 to eliminate most restrictions on white men's suffrage but retained property qualification for Negroes. Constitutional conventions in Tennessee in 1834 and North Carolina in 1835 extended white suffrage while eliminating black voting. Pennsylvania's constitutional convention of 1837 likewise disfranchised black voters, an action ratified by the state's voters in 1838. A Democratic leader summed up the contradictory assumptions of the majority: "I should rejoice to see adopted in this commonwealth a constitution which would give every citizen—I use the word *citizen* as not embracing the coloured population—whether in poverty or affluence, that right, sacred and dear to every American citizen—the right of suffrage." The only successes for black voting rights came in the New England states of Maine and Rhode Island, where voting rights were extended to black men in 1842.

Struggle for Rights. After 1845, when Frederick Douglass achieved fame as the author of *The Narrative of the Life of Frederick Douglass, An American Slave*, free blacks gained significant political and civil rights in the North, though not without bitter struggle. As Paul Finkelman has shown, most racial restrictions on the legal right to testify in court had been removed by 1860, with Illinois, Indiana, Oregon, and California the only free states to forbid Negro testimony. During the 1840s and 1850s every northern state except Minnesota and Oregon guaranteed even runaway slaves the right to counsel, a jury trial, and the protections of the writ of habeas corpus. Only Indiana denied black residents access to public schooling, while Iowa, Massachusetts, some areas of New York, Rhode Island, and Ohio provided racially integrated schools.

Northern Republicans attempted to extend black voting rights, placing the issue on the ballot in Iowa (1857) and New York (1860), but a majority of voters rejected these proposals. Even as New York voted for Abraham Lincoln, the state's electorate voted down the Negro suffrage referendum, much to Douglass's disgust. "The black baby of Negro Suffrage," he complained, had been "stowed away like some people put out of sight their deformed children when company comes."

"The Shackle Broken—by the Genius of Freedom." A commemoration of a famous speech supporting the Civil Rights Act, delivered in the House of Representatives on 6 January 1874 by Robert B. Elliott of South Carolina (center). The banner hanging from the ceiling is a quotation from his address. The other images are a scene from the Civil War (top); statues of Lincoln holding the Emancipation Proclamation (middle left) and Charles Sumner holding the civil rights bill (middle right); and black soldiers (bottom left) and sailors (bottom right) flanking a farm owned by an African American. (Library of Congress.)

Ohio in the late antebellum allowed mulattoes to vote, as readers of *The Adventures of Huckleberry Finn* will remember. (In a richly ironic passage, Huck's father announces that "I'll never vote again" after he learns that a visiting professor "most as white as a white man," well-dressed and knowing "all kinds of languages," was allowed to vote when he was back home in Ohio.) In 1855 John Mercer Langston was elected town clerk in Brownhelm, Ohio, thus becoming, according to Steven Hahn, "the first African American ever elected to political office in the United States."

Black Politics during the Civil War. During the American Civil War, the issue of black citizenship took on new significance, especially as the federal government considered asking black men to fight. For a citizen-soldier to take up arms to defend his country was, for nineteenth-century Americans, the highest symbol of democratic responsibility, undeniable evidence that a man had political rights. Douglass recognized the direct relationship between military service and citizenship: "Once let the black man get upon his person the brass letters, U.S., let him get an eagle on his button, and a musket on his shoulder and bullets in his pocket, and there is no power on earth which can deny that he has earned the right to citizenship in the United States."

With the beginning of the regular recruitment of black soldiers in August 1862, and their baptism by fire in mid-

1863 in battles ranging from Milliken's Bend and Port Hudson to Fort Wagner, many northern leaders were willing to consider a broader definition of black rights than ever before. By the end of the war Lincoln was quietly suggesting that at least "the very intelligent" negroes, "especially those who have fought so gallantly in our ranks" should receive voting rights. This cautious suggestion was a radical change from any policy Lincoln had been willing to endorse before the war.

Black leaders tied the basic goal of abolishing slavery to the issue of political rights for African Americans. In a continuation of the antebellum black convention movement, a national convention of leading negroes met in Syracuse, New York, a few weeks before Lincoln's reelection in 1864. Because blacks had loyally fought for the Union, declared the delegates, they should now receive the "full measure of citizenship."

Reconstruction: The High Point of Black Citizenship. The struggle for black citizenship reached a triumphant conclusion after the Civil War with the abolition of slavery in 1865 and the passage of the Fourteenth and Fifteenth Amendments. By the time of the presidential election of 1872 "colored men" had a legal right to vote everywhere in the Union. This dramatic expansion of black suffrage began in 1866, when black men gained the right to vote in the territories and in the District of Columbia, followed by the Reconstruction Act of 1867, which required that black males be allowed to vote in the election of the new constitutional conventions the act mandated in ten former Confederate states. By 1868 suffrage for black men had expanded to Minnesota, Iowa, Nebraska, and Wisconsin, as well as to the New England states and New York (though still with a property qualification). Ulysses Grant's margin of victory in that year's presidential election was significantly smaller than the estimated half million black voters in the nation, an overwhelming majority of whom supported the Republican nominee.

The platform upon which Grant campaigned was remarkably inconsistent on the subject of black voting rights, proposing one policy for the South and a different one in the North. "The guarantee by Congress of equal suffrage to all loyal men at the South was demanded by every consideration of public safety, of gratitude, and of justice, and must be maintained," declared the Republican platform of 1868, "while the question of suffrage in all the loyal States properly belongs to the people of those States."

Grant's party moved toward consistency after the election by drafting a proposed Fifteenth Amendment, which in carefully limited language barred any racial limitations on suffrage. Without taking the control of voting standards away from the states, the amendment, ratified in 1870, directed the states not to deny the right to vote "on account of race, color, or previous condition of servitude." Strictly speaking the amendment did not give the right to vote to anyone; rather it merely made one potential type of suffrage restriction illegal. A carefully crafted compromise, the amendment was, according to Henry Adams, "more remarkable for what it does not than what it does contain." As a matter of practice, however, many black Americans, especially in the North, gained the right to vote as a result of its passage.

For many Republican leaders Negro suffrage was "the civil panacea," as the eminent abolitionist Wendell Phillips declared in 1869. "A man with a ballot in his hand is the master of the situation," as Phillips saw it. "As soon as the negro holds the ballot at the South, whatever he suffers will be largely now, and in future wholly, his own fault." Such thinking shaped Republican policy for the South, making the Fifteenth Amendment a substitute for a long-term, radical restructuring of southern society.

The Fifteenth Amendment was also important in the North, since by 1870 southern blacks had already secured the vote. In the closely fought elections of the 1870s and 1880s a few thousand Negro voters could spell the difference between victory and defeat in crucial states. For example fewer than 10,000 votes separated the winner from the loser in the presidential election of 1880, and northern black votes were essential to Republican victory. In 1888, when Benjamin Harrison carried President Grover Cleveland's home state of New York, it is reasonable to assume that the state's 20,000 black voters played a role in his narrow 14,373-vote victory. In the disputed election of 1876 Rutherford B. Hayes eked out an even narrower 7,513-vote victory in Ohio, a state with approximately 15,000 black voters.

Although some black leaders, including Douglass, favored extending the franchise to women, all proposals to that end were unsuccessful. Yet the elimination of white-only voting standards held wide significance for all African Americans, female as well as male. The new possibilities for black citizenship affected even women, who were quick to take advantage of the changed environment in order to attend political meetings, agitate on behalf of specific candidates or causes, and promote community solidarity.

Black Officeholding. The expansion of black voting rights led immediately to an unprecedented number of black elected officials. All of the constitutional conventions mandated under Congressional Reconstruction had some black delegates, with African Americans holding an absolute majority in South Carolina and half the seats in Louisiana. Despite being mocked by their political oppo-

"Marshal Frederick Douglass, in His office at the City Hall, Washington, D.C.—the New Administration." This wood engraving, from *Frank Leslie's Illustrated Newspaper* of 7 April 1877, shows "colored citizens paying their respects—sketched by our special artist." (Library of Congress.)

nents as "black and tan" convocations, these conventions did not have a disproportionate number of Negro delegates. Indeed white natives made up a majority of the delegates in six of the ten constitutional conventions held in the former Confederate states in 1867–1868.

The reconstructed state governments elected under these new constitutions also included a remarkable number of black officers, though never equal to overall black voting strength. No black man was elected governor, not even in such heavily black states as South Carolina, Mississippi, or Louisiana. Six black lieutenant governors won office in three different states, and one of them, P. B. S. Pinchback, was acting governor of Louisiana for a month. Black politicians held several other important offices including superintendent of education in Florida and Mississippi, and secretary of state in Mississippi. Francis Cardozo served for four years (1868–1872) as South Carolina's secretary of state and four more years as state treasurer. In addition more than 600 black men served as legislators, with particular political success in South Carolina and Mississippi and limited influence in Arkansas, Texas, and Florida.

Sixteen African Americans won election to Congress during Reconstruction, including the Mississippi senators Hiram Revels (elected to fill the unexpired term of Jefferson Davis) and Blanche K. Bruce (elected to a full term in 1875). Fourteen black men were elected to the House, representing districts in South Carolina, Mississippi, Florida, Alabama, North Carolina, and Louisiana.

Black participation in local government was particularly significant. For the average southerner, the hub of political life was not in Washington or the state capital, but in the county seat. Thus black justices of the peace, recorders of deeds, school committeemen, and county commissioners represented dramatic change and potential controversy. The rare black sheriff or prosecuting attorney was even more unsettling to white voters.

In some cases the symbolism of black political responsibility outweighed more practical considerations. For example when James O'Hara was selected in 1876 for the unpaid, largely ceremonial post of presidential elector in North Carolina, Democrats reacted with such fury that he was eventually forced to resign to prevent their appeal to "caste prejudice" from hurting the Republican ticket.

Erosion of Black Politics. By the time of Frederick Douglass's death in 1895 black political rights were again under attack in the South, though even a careful observer would not yet discern the full extent of the decline of black politics, a retreat that would reach its culmination by 1915, during the Woodrow Wilson administration.

From the end of Reconstruction to about 1890, black political participation seemed relatively secure, with most observers accepting black voting as a permanent achievement of Reconstruction. In crucial races or closely balanced districts, it is true, southern Democrats sometimes partially suppressed the black vote or manipulated election returns, but few expected that black political influence could be entirely eliminated. Running in gerrymandered districts, black candidates, including John R. Lynch in Mississippi (1880), John Mercer Langston in Virginia (1888), and James O'Hara in North Carolina (1882, 1884), occasionally won election to Congress. Scattered independent movements, such as Virginia's "Readjusters," allied with black voters to win significant victories.

Republican platforms regularly promised, in the words of the 1888 platform, to uphold the "sovereign right" of every citizen, "rich or poor, native or foreign born, black or white," to cast a free ballot "and to have that ballot duly counted," and Republican Federal attorneys continued to defend black suffrage by invoking the Enforcement Acts—laws not repealed until 1894. In 1889 the House of Representatives passed the Lodge Federal Election Bill, designed to give the federal government new authority to combat vote fraud, only to see the bill die in the Senate amid Republican second thoughts and vehement southern protest against "the Force Bill."

Although Frederick Douglass rejected the Supreme Court's reasoning in the Civil Rights Cases (1883), both he and the judges thought of the post-Reconstruction era as a return to normal conditions. "An abnormal condition, born of war, carried [the Negro] to an altitude unsuited to his attainments," wrote Douglass in 1884. "He could not sustain himself there." The majority opinion in the Civil Rights Cases went further, declaring that "When a man has emerged from slavery, and by the aid of beneficent legislation shaken off the inseparable concomitants of that state, there must be some stage in progress of elevation when he takes the rank of mere citizen, and ceases to be the special favorite of the laws." (In dissent Justice Harlan defended the Civil Rights Act of 1875 as, in fact, designed "to enable the black race to take the rank of mere citizens.")

Beginning in 1889 with the passage of Tennessee's laws to restrict suffrage, black political rights in the South began to erode rapidly. Using residency requirements and a strange literacy test (requiring potential voters be able to "read *or* understand" the state's constitution), Mississippi revised the state constitution in 1890 to get around the Fifteenth Amendment—with the result that of the state's 76,000 qualified voters in 1892 only 8,600 were African Americans. Other states would find Mississippi's approach appealing, especially in the face of a strong Populist challenge in the 1890s. Frederick Douglass did not live to see South Carolina's disfranchising convention (1895), in which six black delegates resisted in vain the tide of disfranchisement. One southern state after another followed suit, using constitutional conventions or amendments or statutory means such as poll taxes, until the process was completed in Georgia in 1908. Not until 1915 did the Supreme Court rule that "grandfather clauses" were unconstitutional under the Fifteenth Amendment. Although Republicans intermittently threatened to reduce southern representation in Congress under the terms of the Fourteenth Amendment, they failed to act.

The weakening of black political rights was accompanied by other forms of oppression. Mob violence against Negroes intensified in the 1890s, with more than a hundred southern blacks killed by vigilante attacks in each year of the decade. By law and by custom, blacks were more and more isolated, systematically subjected to a pervasive "color line." By the end of the century in 1900 much of the progress of Frederick Douglass's lifetime was threatened. His earlier conclusion that his people were "steadily rising" faced persistent challenge, especially in the area of political rights.

In the two decades after Frederick Douglass's death black political participation (strictly defined) was largely restricted to the North, where blacks continued to vote, seek patronage, and advocate legislation. In the South black citizenship was so sharply restricted that political activity had to find new channels. Scholars seeking evidence of black political aspirations in this era of southern history have been forced to redefine their understanding of politics, looking to such diverse subjects as the politics of education, the social influence of philanthropy, the ideology of black women's organizations, and the paradoxical power of black religious denominations to understand the citizenship of African Americans.

BIBLIOGRAPHY

Anderson, Eric. *Race and Politics in North Carolina, 1872–1901: The Black Second.* Baton Rouge: Louisiana State University Press, 1981.

Finkelman, Paul. "Rehearsal for Reconstruction: Antebellum Origins of the Fourteenth Amendment." In *The Facts of Reconstruction: Essays in Honor of John Hope Franklin*, edited by Eric Anderson and Alfred A. Moss Jr. Baton Rouge: Louisiana State University Press, 1991.

Foner, Eric. *Reconstruction: America's Unfinished Revolution, 1863–1877.* New York: Harper & Row, 1988.

Franklin, John Hope, and Alfred A. Moss Jr. *From Slavery to Freedom: A History of African Americans.* New York: Knopf, 2000.

Gilmore, Glenda Elizabeth. *Gender and Jim Crow: Women and the Politics of White Supremacy in North Carolina, 1896–1920.* Chapel Hill: University of North Carolina Press, 1996.

Hahn, Steven. *A Nation Under Our Feet: Black Political Struggles in the Rural South From Slavery to the Great Migration.* Cambridge, MA: Belknap Press, 2003.

Litwack, Leon F. *North of Slavery: The Negro in the Free States, 1790–1860.* Chicago: University of Chicago Press, 1961.

Perman, Michael. *Struggle for Mastery: Disfranchisement in the South, 1888–1908.* Chapel Hill: University of North Carolina Press, 2001.

Rabinowitz, Howard, ed. *Southern Black Leaders of the Reconstruction Era.* Urbana: University of Illinois Press, 1982.

Xi Wang. *The Trial of Democracy: Black Suffrage and Northern Republicans, 1860–1910.* Athens: University of Georgia Press, 1997.

—Eric Anderson

BLACK PRESS. The oppressed black communities of the antebellum North produced a variety of published materials. Benjamin Banneker's almanac was one of the earliest black periodicals. In the years preceding the advent in 1827 of the first black newspaper, *Freedom's Journal*, African American activists and orators published pamphlets protesting slavery and racial segregation, exclusion, and disfranchisement. Black pamphlets were prototypical

George Parker, in a studio portrait photograph of the 1870s, made by Hossack's Palais Royal Gallery at 4 East 14th Street in New York City. The caption read: "Geo. Parker, Editor 'The Freeman,' now 'N.Y. Age.'" (New York Public Library, Photographs and Prints Division, Schomburg Center for Research in Black Culture; Astor, Lenox, and Tilden Foundations.)

media platforms for the public protest that black newspapers would later embody.

Among the most important pamphlets of the era was *A Narrative of the Proceedings of the Black People, during the Late Awful Calamity in Philadelphia*, published by Absalom Jones and Richard Allen in 1794. In the pamphlet Jones and Allen, prominent African American community leaders and the founders of the African Methodist Episcopal (AME) Church, praised the conduct of Philadelphia's black community during a cholera epidemic and thus countered charges of looting and pilfering. Prince Hall, the founder of a black Masonic chapter, published *A Charge Delivered to the Brethren of the African Lodge* in 1797, calling for African Americans to unify in protest against the racism of the era.

The abolition of the slave trade in 1808 inspired numerous celebratory orations, most of which were published. These speeches included Absalom Jones's "Thanksgiving Sermon on Account of the Abolition of the African Slave Trade," Peter Williams Jr.'s "Oration on the Abolition of the Slave Trade," and Joseph Sidney's "Oration, Commemorative of the Abolition of the Slave Trade." All recounted the horrors of the slave trade and praised its abolition. Daniel T. Coker and James Forten, two of the most important black activists of the era, published pamphlets in 1810 and 1813—*A Dialogue Between a Virginian and an African Minister* and *Letters from a Man of Colour*—respectively, exposing the inequities and absurdities of slavery and calling on enlightened whites to aid in its abolishment. Russell Parrott's pamphlet, titled *An Oration on the Abolition of the Slave Trade* and published in 1814, like earlier orations celebrated the end of the slave trade and further called for the end of slavery. These and many other pamphlets provided the earliest outlets for African American protest in the early national period and were inspirations for the antislavery movement.

African Americans soon needed more elaborate outlets in order to protest and to see their lives and accomplishments reported, which white newspapers would not do. Indeed, white newspapers published only the most negative African American news and constantly editorialized on the innate inferiority of African Americans. The most notorious example of this was the *New York Enquirer*, which harshly criticized free blacks and called for their exile to Africa; the *Enquirer* became the focal point of African American protest against racism in New York City.

In early 1827 a group of African American leaders met in New York City at the home of Boston Crummell to discuss what to do about the *Enquirer*. Those present included Nathaniel Paul, a Baptist minister from Albany; Richard Allen, a cofounder of the AME Church; Samuel Cornish, a Presbyterian minister and vocal abolitionist; and John Brown Russwurm, the third African American to graduate from an American college, having received his degree from Bowdoin, in Maine, in 1826. The men present at the meeting decided to establish a newspaper that would give fair and balanced reportage of the black community, crusade for the abolition of slavery, and oppose the American Colonization Society, which was founded in 1816 to advocate sending free blacks to Africa.

Freedom's Journal first appeared in New York City on 27 March 1827. It was four pages long, with four columns of news and opinion; the paper would be issued weekly. Cornish served as the senior editor and Russwurm as the junior editor. Cornish, in fact, also helped establish the American Anti-Slavery Society. He was aware of how newspapers had helped unite colonists in their struggle against British rule and believed that black newspapers could similarly unite readers in the struggle against racist oppression. Cornish had expressed antislavery and black uplift viewpoints in articles written for white newspapers before doing likewise with *Freedom's Journal*. Russwurm, too, had become active in the antislavery movement prior to the black newspaper's publication.

Freedom's Journal covered local, national, and international news and published African American birth, death, and wedding announcements in New York City. To inspire its audience, the paper published biographies of a variety of prominent blacks, such as the poet Phillis Wheatley, the shipbuilder Paul Cuffe, and the Haitian revolutionary Toussaint Louverture. *Freedom's Journal*'s essays and editorials not only protested racial oppression in New York and elsewhere but also lectured readers on behavior and deportment, emphasizing chastity, thrift, industry, and piety. As a weekly, most of the journal's news coverage resembled that of a magazine more than that of a newspaper; this style of reporting became the norm for black newspapers.

As the publishers wanted *Freedom's Journal* to be more than a local publication, they distributed the paper throughout the North. Among those who aided in the distribution was David Walker, a free black Boston clothing salesman whose pamphlet *Appeal to the Coloured Citizens of the World* jump-started the antislavery movement. *Freedom's Journal*'s weekly circulation was eight hundred, which was not a low number given that the free black population in the 1820s North was insubstantial, totaling less than 300,000—with the number of literate blacks even lower. Also, white dailies in the North did not have high circulations either; the largest New York daily had a circulation of 4,000.

When Cornish left *Freedom's Journal* in September 1827 to concentrate on his church work, Russwurm became the sole publisher. Over time, Russwurm, disillusioned by American racism, began favoring the ideas put forth by the American Colonization Society. Pro-colonization editorials and essays started appearing in *Freedom's Journal*, fatally alienating readers. Consequently, *Freedom's Journal* folded in March 1829. Russwurm then joined the American Colonization Society and immigrated to Liberia, where he eventually became the governor of Maryland County. The development was ironic, considering that *Freedom's Journal* had been founded in part to combat the American Colonization Society. Samuel Cornish tried to revive *Freedom's Journal* through a new version called *Rights of All* in May 1829. However, he had neither the time nor the resources to sustain the newspaper, which ceased publication in October of that year.

Freedom's Journal did not last long—only two years—foundering in the end due to the instability of its publishers. Yet, in its news and editorial format, its wide distribution, and its themes of protest against racism, the paper inspired its African American readers, instilled them with middle-class values, and set the pattern for the many black newspapers that would follow throughout the nineteenth century. As such, *Freedom's Journal* may have been the most influential African American newspaper of all. After the collapse of *Freedom's Journal* and its successor, the *Rights of All*, in 1829 no known black newspaper appeared in the North until the *Colored American* in 1837. There may have been attempts to create black newspapers in the years between 1829 and 1837, but no copies of such publications exist.

Taking up the slack in those years were two publications. One was *Walker's Appeal*, authored by David Walker, a black clothing dealer and *Freedom's Journal* agent in Boston. In 1829 he published an expanded version of a speech in a seventy-six-page pamphlet he called the *Appeal to the Coloured Citizens of the World*. In it he denounced not only slavery but also Thomas Jefferson's racist beliefs, which Walker claimed spread ideas of black inferiority throughout the world. Walker called for immediate and complete civil, political, and social equality for African Americans—a goal he saw as a fulfillment of God's will. If necessary, he argued, blacks should resort to violence to overthrow slavery and racial oppression.

In the decades preceding the Civil War the free black community in the North struggled both for their own freedom from racial oppression and for the freedom of their enslaved southern brethren. Black newspapers reflected these twin struggles in their own fight for survival—a fight that most black newspapers in the antebellum era lost in a relatively short time. Northern black communities were too poor to give long-term support to black newspapers or magazines; and such enterprises had no chance of existing in the South, where the population of free, literate blacks was even smaller and any opinion challenging slavery and white supremacy was quickly suppressed. Nonetheless, black journalists in the years leading up to the

Civil War strove against all odds to create viable newspapers that would serve their communities. Thirty black newspapers were published between 1827 and 1861.

Though it was not a newspaper, David Walker's *Appeal* was the most explicit antislavery publication of its time and eloquently expressed the rage and frustration of black Americans. Later these feelings found an outlet in the black press. Walker's *Appeal* quickly became notorious throughout the United States. It was banned in the South and denounced by white officials in the North. Its publication probably led to Walker's mysterious death in Boston a year later. Still, the *Appeal* was openly and widely circulated throughout black communities in the North and secretly read by both free and enslaved blacks in the South. It encouraged black abolitionists and helped generate black support for the first antislavery newspaper, the *Liberator.*

While also not technically a black newspaper, the *Liberator* filled a void in the black community. Its editor and publisher, William Lloyd Garrison, was active in the antislavery movement beginning in 1828 and was a supporter of *Freedom's Journal.* Seeing that the movement needed a media outlet, Garrison established the *Liberator,* printing the first issue on 1 January 1831. By that time the antislavery movement was gaining momentum in the North, and the *Liberator* became the voice of proponents of immediate abolition. Eighty percent of its initial subscribers were African American, and they provided the majority of its readership from that time forward. (The newspaper sent African American agents throughout northern black communities to solicit subscriptions.) Northern black organizations also supported the *Liberator* through block subscriptions and donations.

The *Liberator* gained African American support by attacking southern slavery and northern racism in its editorials and emphasizing African American achievements and events in its news sections. It also published black birth, death, and wedding announcements and carried advertising from black businesses. The black support the *Liberator* gained in its early years was necessary to its survival because whites constituted only 30 percent of its readers. As the abolition movement gained momentum in the North, however, the *Liberator* gained white readers, and its coverage of African American activities dropped accordingly. At the same time, Garrison guarded his standing as the voice of the antislavery movement carefully and discouraged any and all competitors, especially those who were black.

The *Colored American* and Its Successors. The *Liberator* could not completely fill the vacuum left by the absence of a regional or national black newspaper. To meet this need, the *Colored American* appeared in 1837. It was originally named the *Weekly Advocate* and was published by Philip Bell, who had been chosen for the position by a committee of black abolitionists in New York City. Its first issue appeared on 7 January 1837 and was four pages long. Like its predecessor, *Freedom's Journal,* the *Weekly Advocate* struggled to gain enough subscriptions and circulation to make it viable.

Then Samuel Cornish, returning to journalism after a seven-year hiatus, joined the *Weekly Advocate* and changed its name to the *Colored American.* As he did with *Freedom's Journal,* Cornish justified the *Colored American's* existence by proclaiming the need for a newspaper that would protest slavery in the South and racism in the North, provide a media outlet for the African American population of the North, and uplift the African American community it served socially, morally, and intellectually. The *Colored American* criticized racism in the antislavery movement and monitored the white press's coverage of African Americans. Like *Freedom's Journal,* the *Colored American* covered the everyday lives of its readers, providing them with a positive reflection of their lives—something they did not find in the white press.

The *Colored American* always operated on a shoestring, lacking sufficient subscription revenue, circulation, and advertising to make it prosperous. It survived from 1837 to 1842 through donations from black community groups and the personal financial contributions of its editors and publishers: Philip Bell, Samuel Cornish, and Charles Bennett Ray. Its financial problems became terminal in December 1841, however, and it ceased publication. The *Colored American* lasted twice as long as *Freedom's Journal,* and its example spawned several black newspapers and magazines in the antebellum North.

At the same time the *Colored American* was being published, two black magazines appeared: the *Mirror of Liberty* and the *National Reformer.* The *Mirror of Liberty* was published by David Ruggles and was devoted to promoting antislavery causes and issues; it featured poetry, politics, women's issues, and letters to the editor. David Ruggles's poor health kept him from putting out more than five issues in three years.

The *National Reformer* apparently operated out of Philadelphia and was published by William Whipper, one of the richest black men of the era. As the voice of a black uplift group called the American Moral Reform Society, the *National Reformer* called for black self-help and self-improvement as well as full civil and political rights for African Americans and complete racial integration. It filled sixteen pages and had a layout similar to that of the *Mirror of Liberty.* Distributed up and down the East Coast, the magazine lasted only two years, between 1838 and 1839, despite having more resources to support it than did most black publications. Other black newspapers and magazines that emerged in the 1840s included the *Peoples' Free Press* (1843–1844), the *Mystery* (1843–1847), *Ge-*

nius of Freedom (1845–1847), the *Evangelist* (1845–1848), and the *Ram's Horn* (1847–1848). The *Ram's Horn* was the first newspaper believed to have employed Frederick Douglass.

Frederick Douglass, Journalist. As the leading African American voice of the antislavery movement, Frederick Douglass wanted a newspaper to publicize his antislavery activities, express his opinions of the African American freedom movement, and compete with William Lloyd Garrison's *Liberator*. After supposedly working for the *Ram's Horn* for a short time to gain experience, Douglass started the *North Star* in Rochester, New York, in December 1847. Determined to avoid the failures of previous black newspapers, Douglass amassed sufficient capital and printing equipment to keep his newspaper going for thirteen years—and hired talented staffers such as Martin R. Delany, who had founded the *Mystery*. The *North Star* emphasized the antislavery movement in its news coverage, but like other black newspapers, it covered black community activities throughout the North and published verse, fiction, and book reviews as well as births, deaths, and society news. Douglass was not shy about editorializing, so his columns dotted the paper.

In 1851 the *North Star*, needing an infusion of funds, merged with the *Liberty Party Paper*, the newspaper of the antislavery Liberty Party, to form *Frederick Douglass' Paper*. This publication continued Douglass's crusade for abolition and enabled him to become the symbol of the antislavery movement. Douglass's newspapers became the most well known and widely read of all black publications during the years before the Civil War.

[*See also* Abolitionism; Allen, Richard; American Colonization Society; Antislavery Press; Banneker, Benjamin; Bell, Philip Alexander; Black Abolitionists; Black Church; Black Uplift; Civil Rights; Coker, Daniel T.; Cornish, Samuel; Cuffe, Paul; David Walker's *Appeal*; Delany, Martin Robison; Douglass, Frederick; Economic Life; Entrepreneurs; Forten, James; *Frederick Douglass' Paper*; *Freedom's Journal*; Free Speech; Garrison, William Lloyd; Garrisonian Abolitionists; Hall, Prince; Jones, Absalom; Language; Liberty Party; Literacy in the Colonial Period; Literature; Newspapers; *North Star*; Oratory and Verbal Arts; Parrott, Russell; Paul, Nathaniel; Political Participation; Racism; Ray, Charles B.; Reform; Ruggles, David; Russwurm, John Brown; Slave Trade; Toussaint Louverture; Walker, David; Whipper, William; Williams, Peter, Jr.; *and* Work.]

BIBLIOGRAPHY

Blight, David. *Frederick Douglass' Civil War: Keeping Faith in Jubilee.* Baton Rouge: Louisiana State University Press, 1989. The standard account of Frederick Douglass's activities during the Civil War.

Bruce, Dickson D., Jr. *The Origins of African American Literature, 1680–1865.* Charlottesville: University Press of Virginia, 2001. A comprehensive analysis of African American fiction, nonfiction, poetry, autobiographies, and other writings from the colonial era through the Civil War.

Dann, Martin E., ed. *The Black Press, 1827–1890: The Quest for National Identity.* New York: Putnam, 1971. A collection of articles from black newspapers; exhaustive and comprehensive and gives a vivid picture of the ideologies put forth by nineteenth-century black journalists.

Douglass, Frederick. *Life and Times of Frederick Douglass* (1881). New York: Collier, 1962.

Horton, James O., and Lois E. Horton. *In Hope of Liberty: Culture, Community, and Protest among Northern Free Blacks, 1700–1860.* New York: Oxford University Press, 1997. Now the standard history of the antebellum free black community in the North.

Hutton, Frankie. *The Early Black Press in America, 1827 to 1860.* Westport, CT: Greenwood, 1993. A well-written analytical account of black newspapers, their publishers, and the strains endured in creating and maintaining their publications.

Newman, Richard, Patrick Rael, and Philip Lapsansky, eds. *Pamphlets of Protest: An Anthology of Early African-American Protest Literature, 1790–1860.* New York: Routledge, 2001. All the major black protest writing of the antebellum era is anthologized and analyzed.

Porter, Dorothy, ed. *Early Negro Writing, 1760–1837.* Boston: Beacon Press, 1971. Still the standard collection of early national African American writings.

Pride, Armistead S., and Clint C. Wilson II. *A History of the Black Press.* Washington, DC: Howard University Press, 1997. A comprehensive survey of the black press from its beginnings to the present, emphasizing the publishers of black newspapers and their activities on behalf of black advancement and uplift.

—HAYWARD "WOODY" FARRAR

BLACK SEAFARERS. Throughout the early modern era (1550–1830), blacks participated in the maritime trades and served in navies. By examining crew lists, port authority records, travel narratives, and autobiographies, historians have uncovered a "Black Atlantic." The colonies of early America were established and continually resupplied by sea. Merchant-ship owners needed men to tend to the work of the ship, whether hauling nets, spearing whales, or serving as shipyard carpenters or privateers. Lured by the promise of financial reward and freedom from bondage, blacks took to the sea.

Black slaves joined with their masters and became a "fine, bold race of seamen," carrying fish from the Newfoundland banks eastward or procuring porcelain, tea, and spices from India and bringing them back to colonial ports. The number of black seamen working and sailing from colonial ports totaled tens of thousands. The research of historians gives the number of black sailors recorded in a given year or the number who sailed with a particular ship. However, it is difficult—perhaps impossible—to know the total number of black sailors in the early modern era. Therefore, because of the way that records were kept, it is not known how many black sailors were slaves and how many were free. Similarly, the aggregate number of black seafarers by region is unknown.

The black seaman Briton Hammon wrote *Narrative of the Uncommon Sufferings, and Surprizing Deliverance of Briton Hammon, a Negro Man* in 1760, providing an account of his departure on a ship bound for Jamaica, his time spent on the capes of Florida, the alleged murder of the ship's crew by Indians, and Hammon's eventual return to the port of Boston. Whether Hammon was a servant or slave remains a mystery, but his book appears to be the first voyage account and captivity narrative by an African American.

Hammon's work marked the start of a literary tradition for black seafarers. Those who recounted their harrowing travels in writing educated literate Americans about the toil of African slavery and about blacks themselves. Henry Louis Gates Jr. writes, "The production of literature was taken to be the central arena in which persons of African descent could establish and redefine their status within the human community." The narrative written by the former slave and preacher John Jea tells of his life enslaved to a plantation owner in New York, his conversion to Christianity, and the freedom he acquired as a result of his baptism, in accordance with New York law. Jea also tells of his harrowing experiences crossing the Atlantic in the 1790s to forge a career in England as a preacher. When he published his memoir in 1812, he followed in the footsteps of blacks who used autobiography to make visible both their hardships and their triumphs.

Black slaves who sailed the Caribbean contended with the regulations of mercantile slavery. For instance, two black seamen—who were detained and removed from a Spanish ship, judged as slaves, and thus considered to be commerce—helped incite a slave revolt in New York in April 1712. In reprisal, the colony executed twenty-one slaves, some by hanging and others by burning. As a result of the revolt, New York passed the 1712 Slave Act, Massachusetts issued a law against further importation of slaves, and Pennsylvania responded by levying high taxes to reduce slave importation.

Just before the American Revolution, black seamen made up one-third of all laborers linked to the trade be-

Present State of Potter Jackson's back.   *The manner the Captain and Mate Flogged Potter Jackson.*

Potter Jackson (b. 1774) was a free African American who worked as a seaman. He was tied to the rigging of his ship and whipped by the captain and another officer. This illustration is from *The Remarkable Case of Potter Jackson.* (Library of Congress.)

THE REMARKABLE

CASE

OF

POTTER JACKSON,

(Formerly Steward of the Echo Sloop of War)

GIVING AN ACCOUNT

OF

THE MOST CRUEL TREATMENT,

HE RECEIVED FROM

CAPTAIN LIVESLY,

(Commander of the LORD STANLY-...e-hip)

AND HIS CHIEF MATE;

BY ASSAULTING, IMPRISONING, PUTTING IN
IRONS, AND CRUELLY FLOGGING HIM:

Which caused Blood to burst from his Eyes and Breast,
and large Pieces of Flesh to come from his Back,

OCCASIONED

BY THE UNMERCIFUL FLOGGING,

HE RECEIVED, OF

UPWARDS OF ONE THOUSAND LASHES.

WRITTEN BY HIMSELF.

WITH THE TRIAL,

BEFORE

The Right Hon. LORD ELLENBOROUGH

In the Court of King's Bench, Guildhall, London,

On *THURSDAY, JULY* 10, 1806;

When the Jury returned a Verdict,

FIVE HUNDRED POUNDS DAMAGES!!

LONDON.

Printed for and Sold by the unfortunate Sufferer, at
R. BUTTERS', 22, FETTER-LANE, FLEET-STREET.

[PRICE ONE SHILLING.]

"The Remarkable Case of Potter Jackson," title page—which vividly summarizes the entire episode. The date of publication was c. 1807. (Library of Congress.)

tween North America and the West Indies. Black and white seamen shared quarters and worked side by side in the U.S. navy, but blacks could not be commissioned officers throughout the nineteenth century. In 1779 George Washington paid a total of one thousand dollars to "Negro pilots" who transported his army along the waterways of the Chesapeake region. Thomas Jefferson, in an effort to make even more expansive the naval program of Washington and John Adams, established policies that led to greater numbers of black servicemen. Unlike the Continental army, the navy drafted both free and enslaved blacks.

On the surface, laws proved troublesome to African American military servicemen. The Militia Act of 1792 excluded blacks from state volunteer service, and in 1798 a congressional mandate, executed by the secretary of the navy, Benjamin Stoddard, stated that "no Negroes or Mulattoes are to be admitted." Although the exclusion of blacks remained official military policy until 1807, a lack of formal restrictions or quotas on the docks guaranteed that blacks could travel and work by the sea. Moreover, empowered by "letters of marque," African Americans aboard private ships could seize enemy merchantmen in the course of normal trade. In 1807 Maryland passed laws to prevent slaves from escaping on ships. This may reveal "why almost twice as many black seamen claimed Maryland residency as were born there." When Frederick Douglass, once a ship caulker in Baltimore, made his famed escape from slavery in 1838, he donned a sailor's uniform.

The port could be a key site of resistance to slavery. For example, Denmark Vesey, once owned by a ship captain, purchased his freedom after winning a lottery in 1799 and set up a carpentry shop in Charleston, South Carolina. He was a member of the all-black African Methodist church in nearby Hampstead, where 140 members were arrested in 1818 by city guards who cited an 1800 statute that forbade assemblies of free blacks and slaves without the presence of whites. In the spring of 1822 Vesey organized a general insurrection of hundreds of blacks; he and his rebel followers traveled in canoes to spread word of the plot. Although Vesey's conspiracy was ultimately revealed to authorities, it helped fuel a growing abolitionism in the mid-nineteenth century.

Some black seamen gained great economic success. For example, Paul Cuffe, a merchant captain and self-described "Marineer," sailed from Boston to the West Indies and Europe. Each year, Cuffe invested the profits of a previous voyage into building a larger vessel. His plan was to bring skilled free blacks to West Africa and open up trade in native products between Africa, the United States, and Europe. During the War of 1812, Cuffe petitioned the president and Congress to permit emigration from the United States to Sierra Leone. The resulting bill failed, but when the war ended, Cuffe funded and led a voyage to Sierra Leone for nine black families. Although the emigrants' efforts in their African colony did not bring the prosperity they and Cuffe dreamed of, his death in 1817 was not forgotten. He was eulogized in New York and Boston and beloved for his daring, inventive example.

The Nineteenth Century. During the nineteenth century, black seafarers at port often stayed at boardinghouses. These lodgings, which were close to the sailing vessel, served as residence ashore. Seafarers rarely found time to spend with family, although records indicate that many seamen did fulfill financial obligations to their dependants. Boardinghouse keepers posted advertisements seeking "Colored Seamen" in periodicals like William Lloyd Garrison's *The Liberator*, which began publication in 1831. In Boston some blacks found shelter through the Seamen's Aid Society.

As abolitionism intensified during the nineteenth century, efforts to challenge slavery at sea were emboldened. In the summer of 1839 the British ship *HMS Buzzard* escorted two American slaving ships into New York harbor; the British unsuccessfully attempted to force the Americans to enforce its laws against slave trading. In 1841 black slaves seized the brig *Creole* during a voyage from Virginia to New Orleans. The rebels forced the crew to sail to Nassau, Bahamas, where British authorities took some into custody but freed the remainder, given England's decision to abolish slavery in the British West Indies in 1833. In turn U.S. Secretary of State Daniel Webster called on the British to indemnify the freed slaves, but to no avail.

Despite the activities of individual politicians, the U.S. government actually aided sea travel by issuing protection certificates to black seafarers, guarding them to some extent against the risks of impressment or capture. One such order issued in 1854 for a young man named Samuel Fox described him as having a "light African complexion, black woolly hair and brown eyes."

African Americans served in the Union Navy during the Civil War. Unlike the Army, the Navy did not segregate, nor did it create a separate administrative bureau. Research by Joseph P. Reidy suggests that as many as 25 percent of the sailors were black. The number of black crewmen increased during the course of the war. Most were born in the southern United States, and about four-fifths of them had been escaped slaves. African Americans were often placed in low-wage, low-prestige positions, such as cook or steward. Still, six black seamen were awarded the Medal of Honor by the war's end.

By the late nineteenth century, black seafarers could be found on both coasts. They worked hard jobs as whalers in New Bedford, California, and, in the 1870s, in San Francisco. Despite the restriction on blacks becoming commissioned officers, Michael Healy commanded the *Bear*, a ship that served the Revenue Service, forerunner of the modern Coast Guard. Rising to the rank of captain in 1883, Healy led patrols through the Bering Sea, North Pacific, and Arctic Ocean.

Though less common, it must be noted that black women may also have served as sailors. Given the tradition of women "passing" as men to gain entrance to male-dominated fields, it is important that researchers consider the existence of black women seafarers. In addition black women may have worked on ships, sailed along as stow-aways, or been slaves held captive at sea. Further research can only shed light on this largely unexamined topic.

[*See also* Abolitionism; Adams, John, on African Americans; African Methodist Episcopal Church; American Revolution; Autobiography; Baptism; Black Nationalism; Caribbean; Class; Cuffe, Paul; Denmark Vesey Conspiracy; Free African Americans to 1828; Hammon, Briton; Jea, John; Jefferson, Thomas, on African Americans and Slavery; Laws and Legislation; Literacy in the Colonial Period; Literature; Maritime Trades; New York Slave Revolt of 1712; Pennsylvania; Religion; Resistance; Riots and Rebellions; Slave Rebellions and Insurrections; Slave Narratives; Slave Trade; Vesey, Denmark; War of 1812; Washington, George, and African Americans; *and* Work.]

BIBLIOGRAPHY

Bolster, W. Jeffrey. *Black Jacks: African American Seamen in the Age of Sail*. Cambridge, MA: Harvard University Press, 1997.

Farr, James Barker. *Black Odyssey: The Seafaring Traditions of Afro-Americans*. New York: Peter Lang, 1989.

Gates, Henry Louis, Jr., and William L. Andrews, eds. *Pioneers of the Black Atlantic: Five Slave Narratives from the Enlightenment, 1772–1815*. Washington, DC: Civitas, 1998.

Harris, Sheldon H. *Paul Cuffe: Black America and the African Return*. New York: Simon and Schuster, 1972.

Pendleton, Leila Amos. *A Narrative of the Negro*. Washington, DC: Press of R. L. Pendleton, 1912.

Putney, Martha S. *Black Sailors: Afro-American Merchant Seamen and Whalemen Prior to the Civil War*. New York: Greenwood, 1987.

Ramold, Steven J. *Slaves, Sailors, Citizens: African Americans in the Union Navy*. DeKalb: Northern Illinois University Press, 2002.

Stillwell, Paul, ed. *The Golden Thirteen: Recollections of the First Black Naval Officers*. Annapolis, MD: Naval Institute Press, 1993.

—MILLA ROSENBERG

BLACK SEPARATISM. After 1820, when the political climate in the United States began to turn more strongly against black people, black separatism and full integration into American society were the two main trends of discussion among African Americans. Some black people advocated leaving the United States and going to Africa or to other places of freedom, while others—most notably, the black abolitionist Frederick Douglass—suggested that they should stay in America and fight for equality.

In 1792 several hundred black Americans went to Sierra Leone to join a British-governed African resettlement, and in 1815 more blacks joined them under the leadership of Paul Cuffe. The act of emigration was seen as a legitimate and progressive response to the oppressive conditions of the slave system, especially since many slaves were born in Africa. The main criticism of these emigration efforts, voiced by African Americans like Douglass, was that the institution of slavery would remain intact and that emigration would serve only the interests of a few middle-class free blacks who could afford the travel and whites who wanted blacks out of the United States.

One of the most prominent advocates of black emigration was Martin Robison Delany. A Harvard-educated physician, Delany was seen as an articulate spokesperson opposing Douglass's views. He did not share Douglass's belief that America would allow blacks to become citizens and disagreed with Douglass about blacks' staying in America. He urged black Americans to immigrate to Canada, various countries in Central and South America, or the West Indies, saying that the people of those countries were in the same plight as African Americans. Delany knew not to believe the reports that Africa was the "dark continent" and that the African people were without science, arts, and knowledge of government, as similar comments were made about black Americans. He felt that the ignorance of Africa could be conquered, black nations and African Americans could profit and learn from one another, and all would grow as people. Delany saw whites as the oppressors.

As a leading advocate of black separatism, he believed that blacks had a duty to establish their own society where they would be free to enjoy the privileges of citizenship. With the publication of his 1852 book *The Condition, Elevation, Emigration, and Destiny of the Colored People of the United States*, Delany became the embodiment of radical emigrationist politics, much to the displeasure of Douglass, who advocated social integration. "No people can be free who themselves do not constitute an essential part of the ruling element of the country in which they live," Delany said.

Henry Highland Garnet, a Presbyterian minister and abolitionist, urged slaves to take action to gain their own freedom, telling them "you are far better off dead than to live as slaves." As a proponent of emigration, Garnet advocated any destination that would provide blacks with justice and dignity, but he favored Liberia. Henry Turner, a bishop of the African Methodist Episcopal Church in Georgia, was one of the main proponents of the idea that African Americans emigrate from the United States and go to Africa. Although he inspired much enthusiasm among southern blacks, his efforts were doomed by transportation problems, reports of a harsh life in Africa, inadequate financial backing, and a lack of interest on the part of the black middle class and the educated black elite.

Blacks who agreed with Douglass and advocated staying in America to fight for equality included Maria Stewart. One of a handful of African American women on the lecture circuit, Stewart argued that the goal of blacks in America was to improve their lives and eventually become an integral part of American life. She maintained that blacks were disadvantaged not because of natural inferiority but because of prejudice and slavery. Once those impediments were abolished, education and opportunity would remedy the situation.

Frederick Douglass, as a staunch integrationist, shared Stewart's optimism. He did not support armed resistance or resettlement in African or Latin American countries. In Baltimore, Maryland, where Douglass had lived as a young man, the churches were the bulwark of society, and it was common for black churches to have open forums on the plight of black Americans. There the merits of colonization and emigration were discussed and debated as the only schemes for ending slavery that were acceptable to whites. These issues were deliberated cautiously in southern black churches much as they were in churches in the North; like their counterparts in the North, southern black churchgoers were circumspect enough not to allow their discussions to leave their neighborhoods. Internally and privately, however, most members of black churches condemned colonization and emigration and called for the immediate freeing of slaves.

As a slave, Douglass sometimes had attended black churches in Baltimore, and there his opposition to colonization, emigration, and separation was first formed. As an advocate of freedom and civil rights for all African Americans, Douglass assailed the idea of shipping blacks to Africa. In his speeches and writings he argued that "contact with the white race, even under the many unjust and painful restrictions to which we are subject, does more toward our elevation and improvement, than the mere circumstances of being separated from them could." He invoked the American Dream, in which people of all races find security and enjoy the right to pursue happiness in freedom and equality, and he spent his life in struggle, first for the abolition of slavery and later for the uplift and betterment of all blacks. He envisioned equality for all in a mixed society. As an orator, Douglass used many rhetorical strategies to effectively communicate with his multiracial audiences. Within the antislavery movement were two overlapping movements, "one white and one black, one of integration, and one of emigration." Voicing his position as a mediator between black and white abolitionists, he came to embody a multiracial antislavery movement:

> Laying aside all prejudice in favor of or against race, looking at the Negro as politically and socially related to people generally, and measuring the forces arrayed against him, I do not see how he can survive and flourish in this country as a distinct and separate race, nor do I see how he can be removed from the country either by annihilation or expatriation. (Doughty, p. 438)

As Douglass matured as a speaker and as he questioned the concept of "freedom" for himself and other African Americans, he grew more philosophical and educated in his talks. Aware of rising resistance to the terrors of slavery, riots and rebellions among slaves and free blacks, the free black community's assistance to fugitive slaves, and other incidents of protest activity among black Americans, Douglass understood that the question of how blacks should obtain their freedom was multifaceted. However, throughout the 1840s Douglass was optimistic about the future of blacks. He believed that through constant preaching, political lobbying, and hard struggle blacks would eventually find liberty in America. Whenever he could, he spoke against violence and voiced his disfavor of any plan to send blacks to Africa. "You must be a man here," he said. "And force your way to intelligence, wealth and respectability. If you can't do that here, you can't do it there."

In the 1850s black separatism grew in popularity and became a platform from which to maintain a sense of identity and individual worth. Douglass steadfastly maintained his disapproval, claiming that as Americans, it made no sense for African Americans to be separate. The Fugitive Slave Law of 1850 provoked such disillusionment among blacks that some considered the United States to be a "promised land of evil." The law forced blacks accused of being fugitives to prove their free status, not to a jury but to a special commissioner who was paid more (ten dollars) for returning a slave to his or her alleged owner than for setting a slave free (five dollars). The law also compelled northerners to hunt down and turn in runaway slaves. As slave hunters, known as "kidnappers," flooded the North seizing fugitives, many blacks fled to Canada.

Throughout his career, Douglass's inclusive views led him to reject black separatism as a solution to the racial problems plaguing the United States. He always believed that emigration movements would undermine blacks' efforts to gain the right to citizenship in the United States. As he remarked in the January 1859 issue of *Douglass' Monthly*, "Now, and always, we expect to insist upon it that we are Americans; that America is our native land; that this is our home, that we are American citizens; that it is our highest wisdom thus to recognize ourselves; and that it is the duty of the American people so to recognize us."

[*See also* Abolitionism; Africa, Idea of; Antislavery Movement; Black Abolitionists; Black Church; Black Nationalism; Black Politics; Black Uplift; Canada; Civil Rights; Colonization; Delany, Martin Robison; Discrimination; Douglass, Frederick; *Douglass' Monthly;* Education; Emigration to Africa; Free African Americans before the Civil War (North); Free African Americans before the Civil War (South); Fugitive Slave Law of 1850; Garnet, Henry Highland; Identity; Integration; Liberia; Oratory and Verbal Arts; Political Participation; Progress; Race, Theories of; Racism; Resistance; Riots and Rebellions; Segregation; Slavery; *and* Voting Rights.]

BIBLIOGRAPHY

Doughty, Francis Albert. "The Future of the Colored Race." *North American Review* 142.354 (May 1886): 437–440.

Douglass, Frederick. "Horace Greeley and Colonization." In *The Frederick Douglass Papers*. Series 2, *Autobiographical Writings*. Vol. 2, *My Bondage and My Freedom*. Edited by John W. Blassingame, John R. McKivigan, and Peter P. Hinks. New Haven, CT: Yale University Press, 2003.

Gardiner, Charles A., John T. Morgan, Frederick Douglass, et al. "The Future of the Negro." *North American Review* 139.332 (July 1884): 78.

Levine, Robert S. *Martin Delany, Frederick Douglass, and the Politics of Representative Identity.* Chapel Hill: University of North Carolina Press, 1997.

Ripley, C. Peter. *The Black Abolitionist Papers.* Vol. 4, *The United States, 1847–1855.* Chapel Hill: University of North Carolina Press, 1991.

—FRED LINDSEY

BLACK THEOLOGY. The emergence of independent black churches in the nineteenth century was more than the simple establishment of black congregations led by black ministers. As would prove essential to their black identity, black ministers began not only to preach but also to publish a system of religious thought—a theology—which, though based upon Christian principles and the Bible, took on a decidedly African American flavor. In the antebellum period, black religious thought was of two strains: first, a black interpretation of existing Protestant theology and, second, a protest theology that attacked the institution of slavery on religious grounds. In the aftermath of the Civil War, black ministers continued to preach their respective versions of Christian theology while changing the target of their protest theology from slavery to institutionalized racism against their black congregations. This was the rise of the black social gospel.

Roots of Black Theology. Initially, both ministers of independent black churches and slave preachers on plantations based their sermons and limited writings upon the theology of the Protestant Christian Church, with which they were or had been affiliated. Protestant Christian theology of the early nineteenth century was essentially either Calvinist or Arminian. Calvinist theology, conceived by John Calvin in Geneva, Switzerland, in the late 1500s, became the theology of the Reformed, Baptist, and Presbyterian churches. Its central premise was that human beings were essentially evil and could be saved only by the grace of God. God had predetermined the fate of each man and woman—to end up in either heaven or hell—before the beginning of time. Calvin's point was that humans could do nothing to save or damn themselves. This fatalistic theology was challenged in the early seventeenth century by the Dutch minister and theologian Jacobus Arminius. He believed that Jesus Christ had died for everyone; thus, saving grace was available to everyone, and each person had the ability to accept or reject that grace. This teaching became the basis for the theology of the "New Light" factions of the Presbyterian, Congregational, and Baptist churches. It was also similar to the theology of the Catholic and Anglican churches.

One of the earliest black exponents of Calvinist thought was George Liele, who had been born a slave in Virginia and as a young man was transported to South Carolina. There he participated in a revival and converted to the Baptist faith. He served for a time as a slave preacher at the plantation where he lived, as well as for those nearby. Because of his vehement dedication to his new religion, his master freed him. He established one black Baptist congregation on the South Carolina bank of the Savannah River near Augusta, Georgia, and, later, one in Savannah, Georgia. Near the end of the Revolutionary War, because he had supported the British, he fled to Jamaica and established the first Baptist church on the island.

Liele is credited with the development of an "Afro-Baptist Sacred Cosmos," which he described in the following terms: "I agree to election, redemption, the fall of Adam, regeneration, and perseverance, knowing the promise is that all who endure, in grace, faith, and good works to the end shall be saved." This statement is a hodgepodge of theologies and religious traditions. The term *election* is clearly used in the Calvinist tradition, but the reference to "good works" seems to denote an Arminian tendency. The use of the terms *fall*, *regeneration*, and *endure*, although they certainly exist in Christian theology, embody African concepts of life after death, where salvation results from one's perseverance and good works.

While this description is representative of an African Arminian theological interpretation, such an interpretation did not dominate early black theology. When Liele was in Savannah, he baptized one Andrew Bryan, who established a black Baptist congregation in that city; Bryan was succeeded by Andrew Marshall. Early in his career Marshall adopted African Arminianism, even going so far as to affiliate with Alexander Campbell, an early leader of the Restoration Movement. By the late 1830s, however, he returned to strict Calvinist thought. He became a staunch advocate of the Calvinist doctrines of election and

God's saving grace while rejecting the idea of man's free will in regard to his acceptance of God's saving grace.

African Americans moved quickly and with some self-assuredness to redefine the Methodist tradition in their own terms. In 1816, immediately after the establishment of the African Methodist Episcopal (AME) Church, its founder, the Reverend Richard Allen, and his disciple and a cofounder of the church, Jacob Tapisco, published *The Doctrines and Disciplines of the African Methodist Episcopal Church*. This work became the catechism of the AME Church. Much of what these founders wrote was a restatement of the theology of John Wesley, the founder of Methodism. They focused upon the Wesleyan concerns for justification and sanctification and hoped for witnessing of the Spirit and Christian perfection. Allen also emphasized a holiness resulting from charity and good works. The text presented an evangelical emphasis, with an Arminian flavor, within the framework of Wesleyan theology.

Protest Theology. The theological battle over slavery raged from early colonial times until the Civil War. Among the early Puritans, critics included the great Puritan theologian and minister Cotton Mather. Arguments on this topic centered on biblical interpretation. A good example of this was the 1700 debate between Samuel Sewall and John Saffin, both Boston lawyers, who argued over the justness of slavery based upon the Bible, with Sewall opposing the practice and Saffin supporting it. This bipolar argumentative model extended through early American history between groups who vehemently attacked the practice of slavery, such as the Mennonites and Quakers, and the supporters, who were often clergy from several other denominations, including the Anglican and Baptist faiths.

Black ministers entered this debate only in the late eighteenth century, and although they were certainly part of the larger theological debate over slavery, there were significant differences in the nature of their participation. First, much of black protest theology was not offered as part of the larger argument; rather these black arguments were aimed at black congregations. The purpose was to bring the black community to a greater appreciation of their self-worth. In July 1794 the African Episcopal Church of Saint Thomas, the first black church in Philadelphia, opened its doors. The church was directed by Absalom Jones, who was a qualified Episcopalian minister. Reverend James Abercrombie presided over the first day's service, and Reverend Samuel Magaw gave the sermon; both were white Episcopalian ministers. In his sermon to the black congregation, Reverend Magaw took great pains to explain their debt not only to God but also to the white community of Philadelphia and their need for humility, saying that "pride was not made for man, in any, even the highest stations in life; much less for persons who have just emerged from the lowest."

Such a paternalistic charge sparked Absalom Jones to write a response to his congregation, entitled "The Causes and Motives for Establishing St. Thomas's African Church of Philadelphia." The statement appeared approximately one month after Reverend Magaw's sermon and was confirmed by the church trustees. Jones clearly set forth the congregation's purpose:

> And in order the more fully to accomplish the good purposes of God's will, and organize ourselves for the purpose of promoting the health [of] the people all, but more particularly our relatives, of color. We, after many consultations, and some years deliberation thereon, have gone forward to erect a house for the glory of God, and our mutual advantage to meet in for clarification and social religious worship. And more particularly to keep an open door for those of our race, who may be into assemble with us, but would not attend divine worship in Other places.

Jones wrote of the need to establish "christian-like government" in the congregation and concluded by resolving,

> We dedicate ourselves to God, imploring holy protection; and our house to the memory of St. Thomas, the Apostle, to be henceforward known and called by the name and title of St. Thomas's African Episcopal Church of Philadelphia; to be governed by us and our successors for ever as follows.

This was a respectful statement of self-worth and a declaration of independence for the congregation. Jones sought not only to have his congregation appreciate the value that they had in the eyes of God but also to have the outside Episcopal Church understand that Saint Thomas's was not its slave.

The political element of protest theology, which had been implicit in Jones's "Causes and Motives," was explicitly addressed in Richard Allen's "Address to the Free People of Colour of These United States." Allen, founder and eventually presiding bishop of the AME Church, took the opportunity in 1830 to announce his church's opposition to the plans of the American Colonization Society. The society was founded in 1816 and included among its members prominent politicians, slave owners, and anti-slavery advocates. The goal of the society was to transport freed slaves back to Africa. Allen's "Address" was written in the form of an open letter to his fellow church members. The "Address" opened with a clear reference to the Declaration of Independence:

> Impressed with a firm and settled conviction, and more especially being thought by that inestimable and invaluable instrument, namely the Declaration of Independence, that all men are born free and equal, and consequently are endowed with unalienable rights, among which are the enjoyments of life, liberty, and the pursuits of happiness.

This was an attempt to invoke the political equivalent of the Bible; both were implicitly seen as the highest statements of moral authority.

Based upon this authority, Allen then rejected the American Colonization Society's proposal:

> However great the debt which these United States may owe to injured Africa, and however unjustly her sons have been made to bleed, and her daughters to drink of the cup of affliction, still we who have been born and nurtured on this soil, we whose habits, manners, and customs are the same in common with other Americans, can never consent to take our lives in our hands, and be the bearers of the redress offered by the Society to that much afflicted country.

Allen concluded by recognizing that blacks had often lacked the unity necessary to improve their "precarious and degraded conditions" and called for his "fellow-citizens" to establish societies that would foster "agriculture and mechanical arts" among blacks, thereby "raising the moral and political standing" of blacks in the United States. This statement was not the standard protest theology in either tone or substance. In tone, it was blatantly political; in substance, it addressed worldly issues. Nevertheless, it was a clear pedagogical statement aimed at advancing both the self-worth and independence of African Americans of the time.

Not all antebellum African American protest theology was of the political nature exhibited by Jones and Allen. Many other black ministers utilized biblical rhetoric more common to the white theological debate over slavery. These ministers drew upon biblical stories such as the enslavement of the Israelites, the plagues visited upon the Egyptians by a just and all-powerful God, and, finally, the Israelite slaves' flight from Egypt.

In his *Dialogue between a Virginian and an African Minister*, published in 1810, David Coker, a contemporary of Richard Allen and a cofounder of the AME Church, relied heavily upon a number of biblical references to demonstrate to blacks and other readers that black ministers, too, were quite knowledgeable about the Bible. David Walker took a very aggressive position in 1829 in his *Appeal to the Coloured Citizens of the World*. He argued that God, seeking just vengeance, would bless even violent attempts to overthrow slavery. This violent strain of protest theology was also adopted by the black Presbyterian minister Henry Highland Garnet. In his 1843 address to the Negro Convention in Buffalo, New York, he justified violent resistance to the institution of slavery as the acts of a vengeful God doing justice for his people.

Possibly the most startling condemnation not only of slavery but also of "false" white Christians came from Frederick Douglass. Douglass had been born a slave, taught himself to read, and escaped from slavery. He became a minister in the African Methodist Episcopal Zion Church and the most famous and vehement black opponent of slavery. Writing in his *Narrative of the Life of Frederick Douglass* (1845), Douglass relied little on biblical references; rather his criticism was sharp and straightforward:

> I love the pure, peaceable, and impartial Christianity of Christ; I therefore hate the corrupt, slave-holding, women-whipping, cradle-plundering, partial and hypocritical Christianity of this land. . . . The warm defender of the sacredness of the family relation is the same that scatters whole families,—sundering husbands and wives, parents and children, sisters and brothers,—leaving the hut vacant, and the hearth desolate. . . . Revivals of religions and revivals in the slave-trade go hand and hand together. (Noll, 117)

Although this passage lacks the biblical imagery of his contemporaries, the power of Douglass's denunciation of white hypocrisy cut deeply into the smugness of white Christians of the North while implicitly justifying the independence of black Christians and their churches.

Black Social Gospel. In 1862, as the Civil War raged, Congress ended the practice of slavery in the District of Columbia. The black congregation at the African Methodist Episcopal–Ebenezer Chapel in the Georgetown area of the District held a "day of Thanksgiving and Prayer" to commemorate Congress's action. The sermon was given by Bishop Daniel A. Payne, and it was later published in pamphlet form, at the request of the elders of the congregation, under the title of *Welcome to the Ransomed; or, Duties of the Colored Inhabitants of the District of Columbia*. Payne told his congregation, "We are gathered to celebrate the emancipation, yea, rather, the *Redemption* of the enslaved people of the District of Columbia. . . . Our pleasing task is to welcome to the Churches, the homesteads, and the circles of free colored Americans, those who remain to enjoy *the boon of holy Freedom*." He then proceeded to instruct the newly freed on what was necessary for them to do in their new capacity as free people: "To the adults we say, enter the Sunday Schools and the Night Schools. . . . Keep your children in the schools, even if you have to eat less, drink less and wear coarser raiments. . . . Let the education of your children penetrate the heart." He also advised them as to what was necessary for a better life:

> Let us advise you respecting money. Some people value it too much, others too little. Of these extremes take the medium: for money has its proper value. . . . But how are we to get money? Get it by diligent labor. Work, work, work! Shun no work that will bring you an honest penny. . . . You can save your pennies—yea, dollars—if you will *run away* from whiskey, rum and tobacco. (Payne, p. 9)

These were surely good words of advice, but, more important, Bishop Payne's sermon marked a change in the purpose of the black churches. Before the Civil War many of the various black congregations and churches had focused on ending the slavery that held so many of their people in its grip. With the Emancipation Proclamation of 1863 and the ratification of the Thirteenth Amendment in 1865, all blacks were free. What, then, many asked, would become of the purpose of the black churches? Could they limit themselves to preaching the gospels and imploring their people to act properly? African American people were free, but they still needed direction and assistance in obtaining the material things necessary for life. Payne's themes on the importance of education, work, thrift, and family were the new tenets of the black church. It would become the responsibility of the churches to make freedmen understand the importance of these particular aspects of life. Indeed, if black churches were to save the souls of their people, they needed to better their lives.

The post–Civil War period was characterized by the black churches' emphasis upon a social gospel that permeated all aspects of the emerging black society, especially family, education, and politics. As missionaries from the independent black churches fanned out across the South, they sought to restore order among the shambles of family life that had been produced by slavery. Laws associated with slavery had refused to recognize marriages between slaves, which resulted in a declining interest among freedmen to participate in any religious or legal marriage ceremonies. As such, missionaries preached to their new congregations the need to legalize and formalize their marriages. This was the first step in the churches' attempts to develop structure and organization in black society. To do this, many ministers returned to the Bible and the stories of "good fathers"—notably, Abraham and, of course, God himself.

In his *Apology for African Methodism*, Benjamin T. Tanner, a bishop in the AME Church, wrote,

> For it is one of the brightest pages in the history of our Church, that while the Army of the Union were forcing their victorious passage through the southern land and striking down treason, the missionaries of our Church in the persons of Brown, Lynch, Cain, Handy, Stanford, Steward, and others were following in their wake and establishing the Church and the school house. (p. 251)

This history of this black church indicates that Payne's words from 1862 were taken seriously by black ministers, who charged their people with the responsibility to educate themselves and their children and who labored to provide the institutions that would educate future black generations. A shining light in this respect was Bishop

Payne. He served as the first president of what is now known as Wilberforce University in southwestern Ohio, which has educated blacks since 1856.

Black ministers also served as important leaders of black communities. Hiriam R. Revels, a minister in the AME Church, organized regiments of black soldiers from Maryland during the Civil War. After the war he worked in the Freedmen's Bureau to provide for the physical needs of his people and was later elected a U.S. senator from Mississippi. Likewise, Bishop Henry M. Turner of the AME Church organized the Republican Party in Georgia and later served in the Georgia legislature. Finally, Bishop James W. Wood of the AME Zion Church served as the deputy collector of internal revenue for the United States and later as the assistant superintendent of public instruction for North Carolina. These are only a few examples of talented black ministers who sought to address the physical needs of their people and to provide the leadership needed for them to attain their rights.

The end of Reconstruction in 1877 did not mean that the effects of the war and of slavery had been addressed. Unfortunately, it simply meant that the United States had decided to thenceforth ignore the needs of the poor and oppressed, many of whom were newly freed slaves. The black churches, however, did not stray from their social gospel. The ministers called upon their congregations to be sensitive to the needs of their members. The recurring themes in sermons came to revolve around charity and love of one's neighbor. In response, churches and individual congregations established organizations and societies to help provide food and assistance in times of need, especially regarding sickness, death, and other crises, to their members. In fact, such beneficial societies permeated black communities. Between the 1860s and 1900 nine beneficial societies were established in Atlanta; six of them were associated with black churches.

Holiness: The Roots of the Future. In the 1840s and 1850s a movement characterized as "Holiness" arose, mainly in the Methodist tradition. Simply put, Holiness was the outward manifestation of the conversion that was accomplished by the grace of God. It was characterized by feelings of serenity and the personal assuredness of salvation. The movement was formally recognized with the organization of the National Camp Meeting Association for the Promotion of Holiness in 1867.

The close of Reconstruction in 1877 saw the rise of Jim Crow laws that institutionalized the segregation of the races in much of the United States, which practices would last until the civil rights revolution of the late 1950s and 1960s. Segregation had a serious impact upon black communities in that it limited both employment and education. Such problems were made worse by a series of crop failures beginning in the 1890s, which forced many blacks to leave their rural homes in the South and move into the urban centers of the North. As a result, membership in black churches in Boston, Detroit, Cincinnati, and Philadelphia rose dramatically; in this climate, newly formed churches that emphasized revivalistic practices also attracted many blacks. These groups preached a gospel that made prominent "baptism by the Holy Spirit" and often spoke in tongues.

One such church was the Church of God in Christ, founded by Charles Harrison Mason. Mason was the son of former slaves, who themselves had converted during the antebellum period. He believed that he was destined by God to be a preacher, and after he was cured of tuberculosis, he attended the Arkansas Baptist College with the intent to pursue his calling. After only a brief time he left the college because he saw little value in this formal education. Nevertheless, he was licensed as a preacher by the Baptist Church in 1893. His connection with the Baptist Church was cut short four years later, however, when he was ordered from his pulpit for preaching "Holiness" doctrines. He then preached throughout the South and developed a substantial following. His Church of God in Christ was formally incorporated in 1897, but it was not until he was touched by the Holy Spirit at an Asuza Street revival in Los Angeles in the early 1900s that his church took on its Pentecostal practices. It was there that he was introduced to speaking in tongues by the black Holiness preacher William J. Seymour. These two men opened the Pentecostal movement to blacks, which would become an important aspect of black theology in the twentieth century.

[*See also* African Methodist Episcopal Church; American Colonization Society; Bible; Black Church; Black Family; Black Politics; Black Uplift; Civil Rights; Civil War, Participation and Recruitment of Black Troops in; Colonization; Douglass, Frederick; Education; Emancipation Proclamation; Emigration to Africa; Freedmen; Freedmen's Bureau; Garnet, Henry Highland; Identity; *Narrative of the Life of Frederick Douglass*; Oratory and Verbal Arts; Payne, Daniel A.; Reconstruction; Religion; Religion and Slavery; Republican Party; Resistance; Segregation; Society of Friends (Quakers); Thirteenth Amendment; *and* Walker, David.]

BIBLIOGRAPHY

Allen, Richard. "Address to the Free People of Colour of These United States." In *Minutes of the Proceedings of the National Negro Conventions, 1830–1864*, edited by Howard Holman Bell. Rpt. New York: Arno, 1969. http://www.pbs.org/wgbh/aia/part3/3h512t.html.

Frazier, E. Franklin / Lincoln, C. Eric. *The Negro Church in America / The Black Church since Frazier*. New York: Schocken Books, 1974. The classic study of the black church from a sociological perspective; originally published in 1964, followed by the supplemental work that brings the subject up to date.

Holifield, E. Brooks. *Theology in America: Christian Thought from the Age of the Puritans to the Civil War*. New Haven, CT: Yale University Press, 2003. An intellectual study of religion in early America that includes chapters on African American contributions.

Jones, Absalom. "The Causes and Motives for Establishing St. Thomas's African Church in Philadelphia." In *Annals of the First African Church in the United States of American now Styled the African Episcopal Church of St. Thomas, Philadelphia*, edited by William Douglass. Philadelphia: King and Baird Printers, 1852. http://www.pbs.org/wgbh/aia/part3/3h512t.html.

Lincoln, C. Eric, and Lawrence H. Mamiya. *The Black Church in the African American Experience*. Durham, NC: Duke University Press, 1990. A very good study of black churches with an emphasis on the post–Civil War period.

Noll, Mark A. *The Old Religion in a New World: The History of North American Christianity*. Grand Rapids, MI: Eerdmans, 2002. A text on American religions that gives a very good background for the discussion of black churches.

Payne, Daniel A. *Welcome to the Ransomed; or, Duties of the Colored Inhabitants of the District of Columbia*. Baltimore: Bull and Tuttle, 1862.

Tanner, Benjamin T. *An Apology for African Methodism*. Baltimore, privately printed, 1867.

—THOMAS E. CARNEY

BLACK UPLIFT. African American activists in the antebellum and post–Civil War eras invoked a language and political strategy of black uplift or elevation. Composed of ideas and actions about physical, mental, or intellectual and personal morality and the realm of the soul, black activists, through speech and literature, used uplift as a general program to improve the race. Uplift was also intended to refute white racism prevalent in the literature and public activities of the nineteenth century. Accordingly, two key components were respectability and self-help. Frederick Douglass, for one, noted that only racism kept "the avenues of wealth and honor" from being open to all who chose to enter them. Respectability and wealth were not just accessories to wealth and fame, but required individual action, particularly virtuous assistance to the race or against slavery as well as a purer soul. Blacks also shared the general anxiety over confidence men or tricksters and so urged an "uprightness of character." Black elites thus condemned criminality, ludicrous or showy clothing, and laziness. Austin Steward, for example, sought and gained editorial censure of Israel Lewis for embezzling funds from the struggling Wilberforce Colony in Upper Canada.

Black uplift emphasized literacy and education. David Ruggles wrote a series of articles in the January and February issues of the *Emancipator* extolling the virtues of a free press, especially an antislavery one, and urging African Americans to support the *Emancipator* and others like it through subscriptions and to read it constantly. Blacks formed literary societies in many cities from the 1820s until the end of the century, founded high schools and universities, and touted teaching to be a highly honorable profession. Influenced by the popularity of Benjamin Franklin during the antebellum period and by their own aspirations, black elites extolled as well the virtues of labor. Innumerable slave narrators recalled their own efforts to educate themselves and described themselves as the hardest workers on a plantation by rising to positions of leadership and sometimes even purchasing themselves. Even after escaping to the North, African American narrators prided themselves on hard work. In time, as the example of Douglass's *North Star* shows, blacks tied work and activism together.

Adoration of Franklin and the need to create their own community in a racist society meant African Americans sought uplift through organizations. Mutual societies, benevolent organizations, and literary societies were to inspire a more elevated black citizenry. One key element was temperance. As in white society, black leaders castigated excessive drinking and compared it with slavery. Another source of worry was ostentatious dress in part because it attracted racist ridicule but also because black elites contended that merit was far more significant than fancy dress.

African Americans found themselves in a paradoxical situation within black uplift. As did their male counterparts, black women experienced harsh racism and derision in public discourse. Within black society they were expected to support men and to avoid competition for leadership. As "Ellen" wrote in the *Colored American*, black women should best influence their men by the fireside and provide solace over the hardness of life. Later, Francis Ellen Watkins argued that the home should be the birthplace of affections where women could support and transform their husbands. Other black women urged more public roles by forming benevolent societies and organizations such as the Dorcas Literary Society and by teaching in public schools.

Black uplift was a response to the scurrilous racism of the nineteenth century. Experiencing anxiety over the vulgar representations of black society and politics in the popular press, black activists used self-elevation as a tool to counter such prejudice. Black conventions urged reform of the white press and urged the creation of a black media to counter racist imagery. Worrying about the many evils among themselves, black uplifters condemned the antics of the black poor as much as they resented the insults of white racists. One curative was to leave the cities. Douglass's *North Star* editorialized that a cause for

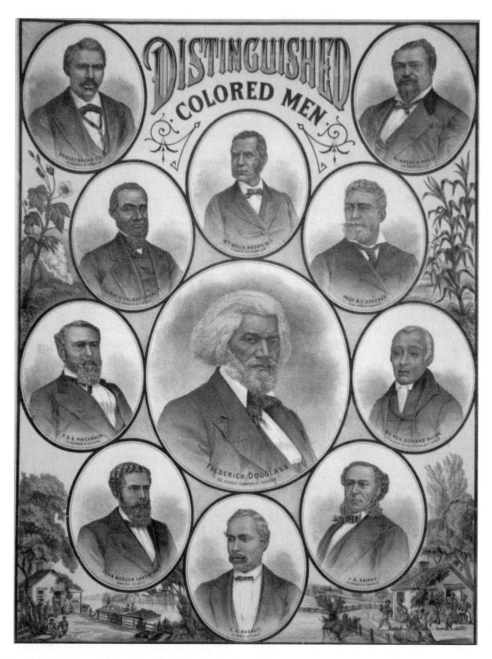

"Distinguished Colored Men," chromolithograph published by A. Muller of New York in 1883. The portraits are: Frederick Douglass (at center); Robert Brown Elliott (top left); Blanche K. Bruce (top right); and (clockwise around Douglass, starting at twelve o'clock) William Wells Brown, Richard T. Greener, Richard Allen, J. H. Rainey, E. D. Bassett, John Mercer Langston, P. B. S. Pinchback, and Henry Highland Garnet. (Library of Congress.)

the degradation of blacks was overcrowding in the city and urged them to move to the countryside and follow the example of the virtuous yeoman farmer. Black conventions later pushed the need for more black-owned businesses.

The drive toward uplift was critical in the fight against slavery and for black civil rights. As blacks declared themselves independent and virtuous people, they made slavery seem all the more oppressive and the denial of civil rights all the more evil. Respectability became a form of resistance to the tyranny of the slave power. After the Civil War, black uplift, along with service in the war and the renewed egalitarianism of white society, became the key arguments for black citizenship.

[*See also* Black Abolitionists; Black Politics; Black Press; Canada; Civil Rights; Civil War; Douglass, Frederick; Entrepreneurs; Franklin, Benjamin; *North Star*; Racism; Ruggles, David; Slave Narratives; Slavery; *and* Temperance.]

BIBLIOGRAPHY

Rael, Patrick. *Black Identity and Black Protest in the Antebellum North.* Chapel Hill: University of North Carolina Press, 2002.

—GRAHAM RUSSELL GAO HODGES

BLAINE, JAMES G. (b. 31 January 1830; d. 27 January 1893), a Speaker of the House of Representatives and the secretary of state under two presidents. One of the most polarizing political figures in American history, James Gillespie Blaine, "the Plumed Knight of Maine," was the most prominent presidential candidate of the late nineteenth century never to be elected. His chameleon-like character kept him at the top of the Republican Party machinery during both Reconstruction and the Gilded Age. He supported the Union during the Civil War and the Radical cause in the late 1860s, took a conciliatory view of the southern question in the early 1870s, and ultimately all but abandoned the African American civil rights agenda in the late 1870s and thereafter. As much as any other Republican, he influenced the course of the party in selling out African Americans after Reconstruction for the joint benefits of sectional reconciliation and national business interests. He did so, however, without necessarily alienating black voters or friends. Frederick Douglass, for instance, supported him throughout his career, sometimes quite enthusiastically, which is a testament to Blaine's unusual acumen as a statesman and demagogue.

Born in western Pennsylvania when it was still largely a frontier region, Blaine graduated from Washington College (later called Washington and Jefferson College) in 1847, moved to Kentucky for a brief time, and then relocated to Philadelphia to continue teaching and studying law. In 1854 he resettled in Maine, where he became a newspaper owner and editor. By 1862 he had worked his way through the ranks of state politics and into Congress. He served as the Speaker of the House from 1869 to 1875; during this time he became the leader of the Half-Breed faction of his party, unsuccessfully opposing the Stalwarts, who favored President Grant's reelection in 1872.

In 1876 Blaine made the leap across Capitol Hill to the Senate, where he served for the next four years. On the election of James Garfield in 1880, Blaine accepted the post of secretary of state, which he held for less than one year, resigning because Garfield's assassination ele-

vated Chester Arthur, a member of the Stalwart faction, to the presidency. In 1884 on his third attempt, Blaine finally received the Republican nomination for president, running against and losing to the Democrat Grover Cleveland in a bitterly fought, controversial, and close election. Many Republican supporters called for Blaine's renomination for the presidency in 1888, but he refused to be considered. Instead, he threw his support behind Benjamin Harrison, who won the race and rewarded Blaine with a second stint as the secretary of state, his last political office. Although he resigned the post in 1892 to run against Harrison for the Republican nomination, he was unsuccessful, and he died shortly thereafter.

It was during the campaign of 1872 that Blaine and Frederick Douglass first met. Blaine invited Douglass to his home in Maine, and Douglass accepted. Although Douglass clearly wanted the Republican Party to address the race problem as its primary issue, Blaine, the consummate

James G. Blaine, the "plumed knight of Maine," was also called—by his opponents in the election of 1884—"Blaine, Blaine, James G. Blaine, the continental liar from the state of Maine." This photograph, c. 1865–1880, is from the Brady-Handy collection, which consists of original glass plate negatives by Mathew Brady and Levin C. Handy studios. (Library of Congress.)

compromiser, explained the political inexpediency of such a stance and managed to keep Douglass pacified as a nominal supporter. The two spoke on the same stage at the Republican National Convention in Cincinnati in 1876. Four years later, both men supported James Garfield for president. Garfield rewarded Blaine with the office of secretary of state, and though he had promised the post of United States marshal for the District of Columbia to Douglass, he tried to renege to avoid stirring racial animosity. Douglass appealed to Blaine for help, Blaine spoke to Garfield on Douglass's behalf, and Douglass got the job. Moreover, Blaine solicited the advice of Douglass in making other federal appointments of African Americans.

Although their positions on the race issue differed, Douglass backed Blaine in the campaign of 1884 out of loyalty to the Republican Party. Douglass urged Blaine to take a stance in support of civil rights, but Blaine refused. Thus, the only issue that really separated the Republicans from the Democrats in the election was the tariff. When the Republican ticket lost, Douglass blamed the defeat on Blaine's refusal to stand apart from the Democrats on the issue of race, which had always been the party's bread and butter. Douglass said Blaine had thus defeated himself. Blaine accepted the criticism in good faith, and the two men continued their professional political relationship, aware that they might need each other in the future.

Harrison's election in 1888 saw both Blaine and Douglass rewarded with government jobs. With Blaine serving as the secretary of state and Douglass as a minister to Haiti, the two interacted regularly, exchanging at least nine letters from 1889 to 1891, before Douglass resigned his post. Blaine and Harrison wanted to secure a naval base on Haiti from the regime of Louis Modestin Florvil Hyppolite, who had recently taken power there. Contemporary reports held that Blaine had charged Douglass with arranging the deal for the base, but Douglass denied that he was assigned that duty. Historical accounts of the Haitian affair have consequently differed. Whatever the circumstances, about a year after Douglass assumed his post, Rear Admiral Bancroft Gherardi was appointed to work with Douglass to secure the base. Gherardi, an outspoken racist, did not like Douglass, considered him a weak negotiator at a time when an intimidating presence would have proven more effective, and demanded his replacement. Douglass urged Blaine to have Gherardi cease his intimidation tactics, saying the Haitians' fear of American imperialism was already acute enough without such bellicosity. The white naval officer got the better of the argument, however, and Douglass resigned. The Harrison administration never did acquire the base, and Blaine and Douglass never had the opportunity to work together again.

[*See also* Cleveland, Grover; Douglass, Frederick; Garfield, James A.; Gherardi, Bancroft; Grant, Ulysses S.; Haiti; Haitian Revolutions; Harrison, Benjamin; Hyppolite, Louis Modestin Florvil; Race, Theories of; Racism; Reconstruction; *and* Republican Party.]

BIBLIOGRAPHY

Muzzey, David S. *James G. Blaine: A Political Idol of Other Days*. New York: Dodd, Mead, 1935.

Spetter, Alan B. and Homer E. Socolofsky. *The Presidency of Benjamin Harrison*. Lawrence: University Press of Kansas, 1987.

Tyler, Alice F. *The Foreign Policy of James G. Blaine*. Minneapolis: University of Minnesota Press, 1927.

Volwiler, Albert T. *The Correspondence Between Benjamin Harrison and James G. Blaine, 1882–1893*. Philadelphia: American Philosophical Society, 1940.

—THOMAS ADAMS UPCHURCH

BLANCHARD, JONATHAN (b. 19 January 1811; d. 14 May 1892), educator and social reformer. Jonathan Blanchard would become an heir of the principles of the evangelical postmillennial Christianity exemplified in America's Benevolent Empire of the early 1800s, wherein activists sought to reform American society through education and religious missions. Blanchard was born the eleventh of fifteen children, near Rockingham, Vermont, to Polly Lovell and the farmer Jonathan Blanchard Sr. The young Jonathan was able to take advantage of a variety of educational opportunities, eventually graduating from Middlebury College, after which he enrolled in Andover Theological Seminary.

Blanchard left Andover in September 1836, because it failed to stand against slavery, and became an abolitionist lecturer for the American Anti-Slavery Society. He was one of Theodore Dwight Weld's "Seventy," preaching the "sin of slavery" throughout Pennsylvania with the hopes that the consciences of slaveholders would be pierced over their treatment of those whom Blanchard, echoing the words of Jesus, lamented as the "least of these my brethren."

In late 1837 Blanchard enrolled in the Lane Theological Seminary in Cincinnati, Ohio, heeding Lyman Beecher's *Plea for the West* to capture this region for Protestant Christianity. After graduation Blanchard was ordained by Beecher and Calvin Stowe and became the pastor of the Sixth Presbyterian Church, which was formed as a result of a slavery-related schism at Cincinnati's First Presbyterian Church. In this capacity Blanchard continued his abolitionist involvement and served as a delegate from the Ohio State Anti-Slavery Society to the World's Anti-Slavery Convention in London in 1843, where he was elected a vice president. For four days in October 1845 he debated the sinfulness of slavery with the nationally known Reverend Nathan L. Rice.

Blanchard later became the president of Knox College, in Galesburg, Illinois, remaining a champion of abolitionist thought. In 1850 he rebuked the senator Stephen A. Douglas in a massive open letter for aiding passage of the Compromise of 1850, with its Fugitive Slave Law. Later, he openly opposed Douglas for the popular sovereignty views he espoused in the Kansas-Nebraska Act, which revived the possibility of slavery in the territories, brought about the weakening of the Whig Party, and, in the end, fostered the Republican Party. Blanchard's challenges to Douglas culminated in a public debate in Knoxville, Illinois, on 13 October 1854. The following year Blanchard was lecturing against slavery throughout Kentucky, traveling with John Fee, the founder of Berea College, and Cassius M. Clay, a Yale graduate and nephew of the statesman Henry Clay. After Knox College, Blanchard assumed the presidency of the struggling Wheaton College in Wheaton, Illinois, fashioning it into a strong and vital reform institution. He restructured the trustee board and named Owen Lovejoy, the brother of the abolitionist martyr Elijah P. Lovejoy, to a seat.

After the Civil War Blanchard shifted his focus from antislavery work to antisecretism. In an April 1869 letter to the abolitionist Gerrit Smith, Blanchard expressed his belief that the curse of secret societies was deeper than slavery, believing that Freemasonry played a role in advancing slavery and fostering the Civil War.

Like many others, Blanchard sought to draw Frederick Douglass into joining forces with his causes, which for Blanchard was the ensnarement and captivity of former slaves into the ranks of Masonry and the like. Blanchard sought the assistance of Douglass by asking him to serve as his vice presidential running mate on the 1884 ticket of the third-party anti-Masonic American Party (as distinguished from the earlier Know-Nothing Party). Blanchard met with Douglass numerous times in efforts to persuade him; in the end Douglass unyieldingly told Blanchard not to put his name on the ticket.

However, the rebuff did not diminish Blanchard's respect for Douglass or his involvement with him, nor did it preclude Douglass from speaking at a later American Party convention. As was the practice of the day, Blanchard's newspaper, the *Christian Cynosure*, republished materials that were available in other venues, such as other newspapers or correspondence. Blanchard reprinted Douglass's thoughts on the Supreme Court's decisions on the Civil Rights Act of 1875 (in 1883) and on John Brown (in 1887). Blanchard even gave favorable press to Douglass's 1884 interracial marriage to Helen Pitts, stating, "God had made of one blood all nations of men."

Blanchard was a jeremiad to his culture as he forged a Christian vision of human equality. However, despite all of his progressiveness, Blanchard still exhibited stains of America's premier sin: racism. In rare moments, his private correspondence exhibits the use of the racist label "darkies." Sadly, this speaks as much about the endemism of American racism as it does about Blanchard. Over time Blanchard's strong character and unflinching efforts for equality and reform put him at odds with many. His shift in focus from significant social problems to peripheral ones caused the biographer Clyde S. Kilby to call him a "minority of one." Though marginalized by his temperament, Blanchard maintained correspondence with his former abolitionist associates for many years.

[*See also* American Anti-Slavery Society; Antislavery Movement; Brown, John; Civil Rights Act of 1875; Civil War; Clay, Cassius M.; Clay, Henry; Compromise of 1850; Douglas, Stephen A.; Douglass, Frederick, Fugitive Slave Law of 1850; Know-Nothing Party; Lane Theological Seminary; Racism; Smith, Gerrit; Supreme Court; *and* Weld, Theodore Dwight.]

BIBLIOGRAPHY

Blanchard, Jonathan, and Nathan L. Rice. *A Debate on Slavery, Held in the City of Cincinnati, on the First, Second, Third, and Sixth Days of October, 1845, upon the Question: Is Slave-holding in Itself Sinful, and the Relation between Master and Slave, a Sinful Relation?* New York: Negro Universities Press, 1969.

Fischer, Raymond P. *Four Hazardous Journeys of the Reverend Jonathan Blanchard, Founder of Wheaton College.* Wheaton, IL: Tyndale House, 1987. Written by a grandson, this work looks at four events from Blanchard's life and utilizes materials from family records previously unavailable to other biographers.

Kilby, Clyde S. *Minority of One: The Biography of Jonathan Blanchard.* Grand Rapids, MI: Eerdmans, 1959. From a sympathetic perspective, this is the only critical biography available.

Taylor, Richard S. "Seeking the Kingdom: A Study in the Career of Jonathan Blanchard, 1811–1892." PhD diss., Northern Illinois University, 1977.

—DAVID B. MALONE

BLUCKE, STEPHEN (b. c. 1752; d. c. 1795), black Loyalist leader. Born free in Barbados, Stephen Blucke moved to New York City sometime before 1770. There Blucke married Margaret Coventry, who was his elder by nine years. She claimed to have purchased her own freedom in 1769, from Mrs. Coventry's family in New York City, as well as that of a six-year-old girl, Isabel Gibbons, who was probably her daughter. Blucke joined the Church of England, which gave him some prominence in the black community of New York City and in rural New Jersey. He chose to remain loyal to the English cause at the outbreak of the American Revolution and gained a patron in Stephen Skinner, a wealthy Loyalist. Stephen Blucke became a commander of the Black Pioneers, an informal black military organization that provided logistical support to the British army.

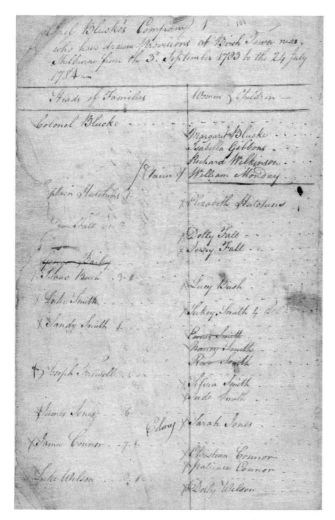

Muster Roll of Colonel Stephen Blucke's Company at Birchtown, Shelburne County: a black settlement in Nova Scotia, 1784. Birchtown was one of several communities of African American loyalists established in Nova Scotia at the time. In 1792, as a result of local hostility and difficult conditions, nearly half its residents left for Sierra Leone. (Violet Keene/Library and Archives Canada/ C-001018.)

On 31 July 1783 Stephen Blucke and his family left New York City on HMS *Peggy* bound for Saint John's River, Nova Scotia. They traveled with one of the certificates offered by General Samuel Birch, which were the first passports ever awarded to African Americans. Upon arrival in Nova Scotia, Blucke was placed in charge of the construction of Birchtown, a small, coastal community designated for the black Loyalist settlement. Captain Booth of the Royal Engineers described Blucke as "a man of surprising address, being perfectly polite and [who], I believe, has had a superior education." Within a year Blucke was commissioned as a lieutenant colonel and commanded twenty-one companies of Black Pioneers.

In his position as commander Blucke personified government authority. As a demonstration of his power he ended the wartime privileges of private cutting and sale of firewood, a practice by which black Loyalists had profited in New York City but which had become a liability in Nova Scotia. Blucke ordered a jail built to house offenders. His leadership soon helped him prosper. He received a land grant of two hundred acres and a home, both of which marked him as highly privileged. Blucke's reputation soared when he entertained Prince William Henry, later King William IV, at his home in Birchtown. Blucke acted as a conduit between white philanthropists such as Stephen Skinner and needy blacks. Blucke became the first African American to rent a pew at the Shelburne Anglican Church.

In 1785 Blucke became master of the Birchtown school, operated by Dr. Bray's Associates, part of the missionary wing of the Society for the Propagation of the Gospel in Foreign Parts, which was devoted to the education of enslaved people. The school was badly underfinanced, and Blucke complained bitterly to authorities in London. The school's budget was the first of many vexing problems for Blucke. Land distribution lagged badly, as did jobs for black settlers. Tired of broken promises from the English colonial authorities, over one thousand black Nova Scotians petitioned to migrate to Sierra Leone. The leaders of this effort, including David George, John Marrant, and Thomas Peters, represented a more militant black identification with radical Methodism. After the departure of the majority of resettled black Loyalists to Sierra Leone in 1791, Blucke's empire shrank to less than fifty people. In 1794 he was charged with embezzlement of funds and disappeared. Legend held that he was eaten alive by a savage animal, a fate that reflected his moderate stance at a time of rising racial tensions.

[*See also* American Revolution; Black Brigade; Black Loyalists; Black Migration; Episcopalians (Anglicans) and African Americans; George, David; Marrant, John; Methodist Church and African Americans; *and* Society for the Propagation of the Gospel in Foreign Parts.]

BIBLIOGRAPHY

Hodges, Graham Russell, ed. *The Black Loyalist Directory: African Americans in Exile after the American Revolution.* New York: Garland, 1995.

—GRAHAM RUSSELL GAO HODGES

BOEN, WILLIAM (b. c. 1735; d. 12 June 1824), a freed slave who became a Quaker. Born a slave in Rancocas, New Jersey, William Boen belonged to a Quaker master. As a young man he met and became friends with John Woolman, the Quaker minister known for his continuing efforts to end slavery. It was most likely Woolman who encouraged Boen to attend worship at the Mount Holly Monthly Meeting of the Society of Friends. *Anecdotes and Memoirs of William Boen, a Coloured Man, Who Lived and Died Near Mount Holly, New Jersey. To which is Added, The Testimony of Friends of Mount Holly Monthly Meeting Concerning Him* was a memorial written by Quakers from Mount Holly for Boen, who was a member of the Society of Friends from 1814 until his death in 1824. The authors of the memorial stated that although they rarely felt called upon to "record the virtues of any of this afflicted race of

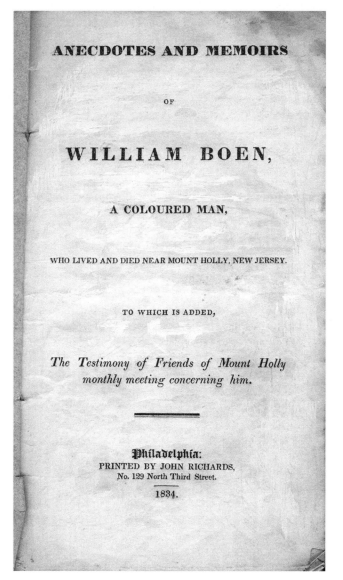

Anecdotes and Memoirs, title page. This work was a memorial written by Quakers from Mount Holly for William Boen, who was a member of the Society of Friends from 1814 until his death in 1824. (University of North Carolina, Wilson Library.)

people," they thought Boen was an exception, in that he had lived his life in a manner that exemplified the beliefs of the Quaker faith, demonstrating that a man's skin color was of no importance to God in his selection of faithful followers. However, the same Mount Holly Monthly Meeting also denied Boen's membership request for almost fifty years following his initial petition, apparently on account of his skin color.

William Boen was often asked to explain the circumstances of his religious awakening. He reported that while he was a young man, his master had sent him to an isolated hillside in Mount Holly, New Jersey, with instructions to cut down all the trees that grew there. But there were Indians in that area who were reportedly killing and scalping people, and Boen feared they would hear the sound of his ax and come to kill him. Even greater than his fear of death, however, was his concern that he was not "fit" to die. One day on the hillside, while standing very still, he said that he felt as if he had been filled with what the Quakers described as the "light" that God places in souls that allows people to distinguish right from wrong. Boen believed that following this light would make him worthy to die in peace, and from that point on he adhered to the ways of the Quakers by responding to "that within me that inclined me to good."

In 1763, when Boen was twenty-eight years old, his master informed him that he would soon gain his freedom. Shortly thereafter Boen became engaged to Dinah ("Dido"), a free colored woman who was employed in the nearby town of Chesterfield. Although at that time neither Boen nor his prospective wife belonged to the Society of Friends, he expressed his desire to be married in a Quaker ceremony. To accommodate this wish, his friend John Woolman convened a number of Friends at the home of Dinah's former employers, the Burrs of Peachfield, where both Quaker and African American witnesses signed the marriage certificate. Not long after his marriage Boen applied for membership in the Society of Friends, but he had to wait until he was almost eighty years old before receiving approval. Until his death ten years later he faithfully attended meetings for worship.

Throughout his lifetime Boen's contemporaries described him as an exemplary member of the Society of Friends: diligent, industrious, truthful and sincere, yet plain and straightforward in all he said and did. It was his continued adherence to these principles, Boen explained, that resulted in the peace and clarity of mind that he maintained until the day he died at ninety years of age.

[*See also* Autobiography; Religion; Society of Friends (Quakers) and African Americans; Spirituality; *and* Woolman, John.]

BIBLIOGRAPHY

Anecdotes and Memoirs of William Boen, a Coloured Man, Who Lived and Died Near Mount Holly, New Jersey. To which is Added, The Testimony of Friends of Mount Holly Monthly Meeting Concerning Him. Philadelphia: J. Richards, 1834. http://docsouth.unc.edu/neh/boen/title.html.

Cadbury, Henry. "Negro Membership in the Society of Friends." *Journal of Negro History* 21.2 (1936): 180–209. http://www.qhpress.org/quakerpages/qwhp/hcjnh3.htm.

—PENNY ANNE WELBOURNE

BOSTON. Boston, sometimes called the "Cradle of Liberty," was the birthplace of the American Revolution. Before the Civil War the city was home to the most radical and vocal opponents of slavery, a (usually safe) haven for fugitive slaves, and the largest city in which blacks had full political and legal equality. For blacks nineteenth-century Boston was a place of promise and hope, but it was not always a place where promises could be fulfilled or hopes realized. Even in Boston there was racism and segregation.

The first black known in Boston arrived in 1638. Most, but certainly not all, slaves in the Massachusetts colony were urban, living in Boston, Cambridge, and Newberry-port. In 1750 slaves constituted 20 percent of the Cambridge population. Slave owners tended to be merchants and artisans who used slaves as laborers and skilled workmen. The maritime industry was also the destination of many Boston slaves. By the 1740s about 20 percent of all male slaves in the county belonged to sea captains, shipwrights, and others associated with the ocean. Boston never had a large slave or black population, although some Bostonians, including the Faneuils and the Waldos, made substantial profits from the African slave trade. By 1752 Boston's 1,500 blacks, most of whom were slaves, represented 10 percent of the city's population. Three slaves in Boston achieved significant fame: the poet Phillis Wheatley, the mariner Briton Hammon, who wrote one of the earliest slave narratives, and the portrait painter Scipio Moorehead. Despite discriminatory legislation and practices, blacks seemed to mingle with whites, at least in the streets and taverns of the city. In March 1770 the mob that harassed British soldiers in Boston included a former slave, Crispus Attucks. When the fearful British soldiers fired on the crowd, touching off the Boston Massacre, Attucks became the first patriot to die in what would become the American Revolution.

When General George Washington arrived in the Boston area to take command of the Revolutionary army he was shocked to see so many black faces in the Massachusetts militia. Among them was Peter Salem from nearby Framingham, who had already seen service at Lexington and Concord. Probably a dozen or more other blacks fought in that battle, and one, Prince Estabrook, lost his life. Peter Salem and a number of other blacks fought at the Battle of Bunker Hill, where Salem Poor was commended by fourteen officers for his bravery. Poor remained in the Continental Army, seeing action at the Battle of White Plains and serving at Valley Forge. During the Revolution slavery largely collapsed in Boston as many male slaves joined the army and male and female slaves asserted their own rights to liberty. In 1780 Massachusetts abolished slavery, an act that reflected hostility to the practice dating at least from 1700 when the Boston lawyer Samuel Sewell published *The Selling of Joseph.* Another Bostonian, Elihu Colman, published *Testimony Against the Antichristian Practice of Making Slaves of Men* in 1733.

The most important black in Boston during the period was Prince Hall, a former slave, who became the leader of the black Masons in the United States. In 1775 Hall was initiated as a Mason and during the Revolution formed an all-black lodge in Boston. In 1777 Hall and seven other blacks petitioned the legislature to end slavery in the new state. After the Revolution Prince Hall would continue to petition the state government on a variety of issues as he became the acknowledged leader of the city's black community. After failing to get city or state support for a public school for blacks, Hall opened one in his home in Boston in 1798. Less than a decade later the school flourished and moved to the larger quarters of the African Meeting House.

By 1800 Boston had about 1,100 blacks, most living below Beacon Hill. Many worked in service industries, while others were involved in the maritime industries. Blacks built churches, continued to run schools, and persistently petitioned and agitated for full civil rights. In 1815 a white benefactor, Abiel Smith, left an estate of $4,000 to the African school, which was renamed the Smith School, and in 1820 the City of Boston began to provide a small amount of funding for the school. By the early 1830s the city funded two other black schools, but the education was inferior to that of whites. In the 1840s black leaders, led by William C. Nell, began to agitate for integrated public schools. After petitions to the school board failed, blacks initiated a lawsuit, with Charles Sumner as lead counsel and, significantly, with Robert Morris, one of the first black attorneys in the nation, as co-counsel. When in *Roberts v. City of Boston* (1850) the Massachusetts Supreme Judicial Court upheld the right of the city to maintain segregated schools, black leaders turned to the state legislature, which in 1855 prohibited segregated education in the state, thus forcing Boston to integrate its schools. Meanwhile, in 1853, Nell and two black abolitionist women—Sarah Remond Parker and Caroline Remond Putnam—successfully sued a Boston theater for refusing to seat them with whites. Persistent struggles by blacks in Boston led to an end to all formal, and a good deal of informal, segregation by 1860. That year the census found 2,261 blacks in the city, though it is likely that hundreds of fugitive slaves living in Boston were not counted.

Hundreds of fugitive slaves came to Boston, where they found employment, education, and a black community ready to help them. In 1842 Boston police seized a fugitive slave named George Latimer. The state's courts would not intervene on his behalf, but political pressure forced the sheriff to refuse to keep Latimer in his jail, while Latimer's owner, James B. Gray, waited for proof of his claim to arrive from Virginia. Having no place to incarcerate him, Gray "sold" Latimer to a group of abolitionists for a modest sum. These actions led Massachusetts and other states to pass "Latimer Laws," prohibiting the use of state facilities to house fugitive slaves. The first attempt to seize a slave in Boston under the 1850 Fugitive Slave Law came in February 1851 with the arrest of a man known as Shadrach. Among those representing Shadrach at his hearing was the black lawyer Robert Morris. In the middle of the hearing a mob, mostly made up of blacks, stormed the courtroom, whisking Shadrach to freedom. Later that year mobs were unable to prevent the return of Thomas Sims. In 1854 the Federal government succeeded in removing Anthony Burns from Boston, but only by deploying federal troops, hiring a huge number of newly minted federal deputies, and spending vast sums of money. Burns would be the last slave taken out of the city. Other fugitive slaves, such as Henry "Box" Brown and William and Ellen Craft, passed through Boston on their way to safety in England.

Starting in the 1830s Boston was the center of the antislavery movement in the nation. In 1829 David Walker, who operated a used clothing store, published one of the most radical antislavery tracts in the nation's history, the *Appeal to the Colored Citizens of the World*. In 1830 Walker died from lung disease, probably tuberculosis, though at the time it was suspected that he was murdered by Southerners infuriated by his publication. In 1831 the white abolitionist William Lloyd Garrison began publishing *The Liberator*, which quickly became the most important antislavery newspaper in the nation. Many, perhaps a majority, of Garrison's subscribers were black. By 1840 William C. Nell, who was then only twenty-four, had become Garrison's typesetter. Garrison's organizations—the American Anti-Slavery Society and the Massachusetts Anti-Slavery Society—hired a number of black agents and lecturers from Boston. Many of the most important black and white critics of slavery lived in the city at one time or another, including Frederick Douglass, William Wells Brown, Lewis Hayden, and Charles Lenox Remond. Antebellum Boston also became a fertile ground for a small group of black professionals and intellectuals. Martin Delaney studied medicine across the river at Harvard in 1850, and in 1854 John DeGrasse became the first black admitted to a state medical society. Dr. John Rock was a successful dentist before turning to the law in 1861. Rock would eventually become the first black attorney admitted to the bar of the Supreme Court. Edward Garrison Walker, the son of David Walker, was also admitted to the bar in Boston in 1861. In 1866 he would win a seat in the Massachusetts state legislature, becoming the first black in the nation to hold such office.

When the Civil War began, Boston's blacks immediately offered their services, but blacks were not allowed into the army until late 1862. The first unit of Northern blacks was organized as the 54th Massachusetts Infantry Regiment under the command of a white Bostonian, Robert Gould Shaw. A second regiment, the 55th, was led by another white officer, Colonel Alfred S. Hartwell. Both regiments fought in a number of engagements. The 54th caught the attention of the whole nation for its heroic but futile charge at Fort Wagner in South Carolina in the summer of 1863. The regiment suffered extensive casualties, including its commander, Colonel Shaw, who died in the attack. The Confederates insisted on burying Shaw with his black troops as a way of insulting him. But throughout the United States their action had the opposite effect, and Shaw became a hero among Northerners of all races.

After the war Boston continued to be a center of black intellectual leadership. There were more than 5,000 blacks in the city by 1870, though they remained a tiny percentage of the entire population. The black population would reach about 10,000 by 1900. Blacks generally lived in a few neighborhoods, some in Boston, some in neighboring Chelsea and Cambridge. Nowhere did blacks have sufficient votes to win elections if the ballots were cast along racial lines. However, starting in 1866, Edward Garrison Walker and later Charles L. Mitchell served in the lower house of the state legislature while Cambridge sent Joshua Smith to the state senate in 1873. Other blacks held various city offices during the rest of the century. In 1866 Richard Greener became the first black undergraduate at Harvard, and in 1869 George L. Ruffin became the first black to graduate from that university's law school. At the end of the century William Monroe Trotter became the first black to be elected to Phi Beta Kappa at Harvard, setting the stage for his career as a newspaper editor in the early twentieth century. Similarly, in 1888, W. E. B. Du Bois came to Harvard where he earned a BA and then in 1895 a PhD, initiating his important career as a black intellectual in the twentieth century. Symbolic of the freedom blacks found in Boston, as well as the price in blood and sweat they paid for that liberty, in 1893 the city erected a huge monument on Boston common to honor the 54th Massachusetts Infantry Regiment.

[*See also* Abolitionism; Attucks, Crispus; Emerson, Ralph Waldo; Faneuil Hall (Boston); Fifty-fifth Massachusetts Infantry Regiment; Fifty-fourth Massachusetts Infantry Regiment; Fugitive Slave Law of 1793; Fugitive Slave Law of 1850; Garrison, William Lloyd; Hall, Prince; Underground Railroad; Walker, David; *and* Wheatley, Phillis.]

BIBLIOGRAPHY

Daniels, John. *In Freedom's Birthplace.* Boston: The South End Association, 1914.

Finkelman, Paul. "Not Only the Judges' Robes Were Black: African-American Lawyers as Social Engineers." *Stanford Law Review* 47 (1994): 161–209.

Horton, James Oliver, and Lois E. Horton. *Black Bostonians: Family Life and Community Struggle in the Antebellum North.* New York: Holmes and Meier, 1979.

Quarles, Benjamin. *The Negro in the American Revolution.* Chapel Hill: University of North Carolina Press, 1961.

—PAUL FINKELMAN

BRADBURN, GEORGE (b. 1806; d. 1880), abolitionist and minister. A devout and charitable Unitarian minister, George Bradburn worked tirelessly within the antislavery movement. While his name is virtually unknown in historical discourse, one has only to search the works of Frederick Douglass and other notable abolitionists to find evidence of Bradburn's defense of those socially and politically wronged. Douglass commented on "his keen wit and his hearty hatred for all manner of baseness" in the 30 October 1851 issue of the *Frederick Douglass' Paper.* In eulogizing his lifelong friend, Lysander Spooner, the author of the *Unconstitutionality of Slavery,* wrote, "Of the strong men of the anti-slavery cause, in its days of trial—of those in whose ability, fidelity, and courage most reliance was placed—George Bradburn was one of the select few."

As a youngster, Bradburn's character was greatly influenced by his mother's stoical and religious doctrine. Born in Attleboro, Massachusetts, he was raised by Sarah Leach Hovey and James Bradburn, who lived according to Quaker beliefs. His mother was a great influence, and by the time of her death, when Bradburn was nine, she had endowed him with the desire to make a lifelong commitment to helping others. The early death of loved ones was all too prevalent in Bradburn's life. At age thirty in 1836 he married Lydia Barnard Hussey, who died in 1837, seventeen days after the birth of their daughter, who died the following year. In 1850 he married Frances Parker.

Bradburn, a white man raised in Massachusetts, and Douglass, a black man once enslaved in Maryland, shared a common belief in the antislavery movement, but for dif-

ferent reasons, which ultimately reflected their individualism. The black, self-educated, fugitive former slave saw authority as oppressive; worlds apart in social class, the white, religiously bred New Englander embraced authority as a cultural norm. Bradburn fought his antislavery battle within a system that he hoped to change, whereas Douglass vehemently disliked any kind of class abasement and held the system itself responsible for the slavery of his people. As a freedman, Douglass shared a bond of kinship with those still enslaved; as a dutiful son, Bradburn shared an emotional link to his mother's legacy of helping others. Thus, two very different men shared similar familial values. At age seventy-four, as death neared, Bradburn agonized over the measure of success with which he had met in attempting to fulfill his mother's wishes.

In 1841, at an abolitionist meeting in New Bedford, Massachusetts, the young Douglass greatly impressed John A. Collins, the general agent for the Massachusetts Anti-Slavery Society, and William Lloyd Garrison, the founding father of the movement for immediate abolition with his passionate discourse against slavery. When they hired Douglass as a lecturing agent, Bradburn respected their judgment. However, later working closer together on lecturing tours, Bradburn and Douglass would encounter political differences of opinion.

As a conscientious member of both the Massachusetts and American antislavery societies, Bradburn was diligent in his activities to aid those victimized by an ignorant and biased system of oppression. He worked tirelessly as a lecturing agent for the American Anti-Slavery Society (AASS) and was chosen as a representative to the World's Anti-Slavery Convention in London in 1840, where he defended the eight American women delegates whom Englishmen had failed to recognize. Bradburn's reputation as a valiant critic of slavery during his term as Nantucket's representative in the Massachusetts legislature from 1839 to 1842 cost him the reelection nomination when Whig opponents deceitfully plotted against him.

As one of the six lecturing agents in the One Hundred Conventions (June–December 1843), which were organized by the Massachusetts Anti-Slavery Society, Bradburn was paired with the abolitionist William A. White as well as Douglass. On June 23, at an antislavery meeting in Nantucket before the tour, Douglass aggressively criticized Bradburn's defense of the Constitution against an antislavery attack. Bradburn resented his peer's self-assertive manner and abruptly left the meeting; Douglass would be publicly chastised for his "ungentlemanly" rebuttal.

Along the tour, Douglass had problems with racist remarks while traveling on trains, and on three separate occasions Bradburn left him to lecture alone. On 16 September in Pendleton, Indiana, Douglass and White were seriously injured during an attack by a drunken mob. Bradburn was present but escaped the mayhem and remained unhurt.

During his career Bradburn edited two brief-running Free-Soil newspapers: the *Pioneer and Herald of Freedom* and the *True Democrat*. Beginning in 1861 he was appointed to a position with the Boston Customs House. He held this post until his retirement in 1875; he died in 1880.

[*See also* American Anti-Slavery Society; Antislavery Movement; Collins, John A.; Douglass, Frederick; *Frederick Douglass' Paper*; Free-Soil Party; Garrison, William Lloyd; Lynching and Mob Violence; Massachusetts Anti-Slavery Society; One Hundred Conventions; Society of Friends (Quakers); *and* Whig Party.]

BIBLIOGRAPHY

Douglass, Frederick. *Frederick Douglass: Autobiographies*. New York: Libraries of America, 1994. This one volume has all three autobiographies: *Narrative of the Life of Frederick Douglass, an American Slave*; *My Bondage and My Freedom*; and *Life and Times of Frederick Douglass*.

Lampe, Gregory P. "The Hundred Conventions Tours of the West: Independence and Restlessness, June–December, 1843." In *Frederick Douglass: Freedom's Voice, 1818–1845*. East Lansing: Michigan State University Press, 1998. A well-written account of the One Hundred Conventions.

Liberator, 14 July 1843, 110. Proceedings of an antislavery convention meeting in Nantucket assembled on June 23, prior to the One Hundred Conventions tour.

—GLORIA GRANT ROBERSON

BRAZIL. Compared with other countries in the Americas, Brazil has the largest number of people of African descent. This demographic reality dates back to the era of the slave trade, and it largely ensured that African cultural practices survived relatively more intact and institutionalized in Brazil than in other areas of the Americas. In earlier times African Americans viewed Brazil, despite its relatively longer history of involvement in the Atlantic slave trade, as a desirable racial paradise where people of all colors lived together in harmony with equal opportunities. This perception stemmed from several factors, including the strong show of African Brazilian culture that brings Brazilians of all backgrounds together, especially during carnivals. The image of Brazil as a racial paradise however, has been challenged and ultimately rejected by scholars, who increasingly note the contradictions in Brazilian society. Even though a growing number of African Americans no longer view Brazil's racial situation as desirable, they still recognize that the country has a relatively more pronounced survival of African cultural practices. For this reason Brazil has become a center of pilgrimage for African Americans seeking relevant sociocultural practices with which to enhance their African identity. In a sense, therefore, the foundation of the relationship between African Americans and Brazil was laid during the era of the Atlantic slave trade, in which the latter was involved from 1538 to 1850.

Brazil's involvement in the Atlantic slave trade began soon after the Portuguese crown colonized the territory in the first quarter of the sixteenth century and initiated the pattern of parceling out large landholdings to nobles or established individuals. Specifically, the large estates that emerged at the birth of the colony created an increasing need for agricultural labor, which in turn gradually resulted in the enslavement of Africans through the slave trade. Over the next three centuries an estimated 4 million African slaves were transported to Brazil. They constituted 40 percent of all Africans enslaved in the New World through the slave trade. In the sixteenth century most were obtained from Guinea and the Gold Coast. In the seventeenth and eighteenth centuries, however, the majority of Africans were imported from Madagascar, Zanzibar, and other areas along the Indian Ocean coast, as well as Angola and Congo. Angola supplied three-quarters of the slaves received in Brazil in the eighteenth century. A significant number of slaves in the nineteenth century came from the Bight of Benin, although Angola remained by far the major source of supply.

African slaves arriving in Brazil were predominantly male. Initially, the majority of them were settled around the northeastern regions of Pernambuco and Bahia, where they were involved in the production of sugar, largely for the European market. The sugar business expanded significantly between the sixteenth and late seventeenth centuries but declined thereafter. Despite this decline, slave imports intensified, owing largely to the discovery of gold and diamonds in southwestern Brazil. Important centers involved in the production of these minerals include the interior regions of Minas Gerais and Mato Grosso, and these regions utilized a growing number of Africans in mining activities from the late seventeenth to the late eighteenth century. Thereafter, the gold and diamond trades became less lucrative while sugar production revived briefly between 1787 and 1820. Although this sugar production required the use of more slaves in the coastal regions, it was the growing importance of coffee coupled with the diversification of crops in the central and southern parts of Brazil that largely sustained the continuation of the slave trade from the 1820s to the abolition period.

From the socioeconomic point of view, colonial Brazil was not simply a producer of major export commodities; other, relatively less prominent export commodities also significantly influenced the slave trade to Brazil. African

"Negro Slaves of Various Nations," an illustration by the French artist Jean Baptiste Debret from his book (published 1834–1839) about his experiences in Brazil during the years 1816 to 1831. Debret produced many valuable lithographs depicting the peoples of Brazil. (New York Public Library; Print Collection, Miriam and Ira D. Wallach Division of Art, Prints, and Photographs; Astor, Lenox, and Tilden Foundations.)

dependence upon substandard tobacco produced in Brazil, for example, contributed to an expansion in slave supply to the South American society. More important, however, the major export commodities themselves engendered diverse activities, including internal commodity trade. For instance, the tendency toward specialization in sugarcane planting created a continuous scarcity of foodstuffs, which in turn gave rise to their domestic production. This was especially evident in the growing of manioc. Cattle raising was also linked in part to the needs of the sugar economy. In short, internal commodity trade, export trade, the trade of African slaves to Brazil, and the use of slave labor were intrinsically related.

While the slave trade lasted, there was no significant migration of African Brazilians to North America. The best-documented account of a slave of African descent who moved from Brazil to North America is that of Mahommah Gardo Baquaqua. Baquaqua originally came from Djougou in what is today the Republic of Benin. As a youth he was enslaved in Africa and eventually shipped to the Pernambuco region of Brazil in 1845.

Two years later Baquaqua was transferred to a ship captain in Rio de Janeiro for a fee. Eventually he sailed on his master's ship to New York, where he fought for his freedom. It was mainly through the assistance of the abolitionist New York Vigilance Society, however, that Baquaqua achieved his freedom. He then moved to Haiti under the auspices of the American Baptist Free Mission Society. In 1849 Baquaqua moved back to North America, and from 1850 to 1853 he attended New York Central College in McCrawville. Baquaqua wrote his memoirs in 1854 while living in Canada. They shed light on many issues, including Baquaqua's desire to return to Africa.

[See also Abolitionism; Autobiography; Festivals; Identity; South America; and Slave Trade.]

BIBLIOGRAPHY

Fausto, Boris. A Concise History of Brazil. New York: Cambridge University Press, 1999.

Hellwig, David J., ed. African-American Reflections on Brazil's Racial Paradise. Philadelphia: Temple University Press, 1992.

Law, Robin, and Paul E. Lovejoy, eds. *The Biography of Mahommah Gardo Baquaqua: His Passage from Slavery to Freedom in Africa and America*. Princeton, NJ: Markus Wiener, 2001.

—MOHAMMED BASHIR SALAU

BRIGHT, JOHN (b. 16 November 1811; d. 27 March 1889), English reform politician principally known for campaigning against the unpopular, restrictive Corn Laws, supporting free trade and peace abroad, and seeking parliamentary reform. John Bright was born into a Quaker family in the mill town of Rochdale, Lancashire, England. His father, Jacob, established a cotton mill in Greenbank in 1809, having moved to the small town in England's Lake District in 1802. By the time of John Bright's birth the mill was well established, allowing for a comfortable upbringing.

After traveling throughout Europe in the mid-1830s, Bright befriended Richard Cobden; the two men quickly became a formidable partnership in Victorian reform politics. Cobden invited Bright to join the Anti–Corn Law League when it was organized in 1839. The end of the Napoleonic Wars in 1815 had threatened a flood of cheap foreign imports of grain into England, and the Corn Laws were designed to protect the interests of English landholders by artificially maintaining high corn prices. Bright quickly became a leading spokesperson and widely respected orator in opposition to the Corn Laws, appealing to both the working and middle classes in a campaign that was married to his beliefs in establishing free trade and ending the power of the landed aristocracy. Economic depression in the early 1840s, combined with the failure of the Irish potato crop in 1845, contributed to the prime minister Robert Peel's repealing of the duties in early 1846. Bright and Cobden were widely celebrated for their role in the repeal movement.

During the repeal campaign, Bright was elected as the member of Parliament for Durham; in 1847 he achieved the same position for Manchester. Increasingly vocal on foreign affairs, he was an opponent of Britain's colonial policy. He became an expert on Indian affairs, supported Indian self-rule, and opposed many midcentury wars. During the Crimean War (1854–1856) he delivered his most famous speech, the antiwar "Angel of Death" speech, which with Biblical references to Exodus discussed the ravages of war, including the terrible loss of life. However, the Crimean War proved popular, and the criticism Bright received against his "peace at any price" stance led to his nervous breakdown in 1855 and his loss of a reelection bid in 1857. Five months later, however, he was elected to Parliament for Birmingham in a special election held to fill a vacancy.

Both Bright and Cobden held the United States in high regard, especially admiring its economic growth. Other members of Parliament would eventually jokingly refer to the two men as "the two members for the United States." Bright advocated the abolition of slavery on both religious and economic grounds and welcomed the visits to England of prominent abolitionists, including Frederick Douglass. During Douglass's 1840s tour, Bright invited the abolitionist to his home, and as a member of London's Free Trade Club, Bright corresponded with the American advocate of free trade. Douglass thought highly of the Englishman, remarking on his wit, expressiveness, and fluency in oratory. In addition, having witnessed the success of the campaign against the Corn Laws, Douglass was impressed by the influence that could be exerted by a protest campaign.

Ellen Richardson, the Newcastle abolitionist who had resolved to purchase Douglass's freedom before he returned to America, sought Bright's help; she felt that his support for abolition and growing political stature would lend great prestige and legitimacy to the campaign. Bright contributed fifty pounds—a third of the figure required. Bright's opposition to slavery led to his support of the Union during the American Civil War. He and Cobden corresponded with Charles Sumner, who passed letters on to Abraham Lincoln that provided unofficial commentary on the British position on the war.

In 1858 Bright observed that only one in six adult males could vote; he continued campaigning for universal suffrage, calling for the introduction of the secret ballot. He also supported the Second Reform Act of 1867, which redistributed parliamentary seats more equitably and enfranchised virtually all men in the country, before retiring owing to ill health in 1870. He returned to politics briefly but resigned in 1882 in protest against Britain's attack on Egypt. Upon Bright's death in 1889, the prime minister William Gladstone delivered a eulogy to the reformer, declaring that Bright had elevated politics to loftier standards.

[*See also* Abolitionism; Douglass, Frederick; Free Trade; Richardson, Anna and Ellen; *and* Sumner, Charles.]

BIBLIOGRAPHY
Robbins, Keith. *John Bright*. London: Routledge, 1979. Allows for an understanding of the consistency of Bright's antislavery position.

—SAM HITCHMOUGH

BRITISH CARIBBEAN. *See* Caribbean.

BROWN, HENRY "BOX" (b. c. 1815; d. ?). Henry "Box" Brown was born a slave in Louisa County, Virginia, probably around 1815. By 1830 he was living in Richmond, where his master hired him out to work in a tobacco factory. Around 1836, when he would have been about twenty-one, Brown married a slave named Nancy, who was owned by a bank clerk. The owner promised not to sell Nancy but soon did so anyway. She was later resold to a Mr. Cottrell, who persuaded Brown to give him fifty dollars of the purchase price. Cottrell also promised never to sell Nancy, but in 1848 he sold her, and her children with Henry, to slave traders, who removed them from the state. Brown pleaded with his own master to buy Nancy and the children. As Brown wrote in his autobiography, "I went to my *Christian* master . . . but he shoved me away from him as if I was not human."

With his wife and children sold, Brown resolved to escape from slavery. He sought the help of an unnamed white keeper of a tobacco shop and Samuel A. Smith, a white friend who sang with Brown in a church choir. The shopkeeper suggested numerous means of escape, but Brown did not like them. According to his autobiography, he was at work at the tobacco factory in March 1849 "when the idea suddenly flashed across my mind of shutting myself *up in a box*, and getting myself conveyed as dry goods to a free state." A free black, J. C. A. Smith, helped Brown procure and outfit a box three feet one inch long, two feet wide, and two feet six inches high. Samuel Smith and the storekeeper then boxed up Brown, and Samuel Smith and J. C. A. Smith took him to an express company. He was bounced around, sometimes on his head, sometimes not. The box containing Brown went by train from Richmond to Washington and then on to Philadelphia. On 30 March 1849 the box arrived and was taken to the office of the American Anti-Slavery Society, where a crowd of abolitionists opened it. Brown stood up, said, "How do you do, gentlemen?" and then passed out. Revived with a glass of water, he stood up again and sang

"The Resurrection of Henry Box Brown at Philadelphia, Who Escaped from Richmond Va. in a Box 3 Feet Long, 2 1/2 Ft. Deep, and 2 Ft. Wide." The onlooker at left, holding the claw hammer, is William Still. Lithograph published by A. Donnelly, New York, 1850. (Library of Congress.)

his own rendition of Psalm 40, beginning, "I waited patiently, I waited patiently for the Lord, for the Lord."

Brown became an instant celebrity. The novelty of his escape caught the attention of abolitionists around the country. Two months after his escape he sang his psalm before an antislavery convention in Boston. Within months of his escape a narrative of his life and escape appeared, written mostly by the white abolitionist Charles Stearns. Woodcuts of Brown emerging from his box were printed and reprinted; his story even appeared in a children's book that year.

Brown quickly began a career as an abolitionist speaker and entertainer. With his friend J. C. A. Smith, who had left Virginia, he traveled in the North telling his story, selling copies of the 1849 edition of his narrative, and singing not only psalms but also lyrics of his own creation to the tune of the popular composer Stephen Foster's song "Uncle Ned," about a dead slave. The chorus for Brown's new song focused on his escape:

> Brown laid down the shovel and the hoe,
> Down in the box he did go;
> No more Slave work for Henry Box Brown,
> In the box by Express he did go.

Brown's parody of "Old Ned" was also published as a broadside, which he probably sold along with his narrative when he gave lectures. Brown soon was giving a lecture, "The Condition of the Colored People in the United States," which had been written for him by the black activist Benjamin F. Roberts. He delivered this lecture in front of a huge panorama by the white painter Josiah Wolcott that depicted the history of slavery in the nation.

Brown left the United States in 1851, after the passage of the Fugitive Slave Law of 1850. He resumed his career as an abolitionist speaker in England, where he also became more of a popular entertainer. In 1851 he published a new autobiography, *Narrative of the Life of Henry Box Brown*, which reflected his own words rather than those of the ghostwriter Stearns. At this point he had a falling out with J. C. A. Smith, who reported to abolitionists in the United States that Brown had begun to lead a dissolute life that might have included drinking, swearing, smoking, and "many other things too Bad" to name.

In fact, it appears that Brown had become something of a successful entertainer in England. He married an Englishwoman, rather than attempting to use his earnings to buy his wife and children out of slavery. For the rest of the decade he toured the British Isles lecturing on the history of slavery as well as acting and singing. He used a large moving panorama to depict the history of blacks in Africa and America, as he lectured on "African and American Slavery." He often appeared as an "African Prince" as he melded antislavery sentiments with propaganda, popular history, and entertaining theatrical production. In 1862 he developed a new lecture and panorama called the "Grand Moving Mirror of the American War." However, by this time his career as a political speaker was beginning to play itself out, and he moved into other forms of entertainment. In 1864 he was billed as "Mr. H. Box Brown, the King of all Mesmerisers" although he continued to perform his "Panorama of African and American Slavery."

In 1875 the sixty-year-old Brown returned to the United States with his wife and daughter, Annie, performing as a magician and mesmerist. Billed as Prof. H. Box Brown, he toured New England in the mid- and late 1870s with a show called the "African Prince's Drawing-Room Entertainment." He still advertised himself as the man "whose escape from slavery in 1849 in a box 3 feet 1 inch long, 2 feet wide, 2 feet 6 inches high, caused such a sensation in the New England States, he having traveled from Richmond, Va. to Philadelphia, a journey of 350 miles, packed as luggage in a box." No record has been found of Brown's life after 1878.

Brown's escape was a dramatic moment in the antislavery movement. It was brave and striking; he emerged from the "box" of slavery to become an icon for those who loved liberty. Yet there was also a darker lining to the silver cloud of Brown's story. After Brown's successful escape, Samuel Smith tried the same method with another slave, but Richmond authorities were now well aware of the trick. Smith was arrested and spent six years in the penitentiary. He was feted in the North after his release but soon disappeared from view. Nevertheless, it is striking that while Brown was entertaining audiences in Britain, the man who had sent him on to freedom was himself in prison.

The abolitionist orator Frederick Douglass, a runaway slave, was somewhat disdainful of Brown for exposing the way he had escaped. In his own *Narrative*, Douglass was careful not to reveal the method by which he had fled slavery, lest someone else be unable to use the same method or lest it might imperil those who had helped him. That was certainly the case with Brown, as Samuel Smith was arrested shortly after Brown's escape. However, it was hardly Brown's fault that his escape became famous. Abolitionists were thrilled with its novelty and audacity. They promoted the fugitive Brown into the celebrity Henry "Box" Brown.

[*See also* Abolitionism; American Anti-Slavery Society; Douglass, Frederick; Foster, Stephen S.; Fugitive Slave Law of 1850; Literature; *Narrative of the Life of Frederick Douglass* (1845); Slave Narratives; *and* Visual Representations of Slavery.]

BIBLIOGRAPHY

Brown, Henry Box. *Narrative of the Life of Henry Box Brown* (1851). New York: Oxford University Press, 2002.

Ruggles, Jeffrey. *The Unboxing of Henry Brown*. Richmond: Library of Virginia, 2003.

—PAUL FINKELMAN

BROWN, JOHN (b. 9 May 1800; d. 2 December 1859), abolitionist. John Brown was born in Torrington, Connecticut, the third of six children of Ruth Mills and Owen Brown, a tanner. The family moved to Hudson, Ohio, in 1805, and soon after his mother's death in 1808, John, who was an indifferent scholar, went to work in his father's tannery. Although he never joined any official abolitionist societies, Brown was opposed to slavery from a very early age, having been taught by his deeply religious father that slavery was a sin against God. Brown witnessed the real meaning of his father's lessons when he traveled alone to Michigan during the War of 1812 to deliver some of his father's cattle to the U.S. Army. During a visit to a farm, Brown saw the farmer beat a slave who was about Brown's age. Deeply affected by the incident, Brown declared himself an enemy of slavery.

In 1820 Brown married Dianthe Lusk in Hudson, Ohio; together they had seven children. Following her death in 1832 he married Mary Ann Day and fathered thirteen more children. Brown and his growing family moved often, living in Ohio, Pennsylvania, Connecticut, Massachusetts, and New York. Between moves Brown tried and failed at many trades: operating a tannery, raising sheep, farming, and land speculation, among others. In the meantime, despite his struggles to support his large family and a habit of declaring bankruptcy, Brown's hatred of slavery did not wane. In November 1837 in Hudson, Ohio, for example, he attended a prayer meeting to honor Elijah Lovejoy, an antislavery journalist who had been killed by a proslavery mob in Alton, Illinois. According to witnesses at the meeting, Brown suddenly stood at the back of the room and, raising his right hand, dramatically vowed to destroy slavery. However, it was in Springfield, Massachusetts, that Brown's abolitionist sympathies became the central focus of his life. Brown moved his family to Springfield in 1847, attended a black church there, and made friends with free blacks who were active in the antislavery cause—men like Augustus Washington, an educator and photographer, and Thomas Van Rensselaer and Willis Hodges, publishers of the *Ram's Horn*, a New York–based newspaper that called for an aggressive approach to black suffrage. It was in Springfield, too, where Brown first met Frederick Douglass.

John Brown, photographed by Levin C. Handy. The image is annotated (possibly by the donor, Thomas Featherstonhaugh), "from a daguerrotype loaned me by Annie Brown. Regarded as the best picture by the family." (Library of Congress.)

Brown's Influence on Douglass. At first glance it would appear that the two men had little in common. John Brown, the white northerner who had failed in every business he ever ventured into, was seventeen years older than Frederick Douglass, the former slave from the South who had become a successful speaker, writer, and editor. However, the two men's backgrounds were similarly humble: neither had a formal education, and both shared strong religious convictions and held an abiding commitment to end the institution of slavery. Douglass had close ties to a number of white abolitionists, but his relationship with Brown seems unparalleled because of Brown's unusual attitude toward blacks. In 1849, for example, Brown moved his family to Timbucto, an African American community started by the wealthy abolitionist Gerrit Smith in North Elba, New York. Brown became a sort of patriarch in Timbucto, mingling with his neighbors on an equal basis, sharing his knowledge of farming with them, eating meals with them, and addressing them respectfully using formal titles.

Unlike other white abolitionists, many of whom believed that blacks were by nature submissive, Brown advocated force to end slavery and believed that blacks were not only willing but also obligated to fight for their freedom. Brown's behavior and attitude toward blacks was quite unique at the time, and in his newspaper, the *North Star*, Douglass noted this uniqueness, describing Brown as "in sympathy a black man, and as deeply interested in our cause, as though his own soul had been pierced with the iron of slavery." In 1848, shortly after his first meeting with Douglass, Brown's ability to identify himself with blacks and their cause was further underscored when his essay "Sambo's Mistakes" was published anonymously in the *Ram's Horn*. "Sambo's Mistakes" is a first-person narrative purporting to be the confessions of a northern black man who comes to realize that he has sold out to white society by turning the other cheek rather than resisting racism. The essay criticizes free blacks for what Brown saw as their unwillingness to become involved more completely in ending slavery.

In his third autobiography, *Life and Times of Frederick Douglas*, Douglass describes his first visit to Brown's home in November 1847. Soon after arriving Douglass realized that Brown had invited him to recruit his support for a plan to free slaves. Brown told Douglass that he had been disappointed in his search for black men with whom he could share his militant plan to end slavery but that he had now met men who, like Douglass, "possessed the energy of head and heart to demand freedom for their whole people." Soon after dinner they began a discussion that lasted most of the night. Brown expressed his belief that moral suasion, the program advocated by the Garrisonian abolitionists (including Douglass at that time) for peacefully changing proslavery thought, would never succeed in ending slavery. Instead, Brown asserted, the only way to liberate slaves was through force. He justified the use of violence by insisting that because they owned slaves, slaveholders had no right to live. Brown also outlined his plans for freeing the slaves. Pointing to his studies of guerrilla warfare and his firsthand knowledge of the Allegheny Mountains, Brown proposed placing five bands, each comprising five armed men, in strategic camps; from each camp one or two men would visit slaves in plantation fields and recruit the strongest and bravest to join them in the mountains. Eventually, with the help of these recruits, more and more slaves would be recruited, with the weaker ones being moved north via the Underground Railroad and the strongest remaining behind to continue the "war." Douglass was impressed by the plan, especially because Brown was not suggesting a massive and violent slave in-

surrection, but he expressed serious doubts about its success, suggesting that white southerners would follow Brown into the mountains and hunt him down or at least cut him off from his provisions. Brown seemed oblivious to every objection, however, and finally said that "if the worst came he could but be killed, and he had no better use for his life than to lay it down in the cause of the slave."

Douglass came away from this first meeting with a profound respect for Brown, and subsequently Brown's influence on Douglass became apparent. Indeed, Douglass admitted that his writings and speeches "became more and more tinged by the color of this man's strong impressions." By June 1849, in speeches in Salem, Ohio, and in Boston, Douglass openly advocated the use of violence to end slavery. In Salem his friend Sojourner Truth, shocked by the change in Douglass's thinking, asked him, "Frederick, is God dead?" His response was, "No, and because God is not dead slavery can only end in blood." According to the biographer Philip S. Foner, Douglass's eventual abandonment of moral suasion as the chief means to end slavery and his acceptance of violence to combat slavery helped lead to his break with the Garrisonian abolitionists.

Bleeding Kansas and Harpers Ferry. Following that fateful first meeting, Douglass and Brown often visited each other's homes and continued to discuss Brown's plan. In the ensuing years Douglass gradually became convinced that the plan might actually succeed, not in ending slavery but in undermining and drawing attention to it. As the relationship continued, Douglass also supported Brown's activities in what came to be known as Bleeding Kansas. Douglass was present at a Radical Abolitionist meeting in June 1855 when Brown appealed for funds to aid free-soil settlers who were trying to ensure that the territory of Kansas would come into the Union as a free state. In 1855 and 1856 Brown and five of his sons were active on the side of the free-soil advocates against the proslavery elements in Kansas. Brown's philosophical advocacy of violence became all too real in May 1856, when he avenged proslavery settlers' attack on the town of Lawrence by ordering the murder of five men at Pottawatomie Creek. In Bleeding Kansas, Brown became a wanted man.

Following his activities in Kansas, Brown turned once again to his dream of invading the South, but by this time his plans had evolved to include an attack on the federal arsenal at Harpers Ferry, Virginia (now West Virginia). In the summer of 1859, with his plans in place, he asked Douglass to meet with him in Chambersburg, Pennsylvania, to invite him to join in the raid. Although Douglass had been in favor of Brown's plan as originally conceived—to recruit a few slaves at a time—he refused to take part in the raid, believing that it was doomed to failure. The two men parted, never to see each other again.

On Sunday, 16 October 1859, Brown and twenty-one followers attacked Harpers Ferry. At first the raid proved successful. They gained possession of the railroad bridge leading from Maryland to Harpers Ferry and soon controlled the armory. They also took hostages, including Colonel Lewis W. Washington, great-grandnephew of George Washington, and recruited a few slaves. Brown's initial success was short-lived, however. Colonel Robert E. Lee arrived with a company of U.S. Marines on the following day, and on the morning of 18 October they attacked the armory's firehouse, into which Brown and his men had retreated. After Brown's capture he and four of his men were taken to Charles Town, Virginia, to stand trial for conspiring with slaves to commit treason and murder. During the trial Brown took advantage of the presence of reporters to speak out as a witness against the evils of slavery. Among southern whites his words carried no weight, but many northerners, including Henry David Thoreau and Ralph Waldo Emerson, came to regard Brown as a martyred saint. Regardless of public sentiment in the North, Brown was found guilty and hanged on 2 December 1859. In a note given to his jailer just before his execution, Brown wrote the following prophecy: "I, John Brown am now quite certain that the crimes of this guilty land will never be purged away but with blood."

Brown's raid on Harpers Ferry has often been labeled a catalyst of the Civil War. Indeed, following the raid, the South began to arm itself, and following Lincoln's election less than a year later, the die was cast. By April 1861 Brown's prophecy was fulfilled, and soon Northern soldiers were singing "John Brown's Body" as they marched to war. Brown had already become a legendary and controversial figure, blamed by Southerners for starting the Civil War, praised by Northerners for his martyrdom, and criticized by some for his use of violence to attain his goals.

One man who did not criticize Brown was Frederick Douglass, whose opinion of his old friend is best expressed in a speech titled "Address at the Fourteenth Anniversary of Storer College," given in 1881 in Harpers Ferry, West Virginia: "His zeal in the cause of my race was far greater than mine . . . mine was bounded by time, his stretched away to the boundless shores of eternity. I could live for the slave, but he could die for him."

[*See also* Abolitionism; Antislavery Movement; Black Abolitionists; Black Press; Crime and Punishment; Douglass, Frederick; Emerson, Ralph Waldo; Free African Americans before the Civil War (North); Free African Americans before the Civil War (South); Free-Soil Party; Freedmen; Garrisonian Abolitionists; Harpers Ferry Raid; *Life and Times of Frederick Douglass*; Moral Suasion; North Elba, New York; *North Star*; Proslavery Thought;

"John Brown Meeting the Slave Mother and Her Child on the Steps of Charlestown Jail on His Way to Execution." Currier and Ives lithograph, 1863, from a painting by Louis Ranson of an apocryhal incident. The caption continues: "The artist has represented Capt. Brown regarding with a look of compassion a slave-mother and child who obstructed the passage on his way to the scaffold.—Capt. Brown stooped and kissed the child—then met his fate." The story of Brown kissing the child is based on a fanciful newspaper account; it is possible, however, that before Brown left the jail where he was being held, he may have kissed one of the slave children owned by the jailer. Nevertheless, this story and the lithograph shown here helped create a powerful legend about Brown that painted a sympathetic portrait of him, which proved useful to opponents of slavery on the eve of the Civil War. (Library of Congress.)

Race, Theories of; Racism; Radical Abolitionist Party; Resistance; Riots and Rebellions; Slave Insurrections and Rebellions; Slave Resistance; Slavery; Smith, Gerrit; Stereotypes of African Americans; Truth, Sojourner; Underground Railroad; Violence against African Americans; *and* Voting Rights.]

BIBLIOGRAPHY

DeCaro, Louis A., Jr. *"Fire from the Midst of You": A Religious Life of John Brown*. New York: New York University Press, 2002.

Du Bois, W. E. B. *John Brown* (1909). New York: International Publishers, 1962.

Finkelman, Paul, ed. *His Soul Goes Marching On: Responses to John Brown and the Harpers Ferry Raid.* Charlottesville: University Press of Virginia, 1995.

Foner, Philip S. *Frederick Douglass* (1930). New York: Citadel Press, 1964.

Oates, Stephen B. *To Purge This Land with Blood: A Biography of John Brown.* 2nd ed. Amherst: University of Massachusetts Press, 1985.

Quarles, Benjamin, ed. *Blacks on John Brown.* Urbana: University of Illinois Press, 1972.

Quarles, Benjamin. *Frederick Douglass.* New York: Atheneum, 1968.

Russo, Peggy A., and Paul Finkelman, eds. *Terrible Swift Sword: The Legacy of John Brown.* Athens: Ohio University Press, 2005.

Sanborn, Franklin B., ed. *The Life and Letters of John Brown, Liberator of Kansas and Martyr of Virginia* (1885). New York: Negro Universities Press, 1969.

Stauffer, John. *The Black Hearts of Men: Radical Abolitionists and the Transformation of Race.* Cambridge, MA: Harvard University Press, 2002.

—PEGGY A. RUSSO

BROWN, MORRIS (b. 12 February 1770; d. 9 May 1849), the second bishop of the Mother Bethel African Methodist Episcopal (AME) Church in Philadelphia. Morris (or Maurice) Brown was born free in Charleston, South Carolina, to a black woman and a father of Scots ancestry. Brown never learned how to read, but as a young man he was trained as a bookmaker. According to Henry Highland Garnet, Brown was "tall and portly, his complexion was yellow, his forehead lofty." As a young man Brown married a bondwoman named Bella, with whom he had five children; because she was enslaved, all of his children were born slaves as well. After years of laboring and saving, in August 1810 Brown bought his wife, three daughters, and two sons from Hannah Lesense for £650. Having purchased his family, Brown continued to use his earnings to liberate other Charleston slaves, for which he later served twelve months in the city's workhouse.

In early 1816 Brown, a pious Methodist, journeyed north with Henry Drayton, a former Carolina slave, to confer with the Reverend Richard Allen about the formation of a branch of the Philadelphia AME Church in Charleston. He may even have been in Philadelphia when delegations from several mid-Atlantic cities met with Allen to confederate their congregations into a united church. Brown and Drayton returned south in 1817 to discover that Anthony Senter, an influential white Methodist leader, was attempting to reassert control over the black Methodist majority and the disbursement of their collection plates and revenues. In a show of force, white trustees voted to construct a hearse house atop a small black cemetery adjoining the Bethel Methodist Church. In response, 4,376 slaves and free blacks quit the church in protest and began construction of an independent African church. Having been ordained by Allen in Philadelphia, Brown was placed at the head of the con-

gregation. By 1822 the number of church members reached nearly 3,000.

Despite the persistent fears that an African Methodist leader would emerge as a latter-day Moses, Morris Brown's eloquent sermons ultimately failed to deliver a theology of liberation. For all of their facility in fusing the powerful creation stories of their ancestral home with the egalitarian spirituality of their native land, southern AME clergymen rarely spoke of a promised land on this earth. The Reverend Brown was a pragmatist who believed that his first responsibility was to protect his black flock and preserve their sense of hope for the future. White authorities often threatened to close his church. Such concerns forced Brown and Drayton to surrender the principle of political leadership in the hope of keeping their church doors open. Although most enslaved congregants appreciated his precarious position, some of the more radical members of his church regarded him as a good man deserving of respect, but not a safe man worthy of trust. It helped little that Malcolm Brown, his eldest son and one of the six church trustees, was a member of the accommodationist Brown Fellowship Society.

Reverend Morris Brown of Philadelphia. This portrait appeared in Daniel Payne's *History of the African Methodist Episcopal Church,* 1891; it was also included in James M. Handy's *Scraps of African Methodist Episcopal History,* 1902. (Library Company of Philadelphia.)

In June 1818 six bishops and ministers from the parent church in Philadelphia arrived in Charleston. In response, city authorities swept into the church and arrested 140 "free Negroes and Slaves," one of them Morris Brown. Confined for the night, the Charleston and Philadelphia blacks were released the next morning only after the city magistrates explained that under a state law of 1803, "the majority of [the congregation] shall be white persons." On the following Sunday, Morris organized a large service in a private home in the suburbs. Again the city guard invaded the service and arrested the congregants; eight unnamed Charleston churchmen, one of them presumably Brown, were sentenced "to receive ten lashes" or pay a fine of five dollars.

Following the assault on the church, Denmark Vesey, a class leader, began to plot a massive exodus of blacks out of the city. Planned for July 1822, the rebels hoped to slay their masters and set sail for Haiti, which was in need of both capital and skilled labor. Vesey "expressly cautioned" his followers not to breathe a word of the plan to Brown or Drayton, and Monday Gell, one of Vesey's chief lieutenants, had no doubts that Brown "would betray [them] to the whites." Even so, as a decided majority of the revolutionaries were congregants in his church, Brown must have been aware that something of great importance was being discussed behind his back.

The conspiracy collapsed in May when several mulatto domestics informed their masters of the plot. Vesey and thirty-four rebels were hanged, with another thirty-seven transported to the Caribbean. Local whites believed Brown to be complicit, but Mayor James Hamilton thought that he was innocent. According to Daniel A. Payne, Hamilton hid Brown in his own home "for a certain time, [and then] gave him safe passage" to Philadelphia. Brown was, however, in violation of the state law that forbade free blacks from reentering South Carolina upon leaving, and circumstantial evidence does indicate that Brown was brought before the court on charges, to ensure that he would not again return to Charleston. Authorities razed the African Church, and Drayton moved north with Brown.

Upon reaching Philadelphia, Brown assisted the aging Allen. For years Allen had disliked travel, and the more vigorous Brown, often by horseback, helped organize new AME congregations in Pennsylvania and Ohio. In recognition of his abilities, on 25 May 1828 the AME General Congregation chose Brown to be their second bishop despite the fact that he remained illiterate. When Allen died in 1831, Brown was elevated to the role of superintendent. Aware of the hostility of the white South to his church, Brown instead expanded west and north. In 1830 he organized the Pittsburgh Conference, which included the state of Ohio, and a decade later he created the Indiana

Conference. According to his secretary, Payne (who became the third bishop), Brown was developing a conference in Toronto, Canada, in 1844 when he was "struck by paralysis." Although Brown was carried back to Philadelphia and lived until 9 May 1849, he never regained his mobility. By the time of his death, however, the Philadelphia church boasted congregations in fourteen states and Canada, with a combined association of seventeen thousand members.

[See also African Methodist Episcopal Church; Allen, Richard; Brown Fellowship Society; Denmark Vesey Conspiracy; Free African Americans to 1828; Methodist Church and African Americans; and Vesey, Denmark.]

BIBLIOGRAPHY

Egerton, Douglas R. *He Shall Go Out Free: The Lives of Denmark Vesey.* Madison, WI: Madison House, 1999.

Koger, Larry. *Black Slaveowners: Free Black Slave Masters in South Carolina, 1790–1860.* Columbia: University of South Carolina Press, 1994.

Payne, Daniel Alexander. *The Semi-Centenary and the Retrospection of the African Methodist Episcopal Church* (1866). Freeport, NY: Books for Libraries Press, 1972.

—DOUGLAS R. EGERTON

BROWN, WILLIAM WELLS (b. c. 1814; d. 6 November 1884), an author and social reformer. William Wells Brown was the son of Elizabeth, a slave on a plantation near Lexington, Kentucky. Because of his mother's status, William was also a slave, even though his father was the white half brother of the plantation's owner. While William was still an infant, his master, Dr. John Young, acquired a farm in Missouri, and the boy and his mother were taken there. At the age of eight, William worked as an assistant in Young's medical practice, where he continued to work until he was twelve. At that point the doctor was elected to the state legislature, and the young slave was forced to work in the fields.

Because Young was frequently in need of money, he would lease William to other masters, many of whom had overseers who beat and humiliated the young man. One who did treat him well was Elijah P. Lovejoy, who published a religious newspaper in Saint Louis, Missouri, before he became the editor of an abolitionist newspaper in Alton, Illinois. Brown later said that he was "chiefly indebted to [Lovejoy] and to my employment in the printing office, for what little learning I obtained in slavery." Yet because Young still owned him, William inevitably had to return to Young's plantation. He continued to be Young's property until, following a failed attempt at escape, Young sold William to Captain Enoch Price, a commission merchant and owner of several steamships. While accompanying the Price family on a pleasure trip aboard a steamboat bound for Ohio, William successfully made his escape when they docked in Cincinnati.

After spending almost a week running at night and hiding by day, William realized that he would need assistance if he were to successfully escape to Canada. He found temporary refuge in the home of a Quaker, Wells Brown, with whom he stayed for almost two weeks. Before he left, the Quaker told William to take the name of Wells Brown as his own, thus providing William with a surname for the first time in his life. Thirteen years later, when writing his autobiography, *Narrative of William W. Brown, an American Slave* (1849), he dedicated the work to the Quaker:

> I was a stranger, and you took me in. I was hungry, and you fed me. . . . You bestowed upon me your own [name]. . . . In the multitude that you have succored, it is very possible that you may not remember me; but until I forget God and myself, I can never forget you. (http://docsouth.unc.edu/brownw/menu.html)

In 1834 Brown arrived in Cleveland where, having met and married a free black woman named Elizabeth Schooner, he decided to remain. He later moved his family to Buffalo, New York. He found work aboard a steamboat on the Great Lakes and became an active member of the Underground Railroad, using his new position to help other fugitive slaves escape to Canada. Already familiar with antislavery newspapers such as the *Liberator* and the *Emancipator*, Brown firmly believed that the most realistic means by which slaves would become free were by following the tenants of William Lloyd Garrison and his followers; that is, that the U.S. Constitution was a proslavery document, that all slaves should be emancipated immediately, and that it was important to remain apolitical. In later years this unwavering support for Garrison became the cause of a major controversy between Brown and Frederick Douglass, when the latter estranged himself from the Garrisonian abolitionists and began to advocate using the Constitution as a weapon against slavery. Brown also became involved in other universal reform movements, particularly the temperance movement, organizing the Union Total Abstinence Society in Buffalo and serving as its president for three years.

In the summer of 1843 Buffalo hosted a national antislavery convention as well as the National Convention of Colored Citizens, both of which Brown attended. There he met and became friends with Frederick Douglass, who also rejected the use of violence. That autumn Brown joined the Western New York Anti-Slavery Society and began to publicly lecture and speak out against slavery, his two primary topics being slavery in the South and the prejudice against African American people that existed in the North, with Buffalo and New York City being among the worst areas. Despite the successes he was meeting in his public life, however, Brown's personal life took a turn for the worse in 1847 when his wife left him and their two daughters. He and the girls moved to Boston, where he became a paid lecturer for the Massachusetts Anti-Slavery Society and the American Anti-Slavery Society, working alongside Garrison and Wendell Phillips. In 1849 Brown published his autobiography, which sold more than ten thousand copies. The book was positively reviewed and advertised by Frederick Douglass in his *North Star*. In the same year Brown also compiled *The Anti-Slavery Harp*, a collection of forty-six antislavery songs.

In 1849 Brown was invited to lecture on the antislavery cause in Great Britain. Learning of Brown's invitation, the president of the American Peace Society elected Brown as a delegate to represent them at the Peace Congress in Paris, providing him with letters of introduction to present to some of the most important men and women in Europe. His reputation as a public speaker continued to grow as a result of his attendance at the Peace Congress, where he was welcomed by its president, the writer Victor Hugo, as well as by other distinguished representatives.

Meanwhile, in 1850 the Fugitive Slave Law was passed in America. As a result, Brown and many other blacks residing in Europe felt that they could not go back to their own country. When he returned to London, Brown sent for his daughters and enrolled them in European schools. Together with William and Ellen Craft, two fugitive slaves whom he had assisted while in America, he toured northern England and Scotland, speaking out against slavery. An article in the Liverpool *Mercury* said of the three fugitives, "all who see and talk with them cannot but feel a deep thrill of indignation at a system that would rob such persons of their humanity." Brown began to write for the English press in 1852, focusing primarily on questions regarding the United States. That autumn he published *Three Years in Europe; or, Places I Have Seen and People I Have Met*, which is considered by many to be the first travelogue ever written by an African American and for which he was paid well. A review in the *Morning Chronicle* observed, "That a man who was a slave for the first twenty years of his life, and who has never had a day's schooling, should produce such a book as this, cannot but astonish those who speak disparagingly of the African race." *Clotel; or, The President's Daughter: A Narrative of Slave Life in the United States*, published in the spring of 1853, fictionalized Thomas Jefferson's relationship with his slave mistress and is generally regarded as the first novel written by an African American. The book brought Brown acceptance into the English literary society, and he was invited to become a member of the London Metropolitan Athenaeum.

Brown remained in Europe for five years, traveling, as he said, to "nearly every town in the kingdom." By 1854 he had delivered more than one thousand antislavery lectures. That spring several English women with whom Brown was acquainted purchased his freedom by paying Brown's former slave master three hundred dollars. On learning that he was no longer in danger of being captured, Brown made plans to return to America, because "what was ease and comfort abroad, while more than three millions of my countrymen were groaning in the prison-house of slavery in the Southern states?" Landing in Philadelphia in 1854 he was given a reception attended by crowds of individuals who welcomed him back as both a lecturer who had represented the plight of slaves in America as well as an author who wrote to enlighten others about the horrors of slavery.

By 1858 there was renewed interest in the idea of African Americans immigrating to Haiti to seek the freedom they were denied in their own country. "Haytian Emigration," as it was called, had become a particularly attractive concept to American blacks. Between 1861 and 1862, and despite his earlier opposition to colonization movements, Brown lectured widely, including throughout Canada, on the benefits blacks could expect to find by immigrating to Haiti. Eventually, however, he ceased to support the idea because visitors to Haiti were returning with less-than-glowing tales of their experiences in that country, and it appeared that the Civil War would be a lengthy and embittered battle.

In April of 1860, a year before the Civil War began, Brown married Anne Elizabeth Gray of Cambridgeport, Massachusetts, an active participant in the temperance movement. Following the war's end, Brown's primary purpose in writing was to destroy popular myths about the inferiority of African Americans. He wanted to "aid in vindicating the Negro's character . . . and show that he is endowed with those intellectual and amiable qualities which adorn and dignify human nature." The first such work, *The Black Man, His Antecedents, His Genius, and His Achievements*, appeared in 1863 and presented biographical information about more than fifty blacks who had been successful in American society on the basis of hard work and diligent effort. In the next three years the book ran through ten editions. In 1867 he wrote *The Negro in the American Rebellion, His Heroism and His Fidelity*, considered to be the first military history of African Americans. This work was reprinted in 1880 and 1885 by A. G. Brown and Company (Mrs. Anne Gray Brown). In 1880, Brown wrote his last book, *My Southern Home; or, The South and Its People*. He died in Chelsea, Massachusetts.

[*See also* Abolitionism; American Anti-Slavery Society; Antislavery Movement; Black Abolitionists; Canada; Colonization; Constitution, U.S.; Douglass, Frederick; Fugitive Slave Law of 1850; Garrison, William Lloyd; Garrisonian Abolitionists; Haiti; Literature; Massachusetts Anti-Slavery Society; National Conventions of Colored Men; Oratory and Verbal Arts; Phillips, Wendell; Society of Friends (Quakers); Stereotypes of African Americans; Temperance; Underground Railroad; *and* Western New York Anti-Slavery Society.]

BIBLIOGRAPHY

Brown, William Wells. *The American Fugitive in Europe: Sketches of Places and People Abroad*. Boston: John P. Jewitt, 1855. http://docsouth.unc.edu/neh/brown55/menu.html.

Brown, William Wells. *Narrative of William W. Brown, an American Slave*. London: C. Gilpin, 1849. http://docsouth.unc.edu/brownw/menu.html.

Farrison, William Edward. *William Wells Brown: Author and Reformer*. Chicago: University of Chicago Press, 1969. Details Brown's life as a fugitive slave, novelist, playwright, historian, essayist, lecturer, and abolitionist, as well as describing the historical times in which he lived.

—PENNY ANNE WELBOURNE

BROWN FELLOWSHIP SOCIETY. Founded by James Mitchell and four other "free brown men" on 1 November 1790, the Brown Fellowship Society of Charleston was the ultimate expression of South Carolina's racial exceptionalism. In that year, only 1.7 percent of the state's nonwhite population was free—compared with 30.5 percent in Delaware—and most of that number were mulattoes. Over the course of the eighteenth century a three-caste system of racial stratification emerged in Charleston that was more typical of the Caribbean than of other parts of the Old South outside New Orleans, Louisiana. When several mulattoes were denied funerary rights in the grounds of Saint Philip's Protestant Episcopal Church, the Reverend Thomas Frost, the white pastor of the congregation, encouraged several mixed-race members of his flock to create an exclusive mulatto fraternal organization.

By its charter, the society was open to no more than fifty men; each had to pay a prohibitive initiation fee of fifty dollars besides monthly dues. The general fund supported aged members who were too ill to work, and the group also assisted widows and orphans of its members. Upon their death, associates were guaranteed an impressive funeral and interment in the society's private cemetery on Boundary Street. But social advancement and economic security for the colored elite, not philanthropy for the state's enslaved majority, were the goals of the organization. Despite its motto of "Charity and Benevolence," the society existed for the purpose of drawing biologically constructed lines of demarcation between the wealthy browns (as they styled themselves) and Charleston's sizable black community, whether bond or free. Slaves, even if mixed race, were denied membership, as were free blacks who could not prove a partial white ancestry.

The immediate success of the society indicated a growing awareness among the Lowcountry's free mulatto population that they were a socially distinct group with a unique position in the city. Although they were denied access to South Carolina's white institutions and cultural life, the free Creoles were neither slaves nor Africans at a time when the state continued to import thousands of African bondpeople every year. Many enjoyed the open patronage of their white fathers, but they occupied a tenuous position in the early national South. Even their chosen term of identification, browns, was designed to remind the city's political elite that they were a group apart from the black majority.

Although black fraternal organizations in Philadelphia routinely purchased slaves for the purposes of manumitting them, no evidence indicates that the Brown Fellowship Society ever did so. Extant records do not reveal the percentage of members who owned slaves, but many of its leading members owned bondpeople. (In Charleston, fully 85 percent of nonwhites who owned slaves were mulattoes.) William Penceel owned fifteen slaves, whom he employed as apprentices in his plate business, and Samuel Holman, a former slave trader who had amassed his fortune in Rio Pongo, West Africa, owned a large plantation at Saint James Santee where he kept forty slaves. Several members even married into the Lowcountry's planter aristocracy. James Pendarvis, the son of planter Joseph Pendarvis and Parthena, Joseph's black mistress, married a poor but respectable white woman, and both of their daughters married prosperous white planters. By the time of his death, Pendarvis owned 150 bondpeople.

The determination of wealthy mulattoes to identify with their fathers' caste was evidenced in other ways as well. On occasion, the free brown aristocracy even fought to protect Charleston's social structure. Conscious of the fact that their mixed ancestry made them suspect in the eyes of many proslavery theorists, who believed that African blood was both dissimilar and inferior to Euro-American blood, Carolina mulattoes sought to prove their worth in times of crisis. During the War of 1812, at a time when Chesapeake slaves fled toward the British invaders, Charleston mulattoes helped man the defense of the city. Five years later, in 1817, the Brown Fellowship Society publicly expelled a member who was implicated in a slave conspiracy, and in 1822 Penceel was instrumental in revealing the Denmark Vesey conspiracy. The cost of white protection, one society member admitted, was that the colored elite "had to be in accord with [whites] and stand

for what they stood for." As recompense for their service against Britain, Mayor Robert Y. Hayne commended the organization's purpose and declared its members exempt from the ordinance requiring the attendance of a white man at any meeting of more than six people of color.

In the hope of democratizing the organization, Thomas Smalls, a free black, applied for membership but was rejected because his hair was not straight enough. In retaliation, Smalls organized a rival fraternal society, the Society for Free Blacks of Dark Complexion, which was later renamed the Brotherly Society. To better make his point, Smalls purchased a lot next to the Brown's cemetery for his group's burial grounds and announced that his graveyard was available only to those of "pure African descent."

Because of this competition, and because the post–Civil War black codes of 1866 briefly tended to erase old distinctions between blacks and browns, the Brown Fellowship Society attempted to change its image of exclusiveness by admitting women. Finally, in 1892, in celebration of its centennial, the society eliminated the word "brown" from its name by becoming the Century Fellowship Society. During World War II, white Charlestonians passed an ordinance that banned private organizations from maintaining graveyards within the city's boundaries. Although the Brown Fellowship Society was no longer the influential organization it had once been, the elimination of the group's original reason for existence essentially marked its termination.

[See also Cemeteries and Burials; Denmark Vesey Conspiracy; Fraternal Organizations and Mutual Aid Societies; Louisiana; Marriage, Mixed; Race, Theories of; Skin Color; South Carolina, Colony and State to 1828; Vesey, Denmark; and War of 1812.]

BIBLIOGRAPHY
Berlin, Ira. *Slaves without Masters: The Free Negro in the Antebellum South.* New York: Pantheon House, 1974.
Egerton, Douglas R. *He Shall Go Out Free: The Lives of Denmark Vesey.* Madison, WI: Madison House, 1999.
Koger, Larry. *Black Slaveowners: Free Black Slave Masters in South Carolina, 1790–1860.* Jefferson, NC: McFarland, 1985.
Powers, Bernard E., Jr. *Black Charlestonians: A Social History, 1822–1885.* Fayetteville: University of Arkansas Press, 1994.
—Douglas R. Egerton

BRUCE, BLANCHE KELSO (b. 1 March 1841; d. 17 March 1898), the first black senator from Mississippi. Blanche Kelso Bruce, the son of a black mother and white planter father, was born into slavery in Prince Edward County, Virginia. He escaped in 1861 while in St. Louis and in 1869 went to Mississippi, where over time he served as a supervisor of elections, the tax collector, the superintendent of schools, the sergeant-at-arms of the Mississippi State senate, the county assessor, and a member of the Board of Levee Commissioners of the Mississippi River. His public service brought him sufficient wealth to buy a large plantation in Floreyville. Bruce sided with other prominent blacks in their belief that freedmen should earn the money to buy land rather than receive acreage as a form of compensation.

When asked in 1873 to head the Republican ticket as a candidate for governor because of his popularity as sheriff of Bolivar County, Bruce declined. Instead he was elected to the U.S. Senate and remained the only black to serve a full term until Edward Brooke of Massachusetts served two terms from 1967 to 1979. In the Senate, Bruce worked diligently and quietly on general-interest issues related to his assignments to the Manufactures, Education, and Labor Committee and the Pensions Committee. He also chaired a Senate investigation into the failure of the Freedman's Savings and Trust Company, lobbied for improved navigation on the Mississippi River, and fought fraud and corruption in federal elections. As an advocate of minority rights, he was a critic of the government's treatment of Native Americans and the policy that excluded Chinese immigrants. A fine orator, Bruce spoke in support of accepting P. B. S. Pinchback to the Senate, but his fellow black politician from Louisiana was denied a seat because of election irregularities.

In the late 1870s Frederick Douglass was the marshall of the District of Columbia and worked with Bruce on various occasions. When Bruce left the Senate, the Massachusetts senator George Frisbie Hoar, the head of the National Republican Convention, asked Bruce to assist him. Douglass saw this act as a blow against prejudice and thanked Hoar for it. Because Bruce's political base dissipated with the end of Reconstruction, he stayed in Washington and became a register of the Treasury from 1881 to 1885 and again from 1895 to 1898. He was also a trustee of Howard University.

Douglass and Bruce both held the job of recorder of deeds for the District of Columbia at various times. Douglass had wanted the job in 1889, but the power of formerly prominent black politicians had waned, and the recorder's position was virtually the only one still in their control; the appointment went to Bruce, who stayed in the office until 1895, and Douglass became the minister to Haiti at the appointment of President Benjamin Harrison. While Bruce held the recorder's office, the Douglass family asked him to provide a job for Frederick Douglass Jr., who was despondent over his wife's terminal illness. Also during this time the Seventh and Eighth battalions of the African American National Guard were scheduled for disbandment. As a public official Bruce condemned this troop reduction as a major error. Bruce died in Washington, D.C., shortly after his fifty-seventh birthday.

[*See also* Douglass, Frederick; Douglass, Frederick, Jr.; Entrepreneurs; Freedman's Savings and Trust Company; Freedmen; Howard University; Native Americans and African Americans; Pinchback, P. B. S.; Political Participation; Reconstruction; *and* Republican Party.]

BIBLIOGRAPHY

Johnson, Charles. *African American Soldiers in the National Guard: Recruitment and Deployment during Peacetime and War*. Westport, CT: Greenwood, 1992. A comprehensive history of race relations in the National Guard.

Sterling, Philip, Logan Rayford, and Charles White. *Four Took Freedom*. Garden City, NY: Doubleday, 1967. Covers the lives of Bruce, Douglass, Harriet Tubman, and Robert Smalls.

Swain, Charles. *Blanche K. Bruce, Politician*. London: Chelsea House, 1995. Probably the only biography of Bruce in print.

—LOIS KERSCHEN

BUCHANAN, JAMES (b. 23 April 1791; d. 1 June 1868), Pennsylvania Democratic politician and fifteenth president of the United States. Hailing from Mercersburg, Pennsylvania, James Buchanan was the son of the storekeeper James Buchanan and Elizabeth Speer. Following a local school education, Buchanan read law and was admitted to the Pennsylvania bar in 1812. Buchanan never married, instead concentrating his energies on his political career. He began in the Pennsylvania state legislature, serving a single term from 1814 to 1816, and was later elected to the U.S. House of Representatives, where he served five terms starting in 1821. Buchanan began his political career as a moderate Federalist, but by the early 1830s he was an ardent supporter of the seventh president, Andrew Jackson, and the newly forming Democratic Party. Jackson rewarded his loyalty by appointing him as minister to Russia in 1832. Upon his return to the United States in 1833, Buchanan was appointed by the Pennsylvania legislature to fill the U.S. Senate seat vacated when William Wilkins resigned from the Twenty-third Congress. Buchanan remained in the Senate until 1845.

In 1844, 1848, and 1852 Buchanan sought, but was denied, the Democratic Party's nomination for president. Instead, he served as secretary of state under President James K. Polk, yet he did not have the president's confidence. Buchanan's indecisive nature apparently led Polk to often take matters of foreign affairs into his own hands, confiding to his diary that the secretary sometimes "acts like an old maid." During his service in Congress, Buchanan gained a reputation for his prosouthern position on many issues; as secretary of state he waffled on the amount of territory that should be annexed following the Mexican War and ardently opposed the Wilmot Proviso, a proposal by Buchanan's fellow Pennsylvania Democrat David Wilmot to exclude slavery from all territory seized during that war. Rather, Buchanan supported the allowing of slavery in the Mexican Cession territory through the extension of the line established by the Missouri Compromise to the Pacific Ocean. Enacted in 1820, the Missouri Compromise had divided the territory acquired in the Louisiana Purchase into free and slave regions along the latitude 36°30′ north.

After failing to secure the Democratic nomination for president in 1848 at the end of Polk's term, Buchanan temporarily retired to private life. He lost another bid to head the party ticket in 1852 but was appointed minister to Great Britain by the Democratic President Franklin Pierce. While serving as minister, Buchanan was one of three authors of the Ostend Manifesto, which advanced a plan to purchase Cuba from Spain or, failing that, to seize the island by force. The manifesto once again demonstrated Buchanan's prosouthern leanings, for at the root of the urge to obtain Cuba for the United States lay the fear that Spain was about to abolish slavery on the island. News of the manifesto leaked into the press, and the subsequent scandal proved the end of the scheme; Buchanan held on to his diplomatic post until resigning in early 1856.

Tensions surrounding the 1854 Kansas-Nebraska Act—which repealed the Missouri Compromise and allowed residents of those territories to determine whether their new states would be free or slave—made those closely involved in the bill's passage, namely, President Franklin Pierce and the Illinois Democrat Stephen Douglas, unlikely presidential candidates in 1856. Instead, the Democratic Party finally turned to Buchanan, who was out of the country during the events and thus not associated with the controversy. The 1856 election pitted Buchanan against the nominee of the new Republican Party, John C. Frémont. Sectional tensions pointed to a growing political crisis when some southerners threatened to secede from the Union should Frémont win the election. Because the Republicans represented northern interests and opposed the extension of slavery, Buchanan gained wide support across the South to secure his election as the fifteenth president of the United States.

Upon his inauguration in March 1857, Buchanan faced the challenge of holding the Democratic Party as well as the nation together amid growing distrust and sectional tensions. His actions as president demonstrated his continued support for prosouthern issues, which had already led Buchanan's opponents to label him a "doughface," or northern politician who supported the South. Among the controversies faced by Buchanan early in his presidency was the extension of slavery into the western territories.

The official Democratic Party position supported popular sovereignty, which allowed residents to decide if slavery would be introduced into their territory. However, when applied in Kansas, the principle quickly devolved into a fierce partisan struggle between factions seeking to make Kansas a free or slave state. Buchanan hoped that the Supreme Court's pending decision in the *Dred Scott* case, which eventually denied citizenship to African Americans regardless of extended residency in supposedly free territories, would put the issue to rest; even before taking the oath of office, Buchanan worked behind the scenes to influence members of the Court to issue a prosouthern decision. When the decision was announced in March 1857, the Court ruled that because slave property was protected under the U.S. Constitution, Congress could not exclude slavery from the territories. Instead of solving the problem, the decision served only to heighten sectional tensions, weaken the principle of popular sovereignty, and lead more northerners to believe in a "slave power" conspiracy.

The controversy surrounding the *Dred Scott* decision made Buchanan more determined to resolve the issue of slavery's expansion, which was then manifested in the struggle within the Kansas territory. Kansas was first open to American settlement in 1854, and by 1857 most Kansas residents opposed slavery. But proslavery elements within the territory organized their own legislature and created the proslavery Lecompton Constitution. This document proposed making Kansas a slave state and included a controversial clause that prevented the amendment of the document to abolish slavery. True to his prosouthern leanings, Buchanan abandoned promises to support popular sovereignty and endorsed the Lecompton Constitution. He managed to use his influence to gain the bill's approval in the Senate, but it failed in the House, even after Buchanan reportedly offered various incentives—including cash—to representatives. Instead, Democrats managed to arrange for a new Kansas election that defeated the Lecompton Constitution and proved to be a resounding defeat for Buchanan.

Buchanan's actions during the Kansas controversy further alienated northerners and bitterly disappointed his southern supporters, leading to the fracturing of the Democratic Party. The resulting disarray left room for Republicans to gain congressional seats in the 1858 midterm election, further weakening the hold of Democrats in the North. Stephen Douglas, the Democratic senator from Illinois who devised the Kansas-Nebraska bill, joined with southern party members in an assault on the president. Scandals also plagued Buchanan's administration, reportedly one of the most corrupt presidencies in U.S. history. One investigation revealed that campaign contributions were rewarded with naval contracts and that bribes could buy government printing contracts. Another investigation found that John Floyd, Buchanan's secretary of war, covered up the embezzlement activities of a relative and sold government lands at a discount to friends of the administration.

Despite his unpopularity with both northern and southern Democrats by the end of his term in office, Buchanan tried to prevent Stephen Douglas's nomination at the 1860 Democratic convention. Instead of healing the party's wounds, the convention further aggravated divisions, leading a number of southern delegates to walk out. As a result, the Democratic Party split its nomination between a northerner, Stephen Douglas, and a southerner, the vice president John C. Breckenridge. This split helped pave the way for the election of the Republican Abraham Lincoln and led seven states to secede from the Union even before Buchanan left office. When Buchanan left Washington in March 1861, the nation was on the brink of an inevitable civil war.

Frederick Douglass, a strong supporter of the Republican Party, denounced the actions of James Buchanan and the Democratic Party, whom he believed had together "betrayed the government into the hands of secession and treason." Douglass strongly opposed Buchanan's attempts to admit Kansas to the Union under the fraudulent Lecompton Constitution but also had personal reasons to fear the president's retribution. Following the radical white abolitionist John Brown's 1859 raid on the federal arsenal at Harpers Ferry, Virginia, Douglass was among those accused of conspiring to support the raid and of trying to incite a slave insurrection. Convinced that President Buchanan sought to arrest him for treason, in late 1859 Douglass temporarily fled the country, first to Canada and then to Great Britain. He returned in time for the 1860 election and celebrated the Republican triumph: "Happily for the country, happily for you and for me, the judgement of James Buchanan, the patrician, was not the judgement of Abraham Lincoln, the plebian."

[See also African Americans and the West; Democratic Party; Douglas, Stephen A.; Douglass, Frederick; Dred Scott Case; Harpers Ferry Raid; Kansas-Nebraska Act; Laws and Legislation, Antebellum; Lincoln, Abraham; Mexican-American War; Pierce, Franklin; Polk, James K.; Republican Party; Slavery and the U.S. Constitution; Supreme Court; and Wilmot Proviso.]

BIBLIOGRAPHY

Birkner, Michael, ed. *James Buchanan and the Political Crisis of the 1850s*. London: Associated University Presses, 1996. This collection of essays by leading political historians focuses around the growing sectional divisions of the 1850s.

Smith, Elbert B. *The Presidency of James Buchanan*. Lawrence: University Press of Kansas, 1975. A brief, critical appraisal of Buchanan's single term as president.

Stampp, Kenneth. *America in 1857: A Nation on the Brink*. New York: Oxford University Press, 1990. Examines the turmoil faced by the United States during Buchanan's presidency, including the Kansas-Nebraska controversy and the Supreme Court's *Dred Scott* decision.

—L. DIANE BARNES

BUFFALO SOLDIERS. African American involvement with the U.S. military unofficially dates back to the American Revolution; officially, black soldiers began serving in the army during the Civil War. With the success of segregated units like the Fifty-fourth Massachusetts Infantry, African Americans solidified their place as a part of the U.S. Army. From this foundation arose the Buffalo Soldiers.

The Buffalo Soldiers consisted of the Twenty-fourth and Twenty-fifth Infantries and the Ninth and Tenth Cavalries. These African American units served all along the frontier, from Texas, New Mexico, and Arizona in the South all the way to the Dakota territories in the North. From 1865 until 1916 these soldiers defended the people of the American West. The majority of the black males who enlisted were eighteen and nineteen years old; the young men, most of whom had never before been away from home, found themselves stationed on the border of the frontier, serving for five years and receiving twelve dollars a month. The African American soldiers possessed a wide range of reasons for joining the military: some wanted to leave farming; others sought to find better-paying jobs, travel the West, learn a trade, or escape the racial segregation of the South.

The Buffalo Soldiers primarily provided protection for white settlers. They served as a frontier police force and an Indian buffer and recovered lost cattle and property. The black soldiers in the West also assisted Native Americans living in the Indian Territory, which later became the state of Oklahoma. Native groups that resisted relocation, like the Comanches, attacked the farms of the Native Americans who signed reservation treaties; the role of protecting the settled tribes fell on the Buffalo Soldiers. They also defended the inhabitants of the Indian Territory against violence perpetrated by white settlers. Through this extensive contact with Native Americans, the black soldiers received the name "Buffalo Soldiers." The native groups bestowed the title because of the hair of African Americans and as a sign of respect for the soldiers' fortitude.

While the primary duties of the Buffalo Soldiers involved peacekeeping, they also participated in some of the important clashes of the period. The Ninth Cavalry was involved in the Ghost Dance campaign of 1889–1890,

Buffalo Soldiers of the Twenty-Fifth Infantry, some wearing buffalo robes, photographed in 1890 by Chr. Barthelmess in Fort Keogh, Montana. In 1992, Colin Powell, then chairman of the Joint Chiefs of Staff, dedicated a memorial to the Buffalo Soldiers at Fort Leavenworth, Kansas, where one of the regiments had originated. (Library of Congress.)

when the soldiers worked to suppress the Ghost Dance, a religious activity that promised the removal of all whites and the return of the North American continent to the Native Americans. The Buffalo Soldiers' last major assignment was as a part of General John J. Pershing's force that journeyed into Mexico in 1916 to capture Pancho Villa, after the Mexican revolutionary attacked Columbus, New Mexico.

While many African Americans saw military service in the West as a way to escape prejudice, black soldiers dealt with many of the same racial problems that they had faced in the South. The Buffalo Soldiers met with both animosity and violence from white civilians; in 1867 whites in Fort Hayes, Kansas, lynched three black soldiers. The hostility toward African American soldiers proved particularly fierce in Texas after the Civil War, where the presence of black soldiers increased the hatred felt by many whites in the former Confederate state toward the North and the Republican government.

With the onset of the Spanish-American War, the history of the Buffalo Soldiers came to a virtual end. Some black soldiers remained in the West until World War I; by 1920 the African American military presence in the West had disappeared.

[*See also* African Americans and the West; Fifty-fourth Massachusetts Infantry Regiment; Lynching and Mob Violence; Mexican-American War; Military; Native Americans and African Americans; *and* Violence against African Americans.]

BIBLIOGRAPHY

Leckie, William H. *The Buffalo Soldiers: A Narrative of the Negro Cavalry in the West.* Norman: University of Oklahoma Press, 1967. This classic work provides an in-depth history of the Buffalo Soldiers.

Taylor, Quintard. *In Search of the Racial Frontier: African Americans in the American West, 1528–1990.* New York: Norton, 1998.

—ROB FINK

BUFFUM, JAMES N. (b. 1807; d. 1887), abolitionist and financier. James Needham Buffum was born in North Berwick, Maine, to Quaker parents. Buffum trained as a carpenter and established his own business as a house contractor in Lynn, Massachusetts. He grew wealthy through his business pursuits, which he expanded to include activities as a real estate speculator and financier. Dissatisfied with Quaker positions on reform, Buffum became an advocate of immediate abolition and a strong supporter of William Lloyd Garrison. Having independent means, Buffum traveled widely in the company of Garrison, Frederick Douglass, and others on the antislavery lecture circuit. He withdrew from the Society of Friends and adopted a radicalism that rejected established religion and politics as tools available to the abolitionist. Garrison mentioned Buffum frequently in his correspondence, often calling him "my true-hearted friend." Buffum joined a variety of antislavery organizations, serving as chair of the finance committee and as a vice president of the New England Anti-Slavery Society. He was also treasurer of the Essex County Anti-Slavery Society and vice president of the Fourierist organization Friends of Social Reform.

As a longtime resident of Lynn, Massachusetts, and an active abolitionist, Buffum probably met Douglass soon after the Douglass family moved to that city in 1842. When Douglass and other African Americans challenged the segregation practices of the Eastern Railroad, which made African Americans ride in separate "Jim Crow" cars, Buffum was among the Lynn residents who denounced the practice and supported Douglass's resistance tactics. Buffum and other activists joined together in "ride-ins" that deliberately challenged the railroad's discrimination practices.

Buffum accompanied Douglass on his tour of Great Britain and Ireland from 1845 to 1847. The pair departed Lynn aboard the *Cambria*, a ship in the British Cunard Line, in late August 1845 and arrived in Liverpool, England, eleven days later. Buffum and Douglass then traveled to Dublin, where they remained in the home of an Irish abolitionist for five weeks. Together the pair toured Ireland, Scotland, and finally England. While in Dundee, Scotland, Buffum spoke out against the Free Church of Scotland's efforts to raise funds among Presbyterians in the slaveholding states. The two then moved on to Edinburgh, where they addressed the annual meeting of the British and Foreign Anti-Slavery Society. Buffum left Britain ahead of Douglass, sailing for the United States in late June 1847.

Douglass and Buffum retained their friendship even after Douglass moved his family to Rochester, New York, to begin publishing his own antislavery newspaper, the *North Star*, in late 1847. The pair appeared together at the annual meeting of the Rhode Island Anti-Slavery Society in November 1848, and by the following year Buffum was acting as a general agent for the *North Star*. In 1849 Buffum and Douglass appeared together again, along with other prominent abolitionist speakers, at the annual meeting of the New England Anti-Slavery Society.

During the Civil War, Buffum abandoned his position on aggressive nonresistance and supported troop enlistments for the Union cause. Following the war he acted as the director of Charles Stearns's Laborers' Homestead and Southern Emigration Society, which purchased land in Virginia for resale to freed men and women. Late in his career, Buffum entered the political arena. In 1868 he was chosen as a presidential elector and in 1869 was elected mayor of Lynn. In 1873 he was elected to a term in the Massachusetts legislature. James N. Buffum served as Lynn's mayor until 1875; he died in 1887.

[*See also* Antislavery Movement; Garrison, William Lloyd; Jim Crow Car Laws; Lynn, Massachusetts; Nonresistance; *North Star*; *and* Society of Friends (Quakers).]

BIBLIOGRAPHY

Blassingame, John, John R. McKivigan, and Peter P. Hinks, eds. *The Frederick Douglass Papers: Series 2, Autobiographical Writings.* Vol. 2: *My Bondage and My Freedom.* New Haven, CT: Yale University Press, 2003.

Douglass, Frederick. *Life and Times of Frederick Douglass* (1892). New York: Collier, 1962.

Mabee, Carleton. *Black Freedom: The Nonviolent Abolitionists from 1830 through the Civil War.* New York: Macmillan, 1970.

—L. DIANE BARNES

BURNED-OVER DISTRICT, NEW YORK. The Burned-Over District was a region of Upstate New York significant to American social and religious history in the first half of the nineteenth century. Beginning around 1790, New Englanders moved west, bringing a culture that embraced religious enthusiasm to the fertile New York farmlands beyond the Catskill and Adirondack mountains. The agrarian villages and small cities populated by the migrants also reflected a traditional Puritan concern for morality and community values. Religious innovations and social movements nurtured in the district influenced the course of American progress well beyond the district's geographical and chronological boundaries.

Named for the intense "fires" of religious enthusiasm that erupted there regularly, the Burned-Over District was a national center for the series of revivals marking the Second Great Awakening, which occurred in the early decades of the nineteenth century. Mass conversions and social change characterized the venues of the revivals, typically in rural areas and small cities. Protestant assemblies across the North vied to host the era's most dynamic and influential preacher, the Presbyterian revivalist Charles Grandison Finney. Using congregation-building doctrinal innovations called New Measures, Finney sparked especially intense revival blazes in 1825 in western New York, and in 1831 in Rochester—where Frederick Douglass lived from 1847 until the early 1870s.

The environs near the Erie Canal, completed in 1825, developed very rapidly. An advancing market economy accelerated the district's transition from a frontier to a mature region; involvement in the revivals became a common response in families hoping to find stable footing in an evolving middle class. Women concentrated on elevating the moral and religious consciousness of their husbands and children. By associating with the revivals, men demonstrated the character and habits consistent with social values that encouraged the success of nascent capitalism.

Theological changes accompanying the Second Great Awakening placed increasing emphasis on the human ability to effect personal and social change. Men and women alike found expression for new moral imperatives in the benevolent and voluntary associations that marked the Burned-Over District as a major center for social reform. Eastern missionary organizations ministered to the early migrants, and eventually New Yorkers also supported the many Bible, tract, temperance, and home mission associations that flourished in the region. Abolitionists, including Frederick Douglass, found ready allies there.

A popular religious focus on perfectionism and millennialism motivated many reformers to strive toward perfecting themselves and society. These and other "ultraist" experimental views were perhaps held more intensely in the Burned-Over District than anywhere else in the country. Consequently, the area was home to a number of utopian groups, including Fourier socialists and John Humphrey Noyes's Oneida Community, controversial for its system of "complex marriage." Spiritual fads, such as mesmerism, phrenology, and Swedenborgianism, also flourished.

In the district's culture, the Mormon founder and local son Joseph Smith rapidly attracted others who believed in his visions. His writings incorporated myths and religious issues familiar to the region. Barely noticed there, Smith gathered a hundred adherents and removed to Ohio in 1831. Although Adventism originated outside the Burned-Over District, it stirred the area to fever pitch; fifty thousand followers nationwide joined the founder William Miller in predicting and eagerly anticipating Christ's return around 1843. These two movements, combined with the theological and stylistic changes encouraged by Finney's revival pulpits, represent some of the most enduring influences to emanate from the Burned-Over District.

[*See also* Bible; Douglass, Frederick; Perfectionism; Reform; Religion; *and* Rochester, New York.]

BIBLIOGRAPHY

Barkun, Michael. *Crucible of the Millennium: The Burned-Over District of New York in the 1840s.* Syracuse, NY: Syracuse University Press, 1986. One of the more recent texts on the topic and a good overview of utopian and apocalyptic enthusiasm in the region.

Cross, Whitney. *The Burned-Over District: The Social and Intellectual History of Enthusiastic Religion in Western New York, 1800–1850.* New York: Harper Torchbooks, 1965. Originally published in 1950, this text remains the classic and most comprehensive work on the topic.

Johnson, Paul E. *A Shopkeeper's Millennium: Society and Revivals in Rochester, New York, 1815–1837.* New York: Hill and Wang, 1978. A social history of Rochester in the era of religious enthusiasm with noteworthy observations on relationships to developing capitalism.

Ryan, Mary P. *Cradle of the Middle Class: The Family in Oneida County, New York, 1790–1865.* Cambridge, U.K.: Cambridge University Press, 1981. A history of one area in the Burned-Over District, with helpful insights regarding changing social roles.

—CATHY RODABAUGH

BURNS, ANTHONY, TRIAL OF. On 24 May 1854, after leaving the secondhand clothing shop owned by Coffin Pitts on Boston's Brattle Street, Anthony Burns was arrested by the notorious slave catcher Asa Butman and several associates on trumped-up charges of petty theft. They took Burns to the courthouse and held him in a third-floor jury room. Burns's former owner, Colonel Charles Suttle of Virginia, and his agent, William Brent, joined Burns in the room, thus beginning Boston's last and most famous fugitive slave case.

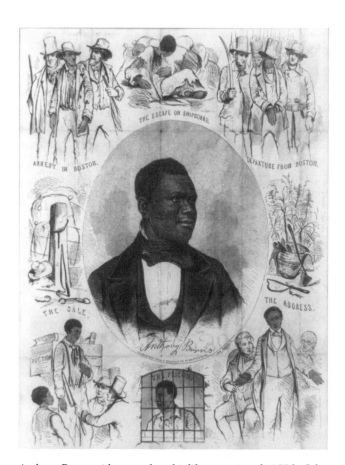

Anthony Burns, with scenes from his life, engraving of 1855 by John Andrews, printed in Boston. It was copyrighted under Burns's name, although by this time Burns had been returned to Virginia; such copyrighting was a common abolitionist practice. (Library of Congress.)

Burns's arrest and trial fueled northern resentment of the Fugitive Slave Law of 1850, which had been evident in earlier fugitive slave cases. Renowned for their participation in the Underground Railroad, Boston abolitionists spirited many fugitive slaves to freedom, including William and Ellen Craft and Frederick (Shadrach) Minkins. Several Bostonians had also voiced their support of the daring Jerry Rescue in Syracuse in 1851. Although the city's antislavery activists had been unable to rescue the fugitive slave Thomas Sims, arrested in Boston in the same year, they mounted strong opposition to his rendition and publicized the heavy-handed tactics used by federal authorities to return him to bondage in Georgia. They portrayed the Fugitive Slave Law as a flagrant violation of both Massachusetts personal liberty laws and the U.S. Bill of Rights guarantees of the rights to life and liberty and to trial by jury. Antislavery leaders argued that the Fugitive Slave Law was not only inconsistent with the nation's founding principles but also was evidence that in federal politics the power of the slaveholding South compromised the interests of free states. On the heels of the Kansas-Nebraska Act, which repealed the Missouri Compromise of 1820, wherein slavery had been prohibited north of latitude 36°30', Burns's arrest appeared to confirm the worst fears of northern abolitionists.

The day after Burns's arrest the young attorney Richard Henry Dana Jr., walking through the courthouse, noticed a hearing involving a black man before the federal slave commissioner Edward Greely Loring. Dana immediately entered the courtroom, insisted on acting on behalf of the distraught Burns, and obtained a postponement of proceedings from Loring. The Reverend Leonard Grimes and Deacon Pitts of Boston's Twelfth Baptist Church quickly spread the news of Burns's arrest among their black congregation and antislavery whites.

Although Boston's Vigilance Committee was divided between moderates, who called for an orderly trial, and Thomas Wentworth Higginson, Theodore Parker, and other radical abolitionists, who favored a rescue attempt, the committee organized a mass rally at Faneuil Hall in support of Burns on the evening of 26 May. After several stirring orations by leading abolitionists, an unidentified man shouted from the back of the hall that an attempt to rescue Burns was under way. The crowd, numbering about five thousand, dispersed; some headed toward the Boston courthouse, where Higginson, Martin Stowell, and several black Bostonians led a charge to free Burns, precipitating Boston's legendary Courthouse Riot. Federal deputies quashed the assault after the death of a guard named James Batchelder and the arrest of several militants. Fearing another rescue attempt and civil disorder, Watson Freeman, the U.S. marshal overseeing the Burns case, requested reinforcements, and the Pierce adminis-tration complied. Several thousand soldiers, marines, and voluntary militia transformed Boston's courthouse into a veritable fortress for the duration of the Burns trial.

On Saturday, 27 May, Dana and his associate, Charles Ellis, succeeded in obtaining an additional delay in proceedings until the following Monday, and the Reverend Grimes approached the former owner Suttle's lawyers, Seth Thomas and Edward Parker, to inquire whether the Virginian would consider an offer by several Bostonians to purchase Burns's freedom. Suttle consented to sell Burns for twelve hundred dollars, but the marshal Freeman successfully delayed the transaction until the stroke of midnight. He then declared that it was Sunday, and no sale could take place on that day. By Monday, Freeman and the U.S. attorney Benjamin Hallett had persuaded Suttle not to sell Burns.

The trial captured the nation's attention, making headlines in newspapers throughout the North and South. The commissioner Loring dismissed Dana's opening argument averring that the Fugitive Slave Law was unconstitutional. Citing an earlier opinion by Justice Lemuel Shaw, Loring ruled that the unpopular federal legislation was constitutional and asserted that the only points to be clarified in the Burns case were the identity of the prisoner and whether or not he owed service to Suttle. The Virginian's lawyers called on Suttle's agent, Brent, who identified Burns by a scar on his face and a disfigured right hand. Brent also stated that Burns had been seen in late March in Virginia—an erroneous claim, since Burns had fled the South the month before; several witnesses testified that he was at work in Boston in February. Suttle's attorneys used statements made by Burns on the night of his arrest that confirmed his status as a slave and Suttle's ownership of him. Although Burns's lawyers objected to the use of these statements on the grounds that the Fugitive Slave Law explicitly excluded the use of testimony by alleged fugitives, Loring admitted Burns's remarks as evidence against him.

With a crowd of several thousand milling about the Boston courthouse, Loring delivered his ruling on the morning of 2 June 1854. Disregarding the testimony of several witnesses and the objections of Burns's attorneys, Loring based his decision on the fugitive's own statements, which he considered to have established the prisoner's identity. Later the same day, dressed in a top hat and tails similar to the outfits worn by slaves at auctions in southern slave pens, Burns was escorted by an armed guard to Boston's T wharf to begin his trip southward. A crowd of some fifty thousand persons, held in check by several thousand troops and militia, lined the route between the courthouse and the waterfront. Bells tolled, stores were closed, windows were draped in black, and flags were lowered in mourning.

Burns's voyage to the South ended in the infamous Lumpkin slave jail in Richmond, Virginia, where he was held in solitary confinement for several months before being sold to a North Carolina slave trader named David McDaniel for $905. Hearing of Burns's fate, the Reverend Grimes and members of the Twelfth Baptist Church, with the assistance of the Reverend G. S. Stockwell of Amherst, Massachusetts, purchased his freedom for a price of $1,300. Afterward, Burns studied at Oberlin College and became the pastor of a Baptist church in Saint Catherines, Ontario, Canada. There were several fugitive slaves in his congregation.

The shadow of the Burns trial lingered over an increasingly divided nation. Burns's rendition underscored increasing northern resistance to the federal defense of southerners' rights to human property. Abolitionists used the Burns story to fan antislavery sentiment; at a Fourth of July antislavery gathering one month after the trial, William Lloyd Garrison ceremoniously burned a copy of Loring's decision and Suttle's claim to his ownership of Burns along with copies of the Constitution and the Fugitive Slave Law. The Burns drama and the role played by the Reverend Grimes and the congregation of the Twelfth Baptist Church also sent a unique message to black communities in the North—one that called for African Americans to unite, build their own institutions, and look out for themselves. Reflecting on the Burns case, Frederick Douglass remarked that African Americans had "a special mission to perform in the United States—a mission which none but themselves could perform."

Anthony Burns died of consumption at only twenty-nine years of age. He was buried in the cemetery adjacent to his church in Saint Catherines.

[See also Faneuil Hall (Boston); Fugitive Slave Law of 1850; Higginson, Thomas Wentworth; Jerry Rescue; Kansas-Nebraska Act; Massachusetts Anti-Slavery Society; Oberlin College; Parker, Theodore; and Phillips, Wendell.]

BIBLIOGRAPHY

Finkelman, Paul. "Legal Ethics and Fugitive Slaves: The Anthony Burns Case, Judge Loring, and Abolitionist Attorneys." *Cardozo Law Review* 17 (1996): 1793–1858.

Pease, Jane H., and William H. Pease. *The Fugitive Slave Law and Anthony Burns: A Problem in Law Enforcement*. Philadelphia: Lippincott, 1975.

Von Frank, Albert J. *The Trials of Anthony Burns: Freedom and Slavery in Emerson's Boston*. Cambridge, MA: Harvard University Press, 1998.

—GORDON S. BARKER

BURR, AARON, AND AFRICAN AMERICANS.

Aaron Burr's legacy to African Americans is mixed. He supported the eventual end of slavery in his home state

Aaron Burr, painted by J. Vandyke. This print bore Burr's signature and the statement: "I certify that the Portrait by Vandyke is the best Likeness ever painted of me since 1809. New York, 1st Jan., 1834." (Library of Congress.)

of New York but was unwilling to confront the issue on the national stage.

Burr was born into a distinguished family of clerics that included his uncle, Jonathan Edwards, the great New England theologian and an early questioner of the morality of slavery. Burr's mother, Esther Edwards Burr, married Aaron Burr Sr., who was the pastor of the First Presbyterian Church in Newark, New Jersey, and the president of the fledgling College of New Jersey (later Princeton). While Jonathan and other members of the family were ardent opponents of slavery, the Burr household owned several. His mother once complained to a friend about her servants: "Exceedingly busy, expect company, and our Negroes are gone to seek a master. Really, my dear, I shall be thankful if I can get rid of them." Enslaved blacks searched for new masters when relations with old ones had failed; thus the quote suggests that enslaved blacks were unhappy members of the Burr family. Despite the antislavery attitudes of several Presbyterian ministers, the church generally accommodated slavery and did not share the antislavery position of neighboring members of the Society of Friends.

Aaron Burr approached the issue of slavery as he did most affairs: with an eye on politics. His action on the abolition of slavery is an example. Burr was a member of the New York legislature in January 1785, when the two houses considered a measure to end slavery in the state. The original proposal sought to institute gradual emancipation for all enslaved blacks born after the passage of the law. Burr introduced an amendment that would have entirely abolished slavery after a specified date—a motion that he knew would alarm legislators, who quickly voted down his amendment. Burr supported the original measure, which passed but, as he expected, failed to override Governor George Clinton's veto.

Although Burr maintained his opposition to slavery in the state, he continued to own his own bond servants. The first federal census in 1790 lists five enslaved persons living at his New York City residence. Burr was also a member of the New York Manumission Society—owning slaves while belonging to the abolitionist society was a contradiction that Burr shared with the statesmen John Jay and Alexander Hamilton. The paradox stemmed from their parvenu status as young lawyers who felt that ownership of slaves elevated them to the status of gentry. Burr emancipated his slaves just before the enactment of the bill instituting gradual emancipation in New York State for African Americans born after 4 July 1799. During his runs for governor of the state, Burr's association with the manumission society hurt his reputation among rural citizens. Later, when Burr contested for the office in 1802 while serving as vice president of the United States, the scurrilous editor James Cheetham accused him of entertaining "twenty gentlemen of color" on the night before the election to obtain the black vote in New York.

Unlike Jay, Burr had little compunction about defending the rights of slaveholders. During the senate negotiations over the controversial Jay Treaty of 1795, Burr introduced several amendments, one of which instructed the treaty negotiators to seek compensation for the value of "Negroes and other property" carried away by the British in 1783, contrary to article 7 of the Treaty of 1783, which ended the American Revolution. Ever since the end of the war southern slaveholders, in particular, had been pressing for compensation for the eight thousand or more escaped slaves who had left with the Loyalists for the West Indies and Nova Scotia, Canada. Jay had not bothered to raise the issue in his London negotiations; Burr sought to reinvigorate it. Burr's proposal was defeated, however, as were several subsequent motions by southern politicians.

Burr also profited from the degradation of enslaved African Americans. In his legal practice Burr regularly served as a prosecutor for county courts in New York City, Westchester, and Albany in cases involving crimes by slaves. In 1789 he and Richard Varick, who was about to be sworn in as the mayor of New York City, prosecuted in absentia a man by the name of Jacob, who was owned by Teunis Slingerland, for murder. The following year Burr led the people's prosecution of Gabe, a slave living in Dutchess County, for rape. In 1791 he met with success in the trial against Pompey and Tom, two slaves accused of burglary in Albany. More than forty such legal cases fill Burr's files.

As vice president, Burr upheld President Thomas Jefferson's actions opposing the Haitian Revolution. Nevertheless, there is tantalizing evidence that blacks viewed Burr positively. In response to allegations of Burr's conspiracy to separate Louisiana from the United States in 1806, slaves cheered the mention of Burr's name; southern planters became alarmed and worried that the conspiracy might generate a rebellion by their bondpeople. Not much evidence suggests that Burr was seriously concerned with the fate of either enslaved or free African Americans, however.

An incident late in Burr's life indicates that he valued union over black freedom. In 1831, just after William Lloyd Garrison began publication of the *Liberator*, which was destined to become the most influential of the abolitionist newspapers, Burr requested a meeting with Garrison. Garrison had also recently begun advocating immediatism, a position on the abolition of slavery that Burr had once espoused in New York State. On this occasion, however, as Garrison remembered, Burr "received me with . . . suavity and politeness . . . and . . . undertook to dissuade me from the antislavery cause and from publishing the Liberator." Burr argued that Garrison's immediatism was hopeless and dangerous to him personally and that general emancipation would imperil the country because of the "power and spirit of the slave oligarchy." Garrison found Burr to be patronizing, though he also perceived Burr to have the most remarkable eyes: "more penetrating, more fascinating, than any I had ever seen." Garrison believed that Burr regarded the abolitionists' obedience to higher law to be "fanaticism." Burr did not argue the rightfulness of slavery but seemed more interested in preservation of the Union than in the freedom of African Americans. In that way he shared the political convictions of many contemporary white Americans.

[See also Abolitionism; American Revolution; Crime and Punishment; Gradual Emancipation; Haitian Revolution; Hamilton, Alexander, and African Americans; Jay, John, and Slavery; Jefferson, Thomas, on African Americans and Slavery; Laws and Legislation; New York City; New York Manumission Society; Presbyterians and African Americans; *and* Society of Friends (Quakers) and African Americans.]

BIBLIOGRAPHY

Burr, Aaron. *Memoirs of Aaron Burr: With Miscellaneous Selections from His Correspondence.* 2 vols. Edited by Mathew L. Davis. Freeport, NY: Books for Libraries Press, 1970.

Burr, Aaron. *The Political Correspondence and Public Papers of Aaron Burr.* 2 vols. Edited by Mary-Jo Kline. Princeton, NJ: Princeton University Press, 1983.

Lomask, Milton. *Aaron Burr: The Conspiracy and Years of Exile, 1805–1836.* New York: Farrar, Straus, and Giroux, 1982.

Lomask, Milton. *Aaron Burr: The Years from Princeton to Vice President, 1756–1805.* New York: Farrar, Straus, and Giroux, 1979.

—GRAHAM RUSSELL GAO HODGES

BUTLER, BENJAMIN FRANKLIN (b. 5 November 1818; d. 11 January 1893), governor of Massachusetts and Civil War general. Born in New Hampshire during the same year Frederick Douglass is thought to have been born in Maryland, Benjamin Franklin Butler led a life parallel to Douglass's in several respects. The two shared mutual respect, friendship, and a working relationship. It is unclear when the two men first met, but they interacted frequently from 1866 to 1890 and almost always agreed on racial issues.

Butler first received national acclaim for his military exploits during the Civil War, but he also made his mark in the political arena afterward. Contemporaries found his penchant for changing his political allegiance enigmatic. He supported the Democrats before the war, the Republicans during Reconstruction, the Democrats again briefly thereafter, and finally various third parties for the last decade of his life. As a Union general, Butler was considered a maverick by the Lincoln administration. In 1861 he unilaterally declared that slaves who sought refuge with Northern troops were to be considered "contraband" of war; in 1862 he issued his infamous "Order No. 28" which stated that women in New Orleans who insulted Union soldiers would be treated as prostitutes. As a lawyer and legislator in civilian life, Butler also displayed a knack for originality. He led the crusade in New England to reform labor laws for factory workers in the 1850s and afterward managed the prosecution's case during the impeachment trial of President Andrew Johnson in 1868.

Douglass's first public comment about Butler came in response to Lincoln's demoting him from brigadier general of the Massachusetts militia to army recruiter as a result of his controversial command in Virginia in 1861. Douglass did not approve of the term that Butler had chosen to describe the black refugees, as it reduced the status of the unfortunate human beings in question to that of mere property. He also did not appreciate that Butler had warned slaves not to escape or instigate rebellion. He nevertheless supported Butler's generosity and compas-

Benjamin Franklin Butler, photographed by Mathew B. Brady Studio c. 1861—about the time when Butler declared, controversially, that slaves who sought refuge with Northern troops were to be considered "contraband" of war. Frederick Douglass, among others, disapproved of this designation, but he praised Butler's generosity and compassion toward refugees who reached the Union lines. (© Medford Historical Society Collection/Corbis.)

sion toward the refugees once they had fled to Union lines, and he criticized Lincoln openly for removing Butler from command. Although Butler had no notable record as an abolitionist before the Civil War, during the conflict Douglass considered him to be one of the few men among the Union army's high command with both antislavery and egalitarian ideals. After the war Douglass lauded Butler as one of the founding fathers of the civil rights revolution then taking place. At the National Loyalist Convention in Philadelphia in 1866, Butler was one of only two white men to show Douglass any common courtesy.

Douglass and Butler campaigned together in 1872 on behalf of the incumbent president Ulysses S. Grant and again in 1884 in opposition to the Republican nominee James G. Blaine's anti–civil rights plank. When the two shared a stage, Douglass never squandered an opportunity to praise Butler. Douglass described him as "honest," "glorious," "generous," "brave," and "sturdy." On two occasions—in public addresses in 1870 and 1872—Douglass called for and received three cheers from the crowd for Butler. Even after Butler reverted to the Democratic Party, Douglass still respected him, saying he was perhaps the only candidate who could run on the Democratic ticket and hope to get a substantial number of black votes. Douglass's assessment of Butler seems accurate, for the controversial New Englander made several notable contributions to the betterment of life for African Americans and undoubtedly ranks among the most significant proponents of civil rights and racial equality in American history.

[*See also* Civil Rights; Civil War; Grant, Ulysses S.; Johnson, Andrew; Labor Movement; Lincoln, Abraham; *and* Military.]

BIBLIOGRAPHY

Douglass, Frederick. *Autobiographies*. New York: Library of America, 1994.

Quarles, Benjamin. *Frederick Douglass*. Washington, DC: Associated Publishers, 1948. Contains some information about Douglass that later biographies do not.

Werlich, Robert. *"Beast" Butler: Biography of Union Major General Benjamin Franklin Butler*. Washington, DC: Quaker Press, 1962. The standard biography of Butler, despite its age.

—THOMAS ADAMS UPCHURCH

BYRON, GEORGE GORDON (LORD) (b. 22 January 1788; d. 19 April 1824), one of the most famous English Romantic poets and a supporter of liberal causes. George Gordon Noel Byron was born in London, England, with a club foot, a deformity that is thought to have affected his personality, particularly his attitudes to certain issues such as those confronting the disadvantaged and the oppressed. His contemporaries included another famous poet, Percy Bysshe Shelley, with whom he formed a close friendship. Byron's principal works include *Childe Harold's Pilgrimage* (1812–1818), a lengthy narrative poem, and the epic poem *Don Juan* (1819–1824). The Byronic hero was a central figure in the poet's work, a romanticized and idealized rebel who often opposed or resisted the prevailing social and religious institutions. Dying as a participant in the Greek struggle for independence from the Ottoman Empire, Byron became a poet much admired by many in the American abolitionist

movement. Frederick Douglass often referred to and quoted from Byron in his speeches urging resistance to the institution of slavery. *Childe Harold's Pilgrimage*, in particular, was a work that Douglass often mentioned.

Byron spent his early years in Scotland, inheriting the title of baron and an estate, Newstead Abbey, from his great-uncle at the age of ten. After completing his education at Harrow and Cambridge University, he had his earliest poems printed privately in 1806. This was a collection entitled *Fugitive Pieces*, and it was followed by the publication of *Hours of Idleness* in 1807. *Hours of Idleness*, however, received poor reviews. Byron took his seat in the House of Lords in 1809, when he reached the age of twenty-one. He then set out on the so-called grand tour, which was considered an essential part of an English aristocrat's education in the late eighteenth and early nineteenth centuries. The tour's traditional scope had been restricted by England's wars with Napoleonic France; consequently, Byron journeyed straight to Spain and across southern Europe, spending time in Greece and Albania. He began the autobiographical *Childe Harold's Pilgrimage* during his trip abroad. Byron returned to England in 1811 and made his first speech in the House of Lords in February 1812; the speech reflected a politically liberal point of view, as would subsequent speeches. That same year he published the first and second cantos of *Childe Harold* to excellent reviews.

Thrust under the spotlight of London's curiosity and interest, Byron had a series of affairs with society women and an incestuous relationship with his half-sister Augusta Leigh. At Leigh's urging, Byron married Anne Isabelle (Annabella) Milbanke in 1815, but the marriage quickly buckled under the weight of the poet's spiraling debts and gossip about his extramarital affairs. Lady Caroline Lamb, one of Byron's lovers, famously described the poet as "mad, bad, and dangerous to know." Annabella left with their daughter (Augusta Ada, born in December 1815) in January 1816, seeking a permanent separation from her husband. Rumors flew about the collapse of the marriage, many speculating about Byron's relationship with Leigh. After signing formal separation papers, Byron left England on 24 April 1816. He never returned from his self-imposed exile in Europe.

Byron traveled to Switzerland with his fellow poet Percy Bysshe Shelley, Shelley's wife-to-be Mary Wollstonecraft Shelley, and Claire Clairmont, Mary's stepsister. Clairmont had an affair with Byron and returned to England, where she gave birth in January 1817 to a daughter named Allegra. Byron then moved to Italy, where he joined the Carbonari, an Italian revolutionary movement, in 1820. Byron's poetic output continued during his stay in Italy. He completed the later cantos of *Childe Harold's Pilgrimage* and *Don Juan*, which some readers consider his finest work.

Byron sailed to Greece in 1823 to aid the country in its struggle for independence from the Ottoman Turks. He made plans to attack a Turkish fortress with Prince Alexandros Mavrokordatos, the leader of the Greek rebels. Byron fell ill with a fever in February 1824; his illness was made worse in April by the bleeding that his doctors insisted on performing, and he died on 19 April. He was lionized by the Greeks, and his heart was removed and buried under a tree at Missolonghi before his body was embalmed and sent to England. The dean of Westminster Abbey refused to bury Byron, owing to his reputation as a libertine, and he was finally laid to rest in the ancestral vault at the Hucknall Parish church, not far from Newstead Abbey. Westminster Abbey finally placed a memorial to the poet in 1969. Byron's widow became a committed abolitionist and admirer of Douglass.

[*See also* Douglass, Frederick *and* Oratory and Verbal Arts.]

BIBLIOGRAPHY

MacCarthy, Fiona. *Byron: Life and Legend*. London: John Murray, 2002.

—SAM HITCHMOUGH

C

CALHOUN, JOHN C. (b. 18 March 1782; d. 31 March 1850), politician and ardent defender of slavery and states' rights. Calhoun did more than anyone else to chart the Slave South's increasingly defiant course from the 1830s onward; the trajectory of his career closely mirrors that of his region. Born into a family of ardent patriots and Revolutionary War veterans, Calhoun's early nationalism steadily gave way to the need to construct ever-more-elaborate defenses of the South's slave society. Ironically, in doing more than perhaps any other individual to set the stage for the Civil War, this "father of secession" and unapologetic slaveholder became a great practical force in the bringing about of Emancipation.

John Caldwell Calhoun was born just outside the town of Abbeville in the South Carolina Upcountry. After studying at Yale and then the Litchfield Law School, Calhoun began his meteoric rise to political prominence with a promising stint in the South Carolina state legislature. In 1811 he married his cousin Floride Bonneau Colhoun [sic], a Lowcountry heiress whose frailties were not optimally suited to the role of wife of a political giant. That year the twenty-nine-year-old Calhoun entered Congress as a committed nationalist and war hawk. There followed an eight-year stint as a competent but frustrated secretary of war under James Monroe and two controversy-filled terms as vice president, first under John Quincy Adams and later under Andrew Jackson.

His stellar résumé notwithstanding, Calhoun never realized his ambition of being president, in large part because he became the leading proponent and expositor of nullification—the idea that a state could refuse to enforce a national law within its borders—during his tenure in Jackson's administration. From 1829 to 1833 the central target of the nullifiers' venom had been the tariff. Were nullification to stand, it would not only vitiate the tariff but also undermine all national laws. Nullification, and Calhoun's later proposal that some laws require a concurrent majority, provided the theory for the ultimate protection of slavery—that the South could nullify or veto any law that threatened the institution. It was no accident that the North's first viable abolitionist movement emerged during the storm over nullification. Calhoun was keenly aware of the stakes; he resigned as vice president in protest of Jackson's policies, and in his subsequent career of nearly twenty years as a South Carolina senator—with a brief stint as secretary of state in President John Tyler's administration—he continued to fight against Jackson's Force Act, which explicitly endowed the chief executive with the power to enforce Congress's laws in all states.

The nullification crisis marked the watershed in Calhoun's career. Thereafter he never wavered in his resistance to the twin demons of abolitionism and federal power. He opposed the Mexican-American War because he feared, correctly, that the war would lead to a political firestorm that would threaten slavery. When the Pennsylvania congressman David Wilmot proposed to keep slavery out of the Mexican Cession, Calhoun came up with his Common Property Doctrine, later to be codified in the *Dred Scott* decision, which argued contra the Northwest Ordinance of 1787 and the Missouri Compromise that since the territories were the common possessions of all the states, no slave-owning American could legally be prevented from taking his chattel into them. Calhoun later lobbied unsuccessfully for the formation of a southern political party and published his impressive *Disquisition on Government*, attacking the perils of unchecked majority rule. By 1850 he could see little alternative to a sectional rupture. Even when his old adversaries Henry Clay and Daniel Webster plied him with a more stringent Fugitive Slave Law, the dying man refused to endorse a Union-saving compromise.

Calhoun did not live to see his greatest dream—and worst nightmare—realized a decade later, when his fellow South Carolinians followed his theories on state sovereignty to their logical conclusion by seceding from the Union, setting in motion the nation's terrible tragedy as well as, incidentally, the freeing of African American slaves. Not quite a contemporary, Frederick Douglass began his life as an abolitionist luminary during the twilight of Calhoun's career as the Slave South's foremost champion. Douglass naturally abhorred the man and his sophistries and spent his every energy exposing the brutality of the system Calhoun endorsed.

[*See also* Adams, John Quincy; Civil War; Clay, Henry; Douglass, Frederick; *Dred Scott* Case; Emancipation; Fugitive Slave Law of 1850; Laws and Legislation; Mexican-American War; Tyler, John; *and* Wilmot Proviso.]

BIBLIOGRAPHY

Bartlett, Irving H. *John C. Calhoun: A Biography.* New York: Norton, 1993.

Niven, John. *John C. Calhoun and the Price of Union: A Biography.* Baton Rouge: Louisiana State University Press, 1988.

Wiltse, Charles M. *John C. Calhoun.* 3 vols. Indianapolis, IN: Bobbs-Merrill, 1944–1951.

—CHAD MORGAN

CALIFORNIA. Spanish soldiers, priests, and settlers brought slaves and free blacks into California in the eighteenth century, and it is estimated that by the 1780s half of the non-Indian residents of Los Angeles were black, and most of these were slaves. A Spanish census in 1790 found that 18 percent of the colony was of African origin. Mexico abolished slavery following independence, and by the time of the Mexican War (1846–1848) the black population was a tiny percent of the total population. In 1845 William Leidsdorff, whose father was Danish and whose mother was a West Indian slave, was briefly in the American diplomatic corps, representing the interests of the United States government in California.

The gold rush led to a huge growth in the population, and some southerners seeking to make their fortune brought their slaves with them. The status of slavery in California illustrated the tension between slavery and freedom throughout the entire nation. Southerners wanted to bring slaves with them in their hunt for gold, but were fearful of losing them if Congress adopted the Wilmot Proviso, which would have prohibited all slavery in the territories acquired from Mexico. The debate over slavery in the new territories stalemated Congress, even as thousands poured into California in search of new wealth. The resulting crisis in Congress prevented the formal organization of a territorial government, but by 1850, with over 90,000 residents, California asked for immediate admission to the Union.

California's statehood was part of the complicated bargain that became the Compromise of 1850. The Compromise brought California into the Union as a free state, thereby signaling the end to parity between slave states and free. Since there were no potential slave states to be brought into the Union at the time, after California entered the Union the free states would have a permanent majority in the Senate. Southerners were displeased, and in 1852 the diplomat James Gadsden sent the state legislature a petition signed by 1200 people from Florida and South Carolina asking for permission to bring their slaves to the state.

At the time of California's statehood the census recorded only 962 blacks in the state, constituting about 1 percent of the total population. It is likely far more were there, including hundreds claimed as slaves by southerners. A decade later there were over 4,000 blacks in the state, or 1.1 percent of the state's population. Southern masters continued to bring slaves into the state, and during this decade a number of slaves sued for their freedom, or gained formal manumission from their masters. In *Ex parte Archy* (1858) California's supreme court justices declared, in dicta, that a slave brought into the state was freed, but at the same time (and in contradiction to this dicta) upheld the right of a master to seize his slave (Archy) in California, even though the master had voluntarily brought Archy into the state. However, a lower court judge later issued a writ of habeas corpus, arguing that the Supreme Court decision had not actually decided Archy's status. Archy was set free and never returned to bondage. After this case southern masters no longer attempted to bring slaves into the state or control them if already there.

At statehood California prohibited blacks from voting and testifying against whites but did not prevent them from moving to the state (as Oregon would in 1859). In 1852 California blacks organized the Franchise League to protest this discrimination and in 1855 held a Colored Citizens Convention to continue to fight for full equality. During the Civil War the Republican-dominated legislature repealed the ban on black testimony but lacked the power (or the votes statewide) to open the ballot box to blacks. That would only come with the adoption of the Fifteenth Amendment to the U.S. Constitution in 1870. In 1869–1870 California adopted legislation to created segregated schools, but the state repealed the law in 1880. In *Wysinger v. Crookshank* (1890) the California supreme court ordered a local school district to admit a black student, in spite of the local custom against integration. At the same time it was giving blacks equal access to schools, California adopted legislation allowing the segregation of Asians and Indians in schools. This mirrored California's testimony law, which had been modified in 1862 to allow blacks to testify against whites, but not to allow Indians or Asians to do so. In 1890 Asians were more than 6 percent of the state's population and clearly threatened the white majority far more than did blacks.

In 1890 the census records only 11,322 blacks in the state, and in 1900 that had dropped to 11,045. At no time in the nineteenth century were blacks more than 1.1 percent of the population, and by the end of the century they were only 0.7 percent. Though few in number throughout the nineteenth century, blacks participated in California society in a variety of ways. Some were successful gold miners; a few were riders for the Pony Express, while the ex-slave Biddy Mason became one of the wealthiest women in the state through shrewd acquisition of land. By the 1880s the black San Francisco artist Grafton Tyler Brown had become a well-known painter of western landscapes. However, most California blacks were relegated to menial jobs, sometimes facing discrimination in housing, education and employment. They were never fully equal citizens in the Golden State, but they also were not oppressed by the violence and racism that the overwhelming majority of African Americans faced in the postwar South.

BIBLIOGRAPHY

Finkelman, Paul. "The Law of Slavery and Freedom in California, 1848–1860." *California Western Law Review* 17 (1981): 437–464.

Katz, William L. *The Black West*. New York: Anchor, 1973.

Lapp, Rudolph. *Blacks in Gold Rush California*. New Haven: Yale University Press, 1977.

—PAUL FINKELMAN

CAMBRIA INCIDENT. In August 1845, shortly after the publication of his first autobiography, *Narrative of the Life of Frederick Douglass*, the author boarded the steamship *Cambria* of the Cunard Line for Great Britain. The voyage served a dual purpose for Frederick Douglass. First, he was embarking on a speaking tour during which he would gain financial and moral support for the antislavery movement. Second, and perhaps just as important, the trip would get Douglass out of the country, as the publication of his *Narrative* would not only bring attention to the horrors of slavery but would also garner the attention of slave catchers bent on reenslaving Douglass.

Prior to boarding the *Cambria*, Douglass was notified by his traveling companion, James N. Buffum, that he would not be able to board the ship as a cabin passenger but would be consigned to the steerage section, or second class. Douglass notes in his second autobiography, *My Bondage and My Freedom* (1855), that while on the ship he was "an object of more general interest than [he] wished to be." Douglass received many visitors on his "rude forecastle deck," where he was "treated with every mark of respect, from the beginning to the end of the voyage, except in a single instance." The single instance concerned a faction of passengers from Louisiana and Georgia.

These southern passengers took offense when the ship's captain, Charles Judkins, asked Douglass to deliver a lecture on slavery. According to Douglass, the protesting group considered Douglass's invitation to speak as "insult offered to them." They wanted to avoid embarrassment and threatened to throw Douglass overboard in an attempt to keep him silent. Douglass, not wanting any trouble, offered not to proceed with the lecture, but Captain Judkins wanted to see if the group would act on their threat. While Douglass does not give a specific account of the ensuing incident, he describes the scene as one with "tragic and comic peculiarities." The incident ended when Captain Judkins called for the men to be placed in irons, whereby they disbanded. The remainder of the trip proceeded without further incident.

The "melee" became quite notorious in Liverpool shortly after the *Cambria* docked, when the group of southerners, "snubbed in their mediated violence," reported the story to the press. According to Douglass, the ploy backfired on the men, whose goal was to denounce both Douglass and Captain Judkins. Douglass referred to the incident aboard the *Cambria* as "a sort of national announcement of my arrival in England."

On 5 December 1845 Douglass addressed a group in Belfast, Ireland, and discussed, among other topics, the *Cambria* incident. On 9 December 1845 the *Banner of Ulster* and the *Northern Whig*, both of Belfast, published articles on the speech, including Douglass's account of the mob scene aboard the *Cambria*. The newspapers referred to the group of angry southerners as "slaveholders, apologists for slavery, and democratic mobocrats." The papers also reported that the interest created by Douglass's appearance on board had more to do with his having been a slave than his efforts as an author and antislavery advocate. Noted in these articles, unlike in Douglass's narrative, is the fact that the angry mob was "cursing and swearing, and uttering the most horrid sentiments" at Douglass as well as accusing him of telling "lies" about slavery. The mob continued for some time shouting "threats of the most bloody character."

Douglass then established authority by reading laws from the "Slaveholder's Code of Regulations," which outlined "the most cruel and barbarous punishments" against slaves. According to the articles published in the *Banner* and in the *Whig*, the southerners attending Douglass's impromptu lecture "writhe[d] in utter agony" on hearing this information read aloud; that is, it became clear to those present on the *Cambria* that the mob of southerners had wanted "to keep their system of slavery covered up." Another fact noted in the *Banner* and *Whig*—and not in Douglass's second autobiography—was that a large Irishman named Gough intervened on Douglass's behalf, intimidating the southern gentlemen by offering to personally throw them overboard. The crowd present in Belfast was amazed and amused and heartily cheered Douglass during his account of the *Cambria* incident.

Back in the United States the *Liberator* published several letters written by Douglass to his friend William Lloyd Garrison, the editor of the paper, in which he recounted the

Cambria incident. In one letter, dated 1 January 1846, Douglass writes that while in Liverpool he visited the residence of the marquis of Westminster, Eaton Hall. Douglass's group had to wait in line before entering and there encountered a group of Americans who had been aboard the *Cambria*. The Americans were offended that Douglass was allowed "equal footing" with whites on entering Eaton Hall.

In the spring of 1847, after British friends helped secure his freedom, Douglass returned to the United States, once again aboard the *Cambria*. On this trip Douglass paid his cabin fare in advance, but on boarding the ship he learned that another passenger had been given his cabin. Douglass was notified that he would not be allowed to board the ship unless he forfeited his berth, agreed not to visit the ship's saloon, and took his meals alone. Douglass indeed agreed to the terms but was outraged at the treatment. On 3 April 1847, just prior to sailing, Douglass wrote a letter to the London *Times* calling the incident "disgusting tyranny." The British press responded with outrage at the actions taken by the *Cambria*'s agents. In response, Samuel Cunard, the owner of the Cunard Line, published a letter in the British presses voicing regret over the actions taken against Douglass and announcing that such occurrences would never again take place on any ship in his line.

Many note that the importance of the *Cambria* incident centers on the dichotomy between Douglass's reception aboard the *Cambria* and his reception in Great Britain. While Douglass was celebrated in Great Britain as a champion of the antislavery movement, aboard the *Cambria*, both coming and going, he was treated "in the harshest possible manner." Inspired by Douglass's emotional appeals and fiery rhetoric, the British were horrified at the treatment to which Douglass was subject aboard the *Cambria*. Public outcries by the British regarding the incidents sharply contrasted with the segregationist sentiments being expressed in America at the time.

[*See also* Antislavery Press; Buffum, James N.; Discrimination; Douglass, Frederick; Garrison, William Lloyd; *My Bondage and My Freedom*; *Narrative of the Life of Frederick Douglass*; Proslavery Thought; Racism; Segregation; *and* Violence against African Americans.]

BIBLIOGRAPHY

Burke, Ronald K. *Frederick Douglass: Crusading Orator for Human Rights*. New York: Garland, 1996.

"The Cambria Riot, My Slave Experience, and My Irish Mission: An Address Delivered in Belfast, Ireland, on December 5, 1845." Gilder Lehrman Center for the Study of Slavery, Resistance, and Abolition. Yale Center for International and Area Studies. http://www.yale.edu/glc/archive/1062.htm.

Douglass, Frederick. *Autobiographies*. New York: Library of America, 1994. Includes all three of Douglass's autobiographies.

Lampe, Gregory P. *Frederick Douglass: Freedom's Voice, 1818–1845*. East Lansing: Michigan State University Press, 1998.

—DENISE R. SHAW

CANADA. The passing of the Fugitive Slave Law of 1850 created an atmosphere of anxiety and urgency for abolitionists, who encouraged many slave men, women, and children to leave the South and travel north. Roused with news of the Underground Railroad—a network of antislavery advocates who would provide guidance, food, and shelter along the way—slaves gathered together in secret to plan escape. Comforted by news of blacks living free in Canadian settlements with housing, employment, and dignity, those who were resolute prodded the undecided. Runaways were instructed to travel under the cover of darkness—over mountains, through forests, across waterways—always heading north, where liberal sentiments promised to shield them from the slaveholders' encroachment on their right to be free. But was Canada really the utopia that abolitionists promised and enslaved men and women imagined?

The efforts of people who labored on the Underground Railroad to deliver fugitive slaves to Canadian shores truly represented "dedication in motion." Many abolitionists were Quakers who deplored slavery and were honest in their efforts to ease human suffering. They felt that it was against Christian values to exploit, brutalize, and enslave a race of people for personal gain. In an earnest attempt to help, abolitionists believed that it was crucial to put

"To Canada." Political cartoon of the 1850s showing Frederick Douglass fleeing attacks by Governor Henry Wise of Virginia. The caption quoted a letter from Douglass to the Rochester papers: "I have always been more distinguished for running than fighting." (© Corbis.)

distance between the slaves and their oppressors by escaping. Many within the antislavery movement truly believed that race relations in Canada mirrored the racial cooperation and integration evident within the movement. Although there was a sizable group of antislavery sympathizers in Canada, not every Canadian citizen had positive attitudes toward blacks. By escaping to America's northern neighbor, slaves could find the freedom they longed for, but emigration did not guarantee integration or acceptance.

Interwoven into the Canadian history of the late seventeenth and early eighteenth centuries is the presence of free black Canadians as well as enslaved blacks in Canada. In his thought-provoking book on Canadian history, Silverman cited Winks, who wrote, "to dismiss the many thousands of Negroes that have walked across the Canadian stage since 1628 . . . is to dismiss a human, interesting, and clearly visible segment of the wider Canadian history." However, in order to understand the complexities surrounding the arrival of blacks in Canada, one must recognize the rivalry between France and Britain, coupled with the double standards that fueled those rivalries. Each European power played a different but significant role in the founding of Canada, bringing to the region social and political problems from two diverse cultures. Each vied for colonizing power in North America, and each had Canadian settlements in their colonial empires. Consequently the Canadas (as they were called) were infused with cultural interrelations of two languages (French and English); two religious groups (Catholics and Protestants, called Huguenots); two legal systems (civil law and common law); two diverse economic systems; two opposing political constitutions; and two quite different philosophies on the ethics of slave trading. For example, beginning in 1605, eastern and central Canada, as well as the settlement of Port Royal (colony of Arcadia) and later Quebec (known collectively as New France) were under civil law as part of France's colonial empire. In contrast other Canadian territories like Newfoundland, Prince Edward Island, New Brunswick, and Nova Scotia were British colonies under common law. As the friction between France and Britain increased, so did battles for military dominance. There were four colonial wars; King William's War (1689–1697), Queen Anne's War (1702–1714), King George's War (1744–1748), and the Seven Years War (1756–1763), called in America the French and Indian War for the Native American tribes allied with France.

Only after the British occupation in 1632 was there slavery in New France. Desiring a French settlement on the Saint Lawrence valley (northeast North America), Henri IV elicited the support of the explorer and geographer Samuel de Champlain who founded the Province of Quebec in 1608. Under French rule until 1629, the Province of Quebec temporarily came under the British when the Kertks brothers of London defeated Champaign in battle. Former members of a French Protestant family, they had been forced out of New France by the religious wars that divided the people. However, in 1632, Champlain's quest to regain control of Quebec was finally realized when the Treaty of Saint-Germain-en-Laye restored French rule in Quebec. Leaving for England, the British Commander David Kertk sold his Afro-Madagascarian slave boy. This sale of young Olivier Le Jeune, reared and baptized by Father Paul Le Jeune, superior of the Jesuits of Quebec, was the first recorded transaction of its kind in Canadian history. Ironically the first black to arrive on Canadian soil came earlier, in 1605, when Mattieu da Costa served as interpreter for the expedition headed by Pierre de Gua, sieur de Monts, the founder of Port Royal (Arcadia).

In 1627 French fur traders founded the Company of New France; in 1670 they established the Hudson Bay's Company. Canada was under company rule from 1608 to 1663. In Canada's infancy, the larger part of its social, economic, and political views, especially those having to do with slavery, were dominated by the French whose Catholic faith and religious promotion was evidenced throughout the region. The realization that slave labor could be profitable to the economy of New France, prompted members of the royal cabinet to petition Louis XIV to legalize slavery. The plan was to bring slaves from the islands, but recurring battles in 1687 and 1701 made traveling across the waterways dangerous, an eventuality that thwarted the king's proclamations in support of importing slaves. In 1724 the Code Noir (Black Law) set boundaries for slaves in the French Caribbean islands, but barely affected New France. The French aristocrats had slaves, and one of the early slave narratives is the story surrounding the death in 1734 of Marie-Joseph Angelique, a Portuguese-born slave in New France who set fire to her master's house and subsequently burned forty buildings in close proximity. When caught she was tried, tortured, and burned in the public square.

The slave population in New France drastically changed when the Treaty of Paris (1763) gave Britain all French territories east of the Mississippi, including New France (Quebec), thereby flooding the province with indentured servants, as well as abolitionists fighting for their freedom.

Eighteenth-Century Policies and Attitudes toward Blacks. Both the Catholic Church and the British Parliament had sent the message to Canada that slavery was deplorable. Thus, in theory, Canadians considered abject oppression to be socially, politically, and judicially incorrect and would frown on covert attitudes of discrimination. In reality, every society implements national policies that adversely affect the economic and social standing of its constituents. Canadian history is replete with mandates that served government but indirectly compromised race relations among its citizenry.

For example, during the American Revolutionary War, slaves were considered "untapped manpower," and both British loyalists and colonists were slaveholders. In 1775 Lord Dunmore, the royal governor of Virginia, issued a proclamation offering freedom to all slaves willing to fight for Great Britain. At the end of the war, blacks who had joined the loyalist forces were evacuated to Canada, along with whites, with the expectation of receiving land grants. The disposition of the promised grants created dissatisfaction for all parties involved. Because the citizens of Canada affected by Dunmore's proclamation had no mechanism for protesting the action, sentiments of hopelessness and frustration prevailed, and hostility toward blacks took root. The land grants promised to the black loyalists did not materialize. Thomas Peters, one of the black emigrants, filed many petitions on behalf of all the former black loyalists in an attempt to get their land grants, but all his requests were denied. In 1791 Peters traveled to England and filed a complaint citing prejudice with the secretary of state for the colonies. Official communication to the Canadian governors arrived with reprimands and orders to investigate and take action against anyone who discriminated against the blacks.

After the American Revolutionary War, British North America consisted of Newfoundland, New Brunswick, Nova Scotia, Lower Canada (Quebec), and Upper Canada (Ontario). At the first legislative assembly of Upper Canada, John Graves Simcoe, the lieutenant governor of the newly created province, proposed legislation to end slavery in that region. Motivated more by economic self-interest than by biogtry, landowners in the assembly fought against the legislation because it gave no thought to their economic conditions after the loss of slave labor. On 19 June 1793 a compromise was reached when the legislative assembly of Upper Canada passed an antislavery act, halting the importation of slaves but preserving the legalization of slavery. The act mandated that all children be released from slavery at age twenty-five, but all adults were to remain slaves until death.

Ironically, three months earlier, in the Lower Canadian House of Assembly, there had been efforts to end slavery, but the efforts lacked legislative support, and nothing happened. Antislavery sentiments were evident in the court decisions of Chief Justice James Monk and in the *Quebec Gazette* by its proprietor, William Brown. Chief James Osgoode of Montreal is credited with making the decision to abolish slavery in Lower Canada in 1803, but research shows that he never held such a position and that he went to England in 1801. Therefore, Upper Canada has the distinction of being the only and "first province" to strike a blow against slavery.

Slavery Ends, but Racism Lingers. In 1807 the British parliament and the U.S. Congress both passed legislation to abolish the importation of slaves from Africa, but the two governments were still worlds apart on the oppression issue. The colonies of the southern United States continued to rely heavily on slaves to maintain social and financial stability, whereas British colonists' use of "indentured servants" waned. The brutal treatment that slaveholders in the South inflicted on their slaves was nonexistent among the slaves in the British colonies. According to the historian Jason Silverman, the "benevolent form of slavery that developed in Canada may have discouraged mistreatment, but the fundamental inhumanity of slavery remained."

By 1833, when the Quaker social reformer Thomas Fowell Buxton presented the Slavery Abolition Act before the British parliament, the institution of slavery in Canada was almost nonexistent. The act passed, freeing almost 800,000 slaves in the British colonies when it became effective on 1 August 1834; barely fifty of the freed slaves were held in the colonies of British North America. It is interesting to note that the Slavery Abolition Act excluded Upper and Lower Canada, so confident was Parliament that slavery had been progressively eradicated in that region. This fact alone denotes responsible government, conscientious citizenry, and a committed antislavery movement. Silverman notes that "blacks were barely visible in Canadian society as a whole. Not until the refugees from the War of 1812 arrived were there overt signs of tension between the races." History records that black seafaring men were on ships during the War of 1812.

In the early nineteenth century, racial tension was brewing in northern U.S. cities such as Cincinnati, Ohio, where stringent black laws enacted in the first decade of the century were intended to limit the activities of free blacks. Initially, the laws were loosely enforced, but by 1829 the population of free blacks in Cincinnati exceeded two thousand, a fact that alarmed many whites in the city. That year mobs of whites began roaming black neighborhoods, burning homes and beating African Americans. Roughly half the city's population sought refuge in Upper Canada. Other events like the 1829 Cincinnati riot carried important implications for race relations in Canada, as resentment grew between races.

In 1840 the Act of Union united Upper and Lower Canada under one governor and one legislature. In 1849 the Reverend William King, a Canadian Presbyterian minister and former slave owner, purchased nine thousand acres on the north shore of Lake Erie to establish a refuge, the Elgin Settlement, for blacks fleeing the oppression of northern U.S. cities. White citizens of the nearby town of Chatham, Ontario, complained about the effect of the settlement on property values and property taxes, as well as its proximity to their homes and families. In the words of one slave, "a white farmer in the vicinity of Chatham manifested in conversation a great dislike of the colored residents." However, formal protests against the Canadian legislature failed, and plans for the Elgin Settlement went ahead.

Effects of the Fugitive Slave Law of 1850. Meanwhile, the profitability of U.S. slave labor was steadily growing in the South, and the numbers of runaways created problems of national consequence. Pressured for solutions, President Millard Fillmore, on 18 September 1850, signed the Fugitive Slave Law, which took away the "free" status of runaway slaves entering northern states. Newly enacted laws clearly stated that the North could no longer extend asylum to any fugitive escaping from a southern plantation. Northern law officials were compromised by a federal mandate requiring them to aid and abet southern slave owners or their agents in recapturing runaways who were officially deemed fugitives from justice. Unquestionably, the Fugitive Slave Law of 1850 had a direct impact on the migration of African Americans to Canada between 1850 and 1860, but the reported figures contradict reason. The problem lies in the demographic inconsistencies inherently found in census data for nonwhites, coupled with the subjectivity of statistical bias. In reality, white communities were being saturated with blacks, threatening the economic self-interest of white Canadians.

On both sides of the border there was outrage at the authority given to slaveholders in free states, but for different reasons. Frederick Douglass, one of the many voices of opposition, was against the Canadian migration movement. In a rather unlikely alliance, many Canadians shared Douglass's point of view, but abolitionists who supported immigration were in the majority. On 1 April 1851, less than a year after the passage of the Fugitive Slave Law, during a lecture series sponsored by the Anti-Slavery Society of Canada at the Saint Lawrence Hall in Toronto, Douglass spoke against the migration of blacks to Canada. The audience of mostly white Canadian abolitionists was disheartened to hear Douglass's views that African Americans should not leave their homes but should stay and fight for their civil rights. The great orator knew that his remarks were unpopular with abolitionists and cut them from his lecture the following evening. In contrast, George Thompson, a British Garrisonian abolitionist and a member of Parliament, promoted Canada as a good place to live. On 21 and 22 June 1854 Douglass spoke again at the Anti-Slavery Society's annual meeting in the Saint Lawrence Hall, where a large audience of supporters cheered his introductory remarks praising Canada's good work against slavery.

Last Stop on the Underground Railroad. After 1850 the Underground Railroad was busy charting new routes toward Canada, and its conductors provided safe houses, food, clothing, and comfort for fugitive slaves. As a runaway slave himself, Frederick Douglass had lived with the burning desire to be unleashed from oppression. Thus, despite his personal views against a legislatively motivated exodus across the border, he willingly took an active role as an Underground Railroad conductor. With his home near the Canadian border in Rochester, New York, he and his wife, Anna Murray Douglass, had the means to help many fugitive slaves by supplying food and shelter. In addition, Douglass's weekly abolitionist newspaper was named the *North Star*, the star that fugitive slaves followed to freedom.

The cities of Buxton, Dresden, Chatham, and Windsor in southwestern Ontario attracted many slaves who fled from the South. In addition, Amherstburg, a small town on the banks of the Detroit River, became a key place of entry into Canada and an important depot for the Underground Railroad. Blacks had lived in the western Ontario town since the end of the eighteenth century, and it served as a stronghold of the Canadian antislavery movement after the Fugitive Slave Law of 1850 was enacted. However, the arrival of more and more blacks in Canada lessened racial tolerance and heightened the prejudice of white Canadians as overcrowding became a constant problem.

Extradition of fugitive slaves often set the tone for relations between the United States and Canada. One highly publicized case occurred in 1860. John Anderson, a fugitive slave living in Windsor, had killed a man in Detroit in 1853 while attempting to flee from enslavement in Missouri. Seven years later he was arrested, and the Canadian court ruled that he should be sent back to the United States to be tried for murder there. In both countries media outcry and protest rallies followed the court's judgment. The 19 May 1861 edition of the *New York Times* published a letter from an officer of the Canadian government that stated the following:

> The case of Anderson is one of the gravest possible Importance, and Her Majesty's Government are not satisfied that the decision of the court at Toronto is in conformity with the view of the Treaty which has hitherto guided the authorities in this country. I have, therefore, to instruct you to abstain in any case from completing Extradition. (p. 6)

This indicates interest long after Anderson had been acquitted, on 19 February 1861.

In October 1859 Douglass took refuge across the border when a warrant was issued for his arrest. He was acquainted with John Brown, the radical abolitionist who orchestrated a raid on Harpers Ferry on 16 October 1859. Douglass had advised Brown to abandon his ill-fated plan. However, the discovery of a letter documenting their friendship caused federal marshals to issue an arrest warrant for Douglass, citing conspiracy. Douglass left New York to escape imprisonment. After only a short time in Canada, he sailed from Quebec on the *Nova Scotian* to Liverpool, England, to begin a lecture tour in November. In March 1860 Douglass's eleven-year-old daughter, Annie, died, and the grieving father immediately returned home.

Although discrimination did exist in Canada, it also offered freedom from the horrors of slavery. James W. Sumler, a runaway slave who arrived in Canada on 3 March 1865, expressed the sentiments of many black emigrants when he said, "I enjoy myself here more than I did in slavery. I believe that liberty is the true and proper state for the colored man, and for every man."

[*See also* Abolitionism; American Revolution; Antislavery Movement; Black Abolitionists; Brown, John; Civil Rights; Colonialism; Colonization; Crime and Punishment; Demographics; Detroit; Douglass, Anna Murray; Douglass, Frederick; Foreign Policy; Free African Americans before the Civil War (North); Free African Americans before the Civil War (South); Freedmen; Fugitive Slave Law of 1850; Garrisonian Abolitionists; Harpers Ferry Raid; Laws and Legislation; Lynching and Mob Violence; *North Star*; Proslavery Thought; Racism; Religion and Slavery; Resistance; Riots and Rebellions; Rochester, New York; Slave Resistance; Slavery; Society of Friends (Quakers); Underground Railroad; *and* Violence against African Americans.]

BIBLIOGRAPHY

"Anderson Case." *New York Times*, 19 May 1861, p. 6.

Landon, Fred. "Negro Migration to Canada after the Passing of the Fugitive Slave Act." *Journal of Negro History* 5.1 (January 1920): 22–36.

Landon, Fred. "The Anti-Slavery Society of Canada." *Journal of Negro History* 4.1 (1919): 33–40.

Martin, Waldo E., Jr. *The Mind of Frederick Douglass*. Chapel Hill: University of North Carolina Press, 1984. Excellent source for understanding Douglass's thoughts about the Fugitive Slave Law of 1850 and the southern exodus across the border.

Mitchell, William M. *The Underground Railroad from Slavery to Freedom* (1860). Westport, CT: Negro Universities Press, 1970.

Silverman, Jason H. *Unwelcome Guests: Canada West's Response to American Fugitive Slaves, 1800–1865*. Millwood, NY: Associated Faculty Press, 1985.

Wade, Richard C. "The Negro in Cincinnati, 1800–1830." *Journal of Negro History* 39.1 (January 1954): 43–57.

Williams, Eric. "The Golden Age of the Slave System in Britain." *Journal of Negro History* 25.1 (January 1940): 60–106.

Winks, Robin W. "The Attack on Slavery in British North America, 1793–1833." In his *Blacks in Canada*. Montreal: McGill-Queens's University Press, 1971. In this chapter Winks elaborates on the contradictions about Lower Canada and abolishment of slavery.

—GLORIA GRANT ROBERSON

CAPITEIN, JACOBUS (b. c. 1717; d. 1 July 1747), minister and missionary of the Dutch Reformed Church. Jacobus Capitein was one of the first Africans to be educated in Europe, ordained in a Protestant denomination, and commissioned to return to his homeland as a missionary. Although little is known of his African heritage, Capitein was probably born in what is now central Ghana. Orphaned or otherwise separated from his parents, he was enslaved and obtained by Dutch traders when he was about eight years old. His enslavement ended in 1728, when his owner took him to the Netherlands to learn a trade. Capitein's tutors recognized his intellectual gifts, and with the understanding that he would return to Africa as a missionary, his theological studies were supported by Dutch patrons. In 1737 he received a scholarship to the University of Leiden, where he excelled as a student. Capitein completed his studies in March 1742 and was ordained in the Dutch Reformed Church in May. In July 1742 he sailed for Africa to fulfill his missionary vocation.

From his arrival in October 1742 until his death, Capitein served as chaplain to the post of the Dutch West India Company in Elmina (present-day Ghana). The primary purpose of the company was commerce, including slave trading; evangelization was not a significant activity. Capitein's ministry was marred by conflicts with the Europeans in Elmina and officials in the Netherlands. Church authorities questioned aspects of Capitein's translations of Christian materials into Fanti, an African language, and strongly objected to his intentions to marry an unconverted African. After his engagement met with resistance, Capitein married a white woman who was apparently sent from the Netherlands to be his wife. His evangelization efforts were largely unsuccessful, yet the Ashanti chief Opoku Ware I was so impressed with Capitein's accomplishments that he wanted several of his young people to be educated in the Netherlands. Capitein died heavily in debt and, in all likelihood, greatly disillusioned.

Capitein's reputation stems mainly from his dissertation, which addresses the question of whether slavery is compatible with Christian liberty. Although he may have written the work to support his missionary vocation, his treatise has long been viewed as a defense of slavery. Relying on a standard distinction between physical and spiritual freedom, Capitein maintains that slavery does not impede conversion and may actually facilitate it. In his own case he sees the hand of providence in his enslavement and conveyance to the Netherlands. He rejects all theories of slavery based on inherent differences between individuals and peoples, and he insists that Christians practice charity to their slaves, which may include manumission. However, he argues that slaveholders have no obligation to free slaves who convert to Christianity and concludes that Christians can own slaves without com-

Jacobus Elisa Joannes Capitein. The text reads: "African Moor. Appointed preacher at the castle of Saint George in Elmina. Beholder, look at this Moor: his skin is black, but white his soul, because Jesus himself, as priest, prays for him. He goes to teach the Moors Faith, Hope, and Love, so that they, made white, may always, like him, worship the Lamb." (Rijksmuseum, Amsterdam.)

promising their religious convictions. Published after he completed his studies, Capitein's dissertation was especially satisfying to proponents of slavery, who perceived it as a defense of slavery written by a former slave. His apparent endorsement of slavery has made Capitein an unsettling historical figure.

[*See also* Dutch Reformed Church and African Americans.]

BIBLIOGRAPHY

Kpobi, David Nii Anum. *Mission in Chains: The Life, Theology and Ministry of the Ex-Slave Jacobus E. J. Capitein (1717–1747) with a Translation of His Major Publications.* Zoetermeer, Netherlands: Uitgeverij Boekencentrum, 1993.

Parker, Grant, ed. and trans. *The Agony of Asar: A Thesis on Slavery by the Former Slave, Jacobus Elisa Johannes Capitein, 1717–1747.* Princeton, NJ: Markus Wiener Publishers, 2001.

—Susan J. Hubert

CAREY, LOTT (b. c. 1780; d. 1828), pioneer African American missionary to Africa. Lott Carey (also known as Lott Cary) was the only child of parents who were held as slaves of William A. Christian in Charles City County, Virginia. His exact birth date is unknown, but Carey believed that it was around 1780. Lott's father was active in the Baptist Church and regularly taught young Lott biblical doctrine. In 1804 Lott's owner sent him to Richmond, where he was hired out at the Shockoe Tobacco Warehouse.

Despite his upbringing, Carey lived a life of dissipation for several years; he was frequently intoxicated and profane. Sometime during 1807 in the First Baptist Church of Richmond, Lott heard a sermon that led to his conversion. Soon afterward Lott was profoundly moved by another sermon preached by his pastor on the third chapter of John's Gospel. Lott was illiterate, but he ardently desired to learn to read the section of the Bible that had riveted his attention, the story of Nicodemus coming to Jesus by night. Men in his church and in the warehouse where he worked assisted him in his initial steps toward literacy. After he was able to read, he began to learn to write.

Observing Carey's expanding education and efficiency at work, because he was learning to keep written accounts, Carey's employer promoted him to shipping clerk and increased his salary. Carey worked so diligently that tobacco orders were correctly prepared and shipped promptly. As further encouragement, his employer gave him waste tobacco that Carey could sell for his own benefit. Carey's first wife died before he was able to amass enough earnings from his job to purchase her freedom. However, with his rising salary and bonuses, he was able to purchase his own freedom and that of his two children in 1813. He also bought a home valued at fifteen hundred dollars. Later, Carey enrolled in a school organized in 1815 as a triweekly night school for people of color in the African Church of Richmond. Carey's mind opened to many new avenues of learning, and he read books on many subjects. One observer mentioned that he noticed Carey reading Adam Smith's *Wealth of Nations*.

When Carey felt called to the ministry, the First Baptist Church of Richmond licensed him to preach. Contemporaries praised his preaching. One observer stated that "a sermon which I heard from Mr. Carey . . . was the best extemporaneous sermon I ever heard. It contained more original and impressive thoughts, some of which are distinct in my memory, and never can be forgotten." Eventually Carey formed his own church in Richmond, while he continued working in the tobacco warehouse.

Carey strongly supported African mission efforts and in 1815 aided in the formation of the Richmond African Missionary Society. The British had established Sierra Leone in West Africa as a settler colony in 1787 for blacks in their territories. U.S. government officials inquired about settling free blacks from the United States in the colony but were rebuffed. Inspired by Sierra Leone and the colonizing efforts of a black shipowner named Paul Cuffe, the American Colonization Society (ACS) was officially organized in Washington, D.C., in 1817 to help free blacks who wanted to return to their ancestral homeland. The founders of the organization had a mix of benevolent and racist motives for their participation, but some of them were indeed eager to sponsor missionary endeavors in Africa.

Carey carefully followed the reports about Sierra Leone and the ACS and, inspired by this missionary work, eventually decided to immigrate to Liberia. He wrote that he longed "to preach to the poor Africans the way of life and salvation." Carey, his family (including his second wife), and some members of his church and community began to make plans to immigrate. Local churches and missions groups gave them spiritual and monetary support.

After several discouraging delays, the Richmond emigrants, along with twenty-eight others from the Norfolk area, sailed on 23 January 1821 from Norfolk, Virginia, on the brig *Nautilus*. Carey preached and taught regularly during the voyage. The party arrived in Sierra Leone in early March after a forty-four-day voyage. The emigrants met with disappointments at every turn. Carey's second wife died, leaving him with three children to tend. Nevertheless, Carey preached. He held his church's first communion on 22 March and attempted to establish a mission among the Mandingo.

In December 1821, with the help of Captain Robert Stockton of the schooner *Alligator* and the ACS agent Dr. Eli Ayers, some of the disgruntled settlers traveled farther down the West African coast and, Stockton reported, forced a treaty at gunpoint with King Peter, a tribal chief, at Cape Mesurado. In April 1822 Carey and his family moved to an island off the cape. The new ACS agent, Jehudi Ashmun, moved to Cape Mesurado in August. The settlement formed at the cape on the mainland was called Monrovia, after the U.S. president James Monroe, and the country was named Liberia, meaning "liberty." Carey married there for the third time.

The ACS intended for its white agents to govern the settlers, but African fevers struck the agents so frequently and forcibly with debility or death that the settlers had no choice but to assume leadership positions. Additionally, the settlers faced periodic skirmishes with neighboring Africans who resented their presence and their hindrance of the lucrative slave trade. Although Carey intended to spend the majority of his time preaching, he more often found himself tending the sick at his own expense.

With support from the Virginia Baptist mission board, Carey was able to hold several services a week, establish schools for settler and African children, and preach to Africans in surrounding towns. At first Carey received no salary from the ACS and contended with Ashmun on land and food distribution issues, but ultimately Ashmun praised Carey's intellect and leadership abilities and named him health officer and vice agent. Ashmun admitted that he probably would not have survived if it had not been for Carey's ministrations.

Carey's life was cut short by an accident in the fall of 1828. While preparing gunpowder to defend against an attack by neighboring Africans, a candle fell and the powder exploded, taking the life of ten men, including Carey. A number of Carey's letters and reports are available in print. Many evangelicals have celebrated Carey's life and work as a pioneering missionary. A Baptist missionary association is named in his honor.

[*See also* American Colonization Society; Baptists and African Americans; Cuffe, Paul; Health and Medicine; *and* Missionary Movements.]

BIBLIOGRAPHY

American Colonization Society. *African Repository and Colonial Journal*. The journal of the ACS; see various issues from 1825 to 1830.

Fisher, Miles Mark. "Lott Cary, the Colonizing Missionary." *Journal of Negro History* 7.4 (October 1922): 380–418.

Fitts, Leroy. *Lott Carey: First Black Missionary to Africa*. Valley Forge, PA: Judson Press, 1978.

Gurley, Ralph Randolph. *Life of Jehudi Ashmun, Late Colonial Agent in Liberia; with an Appendix Containing Extracts from His Journal and Other Writings; with a Brief Sketch of the Life of the Rev. Lott Carey* (1839). New York: Negro Universities Press, 1969.

Hill, Adelaide Cromwell, and Martin Kilson, eds. *Apropos of Africa: Sentiments of Negro American Leaders on Africa from the 1800s to the 1950s*. New York: Humanities Press, 1969.

Miller, Floyd J. *The Search for a Black Nationality: Black Emigration and Colonization 1787–1863*. Chicago, University of Illinois Press, 1975.

—DEBRA NEWMAN HAM

CARIBBEAN. [*This entry contains two subentries dealing with the Caribbean from 1492 through 1895. The first article discusses the Caribbean slave trade, the transmission of cultural identities, and the Caribbean's influence on North America, while the second article discusses the 1834 emancipation of slaves in the Caribbean and annual celebrations of subsequent years.*]

European Colonization and Cultural Exchange

The area of the Western Hemisphere known as the Caribbean is an archipelago that stretches from the coast of South America to the Gulf coast of Central America and the Atlantic coast of North America. This grouping of islands entered the European imagination when

Columbus landed in what is now called the Bahamas on 12 October 1492. Columbus referred to the inhabitants as "Indians," confident in the belief that he had landed in the coveted "spice islands" somewhere off the coast of Asia. Columbus made four journeys to the region. He established settlements on two of the four islands that constitute the Greater Antilles (Hispaniola and Jamaica) and laid claim to Trinidad and the smaller islands in the Lesser Antilles (including Antigua, Barbados, and Saint Vincent) for Spain.

Hispanic Caribbean. Columbus claimed the entire region, but the islands had been occupied by indigenous or Native Americans (such as the Ciboney, Calusa, Arawak, and Carib) long before he arrived. Archaeological evidence (spear points and charcoal) suggests that the original inhabitants were hunter-gatherers who crossed the sea from Central America (Ciboney) to occupy Cuba and Jamaica and from Florida to the Bahamas (Calusa) about five thousand years ago. They were followed by the Arawaks, who migrated up the island chain from South America to occupy Trinidad, Puerto Rico, Hispaniola, Jamaica, and Cuba. The Carib were the last to arrive. Like the Arawak, they originated in the Amazon and hopped islands up the Lesser Antilles, reaching Puerto Rico at about the same time that Europeans arrived. They derived their name from Columbus, who witnessed an encounter between the Arawak and Carib in which the former consumed the latter in a ritual feast; the term *Caribbean* originally referred to those islands under Carib dominion.

Hispaniola was the focal point of activity during the early or initial phase of colonization, when the search for gold and spices occupied the attention of Columbus and those who accompanied him. The Spanish parceled out Jamaica, Hispaniola, Cuba, and Puerto Rico into *encomiendas* ("land grants") when it became apparent that they were not the "spice islands." They introduced cattle, horses, pigs, goats, and tropical commodities such as sugarcane, bananas, and citrus from their African (Canary Islands and Morocco) and Mediterranean (Madeira, Majolica, and Sicily) colonies. They subdued the Arawak; extracted cotton, cassava (tapioca), and other local products from Arawak *conucos* ("gardens"); and relied upon natives to labor on the *encomiendas*. The Arawak population plummeted, and the Spanish began replacing them with enslaved Africans early in the sixteenth century. Spanish interest in the Caribbean waned after the conquests of Mesoamerica (1524) and Peru (1540), and the islands functioned as ports of call that supplied the flotas and galleons that crossed the Atlantic.

Cockpit of Europe. Spanish sovereignty was not unchallenged. Spain occupied the larger islands but not the smaller islands, and the Dutch, French, and English began seizing island after island in the Lesser Antilles during the seventeenth century. The Dutch occupied Saint Maarten, Saint Eustatius, and Saba in the Leewards and they seized Aruba, Bonaire, and Curaáao off the coast of South America and traded with Spanish colonists in Venezuela and Colombia. The French occupied Martinique, Guadeloupe, and Dominica in the Windward Islands, and they seized and transformed the western half of Hispaniola into Saint Domingue (1630). The English settled Saint Kitts (1623), Barbados (1625), and Nevis (1628) and invaded and annexed Jamaica (1655).

The Dutch, French, and English were less concerned with establishing settlements than with buccaneering, or raiding Spanish treasure fleets. The term *buccaneering* is a neologism that was created in the New World. It has at its root the Arawak word *boucan*, which referred to grills used to "barbeque" (that is, to dry and season) native food products fashioned from the lignum vitae (ironwood) that grew on the islands. The Spanish released livestock on the smaller islands for shipwrecked sailors, and the word was borrowed from the Arawak and became associated with the pigs, goats, and cattle they barbequed while awaiting rescue. The noun became a verb when the activity associated with buccaneering shifted from subsistence to piracy. The Dutch, French, and English licensed individuals to raid the treasure fleets and coastal ports, and for the next century the Caribbean became known as the "cockpit of Europe," owing to the activity of buccaneers such as Francis Drake and Henry Morgan.

Although these buccaneers remained active, buccaneering was superseded in the late seventeenth century by the cultivation of tobacco and sugar. The decline of the treasure fleets, coupled with an increase in the consumption of tobacco and sugar, accelerated the transition, and the Dutch, French, and English islands were parceled into "plantations." Plantations were rural factories that produced commodities for mass consumption in Europe. The islands of Jamaica and Haiti became crown jewels in the English and French Caribbean because, besides producing more sugar than their Lesser Antillean counterparts, they became entrepôts in what was known as the "triangular trade," a commercial network that included Africa and North America along with Europe and the Caribbean. Sugar, rum, and coffee were produced or "manufactured" on plantations and transported to North America and Europe, where they were sold or exchanged for commodities (such as barrels, corn, iron, or slaves), which in turn were sold or exchanged in a circuit or triangular trade that united the Old World and the New.

Slavery in the Caribbean. The Dutch, French, and English looked to Europe and initially relied upon indentured or contract labor as a source of supply. Indentured laborers were those who agreed to toil for a specific number of years (usually seven) in exchange for the opportunity to begin life anew in the Americas. Unable to procure indentured labor in sufficient quantities, the Dutch, English, and French followed the lead of their Iberian counterparts and looked to Africa first as a supplemental and, later, a primary source of labor. The Portuguese had established trading stations, or "factories," along what became known as the Ivory, Gold, and Slave Coasts, where they grew sugar and exchanged commodities (iron and paper for gold, ivory, and grain) with local polities such as the Mandingo, Fanti, Eboe, and Kikongo a century before Columbus embarked on his journey.

The Dutch, French, and English acquired Africans from factories they seized (at El Mina, Cape Coast, Whydah, Popo, Kromanti, and Axim) and transported them to the New World. Precise accounts are difficult to ascertain (and range from an estimated 1 million to 100 million souls before the trade was halted in 1807), but the volume was such that by the middle of the eighteenth century Jamaica and Saint Domingue developed the pyramidal, three-tier, color-caste (white, brown, and black) demographic typically associated with plantation societies. In Jamaica, for example, a white or European faction of 15,000 (with 7,000 "absentees" living abroad) dominated a social formation consisting of 20,000 free people of color (mulattoes, quadroons, and octoroons) and 325,000 enslaved Africans.

Creoles and Maroons. Enslaved Africans replaced indentured Europeans in the social and occupational hierarchy associated with plantations. The organization of production was divided into two broad occupational categories: predial (or field laborers), who planted, maintained, and cut cane, and nonpredial (or skilled mechanics), who worked in the boiling houses and as domestics and servants in the great houses and domiciles of the managers, attorneys, and overseers. Africans replaced their indentured counterparts in the field, and as production increased and mortality rose, they toiled as blacksmiths, carpenters, and masons as well as teamsters, domestics, and valets.

Africans were by no means minor or passive actors. Although they were enslaved and disenfranchised, they constituted the single largest faction on most islands, and they exerted an extraordinary influence on the formation of Creole society throughout the region. Similar to the etymology of buccaneer, the term *Creole* is a compound formed from the Spanish *criar* ("to create") and *colono* ("colonist") and refers to a process of formation (creolization) in which a host of disparate social and cultural elements were fused to create something new. Africa is a large continent, and while Europeans sought cheap labor (skilled and unskilled), the multitudes they purchased were a heterogeneous lot (including Akan, Yoruba, Eboe, Mandingo, Congo, and Bantu) and carried with them a diverse ethnic, linguistic, and cultural heritage.

Along with manufacturing commodities, Africans fused and combined this diversity into a host of African-Caribbean folk religions (such as Obeah; Vodun, or voodoo; and Santeria), local or insular festivities (such as Carnival, Jonkunnu or Jon Kannoe, and Gombay), and a number of Creole or spoken languages (Dutch, English, and French) that became the primary means of communication on such islands as Aruba, Barbados, and Martinique. These New World religions, festivals, and languages superseded their ethnic or Old World counterparts as a "Creole," or Caribbean-born, generation replaced a "saltwater," or African-born, generation. The arrival of African Americans or black Loyalists after the American Revolution added African Christian notions concerning "sufferation and redemption," or enslavement and emancipation, to the pepper pot of creolization, so that by the turn of the century the islands had developed a character and identity that was neither African nor European but instead uniquely Caribbean.

These cultural formations were by no means apolitical and were linked to a tradition of resistance, that is, Maroon wars and slave rebellions, that date to the early years of Spanish colonization. Like "Creole," the term *Maroon* is Spanish in origin (*cimarron*) and initially referred to the reddish color of the feral livestock the Spaniards released and consumed for subsistence. It was later used to describe enslaved Africans who escaped and ran away to form *palenques*, or communities scattered throughout the interior of many island and mainland societies. Communities formed in Jamaica and Hispaniola before their seizure and these "Maroon towns" were supported by the Spanish during the guerrilla war that accompanied their occupation by the English and French.

Similar communities formed on the smaller islands (Saint Kitts), in Brazil (Quilombo), and in the Dutch and French Guianas, and they became magnets or destinations for runaways. Some were short lived, but others, such as those in Jamaica and Dutch Guiana (Surinam), were officially recognized as semi-autonomous polities and remain extant. Few years passed in the Caribbean without some sort of insurrection or rebellion by those remaindered to plantations. Whereas most islands experienced such activity, Saint Domingue and Jamaica are unique in that what began as a Vodun-inspired slave revolt in 1790 led to the emergence of Haiti as the first black nation-state in the New World in 1804, and what began as a strike, or labor action, organized by itinerant or African Christian preachers precipitated the Christmas (or Baptist) Rebellion of 1831, emancipation, and the termination of slavery throughout the British Empire in 1834.

North American Focus. The Caribbean ceased to be the cockpit of Europe by the end of the nineteenth century. European interest and investment dissipated rapidly as the focal point of the British, Dutch, and French empires shifted eastward to Africa, Asia, and the Pacific, opening a door for North America. North America was a focal point in the triangular trade, and several island societies became homes away from home for black Americans (enslaved and free). However, as the region slipped from the core of the first to the periphery of the second, or "imperial," phase of empire building, the United States eclipsed Europe politically, economically, and culturally, initiating a new phase in the process of creolization.

On the one hand, termination of the Spanish-American War led to the independence of Cuba, commonwealth status for Puerto Rico, and inclusion of the Caribbean within an expanding American geopolitical sphere of influence. On the other hand, completion of the canal project and creation of the Canal Zone provided a source of employment and became a conduit through which elements of American culture entered and mixed with Caribbean culture. Whereas enslaved Africans forged a unique Creole culture from a diverse ethnic heritage in the eighteenth century, those in the twentieth century combined elements of South American (Brazil), African (Congo), and North American (jazz and blues) with the Caribbean to once again create something new.

The Spanish-, English-, and French-Creole–speaking islands became cultural generators that produced one musical style or genre (such as rumba, meringue, salsa, calypso, soca, reggae, and zouk) after another before, during, and after the world wars. And unlike the eighteenth century, these forms and expressions were not confined to local society but were assisted by print and electronic media that were carried around the world as African Caribbean people of all linguistic and island affiliations immigrated to Paris, London, Toronto, New York, and elsewhere.

[*See also* Black Loyalists; Brazil; Dance; Festivals; Fugitive Slaves; Haitian Revolution; Indentured Servitude; Jamaica; Jon Kannoe; Language; Maroons; Music; Native Americans and African Americans; Religion; Riots and Rebellions; *and* South America.]

BIBLIOGRAPHY

Burton, Richard D. E. *Afro-Creole: Power, Opposition, and Play in the Caribbean*. Ithaca, NY: Cornell University Press, 1997.

Knight, Franklin W. *The Caribbean: The Genesis of a Fragmented Nationalism*. New York: Oxford University Press, 1990.

Lowenthal, Davis. *West Indian Societies*. New York: Oxford University Press, 1972.

Watts, David. *The West Indies: Patterns of Development, Culture, and Environmental Change since 1492*. Cambridge, UK: Cambridge University Press, 1987.

—JOHN W. PULIS

The Abolition of Slavery in the Caribbean

The term *West Indies* applies to British colonies in the Caribbean basin, including Jamaica, Barbados, British Guiana, Saint Kitts, Nevis, and British Honduras. The West Indies were the focus of the Atlantic slave trade in the eighteenth century and were the first colonies to emancipate their slaves, which occurred on 1 August 1834. West Indian emancipation was celebrated as an example of enlightenment by the American abolitionist movement, including Frederick Douglass, for many years afterward.

England acquired most of its Caribbean colonies in the seventeenth century and established sugar plantations as the base of colonial economic output because sugar became a popular commodity in Europe in the seventeenth century. In an era before mechanized production processes, sugarcane was a labor-intensive crop. Once the ripened plant is cut down, its liquid center—the source of sugar—hardens within a matter of hours, at which point the process of granulation is impossible. Therefore, before the availability of machine assistance, sugar production required a large labor force to cut the ripe cane and rush it through the crushing, heating, and cooling processes necessary for granulation. Because the Portuguese had already tapped the African slave trade as a source of cheap and plentiful labor in Brazil, the English were quick to become involved in the slave trade to supply their plantations with the necessary workforce. By the early eighteenth century, the slave trade was profitable enough for the British to demand the right to supply slaves to the huge Spanish empire in America, and an estimated 6 to 7 million African slaves were brought to the Caribbean and the Americas throughout the century.

As the center of Britain's slave trade in the eighteenth century, the Caribbean was also the focus of Britain's abolitionist movement, which gained support over the latter part of the century. A Quaker antislavery society, the Committee for the Abolition of the Slave Trade, lobbied the British Parliament to end the continued transfer of slaves across the Atlantic, hoping to stem slavery by cutting off its source. The group was also known as the Clapham Sect, for the London suburb where most of its founding members lived. Antislavery forces were opposed in the House of Commons by a number of West Indian absentee plantation owners, often derisively referred to as "sugar kings." In accordance with contemporary practice, these men had bought seats in the Commons to protect their livelihoods. The plantation owners also had their own lobbying committee, the West India Association. Many of these London-based planters brought slaves from the Caribbean as personal servants, providing a visual shock to polite London society and reminding it of the reality of slavery in the colonies of the West Indies.

As the Napoleonic wars began in the eighteenth century, Britain's imperial trading interests shifted away from the Caribbean colonies toward India, which was easier to protect and produced cotton, tea, coffee, and sugar without the use of slave labor. Further, the sheer number of slaves in the Caribbean had increased the production of sugar, driving prices down and reducing the profits of the plantation owners. Consequently, in 1807 the British Parliament passed the Abolition Act, ending the slave trade on 1 January 1808. Although the abolitionist movement assumed that the end of slavery would come soon after, they were wrong. As slaves died, they were not replaced—the vast majority of Africans brought to the Caribbean colonies were male, and the paucity of African women meant that there were few opportunities to replenish the population through natural increase. The smaller the slave population got, the lower costs became. Less sugar was produced, and higher profits resulted for plantation owners. They fought harder than ever to keep slavery legal in the empire after the abolition of the slave trade.

Nevertheless, the abolitionist movement gained momentum. In 1823 the West India Association proposed a series of improvements in the condition of slaves, as a compromise to avoid abolition. Suggestions were made to the governors of the colonies that they pass local laws limiting the whipping of slaves, encouraging religious instruction, prohibiting the separation of slave families when they were sold, and even allowing slaves to buy their own freedom. These proposals, however, met with fierce resistance in the colonies. Barbados put down a large slave rebellion in 1816, and Jamaica experienced a similar rebellion in 1831. Both events encouraged plantation owners and managers to be even harsher with their slaves. Protestant missionaries were blamed for inciting slaves to riot, which proved to be a very bad error in public relations for the plantation owners.

Finally, the Reform Act of 1832 allowed millions more middle-class citizens to vote in Britain. The result of this was that the House of Commons experienced a significant change in composition, and most of the sugar kings lost their seats. The new Commons was decidedly abolitionist in makeup and interested in abolishing the sorts of tariffs that protected the sugar plantations' income—they would not protect the income of slaveholders in the West Indies if it meant that British subjects had to pay more for the sugar the slaveholders produced. As a result, the Emancipation Act was passed and put into effect on 1 August 1834. All slaves in the British Empire were freed on that date, with the plantation owners being compensated a total of 20 million pounds for the loss of their property and labor.

The abolition of slavery in the British West Indian colonies became the focus of celebration for the growing abolitionist movement in the United States, as an example of their goals for the future. For twenty-five years after the date of British emancipation, abolitionists in the United States celebrated 1 August as West Indian Emancipation Day, and Frederick Douglass was a prized speaker at such events. He used his speeches to emphasize the righteousness of abolitionism and the invariably peaceful nature of the celebrations, which he pointed to as indicative of the responsible nature of African Americans in general.

[*See also* Abolitionism; Antislavery Movement; Colonialism; Foreign Policy; Slave Trade; *and* Slavery.]

BIBLIOGRAPHY

Eudell, Demetrius Lynn. *The Political Languages of Emancipation in the British Caribbean and the U.S. South.* Chapel Hill: University of North Carolina Press, 2002.

Hamshere, Cyril. *The British in the Caribbean.* Cambridge, MA: Harvard University Press, 1972.

Mintz, Sidney. *Sweetness and Power: The Place of Sugar in Modern History.* New York: Viking Penguin, 1985.

Morris, James. "High and Holy Work." In *Heaven's Command: An Imperial Progress.* New York: Harcourt Brace, 1973.

—DAVID SIMONELLI

CATHOLIC CHURCH AND AFRICAN AMERICANS.

The Roman Catholic Church has a long history regarding the institution of slavery and blacks. The church was founded during the decline of ancient Roman society, in which slavery was endemic and tolerated. Indeed, the church found the practice, at least with respect to black Africans, acceptable well into the nineteenth century. This was so despite the fact that the Catholic Church had an institutional presence in sub-Saharan Africa as early as the beginning of the sixteenth century. The European church's understanding of the nature of slavery, however, differed considerably from the practice as it developed in the British North American colonies and the early United States of America. Pursuant to the official teachings of the Roman Catholic Church, slavery had to operate within the confines of natural law, which limited a master's ownership rights to the slave's labor, not to the slave, and further required that the owner treat his slaves humanely. Consistent with this position and in recognition of its obligations to the slaves, the church carried on an active missionary effort among the African slaves and slave communities. This work was pursued in the seventeenth century by such notable figures as Saints Vincent de Paul and Peter Carver, whose recognition by the church was the result of their dedicated service to African slaves.

Although members of the Roman Catholic Church came to what would later become the United States very early in the exploration of North America, even by the colonial and Revolutionary periods of American history Catholics were numerically few, and their presence was limited mainly to Maryland and Louisiana. In 1783 over 65 percent of the Catholic population resided in Maryland, and as late as 1830 Catholics represented only 5 percent of the total population of the United States. The formal institutional presence of the Catholic Church in the United States began in 1789 with the establishment of the Diocese of Baltimore, followed by the Diocese of New Orleans in 1793. The number of Catholic dioceses increased to six in 1829 and to ten by 1834.

The official position of the U.S. Catholic Church regarding slavery was largely consistent with the position of the church in Europe. It opposed abolitionism and viewed slavery as a means to provide for the religious salvation of the blacks. Not surprisingly, the church, through its emissaries, engaged in the practice of slavery very early on. The Ursulines, a French order of nuns, who were the first order to establish themselves in New Orleans, in 1727, were given and accepted eight slaves. These black slaves served as domestics and worked on the small plantation that the order owned. In compliance with the church's teachings, the nuns carefully provided the slaves (and Native Americans) with religious training.

The earliest and best documentation of the Catholic Church's involvement in slavery in the United States focuses on the Jesuits in Maryland. The ownership of slaves by the Jesuits can be documented from 1717; the number of slaves owned by the Jesuits grew from 192 in 1765 to 272 in 1838. When the Jesuits abandoned the practice of owning slaves in 1838, they held more than eleven thousand acres of land that were worked by slaves. Many (if not most) of the slaves came to the Jesuits as gifts from the Catholic laity. Some historians have argued that the Jesuits originally had hoped to utilize white indentured servants to work their plantations, thereby providing a means to support and enlarge the Catholic population in Maryland. However, the decline of indentured servants in the late seventeenth and early eighteenth centuries prompted the Jesuits increasingly to use black slaves.

The Ursulines and the Jesuits were not the only slaveholders in the early American Catholic Church. The several orders of priests that owned slaves included the Vincentians in Missouri, the Sulpicians in Baltimore, and the Capuchins in Louisiana. The orders of nuns that owned slaves included the Carmelites in Maryland and the Sisters of Charity and the Sisters of Loretto in Kentucky. Slaves often came to the communities of nuns as part of the dowry that each new candidate brought to her convent.

The early American church, through its leadership, was committed to a "Christian" form of slavery. Archbishop John Carroll, the first bishop of the Diocese of Baltimore, criticized Catholic slaveholders who failed to provide for their slaves' faith and morals. This condemnation was repeated by his successor, James Whitfield. In 1791 Archbishop Carroll arranged for the Sulpicians, a French order of priests, to come to Baltimore. By 1796 the Sulpicians were providing religious instruction to free blacks at Saint Mary's Seminary in Baltimore. After 1809 they were assisted by the newly formed Daughters of Charity of Saint Vincent de Paul. Other American bishops also fostered this work among the black Catholics. Bishop John England of Charleston, South Carolina, established a school for free black children that was run by the Sisters of Our Lady of Mercy. In 1829, however, local prejudice and violence forced Bishop England to close the school.

The most significant event in the history of blacks in the Catholic Church in the early United States occurred in Baltimore. In the years following the revolution led by Toussaint Louverture that began in 1791 on the island of Hispaniola (present-day Haiti and the Dominican Republic), significant numbers of blacks and mulattoes fled to the United States. Many of these exiles came to Baltimore. One of them, Mary Elizabeth Lange, was a French-speaking Creole and the granddaughter of a wealthy plantation owner. She was born to Haitian parents in Cuba, came to the United States in 1817, and soon settled in Baltimore. In 1818 Lange and Marie Madeline Balas, another Haitian refugee, established a school for the free black girls of Baltimore. The two women were later joined by another Haitian refugee, Rosine Boegue, and by 1828 they had purchased a house and had eleven boarding students and nine day students. The ultimate goal of the women, however, was to establish an order of black sisters.

The women, along with other black Catholics in Baltimore, attended segregated religious services in the basement chapel of Saint Mary's Seminary on Paca Street. Most Catholic churches in both the North and the South were segregated in the early nineteenth century, although in the District of Columbia they were integrated, because of the large free black Catholic population. In their basement chapel the women first met the Sulpician priest Father Jacques Hector Nicholas Joubert de la Muraille, who had been born in France and later served as a government official in Haiti. After fleeing Haiti, he entered Saint Mary's Seminary in 1805 and was ordained in 1810. Father Joubert was searching for someone to teach catechism to the young black children of Baltimore. The goals of the priest and the women overlapped. With the intercession of the French priest, Bishop James Whitfield of Baltimore encouraged the women, who in 1829 formally began to establish their order of sisters. In 1831 Pope Gregory XVI officially recognized Mother Mary Elizabeth Lange's Oblate Sisters of Providence, who became the first black order of nuns established in the Catholic Church. The order continues in existence, providing education to poor black children in Baltimore and elsewhere.

The first black men ordained as priests in the U.S. Catholic Church were the brothers James Augustine Healy (1854), Alexander Sherwood Healy (1858), and Patrick Francis Healy (1864). All rose to prominence in the church. James was appointed bishop of Portland, Maine, in 1875; Patrick was president of Georgetown University from 1874 to 1882; and Alexander served as the personal theologian to Bishop John Williams of Boston at the First Vatican Council in 1867.

The establishment of the black Oblate Sisters of Providence and the ordination of the Healy brothers were the results of a marked change in church policy and theology that occurred in the late 1830s. The Jesuit decision to end its involvement with slavery was followed by the Roman Catholic Church's first clear rejection of the practice. In 1839 Pope Gregory XVI issued his apostolic letter *In Supremo Apostolatus Fatigo*, in which he condemned the practice of slavery: "[We] do . . . admonish and adjure in the Lord all believers in Christ, of whatsoever condition, that no one hereafter may dare to molest Indians, Negroes, or other men of this sort; or to spoil them of their goods; or to reduce them to slavery." Despite this clear condemnation of slavery by the Supreme Pontiff, the U.S. Catholic Church, at least in the South, firmly held to the practice. Bishop England of Charleston argued that the condemnation was not aimed at Americans but at the Portuguese and Spanish. In the end, some U.S. Catholics joined with some of their Protestant neighbors to support slavery in America until the Thirteenth Amendment ended the practice in 1865.

There is evidence that a vibrant black Catholic laity existed before the Civil War. In 1843 the Holy Family Society of Colored People was established in Baltimore. The Society, whose members included both black laymen and women and probably slaves, numbered approximately 270. The meeting agenda consisted of an opening prayer, a sermon by the group's spiritual advisor, Father John F. Hickey, and hymns (which reflected the group's African roots). The dues paid by the members, 6 1/4 cents a month, provided for the rent for the meeting hall and for masses to be said for deceased members. The group also established a lending library. In September 1845 Calvert Hall, the parish hall that was attached to the cathedral and was the meeting place for the Society, was given over to the Brothers of the Christian Doctrine, thereby displacing the Society. The abruptness of this action caused resentment on behalf of the members, and the Society was dissolved soon after.

In the aftermath of the Civil War, as black and white Protestant ministers and missionaries poured into the South to aid and proselytize the newly emancipated slaves, the American Catholic Church hesitated and then stopped to ponder its relationship to blacks. A few Catholic bishops, Archbishop Martin J. Spalding of Baltimore, Bishop Augustin Verot of St. Augustine, and Bishop William Gross of Savannah, did endeavor to advance an apostolate for blacks. Archbishop Spalding attempted to make the church's position on the new freedmen the primary issue of the Plenary Council of 1866. Despite the efforts of these bishops to establish "an ecclesiastical man" who would take charge of addressing the interests of blacks in the United States, most bishops objected to the proposal, and it was rejected. Instead the bishops choose simply to permit each bishop to address the concerns of blacks in his respective diocese.

Regardless of the American Catholic bishops' unofficial policy of neglect, a strong black Catholic laity continued to grow. In the summer of 1888 Daniel Rudd, a former slave and the publisher of the black Springfield, Ohio, newspaper the *American Catholic Tribune*, proposed a national meeting of black Catholics. In a letter to Reverend John Slattery, S.S.J., he wrote, "Let the leading Colored Catholics gather together from every city in the Union in some suitable place, where under the blessings of Holy Mother Church they may get to know one another and take up the cause of the race" (Davis, p. 171). On 1–4 January 1889 the first Congress of Colored Catholics convened in Washington, D.C. The meeting was blessed by Pope Leo XIII through his Secretary of State, Cardinal Rampolla. The participants were addressed by Cardinal James Gibbons of Baltimore and Archbishop William Henry Elder of Cincinnati and visited the White House at the invitation of President Grover Cleveland. In their closing statement the group called for more Catholic schools to educate black Catholic young people and condemned the growing problem of segregation.

The Congress met annually from 1889 until 1894. It continued its emphasis upon education and chided Catholic bishops for not being as aggressive as the Protestant denominations in their efforts to support and convert blacks. The group also investigated the racist and segregationist practices of the southern Catholic dioceses. The Congress met in 1894 but would not meet again until 1987. Commenting upon the Congress, one historian observed that "they demonstrated beyond a doubt not only that a black Catholic community existed but that it was active, devoted, articulate, and proud." (Davis, p. 193)

[*See also* Education; Haitian Revolution; Missionary Movements; Religion; Toussaint Louverture; *and* Violence against African Americans.]

BIBLIOGRAPHY

Davis, Cyprian. *The History of Black Catholics in the United States.* New York: Crossroad, 1990.

Fialka, John J. *Sisters: Catholic Nuns and the Making of America.* New York: St. Martin's Press, 2003.

Maxwell, John Francis. *Slavery and the Catholic Church: The History of Catholic Teaching concerning the Moral Legitimacy of the Institution of Slavery.* Chichester, U.K.: Barry Rose, 1975.

Morrow, Diane Batts. *Persons of Color and Religious at the Same Time: The Oblate Sisters of Providence, 1828–1860.* Chapel Hill: University of North Carolina Press, 2002.

Murphy, Thomas. *Jesuit Slaveholding in Maryland, 1717–1838.* New York: Routledge, 2001.

—THOMAS E. CARNEY

CAULKER'S TRADE. As a caulker in Baltimore, Maryland, a major site of American shipbuilding, from 1836 to 1838, Frederick Douglass put sealant between the boards of hulls to make ships watertight. He learned the caulker's trade while enslaved in Baltimore, and the experiences Douglass gained in the shipyards there proved instrumental in his escape from slavery.

Douglass's career as a caulker began when Hugh Auld, his master and shipbuilder, apprenticed the young Douglass in the shipyard of William Gardiner. As his apprenticeship began, Douglass witnessed black and white carpenters working shoulder to shoulder; however, as white employment in shipyards became increasingly difficult because of immigration and the arrival of both free and enslaved blacks in Baltimore, white carpenters threatened to strike unless all black carpenters were fired and white carpenters hired in their stead. Under a highly profitable contract to build warships for the Mexican government, Gardiner fired all his black carpenters to prevent a strike and the loss of money. As a caulker, Douglass was not fired; yet antiblack sentiments remained in the shipyard, and twice Douglass thwarted physical attacks, showing his impressive strength, before being severely beaten by four of his fellow white caulkers. Other white shipbuilders looked on during the attack and intervened only when Douglass attempted a counterattack. Douglass was not allowed to prosecute his attackers because, under the laws of Maryland, a black person, whether slave or free, could not testify against a white person.

Seeing the attack on Douglass as a personal attack on his "property," Auld gained an alternate apprenticeship for Douglass in Asa Price's shipyard, also in Baltimore. Having lost his own shipbuilding business on the City Block, Auld then worked as a foreman for Price. At Price's shipyard Douglass completed his apprenticeship as a caulker and became a journeyman caulker—a skilled worker who could practice his craft in any shipyard. Within a year Douglass commanded the highest wages paid journeymen caulkers—one dollar and fifty cents a day. In any given week Douglass earned from six to nine dollars; yet while inching toward his own freedom, Douglass unwittingly helped caulk three slave ships: *Delorez*, *Teayer*, and *Eagle*. These ships, built in the Price shipyard, held freshwater in the ballast as opposed to seawater, giving the human cargo a supply of water during passage, and had shallow but wide storage areas for those humans beneath the decks.

Having left behind plantation labor and taken up his caulking tools, Douglass was introduced to a wider world in the Baltimore shipyards. Early nineteenth-century American shipbuilding owed its boom to the slave trade in the Caribbean and South America and to revolutionary efforts in Central and South America and Greece, as well as to the war effort in Mexico. In the shipyards Douglass met other black caulkers and black mariners, free black men who in the early nineteenth century made up one-fifth of the more than 100,000 American mariners.

Thus caulking gave Douglass a trade, put him in contact with other free blacks, and also helped him pocket the money necessary for his planned escape to the North. Early in his career as a caulker Douglass handed over all of his wages to Auld, keeping nothing himself. While working in the Price shipyard, Douglass made arrangements to pay Auld three dollars a week; in return Douglass would provide for his own room and board as well as cover the expenses for his caulking tools. With this arrangement Douglass gained an increase in liberty and was able to keep up to six dollars a week.

In his escape from slavery, Douglass dressed as a sailor and carried a Seamen's Protection Certificate that he had acquired from a black sailor. Yet freedom for Douglass proved precarious; the open sky of the North closed when, after his New York City marriage to Anna Murray, he arrived in the whaling port city of New Bedford, Massachusetts, and was denied work as a caulker because of the color of his skin. Life for Douglass remained a struggle, even on free soil. Instead of gaining employment in the specialized trade of the caulker, he eventually worked as a common laborer, for which he earned a dollar a day—half of what he would have earned as a caulker.

In the shipyards of the antebellum United States, African American men dominated the caulking trade; their dominance persisted until after the Civil War. Douglass's own career as a caulker, one that saw opportunity as well as racism and the denial of opportunity, touched on many of the ambiguities concerning African Americans and ships—vessels of slavery as well as freedom.

[*See also* Auld Family; Baltimore, Maryland, Slavery in; Civil War; Douglass, Anna Murray; Douglass, Frederick; Free African Americans before the Civil War (North); Mexican-American War; Racism; *and* Slave Trade.]

BIBLIOGRAPHY

Chapelle, Howard I. *The Search for Speed under Sail, 1700–1855*. New York: Norton, 1967.

Douglass, Frederick. *Autobiographies: Narrative of the Life; My Bondage and My Freedom; Life and Times*. Edited by Henry Louis Gates Jr. New York: Library of America, 1994.

McFeely, William S. *Frederick Douglass*. New York: Norton, 1991.

—DELANO GREENIDGE-COPPRUE

CEMETERIES AND BURIALS. The inescapable culmination of life is mortality, and every community must deal with the death of its members, marking the event appropriately, disposing respectfully of mortal remains, offering condolence to the living, and returning life among survivors to normal. Few human communities have faced greater challenges in this regard than those African Americans enslaved in North America, as well as free blacks, during the colonial and early national periods. African American mortuary practices preserved, synthesized, and reworked African traditions and adapted New World customs imported to America by white European Christian colonists.

There is much about which we cannot be certain, given the limited records and archaeological evidence available to us, and considerable diversity characterized the people of African descent throughout North America during this era. But it is clear that African American funerals and interments were creative, hybrid practices—expressions of African American culture that signaled the worth and dignity of black individuals and communities; built and helped maintain unity; and cultivated endurance, defiance, and transcendence, often in the face of extreme callousness or outright repression by white masters, authorities, or neighbors.

Segregated Burial. Although some slave owners displayed a patriarchal concern for the slave dead and encouraged or tolerated funerals and decent burials for their bondpeople, many showed little regard for the deceased or the bereaved family and community, instead limiting or curtailing mourning rites and sometimes even indulging in cruel repression. In the North, even after emancipation in some states, ordinances often restricted African American mortuary practices, and burial grounds were typically segregated. As the perceptive observer Alexis de Tocqueville wrote in the 1830s, "The gates of heaven are not closed against him [the Negro], but his inequality stops only just short of the boundaries of the other world. When the Negro is no more, his bones are cast aside, and some difference in condition is found even in the equality of death."

In the North, African Americans usually were interred in outlying potter's fields, among strangers, criminals, and other "undesirables," rather than in churchyards available to white church members. Although blacks could be baptized at Trinity Church in New York City by the late seventeenth century, for example, they could not be buried there. Instead, they were laid to rest in a swampy area north of town, and even this cemetery was denied sanctity, as black burial grounds were repeatedly relocated as the city encroached northward. Similarly, in Philadelphia, deceased African Americans were excluded from white Protestant and Catholic church graveyards and interred in a separate section of the Strangers' Burial Ground. Even Quakers, pioneers in the antislavery movement, whose commitment to equality militated against the use of marking stones in their own burying grounds, nonetheless usually designated separate plots for blacks.

Segregation of the mortal remains of African Americans reflected the racism and discrimination pervasive in this era and beyond. It also enabled and demanded the resourceful development of separate funerary and burial practices among African Americans—slave and free, South and North—which expressed African American culture and served the particular social needs of black communities. White participation in black funerals and interment rites was a mixed blessing at best; the material contributions of slave masters (of coffins, shrouds, food, or drink) might assist the bereaved to conduct a decent burial, but the attendance of masters (though sometimes inspired by their own sense of loss) was typically an act of supervision and control rather than one of mourning. Their presence often reflected white suspicion and wariness regarding the potential for memorial rites to precipitate acts of transgression or even insurrection.

Legislation often codified such fear and repression, including a 1687 ban on public funerals for slaves in Virginia's Northern Neck and various laws enacted throughout the South in the eighteenth and early nineteenth centuries limiting the number of slaves allowed to assemble on such occasions. Legislators believed that "the frequent meetings of considerable numbers of Negro slaves under the pretense of . . . burials is dangerous"; in response, they enacted strict pass and patrol systems. In the North as well—in New York City and Boston, for example— ordinances required that slave or free black funerals be held only during daylight hours and that attendance be

"The African Burial Ground," by Charles Lilly, 1994. This cemetery in lower Manhattan, New York, was used from the late 1600s to 1795 and was excavated by archaeologists in 1991. Some 20,000 enslaved Africans had been buried there, and the remains of more than 400 men, women, and children—shrouded and mostly in hexagonal coffins—were found, along with numerous coins and artifacts. (New York Public Library, Arts and Artifacts Division, Schomburg Center for Black Culture; Astor, Lenox, and Tilden Foundations.)

limited, in eighteenth-century New York to no more than ten people at slave wakes.

These limitations and controls, however, failed to forestall African American burial rites. Indeed, their limited impact, despite the efforts of some whites, testified to the vitality and creativity of African American culture and society in slavery and freedom. The graveyard may have been the first fully African American institution in mainland North America. In the northern colonies, and particularly with emancipation in the northern states, quasi-religious benevolent associations—such as the Free African Society of Newport, Rhode Island (founded in 1780)—emerged in part to procure decent burial grounds for community members. Having fulfilled the last great necessity of life, these associations assumed additional responsibilities and sometimes evolved into more substantial African American institutions. In Philadelphia, for example, the Free African Society (founded in 1787) laid the groundwork for the organization of a Union Church, which developed into Saint Thomas's African Episcopal

Church in 1794, led by Absalom Jones, as well as a congregation led by Richard Allen, "Mother Bethel" of the African Methodist Episcopal Church.

Burial Practices. Few descriptions of African American burials survive from the colonial and early national periods, and these are too often chronicles penned by outsiders unsympathetic to those in mourning. Yet we can tentatively sketch a picture of the diverse rites employed by African Americans during these years.

Slave funerals (as well as those among free blacks) usually occurred at night, in part because masters refused to allow interruption of work but also because slaves themselves generally preferred nighttime burials, an expression of continuity with West African traditions. Sundays (slaves' lone day of rest) could also serve the needs of mourners, who sometimes lived on distant plantations and could not always assemble quickly, given the constraints of their bondage and the difficulty of travel. In some cases the bereaved held "second burials," actually memorial services that took place after initial interments, in a fashion echoing some West African mortuary traditions. This practice also accommodated the imperative to bury an unembalmed body quickly, yet still provide an appropriate funeral with full attendance. In some cases, memorial ceremonies could mourn the passing of two or more loved ones at a time when traveling mourners found it possible to convene.

Families themselves, particularly women, prepared bodies by washing and dressing or shrouding them and keeping watch. Coffins were typically plain, often homemade pine boxes that were sometimes painted or covered with crepe, and they were carried to grave sites by processions that could include as many as three hundred to seven hundred mourners in densely populated slave regions. A moving rite of communal sorrow and expression of farewell, including singing and chanting, clapping and praying, preceded the final procession to the grave, which often commenced around midnight in a deliberate march accompanied by solemn, rhythmic hymns.

At the burial site, mourners continued to voice their songs and "shouts" and listened to the moving words of black preachers (who appeared sometimes even when they were officially banned) or other respected community members, who spoke not merely of otherworldly rewards but also of hope, unity, and sometimes defiance among the living. The return procession usually displayed less solemnity and was often marked by ceremonial drumming and capped with a boisterous dinner that could feature vigorous singing and dancing. Although white observers denigrated these customs as "heathenish" or "savage," they were important rites of solidarity and revitalization, which showed respect for the living as well as the dead and served to link them in ways that celebrated the life of the community, declaring its humanity, value, and self-respect. Despite the presence of skeptical or critical whites, African Americans usually succeeded in controlling their own services.

African Continuity and African American Hybridity. African American cemeteries and individual graves reflected profound continuities with West African traditions. Like mourners in Africa, the bereaved in America often dug graves along an east-west axis, with the head of the deceased placed in a western position, not "crossways the world" but oriented to see the dawn (and perhaps the ancestral homeland, to which some believed they would return). Often mourners threw individual handfuls of dirt into the grave, a gesture typical of West African custom, which some white observers called "the Negro practice." In addition, graves could include burial goods—food and drink, clothes, tools and other items necessary for a journey—which propitiated the dead, aided their passage to the spirit world, prevented their wandering, and dissuaded them from returning to haunt the living.

Mourners often decorated graves with broken earthenware, carved and painted wooden grave markers, upturned bottles, seashells, plants, and other practical and symbolic items, a practice common in West Africa but without analogues among America's European peoples. As among Kongo peoples (referring broadly to the inhabitants of the entire west coast of Central Africa), African Americans sometimes adorned graves with the last objects touched or used by the deceased, which they believed possessed the last strength and traces of the spirit of the dead, according to the art historian Robert Farris Thompson. Such offerings directed the spirit to rest in peace and honored its power on earth. Likewise, African American seashell grave decoration may echo the Kongo belief that seashells enclosed the soul's immortal presence and represented the sea, the land of demise, and purity.

African American burials expressed a vital, resourceful African American culture, which blended African traditions with New World adaptations, including the ideas and practices of Christianity. Mortuary rites, creatively fashioned under the most stressful conditions, did not merely honor the dead and aid their otherworldly journey but testified to the living that they were a worthy, independent human community, deserving of redemption on earth as well as in heaven.

[*See also* African Methodist Episcopal Church; Allen, Richard; Fraternal Organizations and Mutual Aid Societies; Free African Society; Jones, Absalom; Segregation; *and* Spirituality.]

BIBLIOGRAPHY

Berlin, Ira. *Many Thousands Gone: The First Two Centuries of Slavery in North America.* Cambridge, MA: Belknap Press, 1998.

De Tocqueville, Alexis. *Democracy in America.* Edited by J. P. Mayer and translated by George Lawrence, vol. 1. Garden City, NJ: Anchor Books, 1969.

Egerton, Douglas R. "A Peculiar Mark of Infamy: Dismemberment, Burial, and Rebelliousness in Slave Societies." In *Mortal Remains: Death in Early America,* edited by Nancy Isenberg and Andrew Burstein, 149–160. Philadelphia: University of Pennsylvania Press, 2003.

Frey, Sylvia R., and Betty Wood. *Come Shouting to Zion: African American Protestantism in the American South and British Caribbean to 1830.* Chapel Hill: University of North Carolina Press, 1998.

Morgan, Philip D. *Slave Counterpoint: Black Culture in the Eighteenth-Century Chesapeake and Lowcountry.* Chapel Hill: University of North Carolina Press, 1998.

Roediger, David R. "And Die in Dixie: Funerals, Death, and Heaven in the Slave Community, 1700–1865," *Massachusetts Review* 22 (Spring 1981): 163–183.

Thompson, Robert Farris. *Flash of the Spirit: African and Afro-American Art and Philosophy.*

—MATTHEW DENNIS

CHAPLIN, WILLIAM LAWRENCE (b. c. 1798; d. 28 April 1871), white radical political abolitionist and Underground Railroad operative. William Lawrence Chaplin was born in Groton, Massachusetts, where his father, Daniel Chaplin, was a Congregationalist minister. William, who attended Andover Academy and Harvard College, practiced law in Groton during the 1820s.

Tall, muscular, energetic, well mannered, religious, and generous, Chaplin began a career in reform as a temperance advocate in 1819. With the formation of the American Anti-Slavery Society in 1833, he became increasingly involved in abolitionism. He gave up his law practice and in 1837 moved to Utica, New York, to become the general agent of the New York Anti-Slavery Society. Respected for his administrative activities, Chaplin became known among New York abolitionists as "General Chaplin."

In New York, Chaplin joined a group of radical political abolitionists, headed by the wealthy philanthropist Gerrit Smith; this group formed the Liberty Party in 1840. Like other members of this group, Chaplin contended that slavery was always illegal and that abolitionists must help slaves escape. Chaplin admired the slave rescuer Charles T. Torrey, who was arrested in Baltimore in 1844 and died two years later at the Maryland Penitentiary. In December 1844 Chaplin succeeded Torrey as editor and Washington correspondent of the *Albany Patriot*.

When Chaplin arrived in Washington, D.C., he hoped that as an alternative to risky escape attempts he could organize an agency for purchasing the freedom of slaves, but by early 1848 he was cooperating with African Americans who sought to escape. In April of that year he arranged for the schooner *Pearl* to carry about seventy-seven slaves north from Washington. When this escape attempt failed and the recaptured slaves were sold to traders, Chaplin raised funds to purchase the freedom of several of them. He continued to aid escapees until August 1850, when, following a furious gunfight, Washington police arrested him as he drove a carriage northward with two slaves on board.

Shortly after Chaplin's arrest, Frederick Douglass presided at a Fugitive Slave Convention in Cazenovia, New York. Those assembled, including about fifty fugitive slaves, praised Chaplin's efforts and nominated him for president of the United States. The convention also created a committee to free Chaplin from jail by raising funds to pay his District of Columbia and Maryland bail bonds, which totaled an astounding twenty-five thousand dollars. The committee succeeded in raising the money, with Gerrit Smith and the Washington attorney David A. Hall pledging most of it. Chaplin left the jail in Rockville, Maryland, in December, never to return for trial. His supporters hoped he would undertake a speaking tour to rally antislavery forces and to raise funds to repay the forfeited

bail money, but his frightening experience had damaged his psyche. Chaplin retired from antislavery work and joined his new wife, Theodosia Gilbert, in operating a water-cure sanatorium in Glen Haven, New York.

Chaplin exemplified the aggressiveness of New York abolitionists in confronting slavery on its own ground. In 1871 Douglass remembered him fondly enough to publish his obituary in the *New National Era*. Yet Chaplin's abrupt retirement suggests the price sometimes paid by those who physically challenged slavery.

[*See also* Abolitionism; American Anti-Slavery Society; Douglass, Frederick; Liberty Party; *Pearl* Incident; Smith, Gerrit; Temperance; *and* Underground Railroad.]

BIBLIOGRAPHY

Friedman, Lawrence J. *Gregarious Saints: Self and Community in American Abolitionism, 1830–1870*. New York: Cambridge University Press, 1982. Describes Chaplin's role in the Gerrit Smith circle of New York abolitionists.

Harrold, Stanley. *Subversives: Antislavery Community in Washington, D.C., 1828–1865*. Baton Rouge: Louisiana State University Press, 2003. Analyzes Chaplin's antislavery activities in and around Washington, D.C.

—STANLEY HARROLD

CHARTISM IN GREAT BRITAIN. Chartism was a petition movement in Great Britain that was most pronounced from 1837 to 1848. Participants in the movement were dedicated to political reform in favor of working-class involvement in parliamentary politics. In 1837 the London Workingmen's Association, an artisanal workers' support movement, drew up a "People's Charter" demanding reforms in the British political system. The charter proposed six points as a basis for future parliamentary legislation: universal manhood suffrage; annually sitting parliaments; voting by secret ballot; parliamentary districts with equal population distributions; abolition of property requirements in order to sit in Parliament; and salaries for members of Parliament. Though such demands seem commonplace in contemporary Western democracies, they were considered radical at the time.

The Workingmen's Association was made up mostly of independent artisans put out of work by new industrial inventions. The workers believed that recent efforts to extend the franchise in Britain, such as the 1832 Reform Act, did not go far enough toward the democratization of the nation, and that other reforms which restricted state aid for the unemployed—such as the 1834 Poor Law Amendment Act—were unduly harsh. Since the association's members believed that only full participation in the parliamentary political system would allow them to obtain redress for their grievances, they drew up the People's Charter as a blueprint for future legislation in favor of Britain's working classes.

To apply pressure on the House of Commons to accept the charter, workers held mass rallies to gather signatures on petitions as evidence of popular support—a common lobbying tactic dating back to eighteenth-century reform movements. The first of three such petitions was presented to the House of Commons in 1839 with nearly 1.3 million signatures; the Commons rejected the charter's provisions out of hand. A second petition went to the Commons in 1842, this time with over 3 million signatures—one for every nine people, with much higher concentrations of industrial and agricultural workers, in England, Scotland, Wales, and Ireland—yet it, too, was rejected at once. These refusals posed a dilemma to the Chartists as to how to compel the government to pay attention to their political interests. The movement then divided among those who wanted to simply come up with more signatures, those who wanted to form an alternative National Assembly to challenge the government's authority, and the few who argued that only violent revolution would bring about the adoption of their political principles. Occasional outbreaks of violence throughout England accompanied both petitions, lending credence to the popular idea that Chartism was a movement headed toward revolution—an idea only a select few in the actual movement were willing to even consider.

In 1848, a year of several political revolutions in Europe—such as in the Austrian Empire and Prussia—the Chartists were led by a fiery orator named Feargus O'Connor and assembled their most inflammatory petition drive to date. With 2 million signatures in hand—some of them forged, such as "Victoria Rex" (the Queen ordinarily signed her name "Victoria Regina"), the "Duke of Wellington" seventeen times, and people like "Mr. Punch" and "Flatnose"—the Chartists gathered 100,000 people, as estimated by O'Connor, on Kennington Common in London and prepared to march to the houses of parliament in order to demand that the Commons accept the petition. The petitioners intended to form an alternative government and ignore Parliament in the event that the petition was rejected. Unlike other European governments that year, however, the British government did not flee the capital; instead, British officials deputized some eighty-five thousand Londoners, most of them middle-class citizens, and ordered O'Connor to disband the meeting before it marched on London. Never as fiery a revolutionary as he was an orator, O'Connor sent the Chartists home and had the petition delivered in three hansom cabs to Parliament—which promptly rejected the document again. This third failure was the end of Chartism as a movement. Nonetheless, it had set a precedent; its organization of workers in generally peaceful demonstrations to promote their political interests became a model for future movements. Although Great Britain took longer than several other European nation-states, it eventually adopted all of the reforms listed in the People's Charter in an entirely peaceful fashion.

Douglass was living in England during the waning years of Chartism, before the final charter was assembled in 1848. Chartism was considered the English movement with the most revolutionary potential since the 1832 Reform Act and the riots and demonstrations that preceded it; yet the potentially dangerous nature of Chartism and its minority advocacy of political violence kept Frederick Douglass at a respectful and wary distance from the movement. Many of the Chartist leaders had identified with the abolitionist movement, and Douglass himself was present when a British antislavery league was founded in the mid-1840s with some Chartists as members. But he repudiated the angry speeches of figures like O'Connor in the pages of the *North Star*, believing that violence was not an answer to the political questions of either chattel or wage slavery. The collapse of Chartism after 1848 coincided with rising tensions in the United States regarding the crisis over slavery; consequently, Douglass's demands for decorum in matters of political protest fell on increasingly deaf ears.

[*See also* Antislavery Movement; Douglass, Frederick; *North Star*; Political Participation; Voting Rights; *and* Work.]

BIBLIOGRAPHY

Boston, Ray. *British Chartists in America, 1839–1900*. Totowa, NJ: Rowman and Littlefield, 1971.

Bradbury, Richard. "Frederick Douglass and the Chartists." In *Liberating Sojourn: Frederick Douglass and Transatlantic Reform*, edited by Alan J. Rice and Martin Crawford, 169–186. Athens: University of Georgia Press, 1999.

Saville, John. *1848: The British State and the Chartist Movement*. New York: Cambridge University Press, 1987.

—DAVID SIMONELLI

CHASE, SALMON PORTLAND (b. 13 January 1808; d. 7 May 1873), politician and jurist. Salmon Portland Chase was born in New Hampshire. He graduated from Dartmouth College in 1826 and eventually set up a successful law practice in Cincinnati, Ohio. After defending the freedom of several escaped slaves in Ohio, Chase became more involved in the growing antislavery movement of the 1830s and 1840s. He first affiliated himself with the Liberty Party and attempted to shape it into more than a single-issue antislavery organization. Throughout his political career, Chase was able to hold a curious balance between political idealism and aggressive self-promotion.

Salmon P. Chase, engraving after a photoprint by Mathew Brady that appeared in *Harper's Weekly* on 23 March 1861, at the time when Chase was made secretary of the treasury. As a member of Lincoln's cabinet, he influenced the wording of the Emancipation Proclamation, persuading the president to conclude it with an invocation of the "gracious favor of Almighty God." (Library of Congress.)

His performance in the 1848 convention that resulted in the formation of the Free-Soil Party was a case in point. Chase gained national prominence in his role as chair of the convention and proved to be an effective coalition builder. Although he was not satisfied with the narrow goals of the Free-Soil movement, he was willing to use it as a way to further his own political career. In 1849 Chase won election to the U.S. Senate, where he espoused antislavery ideas and sought to build bridges between Free-Soilers and the Democratic Party.

As a senator, Chase fought against any compromise between free and slave states. But despite strong credentials in abolition and a formidable record of denouncing racial injustice, he was bound by the paternalistic attitudes so common among nineteenth-century politicians. Chase and black abolitionists like Frederick Douglass could be close in their rejection of political compromise with slaveholders but did not see eye to eye on all issues involving race. For example, in 1850 Chase wrote Douglass, arguing that blacks and whites were "adapted to different latitudes and countries" and that therefore colonization was the best postslavery remedy. Although he believed that former slaves should not be forced out of the nation against their will, Chase supported the idea of repatriating emancipated slaves in the West Indies or South America. Given Chase's adamant defense of fugitive slaves throughout his legal and political career, his embrace of colonization seems philosophically, if not politically, incongruous.

Chase's attempts to unite antislavery and mainstream politics never caught wind in the early 1850s. This situation changed in 1854, when Senator Stephen Douglas of Illinois introduced legislation that repealed the Missouri Compromise of 1820 and opened up the new territories of Nebraska and Kansas to slavery under the guise of "popular sovereignty." The Kansas-Nebraska Act thus offered antislavery politicians both a common cause and a rallying cry for further opposition to the "Slave Power" forces at work in Congress. Chase found this legislation an "atrocious plot" to turn the territory into a "dreary region for despotism, inhabited by masters and slaves."

The following year Chase parlayed his opposition to the Kansas-Nebraska Act to help fuse antislavery elements of the Know-Nothing, Whig, and Democratic parties into a fusion ticket in Ohio, with himself as the gubernatorial candidate. He then steered his newfound supporters into the burgeoning Republican Party. He was a strong contender for the Republican presidential nomination in 1860, but his staunch antislavery credentials actually damaged his chances for national office. Instead, Chase's supporters won him a seat in the Senate in 1860.

Although antislavery dominated Chase's early political career, in 1861 things took a different turn when Abraham Lincoln chose him as his treasury secretary. With energy and innovation Chase attacked the fiscal crisis facing the federal government in the midst of the Civil War. He pushed for programs sponsoring federal "greenbacks," war bonds, and increased taxes to help cover the cost of the war; all these programs had a lasting impact on the financial system of the United States. Despite these successes, Chase fell out of favor with Lincoln and even sought to replace him as the Republican candidate for president in 1864. After a series of political clashes, Lincoln accepted Chase's resignation as secretary of the treasury and appointed him chief justice of the U.S. Supreme Court.

Chase's career on the Supreme Court began with a strong commitment to radical Reconstruction. For example, he advocated removing racial barriers to suffrage and ruled that Confederates had forfeited certain civil rights when they attempted to secede from the Union. When Chase presided over President Andrew Johnson's impeachment trial with impartiality, his relationship with Radical Republicans, including Douglass, was strained. He continued to lead the Supreme Court until his death in 1873, although his decisions took a more conservative tone later in his career.

[*See also* Antislavery Movement; Caribbean; Civil War; Colonization; Democratic Party; Douglas, Stephen A.; Douglass, Frederick; Free-Soil Party; Johnson, Andrew; Kansas-Nebraska Act; Know-Nothing Party; Liberty Party; Lincoln, Abraham; Republican Party; Supreme Court; *and* Whig Party.]

BIBLIOGRAPHY

Blue, Frederick. *Salmon P. Chase: A Life in Politics*. Kent, OH: Kent State University Press, 1987.

Maizlish, Stephen E. *The Triumph of Sectionalism: The Transformation of Ohio Politics, 1844–1856*. Kent, OH: Kent State University Press, 1983.

Niven, John. *Salmon P. Chase: A Biography*. New York: Oxford University Press, 1995.

—SEAN PATRICK ADAMS

CHAVIS, JOHN (b. 1763; d. 13 June 1838), a clergyman and teacher. John Chavis was born into a free African American family in Granville, North Carolina—a circumstance that alone made him historically unusual. He served, while a teenager, as a soldier in the Revolutionary War. Early accounts of his life state that he attended Princeton University, then known as the College of New Jersey. The historian Edgar W. Knight, in preparing a biography of Chavis in 1929, asked that institution to confirm his attendance. Princeton replied that although they had no actual records to verify that Chavis was a student, they believed that he had been and listed him as a nongraduate. Scholars now believe that Chavis was a private student of the college president, John Witherspoon, until that scholar's death in 1794. In 1795 Chavis began studies at Liberty Hall Academy (later Washington Academy and then Washington and Lee University) in Lexington, Virginia. Although this was unusual for an African American, it was not completely unheard of at the turn of the century, before the confluence of Eli Whitney's cotton gin, the ban on the slave trade, and the contradiction between slavery and the Enlightenment values of the American Revolution caused the hugely increased oppression of black Americans during the antebellum period in the South. He graduated no later than 1800, when the Presbyterian Church granted him a license to preach.

In 1801 the Acts and Proceedings of the General Assembly of the Presbyterian Church in the United States resolved that "Mr. John Chavis, a black man of prudence and piety, who has been educated and licensed to preach by the Presbytery of Lexington in Virginia, be employed as a missionary among people of his color, until the meeting of the next General Assembly." Chavis was the first African American ordained as a missionary minister in the Presbyterian Church. For the next thirty years he served as a circuit rider, preaching in churches all over North Carolina. To support himself, he opened a school, teaching both black and white, slave and free children. He separated the races when white parents complained, teaching white children by day at a rate of $2.50 per quarter and black children in the evening for a quarterly rate of $1.75. Among his white students were two future governors: Charles Manly of North Carolina and Abram Rencher of New Mexico. He formed a lifelong friendship with another white student, the future U.S. senator Willie

Portrait bust representing John Chavis, by Richard Weaver. Washington and Lee University commissioned the bust in 2002 for the Chavis Board Room. Since there were no extant pictures of Chavis, the artist's model was a man he saw on a street in Charlotteville and persuaded to sit for him. (Courtesy of Washington and Lee University.)

P. Mangum of North Carolina, who regarded him as a mentor and adviser. Unfortunately, the names of his African American students have not been preserved.

Throughout this time John Chavis was a respected member of his community, preaching in white churches and visiting in white homes. George Wortham, a white lawyer who was familiar with his sermons, wrote that "his manner was impressive, his explanations clear and concise, and his views, as I then thought and still think, entirely orthodox." Wortham also attested to Chavis's learning in theology, Latin, and Greek.

In August 1831 the antislavery rebellion led by Nat Turner in Southampton County, Virginia, triggered repressive measures across the South. In reaction to the insurrection the North Carolina legislature passed a law in 1832 forbidding any preaching by African American ministers. The Proceedings of the Orange Presbytery for that year contain that body's response to the situation in which this law put their black minister:

> A letter was received from Mr. John Chavis, a free man of color, and a licentiate under the care of the Presbytery, stating his difficulties and embarrassments in consequence of an act passed at the last session of the legislature of this state, forbidding free people of color to preach: whereupon, Resolved, That the Presbytery, in view of all the circumstances of the case, recommend to their licentiate to acquiesce in the decision of the legislature referred to until God in His providence shall open to him the path of duty in regard to the exercise of his ministry. (Weeks, p. 103)

John Chavis, by all accounts, never preached again.

The resultant loss of income put Chavis and his wife in financial difficulties, and he more than once turned to Mangum for help. Chavis's close relationships in the white community and his political conservatism have left him open to criticism by those who fail to consider all the circumstances of his life. His contemporaries, however, regarded him as a man of great intelligence and integrity who greatly benefited the community in which he lived.

[*See also* American Revolution; Colleges and African Americans; Education; Free African Americans to 1828; Missionary Movements; North Carolina, Colony and State; Presbyterians and African Americans; *and* Religion.]

BIBLIOGRAPHY

Berlin, Ira. *Slaves without Masters: The Free Negro in the Antebellum South*. New York: Oxford University Press, 1974.

Brawley, Benjamin. *Negro Builders and Heroes*. Chapel Hill: University of North Carolina Press, 1937.

Chavis-Othow, Helen. *John Chavis: African American Patriot, Preacher, Teacher, and Mentor (1763–1838)*. Jefferson, NC: McFarland, 2001.

Franklin, John Hope. *The Free Negro in North Carolina, 1790–1860*. Chapel Hill: University of North Carolina Press, 1943.

Kaplan, Sidney, and Emma Nogrady Kaplan. *The Black Presence in the Era of the American Revolution*. Rev. ed. Amherst: University of Massachusetts Press, 1989.

Knight, Edgar W. "Notes on John Chavis." *North Carolina Historical Review* 7 (1930): 326–345.

Weeks, Stephen. "John Chavis: Antebellum Negro Preacher and Teacher." *Southern Workman* (February 1914): 101–106.

—KATHLEEN THOMPSON

CHILD, LYDIA MARIA (b. 11 February 1802; d. 20 October 1880), writer, reformer, suffragist, and abolitionist. Lydia Maria Child's name was a household word in America for nearly fifty years, beginning in 1824 with the publication of her best-selling and controversial novel about interracial marriage, *Hobomok: A Tale of Early Times*. Child's pioneering work in many realms combined her passions for literary excellence and for social justice. In the literary arena she worked as a novelist, short-story writer, essayist, women's-advice book writer, children's writer, and magazine editor. As an activist and reformer she became a prominent advocate for both Native American and women's rights. Her path and passions crossed with those of Frederick Douglass through her work as an antislavery activist and as the editor of Harriet Jacobs's slave narrative *Incidents in the Life of a Slave Girl* (1860), the work for which she is probably best known today.

Child's writing about abolition began in 1833, when she published *An Appeal in Favor of That Class of Americans Called Africans*. The Child biographer Carolyn L. Karcher notes that *Appeal* "destroyed her literary popularity but propelled her to the forefront of the Abolitionist movement." Child seemed aware of the potential power—both constructive and destructive—of her text when she wrote in the preface to *Appeal*, "I am fully aware of the unpopularity of the task I have undertaken; but though I expect ridicule and censure, it is not in my nature to fear them." When her friendship with her close friend and fellow writer Catharine Sedgwick ruptured over this issue, she insisted in a letter to Sedgwick, dated 30 May 1834, that abolition had already become a total commitment for her:

> To the last hour of my life my voice and my pen shall be given to the work—by the way-side and by the fire-side—at the corners of streets, in the recesses of the counting room—in the publicity of the stage-coach, and the solitude of prayer. For this cause I wish to live—for this cause I am willing to die.

Child's powerful and persuasive indictment of slavery was the first major American work by a woman advocating immediate emancipation for all held in bondage, an end to all forms of discrimination, and racial equality and integration. The prominent editor and abolitionist Thomas Wentworth Higginson credited Child's *Appeal* in

Lydia Maria Child, photographed c. 1870. Although she is most famous for her antislavery writings, Child was interested in social reform in general, including education, religious tolerance, and the rights of Native Americans and women. She also wrote poetry, including the famous verse "Over the river, and through the wood, / To grandfather's house we go; / The horse knows the way, / To carry the sleigh, / Through the white and drifted snow." (Library of Congress.)

his memoirs as the text that converted him to the cause of abolition.

Child continued her abolitionist work through both her writing and her editing. She and her husband, David Lee Child, served as editors of the Garrisonian *National Anti-Slavery Standard* from 1841 to 1843, and her popular column for the *Standard* was published as a book—*Letters from New York* (1843). Child's antislavery activism reached its height during the controversy surrounding John Brown's 1859 raid on the federal arsenal at Harpers Ferry, Virginia. She wrote passionately in praise of Brown's heroism—although it should be noted that she objected to his methods—in her most widely distributed antislavery tract, *Correspondence between Lydia Maria Child and Gov. Wise and Mrs. Mason, of Virginia* (1860), which sold 300,000 copies. Child argued that there was no more time to hope for compromise with the South and urged northerners not to yield any further on the issue of slavery, even if it meant civil war.

Near the end of her life, in a letter dated 10 July 1880 to Theodore Dwight Weld, Child writes fondly and nostalgically about the early days of the abolitionist movement. She makes special mention of the power of Douglass's life and oratory: "Politicians said, 'The abolitionists exaggerate the evil; they do not know whereof they affirm'. . . . Then, like a cloud full of thunder and lightning, Frederic Douglass loomed above the horizon. *He* knew whereof he affirmed; for he had *been* a slave."

Douglass and Child shared the belief that the causes of women's rights and abolition were intertwined as issues of social justice and human rights. As the historian Waldo E. Martin Jr. explains, "The emancipation struggles of slaves and women became increasingly symbiotic as the tactics and ideology of antislavery began to function as a primary basis for those of women's rights." Douglass and Child thought that women should be accepted as equal participants in the abolitionist cause and should be eligible to serve in positions of leadership, rather than being confined to work in auxiliary societies—issues that split the U.S. abolitionist movement into several factions. In 1840 Child, along with Lucretia Coffin Mott and Maria Weston Chapman, was voted onto the executive committee of the American Anti-Slavery Society.

Child's final piece of nonfiction abolitionist writing was the reader *The Freedmen's Book* (1865), which was intended to encourage newly emancipated slaves' self-improvement. As Karcher explains, *The Freedmen's Book* is a "primer, anthology, history text, and self-help manual rolled into one . . . [that] anticipates twentieth-century educators in conceptualizing the teaching of literacy as a process that starts with the cultivation of students' pride in their own identity." Child includes an extended biography of Douglass in *The Freedman's Book* to show newly freed slaves the ways in which Douglass's life exemplified the overcoming of the evils of slavery. Interestingly, the Douglass biographer William S. McFeely notes that years earlier Child was one of many suspected of having been the ghostwriter for *Narrative of the Life of Frederick Douglass* (1845), as many critics and readers of Douglass's autobiography believed that "a slave boy could not have written the book."

Douglass wrote to Child on 30 July 1865 in response to her request to make use of materials from his autobiographical writings. Therein he agrees to allow her to do so and adds a strong statement about his belief that African Americans needed the right to vote: "I am just now deeply engaged in the advocacy of suffrage for the whole colored people of the South. I see little advantage in emancipation without this. Unfriendly legislation by a state may undo all the friendly legislation by the Federal Government." Douglass also pays tribute to Child in the chapter "Honor to Whom Honor" in his final autobiography, *Life and Times* (1892), which focuses on his benefactors. He writes:

> Kindred in spirit with Mrs. Mott was Lydia Maria Child. They both exerted an influence with a class of the American people which neither Garrison, Phillips, nor Gerrit Smith could reach. Sympathetic in her nature, it was easy for Mrs. Child to "remember those in bonds as bound with them"; and her "appeal for that class of Americans called Africans," issued, as it was, at an early stage in the anti-slavery conflict, was one of the most effective agencies in arousing attention to the cruelty and injustice of slavery. When, with her husband, David Lee Child, she edited the *National Anti-Slavery Standard*, that paper was made attractive to a broad circle of readers, from the circumstance that each issue contained a "Letter from New York," written by her on some passing subject of the day, in which she always managed to infuse a spirit of brotherly love and goodwill, with an abhorrence of all that was unjust, selfish and mean, and in this way won to antislavery many hearts which else would have remained cold and indifferent. (pp. 470–471)

Clearly, Douglass and Child were linked through their shared beliefs about universal human rights and human dignity and in their shared ability to express ideas both powerfully and persuasively.

[*See also* Abolitionism; American Anti-Slavery Society; Brown, John; Douglass, Frederick; Emancipation; Garrison, William Lloyd; Harpers Ferry Raid; Higginson, Thomas Wentworth; Jacobs, Harriet; *Life and Times of Frederick Douglass*; Mott, Lucretia Coffin; *Narrative of the Life of Frederick Douglass*; Oratory and Verbal Arts; Slave Narratives; Suffrage, Women's; Voting Rights; Weld, Theodore Dwight; Weston Sisters; *and* Women.]

BIBLIOGRAPHY

Child, Lydia Maria. *An Appeal in Favor of Americans Called Africans.* New York: Arno, 1968.

Child, Lydia Maria. *The Freedmen's Book.* New York: Arno, 1968.

Douglass, Frederick. "Letter to Lydia Maria Child." 30 July 1865. Letter 76, University of Rochester Frederick Douglass Project. http://www.lib.rochester.edu/rbk/douglass/letter76.stm.

Douglass, Frederick. *Life and Times of Frederick Douglass: His Early Life as a Slave, His Escape from Bondage, and His Complete History.* New York: Collier, 1962. Includes an introduction by Rayford W. Logan.

Karcher, Carolyn L. "Lydia Maria Child." In *American Short Story Writers before 1880*, edited by Bobby Ellen Kimbel. Vol. 74. Ann Arbor, MI: Gale, 1988: 43–53.

Karcher, Carolyn L., ed. *A Lydia Maria Child Reader.* Durham, NC: Duke University Press, 1997.

Martin, Waldo E., Jr. *The Mind of Frederick Douglass.* Chapel Hill: University of North Carolina, 1984.

McFeely, William S. *Frederick Douglass.* New York: Norton, 1991.

Meltzer, Milton, and Patricia G. Holland, eds. *Lydia Maria Child: Selected Letters, 1817–1880.* Amherst: University of Massachusetts Press, 1982.

Sedgwick, Catharine Maria. *Catharine Maria Sedgwick Papers, 1798–1867.* 3 collections. Boston: Massachusetts Historical Society, n.d.

—STEPHANIE A. TINGLEY

CHILDHOOD. The reconstruction of childhood as experienced by black girls and boys in early America is vastly instructive. Much can be told about the lives of children who were kidnapped in Africa, transported across the Atlantic Ocean, and sold in the Americas, and who survived to join labor forces, marry shipmates, form families, and create a lasting culture.

From Africa to North America. Girls and boys under eighteen years of age constituted a significant portion— an estimated 25 to 33 percent—of the more than 10 million Africans transported to the Americas between the seventeenth and nineteenth centuries. The majority of them had been born in West Africa and had previously spent their days performing simple chores, such as chasing birds from fields of grain, carrying water, and gathering kindling for their own families or for persons who owned them.

The African-born Ottobah Cugoano published a 1787 narrative chronicling the events leading to his enslavement in America. He begins, "I WAS early snatched away from my native country." He and eighteen or twenty other children had ventured into the woods to gather fruit, catch birds, and amuse themselves. Their idyllic childhood ended when several "great ruffians" detained them and accused them of infractions. The frightened children attempted to run away, but the assailants threatened them with weapons. Instead of answering charges at a hearing, the children were later sold to traders. The kidnappers exchanged Cugoano for a gun, cloth, and lead, catapulting him into the Middle Passage and bondage in America.

Several young Middle Passage survivors, including James Albert Ukawsaw Gronniosaw, Venture Smith, and Florence Hall, provided recollections of their early childhoods in Africa, enslavement in America, and the impact of separation from loved ones. Perhaps the most detailed and controversial of accounts was *The Interesting Narrative of the Life of Olaudah Equiano, or Gustavus Vassa, the African*. The work appeared in 1789, and questions persisted as to whether the author was indeed the West African–born Olaudah Equiano or the South Carolinian Gustavus Vassa. Regardless, the firsthand account could not be dismissed, because it was not at variance with other

"Kidnapping," engraving by Charles Goodman and Robert Piggot after Alexander Rider, 1822. This scene is depicted in Jesse Torrey's *American Slave Trade*, originally published in 1817. Between 1770 and 1820, as the northern states were dismantling slavery, numerous people were sold south, including free men and women who had been kidnapped by slave traders. (© Corbis.)

narratives describing the kidnappings, sales, and transoceanic voyages of Africans to America.

Unlike the adults—shackled men were confined to the ship's hold, and women traveled on the quarter deck—young boys and girls in the Middle Passage walked about the decks unfettered. Virtually all survivors' narratives mention some facet of the horrid conditions experienced during the passage, particularly the torrid weather, the rough seas, the poor quality of food, and sexual exploitation, along with high incidences of morbidity and mortality. Mutinies occurred on 10 percent of the voyages, during which 10 percent of the Africans present died.

In 1734 Samuel Waldo, the owner of the Massachusetts slaver *Affrica*, issued (with orthographic originality) a warning to the ship's captain, Samuel Rhodes, regarding the possibilities of trouble: "For your own safety as well as mine, putt not too much confidence in the Women nor Children lest they happen to be Instrumental to your being surprised which might be fatall." The owner of the British vessel *Henrietta Marie* was evidently mindful of potential mutinies supported by youngsters: he equipped his

eighteenth-century slaver with more than eighty pairs of shackles for child-size hands.

In fact, Cugoano's description of his Atlantic crossing refers to a plot among the boys and women to destroy the ship and die together; Cugoano claimed that his shipmates preferred death over life. A woman on board betrayed the potential mutineers, however, foiling their plan. The Africans aboard the Rhode Island slaver *Little George*, on the other hand, succeeded in gaining control of the sloop, killing several crew members and sailing back toward Africa in 1730. When Captain George Scott realized the peril he and the remaining crew faced, he sent the cabin boy, a lad of about ten years of age and probably African, up to the deck to negotiate with the African leaders. "But," wrote Scott, "they little Regarded our Message." While the young messenger came away from the ordeal physically unscathed, his psychic health was no doubt less secure.

With little to no concern for their captives' physical and mental welfare, traders transported innumerable girls and boys across the Atlantic and into bondage. Occasionally, children made up the majority of a slaver's cargo. In 1734 the *Margarita* carried ninety-three Africans: 87 percent were sixteen years old or younger, for an average age of 13.4 years. In 1790 the *Maria* sailed with eighty Africans on board: over 90 percent—forty-nine males and twenty-five females—were listed as children.

Becoming African Americans. The greater number of Africans transported to the Americas, irrespective of age, were males, making it difficult for men to find partners of African descent and form families if they so desired. Partly as a result, sexual intimacy often occurred between African men and white or Indian women. The question as to the status of their offspring—dubbed the "spurious issue"—was of great concern to Virginia's legislators. In 1662 the Virginia Assembly declared that all children born in the Old Dominion were bound or free according to the condition of their mothers; other colonies would later follow Virginia's lead. Enslaved black women bore enslaved black children, regardless of the status or color of the fathers, while the offspring of white or Indian women and enslaved African men were free—though still considered black.

By the time Virginia enacted its 1662 statute, the legal status of Africans in North America was becoming more and more clearly delineated. Rather than working several years as indentured servants and earning freedom after satisfying certain obligations, the majority of Africans were being relegated to bondage in perpetuity. By 1790 the number of free blacks stood at 59,557, while the enslaved population had escalated to 697,624.

While slavery and freedom existed concurrently in eighteenth-century North America, bondage in any capacity was not compatible with the increasingly popular natural rights ideology embracing liberty and equality. This incongruence became glaring in Revolutionary America, when the colonies waged war against England's "tyrannical hand." The African-born Phillis Wheatley, who was seven years old when she was taken from Africa and sold in New England, was well aware of the disjuncture, as evidenced by her poem "To the Right Honorable William, Earl of Dartmouth," which was included in her *Poems on Various Subjects* (1773). Wheatley posited that God had "implanted a Principle" called "Love of Freedom" in every breast and that this principle was "impatient of oppression and pants for Deliverance." The ideology behind the Revolutionary War and the efforts of slavery's opponents, especially Quakers—including Anthony Benezet and John Woolman—ultimately prevailed; states north of Delaware either ended slavery or made provisions for gradual abolition. While it appeared that the Revolutionary spirit had flowed generously from newly independent lawmakers to enslaved persons, such was not quite the case. New York, for example, granted unconditional freedom to blacks born before 1799; however, females born afterward remained in servitude until they reached twenty-five years

of age, while males were not free until they turned twenty-eight. New Jersey, Rhode Island, and Connecticut, meanwhile, granted freedom at eighteen years of age.

By contrast, the southern states made no provisions for abolition en masse, though possibilities for the individual attainment of freedom did exist. Self-purchases, legal suits, and public or private manumissions all contributed to increases in the free black population.

African American Childhoods. Despite legal differences in the statuses of free and unfree children, many commonalities existed in their parents' child-rearing practices, owing to their shared African heritage. Moreover, a significant number of freed persons had been slaves, and few of them could not count a relative or friend who remained in bondage. Female black newborns received their grandmothers' names more frequently than their own mothers'. A firstborn male often received either his father's given name or that of a grandfather. African naming traditions—like that of naming children for the day on which they were born—faded with the passing of time and as Africans began creating new cultural patterns in America.

In large southern agricultural households, enslaved mothers returned to work one month after giving birth to enslaved children. Their children ordinarily received care at the hands of persons too old or too young to assume full labor responsibilities. Black women who were enslaved in small households or who were free made other provisions for child care or simply carried offspring along.

Until they were old enough to assume work responsibilities equivalent to those of adults, children gathered kindling, hauled water, swept yards, or minded children younger than themselves. As youths matured, they were gradually introduced to agricultural, industrial, or domestic labor. Boys and girls not engaged in farmwork performed gender-specific chores: selected males learned the skills of artisans, while some females learned the skills associated with housewifery.

Adult family members or fictive kin—that is, people not related by blood but who shared "familial" relationships—across geographical regions taught enslaved and free youngsters alike behavior appropriate for children. Additionally, girls and boys learned to complete chores satisfactorily and avoid arbitrary punishment from owners, overseers, or employers. Many poor black children in the North, regardless of their status as free or enslaved and destined for freedom, did not live with their parents but served as apprentices in white families until they came of age. In the meantime they received food, clothing, shelter, and the fundamentals of common and religious educations in exchange for their labor.

Disaffection with work prompted some children, whether free or enslaved, to run away. A January 1780 advertisement in a New York paper offered a reward for the

"Slave Scene," woodcut c. early 1800s by Alexander Anderson (1775–1870), who has been described as the father of American wood engraving. His pleasant pastoral view contrasts sharply with the grim incident depicted by Goodman and Piggot. (Library of Congress.)

return of York, a twelve-year-old chimney sweep. Chimney sweeps, mostly small boys, worked under particularly harsh conditions: those who conquered fears of height were still subject to injuries from falling or from scraping against the rough mortar inside chimneys. Sores and bruises were marks of the trade. Chimney sweeps' bodies typically became calloused from lacerations, and the young boys had a tendency to suffer from cancer of the scrotum or tuberculosis.

Although the average runaway was a young male who fled alone, young females became fugitives as well. An eighteenth-century advertisement in New York's *Royal Gazette* sought "a Mulatto, or Quadroon Girl, about 14 years of age, named Seth, but calling herself Sall." According to the advertisement, the girl was given to claim

that "she is white and often paints her face to cover that deception." The girl certainly understood the social construction of race: black skin, of course, was associated with slavery, and white skin signaled freedom. The majority of children did not run away from slavery. Instead, through socialization processes at the hands of loved ones, black children learned to cope with the worst abuses of slavery or apprenticeships. Children benefited from the wisdom of elders; folktales told at nightfall offered entertainment and valuable lessons for survival, and religion provided solace.

The well-known abolitionist, author, and diplomat Frederick Douglass was born Frederick Augustus Washington Bailey to an enslaved woman on Maryland's Eastern Shore in 1818. In his second autobiography, *My*

Bondage and My Freedom (1855), Douglass wrote, "Children have their sorrows as well as men and women; and it would be well to remember this in our dealings with them. SLAVE-children *are* children, and prove no exceptions to the general rule."

As Douglass experienced the most horrific aspects of bondage—physical abuse and separation from loved ones—before reaching adulthood, his observation illuminates the fact that the majority of black children in nineteenth-century America did not enjoy a childhood, or an idyllic period during which they were sheltered from color- or class-based discrimination and adult responsibilities. In acknowledging the fragility of youth, Douglass seems to be making a case for protecting children, including enslaved ones, from social and economic pressures that would encroach upon their childhoods.

By the time Douglass was born the legal importation of Africans into the United States had ended (in 1808); the slave population was growing through natural increase, and the gender ratio among black Americans was showing greater parity. The number of enslaved people increased from 893,602 in 1800 to 1,538,022 in 1820; the free black population grew from 108,435 to 233,634 in the same time span. With that population growth the possibilities for creating African American communities and families became more favorable than they had been in the eighteenth century.

Douglass's earliest recollections with respect to his own family were of his affectionate maternal grandmother, Betsey Bailey, rather than of his immediate family. He had no associations with his father, whose identity was uncertain, and, his older siblings, Perry, Sarah, and Elizabeth, lived elsewhere. Douglass did not even remember ever seeing his mother during the day, as she worked twelve miles away. Despite the distance, she did make sporadic, brief visits to see her son after the workday ended, leaving early the following morning to arrive at her place of residence in time for work. Separations from enslaved mothers were less common than separations from fathers. An estimated 50 percent of children in bondage grew up without their fathers because the men were owned by someone else, had died, or were white and did not acknowledge paternity. Among the former slaves interviewed by Works Progress Administration (WPA) in the late 1930s, 10 percent claimed that their fathers were white.

In 1824 Douglass's owner ordered Betsey Bailey to carry her young grandson to another plantation, where he was to perform tasks considered appropriate for his age. The separation from his grandmother and poor treatment by that plantation's cook rendered him, a stranger in a strange land, inconsolable. The children around him, especially his own siblings, understood his plight, as they

had experienced similar dislocations as soon as they were old enough to work. Perry attempted to console Frederick with peaches and pears, but the distraught seven-year-old threw the fruit away. Afterward, their mother paid Douglass a memorable visit. Her intercession with the cook on his behalf taught him that he was not just a child but *"somebody's* child." He declared that being upon his mother's knee at that time made him more proud than a king upon a throne. The visit, her last, was short; Douglass was more alone than ever when she died in 1825.

Separations could be as socially chilling as death. Once relations parted, regardless of the causes, there were no

Two emancipated children, Isaac and Rosa, photographed in 1863. The mounting of the photograph is annotated "Proceeds for benefit of colored people." (Library of Congress.)

guarantees of reunions. Slave owners were aware of the impact of such disconnections and on occasions refrained from telling bound servants of pending moves. According to one owner, such news would "set them to crying and howling." The threat of separation—sometimes used as a control mechanism to force slaves, young and old, to toe the line—also heightened anxiety levels.

Some owners were sensitive to the emotional distress caused by separations and the threat thereof and sought to keep children and parents together. Ultimately, owners' interests in their own economic welfare and productivity determined whether enslaved families or communities would remain undisturbed. This was an aspect of slave ownership that the planter and founding father George Washington certainly would have taken into consideration; in 1799 he owned 316 men, women, and children, all scattered across five farms within his Mount Vernon estate. Brenda Stevenson, the author of *Life in Black and White*, concludes that the Virginian's priorities fostered the development of "a slave community characterized by a diversity of marriage styles and family and household structures." Marital unions with men and women owned by different persons, or "abroad marriages," single parenthood, and structural and functional matrifocality were not uncommon in Washington's household. Only 27 percent of the ninety-six slaves at his Mansion House Farm lived in traditional family units; none of the thirty-six slaves at his Union Farm lived in nuclear families.

Black Families and Parent-Child Relationships. Some free children lived in nuclear families, but those born to free mothers and enslaved fathers often lived in female-headed households. Such families could be unified if the women garnered sufficient resources to purchase their partners, the men purchased themselves, or owners emancipated them. In other cases two-parent households were disrupted when men accepted jobs that necessitated absences. For example, black men held 17 percent to 22 percent of the seafaring jobs based in Philadelphia between 1800 and 1820; percentages were comparable for black men in seafaring jobs in Providence, Rhode Island, and in New York City. The numbers of free black girls and boys under fourteen years of age in 1820, many of whom may have been sorely affected by paternal absences, were 45,027 and 46,848, respectively.

Black parents, enslaved and free and across geographical regions, certainly tried to prevent encroachments on their children's well-being, as evidenced by statements made in the WPA interviews and other sources. In these parents' views, innocuous behavior could stave off hardships. One enslaved parent wrote, "I want Elizabeth to be a good girl." Another cautioned his wife, "Raise your child up rite. . . . Learn them to be Smart and deacent and alow them to Sauce no person." Testimony from Henry Green, who was born in 1845, appeared in *God Struck Me Dead*, affirming that his father told him, "Whatever you do treat people right." It was generally perceived that "good," "smart," decent, and polite children who were predisposed to "treating people right" were not likely to incur the wrath of owners, overseers, or employers.

While an abundance of data about child rearing in the slave quarters can be found in the thousands of WPA interviews, no comparable body of information exists regarding the masses of free persons. Despite the void, it is reasonable to assume that particular facets of black culture and social mores, such as child-naming patterns, deference to elders, taboos against sexual intimacy with close relatives (including first cousins), and social responsibility to others, did not differ vastly according to legal status. Such an assumption is reasonable because blacks shared a common heritage and passed cultural values from one generation to another through socialization processes. Furthermore, many enslaved persons were emancipated before 1865, and few free African Americans could not count a relative or friend among those in bondage. For example, the freed North Carolinian Molly Horniblow cared for the enslaved children of her granddaughter, Harriet Jacobs, who would become one of the first black female autobiographers, for nearly seven of their formative years while their mother was in hiding.

Also of interest are the many northern black families who were affected by the gradual abolition laws instituted in the Revolutionary War era. Rhode Island and Connecticut passed laws declaring that the offspring of enslaved women born after 1 March 1784 would be legally free. In Connecticut these "freeborn" children were to provide uncompensated service to their mothers' owners until they reached twenty-five years of age. Rhode Island required shorter periods of service: eighteen years for girls and twenty-one for boys. Until the children came of age, of course, they, like their mothers, were essentially slaves. Afterward, the children were at liberty while their parents remained in bondage. Interactions and relationships between enslaved and free persons under such conditions doubtlessly excluded the possibility of separate and distinct patterns of socialization. Slavery had disappeared in the North by 1860, but it is unlikely that all freed persons or their offspring had erased their slave heritage by that time.

Workplace. The performance of obligatory chores truncated the childhoods of many black boys and girls. When Frederick Douglass initially entered the workforce, he was not mature enough to perform the most demanding tasks. He herded cows, swept the yard, and ran errands. His chores, like those of hundreds of thousands of other en-

Slave woman pleading for the return of her two small children. An illustration from Austa Malinda French's *Slavery in South Carolina and the Ex-Slaves; or, The Port Royal Mission*, 1862. At the time, a reviewer for *Continental Monthly*, though praising the content, observed: "The work is fairly printed, but, we regret to add, is disfigured by a mass of wretched woodcuts of the worst possible design, which look as if they had been gleaned from old Abolition tracts, and which we trust will be omitted from the next edition." (New York Public Library, Manuscripts, Archives, and Rare Books Division, Schomburg Center for Black Culture; Astor, Lenox, and Tilden Foundations.)

slaved children, were not uniform. Like the institution of slavery itself, tasks were not monolithic but varied according to age, gender, and the size of an owner's household. Additionally, geographical regions determined whether children picked cotton, cut sugarcane, harvested hemp, winnowed rice, or suckled tobacco. Finally, the jobs of enslaved children in urban areas necessarily differed from those of enslaved children in the countryside.

Variations aside, young laborers were expected to fulfill demands in a timely manner. In *My Bondage*, Frederick Douglass remembered of his adolescence, "We were worked in all weather. It was never too hot or too cold; it could never rain, blow hail, or snow, too hard for us to work in the field." If tasks were not performed satisfactorily, laborers were subjected to punishment.

In the end Douglass preferred Baltimore, Maryland, over plantations. That city—where he lived for a brief period in 1826 and then again in the late 1830s—and other urban areas were centers of wider varieties of activities and opportunities. Baltimore itself was a unique southern city in that its population of free blacks was larger than that of slaves. Term slaves, or people who were not free but served owners for specified periods before being emancipated, were common in Baltimore. The combina-

tion of the large free black population and term slavery made it nearly impossible to maintain the traditional institution of slavery in the port city; fugitives young and old faded into anonymity with the help of free blacks.

Many free black children in Baltimore and elsewhere performed chores for hire and returned to their humble abodes when finished; other children lived in the homes of employers. In 1814 the fourteen-year-old Nancy Prince accepted a "service" job with a Massachusetts family of seven. In her narrative Prince claims that the employer was unkind and describes the work, especially the laundry, as "very severe." She remained on the job for only three months before it took a toll on her health. Another account of a child in domestic service, albeit in historical fiction—Harriet Wilson's 1859 *Our Nig; or, Sketches from the Life of a Free Black, in a Two-Story White House, North, Showing That Slavery's Shadows Fall Even There*—contains similarities to Prince's narrative. *Our Nig* focuses on the protagonist Frado, a young, free, black servant who experiences abusive treatment at the hands of white employers in the North. Taken together, Prince's narrative and Wilson's fictional autobiography offer suggestions about the lives of northern free children, particularly girls, in domestic service.

Boys often entered apprenticeships that involved agricultural work or craft skills. The story of the talented Robert S. Duncanson, born in Seneca County, New York, is informative. Born into a family of carpenters and house painters in 1821, Robert and three of his four brothers gained skills and work experience as apprentices. In 1838 Robert and a friend, John Gamblin, placed a long-running advertisement in the *Monroe Gazette* (Missouri) announcing the establishment of "A New Firm" and soliciting business as "painters and glaziers." Duncanson's creative talent and interest in fine art eventually led him into a career as a landscape artist in the traditions of the Hudson River and Ohio River valleys. Few apprenticeships led to such distinguished careers as those of Duncanson or the slave-born South Carolinian William "April" Ellison, who became a successful cotton gin manufacturer, but indentures at least offered possibilities for gaining useful skills and literacy.

Educational Opportunities. Frederick Douglass first received reading lessons from his "young mistress" Sophia Auld; when the lessons ended because her disapproving husband learned about them, Douglass furthered his own education. Whenever he met white boys whom he knew to be literate, Douglass bragged that he could read and write as well, or better. This ploy at one-upmanship set the stage for his advancement. Many enslaved boys and girls learned from white children, such as the former slave and autobiographer Susie King Taylor, who attributed her literacy to lessons given over several months by Katie O'Connor.

Following the 1831 insurrection led by the literate, enslaved preacher Nat Turner, many southern legislatures prohibited the teaching of blacks to read and write. Enforcement was never uniform; by 1860 an estimated 5 percent of the enslaved population had become literate. An untold number kept their literacy secret out of the fear of being punished if their abilities were verified. One former slave specifically told WPA interviewers that "the White folks feared" slaves' attaining an education; in the view of white owners, knowledge would make blacks unfit for slavery.

Regardless of owners' opinions, many enslaved children put forth herculean efforts to learn to read and write. Literacy was liberating and could unlock the mysteries of religion and science and lead to a life unfettered by ignorance. An early reading lesson exposed Frederick Douglass to *The Columbian Orator*, a schoolbook containing, among

A freed slave escorting her children to school. From Austa French's *Slavery in South Carolina and the Ex-Slaves; or, The Port Royal Mission.* The "Port Royal experiment" began a few months after federal forces had seized the area in 1861, when some fifty abolitionists arrived there to tutor the freed African Americans. Austa French was the wife of a leading member of this program, Reverend Mansfield French; her book, appearing in 1862, was an early account of the project. (New York Public Library, Manuscripts, Archives, and Rare Books Division, Schomburg Center for Black Culture; Astor, Lenox, and Tilden Foundations.)

other speeches, a brief dialogue between a slave and slaveholder that effectively served as a forum for pro- and antislavery arguments. Reading the text, in addition to interacting with white boys who rather than defending slavery encouraged him to think he would eventually be free, made Douglass restive.

Through literacy black children learned much about the abridgment of their rights, which many sought to end. In 1855 Matilda A. Jones, once a pupil at Myrtilla Miner's School for Colored Girls in Washington, D.C., understood that the black community expected free persons to acquire an education and use it in the interest of their people. "Knowledge," said the black activist Maria W. Stewart, an advocate of the higher branches of education, "is power."

The acquisition of an education for many free children in the North and the South was haphazard at best. Black nuns, such as the Oblate Sisters of Baltimore and the Sisters of the Holy Family in New Orleans, proselytized through education and succeeded in teaching many children but did not appeal to persons unwilling to accept Catholicism. Other private schools were available, but tuition costs were often prohibitive.

Public schools certainly existed in some northern cities but were generally segregated. Benjamin Roberts sued the city of Boston in 1849 on behalf of his five-year-old daughter Sarah, who had to walk past five white elementary schools before reaching the overcrowded and badly deteriorated Smith Grammar School for blacks. Roberts based the suit on an 1845 statute saying that children unlawfully excluded from the city's schools could seek relief. Charles Sumner and the black lawyer Robert Morris represented the plaintiff in *Roberts v. City of Boston* (1849) before the Supreme Judicial Court of Massachusetts, then headed by the chief justice Lemuel Shaw. Sumner argued not only that Sarah was disadvantaged by attending Smith Grammar School but also that white children were harmed by segregation: "Their hearts, while yet tender with childhood, are necessarily hardened by this conduct," said Sumner, and "their subsequent lives, perhaps, bear enduring testimony to this legalized uncharitableness."

Chief Justice Shaw, a former member of the Boston School Committee, disagreed and maintained that segregation was for the good of both black and white children. In his opinion, the school committee, which supported the doctrine of "separate but equal," was solely responsible for the operation of the city's schools. Roberts did not win relief through the suit; however, in 1855 the state legislature voted to end segregation in Boston's public schools.

Rather than fighting in court or having their children endure local segregation, black families with resources often sent their offspring to schools elsewhere, as was the case with Fredrick Douglass's daughter, Rosetta. Charlotte Forten, the freeborn granddaughter of James Forten, the prosperous Philadelphia sailmaker and abolitionist, attended school in Salem, Massachusetts, in the 1850s; to do so she boarded with the well-known abolitionist Charles Lenox Remond and his wife. Incidentally, Remond's parents, John and Nancy, had moved to Newport, Rhode Island, in the 1830s to provide their children, Charles and Sarah, with better educational opportunities.

The curricular offerings in public and private schools included traditional courses in reading, writing, arithmetic, geography, and spelling. At Philadelphia's Institute for Colored Youth, a classical high school founded in 1837 by the Society of Friends, pupils studied a greater variety of subjects. The freeborn Sarah Mapps Douglass, the highly respected teacher in charge of the girl's department at the institute, enrolled in medical classes at the Ladies Institute of Pennsylvania Medical University between 1855 and 1858 to introduce new subjects, including physiology, into the Institute for Colored Youth's curriculum.

Based on comments about her final examinations, Helen Amelia Loguen studied an expansive curriculum. The daughter of the slave-born Jermain Wesley Loguen, an African Methodist Episcopal Zion bishop, and a resident of Syracuse, New York, Helen wrote on 10 April 1862:

> Spring has brought with it as usual, the ever dreaded, yearly school examinations, *dreaded* because they are so *very tedious*. Monday I thought of nothing but Chloride of Sodium, Nitrate of Silver detection of arsenic, uses of Zinc etc etc; Tuesday, Parlez-vous franáais? Comment-vous appelez-vouz? And Je me porte tres bien, yesterday oh! terrible thought Plane Trigonometry; do you wonder then that last night I dreamed of being in France . . . trying to show that Chemistry is one of the most useful and interesting studies imaginable and lastly I was alone in some queer place trying to accertain the height of a 'fort on a distant hill inaccessable on account of an intervening swamp.' O! how refreshing on awaking this morning to know that all *such* is for a time past and that vacation is close at hand. (Woodson, p. 541)

Loguen's curriculum appears free of gender-bound notions suggesting that girls were not suited for study of the sciences. She married Frederick Douglass's son Lewis in 1869 and graduated from the Syracuse University College of Medicine in 1876.

Abolition. Black children in northern schools often endured hostile treatment from classmates and the larger community. In 1832 Prudence Crandall, a Quaker who had a well-established reputation as an educator, admitted the seventeen-year-old African American Sarah Harris to her Canterbury, Connecticut, school. When white parents protested by withdrawing their daughters, Crandall filled their places with African Americans. Had she opened a "college for the spread of contagious diseases," wrote one journalist, the community would not have been more agitated. Crandall received one insult after another, ranging from local merchants refusing to sell her the supplies she needed to unknown persons dumping manure into her well. Crandall was arrested for violating the hastily passed 1833 Black Law prohibiting the founding of schools for blacks. The town's hostility eventually forced the Quaker woman to give up her idea of educating blacks. Given the circumstances, Charlotte Forten expressed amazement at the fact that blacks were not misanthropes as a result of the ubiquitous racism and violations of their civil rights. She hoped to be a writer and promised that if ever favored by the muse, her first effort would be to erect a literary shrine of liberty for her people.

Forten's commitment to social reform was not unusual in a family dedicated to abolition over three generations. Children who came of age in homes where parents and other influential relatives advocated the abolition of slavery were likely to join in the movement. Thomas and Susan Paul, Isaac and Mary Ann Shadd, Charles Lenox and Sarah Parker Remond, and Frances Ellen Watkins could all link their social consciousness to adult reformers or abolitionists who recognized societal ills and attempted to eradicate them.

Abolitionists played a crucial role in sensitizing the public to the wrongs of slavery and met with some success in drawing attention to and thwarting the destruction of families, the mistreatment of children, and the abuse of women. Abolitionist involvement with the 1848 case concerning two young black girls, Emily and Mary Edmondson, who fell into the hands of slave traders after a failed escape attempt, gained widespread attention. Traders in Alexandria, Virginia, had set an unusually high price on the thirteen- and fifteen-year-old girls designated as "fancy girls" for "southern connoisseurs in sensualism." Through the combined efforts of certain churches in Washington, D.C., as well as Henry Ward Beecher and the New York Anti-Slavery Society, the Edmondsons were purchased and freed. While publicity led to the removal of these two girls from enslavement and certain sexual abuse, an untold number of other enslaved girls and boys were subject to exploitation at the hands of lecherous owners.

The day-to-day activities of abolitionists involved with the Underground Railroad, which assisted fugitives in their flight, received less publicity because of the secret nature of the operations. William Still, an Underground Railroad conductor in Philadelphia, recorded notes about the "hairbreadth escapes and death struggles" of fugitives of all ages. His massive tome entitled *The Underground Rail Road*, published in 1872, mentions Susan Stewart and Josephine Smith. The twelve-year-old Smith, a perpetual runaway, feared being sold again but offered no explanation for her companion, Josephine; regardless, the girls fled together and perhaps comforted each other.

Based on the extant number of slaveholders in 1860, as many as fifty thousand slaves may have run away annually if at least one person per owner fled. Regardless of the size of the fugitive population, the majority, unlike Frederick Douglass, failed to permanently liberate themselves, while their owners simultaneously failed to eradicate their slaves' collective desire for freedom. Nevertheless, neither slaves nor slave owners ever ceased trying to fulfill their own desires and interests as long as slavery existed.

Civil War and Reconstruction. By 1860 the enslaved population had increased to nearly 4 million, and 56 percent of slaves were less than twenty years of age. Many were too young to understand the reality of the Civil War and the tumultuous conditions it created; others viewed Union soldiers as liberators and thus emancipated themselves by fleeing to Union lines. A small number of young boys became drummers and accompanied soldiers on maneuvers.

In the midst of the Civil War, President Abraham Lincoln issued the Emancipation Proclamation, effective 1 January 1863, which freed slaves in areas in rebellion against the U.S. government. Pick Gladdney, born 15 May 1856, remembered the 1 January 1863 "speeching" in Maybinton, South Carolina, where he climbed a tree for a better view. He claimed to remember nothing about the reading of the proclamation but had vivid recollections of "the brass band what let out so much music"—the first he had ever seen. Considering his age of six years and his fascination with a melody rather than the message, it is understandable that he said, "Being free never meant nothing to us chaps, cause we never had no mind fer all such as that nohow."

Like many of his young enslaved contemporaries, Gladdney had probably yet to endure the harshest realities of bondage—arduous labor, physical and emotional abuse, and family separation. The December 1865 passage of the Thirteenth Amendment, which constitutionally abolished involuntary servitude, ensured that Pick Gladdney, his peers, and their offspring would never experience the harshest realities of bondage.

Newly freed blacks were ostensibly at liberty to form families, earn livings, attend churches of their choice, and learn to read and write without interference from whites. Yet, while the U.S. Constitution no longer sanctioned the ownership of human beings, some whites refused to acknowledge this monumental economic and social change. In their efforts to build a future based on the past, an untold number of former slave owners bound thousands of

"Christmas Eve—Getting Ready for Santa Claus," wood engraving from *Harper's Weekly*, 30 December 1876. (Library of Congress.)

newly freed children to lengthy indentures. Court officials and agents for the Bureau of Refugees, Freedmen, and Abandoned Lands, commonly called the Freedmen's Bureau, were quick to "apprentice" youngsters, who were considered "orphans" if separated from parents or if officials deemed the parents incapable of providing financial support. Such arbitrary actions based on insidious motives were tantamount to reenslavement.

Complaint books kept by Freedmen's Bureau agents in the Old South teem with children's protests regarding the arduous work and physical abuse they endured. Additionally, many parents, male and female, objected to the conditions under which their children lived or worked and registered their disaffection. Abused children were quick to run away, and parents made haste to prevent their return to hateful "masters" and "mistresses."

Black children who were subjected to such negative circumstances obtained new dimensions of freedom following the passage of the 1866 Civil Rights Act and the outlawing of black codes—southern statutes passed immediately after the Civil War that were designed primarily to circumscribe the liberty of newly freed people. In the meantime the North Carolina Supreme Court's decision in the case concerning Harriet and Eliza Ambrose in 1867 signaled the death knell for apprenticeships in the Tar Heel State. That case began in December 1865 when Daniel Lindsay Russell Sr., a planter, judge, and state legislator, bound Eliza, Harriet, and John Allen in apprenticeships without the consent of their parents, Hepsey Saunders and Wiley Ambrose, whom he had once owned.

Russell's actions violated the Civil Rights Act of 1866; Freedmen's Bureau lawyers represented the children in the case officially designated *In the Matter of Harriet Ambrose and Eliza Ambrose*. The lawyers claimed the girls to be members of a legitimate household and not legally subject to indentures. The attorneys entered a second plea highlighting the children's rights as citizens.

The court declared that all persons involved in apprenticeship negotiations, including children, had to be present at the time of binding for the "agreement" to constitute a legal contract; otherwise the indentures were null and void. The 1867 decision recognized the rights of children and ended the binding of freed children in the same manner as had emancipation. Once entirely independent of forced servitude in North Carolina and elsewhere, former slaves were more at liberty to enjoy the fruits of emancipation. Children, along with their parents and other loved ones, were free to determine how they would spend their lives as American citizens.

[*See also* Africanisms; Auld Family; Bailey Family; Beecher, Henry Ward; Benezet, Anthony; Black Family; Class; Cugoano, Quobna Ottabah; Demographics; Education; Emancipation; Equiano, Olaudah; Folklore; Forten, James; Free African Americans to 1828; Free African Americans before the Civil War (North); Free African Americans before the Civil War (South); Freedmen; Fugitive Slaves; Gender; Gronniosaw, Indentured Servitude; Jacobs, Harriet; James Albert Ukawsaw; Kidnapping; Literature; Loguen, Jermain Wesley; Manumission Societies;

Marriage, Masculinity; Mixed; Racism; Remond, Charles Lenox; *Roberts v. City of Boston*; Sexuality; Skin Color; Slave Narratives; Slave Trade; Slavery; Smith, Venture; Still, William; Thirteenth Amendment; Underground Railroad; Urbanization; Violence against African Americans; Wheatley, Phillis; Women; Woolman, John *and* Work.]

BIBLIOGRAPHY

Andrews, William L. *To Tell a Free Story: The First Century of Afro-American Autobiography, 1760–1865*. Urbana: University of Illinois Press, 1986.

Andrews, William L., ed. *Sisters of the Spirit: Three Black Women's Autobiographies of the Nineteenth Century*. Bloomington: Indiana University Press, 1986. The autobiographical writings include some discussions of the childhoods of free persons.

Curtin, Philip D., ed. *Africa Remembered: Narratives by West Africans from the Era of the Slave Trade*. Madison: University of Wisconsin Press, 1967. A useful anthology with firsthand accounts.

Douglass, Frederick. *My Bondage and My Freedom* (1855). New York: Dover, 1969.

Equiano, Olaudah. *The Interesting Narrative of the Life of Olaudah Equiano, Written by Himself*. Edited by Robert J. Allison. Boston: Bedford Books of St. Martin's Press, 1995. A detailed account of Middle Passage experiences by a survivor who endured the voyage as a child.

Forten, Charlotte L. *The Journals of Charlotte Forten Grimké*. Edited by Brenda Stevenson. New York: Oxford University Press, 1988. Valuable as commentary by a young girl both before and during the Civil War.

Franklin, John Hope, and Loren Schweninger. *Runaway Slaves: Rebels on the Plantation*. New York: Oxford University Press, 1999. An excellent study of fugitive slaves across geographical and chronological boundaries.

Johnson, Clifton H., ed. *God Struck Me Dead: Religious Conversion Experiences and Autobiographies of Ex-slaves*. Philadelphia: Pilgrim Press, 1969.

Jones, Howard. *Mutiny on the "Amistad": The Saga of a Slave Revolt and Its Impact on American Abolition, Law, and Diplomacy*. New York: Oxford University Press, 1987. Chronicles a mutiny and offers insight about several children on board the ship.

Mannix, Daniel P., and Malcolm Cowley. *Black Cargoes: A History of the Atlantic Slave Trade, 1518–1865*. New York: Viking Press, 1962.

King, Wilma. *Stolen Childhood: Slave Youth in Nineteenth-Century America*. Bloomington: Indiana University Press, 1995.

Melish, Joanne Pope. *Disowning Slavery: Gradual Emancipation and "Race" in New England, 1780–1860*. Ithaca, NY: Cornell University Press, 1998. An essential text for discussion of northern slavery and its demise.

Mintz, Steven. *Huck's Raft: A History of American Childhood*. Cambridge, MA: Harvard University Press, 2004. A comprehensive study placing African American children in historical context.

Morgan, Edmund S. *American Slavery, American Freedom: The Ordeal of Colonial Virginia*. New York: Norton, 1975. Presents an excellent discussion of the development of slavery.

Nash, Gary B. *Forging Freedom: The Formation of Philadelphia's Black Community, 1720–1840*. Cambridge, MA: Harvard University Press, 1988. An excellent source regarding the building of a black community and the presence of enslaved and emancipated persons.

Palmer, Colin A. *Human Cargoes: The British Slave Trade to Spanish America, 1700–1739*. Urbana: University of Illinois Press, 1981.

Rhodes, Jane. *Mary Ann Shadd Cary: The Black Press and Protest in the Nineteenth Century*. Bloomington: Indiana University Press, 1998.

Sheinin, David. "Prudence Crandall, *Amistad*, and Other Episodes in the Dismissal of Connecticut Slave Women from American History." In *Discovering the Women in Slavery: Emancipating Perspectives on the American Past*, edited by Patricia Morton. Athens: University of Georgia Press, 1996: 132–133.

Sterling, Dorothy, ed. *We Are Your Sisters: Black Women in the Nineteenth Century*. New York: Norton, 1984. Contains primary accounts from enslaved and free women, with insight into social, political, and economic conditions.

Still, William. *The Underground Rail Road: A Record of Facts, Authentic Narratives, Letters, Etc., Narrating the Hardships, Hairbreadth Escapes and Death Struggles of the Slaves in Their Efforts for Freedom, as Related by Themselves and Others, or Witnessed by the Author; Together with Sketches of Some of the Largest Stockholders, and Most Liberal Aiders and Advisers, of the Road*. Philadelphia: Porter and Coates, 1872.

Woodson, Carter G., ed. *The Mind of the Negro as Reflected in Letters Written during the Crisis, 1800–1860*. New York: Russell and Russell, 1969.

—WILMA KING

CHRISTIANA INCIDENT. On 11 September 1851 in Christiana, Lancaster County, Pennsylvania, a violent confrontation broke out between proslavery and antislavery forces. Commonly referred to as the Christiana Riot, the encounter had its roots in the escape of four slaves—Noah Buley, Nelson Ford, George Hammond, and Joshua Hammond—from the Maryland plantation owned by Edward Gorsuch. Although Gorsuch reputedly was a good master, the slaves fled across the state line to Pennsylvania on 6 November 1849 after Gorsuch learned that they were stealing wheat from the plantation's storehouse. A resident of Christiana informed him a short time later that his slaves were taking refuge in the small town.

In Lancaster County the escaped slaves plunged into a volatile world of white slave catchers and armed black defenders. Many Pennsylvanians were weary of slaves' escaping from Maryland. Whites from Lancaster County formed a vigilante group to apprehend runaways around the time of the passage of the federal Fugitive Slave Law in September of 1850. On the other hand, Pennsylvania's large Quaker population had long participated in antislavery activities, and many Quakers openly aided runaway slaves, including Gorsuch's. To add to this mix, a Christiana resident, William Parker, himself a runaway slave from Maryland, had formed a black self-defense group to counter the vigilantes. Parker shielded Buley, Ford, and Joshua Hammond in his home, and they soon joined his defensive group to prevent the capture of runaways, themselves included.

The forces of the proslavery vigilantes and the antislavery Quakers and Parker's defensive group came into conflict in September of 1851 when Edward Gorsuch mounted a well-armed expedition to reclaim his slaves.

"The Christiana Tragedy," wood engraving from William Still, *The Underground Rail Road*, 1872. African Americans are shown firing on slave-catchers at the home of William Parker on 11 September 1851. Two of the slave hunters—Edward and Dickerson Gorsuch—were killed. (Library of Congress.)

Gorsuch secured the assistance of his son Dickinson, his cousin Joshua Gorsuch, his nephew Thomas Pearce, and two neighbors. The men arrived in Philadelphia on 8 September and obtained four arrest warrants for the slaves under the edicts of the Fugitive Slave Law. A deputy U.S. marshal, Henry Kline, assumed leadership of the posse and hired two Philadelphia police officers to aid in the fugitives' capture.

The men traveled in four groups to conceal their approach to Christiana, but the expedition was fraught with problems. Kline was a well-known slave catcher, and local people warned Parker of the impending danger. Along the way, the two policemen abandoned the posse and returned to Philadelphia. To add to their tribulations, the party took longer to reach Parker's home than planned. When they finally arrived, it was nearly daylight on the morning of 11 September. The final setback occurred when Nelson Ford stumbled upon Gorsuch at the outskirts of Parker's property. Ford ran back to the house to arouse his associates. With his presence revealed, Gorsuch brazenly entered the house and demanded that Parker return his slaves. Parker denied that any of the slaves were present, but Gorsuch had seen Ford and was determined to retrieve him. Gorsuch and Kline attempted to ascend the stairs to the second story, where the black defenders had secured themselves, but a barrage of items thrown by the occupants repelled the two men. Parker then instructed his wife to sound the alarm to alert the surrounding community of the impending attack. When she did so, the posse opened fire on her. The defenders returned fire.

The noise alerted local residents, and over seventy people rushed to Parker's home, including Buley. Kline insisted that the posse retreat, but Gorsuch refused. At a pause in the shooting, one of the former slaves exchanged angry words with Gorsuch. The dialogue led the man to pistol-whip Gorsuch, who fell to the ground. Other blacks then attacked Gorsuch, and he was beaten and shot repeatedly. Dickinson rushed to his father's aid, but he, too, was clubbed and shot. Kline and the other members of the posse beat a hasty retreat. Pearce was shot five times as he fled. Joshua Gorsuch received innumerable blows from the crowd as he ran from the scene, but he was not shot. The group of defenders chased the men out of the town. Edward Gorsuch died at the scene.

After the battle, the fugitives from Gorsuch's plantation escaped to safety in Canada. Parker and several other former slaves fled to New York, where the renowned black abolitionist Frederick Douglass aided their escape to Canada. For Douglass, the response of Christiana's residents exemplified his opinions regarding slavery. He equated the actions of those involved in the incident with those of the American revolutionaries, particularly the Minutemen. Further, the episode demonstrated the hypocrisy of the Fugitive Slave Law, which rewarded slave owners and slave catchers and punished those in search of freedom. Above all else, for Douglass and many other Americans, the Christiana Incident confirmed the slaves' desire for freedom and their willingness to fight for it.

A number of the Christiana defenders were later arrested for treason for violating the Fugitive Slave Law. Treason proved a difficult charge for the prosecution to substantiate. Robert C. Grier, a U.S. Supreme Court justice who presided over the case as a circuit justice, noted that the participants in the Christiana Incident were clearly guilty of riot and murder. But Grier acknowledged that the prosecution had offered no proof of a conspiracy to resist the laws of the United States and that opposing the Fugitive Slave Law did not constitute treason. A jury took fifteen minutes to find the defendants not guilty.

[*See also* Canada; Frederick Douglass; Fugitive Slave Law of 1850; Riots and Rebellions; *and* Society of Friends (Quakers).]

BIBLIOGRAPHY

Bacon, Margaret Hope. *Rebellion at Christiana.* New York: Crown, 1975.
Finkelman, Paul. "The Treason Trial of Castner Hanway." In *American Political Trials*, edited by Michael R. Belknap. Westport, CT: Greenwood Press, 1994.
Katz, Jonathan. *Resistance at Christiana: The Fugitive Slave Rebellion, Christiana, Pennsylvania, September 11, 1851; A Documentary Account.* New York: Thomas Y. Crowell, 1974.
Slaughter, Thomas P. *Bloody Dawn: The Christiana Riot and Racial Violence in the Antebellum North.* New York: Oxford University Press, 1991.

—BRIAN D. BEHNKEN

CHRISTIAN RECORDER.

The *Christian Recorder*, which began publication in Philadelphia in July 1852, was not the first African American newspaper; nevertheless, it was an important milestone in the history of black American journalism. The newspaper was purchased from Martin Delany, one of the nineteenth century's most dedicated and independent-minded black community builders. Drawing its financial support and editorial leadership from the African Methodist Episcopal (AME) Church rather than relying entirely upon subscribers, philanthropists, or the variable fortunes and interests of an individual owner, the *Christian Recorder* was the first black paper sponsored by an organization. The AME sponsorship allowed the paper to develop and maintain a consistent mission and distribution network and also to withstand the economic difficulties and editorial limitations that plagued many nineteenth-century newspapers. The *Christian Recorder* was the only black newspaper to publish through the Civil War, providing an array of information and services that gained it a loyal following. With only short interruptions, the *Christian Recorder* published continuously into the twenty-first century.

Freedom's Journal, the first African American newspaper, began publication in 1827 and foundered a few years later when its editors, Samuel Cornish and John Brown Russwurm, parted over the question of whether black Americans should settle in Africa. Then came the *Colored American*, begun in 1837, which survived only five years. In 1843 Martin Delany, a renowned leader among African Americans, became concerned that with the demise of the *Colored American* the black community had no published voice. He therefore founded the *Mystery*, but it, too, ran into economic difficulties, as there were simply not enough black people who could read and who had the economic resources to support the paper.

Delany had close ties with the AME Church, which relaunched the publication, renaming it the *Christian Recorder*. The first editor was the Reverend M. M. Clark, one of the few AME ministers with a college education. Unable to make the paper economically stable, Clark resigned after two years and nineteen issues. Determined to keep a black voice alive, the AME leadership assigned a new editor, the Reverend Jabez Pitt Campbell, who lasted two years and twenty-four issues. The AME Church then considered redesigning the paper to become a monthly magazine but felt that there was sufficient commitment to more frequent publication and to news reporting, rather than simply to Christian doctrine, for it to maintain the newspaper format—even though editors changed frequently and economic stability would not come until after the Civil War.

From the outset the *Christian Recorder* developed and maintained a focused mission: to not only discuss religion but also educate its readership, publishing articles about science, literature, and morality in a voice and from a perspective that would appeal to all of the black community. While serving as editor, Clark declared that the paper would make no "social or geographical distinction among our people of East or West or North or South, but shall be the equal friend of all." The editor's vision was large: "that families and individuals may have books made of it and preserved for historical reference."

Though the majority of African Americans could not read, the messages of black unity, industry, and the struggle for civil rights that were published in black newspapers were in turn distributed through the conversations of those who could read. Black newspapers were mostly distributed throughout the North, but by the mid-nineteenth century the *Christian Recorder* could be found in AME churches in the South as well. Articles by women as well as by men discussed black education, politics, and the struggle for the vote. Always, however, the underlying theme was the importance of African American unity and the need for black Americans to embrace northerners and southerners, educated and "unfortunate," as one community.

By the late 1850s the newspaper was also part of the AME mission effort in Liberia, and during the Civil War and Reconstruction the paper quoted and encouraged black politicians, many of whom were leaders in the AME denomination. The AME bishop Henry McNeal Turner, whose efforts to encourage emigration to Africa culminated in the 1878 plan to sail the *Azor* to settle freed people there, also served as the business manager of the *Christian Recorder* in the 1870s. It was Turner's skill that finally stabilized the paper's finances, and he published frequently in its pages, encouraging emigration. True to its mission to serve all, the *Christian Recorder* also published the ideas of those who opposed emigration. In these years the paper engaged in discussion about whether to use the word "African" in its name or to stress the fact that black people were Americans.

Perhaps the most critical work of the *Christian Recorder* occurred during the Civil War and Reconstruction. Though publication remained erratic, advertisements from family members looking for lost children, parents, or siblings were so useful that the service continued for decades after the war. Reports of black conventions, poetry, and of missionary work across the South filled the pages of the paper, as did encouragement for black Americans to seek education.

The value of the *Christian Recorder*, both in its inception and in its modern form, is that it provides a window into a black religious denomination over time as well as into a wide range of secular issues. The publication has provided the contemporary reader and the historian alike with insight into black perspectives that would have otherwise been unavailable.

[*See also* African Methodist Episcopal Church; Black Church; Black Press; Civil War; Colonization; Emigration to Africa; Entrepreneurs; Liberia; Literature; Moral Suasion; Religion; *and* Russwurm, John Brown.]

BIBLIOGRAPHY

Dann, Martin E., ed. *The Black Press, 1827–1890: The Quest for National Identity*. New York: Putnam, 1971.

Seraile, William. *Fire in His Heart: Bishop Benjamin Tucker Tanner and the A.M.E. Church*. Knoxville: University of Tennessee Press, 1998

Sterling, Dorothy. *The Making of an Afro-American: Martin Robison Delany, 1812–1885*. New York: Da Capo, 1996.

Walker, Clarence Earl. *A Rock in a Weary Land: The African Methodist Episcopal Church during the Civil War and Reconstruction*. Baton Rouge: Louisiana State University Press, 1982.

Williams, Gilbert Anthony. *The Christian Recorder, Newspaper of the African Methodist Episcopal Church: History of a Forum for Ideas, 1854–1902*. Jefferson, NC: McFarland, 1996.

—EMMA J. LAPSANSKY-WERNER

CIVIL RIGHTS. [*This entry contains three subentries dealing with civil rights from 1619 to 1895. The first article provides a discussion of the topic during the colonial period through the American Revolution; the second article discusses the topic up to the beginning of the Civil War in 1861; and the third article discusses civil rights during the war and after—especially focusing on the effects of Emancipation and Reconstruction on civil rights in the United States.*]

Civil Rights in the Colonial Period

The first Africans to land in Jamestown, Virginia, in 1619 entered into the labor system of the day, becoming indentured servants who generally worked out a term of labor before earning their freedom. In this manner many indentured Africans became free in the colonies, in some cases going on to hire their own indentured servants. The system did not see the exclusive employment of blacks in the early to mid-seventeenth century, as a multiracial workforce of Native Americans and whites was also commonly indentured. Not until the late 1600s and early 1700s was the stipulation *durante viva* ("for life") applied to terms of labor.

For the black population of approximately 170 in 1640, there were a number of ambiguities regarding their status; their identity as Africans had not yet resulted in their being singled out for different treatment. In some cases, blacks as well as other indentured servants could ask for payment, marry, become free, own property, and have their own servants. The last two possibilities in this list were often linked together under the colony's "headright" system, wherein free men were allotted fifty acres of land for every worker they brought into the colony. The system yielded circumstances such as those of Richard Johnson, a black man who imported two white servants and gained one hundred acres of land, and Anthony Johnson, another black man, who arrived in the 1620s and by 1640 had acquired five servants and 250 acres. In general, on the other hand, many more indentured whites than blacks had legitimate contracts and subsequently had more legal recourse than blacks, whose arrival in the colonies often resembled more of a spurious sale that did not institute as much legal protection.

Nevertheless, case records suggest that blacks had legal rights. There are examples from the 1620s where black men testified against whites in court (as did John Philip in 1624) and where black servants were awarded regular payments. The experiences of blacks certainly did not conform to any one common experience. Some blacks worked out their terms and gained freedom, while others were looped back in to the system and never escaped, as terms could be extended for any number of "infringements," such as theft or attempted escape. Such irregularities were not exclusive to blacks and became more common as the century progressed.

Racialization of Slavery and Erosion of Rights. Blacks who had previously benefited from inconsistencies in indentured servitude increasingly fell victim to the tightening up of regulations, as a system that had borne a purely economic appearance assumed characteristics that were more and more frequently based on race and racism. This was reflected in a variety of ordinances, laws, and court sentences expanding the fledgling pattern wherein blacks were treated differently from whites, as well as in terminology itself, as blacks were increasingly referred to as slaves as opposed to servants. The racialization of the colonial landscape also spilled over into social attitudes, with states such as Virginia and Maryland introducing restrictions on interracial sex and marriage. By the late 1600s Africans, and their children, were classed as slaves for life, as Native Americans and whites were slowly phased out of the indentured labor system. Nevertheless, the need for cheap, coerced labor—and thus the need to procure more slaves from Africa—continued, yielding a black population of around 500,000 by 1770.

As the volume of slaves increased, the institution expanded in legal terms so as to embrace this growth. Colonial officials began adopting "slave codes" that were in many cases modeled on the codes employed in the Caribbean slave system. The codes dismantled the rights of slaves as human beings, redefining them as property. Typical codes prevented slaves from owning property or meeting in large groups, placed tight restrictions on mobility and judicial representation, and banned participation in commercial activity. Murder, rape, and repeated theft were defined as capital offenses, all carrying the sentence of death by hanging. Robbery might result in a slave's being whipped or else having his ears pinned to posts or cut off. A lesser whipping or branding would be given to those who lied or were disobedient. The law was also sympathetic to slave owners' killing of unruly slaves. Anxiety and fear over the swelling slave population created an atmosphere in which it became desirable and acceptable to further control as many dimensions of slave life as possible. The Negro Act (1735) in South Carolina prescribed particular clothing for slaves. There was widespread use of leg irons, chains, and whips to atomize slave populations and maintain control.

Such activity occurred throughout the colonies, with northerners also seeking to suppress slave autonomy. Any fugitive slave originating in Albany, New York, and caught more than forty miles away was subject to the death penalty. Whites became particularly concerned about the possibility of blacks attacking whites. Consequently, many laws were enacted severely punishing blacks for "striking" whites or even, as was the case in Boston, prohibiting blacks from carrying sticks or canes that could be used as weapons. While slave codes bore certain common characteristics across the colonies, they were generally more regulatory and harsh in the southern colonies. Special slave courts were common in southern colonies; these courts would hand out sentences such as branding, nose slitting, extraction of teeth, amputation of ears, toes, and fingers, castration, and burning at the stake.

Overall, in terms of civil rights in pre-Revolutionary America, a system that defined blacks as property or chattel evolved and became entrenched. The system was initially one in which other racial groups were also held under contracts of indentured service; as the colonies expanded, the perceived economic necessity of the continuation of slavery and the growth of racist ideologies twisted the system into one of lifelong slavery for Africans. Rules revolved around the sale of blacks as commercial property, and slave codes further disempowered them. As many historians have observed, the situation was somewhat paradoxical. While blacks were enslaved and classed as property in lieu of being given human and civil rights, some laws implicitly acknowledged blacks as individuals capable of making moral decisions. Slaves were given accountability and responsibility for their actions, yet they had nothing to gain from their situation; their humanity was recognized only in punishment. America had become a fully fledged slave society, with slave labor and the denial of civil rights to blacks underpinning the economy and the social order.

American Revolution. The American Revolution provided the first challenge to slavery and the rise of a common will to improve upon the negligible civil rights of blacks. The net results of the war included the abolition of slavery in the North, an increased free black population in the Upper South, and the eventual end, in 1808, to the international African slave trade. The philosophical currency of human rights that swept the North had beneficial consequences for northern slaves; in the South, however, civil rights continued to be severely repressed, as the colonial era gave way to an antebellum slave era in which the withholding of civil rights from blacks was seen by some as ultimately protecting wayward, uncivilized children.

In the North, many blacks appropriated Revolutionary rhetoric and petitioned for their freedom, such as Boston blacks in 1773. Many took advantage of the rhetoric of American colonists who spoke of being enslaved by the British to bolster their claims; petitions and street protests became increasingly common. These actions aimed to enhance civil rights, as did, in a sense, the actions of Crispus Attucks, the runaway slave who died during the Boston Massacre in 1770. He had become involved in a protest against British troops who were taking extra civilian work away from the black working class.

In 1774 the Continental Congress voted to outlaw further slave trading, and several states independently imposed the prospective ban (such as Rhode Island and Connecticut) or else imposed extra tariffs that were so high that they all but stopped further trade (such as Pennsylvania); however, the Constitution as drafted in 1787 in Philadelphia made significant concessions to slave owners and thus only served to reinforce the institution. As a further reflection of conflicting sentiments with regard to slavery, when Thomas Jefferson, then a delegate from Virginia to the Second Continental Congress, expressed the notion that slavery was a violation of basic human rights of life and liberty in an early draft of the Declaration of Independence, the sentiments were overridden by proslavery factions. Indeed, the finalized document, however iconic, panders to powerful slave interests; the statement "all men are created equal" was not, at the time, intended to include blacks.

Nevertheless, the new state constitutions of Delaware, Maryland, Kentucky, North Carolina, and Tennessee gave blacks the vote, subjecting them to the same property requirements as they did white men, while Virginia, Delaware, and Maryland made it easier for individual slave owners to manumit their slaves; the easing of manumission restrictions spread across the Upper South. Vermont prohibited slavery through its 1777 constitution, and Massachusetts followed suit, in large part owing its speed in doing so to the series of freedom suits brought by black Bostonians.

The Northwest Ordinance of 1787 legally articulated growing antislavery sentiments by prohibiting slavery north of the Ohio River. The ban drew attention to some issues lurking beneath the surface. While northern states such as Illinois and Indiana indeed outlawed slavery, it quickly became apparent that the translation of words on paper to reality was a process wherein the actual concession of rights to blacks would be slow to match the promises of such. Many states where slavery was prohibited introduced strict limits on the entry of free blacks as well as policies reflecting ever-present racism.

Revolutionary Aftermath. Despite the Revolution and the Northwest Ordinance, the emancipation of slaves across the northern states was not immediate, with different states abolishing slavery at different times and in different forms. During the three decades following the Revolution, every northern state either abolished slavery outright or initiated proceedings to phase it out through acts of gradual emancipation.

The violation of civil rights continued, however, through the introduction of alternate legal restrictions. In the midst of emancipation, many northern states installed harsh restrictions on black voting, legislated against interracial marriage, and severely limited interstate travel. Even in the states that had been among the first to abolish slavery, restrictions of black civil rights could be found. Ohio passed a law requiring free blacks to provide proof of their freedom when entering the state in 1804, then made a five-hundred-dollar bond a prerequisite to entry in 1807. Individual states introduced a variety of bonds, restrictions, and poll taxes, and in 1790 the federal government followed the trend by placing limits on naturalization, such that foreign white immigrants could gain citizenship but blacks could not. The government disallowed blacks from joining the federal militia in 1792, prevented blacks from delivering U.S. mail in 1810, and took the vote away from free blacks in Washington, D.C., in 1820.

The U.S. Constitution of 1787 did nothing to counter this usurpation of black civil rights; instead, it safeguarded the international slave trade for two decades, increased the representation of southerners in Congress by counting each slave as three-fifths of a free person, and implicitly recognized the right of slave owners to retrieve fugitive slaves—all while carefully avoiding the use of the word "slavery." White American attitudes toward the black population had not substantially changed; many now perceived free blacks as undesirables—as misfits who would be better removed from the country than allowed to remain to create social and racial tension. The American Colonization Society became popular on the back of such sentiments in the early 1800s.

State constitutions continued to be revised throughout the period, regularly undermining black civil rights. Save Tennessee and North Carolina, southern states completely disenfranchised blacks, while free blacks seeking to cross state lines found legal obstacles in their path in Virginia, Georgia, Kentucky, Maryland, and the Carolinas. Most states began issuing a range of permits and passes needed for travel and for participation in a variety of activities such as trading. In the southern states, harassment and day-to-day discrimination were endemic; there were many cases of free blacks being kidnapped and sold into slavery.

Blacks struggled to maintain existing civil rights and to secure more of them. Examples from the post-Revolutionary era display an extensive rhetorical campaign for increased civil rights, as African Americans petitioned for equal access to education (as in a 1787 Boston petition) and equalized taxation. They also fought against specific state laws that were deemed unacceptable, such as in the 1797 civil rights action taken by North Carolinian free blacks: The state had ruled that any free black manumitted without state approval would be reenslaved; four men moved out of state to file what many regard as the first petition presented to the U.S. Congress by black Americans. Jacob and Jupiter Nicholson, Job Albert, and Thomas Pritchet sought federal protection of their rights; the issue raised by their petition was referred to the discretion of individual states.

As the South became immersed in a defense of slavery in the early to mid-nineteenth century, the civil rights of free blacks were relentlessly violated. In the North, the gains introduced as a result of the Revolution were in most cases reversed in the early 1800s, as northern racism proved nearly as pervasive as that in the South. The "freedom" possessed by many blacks was largely cosmetic.

[See also American Colonization Society; American Revolution; Attucks, Crispus; Black Codes and Slave Codes, Colonial; Constitution, U.S.; Constitutional Convention, African Americans and; Declaration of Independence; Discrimination; Gradual Emancipation; Indentured Servitude; Inheritance and Slave Status; Jefferson, Thomas, on African Americans and Slavery; Kidnapping; Laws and Legislation; Petitions; Political Participation; Race, Theories of; Segregation; and Slave Trade.]

BIBLIOGRAPHY

Franklin, John Hope, and Alfred A. Moss Jr. *From Slavery to Freedom: A History of African Americans.* 8th ed. Boston: McGraw-Hill, 2000.

Green, Robert P., Jr., ed. *Equal Protection and the African American Constitutional Experience: A Documentary History.* Westport, CT: Greenwood, 2000.

Jordan, Winthrop D. *White over Black: American Attitudes toward the Negro, 1550–1812.* Chapel Hill: University of North Carolina Press, 1968.

Kolchin, Peter. *American Slavery, 1619–1877.* London: Penguin, 1995.

Morris, Thomas D. *Southern Slavery and the Law, 1619–1860.* Chapel Hill: University of North Carolina Press, 1996.

Trotter, Joe William, Jr. *The African American Experience.* Boston: Houghton Mifflin, 2001.

—SAM HITCHMOUGH

Civil Rights in Antebellum America

Under the U.S. Constitution of 1787 civil rights were largely left to the states. The Constitution never set out what the requirements should be for voting, instead merely providing that those who could vote for the lower houses of their state legislatures were entitled to vote for members of the federal Congress. Similarly, while the Constitution mentioned both citizens of the states and citizens of the United States, it never defined the requirements for either, except to note that after the adoption of the Constitution only "natural born" citizens could be elected president. The authors of the Constitution did posit that foreigners could be naturalized and hold any public office except that of president. While article 4 of the Constitution provided that the "Citizens of each State shall be entitled to all Privileges and Immunities of Citizens of the several States," the Constitution did not spell out what these privileges and immunities were or how the states were to define citizenship.

Before the Civil War most blacks—almost 90 percent of the nation's African American population—were slaves and as such had virtually no civil rights. Some minimal legal provisions were made on behalf of slaves: By 1860 the southern states had made it a crime for whites, even masters, to torture, mutilate, or murder slaves. It was also a crime for someone who was neither the owner nor the overseer of a slave and who had no legal authority over a slave to beat, whip, or attack him or her. However, because slaves could never testify against whites, batteries or even murders of slaves might go unpunished, as the only witnesses might be other slaves. Aside from their rights not to be murdered by anyone or beaten by strangers, enslaved blacks had no rights under either the Constitution or the laws of the states. Thus, "civil rights" as applied to African Americans before the Civil War can be understood only in the context of the rights of free blacks.

Political Rights. As the new Republic emerged, the states defined civil rights according to their own needs and desires. In the antebellum period there was enormous diversity throughout the nation on this issue. The New England states were the most expansive in their approaches to civil rights. Massachusetts, Vermont, New Hampshire, and Maine allowed all adult males to vote, without regard to race or property qualifications. Rhode Island did the same when it adopted its first constitution in 1842. By the eve of the Civil War, Connecticut was the only New England state to deny suffrage to blacks. These New England states also did not discriminate with respect to the right to hold office, and by 1860 a few of the region's blacks had held minor governmental positions.

In the wake of the American Revolution blacks initially found themselves able to vote in New York and Pennsylvania. Some blacks also may have voted in New Jersey, but suffrage there was revoked by 1820. In 1821 New York revised its constitution, eliminating a property requirement for white males—but not for blacks. Thus, until the Civil War, African Americans could vote in New York only if they owned sufficient property. In some parts of the state this rule was ignored; registrars simply asked black voters if they "met the requirements of being able to vote," and when they said that they did, they were permitted to cast their ballots. For the most part, however, the restriction effectively limited black suffrage in the state. As a property owner in Rochester, Frederick Douglass could vote, and in both 1860 and 1864 he cast his ballot for Abraham Lincoln; Douglass also served as a presidential elector in 1860. Blacks were allowed to vote in Pennsylvania until 1837, when the legislature and then a new constitution took suffrage away from them.

The southern states of North Carolina and Tennessee allowed free African Americans to vote until the mid-1830s, when both states disenfranchised them. Some blacks may have voted in Maryland after the Revolution, but by 1820 the state no longer allowed it. None of the other southern states allowed blacks to vote before the Civil War. Likewise, with a few minor exceptions, all the midwestern and far western states denied blacks access to the ballot box. The Ohio Supreme Court ruled that men of mixed ancestry who were more than half white could vote, and both Ohio and Michigan did allow blacks to vote in some school board elections. Oddly, Ohio did not prohibit blacks from holding office, and at least one man of mixed ancestry, John Mercer Langston, was elected to office in the 1850s.

No southern state allowed slaves to testify in court against whites. The southern states also prohibited free blacks from testifying against whites, as did Indiana and Illinois; from statehood until 1849 Ohio maintained the same restriction, but in that year the state changed the law to allow black testimony in all cases. In 1862 Oregon gave blacks the right to testify against whites, and California did the same in 1863 (although, significantly, neither of these two Pacific Coast states extended this right to Asians or American Indians). The Middle Atlantic, New England, and Upper Midwest states, meanwhile, never prohibited free blacks from testifying. Because jury service was typically tied to the franchise, blacks could serve on juries in states where they could vote. However, there is no indication that blacks were jurors in North Carolina and Tennessee, even though they could vote in those states until the 1830s. Blacks had served in the Continental army and in northern colonial militias during the Revolution, but after the Constitution went into effect, Congress pro-

hibited blacks from serving in the military, as did a number of states. By 1863 most northern states were actively recruiting black soldiers to serve in state regiments, yet all of these regiments were segregated—and invariably led by white officers.

Employment, Public Services, and Property Rights. Free African Americans in the antebellum period faced racism in much of daily life. In the South they had to carry passes to prove their status as free, and most states required that they obtain permission from local authorities to move from one county to another. In various southern states blacks could not hold certain jobs or enter certain professions; they were sometimes explicitly banned from becoming pharmacists, lawyers, teachers, gunsmiths, or printers. In general, free blacks were rarely able to compete with whites for employment. When the young slave Frederick Douglass tried to hire out his own time on the docks of Baltimore—essentially acting as if he were free—he faced discrimination and even violence from white laborers.

African Americans could hold no public office, although they might be hired by the government to perform menial labor. Free southern blacks did have the right to marry each other and raise their own children, a right denied to slaves. They could also own personal property—as did many free blacks in Virginia, South Carolina, and Louisiana, in particular—and in some states they could own real estate. On the other hand, some states, like Mississippi and Georgia, denied free blacks the right to own various types of property in their own name, requiring that they have white guardians. Inns, hotels, and restaurants were free to refuse to serve free blacks, while railroads, steamboats, and other public conveyances segregated them, as no laws prevented them from doing so.

In most southern states free African Americans could not form churches or hold religious services without the permission of local authorities, and in some places, such as South Carolina, they could hold their own religious services only if a white person were present. No southern state provided public education for free blacks, and most, in fact, prohibited, or virtually prohibited, them from getting any education at all. In 1860 only 3 percent of all free black children in the South attended school; in the eleven states that later became the Confederate states, less than 2 percent of the free black children attended school. Only 0.2 percent of Virginia's twenty-two thousand free black children attended school. In the antebellum South the notions of segregation and integration were irrelevant with respect to education, because blacks were simply denied any meaningful access to the institution.

The rights of northern African Americans were more complicated. They also faced discrimination in public accommodations and in access to public facilities, but they fought back with boycotts and lawsuits and were sometimes successful. In 1853 William Cooper Nell, Sarah Remond Parker, and Caroline Remond Putnam successfully sued a Boston theater when they were denied the seats they had paid for. Similarly, in 1859 a black woman in Ohio won monetary damages from a streetcar conductor who forced her off a car because she was black. On a number of occasions in the 1840s and 1850s Frederick Douglass resisted being forced to sit in the "Negro cars" of trains in New England and New York.

In 1845 Douglass went to England aboard the *Cambria*, a British ship owned by the Cunard Line. When his supporters tried to book him a cabin, they were told that as a black, Douglass would have to cross the ocean in steerage. He later wrote in his second autobiography, *My Bondage and My Freedom* (1855), "American prejudice against color triumphed over British liberality and civilization, and erected a color test and condition for crossing the sea in the cabin of a British vessel." Douglass further noted, "The insult was keenly felt by my white friends, but to me, it was common, expected, and therefore no great consequence, whether I went in the cabin or in the steerage."

Douglass's perspective suggests how common segregation was in the North in the early 1840s. On his return voyage, in 1847, Douglass faced a similar insult when the Cunard agent in Liverpool refused to honor his ticket for a first-class cabin. After two years of living in England, where he did not face such discrimination, Douglass vigorously protested the treatment; by that time he was a famous lecturer and so "took occasion to expose the disgusting tyranny, in the columns of the London Times." The result was an apology from Samuel Cunard himself and a change in the shipping company's policy.

After his return to America, Douglass more aggressively challenged segregation on trains and was on more than one occasion forcibly removed when he would not sit in Jim Crow cars. In the end, his protests and those of other blacks and their white allies paid off. The politician Charles Francis Adams proposed legislation to force the integration of all trains in Massachusetts, and the threat of legislation led the railroads to independently change their policies. In 1855 Douglass was able to note that "the 'Jim Crow car'—set up for the degradation of colored people—is nowhere found in New England." Nevertheless, Douglass and other blacks continued to face such discrimination and indignities in the Midwest and other parts of the North. Unlike their southern counterparts, at least, northern blacks did not have to carry papers to prove their freedom or worry about being arrested by local officials and held as fugitive slaves.

Antebellum northern blacks faced discrimination in employment, but this was almost always a function of discrimination by employers or by whites who refused to work alongside them. By 1860 blacks had entered every profession in the North, including law, medicine, pharmacy, the ministry, teaching, and publishing. Northern blacks were free to acquire any property they could afford—although whites were also free to refuse to sell land or rent space to blacks. Blacks in the North built churches, schools, and buildings for social and fraternal organizations. They published newspapers; filed lawsuits; and persistently, and sometimes successfully, protested segregation on railroads, passenger boats, and streetcars and in schools.

In 1849 blacks in Boston initiated the first school desegregation case in the United States. Benjamin Roberts sued on behalf of his five-year-old daughter, Sarah, who was not allowed to attend the public school nearest to her home. Roberts was represented by the abolitionist lawyer and politician Charles Sumner and Robert Morris Jr., one of the first black attorneys in the nation. At the time, schools throughout Massachusetts were integrated; only Boston maintained separate schools for blacks. In *Roberts v. City of Boston* (1850) the Massachusetts Supreme Court rejected Sumner's argument that segregation violated the state constitution; however, blacks in Boston, led by William Cooper Nell, did not give up. In 1855, after five years of petitions and lobbying, the state legislature banned segregated schools.

By this time most public schools in the rest of New England were also integrated, although some places, like Hartford, Connecticut, had separate schools for blacks until after the Civil War. The motivation for some separate schools may have come in part from blacks themselves, who understood that segregated schools would provide jobs for black teachers, while integrated schools might hire only whites. By 1852 the black schools in Hartford were receiving more tax dollars than were paid by the black community, suggesting that at least some deemed segregated education a benefit to the poorer community.

By the 1830s most northern states provided public education for blacks, though usually in separate schools; generally, educational opportunities varied by state and by localities within states, because education was typically controlled by local officials. In New York, schools in Rochester, Syracuse, and Utica were integrated by the 1850s, while Albany, Buffalo, and New York City maintained segregated schools. In Ohio, by the eve of the Civil War, schools in Cleveland, Toledo, Ashtabula, Oberlin, and Greene County were integrated, while those in Cincinnati, Columbus, Dayton, and most of the southern part of the state remained segregated.

While most African Americans in the North probably attended all-black schools, by 1860 most were able to attend public schools, which were supported by tax dollars that came from white as well as black taxpayers. In 1850, 31 percent of all black children in the North attended school; this figure had increased to 35 percent by 1860, when more than 29,000 black children were enrolled in northern schools. In 1860, 46 percent of Michigan's 2,414 black children were in school. These statistics contrast dramatically with those from the South. The total of 1,105 black schoolchildren in Michigan exceeded the entire number of blacks attending school in the eleven states that would later form the Confederacy, where more than 50,000 free black children lived. Aside from primary and secondary education, by 1860 some northern colleges were integrated, and a few, like Wilberforce in Ohio, had been founded specifically to provide higher education for blacks.

Right to Settle in or Visit a State. The right to move, travel, and settle in a new place was also a fundamental civil right regulated by the states. Significantly, the national government might have regulated this under the commerce clause, which gave Congress the power to regulate "commerce among the several states." In *Gibbons v. Ogden* (1824) the U.S. Supreme Court acknowledged that the power to regulate commerce included the power to regulate interstate travel. Similarly, the slave trade clause (article 1, section 9, of the Constitution) prohibited Congress from regulating the "migration or importation" of people before 1808, meaning that after 1808 Congress could regulate both the slave trade and domestic and foreign immigration and migration. Nevertheless, before the Civil War the Supreme Court never interfered in the rights of the states to regulate who entered their domains, and Congress, bowing to southern pressure, never did either. The result was that almost all the slave states and some free states limited or banned free blacks from entering their boundaries.

In 1804 and 1807 Ohio passed laws designed to inhibit black migration. Blacks entering the new state were required to prove their status as free people, register with county authorities, and find sureties to guarantee their good behavior and their support if they could not support themselves. Had this law been strictly enforced, free blacks would have faced enormous—perhaps insurmountable—obstacles in entering the state. In fact, however, the law was rarely drawn upon, and from 1804 until its repeal in 1849 the state's black population grew dramatically. In 1800 Ohio Territory had only 337 blacks; by 1850 there were over 25,000 in the state—clearly, immigration restrictions were not followed. Illinois and Indiana had similar restrictions, which for the most part

were equally ineffective: Indiana's black population went from 630 in 1810 to over 11,000 in 1850, at which point it stagnated for a decade, as the Hoosier State banned all black immigration. Illinois had about 780 blacks in 1810 and then more than 5,400 in 1850. In the last antebellum decade Illinois passed more restrictive legislation, but the black population nevertheless grew by over 40 percent, to 7,628, by 1860.

In 1851 the Iowa state legislature imposed heavy fines of two dollars per day on any blacks who moved into the state, but it is unclear whether the law was properly adopted. In any event, the statute did not stop the black population from tripling before the legislature deleted it in 1860; in the only known attempt to enforce the law, a state judge declared it unconstitutional. Oregon banned black immigration in its 1859 constitution, but, again, the law was apparently never enforced, and the few blacks who found their way to that Pacific Coast state were allowed to remain. All other northern states allowed blacks to immigrate without any legal impediments. This was an important civil right that by 1860 was available to blacks in every free state in the North except Indiana and perhaps Illinois. In the 1850s the black population in Wisconsin nearly doubled, while in Michigan it grew by more than 250 percent.

The South, on the other hand, consistently restricted the movement of free blacks, and some states made it impossible for them even to reside within their boundaries. By 1860 it was illegal for any free black to move into any of the slave states except Maryland, Delaware, and Kentucky. Every coastal southern state from Virginia to Texas prohibited free black sailors from landing at their ports, with the exception of Mississippi, which had no true port. In fact, free black sailors from the North or from other countries who entered such cities as Norfolk, Charleston, Mobile, Savannah, and New Orleans were subject to being jailed while their ship was in port. When the ship was ready to leave, the captain was required to pay the jailor for providing food and lodging to the free black sailor, who was only then permitted to leave the state. If their "bill" at the jail was not paid, or if their ship left port without them, such free blacks sailors could be sold into limited servitude or, if repeat offenders, made into permanent slaves.

In the early national period a number of slave states allowed masters to free their slaves within the state; by the 1850s, however, the eleven slave states that soon created the Confederate States of America no longer allowed this. Virginia's 1852 constitution specifically prohibited manumitted slaves from remaining in the state. In most of these states free blacks needed the permission of local courts simply to reside in the state. In the late 1850s Charleston, South Carolina, began to crack down on the many free blacks who were living in the city without the proper paperwork. In 1859 the Mississippi Supreme Court ruled in *Mitchell v. Wells* that if a master freed his slave outside the state, that freed black could be reenslaved if he or she returned to Mississippi. In 1860 Arkansas passed legislation that required all free blacks to leave the state; had the Civil War not begun, it is likely that other southern states would have followed suit.

Southern laws denying any rights to free blacks from other states or countries clearly infringed upon the power of the national government to regulate interstate and international commerce, yet the federal courts refused to intervene in such cases. Moreover, with its decision in *Dred Scott v. Sandford* (1857), the Supreme Court made clear that it would not protect the rights of free blacks. In that case the Court held that free blacks, even if they were full citizens of northern states, could not claim rights under the U.S. Constitution and could not litigate in federal court to protect their liberty, property, or civil rights.

Civil Rights, Federal Law, and Personal Liberty.

While the states had the authority to regulate civil rights for most Americans, the federal government had the power to do so for people living in the national capital and the territories. Before 1861 Washington, D.C., was a slaveholding city, with laws borrowed from Maryland and Virginia, and free blacks there had very few civil rights. Congress banned slavery in most of the western territories in the Missouri Compromise (1820), but the Compromise of 1850, the Kansas-Nebraska Act (1854), and the decision in *Dred Scott v. Sandford* opened up almost all the federal territories to slavery. As such, civil rights would be limited for blacks in territories in the West, as slavery undermined freedom.

In the antebellum period the federal government denied blacks passports, thus effectively limiting their claims to U.S. citizenship. In an age when military service was a mark of citizenship Congress prohibited blacks from serving. Finally, in *Dred Scott v. Sandford* the Supreme Court held that blacks could never be citizens and could not sue in federal courts to protect their rights. They were, in effect, a people without rights at the national level.

The capture and return of fugitive slaves further undermined black civil rights. The Constitution prohibited states from emancipating runaways, instead requiring that they be "delivered up on Claim of the Party to whom such Service or Labour may be due"; the Fugitive Slave Law of 1793 fully authorized all states and federal courts to enforce this provision without providing for jury trials or any other due process protections for alleged slaves. Most northern states independently passed personal liberty laws to protect free blacks from mistakenly being seized as fugitive slaves, but in *Prigg v. Pennsylvania* (1842) the Supreme Court struck down these laws as interfering with the constitutional right of masters to recover fugitive slaves. After this decision many northern states refused to cooperate in the return of fugitive slaves, leading to the Fugitive Slave Law of 1850, which set up commissioners in every county to hear fugitive slave cases. The 1850 law prohibited alleged slaves from even testifying at their own hearings; the law seriously jeopardized the liberty of all free blacks in the North.

Civil Rights on the Eve of the Civil War.

By the time of Lincoln's election free blacks in the North generally had basic legal protections. They could testify against whites and were free to move where they wished in all but a few states. They could own property and enter whatever professions they chose. In New England and some places in the Middle Atlantic states they were treated equally on public accommodations. In some of the northern states whites and blacks were free to intermarry. However, in only a few states could blacks serve on juries, and throughout most of the North outside New England they faced discrimination in schooling and on public accommodations. They were barred from state militias and in most places could not vote.

In the South most African Americans were slaves, and except for the right not to be murdered or tortured, they had almost no civil or legal rights. Free blacks in the South could be married either to each other or, informally but not legally, to slaves. In most of the South free blacks could own property. They could travel within their own state, but only with caution, as they might be arrested or kidnapped and sold as slaves if they were found where they were not known. Generally, blacks could not move to other slave states. They had no access to public education and almost no access to private education. In many slave states they were prohibited from even learning to read and write.

At the national level the Supreme Court and existing public policy generally placed free blacks outside the protection of the law. Chief Justice Roger B. Taney declared in *Dred Scott* that blacks

> are not included, and were not intended to be included, under the word "citizens" in the Constitution, and can claim none of the rights and privileges which that instrument provides for and secures to citizens of the United States. On the contrary, they were at that time considered as a subordinate and inferior class of beings, who had been subjugated by the dominant race, and, whether emancipated or not, yet remained subject to their authority, and had no rights or privileges but such as those who held them power and the Government might choose to grant them.

Blacks, he declared, were "so far inferior" both at the time of the writing of the Constitution and at the time of the *Dred Scott* decision that "they had no rights which the white man was bound to respect." Taney assumed this would forever be the status of African Americans in the United States, but, of course, conditions in both the North and the South changed dramatically after 1861.

Civil Rights from the Civil War to the Age of Segregation

Secession and the Civil War profoundly altered the nature of civil rights in the United States. The war not only destroyed slavery but also changed perceptions of African Americans and notions of civil rights. The war began as a white man's war to save the Union; blacks were excluded from the army, and the federal government had no intention of interfering with the institution of slavery in the states where it existed. But, as Abraham Lincoln noted in his second inaugural address, "all knew" that slavery "was somehow the cause of the war." By the end of the Civil War slavery had been destroyed in most of the nation and by the end of 1865 slavery was constitutionally prohibited everywhere in the country.

The ending of slavery through presidential proclamation and constitutional amendment nationalized, to some extent, civil rights. Reconstruction brought constitutional change that guaranteed the rights of former slaves and their descendants. The period also brought new legislation that provided federal protection for civil rights. After 1876, however, African Americans saw their rights gradually erode, as the South was "redeemed" by white conservatives, who did their best to undermine black political and civil rights.

Slavery, Emancipation, and the Civil War. In 1861 there were about 4 million blacks in the United States. Almost 90 percent of African Americans, about 3.5 million, were slaves living in fifteen southern states. Slightly more than half of the remaining 10 percent were free blacks living in the South, and the rest were free blacks living in the North. As slaves, most blacks had no civil rights at all, and the 260,000 or so free blacks in the South had only the most minimal rights. The 240,000 northern free blacks had far greater rights than their southern counterparts, although only in a few states did they have true legal equality. Nowhere at this time, or indeed at any time during the nineteenth century, did blacks have true social equality with whites.

Throughout the Civil War free African Americans in the North agitated for greater rights and an end to slavery. Blacks tried to enlist in the U.S. Army at the beginning of the war but were rebuffed by a whites-only policy. Frederick Douglass was one of many black leaders who constantly demanded that the army accept black soldiers, which it did starting in 1862. Blacks also organized during the war to fight for other civil rights. In 1864, for example, blacks from around the country met in Syracuse, New York, to form the National Equal Rights League, electing the black lawyer John Mercer Langston as the organization's president. Langston continued in that capacity until 1868.

Indeed, regardless of Lincoln's original notion that his only goal was to preserve the Union, the Civil War can be seen as a civil rights struggle that led to the emancipation of about 3.5 million slaves. Becoming free—ceasing to be property owned by someone else—was, of course, the most fundamental civil right of all. For the newly emancipated slaves, freedom brought mobility, the right to earn money, and the right to acquire property. Most important, perhaps, freedom allowed former slaves to marry and raise their children without the fear, or the possibility, that their families would be destroyed by sale or forced migration.

Freedom came early in the war to those slaves who abandoned their masters and presented themselves to U.S. Army troops. Union commanders responded to slavery in different ways. In Missouri, General John C. Frémont declared that all slaves owned by Confederate supporters were free, but President Lincoln countermanded that order, as he understood that any moves against slavery would push the four loyal slave states into the Confederacy. In the East, General Benjamin F. Butler dealt with the issue more shrewdly. When slaves fled to his camp, he refused to return them to their Virginian masters, declaring them "contraband of war"; this soon became standard U.S. Army policy, and any slaves who escaped to Union lines were emancipated and employed by the army.

By the beginning of 1862 the war was bringing freedom—the most fundamental civil right—to thousands of slaves. Over the course of the war Congress ended slavery in all federal territories and the District of Columbia. Finally, in January 1863, Lincoln issued the Emancipation Proclamation, declaring that all slaves living in the Confederacy were free. By the end of the war slavery was all but dead throughout the nation, and the Thirteenth Amendment was presented before the states. When it was ratified in December 1865, that amendment forever ended slavery in the American Republic.

While slavery was being abolished, free blacks gained other new civil rights. Starting in 1862 blacks were allowed to serve in the military; while they initially did not receive equal pay, by the end of the war this slight had been rectified, and soldiers who were previously underpaid were retroactively compensated. Serving in the military was a particularly important step toward civil rights in that military service was often tied to citizenship and the right to claim equality of citizenship. By the end of the war more than 200,000 blacks had served in the army and navy. In 1864 the federal government repealed the Fugitive Slave Laws of 1793 and 1850, thus securing for all blacks greater civil rights and protections.

During the war some jurisdictions also altered discriminatory laws, perhaps in recognition of the facts that the war was about slavery and that blacks were making important contributions to saving the Union and upholding the Constitution. In 1862 Oregon repealed its ban on black testimony against whites, and California did likewise in 1863. Indiana leveled the legal playing field to a lesser extent with a statute declaring that in cases where the testimony of a black or Native American was excluded, that of "his opponent shall also be excluded." Thus, in a suit between a white and a black, neither would be able to testify. More progressively, in March 1861 Indiana formally guaranteed the right of blacks to own land and "legalized" all previous sales to blacks and Native Americans. Despite such changes, both Indiana and Illinois continued to legally prohibit the immigration of blacks; Oregon also retained its ban on black immigration.

These three jurisdictions were aberrations, however, as all other free states allowed the free migration of blacks. In 1865, as the war ended, Illinois repealed all its black laws, and Wisconsin extended suffrage to blacks. Indiana, meanwhile, created public schools for blacks, though on a segregated basis; still, for a state that had only a year earlier banned black immigration and had never supported black education this was a huge step toward equality. Other northern states moved to eliminate discrimination in the wake of the war. In 1867, for example, Michigan banned segregation in its public schools.

At the federal level, civil rights also began to evolve. In May 1862 Congress created the first public school system in the District of Columbia, limiting the schools to white children; the next day Congress passed a law to create a school system for black children in the District. By modern standards the creation of a segregated school system would be a sign of racism and discrimination, but at that time it was a major step forward: for the first time in the country's history the national government had provided for the education of blacks within a federal jurisdiction. Washington, D.C., was a southern city, surrounded by slave states, creating a public school system for blacks.

Equally important, this new law made all African Americans in the District "subject and amenable to the same laws and ordinances to which white persons are or may be subject or amenable." While the District's blacks were still unable to vote or serve on juries, they would at least be subject to the same forms of trial and punishment as whites, as the city's old black code disappeared from the statutes; in theory, at least, blacks were almost equal to whites. The revolution in law became more apparent in March 1863, when Congress issued a new charter for the Alexandria and Washington Railroad providing that "no person shall be excluded from the cars on account of color." Congress put similar provisions on other railroad charters during the war, and in 1865 it banned segregation on the capital city's streetcars. In 1864 Congress authorized the admission of any patient to the hospital for the insane in the District of Columbia, without regard to race.

Institution of Black Codes. Unfortunately, the end of the war did not bring equal rights to former slaves. On the contrary, in the immediate aftermath of the war southern blacks faced a plethora of new laws designed to reduce them, at best, to permanent second-class citizens. Southern whites, almost all of whom were former Confederates, controlled southern state legislatures. In the fall of 1865 and the early winter of 1866 almost every southern state passed statutes known as black codes, which at least acknowledged that slavery was over and blacks were free. They also recognized slave marriages, allowing former slaves to formalize and legalize the unions they had consummated during slavery. These laws also legitimized all children born to such unions. For people who had never had any civil rights, freedom and legalized family relations were important gains.

Other aspects of these laws, however, were designed to limit black rights as much as possible. The laws allowed blacks to sign contracts—something slaves had been able to do—but these contract provisions were then turned back on the former slaves in attempts to force them to remain agricultural laborers tied to the land, unable to move about freely or explore other economic opportunities. Other laws simply prohibited blacks from living in towns or cities, thus forcing them to remain rooted in plantation agriculture. Some laws required that blacks sign one-year work contracts, specifying that if they did not fulfill the entire contract the employer did not have to pay them anything. Vagrancy laws allowed police to arrest any blacks who did not have labor contracts. These blacks might then be sent to chain gangs, fed only bread and water for up to a week, or auctioned off to work for whoever might pay their fine.

Mississippi, for example, prohibited blacks from buying or renting farmland and required that all agricultural labor contracts be for one year. The state's "Civil Rights Act" of 1865 authorized state officials to "arrest and carry back to his or her legal employer any freedman, free ne-

THE CRUEL UNCLE AND THE VETOED BABES IN THE WOOD.

"The Cruel Uncle and the Vetoed Babes in the Wood," a cartoon from *Frank Leslie's Illustrated Newspaper*, 12 May 1866. Andrew Johnson is the cruel uncle; the hapless infants are "civil rights" and "bureau," that is, the Freedmen's Bureau. Congress passed the civil rights bill over Johnson's veto—it became the Civil Rights Act of 1866. Congress also overrode a veto by Johnson in 1866 regarding the bureau, which remained in operation until June 1872. (Library of Congress.)

gro or mulatto, who shall quit the service of his or her employer before the expiration of his or her term of service." This was, in effect, a fugitive laborer law.

Most southern states prohibited blacks from owning firearms or large knives and from selling liquor; whites who sold liquor or weapons to blacks could also be jailed or fined. Blacks who violated almost any noncapital-offense laws were to be fined or jailed, and if they could not pay their fines, they would be "hired out" at public auctions to anyone who would pay their fines for them. The goals of these laws were to replicate slavery as much as possible and to retain full control over black labor, while at the same time leaving blacks with the burden of responsibility in obtaining food, shelter, and clothing for their families.

The new codes typically limited black testimony. In 1865 both Georgia and Alabama enacted codes that allowed blacks to testify in court only if a black was party to a civil case or, in criminal matters, if a black was the victim of a crime. Under this law, white vigilantes and terrorists, such as members of the Ku Klux Klan, could murder other whites—such as teachers in Freedmen's Bureau schools or white politicians seeking alliance with blacks—in front of black witnesses, knowing that those blacks could not testify against them. Some southern states altogether banned black testimony against whites. The former Confederate states also either directly prohibited blacks from serving on juries or did so indirectly, by continuing to tie jury service to the franchise, which former slaves did not have.

Toward Reconstruction. In December 1865 Congress authorized the Joint Committee on Reconstruction to investigate conditions in the South. The committee members interviewed scores of people, including former slaves, slave owners, Confederate leaders, U.S. Army officers, journalists, and others throughout the South. In its massive report—some eight hundred pages in length—the committee reminded the nation that the former slaves had "remained true and loyal" throughout the Civil War and "in large numbers, fought on the side of the Union." The committee concluded that it would be impossible to "abandon" the former slaves "without securing them their rights as free men and citizens." Indeed, the "whole civilized world would have cried out against such base ingratitude" if the U.S. government failed to secure and protect the rights of the freedpeople.

The Joint Committee on Reconstruction also found that southern leaders were still given to "defend the legal right of secession, and the doctrine that the first allegiance of the people is due to the States." Noting the benevolent "leniency" of the policies of Congress and the president after the war, the committee declared that "in return for our leniency we receive only an insulting denial of our authority." Rather than accept the outcome of the war, southern whites were using local courts to prosecute "Union officers for acts done in the line of official duty" and others who had been loyal to the North, and "similar prosecutions" were "threatened elsewhere as soon as the United States troops [were] removed."

The committee detailed the denials of civil rights by new southern state governments and printed large excerpts from new statutes and state constitutions. In addition, the committee described the violence perpetrated against blacks as white vigilantes and state officials worked together to deny them civil rights. Major General Edward Hatch testified that whites in much of Tennessee were unwilling to accept black liberty. He noted that "the negro is perfectly willing to work, but he wants guarantee that he will be secured in his rights under his contract" and that his "life and property" also will be "secured." Indeed, blacks understood that they were "not safe from the poor whites." Hatch noted that whites, meanwhile, wanted "some kind of legislation" to "establish a kind of peonage; not absolute slavery but that they can enact such laws as will enable them to manage the negro as they please—to fix the price to be paid for his labor." Hatch further observed that if blacks resisted this reestablishment of bondage, "they are liable to be shot."

Major General Clinton Bowen Fisk, for whom one of the nation's first black colleges—Fisk University, in Nashville, Tennessee—would be named, testified about the murderous nature of former "slaveholders and returned rebel soldiers." Such men, he declared, "persecute bitterly" the former slaves, "pursue them with vengeance, and treat them with brutality, and burn down their dwellings and school-houses." Notably, such behavior was occurring even in Tennessee, which was universally recognized as the former Confederate state with the strongest Unionist sentiment. When Lieutenant Colonel R. W. Barnard, one of Fisk's field officers, was asked if it was safe to remove troops from Tennessee, he replied,

> I hardly know how to express myself on the subject. I have not been in a favor of removing the military. I can tell you what an old citizen, a Union man, said to me. Said he, 'I tell you what, if you take away the military from Tennessee, the buzzards can't eat up the niggers as fast as we'll kill 'em.' (Report of the Joint Committee on Reconstruction, part 1, page 121)

Barnard thought this might have been an exaggeration but nevertheless told the committee, "I know there are plenty of bad men there who would maltreat the negro." He did not need to emphasize that the threat to black life he had heard came not from a "bad" man but from a Unionist.

Thus, while the dangers to blacks were great in Tennessee, where loyal Union men were most common, in other states the dangers were extraordinarily greater. Major General John W. Turner reported that in Virginia "all of the people" were "extremely reluctant to grant to the negro his civil rights—those privileges that pertain to freedom, the protection of life, liberty, and property before the laws, the right to testify in courts, etc." Turner noted that whites were "reluctant even to consider and treat the negro as a free man, to let him have his half of the sidewalk or the street crossing." They would only "concede" such rights to blacks, "if it is ever done, because they are forced to do it." He noted that poor whites were "disposed to ban the negro, to kick him and cuff him, and threaten him."

The Virginia farmer George B. Smith, in turn, admitted that whites in the state "maltreat [blacks] every day" and that blacks had "not a particle" of a chance "to obtain justice in the civil courts of Virginia." He declared that a black or "a Union man" had as much chance of obtaining justice in Virginia as "a rabbit would in a den of lions." The white sheriff of Fairfax County noted that the state was "passing laws" to "disfranchise" black voters and "passing vagrant laws on purpose to oppress the colored people and to keep them in vassalage, and doing everything they can to bring back things of their old condition, as near as possible."

The U.S. district judge John C. Underwood, who had lived in Virginia since the 1840s, believed that freedmen were safe only because the U.S. Army would intercede to protect them. If the army abandoned the state, leaving the fate of the freedmen to the native whites of Virginia, the situation would be radically altered. Underwood quoted a "most intelligent" man from Alexandria who declared that "sooner than see the colored people raised to a legal and political equality, the southern people would prefer their total annihilation."

Similarly, testimonies revealed the murders, beatings, and rapes of blacks throughout the South. Lieutenant Colonel Dexter H. Clapp told the committee about a gang of North Carolina whites who "first castrated" and then "murdered" a black; when the culprits escaped from jail, the local police refused to even attempt to capture them. This gang then shot "several negroes." One of these men, a wealthy planter, later killed a twelve-year-old African American boy and wounded another. A local police sergeant, meanwhile, "brutally wounded a freedman . . . in his custody": while the man's arms were tied behind his back, the policeman struck him on the back of his head with a gun. It was later shown that this man had "committed no offence whatever." This policeman later "whipped another freedman" so that "from his neck to his hips his back was one mass of gashes"; the policeman then left the bleeding man outside overnight. One African American who defended himself when assaulted by a white was given twenty-two lashes with a whip over a two-hour period; was then "tied up by his thumbs for two hours, his toes touching the ground only"; and was finally "given nine more lashes and then tied up by his thumbs for another two hours." A planter in the same area whipped two black women until their backs were "a mass of gashes." Clapp asserted that away from military posts, "scenes like these" were "frequent occurrences" in "portions" of North Carolina. An army general in Georgia reported that a gang of whites there was kidnapping black children in order to sell them as slaves in Cuba.

Legislation of Reconstruction. In 1866 Congress, shocked by the repressive laws of the South, responded with the Civil Rights Act of 1866. As was indicative of the dangers to black civil rights, while Congress was debating the act, Senator Charles Sumner of Massachusetts received a box containing the finger of a black man. The accompanying note read, "You old son of a bitch, I send you a piece of one of your friends, and if that bill of yours passes I will have a piece of you." Congress nevertheless passed the bill, then enacting it by overriding President Andrew Johnson's veto. The Civil Rights Act of 1866 made African Americans citizens of the United States and of the states in which they lived. It declared that blacks would have all of the rights already held by whites:

> to make and enforce contracts, to sue, be parties, and give evidence, to inherit, purchase, lease, sell, hold, and convey real and personal property, and to full and equal benefit of all laws and proceedings for the security of person and property, as is enjoyed by white citizens, and shall be subject to like punishment, pains, and penalties.

The law provided for fines of up to one thousand dollars and punishments of up to one year in jail for anyone acting "under color of law" who denied any legal rights to blacks. At the same time, Congress wrote the Fourteenth Amendment, which, when ratified in 1868, constitutionalized the legal principles set out in the Civil Rights Act.

Between 1866 and 1871 Congress passed a plethora of additional pieces of legislation to protect black freedom, including the first Reconstruction Act of 1867. The Second Reconstruction Act of 1867, which, like the first, was passed over Johnson's veto, authorized the military to register black voters in the South. This marked the beginning of a revolution in southern life and politics. Southern legislatures were soon integrated, and they quickly repealed most discriminatory legislation in the South. Some southern states passed laws allowing for interracial marriage. Louisiana's Reconstruction-era constitution prohibited racial discrimination in public accommodations, and in 1869 the state gave victims of such discrimination the right to sue those who had mistreated them. Southern whites reacted to this new order with violence; in turn, Congress responded with three Force Acts in 1870 and 1871, giving the army and the federal courts the power to implement the new laws and amendments—including the Fifteenth Amendment, ratified in 1870, which prohibited discrimination with regard to voting rights on the basis of race. The third Force Act, also known as the Ku Klux Klan Act, allowed the president to suspend the writ of habeas corpus to suppress the Klan and other white terrorist organizations.

Throughout the South, the newly integrated state governments repealed black codes and created formal equality to guarantee the civil rights of all Americans. Most southern states eliminated discriminatory legislation, and some, like Louisiana, required that railroads and steamboats provide equal and integrated accommodations to all people. A number of the southern states allowed interracial marriages. Indeed, most Reconstruction legislation was directed at ending repression by southern governments or at suppressing violence and terrorism. The Civil Rights Act of 1875 sought to prevent private discrimination in public accommodations. Although the bill was introduced in Congress by Senator Sumner, it was shaped by black activists, including Langston, who helped draft it. In 1875 Congress also changed the nation's naturalization laws to allow foreign-born blacks to become American citizens. Sadly, the Civil Rights Act of 1875 represented the last gasp of federal intervention on behalf of blacks in the Reconstruction era.

Regression. In 1877 Reconstruction formally came to an end, although in most of the South it had already informally ended. In 1870, for example, Virginia passed legislation creating a public school system wherein blacks were specifically prohibited from attending the same schools as whites. Throughout the South, legislatures that were now dominated by southern-born whites, often the sons of former planters, began to repeal civil rights laws and limit the rights of blacks. More important, white-dominated southern governments ignored violence perpetrated against blacks. Lynching became common and was often used to terrorize blacks so that they would not vote or participate in public affairs.

Even before the end of Reconstruction the Supreme Court had begun to chip away at black civil rights. In the *Slaughterhouse Cases* (1873) the Court held that the states, and not the federal government, were primarily responsible for protecting civil rights. More disastrous were the decisions in the *Civil Rights Cases* in 1883. Here the Supreme Court struck down the Civil Rights Act of 1875, which had guaranteed blacks equal access to public accommodations and places of public entertainment, like theaters and concert halls. The Court ruled that the Fourteenth Amendment banned only state action that discriminated and did not empower Congress to regulate private discrimination. In a stinging and prophetic dissent—but one that had no impact at the time—Justice John Marshall Harlan pointed out that the state, in fact, regulated theaters, hotels, restaurants, and public transportation, and thus there was surely enough state action on these issues to merit federal regulation. He argued that the Court's distinction between "private" and "state" action was a false distinction, because the state was already regulating public accommodations and transportation.

African Americans responded to these decisions with anger and protests. After the decisions in the *Civil Rights Cases*, the black journalist T. Thomas Fortune wrote in the *New York Globe* that "the colored people of the United States feel to-day as if they had been baptized in ice-water," while Langston, who had helped write the original act, said that the Court seemed "desirous of remanding us back to that old passed condition." He found the decision "incomprehensible." Douglass remarked that the decision "grievously wounded" African Americans, comparing it to the Fugitive Slave Law of 1850 and the *Dred Scott* decision. He asserted in a speech in October 1883 that "in humiliating the colored people of this country, this decision has humbled the Nation. It gives to a South Carolina or a Mississippi Railroad Conductor more power than it gives to the National Government." Douglass longed "for a Supreme Court which shall be as true, as vigilant, as active, and exacting in maintaining laws enacted for the protection of human rights, as in other days

was the Court for the destruction of human rights!" In 1887 blacks in Baltimore formed the Brotherhood of Liberty, which might be considered the nation's first civil rights organization. In 1889 the Brotherhood of Liberty published *Justice and Jurisprudence: An Inquiry Concerning the Constitutional Limitations of the Thirteenth, Fourteenth, and Fifteenth Amendments*. At more than six hundred pages, this ambitious tome was designed to convince lawyers and jurists of the legitimacy of federal protections for civil rights.

In denying that the federal government could protect basic civil rights, the Court in both the *Slaughterhouse Cases* and the *Civil Rights Cases* left the states free to regulate those rights. Most northern states then did what they deemed necessary, passing new laws throughout the last quarter of the nineteenth century to protect blacks from racial discrimination. Pennsylvania's 1887 law, for example, provided for a fine of fifty to one hundred dollars for those denying equal access to public transportation, theaters, hotels, restaurants, concerts, or any other "place of entertainment or amusement"; one hundred dollars was at that time worth the same as at least two thousand dollars in the year 2000. New York and New Jersey passed similar laws. New Jersey's 1884 act provided for fines of between five hundred and one thousand dollars for those denying blacks access to public places, such as restaurants and theaters. The law also recognized the right of the complaining witness to pursue private action for up to five hundred dollars and provided for the possibility of jailing offenders for up to one year. In addition, the law protected the right of all citizens to serve on juries, allowing a fine of up to five thousand dollars for any officials who refused to call blacks for jury service.

Ohio saw similar legislative and judicial confirmation of black civil rights. In 1881 a Cincinnati jury awarded a black woman one thousand dollars—an enormous sum of money under the circumstances—when a railroad forced her to ride in a smoking car instead of honoring her ticket for the first-class car. Three years later Ohio adopted a new civil rights law, declaring that all its citizens were "equal before the law"—and noting that such a status was "essential to just government." The statute prohibited private businesses from discriminating, specifically banning discrimination in all "inns, public conveyances on land or water, theaters and other places of public amusement." A second act passed later that year amended this law to also cover "inns, restaurants, eating-houses, and barber-shops, and all other places of public accommodation and amusement."

Three years later Ohio repealed its last remaining black laws with the passage of the "Arnett bill," sponsored by Benjamin Arnett, a black state legislator who represented the predominantly white Green County. In 1894 Ohio strengthened its civil rights laws, raising the maximum fines for violations from one hundred to five hundred dollars, increasing the maximum jail time from thirty to ninety days, and, most important, providing for the first time a statutory minimum for violators of either a fifty-dollar fine or thirty days in jail. In 1896, the same year the Supreme Court upheld the separate-but-equal doctrine in *Plessy v. Ferguson*, Ohio passed a tough anti-lynching law.

Other midwestern states also passed various civil rights laws in the 1880s and 1890s, legalizing interracial marriage, guaranteeing blacks equal access to public accommodations and other facilities, and even attempting to require that insurance companies charge the same premiums for blacks as they did for whites. In contrast, in 1883 the U.S. Supreme Court, in *Pace v. Alabama*, upheld the prosecution of an Alabama couple for violating the state's ban on interracial marriage. That same year Michigan repealed its own law prohibiting interracial marriage. In 1885 Michigan also passed a strong civil rights law, banning discrimination in restaurants, hotels, and other public places.

That year Nebraska also passed a law to protect the civil rights of all citizens. In 1896 Wisconsin passed a law "to protect all citizens in their civil and legal rights." Throughout the Northeast and Midwest, states passed such laws in the 1880s and 1890s, at the very time that states across the South were beginning to enact mandatory segregation laws. Moreover, these laws were passed after the Supreme Court struck down the federal Civil Rights Act of 1875 in the *Civil Rights Cases*. In other words, the northern response to the Court's rejection of racial fairness in the *Civil Rights Cases* was to adopt state laws to accomplish what the Court would not let Congress accomplish.

The Republican Party also remained formally committed to black rights, even though it was no longer able to protect them through legislation because of the opposition from Democrats in Congress. In 1892 the Republican Party platform denounced lynching, described as "continued inhuman outrages perpetrated upon American citizens for political reasons in certain Southern States of the Union." The Republican platform also directly asserted the rights of black voters:

> We demand that every citizen of the United States shall be allowed to cast one free and unrestricted ballot in all public elections, and that such ballot shall be counted and returned as cast; that such laws shall be enacted and enforced as will secure to every citizen, be he rich or poor, native or foreign-born, white or black, this sovereign right, guaranteed by the Constitution. The free and honest popular ballot, the just and equal representation of all the people, as well as their just and equal protection under the laws, are the foundation of our Republi-can institutions, and the party will never relax its efforts until the integrity of the ballot and the purity of elections shall be fully guaranteed and protected in every State. (Republican Party Platform of 1892)

While the northern states and the Republican Party pushed forward to protect the civil rights of blacks, the Supreme Court generally, but not always, supported southern restrictions on civil rights. In *Ex parte Yarbrough* (1884), also known as the *Ku Klux Klan Cases*, the Court upheld prosecutions of Tinsley E. Yarbrough and other Klansmen who had beaten a former slave in Georgia to prevent him from voting in a congressional election. The Court reasoned that the Fifteenth Amendment gave Congress the power to protect voters from private as well as state action. However, the Court would abandon this position two decades later in *James v. Bowman* (1903).

The last decade of the century signaled an end to any hope of committed civil rights protection from the Court. Over the objections of the local railroads and streetcar companies themselves, southern states increasingly required segregation on public transportation. In *Louisville, New Orleans, and Texas Railroad Company v. Mississippi* (1890), the Court upheld a Mississippi law requiring segregation on trains that operated in interstate commerce. The Court had previously denied the right of states to require integrated transportation, finding in *Hall v. DeCuir* (1878) that a Louisiana law on this subject interfered with federally regulated interstate commerce; now, however, the Court allowed such segregation. This case set the stage for a fully segregated South just as the age of Frederick Douglass came to an end. Douglass died in 1895, and the following year the Court would give its final blessing to racial segregation in *Plessy v. Ferguson*.

[*See also* African Americans and the West; American Revolution; Baltimore, Maryland, Slavery in; Black Church; Black Politics; Black Press; Butler, Benjamin Franklin; *Cambria* Incident; Civil Rights Act of 1866; Civil Rights Act of 1875; Civil War; Civil War, Participation and Recruitment of Black Troops in; Confederate States of America; Compromise of 1850; Constitution, U.S.; Crime and Punishment; Democratic Party; Discrimination; Douglass, Frederick; *Dred Scott* Case; Education; Election of 1860; Emancipation; Emancipation Proclamation; Fifteenth Amendment; Fisk, Clinton Bowen; Fourteenth Amendment; Free African Americans before the Civil War (North); Free African Americans before the Civil War (South); Free Speech; Freedmen; Freedmen's Bureau; Fugitive Slave Law of 1793; Fugitive Slave Law of 1850; Integration; Jim Crow Car Laws; Johnson, Andrew; Kansas-Nebraska Act; Langston, John Mercer; Laws and Legislation; Lincoln, Abraham; Lynching and Mob Violence; Marriage, Mixed; Military; Mulattoes; *My Bondage and My Freedom*; Native Americans and African Americans; Nell, William Cooper; Political Participation; Racism; Reconstruction; Republican Party; *Roberts v. City of Boston*; Rochester, New York; Segregation; Sharecropping; Slavery; Slavery and the U.S. Constitution; Supreme Court; Sumner, Charles; Taney, Roger B.; Union Army, African Americans in; Violence against African Americans; Voting Rights; *and* Work.]

BIBLIOGRAPHY

Anderson, Eric, and Alfred A. Moss Jr. *The Facts of Reconstruction: Essays in Honor of John Hope Franklin.* Baton Rouge: Louisiana State University Press, 1991.

Cohen, William. *At Freedom's Edge: Black Mobility and the Southern White Quest for Racial Control, 1861–1915.* Baton Rouge: Louisiana State University Press, 1991.

Finkelman, Paul. "Civil Rights in Historical Context: In Defense of Brown." *Harvard Law Review* 118.3 (2005): 973–1027.

Finkelman, Paul. "Prelude to the Fourteenth Amendment: Black Legal Rights in the Antebellum North." *Rutgers Law Journal* 17 (1986): 415–482.

Franklin, John Hope, and Alfred A. Moss Jr. *From Slavery to Freedom: A History of African Americans.* 8th ed. New York: McGraw Hill, 2000.

Gerber, David A. *Black Ohio and the Color Line, 1860–1915.* Urbana: University of Illinois Press, 1976.

Justice and Jurisprudence: An Inquiry Concerning the Constitutional Limitations of the Thirteenth, Fourteenth, and Fifteenth Amendments. Philadelphia: J. B. Lippincott, 1889.

Klarman, Michael. *From Jim Crow to Civil Rights: The Supreme Court and the Struggle for Racial Equality.* New York: Oxford University Press, 2004.

Logan, Rayford W. *The Negro in American Life and Thought: The Nadir, 1877–1901.* New York: Dial Press, 1954.

McBride, David. "Mid-Atlantic State Courts and the Struggle with the 'Separate but Equal' Doctrine: 1880–1939." *Rutgers Law Journal* 17 (Spring–Summer 1986): 569–589.

Morris, Thomas D. *Southern Slavery and the Law, 1619–1860.* Chapel Hill: University of North Carolina Press, 1996.

Murray, Pauli, ed. *States' Laws on Race and Color.* Athens: University of Georgia Press, 1997.

Nieman, Donald. *Promises to Keep: African Americans and the Constitutional Order, 1776 to the Present.* New York: Oxford University Press, 1991.

Rabinowitz, Howard. *Race Relations in the Urban South, 1865–1890.* New York: Oxford University Press, 1978.

Report of the Joint Committee on Reconstruction at the First Session Thirty-Ninth Congress. Washington, DC: Government Printing Office, 1866.

"Republican Party Platform of 1892." The American Presidency Project. http://www.presidency.ucsb.edu/showplatforms.php?platindex=R1892.

Urofsky, Melvin I., and Paul Finkelman. *A March of Liberty: A Constitutional History of the United States.* 2nd ed. New York: Oxford University Press, 2002.

Waldrep, Christopher. *Roots of Disorder: Race and Criminal Justice in the American South, 1817–1880.* Athens: University of Georgia Press, 1998.

Wang, Xi. *The Trial of Democracy: Black Suffrage and Northern Republicans, 1860–1910.* Athens: University of Georgia Press, 1997.

Williams, Lou Falkner. *The Great South Carolina Ku Klux Klan Trials, 1871–1872.* Athens: University of Georgia Press, 1996.

—PAUL FINKELMAN

CIVIL RIGHTS ACT OF 1866. Immediately after the Civil War many of the defeated former Confederate states passed new laws, known as "black codes," to control the recently freed slaves. Some of the laws prohibited blacks from living in towns, owning guns or dogs, or testifying against whites in some trials. Vagrancy laws required that former slaves have work contracts and allowed planters—often their former masters—to force them to labor if they did not have work contracts. Blacks who committed minor crimes could be hired out to planters or forced to work on chain gangs. If black parents were unemployed or deemed unfit in other ways, their children could be seized and "apprenticed" until they turned eighteen. The goal of all such laws was to reduce the freed people to a state as close to slavery as possible. Congress authorized the Joint Committee on Reconstruction to investigate these laws, as well as other conditions in the South, and recommend legislation. The committee suggested two remedies: the Civil Rights Act of 1866 and what became the Fourteenth Amendment to the Constitution.

In March 1866 Congress first passed the Civil Rights Act. The law overruled *Dred Scott v. Sandford* (1857), in which the Supreme Court had declared that blacks, even if free, could *never* be citizens of the United States. The first line of the new act stated that "all persons born in the United States . . . are hereby declared citizens of the United States" and that

> such citizens, of every race and color, without regard to any previous condition of slavery or involuntary servitude . . . shall have the same right, in every State and Territory in the United States, to make and enforce contracts, to sue, be parties, and give evidence, to inherit, purchase, lease, sell, hold, and convey real and personal property, and to full and equal benefit of all laws and proceedings for the security of person and property, as is enjoyed by white citizens, and shall be subject to like punishment, pains, and penalties.

The law made it a crime to deprive any person of his or her federal civil rights and gave the federal government the power to enforce these rights. Congress acted under section 2 of the Thirteenth Amendment, which empowered it to pass laws to implement the amendment.

President Andrew Johnson vetoed the act on 27 March 1866. Johnson argued that the act violated the rights of the states and that Congress was not authorized to pass such a law. He asserted that the Congress could not make blacks citizens of the United States or of the states and could not tell the states how to regulate their courts or in any other way interfere with what were generally called the "police powers" or "domestic institutions" of the states.

Congress overrode Johnson's veto on 9 April 1866. However, some supporters of the bill, including Representative John Bingham of Ohio, were uncertain whether Congress did, in fact, have power to pass the law. The

Thirteenth Amendment had ended slavery in the United States, and Republicans like Bingham wondered whether protecting civil rights was an element of ending slavery. Thus, led by Bingham, the Congress also passed the Fourteenth Amendment, which duplicated some of the Civil Rights Act—most important in guaranteeing national and state citizenship for all former slaves and all other persons born in the United States. Acting under the enforcement provisions of the Fourteenth Amendment and the Fifteenth Amendment (which prohibited discrimination in voting on the basis of race), Congress reenacted the Civil Rights Act in 1870.

The Civil Rights Act of 1866 was the first federal statute designed to protect individual rights and liberties at a national level. States resisted the law. In *Bowling v. Commonwealth* (1867), for example, Kentucky's highest court declared the act unconstitutional. Other states avoided the law or reinterpreted it. In order to preserve bans on interracial marriage, some states held that a marriage was not a contract as set out in section 1 of the 1866 act. While under national control during Reconstruction and with an integrated Republican Party in control of the state government, courts in two former Confederate states—Alabama (1872) and Louisiana (1874)—struck down their state antimiscegenation laws. However, after Reconstruction these states joined the rest of the South in banning interracial marriage.

By the 1880s the national government was doing little to protect black civil rights in the South. Enforcement of the 1866 act waned after Reconstruction formally ended in 1877. The Supreme Court, meanwhile, eviscerated congressional power to protect black freedom. In the *Slaughterhouse Cases* (1873) the Court gave a cramped and restricted interpretation of the Fourteenth Amendment. In the *Civil Rights Cases* (1883) the Court found that Congress had no power to regulate private discrimination under the 1875 Civil Rights Act. While not interpreting the 1866 act, this decision nevertheless undermined its enforcement. Indeed, by this time the Civil Rights Act of 1866 was mostly a dead letter. However, the act remained on the books and would be resurrected in the mid-twentieth century as a tool for civil rights enforcement.

[*See also* Civil Rights; Civil Rights Act of 1875; Compromise of 1850; Confederate Policy toward African Americans and Slaves; *Dred Scott* Case; Fifteenth Amendment; Fourteenth Amendment; Johnson, Andrew; Marriage, Mixed; Reconstruction; Supreme Court; Thirteenth Amendment; *and* Voting Rights.]

BIBLIOGRAPHY

Nieman, Donald G. *Promises to Keep: African-Americans and the Constitutional Order, 1776 to the Present*. New York: Oxford University Press, 1991.

—Paul Finkelman

CIVIL RIGHTS ACT OF 1875. Charles Sumner's proposed civil rights bill aimed to ensure that the rights of African American freedmen would be honored. Placed before the Senate on 13 May 1870, it was the first national desegregation measure in U.S. history. To Sumner, the Reconstruction measures already adopted did not provide blacks with the full range of rights to which, in his view, they were entitled as citizens. Sumner's bill called for an end to segregation of public accommodations, schools, and church organizations and for the right of African Americans to serve on juries. The first section reads:

> All persons within the jurisdiction of the United States shall be entitled to the full and equal enjoyment of the accommodations, advantages, facilities, and privileges of inns, public conveyances on land or water, theaters, and other places of public amusement; subject only to the conditions and limitations established by law, and applicable alike to citizens of every race and color, regardless of any previous conditions of servitude.

Sumner's first attempt to pass a civil rights bill faced the opposition of Senator Lyman Trumbull, the chairman of the Senate Judiciary Committee. Trumbull recommended the bill's "indefinite postponement." On 20 January 1871 Sumner made a second attempt to have the bill considered by this committee, but the Senate continued to balk. In view of this development, on 9 March 1871 Sumner chose to have the bill considered not by the Judiciary Committee but by the entire Senate. He pleaded before the first session of the Forty-second Congress to consider the bill on the ground that it "conformed to the Declaration of Independence and the Constitution." To Sumner, if the statement that "all men are created equal" did not have any legislative power, then the words were empty. The Senate ignored his request and sent the bill back to the Judiciary Committee. When the Senate met in December 1871 for the year's second session, the House was considering an amnesty bill advocating forgiveness for former Confederate leaders. Sumner decided to enter his bill as an amendment to the amnesty bill, hoping this would increase the chances for his bill to succeed. Furthermore, on 15 January 1872 Sumner presented a long argument emphasizing his views that the equal protection clause of the Fourteenth Amendment applied to public accommodations and schools. He related the humiliating experience that the abolitionist Frederick Douglass endured when, after returning from a government assignment in Santo Domingo, the Dominican Republic, he was not allowed to ride in the first-class railway car because of his race.

During Sumner's absence from the Senate because of illness, the Republican Senator Matthew Carpenter of Wisconsin spearheaded a series of political maneuvers that resulted in the civil rights bill being modified to ex-

"Death at the Polls, and Free from 'Federal Interference.'" Cartoon by Thomas Nast from *Harper's Weekly*, 18 October 1879. The skeleton, labeled "solid southern shotgun," is preventing African Americans from voting. (Library of Congress.)

clude two of its most controversial aspects: desegregation of schools and participation of blacks on juries. In spite of the changes the Republicans were unable to obtain the two-thirds majority for the bill's passage.

When the Forty-third Congress resumed activities, Sumner renewed efforts to pass the civil rights bill. He restated his arguments with customary passion despite having been ill. His focus now was to substantiate the fact that each of the institutions named in the rider was already subject to a common-law duty to treat all applicants equally. Furthermore, according to Sumner, the duties and obligations of national citizenship superseded state citizenship. He asserted that it was therefore "perfectly constitutional for Congress to say to the states, 'the regulation of the relations between all these institutions and the public is with you, but you shall treat citizenship as citizenship, every-where.'" Therefore, the Fourteenth

Amendment's equal protection clause was to be honored by all the states and could not be violated by any state law under any circumstances. Sumner stated, "All citizens, without regard to race or color, shall have the same rights, in every State and Territory in the United States."

Sumner died on 11 March 1874 without seeing his bill passed. In the House the bill was finally passed on 4 February 1875, omitting the desegregation of schools clause. The bill was approved in the Senate on 27 April 1875. Eight years later the U.S. Supreme Court, on 15 October 1883, declared the bill unconstitutional. The historian Bertram Wyatt-Brown asserts that "the members of [Sumner's party] were losing their enthusiasm for aggressive racial reform." The Court gave way to the northern mood for conciliation with the South and to the South's racist views. In the process of forgiving and forgetting, the freedmen were forgotten.

Douglass reacted to the Supreme Court's decision with a mixture of anger and sadness, as expressed in several speeches and in his writings: "The Supreme Court decision has hauled down this flag of liberty in open day, and before all the people, and has thereby given joy to the heart of every man in the land who wishes to deny to others what he claims for himself." In a public meeting after the decision Douglass asserted, "The enemies of justice rejoice, the friends of freedom mourned." It would take nearly a century before a movement to guarantee the civil rights of African Americans and other people of color would begin.

[*See also* Black Politics; Civil Rights; Civil Rights Act of 1866; Discrimination; Douglass, Frederick; Fourteenth Amendment; Freedmen; Laws and Legislation, Civil War and After; Political Participation; Racism; Reconstruction; Reform; Republican Party; Segregation; Sumner, Charles; *and* Supreme Court.]

BIBLIOGRAPHY

Avins, Alfred. "The Civil Rights Act of 1875: Some Reflected Light on the Fourteenth Amendment and Public Accommodations." *Columbia Law Review* 66 (May 1966): 873–915.

Foner, Eric, and Olivia Mahoney. *America's Reconstruction: People and Politics after the Civil War.* New York: HarperPerennial, 1995.

Wilson, Kirt H. *The Reconstruction Desegregation Debate: The Politics of Equality and the Rhetoric of Place, 1870–1875.* East Lansing: Michigan State University Press, 2002.

Wyatt-Brown, Bertram. "The Civil Rights Act of 1875." *Western Political Quarterly* 18.4 (December 1965): 763–765.

—ALICIA RIVERA

African American soldier, tintype, 1862–1865. The second Confiscation Act of 17 July 1862, which freed slaves owned by rebels, also empowered the president to enlist black soldiers. By the end of the Civil War, some 200,000 blacks had served in the U.S. military. (Library of Congress.)

CIVIL WAR. Few events in American history are more significant than the Civil War. The four years of conflict from 1861 to 1865 changed the nation more profoundly than any other single event. The bloody war finally laid to rest the contentious issue of slavery, ending half the nation's horrendous reliance on the buying and selling of human flesh. The Union's industrial power, which the war only provided a glimpse of, grew and strengthened throughout the rest of the nineteenth century. The way Americans saw themselves also changed. The war brought a new sense of nationalism, especially to the Union; Americans began to refer to "*The* United States" as opposed to "*These* United States." Americans also started to view the federal government and the presidency differently. Instead of being some entity in far-off Washington, D.C., during and after the war the federal government came into much closer contact with the average citizen than ever before. The presidency also began to assume more importance than it had in the past; over time, Americans grew to expect strong leadership from their president.

Women found themselves in new roles; many were involved in some aspect of public service, in the workforce, or in running the family farm for the very first time.

More has been written on the Civil War than on any other single event in American history. Historians are still debating the causes of the conflict that tore the nation apart in April 1861. The institution of slavery, however, is the key to understanding why North and South literally came to blows. As the North eagerly industrialized in the first half of the nineteenth century, the South remained basically agrarian. There was some industry in the South, but for the most part, it was a much smaller part of the economic system compared with the system in the North. Without slavery, the North relied more on immigrant labor; thus, such new industries as textiles, iron, and coal mining drew many newcomers. The South, with its pool of slave labor, was not as attractive as the North to these immigrants.

The increasing numbers of immigrants led to a greater degree of urbanization in the North; the established eastern cities grew rapidly, as did new western cities like Cincinnati, Chicago, and St. Louis. The progressively more disparate cultures of the North and South made the latter far more defensive about such issues as slavery and states' rights. These different patterns of development, coupled with the perceived strength of abolitionism, the Mexican-American War, the Compromise of 1850, the Kansas-Nebraska Act, the *Dred Scott* decision, and John Brown's raid on Harpers Ferry, supplied the makings of the conflagration of the Civil War. The election in 1860 of Abraham Lincoln, who many southerners viewed as a dangerous and radical abolitionist, was the final straw and led to the secession of the Lower South beginning in December 1860. Despite attempts at compromise, the war began on 12 April 1861, after Lincoln tried to resupply Fort Sumter in South Carolina. Following Lincoln's subsequent call for seventy-five thousand volunteer troops, four additional states in the South seceded, giving the Confederate States of America a total of eleven states.

Major Battles and Campaigns. From the outset, both sides set as their goal the capture of each other's capital. There was also a general belief in the North and South that the war would be over in ninety days. The first major engagement of the war took place on 21 July 1861 at the battle of Bull Run, where the Union suffered a humiliating defeat at the hands of Generals Joseph E. Johnston and P. G. T. Beauregard. For more than a year thereafter, the Union was hard-pressed to win a battle in the eastern theater. In the West the Union had two goals: to keep the border states loyal to the North and to gain control of the full length of the Mississippi River; both efforts proved to be successful. Union victories in 1862 at Shiloh in Mississippi and Forts Donelson and Henry in Tennessee, as well as the capture of New Orleans by Commander David Farragut, helped strengthen the Union position in the West.

For the most part, the eastern theater in 1861 and 1862 was a disaster for the federal forces, with major losses in the peninsula campaign under the leadership of General George McClellan. A Union victory in the East finally came at the battle of Antietam in September 1862. Although the Union won at Antietam, McClellan failed to follow Robert E. Lee's army back to Virginia—a display of indecisiveness that infuriated Lincoln. For his part, Lincoln used the victory at Antietam as justification for issuing his preliminary Emancipation Proclamation, which freed the slaves in areas still in rebellion on 1 January 1863. Meanwhile, Lincoln continued his search for a general who would fight and replaced McClellan in November 1862 with Ambrose E. Burnside, the "hero" of Antietam.

Burnside, however, suffered a major defeat at Fredericksburg, Virginia, in December 1862. Continuing the string of Union disasters, Lee again defeated the federal forces under the command of Joseph J. Hooker at Chancellorsville in the spring of 1863. Although Lee won the battle, the death of Thomas J. "Stonewall" Jackson proved to be a major loss for the Confederacy. Lee's decision the following summer to invade the North provided one of the major turning points of the war. The battle of Gettysburg on 1–3 July 1863 pitted the two sides in a horrendous encounter outside a small town in southern Pennsylvania, which resulted in a major Union victory. The federal troops under General George G. Meade did not push their advantage, however, and pursue Lee's army back across the Potomac. At the same time as the battle of Gettysburg, Union troops under the command of Ulysses S. Grant finally took the town of Vicksburg, Mississippi, after a long siege. The capture of Vicksburg essentially cut off the western section of the Confederacy from its eastern sector by putting control of the Mississippi River in Union hands. Grant's success led Lincoln to promote him to the rank of lieutenant general and place him in command of all Union armies.

Under the command of General William Tecumseh Sherman, the Army of the Tennessee began its move east. Sherman pursued Confederate troops through Georgia in the famous Atlanta campaign during the summer and early fall of 1864, capturing the major railroad terminus of Atlanta in early September. Throughout the fall, Sherman conducted his scorched-earth "march to the sea" and captured the city of Savannah in December. While Sherman's troops devastated the countryside of Georgia and the Carolinas, General Philip H. Sheridan and the Union cavalry wreaked havoc on the Shenandoah Valley of Virginia. From 31 May through 12 June 1864, Lee and Grant engaged in the bloody battle of Cold Harbor, Virginia. A few days later both sides were bogged down in the siege of Petersburg, which lasted until April 1865. In early April the Confederate government evacuated Richmond and the federal troops then occupied the capital. Lee surrendered his forces to Grant at Appomattox Court House, Virginia, on 9 April 1865, essentially ending the Civil War. Sporadic fighting continued in the West, however, through 26 May 1865.

Struggle for Emancipation. The path to Emancipation was not straightforward. Responding in August 1862 to the reformer Horace Greeley's famous editorial in the New York Tribune, "The Prayer of Twenty Millions," Lincoln declared that this conflict was a war to preserve the Union.

My paramount object in the struggle *is* to save the Union, and is *not* either to save or destroy slavery. . . . If I could save the Union without freeing *any* slave I would do it, and if I could save it by freeing some and leaving others alone, I would also do that. (Donald et al., pp. 331–332)

Frederick Douglass, however, preferred to let the Union "perish" if the only way to keep it together was to make concessions to slave owners. The former slave believed that the war to save the Union was inextricably linked to the elimination of slavery. Indeed, while abolitionists wanted this conflict to focus on ending slavery, most were not overtly critical of Lincoln and his administration, at least in the beginning. Generally, abolitionists felt that battling the "slave oligarchy," as William Lloyd Garrison put it in a letter of 1861, would destroy slavery in the end. Douglass vehemently disagreed with this position, noting that fighting slaveholders without the ultimate goal of Emancipation was "a half-hearted business and paralyzes the hands engaged in it." Agreeing with Lincoln that the South had had no right to secede from the Union, Douglass saw the war as the opportunity to build a new nation in which African Americans were free and equal citizens.

Throughout 1861 and 1862 Republicans and abolitionists, including Douglass, pressed Lincoln to commit himself publicly to ending slavery. The president's silence perturbed many, especially Douglass, who believed Lincoln to be the "tool" of "traitors," meaning those who opposed Emancipation, especially northerners. For his part, Lincoln tried to soften opposition to ending slavery by coupling Emancipation with a plan for colonization in Central America. Lincoln believed that whites and blacks could not live together and proposed establishing a colony in Central America where American blacks could resettle and have more opportunities. One of Lincoln's main concerns was not alienating the border states, lest those that permitted slaveholding leave the Union. The proponents of Emancipation, however, argued that freeing the slaves would help to defeat the Confederacy because it would eliminate an important labor source for the South. In the first two years of the war, slaves had been put to work building fortifications, delivering supplies, working in mines and factories, and digging trenches, thus freeing up white Southerners for combat service.

Moreover, the realities of frontline combat forced the federal government to deal with the issue of slavery. As the Union armies pushed forward, slaves either were captured or fled behind Union lines. General John C. Frémont, who tried to contain rampant guerilla warfare in Missouri by declaring martial law, also decreed, on 30 August 1861, that all the slaves in Missouri were now free. Lincoln revoked Frémont's orders and removed him from command, dashing the hopes of Douglass and other abolitionists. General Benjamin F. Butler set a precedent when he began treating captured slaves as "contraband of war," considering them to be property forfeited by owners who were in rebellion against the United States. As more slaves found themselves in Union hands, the ques-

tion of their status became a pressing issue. Were they still slaves? Were they free?

Congress responded by passing the First Confiscation Act in August 1861, which declared that slaves could be seized as rebel property if they were employed to aid the war effort. Slavery was finally abolished in the District of Columbia in April of the following year. The second Confiscation Act of 17 July 1862 freed the slaves owned by rebels and also empowered the president to enlist black soldiers. The same day, Congress passed the Militia Act, which freed "soldier slaves" of all owners, including slaveholders loyal to the Union, who would receive compensation for the loss of their former slaves. These pieces of legislation were steps on the way to Lincoln's announcement of the preliminary Emancipation Proclamation on 22 September 1862, following the Union victory at Antietam.

Two months before the September announcement, Lincoln read his proposal for Emancipation to his cabinet. Only Montgomery Blair, the Postmaster General, was completely opposed to the president's proposal. Blair believed that declaring Emancipation would cost the Republicans control of Congress in the upcoming elections. Lincoln invited a group of free African Americans to the White House in August 1862, when he gave a speech on colonization. In this speech, Lincoln essentially cited the presence of blacks in the United States as the reason for the war. He also stated that he believed that racial equality was impossible and that the two races could not live together harmoniously. An irate Frederick Douglass reprinted Lincoln's words in his newspaper, *Douglass' Monthly*, in September 1862, followed by a scathing commentary. Douglass wrote that Lincoln's view was like "a horse thief pleading that the existence of the horse is the apology for his theft"—a classic instance of blaming the victim. In his speech, Lincoln also reiterated his scheme for colonization, which struck great fear into Douglass's heart. Clearly the Emancipation Proclamation was only one step in the direction of full Emancipation and equality when it finally took effect on 1 January 1863.

Douglass rejoiced, however, when news of the Emancipation Proclamation reached Boston, where he spoke on this momentous occasion. The former slave later wrote of this great day of jubilee: "We were waiting . . . as for a bolt from the sky, which should rend the fetters of four million slaves; we were watching . . . by the dim light of stars, for the dawn of a new day, we were longing for the answer to the agonizing prayer of centuries." The Emancipation Proclamation finally turned the Civil War into the holy cause Douglass believed it should have been all along; as he had stated in *Douglass' Monthly* in July 1861, "not a slave should be left a slave in the returning footprints of the American army gone to put down this slave-

African Americans with Meade's army in Culpeper, Virginia, photographed by Timothy H. O'Sullivan in November 1863. For three years during the Civil War, working for Alexander Gardner, O'Sullivan photographed soldiers before and after battle. His images were included in *Gardner's Photographic Sketchbook of the War*, 1866. (Library of Congress.)

holding rebellion. Sound policy, not less than humanity, demands the instant liberation of every slave in the rebel states."

Slavery and Emancipation then became a key issue in the presidential election of 1864. Lincoln interpreted the Republican victory in that election as a mandate for ensuring the end of slavery once and for all with the passage of the Thirteenth Amendment to the Constitution. Congress passed the amendment on 31 January 1865, and ratification by the necessary twenty-seven states was completed by 6 December 1865.

Blacks in the Military. From the beginning of the Civil War, not only did the issue of slavery consume the thoughts of participants on both sides, so did the question of black combatants. After Fort Sumter, many blacks in the North tried to enlist in the armed forces on the Union side in the hope that slavery would end with the defeat of the Confederacy. At the time, the U.S. government refused their help. Frederick Douglass strongly supported the enlistment of African Americans to fight the war, stating, "Let the slaves and colored people be called into service, and formed into a liberating army to march into the South and raise the banner of Emancipation among the slaves." Several Union commanders, including Benjamin Butler, David Hunter, and James Lane, took it upon themselves to organize black troops into combat units. Hunter, who commanded the Department of South Carolina, was the first to allow blacks to fight for their own cause. The Union formally created regiments of black troops in August 1862; however, these units were to be led by white commanders.

While the recruitment of black soldiers made sense to many Northerners, the persistent racism of some people engendered a distrust and even fear of such forces. Once in military service, blacks were segregated into their own units and used primarily not for actual combat duty but to build fortifications and perform other general labor duties. The only exception to the racially segregated armed forces was in the Union navy, in which twenty thousand black sailors served alongside their white comrades. African American soldiers were also discriminated against

Burial party in Viriginia, April 1865. These African Americans were collecting bones of Union soldiers killed nearly a year earlier, in June 1864, in the battles of Gaines Mill and Cold Harbor. Sixty thousand men died or were wounded here—so many that the local residents had not been able to bury the dead as was the usual custom. The photographer, John Reekie, worked for Mathew Brady's studio; some of his images appeared in Alexander Gardner's *Photographic Sketchbook of the War*. (Library of Congress.)

in terms of salary (although Congress eventually authorized equal pay for black soldiers in 1864), reenlistment bonuses, and even medical care. Yet despite these obstacles, the United States Colored Troops served their country valiantly.

The Fifty-Fourth Massachusetts Infantry Regiment, commanded by Robert Gould Shaw, was one of the most famous regiments of black soldiers. Among its numbers were two of Frederick Douglass's sons, Charles and Lewis, who served with distinction. The Fifty-Fourth Massachusetts lost 40 percent of its men as they fought courageously in the battle of Fort Wagner, South Carolina, in July 1863. The performance of the Colored Troops at Fort Wagner as well as in other engagements did much to dissipate objections to black soldiers and, in fact, gained them respect and admiration. Douglass actively recruited African Americans for military service, throwing himself into this activity with the same conviction and enthusiasm as he had done with abolitionism.

Douglass used his considerable oratorical skills to convince black men that they would be able to contribute to the destruction of slavery by enlisting in the armed forces.

As he put it, "Once let the black man get upon his person the brass letters, U.S. . . . and there is no power on Earth which can deny that he has earned the right to citizenship in the United States." He held on to his dream that African Americans would receive the full benefits of American citizenship and equal treatment before the law by serving the United States in a time of crisis. While Douglass understood the depth of racism in nineteenth-century America, he also believed that the loyalty and dedication his people showed toward the Union would help soften at least some of the hostility and mistrust of his race and eventually lead to full equality.

By the end of the war, more than 200,000 African-Americans had served in the U.S. army and navy, with about 37,000 casualties. Black soldiers made up about one-ninth of the Union army by the summer of 1864. It is clear that the United States Colored Troops made, as Douglass and others insisted, significant contributions to the Union's victory. Besides participating in over forty engagements, in which they often made the difference between defeat and victory, black soldiers also provided much of the labor that supported the troops in the field, such as guarding and delivering supplies, building defenses, driving supply trains, and numerous other vital tasks. The Colored Troops also provided a psychological advantage for the Union. The idea of so many armed African Americans, many of whom were former slaves, struck fear into the hearts of many Southerners. For countless years, Southerners had trembled at the thought of slave rebellions; now it looked as if those nightmares were becoming reality. The opportunity to fight the Confederacy also inspired numerous slaves to make their way to Union lines and join the Union army—not only swelling the federal ranks but at the same time depriving the Confederacy of an important source of labor. Although there were many after the war who tried to belittle the contributions of the Colored Troops to the North's war effort, it is clear that black soldiers and sailors were important to the Union's final victory.

When the Civil War began, Frederick Douglass had high hopes for a better future for African Americans. He believed that the conflict was a war against slavery and that a Union victory would mean more than freedom for his people—he believed that despite the deep racism harbored by many white Americans, African Americans would be able to participate fully as American citizens. Late in the war, Douglass summed up his feelings for the future:

I end where I began; no war but an abolition war; no peace but an abolition peace; liberty for all, chains for none; the black man a soldier in war; a laborer in peace; a voter in the South as well as the North; America his permanent home, and all Americans his fellow countrymen. (Donald et al., pp. 345–346)

The war did end slavery, but equal justice for all was a promise deferred.

[See also Antislavery Movement; Black Militias; Brown, John; Buffalo Soldiers; Butler, Benjamin Franklin; Civil War, Participation and Recruitment of Black Troops in; Colonization; Compromise of 1850; Confederate States of America; Constitution, U.S.; Douglass, Charles Remond; Douglass, Frederick; Douglass, Lewis Henry; *Douglass' Monthly*; *Dred Scott* Case; Election of 1860; Emancipation; Emancipation Proclamation; Fifty-Fourth Massachusetts Infantry Regiment; Grant, Ulysses S.; Greeley, Horace; Harpers Ferry Raid; Immigrants; Kansas-Nebraska Act; Laws and Legislation; Lincoln, Abraham; Mexican-American War; Military; Racism; Republican Party; Segregation; Slavery; Slavery and the U.S. Constitution; Taney, Roger B.; Thirteenth Amendment; Union Army, African Americans in; Union Army, African Americans in; *and* Women.]

BIBLIOGRAPHY

Blight, David W. *Frederick Douglass' Civil War: Keeping Faith in Jubilee*. Baton Rouge: Louisiana State University Press, 1989. The single best source on Frederick Douglass and the Civil War. Blight examines Douglass's role in the Civil War and studies his motivations as well as his religious beliefs.

Clinton, Catherine, and Nina Silber, eds. *Divided Houses: Gender and the Civil War*. New York: Oxford University Press, 1992. A book of essays detailing the impact of the Civil War on gender roles, exploring topics such as manhood and soldiering, women as nurses, and freedwomen during Reconstruction.

Donald, David Herbert, Jean Harvey Baker, and Michael F. Holt. *The Civil War and Reconstruction*. New York: Norton, 2001. An updated edition of the classic one-volume history of the war and its aftermath.

Glatthaar, Joseph T. *Forged in Battle: The Civil War Alliance of Black Soldiers and White Officers*. New York: Free Press, 1990. Details the role of black soldiers in the Civil War and uncovers their significant—and often neglected—contribution to the Union victory.

McPherson, James M. *Battle Cry of Freedom: The Civil War Era*. New York: Oxford University Press, 1988. One of the best one-volume works on the Civil War and winner of the Pulitzer Prize for history.

McPherson, James M. *The Struggle for Equality: Abolitionists and the Negro in the Civil War and Reconstruction*. Princeton, NJ: Princeton University Press, 1964. Looks at the role of African Americans in the war and also examines what abolitionists and blacks hoped to achieve in the aftermath.

Paludan, Phillip Shaw. *"A People's Contest": The Union and Civil War 1861–1865*. New York: Harper and Row, 1988. Looks at the North during the Civil War and examines, in particular, how industrialization transformed the United States into a modern nation through its forging in battle.

Quarles, Benjamin. *The Negro in the Civil War*. Boston: Little, Brown, 1953. One of the earliest works to study African Americans and the Civil War.

—DONNA M. DEBLASIO

CIVIL WAR, PARTICIPATION AND RECRUITMENT OF BLACK TROOPS IN.

Frederick Douglass considered the Civil War to be both a millennial event and a regenerative force in American life. He believed that a redeeming God would use the war as a crucible to free the South's 4 million slaves. After years of personal and collective protest against slavery, Douglass framed the war's meaning—its suffering and its mandate—in apocalyptic terms.

Central to Douglass's understanding of the war was his vision of free blacks and former slaves' fighting to free their slave brethren. In May 1861 he clamored for "carrying the war into Africa [the South]"; he declared, "Let the slaves and free colored people be called into service, and formed into a liberating army." In January 1862, while waiting impatiently for the government to free and arm the slaves, Douglass remarked, "Slavery has been, and is yet the shield and helmet of this accursed rebellion." President Abraham Lincoln listened to but was unmoved by Douglass's appeals.

Since the war's outbreak in April 1861 the president had insisted that the conflict was a constitutional struggle to

Band of the 107th U.S. Colored Infantry at Fort Corcoran, Arlingston, Virigina, c. 1862–1865. Congress established no standard band instrumentation, but most bands—like this one—used all brass, since brass instruments stood up best in outdoor conditions. (Library of Congress.)

keep the Union intact, not a war to destroy slavery or to arm blacks. Lincoln understood that emancipation, the use of armed black soldiers, and the possibility of placing blacks on a social and political par with whites would all challenge the nation's racial status quo: white supremacy. Thus, such actions would fuel the racial phobias of conservative Democrats and Republicans and discourage white enlistment. Lincoln also worried that emancipation would alienate nonslaveholders as well as slaveholders in the loyal border states and might further solidify opposition to the Union in Confederate states.

Nevertheless, Douglass became disgusted by what he considered to be Lincoln's inaction. In a 4 July 1862 speech, Douglass charged that Lincoln's policies had "been calculated . . . to shield and protect slavery" and that the president had "scornfully rejected the policy of arming the slaves, a policy naturally suggested and enforced by the nature and necessities of the war." Two months later, in a blistering editorial in *Douglass' Monthly*,

the black leader branded Lincoln as little more than "an itinerant Colonization lecturer, showing all his inconsistencies, his pride of race and blood, his contempt for Negroes and his canting hypocrisy." Despite Lincoln's professed antislavery views, Douglass blasted him as "quite a genuine representative of American prejudice and Negro hatred and far more concerned for the preservation of slavery, and the favor of the Border Slave States, than for any sentiment of magnanimity or principle of justice and humanity." Specifically, Douglass complained that Lincoln, lacking "courage and honesty," had failed to enforce the Second Confiscation Act of July 1862. The president had

evaded his obvious duty, and instead of calling the blacks to arms and to liberty he merely authorized the military commanders to use them as laborers, without even promising them their freedom at the end of their term of service . . . and thus destroyed virtually the very object of the measure. (Foner, vol. 3, p. 269)

Lincoln's decision to issue the final Emancipation Proclamation in January 1863 forced Douglass to change his tune. By that time the president had concluded that the destruction of slavery had become both a military necessity and a major Union war aim. The enlistment of black troops was inextricably linked to Lincoln's emancipation policy.

Douglass congratulated Lincoln on the "amazing change" regarding emancipation, calling it an "amazing approximation toward the sacred truth of human liberty." Douglass added that "we are all liberated" by the Emancipation Proclamation; "the white man is liberated, the black man is liberated, the brave men now fighting the battles of their country against rebels and traitors are now liberated, and may strike . . . the Rebels, at their most sensitive point." Convinced that black troops would help turn the tide in the direction of Union victory, Douglass predicted that "whoever sees fifty thousand well drilled colored soldiers in the United States, will see slavery abolished and the union of these States secured from rebel violence."

Determined to do his part to recruit black troops, in 1863 Douglass joined such leading abolitionists as George Luther Stearns, Richard P. Hallowell, Martin Robison Delany, William Birney, Henry McNeal Turner, and John Mercer Langston in traversing the Northern states to gather enlistees. Douglass admonished black recruits "to fly to arms, and smite with death the power that would bury the government and your liberty in the same hopeless grave." Douglass's dream of "carrying the war into Africa" became a reality in May 1863 when African Americans fought heroically at the battle of Port Hudson, Louisiana, the first significant assault by black troops in the war.

Two months later, when addressing a mass meeting in Philadelphia, Douglass explained the importance of black men brandishing their swords to defeat the Rebels:

> Never since the world began was a better chance offered to a long enslaved and oppressed people. The opportunity is given us to be men. With one courageous resolution we may blot out the hand-writing of the ages against us. Once let the black man get upon his person the brass letters U.S.; let him get an eagle on his button, and a musket on his shoulder, and bullets in his pocket, and there is no power on earth or under the earth which can deny that he has earned the right of citizenship in the United States. I say again, this is our chance, and woe betide us if we fail to embrace it. (Foner, vol. 3, p. 365)

Douglass realized, however, that the U.S. Colored Troops confronted twin obstacles generally unknown to white Union soldiers. Confederate President Jefferson Davis threatened to enslave black troops captured in battle and to execute their white officers. African American soldiers also had to combat the across-the-board second-class status accorded them by the U.S. government. Lincoln's administration and acts passed by Congress denied blacks commissions as officers; provided them with inferior pay, equipment, and medical care; and largely denied their families the humanitarian relief provided to white soldiers' families.

Douglass exploded with anger when he learned of the Confederates' treatment of the Fifty-fourth Massachusetts Infantry Regiment at Battery Wagner on 18 July 1863. Although the black soldiers fought heroically "and vindicated their sponsors, the abolitionists," the regiment paid a heavy price for its valor. Almost one half of the six hundred men who attacked the Confederates were killed, wounded, or captured.

Douglass admonished George L. Stearns,

> Think of its noble and brave officers literally hacked to pieces while many of its rank and file have been sold into a slavery worse than death, and pardon me if I hesitate about . . . raising a fourth Regiment until the President shall give the same protection to them as to white soldiers. (Foner, vol. 3, p. 369)

Further, Douglass complained, "the slaughter of blacks taken as captives seems to affect him as little as the slaughter of beeves for the use of his army." He wrote in August 1863, "Colored men have a right not only to ask for equal pay for equal work, but that merit, not color, should be the criterion observed by Government in the distribution of places."

While sympathetic to the injustice accorded black soldiers in terms of their unequal pay, Lincoln urged them to be patient. According to Douglass, in August 1863 the president reminded him that many whites still doubted the wisdom of enlisting black troops, that many whites still considered the idea of black soldiers offensive, and "the fact that they were not to receive the same pay as white soldiers seemed a necessary concession to smooth the way to their employment at all as soldiers." In a reportedly patronizing tone, Lincoln informed Douglass that because black men "had larger motives for being soldiers than white men . . . they ought to be willing to enter the service upon any condition." Lincoln eventually assured Douglass that the government would equalize the pay of black and white soldiers—but the men would have to wait.

Douglass and African American troops, however, were losing "patience and faith" with Lincoln. As late as September 1864, the black leader, writing in the *Liberator*, remained dismayed at the government's

> treatment of our poor black soldiers—the refusal to pay them anything like equal compensation, though it was promised them when they enlisted; the refusal to insist upon the exchange of colored prisoners, and to retaliate upon rebel pris-

oners when colored prisoners have been slaughtered in cold blood, although the President has repeatedly promised thus to protect the lives of his colored soldiers. (p. 1)

Though the black soldiers held on, they remained impatient and seethed with indignation, especially over their unequal wages. Back home, their families suffered from lack of support. Not until 3 March 1865 did Congress finally grant full retroactive pay to all black soldiers who had been promised equal pay upon mustering into the service.

Although Douglass never joined the U.S. Colored Troops—the secretary of war, Edwin M. Stanton, reportedly promised him a commission that never came to pass—two of his sons, Charles and Lewis, served in the Fifty-fourth Massachusetts Infantry Regiment. A third son, Frederick Douglass Jr., recruited black troops in Mississippi. By the war's end, with Douglass's assistance, the army had raised 178,975 African American soldiers. His prediction that the war would forever change African Americans' relationship to white Americans had proven true.

[*See also* Black Militias; Civil War; Confederate Policy toward African Americans and Slaves; Confederate States of America; Delany, Martin Robison; Discrimination; *Douglass' Monthly*; Douglass, Frederick; Emancipation; Emancipation Proclamation; Fifty-fifth Massachusetts Infantry Regiment; Fifty-fourth Massachusetts Infantry Regiment; Integration; Langston, John Mercer; Lincoln, Abraham; Military; Religious Beliefs, Frederick Douglass and; Stearns, George Luther; *and* Union Army, African Americans in.]

BIBLIOGRAPHY

Blight, David W. *Frederick Douglass' Civil War: Keeping Faith in Jubilee*. Baton Rouge: Louisiana State University Press, 1989.

Douglass, Frederick. "Frederick Douglass on President Lincoln." *Liberator* 16 September 1864, 1.

Douglass, Frederick. *Life and Times of Frederick Douglass* (1881). New York: Random House, 1993.

Foner, Philip S., ed. *The Life and Writings of Frederick Douglass*. 5 vols. New York: International Publishers, 1950–1975. See, in particular, volume 3, *The Civil War*.

Smith, John David. "Let Us All Be Grateful That We Have Colored Troops That Will Fight." In *Black Soldiers in Blue: African American Troops in the Civil War Era*, edited by John David Smith, 1–77. Chapel Hill: University of North Carolina Press, 2002.

—JOHN DAVID SMITH

CLARKSON, THOMAS (b. 28 March 1760; d. 26 September 1846), an English publicist and leader in the abolitionist movement. Thomas Clarkson single-mindedly devoted his life to ending the slave trade and slavery. Clarkson was born in Wisbech, Cambridgeshire, England.

His father, the Reverend John Clarkson (who died suddenly when Thomas was only six years old) was headmaster of the Wisbech Free Grammar School; his mother, Anne Ward, came from a genteel background. From an early age Clarkson was raised in the Anglican faith, which was to inspire his tireless abolitionist activities in later life.

Clarkson, who initially pursued a career in the church, was a diligent and brilliant student. After attending Saint Paul's School in London, he earned a bachelor's degree at Saint John's College, Cambridge, in 1783. In 1785 he won first place in a Latin dissertation contest at Cambridge for which the given subject was *Anne liceat invitos in servitutem dare?* (Is it lawful to make slaves of others against their will?). The following year Clarkson expanded his dissertation, translated it into English, and published it as a book, *An Essay on the Slavery and Commerce of the Human Species, Particularly the African*. Clarkson's researching and writing the essay had a profound impact on the direction of his career. Even though he had already been ordained a deacon, he decided to commit his life to the antislavery movement.

With a group of abolitionists in Great Britain, Clarkson helped to lobby the British parliament to first outlaw the slave trade and then later to emancipate slaves in the colonies. In 1787 he joined the Committee for the Abolition of the Slave Trade, which at the time consisted largely of Quakers. To pass a bill to abolish the slave trade, he teamed up with the member of Parliament William Wilberforce. While Clarkson toured Britain to gather information to support the abolition of the slave trade, Wilberforce worked on legislative matters in Parliament. Through persistent petitions by the antislavery lobby, Parliament finally passed the Bill for the Abolition of the Slave Trade in 1807. In the 1820s Clarkson worked with Thomas Buxton, who succeeded William Wilberforce as the leader of the antislavery campaign in the House of Commons, to organize his own country's Anti-Slavery Society with the mission of ending slavery in British colonies. The society's goal was attained in 1833, when Parliament passed the Emancipation Bill. Through his many publications and wide correspondence, Clarkson became a father figure among abolitionists throughout the world, especially in the United States.

In the 1830s and 1840s Clarkson shifted his attention to the slavery issue in the United States, corresponding with leading American abolitionists and writing pamphlets on slavery in America. Many abolitionists sought his advice and endorsement. In 1831 the American philanthropist Elliott Cresson visited Clarkson to obtain his endorsement for a plan by the American Colonization Society, which wanted to manumit slaves in America and have them immigrate to Liberia. Persuaded by Cresson, Clarkson initially supported the plan but eventually canceled his endorsement because he thought the plan was unpractical. In 1833 Clarkson was visited by William Lloyd Garrison, the founder of the New England Anti-Slavery Society and the editor of the weekly antislavery publication *Liberator*. Garrison was campaigning for an immediate end to slavery in America. Even though Clarkson admired Garrison's passion, he believed the American was distracted by too many other liberal issues, such as women's suffrage and pacifism. Clarkson criticized the proslavery stance of the clergy and members of many American Christian churches in several pamphlets, including *Letter to the Clergy of Various Denominations and to the Slave-Holding Planters in the Southern Parts of the United States* (1841) and *Letter to Such Professing Christians in the Northern States of America as Have Had No Practical Concern with Slave Holding* (1844). In 1842 Clarkson played an influential role in exempting fugitive slaves in Canada from the Webster-Ashburton Treaty, which extradited criminals between Great Britain and the United States.

On 20 August 1846, shortly before his death, Clarkson was visited by three fellow abolitionists: the Scotsman George Thompson and the Americans Frederick Douglass and Garrison. Douglass was touring Britain to lecture on American slavery and to establish contact with prominent abolitionists. From his correspondence with American abolitionists, Clarkson knew about Douglass's background and activities. In his third autobiography, *Life and Times of Frederick Douglass* (1881, 1892), Douglass recounted his brief encounter with Clarkson, who at the time was seated at a table busily writing a letter to America against slavery: "He took one of my hands in both of his, and, in a tremulous voice, said 'God bless you, Frederick Douglass! I have given sixty years of my life to the emancipation of your people, and if I had sixty years more they should all be given to the same cause.'" Clarkson died at Playford Hall, Suffolk, at the age of eighty-six.

[*See also* Abolitionism as a Concept; American Colonization Society; Antislavery Movement; England, Frederick Douglass and; Garrison, William Lloyd; Liberia; *and* Thompson, George.]

BIBLIOGRAPHY

Griggs, Earl Leslie. *Thomas Clarkson: The Friend of Slaves*. 2nd ed. Westport, CT: Negro University Press, 1970. Contains a bibliography that includes the works of Thomas Clarkson.

Wilson, Ellen Gibson. *Thomas Clarkson: A Biography*. London: Macmillan, 1989. Well researched and documented but lacks a bibliography.

—MAX KENT

CLASS. The discussion of class among African Americans in the centuries before the industrial revolution en-

countered significant conceptual difficulties. Did "class" as the philosopher Karl Marx described it exist among a people who were almost entirely enslaved? African Americans were industrial laborers in parts of the early United States, but the vast majority were agricultural workers, whose skills and statuses seem superficially to have been interchangeable. At the same time, the great transformation occurring in white society "from feudalism to capitalism" entailed the commodification of money, land, and labor. African Americans' lives were inextricably entwined in each of these changes. Undoubtedly, exploitation helped create the capital value of landowner and merchant. African Americans also made themselves. African American slaves can be viewed as the first true proletarians in America. A leading scholar of early African American business argues cogently that race, not class, was the key variable for African Americans. Examination of a number of categories reveals how, despite general economic weakness, some blacks were initially able to carve out higher status and, in the early Republic, create a staunch middle class.

Seeking Status. Africans arriving in the New World came with common perceptions of status. Many had lived in kingdoms and regarded themselves as holding ranks appropriate to their occupation and skills. In Africa the key to wealth was not to own land, which was often held in common or belonged to the king, but rather to acquire labor, which could be accomplished through marriage, by the subordination of women, or through a widespread internal slave trade. Purchasing slaves and making them do agricultural work often made enslaved Africans the equivalent of hired workers or peasant cultivators in Europe. In North America enslaved people were at the center of visibility and power in settler society.

Among the "ranks" of European settlements in North America, enslaved Africans seemed to be at the bottom, beneath the sailors, indentured servants, landless laborers, and soldiers, who made up the lower ranks of white society, further below the artisans, who constituted the middle, and far under the merchants, gentry, professionals, and government officials, who were the elite. Still, there were some who crossed these boundaries.

In the early seventeenth century a few African Americans, termed "Creoles" by Ira Berlin in his influential study *Many Thousands Gone*, made the transition from servitude to freedom and landownership. By 1650 only Massachusetts Colony had created a Code Noir or system of slavery, and even there the numbers of African American servants remained low. By 1664 slavery in New Amsterdam was beginning to take hold, with about eight hundred Africans, of whom over one hundred were free and about forty owned land. Virginia still combined indentured servitude and some slavery. As in New York, blacks who had worked out their indentures received freedom papers, and some acquired land, planted tobacco, owned cattle and hogs, and intermarried with whites. Virginia was more hospitable to free blacks than was New York, but in both places the key to higher status lay in landownership. As restrictive laws in both colonies placed onerous demands on free blacks, many moved on, trying to stay ahead of the expanding jaws of slavery.

A second mark of status was ownership of slaves. In New England Bastian Ken purchased his own freedom and then bought the slave Angola and manumitted him for humanitarian reasons. Ken even mortgaged his home to buy and free Angola. Other black slave owners were less charitable. In the 1640s Anthony Johnson, a free black in Virginia, owned slaves. He even went to court in the mid-1650s to reclaim the labor of his slave, John Castor, who claimed to have worked out a term as an indentured servant. Castor initially won his freedom, but Johnson prevailed on appeal because Castor was not from a Christian nation.

Newer colonies such as South Carolina and New Jersey installed systems of black slavery in their earliest phases of development. Even in South Carolina a free, black, land-and-slave-holding class had emerged by the mid-eighteenth century. By the late 1790s there were 59 black slaveholders owning around 357 slaves in South Carolina; these numbers increased steadily to over 450 black masters by 1830, who owned over 2,400 slaves, the peak number before the Civil War.

African Americans could hold occupations that brought them income and prestige above the level of ordinary slaves. Carpenters, brick makers, painters, lime makers, and even gunsmiths worked first as slaves and then possibly as free people. Craftsmen knew the value of their labor and could eke out better working conditions and pay, which they used for self-purchase and then for buying slaves. Such slaves were also adept at hiring themselves out, often working out arrangements with their masters that allowed for nearly complete autonomy after paying an agreed-on annual sum.

House servants or domestics could also take on the trappings of higher status. Though historians have cautioned that house servants suffered from proximity to their masters, who abused them sexually and psychologically, they had certain advantages over other slaves. Anglophilic masters were anxious to own educated, well-groomed servants who could reflect well on their cosmopolitan self-images. In the North and the South masters paid for the medical and clothing bills of their slaves and sent them to Anglican catechism schools. In New York such classes produced a class of clerics capable of leading services and ready to assume leadership in a nascent black community. Their religious training and closeness to their masters gave house servants an additional advantage. On rare occasions in the colonial period, servants could appeal to dying masters to bequeath to them their freedom. Hardly widespread, such practices nevertheless created lifelong aspirations and led to gradual emancipation. Historians debate the extent to which house servants gained emancipation, but there was an advantage to being enslaved by single women or widows, because they were more likely to manumit slaves.

"Fortunate" Slaves. A more rarefied type of servant was the "fortunate slave," who had extraordinary talents that might earn freedom and fame. Such were the lives of the writers Phillis Wheatley and Jupiter Hammon (though he spurned emancipation) or the Afro-Englishmen Charles Ignatius Sancho, Quobna Ottobah Cugoano, and Olaudah Equiano. Scientists such as the free black mathematician Benjamin Banneker likewise fall into this category. After the American Revolution such talented blacks were part of an international controversy. Thomas Jefferson, in his famous *Notes on the State of Virginia* (1785), denied that African Americans had the imagination or creative abilities of whites and therefore fortunate slaves were either overrated or freaks of nature. Contesting Jefferson's racism was Bishop Henri Grégoire's *The Cultural Achievements of Negroes* (1810), which listed many writers and scientists. African Americans used Grégoire's book to create a pantheon of black greatness.

These individuals gained their fame and status from external forces. Within the colonial African American world, rank came in different ways. In New England blacks annually selected a king on Negro Election Day. The king, often belonging to a prosperous family, dressed in elaborate clothing and presided over a parade. Similar elections to leadership accompanied Pinkster celebrations in New York and New Jersey. Other African American leaders came from more clandestine routes. Runaways were seen as bold and adventurous. At times they would take on the trappings of leadership. Simon, who ran away from James Leonard in Middlesex County, New Jersey, in 1740, was described as "Pretending to be a Doctor and very religious and says he is a Churchman." Mark, who fled from Major Prevost in Bergen County, New Jersey, in 1775, was "serious, slow of speech, rather low in stature, reads well, is a Negro Preacher, about 40 years of age." During the American Revolution, leaders emerged. Colonel Tye struck fear into the hearts of Patriots around New York City. David George, Stephen Blucke, and Boston King were important black Loyalist leaders. Revolutionary War service enabled some Patriot blacks to retain prestige after the conflict, including Peter Williams Sr., James Forten, and Jude Hall, all of whom used Revolutionary War credentials to embellish their careers.

There were a few famous athletes among early African Americans. Long before the democratization of fame,

Tom Molineaux and Bill Richmond were internationally acclaimed boxers. Far more noted were the innumerable fiddlers or "physicianers" who played airs from many ethnicities for frolics and dance halls. After the American Revolution black dancers at the Catherine Market in New York became nationally famous, as did actors at the African Grove Theater in the 1820s.

African American class and status after the American Revolution built on cultural scaffolding evident in the colonial period. Education, occupation, special skills, and the power of community organizations all were avenues to higher status among African Americans in the early national period. One of the best occupations for ambitious free blacks was that of minister. Richard Allen, Absalom Jones, Peter Williams Jr., and other eminent African American divines enjoyed leadership within the black community and had extensive contact with educated and, at times, liberal whites. A few African Americans were actually prosperous, but middle-class status based on education and community leadership was more common. Philadelphia and New York City were the homes of such members of the black elite. In both cities interlocking membership in mutual societies, Masonic halls, African societies, and the emerging independent black churches sustained black middle classes composed of ministers and skilled tradesmen. Few had substantial incomes, although James Forten of Philadelphia became wealthy. Rarer was the genuine wealth of Paul Cuffe, the shipmaster from New Bedford, Massachusetts. Cuffe was the best example of the northern elite's ambivalent attitude toward America and Africa. Although highly patriotic and insistent on civil rights, Cuffe (as did other members of the black elite) favored colonization of Africa as the future of black Americans. After Cuffe's death in 1817 and the founding of the whites-only African Colonization Society, which proselytized removal of all free blacks, the black elite's attitude toward colonization changed sharply and negatively.

In the American South skin color and slave ownership added to the middle-class memberships common in the North. In Charleston, South Carolina, the Brown Fellowship Society, formed in the 1790s, was at once a mutual benefit and burial society, much like the Free African Society of Philadelphia and the New York African Society of Mutual Relief. Unlike those institutions, however, admission to the Brown Fellowship Society was reserved for free mulattoes and their descendants. Other Charleston groups such as the Society of Free Dark Men, the Unity and Friendship Society, and the Humane Brotherhood disdained the mulattoes' organization.

Overall, urban organizations, whether benevolent, religious, or political, emphasized education, self-help, morality, and a sense of obligation to assist poorer blacks through schools, church attendance, and personal uplift.

As the nineteenth century wore on, the inclusion of antislavery politics made northern societies more racially conscious. Whether these middle-class organizations consciously borrowed from white institutions, or reflected the class attitudes within the black community, is a matter of intense debate.

The previously mentioned societies were for males only, although New York City's African Dorcas Society, which was devoted to black literacy, is an exception. Black women were able to attain middle-class status in the early Republic either through marriage or by work. Women made economic gains in food production, dressmaking and fashion, health services, hair care, boardinghouse keeping, and property ownership. Black women also owned slaves, as in the case of Philada Turner, a well-known Charleston seamstress, who bought and later sold a female slave. Census reports have revealed that of sixteen free black seamstresses in Charleston, thirteen owned slaves.

Class may not have been as important a variable as race in determining an African American's individual status or occupation in early America, but there were significant examples of upward mobility and status, and even of class exploitation. During the lifetime of Frederick Douglass (1817–1895), class among African Americans remained tied to differences in status, color, and culture. In keeping with America's emerging market economy, class relations also developed into capitalist relations within and outside of black society. Free black Americans generally shared income status and skills with white artisans. Just as white skilled workers bifurcated into master/capitalists and journeymen/employees, so too did African Americans experience changing economic relations. As the United States embraced capitalist economic relations, enslaved African Americans, who by definition did not own the means of production or their own labor, became true proletarians. After the demise of slavery in the North, free African Americans often found gains in the region's market economy out of reach. Some historians have argued that capitalists in the North sought the end of slavery in the region largely in order to institute free labor without the paternalist trappings of colonial servitude. However, while many free blacks were exploited, there was also a class of black entrepreneurs and capitalists. African Americans joined white Americans in pursuit of middle-class dreams of equality and good jobs. Few blacks, though, gained sizable wealth, and black capitalists normally sustained close relationships with their laborers.

African American Slave-Owners. Of the two and a half million African Americans living in the United States in 1850, the vast majority was enslaved. There were variations in status among slaves earlier in the century, but over time worsening racism and job discrimination, combined with white anxieties about the possibility that skilled blacks might inspire revolution, made relative success harder for ambitious slaves. Class-based organizations such as the African Society for Mutual Relief in New York City and the more conservative Brown Fellowship Society in Charleston, South Carolina, continued from the early nineteenth century.

Although racial lines hardened in the nineteenth century, race did not hinder some blacks from becoming slave owners. There were 242 black planters, defined as property owners with more than twenty slaves, in the American South in 1850. Five African American sugar planters in Louisiana held seventy or more slaves. Another family, the Metoyers of Louisiana, owned cotton plantations with 287 slaves in 1830. The matriarch of the Metoyer family was Coincoin, the American-born daughter of two Africans brought to Louisiana in the mid-eighteenth century. She inherited a plantation and built it into a short-lived empire. Another black Louisiana family, the Ricauds, owned over 130 slaves in the antebellum years. As a Dun and Bradstreet report announced about these large planters, who were among the most prosperous people in the country, "They are capitalists."

Southern cities were home to other black slave-owners, though normally on a much smaller scale. In 1830 New Orleans was the home of 753 free black slave-masters who owned 2,363 slaves, with an average of slightly over three chattel per holding. In Charleston, South Carolina, 262 blacks, or about 12 percent of the free black population, owned 1,324 slaves, with an average holding of just over five. Among these holders were a number of black women. Most of these African American slave-owners were of mixed ancestry and many of them had inherited slaves from white families. In Louisiana African American slave-owners of mixed ancestry were known as *libre gens de couleur* (free men or women of color).

Many of these free blacks held conservative attitudes. The Brown Fellowship Society in Charleston, South Carolina, for example, prohibited discussion of political or church-based issues at its meetings, a ruling that allowed the fellowship to survive amid restrictive laws.

Building Wealth. In the northern states, gradual emancipation ended slavery. Only a few blacks in New Jersey and Delaware owned slaves. Given civil freedom but lacking political or economic power, newly freed blacks in the North sought to extend gains made in the post-Revolutionary period. The mutual society movement, initiated in the early nineteenth century, sustained itself by careful deposits in the United States Bank. Discriminatory laws made it difficult for individual African Americans to own stock, but a few did. Julien Lecroix of New Orleans was

worth over $250,000 in 1854. In the North and South, wealthy blacks operated as private bankers, making loans and discounting private bank currency. The Pennsylvanians Stephen Smith and Joseph Cassey became wealthy handling money exchanges between the bewildering banknote systems. Smith also invested heavily in railroad and bridge stocks. Laws in the South and discrimination in the North made such investments more difficult, so blacks returned to the collective aid organization. The National Negro Convention, which in the 1830s invested small sums, created an elaborate plan in 1855 to create venture capital. Blacks also found investing in urban real estate profitable. New Orleans real estate investors led the way. In 1860 free blacks owned over one-fifth or $22 million of taxable property in the city. Among the wealthiest investors in the city were Drausin Macarty, Julien Lacroix, and Julien Colvis.

In the North and West, some African Americans owned and operated small factories. These petty producers dominate Martin Delany's 1852 list of black male entrepreneurs, which included examples of merchants of myriad commodities, a jeweler, a resort owner, bandleader, restaurateurs, and many skilled craftsmen. Anthony Weston of Charleston, South Carolina, owned a millwright manufactory. Robert Banks of Detroit was a clothing merchant.

Generally, black economic success was difficult in the North. Largely shut out of the classes of industrial laborers and hindered from credit by racism, black New Yorkers found space for their class aspirations in education and other forms of personal uplift. African American activists sought to reform the paternalist charity schools of the colonial and early national periods and to create public schools with black teachers. They were partly successful, but poor funding and unfair treatment undercut their efforts. The same was true for efforts to establish black colleges. In 1850 nearly 10 percent of the students at New York Central College in McGrawville, New York, were black; smaller numbers attended Oberlin College and the Oneida Institute and a few other northern colleges. Middle-class blacks in the North prided themselves on their education, moral demeanor, and culture.

Civil Rights and Political Success. One of the greatest forms of pride among northern African Americans was their activism. As scholars have argued, definitions of black manhood and femininity in the antebellum period included antislavery activism and efforts to improve civil rights. Closely with the education movement, black societies worked assiduously to end slavery and to fight for improved rights. Black convention movements, antislavery societies, temperance groups, and reading groups all strove for self-improvement. Though often factious, these black organizations formed the backbone of the abolitionist movement that eventually shook the country in two.

Though the Civil War devastated the American South, it created new opportunities for free black people. In addition to a new freedom of mobility, the war created chances for skilled blacks. In an 1865 census of the South, skilled blacks outnumbered whites 100,000 to 20,000. The census of 1870 indicated growing numbers of black coopers, carpenters, blacksmiths, mechanics, shoemakers, brick masons, and small tradesmen, all of whom owned homes. While black skills and prewar ambitions should have created a stronger middle class, racist terror in the South and racism in the North curbed black prospects. Skilled blacks suffered from this racism and terror and gradually lost the advantages of Reconstruction.

The older black elite in New Orleans also suffered. The Lacroix brothers fell from great wealth into failure, as did Pierre Casenave and Francis Dumas. On the plantations the ambitious efforts of Benjamin Montgomery to purchase and operate two farms owned by the former Confederate president Jefferson Davis succeeded for a number of years, then fell victim to the Panic of 1873, natural disasters, a suit by Davis to regain his property, and, finally, Montgomery's death in 1877. Petty business operators in the South suffered from poor credit ratings and doubts about their abilities from both races. Even though black purchasing power was better than in the prewar period, few small businesses survived. Blacks did do better at commercial farming, with notable successes in Louisiana, in Alabama, and in the North and West. In Kansas, Junius P. Groves was known as the Negro Potato King.

The greatest accomplishments during Reconstruction came from cooperative efforts. To overcome their limited funds, blacks pooled money in cooperative enterprises in manufacturing, real estate, banking, and insurance. Harsh black codes limited black entrance into many businesses, especially in South Carolina and Mississippi. Better successes came from the Black Towns Movement, which in Kansas and Oklahoma created a uniform class based upon race. The best-known black town was Mound Bayou, Mississippi, founded in 1887 by Isaiah Montgomery, the son of Benjamin Montgomery. The town was highly successful for several decades, although Montgomery was criticized by blacks nationwide after he accepted the disenfranchisement of blacks in Mississippi. Lack of political power hampered African Americans in the North as well. There, free enterprise also failed them and curbed the future of the black middle class. Business areas such as catering survived by embracing the cooperative movement.

The most notable political successes of blacks in the South also came from cooperative efforts. Kinship, labor, and networks of communication set the stage for grassroots mobilization. Not always apparent until the twentieth century, these fledgling political efforts identified self-governance as the primary goal. Black political leaders made enormous strides immediately after the Civil War. In 1868 in South Carolina, the cradle of the Confederacy, fully 55 percent of the entire state legislature was black. At the local level, the changes in power promised to be even more massive. There, blacks could hold public office as county commissioners, tax assessors, constables, and even sheriffs, possibilities that horrified whites. At one time or another, blacks held virtually every office available at the local level in the South including coroner, surveyor, tax collector, jailer, registrar of deeds, police officer, and even mayor. Even if these gains were later lost, they reflected extraordinary community and class development.

As part of this effort, African Americans sought to create cultures of class. During the 1880s, African Americans began establishing their own historical societies and professional associations. In 1880 black leaders from religious and secular publications formed the Colored Press Association, followed in short order by the Bethel Literary and Historical Association of Washington, D.C. Ten years later, black intellectuals in Boston formed the Society for the Collection of Negro Folklore; other influential organizations included the National Medical Association, the National Federation of Afro-American Women, and the National League of Women's Clubs. The latter two consolidated in 1896 to form the National Association of Colored Women. The culminating organization of black historical societies was the American Negro Academy, led by its first president, Alexander Crummell.

Middle-class African Americans vied to consolidate their position through historical compendiums and encyclopedias. Built upon seminal works such as Henri Grégoire's *On the Cultural Achievements of Negroes* (1810) and William C. Nell's *Colored Patriots of the American Revolution* (1855), black scholars in the late nineteenth century compiled huge biographical studies of notable men of achievement. Building on Nell's work was George Washington Williams's *A History of the Negro Troops in the War of the Rebellion, 1861–1865* (1888), to which Williams appended a review of military service by blacks dating back to ancient times. William J. Simmons's compendium of biographies, *Men of Mark: Eminent, Progressive, and Rising* (1887), included over one hundred seventy-five chapters on eminent blacks. The vast majority of the subjects were ministers, but scholars, missionaries, lawyers, and a few politicians were also included.

Despite the difficulties blacks faced, and with worse conditions on the horizon, African Americans did make some progress in achieving middle-class status. The numbers of blacks owning homes jumped from 9,000 in 1863 to 210,000 by 1893; the number owning farms went from 20,000 to 550,000 during the same period. Black businesses jumped from 2,000 to 17,000, while the overall wealth of the African American community rose from about twenty million to seven hundred million dollars. These gains were especially noticeable among former slaves in the upper South. Still, the disappointments of the Reconstruction period and the Gilded Age left most blacks impoverished. African American middle classes strove valiantly to sustain the status they had gained in the antebellum period.

[*See also* African Colonization Society; Allen, Richard; Banneker, Benjamin; Black Church; Black Loyalists; Black Uplift; Blucke, Stephen; Brown Fellowship Society; Civil Rights; Colonel Tye; Crummell, Alexander; Cuffe, Paul; Cugoano, Quobna Ottobah; Delany, Martin Robison; Education; Entrepreneurs; Equiano, Olaudah; Forten, James; George, David; Grégoire, Bishop Henri; Fraternal Organizations and Mutual Aid Societies; Free African Americans to 1828; Free African Americans before the Civil War (North); Free African Americans before the Civil War (South); Free African Society; Hammon, Jupiter; Indentured Servitude; Jon Kannoe; Jones, Absalom; Molineaux, Tom; Negro Election Day; New York African Society of Mutual Relief; Pinkster; Poverty; Race, Theories of; Reconstruction; Sancho, Charles Ignatius; Skin Color; Virginia; Wheatley, Phillis; Williams, George Washington; Williams, Peter, Jr.; *and* Williams, Peter, Sr.]

BIBLIOGRAPHY

Berlin, Ira. *Many Thousands Gone: The First Two Centuries of Slavery in North America.* Cambridge, MA: Harvard University Press, 1998.

Boubacar, Barry. *Senegambia and the Atlantic Slave Trade.* Translated by Ayi Kwei Armah. New York: Cambridge University Press, 1998.

Hahn, Steven. *A Nation Under Our Feet: Black Political Struggles in the Rural South, from Slavery to the Great Migration.* Cambridge, MA: Harvard University Press, 2003.

Schweninger, Loren. *Black Property Owners in the South, 1790–1915.* Urbana: University of Illinois Press, 1990.

Walker, Juliet E. K. *The History of Black Business in America: Capitalism, Race, Entrepreneurship.* New York: Macmillan, 1998.

—GRAHAM RUSSELL GAO HODGES

CLAY, CASSIUS M. (b. 19 October 1810; d. 22 July 1903), abolitionist and politician. "I do not set up for being perfect: far from it!" wrote the Kentucky antislavery agitator Cassius Marcellus Clay to the abolitionist John Fee in 1855. "I wish I were," he continued, but "a good balance sheet of good against evil is all I aspire to!" Judged by his own standards as well as by those of black and

Cassius Marcellus Clay. Daguerreotype, c. 1844–1860, produced by Mathew Brady's studio and possibly by Albert Sands Southworth and Josiah Johnson Hawes of Boston, who were partners from 1843 to 1862 and are considered the first great masters of photography in America. The image may have been made at the time of Clay's appointment as U.S. minister to Russia in 1861. (Library of Congress.)

white antislavery advocates, Cassius Clay succeeded in fulfilling his ambition, through his battles against the evil of slavery. A former slaveholder and one of the few antislavery leaders to remain in the South after 1830, Clay became something of a hero to northern abolitionists, who appreciated his willingness to challenge slaveholders on their own turf.

Cassius Clay was born in Kentucky's Bluegrass region to the planter Green Clay and his wife, Sally, in Clermont. Clay lived to the age of ninety-three and spent much of his life immersed in the nation's battles over the meanings of race, slavery, and freedom. As a young man, Clay lived the life of a Kentucky planter's son; on his father's death in 1828 Clay inherited seventeen slaves and vast landholdings. His rise into the planter class took an abrupt turn when in 1831 he enrolled at Yale University and happened upon a speech by the abolitionist William Lloyd Garrison. When Clay returned to Kentucky, the contrast between free labor in New England and the slave society in Kentucky struck him particularly hard; he was soon convinced that slavery was the source of the ills plaguing whites in the South.

Clay entered Kentucky politics in the late 1830s, championing economic diversification in Kentucky and the gradual abolition of slavery. His attacks against slaveholders and the debilitating effects of slavery outraged opponents, who frequently resorted to violence in failed efforts to silence him. Never one to back down from a fight—Clay regularly engaged in physical brawls with political opponents, once nearly killing a man whom political opponents had hired to assassinate him—he became more determined in his opposition to planters and more defiant in his denunciations of slavery. By 1841 his political career in Kentucky was at an end. Refusing to be silenced, he soon became the preeminent spokesperson for gradual abolition in Kentucky.

In 1845 Clay established an antislavery newspaper in Lexington, the heart of Kentucky's Bluegrass plantation country. The *True American* would commit itself "to gradual and constitutional emancipation," Clay explained in the paper's prospectus. The thought of an abolitionist newspaper in Kentucky, no matter how reasonable and gradual its proposals, infuriated slaveholders, who threatened Clay with further violence and even death if he insisted on publishing his newspaper. Clay responded by turning his printing office into a fortified arsenal, complete with two cannons trained on the front door. Only after a bout of typhoid fever weakened Clay did a Lexington mob successfully break into his shop; the press would be sent to Cincinnati, where Clay resumed the *True American*'s publication.

After 1845, whenever Clay spoke against slavery in Kentucky, he armed himself with pistols and a knife. In 1849, while Clay campaigned for a state constitutional convention, a proslavery mob attacked and nearly killed him—the second attempt on his life in less than a decade. During this period Clay became friends with Horace Greeley, the editor of the *New York Tribune*. Greeley began publishing stories of Clay's antislavery exploits, and tales of his bravado and physical courage made him a southern antislavery hero among northern abolitionists. By the 1850s, with slavery now at the center of politics, the one-time slaveholder became a valued antislavery speaker for the emerging Republican Party. In 1854 Clay and the abolitionist and writer Frederick Douglass shared the same stage at a Chicago antislavery meeting, and through 1860 Clay stumped extensively for Republican candidates, following much the same circuit as Douglass.

Clay's willingness to use racism to advance the cause of antislavery in the 1830s and 1840s, along with his ever-shifting tactics, earned him persistent critics among some contemporaries and later historians. Still, Clay never deviated from his conviction that slaves were entitled to freedom, and black abolitionists in the North praised Clay, holding him in the same high regard as they did Garrison. Writing in the Massachusetts antislavery publication *Liberator* in 1853, the black abolitionists Charles Lenox Remond, William Cooper Nell, and Lewis Hayden hailed Clay as emancipation's "unflinching advocate, in its application to all who are pining in bondage at the South." Despite his flaws, in the end Clay managed to obtain a "good balance sheet of good against evil."

[*See also* Antislavery Movement; Antislavery Press; Douglass, Frederick; Garrison, William Lloyd; Greeley, Horace; Nell, William Cooper; Remond, Charles Lenox; *and* Republican Party.]

BIBLIOGRAPHY

Clay, Cassius M. *The Life of Cassius Marcellus Clay: Memoirs, Writings, and Speeches Showing His Conduct in the Overthrow of American Slavery, the Salvation of the Union, and the Restoration of the Autonomy of the States* (1886). New York: Negro Universities Press, 1969. Contains many of Clay's antislavery writings and speeches.

Smiley, David L. *Lion of White Hall: The Life of Cassius M. Clay*. Madison: University of Wisconsin Press, 1962. A fact-filled and well-documented biography that overstates the importance of racism to Clay's antislavery beliefs and activities.

Tallant, Harold D. *Evil Necessity: Slavery and Political Culture in Antebellum Kentucky*. Lexington: University Press of Kentucky, 2003. See, in particular, chapters 5–8 for an examination of Clay's antislavery agitation in Kentucky and his antislavery beliefs.

—JOHN CRAIG HAMMOND

CLAY, HENRY (b. 12 April 1777; d. 29 June 1852), American politician. Henry Clay was born in Hanover County, Virginia. His father, John, a Baptist minister, died in 1781. His mother married Henry Watkins the following year and followed her new husband to Kentucky. Henry Clay remained in Virginia, where he later studied law with George Wythe. Finishing his studies in 1797, Clay followed his family to Kentucky and settled outside of Lexington. There he married Lucretia Hart, the daughter of a prominent Kentucky businessman, on 11 April 1799 and purchased a plantation near Lexington, which he named Ashland. Clay and his wife had eleven children, although only four outlived their father. After a long and illustrious career, Clay died in Washington, D.C. He was buried in Lexington, Kentucky, where a statue to his memory stands.

Clay's national political career began in 1806 when the Kentucky legislature selected him to complete an unexpired term in the U.S. Senate at the age of twenty-nine. Four years later he was elected to the House of Representatives, becoming the Speaker of the House during his first term in 1811; he would hold that position three different times, presiding over six different congresses. He was one of six delegates to negotiate the Treaty of Ghent, which ended the War of 1812. In 1820–1821 Clay played an integral part in the passing of the Missouri Compromise, which temporarily quelled arguments over the extension of slavery and earned him the nickname the "Great Compromiser." The compromise stated that Maine would enter the Union as a free state, Missouri would enter as a slave state, and there would be no slavery above the 36°30′ parallel. Throughout his congressional career Clay advocated his political beliefs through a coherent program known as the American System. This system supported federal funding for road and canal construction, a national bank, protective tariffs, the gradual emancipation of slaves, and the colonization of freed blacks to Africa.

After his own failure in the 1824 presidential election, Clay backed John Quincy Adams, who defeated Andrew Jackson and was named president in 1825. Adams appointed Clay as secretary of state, and Jackson's supporters immediately argued that a "corrupt bargain" had transpired between Clay and Adams. While the charges were false, they followed Clay for the rest of his life and created deep animosity between him and Jackson. Clay ran for president twice more, in 1832 and 1844, but was defeated on both occasions. The Kentucky legislature returned him to the Senate in 1849.

In 1850 Clay again proposed a compromise to keep the Union from splitting over the issue of slavery. The terms of the compromise were as follows: Texas would be given money to pay its debts to Mexico; New Mexico, Nevada, Arizona, and Utah would be organized without slave restrictions, allowing inhabitants to decide at a later time whether or not to permit slavery; the slave trade in Washington would be abolished, but slavery would still be legal; California would enter the Union as a free state; and a new, stiffer Fugitive Slave Act would be added to pacify southern politicians. The Fugitive Slave Act required citizens to help masters reclaim runaway slaves and denied a fugitive's right to a jury trial. Clay proposed the measure as an "omnibus" bill, which was defeated in July 1850. Each resolution did eventually pass, however, when introduced as separate measures by Clay's fellow senator Stephen A. Douglas.

Clay's own views on slavery were varied and controversial. He favored the eventual emancipation of slaves yet was a slave owner himself. He had inherited his first slaves at the age of four, upon the death of his father, and later purchased more to work on his Lexington plantation. He freed a handful of his slaves during his life but did not free the rest upon his death. Perhaps Clay's most controversial involvement with slavery was his role in the American Colonization Society (ACS). Founded in 1816, the ACS aimed to remove free blacks from the United States. Clay thought gradual emancipation and the re-

moval of African Americans would solve the slavery problem, but the majority of the members of the ACS were southerners who worried about the effect free blacks would have on their society and wanted to remove the threat. Clay became the president of the ACS in 1836 and held that position until his death.

Frederick Douglass did not care for Clay; he called him a notorious man stealer and frequently criticized his attitudes and actions on the issue of slavery. He considered Clay a hypocrite for owning slaves while speaking out in favor of gradual emancipation. Douglass used Clay's actions and words to rouse support from antislavery crowds, who also opposed Clay's views on slavery. Douglass particularly disliked that Clay was involved in the ACS, an organization Douglass considered a dangerous enemy to all blacks in the Union, enslaved or free.

Henry Clay was a slave-owning politician who favored the removal of blacks to Africa; his integral role in American politics cannot be denied. His moral actions may have been reprehensible, but his political prowess twice kept the nation from fighting a civil war. He was one of the most powerful and important legislators of his era.

[*See also* African Americans and the West; American Colonization Society; Douglas, Stephen A.; Douglass, Frederick; Fugitive Slave Law of 1850; *and* Laws and Legislation, Antebellum.]

BIBLIOGRAPHY

Clay, Henry. *Papers*. Edited by James F. Hopkins. 11 vols. Lexington: University of Kentucky Press, 1959–1992. The best compilation of Clay's numerous letters and papers available.

Mayo, Bernard. *Henry Clay: Spokesman of the New West* (1937). Hamden, CT: Archon, 1966. The first comprehensive biography of Clay's life and career.

Remini, Robert V. *Henry Clay: Statesman for the Union*. New York: Norton, 1991. The most readable and comprehensive account of Clay's life, focusing mainly on his political career.

—KATE GIGLIOTTI-GORDON

CLEVELAND, GROVER (b. 18 March 1837; d. 24 June 1908), the twenty-second and twenty-fourth president of the United States. Stephen Grover Cleveland came of age in western New York after the premature death of his father, a Presbyterian minister. He became involved in the Democratic Party at an early age and, after becoming a lawyer in 1859, served in a number of local offices in Buffalo. Having quickly developed a reputation as a reformer and party official willing to take on corruption in public affairs, Cleveland successfully campaigned to become mayor of Buffalo in 1881. Just two years later he entered the statewide spotlight and was elected governor of New York. In that position Cleveland continued his crusade for political reform. His attempt to clean up New York City's municipal government garnered the ire of the powerful and corrupt Tammany Hall political machine, but Cleveland survived attacks on both his policies and character to emerge as one of the leading reformers of the Gilded Age.

In 1884 Cleveland's political star continued to rise with his nomination for president on the Democratic ticket. His campaign, however, was besieged by the accusations that he had fathered an illegitimate child, that he had shirked military service during the Civil War, and that the Democratic Party was the party of "rum, Romanism, and ruin." The election of 1884 was a close one, with Cleveland and his Republican rival, James G. Blaine, splitting the popular vote of the nation in half. Cleveland, however, won the electoral vote by a margin of 219 to 182, thus carrying the election; in 1885 he became the first Democratic president to be sworn into office since James Buchanan in 1857. His administration largely focused on civil service reform, healing the sectional wounds of the Civil War, and lowering tariffs. By promoting these policies Cleveland aroused a great deal of political controversy, and although he won the nomination of his party for a second term, he lost the presidency in yet another close election in 1888. In that bid for reelection, he won the popular vote but lost in the Electoral College to the Republican candidate, Benjamin Harrison.

Cleveland retired to a private law practice in 1889, but the unpopularity of the Harrison administration, particularly its Republican stance on high protective tariffs, spurred interest among Democrats in nominating Cleveland for a third time. In 1892 Cleveland came back to win the presidency from Harrison and became the only American president to be elected to two nonconsecutive terms. Almost as soon as he was inaugurated, however, the nation's economy spun into a major depression. Cleveland responded conservatively to the crisis throughout his second administration. In 1894, for example, he sent in federal troops to quell the strike of the American Railway Union outside Chicago. Moreover, throughout that second term Cleveland remained wedded to the gold standard for American currency. By 1896 the Democratic Party as a whole had moved on to a platform promoting silver and a fusion ticket with the emergent Populist Party. Cleveland again retired to private life.

During Cleveland's two terms as president his record on civil rights and his relationship with Frederick Douglass were mixed. Because Cleveland was the leading Democratic politician in the post-Reconstruction years, many African Americans were skeptical of his intentions toward them when he entered the White House. Although he retained Frederick Douglass in the post of recorder of deeds in the District of Columbia, eventually replacing him with another African American official, Cleveland did not have a strong record of supporting racial equality while in office. In fact, a great deal of racial discrimination within the federal government occurred during both of Cleveland's terms, as he believed African Americans needed to take gradual steps toward equality with whites. Despite Cleveland's denouncement of racial violence in the South, Frederick Douglass argued in 1886, "he has done nothing in his position as commander-in-chief of the army and navy to put a stop to such horrors." The legacy of Cleveland in the area of racial justice was much like his legacy in other fields. Although he had developed a reputation as a progressive reformer in his early political career, Grover Cleveland ultimately became known as a conservative figure in American politics.

[*See also* Blaine, James G.; Civil Rights; Democratic Party; Discrimination; Harrison, Benjamin; Reconstruction; *and* Reform.]

BIBLIOIGRAPHY

Hollingsworth, J. Rogers. *The Whirligig of Politics*. Chicago: University of Chicago Press, 1963.
Welch, Richard. *The Presidencies of Grover Cleveland*. Lawrence: University of Kansas Press, 1988.

—SEAN PATRICK ADAMS

CLOTHING. African Americans wore myriad varieties of clothing in early America, with the predominant types identifying them as workers. Enslaved and free blacks made their own clothing, received allotments from masters and employers, accepted hand-me-downs, and stole finery. Clothing was not strictly functional, however; early blacks refashioned clothing styles to fit their self-perceptions and to make political and religious statements. In urban centers, during the Revolutionary period and afterward, blacks—especially women—created an aesthetic that reflected a newfound sense of freedom and identity.

The most common evidence with regard to black clothing comes from the thousands of runaway notices that white masters published in colonial newspapers in the hope of retrieving "blacks that stole themselves." The earliest such announcements were public warnings made before the introduction of newspapers. One such hue and cry from 1664 described a particular fugitive's attire, including "a red wastecoat, with a sad colour'd Coate over it, a paire of lineen breeches, somewhat worne, and a grey felt hat, but no shoes or stockings"; the secondhand quality of slave clothing was consistent throughout the colonial period. Common clothing included oznabrig shirts—made of coarse, unbleached linen—which were imported strictly for slave attire and worn by newly arrived and American-born slaves alike. One slave, as described in the *Virginia Gazette* in 1751, wore "a new strong Oznabrig Shirt, a blue

Penneystone wastecoat, Sew'd Up at the Side, the Whole Breadth of the Cloth and a new Scotch bonnet."

Although the European style of clothing may have seemed unfamiliar to many of those wrenched from their lives in Africa by the slave trade, they soon adapted and made their own garments. Enslaved peoples made their own "leather breeches," shoes, and homespun stockings; such makeshift attire immediately identified the wearer's second-class status. Others strived to comport themselves with higher fashion by wearing used beaver hats, silk cloaks, and heavy wool coats; black women became skilled at dying clothes to add color. Some, such as a man by the name of Storde, who decamped from a privateer in New York harbor, owned a "large pair of silver shoe buckles, and a pair of Gold sleeve buttons"—which he intended to sell to finance his freedom.

Storde was hardly the only enslaved person to use clothes as currency. A bond servant who ran away from an ironworks in 1750 took from his master "a new broadcloth jacket and a fine Holland check'd shirt as well as trousers and other garments," either for personal use or to sell in the used clothing markets located in port cities. Occasionally, self-emancipated slaves left wearing new clothes, as did Cato, who fled his master in 1757 and took new shoes, a fine shirt, and a wool hat. Fugitive blacks also used clothing to identify their beliefs. Andrew Saxon, who fled his master in New York in 1733, marked his shirts with a cross on his left breast, to announce his Roman Catholic affiliation—a brave statement at a time when that faith was illegal in the colony. South Carolina was but one of several colonies to insert clauses prohibiting enslaved peoples from wearing fine dress. A Maryland legislator linked a crime wave to the insatiable desire of blacks to raise money to buy fine clothing. The failure of such laws to restrict African American desires for clothing is evident in the inventory that one Bacchus took with him upon fleeing: "two white Russia drill coats . . . , blue plush breeches, a fine Cloth pompadour waistcoat," several expensive summer jackets, many pairs of fine stockings, five or six shirts, shoes, silver buckles, and a quantity of other luxurious garments. Certainly, the sight of a well-dressed slave would arouse the suspicions of white viewers; indeed, urban markets included flourishing secondhand clothing booths.

Black women wearing fine clothes spurred accusations of prostitution. Yet, the meaning of their outfits could be ambiguous. During the American Revolution, African American women displayed their newfound assertiveness through dress—to the anger and scorn of white observers. One Hessian chaplain observed that "even the lovely female Negroes were given time off by their mistresses, and appeared in such finery that, when seeing them from the rear, we were immediately prepared to pay our respects."

Realizing his mistake, the Hessian was amused "to see a pitch-black person wearing a white summer dress with a white velvet sun hat and black velvet gloves." Blacks also incorporated military uniforms into their apparel, sometimes to demonstrate resistance, at other times simply for warmth.

While rural blacks still dressed in the drab garb of the subsistence farmer, young urban African Americans celebrated their freedom with ostentatious apparel; from the late colonial period onward, blacks were consumers of fine fashions. The visitor C. F. Arfwedson noted that black women in 1820s New York wore "bonnets, decorated with plumes, ribbons, and flowers of a thousand different colors." He observed how the men wore "their coats so open [that] the shirt sticks out of the armpits; the waistcoats are of all colours of the rainbow; the hat is carelessly put off to one side; the gloves are yellow, and every dandy carried a smart cane." White artists soon satirized black clothing in series of racist cartoons. In response, such black leaders as David Ruggles and Sojourner Truth affected the plain clothes of the Society of Friends. For some of the educated black elite, the adaptation of contemporary business clothing became a sign of much-desired respectability. In fact, there emerged a class of black urban dandies who were simply showing their desire to be fashionable. By 1830, despite the scorn of anxious whites and a disapproving black elite, young blacks wearing gaudy or simply classy outfits enlivened both the city streets and their own culture.

Clothing after 1830. The gap of freedom between north and south found expression in the clothing that African Americans wore. In the north the industrial revolution transformed the textile trade early and made available inexpensive varieties of clothing. Unlike the homemade cow skin trousers, oznabrig shirts, and shoddy footwear of the colonial era, free blacks— their numbers always increasing due to the abolition of slavery in their respective states, manumission through bargaining with masters or through bequests, or self-emancipation—expressed their liberty in clothing. Middling rank blacks, defined as educated and steadily employed, often chose to reflect their seriousness about life in clothing similar to that of their white counterparts. Both races discarded the colonial waistcoat, pantaloons, and wigs for Victorian-era business suits, white shirts, stovepipe hats, formal boots, and overcoats. Antebellum middle-class black women dressed in bustled full-length dresses and shoes, adding bonnets and long coats for inclement weather. In a century during which English middle-class fashions prevailed in America, blacks as well as whites took on standard outfits. The major exceptions to such conformity were young belles and their beaux. Much satirized in racist caricatures printed in northern urban centers, young African American men and women celebrated their new freedom with extravagant outfits, much to the disgust and anger of white observers and to the discomfort of middle class African Americans. White observers derisively described blacks dressed in "blue coat, fashionably cut; red ribbon, and a bunch of pinch-beck seals; white pantaloons, shining boots, gloves, and a tippy rattan." The man's female companion wore "pink kid slippers; her fine Leghorn, cambric dress with open work; corsets well fitted; reticule hanging on her arm." Bothersome to many whites, such young dandies anticipated and influenced the dress codes of working class whites known as "Bowery Bhoys" and "Ghals." Another, more insulting piece of entertainment that emerged from the racist ridicule of black pretensions was the coon show, a racially charged stage performance that lasted into the twentieth century and was a staple of white vaudeville acts. Featuring whites in blackface, African American dress habits became a vehicle for white voyeurism and contempt.

In the southern states, where the "cotton revolution" made blacks a commodity, clothing was simpler. Usually male field hands received one shirt and pair of pants per year while women wore dresses and children were attired in long shirts. The fabric was rough oznabrig or "Negro cloth" that was purchased from northern retailers. Frederick Douglass recalled his gratitude toward his older brother for wearing this cloth until it softened before passing it to his younger sibling. Crude shoes made in the north were shipped to the slave south. On more remote plantations blacks wore homemade clothing and leather trousers. Children often went naked until ten years of age.

While masters sometimes purchased special shirts, trousers, and dresses for holidays and church services, better-quality clothing was available through theft. Self-emancipated or runaway slaves commonly took as much their masters' or mistresses' clothing as possible, for personal use or for sale in the used-garment markets in the cities. While enslaved blacks often wore plantation clothing, advertisements for their return described new "freedom garments." One Virginia slave named Laban fled with a gray lambskin coat, white trousers, a double-breasted gray coat, a black cape, and "sundry other clothes." One Kentucky field hand incongruously wore a cashmere coat, nice pants, shoes, stockings, and a fur hat. A southern master wrote that a female slave was fond of clothing and took four sets with her. A Mississippi slave had several gold rings, and a "fine stock of clothes." The vagaries of the internal slave trade could mean that not all these clothes and accoutrements were stolen, but were rather the gleanings of past lives. In contrast to their country cousins, urban enslaved people wore uniforms, more fashionable clothing, and often "had the appearance of a dandy." Walley, who ran away from his Charleston master, wore a blue coat, with yellow buttons, thin black pants, and a black fur hat, and carried extra jackets and pants wrapped in a carpet.

The Civil War brought freedom and obviated the need to flee slavery. During the Reconstruction era, blacks celebrated their new liberty with elegant military uniforms that angered the defeated whites of the south. One troubled white regarded a parade of black horsemen followed by a "patriarch" wearing an apron of black and gold, a pair of trousers with a gold stripe down the sides, and a black, feathered hat. Next came a band in full regalia followed by hundreds of field hands in ordinary clothing. White supremacists felt humiliated by such drill teams occupying the cities. As was the case in the antebellum north, middle class blacks in the postwar south wore formal business attire. But for the newly freed blacks, clothing allowed assertive messages. Black parades featured former slaves "dressed in new flashy sports attire, fancy expensive silk shirts, new pants, hats, ties, with every color of the rainbow." By the end of the century, the repression of southern rural blacks into sharecropping was expressed in their work clothing while urban blacks, north and south, demonstrated their class with elegant attire. Examples can be seen in the widely circulated photographs of the carefully dressed, elegant black leader W. E. B. Du Bois. An exception to these rules were the black dandies, epitomized by the protagonist of the urban saga of Frankie and Johnnie in which the killer Stagger Lee (also known as Stagolee or Stackolee) wore fancy clothing and, most tellingly, a broad-brimmed hat, in styles still worn by rap and hip-hop performers of the late 1990s and into the twenty-first century.

[See also American Revolution; Arts and Crafts; Free African Americans to 1828; Fugitive Slaves; Society of Friends (Quakers) and African Americans; and Urbanization.]

BIBLIOGRAPHY

Franklin, John Hope, and Loren Schweninger, *Runaway Slaves: Rebels and the Plantation.* New York: Oxford University Press, 1999.

Hodges, Graham Russell, and Alan Edward Brown, eds. *"Pretends to Be Free": Runaway Slave Advertisements from Colonial and Revolutionary New York and New Jersey.* New York: Garland, 1994.

Smith, Billy G., and Richard Wojtowicz, eds. *Blacks Who Stole Themselves: Advertisements for Runaways in the "Pennsylvania Gazette," 1728–1790.* Philadelphia, 1989.

White, Shane, and Graham White. *Stylin': African American Expressive Culture from Its Beginnings to the Zoot Suit.* Ithaca, NY: Cornell University Press, 1998.

Windley, Lathan A., ed. *Runaway Slave Advertisements: A Documentary History from the 1730s to 1790.* 4 vols. Westport, CT: Greenwood, 1983.

—GRAHAM RUSSELL GAO HODGES

CLYDE, WILLIAM PANCOAST (b. 11 November 1839; d. 1923), New York steamship and railway industrialist. William Pancoast Clyde was born in Claymont, Delaware, the son of Thomas Clyde and Rebecca Pancoast. His father, a Scottish immigrant, settled in Chester, Pennsylvania, where he worked as a civil and marine engineer. In 1844 Thomas Clyde built America's first screw propeller steamship and launched the Clyde Steamship Line, which became the nation's largest coastal steamship company.

William Clyde attended Trinity College in Connecticut, but at the outbreak of the Civil War in 1861 he left his studies to join the Union forces as a Philadelphia Gray Reserve. In 1865 he married Emeline Field, with whom he had seven children, and entered the merchant shipping business in which his father had prospered. At the age of thirty-four, Clyde became president of the Pacific Mail Steamship Company, enabling him to dominate American shipping on the Pacific coast while his father dominated shipping on the Atlantic coast. Clyde became a leading figure in steamship transportation between New York and San Francisco, as well as in the Panama railroad through Central America that linked that nation's Pacific and Atlantic shores before the completion of the Panama Canal in August 1914. He was also active in the expansion of railroads in the southern United States and, for a time, controlled the Richmond and Danville Railroad System.

In 1878 Clyde established his West India Line to the Caribbean. Ten years later a civil war in Haiti pitted François Denys Légitime's forces in Port-au-Prince against Florvil Hyppolite's rebels at Cap-Haïtien in the north. The Democratic administration of President Grover Cleveland maintained a policy of neutrality, but American merchants were eager to profit from the two Haitian rivals, who sent their agents abroad to purchase weapons. The United States sent naval vessels off the coast of Haiti to guard American merchant ships. Clyde sold armaments to Hyppolite's forces under the protection of Rear Admiral Bancroft Gherardi, the commander of the U.S. North Atlantic Squadron, which rendered ineffective Légitime's blockade of Haiti's northern ports.

With the election of President Benjamin Harrison, the American effort to supplant European influence in the Caribbean accelerated. Harrison's secretary of state, James G. Blaine, favored the strengthening of commercial ties with Latin America and the Caribbean and the construction of U.S. naval bases in the region. Clyde, an influential man in New York Republican circles, gained further access to national power holders when Benjamin Franklin Tracy, a Brooklyn lawyer, became Harrison's secretary of the navy. Tracy's law firm was employed as legal counsel for Clyde. Through Tracy, Clyde influenced Blaine's and Harrison's decisions regarding the Caribbean.

President Harrison appointed Frederick Douglass to be minister resident and consul general to Haiti, but Blaine, Tracy, Gherardi, and Clyde formulated strategies to which Douglass was not privy because of the assumption that he was too enamored of the Caribbean's only black republic to negotiate forcefully with Haitians. Douglass's arrival in Port-au-Prince in 1889 coincided with Hyppolite's presidential inauguration. Captain E. C. Reed of South Carolina, an agent for the Clyde Steamship Line, also arrived seeking a shipping concession, Clyde's reward for helping Hyppolite defeat Légitime.

Douglass favored the concession, assuming that ordered and regular transportation service between the United States and Haiti would benefit both countries. Yet, Clyde believed that Douglass, who insisted on treating the Haitians as equals in negotiations with the powerful United States, did not sufficiently pressure the Haitians. Douglass, offended by the suggestion that he serve the private interest of one U.S. industrialist rather than the interests of all U.S. citizens, refused Reed's request to renounce all other private American initiatives in Haiti if the concession was granted. The press reported the refusal unfavorably against Douglass. Clyde tried to have him removed from his post.

Blaine and Tracy sought to use the Clyde contract to gain access to Môle Saint-Nicolas, the deepwater harbor on Haiti's northwest coast, for a U.S. naval base. They authorized Gherardi to negotiate a contract with the Haitians that gave Clyde a five-year subsidy and provided certain exclusive privileges for the Clyde Steamship Line. Clyde then submitted to the Hyppolite government a revised version of the contract asking for a ten-year subsidy at a higher rate, plus a ninety-nine-year lease of Môle Saint-Nicolas that stipulated only American ships be allowed to use the harbor.

After the Haitian assembly adjourned without considering the contract, Blaine instructed Douglass to assist Gherardi in a formal diplomatic effort for Môle Saint-Nicolas. In 1891 Douglass returned home, resigned, and published his side of the story concerning the many reasons the negotiations had failed. He argued that the strategy of seeking the Clyde concession before negotiating for Môle Saint-Nicolas had hindered U.S. efforts to acquire a naval base in Haiti.

[*See also* Blaine, James G.; Civil War; Cleveland, Grover; Douglass, Frederick; Foreign Policy; Gherardi, Bancroft; Haiti; Haitian Revolutions; Harrison, Benjamin; Hyppolite, Louis Modestin Florvil; Môle Saint-Nicolas (Haiti) Annexation; *and* Tracy, Benjamin Franklin.]

BIBLIOGRAPHY

Douglass, Frederick. *Life and Times of Frederick Douglass*. Grand Rapids, MI: Candace Press, 1996.

Heinl, Robert Debs, Jr., and Nancy Gordon Heinl. *Written in Blood: The Story of the Haitian People, 1492–1995.* 2nd ed., revised and expanded by Michael Heinl. Lanham, MD: University Press of America, 1996. One of the best general histories of Haiti in English.

McFeely, William S. *Frederick Douglass.* New York: Norton, 1991. A treatment of Douglass's activities in Haiti can be found in chapters 25 and 26.

—DAVID M. CARLETTA

COKER, DANIEL T. (b. 1780; d. 1846), African American preacher, teacher, and missionary to Africa. Daniel Coker was born Isaac Wright in 1780, probably in Frederick County, Maryland, to the enslaved African Edward Wright and the white indentured servant Susan Coker. Isaac's mother also had an older white son, named Daniel Coker, who refused to go away to school unless Isaac could accompany him. While with his half brother, Isaac received a rudimentary education and ran away to New York, where he assumed his brother's name.

The mixed-race Coker was active in the Methodist movement under the traveling bishop Francis Asbury. Coker became a minister in a Baltimore Methodist church that was modeled after the Reverend Richard Allen's church in Philadelphia and opened a school in about 1800. Despite the fact that early Methodists were encouraged to free their slaves, welcome African American members, and support abolition, many white preachers, trustees, and churchgoers treated African American members of their congregation unjustly or discourteously. In response, Coker published a forty-three page pamphlet containing one of his 1810 sermons protesting African slavery: *A Dialog between a Virginian and an African Minister.* Therein he describes himself as a "Minister of the African Methodist Episcopal Church in Baltimore" and in an appendix lists the names of African ministers "who are in holy orders" as well as local African preachers, churches, and "names of the descendants of the African race, who have given proofs of talent."

In the introduction to the 1817 publication *Doctrines and Discipline of the African Methodist Episcopal Church,* Daniel Coker, Richard Allen, and the Philadelphia minister James Champion explain how they responded to their mistreatment by white Methodists after a number of years of dissatisfaction. They state that the African American members of their church were "disposed to seek a place of worship for themselves" rather than seek legal redress against white Methodist preachers and trustees, who repeatedly tried to prevent them from attaining equality with white congregants or from worshiping solely among people of their own race. African American Methodists from Baltimore, Philadelphia, and other places met together "to secure their privileges [and] promote union and

Reverend Daniel Coker, in a portrait included in James A. Handy's *Scraps of African Methodist Episcopal History,* 1902. Handy wrote of Coker: "For several years he was the most popular, if not the only school-master among the colored people in the Monumental City (Baltimore), and has been the honored instrument of preparing some of the most gifted among the youth of that day, for usefulness on earth, and glory in heaven." (University of North Carolina, Wilson Library.)

harmony among themselves." In April 1816 they formed the African Methodist Episcopal Church in the "fear of God, the unity of the Spirit and the bonds of peace, and to preserve us from that spiritual despotism which we have so recently experienced."

Coker was elected the first bishop of the AME Church, but he declined; the group then elected the Reverend Richard Allen to the post. In addition to serving as a pastor, Coker established the church's Bethel Charity School; several generations of blacks benefited from the teachers and preachers trained in this school. The Baltimore church reported 1,066 members in 1818, 1,388 in 1819, and 1,760 in 1820. Coker was removed from the church in 1818—he evidently decided that he wanted to be a missionary to Africa—but restored a year later. In addition to serving as a pastor and teacher, Coker underwent several other important experiences. Several years prior to the formation of the AME Church, Coker became very interested in developments in Sierra Leone, in West Africa. During the Revolutionary War many slaves fled to British lines because Lord Dunmore, the governor of Virginia, offered them freedom; at the end of the conflict British troops took thousands of blacks out of the United States and settled them in Nova Scotia, the Caribbean, and the British Isles. In 1787 British abolitionists and philanthropists established Sierra Leone as a homeland for the "black poor" living in their territories. Some Americans closely followed the development of this West African colony, and some further tried to negotiate for the settlement of African Americans there. Paul Cuffe, the son of an African father and an Indian mother, was a ship owner and builder from Massachusetts. He traveled to Sierra Leone to see the colony and to inquire about the possible immigration of blacks and the development of a black-owned transatlantic shipping business.

Cuffe, a Quaker, formed the Friendly Society with John Kizzell, a U.S. Revolutionary War veteran who had lived in England and migrated to Sierra Leone. Cuffe and Kizzell made arrangements for an African American settlement off the coast of Sierra Leone on Sherbro Island. Cuffe then attempted to negotiate with the British and U.S. governments for funding as well as with potential African American immigrants. Cuffe's negotiations with the U.S. government failed because his petition came before Congress during the War of 1812, when there was an embargo against the British; additionally, free blacks in the cities he visited were largely opposed to his plan. During his travels, Cuffe became friends with Coker. At the end of the War of 1812, shortly before his death, Cuffe wrote to his "Estemed friend Daniel Coker" from Westport, Connecticut, "3d mo 13th 1815" (spelling and capitalization Cuffe's):

> May we unite in greatful acknowledgement to Almighty God that the sword is again stayed in this quarter of the Globe, and peace expirenced I now call thy attention to arouse in the minds of Citizens of Baltimore of the ancestors of africans who have to do or may feel their minds Zealously inguaged for the good of their fellow creators in africa and have a mind to Visit or remove to that Countery to give their names as I have written to the Institution in London for their aid in accomodating in their passage and also in making suitable provisions for receiving them when arriving in Africa. I do not see that the voyage Can be entered into until about the 10th mth next which will give proper time for all readyness to be made.
> I am thy ashured friend
> Paul Cuffe (Wiggins, p. 322)

Having received little or no support from those to whom he applied, Cuffe finally sent a small group of willing setters to Sherbro Island at his own expense. Sev-

eral white U.S. government officials, preachers, and slaveholders carefully monitored the development of Sierra Leone and were extremely interested in Cuffe's colonizing efforts. This group of men met in Washington, D.C., in December 1816 and formed the American Colonization Society (ACS) in January 1817 to help colonize willing free blacks. While the founders of the organization had a mix of benevolent and racist motives guiding their participation, some were indeed eager to sponsor missionary endeavors in Africa. Congress finally agreed to provide funding for shelters to be built for Africans who were captured from slave ships (called "recaptives") and returned to West Africa before they could be sold in the Western Hemisphere. African American "workers" were sent on board the ship *Elizabeth* in 1820 to build shelters and care for recaptives until they could return to their homelands or find somewhere to settle permanently.

Although the vast majority of African Americans were adamant about remaining in the U.S., most blacks who truly desired to return to Africa had dual motives: liberation and evangelism. Much to the dismay of Bishop Richard Allen and other black leaders, Coker decided that he and his family would partner with the ACS to return to Africa as missionaries. He kept a journal during the voyage and the settlement at Sherbro. Part of it was published in 1820 as *The Journal of Daniel Coker, a Descendant of Africa, from the Time of Leaving New York, in the Ship "Elizabeth," Capt. Sebor, on a Voyage for Sherbro, in Africa, in Company with Three Agents and About Ninety Persons of Colour* (1820).

The ninety *Elizabeth* emigrants met with disappointments at every turn. The settlers resented the presence of the white ACS agents on board the *Elizabeth* only slightly more than that of the half-white Coker. The Sherbro Island settlement itself was a disaster. Kizzell proved unreliable, the water was of poor quality, and the island was infested with insects. Many settlers became sick; some died. The ACS intended for its white agents to govern the settlers, but when the last surviving white agent was struck with "African fever," he appointed Coker to lead. Coker wrote to the secretary of the navy from Yonie, Sierra Leone, on 26 May 1820:

> Honourable Sir:
> Your Honour may think it strange that I (who am an entire stranger to you) should take the liberty of writing to you at this time. . . . I having come out from America with the Agents of the United States, the Reverend Mr. Samuel Bacon, and Mr. J. P. Bankson, have had to witness with much pleasure, the zeal and ability with which they prosecuted the business of their Agency . . . from the time of their arrival until the day of their death. For permit me to inform you that they are both dead. (Huberich, vol. 1, p. 135)

The letter further explained the state of the colonists. The settlers resented Coker's leadership, but he continued to serve until another white ACS agent arrived. The settlers moved to several other locations before finally relocating to Freetown, the capital of Sierra Leone. When some of the settlers decided to move down the coast to found Liberia in 1822, Coker elected to remain in Sierra Leone, where he ministered until his death in 1846. The ACS agents and naval officers with whom he came in contact extolled "his qualities as a man, as an administrator and as a leader of his people." The ACS paid Coker $150 for the time he served as an agent.

[*See also* Africa, Idea of; African Methodist Episcopal Church; Allen, Richard; American Colonization Society; Black Church; Black Loyalists; Cuffe, Paul; Methodist Church and African Americans; Missionary Movements; Murray, John (Lord Dunmore); *and* Society of Friends (Quakers) and African Americans.]

BIBLIOGRAPHY

African Methodist Episcopal Church. *The Doctrines and Discipline of the African Methodist Episcopal Church.* Philadelphia: printed by Richard Allen and Jacob Tabisco, 1817.

American Colonization Society. *The Fourth Annual Report of the American Society for Colonizing the Free People of Colour of the United States.* Washington, DC: Davis and Force, 1821.

Coker, Daniel. *Journal of Daniel Coker, a Descendant of Africa, from the Time of Leaving New York, in the Ship "Elizabeth," Capt. Sebor, on a Voyage for Sherbro, in Africa, in Company with Three Agents, and about Ninety Persons of Colour.* Baltimore, MD: Edward J. Coale, 1820.

Huberich, Charles Henry. *The Political and Legislative History of Liberia.* 2 vols. New York: Central Book, 1947.

Smith, Jessie Carney, ed. *Notable Black American Men.* Detroit, MI: Gale, 1999.

Wiggins, Rosalind Cobb. *Captain Paul Cuffe's Logs And Letters, 1808–1817: A Black Quaker's "Voice from within the Veil."* Washington, DC: Howard University Press, 1996.

Woodson, Carter G. *The History of the Negro Church* (1921). Washington, DC: Associated Publishers, 1992.

—Debra Newman Ham

COLFAX MASSACRE. On 13 April 1873 a unit of the Louisiana state militia headed by a former slave named William Ward confronted a large number of armed white men from Grant Parish and neighboring locales at the parish seat of Colfax. In what came to be known as the Colfax Massacre, fifty-nine black militiamen, including Ward, were gunned down after fleeing the town's courthouse, which the white gang, many of whom were reputedly members of the White League, or the Ku Klux Klan, had set ablaze. The militia had taken a defensive position inside the building after the whites demanded they lay down their arms. Ward and his militia had provoked the ire of local whites after attempting to arrest several reputed Leaguers.

The political problems that gave birth to the Colfax Massacre were ones Republicans suffered throughout the South during Reconstruction. Having lost most of the Louisiana backcountry in the election of 1868 when the Klan's campaign of terror kept many voters away from the polls, Governor Henry Clay Warmoth devised a plan to ensure Republican success in the future. Under his influence, the Louisiana legislature created nine new parishes whose officials were to be appointed by the governor. One of these was Grant Parish, named in honor of the newly elected U.S. president, Ulysses S. Grant. Deep in the Red River Valley, Grant Parish was evenly divided along racial lines; therefore, Republicans could count on a sizable black vote come election time. William Calhoun, a powerful planter and Republican leader, dominated Grant Parish politics and proved a loyal ally to the governor in the state legislature. In fact, the town of Colfax was not really a town at all—it was one of Calhoun's five plantations in the parish; a stable served as the courthouse.

William Ward, a native of Virginia, had come to Louisiana as a soldier in the Union army. Like many black veterans, he attained a great deal of respect and political authority within the black community after the war. He quickly rose to the rank of captain in the state militia. Not one to toe the line when it came to pleasing party leaders, Ward became a political force in his own right, using his militia to pursue the murderers of his Republican allies and round up other white conservatives he suspected of supporting political terrorists. Warmoth, who was trying desperately to build an alliance of moderate-conservative white Republicans and Democrats, felt threatened by such displays of political independence and ordered Ward's company disbanded. Ward refused and continued to drill his men as well as gather black support for a radical ticket he headed up in the 1872 local elections.

Fraud, intimidation, and intraparty rivalry between the Fusionist Warmoth faction and the radicals now led by William Pitt Kellogg resulted in a chaotic election. Vote counts were unreliable, and each party claimed victory. Throughout the winter and early spring of 1873 dual governments existed in Louisiana, Kellogg and the Democrat William McEnery vying for control. The political futures of Ward and his men in Grant Parish also hung in the balance, since the Fusionist ticket claimed victory there. Finally, President Grant recognized Kellogg as governor, and Ward made his move to oust the Fusionists in Grant Parish.

Local whites organized to deal with Ward and his militia in early April. By Easter Sunday men from as far away

"Negroes Hiding in the Swamps of Louisiana," wood engraving by James L. Langridge from *Harper's Weekly*, 10 May 1873; the artist was William Ludwell Sheppard. This image illustrated an account of the Colfax massacre with the headline "The Louisiana Murders." The journalist noted, "The first reports of that atrocity were not exaggerated," and ended by saying that in the aftermath of the incident, "A general feeling of insecurity prevails among the colored people of Louisiana, and hundreds are seeking safety in the swamps and forests." (New York Public Library/Art Resource, N.Y.)

as Texas and Arkansas had assembled at the Colfax courthouse to demand Ward's surrender. He refused, even though there were only eighty men inside the courthouse to face the nearly three hundred armed and mounted whites waiting outside. Federal troops were two days away in New Orleans, and although Ward sent word to Governor Kellogg that he needed assistance, it was too late. Ward's militia managed to keep back the onslaught for nearly two hours, but soon the courthouse was in flames, and those remaining fled outside to surrender. Later that evening forty prisoners were taken to a nearby field and shot. In all, more than one hundred African Americans were killed.

The federal government prosecuted several of the vigilante ringleaders. In *U.S. v. Cruikshank*, the prosecutors argued that the white mob had violated Ward and his men's civil rights by conspiring to deny them the right to bear arms. The Supreme Court rejected this argument and accepted the defense's claim that Ward's militia, having been disbanded by Governor Warmoth, was not an official part of the state forces and therefore had no right to be protected as such. No one ever served jail time for the murders at Colfax.

[*See also* Black Militias; Reconstruction; Supreme Court; *and* Violence against African Americans.]

BIBLIOGRAPHY

Hahn, Steven. *A Nation under Our Feet: Black Political Struggles in the Rural South from Slavery to the Great Migration*. Cambridge, MA: Harvard University Press, 2003.

Lonn, Ella. *Reconstruction in Louisiana after 1868* (1918). Gloucester, MA: Peter Smith, 1967.

Taylor, Joe Gray. *Louisiana Reconstructed, 1863–1877*. Baton Rouge: Louisiana State University Press, 1974.

—CAROLE T. EMBERTON

COLLINS, JOHN A. (b. 1810; d. 1879), abolitionist and reformer. Little is known of the youth or parentage of John Anderson Collins other than that he was born in Manchester, Vermont. He attended Middlebury College and then, like his abolitionist colleague Parker Pillsbury, Andover Theological Seminary. Unlike Pillsbury, who went into the ministry before fully committing himself to the abolitionist movement, Collins left the seminary and began working with the Massachusetts Anti-Slavery Society, soon becoming its general agent. It was in this role that he seems to have actively fought the attempts of conservative clergymen like Amos Phelps and Charles Torrey to take control of the group from more radical abolitionists like William Lloyd Garrison.

Anderson became a trusted ally of Garrison and went to Great Britain in 1840 in the hope of drawing economic and philosophical connections between the American Anti-Slavery Society (AASS) and the British and Foreign Anti-Slavery Society. In Britain, however, Collins's strong opinions—especially his questioning of organized religion—alienated several British abolitionists, and the trip was not a success.

Returning to the United States, Collins threw himself into organizing and lecturing. In addition to editing the *Monthly Garland* (1840–1841), an abolitionist periodical, he collected material for an anthology, *The Anti-Slavery Picknick* (1842), and was probably the originator of the antislavery picnics that took place on 1 August throughout the antebellum period, which celebrated West Indian emancipation. He lectured all over New England and tirelessly supported other lecturers. He met Frederick Douglass at Douglass's first speech at the antislavery meetings in Nantucket, Massachusetts, and with Garrison, Collins attempted to convince Douglass to lecture for the movement. When Douglass eventually accepted an appointment, Collins accompanied him for most of his three-month trial period.

Contemporary scholars generally limit their discussion of Collins's role in this phase of Douglass's development to noting his condescending assertion that Douglass should "give us the facts; we will take care of the philosophy." Still, Collins undoubtedly did a great deal to introduce Douglass to antislavery politics and rhetoric and to the rigors of the life of an itinerant lecturer. Collins and Douglass grew to be friends; when a railroad conductor had Douglass forcibly removed to a Jim Crow (racially segregated) car in September 1841, Collins almost started a riot in insisting that he, too, would go. Two weeks later on the same train, both men refused to give up their seats and were supposedly removed only after a handful of men ripped up the floorboards under their seats.

In 1842 Collins, now a general agent of the American Anti-Slavery Society, arranged a massive lecture tour of New York that employed eight agents, who would deliver over six hundred lectures in twelve weeks. While Collins initially denoted Douglass as the tour's drawing card, it was Abby Kelley, lecturing widely for the first time, who captured the interest—and sometimes the invective—of the press and many listeners. From the widespread attention paid to this tour, Collins went on to plan the One Hundred Conventions movement, a series of meetings across the North and the West on abolition.

Collins, though, was already chafing from the narrow focus of the AASS. Introduced to international social reform movements in 1840, Collins was fast becoming a devotee of utopian anticapitalists like Robert Owen and Charles Fourier. During the 1843 tour Collins often insisted on following—and later preempting—the abolitionist meetings with conversations on Fourierism and especially on the antiproperty movement. Slavery, he began to argue, was but an individual symptom of the larger problem of a society based around property.

Collins's stance created noticeable tension among him and his lecturing partners, culminating in a fiery exchange with Douglass and the black abolitionist Charles Lenox Remond at a meeting in Syracuse, New York. Douglass, Remond, and a fiercely angry Abby Kelley wrote letters to Maria Weston Chapman, the society's corresponding secretary, denouncing Collins, but Chapman—seemingly with some of the same racist paternalism that shaped Collins's later interactions with Douglass—reprimanded Douglass and allowed Collins to continue as general agent.

Still later in 1843 Collins formed his own Society of Universal Inquiry and Reform; he tendered his resignation from the AASS in January 1844. Collins moved to Skaneateles, New York, where he founded a utopian community focused on socialism, temperance, and vegetarianism. Yet after only two years the community fragmented and then dissolved. Collins's life after this is hazy and underresearched. He worked briefly with a Whig newspaper in Ohio before settling in California in 1849. He was involved in both mining and mine speculation and may have practiced law in San Francisco. He seems, though, to have left radical politics behind. His family life is similarly unclear: one source reports that an unnamed wife died as early as 1840, but as late as 1843 a wife named Eunice wrote to Chapman about Collins's health and travels. He may have married again in California.

[*See also* American Anti-Slavery Society; Antislavery Movement; Douglass, Frederick; Garrison, William Lloyd; Jim Crow Car Laws; Massachusetts Anti-Slavery Society; One Hundred Conventions; Oratory and Verbal Arts; Pillsbury, Parker; Remond, Charles Lenox; Temperance; Weston Sisters; *and* Whig Party.]

BIBLIOGRAPHY

Lampe, Gregory P. *Frederick Douglass: Freedom's Voice, 1818–1845.* East Lansing: Michigan State University Press, 1998. This study of

Douglass's early oratory contains the most detailed discussion of Douglass's interactions with Collins.

Mabee, Carleton. *Black Freedom: The Nonviolent Abolitionists from 1830 through the Civil War*. New York: Macmillan, 1970. This general history of the movement contains a useful discussion of Collins, including his break with Garrison.

Sernett, Milton C. "Collins, John Anderson." In *American National Biography*, edited by John A. Garraty and Mark C. Carnes, vol. 5. New York: Oxford University Press, 1999. This is one of the more complete biographical entries on Collins.

—ERIC GARDNER

Runaway ad for Titus, posted in 1775. Titus had fled after Lord Dunmore, the royal governor of Virginia, made a famous proclamation offering freedom to enslaved blacks who joined the British forces. (American Antiquarian Society, Worcester, Massachusetts.)

COLONEL TYE (b. c. 1755; d. September 1780), black Loyalist and guerrilla warrior. The son of unknown parents, Titus Corlies was born on the farm of John Corlies, a Quaker farmer and slave owner in Shrewsbury, New Jersey. John Corlies resisted the determination of Quakers to free members' slaves. When elders of the Shrewsbury Meeting visited Corlies at his farm in 1775, he angrily refused to manumit his slaves. Titus Corlies, then about twenty years old, was listening carefully.

After Lord Dunmore, the royal governor of Virginia, made his famous proclamation offering freedom to enslaved blacks who joined the British forces, Titus fled. John Corlies described the self-emancipated fugitive as "not very black near 6 feet high, had on a grey homespun coat, brown breeches, blue and white stockings"; he also noted that Titus took along a quantity of clothes. The fugitive slave perhaps joined Dunmore's Ethiopian Regiment when it arrived at Staten Island, New York, in December 1776. Little was heard of him until the battle of Monmouth, fought near Freehold, New Jersey, on 28 June 1778. Titus, then known as "Captain Tye"—he would become "Colonel Tye" by 1779—was cited by British officials for capturing Elisha Shepard, a captain in the Monmouth County Militia, and moving him to imprisonment in British-occupied New York City.

Tye's endeavors were part of a Loyalist effort to support the British military in New Jersey; over the next two years Tye consistently terrorized the Patriots of that state. On 15 July 1779 Tye commanded "fifty Negroes and refugees [white Loyalists] in a daring raid on Shrewsbury." The "motley crew," as the interracial force was known, plundered Patriots of cattle, horses, clothing, and furniture and captured several American sympathizers. The raid established a pattern: Tye, accompanied by black and white Loyalists, repeatedly raided Patriot towns and took prisoners, provisions, and animals. The British forces paid Tye handsomely for his feats, once rewarding him with five guineas—nearly half a year's wage.

Over the harsh winter of 1779–1780 Colonel Tye helped the beleaguered British garrison in New York City survive by providing fuel and food, which his forces seized from Corlies and his neighbors. During the spring of 1780 Tye regularly commanded forces that captured leaders of county militias. In the second week of June 1780 alone, he and his men raided Monmouth County three times. In one battle they captured Barnes Smock, a local captain, and spiked his cannon, a symbolically disheartening act for the Patriots; Smock and two of his brothers were imprisoned in New York City. Tye's incursions frightened local Patriots so much that they petitioned New Jersey's wartime governor, William Livingston, to declare martial law. Even that action failed to halt Tye's incursions, however, which continued throughout the summer.

Tye's most famous venture came on 1 September 1780, when he commanded a small army of blacks, whites, and Queen's Rangers (an elite corps of British soldiers) against the stronghold of Josiah Huddy, a leading Patriot known for quick executions of captured Loyalists. After a fierce two-hour battle, Tye captured Huddy and started taking him back to New York City by boat. Along the way the state militia intercepted Tye's forces. Huddy jumped out of the rowboat in which he was being transported and swam to his rescuers shouting, "I am Huddy," an incident that became legendary. In the fighting, Tye suffered a bullet to the wrist; lacking medical attention, the wound brought about a case of lockjaw that soon killed him.

In the ensuing decades Patriots recognized Tye's courage, affirming that had he fought for the American side, its victory over the British might well have come sooner. Today he represents one of the military choices African Americans made during the American Revolution.

[*See also* American Revolution; Black Loyalists; Fugitive Slaves; Military; *and* Society of Friends (Quakers) and African Americans.]

BIBLIOGRAPHY

Hodges, Graham Russell. *Slavery and Freedom in the Rural North: African Americans in Monmouth County, New Jersey, 1665–1865.* Madison, WI: Madison House, 1997.

—GRAHAM RUSSELL GAO HODGES

COLONIALISM. Colonialism was the effort by nineteenth-century European powers to control, exploit, and inhabit other parts of the world, particularly Africa. Following Britain's abolition of the slave trade in 1807 and the end of slavery in the British colonies starting in 1834, missionaries and explorers made extensive efforts to learn more about Africa, partly to compensate for their earlier enslavement of African peoples. In the process, interest also grew in Africa's vast potential to produce exploitable natural resources and the perceived need to bring the Africans "commerce, civilization and Christianity," in the famous words of the missionary explorer David Livingston.

The earliest manifestations of this interest brought isolated explorers and missionaries into the interior of sub-Saharan Africa; such adventurers mostly set off from the British colonies of Sierra Leone and Cape Colony (South Africa). With the opening of the Suez Canal in 1869 and the creation of the Belgian King Leopold's International Association in 1875 to exploit the ivory and gold trades in the Congo, Africa took on a new strategic and commercial significance in European diplomacy. French generals marched around the western Sahara and coastal West Africa planting the French flag; German industrial magnates influenced their government to declare intentions to claim colonial control over Togo, Cameroon, and what became German Southwest Africa and German East Africa. To protect his interest in the Congo, Leopold called for an international conference, held in 1884 in Berlin, to establish formal procedures for the colonization of the rest of Africa. Major European politicians such as Prime Minister William Gladstone of Britain, Prince Otto von Bismarck of Germany, and Leopold himself came up with a series of rules for controlling African territories: European powers would have to carve out military control over a region and declare intentions to exploit resources to the partial advantage of the African peoples that lived there. Thus, the "scramble for Africa" began.

Between 1875 and 1912 the entire African continent was broken up into European colonies, with only Ethiopia and Liberia (the home of former American slaves repatriated to Africa) remaining independent. The declaration that colonial peoples would benefit from European colonization proved specious almost immediately; in 1890 a second European conference on African colonization limited the sale of alcohol to Africans—a thriving trade at the time—and also declared a ban on the selling of machine guns to Africans, since they could use the weapons to defend themselves from further conquest. African "benefits" from colonization simply meant that native peoples would learn how to become a cheap labor force for British, German, Italian, French, and Belgian entrepreneurs to use in mining and farming useful commodities to be sold on the world market; centuries-old Spanish and Portuguese colonies, meanwhile, gave little to no consideration to any "benefits" of their ruling presence to the native people.

Nearly every colony acquired after 1875 excited quick interest in its resources only to be neglected—along with its people—as more colonies were acquired and European diplomatic rivalries grew at home. By 1912 Africa was a subjugated continent that gained virtually no benefit whatsoever from European colonization, except for the notable exception of the introduction of new medicines, which were necessary for Europeans to survive in the African environment. Thus, Africa became the primary example of colonialism as a disaster for the colonized, as Europeans abused, neglected, and often murdered African peoples in the interest of meager economic exploitation and meaningless power diplomacy.

Oddly, toward the end of his life the abolitionist Frederick Douglass appeared to show little interest in colonialism in Africa and the potential for the further abuse of African peoples. Even after making a grand tour of Europe in the 1880s, he added no references in his *Life and Times* (1881, 1892) to the efforts of the European powers to overrun the same areas in West and Central Africa from which they had extracted slaves a hundred years earlier. A trip to Egypt merely warranted a plea for greater respect for adherents to the religion of Islam—and no discussion of the then-current British battle to subdue Islamic nationalism in Alexandria and the Sudan. Understandably grateful for his reception throughout Europe as a hero of the American antislavery movement, he may not have wished to antagonize his hosts by questioning their motives in the colonization of Africa.

[*See also* Africa, Idea of; Antislavery Movement; Colonization; Douglass, Frederick; Egypt, Frederick Douglass and; Liberia; *Life and Times of Frederick Douglass*; Slave Trade, African; *and* Slavery.]

BIBLIOGRAPHY

Gifford, Prosser, and William Roger Louis, eds. *Britain and Germany in Africa: Imperial Rivalry and Colonial Rule.* New Haven, CT: Yale University Press, 1967.

Gifford, Prosser, and William Roger Louis, eds. *France and Britain in Africa: Imperial Rivalry and Colonial Rule.* New Haven, CT: Yale University Press, 1971. Collections of articles comparing motivations in colonialism among the major powers involved during the era.

Hochschild, Adam. *King Leopold's Ghost: A Story of Greed, Terror, and Heroism in Colonial Africa.* Boston: Houghton Mifflin, 1998. Readable popular history of King Leopold's International Association, which exploited the populations of the Congo basin as slave labor in the extraction of gold and ivory.

Robinson, Ronald, John Gallagher, and Alice Denny. *Africa and the Victorians: The Official Mind of Imperialism.* London: Macmillan, 1961. The classic in the field and one of the best history books of the twentieth century. Argues for the reactionary, strategic nature of British colonization in Africa.

—DAVID SIMONELLI

COLONIZATION. Throughout the nineteenth century, activists of various racial and political backgrounds drafted plans to remove all free blacks and freed slaves from the United States. Sending settlers to Africa was the most commonly proposed means for doing this, but the difficulty and expense associated with back-to-Africa schemes also encouraged similar plans involving Haiti, Mexico, and Canada. Overall, emigration never came close to levels sufficient to reduce the black population in the United States.

The idea of colonization stemmed from the understanding in the Revolutionary period that slavery posed grave threats to the Republic, but that a free black population might also undermine the new nation. Thus, for some Americans, any emancipation had to be tied to expatriation. Ironically, the first steps toward colonization came from the British, who evacuated over 10,000 former slaves from the United States at the end of the Revolution. About 3,500 of these former slaves were colonized in Nova Scotia and then in 1791 about 1,000 were resettled in Sierra Leone. In addition the British resettled some former slaves in Jamaica and other Caribbean islands.

As the Revolution drew to a close Thomas Jefferson wrote in *Notes on the State of Virginia* (1781) that if slaves were freed "they should be colonized to such place as the circumstances of their time should render most proper." Jefferson explained that it would be impossible to "retain and incorporate the blacks into the state" because "deep rooted prejudices, entertained by the whites; ten thousand recollections, by the blacks, of the injuries they have sustained; new provocations; the real distinction which nature has made; and many other circumstances, will divide us into parties, and produce convulsions which will probably never end but in the extermination of one or the other race." Thus, for Jefferson at least, emancipation could never come except with exile. Forty years later, in a famous letter to Congressman John Holmes during the debates over the Missouri Compromise, Jefferson would take the same position, claiming that the "cession of that kind of property, for so it is misnamed, is a bagatelle which would not cost me a second thought, if, in that way, a general emancipation and *expatriation* could be effected;

and gradually, and with due sacrifices I think it might be [Italics in the original]."

Jefferson, however much he claimed to like the idea of colonization, never in fact supported any program for colonization. He understood that there were simply not enough ships to accomplish it. Thus, he wrote to Jared Sparks in 1824 that colonizing all the nation's slaves on the coast of Africa was impossible. Instead, he suggested a system whereby the children of slaves would be raised as free blacks, working for the owners of their mothers "until a proper age for deportation," and then they would be sent to Africa. However, in the end, Jefferson saw little likelihood of such a program being adopted.

Jefferson was not the only early national figure to consider colonization. In 1773 Reverend Samuel Hopkins of Rhode Island first offered to send black missionaries to Africa. In 1787 the British abolitionist Granville Sharp sponsored a first shipment of freed slaves to Sierra Leone, a British colony that later attracted American blacks, most prominently the wealthy ship owner and sea captain Paul Cuffe of Westport, Massachusetts.

The Virginian Ferdinando Fairfax proposed an emigration plan in 1790 that was similar to Jefferson's early ideas. And in 1800, in the wake of the Gabriel Conspiracy, the Virginia legislature considered the possibility of ending slavery and shipping the former slaves to Africa or some other place outside of the United States. Jefferson suggested to the governor James Monroe that blacks be sent to Haiti, but nothing came of this. After the Louisiana Purchase some Americans suggested that slaves might be freed and sent west of the Mississippi. None of these programs ever gained much traction, although the idea of using the west to get rid of unwanted non-whites was soon applied to Indians, and after the War of 1812 the United States embarked on a policy of forcing Indians into what would later become Oklahoma.

In 1817 a group of prominent Americans, including the Kentucky politician Henry Clay, Reverend Robert Finley of New Jersey, and Supreme Court Justice Bushrod Washington, a nephew of the president, formed the American Colonization Society (ACS). Other officers of the ACS included the rabidly proslavery South Carolina leader John C. Calhoun. The founders of the ACS created the society with the intention of shipping free blacks to Africa. In 1821 the ACS purchased land south of Sierra Leone at Cape Mesurdo, and named the colony Liberia, with a capital city, Monrovia, named for president of the United States, James Monroe. Congress, with President Monroe's encouragement, ultimately appropriated almost $100,000 for the society. Some states, especially Maryland, also appropriated money for the society. Support for the ACS varied. Some in the society saw it as a vehicle for ending slavery in the United States. Many of these supporters, particularly in the North, thought it was the most likely vehicle for emancipation. In fact over the next four decades hundreds of masters would emancipate their slaves on condition that they be turned over to the ACS for transportation to Africa. Many supporters of the ACS, however, were uninterested in either abolition in general or in facilitating private manumission. Rather, they saw the ACS as a vehicle for removing free blacks from the county. Ultimately, the ACS sent more than ten thousand black Americans to Liberia from 1816 to 1860; however their efforts declined after the Civil War and the society ceased most of its activities in 1892 due to lack of funds.

Debates about Colonization. Supporters and opponents of colonization encompassed a surprising variety of the political and racial spectrum. White supporters of emigration included both advocates and opponents of slavery. Some slave owners believed that the presence of free blacks in southern states created unrest and that their removal would more closely associate skin color with slave status. Some antislavery advocates, such as Benjamin Lundy, a prominent Quaker and abolitionist who proposed in the 1820s to create a colony of freed slaves in Mexico, believed that racism was so deeply ingrained in the American mind that there was no hope for peaceful racial coexistence. Many religiously minded supporters of colonization hoped that sending freed slaves to Africa would erase America's sinful slave-trading past while also Christianizing Africa. Finally, an overseas colony would provide lucrative trading opportunities, which might offset the cost of transporting and settling the freed slaves.

White opponents of emigration also belonged to both the proslavery and antislavery camps. Slave owners feared that having an outlet for freed slaves would increase demands for emancipation, while abolitionists complained of paying to rid the antebellum South of its unwanted free black population. On a practical level, ships to Africa, and to a lesser extent the Caribbean, were rare and expensive. After Liberia gained independence in 1847, critics focused on the country's unhealthy climate, lack of economic opportunities, unstable politics, and use of slave labor; Haiti's reputation was comparable. Some political idealists also viewed colonization as antithetical to the American anticolonial tradition.

In the late 1820s blacks began to attack the ACS, and the entire idea of colonization, as a racist plot. One of the most important opponents of colonization was the black radical David Walker, whose *Appeal to the Colored Citizens of the World* contained an attack on colonization. In the early 1830s the new abolition movement, led by William Lloyd Garrison, constantly attacked colonization as racist and unfair to blacks. James G. Birney, who would run for president on the Liberty Party ticket, began his

career as a colonizationist, but by the early 1830s had concluded that colonization was really a form of proslavery agitation. He spent most of the rest of his life opposing colonization and supporting an end to slavery, with former slaves living in the land of their birth: the United States.

Before and after the Civil War, black leaders such as Frederick Douglass opposed emigration schemes and advocated general emancipation and integration instead. With the exception of two stays in England and Canada, Douglass chose to remain in the United States after fleeing from the Maryland plantation where he worked as a slave. When the Civil War ended, Douglass supported the Freedmen's Bureau and headed the Freedman's Savings and Trust Company, both agencies designed to help freed slaves succeed in the United States. Douglass opposed colonialism, though his membership in the Republican Party forced him to support attempts to annex the Dominican Republic (1871) and Môle Saint-Nicolas in Haiti (1889–1891).

Most other post–Civil War black leaders, including Booker T. Washington and W. E. B. Du Bois, hoped that blacks would eventually overcome racism by focusing on education and entrepreneurship. Because they fought for the right of black citizens to gain an equal footing in American society, they opposed emigration. They also argued that after two hundred years in the United States, American blacks were no longer Africans and that voluntary emigration could easily turn into forced deportation. The white southern elite concurred, though for a different reason: after slavery was abolished, large agricultural estates suffered from a labor shortage that emigration could only worsen.

The best-known black advocate of emigration after the Civil War was Bishop Henry McNeal Turner (1834–1915) of the African Methodist Episcopal Church, who argued that educated men such as he had no future in a racist society and should flee to Africa. Many lower-class blacks, for whom upward social mobility and racial equality were unlikely prospects in the short term, displayed great interest in Turner's rhetoric. Destitute black southern farmers constituted the bulk of candidates for emigration after the Civil War.

Emigration Schemes for Africa, Canada, and Latin America. In addition to sending former slaves to Africa, colonization schemes often focused on Haiti, a black republic populated largely by former slaves that, after years of revolution, had gained its independence from France in 1804 and was the second-most-favored destination after Liberia. In 1824 the Haitian president, Jean-Pierre Boyer, entered into an agreement with Loring Daniel Dewey, the general agent for the New York Colonization Society and the Society for Promoting the Emigration of Free Persons of Colour to Hayiti, to urge black Americans to leave for Haiti. Similar efforts were led by the Reverend Thomas Paul of Boston's First African Baptist Church and Bishop Richard Allen and by the Philadelphia businessman James Forten's Haytian Emigration Society of Coloured People. (Boyer appropriated enough funds to allow six thousand black Americans to emigrate to Haiti, but most of them returned home within a year.) A more imaginative scheme, engineered by Boyer and the U.S. consul in Cayes, Ralph Higinston, was for U.S. slave owners to buy plantations in Haiti, send some of their black slaves there, and force them to work on the plantations as indentured servants. The Reverend James Theodore Holly of New Haven, Connecticut, also advocated emigration to Haiti in the 1850s, but Faustin Soulouque's brutal reign there hindered emigration at that time. In the 1860s the British-born James Redpath headed the Haytian Bureau of Emigration in the United States, a Haitian-sponsored organization designed to attract black settlers and obtain diplomatic recognition.

Canada was also considered as potential settlement grounds for free blacks before the Civil War. When the Revolutionary War ended, many black supporters of the British fled to Canada. Several all-black communities, such as Dawn, Elgin, and Wilberforce, sprang up, the latter after an 1829 race riot in Cincinnati forced many blacks to leave. The 1850 Fugitive Slave Law, which required authorities in abolitionist states to collaborate with slave catchers, prompted another wave of black emigration from the northern United States to Canada.

During the Civil War, President Abraham Lincoln seriously considered exiling all emancipated slaves. One plan involved sending settlers to Panama; few blacks volunteered, however, and Latin American hostility doomed the plan. An 1862 law stipulated that one-quarter of all proceeds from the sale of abandoned land in the South would go toward financing emigration. Much of this money was never used. In 1863 Lincoln sent five hundred black settlers to Île-à-Vache just off the Haitian coast; the venture failed, and most of the settlers returned to the United States.

After the Civil War ended in 1865, racial tensions and economic hardship provided many candidates for emigration in the South, but lack of funds doomed most plans. President Ulysses S. Grant, who tried to annex the Dominican Republic in the 1870s, hoped, among other things, to offer the island as a safe haven for former slaves (the U.S. Senate refused to ratify the annexation treaty). In 1878 the black physician and separatist Martin Robison Delany's Liberian Exodus Joint Stock Steamship Company sponsored one ship bound for Africa, the *Azor*. An 1884 bill sponsored by Senator Matthew Butler, a Democrat from South Carolina, would have appropriated five million dollars of federal money to provide transportation to any African Americans desirous to leave, but the Republican majority killed the bill.

Throughout the 1880s another Democratic senator, John T. Morgan of Alabama, ardently lobbied for the Belgian king Leopold II's Congo Free State, with the hope that a successful Belgian colony in Africa would attract black Americans. Headed by the Reverend Benjamin Gaston, a black Baptist preacher, the Congo National Emigration Company (founded 1886) succeeded in sponsoring only a forty-two-person group that left for Liberia in 1894. The International Migration Society, founded in 1894, sent a total of five hundred emigrants to Africa in 1895 and 1896 aboard two ships, the *Horsa* and the *Laurada*. In 1894 William H. Ellis, a businessman from San Antonio, Texas, contracted with the Mexican government to send up to ten thousand blacks to Mexico; a lone group of 816 arrived in 1895. These were the last notable emigration plans until Alfred C. Sam's and Marcus Garvey's efforts in the twentieth century.

[*See also* American Colonization Society; Black Nationalism; Black Separatism; Canada; Delany, Martin Robison; Dominican Republic, Annexation of; Emancipation; Emigration to Africa; Forten, James; Freedman's Savings and Trust Company; Freedmen; Freedmen's Bureau; Fugitive Slave Law of 1850; Haiti; Jefferson, Thomas; Liberia; Lincoln, Abraham; Lundy, Benjamin; Môle Saint-Nicolas (Haiti) Annexation; *and* Racism.]

BIBLIOGRAPHY

Dixon, Chris. *African America and Haiti: Emigration and Black Nationalism in the Nineteenth Century*. Westport, CT: Greenwood Press, 2000. Covers the rarely studied, but notable movement favoring emigration to Haiti.

Kinshasa, Kwando Mbiassi. *Emigration vs. Assimilation: The Debate in the African American Press, 1827–1861*. Jefferson, NC: McFarland, 1988. Analyzes opposition to emigration within the black community.

Redkey, Edwin S. *Black Exodus: Black Nationalist and Back-to-Africa Movements, 1890–1910*. New Haven, CT: Yale University Press, 1969. Argues that the low number of emigrants after the Civil War was due to financial problems rather than lack of interest among poor southern farmers.

Staudenraus, P. J. *The African Colonization Movement, 1816–1865*. New York: Columbia University Press, 1961. Focuses mostly on the American Colonization Society and Liberia.

Wilson, Moses J. *The Golden Age of Black Nationalism, 1850–1925*. New York: Oxford University Press, 1988.

—Philippe R. Girard
—Paul Finkelman

COLUMBIAN ORATOR, THE. Nineteenth-century America may justly be called the golden age of oratory. While aspiring authors struggled to claim a distinctive literary tradition, no one doubted American achievements when it came to the spoken word. An expanding electorate, increasing rates of literacy, and rapid population growth combined with issues of great interest to create a volatile public environment. It is no surprise, then, that the ability to speak persuasively was held at a premium, for to wield language in such a world was to wield power itself. And where there was demand, there was supply: textbooks designed specifically to cultivate the arts of oratory and eloquence were numerous and popular. Among them, Caleb Bingham's *Columbian Orator* was the foremost book of its kind. First published in 1797, the volume was subsequently reissued in scores of editions and became the most influential guide to public speaking in the early Republic and antebellum eras.

As popular as it was, *The Columbian Orator* may well have remained a historical footnote if not for Frederick Douglass. One of the greatest orators of the century, Douglass recalls in each of his three autobiographies that serendipitous event when, at age twelve, he purchased a copy of *The Columbian Orator* for a hard-earned fifty cents. There on the streets of Baltimore, behind the sheds or under the blankets, the young Douglass first came into contact with a world heretofore unknown. It was, he writes, a pivotal experience, indeed a definitive moment in his development not only as an advocate but also as a person.

Typically, one does not think of textbooks as possessing this kind of power. What was it about Bingham's volume that so moved Douglass? Several answers can be readily found in his autobiographical accounts. The book arrived in Douglass's hands just as he was learning how to read and write beyond the basics; it was thus a primary medium of his emerging literacy. But more than an educational vehicle, the text contained material that opened up entire vistas, in which Douglass discovered that he was not alone, that others, too, had sought freedom, resisted tyranny, and imagined better worlds. *The Columbian Orator* was thus a means through which Douglass could join, if for the moment only through its pages, a community of people and ideas otherwise absent. Finally, here was proof positive that language mattered, that those who commanded its resources might command the weapons of change.

Running to more than three hundred pages, *The Columbian Orator* is a compilation of eighty-one examples of eloquence. Besides an introductory essay on the principles of effective speaking, the volume features a broad assortment of religious, occasional, legal, and political themes. The pedagogical aim of these entries is to inspire and to provide a basis for emulation, and to this end Bingham offers up a veritable feast. Hungry as he always was, Douglass read and reread orations on Independence Day, Marcus Porcius Cato before the Roman Senate, sermons on the existence of God, and Marcus Tul-lius Cicero declaiming against Lucuis Sergius Catilina. He was especially taken, he writes, with the performances of Richard B. Sheridan, Lord Chatham, William Pitt, and Charles J. Fox—those icons of British liberty in whose words Douglass found inspiration and models aplenty. One piece he found particularly compelling was John Aikin's "Dialogue between a Master and Slave." There, he discovered many of the commonplaces he would later encounter in adult life: the master's profession that slavery was benign, sanctioned by scripture, and morally tenable as well as the protests of the slave, whose appeal to a kinder God, to law, and to humanity would fund so much of Douglass's public speaking in the years to come.

A boy and his book, each bringing to the other little more than a promise that here was not just a boy or just a book. *The Columbian Orator* gave Douglass a reason to believe that, given the powers of speech, the boy might become a force for change in a benighted world. And Douglass gave to the book a reader who, though anxious to emulate, was to give singular expression to the prospects of human freedom.

[*See also* Douglass, Frederick; Literacy in the Colonial Period; Literature; *and* Oratory and the Verbal Arts.]

BIBLIOGRAPHY
Bingham, Caleb. *The Columbian Orator*. Edited by David W. Blight. New York: New York University Press, 1998. An accessible and informative edition by the distinguished Douglass scholar.
Lampe, Gregory P. *Frederick Douglass: Freedom's Voice, 1818–1845.* East Lansing: Michigan State University Press, 1998. This text pays special attention to Douglass's career as an orator.
McFeely, William S. *Frederick Douglass*. New York: Norton, 1991. Comprehensive and highly readable biography.

—STEPHEN HOWARD BROWNE

COME-OUTERISM. For many abolitionists, one of the core motivating factors for their involvement in the antislavery movement was their deeply held religious beliefs. This was especially true after 1831, when antislavery proponents insisted that slavery was a sin and that slaveholders were sinners. Indeed, throughout the antebellum period organized religion was a bone of contention between abolitionists and proslavery advocates. Many denominations became battlegrounds, where the debate over slavery often tore congregations apart. Abolitionists, especially the more radical Garrisonians, argued that by not condemning slavery outright and chastising the slave owners, most denominations were guilty of abetting the "peculiar institution." The fact is that religious denominations included people from all walks of life, including slave owners, which made denunciation of slavery and its advocates difficult. Indeed, while some denominations did agree that slavery was wrong, they would not go so far as to condemn the institution or its participants. The hard-line stance of many abolitionists often resulted in either a split within the denomination or, in some instances, a complete withdrawal on the part of the abolitionists themselves. Abolitionists who advocated seceding from the churches they deemed proslavery were referred to as "come-outers," taking literally the biblical admonition, "Come out from among them, and be ye separate, and touch not the unclean thing."

Come-outerism took various forms. Some come-outers severed all ties with any religious institution, while others formed their own abolitionist sects specifically condemning slavery. For the come-outers, leaving their various denominations was an overt act of protest, exposing the hypocrisy they believed existed within their churches. The most radical come-outers, including Stephen S. Foster; his wife, Abby Kelley Foster; and Parker Pillsbury, took their opposition to the perceived proslavery churches to the extreme. They interrupted Sunday services and commenced lecturing on abolitionism, which usually resulted in their being physically removed from the church. While not condoning the behavior of the radical few, many come-outers believed that such actions called attention to the contradictions inherent in religious institutions that preached the word of God, yet refused to take an overt antislavery stance.

Come-outerism was not limited to separation from churches; the Garrisonians upheld the *Liberator*'s declaration of "No Union with Slaveholders." Come-outers generally held the state to the same standards as the church. Garrisonians were convinced that the U.S. Constitution was a proslavery document and, according to the Ohio abolitionist Betsy Mix Cowles, the only way to finally abolish slavery was to "make a *post mortum* [*sic*] of [the] government, its constitution and its laws."

Frederick Douglass, himself a radical Garrisonian abolitionist, was until 1851 a come-outer from the church. Although he professed deeply held religious beliefs, the former slave agreed that most churches supported slavery either outright or by their cowardly failure to speak out against it and slave owners. At one point Douglass parodied those ministers who admonished the men and women in bondage to embrace their enslavement because, according to the Bible, slaves were commanded to "obey their masters." Douglass was, to the end, a staunch come-outer; in 1860 only he, William Lloyd Garrison, and a few others supported the candidacy of Gerrit Smith of the Radical Abolitionist Party, who espoused a "Religion of Reason."

[*See also* Abolitionism; Antislavery Movement; Bible; Constitution, U.S.; Douglass, Frederick; Foster, Abby Kelley; Foster, Stephen S.; Garrison, William Lloyd; Garrisonian Abolitionists; Pillsbury, Parker; Proslavery Thought; Radical Abolitionist Party; Religion; Religion and Slavery; Slavery and the U.S. Constitution; *and* Smith, Gerrit.]

BIBLIOGRAPHY

Mayer, Henry. *All on Fire: William Lloyd Garrison and the Abolition of Slavery*. New York: St. Martin's Press, 1998. Mayer discusses come-outerism among the Garrisonian abolitionists as well as Douglass's come-outer beliefs. He relates the story of Douglass's parody of religion.

McKivigan, John R. *The War against Proslavery Religion: Abolitionism and the Northern Churches, 1830–1865*. Ithaca, NY: Cornell University Press, 1984. McKivigan's work contains much information on the come-outers, including the various sects that they established after leaving their respective churches.

—Donna M. DeBlasio

COMPROMISE OF 1850. Geographic expansion following the annexation of Texas and victory in the Mexican-American War accentuated differences between Americans on the issue of slavery and sowed seeds of division between North and South. Just as the territory of Missouri's application for statehood precipitated a crisis that was resolved by the Missouri Compromise of 1820—which prohibited slavery north of latitude 36°30′ and maintained the balance between free and slave states with the admission of Maine (as a free state) and Missouri (as a slave state) to the Union—so the Mexican Cession and California's request to be admitted to the Union forced Americans to revisit the question of slavery.

In the North, the rapid population growth, a rising tide of antislavery sentiment, and the enactment of personal liberty laws designed to impede the return of fugitive slaves precipitated increasing anxiety among slaveholders about the balance of power between free and slave states. President Zachary Taylor's plan to admit California as a free state exacerbated the concerns of slaveholders, as did his stance on New Mexico. The president supported New Mexicans in their boundary dispute with Texas and rejected the Lone Star State's claim to that portion of the New Mexican territory east of the Rio Grande, thus limiting the expansion of slavery. He also encouraged New Mexicans to organize for statehood and supported their right to decide the issue of slavery on the basis of popular sovereignty.

With Californians demanding admission as a free state and Texans poised to exercise their claim despite Taylor's vow to use federal troops to thwart them, the Thirty-first Congress confronted a crisis. Antagonism mounted between southern diehards, who branded their fellow southerner in the White House a traitor and threatened secession if California entered the Union as a free state, and antislavery northerners, who were intent on establishing the Mexican Cession (the land ceded to the United States by Mexico at the end of the Mexican War) as free soil and

"Union," symbolic group portrait engraved by H. S. Sadd from a painting by T. H. Matteson, 1852. It commemorates legislative efforts to save the Union, in particular the Compromise of 1850. Front row, left to right: Winfield Scott, Lewis Cass, Henry Clay, John Calhoun (who had, however, opposed the compromise), Daniel Webster, and (holding the shield) Millard Fillmore. Calhoun and Webster stand with a bust of George Washington between them. Left background, left to right: Speaker of the House Howell Cobb of Georgia, Virginia representative James McDowell, Thomas Hart Benton of Missouri, and former secretary of state John M. Clayton of Delaware. Second row at right: Ohio senator Thomas Corwin, James Buchanan, Stephen A. Douglas, attorney general John J. Crittenden, and senators Sam Houston of Texas and Henry Foote of Mississippi. Behind are senators Willie P. Mangum of North Carolina and W. R. King of Alabama. At far right, below the eagle, are Daniel S. Dickinson of New York, Supreme Court justice John McLean of Ohio, and senators John Bell of Tennessee and John C. Fremont of California. (Library of Congress.)

abolishing slavery in the nation's capital. These events set the stage for the drama that ended in the Compromise of 1850.

Believing that the urgency of congressional support to save the Union outweighed sectional differences on individual measures, Henry Clay of Kentucky presented a package containing eight provisions designed to resolve the sectional disputes on slavery. Addressing the Senate in late January 1850, the "Great Compromiser" called for the admission of California as a free state, the organization of the balance of the Mexican Cession as territories subject to no restrictions on slavery, settlement of the New Mexico–Texas boundary dispute in favor of New Mexico and federal assumption of the preannexation Texas debt,

abolition of the slave trade in the District of Columbia coupled with a guarantee that slavery itself would not be abolished in the nation's capital without the consent of its citizens and those in neighboring Maryland, no congressional interference with the domestic slave trade elsewhere, and a stronger Fugitive Slave Law.

Following Clay's proposals, the Senate became the scene of great debate. In early March a deathly ill John C. Calhoun of South Carolina made his way to the chamber to make his last speech to Congress championing the South's right to their "peculiar institution." Read by Senator James Mason of Virginia, the speech questioned congressional jurisdiction over slavery in the territories, suggested the need for a constitutional amendment to protect the property of slaveholders, and raised the specter of disunion if the equilibrium between slave and free states was not maintained. Daniel Webster of Massachusetts, having conferred with Clay, responded but incurred the wrath of antislavery northerners by advocating compromise with Southern slave owners. Days later, William H. Seward of New York, one of Taylor's most influential advisers, piqued the ire of southern slaveholders by calling for the recognition of a law higher than the Constitution and demanding the abolition of slavery. Amidst unprecedented sectional bickering, Clay's package was turned over in mid-April to a committee of thirteen senators, chaired by the aging senator himself.

In May the committee presented a comprehensive legislative package that was quickly dubbed the Omnibus Bill. Basically unchanged from Clay's original proposals, it precipitated a deluge of amendments and motions that left the Senate deadlocked along sectional lines and increased tensions on the eve of a convention of southern states at Nashville that embraced the extension of the 36°30′ line westward as a minimum condition for resolving the slavery issue. The stalemate in Congress continued, and the Texas–New Mexico boundary dispute threatened to erupt in violence, until Taylor's unexpected death suddenly put New York's Millard Fillmore in the White House in July.

By August the Omnibus Bill, stripped of all its provisions except for the territorial organization of Utah, was moribund. Recognizing that the packaging of measures that individually had the support of a near majority into one bill had united opposition against the proposed legislation, Senator Stephen Douglas of Illinois, supported by fellow Illinoisan John McClernand in the House and a new president willing to compromise, unpacked the Omnibus Bill and began to steer Clay's proposals through Congress as distinct measures. By mid-September, when the bill abolishing the slave trade in the District of Columbia and the new Fugitive Slave Law was enacted, the Compromise of 1850 had been passed as a series of individual measures—and disunion had seemingly been averted.

The Compromise of 1850, however, was a flawed solution to the crisis over slavery; it postponed rather than resolved the issues surrounding the South's peculiar institution. Indeed, it is perhaps best considered as only an armistice. In an era of remarkable expansion, the Compromise of 1850 failed to address deep-rooted differences in the attitudes of Americans regarding the future of slavery. The opposition of northern Whigs and southern Democrats to the compromise helped to accelerate the demise of America's second-party system, paving the way for further polarization along sectional lines. Southern diehards continued to refuse to acknowledge congres-

sional jurisdiction over slavery in the territories, and antislavery activists denounced concessions to slaveholding power.

Frederick Douglass assailed the Compromise of 1850 as part of an "iniquitous combination" designed to ensure the "peaceful perpetuity" of a monstrous institution. In particular, he attacked the new Fugitive Slave Law, which made it an offense for citizens to help fugitives and created a federalized enforcement apparatus that extended the tentacles of slavery to the North. He campaigned for resistance to this oppressive federal legislation, which he argued violated the "plainest principles of justice." During fugitive slave crises—notably, the rendition of Anthony Burns, when President Franklin Pierce authorized a show of force that was unprecedented in peacetime—Douglass called on northerners, black and white, to make the Fugitive Slave Law the dead letter that it, and the Compromise of 1850, soon became.

[*See also* Antislavery Movement; Burns, Anthony, Trial of; Calhoun, John C.; Clay, Henry; Democratic Party; Disunionism; Douglas, Stephen A.; Fugitive Slave Law of 1850; Laws and Legislation, Antebellum; Mexican-American War; Pierce, Franklin; Seward, William Henry; Slavery; *and* Whig Party.]

BIBLIOGRAPHY

Holt, Michael F. *The Political Crisis of the 1850s*. New York: Wiley, 1978.

Potter, David M. *The Impending Crisis, 1848–1861*. Edited and completed by Don E. Fehrenbacher. New York: Harper and Row, 1976.

Waugh, John C. *On the Brink of Civil War: The Compromise of 1850 and How It Changed the Course of American History*. Wilmington, DE: Scholarly Resources, 2003.

—GORDON S. BARKER

CONFEDERATE POLICY TOWARD AFRICAN AMERICANS AND SLAVES. The eleven Southern states that formed the Confederate States of America seceded from the Republic in order to protect the institution of slavery. The delegates of the conservative rebellion gathered on 5 February 1861 to frame a constitution for the new nation that would protect the practice of human servitude and an economy dependent on the importation of agricultural products. The authors of the Confederate constitution considered their product to be an improved version of the U.S. Constitution; therein they outlined a defense of the institution of slavery and openly declared its value, legally protecting and codifying the idea of human servitude.

From the U.S. Constitution the Confederate constitution adopted the three-fifths clause, which stated that each white citizen and three-fifths of all slaves counted toward determining the representation for each state; the clause also affected the amount of taxation levied on white citizens. In adopting the three-fifths clause, the Confederate Congress ensured that slavery was retained as an integral part of the structure and governance of the Confederate States of America.

The difficulties regarding the movement of slaves also received attention in the Confederate constitution. The document stipulated that slaves, as the property of their owners, could be transported into new territories and lands. Thus, the issue of the expansion of slavery either south or west was settled through the formation of the new nation and protected as a point of national policy. The Confederate constitution banned the importation of foreign slaves, despite the desire of fire-eaters in South Carolina and other states to not just reinforce but also expand slavery. The provision increased the value of slaves already in the Confederacy and aided in the development of diplomatic relations in Europe. Finally, the fugitive slave provision in the U.S. Constitution was adopted in the Confederate constitution. Unlike the U.S. version of the law, however, the Confederate article made the governor of a state receiving a runaway slave responsible for either returning the slave or financially compensating the owner.

Blacks and Confederate Communities. On the surface, the lives of free blacks and slaves did not change immediately after the creation of the Confederate States of America. African Americans already lived under oppressive restrictions imposed by state and local communities in response to the threat of slave rebellions and outside agitation. They continued to be monitored with respect to their practices of religion, education, and social relationships. On plantations, overseers regulated slaves' work habits and adjusted their schedules based on the seasons and levels of crop production. The movements and assemblies of urban blacks were controlled as a preventive step to forestall any formation of a slave revolt. John Brown's raid on the federal arsenal at Harpers Ferry, Virginia, in 1859 had convinced many southerners that black communities needed to be controlled and monitored daily. In many cases laws were passed to restrict blacks' movements, prevent assemblies of groups of black individuals, and monitor possible abolitionists in the slave communities. Further, slave owners and contractors were required by law to register their slaves' movements in and out of urban areas while under commission to fulfill craft and trade agreements. Slave patrols were created out of local militia units to monitor both urban and rural areas and watch for possible rebellions. If a rumor identified an individual or a group of slaves as a threat, at the local level the potential revolt was quelled swiftly and cruelly.

As the Civil War progressed and its impact on the social makeup of the South increased, Southern communities and black populations began to change. With the passage of the first conscription act in April 1862, large numbers of white men were drafted into the Confederate army. The displacement of the controlling factors in Southern communities forced many slaveholding families into new relationships with their slaves. Farming families were forced to either hire new overseers or call on other men in the family—those younger or older than the Confederate conscription age of eighteen to thirty-five years (later seventeen to forty-five years)—to manage the slave labor force. In addition, farmers' wives assumed more dominant roles in controlling the slaves or directing the overseers than was customary. Such changes began to affect production on farms scattered throughout the Confederacy. Control over the movement of slaves began to wane as slave patrols lost members to conscription. Yet, despite reductions in local control, no major slave revolts occurred during the war.

Throughout the Confederacy's existence Southern cities and towns experienced great surges in population. Businesses were being created to bid and produce items for military contracts for the Confederate government; military supply depots and hospitals were set up in communities connected by rail to major urban centers. With the influx of workers for these operations, refugee families entered cities and towns to circumvent the movement of the armies. These families brought their slaves with them, and those slaves were soon being incorporated into the urban workforce. Large numbers of free blacks and slaves resided in cities like Atlanta, Georgia, and Richmond, Virginia, working in government departments, tending the wounded in hospitals, and assisting in the movement of supplies. These black workers became competition for the poor whites and immigrants who provided manual labor in the urban labor pool. In several instances black workers were used as strikebreakers when white workers attempted to gain better wages through strikes.

The realities of the Civil War were harshest for black communities. Both sides of the conflict committed abuses against free blacks and slaves because of the perception that blacks were lower in value than other races. The Confederate army committed numerous crimes against blacks in the midst of military operations. Farm hands were shot by roving bands of Confederate cavalry and partisans. Soldiers raped black women while on the march or after deserting their units in the field. Death was often the outcome for a Northern black soldier taken captive on the battlefield; many black Union soldiers and their white officers were shot during the process of surrendering or while lying wounded in field stations behind the lines. If a soldier was lucky enough to survive his initial capture, he might become a slave and be put to work on constructing military projects or burying the numerous dead. Several Southern newspapers reported accounts where runaway slaves joined with deserters to form criminal gangs in 1865.

Blacks and the Confederate Military Effort. The Confederate army stemmed from the provisional army of the Confederate States, which comprised militia units gathered together when the Southern states seceded. Nowhere could free blacks serve as members of county militia units because a militia private was required to be a tax-paying citizen of the county. The only militia open to black men was the Louisiana Native Guards, a private militia company made up of elite men of mixed ancestry, known as free men of color. This militia unit offered its services to the state and the Confederacy, but Louisiana rejected the offer. Slaves could not keep firearms by law, and if any slave did need a weapon, it had to be registered with the superior court in the county in question.

Some blacks did serve as soldiers in Confederate army units. In each case the subjective definition of the man's skin color as either white, black, mulatto, or Native American affected his enrollment. Black Confederate soldiers would have joined units voluntarily and would have avoided the controls established in the three Confederate conscription laws; under these controls a possible conscript had to register through the county justice of the peace, undergo a medical examination, and experience further induction by a Confederate officer at a camp of instruction.

Southern blacks' greatest contribution to the Confederate war effort was a forced one that came through the impressment of slaves as laborers for the Confederate army. The Confederate president Jefferson Davis and others saw the resource of the slave population as a valuable means to free white soldiers for combat duty. The idea of impressing slaves for manual labor originated in January 1862, owing to the failure of Confederate states to provide necessary labor for Confederate military operations. In Richmond, roughly two thousand slaves and seven hundred free blacks were pressed into service to build fortifications to protect the Confederate capitol. Slave owners were compensated for the time spent by their slaves performing military labor. This ready source of labor was especially desirable in those localities where trenches and fortifications were needed to blunt possible Union advances.

President Davis also wanted the Confederate Congress to authorize free blacks and slaves for noncombatant military positions like teamsters, cooks, and hospital assistants, thereby freeing more white soldiers to reinforce battered Confederate regiments in the field. Beginning in 1862 many blacks served as support personnel to Confederate army combat units. With the failure of the first conscription act to provide adequate manpower to the Confederate armies, the idea of impressing more blacks began to be discussed in the Confederate Congress in March 1863. Several states were opposed to the idea because impressment would pull slaves from crop production and harvest. In the third Confederate conscription act in February 1864, the Confederate Congress agreed to set the number of impressed free blacks and slaves at twenty thousand. By 6 December 1864 the Confederate Congress was again ready to double the number of black laborers. The law enacted on 28 February 1865 left the final number of slave impressments up to the War Department.

The failure of the conscription acts to provide enough soldiers for regiments in the field convinced several Confederate officers that blacks were a legitimate source of men for the battlefield. On 2 January 1864 Major General Patrick Cleburne decided that it was time to tap into this potential manpower source. As an infantry division commander in the Confederate army in Tennessee, he proposed to a group of fellow officers that slaves be enlisted as soldiers with the promise of freedom for them and their families upon the winning of the war. He suggested that the group of officers sign a petition requesting legalized black enlistment in the Confederate army. While several of the officers were shocked by the Irish American's idea, Cleburne's brigade commanders agreed to sign the document. However, Cleburne's army commander, General Joseph E. Johnston, decided to ignore the written proposal, since he considered it a political matter that could adversely affect Cleburne's military career. Despite the efforts of the rival major general William H. T. Walker to discredit Cleburne by sending his petition to President Davis, the president dropped the matter to save the reputation of one of the Confederacy's best battlefield commanders.

On 7 November 1864 President Davis asked the Confederate Congress to authorize the purchase of forty thousand slaves for service to the Confederacy. He did not specify that these slaves would be used as soldiers, but the stage was set for a proposal of black enlistment. On 10 February 1865 a bill was introduced to arm the slaves as soldiers. Several days later, in his new role as the commanding general of all armies in the field, Robert E. Lee endorsed the idea of black enlistment. In March the Confederate Congress finally passed a bill to enlist African Americans into the Confederate army, and General Order Fourteen regarding black enlistment was issued by the Confederate War Department. On 25 March 1865 Richmond newspapers noted the appearance of a black military company, and General Lee launched his final attempt to break the Union lines at Fort Stedman. His attempt failed, and several weeks later the Union's spring offensive forced the evacuation of the capital of the Confederate States of America.

[*See also* Black Militias; Brown, John; Civil War; Civil War, Participation and Recruitment of Black Troops in; Confederate States of America; Constitution, U.S.; Crime and Punishment; Discrimination; Foreign Policy; Free African Americans before the Civil War (South); Freedmen; Fugitive Slave Law of 1850; Harpers Ferry Raid; Immigrants; Integration; Laws and Legislation; Lynching and Mob Violence; Military; Mulattoes; Proslavery Thought; Race, Theories of; Racism; Segregation; Slave Insurrections and Rebellions; Slave Trade; Slavery; Slavery and the U.S. Constitution; Stereotypes of African Americans; Strikes; Union Army, African Americans in; Urbanization; Violence against African Americans; *and* Work.]

BIBLIOGRAPHY

Alexander, Thomas B., and Richard E. Beringer. *The Anatomy of the Confederate Congress: A Study of the Influences of Member Characteristics on Legislative Voting Behavior, 1861–1865*. Nashville, TN: Vanderbilt University Press, 1972.

Brewer, James H. *The Confederate Negro*. Durham, NC: Duke University Press, 1969.

Rollins, Richard, ed. *Black Southerners in Gray: Essays on Afro-Americans in Confederate Armies*. Redondo Beach, CA: Rank and File Publication, 1994.

Smith, John David, ed. *Black Soldiers in Blue: African American Soldiers in the Civil War Era*. Chapel Hill: University of North Carolina Press, 2002.

Thomas, Emory M. *The Confederate Nation: 1861–1865*. New York: Harper and Row, 1979.

Wiley, Bell I. *Southern Negroes, 1861–1865*. New Haven, CT: Yale University Press, 1938.

—WILLIAM H. BROWN

CONFEDERATE STATES OF AMERICA. From the Revolution until the Civil War, sectionalism was a factor in American political life. While debating the Articles of Confederation, the 1781 document that preceded the Constitution, Thomas Lynch of South Carolina suggested that his state would leave the new nation if anyone questioned the rights of southern masters to own slaves. During the Constitutional Convention some delegates, again from South Carolina, hinted that they could not support the Constitution unless it gave specific protections to slavery. In the early 1830s South Carolina attempted to nullify a federal tariff, essentially declaring that the state could ignore the collective will of the nation. Despite threats of secession and disunion, the nation managed to resolve through compromises various crises that were fueled by sectionalism. For example, the 1820 Missouri Compromise and the Compromise of 1850 both temporarily settled the issue of the status of slavery in U.S. territories. Time after time, national political party membership offset sectionalism and made compromise possible.

However, in the election of 1860 the Democratic Party split, and the Republican Party was able to put a president, Abraham Lincoln, in the White House on a national platform dedicated to stopping the spread of slavery into the territories and preventing any new slave states from entering the Union. The election itself was geographically skewed, with four parties competing for the White House but only two candidates running nationwide campaigns: the "regular" Democrat Stephen A. Douglas of Illinois and the standard-bearer of the newly created Constitutional Union Party, John Bell of Tennessee. John Breckenridge of Kentucky ran as the "southern" Democrat; he campaigned almost exclusively in the fifteen slave states. Lincoln appeared on the ballot in only the eighteen free states and some of the border slave states. Nevertheless, Lincoln carried all of the northern states, a plurality of the popular vote, and a huge majority in the electoral college, and he took the election. As both candidate and president-elect, Lincoln asserted on a number of occasions that he had no power to or interest in interfering with slavery in the states where it already existed but that he would not allow any new slave states to be created.

Nevertheless, as soon as Abraham Lincoln was elected, southern states began to secede from the Union. In the months before Lincoln's inauguration, the incumbent president, James Buchanan, did nothing to interfere with secession—or with the flow of military weapons to southern militias. South Carolina seceded first, on 20 December 1860, proclaiming itself an independent state. By 1 February 1861 Mississippi, Florida, Alabama, Georgia, Louisiana, and Texas had also left the Union. The leaders of the these states, all in the Deep South, trusted neither Lincoln's claims that he was not interested in harming slavery where it already existed nor the Republican Party, which they viewed as radically abolitionist. Some of the states claimed the right to secession based on the concepts of state rights and state sovereignty, while others cited the principles of the Declaration of Independence. While state sovereignty might have provided the theory to support secession, the cause was slavery. Shortly after the putative new nation, the Confederate States of America, was formed, its vice president, Alexander Stephens, declared that "the cornerstone" of the Confederacy was slavery.

A month after Lincoln took office Confederate forces attacked Fort Sumter, a U.S. Army installation in the Charlestown harbor. Lincoln then called for seventy-five thousand soldiers to protect and preserve the Union. This led to a second wave of secession as Virginia, Arkansas,

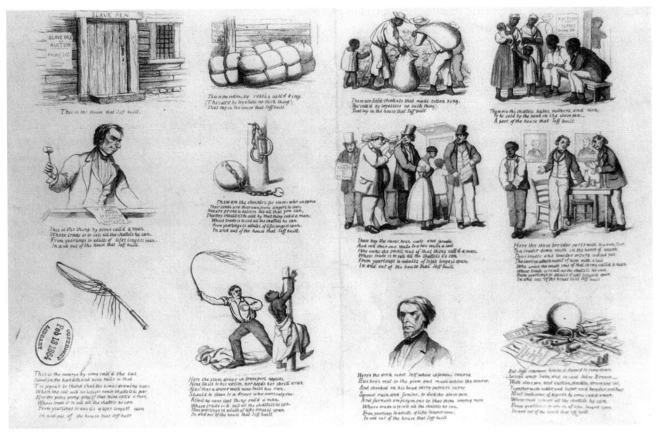

"The House That Jeff Built, vignettes indicting Jefferson Davis and southern slavery, etched by David Claypool Johnston, Boston, 1863. Left to right, top row to bottom: (1) door to a slave pen; (2) bales of cotton; (3) slaves picking cotton; (4) slave families awaiting auction; (5) auctioneer; (6) shackles; (7) slave merchants; (8) slave breeder negotiating with a merchant; (9) cat-o-nine-tails; (10) slave driver flogging a woman; (11) Davis; (12) dismantled symbols of slavery, with an envisioned notice of Davis's execution. The accompanying verses are modeled on the nursery rhyme "The House That Jack Built." (Library of Congress.)

Tennessee, and North Carolina joined the Confederacy, bringing the number of rebelling states to eleven. By mid-1861 all of the states that were to make up the Confederacy were in place. The people of these states were afraid that the North would pass laws that would ruin the South, and they saw the election of Lincoln as a deliberate attack on their honor. Consequently, they set out to create a new nation in which they could gain greater representation. Jefferson Davis, the president of the Confederacy, explained that all that they desired was to be left alone.

The Confederate Constitution was similar to that of the United States but differed significantly on the issues of slavery and federal power. For example, the right to own slaves was detailed more completely in the Confederate than in the U.S. Constitution, and the fugitive slave clause was strengthened. In addition, Confederate citizens were guaranteed the perpetual right to travel into other Confederate states with their slaves. However, unlike its counterpart, the Confederate Constitution prohibited any fur-

ther slave importation; also, although it emphasized state rights, it vested the national government with important powers. For example, before the Civil War states' rights advocates had consistently opposed the "necessary and proper clause" (Article I, Section 8) of the U.S. Constitution because it gave the national government too much flexibility and too much power. Congress and various presidential administrations had used this clause to enhance the federal government and to create national institutions not specifically called for in the Constitution— such as the Bank of the United States. Many southerners opposed this sort of open-ended power and wanted a national government that was more clearly limited by the Constitution.

The Confederate framers also gave their national government the power to protect the institution of slavery in any state or territory of the Confederacy. Other significant differences in the Confederate Constitution included the granting to the president an item veto, the limiting of the terms of the president and vice president to one six-year term without the possibility of reelection, and the prohibition of any protective tariffs. Also, borrowing an idea from the British system, cabinet officers were given seats on the floors of both congressional houses in order to facilitate the discussion of measures before the Confederate Congress at any given time.

The Confederate Congress followed the basic U.S. model. In fact, some of the people who served in the Confederate Congress had previously served in the U.S. government. The departments that the Confederate Congress created, such as the State, Treasury, War, and Navy departments, were largely similar to the U.S. departments. The Postal Department, for example, remained unchanged, with U.S. postal employees simply becoming Confederate postal employees at the moment secession took place. Other great similarities stemmed from the fact that the Provisional Congress reenacted all U.S. laws not inconsistent with the Confederate Constitution. Overall, while there were many differences between the governments of the Confederacy and the United States, the similarities outnumbered the differences.

In 1861 Frederick Douglass was convinced that the Confederacy had two overriding goals: the preservation of slavery and the submission of the rest of the country to its will. In Douglass's opinion the Confederacy would not be content until it had captured Washington, D.C., and extended slavery over the entire country, binding even free African Americans. According to Douglass, the two fundamental beliefs of members of the Confederacy were that slavery was right and that whites were superior to blacks. However, by 1863 Douglass had come to see the Confederacy and the war that resulted from its inception as a blessing, which he hoped would one day bring about the abolition of slavery. As the war continued, Douglass witnessed over 200,000 African Americans serving in the U.S. Army and Navy. He also learned of the atrocities against black Union soldiers committed by Confederate troops at Fort Pillow and elsewhere. In the end, the war was about race and freedom in the South.

The Confederacy defended slavery until the war's end. Only in the waning weeks of the war would the government of the South even consider enlisting some blacks, who would be emancipated for the purpose of fighting in the Confederate army. But there was little support even for this. Victory without slavery would have been a failure for the Confederacy, as its cornerstone would have been destroyed. Indeed, the Confederacy was a failed attempt to create a thoroughgoing slaveholders' nation in the American South.

[*See also* African Americans and the West; Buchanan, James; Civil War; Civil War, Participation and Recruitment of Black Troops in; Compromise of 1850; Confederate Policy toward African Americans and Slaves; Democratic Party; Disunionism; Douglas, Stephen A.; Douglass, Frederick; Election of 1860; Laws and Legislation; Lincoln, Abraham; Republican Party; Slavery; Union Army, African Americans in; *and* U.S. Constitution, Slavery and.]

BIBLIOGRAPHY

Davis, William C. *A Government of Our Own: The Making of the Confederacy*. New York: Free Press, 1994. Presents a detailed look at the men who brought the Confederate States of America into existence.

Lee, Charles R. *The Confederate Constitutions*. Westport, CT: Greenwood Press, 1974.

Rable, George C. *The Confederate Republic: A Revolution against Politics*. Chapel Hill: University of North Carolina Press, 1994. An examination of the assumptions, values, and beliefs that created a distinctly Confederate political culture that in many ways differed from its Northern counterpart.

—ROLANDO AVILA
—PAUL FINKELMAN

CONGREGATIONALISM AND AFRICAN AMERICANS. The first decade of Puritan settlement in New England coincided with the arrival of enslaved Africans; slaves would remain in Congregationalist society into the nineteenth century. While never central to Puritan culture, slavery was nevertheless a constant and accepted feature of colonial life until the American Revolution. Puritan ministers and laypeople alike struggled over several generations to reconcile their faith and their idealistic vision of a "city upon a hill" with the realities of racial slavery. Various theologians offered a range of defenses of the institution, while other public voices slowly developed a Christian antislavery position. By the end of the colonial period New England Congregationalists supported the emancipation of the region's slaves, but only after generations of cultural struggle over the religiously interpreted status of slavery.

Congregationalism was the dominant faith in New England in both the seventeenth and eighteenth centuries. Beginning in the 1630s tens of thousands of English Puritans crossed the Atlantic to found the new colony at Massachusetts Bay. Devoted to the theology of John Calvin, Puritan society in the New World was marked by religious orthodoxy, a capitalist economy, and suppression of dissent. Puritan theology exerted powerful influences on colonial New England society, supporting particular systems of education, economy, and family life. Calvinist belief in a community of the elect (God's chosen few) gave rise to strong, homogeneous communities in the New World; dissent was stifled, and difference was viewed as dangerous. Church and state were intertwined, particularly in Massachusetts, where the Congregationalists would retain official government support until the early nineteenth century.

Congregationalist racial thought emerged in the context of recurring seventeenth-century conflict with indigenous peoples. The Pequot War of 1637 and the larger King Philip's War of the 1670s, the two most consequential armed conflicts between Puritan settlers and native tribes in southeastern New England, were important milestones in the development of Puritan attitudes and ideas about other races. New England's Native American population declined precipitously in the course of the first half century of Puritan settlement as a result of the catastrophic spread of disease combined with regular warfare. In this context many white European settlers embraced an ideology declaring it to be God's will that they rule the lands of New England. This evolving worldview was simultaneously used to justify the existence of race-based slavery in the colonies of New England.

Enslaved Africans could be found in every one of the region's colonies until the American Revolution. While the enslaved constituted fewer than 5 percent of the region's colonial population, slaves constituted significantly larger communities in New England's coastal towns. Boston, always the center of the Congregationalist establishment, was home to a particularly important community of enslaved blacks. White Bostonians owned slaves in significant numbers and were leading merchants in the Atlantic trade network in which slaves were central commodities.

The years around the turn of the seventeenth century gave rise to a particularly intense era of Congregationalist debate over the place of slavery in a Christian society. In the aftermath of Britain's bloodless Glorious Revolution of 1688–1689 and the consolidation of parliamentary power; the failure of James II's Dominion of New England and the attempt to assert royal control over the northeastern colonies; and the Salem witchcraft hysteria of 1692, which destabilized the politics and culture of the entire region, local ministers and writers articulated a series of classic statements on the Puritan view of slavery. In 1693 Cotton Mather, the leading New England Congregationalist minister of his generation, sought to reconcile competing ideas about slavery in Massachusetts by organizing a Society of Negroes in Boston. The *Rules for the Society of Negroes* revealed Mather's interest in the education of the local enslaved population; in particular, he took great care to instruct white Congregationalists on the best means for instructing slaves. Mather organized weekly religious classes at his home for area blacks. Later, he hired tutors to educate local slaves in Christian orthodoxy.

Mather and the Boston judge Samuel Sewall wrote the defining Congregationalist texts on slavery. Sewall's 1700 tract, *The Selling of Joseph*, offered the most explicit attack on slavery in the Congregationalist tradition during the colonial era. Sewall wrote in defense of a Boston-area slave named Adam, who was at the time seeking his freedom through the colonial courts. *The Selling of Joseph* makes extensive use of the Old Testament to support a Christian antislavery argument. Anticipating later New England religious voices of reform, Sewall employed scripture to advance a powerful argument for the equality of souls. One year later, in 1701, Sewall's proslavery rival John Saffin—Adam's master—published a lengthy reply, entitled *A Brief and Candid Answer to a Late Printed Sheet, Entitled, the Selling of Joseph*. A leading Bostonian himself, Saffin rejected the broader claims of Sewall's argument and defended his ownership of slaves. Sewall's work and Saffin's response indicate the range of Puritan opinion on the slavery question all through the colonial period.

Cotton Mather published *The Negro Christianized* in 1706, arguing for the humane treatment of slaves in Massachusetts. By no means a condemnation of the colony's slave system, Mather's argument highlighted the need to convert enslaved blacks to Christianity. Both virtue and self-interest would be rewarded, Mather claimed, as Christian slaves would be more productive for their owners. Five years after the Sewall-Saffin exchange, Mather sought to carve out a middle ground for Congregationalists by recognizing the legality of New England's slave system while advocating a thorough moralization of that system. In Boston and in his correspondence with British leaders, Mather consistently made the case for a Christian slave system in New England.

Generations passed before the great turning moment in Congregationalist thinking on slavery occurred. The American Revolution, begun in Massachusetts, had a particularly powerful impact on local thought regarding slavery and freedom. Rhode Island Quakers had grown more explicitly antislavery in the decades before 1775, while other New England Protestants remained largely silent on the question of emancipation. In the 1770s Congregationalist communities across the region gradually turned against the institution of slavery amid the upheavals of war, as the Declaration of Independence's promise of revolutionary equality transformed public opinion. Massachusetts and other New England states with large Congregationalist populations joined Pennsylvania and its large Quaker population in taking the lead in destroying slavery.

Congregationalists after 1830. Although hierarchical and conservative in doctrinal matters, the Congregationalists became firmly antislavery after 1830, forming antislavery organizations, openly assisting self-emancipated slaves, and writing many books against the "peculiar institution." Congregationalists also supplied many leaders and foot soldiers to the abolitionist movement. Geography was a factor as the Congregationalists were rare outside of New England, where antislavery activism was strongest in the nation. Congregational churches across the region embraced abolitionism, just as they did anti-tobacco and temperance reforms designed to free society from evil habits and institutions. Infused with the evangelicalism of the Second Great Awakening, Congregationalists Arthur and Lewis Tappan, and ministers William Ellery Channing, Parker Pillsbury, John Fee, and Charles Goodell wrote antislavery books and organized societies to fight slavery. As Yale and Harvard universities (the two main suppliers of Congregational ministers) became centers of abolitionism, it emerged as church orthodoxy.

Although Congregationalism in New England had fewer African American members, there were noteworthy adherents. Lemuel Haynes was a prominent Congregational minister. The black abolitionist David Ruggles, a fierce opponent of slavery, learned about activism in the Second Congregational Church of Norwich, Connecticut. In turn, he inspired the black Congregationalist ministers Samuel Ringgold Ward and Henry Highland Garnet. The poet Ann Plato followed in the Congregationalist tradition of Phillis Wheatley.

The *Amistad* case of 1839 further radicalized Congregational ministers. In fact, the majority of people who came to the aid of the *Amistad* captives were black and white Congregationalists and radical abolitionists (as many as 20,000 Congregationalists regularly received the newsletter *American Missionary*, an organ of evangelical abolitionists). One of the most famous Congregationalists, the former president John Quincy Adams, ably defended the *Amistad* case and won approbation for the movement. Adams had also been the conscience of the U.S. Congress when he raised antislavery petitions from local congregations across New England and upstate New York in defiance of the infamous Gag Rule.

In 1846 white and black Congregationalists formed the American Missionary Association (AMA). Designed to train southern slaves in a creditable and organized manner, the AMA was both a missionary and abolitionist society that focused largely on educating freed slaves after the start of the Civil War. The AMA opened its first school on the grounds of the Chesapeake Female College across the Hampton River in Virginia on 17 September 1861. In just a few years, the AMA opened three additional schools in North Carolina—in Morehead, Roanoke Island, and Beaufort. By 1868 the AMA had over five hundred teachers and missionaries throughout the south and near the border states. The AMA teachers often lived and worked with black families, yet usually failed to recognize and en-

courage the richness of African American culture. After the Civil War, the AMA's efforts helped found many black colleges and universities including Fisk University, Berea College, Atlanta University, Talladega College, Le Moyne Institute, and Straight University (now Dillard University). Even as northern support for Reconstruction faded, Congregationalist mothers and daughters, in memory of lost husbands, sons, and daughters, continued to travel south to serve as schoolteachers. Congregationalists remained important in the north as well. Sterling N. Brown (father of the poet) was pastor of a Congregational Church in Washington, D.C., and head of the Howard University department of religion in the late nineteenth century.

[*See also* American Revolution; Catholic Church and African Americans; Declaration of Independence; Education; Episcopalians (Anglicans) and African Americans; Massachusetts; Mather, Cotton, and African Americans; Missionary Movements; Presbyterians and African Americans; Race, Theories of; Religion; Slavery: Northeast; *and* Society of Friends (Quakers) and African Americans.]

BIBLIOGRAPHY

Brown, Sterling N. *My Own Life Story*. Washington, DC: Hamilton Printing, 1924.

DeBoer, Clara M. *Be Jubilant My Feet: African American Abolitionists in the American Missionary Association, 1839–1861*. New York: Garland Publishing, 1994.

Jordan, Winthrop D. *White over Black: American Attitudes toward the Negro, 1550–1812*. Chapel Hill: University of North Carolina Press, 1968.

Piersen, William D. *Black Yankees: The Development of an Afro-American Subculture in Eighteenth-Century New England*. Amherst: University of Massachusetts Press, 1988.

—DAVID QUIGLEY
—GRAHAM RUSSELL GAO HODGES

CONNECTICUT. Slavery appeared early in the history of colonial Connecticut. Records indicate that in 1639 an enslaved African was killed by his Dutch owner in Hartford. Unlike Massachusetts and Rhode Island, however, Connecticut conducted its colonial slave trade with merchants and sailors playing only minor roles.

Connecticut's African American population clustered in a few port towns. Almost one-half of all blacks in the colony in 1774 lived in the coastal counties of New London and Fairfield. In that year 49 percent of Connecticut blacks were under the age of twenty, a substantially lower percentage than that of the colony's white community. Across New England, colonial African Americans had low birth rates.

Connecticut stood apart from the rest of the New England colonies in the intensity of its restrictions on the free black community. In 1718 the colonial assembly passed a law denying blacks the right to buy land and enacted legislation prohibiting free blacks from living in the colony's towns. Local jurisdictions were directed to enforce the laws but seemingly never did so. Nevertheless, the laws remained on Connecticut's books throughout the colonial period.

The complexity of free black life in late-eighteenth-century Connecticut is illuminated in the life of Venture Smith. Born in West Africa in 1729, Smith had been brought in slavery to southern New England. He finally gained his freedom in the 1760s and eventually earned enough money to purchase the freedom of his wife and children, to establish several businesses, and to amass more than a hundred acres of property. Settling in East Haddam, Connecticut, Smith took advantage of the freedoms of life on the state's coast but eloquently wrote about the discriminations he and his family faced. His 1798 memoir was published in New Haven and was read by nineteenth-century New Englanders as a classic autobiography of a self-made man.

Before the Revolution blacks commonly served in Connecticut's militia, with at least twenty-five companies that fought in the French and Indian War containing African Americans. Similarly blacks served in Connecticut units when the Revolution began, although not as extensively as in Massachusetts and Rhode Island. In 1777 the legislature allowed men to provide substitutes—including slaves—to fulfill their military service requirement. The slaves would then become free. To further encourage both manumission and enlistments, the legislature provided that masters would not be responsible for the future maintenance of any slaves they manumitted for military service. By the end of the war almost every sizable town in the state had provided black soldiers.

In the wake of the American Revolution, African American demands for freedom intensified, and white Connecticut citizens debated the state's commitment to a system of slavery. Connecticut joined neighboring Rhode Island in adopting a gradual emancipation statute in 1784. All children born after 1 March of that year were not slaves for life but were required to work for twenty-five years for their mothers' owners. This provision meant that slaves can be found in Connecticut census records well into the nineteenth century. At the same time, the gradual abolition act spurred private manumissions. In 1790 about half of the state's 5,572 blacks were slaves, but by 1800 only about 900 of the 6,281 blacks in the state were slaves. The 1810 census found only 310 slaves in the state. In 1840 there were just 17 enslaved blacks in the state, and they would all become free through a statute in 1848.

Even as the rest of New England committed to multiracial citizenship in the early nineteenth century, Connecticut pursued a different route and moved toward establishing second-class citizenship. In 1818 the state was one of the first to rewrite its original eighteenth-century constitution. Republicans pushed hard for a more democratic suffrage clause. Local Federalists had managed to maintain strict property qualifications since the American Revolution. These elitists lost ground in the second decade of the nineteenth century because of their opposition to the War of 1812 and because poor veterans were clamoring for political rights. In addition, some reformers suggested that expanded voting rights would convince some of the state's young men not to migrate westward. The 1818 Connecticut Constitutional Convention voted to remove existing property qualifications and at the same time to insert the word *white* in the new elections clause. As a result, every white male citizen could vote but even blacks with property were barred from voting. In the next two decades most other northern states followed Connecticut's lead, linking the empowerment of poor whites with some form of African American disfranchisement.

At the beginning of the Jacksonian era Connecticut showed little sympathy for the 8,000 or so blacks in the state. In 1832 Prudence Crandall, a Quaker opponent of slavery, allowed the daughter of a prosperous black farmer to enroll in her school in Canterbury. Whites immediately boycotted the school, and Crandall responded by turning her enterprise into a boarding school for African American females. Residents of Canterbury not only boycotted her efforts, but vandalized the school and put manure in Crandall's well, while merchants refused to sell her food and other goods. Meanwhile in May 1833 the Connecticut legislature, at the request of Andrew Judson, a local attorney, passed a law making it a crime to run a boarding school for blacks who came from other states. Crandall defiantly ignored the law and Judson, who was now the county attorney, successfully prosecuted her. In 1834 the state Supreme Court dismissed the charge on a technicality.

Within a few years there was a sea change in Connecticut's treatment of blacks. In 1838 the legislature repealed the anti-Crandall law. In 1837 the state Supreme Court held in *Jackson v. Bulloch* that slaves brought into Connecticut by their masters became immediately free. A year later, in addition to repealing the law used to prosecute Prudence Crandall, the legislature passed a strong personal liberty law, guaranteeing the right of a jury trial for anyone seized as a fugitive slave. In a mere five years Connecticut had gone from opposing blacks coming into the state merely for an education, to protecting the liberty of any black brought into the state, as well as anyone claimed as a fugitive.

A year later one of the most dramatic slavery-related cases arose in the Nutmeg State. In August 1839 the

United States Coast Guard brought the ship *Amistad* to New Haven, Connecticut. On board were thirty-nine Africans who had been illegally imported into Cuba and purchased by Montez and Ruiz, who were also on the ship. Montez and Ruiz were taking their newly purchased slaves by ship to another part of Cuba when they revolted and eventually the ship ended up in Long Island Sound. Once in New Haven Connecticut abolitionists rallied to the cause of the "Amistads," as the Africans were called. Their main attorney was Roger S. Baldwin, who came from a distinguished Connecticut family and would later serve as governor and U.S. senator. Yale professors worked with the Africans to discover what language they spoke (Mende) and to find someone who could help communicate with them. Meanwhile, Ruiz and Montez claimed them as slaves and the Spanish government wanted them returned to be tried for killing the ship captain and others during their revolt. The status of the Amistads was first determined by Andrew T. Judson, who had prosecuted Prudence Crandall earlier in the decade and had since become a U.S. district judge. To the surprise of President Van Buren, and the delight of the antislavery community, Judson ruled the Amistads were illegally taken from Africa and should be returned to Africa. The case would eventually go to the U.S. Supreme Court, where Baldwin would be joined by former president John Quincy Adams in successfully arguing for the freedom of the Africans. They would remain in Connecticut until 1842, when they were finally returned to Africa. This case helped transform Connecticut into strong antislavery state. In 1844 the legislature passed a new personal liberty law, which essentially withdrew all state support for the return of fugitive slaves. And in 1854 passed another law that further distanced the state from the support (in any form) of slavery. During this period a number of black abolitionists lived and worked in the state, including Reverend James W. C. Pennington. In the 1850s Republicans in the state attempted to give blacks the vote, but could only get their legislation through one house of the legislature.

The black population of Connecticut remained stable throughout the first half of the century, growing from 5,600 in 1790 to 7,700 in 1850. At the beginning of the Civil War there were approximately 8,600 blacks in the state; from this population, plus some volunteers from other states, Connecticut organized two black regiments who served in the War, the Twenty-ninth and Thirtieth Connecticut Infantry. Both regiments saw action in Virginia in the last year and a half of the war. The Twenty-ninth Connecticut was the first U.S. Army unit to enter Richmond when the Confederates evacuated the city. After the war, in 1868, blacks successfully agitated for an end to all segregated education in the state. The leader of

this movement was James Ralston, who was the Grand Master of the Prince Hall Masons. Blacks remained active in Republican Party politics for the rest of the century as their population grew to 12,000 in 1890 and 15,000 by 1900. In the late nineteenth century B. Rollin Bowser was appointed U.S. Consul General to Sierra Leone, as reward for helping to turn out the black vote for Republicans in Connecticut. Another significant African American in the state was the Hartford painter Charles Porter, who had the patronage of the city's most famous resident, Mark Twain.

With only 1.7 percent of the state's population, blacks had relatively little influence in politics or public life, though the state had no formal laws that segregated blacks or discriminated against them, and some African Americans worked for large white companies, especially in the insurance industry. Generally, however, blacks in late nineteenth century Connecticut were economically and politically on the periphery of the state. In the 1880s blacks in Connecticut had their own national guard units, but, reflecting the growing segregation in the nation, in 1896 the last black company was disbanded. There was no formal introduction of segregation in the Connecticut national guard, but the guard remained entirely white until well into the next century.

[*See also* American Revolution; *Amistad*; Autobiography; Civil Rights; Discrimination; Free African Americans to 1828; Gradual Emancipation; Laws and Legislation; Massachusetts; Rhode Island; Slavery: Northeast; Smith, Venture; Voting Rights; *and* War of 1812.]

BIBLIOGRAPHY

Adams, James Truslow. "Disfranchisement of Negroes in New England." *American Historical Review* 30.3 (April 1925): 543–547.

Greene, Lorenzo Johnston. *The Negro in Colonial New England*. New York: Columbia University Press, 1942.

Piersen, William D. *Black Yankees: The Development of an Afro-American Subculture in Eighteenth-Century New England*. Amherst: University of Massachusetts Press, 1988.

—David Quigley
—Paul Finkelman

CONSTITUTION, U.S. The U.S. Constitution, written in 1787, did not specifically mention slavery or race. Throughout the Constitutional Convention the delegates talked about "blacks," "Negroes," and "slaves," but the final document avoided these terms because northerners made it clear that using these terms would undermine support for the new form of government among their constituents. As James Iredell, one of North Carolina's delegates, told his state's ratifying convention, "The word *slave* is not mentioned" because "the northern delegates, owing to their particular scruples on the subject of slavery, did not choose the word *slave* to be mentioned, the southerners at the Convention were willing to do without the word *slave*."

Proslavery Provisions of the Constitution. Despite the circumlocution, slavery was sanctioned throughout the Constitution. Five provisions dealt directly with slavery:

Art. I, Sec. 2, Par. 3. The three-fifths clause provided for counting three-fifths of all slaves for purposes of representation in Congress. This clause also provided that if any "direct tax" was levied on the states, it could be imposed only proportionately, according to population, and that only three-fifths of all slaves would be counted in assessing what each state's contribution would be.

Art. I, Sec. 9, Par. 1. Popularly known as the "slave trade clause," this provision prevented Congress from ending the African slave trade before 1808 but did not require Congress to ban the trade after that date. The clause was a significant exception to the general power granted to Congress to regulate all commerce.

Art. I, Sec. 9, Par. 4. This clause declared that any "capitation" or other "direct tax" had to take into account the three-fifths clause. It ensured that if a head tax were ever levied, slaves would be taxed at three-fifths the rate of whites.

Art. IV, Sec. 2, Par. 3. The fugitive slave clause prohibited the states from emancipating fugitive slaves and required that runaways be returned to their owners "on demand."

Art. V. This article prohibited any amendment of the slave importation or capitation clauses before 1808.

Taken together, these five provisions gave the South a strong claim to "special treatment" for its peculiar institution. The three-fifths clause also gave the South extra political muscle—in the House of Representatives and in the Electoral College—to support that claim.

Numerous other clauses of the Constitution supplemented the five clauses that directly protected slavery. Some provisions that indirectly guarded slavery, such as the prohibition on taxing exports, were included primarily to protect the interests of slaveholders. Others, such as the guarantee of federal support to "suppress Insurrections" and the creation of the Electoral College, were written with slavery in mind, although delegates also supported them for reasons having nothing to do with slavery. The most prominent indirect protections of slavery were:

Art. I, Sec. 8, Par. 15. The domestic insurrections clause empowered Congress to call "forth the Militia" to "suppress Insurrections," including slave rebellions.

Art. I, Sec. 9, Par. 5, and **Art. I, Sec. 10, Par. 2.** These clauses prohibited federal or state taxes on exports and thus prevented an indirect tax on slavery (and slaveholders) by taxing the staple products of slave labor, such as tobacco, rice, and eventually cotton.

Art. II, Sec. 1, Par. 2. This clause provided for the indirect election of the president through an electoral college based on congressional representation. This provision incorporated the three-fifths clause into the Electoral College and gave whites in slave states disproportionate influence in the election of the president.

Art. IV, Sec. 4. The domestic violence provision guaranteed that the U.S. government would protect states from "domestic Violence," including slave rebellions.

Art. V. By requiring a three-fourths majority of the states to ratify any amendment to the Constitution, this article ensured that the slaveholding states would have a perpetual veto over any constitutional changes.

Other provisions, such as those giving Congress jurisdiction of the national capital—what became Washington, D.C.—and the federal territories, allowed Congress to regulate slavery but did not require it be done.

All of these clauses dealt with slavery and status and not with race. The most misunderstood of these clauses is the three-fifths clause. This clause provided a mechanism for allocating representation in Congress. Under the clause, representation would be "determined by adding to the whole Number of free Persons . . . three-fifths of all other persons." Thus, all free blacks would be counted as "free People." The "other persons" referred only to slaves. As such, this clause did not say that blacks were three-fifths of a person but rather that representation in Congress would be based on population and that slaves would not be counted in the same way as free people. At the Constitutional Convention southerners pushed for counting slaves fully for representation, while opponents of slavery did not want to count slaves at all for purposes of representation.

During the debates over ratification some opponents of the Constitution (the anti-Federalists) focused on the protections of slavery, especially the provision that allowed the states to import slaves for at least twenty years. The slave trade was not necessarily a sectional issue. Some southerners, especially Virginians, opposed the trade because their state had an abundance of slaves. One New York opponent of the Constitution complained that the document condoned "drenching the bowels of Africa in gore, for the sake of enslaving its free-born innocent inhabitants." A Virginian thought the slave trade provision was an "excellent clause" for "an Algerian constitution: but not so well calculated (I hope) for the latitude of America." George Mason, who was also one of Virginia's delegates to the Convention, thought that importing slaves would "render the United States weaker, more vulnerable, and less capable of defense." This was one of many reasons why he opposed the Constitution. Three Massachusetts anti-Federalists also feared the dangers of slavery. They noted that the Constitution bound the states together as a "whole" and "the states" were "under obligation . . . reciprocally to aid each other in defense and support of every thing to which they are entitled thereby, right or wrong." Thus, they might be called to suppress a slave revolt or in some other way defend the institution. They could not predict how slavery might entangle them in the future, but they did know that "this lust for slavery, [was] portentous of much evil in America, for the cry of innocent blood, . . . hath undoubtedly reached to the Heavens, to which that cry is always directed, and will draw down upon them vengeance adequate to the enormity of the crime."

In the South, however, supporters of the Constitution focused their attention on its proslavery provisions. At the Virginia ratifying convention, Governor Edmund Randolph, who had also represented his state at the Convention and become the first attorney general of the United States, praised the Constitution for protecting slavery. In response to a suggestion that the Constitution might threaten slavery, he challenged opponents of the Constitution to show "*where* is the part that has a tendency to the *abolition* of slavery?" He answered his own question by asserting, "Were it right here to mention what passed in [the Philadelphia] convention . . . I might tell you *that the Southern States, even South Carolina herself, conceived this property to be secure*" and that "there was not a member of the Virginia delegation who had *the smallest suspicion of the abolition of slavery.*" General Charles Cotesworth Pinckney of South Carolina similarly bragged to the South Carolina House of Representatives, "In short, considering all circumstances, we have made the best terms for the security of this species of property it was in our power to make. We would have made better if we could; but on the whole, I do not think them bad." Noting that this was a government of limited power, Pinckney declared, "We have a security that the general government can never emancipate them, for no such authority is granted and it is admitted, on all hands, that the general government has no powers but what are expressly granted by the Constitution, and that all rights not expressed were reserved by the several states." Talking about the fugitive slave clause, Pinckney told his South Carolina neighbors, "We have obtained a right to recover our slaves in whatever part of America they may take refuge, which is a right we had not before."

In the North supporters of the Constitution tried to deflect criticism about slavery. Many argued that the slave trade clause was actually antislavery, because it would allow for the end of the trade in "only" twenty years. James Wilson, the Scottish born lawyer who was part of the Pennsylvania delegation to the Convention and would later serve on the U.S. Supreme Court, exaggerated the importance of this clause, erroneously claiming that the provision would, in fact, lead to an end to slavery in the nation. Many northern supporters of the Constitution implied, and some incorrectly declared, that the slave trade provision *required* that Congress end the African trade in 1808. Such supporters of the Constitution never mentioned the fugitive slave clause.

Implementing the Proslavery Constitution. Shortly after the Constitution went into effect, Congress passed the Fugitive Slave Law of 1793 to implement the fugitive slave clause. There was little controversy over this clause at the time, but opponents of slavery would later argue that Congress had no power to regulate the return of fugitive slaves. In the 1820s a number of northern states passed "personal liberty laws" to prevent the improper removal of free blacks from their jurisdiction under the weak evidentiary rules of the fugitive slave law.

After the Constitution was ratified, Quakers began to petition Congress to end the African slave trade. Southerners denounced these petitions, arguing that people should not be allowed to petition for an unconstitutional law. Ironically, at this time, the early 1790s, none of the states allowed the importation of new slaves from Africa. However, between 1800 and 1 January 1808 the Deep South imported about 100,000 new slaves. On 1 January 1808, however, a federal ban on the slave trade went into effect. It was not entirely successful, and some Africans were smuggled into the country. Congress passed new legislation in 1819, and Justice Joseph Story of the U.S. Supreme Court urged federal grand juries to investigate illegal slaving. But in the end Congress never appropriated enough money to stop the illegal trade, which continued throughout the period.

In this early period Congress also began to regulate race under its constitutional powers. The Naturalization Act of 1790 allowed only whites to become naturalized citizens. Similarly, the Militia Act of 1792 limited membership in that important civil body to white men. These early federal laws, which implemented the Constitution, affected blacks in ways that did not affect whites.

The first constitutional crisis over slavery and race did not emerge until 1819, when Missouri petitioned to enter the Union as a slave state. In 1787 Congress, under the Articles of Confederation, had banned slavery in the Northwest Territory. The language of the law prohibited slavery "north and west" of the Ohio River. In 1789 Congress reenacted this law, under its constitutional authority to regulate the territories. There was little controversy at the time, although in the mid-nineteenth century the U.S. Supreme Court would hold that Congress did not have the power to regulate slavery in the territories. In 1803 Ohio entered the Union as a free state, as did Indiana in 1816. Although some slaves were held in the region until the 1840s, the Northwest Ordinance of 1787 seemed to be leading to an end to slavery north and west of the Ohio River.

No one apparently thought much about the Northwest Ordinance in 1803, when the United States bought the Louisiana Purchase from France. In 1812 Louisiana came into the Union as a slave state. However, when Missouri sought admission as a slave state in 1819, northerners objected. They noted that most of Missouri was north and west of Ohio River, and thus it should be free under the Northwest Ordinance. Southerners argued that the Northwest Ordinance of 1787 extended only to the Mississippi River and that Missourians should be allowed to choose, for themselves, whether they wanted slavery or not. After two years of debate, Congress adopted the Missouri Compromise in 1820. Missouri came in as a slave state, Maine broke away from Massachusetts and entered the Union as a free state, and most important of all, Congress banned all slavery north and west of the southern boundary of Missouri. Many southerners opposed this compromise, arguing that Congress could not constitutionally prohibit citizens from bringing their slaves into the territories. In *Dred Scott v. Sandford* (1857) the Supreme Court would adopt this southern position.

In the 1820s a new issue arose, involving race and commerce. The Constitution gave Congress the sole power to regulate international and interstate commerce. South Carolina, however, passed laws requiring that any free black sailors who entered the state be incarcerated until their ships left. Henry Elkison, a free black from the Caribbean, sailing on an English ship, challenged his incarceration in the U.S. Circuit Court for South Carolina. In *Elkison v. Deliesseline* (1823), Justice William Johnson of the U.S. Supreme Court, while riding circuit, denounced the new South Carolina policy as a violation of the Constitution. Only Congress could regulate interstate or international commerce, including the right of sailors from other states or nations to enter a particular port. However, for technical reasons, Justice Johnson did not order the release of Elkison. By the end of the decade most of the southern Atlantic and Gulf states had passed laws requiring the incarceration of black seamen. The controversy over these laws continued until the Civil War and undermined interstate relations.

By 1830 the Constitution had been in effect for almost half a century. The document had weathered the storm of the Missouri crisis and slavery had not, for the most part, undermined the constitutional order. Congress had exercised its powers to ban the African slave trade and

support the return of fugitive slaves, but neither had been fully implemented. A few laws, such as the Militia and Naturalization Acts, blatantly discriminated against blacks, but by and large there had been little constitutional controversy over slavery and race. The status of blacks under the Constitution changed dramatically during the period from 1830 to 1895. At the beginning of the period most blacks were slaves; at the end they were free people, citizens of the United States, officeholders and voters. The Constitution of 1787 protected slavery in a variety of ways, but between 1865 and 1870 three new amendments revolutionized the constitutional status of African Americans.

These six decades of change can be divided into four periods. The years from 1830 to 1861 were the age of slavery. The Constitution protected slavery in a range of ways. The three-fifths clause gave the southern states extra representation in Congress for their slaves; the fugitive slave clause, and laws passed in 1793 and 1850 to enforce it, allowed masters to recover slaves who escaped to the free states; and the domestic insurrections clause provided federal aid to suppress slave rebellions. Congressional power over the territories made slavery a constant source of political conflict. The issue of slavery in the territories became a major constitutional question during this period. The rights of blacks, as opposed to the status of slaves, became a constitutional issue throughout the decades leading up to the Civil War. The *Dred Scott* case (1857) raised questions about the status of blacks as well as the power of Congress to regulate slavery in the territories. Constitutional issues affected blacks in other ways as well. In the 1830s and 1840s Congress wrangled over whether to receive antislavery petitions. While not directly affecting the lives of African Americans, these debates revealed how slavery interacted with the nature of the Constitution. Meanwhile, abolitionists debated just what that nature was. Was the Constitution a proslavery compact, a "covenant with death and an agreement in Hell," as the white abolitionist William Lloyd Garrison and his followers claimed? Or was it a more flexible document that would allow opponents of bondage to slowly chip away at the peculiar institution?

Secession and the Civil War raised new constitutional concerns. At the beginning of the crisis President Abraham Lincoln correctly argued that he had no power to touch slavery where it existed. The exigencies of war, however, altered political facts and constitutional understandings. By mid-1862 Lincoln found constitutional authority—in his role as commander in chief of the nation's armed forces—to end slavery in the rebellious states. Meanwhile, Congress discovered similar powers when it passed two confiscation acts to take slaves from Rebel masters. Before the Civil War was over, Congress had sent the Thirteenth Amendment to the states. When it was ratified in December 1865, the amendment ended all slavery in the United States.

The third period began with the end of the Civil War. In 1866 Congress passed the Fourteenth Amendment (ratified in 1868), which made all African Americans citizens of the nation and prohibited the states from denying them "due process of the law" or the "equal protection of the laws" while guaranteeing them the "privileges or immunities of citizens of the United States." The Fifteenth Amendment (ratified in 1870) prohibited racial discrimination in suffrage. Furthermore, Congress passed legislation, including the Civil Rights Acts of 1866 and 1875, to implement the new amendments, and various enforcement acts to suppress racist violence from the Ku Klux Klan and other white terrorist groups. No longer the tool of slave owners, the Constitution now reflected the aspirations of the Declaration of Independence, promising that all people would be treated equally and would have full liberty to pursue happiness.

The fourth period began with the end of Reconstruction in 1877, as the nation retreated from its commitment to civil rights and equality. The retreat was gradual, and blacks did not lose all their rights at once. As late as 1890 blacks voted on the same basis as whites in much of the South. However, by this time southern blacks were increasingly losing their civil and political rights. The promises of the new amendments failed to materialize, as discrimination, repression, and segregation became common throughout the South, where more than 90 percent of all African Americans lived.

Slaveholder's Constitution. In 1830, while the young Frederick Bailey (later Douglass) was growing up as a slave in Maryland, the U.S. government remained fully in the hands of supporters of slavery. Since 1788 only two one-term presidents—John Adams and John Quincy Adams—had *not* been slave owners. The slave South had rarely lost a battle in Congress. Constitutionally, slavery was secure from national assault, as all commentators, politicians, and lawyers agreed that the Congress had no power to legislate on slavery in the states. At most, Congress could regulate slavery in the territories and in the District of Columbia. The territorial issue had been settled by the Missouri Compromise, which brought Missouri into the Union and allowed slavery to spread to some of the West but banned it in most of the territory acquired in the Louisiana Purchase. The District of Columbia remained firmly a slave city, with Congress never seriously considering laws to ban the institution in the nation's capital. As part of the Compromise of 1850 Congress banned the sale of people at public slave markets and slave auctions in the District but otherwise did nothing to remove the stain of slavery from the seat of the national govern-

ment. The free black population grew rapidly in the District of Columbia before the Civil War, but free blacks there always lived a precarious legal existence.

In 1831 two events led to a new understanding of the relationship between slavery, blacks, and the Constitution. Nat Turner's rebellion in Virginia shook southerners, when slaves following their charismatic leader, Turner, killed scores of whites. After two days, whites suppressed the rebellion, using the militia, the army, and the navy. The rebellion reminded southerners of the importance of the Constitution, which provided that the national government would help suppress insurrections and rebellions. At the same time, however, the rebellion made southerners wonder about the danger of being in a Union with free states. Many southerners assumed—incorrectly—that Turner had been encouraged by northern opponents of slavery.

The rise of a new opposition to slavery also changed constitutional understandings. In 1831 William Lloyd Garrison began publishing the first abolitionist newspaper in the nation. Garrison demanded an immediate end to slavery. To make matters worse, he began mailing copies of his paper to editors and influential leaders around the nation. Southerners were shocked by this verbal assault on their most important social and political institution. A few years earlier, in 1828, David Walker, a free black in Massachusetts, had published a scathing attack on slavery, urging slaves to revolt. Walker's *Appeal* led southerners to demand his arrest, but officials in Boston refused to help them, noting that he had not committed any offense that could be regarded as a crime in Massachusetts. Walker died under mysterious circumstances only months after publishing the *Appeal*, but the freedom of the press issues raised by Walker's *Appeal* and by Garrison's aggressive use of the press to attack slavery would not go away. Nor did the more global questions of slavery and freedom of expression disappear.

At issue was an understanding of constitutional rights. Officials in Boston may not have liked what Garrison and Walker had to say, but they believed that these men's speech was constitutionally protected. The First Amendment did not yet apply to the states, but the states had their own constitutional protections of free speech. Southern whites, on the other hand, did not believe that freedom of speech included the right to attack slavery. Thus, starting in the late 1820s and early 1830s, there was a profound change in the way northerners and southerners viewed the Constitution and constitutional rights. From the 1830s until the Civil War the South would remain a closed society in which no one, black or white, was free to discuss abolition or any serious opposition to slavery. In 1858 a white North Carolinian, Hinton Rowan Helper, attacked slavery, arguing in his book *The Impending Cri-*

sis that the institution was detrimental to the interests of non-slaveholding whites. Helper was forced to leave the state, fearful that he would be murdered for his views.

In the mid-1830s abolitionists began to petition Congress to limit slavery. The petitions focused on those areas where the federal government could affect slavery: in the territories and the District of Columbia and through enforcement of the ban on the African slave trade and a repeal of the Fugitive Slave Law. The House of Representatives adopted a standing rule—known as the gag rule—that prevented any of these petitions from being read on the floor of the House. This prohibition led to an eight-year battle (1836–1844) in the House, pitting supporters of the right to petition against southerners and their northern allies, who wanted to prevent any debates over slavery. The strongest support for petitioning came from John Quincy Adams, the former president who had been elected to Congress after he left the White House. In the end, the petition campaign highlighted the way in which slavery undermined constitutional rights for whites. After 1844 Congress ceased to bar antislavery petitions. By this time the gag rule had become part of the larger, polarizing debate over the constitutional power of Congress to limit the spread of slavery.

In the 1840s the constitutional debate turned to the territories. Opponents of slavery argued that the annexation of Texas violated the Constitution because it was accomplished by simple legislation rather than a treaty, which would have required the support of two-thirds of the Senate. That would have been impossible to achieve. The annexation led to a war with Mexico, and opponents of slavery tried to ban the institution in the territories acquired in that war. Southerners argued that they had a constitutional right to settle in the new territories—with their slaves.

Conflict over the status of slavery in the new territories led to a national crisis, which was resolved with the Compromise of 1850. Congress regulated slavery in three areas. The compromise banned the slave trade in the District of Columbia, which came under Congress's plenary powers to control the seat of the national government. It allowed slaves to be brought into all of the new territories acquired from Mexico except California, which was admitted as a free state—both of these actions falling under Congress's power to regulate the territories and admit new states. Finally, the compromise contained a new and much harsher fugitive slave law, which created federal commissioners in every county to aid in the return of runaway slaves. This was the first time in the nation's history that Congress had created law enforcement mechanisms at the local level.

All of these matters were at the periphery of slavery, but that was consistent with constitutional understanding at the time. With the exception of a few radical abolitionists, no one believed that Congress had the power to end slavery in the states. Thus, constitutional questions centered on those areas where Congress had power, such as the territories and the fugitive slave clause.

In the modern era, constitutional law is usually understood to be determined by the Supreme Court, but for most of the antebellum period the Supreme Court was rarely involved with slavery. In the 1830s the Court did not hear any significant cases involving slavery. During the next two decades, however, it heard a number of them. In two 1841 cases the Court avoided major constitutional questions. *Groves v. Slaughter* involved a state constitutional provision in Mississippi banning the importation of slaves for resale. This was not an antislavery provision but rather an attempt to limit the outflow of capital from the state. The Court avoided any important constitutional interpretation by holding that the Mississippi provision had never been implemented. In *United States v. the Amistad*, decided in the same year, the Court did not face a constitutional issue either. The issue before the Court concerned an interpretation of a treaty with Spain and the factual question of whether the blacks on the *Amistad* had been born in Africa and illegally brought to the New World or whether they had been born in Cuba and were thus legally held as slaves. The trial court found them to be Africans who had been illegally taken to Cuba, and the Supreme Court agreed. This case had an enormous impact on the growth of the antislavery movement but lacked any significant constitutional issues.

Vastly more important in terms of constitutional interpretation regarding slavery were *Prigg v. Pennsylvania* (1842) and *Dred Scott v. Sandford* (1857). In *Prigg* the Court upheld the constitutionality of the Fugitive Slave Law of 1793 while striking down northern laws that impeded the return of fugitive slaves. In this case the Court struck down state laws designed to prevent the kidnapping of free blacks. The Court ruled that these laws unconstitutionally interfered with the right of masters to recover their runaway slaves. Justice Joseph Story's opinion was a powerful endorsement of the proposition that the Constitution not only sanctioned slavery but also defined slaves as a singular sort of property with special constitutional protection.

Dred Scott v. Sandford was the Court's most important decision on slavery. In an analysis of the Constitution that defied logic and seemed to run counter to the wording of the document, Chief Justice Roger B. Taney held that Congress could not legislate for the territories in any significant way, and thus the portion of the Missouri Compromise that banned slavery in the western territories was unconstitutional. On somewhat stronger ground, Taney held that the Fifth Amendment prevented the emancipation of slaves in federal territories because this would be a taking of private property without just compensation. The Fifth Amendment prohibited the national government from depriving anyone of "life, liberty or property without due process of law." Abolitionists, of course, had argued that this provision meant slavery was unconstitutional because it deprived those in bondage of their "liberty." Taney, however, focused on the "property" provision in the amendment and held that any law freeing a slave in a federal jurisdiction was an unconstitutional taking.

Taney was able to reach this result because he also effectively wrote blacks out of the Constitution. The chief justice found that blacks, even if free, could never be considered citizens under the Constitution. He declared that blacks were not included in the "word 'citizens' in the Constitution, and can therefore claim none of the rights and privileges which the instrument provides and secures to citizens of the United States." Amplifying this assertion, he further claimed that at the time of the Constitution's framing and adoption, blacks were "considered as a subordinate and inferior class of beings who had been subjugated by the dominant race, and, whether emancipated or not, yet remained subject to their authority, and had no rights or privileges but such as those who held the power and Government might choose to grant them." According to Taney, blacks were "so far inferior, that they had no rights which the white man was bound to respect." Thus, he concluded, blacks could never be citizens of the United States, even if they were born in the country and considered to be citizens of the states in which they lived.

The case was an enormous victory for the South and slavery, but it came at a huge price. Many in the North found the decision unacceptable. The *New York Tribune* declared that the decision had as "much moral weight as would be the judgment of a majority of those congregated in any Washington bar-room," while the *Chicago Tribune* suggested that the decision was "part of a grand conspiracy against Freedom." In a speech in New York City, Frederick Douglass called it a "devilish decision—this judicial incarnation of wolfishness." However, Douglass was somewhat optimistic after the decision, believing that it would stimulate northerners to work harder to fight slavery. He predicted that "this very attempt to blot out forever the hopes of an enslaved people may be one necessary link in the chain of events preparatory to the downfall and complete overthrow of the whole slave system."

Douglass was more prescient than he could have imagined. The Court's opinion energized the new Republican Party, which made *Dred Scott* the focus of its campaigns in 1858 and 1860. The most articulate critic of *Dred Scott* was Abraham Lincoln, a virtually unknown Illinois lawyer who had previously served just a single term in Congress.

In 1858 Lincoln mounted a vigorous campaign against Stephen A. Douglas for the U.S. Senate seat from Illinois. In debating Douglas, Lincoln suggested a great conspiracy among Douglas, Taney, and Presidents Franklin Pierce and James Buchanan to destroy American liberties by nationalizing slavery. Lincoln lost the Senate race, but his opposition to *Dred Scott* made him a national figure. Two years later he was elected president on a platform that promised to prohibit slavery in the territories.

A year before the 1860 election, the abolitionist John Brown invaded Virginia with a handful of followers, hoping to start a great slave rebellion. Brown's band was trapped at Harpers Ferry, Virginia (now West Virginia), and most were killed or captured by a contingent of United States Marines led by Colonel Robert E. Lee of the United States Army. In December 1859 Virginia authorities hanged Brown. The John Brown raid underscored once again the constitutional protections for slavery, as the national government suppressed this attack on the South's peculiar institution.

Civil War Era. Lincoln's election stunned the South. For the first time in American history there was a president who promised to prevent the spread of slavery and otherwise challenged the institution's legitimacy. By the time Lincoln took office, seven states had passed ordinances of secession and claimed to no longer be part of the United States. Lincoln's first inaugural address, given on 4 March 1861, was a mixture of political theory, appeals to patriotism, and a lesson in constitutional law. Lincoln denied that the southern states had the right to secede under the Constitution. He also reminded the South that as president, he could not interfere with slavery there. He declared at the very beginning of his speech, "I have no purpose, directly or indirectly, to interfere with the institution of slavery where it exists. I believe I have no lawful right to do so, and I have no inclination to do so." He also quoted from the Republican Party platform, which reaffirmed "the right of each State to order and control its domestic institutions according to its own judgment exclusively."

Despite Lincoln's pleas, the secessionists maintained their position, and in April 1861 the Civil War began. From the onset Lincoln stated that his goal was to preserve the Union. Slavery, however, was the root cause of the war, and from the beginning the constitutional status of bondage was a critical issue. When the war began, Lincoln made clear again that he had no intention of disturbing slavery where it existed. He quickly countermanded General John C. Frémont's order emancipating all of the slaves in Missouri, a border slave state that had remained in the Union. He similarly rejected pleas from abolitionists to move against slavery in the Confederate states. His first strategy in holding the Union together was to ensure that none of the four loyal slave states—Delaware, Maryland, Kentucky, and Missouri—joined the Confederacy. He feared that if he made the war a crusade against slavery, these states would also leave the Union. When a group of ministers told Lincoln that if he freed the slaves, he would have God on his side, Lincoln allegedly responded that he would like to have God on his side but that he "needed Kentucky."

Meanwhile, slaves acting on their own began to leave their masters and seek the protection of the U.S. Army. Initially, some soldiers returned slaves to their owners, in part because they believed the fugitive slave clause of the Constitution required them to do so. But in May 1861 General Benjamin Butler refused to return fugitive slaves sought by Virginia masters. Butler declared that the slaves were "contrabands of war" and thus could not be returned to masters living in areas claimed by the Confederacy. Lincoln acquiesced in the theory, and slavery began to crumble. Thus, by mid-1861 the Constitution's fugitive slave clause had become a dead letter, at least for slaves escaping from the Confederate states. This development illustrated how the Constitution had protected slavery. While they were in the Union and living under the Constitution, the states of the Slave South could count on federal support for the return of fugitive slaves. But when they left the Union, these states lost not only this protection but also the immense political power they had held in Congress, the courts, and the executive branch to protect slavery.

General Butler's brilliant characterization of slaves as "contrabands" was the beginning of a constitutional revolution. In August 1861 and March 1862 Congress passed the First and Second Confiscation Acts, allowing the slaves of some rebel masters to be seized and freed. In April 1862 Congress passed a law providing financial incentives for loyal masters who would free their slaves. At the same time Congress abolished slavery in the District of Columbia, providing compensation of only three hundred dollars per slave to masters. In September 1862 Lincoln announced the preliminary Emancipation Proclamation, declaring that in one hundred days—on 1 January 1863—he would use his power as commander in chief of the army to free slaves owned by persons in rebellion. On that date he did issue the Emancipation Proclamation, declaring that slaves in areas controlled by the Confederacy were free. Before the war this step would have been an unconstitutional taking of private property without compensation. Now it was considered, at least by Lincoln, to be a constitutionally permissible act necessary to win the war.

The events of 1861–1863 were constitutionally dramatic. Southern secession accomplished what three decades of abolitionist agitation could not accomplish: by leaving the Union, the South created circumstances that allowed for an interpretation of the Constitution that would permit the national government to free slaves not only in federal jurisdictions but also throughout much of the country. In June 1864 Congress repealed the Fugitive Slave Laws of 1793 and 1850. By the end of the war the vast majority of slaves had been freed. The Thirteenth Amendment, proposed in late 1864 and ratified in December 1865, freed the remaining slaves in the United States.

Meanwhile, starting in 1862, the United States began to enlist black soldiers. Frederick Douglass recruited black soldiers throughout the North for the Fifty-fourth Massachusetts Infantry Regiment, in which two of his sons served. By the end of the war more than 200,000 blacks had served in the army and navy, providing vital manpower for the war effort. This military participation gave African Americans an important new claim to constitutional rights. African Americans had fought and died to preserve the Constitution. They now had a right to demand not only that they be protected by it but also that they have full citizenship rights under it.

Reconstructing the Constitution. The Civil War destroyed slavery, but the place of African Americans in the new regime was uncertain. In the months following their defeat, many of the former Confederate states passed repressive laws designed to reduce blacks, as much as possible, to second-class citizenship. The new laws limited the right of blacks to travel, live in towns, practice some professions, testify in court, or engage in various economic activities. Alabama's law "Concerning Vagrants and Vagrancy" allowed for the incarceration in the public workhouse of any "laborer or servant who loiters away his time, or refuses to comply with any contract for a term of service without just cause." Mississippi's Civil Rights Act of 1865 provided that if any laborer quit a job before the end of the contract period, he would lose all wages earned up to that time. Thus, if a black laborer signed a contract to work for a planter for a year and left after eleven months, he would get no wages. This legislation allowed employers to mistreat and overwork laborers, knowing that they dare not quit. Indeed, a shrewd employer could purposely make life miserable for workers at the end of a contract term in the hope that they would quit and forfeit all wages.

Mississippi's law further declared that any blacks "with no lawful employment or business" would be considered vagrants and could be fined up to fifty dollars. Any black who could not pay the fine would be forcibly hired out to whoever would pay it, thus creating another form of unfree labor. The same act created a one-dollar poll tax for all free blacks. Any blacks not paying the tax could be declared vagrants and thus assigned to work for white planters—often the persons who had owned them when they were slaves. These laws also prohibited blacks from renting land or houses in towns or cities, thus, in effect, forcing them into the countryside, where they would be doomed to agricultural labor. Throughout the South blacks faced violent and murderous repression by individuals and bands of white terrorists. General Carl Schurz, after visiting the region in 1865, concluded that although many, perhaps most, southern whites conceded that blacks were no longer the slaves of individual masters, they also intended to make them "the slaves of society."

In December 1865 Congress authorized the Joint Committee on Reconstruction to investigate conditions in the South. The committee consisted of six senators and nine congressmen and included such leading Republicans as Thaddeus Stevens, John Bingham, and Justin Morrill. The committee's report, based on interviews with hundreds of people, was massive, amounting to about eight hundred pages. In it the committee reminded the nation that the former slaves had "remained true and loyal" throughout the Civil War and "in large numbers, fought on the side of the Union" and that the nation had a duty to protect these people. The committee found that southern leaders still "defend[ed] the legal right of secession, and [upheld] the doctrine that the first allegiance of the people is due to the States."

From everywhere in the South the committee heard stories of violence and intimidation. Lieutenant Colonel R. W. Barnard, who was stationed in Tennessee, was asked if it was safe to remove troops from that state. He replied:

> I hardly know how to express myself on the subject. I have not been in a favor of removing the military. I can tell you what an old citizen, a Union man, said to me. Said he, "I tell you what, if you take away the military from Tennessee, the buzzards can't eat up the niggers as fast as we'll kill 'em."

Major General John W. Turner reported that in Virginia "all of the [white] people" were "extremely reluctant to grant to the negro his civil rights—those privileges that pertain to freedom, the protection of life, liberty, and property before the laws, the right to testify in courts, etc." Turner added that whites were "reluctant even to consider and treat the negro as a free man, to let him have his half of the sidewalk or the street crossing." They would only "concede" such rights to blacks "if it is ever done, because they are forced to do it." He noted that many whites were "disposed to ban the negro, to kick him and cuff him, and threaten him."

A Virginia farmer admitted that whites in the state "maltreat [blacks] every day" and that blacks had "not a par-ticle" of a chance "to obtain justice in the civil courts of Virginia." He declared that a black or "a Union man" had as much likelihood of obtaining justice in Virginia as "a rabbit would in a den of lions." United States District Judge John C. Underwood described the cold-blooded murder of a white Unionist by a returning Confederate officer. The state did not prosecute anyone for the crime. Underwood believed that if the army abandoned the state and left the fate of the freedmen to the native whites, the situation would be a disaster. He quoted a "most intelligent" Virginian who declared that "sooner than see the colored people raised to a legal and political equality, the southern people would prefer their total annihilation." Witnesses from the Carolinas and Georgia told about beatings, gruesome torture, and murders of former slaves and about black children who were kidnapped so that they might be sent to Cuba, where slavery was still legal.

In the wake of this testimony the committee wrote the Civil Rights Act of 1866. During debates over this bill Senator Charles Sumner of Massachusetts received a box containing the finger of a black man. An accompanying note read, "You old son of a bitch, I send you a piece of one of your friends, and if that bill of yours passes I will have a piece of you." Congress was not intimidated, passing the law and then enacting it over President Andrew Johnson's veto. The putative authority for the new law was the Thirteenth Amendment, which not only prohibited slavery in the nation but also empowered Congress to enforce the amendment "with appropriate legislation." Some members of Congress, however, were worried that the Civil Rights Act could not be justified under an amendment to end slavery. Thus, in 1866 the committee also drafted the Fourteenth Amendment.

This amendment had a number of purposes. Much of the debate in Congress was over the status of former Confederates. The amendment did not directly enfranchise blacks but instead had a provision to reduce southern representation in Congress if black men were not allowed to vote under the same rules as white men. Section 1 of the amendment explicitly overruled the *Dred Scott* decision, declaring that all persons born in the United States, including former slaves, were "citizens of the United States and of the State wherein they reside." The amendment also prohibited the states from making or enforcing "any law which shall abridge the privileges or immunities of citizens of the United States" and further declared that no state could "deprive any person of life, liberty, or property without due process of law; nor deny to any person within its jurisdiction the equal protection of the laws." The states ratified this amendment in 1868. In 1870 they ratified the Fifteenth Amendment, which provided that "the right of citizens of the United States to vote shall not be denied or abridged by the United States or any State on account of race, color, or previous condition of servitude."

Frederick Douglass was an active supporter of both amendments. He found himself at odds, however, with many former allies—female abolitionists who opposed the amendments because they did not also enfranchise women. Douglass argued that blacks needed special political and constitutional protection at this time and that it was "the Negro's hour." He had been a lifelong supporter of women's suffrage, but he understood that blacks were in desperate need of political power in a way that women were not. White terrorists like the Ku Klux Klan were targeting blacks throughout the South because of their race. Whatever disabilities women faced, they paled in comparison with the threat of lethal violence being directed at blacks.

The new amendments made blacks citizens of the nation and black men voters. Following these amendments Congress passed important legislation to protect these new black voters and suppress the Ku Klux Klan. During Reconstruction more than fifteen hundred blacks held public office throughout the South, serving in state legislatures and state constitutional conventions and as sheriffs, city councilmen, and U.S. congressmen. Two served in the U.S. Senate, one as a governor, one on a state supreme court, and more than a dozen as heads of various state agencies or as statewide officers, such as secretary of state or state treasurer. Frederick Douglass remained a private citizen at this time, editing the *New National Era* in Washington, D.C. However, he remained active in politics and a leader in the Republican Party.

From 1861 to 1870 vast constitutional changes in the nation had come about through war, legislation, and the amendment process. In just nine years there had been a remarkable revolution in constitutional order. Ideas of state sovereignty were dead, never to rise again in a way that would threaten the nation. Slavery was abolished, and African Americans were, at least in theory, full citizens. Congress implemented this constitutional revolution with the Civil Rights Act of 1866, the Freedmen's Bureau Act, and the three Force Acts of 1870 and 1871 (the third is commonly called the Ku Klux Klan Act), which successfully suppressed a great deal of terrorism that had been directed at blacks and their white allies in the South. The Civil Rights Act of 1875 added one more layer of legal protection for the former slaves by guaranteeing them access to public accommodations. As in no other period of the nation's history, constitutional change was not driven by the Supreme Court, which in the postwar decade had little to say about Emancipation or black freedom.

Failure of Constitutional Change, 1877–1895. The presidential election of 1876 ended in chaos, with both the Democrat Samuel Tilden and the Republican Rutherford B. Hayes claiming victory. At issue were disputed votes in South Carolina, Florida, and Mississippi. In all three states intimidation, vote fraud, and violence had prevented many blacks from voting or led to their votes' not being counted. By this time most U.S. troops had been removed from the South and federal supervision of elections was virtually nonexistent. Many former Confederates and their sons had steadily gained political power and reasserted their economic power as landowners in an overwhelmingly agrarian society. They combined to stop many black voters. With the election in the balance, Congress appointed a complicated "electoral commission," which by one vote awarded the disputed electoral votes to Hayes.

The "Compromise of 1877" put Hayes in the White House but led to removal of the last federal troops from the South. Reconstruction was now officially over. Its closure prompted acceleration in the gradual diminution of constitutional rights for blacks. By the time of Frederick Douglass's death in 1895, African Americans would still be citizens of the nation, but in many respects they would be second-class citizens. These changes did not take place all at once, and, indeed, blacks continued to hold political office and participate in politics after the formal end of Reconstruction. Frederick Douglass, for example, held office for the first time under Hayes, serving as the U.S. marshal for the District of Columbia (1877–1881). Under Presidents James Garfield, Chester A. Arthur, and Benjamin Harrison, he would continue to hold federal office as the recorder of deeds for the District of Columbia (1881–1886) and as chargé d'affaires for Santo Domingo and minister to Haiti (1889–1891). Blacks held other offices as well in this period and continued to participate in politics, vote, and serve on juries, but gradually their claim on constitutional equality declined. While political change had much to do with these transformations, the main engine driving the decline of black rights was the United States Supreme Court.

In the *Slaughterhouse Cases* (1873) the Supreme Court offered a cramped interpretation of the privileges and immunities clause of the Fourteenth Amendment. Many supporters of this amendment believed that it would nationalize the Bill of Rights and give the federal courts the power to protect the civil liberties of former slaves. But the Court read the amendment narrowly and found that there were few national privileges and immunities to be protected. In *United States v. Reese* (1876) the Court struck down the Force Act of 1870, which was designed to protect black voters. In *United States v. Cruikshank*

(1876) the Court reversed the convictions of white terrorists who had murdered about one hundred blacks in 1873 in Grant Parish, Louisiana, in what is known as the Colfax Massacre. In *Hall v. DeCuir* (1878) the Court struck down a Louisiana law that required integration on public transportation in the state. The Court said that this requirement interfered with interstate commerce because boats or trains coming from other states would have to integrate their seating patterns once they arrived in Louisiana.

The Court would not allow laws that blatantly discriminated against blacks. Thus, in *Strauder v. West Virginia* (1880) the justices struck down a West Virginia law that prohibited blacks from serving on juries. But in other cases, such as *Virginia v. Rives* (1880), the Court found that black defendants had no special right to have men of their race on their juries. In *Neal v. Delaware* (1881), however, the Court reversed the conviction of a black on the ground that no African Americans had *ever* served on a jury in the state. Thus, even though there was no law banning blacks from juries, the Court accepted the evidence that race discrimination was the rule in that state. In the *Civil Rights Cases* (1883) the Court held that most of the Civil Rights Act of 1875 was unconstitutional. The law prohibited discrimination in public accommodations, but the Court read the Fourteenth Amendment to limit only state action. Congress had no power, the Court declared, to force privately owned theaters or restaurants to serve blacks.

African Americans were appalled by these decisions. After the decision in the *Civil Rights Cases*, the prominent black journalist T. Thomas Fortune wrote in the *New York Globe* that "the colored people of the United States feel to-day as if they had been baptized in ice-water." In Philadelphia there was a huge protest rally after the decision was announced. John Mercer Langston, one of the nation's leading black lawyers, said that the Court seemed "desirous of remanding us back to that old passed condition." He found the decision "incomprehensible." Frederick Douglass said that the decision "grievously wounded" African Americans. He compared it to the Fugitive Slave Law of 1850 and the *Dred Scott* decision. He asserted in a speech in October 1883 that "in humiliating the colored people of this country, this decision has humbled the Nation. It gives to a South Carolina or a Mississippi, Railroad Conductor, more power than it gives to the National Government." Douglass longed "for a Supreme Court which shall be as true, as vigilant, as active, and exacting in maintaining laws enacted for the protection of human rights, as in other days was the Court for the destruction of human rights!"

In 1887 blacks in Baltimore formed the Brotherhood of Liberty, which might be considered the nation's first civil rights organization. In 1889 the Brotherhood published *Justice and Jurisprudence: An Inquiry Concerning the Constitutional Limitations of the Thirteenth, Fourteenth, and Fifteenth Amendments*. At over six hundred pages, this ambitious tome was designed to convince lawyers and jurists of the legitimacy of federal protections for civil rights. The arguments were sound, but they fell on deaf ears in the Supreme Court. Republicans in Congress still tried to protect civil rights. In 1891 Congressman Henry Cabot Lodge of Massachusetts courageously tried to pass a bill known as the "Lodge Federal Elections Bill" or the "Lodge Force Bill." It passed the House but died in the Senate when a few western Republicans defected from their party's support for the bill. The handful of western Republicans opposing the bill were from silver-producing states where virtually no blacks lived, and they voted against black voting rights in return for the support of southern Democrats for free coinage of silver. As the *Nation* noted, the Lodge bill was "buried by a bargain between Democrats and free silverites." A few years later the populist Democrat William Jennings Bryan would rail that "you shall not crucify mankind upon a Cross of Gold." In this instance a few western Republicans and a passel of southern Democrats crucified black rights on a cross of silver.

Throughout the North, states passed their own civil rights acts following the Supreme Court's decision in the *Civil Rights Cases*, striking down the federal civil rights act of 1875. Most of them banned discrimination in public accommodations and on public transportation. A number repealed laws banning interracial marriage, and in 1896, the year after Douglass's death, Ohio passed the nation's first antilynching law. The constitutional rights of blacks were more or less secure in the North, although enforcement did not always comport with the lofty ideals of the statutes. But in 1890 most American blacks—more than 90 percent—lived in the South, where constitutional rights were left to the tender mercies of the former Confederates and their sons, who were intent on reversing, as much as possible, the racial progress achieved between 1861 and 1875.

[*See also* Abolitionism; Adams, John, on African Americans; Antislavery Movement; Antislavery Press; Black Codes and Slave Codes; Black Seafarers; Brown, John; Buchanan, James; Butler, Benjamin Franklin; Caribbean; Civil Rights; Civil Rights Act of 1866; Civil Rights Act of 1875; Civil War; Civil War, Participation and Recruitment of Black Troops in; Compromise of 1850; Constitutional Convention, African Americans and; Democratic Party; Discrimination; Douglas, Stephen A.; *Dred Scott* Case; Emancipation; Fifteenth Amendment; Fourteenth Amendment; Free African Americans to 1828; Free

African Americans before the Civil War (North); Free African Americans before the Civil War (South); Fugitive Slave Law of 1793; Fugitive Slave Law of 1850; Fugitive Slaves; Garrisonian Abolitionists; Harpers Ferry Raid; Hayes, Rutherford B.; Integration; Johnson, Andrew; Langston, John Mercer; Laws and Legislation; Lincoln, Abraham; Lynching and Mob Violence; Military; Missouri Compromise; Pierce, Franklin; Reconstruction; Republican Party; Riots and Rebellions; Slave Insurrections and Rebellions; Slavery; Slavery and the U.S. Constitution; Slave Trade; Stevens, Thaddeus; Sumner, Charles; Supreme Court; Thirteenth Amendment; Turner, Nat; Violence against African Americans; Virginia; *and* Voting Rights.]

BIBLIOGRAPHY

Fehrenbacher, Don E. *The Dred Scott Case: Its Significance in American Law and Politics*. New York: Oxford University Press, 1978.

Fehrenbacher, Don E. *The Slaveholding Republic: An Account of the United States Government's Relations to Slavery*. New York: Oxford University Press, 2001.

Finkelman, Paul. *Dred Scott v. Sandford: A Brief History with Documents*. Boston: Bedford Books, 1997.

Finkelman, Paul. *Slavery and the Founders: Race and Liberty in the Age of Jefferson*. 2nd ed. Armonk, NY: M. E. Sharpe, 2001.

Foner, Eric. *Freedom's Lawmakers: A Directory of Black Officeholders during Reconstruction*. Baton Rouge: Louisiana State University Press, 1996.

Hyman, Harold M., and William M. Wiecek. *Equal Justice under Law: Constitutional Development, 1835–1875*. New York: Harper and Row, 1982.

Morris, Thomas D. *Free Men All: The Personal Liberty Laws of the North, 1780–1861*. Baltimore, MD: Johns Hopkins University Press, 1974.

Nieman, Donald. *Promises to Keep: African Americans and the Constitutional Order, 1776 to the Present*. New York: Oxford University Press, 1991.

Robinson, Donald L. *Slavery in the Structure of American Politics, 1765–1820*. New York: Harcourt Brace Jovanovich, 1971.

Wang, Xi. *The Trial of Democracy: Black Suffrage and Northern Republicans, 1860–1910*. Athens: University of Georgia Press, 1997.

—PAUL FINKELMAN

CONSTITUTIONAL CONVENTION, AFRICAN AMERICANS AND.

As the legend of the founding fathers grew over the course of the nineteenth century, the United States Constitution of 1787 was invented to be the perfect document, the guiding force not only for the new and unique American Republic but also for others that would attempt to emulate the American example. The African American presence was given due consideration at the Constitutional Convention of 1787, in which the nation's founding document was shaped and reshaped. As great as the work of the founding fathers was, by recognizing slavery and co-opting it into the American Republic's institutional fabric, the founders provided the blueprint for national disaster, for black and white Americans alike.

Validation of Slavery. The supreme law of the land validated slavery in two explicit ways. First, in apportioning representation in the House of Representatives and the Electoral College, it counted each African American slave as three-fifths of a white man; this increased southern slave-owning political power by augmenting southern membership in the aforementioned bodies. Second, the Constitution allowed for the extension of the slave trade to at least 1808—a substantial concession, as the number of slaves would grow from some 700,000 in 1790 to nearly 1,200,000 in 1808. Numbers aside, if slavery had ended in 1787, as only a few founding fathers insisted it should, by 1808 the newly sovereign American Republic would have at least begun life with a clean slate, making peaceful racial integration a possibility, however remote. Instead, by 1808 the augmented number of black bond servants and the longterm practice of slavery already in place rendered the permanent institutionalization of slavery complete—and perhaps already irreversible, except through civil war. The perpetuation of slavery was the single most important result of the finalized Constitution for African Americans, who then made up nearly 20 percent of the population but were denied the promise to whites spelled out in the preamble: "to secure the Blessings of Liberty to ourselves and our Posterity." It would be more than three-quarters of a century before the Thirteenth Amendment would finally end the "peculiar institution." The cost in terms of the Civil War alone would be more than 600,000 dead—black and white, men, women, and children.

Why the founding fathers did not resolutely end slavery outright in 1787 is not a complicated question. Many of the delegates, from both the South and the North, owned slaves; slaves were property. Ownership of property—the vested, protected right to property—was not merely a basic value of the founding fathers; it was supreme among all other values in the new nation. Entrepreneurial capitalism was rooted in the pursuit of private gain, such as of property, and capitalist principles were woven deeply into the fabric of the U.S. Constitution. Moreover, the Republic was founded in a post-Enlightenment paternal era: there were the "founding fathers," George Washington was "the father of our country," and James Madison was "the father of the Constitution." The political discourse of the era was rife with such patriarchal language. Male slave owners considered themselves benevolent fathers to their "childlike" slaves. That parallel linguistic universe fed a moral ambiguity that cut deeply into the post-Enlightenment understanding of the meaning and promise of human equality and individual rights—the legacy of the eighteenth century's Age of Reason.

No founding father was more susceptible to this obfuscation than James Madison, the universally acknowledged architect of the Constitution. A Virginian and a slaveholder, he was the author of the Virginia Plan, which for the most part metamorphosed into the finished Constitution in the 1787 debates. Indeed, he displayed an uncharacteristic but wholly understandable moral ambiguity, given his status as a slave owner himself, in dealing with any threats to agreement imposed by the slave issue at the convention. While he was uncomfortable with racially driven human bondage, Madison nevertheless saw slavery—at least economically and politically—as needful of inevitably being protected through the Constitutional Convention. Slavery as an issue, he said, was "distracting" the work of the convention, "agitating and retarding the labors" of the delegates, and had to be dealt with—not as a moral question but as a political problem.

He exemplified this widespread moral disconnect in advocating the need for a free republic based on natural rights, which the Constitution indeed otherwise embodied—a promise made even more explicit in 1776's Declaration of Independence, which explicitly proclaimed that "all men are created equal." Given that Thomas Jefferson was not at the 1787 Constitutional Convention in Philadelphia, as he was serving as America's ambassador to France, no delegate was more guilty of this disconnect than Madison. In fact, he personally facilitated the three-fifths compromise; according to his account, "the northern or antislavery portion of the Country agreed to incorporate" that compromise, "making the Constitution the more acceptable to the slaveholders"—himself included.

As to the slave trade, Madison himself knew that its prohibition would be a nonstarter in Philadelphia, in that South Carolina and Georgia, at least, were "against any restraint" on the importation of slaves and "inflexible" on any compromise that did not explicitly guarantee its continuation. If he had qualms about any of this in the 1780s, they do not appear anywhere in his voluminous public and private writings. Only political solutions with regard to slavery's future were needed, the white fathers concluded, and political solutions were what the 1787 convention delivered.

Allowances and Capitalism. Why did northern delegates who opposed slavery, or at least found it distasteful, agree to its explicit recognition as a permanent component of American life? First, they believed it could not endure much longer in any event—that it would collapse of its own economic and social weight. These fathers selectively failed to consider that circumstances inevitably change. The most brilliant hallmark of the Constitution was its

elasticity; it was created as a living framework for the Republic, adaptable to future transitions within a viable and free society. The myopia over slavery stands as a stark exception to the otherwise flawless historical consideration of the founding fathers. Most northern delegates, like many of the white Americans they represented, did not believe African Americans could ever achieve equality as a free people; the founding fathers were mostly of the opinion that African Americans constituted an inferior race—or at least one that needed to be kept at a distance, whether slavery existed or not. More important, all the delegates, northern and southern alike, were united in their commitment to the sanctity and primacy of private property; the abolition of propertied wealth of any kind, including the ownership of other human beings, was not on the table in 1787.

Even Gouverneur Morris of New York, probably the most outspoken opponent of human bondage at the Constitutional Convention, bought into the argument that an essential aspect to forming the new Republic was defending and facilitating capitalism—which encompassed, in the eyes of the delegates, the sanctity of private property. At the convention the abolitionist crusader Morris intoned that while "life and liberty were generally said to be of more value than property . . . , an accurate view of the matter would . . . prove that property was the main object of Society." If such an enemy of slavery could defend this point of view—one that sustained the sanctity of the belief that slaves were property—what chance did abolition have in Philadelphia?

Of course, almost all southern proponents of slavery at the convention concurred with regard to the primacy of the sanctity of private property. One of those who outspokenly endorsed the extension of the slave trade was Charles Cotesworth Pinckney of South Carolina. He believed that "property in slaves should not be exposed to danger under a Government instituted for the protection of property." Indeed, embracing abolition in the Constitution was never a real possibility; slaves were property, and property was sacrosanct. There remained only the provision of the formula with which to recognize human bondage. In fact, the antislavery proponent Morris was the one who introduced the three-fifths compromise, not only in terms of political representation but in matters of federal taxation as well.

As bad as this state of affairs was, the real nail in the coffin of abolitionist thought in Philadelphia was the extension of the slave trade. Article 1, section 9, stated explicitly that the importation of slaves could not be prohibited by Congress until twenty years after the Constitution's ratification, which turned out to be the year 1808. That time lag provided the window of growth that would add another half million bondpeople to the population—

virtually all of them consigned to the southern states, as gradual emancipation legislation on behalf of states marked the beginning of the end of slavery in the North. Congress finally acted in March 1807, banning the importation of slaves effective 1 January 1808. The "ban," however, was enforced not by the seizure and manumission of illegally arriving slaves but by fines of eight hundred dollars for the purchasers of imported, not U.S.-born, slaves—which fines were almost never imposed.

Thus, the 1808 ban hardly ended the slave trade; indeed, lax enforcement and weak legal remedies guaranteed that slave smuggling would continue, driving up the price per capita and rendering the institution seemingly ever more profitable, especially for slave traders. While historians still debate slavery's ultimate profitability, the historical reality was that the slave establishment that dominated the South in the antebellum nineteenth century, implicitly drawing upon the sustained reality of constitutional recognition, chose to believe that the institution was profitable. Perhaps this was so for psychological reasons, since slavery was in many ways less about money than about the tension-ridden nature of southern society and its psychic and political dependence on the "peculiar institution."

The answer to the question of how the Constitution could have failed African Americans so badly is an ugly one. First and foremost, the large majority of delegates, from the North and the South, were conflicted about slavery in 1787. Slave-owning delegates like Madison and Washington, the president of the convention, chose not to manumit in 1787, or anytime soon thereafter. Even Jefferson was ambivalent; the author of the Declaration of Independence did not free his slaves until his death in 1826. Like Washington, while claiming to abhor slavery in the abstract, he nonetheless accepted as true the notion that African Americans were innately inferior. His fellow Virginian George Mason, who was an influential delegate, did not manumit his own slaves even as he excoriated the institution at the 1787 convention—and he, of course, supported the three-fifths and slave-trade compromises, as did most other nominally antislavery delegates.

The perpetuation of the slave trade had extensive ramifications in the early nineteenth century. Jefferson, as president from 1801 to 1809, clung to the quixotic notion of relocating all slaves to a black republic in the Pacific Northwest rather than confronting the evil in his presidency. As late as 1833 an aged James Madison wrote that union with the slaveholding states was assured in the North, since "as merchants, as ship owners, and as manufacturers" the North's emerging power elite was tied to slavery by bonds of cotton; indeed, even he paid homage to "King Cotton." By this late date, there seemed to be lit-

tle moral ambiguity in the heart of the supreme progenitor of the "free" American Republic.

There can be little wonder, then, that the founding fathers were unable to summon up substantial indignation against the palpably evil institution of slavery in 1787. Even in the face of avowed Enlightenment principles and belief in the already-hallowed Declaration of Independence and its thunderous promises of human freedom and individual rights, slavery was extended into the otherwise bright American future. The innate prejudices of even the most enlightened fathers of the country, as sustained by the imperatives of economic free enterprise and the consequent sanctity of all private property, mattered a great deal. While these men were perhaps comforted by the flawed belief that slavery would die of its own accord, that belief deeply darkened the American future; in this sense, the Constitution of 1787 was profoundly less than perfect.

[*See also* Abolitionism, Early; Constitution, U.S.; Declaration of Independence; Georgia; Jefferson, Thomas, on African Americans and Slavery; Laws and Legislation; Madison, James, and African Americans; Race, Theories of; Slave Trade: Prohibition of; Slave Trade: Revolution to 1808; South Carolina, Colony and State to 1828; Virginia; *and* Washington, George, and African Americans.]

BIBLIOGRAPHY

Bailyn, Bernard. *To Begin the World Anew: The Genius and Ambiguities of the American Founders*. New York: Knopf, 2003.

Farrand, Max, ed. *The Records of the Federal Convention of 1787*. New Haven, CT: Yale University Press, 1911.

Lynd, Staughton. "On Turner, Beard and Slavery." *Journal of Negro History* 48 (1963): 237.

Mitchell, Broadus, and Louise P. Mitchell. *A Biography of the Constitution of the United States: Its Origin, Formation, Adoption, Interpretation*. New York: Oxford University Press, 1975.

Rakove, Jack N. *Original Meanings: Politics and Ideas in the Making of the Constitution*. New York: Knopf, 1996.

—CARL E. PRINCE

CORNISH, SAMUEL (b. c. 1795; d. 6 November 1858), African American minister, journalist, and civil rights activist. Samuel Eli Cornish was born free in Sussex County, Delaware. At the age of twenty Cornish traveled to Philadelphia, where he trained for the ministry under John Gloucester, the founder of the First African Presbyterian Church, and was licensed on probationary status in 1819. After briefly working as a missionary among the enslaved population of Maryland's Eastern Shore, in 1821 Cornish settled in New York City, where he served as a missionary among black residents. Formally ordained in 1822, Cornish established the first African American Presbyterian congregation in New York, at the New Demeter Street Presbyterian Church. Two years later he married Jane Livingston, with whom he would have four children.

In 1827 Cornish became the founding editor of *Freedom's Journal*, the first newspaper in the United States edited by African Americans. Along with his coeditor, John Brown Russwurm, Cornish used *Freedom's Journal* to support the uplift of black Americans. In his own words, the paper aimed to effect the "moral, religious, civil and literary improvement of our injured race." Through his editorial pen Cornish denounced African colonization and promoted a conservative agenda urging African Americans to work hard for their own advancement. Cornish resigned from his editorial post within six months to return full time to his ministry; the newspaper ceased publication in March 1829 when Russwurm shocked Cornish and subscribers by accepting a position as administrator of schools in Liberia. Cornish soon began a second newspaper, the *Rights of All*, published intermittently in New York for about six months in 1829. In 1837 he returned to the world of journalism to establish another weekly, the *Colored American*, with support from the black activist Philip Alexander Bell, financing from the wealthy white abolitionist Arthur Tappan, and the efforts of his coeditor, Charles B. Ray. More successful than *Freedom's Journal*, the *Colored American* published into the early 1840s, although Cornish left his editorship in 1839.

Through his editorial posts and ministry Cornish pushed a conservative agenda of black self-help through education and advocated African American involvement in agriculture. As early as 1828 he supported a venture encouraging African American settlement on two thousand acres of farmland in the Delaware River valley offered at a reduced price through subsidy. Cornish also championed educational opportunities for his race, acting as an agent for the New York African Free Schools in the late 1820s, but chose to leave New York in the 1830s when his own children were denied admission to advanced schools in the city. Removing his family to rural New Jersey in 1838 proved little better, however; his children faced similar discrimination there. The family moved again, to Newark, in 1840.

In addition to his ministerial and editorial responsibilities, Cornish found time for a host of reform activities. He served on the executive committees of the American Anti-Slavery Society and the New York Vigilance Committee (formed to assist fugitive slaves), was active in the American Bible Society, and was a founding member and officer of the American Missionary Association, dedicated to training and educating slaves. Cornish was among the founders of the New York Phoenix Society, a benevolent organization aimed at black moral uplift; it sponsored day and evening schools as well as libraries and reading rooms and encouraged vocational training. Involvement in the black national convention movement in the 1830s brought Cornish into association with the American Moral Reform Society, of which he served for two years as a vice president. In 1840 he and his fellow Presbyterian minister Theodore S. Wright co-wrote an anticolonization pamphlet entitled *The Colonization Scheme Considered, in Its Rejection by the Coloured People*. Late in his life he acted as a board member for the American and Foreign Anti-Slavery Society.

Cornish may have met Frederick Douglass at the very outset of the great abolitionist speaker's career. When Douglass reached New York City in September 1838, just after his escape from slavery, the New York Vigilance Committee offered him refuge in the home of the committee's secretary, David Ruggles. Certainly Cornish provided Douglass with a fine example of African American achievement in journalism and in the cause of civil rights. By the time Douglass ascended to the abolitionist platform as an important orator and activist, however, Cornish's influence was waning. His conservative acceptance of the existing American political system and his refusal to embrace the anticlerical approach of William Lloyd Garrison put him at odds with both black militants and radical white abolitionists. He opposed the formation of an abolitionist political party in 1839, then in a characteristic change of heart argued against the growing black convention movement when it was revived in the late 1840s, now claiming he abhorred racially separate activities. In the 1850s his strong anticolonization views led him to oppose the Pan-African movement supported at the time by the black nationalist Martin Robison Delany and others.

In an era in which reformers and reform organizations grew increasingly more activist and militant, Samuel Cornish remained an advocate of conservative methods to achieve black uplift, equal education, and the abolition of slavery. During his later years in New Jersey he ministered at the Negro Presbyterian Church in Newark. In 1845 he organized another New York congregation, the Emmanuel Church, remaining there until 1847. In 1855 he moved to Brooklyn, where three years later, having outlived his wife and three of his four children, he died.

[*See also* American and Foreign Anti-Slavery Society; American Anti-Slavery Society; American Missionary Association; Bell, Philip Alexander; Black Church; Black Press; Black Uplift; Colonization; Delany, Martin Robison; Education; Entrepreneurs; Garrison, William Lloyd; Liberia; Ray, Charles B.; Ruggles, David; *and* Russwurm, John Brown.]

BIBLIOGRAPHY

Pease, Jane H., and William H. Pease. *Bound with Them in Chains: A Biographical History of the Antislavery Movement.* Westport, CT: Greenwood, 1972. Includes a chapter on the life and works of Samuel Cornish.

Swift, David E. *Black Prophets of Justice: Activist Clergy before the Civil War.* Baton Rouge: Louisiana State University Press, 1989. Cornish is one of six African American clergy featured in an examination of their roles in the various reform movements of the nineteenth century.

—L. DIANE BARNES

COTTAGERS. The term *cottagers* refers to farm workers and their families in a labor system common during the age of gradual emancipation from 1780 to 1830 in Pennsylvania, New Jersey, and New York. Under a contractual arrangement, laborers who were frequently, but not exclusively, former slaves agreed to work for commercial farmers. Contracts helped large landowners obtain badly needed labor at all times and at various wage rates—ordinary tasks, for example, earned less than harvest work. The key for the landowner was a constant supply of semidependent labor.

In return, the system allowed some landless laborers and artisans to avoid poverty and eke out a meager subsistence. The landowner provided them with lodging, fuel, the means to raise some of their own food, and inexpensive access to farm animals, often cows. Laborers were paid wages that were established more by custom than by true market forces. The cottager expected to pay for the use of a plow and horse team in the spring and a wagon and animals for hauling wood or for moving. His wife and children could earn cash for harvest work or flax spinning. Still, the cottager was not an independent wage laborer: the landowner held full power over the contract, regulated the work and pay of the cottager family, and could terminate the arrangement at any time.

For many African American laborers in the mid-Atlantic region, such contracts were halfway between servitude and freedom. In Monmouth County, New Jersey, for example, newly freed slaves often remained on their former master's property under just such an arrangement, with housing and food provided by the master, who also set wages. It was especially difficult for free people to own property in New Jersey or in areas near cities in Pennsylvania and New York. Unimproved or uncultivated land was scarce and expensive. Banking systems were primitive and paternalistic. Few blacks could expect loans from their former owners or other whites; mortgages required from one-third to one-half down payment and full repayment within five years. As subsistence farming became increasingly difficult near cities after the American Revolution, opportunities for independent African American landowners were remote.

As a result of such adverse market pressures, cottagers became numerous. Psychological pressures existed as well. Masters faced with enslaved people about to gain freedom would present an option: remain on the farm and feel assured about a life of work and narrow independence or go out into the world and never cross the master's doorstep again. Although innumerable African Americans chose the latter and crowded into urban centers like New York City and Philadelphia, it is understandable why others chose freedom within the dependency of the cottage system.

[*See also* Gradual Emancipation; Occupations; Urbanization; *and* Work.]

BIBLIOGRAPHY

Clemens, Paul G. E., and Lucy Simler. "Rural Labor and the Farm Household in Chester County, Pennsylvania, 1750–1820." In *Work and Labor in Early America*, edited by Stephen Innes. Chapel Hill: University of North Carolina Press, 1988.

Hodges, Graham Russell. *Slavery and Freedom in the Rural North: African Americans in Monmouth County, New Jersey, 1665–1865.* Madison, WI: Madison House, 1997.

—GRAHAM RUSSELL GAO HODGES

COVEY, EDWARD (b. 2 December 1806; d. 2 May 1875), a Maryland farmer and slave breaker. Edward Covey, about twenty-eight years old in 1834, lived with his wife and infant son, Edward, on a rented farm of 150 acres located about seven miles from Saint Michaels, Maryland. The Covey home was small, unpainted, and hidden nearly a mile from the main road. Before setting up as a small farmer, Covey worked as an overseer, where he may have gained his reputation as a "Negro breaker." In 1834 he rented the services of Frederick Douglass for an entire year. Douglass, nearly sixteen years old, initially submitted to the regular whippings but he eventually fought back and later recorded that this was when he finally felt like a man.

Douglass's owner, Thomas Auld, leased his slave's services to Covey; through this arrangement, Covey would receive low-cost farm labor and Auld could expect a more submissive slave in return. On 1 January 1834 Douglass traveled the seven miles to Covey's farm. He described the "chilling wind and pinching frost" as he carried his personal belongings in a bundle tied at the end of a stick. Douglass's new home was a "small wood-colored building," with the foam of Chesapeake Bay and dense, dark forest serving as its background. This dwelling housed

Covey and his wife and son; Covey's sister, Emma Caulk; and his cousin, William Hughes. The household included three slaves: a cook named Caroline and two hirelings, Bill Smith and Samuel Harrison.

Covey put Douglass to work as a field hand, a new experience for the young slave. Within three days Covey ordered Douglass to travel two miles to obtain a load of wood, giving him a pair of unbroken oxen to complete the chore. This was the slave's first task involving oxen, and his failure to control the beasts resulted in a severe flogging that left significant stripes on his back. Beneath the coarse clothing that Douglass wore, the sores bled for weeks.

Slaves, including Douglass, referred to Covey as "the Snake," a nickname that referenced Covey's ability to crawl though ditches and hide behind bushes to catch and punish slaves who wasted time. Covey's slave-breaking skill quickly wore down Douglass's resolve. "I was somewhat unmanageable at the first," he wrote in his third autobiography, *Life and Times of Frederick Douglass* (1881, 1892), "but a few months of this discipline tamed me. Mr. Covey succeeded in breaking me—in body, soul, and spirit. . . . I was completely wrecked, changed, and bewildered, goaded almost to madness."

Although Covey's nickname corresponded to the Christian symbol of Satan, the farmer was devoutly Methodist, and he conducted lengthy worship services at his home consisting of prayers and hymns. A poor singer himself, Covey insisted that Douglass lead the music. Douglass particularly resented the Christian aspect of his master, finding it hypocritical in light of the fact that Covey, a poor farmer, was seeking to expand his personal wealth by "breeding" Carolyn with Bill Smith; shortly thereafter, Carolyn was pregnant with twins.

Matters worsened one hot August afternoon when Douglass was overcome with a headache, dizziness, and trembling. Staggering into the shade, he became violently ill. Covey investigated and, seeing Douglass not at work, kicked him in the head and then beat him with a slab of wood, gashing him. When Douglass, bleeding profusely, did not rise, Covey walked away.

Once Douglass recovered somewhat, he fled to Auld's farm to plead his case: Even if Auld was not moved to help for humanitarian reasons, perhaps he might resent the damage done to his property. Douglass was only briefly pursued by Covey and, although the journey through the woods was difficult, Douglass made his way home. The result was disappointing. Although he initially seemed concerned over the condition of Douglass, Auld insisted that the slave return to serve out his lease so that Auld would not lose wages owed to him. Auld did not feed Douglass but did allow him to sleep overnight at his farm.

When Douglass returned, he saw that Covey was waiting for him, so he darted back into the woods. Douglass then encountered a friend named Sandy Jenkins, who fed him and sent him back to Covey with a root purported to have magical and protective powers. Douglass returned to Covey's farm on Sunday, the day in which Covey did not whip slaves; on Monday Covey sneaked up behind Douglass and attempted to bind him to punish him. Douglass chose to fight back—and later recalled the fight as lasting two hours. When Covey cried out for help, Carolyn and Smith feigned ignorance. Covey did not seek retribution for Douglass's rebelliousness—perhaps not wanting to admit that he could not control a slave—and he also did not physically chastise Douglass again. On Christmas Day of 1834 Douglass's term of service with Covey ended, and he returned to the home of Thomas Auld.

Starting in 1841 Douglass spoke against slavery, using Covey as the epitome of the cruel slaveholder. Douglass also used him as a source of humor in his speeches, sharing how he had bested this notorious Negro breaker. Douglass also focused on his experiences with Covey as a turning point in his own thinking; although the year with Covey was difficult and numbing, it also helped solidify Douglass's decision to finally escape slavery.

[*See also* Auld Family; Crime and Punishment; Douglass, Frederick; *Life and Times of Frederick Douglass*; Manhood; Proslavery Thought; Saint Michaels, Maryland; Slave Resistance; Slavery; *and* Violence against African Americans.]

BIBLIOGRAPHY

Douglass, Frederick. *Life and Times of Frederick Douglass: His Early Life as a Slave, His Escape from Bondage, and His Complete History, Written by Himself* (1881, 1892). New York: Collier, 1962.

McFeely, William S. *Frederick Douglass*. New York: Norton, 1991.

Preston, Dickson J. *Young Frederick Douglass: The Maryland Years*. Baltimore, MD: Johns Hopkins University Press, 1980.

—KELLY BOYER SAGERT

CRIME AND PUNISHMENT.

[*This entry contains two subentries dealing with law as specifically applied to African Americans from the seventeenth century through the nineteenth century. The first article discusses the development of crimes and punishments related to slavery through 1830, while the second article discusses law and legal penalties as applied to African Americans from 1830 through 1895.*]

Crime and Punishment as Related to Slavery

Enslaved and free African Americans committed large and small crimes and received punishments just as their white

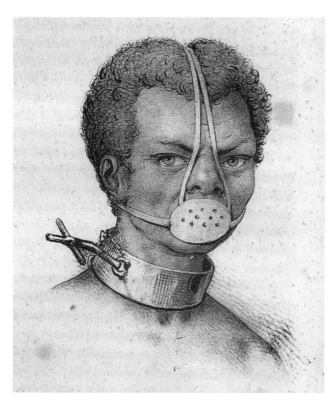

Slave wearing an iron muzzle, as depicted in Jacques Arago's *Souvenirs d'un aveugle* ("Reminiscences of a Blind Man," 1839–1840), about his journeys as the official artist of a French expedition in 1817–1820. This image came from Brazil, where the expedition spent nearly two months. The explanation of the work's title is that by the time it was published, Arago had lost his sight. (University of California, San Diego, Mandeville Special Collections Library.)

counterparts did; the differences lay in the degree of ferocity of the penalties, which could be severe. Some scholars argue that the punishments meted out to blacks were intended to instill fear and create respect for state power; often, however, the barbarity of punishments was simply indicative of a premodern world of torture, especially when crimes were deemed to be assaults on community mores. New Amsterdam provides examples of extraordinary punishments: A homosexual black was burned at the stake while his young lover was whipped during the immolation. Similarly, a white sailor convicted of sodomy was tied in a sack and thrown into the river.

In the seventeenth century enslaved and free blacks convicted of minor crimes such as stealing did not suffer punishments distinct from those of white felons. Whippings were usually the penalty for both races. Gradually, as the colonies began to pass laws regulating full-blown slave codes or supporting white supremacy, black thieves found punishments to be harsher. Besides corporal penalties, blacks could lose precious freedoms; free blacks in New

York in the 1680s were warned that if they received stolen goods or sold liquor to slaves, they would suffer reenslavement. White authorities often followed biblical rules, which limited whippings to thirty-nine lashes; flogging was also used for curfew violations, assembly in excessive numbers, or drunkenness. Whenever white authorities felt the need, they could up the retributive ante with impunity. For example, in 1698 the governor of New York Colony ordered the sheriff to open fire on blacks who refused to disperse. Slave codes also had the effect of curbing or at least placing limits on masters' brutality. Although white authorities were usually loath to do so, masters were sometimes prosecuted for torturing or maiming blacks.

With the establishment of black codes to undergird slavery, the fates of white and black criminals diverged. Virginia cut a new path in 1669 when its legislature decreed that masters who killed slaves while correcting them were immune to prosecution—a practice that South Carolina also instituted in 1690. Virginia's government set up special courts to ensure speedy "justice" for accused slaves. As would become the case in New Jersey and South Carolina, county justices formed a gubernatorial commission for trials of blacks involving execution, the loss of a member, or other severe punishments. In the aftermath of Bacon's Rebellion of 1676, Virginia's new laws for slave trials lasted until the Civil War, ensuring that blacks, slave or free, would not have rights similar to whites. Some slaves were saved from execution only because of their commercial value.

Some crimes were difficult to police. In the late seventeenth century authorities in Virginia, New York, and South Carolina began complaining about unlawful trafficking in stolen goods by slaves and worried about excessive instances of slave hawking and peddling. Laws were passed, and occasional arrests were made, but the regularity with which colonial assemblies sought new legislation, attempted to license petty sellers, and complained about abuses through the colonial era and beyond indicates the overall failure of their efforts. At times their anxieties were well founded, as evidenced by the direct correlation between slave thefts and fencing in the New York conspiracy of 1741.

Philip J. Schwarz's research and analysis of Virginia's colonial legal records indicates how fiercely the commonwealth used the law as an instrument of terror. Between 1706 and 1784 over 300 slaves were sentenced to be hung for crimes against property, 137 were slated for hanging for crimes against persons, and 22 were to have had their bodies or heads displayed for such crimes; three slaves were hanged, drawn, and quartered. Remarkably, the American Revolution and the Enlightenment had little effect on Virginia. Between 1785 and 1865 an astounding 628 slaves were hanged in Virginia for various causes, primarily attacks on persons. Schwarz's studies of various crimes show conviction rates above 70 percent for crimes against property—which figure would be higher if not for a low rate of conviction in cases of receiving stolen goods. Rape prosecutions were successful in over 85 percent of cases, while charges of insurrection were found legitimate 90 percent of the time. In South Carolina individual rape was deemed suggestive of social overthrow and so was punished ferociously. Such obsession with physical violation became an integral part of social control, even as the punishments reflected deeper barbarism.

Such high rates of conviction and resultant capital punishments were not the norm only in the southern colonies. In New York City in 1732 an enslaved man accused of rape was taken up at midnight, tried during the early morning hours, and burned at sunrise. As in the South, rapists were considered threats to the social system and were punished as severely as were conspirators. Rebellious slaves in New York in the revolt of 1712 and the conspiracy of 1741 were broken on the wheel, burned at the stake, and hung in chains. Similar punishments were accorded to white sympathizers in 1741.

As Ira Berlin concludes, the imposition of terror on the enslaved population failed to accomplish its intended goal of cowing slaves into submission. In colony after colony the imposition of slave codes or drastic punishments was followed in a short period of time by a sizable slave rebellion. New York's revolt in 1712 was answered by a harsh code in 1714 that was then answered by years of discontent, petty crimes, and then the disastrous conspiracy of 1741. The Stono Rebellion in South Carolina is another example of this trend.

Masters asked authorities to use the whip to ensure correction of their slaves. It was indeed a common practice in the colonies through the post-Revolutionary period for sheriffs to whip unruly slaves for worried masters. At times the local government took matters into its own hands. New York authorities became so angry about unauthorized gatherings of blacks that nine of them were once apprehended, "committed, try'd, and whipt at the whipping post for assembling and meeting together in an illegal manner."

Royal governors could do little to stop judicial terror because of deeply instilled racial hatred at the local level. A New Jersey case illustrates the power of local behavior and its premodern qualities: In a crime that occurred in Somerset County in 1752, a slave chopped off his master's head with an ax, because the owner had taken his tobacco without permission. The next day the slave was arrested, taken to the decapitated corpse, and forced to touch the head. When blood trickled from the nose and ear, the slave was considered convicted. He was then taken to a spot on the Raritan River and burned at the stake in front of several hundred other slaves who were required to watch. Just as the flames consumed his body, he shouted to the surrounding multitude that the executors had taken the root but left the branches. This was considered by all to be a good death—one in which courage was demonstrated—and was talked about by slaves and free people for years afterward.

Other crimes considered blows against slavery were poisoning and arson. Schwarz assembles data indicating that white authorities were not at all sure how to view accusations of poisoning. In 179 cases considered between 1706 and 1784, 35 slaves were hung, while 44 were given the benefit of the clergy or clerical clemency, and 100 were acquitted or not tried; even when attacks were on white people, slaves accused of poisoning were often declared not guilty.

One of the most frequent crimes committed by slaves was running away, which was considered in all the colonies to be a crime against the system. In most cases a recaptured slave was returned to his or her master for a whipping. A narrative from New Jersey relates how one slave was whipped for a first self-emancipation, whipped again for a second such offense, and the third time finally whipped until he became insensible. When running away touched on military concerns, punishments could be harsher. New York Colony passed a law in 1705 declaring that any fugitive slave caught fifty miles north of Albany would be executed, under the presumption that he planned to join the enemy French.

Runaway slaves often combined "stealing themselves" with other crimes. Theft of clothing was common, as was taking horses, jewelry, boats, and other commodities that might be sold to finance successful flight. Some ads reflect how masters had entrusted slaves with increased freedom only to eventually find that trust abused. Slaves also joined forces with indentured servants to gain their freedom; race mattered little in the picaresque proletariat. The punishment for both was a whipping.

Fugitive slaves were considered a problem throughout the colonial period but never as much as during the American Revolution. British offers of freedom to slaves willing to serve in the king's forces in exchange for freedom enticed nearly 100,000 enslaved blacks to leave their masters during the war. They frequently took along stolen property to raise money on the road. Their numbers were so great that Patriot forces were often helpless to stop them. This mass slave flight struck the system of servitude a mighty blow, from which it never recovered in the North. In the South prolific flight first made masters rethink slavery and then pushed them on the road to harsher restrictions.

The post-Revolutionary period saw a split between North and South in allegations and punishments of crime by blacks. As northern states gradually ended servitude, laws specifically constricting slaves no longer applied; crimes by blacks against property and persons were still enforced but in different manners. In 1796 New York City abandoned the practice by which sheriffs whipped unruly slaves. Prosecutions of blacks continued, but the evolution of the prison system and the increasing unpopularity of public executions meant that blacks who violated state laws were less likely to receive corporal or capital punishment and more likely to be sentenced to prison for lengthy terms. Third offenses for petty theft could merit ten years in prison or longer.

In southern states the creation of prisons for white felons grew; such was not the case for blacks. Even valuable slaves were put to death for crimes for which whites regularly received penitentiary sentences. As is indicative of the common opinion of the era, the southern legal scholar Thomas R. R. Cobb noted in 1858 that the slave "can only be reached through his body"; nor was there much imprisonment for free blacks. Only Louisiana made prison an alternative to hanging for serious crimes. As the North moved from the death sentence toward imprisonment as the primary deterrent to crime, the use of older, premodern methods was maintained in the South.

[*See also* American Revolution; Black Codes and Slave Codes, Colonial; Black Loyalists; Free African Americans to 1828; Fugitive Slaves; Laws and Legislation; Lynching and Mob Violence; New Jersey; New York City; New York Conspiracy of 1741; New York Slave Revolt of 1712; Riots and Rebellions; Stono Rebellion; *and* Violence against African Americans.]

BIBLIOGRAPHY

Ayers, Edward L. *Vengeance and Justice: Crime and Punishment in the Nineteenth Century American South*. New York: Oxford University Press, 1984.

Berlin, Ira. *Many Thousands Gone: The First Two Centuries of Slavery in North America*. Cambridge, MA: Belknap Press, 1998.

Hodges, Graham Russell. *Root and Branch: African Americans in New York and East Jersey, 1613–1863*. Chapel Hill: University of North Carolina Press, 1999.

Morgan, Philip D. *Slave Counterpoint: Black Culture in the Eighteenth-Century Chesapeake and Lowcountry*. Chapel Hill: University of North Carolina Press, 1998.

Schwarz, Philip J. *Twice Condemned: Slaves and the Criminal Laws of Virginia, 1705–1865*. Baton Rouge: Louisiana State University Press, 1988.

Wood, Peter H. *Black Majority: Negroes in Colonial South Carolina from 1670 through the Stono Rebellion*. New York: Knopf, 1974.

—GRAHAM RUSSELL GAO HODGES

Law as Applied to African Americans, 1830–1895

With slaves defined as property, their legal and judicial rights were extremely restricted. Slave owners were the first authority concerning the governance of slaves; the courts were considered the final authority in legal matters regarding slaves and their crimes. Many owners had different opinions concerning the use of courts with regard to the conduct of slaves. Some believed that the courts had no right to rule over their slaves, who were legally their private property; others trusted that the courts would affirm their rights as masters in disputes. The fear of violence or slave rebellions prompted many owners to see the courts and the state as protectors of themselves, their property, and the institution of slavery.

Court and Law. Between 1830 and 1860 slave owners saw the courts as the guardians of their lives and property. To this end, laws were passed to impose restrictions on slaves and their actions in white society. The true fear was not about owners' control of their property but about the possible effects of the outside world in turning loyal slaves into a violent race bent on revenge. Southern society was beginning to feature slaves who were contracted out to work in growing towns, where their increased freedom might encourage illegal activities. In addition, growing fears over literacy and the influence of abolitionists became concerns for slave owners who believed that the road to rebellion was paved with education. To this extent, slave crimes were not merely minor crimes and felonies but violations of rules that were essential in controlling slaves' lives and protecting masters.

Nevertheless, there remained differences regarding what slaves could or could not be prosecuted for in the courts. Some believed in the "natural rights" that should be accorded to all men, no matter their position in life; thus, they sought to liberalize the rigid nature of the slave codes and pushed for greater judicial rights for slaves. Others saw slave codes as necessary to prevent rebellion and sought the courts' assistance in controlling and punishing slaves so as to prevent white bloodshed.

By the time of Nat Turner's revolt, which took place in Virginia in 1831, the typical southern state operated with magistrate courts, superior courts, and a state supreme court. Appointed justices of the peace ran the magistrate courts, whose jurisdiction would normally be over a county or parish. Superior courts handled more serious crimes, particularly those concerning felonies. Last, the state supreme court would handle appeals. After Turner's rebellion, many legal restrictions came into play regarding slaves and their actions. Slaves and free blacks alike were prevented from carrying weapons of any kind; if an owner wanted his slave to be armed for hunting or livestock protection, he would have to file a petition or submit a license to a superior court for judicial approval. Blacks were also legally prevented from gathering in large groups and engaging in inflammatory language. The fear of slave rebellion had clearly created an entire set of laws

"Common Mode of Whipping with the Paddle," wood engraving, 1845, from "Trial and Imprisonment of Jonathan Walker, at Pensacola, Florida, for Aiding Slaves to Escape from Bondage," published in Boston by the Anti-Slavery Office. This was Walker's own account of an episode that made him a national hero: having attempted to help several runaway slaves find freedom, he was tried and convicted as a "slave stealer" and was accordingly branded SS on his right hand. He was an abolitionist in the period preceding the Civil War; after the war he became a farmer in Muskegon, Michigan, where he died in 1878. (Library of Congress.)

to prevent further bloodshed. Violations of these laws would result in some kind of corporal punishment to the offender, often through whipping or branding, to mark a troublemaker. In more serious cases, courts could rule that the purported leaders of plots be publicly executed as a warning to others.

Slave Crimes. Property crimes, including arson, burglary, and larceny, were among the most common crimes committed by slaves during this period. In the case of fires on private property, there were no distinctions made in terms of penalties for the act of arson and the degree of incidental damage caused to structures or crops. In the majority of cases, the convicted person was executed. When death was not the penalty, the convicted slave could be whipped, branded, and transported out of the state. Burglary also carried the penalty of death, but courts often decreed lesser forms of punishment. Most slave crimes qualified as simple larceny, with the penalty determined according to the seriousness of the crime. Minor cases of larceny were punishable by some form of corporal punishment, often whipping by the master or an officer of the court. For more serious acts of larceny, the court nearly always employed capital punishment. Rarely would blacks would be incarcerated as punishment for minor crimes.

Slaves committing homicides and acts of sexual violence were the most severely punished, usually by death. In the mid-1700s several states deemed any homicide of a white person by a slave to be a capital offense, wherein "legal" retribution bore similarities to the lynchings that often occurred after Reconstruction in the 1870s. Questions eventually arose regarding the automatic death penalty, with reformers advancing the idea of qualifying acts as manslaughter in certain cases. The states of North Carolina and Tennessee ruled that manslaughter would be the appropriate verdict when there was no premeditation; unfortunately, however, most southern states did not follow such a humane course of action. To many, the desire to control black populations with an iron fist necessitated the liberal use of the death penalty in cases of homicide. Even cases of assault against whites were considered capital offenses in the eyes of many southern superior courts.

In cases of sexual violence, if a capital penalty was not enforced, castration was used to punish the convicted slave. In North Carolina in the mid-1700s castration was preferred, owing to the cost of applying the death penalty. Yet this form of punishment fell out of favor in many states by the 1850s. One exception was Missouri, which used castration as punishment, according to the general statutes of 1845 until the end of the Civil War. It was found that lower-class women were the main accusers in charges of rape leveled against both slaves and free blacks in southern society. In some state courts, efforts were made to determine whether such accusers were morally capable of preventing sexual advances by black men. Court officials were concerned that the high level of interaction between blacks and lower-class whites generated problems involving loose women who enticed black men into having sex. In court appearances, to justify the charge of rape, women had to proclaim that they had fought back against a slave's advances. White women were protected under the law, but rapes committed against black women, especially slaves, were almost never brought to court. In fact, such cases were legally addressed only in divorce proceedings, where the actions of white men against black female slaves were used as reasons to approve petitions before the court.

In the case of Frederick Douglass, crimes affected his relationship with his master and his attempts to run away from his various employers. Sophia Auld's desire to educate the young Douglass was rejected by her husband, Hugh Auld, who was clearly concerned that education would prompt the young lad to desire his freedom. Later, Douglass's fight with the farmer Edward Covey, to whom he had been hired out as field hand, could have resulted in Douglass's being tried in court for assault on a white person; indeed, this could have been a capital offense in the eyes of the court. Perhaps only Covey's concern that the public accounting of Douglass's behavior would have caused him to lose business as a slave breaker saved Douglass from death. Douglass later attempted to escape from the farm of William Freeland but was captured before that plot could be put into motion. The kind actions of Thomas Auld, who sent Douglass into employment in Baltimore, Maryland, again prevented a more serious penalty from being inflicted on one of the future leaders of African American society. As with most slaves hired out for employment, the lack of constant supervision fostered a sense of freedom, and the opportunity to live and work around free blacks gave Douglass additional impetus to escape.

Once Douglass fled to the North, he discovered the oppressive conditions that still existed for freedmen and escaped slaves. Even many northern states considered the African American a nonperson by law, arresting freedmen for minor offenses like vagrancy and applying unfairly long prison sentences. In trials, black testimony was not allowed, unless a white man could be found to corroborate the story of a black witness. Several states, like New York, did not allow blacks to serve on juries or even bring suits to court. Massachusetts finally allowed freedmen to sit on juries for the first time in 1860. With such a lack of judicial safeguards, African Americans found themselves convicted at higher rates, and northern prisons held disproportionate shares of black inmates. In the 1840s African Americans made up one-third of the prison population in Pennsylvania.

American Civil War, Reconstruction, and Aftermath. The short life of the Confederacy extended the process of spe-

"Wilson Chinn, a Branded Slave from Louisiana, Also Exhibiting Instruments of Torture Used to Punish Slaves." Photograph by Kimball, New York City, 1863. On 30 January 1864, *Harper's Weekly* published a letter from C. C. Leigh with an engraving of emancipated slaves, including Chinn, who had been set free in New Orleans by General Benjamin Franklin Butler. Leigh gave a biographical sketch of each person pictured, noting that Chinn was then about age sixty, had been "raised" by Isaac Howard in Kentucky, and at age twenty-one had been sold to a Louisianian sugar planter, Volsey B. Marmillion, who branded his slaves "like cattle with a hot iron." Chinn's forehead bore the letters "V.B.M." (Library of Congress.)

cialized justice with respect to the slave community. The only basic change in Confederate law was in the severity of punishments inflicted on convicted blacks. In fighting for their political independence, Southern whites saw slave insurrection as a possible war tool of Northern abolitionists and the Republican government. A grip of fear similar to that following the Harpers Ferry raid led to the deaths of hundreds of slaves at the hands of Confederate soldiers, slave owners, and local authorities; in many cases, local white populations attempted to control large slave communities through violence rather than through legal means. During the Civil War, runaway slaves joined with army deserters to form outlaw gangs that terrorized local communities. Several such groups operated in the Carolinas, where local authorities proved ineffective, owing to the loss of men to Confederate conscription.

With the demise of the Confederacy, federal authorities set about recreating the federal and state court systems in the southern states. Some attempts were made to find new justices of the peace who would reflect the new political climate in the South. Leaders in former slave communities were tapped as local representatives in southern counties. In some cases, these new leaders were southern Republicans, black ministers, or returning black veterans, and incoming judicial appointees started to bring about change in the interpretation of criminal laws. Some states did try to put black codes in place to restrict the freedoms of former slaves, but the efforts of congressional Reconstruction blunted those actions. Many of the Reconstruction state governments held constitutional conventions to draft new documents to introduce and protect the new freedoms of both former slaves and poor whites. These documents offered new judicial protections for freedmen, such as the ability to sit on juries and the right to due process under law. New local courts were set up, with commissioners governing the counties. With such protections in place, former slaves became part of the local system of justice instead of a restricted people controlled by fearful white landowners.

With the end of Reconstruction and removal of federal control in 1877, southern whites began to reestablish control over the black population through changes in legal codes. New vagrancy laws allowed county sheriffs to arrest unemployed blacks. In many southern states, penalties were increased for numerous minor crimes, disproportionately affecting blacks. Many of the positive changes made to state courts through postwar constitutions were negated by such increases in penalties. One example was the "pig" law of Mississippi: larceny of livestock valued over ten dollars mandated a five-year prison sentence. Judicial changes led to higher conviction rates for blacks, greatly increasing southern prison populations after 1877.

Also after Reconstruction, the political rights of blacks came to be restricted, as Republican legislators were replaced by ruling members of the former Confederacy. These former Confederates limited the involvement of former slaves in the judicial process, disenfranchising blacks and disallowing them to serve on trial juries.

Violent criminal actions by blacks came to face more severe punishment and retribution. As with the southern white population, a portion of black society saw minor acts of violence as a means of settling minor disputes. These minor acts were placed on the same level as more serious felonies, such as murder and rape. White juries came to hand out more severe punishment for acts of violence, no matter the nature of the crime. Guilty parties were more likely to receive the death penalty for crimes such as manslaughter or second-degree murder. Harsher sentences were also employed in cases of arson and larceny if the victim was white. In cases of murder and rape, southern whites would enforce their own judgment of a black defendant through lynching.

In the July 1881 *North American Review*, Frederick Douglass made a strong statement regarding the treatment of blacks through the legal code in the southern United States. He called into question the masculinity of the white male, who used the law to punish and restrict the lives of blacks. The question of fair trials in the South was a particular point of contention, wherein, all too often, "the murdered man [was] the real criminal, and the murderer innocent."

In the postwar North the judicial treatment of African Americans continued to improve their legal status compared with that of their brothers and sisters in the South. Problems remained with respect to finding representative juries for criminal trials and the application of longer prison sentences for minor crimes. Segregation also remained a major problem facing African Americans in northern states with regard to governmental institutions. Such discriminatory treatment would eventually force African American families into ghettos in northern cities, where law enforcement ruled with a heavy hand. The threat of mob violence continued to be employed by white communities, especially with the rise in Ku Klux Klan membership in midwestern states.

Convict-Leasing System. The use of convict labor was seen as an attempt by southern state governments to bring back the concept of slavery as a form of correction. For the southern states it was a solution to the problem of the large numbers of blacks being moved through antebellum-era penal facilities. The system whereby local prison camps provided labor to local businesses and governments soon became the norm within the region of the former Confederacy. This system was seen as another example of southern white injustice toward the African American community.

During the Civil War, the state-run penitentiary system was severely damaged by the Union forces moving through the South. The collapse of Confederate state governments allowed inmates to scatter across the countryside. During Reconstruction, prison systems had to be rebuilt. Many legislators sought to reestablish the antebellum prison system, but it quickly became apparent that the old system would not accommodate the influx of former slaves into the system. Another perceived solution was the building of larger penitentiaries. This answer soon proved inadequate as well, owing to the enormous costs of construction of buildings to match the growing prison population. Before the Civil War, southern states operated on tight budgets that revolved around providing services for the white populations. Thus, newly reconstituted state governments did not have the revenue base to provide services for hundreds of thousands of freedmen. The financial benefits of the convict-leasing system persuaded even black state legislators to endorse this mode of incarceration. By 1880 all former Confederate states had created a state labor force for hire through the state prison system.

The leasing of convict labor was riddled with corruption and abuse toward the prison population. The need for cheap labor on behalf of southern businesses and the profit margin of the leasing system generated abuses on many governmental levels. State officials made large profits through contracts to local businesses. Indeed, convicts proved to be a very cost-effective labor pool for the South's growing industrial base. In many states "penitentiary rings" became commonplace, with businessmen and prison wardens cutting illicit deals where cash payments were exchanged for the supply of cheap prison labor to companies.

Throughout the South the newly freed black population was seen as a source of additional workers to feed the collective labor mill. Higher conviction rates among former slaves turned the convict leasing system into another form of servitude. With the increased desire for profits by corrupt state officials bent on racial control, the inhuman treatment of prisoners became a serious problem. Many black prisoners faced terrible working conditions, often being beaten by sadistic prison camp overseers and foremen. In some cases, former slaves ended up working for former masters who had contracted for labor to manage large farms or growing textile and tobacco industries. In South Carolina from 1877 to 1879 nearly half of the convicts leased to work for the Greenwood and Augusta Railroad died through either work or disease. Not until the turn of the twentieth century would reformers start to effect change on convict-leasing policies and the cruel treatment of both blacks and the immigrant populations of southern states. The ending of the convict-leasing system, however, merely forced state penal institutions to create chain-gang labor crews, employing prisoners on public works projects.

[See also Auld Family; Civil War; Confederate Policy toward African Americans and Slaves; Confederate States of America; Covey, Edward; Discrimination; Douglass, Frederick; Education; Free African Americans before the Civil War (North); Freedmen; Harpers Ferry Raid; Laws and Legislation; Lynching and Mob Violence; Reconstruction; Republican Party; Resistance; Riots and Rebellions; Segregation; and Turner, Nat.]

BIBLIOGRAPHY

Ayers, Edward L. *Vengeance and Justice: Crime and Punishment in the Nineteenth Century American South*. New York: Oxford University Press, 1984.

Foner, Eric. *Reconstruction: America's Unfinished Revolution, 1863–1877*. New York: Harper and Row, 1988. An excellent primer on Reconstruction.

Franklin, John Hope, and Loren Schweninger. *Runaway Slaves: Rebels on the Plantation*. New York: Oxford University Press, 1999. The definitive work on the subject.

Freehling, William W. *The Road to Disunion*. New York: Oxford University Press, 1990.

Genovese, Eugene D. *Roll, Jordan, Roll: The World the Slaves Made*. New York: Vintage Books, 1976.

Halasz, Nicholas. *The Rattling Chains: Slave Unrest and Revolt in the Antebellum South*. New York: D. McKay, 1966.

Johnson, Guion G. *Ante-bellum North Carolina: A Social History*. Chapel Hill: University of North Carolina Press, 1937. An excellent regional study of antebellum life.

Litwack, Leon F. *North of Slavery: The Negro in the Free States, 1790–1860*. Chicago: University of Chicago Press, 1961.

Miller, Randall M., and John David Smith, eds. *Dictionary of Afro-American Slavery*. Westport, CT: Praeger, 1997.

Morris, Thomas D. *Southern Slavery and the Law, 1619–1860*. Chapel Hill: University of North Carolina Press, 1996. Required reading for any study concerning the development of the legal definitions of slavery.

Myers, Martha A. *Race, Labor, and Punishment in the New South*. Columbus: Ohio State University Press, 1998.

Quarles, Benjamin, ed. *Frederick Douglass*. Englewood Cliffs, NJ: Prentice-Hall, 1968.

Roark, James L. *Masters without Slaves: Southern Planters in the Civil War and Reconstruction*. New York: Norton, 1977.

Tindall, George Brown. *South Carolina Negroes: 1877–1900*. Columbia: University of South Carolina Press, 2003.

Woodward, C. Vann. *Origins of the New South, 1877–1913*. Baton Rouge: Louisiana State University, 1951. The best work on the subject.

—WILLIAM H. BROWN

CROFTS, JULIA GRIFFITHS (b. c. 1821; d. c. 1895), British abolitionist. One of the more controversial figures in the life of Frederick Douglass, Julia Griffiths also proved to be one of his most effective supporters through her financial acumen, British connections, and organizational abilities. Julia was the daughter of Thomas Powis Griffiths, a British barrister who was a member of the British and Foreign Anti-Slavery Society and an attendant at the farewell dinner held for Frederick Douglass in 1847, at the culmination of the black abolitionist's first British tour. Julia Griffiths, herself a member of a London women's antislavery society, had seen Douglass toward the end of that tour. She found herself captivated by him and subsequently devoted her energies to galvanizing the support of English abolitionists behind him. From Griffiths's earliest efforts, many observed that she seemed to identify Douglass as representing the entire antislavery movement—much to the chagrin of the American Anti-Slavery Society and its supporters, of whom she became a significant competitor in fund-raising.

Not satisfied with her own work in England and possibly distressed at rumors of the difficulties that Douglass faced in launching his first newspaper, the *North Star*, Griffiths became interested in traveling to the United States to assist Douglass directly. Taking her younger sister, Eliza, she departed for America from Liverpool on the steamer *Sarah Sands*. The sisters arrived in New York City on 2 May 1849, just in time for the annual meeting of the American Anti-Slavery Society. There, Julia and Eliza presented themselves to Douglass and quickly charmed him. The trio became fast friends, with the bond between Julia and Douglass being particularly strong. Julia had little difficulty in debating Douglass on various points of ideology, and others noted that he bore her differences of opinion with an unusual grace. He invited the sisters to pay him an extended visit at his home in Rochester, New York.

However, companionship between white women and a black man was difficult, both in New York City and on the journey to Rochester. While the three friends were walking down Broadway one day, a group of white men attacked Douglass for being in the company of the sisters. The men retreated only when Eliza managed to persuade a nearby police officer, also white, to intervene. On the journey to Rochester aboard the steamer *Alida*, vocal resistance arose whenever Douglass joined the women for meals or conversation. Rumor had it that Julia, whose cabin adjoined Douglass's, spent inordinate amounts of time alone in his company at improper hours. These events and rumors foreshadowed the difficulties that Griffiths and Douglass would face throughout the course of their friendship.

Once in Rochester, Douglass installed the Griffiths sisters in his home. His wife's reaction to the move was not recorded. Also living in the Douglass household at the time was John Dick, another Briton whom Douglass had hired as the printer for the *North Star*. Within a year Dick and Eliza married and moved to Canada to work in the fugitive slave communities around Toronto. Julia remained unescorted in the Douglass home; she would stay until the rumors surrounding her relationship with Douglass became so vicious that she first removed herself to the home of the Rochester abolitionists Samuel and Susan Porter and eventually went back to England.

Immediately upon her arrival in Rochester, Griffiths began organizing the *North Star*'s finances. Antislavery newspapers, appealing to a small segment of the population, tended to be fiscally unstable during their very short lives. William Lloyd Garrison's *Liberator* was the exception, and even that paper's thirty-four-year run did not make Garrison a rich man. By 1849 the *North Star* carried heavy debts and faced fierce opposition from abolitionist leaders in Boston, Philadelphia, and the Midwest, which impeded Douglass's efforts to appeal to a large abolitionist audience. His independence as the paper's manager was also threatened when the Rochester abolitionists Amy and Isaac Post, his most prominent backers, suggested that he allow a board of directors to oversee the business affairs of the journal.

Griffiths, however, saved the *North Star* from collapse and preserved Douglass's independence. She and her sister purchased the mortgage on Douglass's home and allowed him to repay them at a pace and interest rate that he could manage; they also invested their own money in the *North Star* to stabilize its finances. Julia then separated Douglass's personal financial records from his business financial records, allowing his wife, Anna, to oversee the household budget while Griffiths took over the newspaper's accounts. Once the *North Star*, renamed *Frederick Douglass' Paper* in 1851, became solvent, she pursued subscriptions and donations with an aggression that often embarrassed Douglass. She also contributed a column to its pages.

Following the proven model of the abolitionist women in Boston, Griffiths joined Amy Post in organizing the women of western New York and in conducting a yearly fund-raising fair. She used her connections in England to solicit donations, which were particularly valuable because European items proved in much demand at most bazaars. In this arena, as in her pursuit of English subscriptions for the *North Star*, Griffiths met with substantial resistance from the American Anti-Slavery Society, particularly from the society's female leader, Maria Weston Chapman.

The pool from which an antislavery activist could draw financial support was limited, as was the time and money supporters could give to the cause. The American Anti-Slavery Society, which identified itself as the sole arbiter of abolitionist action, dominated the field if for no other reason than for its longevity. Griffiths, as a backer of the enormously popular Frederick Douglass, presented a significant threat to the influence of the American Anti-Slavery Society in England. The society retaliated by magnifying the existing rumors about the relationship between Douglass and Griffiths and playing on Griffiths's personal eccentricity and assertive behavior, which put off many people, including those who supported her cause. Even after she left Douglass's home, she faced extreme criticism for her influence at the *North Star*. In many ways Griffiths became the scapegoat for abolitionists' anger and frustration at Douglass's defection from the American Anti-Slavery Society over issues surrounding abolitionist tactics, his requests for higher fees for lecturing and writing, and his decision to found his own newspaper against the wishes of the Society's leaders. His opponents could more easily accuse the odd English spinster of dominating and manipulating Douglass into betraying his former allies than they could accept that Douglass had asserted his own independence and taken in Griffiths as an effective partner.

By 1855 the climate in the antislavery movement had become so hostile to Griffiths that even her allies questioned her value to the cause. At that point Douglass was in the process of publishing his second autobiography, *My Bondage and My Freedom*, in which he criticized the American Anti-Slavery Society. As with his earlier autobiography, *Narrative of the Life of Frederick Douglass* (1845), he intended to have a European version published. Having alienated the Irish publisher of the *Narrative*, who sympathized with the society, he found himself in dire need of a new printer. Griffiths seized this opportunity and returned to England to use her influence. She toured the British Isles to bolster support for Douglass by revitalizing the antislavery societies that had formed during his first tour overseas. Although she intended this visit to be temporary, she never returned to the United States.

Griffiths continued to be Douglass's strongest advocate in Britain even after her 1859 marriage to the Methodist minister Henry O. Crofts. Indeed, Crofts supported his wife in her antislavery activities, with the couple acting as the British agents for *Frederick Douglass' Paper*; Julia continued to contribute columns, reporting on the abolitionist movement in England, and exchanged personal correspondence with the paper's editor. In 1859, when Douglass fled the United States in the wake of John Brown's failed raid on Harpers Ferry, Virginia, Henry and Julia Crofts offered him asylum. Decades later—after the cause they both supported had come to fruition in the Civil War, both Henry Crofts and Anna Douglass had died, Douglass had remarried, and Julia had worked in various positions as an educator—the friendship between Douglass and Crofts still flourished. She welcomed him and his second wife, Helen Pitts, into her home when they took a grand tour of Europe in the 1880s. Julia Griffiths Crofts and Douglass died in the same year, 1895.

[*See also* Abolitionism; American Anti-Slavery Society; Antislavery Movement; Antislavery Press; Brown, John; Discrimination; *Douglass, Anna Murray; Douglass, Frederick; Frederick Douglass' Paper*; Free African Americans before the Civil War (North); Garrison, William Lloyd; Harpers Ferry Raid; *My Bondage and My Freedom; Nar-* *rative of the Life of Frederick Douglass*; *North Star*; Post, Amy and Isaac; Racism; Rochester, New York; Segregation; Sexuality; Stereotypes of African Americans; Western New York Anti-Slavery Society; Weston Sisters; *and* Women.]

BIBLIOGRAPHY

Diedrich, Maria. *Love across the Color Lines: Ottilie Assing and Frederick Douglass*. New York: Hill and Wang, 1999.

Palmer, Erwin. "A Partnership in the Abolition Movement." *University of Rochester Library Bulletin* 26 (1970–1971): 1–19.

—LEIGH FOUGHT

CROMWELL, OLIVER (b. c. 1752; d. 24 January 1853), an African American Patriot in the Revolutionary War. Oliver Cromwell was born a free African American in Burlington County, New Jersey, in the town that later became Columbus. He lived with the family of John Hutchin, a farmer, and was expected to become a farmer as well. Little else is known about Cromwell's life before he was twenty, the age at which he enlisted in a company attached to the Second New Jersey Regiment, led by Colonel Israel Shreve. In 1772 free African Americans were permitted to fight in the American Revolutionary War, a practice later reinforced by the passage of the Militia Act of New Jersey in 1777.

Ironically, Cromwell served for six years and nine months under the immediate command of George Washington, who was initially opposed to African Americans' enlisting in the Continental army. Along with another African American, Prince Whipple, on Christmas Eve 1776 Cromwell crossed the Delaware River with Washington to Trenton, New Jersey, where the Patriots successfully attacked the Hessians and claimed a major victory. For an unknown reason, the famous painting of this event by John Trumble includes only one African American soldier, usually identified as Whipple (although some historians believe that the lone figure is Cromwell).

During his time of service from 1776 to 1783 Cromwell also fought at the battles of Princeton and Brandywine (1777), Monmouth (1778), and Yorktown (1781) and claimed to be present at the last killing to take place in the war. On 5 June 1783 Cromwell received an honorable discharge signed by General George Washington, as well as a Badge of Merit for his six years of service as a private in the New Jersey regiment. However, Cromwell was denied his veteran's pension when he applied for it. After several local politicians, lawyers, and judges came to his assistance, Cromwell received a federal pension of ninety-six dollars a year.

He used his pension to purchase a 100-acre farm in Burlington County, New Jersey, where he raised fourteen children. In his later life he moved to a small house in the city of Burlington at 114 East Union Street (which was designated as an historic site in the early 2000s). At the time of his death in 1853 Cromwell had just passed his hundredth birthday and was reportedly a pauper. He was buried near his home in the cemetery of the Broad Street Methodist Church and was survived by several of his children, grandchildren, and great-grandchildren, some of whom still resided in Burlington more than 150 years later.

In 1976, as part of the American bicentennial celebration, a commemorative stamp was issued depicting both Cromwell and Whipple as the African American soldiers who accompanied Washington across the Delaware River. In the early 1980s the Oliver Cromwell Black History Society was formed in Burlington City to research and disseminate information about Cromwell and other African American soldiers who fought in the American Revolution. The group's goal was to bridge the gap between African American history and what has traditionally been categorized as American history to ultimately present a more accurate picture of America's past.

[*See also* American Revolution; Military; New Jersey; *and* Washington, George, and African Americans.]

BIBLIOGRAPHY

Nell, William Cooper. *The Colored Patriots of the American Revolution, with Sketches of Several Distinguished Colored Persons: To Which Is Added a Brief Survey of the Condition and Prospects of Colored Americans.* Chapel Hill: University of North Carolina, 1999. http://docsouth.unc.edu/nell/nell.html.

Quarles, Benjamin. *The Negro in the American Revolution.* Chapel Hill: University of North Carolina Press, 1961.

—PENNY ANNE WELBOURNE

Alexander Crummell, an illustration in James T. Haley's *Afro-American Encyclopaedia* of 1895. Haley said of Crummell: "He is the acknowledged leader of his race, from a theological stand-point. Half a century numbers his years in the ministerial work. He . . . has been the guest of crowned heads of Europe. His writings are chaste and scholarly, instructive and entertaining. They flow from a heart full of tenderness and love toward mankind, and show a simple faith in Christ. . . . He is a true African in color." (New York Public Library, General Research and Reference Division, Schomburg Center for Research in Black Culture; Astor, Lenox, and Tilden Foundations.)

CRUMMELL, ALEXANDER (b. 3 March 1819; d. 19 September 1898), clergyman, educator, and Pan-Africanist. Alexander Crummell was born in New York City, the son of Boston Crummell, said to have been an African prince, and a free mother (whose name is unknown). Crummell, one of the most prominent black nationalist intellectuals and ministers of the nineteenth century, strongly believed that the combination of Christianity and education would elevate blacks in America and Africa to a high level of civilization and prominence as a race. As a youth, Crummell came under the influence of the Reverend Peter Williams Jr., a staunch supporter of back-to-Africa movements. Prior to the Civil War, Crummell was a major supporter of African colonization. Ironically, however, his earliest success as an orator was as an opponent of the American Colonization Society.

Crummell spent the years 1853 to 1872 in Liberia with his family and became a citizen of the country. Upon his arrival there, he worked as a missionary of the Protestant Episcopal Church of America and established a number of churches. He also served as a professor of English and moral science at the College of Liberia. During the Civil War he made three trips to the United States, where he petitioned for support for African colonization. Soon after the war's end he was named a commissioner by the Liberian government and given the responsibility of developing interest in emigration from the United States. Both Crummell and his close friend Edward Wilmot Blyden became major voices for Liberian nationalism.

Crummell was an outspoken and active black nationalist and Pan-Africanist. While he was in Liberia he envisioned the formation of a black Christian republic of freed slaves. However, owing to his disillusionment with political life and turmoil in Liberia, particularly an unfavorable reception of his black nationalist and Pan-African views by Liberian mulattoes and white missionaries, coupled with declining health, Crummell opted to leave Liberia in 1872 and return to the United States. Settling in Washington, D.C., he founded and pastored Saint Luke's Episcopal Church. His missionary activities in the nation's capital and regarding the African continent won him the characterization of "missionary at large." In keeping with this title, he continued to seek greater recognition for blacks within the polity and leadership of the Episcopal Church; for example, in 1883 he led the Conference of Church Workers among Colored People.

Crummell published three major works from the 1860s to the 1890s: *The Future of Africa* (1862), *The Greatness of Christ* (1882), and *Africa and America* (1892). From 1895 to 1897 he taught at Howard University. In 1897 he founded the American Negro Academy, one of the first African American think tanks. Its members ultimately included the prominent black intellectuals Alain L. Locke, Kelly Miller, and W. E. B. Du Bois. Crummell was also a mentor to many prominent African American intellectuals, including Du Bois, William Ferris, and John E. Bruce. In fact, Du Bois characterized Crummell as his "guru" and one of the greatest influences on his intellectual and moral development. Crummell made it his mission to transform the image of blacks in the minds of blacks and whites through admonishing them to embrace Christian redemption.

One of the first encounters between the abolitionist orator and former slave Frederick Douglass and Crummell occurred at the 1847 National Negro Convention, held in Troy, New York. The two worked together on developing the best approach to abolish slavery and caste in America. Crummell also was a staunch Pan-Africanist who believed in the redemption of Africa and a common heritage and destiny of all people of African heritage. Crummell's Pan-African beliefs transcended class and social place.

During the latter part of the nineteenth century, a crisis in black leadership emerged. Following the death of his close friend Henry Highland Garnet in Liberia in 1881, Crummell took it upon himself to rally African Americans around a common leadership. In attempting to garner more support for Douglass, Crummell made a plea for greater solidarity among African American leaders. Douglass's leadership had come into question because he remained loyal to the Republican Party at a time when younger African American leaders were growing disillusioned with the party over several issues, including its dwindling support for black civil rights. Crummell did not view his support of Douglass as motivated by his own career aspirations. Instead, he placed his personal stamp of approval on Douglass in the hope of fostering racial solidarity and solidifying black leadership around a common platform.

In 1885 Crummell delivered an address entitled "The Need of New Ideas and New Aims for a New Era" at Storer College. In it he called for blacks to refocus their thinking from a concentration on the legacy of slavery to ideas of service to the race in the present. Douglass, who was at the lecture, retorted that "a constant recollection of the slavery of their race and [its] wrongs" must always shape the history of black men in America. Douglass did not oppose Crummell's insistence on self-help but was adamant that black Americans should not shoulder the sole responsibility for their condition in the post–Civil War period. Douglass strongly believed that America owed black Americans a debt that in consequence could never be fully repaid. Despite America's unwillingness to acknowledge its debt, he believed that blacks should never forget the horrors of slavery and never stop fighting for freedom in their own country.

As the years progressed, the relationship between Douglass and Crummell became more cordial despite the fact that they never saw eye to eye on many issues. Douglass spoke admiringly of Crummell, and each man demonstrated a very high regard for the other. They differed on the issue of African American representation. Douglass supported individual rights of African Americans to transcend race, while Crummell insisted that blacks represented "a nation within a nation." Crummell encouraged economic solidarity among African Americans, while Douglass counseled against segregation of blacks socially and economically. In terms of policy perspectives, Douglass adopted more of a liberal stance and encouraged blacks to integrate more into American society. He also admonished black supporters of African colonization such as Crummell to come back to the United States and focus their energies on American abolitionism and civil rights.

The historian Wilson Moses asserts that Douglass's motives were primarily individualistic and demonstrated that his personal freedom was paramount. By contrast, Crummell assumed a double consciousness in his social philosophy concerning African Americans. Somewhat paradoxically, he emphasized racial pride and responsibility while also promoting ideas of individual achievement and personal responsibility with respect to his own life.

[See also American Colonization Society; Black Nationalism; Black Politics; Black Separatism; Black Uplift; Civil Rights; Colonization; Douglass, Frederick; Economic Life; Education; Emigration to Africa; Garnet, Henry Highland; Howard University; Liberia; National Conventions of Colored Men; Oratory and Verbal Arts; Republican Party; *and* Segregation.]

BIBLIOGRAPHY

Moses, Wilson Jeremiah. *Alexander Crummell: A Study of Civilization and Discontent.* Amherst: University of Massachusetts Press, 1992.

Oldfield, J. R. *Alexander Crummell (1819–1898) and the Creation of an African-American Church in Liberia.* Lewiston, NY: Edwin Mellen Press, 1990.

Rigsby, Gregory U. *Alexander Crummell: Pioneer in Nineteenth-Century Pan-African Thought.* Westport, CT: Greenwood Press, 1987.

Scruggs, Ottley M. "Two Black Patriarchs: Frederick Douglass and Alexander Crummell." *Afro-Americans in New York Life and History* 6, no. 1 (1982).

—ZACHERY R. WILLIAMS

CUFFE, PAUL (b. 17 January 1759; d. 7 September 1817), wealthy black sea captain and Pan-Africanist. Paul Cuffe was born as Paul Slocum on Cuttyhunk Island, Massachusetts, the seventh child of the freed African slave Kofi and the Wampanoag Indian woman Ruth Moses. A member of the West African Ashanti tribe, Kofi had been a slave for fifteen years before the wealthy and influential Quaker John Slocum freed him. In the 1740s, spurred by the preaching of the Quaker prophet John Woolman, the Society of Friends began to question the institution of slavery. Many Quakers throughout the Eastern Seaboard started freeing their slaves and organizing in opposition to the institution. Paul Cuffe's African heritage and his experiences with Friends would decisively shape his life.

In 1746 the freed Kofi took the name Cuffe Slocum and married Moses. They moved to Cuttyhunk, where Slocum became quite prosperous. By 1766 he had earned enough money to purchase 116 acres of farmland on the continent at Dartmouth, Massachusetts. Seven years later Slocum died; at that time Paul shipped out on a whaling vessel bound for the Gulf of Mexico.

For the next three years Paul Cuffe traveled throughout the Caribbean on whaling and cargo vessels, learning seamanship and navigation. In 1776, with the outbreak of the American Revolution, the British captured Cuffe then released him after three months. Two years later he joined his older brother David in a more dangerous venture: blockade running. The British navy had blockaded the Eastern Seaboard, cutting off supplies to Martha's Vineyard and Nantucket. At great risk to life and liberty Cuffe personally shipped supplies to these two islands throughout the war.

Exposure to Revolutionary ideals may have inspired Cuffe to challenge discrimination against blacks during the war. In 1777 he and his brother John protested taxation on their father's estate, arguing that they were denied

Paul Cuffe, in an engraving from a drawing by John Pole of Bristol, England. Cuffe was one of the richest African Americans of his day, owned a large farm, and built ships large enough to conduct international trade. (© New Bedford Whaling Museum.)

the right to vote and therefore ought not pay taxes. Three years later they joined with other free blacks throughout Massachusetts in opposing such "taxation without representation." Their complaints ultimately resulted in judicial decisions declaring the right of individual towns to grant suffrage to their residents.

At the war's end in 1783 Cuffe married Alice Pequit, a Wampanoag Indian, and began working closely with his sister Mary's husband, Michael Wainer. The two established themselves at the coastal town of New Bedford, associating with the powerful Quaker merchant family of William Rotch. Building their own boats, Cuffe and Wainer traded along the coast as far south as the Carolinas. In the 1790s their business brought them into contact with the growing southern slave economy. Such ventures southward were particularly dangerous for Cuffe and his free black sailors: the Fugitive Slave Law of 1793 made the capture and enslavement of any black suspected of being a runaway legal, with the future of the case entirely dependent upon the claims of the presumed slave owner. In Vienna, Maryland, in 1796 nervous townspeople detained Cuffe's ship for several weeks. By virtue of his connections with William Rotch, he and his sailors escaped without further incident; the experience very likely reinforced Cuffe's opposition to racial discrimination, and despite the risk of false enslavement he continued to trade along the Eastern Seaboard.

Cuffe's efforts soon brought him considerable wealth. By 1810 he was easily among the richest black men in the United States, with a fortune estimated at more than twenty-five thousand dollars. He owned a two-hundred-acre farm near Westport, Massachusetts, and built ships large enough to conduct international trade. In 1800 he constructed the 162-ton *Hero*; six years later he built a ship nearly twice as large, *Alpha*. Also in 1806 Cuffe built the 109-ton vessel that became his favorite, *Traveller*.

Cuffe's personal success did not diminish his commitment to the pursuit of racial equality. His commercial activities brought him into contact with abolitionists and social reformers such as Dr. Benjamin Rush, the black ministers Richard Allen and Absalom Jones, and the black businessman James Forten. Antislavery advocates on both sides of the Atlantic extolled Cuffe's virtues and offered his success as a rebuttal to arguments of black inferiority. His personal experience and the Quakers' strong opposition to slavery drew Cuffe into the Society of Friends; in 1808 he formally joined the Westport Monthly Meeting.

Soon after, perhaps inspired by Quaker ideas about service, Cuffe more fully committed himself to bettering the lives of African Americans in the United States. He came to believe that the development of Africa along Western lines would ultimately end the continent's dependence on the slave trade, thereby benefiting both Africans and African Americans. Fundamental to this development, he opined in his personal journals, would be the settlement of skilled free blacks from the United States as a model for the rest of Africa to follow. Learning of the efforts of British philanthropists to establish the colony for freed slaves known as Sierra Leone, Cuffe saw fit to raise support in the United States for the venture.

In 1811, having gathered the backing of notable Quakers and antislavery advocates for three years, Cuffe launched an expedition to the colony. Pleased by what he saw, he set about making settlement plans of his own. Colonial authorities in Sierra Leone, however, opposed Cuffe and forced him to seek support elsewhere, in London and in the United States. After spending three months at the colony, he traveled back to the United States and sought the assistance of the Madison administration. President James Madison, impressed by Cuffe's presentation, gave the venture his blessing.

The outbreak of the War of 1812 put Cuffe's plans on hold. For the next three years he continued to plan and obtain support for his scheme. Finally, in December 1815,

he returned to Sierra Leone to deposit a cargo of goods and thirty-eight free black pioneers. This proved to be Cuffe's last journey to the colony, as ill health prevented him from leading subsequent trips. He died in Westport, Massachusetts, less than two years later.

In many ways Cuffe's colonization effort prefigures the twentieth-century work of the black nationalist Marcus Garvey and the educator Booker T. Washington. Realizing the plight of black slaves in the United States as well as that of West Africans, Cuffe sought to alleviate the degradation of both. His colonial model recognized that pervasive racism in the United States prevented social equality for African Americans; yet that model also stressed the importance of self-help and industry in resuscitating black self-worth in both the United States and Africa. Although colonization was discredited after Cuffe's death—including by many who once supported him in it—his devotion to the idea reflected his commitment to the achievement of not only social equality but also a measure of dignity for African Americans.

[*See also* Allen, Richard; American Colonization Society; Black Seafarers; Civil Rights; Discrimination; Entrepreneurs; Forten, James; Fugitive Slave Law of 1793; Jones, Absalom; Laws and Legislation; Madison, James, and African Americans; Maritime Trades; Marriage, Mixed; Native Americans and African Americans; Society of Friends (Quakers) and African Americans; Voting Rights; *and* Woolman, John.]

BIBLIOGRAPHY

Harris, Sheldon H. *Paul Cuffe: Black America and the African Return*. New York: Simon and Schuster, 1972.

Murphy, Larry, J. Gordon Melton, and Gary L. Ward. *Encyclopedia of African American Religions*. New York: Garland, 1993.

Thomas, Lamont D. *Paul Cuffe: Black Entrepreneur and Pan-Africanist*. Urbana: University of Illinois Press, 1988.

Wiggins, Rosalind Cobb. *Captain Paul Cuffe's Logs and Letters, 1808–1817: A Black Quaker's "Voice from within the Veil."* Washington, DC: Howard University Press, 1996.

—SCOTT A. MILTENBERGER

CUGOANO, QUOBNA OTTOBAH (b. c. 1757; d. after 1791), slave, freedman, servant, author, and abolitionist. Cugoano, baptized John Stuart in England in 1773, seems to have been born in Fante territory (modern Ghana) around 1757 and seized by African slave traders around 1770. He was held as a slave briefly in the West Indies and then taken to England, where he gained his freedom by means not now known. In the 1780s he became a public opponent of the slave trade in general and West Indian slavery in particular, assisting individual blacks in England, publishing in newspapers, and objecting to plans to resettle London's black poor in West Africa. He noted, accurately as it turned out, that the settlers were at risk and that a colony in Sierra Leone would likely fail in its goal of undermining the slave trade in that region. The black poor suffered a high mortality rate in Sierra Leone, some survivors became slave traders themselves, and the settlement disintegrated, but despite these events the ideal of an African colony was revived in the early 1790s by North American blacks.

In 1787 Cugoano established himself as a major commentator on the Atlantic slave system—the African trade, the Middle Passage, and New World slavery—with a book called *Thoughts and Sentiments on the Evil and Wicked Traffic of the Slavery and Commerce of the Human Species*. *Thoughts* appealed to some members of the English intelligentsia. A shorter edition of 1791, subtitled *Addressed to the Sons of Africa, by a Native*, was the first book that identified black people as its primary audience. Nothing is known of Cugoano's later life.

Thoughts was notable for its aggressive critique of the slave system and its erudite use of biblical and historical material. Indeed, the book modeled the value of literacy and criticized Europeans' misuse of the skill—as when, for example, they used the Bible to legitimate the slaughter and subjugation of the New World's native peoples. Some details from Cugoano's Fante boyhood appeared in *Thoughts*, but most of the book deployed passages from scripture against the slave system. In a time in which the leading abolitionist arguments were based on Christian theology, Cugoano distinguished himself by a more searching use of the Bible than most of his contemporaries.

He shared an understanding of the Bible with other early abolitionists, both English and American. They presupposed a Calvinist hermeneutics, arguing that the slavery that seemed to be allowed in the Old Testament had been intended by God as a symbol of enslavement to sin and that only believers enlightened by New Testament faith could comprehend that human beings were never meant by God to be slaves. The slave system was thus rooted in an outmoded and mistaken understanding of the Old Testament. Cugoano's *Thoughts* excoriated both Islam and Roman Catholicism—the former because (in Cugoano's view) it maintained Old Testament traditions, including slavery, and the latter (in the Protestant polemics of the times) because it had corrupted Christianity.

Thoughts drew on Calvinist theology in another way that Cugoano shared with his abolitionist peers, namely, in the declaration that God worked providentially in the lives of believers. God's providence included predetermination of Christians' suffering and worldly dispossession as a means of purifying their faith and saving them. Cugoano saw himself as one such believer. His black contemporaries, such as Olaudah Equiano, James Albert Ukawsaw Gronniosaw, John Marrant, and Phillis Wheatley, all presented themselves as such exemplars. Another black peer, Lemuel Haynes, wrote little about his own life but did see God's providence at work in the lives of blacks in general.

One tool that Cugoano and other British abolitionists used against the slave trade and slavery was the English constitution—the unwritten summary of laws and court decisions in the national heritage. The eighteenth century saw such significant moves against slavery as the 1772 *Somerset* case, in which Lord Chief Justice Mansfield ruled that a master could not transport a slave from Britain to the colonies against the slave's will. British abolitionists argued that the constitution protected liberty and that Britons were abandoning their own revered legal tradition by tolerating slave traders and slaveholders among their compatriots, whether at home, on the seas, or in the colonies.

In the last quarter of the eighteenth century the Atlantic slave trade was, in fact, at its height, with Britons among the major slavers. As with scripture, the *Thoughts* included a vigorous statement of the antislavery implications of the English constitution. One of Cugoano's reservations about the Sierra Leone colony had been the likelihood that traditional English liberties would not be protected there. His proposals for the abolition of the slave system included national and international resolutions against enslavement, a gradual transition to freedom in the colonies (a maximum of seven years in indentured servitude for former slaves, a form of gradual emancipation), education for those passing from slavery to freedom along with Christian missions in the slave-trading areas of Africa, and prohibition of any further slave trading on the African coast. He envisioned that after the eradication of the slave system, West Indian blacks would be agricultural laborers or servants while West Africans would gradually accept Christianity and participate in a market economy involving trade with Europeans. This new economy was to be a legitimate trade replacing the illegitimate trade in slaves.

Cugoano's writings pose an obvious challenge to modern readers. Fante by birth and a defender of blacks' rights, Cugoano expressed no sense of racial identity apart from his affiliations with Christianity and England. His Calvinist approach to scriptural interpretation and the doctrine of divine providence, particularly the predetermination of suffering, were features of his world, not the modern one. The detailed arguments appealing to the English constitution that characterized the work of eighteenth-century abolitionists, including Cugoano, seem less relevant now than the universal consensus that all people are free and equal.

Cugoano's acceptance of gradual emancipation and servitude for freedmen and freedwomen may well offend modern sensibilities, as might his hostility to Islam and Roman Catholicism and his plan for a Euro-African market economy to supplant the slave system. Yet he never could have imagined attachment to racial identity or African nationalism as the modern world knows them. He certainly knew that an anti-Calvinist liberal religion (which would become typical of nineteenth-century black Christianity) existed, but little or nothing in it or in other religions dovetailed with his experience. He believed that he was obliged to craft religious and constitutional arguments for freedom, not to make emotional appeals to widespread feelings. If modern freedom emerged in part from the destruction of the Atlantic slave trade and New World slavery, Cugoano and his abolitionist peers were among the creators of the modern world even if they never entered it themselves.

[*See also* Abolitionism, Catholic Church and African Americans; Emancipation, Gradual; Equiano, Olaudah; Gronniosaw, James Albert Ukawsaw; Haynes, Lemuel; Literacy in the Colonial Period; Literature; Marrant, John; Muslims; Slave Trade *and* Wheatley, Phillis.]

BIBLIOGRAPHY

Braidwood, Stephen J. *Black Poor and White Philanthropists: London's Blacks and the Foundation of the Sierra Leone Settlement, 1786–1791*. Liverpool, U.K.: Liverpool University Press, 1994.

Carretta, Vincent, ed. *Quobna Ottobah Cugoano: Thoughts and Sentiments on the Evil of Slavery and Other Writings*. New York: Penguin Books, 1999.

—JOHN SAILLANT

D

DANCE. [*This entry contains two subentries dealing with dance from the early eighteenth century through the end of the nineteenth century. The first article discusses the transmission of African dance traditions to North America by slaves and the new expressions that arose, while the second article discusses the movement of African American dance from the plantation to the stage and its influence on all American dance.*]

The First Expressions of African American Dance

African American dance has a rich tradition stemming from West Africa, where people danced for religious and secular reasons. Numerous Europeans described how West Africans danced in rings, clapping their hands and stomping their feet while drums or gourds pulsated a strong beat. Africans retained their cultural dancing practices during the Middle Passage—their transport from Africa to North and South America—but had to modify them under the extreme circumstances. Captains often brought slaves above deck for fresh air and exercise. Bondservants who had some form of exercise fetched higher prices because they were a bit healthier and more fit for work. The white crew also drew amusement from watching slaves dance, which they did only when threatened with the lash. Without their traditional musical instruments, slaves improvised by rattling their chains or thumping on upturned buckets and tubs, perhaps accompanied by the lively jig of a sailor playing the fiddle.

Slave dance on mainland North America at first underwent scant modification from its West African beginnings. Africans in America re-created as many of their musical instruments as possible, and the drum was the most popular accompaniment to dances. White authorities began to prohibit slave gatherings and the use of drums after the 1739 Stono Rebellion, when more than 150 South Carolina slaves seized guns, murdered several white planters, and marched toward Spanish Florida before being attacked and defeated. The Stono slaves had marched to the sound of drums, and masters feared that other slaves would use drums to signal insurrection and communicate subversive ideas. Drums survived, but slaves looked elsewhere for instruments that could accompany a dance. They used tambourines, washtubs, banjos, and fiddles to accompany their dances. Individual dancers also created their own rhythm and syncopation by dancing on boards placed on barrels or stones while wearing hard-soled shoes, hobnailed boots, hollow-heeled shoes, or clogs. This type of dance evolved into what we know today as tap dancing.

Once slaves dispersed in North America, they became familiar with European dance practices. The type of dance practiced in slave quarters fused European and African practices. The African American style stressed movement in the hips, a relaxed spine, a flexible torso, and gliding, dragging, or shuffling steps. The European style was different, favoring precision footwork in a complicated bounding or hopping pattern, an erect spine, and almost no hip movement. Slaves fused these two great traditions into a variety of secular and sacred dances.

Most slave dances took place on plantations. Despite the exhausting monotony of working six days a week, slaves found new energy to celebrate with dances on Saturday nights. These festivals might include slaves from other plantations, a real treat for bondservants. Dance contests served as a way to share important information from the world outside the plantation or became venues to meet eligible marriage partners. Dance, along with activities such as slave religious services and spontaneous gatherings, was also a precious way to retain individuality and personal dignity under the crushing weight of slavery. Slaves could take pride in their own accomplishments—skill at dancing or playing the fiddle rather than having to work for the master.

The ring shout, with origins in West African dance, is probably the most famous African American dance pattern. It combined dance and song in a creative expression of slave culture. The ring shout was a sacred dance that had secular overtones and remained popular in areas of the South until the 1950s. Although this dance took many different forms, it was an important building block for African American cultural identity. In a common version of the shout, slaves moved in a counterclockwise circle, shuffling their feet while clapping their hands. They also "hamboned," or rhythmically slapped their thighs, arms, or torso, using their bodies as drums. The circle gained

"An Old-Fashioned Negro Dance," wood engraving from James Buel's *Metropolitan Life Unveiled, or the Mysteries and Miseries of America's Great Cities*. Although the book dates from 1882–1883, this illustration evidently harks back to a considerably earlier time. (Library of Congress.)

velocity and volume as the dance wore on. In areas with a large number of African-born slaves, the dancers moved in rings by nationality, and white observers were shocked at the tattoos and scarification on the slaves' bodies. Many types of instruments were found at a ring shout, with some variation of African drums being most common.

New Orleans became closely associated with the ring shout, so much so that a weekly dance was held where hundreds of slaves participated. The dance took place in a large, open area known first as the Place Publique, then Circus Square, and then Congo Square. Slaves who did not dance sold the products of their gardens, traded information, or merely enjoyed the atmosphere. There are some accounts that mention voodoo practices associated with the ring shouts in Congo Square, but it appears that most of the activity was secular rather than sacred. Eventually, city authorities banned the ring shout in the 1830s for fear that it would incite slaves to rebel, but public ring shouts resumed in 1845.

Similar to the ring shout is the juba, a dance known as the *djouba* in West Africa. This dance, too, incorporated numerous variations but was mainly a competitive dance of skill. One slave would start the dance, with the others in a circle around him. As in the ring shout, the dancer and others would use their bodies as drums to set the dance rhythm. This was sometimes called "patting juba." Once the dancer had sufficient time to display his prowess, a number of women would join in, and the main dance would be taken up by another member of the circle. The juba dance also involved singing, the most common words being: "Juba this and juba that, juba killed a yellow cat."

Slaves performed such dances as the buck, pigeon wing, or jig on a variety of occasions. African Americans copied pigeons by flapping their arms, kicking their feet, and holding their heads stiff. Others danced the buck dance on a large platform during plantation barbecues. The most athletic and skilled dancers engaged in impromptu contests to determine who was the best dancer. Slave owners might also arrange dance contests, in which they entered their own slaves in the hope of winning prize money.

The cakewalk was originally one such contest. This dance often took place to celebrate the end of the harvest. The cakewalk eventually became a contest where slaves walked a course with a pail of water on their heads. Those who spilled the least amount of water won the prize cake. This dance has survived in many forms to this day. Other water dances were popular, including ones where slaves danced with water glasses on their heads. Only the most athletic and talented dancers could move their feet, legs, and hips while keeping their heads stationary. Some historians believe that this type of contest has its origins in West Africa, where it was common to carry all manner of objects, including water pots, on the head.

All these dances accompanied special occasions, such as Christmas, corn shucking, weddings, and funerals, and special dances also abounded. Many white owners gathered in the slave quarters to present Christmas "gifts," normally the slave's set of clothes, shoes, and blankets for the year. Slaves were expected to dance during such events, partly as an expression of thanksgiving. After a burial service, especially in the Sea Islands of Georgia, some slaves danced around the grave to keep away evil influences and to aid the deceased in his or her transition to the next world.

Slaves danced during other difficult times. White observers often commented that slaves danced either at public auction or while being held in a slave trader's holding pen. At these times, slaves rarely danced as an expression of spontaneous joy but were forced to dance for a purpose, much as their ancestors had done on the decks of slave ships. A dance at a slave auction, often performed on the block itself, was a measure of athletic ability and youthful vigor. It might also have been meant to send a message of contentment with enslavement. Bondservants who were forced to dance in a slave pen usually did so under threat of punishment. Dance was also a way to exercise and maintain health or amuse the jailer.

Northern slaves danced as well, although there is less information about their activities. Slaves in lower Manhattan in the early 1700s gathered together to sell products and then dance in the Catherine Market. The slaves usually brought wooden planks upon which they danced for audiences who paid to see the performance. New York slaves were known to dance on Pinkster, or Pentecost. James Fenimore Cooper, the well-known American novelist, saw a Pinkster dance in 1757. He described hundreds of slaves playing banjos, singing songs, and dancing to drums made of hollow logs.

"Equality Ball," given to the Negroes of Boston by Governor Hancock, 1793. This engraving, in *The Echo, with Other Poems* (1807, a collection of the works of the "Hartford wits"), illustrated satirical verses about the event. Hancock, at left, is being greeted by a dancer called Cuffey; another white man is shown holding his nose—the poet having stressed the "fragrant air" in the ballroom. (Library of Congress.)

[*See also* Africanisms; Cemeteries and Burials; Festivals; Identity; Music; Pinkster; Riots and Rebellions; *and* Stono Rebellion.]

BIBLIOGRAPHY
Emery, Lynne Fauley. *Black Dance from 1619 to Today.* 2nd ed. Princeton, NJ: Princeton Book Company, 1988.
Gomez, Michael A. *Exchanging Our Country Marks: The Transformation of African Identities in the Colonial and Antebellum South.* Chapel Hill: University of North Carolina Press, 1998.
Haskins, James. *Black Dance in America: A History through Its People.* New York: T. Y. Crowell, 1990.

—ROBERT H. GUDMESTAD

African American Dance through the 1890s

During the eighteenth century the dancing of enslaved people developed its own particular character. In the nineteenth century African American dance became a crucial part of the development of dance in America. Moving from the plantation to the stage, it began to influence all forms of popular American dance.

Plantation Dance. Records of the earliest examples of black dance in this country are rare and seldom detailed, but they confirm what we can surmise from surviving dances: The African dance forms that enslaved people brought with them to America gradually took on some of the flavor of a variety of European dances and music, resulting in the creation of a new kind of dance.

There are a few descriptions, written by white spectators, of slave festivals in Manhattan and Albany, New York, during the mid-1600s and into the 1700s. The festivals drew hundreds of black women and men who danced and sang almost continuously, while crowds of white spectators watched and applauded. At these festivals, the singing, dancing, and music making were largely African in nature.

In New Orleans during the early 1800s enslaved women and men gathered each Sunday and on church holy days at a place called Congo Square. The architect Benjamin Latrobe watched these dancers and in 1819 wrote at some length about them in his journal. According to his report the dancing began at about three o'clock in the afternoon and went on until nine o'clock at night. A number of groups, or "tribes," took part, each claiming a section of the square for its own. Each group had its own band, with both male and female musicians who played banjos, drums, and rattles. The groups danced in circular patterns, moving to the music and marking time with their feet. It has long been believed that these dances continued in Congo Square until about 1885, but current research indicates that they may have stopped in about 1870.

In some situations, instead of using instruments—or in addition—the dancers "patted juba" (or juber). This involved tapping the feet to keep a strong rhythm and enhancing that rhythm by clapping hands and slapping thighs. One person, the "juba rhymer," improvised lyrics that were spoken, not sung. On one plantation in Maryland the main juba rhymer was a young woman named Clotilda. In *The Old Plantation, and What I Gathered There in an Autumn Month,* written by James Hungerford and published in 1859, some of Clotilda's juba song lyrics survive. As in square dancing the words dictated the dancers' steps. At the same time they poked fun at people in the community. Hungerford's notes indicate that the people answered back, responding to Clotilda's impudence.

Most of the dancing among slaves was not on view to whites, of course, and most of the dancers were not able to write about it. Fortunately, the oral histories gathered by the Federal Writers' Project in the 1930s preserved the memories of some former slaves. "There was a girl named Cora from over to the Herndon place," Martha Haskins recalled. "Slaves sure would hoop and holler when Cora got to stepping. Gal was graceful as a lily—bend her arms and elbows to the music just as pretty as a picture. Long, tall, slim gal she was and when she 'cut the corner,' tossing her head and rolling her eyes, everybody knowed she was the best."

Other knowledge about early black dance has been gathered by folklorists who found black Americans doing a number of traditional dances well into the twentieth century. The music archivists John and Alan Lomax, for example, attended ring shouts—sacred communal circle dances incorporating singing and percussion—in Louisiana, Texas, and Georgia in the 1930s.

Minstrelsy. By the early nineteenth century the songs and dances of the plantation had made their way to the streets of southern cities. In New Orleans a white performer named Thomas Dartmouth "Daddy" Rice saw the plantation dances and became intrigued. He began to perform black dances onstage at the Park Theatre, where he did short skits between the acts. While doing the dances he wore blackface and affected exaggeratedly "black" speech and movement. Because of the quality and novelty of his material, he became one of the most popular entertainers in the country. Soon many other white entertainers imitated Rice imitating African Americans, and the minstrel show was born. Black dance was now onstage—but black dancers were not, with a few notable exceptions.

William Henry Lane was born in 1825 into a free family in Mississippi. By the time he was a teenager he lived in the notorious Five Points neighborhood of New York City. There he met "Uncle" Jim Lowe, a black dancer who entertained in the mixed-race saloons of the district. Lowe taught Lane the jigs and reels that he specialized in and encouraged the young man to become a buck-and-wing dancer. Lane developed his own style, adding African steps to the jig steps and introducing syncopation and improvisation. Throughout the 1840s he was well known by the name Juba, touring New York, New England, and even London. He was challenged by the Irish step dancer Jack Diamond to a number of competitions and, depending on the account, either defeated Diamond or left an inconclusive series declaring himself the winner. He was one of the first black dancers to tour as a soloist with white dancers.

Lane has been credited with inventing tap dancing and has been called the single most influential dancer of nineteenth-century America. He was probably the dancer described by Charles Dickens in this account in *American Notes for General Circulation*:

> Single shuffle, double shuffle, cut and cross-cut; snapping his fingers, rolling his eyes, turning in his knees, presenting the backs of his legs in front, spinning about on his toes and heels like nothing but the man's fingers on the tambourine; dancing with two left legs, two right legs, two wooden legs, two wire legs, two spring legs—all sorts of legs and no legs—what is this to him? (p. 104)

Other black dancers reached mainstream stages after the Civil War. Like hundreds of white performers, they did minstrel shows, which were the most popular form of entertainment in the country for most of the nineteenth century. So strong was the tradition of minstrelsy that many of the black performers themselves wore blackface, and all enacted the stereotypical depiction of black people that was demanded by the minstrel show audience. It was an appalling price to pay for the chance to perform, as the stereotypes were mean and degrading portrayals that fed the racist attitudes of the time. Yet there were remarkable dancers among the black men of the minstrel stage. (Female characters existed in the shows but were performed by men.) Early stars included Billy Kersands, Sam Lucas, and Tom Fletcher.

Even though minstrelsy was greatly to blame for a degraded image of African Americans, it served to preserve

Cakewalk, shown in a lithograph poster of c. 1897 for an African American minstrel troupe. (Library of Congress.)

a number of plantation dances, such as the walk-around, the Virginia Essence—precursor to the soft shoe—and the cakewalk.

From the Cakewalk to Tap. The cakewalk has a special significance in the history of American dance because it was the first social dance to become a fad in both black and white communities. Its emergence in the 1880s and 1890s set a pattern that would be followed by dozens of other dances in the century to come, and these African American social dances were later at the core of much modern dance choreography.

Originally a parody of formal European dances executed through African dance steps, the cakewalk took the form of a circle of couples with their arms linked at the elbows; the couples alternated short hopping steps with high kicking steps. Inside the circle, dancing couples took turns showing off their steps, vying for recognition as the best dancers—and sometimes for the reward of a cake.

The dancer and choreographer Ada Overton Walker was largely responsible for the immense popularity of the cakewalk. She performed the dance brilliantly herself in

Ada Overton Walker, photographed c. 1895. Walker, who contributed significantly to making the cakewalk popular, gave this dance a new dignity. (New York Public Library, Schomburg Center for Research in Black Culture.)

productions arranged by her husband George Walker and his partner, Bert Williams. She also taught the cakewalk to white New York society, refining the dance, eliminating all traces of vulgarity and buffoonery, and giving it a new dignity to go along with its joy and vitality.

The black musical shows of the 1890s brought other developments in black dance, chief of which was the appearance of women onstage. In addition to Walker, who was certainly the first great star among African American women dancers, there were hundreds of "chorus girls." Individually, most of them are forgotten, but they were a crucial element in the transition from minstrelsy to modern musical comedy. The chorus provided black women—including Florence Mills and Josephine Baker—with the opportunities to perform and to perfect their dancing skills that black men had found in the minstrel show.

By the end of the nineteenth century tap was a well-developed and popular form of dance, as was the soft shoe. Indeed, vaudeville stages were dominated by these outgrowths of black dance, and soon the dance halls of the country would fill with both black and white Americans dancing the fox trot, the Charleston, and the black bottom. It would take another century, however, before the significance of these dance forms and their origins would be recognized.

[*See also* Minstrel Shows; Music; Racism; Stereotypes of African Americans; *and* Women.]

BIBLIOGRAPHY

DeFrantz, Thomas F., ed. *Dancing Many Drums: Excavations in African American Dance.* Madison: University of Wisconsin Press, 2002.

Dickens, Charles. *American Notes for General Circulation.* New York: Harper and Brothers, 1842.

Emery, Lynne Fauley. *Black Dance: From 1619 to Today.* 2nd rev. ed. Princeton, NJ: Princeton Book, 1988.

Harnan, Terry. *African Rhythm—American Dance: A Biography of Katherine Dunham.* New York: Knopf, 1974.

Hine, Darlene Clark, and Kathleen Thompson. *A Shining Thread of Hope: The History of Black Women in America.* New York: Broadway Books, 1998.

Perdue, Charles L., Jr., Thomas E. Barden, and Robert K. Phillips, eds. *Weevils in the Wheat: Interviews with Virginia Ex-Slaves.* Charlottesville: University Press of Virginia, 1976.

Southern, Eileen. *The Music of Black Americans: A History.* New York: Norton, 1971.

—KATHLEEN THOMPSON

DAVID WALKER'S APPEAL. In the fall of 1829 David Walker wrote *Appeal to the Coloured Citizens of the World.* Walker circulated this scathing pamphlet throughout the South in late 1829 and 1830, especially in the coastal regions. Relying on his knowledge of the covert communication networks of African Americans in the South,

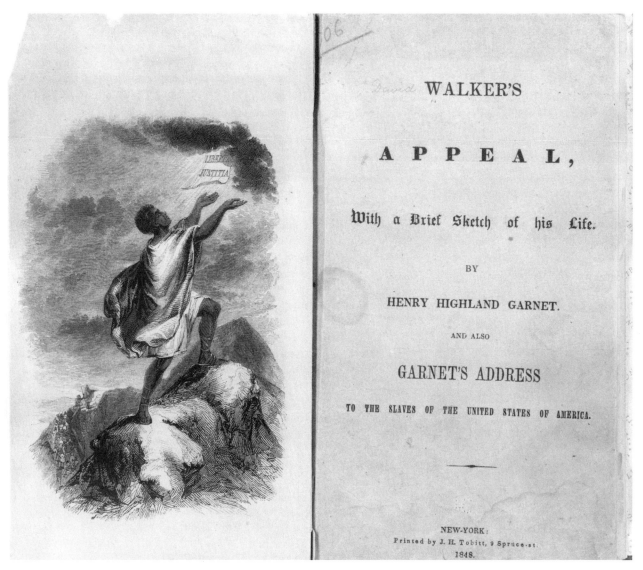

Walker's *Appeal*, frontispiece—with the words "Libertas justitia" appearing in the sky—and title page of an edition published in 1848. Garnet (1815–1882), who provided a short biography and whose own militant "Address" is also included, was a notable African American clergyman and abolitionist. (Library of Congress.)

among whom he had spent his youth, Walker tapped the energies of mariners, runaways, itinerants, preachers, settled free blacks, and slaves to craft a strategy of distribution remarkable for its geographical reach. He aspired to place his pamphlet in the hands of people who shared his convictions and would disseminate its words broadly.

From its opening sentences, Walker's *Appeal* indicted American slavery and all its deepest assumptions of black racial inferiority:

> We Coloured People of these United States, are, the most wretched, degraded and abject set of beings that ever lived since the world began, down to the present day, and, that, the white Christians of America, who hold us in slavery, (or, more properly speaking, pretenders to Christianity,) treat us more cruel and barbarous than any Heathen nation did any people whom it had subjected. (p. 2)

Walker feared that racial prejudice had so pervaded American society by the late 1820s that African Americans, North and South, were becoming overwhelmed by its insidious principles and were coming to accept the degraded station assigned to them exclusively by the mass of white Americans. He encapsulated the force of these principles by highlighting one of the nation's most eminent proponents of them, Thomas Jefferson, who had expounded in the 1780s that "blacks, whether originally a distinct race, or made distinct by time and circumstances, are inferior to the whites in the endowments both of body and mind." Walker grimly challenged his black audience: "Unless we try to refute Mr. Jefferson's arguments respecting us, we will only establish them."

Walker envisioned the *Appeal* as a bold antidote to all such malignant formulations. In the pamphlet he testified to blacks' physical and psychological suffering and to his great fear that they might acquiesce to their relentless overlords. Yet he also heralded their rich and noble heritage as a people of African descent and their ample capacity to surmount their afflictions as a race particularly beloved by God. The *Appeal* is infused with an evangelical summons to all African Americans to submit only to God, who abominated their enslavement and degradation and called to them to destroy those great evils once and for all. Remember, Walker proclaimed, "that your full glory and happiness, as well as all other coloured people under Heaven, shall never be fully consummated, but with the entire emancipation of your enslaved brethren all over the world." The widespread trumpeting of the *Appeal* would be a prime instrument in advancing that divine mission.

The pamphlet first surfaced in Savannah, Georgia, in December 1829, where a white ship steward delivered sixty copies to a prominent local black Baptist preacher, Henry Cunningham, who promptly carried all of them to the local police. In Milledgeville, Georgia, Walker sent twenty requested copies to a local white newspaper editor, Elijah Burritt, who then passed a few on to friends. In early 1830 in Richmond, Virginia, a free black courier introduced at least ten copies into the black population, and later, in Charleston, South Carolina, a white mariner gave at least seven copies to black stevedores. Four blacks were arrested for circulating numerous copies in New Orleans in March 1830. Two of them were slaves, and two were free blacks, including a successful local shopkeeper named Robert Smith.

Walker's efforts were particularly successful in his native North Carolina. Sometime in early August 1830 Wilmington authorities were alerted that the pamphlet was circulating in the town. An investigation soon determined that Jacob Cowan, a local slave, had received two hundred copies from Walker with instructions to distribute them throughout the state. Cowan's owner had allowed him to keep a tavern of sorts in town, which he used as a center for distribution. A local black Baptist preacher and cooper named John Spaulding had a copy of the book, and he loaned it to others, whom whites observed reading it. Soon alarmed, whites aggressively investigated the matter. Spaulding was promptly transported to New York in chains, and Jacob Cowan was sold deep into Alabama.

Cowan and others in Wilmington must have had connections with local runaways, for evidence exists that runaways from settled encampments near the town were in part responsible for carrying the book to other areas of North Carolina. In early November 1830 the wife of a jailer in coastal New Bern overheard a captured runaway, Moses, describe an extensive network of slaves and runaways who were conspiring throughout eastern North Carolina. One branch of this system connected with Wilmington through "a fellow named Derry" who had "brought some of those pamphlets" to New Bern and possibly as far north as Elizabeth City. The men stated that a number of captains had been selected and that runners or messengers "carried word" between Wilmington, New Bern, and Elizabeth City, and reported any doings to the captains.

Runaways proliferated in this swampy and forested region and had plagued authorities and slaveholders for decades. Conspirators were known to congregate at retreats near New Bern that were familiar to all runaways in the district. Advertisements for their apprehension attest to their regular movement between such towns as Wilmington, Fayetteville, and New Bern and their hinterlands and usually with the assistance of their fellow slaves, especially those working the region's innumerable rivers and tributaries.

Many of these runaways had attempted escape more than once, were deeply disaffected with slavery, and found it extremely difficult to manufacture even a veneer of submission to it. They were very familiar with the underground world of runaways and with the network binding them together throughout coastal North Carolina. One of them, Tom Abner, was a skilled artisan who may also have been literate and able to read the *Appeal* to others. The existence of this handful of literate African Americans in the state who were also very rebellious was vital to the dissemination of the pamphlet and its message. Very possibly Abner's exposure to the *Appeal* transformed him from a mere irritant to local slaveholders into a committed ideologue who sought to organize a cadre of similarly motivated runaways to threaten the institution of slavery regionally. Runaways in 1830 found boldness in their numbers and security and mobility in the numerous and interconnected refuges that ran throughout southeastern and coastal North Carolina.

As the holidays approached in December 1830, with the accompanying relaxation of regulations, apprehension mounted in New Bern and the central coastal area. A white Quaker was discovered preaching to a group of blacks in language similar to Walker's. A slave who claimed to be from South Carolina but had a suspicious pass was arrested in New Bern in late 1830 after he made it appear necessary for him to be traveling around Christmas, the time when slaves had the greatest latitude and he could best communicate to them his business. According to newspaper reports on or about 25 December 1830, sixty armed slaves had assembled in a swamp near New Bern and had selected Christmas morning as the time to commence a rebellion. The local militia, however, were alerted, surrounded the swamp, and killed the whole party.

Disturbances also ensued in the Wilmington region, where it was reported that "there has been much shooting of negroes in this neighborhood recently, in consequence of symptoms of liberty having been discovered among them." James Barbadoes, a friend of Walker's in Boston, repeated in the *Liberator* in February 1831 that sixty slaves had been killed in New Bern on the past Christmas and that it was "owing to Walker's inflammatory pamphlet." Employing a variety of individuals and avenues, Walker's innovative strategy illuminated how informal, yet surprisingly effective channels of communication had grown among southern slaves as their numbers and dispersion and mobility extended in the early nineteenth century and as African Americans became more fired with the democratic idealism then sweeping the Atlantic world.

Walker's *Appeal* never did ignite a major social conflagration. It did, however, strike real terror in authorities throughout the coastal South and spurred them to reinforce laws against slave literacy and the circulation of any inflammatory literature. Laws newly written in Wilmington and Savannah—modeled after one passed in Columbia, South Carolina, in 1822 after the failed conspiracy led by Denmark Vesey—required that any free black mariners from the North entering either of these southeastern ports be confined to jails during the term of their ship's presence there. This measure, local authorities hoped, would eliminate contact and exchanges between northern free blacks and local African Americans.

Southern authorities were rightly concerned about the ability of Walker to place his pamphlet in the hands of those who were knowledgeable about the numerous covert communication systems existing among southern slaves. They knew all too well that southern blacks had used similar networks effectively during the Vesey conspiracy as well as the conspiracy led by the slave Gabriel in Virginia. However, Walker expanded on these local and regional applications and used the structures throughout the coastal South to deliver his message of black strength, dignity, freedom, and Christian mission to as many slaves as possible. He envisioned a plan of black empowerment and mobilization that was the most sophisticated and extensive articulated in antebellum America. Walker's influence reverberated throughout the United States and beyond. Some contemporaries even speculated that the evangelical *Appeal* helped spur Nat Turner to his bloody judgments in Southampton County, Virginia, in August 1831.

[*See also* Abolitionism; Africa, Idea of; African Diaspora; Artisans; Baptists and African Americans; Black Church; Black Seafarers; Civil Rights; Declaration of Independence; Denmark Vesey Conspiracy; Discrimination; Free African Americans to 1828; Fugitive Slaves; Gabriel; Gabriel Conspiracy; Identity; Jefferson, Thomas, on African Americans and Slavery; Laws and Legislation; Literacy in the Colonial Period; Literature; Maritime Trades; Race, Theories of; Religion; Resistance; Riots and Rebellions; Slave Rebellions and Insurrections; Slavery: Lower South; Slavery: Mid-Atlantic; Slavery: Upper South; Society of Friends (Quakers) and African Americans; Spirituality; Vesey, Denmark; Violence against African Americans; *and* Walker, David.]

BIBLIOGRAPHY

Eaton, Clement. "A Dangerous Pamphlet in the Old South." *Journal of Southern History* 2 (August 1936): 323–334.

Hinks, Peter P. *To Awaken My Afflicted Brethren: David Walker and the Problem of Antebellum Slave Resistance.* University Park: Pennsylvania State University Press, 1997.

Talmadge, John E. "The Burritt Mystery: Partisan Journalism in Antebellum Georgia." *Georgia Review* 8 (Fall 1954): 332–341.

Walker, David. *David Walker's Appeal to the Coloured Citizens of the World.* Edited with a new introduction by Peter P. Hinks. University Park: Pennsylvania State University Press, 2000.

—PETER HINKS

DECLARATION OF INDEPENDENCE.

In 1776 Congress appointed a committee to draft a statement declaring American independence. The chief draftsman was Thomas Jefferson, a young Virginian, who at the time owned about 150 slaves. The Declaration's preamble contains a clarion call for fundamental equality. This credo of American life provides the basis for subsequent claims to liberty and equality for African Americans from the late eighteenth century to the twenty-first century. The Declaration is also connected to the African American experience because of provisions related to slavery in the final document—as well as a famous provision that was deleted from it.

The most obvious connection between slavery and the Declaration is in the preamble's assertion "We hold these Truths to be self-evident, that all Men are created equal, that they are endowed by their Creator with certain unalienable Rights, that among these are Life, Liberty, and the Pursuit of Happiness." These sentiments undermined the morality of slavery and its legitimacy under natural law; they would later also be used to undermine segregation. From David Walker to the Reverend Martin Luther King Jr., African American activists have quoted the Declaration in their assaults on slavery, segregation, and discrimination. Antebellum opponents of slavery as diverse as William Lloyd Garrison, Frederick Douglass, and Abraham Lincoln relied on this language to bolster their opposition to human bondage. In dedicating the nation to the dismantling of slavery and to a "new birth of freedom," Lincoln harked back to the Declaration, which "brought forth . . . a new nation, conceived in Liberty and dedicated to the proposition that all men are created equal." David Walker ended his *Appeal to the Coloured Citizens of the World* (1829) by demanding of white Americans, "See your Declaration," and asking "Do you understand your own language?" Indeed, after quoting the preamble he asked white Americans to "compare your own language . . . from your Declaration of Independence, with your cruelties and murders inflicted by your cruel and unmerciful fathers and yourselves on our fathers and on us . . . men who have never given your fathers or you the least provocation!"

In his famous speech "What to the Slave Is the Fourth of July?" Frederick Douglass agreed that "the Declaration of Independence is the ring-bolt to the chain of your nation's destiny" and that the "principles contained in that instrument are saving principles." He urged white abolitionists to "stand by those principles, be true to them on all occasions, in all places, against all foes, and at whatever cost." But he could not embrace the Declaration. He rhetorically asked,

> What have I, or those I represent, to do with your national independence? Are the great principles of political freedom and of natural justice, embodied in that Declaration of Independence, extended to us? and am I, therefore, called upon to bring our humble offering to the national altar, and to confess the benefits and express devout gratitude for the blessings resulting from your independence to us? (Blassingame, vol. 2, p. 367)

Thus, for Douglass the Declaration remained a broken promise, a goal unmet, and a lie when presented to African Americans. A century later the Reverend Martin Luther King Jr. asked Americans "whether they believe that the framers of the Declaration of Independence intended that liberty should be divided into installments, doled out on a deferred-payment plan."

While the Declaration generally remained only of theoretical value to most slaves, some white Americans took such documents more seriously. The Massachusetts Constitution of 1780 also declared that all men were born free and equal, and the state's courts eventually interpreted this clause to have ended slavery. The preamble to Pennsylvania's 1780 gradual abolition act ended with a reference to the Declaration and the American Revolution, noting that slavery was ended in the new state "in grateful commemoration of our own happy deliverance from that state of unconditional submission, to which we were doomed by the tyranny of Britain." In the years after the Revolution many people, such as Jefferson's neighbor Edward Coles, freed their slaves because they took seriously the language and ideology embodied in the Declaration itself.

In its main body the Declaration dealt with slavery indirectly and in a way that is inconsistent with the assertions of equality and liberty in the preamble. Before turning to the Declaration itself, however, it is instructive to examine a clause on slavery that Thomas Jefferson proposed but that was left out of the final document. This clause has often been misunderstood as an attack on slavery itself or even as a call for abolition; in fact, it is neither. In his original draft Jefferson complained that the King had "waged cruel war against human nature itself, violating its most sacred rights of life and liberty" by perpetuating the African slave trade. Calling the African trade "piratical warfare," Jefferson complained that "a CHRISTIAN king of Great Britain" was so "determined to keep open a market where MEN" were bought and sold that he suppressed "every legislative attempt to prohibit or to restrain this execrable commerce." While condemning the King for supporting the African trade, Jefferson also denounced him for encouraging slaves to enlist in the British army:

> exciting those very people to rise in arms among us, and to purchase that liberty of which he has deprived them, by murdering the people on whom he also obtruded them: thus paying off former crimes committed against the LIBERTIES of one people, with crimes which he urges to commit against the LIVES of another. (Jefferson, pp. 25–26)

The background of this paragraph was Virginia's attempt to stop the African slave trade before the Revolution. The Virginia legislature had, in fact, passed laws to end the trade, but the King had vetoed them. The Virginia law was not antislavery; the legislature simply wanted to regulate the number of slaves entering the state for economic and prudential reasons. New slaves were a drain on the colony's economy, sending valuable resources to England, which financed most slave-trading operations. In addition, Virginians were beginning to feel they had a surplus of slaves. A temporary end to the trade would raise the value of existing slaves in the colony. Finally, freshly imported slaves were more likely to revolt than those born in the colonies. Thus, reducing the number of new slaves was a prudent move.

Although this "vehement philippic against negro slavery," as John Adams called it, never made it into the final version of the Declaration, it has made it into the public mind as proof of Thomas Jefferson's opposition to slavery. But Adams's characterization of the clause is misleading. Congress deleted this clause for a variety of reasons, including the complaints of Georgia and South Carolina, still active participants in the transatlantic trade. Yet, even without the specific complaints of those states, "the charge," as Jefferson's biographer Merrill Peterson suggests, "simply did not ring true." More to the point, Jefferson was attacking the African slave trade, not slavery itself. The arguments against the African trade were humanitarian but also, again, economic and prudential.

Jefferson certainly fit into the slaveholding class of Virginians. Because he sold human chattel throughout his life, the African trade threatened him economically by undermining the value of his surplus slaves. Similarly, Jefferson always argued for curbs on the growth of America's black population. He almost always tied any discussion of manumission or emancipation to colonization or "expatriation." Ending the African trade would slow the growth of the nation's black population. Thus, the attack on the King dovetailed with Jefferson's negrophobia and his interests as a Virginia slave owner and did not necessarily indicate opposition to slavery itself.

The final Declaration did contain one clause that directly related to slavery; in his very last charge against King George III, Jefferson raised the issue of the institution—the only such mention incorporated into the final document, which is rarely discussed by either biographers of Jefferson or historians of the Declaration. There, Jefferson complains that the King "has excited domestic insurrections against us." For southern slave owners "domestic insurrections" had only one unmistakable meaning: slave revolts. In fact, this clause was a direct reference to Lord Dunmore's proclamation. As the royal governor of Virginia, Dunmore had offered freedom to any slaves who would fight for the British cause—the "domestic insurrection" Jefferson condemned and feared. Ironically, in his original draft of the Declaration, Jefferson complained that the King had enslaved people "against human nature itself," but in the final document he condemned the King for enabling those people to fight for their freedom. Also, Jefferson failed to consider the irony of Americans rebelling against the King while complaining that slaves were rebelling against Americans.

This irony, of course, illustrates the contradiction inherent in both the American Revolution and the Declaration of Independence. All men may have been "created equal" in Jefferson's mind, but clearly black slaves were not entitled to the "unalienable Rights" of "Life, Liberty, and the Pursuit of Happiness." Thus, despite the Declaration's proclamations of universal liberty and equality, slaves were used as mere objects in the propaganda war against the King. Not a few Englishmen read the Declaration and wondered, as did the English Tory and literary figure Samuel Johnson, "How is it that we hear the loudest *yelps* for liberty among the drivers of negroes?"

[*See also* American Revolution; Civil Rights; Constitution, U.S.; David Walker's *Appeal*; Discrimination; Emancipation; Jefferson, Thomas, on African Americans and Slavery; Laws and Legislation; Military; Murray, John (Lord Dunmore); Segregation; Slave Rebellions and Insurrections; Slave Trade: Eighteenth Century to Revolution; Slavery: Lower South; Slavery: Upper South; Virginia; *and* Walker, David.]

BIBLIOGRAPHY

Blassingame, John W., ed. *The Frederick Douglass Papers. Series 1, Speeches, Debates, and Interviews.* 5 vols. New Haven, CT: Yale University Press, 1979–1992.

Finkelman, Paul. *Slavery and the Founders: Race and Liberty in the Age of Jefferson.* 2nd ed. Armonk, NY: M. E. Sharpe, 2001.

Jefferson, Thomas. "Autobiography." In *The Life and Selected Writings of Thomas Jefferson*, edited by Adrienne Koch and William Peden. New York: Modern Library, 1944.

Peterson, Merrill D. *Thomas Jefferson and the New Nation.* New York: Oxford University Press, 1970.

—PAUL FINKELMAN

DELANY, MARTIN ROBISON (b. 6 May 1812; d. 24 January 1885), a prominent African American intellectual of the nineteenth century. Martin Robison Delany was at once a doctor, political activist, journalist, author, and military officer. However, because of his vehement political and social critiques of the United States, Delany is often relegated to the shadows of his contemporary, Frederick Douglass. Like Booker T. Washington and W. E. B. Du Bois in the early twentieth century, Delany and Douglass represent a point-counterpoint in American history. Unlike Washington and Du Bois, however, Delany and Douglass were at times business partners and friends despite their conflicting social views.

Delany was born in Charles Town, Virginia (now West Virginia) in 1812, the son of Pati Peace, a free black woman, and Samuel Delany, a slave father. In 1822 his family moved north to Chambersburg, Pennsylvania. In 1831 Delany went to Pittsburgh to study under the Reverend Lewis Woodson, an ardent black separatist. Delany also began studying medicine under the direction of several Pittsburgh doctors while serving as a cupper and bleeder.

In 1843 Delany began the *Mystery*, a weekly Pittsburgh newspaper that he edited until 1847. This enterprise drew him to Douglass, who was also in the newspaper business. After selling his interest in the *Mystery*, which continued publication under the name of the *Christian Recorder*, Delany remained active in the newspaper business. He and Frederick Douglass began a partnership as co-editors of the *North Star*, with Douglass serving as the paper's agent in Rochester, New York, and Delany as its Pittsburgh agent. Both men supplied the necessary funds to keep the paper in print, an action that drained the resources of both and ultimately led to the end of the business partnership.

The financial burdens that co-editing the *North Star* placed on Delany forced his departure from the enterprise in 1849. He needed money to continue his interest and studies in medicine. After many years of applying and being denied access to a host of medical schools, Delany was accepted into the Harvard Medical School in 1850. His joy over admission was short-lived, however, because within months the school bowed to pressure from fellow students and rescinded its admission offer to Delany and two other African Americans. In less than a year Delany and his two fellow African American students were the first blacks admitted to Harvard and the first dismissed.

The dismissal from Harvard had a profound effect on Delany, an effect that was compounded by the passage of the Fugitive Slave Act of 1850. His criticism of the United States and the institution of slavery became even harsher. Never a person to mince words, Delany responded to the passage of new fugitive slave legislation openly and harshly. In North Pittsburgh he publicly challenged President Millard Fillmore to enforce the law, threatening to kill the president if he attempted to abduct any member of the Delany family. In the decade immediately preceding the Civil War, Delany's activism reached a fevered pitch.

In 1852 Delany published *The Condition, Elevation, Emigration and Destiny of the Colored People of the United States*. Written in response to both the Fugitive Slave Law of 1850 and the sometimes misplaced intentions of white abolitionists, the *Condition* described the plight of African Americans and proposed a remedy. The book attacked the efforts of white abolitionists, particularly William Lloyd Garrison. Citing the absence of African American leadership in national antislavery and abolition organizations, Delany charged that blacks fell into secondary status even among those who purported to aid them. Years of second-class citizenship angered Delany, and he expressed his emotions fully in his book. To elevate their collective status, he argued, African Americans must emigrate from the United States.

White abolitionists harshly reviewed Delany's book, but by that time he cared little for the concerns of white America as they pertained to ending slavery. He clearly and openly advocated separatism as a means to escape oppression. Despite his disregard for white approval, Delany did hope for a favorable endorsement from his friend Douglass. The sought-after endorsement never materialized, however. Douglass disagreed with Delany's emigrationist ideas. But he refused to review Delany's book or even simply to note the book's circulation in his newspa-

Major Martin R. Delany, U.S.A., "Promoted on the Battle Field for Bravery," lithograph, c. 1865. Despite the title provided by the anonymous artist, Delany received his commission in February 1865, following a meeting with President Lincoln, and did not join his unit in the field until two months after the war ended. Significantly, however, his appointment as a major made Delany the first African American field officer of high rank. (National Portrait Gallery, Smithsonian Institution/Art Resource, N.Y.)

per mainly for fear of jeopardizing the financial support of white abolitionists. Unlike Douglass, Delany would not accept funding from whites. He hoped to promote his emigration movement without depending on the economic and political assistance of white America.

The rift between Douglass and Delany widened in the ensuing years. Following the publication of Harriet Beecher Stowe's novel *Uncle Tom's Cabin*, Delany began writing a response to Stowe's best-seller. Convinced that Stowe's work failed to adequately illustrate the horrors of slavery, Delany painstakingly portrayed brutal and sadistic slaveholders in his novel, *Blake; or, The Huts of America*. Unlike Stowe, he gave no quarter to well-intentioned whites in his work. *Blake* was not published until years after Delany's death, however, and thus had no impact on the debate over slavery and little impact on African American history. Meanwhile Douglass, who had achieved celebrity status and appealed to both white and black abolitionists, publicly praised *Uncle Tom's Cabin*.

Douglass continued to court white abolitionist leaders, both to further the abolition movement and to gain vital financial support for his newspaper. With the outbreak of the Civil War, Douglass hoped to parlay his public persona into a weapon for promoting the Union. He approached President Abraham Lincoln to propose the use of black troops in the war effort and to offer himself as the officer to lead those troops. Uninspired by his meeting with Douglass, Lincoln rejected the idea of mustering black troops and did not offer Douglass a commission. The president struggled to maintain the support of border states while turning a blind eye to the continuation of slavery within those states. The timing of Douglass's proposal as well as his public criticisms of Union recruiting efforts moved Lincoln to decline.

As the war progressed and Lincoln's views on black soldiery changed, the opportunity to commission black field officers reemerged. By 1863 Delany was actively recruiting black men from across New England to serve in the Fifty-fourth Massachusetts Infantry Regiment, an all-black unit. Then in 1865 he succeeded where his friend Douglass had failed. Delany persuaded Lincoln to commission black officers to lead black units in the field. Following a meeting with the president in February, Delany received a commission as a major in the Union Army. Not until June 1865, two months after the war ended, however, did Delany join his unit in the field.

In the wake of the Civil War, Delany served as a sub-assistant commissioner in the ill-fated Freedmen's Bureau in South Carolina. The rampant corruption of the Reconstruction South disenchanted Delany, and he soured on the efforts of the Republican Party and the U.S. Army. Just as he had done earlier in his life, Delany took steps to correct what he perceived to be the wrongs perpetrated on African Americans. To the disdain of many blacks, Delany switched his political affiliation to the Democratic Party and backed former Confederates in their quest to regain political power. In 1874 he unsuccessfully ran for lieutenant governor of South Carolina. Nevertheless, his political efforts did not go unrewarded; Governor Wade Hampton appointed Delany to a judgeship in Charleston in 1876, a position he held until 1879. During his tenure on the bench he sponsored an ill-fated attempt at Liberian emigration and published another book, *Principia of Ethnology*, in which he praised African culture and espoused the principles of racial purity. Following his foray into politics Delany returned to practicing medicine. He died on 24 January 1885 in Wilberforce, Ohio.

[*See also* Abolitionism; Africa, Idea of; Antislavery Movement; Antislavery Press; Black Abolitionists; Black Nationalism; Black Politics; Black Press; Black Separatism; *Christian Recorder*; Civil War; Civil War, Participation and Recruitment of Black Troops in; Democratic Party; Discrimination; Douglass, Frederick; Education; Emigration to Africa; Fifty-fourth Massachusetts Infantry Regiment; Free Blacks before the Civil War (North); Free Blacks before the Civil War (South); Freedmen's Bureau; Fugitive Slave Act of 1850; Garrison, William Lloyd; Liberia; Lincoln, Abraham; *North Star*; Political Participation; Race, Theories of; Racism; Reconstruction; Republican Party; Slavery; Stowe, Harriet Beecher; *Uncle Tom's Cabin*; *and* Union Army, African Americans in.]

BIBLIOGRAPHY

Delany, Martin R. *The Condition, Elevation, Emigration and Destiny of the Colored People of the United States* (1852). Salem, NH: Ayer, 1988. An excellent source of information regarding Delany's feelings toward white abolitionists and the conditions facing African Americans in the mid-nineteenth century.

Levine, Robert S. *Martin Delany, Frederick Douglass, and the Politics of Representative Identity*. Chapel Hill: University of North Carolina Press, 1997. An excellent comparison of the writings of Delany, Douglass, and Stowe and how those writings shaped the iconic development of Douglass.

Sollors, Werner, Caldwell Titcomb, and Thomas Underwood, eds. *Blacks at Harvard: A Documentary History of African-American Experience at Harvard and Radcliffe*. New York: New York University Press, 1993. This work gives a general biography of Delany and chronicles his admission and dismissal from Harvard.

Ullman, Victor. *Martin R. Delany: The Beginnings of Black Nationalism*. Boston: Beacon Press, 1971. This somewhat sympathetic biography of Delany explores his significance to the black nationalist movement.

—TIMOTHY KONHAUS

DELAWARE. Delaware occupied a unique place in African American history in that it was a border slave state. The state slowly emerged from a colonial past of plantation slavery, and by 1840 the majority of African Americans were free, yet the state retained the institution of slavery and the white supremacist social order that accompanied it.

In 1639 a Caribbean slave named Anthony became the first African to arrive in Delaware. At least a hundred more Africans were later held as slaves on small Swedish and Dutch settlements in the colony in the middle of the seventeenth century. In 1664, the year that Britain took Delaware away from the Netherlands, slaves made up 20 percent of the population. Their concentration fell, however, as poor white farmers moved into the colony. Seventeenth-century Delaware was not a major destination for slave traders; most of the colony's slaves resembled Anthony in that they came from other New World colonies and were sold in small groups or as individuals.

Slavery in colonial Delaware expanded rapidly between 1725 and 1775, with several factors increasing demand for slave labor: tobacco prices rose; slaveholders abandoned exhausted soils on Maryland's Eastern Shore for fresh lands in neighboring Delaware; and trade opportunities expanded through the port of Philadelphia, located just north of the colony. On the eve of the American Revolution, African American slaves in Delaware numbered approximately ten thousand, accounting for one-fifth of the population. Unlike the charter generation of Delaware slaves who were predominantly African-born, in the late 1700s men and women born in America made up 90 percent of enslaved Delawareans.

In the first half of the eighteenth century most slaves in Delaware cultivated tobacco, which had been brought to the colony by slaveholders from the Chesapeake Bay colonies of Maryland and Virginia. Chesapeake slaveholders had introduced a harsh code of slave discipline that discouraged manumission and restricted the ability of slaves to travel, assemble, and combat cruel treatment.

After 1750 soil exhaustion and falling tobacco prices persuaded planters to grow wheat and corn. The decline of tobacco production decreased the profitability of slavery, and the switch to less labor-intensive grain crops diminished the demand for field hands. These changes led some Delaware masters to free their slaves; others hired their slaves out to poorer neighbors; and a third group assigned their chattels to manufacture goods such as cloth, iron, and bricks.

In the third quarter of the eighteenth century slaves were roughly evenly distributed among Delaware's three counties. Delaware lacked the great plantations and quasi aristocracy of the slaveholding gentry that dominated Virginia and Maryland; consequently, most Delaware slaves lived close to their masters on small farms. The small slaveholdings inhibited the ability of slaves to form stable families. At most, an estimated one-fifth of Revolutionary-era slaves resided with their spouses. As did slaves in other states, those in Delaware dwelled in ramshackle housing; ate monotonous, protein-poor diets; and wore simple clothing.

In the early Republic, African American life changed dramatically as Delaware approached—though did not achieve—an end to slavery. In 1787, during a wave of manumissions, the state legislature banned the importation of slaves. In 1775 only 5 percent of Delaware's African Americans were free; by 1810 the state's 13,136 free blacks made up 76 percent of the African American population. During that thirty-five-year interval Delaware was the only state below the Mason-Dixon Line to experience a net decline (of approximately 5,800) in its slave population. Along with falling tobacco prices, factors promoting emancipation were the growth in industry and seasonal farm work, the disruption of the American Revolution, and libertarian and egalitarian ideas associated with the Revolution and evangelical Christianity.

The route to freedom taken by Richard Allen, the founder of the African Methodist Episcopal (AME) Church, bore similarities to other Delaware manumissions. In 1768, eight years after his birth in Philadelphia, Allen and his family were sold to Stokely Sturgis, a planter living in Dover, Delaware. Debts associated with falling staple-crop profits impelled Sturgis to sell Allen's mother and three siblings to a trader. Later Sturgis's need for cash and his sympathy for Allen's piety persuaded him to let Allen purchase his freedom for two thousand dollars. Over the next six years Allen raised this money by working at various jobs, ranging from bricklaying to hauling cargo. As a free man Allen used his contacts among African American evangelicals to find work as a preacher in Wilmington, Delaware's principal city; urban areas offered more work and social opportunities than did the countryside. Allen later went to Philadelphia, where he founded the AME Church. Other Delaware slaves won freedom through similar means—namely, access to wage labor, help from blacks who were already free, and offers of self-purchase from masters like Sturgis, who were motivated by both economic need and evangelical humanitarianism.

Most free blacks in Delaware, however, did not enjoy Allen's level of success. White lawmakers crafted statues designed to make free African Americans continue to labor for Delaware farmers. An 1811 law denied free blacks the right to live in Delaware if they remained out of state for more than six months. The measure hindered blacks' ability to participate in the larger labor market of the mid-Atlantic. Other laws discouraged nonfarm employment, apprenticed free black children, hired out indigent free black adults, and banned interracial marriage. Laws against African American suffrage and court testimony denied African Americans a voice in government. Although restricted by law after 1787, every decade a few hundred Delaware slaves were sold out of state. As a result, most free blacks worked in agriculture, although many moved to Wilmington to take service-sector jobs.

Despite white racism, free blacks succeeded in building community institutions, beginning with independent churches. Three leaders of the independent black church movement—Richard Allen, Absalom Jones, and Peter Spencer—began their lives as Delaware slaves. Black churches promoted schools and mutual benefit societies and organized against slavery and colonization. Because state government ignored black education, African American churches and white abolitionists privately funded schools. In 1809 Quakers abolitionists founded the African School Society to further this effort. Private schools helped bring Delaware's African American literacy rate to nearly 50 percent by 1860. Free blacks and their allies in Wilmington staffed the last stop in slave territory for fugitives bound out of the South. Working with the renowned fugitive "conductor" Harriet Tubman, Thomas Garrett, a white abolitionist owner of a Wilmington shoe factory, helped smuggle approximately 2,000 escaped slaves to freedom. Another benefit of freedom was the ability African Americans gained to bring husband, wife, and children together under one roof, solidifying family ties.

In 1840 Delaware's proportion of free blacks in its population—22 percent—was the largest of any state in the Union, and it remained so until 1860. By that time free blacks were most numerous in New Castle County, Delaware's northernmost county that included Wilmington, while three-fourths of the state's 1,798 slaves lived in Sussex County, located in the far south with affinities for Chesapeake slavery. Although slavery was near extinction by 1860, its supporters remained influential in Delaware politics. In 1703 and 1847, the legislature considered gradual emancipation bills. Each time, a one-vote majority defeated the proposals. The slaveholding minority, headquartered in Sussex County, benefited from a legislative apportionment system that diluted the power of the more populous, and more antislavery, north.

During the secession crisis of 1860–1861, Delaware decided to remain within the Union, although in the presidential election of 1860 it gave a plurality of its votes to the Southern Rights Democrat John C. Breckinridge. Most voters rejected secession because of Delaware's proximity to the free states, its close ties to Philadelphia's economy, and pride in the state's history as the first to ratify the federal Constitution. Notwithstanding their Unionism, Delaware whites clung tenaciously to slavery throughout the Civil War. In 1861 President Abraham Lincoln proposed compensated emancipation to the Delaware legislature. Proslavery forces charged that emancipation would bring racial equality and embolden free blacks to attack whites. A Democratic victory in the 1862 state legislative elections doomed compensated emancipation. Thereafter, Delaware Democrats blocked all Republican measures related to slavery and black civil rights. Slavery ended in Delaware only with the passage of the Thirteenth Amendment in 1865, which became national law despite Delaware's refusal to ratify it.

Black Delawareans helped the cause of freedom by fighting for the Union and intensifying the efforts of their voluntary organizations. The Federal military enlisted 954 Delaware blacks, most of whom had been free in 1860. These soldiers campaigned in Virginia in 1864 and 1865, and saw combat at Cold Harbor, the Crater, and Petersburg. African Americans also used churches and voluntary associations to promote education and secure civil rights.

Exempted from Reconstruction because of its wartime loyalty, Delaware's government continued to support white supremacy. Civil rights came with the Fourteenth Amendment to the Constitution in 1868 and suffrage via the Fifteenth Amendment in 1870. In defiance of the spirit of these laws, Delaware legislators segregated public space, ignored black education, and enacted more labor controls. Discriminatory poll taxes targeted the estimated 4,500 newly eligible African American voters. Reacting against federal efforts to ban the practice, in 1873 the legislature passed a new tax statute that disfranchised most black voters. Jim Crow prevailed in Delaware for the remainder of the century. Symbolic of racism's hold, the Delaware legislature waited until 1901 to ratify the Thirteenth Amendment.

[*See also* Abolitionism; African Methodist Episcopal Church; Allen, Richard; American Revolution; Black Church; Black Family; Caribbean; Demographics; Discrimination; Education; Emancipation; Food; Free African Americans to 1828; Gradual Emancipation; Jones, Absalom; Occupations; Religion; Slavery: Mid-Atlantic; Spencer, Peter; Urbanization; *and* Work.]

BIBLIOGRAPHY

Allen, Richard. *The Life, Experience, and Gospel Labours of the Rt. Rev. Richard Allen*. Philadelphia: Martin and Boden, 1833. http://docsouth.unc.edu/neh/allen/allen.html.

Baldwin, Lewis V. *"Invisible" Strands in African Methodism: A History of the African Union Methodist Protestant and Union American Methodist Episcopal Churches, 1805–1980*. Metuchen, NJ: Scarecrow Press, 1983.

Essah, Patience. *A House Divided: Slavery and Emancipation in Delaware, 1638–1865*. Charlottesville: University Press of Virginia, 1996.

Hancock, Harold B. *Delaware during the Civil War*. Wilmington: Historical Society of Delaware, 1961.

McGowan, James A. *Station Master on the Underground Railroad: The Life and Times of Thomas Garrett*. Moylan, PA: Whimsie Press, 1977.

Williams, William H. *Slavery and Freedom in Delaware, 1639–1865*. Wilmington, DE: Scholarly Resources, 1996.

—FRANK TOWERS

DEMOCRATIC PARTY. The Democratic Party traces its origins to the political disputes between Thomas Jefferson and Alexander Hamilton in the early 1790s. In its early years the party was known as the "Republican Party." After about 1801 the followers of Jefferson were known as Democratic-Republicans, and after the War of 1812 the same politicians were called National Republicans. Despite these early party labels, there is a continuous line from Jefferson in the 1790s to Jackson in the 1830s and then to the modern Democratic Party. Between 1801 and 1841 every president was, in this sense, the candidate of the Democratic party, although some were known at the time as "Republicans" or "National Republicans." The last president elected under this label was John Quincy Adams in 1824, who was technically a Democrat elected under the banner of the National Republicans, but ideologically was closer to the Whig party which formed in opposition to the Democrats in the 1830s. Indeed, when Adams ran for reelection in 1828 he was the candidate of the National Republicans but the bulk of Jefferson's old party supported Andrew Jackson, running as a "Democrat." After 1828 the National Republicans disappeared, with the followers of the late Jefferson forming the Democratic Party, under the leadership of Andrew Jackson and his chief strategist, Martin Van Buren. From 1800 until 1860 the party dominated American politics, winning all but two presidential elections (1840 and 1848) and invariably dominating Congress. For most of this period Democrats also dominated the Supreme Court. Although every state had some Democratic presence, the party was particularly powerful in the South. It claimed to be the party of the "common man," but its leadership often consisted of wealthy slaveholding southern planters, such as Thomas Jefferson, James Monroe, Andrew Jackson, James K. Polk, John C. Calhoun, and Jefferson Davis. Most Democrats, whether from the North or the South, were hostile to black freedom and black civil rights. As a national institution, the Democratic Party was overwhelmingly proslavery. Secession and the Civil War broke the party's dominance of American politics, and from 1861 until Douglass's death in 1895 Democrats were generally in the minority. Only twice did a Democrat win the presidency, although the death of Abraham Lincoln put a former Democrat, Andrew Johnson, in the nation's highest office. After the Civil War, Democrats continued their hostility toward the rights of blacks, as they fought against constitutional amendments and laws designed to protect black freedom.

From Jefferson to Jackson. The Democratic Party traces its origins to the supporters of Thomas Jefferson in the 1790s. By 1796 the Jeffersonians had organized into a political party whose members called themselves Republicans or Democratic Republicans. With the election of Jefferson in 1801 they emerged as the dominant political force in the new nation. By 1816 the opposition Federalist Party had all but disappeared, and in 1820 President James Monroe ran for reelection with no opposition as a member of what had come to be called the National Republican Party.

The Jeffersonians had a complicated relationship to slavery and race. Their leader and hero, Thomas Jefferson, owned between 175 and 225 slaves from the Revolution until his death in 1826. Due to Jefferson's relationship to

slavery (as well as Madison's and Monroe's, who followed him to the presidency), it would have been hard for early Democrats to oppose slavery. Indeed, with the exception of John Quincy Adams, who was a National Republican but went into the Whig Party after 1829, every Democratic president from 1801 to 1837 was a slaveholding southerner. The southern dominance of the party insured that it would be proslavery and often anti-black. In those states where free blacks could vote, the Democrats often ran blatantly racist campaigns, while working to disfranchise blacks. In the 1821 election, Jeffersonian Democrats led by Martin Van Buren attempted to disfranchise blacks in New York. While unsuccessful in eliminating the black vote, the Democrats managed to remove property requirements for white voters, but not for black voters. Not surprising, in those states where blacks could vote, they were almost universally supporters of the Federalist and Whig Parties until the 1840s and 1850s, when they backed the Liberty, Free Soil, and then the Republican parties.

While utterly unsympathetic to freeing blacks or to ending slavery, Jefferson and other early Democrats did understand that slavery was dangerous to the nation. Thus, Jefferson and his followers favored an end to the African slave trade, which would not harm slavery but would reduce the growth of the nation's black population. In foreign policy Jefferson sought to undermine the independence of Haiti, fearful of a black republic on America's doorstep. Under Monroe the United States pursued an aggressive policy against the Spanish and the Seminole Indians in an attempt to recover runaway slaves.

Except for a brief resurgence during the debates over the Missouri Compromise, the Federalist Party ceased to be much of a force in national politics after about 1813. Jefferson's party, now called the National Republicans, had no serious opposition, although factions within the party jockeyed for power. The absence of any opposition party proved to be destabilizing to the political system, and in 1824 four viable candidates, all theoretically from the same party, competed for the presidency. Andrew Jackson had a plurality of the popular vote and the electoral vote but lacked a majority of the electors. That threw the election into the House of Representatives, where John Quincy Adams, who ran second to Jackson, was chosen as president. In 1828 Adams ran for reelection as a National Republican, but that organization no longer represented the Democratic-Republican tradition of the Jeffersonians. That year Adams lost decisively to Jackson, who ran as a Democrat and, in doing so, claimed the Jeffersonian tradition. The losing supporters of Adams soon formed the Whig Party.

Jackson claimed to be the heir to the legacy of Thomas Jefferson, and in many ways his party and his politics fit this claim. Both men had enormous faith in the "common man" and saw small farmers and urban workers as the base of their political support. Both relied on the South for their main political strength, although both had significant northern support. Jefferson ran with a New Yorker, Aaron Burr, in the election of 1800, and Jackson did the same in 1832, running with Martin Van Buren. Like Jefferson, Jackson generally opposed internal improvements, an expanded federal government, and a policy that enhanced the nation's commercial and manufacturing interests. As the secretary of state, Jefferson had opposed the chartering of the First Bank of the United States; as the president, Jackson vetoed a bill to recharter the Second Bank of the United States. When he purchased Louisiana from France, Jefferson envisioned resettling all eastern Indians on some of this new land west of the Mississippi. As a general and president, Jackson oversaw the removal of most Indians in the Southeast to what later became Oklahoma.

Most important, like Jefferson, Jackson was a proslavery planter who owned hundreds of human beings. Jackson built a party that was southern based, intensely supportive of slavery, and opposed to the rights of free blacks, even while supporting democracy and the "common man." During the age of Jackson, Democrats in Pennsylvania, Tennessee, and North Carolina stripped free black men of the right to vote. Democrats in the Midwest restricted the rights of free blacks. In Congress the Democratic Party vigorously supported a "gag rule" that prevented the House of Representatives from even receiving antislavery petitions. Jackson's attorney general, Roger B. Taney, issued an opinion that the United States should not grant passports to free blacks nor grant them any rights as citizens of the United States. Jackson would later appoint Taney to the Supreme Court, where as chief justice he would consistently oppose rights and legal protections for blacks.

Prewar Platform. Starting with Jackson's victory in 1828, the Democrats dominated American politics until the Civil War. At the state and local levels Democrats in the North and the South were hostile to free blacks. At the national level Democrats generally stood for a limited federal government, low taxes and tariffs, and allowing the states to develop policies as they wished. A key component of the Democratic Party's platform, at least until the 1840s, when the issue mostly disappeared, was opposition to a national bank. Democrats in Congress voted to limit the funding of the U.S. Navy's Africa Squadron, which was sent to patrol the Atlantic to stop the international slave trade. At the same time, Democrats opposed cooperating with England to suppress the African slave trade. Democrats also generally supported states' rights. For example, the Democratic majority on the Supreme Court allowed states to regulate certain aspects of national commerce, including the movement of free blacks into the South or immigrants entering northern ports. Despite their opposition to an active federal government, Democrats favored territorial expansion and in the 1830s and 1840s were strong proponents of manifest destiny.

From Jefferson through Martin Van Buren, Democrats aggressively sought the removal of all Indians from the eastern states. The Indian Removal Act, passed by Congress in 1830 under Jackson's sponsorship and strictly enforced by Van Buren, opened up new lands in the South for cotton cultivation, thus strengthening slavery while removing a large nonwhite population from the region. Democrats pushed for the annexation of Texas, which was accomplished by John Tyler, who had been a Democrat before running for vice president as a Whig. Once in power, however, Tyler mostly adopted Democratic politics. Democrats, led by President James K. Polk, a slaveholding Tennessean like Andrew Jackson, pushed for and advocated war with Mexico to gain new territories. Democrats also advocated strong federal policies to support slavery and to help masters recover fugitive slaves.

Southern Control of the Dominant Party. With a strong base in the South and support from many urban workers and some immigrants—especially those from Ireland—the Democratic Party dominated American politics before the Civil War and lost only two elections before 1860. Both losses were to Whig Party candidates, in 1840 and 1848. The Whigs' first victory was partially undone by the unexpected death of William Henry Harrison only a month after he took office. His vice president, John Tyler, had been a Democrat before running with Harrison and had little interest in the Whig agenda. The second Whig president, Zachary Taylor, also died in office, only to be succeeded by Millard Fillmore, another Whig with minimal commitment to the party. In his home state of New York, Fillmore had opposed the antislavery wing of the Whig Party, which was led by Senator William H. Seward. By the start of the Civil War, Fillmore had become a Democrat. Throughout the three antebellum decades Democrats in the Senate were led by southern fire-eaters like John C. Calhoun of South Carolina, Robert Toombs of Georgia, and Jefferson Davis of Mississippi.

While the Democrats dominated American politics, southerners dominated the Democratic Party. A majority of southern senators were Democrats, and they were always a majority of the Democrats in the Senate. Thus, a northern Democrat who hoped to gain a spot on an important Senate committee was forced to support the party's proslavery agenda. The most successful Democratic presidents—Jackson (1829–1837) and James Knox Polk (1845–1849)—were also slaveholding southerners.

The northern Democratic presidents—Martin Van Buren (1837–1841), Franklin Pierce (1853–1857), and James Buchanan (1857–1861)—were classic "doughfaces," northern men with southern principles.

With Democrats controlling the presidency for twenty-four of the thirty years leading up to the Civil War, the Supreme Court became almost an arm of the party. There was a southern majority, and an overwhelming Democratic majority, on the Court from the early 1830s until the Civil War. In the three decades before the Civil War only one justice, John McLean of Ohio (1830–1861), was a strong opponent of slavery. Joseph Story (1811–1845), a National Republican appointed by James Madison, and Benjamin Robbins Curtis (1851–1857), the only Whig on the Court in this period, were at best moderate opponents of the institution. Story's opposition was particularly timid and muted by the end of his career. The rest of the Court consisted of proslavery southern Democrats and their northern Democratic doughface allies.

This Court consistently supported the fugitive slave laws and in *Dred Scott v. Sandford* (1857) constitutionalized the position of the southern wing of the Democratic Party by declaring that Congress had no power to regulate slavery in the territories and that free blacks, even if they were citizens of northern states, could never be considered citizens of the United States. The *Dred Scott* decision, which declared that blacks had no rights under the U.S. Constitution, was written by the Jackson-appointed Chief Justice Taney and supported by six other justices appointed by Democratic presidents. John McLean, another Jackson appointee, dissented in the case, but by this time McLean had abandoned his support for the Democratic Party largely because of its proslavery stance. The only other dissent in the case came from the lone Whig on the Court, Benjamin R. Curtis.

Slavery Causes Party Division. In the North some Democrats were antislavery, but most expressed no opinion on the issue, took the position that it was a "southern problem," or were openly proslavery. On race, however, almost all Democrats were united in opposing black rights. In the 1850s Democrats in Indiana, Illinois, Oregon, and Iowa banned black immigration, although only in Indiana were such laws effective. Throughout the North, Democrats played the race card in campaigns, accusing their Whig and, later, Republican opponents of favoring racial equality or interracial marriage. By the 1850s this tactic was no longer effective, however, as Republicans correctly accused northern Democrats of being in the palm of the proslavery national party, which forced the Democratic Party to support laws that protected slavery and allowed for its expansion into the West.

Many northern whites may have opposed black rights, but few were sympathetic to slavery. During the Mexican-American War, northern Whigs accused their Democratic opponents of supporting the war to bring new slave states into the Union. In response to this charge, Congressman David Wilmot, a Pennsylvania Democrat, tried to ban slavery in any territory acquired in the war by appending a rider, known as the Wilmot Proviso, to an appropriations bill for the war. Although the proviso passed the House with ease because the huge northern majority voted for it without regard to party affiliation, it died in the Senate, where southerners held a temporary majority.

By the 1850s the proslavery stance of the Democratic Party had undermined its viability in much of the North. Senator Stephen A. Douglas of Illinois attempted to finesse the issue with the Kansas-Nebraska Act of 1854. Douglas argued that western settlers should decide the issue of slavery in the territories through what he called "popular sovereignty." Under this policy Congress opened up most of the western territories to settlement without regard to slavery, thereby repealing a major element of the Compromise of 1820. Douglas's solution to the dilemma of northern Democrats backfired in two ways. In Kansas it led to a mini–civil war: southerners resorted to violence and vote fraud to prevent a northern majority from banning slavery in the territory, and northerners struck back with their own lethal force. For two years the territory was known as "Bleeding Kansas." More significant, the partial repeal of the Missouri Compromise led to a huge backlash by Whigs, antislavery Democrats, and unaffiliated northerners opposed to slavery. The result was a formation of what was first called the Anti-Nebraska Party but soon became known as the Republican Party. By 1860 this new political organization had defeated Democrats throughout the North, taking over state legislatures and governorships.

In 1856 the Democrats managed to win the presidency by running a Pennsylvania doughface, James Buchanan, with a former Kentucky congressman, John C. Breckinridge, as his running mate. The ticket carried the South and a handful of northern states, but eleven northern states sided with the new Republican Party, which was pledged to stop the spread of slavery in the West. In 1860 the Democratic Party divided into northern and southern wings over the issue of slavery in the territories. Douglas ran in the North, and Breckinridge ran in the South. Even if the Democrats had remained unified, however, it is doubtful they could have beaten the new Republican Party. Led by the moderate Abraham Lincoln, the new party carried all the northern states and the election in 1860. The Democratic proslavery stranglehold on American politics was finally broken.

Civil War and Civil Rights. The election of Lincoln led to civil war, with seven states seceding before he even took office. Four more slave states left the Union after Confederate forces fired on Fort Sumter, and Lincoln asked for volunteers to save the Union. Most northern Democrats accepted the argument that secession was illegal, although many, including the outgoing president, James Buchanan, did not believe that Lincoln should use force to hold the Union together. Once the war began, most northern Democrats supported the effort, but they opposed turning the war to save the Union into a war to end slavery. However, a significant minority of the party always opposed the war, arguing that the states were free to leave the Union. These "Peace Democrats" were seen as traitors in the North and were often referred to as "Copperheads," after the poisonous snake that strikes without warning.

By late 1862 many Democrats who had supported the Union became opponents of the war because the Emancipation Proclamation, preliminarily issued in September 1862 and finalized on 1 January 1863, had changed the nature of the conflict. In 1864 the Democrats ran General George B. McClellan as a peace candidate. McClellan promised to end the Civil War, even if it meant a permanent dissolution of the Union. Many northerners considered this former general's campaign to be tantamount to treason, and he was soundly defeated in the free states, carrying only three loyal slave states with a mere twenty-one electoral votes. Throughout the war some Democrats teetered on a fine line between opposing Lincoln's policies and supporting the rebellion. In 1863 the Lincoln administration expelled Clement Vallandigham from the Union because the Ohio Democrat persistently and intemperately spoke out against the administration's war policy and allegedly encouraged draft evasion. Within the party, the "War Democrats" continued to support efforts to suppress the rebellion even as they opposed emancipation, the enlistment of black troops, and, ultimately, black citizenship.

After the war Democrats favored a speedy readmission of the former Confederate States but accepted emancipation as a fact and generally did not oppose the Thirteenth Amendment. The assassination of Lincoln in April 1865 put Andrew Johnson in the White House. Before the war Johnson had been a Democratic senator from Tennessee. He was a slaveholder, a strong supporter of states' rights, and a deeply racist man who opposed any legal rights for blacks. He supported the end of slavery but persistently vetoed civil rights legislation, such as the Freedmen's Bureau Bill and the Civil Rights Act of 1866. In this sense, his policies were those of the Democratic Party, not of the Republicans who had put him in office. Following prewar Democratic ideology, the party became a strong advocate of states' rights after the war. As such, Democrats in Congress, as well as President Johnson until he left office in 1869, opposed the civil rights legislation of the 1860s and 1870s as well as the Fourteenth and Fifteenth Amendments.

In response to the disputed election of 1876, Democrats forced the incoming Republican administration to withdraw all federal troops from the South and end attempts to protect black civil rights in that region. In the 1880s and 1890s Democrats at the state level gradually deprived blacks of many of the rights they had gained during Reconstruction. When the Populist Party tried to create an alliance of blacks and poor whites, the Democratic Party in the South used every means at its disposal to prevent blacks from gaining or retaining political rights and power. At the national level Democrats in Congress vigorously opposed the efforts of the congressman from Massachusetts, Henry Cabot Lodge, to pass a federal law in 1890 to protect the voting rights of African Americans.

Throughout the late nineteenth century blacks naturally gravitated to the Republican Party, not only because it was "the party of Lincoln" and the party of emancipation but also because Democrats opposed black political participation. In the South, Reconstruction ended when white Democratic administrations took over state governments. For the rest of the century the Democratic Party in the South stood for limiting black political power while economically and socially isolating and repressing former slaves and their children. In the North some Democrats tried to woo newly enfranchised blacks, and in the Midwest and Mid-Atlantic states there were some bipartisan efforts to secure civil rights legislation. In general, however, blacks remained loyal to the Republican Party, which in turn offered them some political power and patronage. Black leaders like Frederick Douglass gained political appointment from Republican administrations at the state and federal levels and lost both authority and offices when Democrats were in power.

[See also Adams, John Quincy; Antislavery Movement; Black Politics; Buchanan, James; Calhoun, John C.; Civil Rights; Civil Rights Act of 1866; Civil War; Civil War, Participation and Recruitment of Black Troops in; Confederate States of America; Constitution, U.S.; Douglas, Stephen A.; Douglass, Frederick; *Dred Scott* Case; Election of 1860; Emancipation; Emancipation Proclamation; Fifteenth Amendment; Fourteenth Amendment; Free African Americans before the Civil War (North); Free African Americans before the Civil War (South); Freedmen; Freedmen's Bureau; Fugitive Slave Law of 1793; Fugitive Slave Law of 1850; Immigrants; Jefferson, Thomas; Kansas-Nebraska Act; Laws and Legislation; Mexican-American War; Native Americans and African Americans; Pierce, Franklin; Political Participation; Polk, James K.; Proslavery Thought; Racism; Reconstruction; Republican Party; Seward, William Henry; Slave Trade, African; Slave Trade, Domestic; Slavery; Supreme Court; Taney, Roger B.; Thirteenth Amendment; Union Army, African Americans in; Voting Rights; Whig Party; and Wilmot Proviso.]

BIBLIOGRAPHY

Finkelman, Paul. *Slavery and the Founders: Race and Liberty in the Age of Jefferson*. 2nd ed. Armonk, NY: M.W. Sharpe, 2002.

Ketcham, Ralph L. *Presidents Above Party: The First American Presidency, 1789–1829*. Chapel Hill: University of North Carolina Press, 1987.

Kousser, J. Morgan. *The Shaping of Southern Politics: Suffrage Restriction and the Establishment of the One-Party South, 1880–1910*. New Haven, CT: Yale University Press, 1974.

Rable, George C. *But There Was No Peace: The Role of Violence in the Politics of Reconstruction*. Athens: University of Georgia Press, 1984.

Rutland, Robert Allen. *The Democrats: From Jefferson to Carter*. Baton Rouge: Louisiana State University Press, 1979.

Silbey, Joel H. *A Respectable Minority: The Democratic Party in the Civil War Era, 1860–1868*. New York: Norton, 1977.

Wang, Xi. *The Trial of Democracy: Black Suffrage and Northern Republicans, 1860–1910*. Athens: University of Georgia Press, 1997.

—PAUL FINKELMAN

DEMOGRAPHICS. The demographics of African Americans in early America were influenced significantly by the transatlantic and domestic slave trades, the westward and southwestward expansion of slavery, and steadily improving rates of natural increase. From 1619, when the first Africans arrived in colonial America, to 1830, when the black enslaved population numbered 2 million, a significant social and cultural shift from African-dominated communities to native-born communities occurred.

In 1619 the demographic phenomenon that became black America began in Virginia when "twenty-odd Negroes" arrived on a Dutch sloop. Accorded the status of indentured servants, these Africans planted the roots that would later flower into thousands of black descendants. The first person of African descent to be born in the American colonies, a child named William, was born in 1624. By 1649 a census conducted in the colony enumerated three hundred people of African descent, almost all of whom were indentured servants.

Shortly after that census, however, an important transition occurred in the Chesapeake that altered the evolution of African American society. Long dominated by white indentured servants, the region's labor force underwent a metamorphosis during the 1660s and 1670s that eventually gave it a distinctly black face. A combination of economic and demographic forces made purchasing Africans for life a better investment than purchasing the temporary labor of indentured servants. In particular, with Africans living longer in the New World, African slaves became the laborers of choice for planters in Maryland and Virginia. By the 1690s, when the English government lifted the slave-trading monopoly of the Royal African Company, the supply of Africans for Virginia owners was dramatically increased, which in turn reduced prices for slaves to the point where more owners could afford them.

From 1680, when only 9 percent of Maryland's and 6.9 percent of Virginia's populations were black, to 1700 the enslaved population in the Chesapeake increased considerably. In 1700 the black population in Maryland had expanded to nearly 11 percent; in Virginia the increase was much larger, to 28 percent. The increase in both colonies was almost entirely a result of immigration: of the nearly six thousand Africans shipped to the English colonies of North America between 1675 and 1700, two-thirds went to Virginia, nearly one-third went to Maryland, and the small remainder went to Rhode Island and other New England colonies. The turn toward the use of Africans as permanently unfree laborers had precipitated a huge population boom among people of African descent in the Chesapeake.

Slaves also worked on large wheat-producing estates in New York and Pennsylvania and on farms in Rhode Island. But climate and soil restricted the development of commercial agriculture in the northern colonies, and slavery never became as economically significant as in the South. Slaves in the North were typically held in small numbers, and most served as domestic servants. By 1700 in the North only in New York did African Americans constitute more than 10 percent of the population. New Jersey (6 percent) and Rhode Island (5.1 percent) had notable black populations, but in the remaining northern colonies the percentage of the population that was black was not more than 2.6 percent. Overall, African Americans formed less than 5 percent of the population in the North.

The region where slaves most dominated the population was in the Lowcountry of South Carolina. In 1700 nearly 43 percent of the population was black; by 1720 that proportion had increased to 70 percent. Most of the black population was from West Central Africa. Identified as "Angolans," these slaves toiled hard in the rice fields but also enjoyed the relative semiautonomy that came with having absentee owners. That facet of their life, coupled with the unusually large concentration of Africans from a single culture, resulted in the maintenance of significant elements of their African traditions. Foodways, religion, language, and folklore—while altered because of their New World setting—were maintained by Carolina's Africans.

In 1739 another aspect of this demographic uniqueness was manifested when Angolan slaves organized the Stono Rebellion, which led to the deaths of dozens of whites and slaves. The aim of the conspirators was to reach Spanish Florida, where authorities had developed a policy of freeing runaway slaves from English colonies. While the rebellion was stamped out before any of the participants could reach Florida, the impact on African American demographics in South Carolina was significant. Fearful of similar events, which they believed could occur due to the high concentration of African Americans, owners in the colony adopted policies of diversifying their enslaved population. Subsequent imports of slaves from Africa to South Carolina came from other regions.

Though South Carolina offers the clearest examples of the expression of African culture in the New World, all the colonies of British North America had African-born populations. The peak of the transatlantic slave trade occurred in the eighteenth century, when approximately 215,000 Africans were imported to the United States. South Carolina and Virginia were by far the most common destinations: together they accounted for nearly four-fifths of arrivals. Not surprisingly, other southern colonies—Georgia and Maryland—and the eventual American territories of Louisiana and Mississippi accounted for the bulk of the remainder.

The three most common places of origin for African slaves who arrived in the United States were Senegambia (modern-day Senegal and Gambia), West Central Africa (roughly modern-day Angola), and the Bight of Biafra (modern Nigeria). Over 60 percent of Africans shipped to the United States came from those regions. Additionally, significant numbers came from the Gold Coast (modern Ghana), Sierra Leone, the Windward Coast, and the Bight of Benin. As with the Angolans in South Carolina, in some regions the concentration of slaves from particular African ethnic groups or regions resulted in more homogeneous slave culture than was typical. During the early eighteenth century the Ibo in Virginia and the Bambara in Louisiana became examples of this phenomenon.

Though the figures for transatlantic imports to the United States are high, they constitute only 4 percent of the total traffic of the slave trade during its four-hundred-year history. Given the large population of African Americans in the United States, this fact seems counterintuitive, but the explanation is one of the demographic phenomena of African American life in early America: natural increase. Fundamentally, natural increase is the process of having more births than deaths in a given population. Different regions of colonial America and different ethnic groups in those regions experienced different rates of natural increase. For example, the white, middle-class population of New England, which migrated largely in nuclear-family units, experienced natural population growth within fifteen years of arrival. On the other hand, the overwhelmingly male population of Virginia whites did not experience natural increase until the mid-seventeenth century.

Like their white owners, Africans and their descendants faced two main obstacles to natural population growth: disease and an imbalanced ratio between males and females. In the eighteenth century, although improving among Africans, disease resistance continued to be a significant problem. The problem was exacerbated by the fact that nearly two-thirds of all Africans shipped to British North America were males (this ratio was typical for the entire transatlantic slave trade), resulting in unbalanced sex ratios among blacks in every colony. In the Chesapeake a ratio of 1.5 males to every 1 female prevented the emergence of natural increase; farther south, in South Carolina, the ratio was even higher (1.7 to 1). Thus, it took much longer for black populations to undergo natural increases than for white populations to do so. Nonetheless, as early as the 1730s in the Upper South and during the 1750s in the Lower South natural increase took root among black populations. The result—children born into slavery—provided masters with a steady source for slave labor. After the 1740s most American masters did not have to rely on the transatlantic trade as a source for slaves. Over the next fifty years the black population became younger and decidedly more American.

Revolutionary Period: 1750–1800. During the late eighteenth century two seemingly contradictory processes occurred: the growth in the number of slaves earning their freedom, which produced a larger free black population, and the territorial expansion and political protection of slavery following the invention of the cotton gin by Eli Whitney in 1793.

By 1750 over 90 percent of American slaves lived in the South, where demographic conditions contrasted sharply with those in the North and in the Caribbean. In the northern colonies blacks were few, and slaves were typically held in groups of fewer than five. In the South, by contrast, slaves formed a large minority of the population (in some areas forming the majority), and most lived among small or medium-sized holdings of between five and fifty slaves.

In New England at midcentury every colony except Rhode Island had a black population that accounted for less than 3 percent of the total population. In Rhode Island, where both slavery and slave-trading had become important to the colony's economy, African Americans constituted 10 percent of the population. In the middle colonies, New York maintained the largest black population (14 percent), while New Jersey (7.5 percent) and Pennsylvania (2.4 percent) had smaller ones. Farther south in the Chesapeake, slavery continued its expansion—except in Delaware, where the proportion of blacks in the population actually decreased between 1720 and 1750 from 13 to 5 percent. Slavery's expansion in Maryland and Virginia led to considerably higher black proportions of the population: 31 and 44 percent, respectively. In the Lowcountry, African Americans remained predominant in South Carolina (at 61 percent of the population) while increasing significantly in their share of the total populations of North Carolina (26 percent) and Georgia (19 percent). All told, in 1750 two out of every five people living in Britain's thirteen North American colonies were black.

Over the next quarter century, as the colonists moved toward war with Britain, slavery continued its expansion in the South and became somewhat less important in northern colonies. African Americans in New Jersey and New York, for example, formed significantly smaller proportions of the populations in 1775 than they had in 1750. Conversely, North Carolina and Georgia witnessed considerable increases in their African American populations during that period. In North Carolina blacks formed more than one-third of the 1775 population; the increase was even more pronounced in Georgia, where they constituted nearly half the population.

As important as the changes in population proportions was the shift from an African to an African American slave population. By 1775 only about 20 percent of American slaves were African born. Regional variations existed: the Chesapeake's black population had a significantly smaller African-born proportion than did the Lowcountry; in fact, by the 1770s perhaps as few as one-tenth of Chesapeake blacks had been born in Africa. A similar process was occurring in the Lowcountry, albeit at a slower pace: by the same decade Africans accounted for less than half of all blacks in South Carolina for the first time. As a result, the social and cultural practices of the slave communities in the colonies had become increasingly creolized, mixing African and New World traditions.

Natural increase also accelerated. Typically, slave populations dominated by Africans did not increase naturally; the exceedingly high rate of males in the transatlantic slave trade prevented that from happening. By the late eighteenth century, however, as rates of importation were decreasing, the sex ratios among African Americans began to equalize. In the Chesapeake the sex ratio had nearly reached equilibrium by 1775, and in South Carolina, where the ratio had fallen to 1.2 males for every 1 female, a similar development was well under way. This, in turn, fueled the rates of reproduction and decreased the need to import Africans, resulting in a continued evolution toward an African American culture.

Because African-born slaves had considerably higher mortality rates than American-born slaves, the increased proportion of Creoles in the black population also produced declining mortality rates. Nonetheless, even by the end of the eighteenth century the infant mortality rate for slaves was 50 percent—more than twice that of southerners. Not until the mid-nineteenth century would those horrific rates begin to decline.

Thus, the last half of the eighteenth century was particularly significant for African American demographics, as slavery expanded and was fueled by the accelerated rates of natural increase in the southern colonies. In addition, political interpretations of the American Revolution had a dramatic impact on the lives of some African Americans. As slaves, free blacks, and sympathetic whites attacked slavery as being contradictory to the ideals of the Declaration of Independence, two important consequences evolved. First, almost every northern state legislature adopted some form of emancipation. Though this action took a variety of forms—most commonly "gradual emancipation," whereby slaves were freed at a given age or in a given year—the result was an accelerated geographical shift of the enslaved black population to the South. Second, a rather large population of free blacks emerged, many of whom secured their freedom as a result of the egalitarian principles of the Revolutionary period being applied universally across racial lines. Thus, for the first time in American history, a significant population of free blacks became a visible presence.

In the 1790s approximately sixty thousand free blacks lived in the United States, representing only 8 percent of the black population. Free blacks were particularly concentrated in Upper South urban areas, where opportunities for wage labor were greater than in rural areas. In the 1790s in the North, 40 percent of all blacks were free; in the South, less than 5 percent were free. Though free blacks were not numerous in the Deep South, those in the Upper South constituted over half the population of free blacks in the nation.

Nonetheless, just as the population of free blacks was expanding, and slavery's continued existence in the United States appeared to be under assault, a technological innovation altered the course of these developments. In 1793 the New England schoolteacher Eli Whitney invented the cotton gin while working on a plantation in Georgia. Over the next several years, plantation owners across the South perfected their own versions of the gin, which broke the bottleneck in cotton production that had prevented the crop from becoming a significant part of the southern economy. As more owners turned to cotton as their main enterprise, they looked to the southwest for fresh, fertile soil where slave labor could maximize cultivation. The result was a massive expansion of slavery into new territories—notably Alabama, Mississippi, and Louisiana—and the attendant expansion of the slave population in those areas. As the center of African American population shifted southwestward, the promises of the Revolutionary age receded.

Expansion of Slavery in the Early Republic: 1800–1830. The cotton-fueled expansion of slavery resulted in a significantly larger black population in what was then the southwestern portion of the United States. In 1800 the population of African Americans stood at just over 1 million; as more owners moved southwestward, a higher proportion of blacks shifted to that region. Not surprisingly, the destinations for new cotton producers—Alabama, Mississippi, Louisiana, Arkansas, and Missouri—all became states during this period. The closing of the transatlantic slave trade to the United States in 1808 meant that owners in these territories had to look for domestic sources of slaves. Consequently, the interstate or domestic slave trade replaced transatlantic traffic, as owners from the Upper South sold their bondpeople to those in the Deep South.

By far the most significant demographic force during the first three decades of the 1800s was the domestic slave trade. Between 1800 and 1830 as many as 300,000 African American slaves were sold from Upper South states (Virginia, Maryland, and Kentucky) to the new cotton-producing regions of the Deep South. Continuing the southern movement of slavery's epicenter, which had developed during the eighteenth century, the interstate trade dramatically changed the shape of slavery and of African American demographics in the United States.

Nonetheless, even though slavery was expanding in the early nineteenth century, free blacks, one of the important vestiges of the Revolutionary period, continued their own population expansion. By the 1810s free blacks had increased their share of the black population to 13.5 percent—a figure that would never again be as high while slavery was in existence. In one of the new regions, Louisiana, the free black population accounted for nearly 40 percent of the total black population, as the Spanish practice of self-purchase had dramatically increased its ranks during the late eighteenth century. In cities such as New Orleans, Mobile, Baltimore, and Washington, D.C., free blacks constituted an important share of the African American population.

By 1830 the 25 percent rate of natural increase per decade among African Americans had produced a black population of 2 million. Of those, 319,000 were free, and half of those free blacks lived in the North. Thus, the geographical shift in the concentration of African Americans from the Upper South to the Lower South meant that in addition to dealing with a rapidly expanding population, blacks were constantly altering their social relationships and cultural traditions.

The Antebellum Era: 1830–1861. During the antebellum years the expansion of slavery into the cotton-producing Deep South continued unchecked, sustaining in turn the physical movement of slaves from states in the Upper South, such as Maryland, Virginia, and Kentucky, to those of the Deep South, mainly Georgia, Alabama, Mississippi, and Louisiana. The annexation of Texas in 1845 added yet another frontier for cotton-based slavery. Except for a small population in California, however, the

African American population west of Texas was virtually nonexistent; only at the end of the century would a critical mass of black Americans move into relatively unsettled areas like Oklahoma and Kansas.

In 1830 the total African American population in the United States was 2.3 million. The majority of those, 2 million, were enslaved. The equalizing of the ratio of

PARISHES.	Whites.	Free Colored.	Slaves. Black.	Slaves. Mulatto.	Aggregate.	Cotton Bales of 400 lbs. each.
Ascension..	3,940	168	6,864	512	11,484	684
Assumption	7,189	94	7,041	1,055	15,379	619
Avoyelles..	5,908	74	6,661	524	13,167	20,068
B. Rouge, E.	6,944	532	7,201	1,369	16,046	11,621
B. Rouge, W.	1,859	113	4,890	450	7,312	1,405
Bienville...	5,900	100	4,500	500	11,000	..
Bossier	3,348	..	7,337	663	11,348	40,028
Caddo	4,733	69	6,781	557	12,140	9,385
Calcasieu ..	4,452	305	946	225	5,928	640
Caldwell ..	2,888	..	1,762	183	4,833	7,296
Carroll	4,124	20	12,357	1,551	18,052	84,165
Catahoula..	5,492	46	5,538	575	11,651	25,564
Claiborne..	8,996	4	6,920	928	16,848	18,983
Concordia..	1,242	21	12,205	337	13,805	63,971
De Soto..	4,777	14	7,777	730	13,298	16,554
Feliciana, E.	4,081	23	10,148	445	14,697	23,932
Do. W.	2,036	64	8,363	1,208	11,671	21,361
Franklin...	2,758	2	3,038	364	6,162	9,307
Iberville ...	3,793	188	10,159	521	14,661	179
Jackson....	5,367	..	3,871	227	9,465	10,687
Jefferson..	9,965	287	4,968	152	15,372	..
Lafayette..	4,309	231	5,392	1,071	9,003	11,530
Lafourche..	7,500	149	4,728	1,667	14,044	476
Livingston .	3,120	..	1,240	71	4,431	1,563
Madison ...	1,640	16	11,663	814	14,133	44,870
Morehouse.	3,784	4	5,822	747	10,357	26,982
Natchitoch's	6,306	959	8,806	628	16,699	36,887
Orleans	149,068	10,939	10,891	3,593	174,491	400
Ouichita...	1,887	..	2,757	83	4,727	8,639
Plaquemine	2,595	514	5,284	101	8,494	..
Pt. Coupee.	4,094	721	11,162	1,741	17,718	28,947
Rapides....	9,711	291	13,486	1,872	25,360	49,168
Sabine.....	4,115	..	1,550	163	5,828	5,052
St. Bernard.	1,771	65	2,020	220	4,076	..
St. Charles.	968	177	3,793	389	5,297	..
St. Helena.	3,413	6	3,453	258	7,130	6,484
St. James ..	3,348	61	7,114	976	11,499	..
St. J. Bapt.	3,037	299	4,079	515	7,930	..
St. Landry .	10,703	965	10,116	1,310	23,104	21,198
St. Martin's	5,005	311	6,561	997	12,674	4,717
St. Mary's .	3,508	251	12,532	525	16,816	142
St. Tam'an,	3,153	412	1,636	205	5,406	200
Tensas....	1,479	7	14,536	56	16,078	141,493
Terre Bonne	5,234	72	6,032	753	12,091	195
Union	6,641	3	3,627	118	10,389	10,843
Vermilion..	3,001	7	1,107	209	4,324	14,405
Washington	2,996	22	1,477	213	4,708	2,725
Winn	5,481	41	1,102	252	6,876	2,993
Total...	357,629	18,647	299,103	32,623	708,002	777,738

Census of Louisiana by parishes, 1860, showing four racial categories: whites, "free coloured," black slaves, and mulatto slaves. This statistical table was printed in *Harper's Weekly* of 3 February 1866. (New York Public Library, Photographs and Prints Division, Schomburg Center for Research in Black Culture; Astor, Lenox, and Tilden Foundations.)

males to females, which had begun in the eighteenth century, continued into the nineteenth century, and by 1830 the number of black males living in the United States was almost exactly the same as the number of females. The black population at that time was also decidedly younger than in previous generations: 85 percent of African Americans in 1830 were thirty-five years old or younger; the closure of the transatlantic slave trade in 1808 had prevented adult Africans from entering the population and accelerated rates of natural increase.

The free black population had grown to 312,000 by 1830. Among free blacks the gender ratio was actually slightly skewed toward females. As part of a trend that had developed during the Revolutionary period, the majority of free blacks lived in the North or Upper South. In fact, three-fifths of free people of color lived in only four states: Maryland, Virginia, New York, and Pennsylvania. Nonetheless, in constituting nearly 16 percent of the entire black population, free blacks had reached a record high proportion of their racial group. Subsequent limitations on manumitting slaves, however, would arrest this growing proportion of free blacks, whose relative numbers declined later in the decade. By 1840, although free people of color numbered 386,000, their demographic increase had not kept pace with the rapidly expanding slave population; only 13.4 percent of African Americans in that year were free. The expansion of the "cotton kingdom" in the Deep South had produced an exploding slave population; increasing at nearly a 25 percent rate during the 1830s, that population had swelled to approximately 2.5 million by 1840. These numbers illustrate the economic and territorial expansion of slavery away from the Upper South.

Improved Health. One important factor in the massive increase in the slave population was better health, most of which can be attributed to advances in pre- and postnatal care for both mothers and children. In 1850 the mortality rate among slave women giving birth had decreased to just 1 out of every 167 women—which was even slightly better than the maternal death rate of southern whites. Though the death rate for slave infants was higher, it marked a considerable improvement from the eighteenth century, when one-half of all slave infants died before their first birthdays. In 1850, 183 slaves out of every 1,000 died before reaching the age of one, which was noticeably higher than the white infant mortality rate (146 per 1,000). The infant mortality rate for slaves was much closer to that of southern white infants, whose mortality rate was 177 per 1,000.

Likewise, life expectancy rates were increasing. Largely as a result of better nutrition, the life expectancy for American slaves born in 1850 was thirty-six years; though abysmally low compared with the modern life expectancy, this rate was a marked increase from the eighteenth century and was quite close to the concurrent life expectancy of whites, which was forty years. Moreover, compared with urban industrial workers in both the United States and Europe during the nineteenth century, African American slaves could expect to live significantly longer. The monetary value of slaves, which increased as the cotton kingdom expanded, certainly made owners much more diligent in taking care of them.

The trends in lower infant mortality rates and longer life expectancies for slaves continued through the 1840s. By 1850 the slave population had increased to 3.2 million, which represented a 28 percent increase from 1840. Illustrating the role of natural increase on this population, the gender ratio had by then reached equilibrium. Although the population of free people of color stood at 424,000, their share of the total black population continued to decline, representing just 13.3 percent in 1850. Thus, with a total population of 3.62 million in 1850, African Americans constituted about 16 percent of the U.S. population. This represented a relative decline from 1840, when black Americans accounted for about 17 percent of the total population, and from 1830, when they constituted 18 percent. This small but steady decline in the African American proportion of the population was the result not only of significant rates of natural increase among whites but also of a wave of white immigration, particularly from Ireland.

The last full decade of slavery, the 1850s, was also one of tremendous growth for the black slave population. With nearly 4 million slaves counted in 1860, the enslaved population had grown by 23 percent during the 1850s. Continuing the trend that had begun following the invention of the cotton gin in the 1790s, the slave population had made a decisive shift from the Upper South states of Virginia, Maryland, Kentucky, and North Carolina to the Deep South states of Georgia, Alabama, Mississippi, Louisiana, and Texas. In 1860 nearly one-half of the slave population resided in those five Deep South states; in 1830 only one-quarter of the country's slaves had lived in that region. In the three decades immediately prior to the Civil War, the production of cotton had opened attractive land for potential planters, who then uprooted tens of thousands of slaves from the Upper South.

Between 1830 and 1860 the mechanism for moving slaves from the Upper to the Deep South—the interstate slave trade—had accelerated dramatically in volume. Estimates by decade indicate that the domestic slave trade peaked in the 1830s, when 223,000 slaves were sold from the Upper South to the Deep South. The volume slowed considerably in the 1840s, but the aggregate figure of 149,000 slaves sold to the Deep South still represented an impressive segment of the black slave population. With a further 193,000 slaves sold from the exporting region to the importing region during the 1850s, the demographic shift to the Deep South had been completed. Overall, from 1790 to 1860 approximately 835,000 slaves were sold through the interstate slave trade.

The free black population also continued its growth during this time period, with 488,000 free people of color representing 11 percent of the black population in 1860. Most free blacks continued to live in either the North or the Upper South; in the Deep South free people of color constituted less than 2 percent of the black population. Indeed, 60 percent of free blacks lived in five states: Maryland, Virginia, Pennsylvania, New York, and Ohio; Ohio had become an important destination for free people of color during the 1840s and 1850s. Portending the post–Civil War shift of many African Americans from the South to the Midwest, the increasingly high numbers of free people of color in Ohio laid the social foundations for a black population that would eventually be both numerous and vibrant in the region. On the eve of the Civil War, the black population of 4.4 million represented 14 percent of the nation's total population. Of these, 3.99 million were slaves and 448,000 were free blacks, with all but 250,000 of them living in the South.

Upheaval during the Civil War and Reconstruction. The Civil War (1861–1865) eventually brought the end of slavery, but during and after the conflict significant chaos arose within the African American population; free and enslaved blacks alike were significantly affected by the war. In late 1862, when President Abraham Lincoln issued the Emancipation Proclamation, scores of black slaves left their owners. In areas such as Georgia where the Union armies progressed across Confederate territory, slaves saw the proximity of the blue-clad soldiers as their cue to run away. The result was a tremendous demographic upheaval that split up families and shifted huge populations of slaves between locales.

The 1870 census provides evidence of those demographic changes. The African American population, by then 4.9 million, had grown at a much slower rate during the 1860s than in preceding decades. Although the 11 percent rate of growth represented continued natural increase among black Americans, the disruption to families, considerable migrations, and general chaos following the war all presented serious obstacles to the establishment of the stable relationships that would have produced significantly higher birth rates.

Some migrations, on the other hand, did produce stable, vibrant black communities in places where few African Americans had lived before the Civil War. The African American population in seven states and Washington, D.C., jumped at least 75 percent between 1860 and 1870. Aside from the nation's capital, where the black pop-

ulation of forty-three thousand represented a 303 percent increase from 1860, all the other states were in the Midwest or West. Michigan, Ohio, and Wisconsin proved attractive places for African American migrants, with the black populations of those states increasing by approximately 80 percent during the decade. Other states saw the doubling, tripling, and even quintupling of their African American populations, as abundant farmland and less prominent racism attracted thousands of blacks away from the South. Indiana (the population of which grew twice over to 24,560), Illinois (more than three times over to 28,762), Iowa (five times over to 5,762), and Kansas (twenty-seven times over to 17,108) became the most common destinations for black Americans looking for nonsouthern places to live.

Unlike previous and subsequent internal migrations in the region, the physical movement of African Americans within the South during the late 1860s and early 1870s had no discernible pattern. The most typical migration was actually fairly short, as recently freed slaves filled backcountry roads looking for family members who had been sold to nearby plantations. Moreover, the advent of sharecropping, tenant farming, and the crop lien system kept many former slaves on the very land they had been forced to work as slaves. Tenancy, a system of some change—but also of exploitation, perhaps resembling slavery more than differing from it—had the demographic effect of delaying, if not stopping altogether, the movement of black Americans from one region to another.

By 1870 the numbers of African Americans had actually declined in a handful of states, all in the Upper South, with the exception of Missouri. Virginia, West Virginia, and Kentucky lost approximately 5 percent of their 1860 black populations; in Missouri the African American population declined by only 2 percent. The opportunities in the Midwest, which was a reasonable distance from all four of those states, proved enticing for thousands of former slaves and free blacks who wanted to leave the vestiges of slavery behind.

Migration from the South, 1877–1895. The end of Reconstruction in 1877 sparked a period during which whites reacted to the political and economic gains made by African Americans since the Civil War. Known as "Redemption," this backlash saw the reinstitution of black codes—highly restrictive laws governing the public behavior of African Americans. Eventually known as Jim Crow segregation, this process initiated the first mass exodus of African Americans from the South. Usually occurring in spurts rather than in consistent streams—at least until the Great Migration of the 1910s and early 1920s—these migration patterns considerably altered the demographics of African Americans.

The most famous of these migrations was the Exoduster Movement of 1879, when an estimated twenty thousand African Americans migrated from Louisiana, Texas, and Mississippi to Kansas. Building on the earlier migrations of African Americans to Kansas and the Midwest, promoters like Benjamin Singleton, a former slave who had become a leading advocate for African Americans following the Civil War, established a number of black towns in the region. Advertising by railroad companies and land promoters helped encourage the exodus, but worsening conditions for blacks in the South played a larger part. A sense of impending doom, combined with an idyllic picture of life in the West, evolved into a millenarian vision of Kansas as the new promised land. During the spring of 1879 hundreds and then thousands of black families from all over the South joined the exodus to Kansas. Most of these Exodusters managed to reach Kansas, but their huge numbers and relative penury overwhelmed the resources of the various charitable organizations set up to assist them. Few had enough money to start farming, so most had to turn to wage labor, and some became destitute.

By 1880 the exodus had ended. News of the problems encountered by the first Exodusters, the growing efforts by Kansans to discourage further immigration, and the difficulties of winter travel all broke the momentum. The black population in Kansas had grown to forty-three thousand in 1880 from seventeen thousand in 1870. In 1880 southern Democrats in Congress produced a committee report blaming the migration on enticement by Republicans and promoters. It seems clear, however, that whatever the attractions of the West, the Exoduster Movement of 1879 was primarily a desperate reaction to the economic and political repression faced by African Americans in the South.

By 1880 the African American population in the country had reached 6.6 million, or just over 13 percent of the nation's total population. Nine out of every ten black Americans continued to live in the South; the small stream of migration to the Midwest and West continued, however, as states like Ohio, Indiana, Illinois, Michigan, and Iowa, as well as Kansas, remained the most likely goals for African Americans determined to leave the South.

Yet, in relative terms, these migrations from the South tend to obscure the more common situation of black Americans staying closer to home. The 1870s was a particularly stable one demographically, as rapidly increasing birth rates compensated for the slower growth of the 1860s. The 35 percent rate of increase among black Americans between 1870 and 1880 illustrates the establishment of more stable family units as well as continuing improvement in mortality and life expectancy. In short, while the end of Reconstruction presented significant challenges to African Americans, in demographic terms the late nineteenth century was a period of significant stabilization.

In 1890 about seven thousand blacks from Arkansas joined a mass migration to Oklahoma, which occurred in part because of the popularity of the creation of all-black towns. In 1891 Langston, Oklahoma, was established with the intent of forming the nucleus of an all-black state in the West. Five thousand other African Americans headed west to become cowboys, participating in the great cattle drives that linked Abilene, Texas, and Dodge City, Kansas. The 1890 population of African Americans in Texas, 488,000, represented a 24 percent increase from 1880 and was nearly double that of 1870. As with many Americans, African Americans found the West to have attractive economic opportunities and appealing social freedom.

The result was not only a shift in where African Americans lived but also a change in economic class for most blacks. Though farming in the Midwest and sharecropping in the South had their limitations in producing economic success, African Americans were enjoying much better standards of living than they had under slavery. Some black Americans, primarily those from families who had been free before the Civil War, even enjoyed elite urban professions in cities like Washington, D.C., Baltimore, and New Orleans. For them, new opportunities in higher education provided the path to continued economic and social success. Yet this class of elite African Americans represented only a tiny sliver of the nation's black population, most of which continued to be mired in poverty, albeit with improvements over the 1860s.

Across the board, African American literacy rates had improved dramatically since the Civil War. Largely as a result of the establishment of schools for black children by the Freedmen's Bureau and the end of laws prohibiting African American slaves from reading and writing, the black literacy rate had jumped from 15 percent in 1865 to 50 percent by the 1890s. Though this did not translate into immediate economic gain for many African Americans, it did lay the groundwork for subsequent efforts to improve the lot of blacks in the United States.

By the early 1890s African Americans numbered 7.5 million. Although the South remained the geographical center for the country's black population, migrations to the West and Midwest, as well as to southern cities where economic opportunity was greater than in rural areas, had begun an important long-term shift for black Americans. While the Great Migration was still two decades away, more African Americans found urban areas to be socially hospitable and economically viable. In short, after centuries of being the most demographically unique segment of the nation's population, by 1895 African Americans exhibited the patterns of westward movement, urban migration, and natural increase that characterized all of the late-nineteenth-century United States.

[*See also* Africanisms; African Americans and the West; African Diaspora; Baltimore, Maryland, Slavery in; Black Family; Black Separatism; Colonization; Education; Emigration to Africa; Entrepreneurs; Exoduster Movement; Food; Folklore; Free African Americans to 1828; Free African Americans before the Civil War (North); Free African Americans before the Civil War (South); Freedmen; Freedmen's Bureau; Gender; Gradual Emancipation; Health; Immigrants; Laws and Legislation; New York; Poverty; Race, Theories of; Racism; Segregation; Sharecropping; Slave Trade; Slavery; *and* Urbanization.]

BIBLIOGRAPHY

Berlin, Ira. *Generations of Captivity: A History of African-American Slaves*. Cambridge, MA: Harvard University Press, 2003. A well-received overview of the phases of African American life in the United States up to the Civil War.

Cramer, Clayton E. *Black Demographic Data, 1790–1860: A Sourcebook*. Westport, CT: Greenwood, 1997. A helpful resource that is based largely on census records.

Fogel, Robert W. *Without Consent or Contract: The Rise and Fall of American Slavery*. New York: Norton, 1989.

Fogel, Robert W., and Stanley L. Engerman. *Time on the Cross: The Economics of American Negro Slavery*. Lanham, MD: University Press of America, 1984.

Kolchin, Peter. *American Slavery: 1619–1877*. New York: Hill and Wang, 1993. An excellent synthesis of slavery in the United States.

Kulikoff, Allan. *Tobacco and Slaves: The Development of Southern Cultures in the Chesapeake, 1680–1800*. Chapel Hill: University of North Carolina Press, 1986.

Morgan, Philip D. *Slave Counterpoint: Black Culture in the Eighteenth-Century Chesapeake and Lowcountry*. Chapel Hill: University of North Carolina Press, 1998.

Painter, Nell Irvin. *Exodusters: Black Migration to Kansas after Reconstruction*. Lawrence: University Press of Kansas, 1986.

Steckel. Richard H. *The Economics of U.S. Slave and Southern White Fertility*. New York: Garland, 1985.

Tadman, Michael. *Speculators and Slaves: Masters, Traders, and Slaves in the Old South*. Madison: University of Wisconsin Press, 1996. The definitive source on the domestic slave trade.

—KEVIN D. ROBERTS

DENMARK VESEY CONSPIRACY.

DENMARK VESEY CONSPIRACY. The plot organized in 1822 by Denmark Vesey, a free black carpenter from Charleston, South Carolina, was the largest slave conspiracy in North American history. Although he was brought into the city in 1783 as a slave of Captain Joseph Vesey, Telemaque, as he was then known, purchased his freedom in December 1799 with lottery winnings. For the next twenty-two years, Vesey earned his living as a craftsman and, according to white authorities, was distinguished for his great strength and "activity." It was said that the black community always looked up to him with awe and respect. His last (and probably third) wife, Susan Vesey, was born a slave but became free before Vesey's death. But his first wife, Beck, remained a slave, as did Vesey's sons, Polydore, Robert, and Sandy. Sandy was the only one of his children to be implicated in Vesey's conspiracy.

Stirrings of Rebellion. In about 1818 Vesey joined the city's new African Methodist Episcopal Church congregation. Formed when 4,376 slaves and free blacks resigned from the Methodist fold when church authorities voted to construct a hearse house atop a small black cemetery, the African Church (as both whites and blacks called it) quickly became the center of Charleston's enslaved community. Sandy Vesey also joined, as did four of Vesey's closest friends: Peter Poyas, a literate and highly skilled ship carpenter; Monday Gell, an African-born Ibo who labored as a harness maker; Rolla Bennett, the manservant of Governor Thomas Bennett; and "Gullah" Jack Pritchard, an East African priest who had been purchased in Zinguebar (in present-day Tanzania) in 1806.

The temporary closure of the church by city authorities in June 1818 and the arrest of 140 congregants, one of them presumably Vesey himself, only reinforced the determination of black Carolinians to maintain a place of independent worship and established the motivation for the Vesey conspiracy. In 1820 several blacks were arrested for holding a late-night service at the church. On 15 January 1821, Councilman John J. Lafar warned the Reverend Morris Brown that the city would not tolerate class leaders conducting instructional "schools" for slaves, as "the education of such persons was forbidden by law." The "African Church was the people," Monday Gell replied. He and Pritchard had considered insurrection in 1818, he swore, "and now they had begun again to try it."

At the age of fifty-one Vesey thought briefly about immigrating to the English colony of Sierra Leone. But since his children with Beck remained slaves, Vesey resolved instead to orchestrate a rebellion to be followed by a mass exodus from Charleston to Haiti. President Jean-Pierre Boyer had recently encouraged black Americans to bring their skills and capital to his beleaguered republic. Historians have long argued that Vesey's plan stood little hope of success, as the combined power of the Carolina militia and the federal government could overwhelm black attempts to seize and fortify the city. But Vesey did not intend to tarry in Charleston long enough for white military power to present an effective counterassault. "As soon as they could get the money from the Banks, and the goods from the stores," Rolla Bennett insisted, "they should hoist sail for Saint Doming[ue]" and live as free men. For all of his acculturation into Euro-American society, Vesey, as a native of the West Indies island of Saint Thomas, remained a man of the black Atlantic.

Vesey planned the escape for nearly four years. His chief lieutenants included Poyas, Gell, Rolla Bennett, and Pritchard. Although there are no reliable figures for the number of recruits, Charleston alone was home to 12,652 slaves. Pritchard, probably with some exaggeration, boasted that he had 6,600 recruits on plantations across the Cooper and Ashley rivers. The plan called for Vesey's followers to rise at midnight on Sunday, July 14—Bastille Day and the day blacks in Boston celebrated their freedom—slay their masters, and sail for Haiti and freedom. As one southern editor later conceded, "The plot seems to have been well devised, and its operation was extensive."

Those recruited into the plot during the winter of 1822 were directed to arm themselves from their masters' closets. Vesey was also aware that the Charleston Neck militia company stored their three hundred muskets and bayonets in the back room of Benjamin Hammet's King Street store and that Hammet's slave Bacchus had a key. At length, Bacchus agreed to deliver the weapons on the night of the uprising. Because few slaves had any experience with guns, Vesey encouraged his followers to arm themselves with swords or long daggers, which in any case would make for quieter work as the city bells tolled midnight. Vesey also employed several enslaved blacksmiths to forge pike heads and bayonets with sockets, to be fixed at the end of long poles.

Considerably easier than stockpiling weapons was the recruitment of willing young men. With Vesey and Pritchard employed about the city as carpenters, it is hardly surprising that so many other craftsmen became involved in the plot. Most of all, Vesey and his lieutenants recruited from the African Church. As a class leader, Vesey was respected by the church membership and knew each of them well; he knew whom to trust and whom to avoid. As the former Charleston slave Archibald Grimké later wrote, Vesey's nightly classes provided him "with a singularly safe medium for conducting his underground agitation."

Unraveling and Aftermath. The plot unraveled in June 1822, when two slaves, including Rolla's friend George Wilson, a fellow class leader in the African Church, revealed the plan to their owners. Mayor James Hamilton called up the city militia and convened a special court to try the captured insurgents. Vesey was captured at the home of Beck, his first wife, on 21 June and hanged on the morning of Tuesday, 2 July, together with Rolla, Poyas, and three other rebels. According to Hamilton, the six men collectively "met their fate with the heroic fortitude of Martyrs." In all, thirty-five slaves were executed.

Forty-two others, including Sandy Vesey, were sold outside the United States; some, if not all, became slaves in Spanish Cuba. Robert Vesey lived to rebuild the African Church in the fall of 1865.

In the aftermath of the conspiracy, Charleston authorities demolished the African Church and banished Morris Brown to Philadelphia. The state assembly subsequently passed laws prohibiting the reentry of free blacks into the state, and city officials enforced ordinances against teaching African Americans to read. The city council also voted to create a permanent force of 150 guardsmen to patrol the streets around the clock, at an annual cost of twenty-four thousand dollars. To deal with the problem of black mariners bringing information about events around the Atlantic into the state's ports, in December 1822 the legislature passed the Negro Seamen Act, which placed a quarantine on any vessel from another "state or foreign port, having on board any free negroes or persons of color." Although U.S. Circuit Court Judge William Johnson struck the law down as unconstitutional, a defiant assembly renewed the act in late 1823. It would be no coincidence that many of those in South Carolina who nullified a federal tariff enacted in 1832, which benefited trade in the northern states—including then-governor James Hamilton, who resigned his office in 1833 to command troops in defense of his state's right to resist national tariffs—were veterans of the tribunals that had tried Vesey and his men a decade before.

Although no contemporaneous observer of events, white or black, ever voiced doubts about the reality of a slave conspiracy in 1822, in 1964 the historian Richard C. Wade suggested that the plot was little more than angry "loose talk" on the part of Charleston blacks. Wade's thesis, however, was not based only on the faulty premise that urban slaves had too much to lose by being rebellious; it was constructed on faulty data. Wade misidentified key players in the saga, fused two important mulatto informants into a single person, and carefully crafted his prose in such a way as to imply that white contemporaries, including Governor Thomas Bennett, shared his loose-talk thesis. Michael P. Johnson revived the Wade thesis but added the theory that a small number of white authorities concocted the story to justify closing down the African Church and used Vesey as an innocent fall guy.

The church, however, was already in violation of two South Carolina statutes of 1800 and 1803, which is why city authorities consistently closed it down. As other critics of Johnson's theory have observed, in the Lowcountry black men swung from tree branches every day; city authorities hardly had to resort to elaborate hoaxes to justify their brutality. Johnson also assumes that many of the white ministers who visited the condemned in jail, having previously stood up to city authorities by defending the right of blacks to worship in the African Methodist Episcopal Church, would help perpetuate such a grandiose fraud.

[*See also* African Methodist Episcopal Church; Brown, Morris; Crime and Punishment; Riots and Rebellions; *and* Vesey, Denmark.]

BIBLIOGRAPHY

Egerton, Douglas R. *He Shall Go Out Free: The Lives of Denmark Vesey.* Madison, WI: Madison House, 1999.

Freehling, William W. *The Reintegration of American History: Slavery and the Civil War.* New York: Oxford University Press, 1994.

Lofton, John. *Insurrection in South Carolina: The Turbulent World of Denmark Vesey.* Yellow Springs, OH: Antioch Press, 1964.

Paquette, Robert L. "Jacobins of the Lowcountry: The Vesey Plot on Trial." *William and Mary Quarterly*, 3rd. ser., 59.1 (January 2002): 185–192.

—DOUGLAS R. EGERTON

DETROIT. From its establishment as a territory through its statehood and involvement with the Underground Railroad, Michigan had an intimate relationship with the institution of slavery. The city of Detroit, specifically, was the cornerstone of antislavery activity in Michigan. Known as the gateway or door to freedom, Detroit served as a safe haven for many runaway slaves before they secured their freedom across the Detroit River into Canada. Detroit's significance as a geographical location on the Underground Railroad was further reinforced when Frederick Douglass, John Brown, and many other leading abolitionists met in the city in March 1859 to discuss possible ways of subverting the Fugitive Slave Law of 1850. This meeting, along with the coordinated efforts of others who worked tirelessly on the Underground Railroad, underscores the integral role the people of Detroit played in securing the freedom of thousands of slaves.

Long before European explorers arrived on the shore of the Detroit River, Michigan was inhabited largely by two groups of Indians: the Iroquois, who settled along the south shore of Lake Ontario and the north shore of Lake Erie, and the Algonquins, who settled mostly north of the Saint Lawrence River and along the rims of lakes Huron and Superior. The Iroquois tribes consisted of the Five Nations, the Hurons, and the Neutrals, whereas the Algonquin tribes consisted of the Ottawa, Chippewa, Potawatomi, Sac and Fox, and Miami. Intertribal wars and later competition to gain favor with French fur traders caused representatives from each tribe to migrate and establish posts in Detroit.

The earliest European explorers to arrive in Detroit predicated their missions on converting "heathen" Indians to Christianity, and exploiting natural resources such as copper and animal pelts said to have been abundant in the region. One of the earliest French explorers, Adrien Jolliet, arrived in Detroit in 1669 for the expressed purpose of finding copper and creating a relationship between the French and the Indians. This partnership would later deliver much wealth to the French and much misery to the Indians.

When discussing the early interactions between the French and the Indians, it is extremely important to understand the magnitude of the impact on both parties as well as on Detroit. The fur trade, for the French, was one of the many economic opportunities that had previously stood for Spain and Britain's success in the New World. With the supply of fur exhausted in Europe, and the demands for it ever-increasing, French traders found themselves relying on Indian trappers to obtain rich beaver pelts. In exchange for the pelts, traders, much to the dismay of Jesuit missionaries, offered the Indians French brandy or "firewater," the ramifications of which are still felt today in surviving Indian tribes.

Detroit became a permanent French settlement in 1701 when Antoine de la Moth Cadillac established Fort Pontchartrain on the Detroit River. Cadillac's reasoning was not only economic, but also strategic. *Le Detroit* or "the straits" proved to be advantageous both defensively and offensively in case of an attack. The river's connection to Lake Saint Clair and the Saint Lawrence Strait made the shipping of people and cargo easier and faster, and with the water to their backs, it was very difficult for adversaries to attack the fort in secret. Even after Cadillac's departure, the fort remained strong and under French control for almost sixty years.

However, growing commercial competition between the French and British erupted in the French and Indian War of 1744, which reached the Great Lakes region around 1755. The fort fell to Britain and Sir Jeffrey Amherst on 28 November 1760. The Indians, especially the Ottawas, Hurons, and Pottowatomi had fought alongside the French, and now that the Detroit River was effectively under British control, trading was restricted to British stipulations. Under Amherst's direction, the Indians were left without rum, guns, or ammunition. The growing frustration amongst the Indians led Chief Pontiac to plan a siege of Fort Detroit. Though he and his allies fought the English with some success, French betrayal and disenchantment among the Indians themselves made it impossible for Pontiac to achieve his vision of conquering the British. As more and more settlers came to Detroit and the Northwest after the American Revolution, the land rights to which the Indian tribes had once held claim quickly evaporated into national discussions of how the "new" land would be used by the Americans. However, Detroit, the scene of so much Indian degradation, would become the hope for another oppressed population in the new country.

When the territory of Michigan was officially organized by the United States Congress in 1805, the question of whether this territory would allow slaveholding was widely discussed. Though Article 6 of the Northwest Ordinance of 1787 specifically forbade slavery in the territory, it did allow British and French slaveholders to retain slaves acquired before the passing of the ordinance. This provision both pacified existing slaveholders in Michigan and offered hope to many African Americans seeking refuge from the cruelties of slavery.

Detroit proved to be an almost ideal place of settlement for many free African Americans. Abundant in natural resources and, after the construction of the Erie Canal in 1817, closely connected to the wealth gleaned from extensive trade, the city provided economic opportunity and prosperity for those who actively participated in its commerce. The first generation of African Americans in Detroit found that without the shackles of slavery, it was possible to create flourishing businesses and communities.

The capital generated from these flourishing businesses and communities allowed for the construction of some of Detroit's oldest and most active churches. The participation of congregants from churches like the Saint John–Saint Luke Evangelical Church, the First Congregational Church, and the Second Baptist Church was essential to the success of the Underground Railroad. Tactics such as hiding runaway slaves in coffins and then carrying the coffins to the riverfront in a "funeral procession" to freedom were not uncommon methods used to detract suspicion from curious antiabolitionist onlookers. The Second Baptist Church, founded in 1836 by thirteen former slaves, was the first African American church in Detroit and is believed to have played the largest role in Detroit's Underground Railroad effort.

On 26 January 1837 Michigan achieved statehood and just three months later, on 26 April, the Detroit Anti-Slavery Society was formed. This rapid organization of abolitionists in Detroit leaves little room for doubt regarding their commitment to ensuring that the new state would remain free to all fugitive slaves. The Detroit abolitionists' commitment to the Underground Railroad seems to have become all the more passionate when they employed a radical group, known as the McKensyites, to liberate slaves. The McKensyites, consisting mostly of former prisoners and other social deviants, were known to steal slaves from southern plantations and place them in the hands of the caretakers of the Underground Railroad.

Prior to the Fugitive Slave Law of 1850, Detroit was the final destination for many fugitive and manumitted slaves.

Indeed, slaves such as Henry W. Bibb and John Freeman Wells made their homes in Detroit after harrowing escapes from bondage. This changed after the passage of the Fugitive Slave Law, which stated that runaway slaves could be hunted down and returned to slavery regardless of whether they resided in a free or slave state; Detroit could no longer be considered a safe haven. The city, under the code name "midnight," instead became the last stop on the long journey to freedom in Canada.

The Fugitive Slave Law created an enormous outcry from abolitionists across the country, and on 12 March 1859 some of the most prominent figures in the antislavery movement met in Detroit at the home of William Webb to discuss possible ways of subverting the law's provisions. In addition to Webb, local abolitionists attending the meeting included George De Baptiste, William Lambert, and Dr. Joseph Ferguson, and Brown and Douglass also attended. During this meeting Brown is believed to have first discussed with Douglass his plans to raid Harpers Ferry, a heavily armed U.S. arsenal. Brown believed that the only way to counteract the Fugitive Slave Law was through arming slaves and convincing them to rise up against their masters. Douglass argued that such a mission was not only violent but also foolhardy. He stressed that innocent white bystanders were sure to be injured or killed and that the long-term goals of abolitionism would become more difficult to achieve given the likely repercussions of such an offensive plan. Douglass later reiterated these sentiments in a speech he gave in the churchyard of the Second Baptist Church. Having experienced the horrors of slavery himself, Douglass felt there was no need to compound the immense suffering of many for a moment's gratification.

History proved the assertions that Douglass made in Detroit to be true. Brown's raid on Harpers Ferry was a complete disaster. It ended the lives of many, including Brown, who was tried, convicted, and hung for treason. Even more significant is the fact that the raid on Harpers Ferry stiffened the resolve of many slaveholding politicians and plantation owners to doggedly pursue their runaway property, thereby making it twice as dangerous and difficult for abolitionists and Underground Railroad workers in cities like Detroit to complete their missions in a successful manner.

To commemorate the spirit of freedom, a bronze statue by Ed Dwight depicting a group of fugitive slaves was erected in 2001 on the banks of the narrow waterway separating Detroit from Canada. A mother holding a sleeping baby looks toward Windsor, Ontario, with hopeful eyes. Behind her stands an adolescent male, signaling to other runaways, urging them to hurry toward freedom. This statue honors the first African American Detroiters and their struggles to achieve not only a free state of being but also a free state of mind.

[*See also* Abolitionism; Antislavery Movement; Bibb, Henry W.; Black Church; Brown, John; Canada; Douglass, Frederick; Free African Americans before the Civil War (North); Fugitive Slave Law of 1850; Harpers Ferry Raid; Monuments, Museums, Public Markers; *and* Underground Railroad.]

BIBLIOGRAPHY
Bibb, Henry. *Narrative of the Life and Adventures of Henry Bibb, an American Slave, Written by Himself*. New York: privately published, 1849.
Horton, James Oliver. *Free People of Color: Inside the African American Community*. Washington, DC: Smithsonian Institution Press, 1993.
Katzman, David M. *Before the Ghetto: Black Detroit in the Nineteenth Century*. Urbana: University of Illinois Press, 1973.

—STEPHANIE J. WILHELM

DICKINSON, ANNA ELIZABETH (b. 28 October 1842; d. 22 October 1932), abolitionist and feminist. Born in Philadelphia, Anna Elizabeth Dickinson was the youngest of five children of the devoted Quakers John and Mary Edmondson Dickinson. When Anna was two years old, her father died shortly after giving an antislavery speech. Although it is unlikely that Dickinson remembered her father, she may have been inspired by his legacy.

After John's death the family struggled financially, but Anna still received a quality education, attending the Friends' Select School in Philadelphia and the Greenwood Institute in New Brighton, Pennsylvania; at the latter she was known as an avid reader and questioner. She showed early promise, publishing her first article at age fourteen in the *Liberator*, the newspaper that served as a platform for the radical reformer and abolitionist William Lloyd Garrison.

Following her 1860 address to the Pennsylvania Anti-Slavery Society and her 1861 speech entitled "Women's Rights and Wrongs," Dickinson began receiving speaking invitations from reform groups throughout New England. She was praised for her "combination of eloquence, sarcastic wit, and bold, occasionally outrageous statements." At the outset of the Civil War she worked at the U.S. Mint but was fired for accusing the Union general George B. McClellan of treason when he lost an important battle.

On 1 January 1863, as an orchestra played Beethoven's "Ode to Joy," Dickinson and Frederick Douglass spoke passionately to a crowd anticipating the announcement of the Emancipation Proclamation. When the proclamation was confirmed, there was a "wonderful tumult" among the "mainly black" crowd. On 6 July 1863 the two abolitionists appeared together in Philadelphia to promote "colored enlistments" in the Union army, with Dickinson noting that blacks must "sink, generation after generation, century after century, into deeper depths, into more absolute degradation; or mount to the heights of glory and of fame." Dickinson and Douglass maintained correspondence; in one letter she closed with "always faithfully, your friend."

In January 1864 Dickinson, known then as "America's Joan of Arc," spoke before President Abraham Lincoln in Washington. After the Civil War, Dickinson focused her speeches on the Reconstruction and feminist issues. She also advocated suffrage for men and women of all races, believing universal voting rights would strengthen the country. In 1866 Dickinson spoke beside Douglass in a passionate plea for ratification of the Fourteenth Amendment, which would allow blacks the same rights as whites. Douglass later said that Dickinson was "magnificent in her advocacy" and wrote that his heart was "full to overflowing" for her support.

By the 1870s Dickinson had cut back on public speaking and had begun writing nonfiction books and novels; she also acted in her own plays. When she gave a speech before the Republican Party in 1888 she was not well received. Dickinson eventually experienced difficulty coping with her dwindling power and voice. Her sister Susan led efforts to commit her, and in 1891 Anna was briefly incarcerated in the Danville State Hospital for the Insane. After her release she sued to restore her good name and received damages. She lived out her later years in Goshen, New York, above storefronts on Main Street and then in the home of the hospitable Ackley family. She died in Goshen just a few days before her ninetieth birthday.

[*See also* Abolitionism; Antislavery Movement; Civil War, Participation and Recruitment of Black Troops in; Douglass, Frederick; Feminist Movement; Fourteenth Amendment; Garrison, William Lloyd; Oratory and Verbal Arts; Reconstruction; Society of Friends (Quakers); Suffrage, Women's; Union Army, African Americans in; *and* Voting Rights.]

BIBLIOGRAPHY
Campbell, Karlyn Kohrs, ed. *Women Public Speakers in the United States, 1800–1925: A Bio-Critical Sourcebook*. Westport, CT: Greenwood, 1993.
From Slavery to Freedom: The African American Pamphlet Collection, 1824–1909. Washington, DC: Library of Congress, 2000.
Gallman, J. Matthew. "An Inspiration to Work: Anna Elizabeth Dickinson, Public Orator." In *The War Was You and Me*, edited by Joan E. Cashin, 159–182. Princeton, NJ: Princeton University Press, 2002.
McFeely, William S. *Frederick Douglass*. New York: Norton, 1991.
Papers of Anna E. Dickinson, Library of Congress, Washington, DC.

—KELLY BOYER SAGERT

DISCRIMINATION. [*This entry contains two subentries dealing with discrimination against African Americans from the early seventeenth century through 1895. The first article discusses the evolution of federal laws and abusive perceptions that disenfranchised African Americans to 1830, while the second article discusses the development of separate institutions and organizations through which African Americans fought discrimination.*]

Legislation and African Americans to 1830

Discrimination by whites against African Americans began during the earliest periods of settlement in America. In Virginia in the 1620s the earliest blacks were regarded as indentured servants, but their names appeared at the end of passenger lists, and most did not have a last, or English, name. Before slavery was codified in the 1660s, punishments were harsher for blacks: when seven servants ran away, for example, the whites merely had their terms of service lengthened, while the black was branded and made to wear irons—the assumption being that he would serve for life. Punishment for fornication was greater if interracial sex was involved, and slave codes ensured that children took the status of their mother. By the 1660s blacks were presumed to be slaves, whites to be free.

Rising Free Black Presence. During the colonial period free blacks were allowed to own property, move about freely, and own guns. They were not denied the right to vote, although few probably met the required property qualifications. Pennsylvania, Tennessee, and North Carolina specifically allowed blacks to vote in their first constitutions, but the measures were repealed in the 1830s. One reason for this initial laxity was that there were relatively few free blacks in the British colonies before the American Revolution.

As Revolutionary Americans proclaimed the equality of all men, some masters questioned the justice of slavery. Many freed their slaves, leading to the rise of free black urban communities in both the South and North. Statistics for Virginia, for example, show an eightfold increase in the free black population from 1782 to 1790. There may have been as many as 6,000 free blacks in the United States in 1780, 59,455 in 1790, 108,395 in 1800, and 186,446 in 1810. Most lived in the cities, where they could form communities and escaped slaves could find protection. The rural, predominantly tobacco-based Upper South began to decline economically in the late eighteenth century, causing masters to either manumit slaves or sell them to a flourishing Lower South. Thus, in the Upper South as well as in northern cities, poor whites hoping to obtain employment found themselves threatened by blacks who would usually work for less.

After slaves ran away by the thousands to join the British during the War of Independence and the slaves of Saint Domingue revolted and established an independent black state between 1791 and 1804, whites further began to consider free blacks a potential nucleus for social disorder. Federal laws reflected this evolving attitude. In 1790 the new nation denied naturalization to black immigrants. Although blacks had fought in integrated units during the American Revolution, in 1792 they were forbidden from enrolling in the militia. After 1810 they could no longer serve as mail carriers—white lawmakers feared they would communicate subversive ideas to black communities. Beginning with Ohio in 1803, most states admitted to the Union before the Civil War forbade the presence of free Negroes, although some accepted those who could post considerable amounts of money to guarantee their good behavior.

Congress approved all such prohibitive state constitutions; in general the federal government did not interfere with states' desires for racial control. After Denmark Vesey's real or alleged planned uprising in 1822, South Carolina, followed by other southern states, mandated that black sailors be confined to jail while their ships were in port and that either ship captains pay their expenses or the sailors be sold into slavery. In vain the British government protested against the blacks in its merchant marine being confined, notwithstanding a commercial treaty with the United States prohibiting discriminatory treatment of each other's sailors.

Restriction of Activities. Northern as well as southern states eventually disenfranchised blacks. By the Civil War, only in New England—where blacks composed a much smaller proportion of the population than elsewhere (under 2 percent)—did blacks have equal voting rights. The only other state allowing blacks to vote was New York, which after 1821 required that they possess $250 worth of property, whereas all adult white males could vote.

Several northern states joined the South in prohibiting free blacks as well as slaves from serving on juries or testifying in court in cases involving whites. Black vagrants were subject to harsher penalties than whites; Illinois permitted them to be sold into slavery. Because of widespread black poverty and the prejudices of judges and juries, there were disproportionately greater numbers of black prisoners than white. In 1826 blacks constituted 16.7, 25, and 33.3 percent of the prisoners in Massachusetts, New York, and Pennsylvania, respectively, and only 1.4, 2.8, and 2.9 percent of those states' populations. Black prisoners, like almost all black school students, were segregated in inferior facilities.

Education, too, was denied to blacks. Only twenty-eight blacks graduated from American colleges before the Civil

War, the first from Dartmouth, in New Hampshire, and Wesleyan, in Connecticut. Case Western Reserve and Oberlin, in Ohio, founded by antislavery New Englanders, also admitted blacks; however, most of New England resisted integration. In the early 1830s Prudence Crandall's attempt to found an interracial school in Canterbury, Connecticut, met with physical violence and legal barriers, as did an attempt to start a black men's college in Canaan.

Religious bodies, too, became more racist after the Revolution. White Methodists and Baptists, who had converted blacks and preached to them at integrated meetings during the late eighteenth century, began to insist on segregated churches. Even where the two races worshipped together, as in Quaker meetings, blacks would be relegated to special benches in the rear or on the sides. White denominations rarely ordained black ministers; when they did, as with the Episcopal Diocese of New York in 1819, neither the priest nor the congregation could vote at diocesan conventions. The major spur for the founding of black churches, first autonomously organized in Philadelphia in the 1790s, was the refusal of whites to worship beside blacks who had helped to build and pay for their very churches.

Such concerns were moot for most African Americans, who suffered far more from prohibitions against holding the jobs they had held in the eighteenth century. In the South states and cities passed laws restricting blacks to certain trades; certain such trades, including barbering, bricklaying, shoemaking, and food service, contained sizable numbers of blacks, some of whom acquired considerable wealth. In the North informal pressure from white majorities proved similarly effective in restricting African American employment. In New York City all of the chimney sweeps were black; on the other hand, blacks were gradually excluded from the roles of cartmen or teamsters that they had performed in the eighteenth century.

The majority of free blacks worked in unskilled occupations as laborers (men) or domestic servants (women). While no segregated housing ordinances were passed, in general blacks congregated in certain neighborhoods on the outskirts of cities or in undesirable areas near sewage disposal or docks. In such areas they would typically mingle with the white poor; outside the Deep South—where there were very few free blacks, and a good number of those were well-to-do—those who could afford to do so preferred not to live near blacks. One result of this discrimination was that black urban communities developed their own middle class; black doctors, schoolteachers, ministers, and shopkeepers became community leaders, as few white professionals and merchants would service black clients.

Public accommodations were also segregated. In theaters, blacks sat in galleries if admitted at all. Once in-side, they often had to endure portrayals of themselves by whites in blackface, who depicted them as lazy, ostentatious, ugly, and criminal. Hotels, railroads, steamboats, and omnibuses segregated blacks in inferior accommodations or, again, not at all. White and black workers received different pay, as when both black and white teachers taught at all-black schools. Interestingly, blacks who occupied definitively inferior positions were admitted to the same places as whites: black nurses for white children could go to white hotels, and black janitors and cooks could work at white schools.

Perceptions of African Americans. Perhaps the greatest discrimination suffered by blacks was both psychological and physical abuse. Plays, speakers, newspapers, and other publications all stressed blacks' inferiority and unworthiness for citizenship. Free blacks were frequently whipped for crimes for which whites would be merely imprisoned or fined—a reminder that they were still closer to black slaves than to free whites. Many if not most white Americans would have preferred to send free blacks to Africa, as the literature of the American Colonization Society, founded in 1817, reveals. The society's plans were supported by the U.S. presidents James Madison and Andrew Jackson, the presidential candidates Henry Clay, Stephen Douglas, and Winfield Scott, and the Supreme Court chief justice John Marshall; the society only failed in its efforts because of prohibitive costs and the resistance of African Americans.

Nearly every black community in the nation suffered at one time or another when white mobs, fearful that blacks planned to rise up against them or would otherwise threaten the social order, wreaked havoc with the connivance or complaisance of local authorities. In 1829 white Cincinnatians, fearful of a growing, disorderly black community, decided to exercise the Ohio law forbidding entry to blacks and drove out nearly half the city's two thousand free blacks. Blacks in Philadelphia suffered five major mob actions between 1829 and 1844—most notably the incineration of Pennsylvania Hall, where black and white abolitionists planned to meet, within a few days of its completion. In the South, after learning of Denmark Vesey's purported conspiracy in 1822, white Charlestonians formed vigilante groups that raided black neighborhoods with impunity.

Outside of Louisiana and ports on the Gulf of Mexico, African Americans in the South endured the same forms of discrimination as in the North, in addition to other forms. Black criminals or debtors could be sentenced to slavery by white jurors, and free African Americans had to carry freedom certificates, which had to be produced for examination by any white person at any time, to prove they were not slaves. Cities required free blacks to register upon arrival and would periodically check black churches and neighborhoods for compliance. Municipalities punished blacks who supposedly insulted whites or failed to defer to them—as, for instance, by not stepping out of their way on a sidewalk. The children of free blacks whose parents could not support them or who were orphaned were given apprenticeships, usually at menial jobs, until adulthood. In some states, blacks who owned property were assigned, or sometimes could choose, a white guardian to manage it for them; much like women, they were not regarded as rational creatures capable of handling such matters responsibly.

Some exceptions existed to the general patterns of discrimination. Outside of cities, blacks in New England were so few that, like the Du Bois family of Great Barrington, Massachusetts, they could be accepted with equanimity. Far more blacks enjoyed unusual degrees of freedom in Louisiana and the ports of Mobile and Pensacola. Under French and Spanish rule, few white women came to Louisiana and Florida; as in these nations' Caribbean colonies, white men often married women of color and legitimated their children. Unlike the rest of the South, where free people were considered either white or black— legally, in most cases, if they had one black grandparent— Louisiana, like Latin America, developed a social hierarchy based on a person's degree of whiteness: a mulatto was half black, a quadroon one-quarter black, and an octoroon one-eighth black. To be sure, throughout the country whites generally favored mixed-race, light-skinned ("brown" or "yellow") African Americans over darker blacks, although outside Louisiana such distinctions were of little importance.

Limited Opportunity. When the United States purchased Louisiana in 1803, about one-fourth of the population of New Orleans and one-sixth of what would become the state of Louisiana nine years later consisted of African Americans or people of mixed race. Many of these blacks were well-to-do and socially accepted, having performed both the commercial services and, critically, military service that lower- and middle-class whites did elsewhere. As white, mostly southern immigrants flocked to New Orleans, however, they abolished the black militia and tried to reduce blacks' rights. Nevertheless, at the battle of New Orleans in 1815 the defunct black militia offered its services to General Andrew Jackson in his stand against a British invasion. Their patriotism was such that Louisiana African Americans retained their militia until the 1830s; in addition members of the militia could travel freely and testify in court against whites, and they remained sufficiently well-off to invest heavily in the largest state bank in the country, the Citizens Bank of Louisiana, formed in 1833. Many of those African Americans, in fact, owned

slaves. Elsewhere as well, such as on the section of the Gulf Coast that had once been Spanish Florida, blacks were allowed a variety of the privileges that they were denied in the rest of the South, such as schooling and the right to carry guns. Despite these potential benefits to living in the region, however, most African Americans there were enslaved rather than free.

The military prowess of blacks from New Orleans anticipated what, on a more general scale, would finally cause some of discrimination's barriers to fall. During the Civil War black military participation was a major reason for the desegregation of public transportation and of some schools and public spaces in the North and then in the South under Northern occupation. But as such later landmarks as Jackie Robinson's Major League Baseball debut in 1947 and the Voting Rights Act of 1964 should remind us, the early Republic did little but enhance the racial discrimination that had begun with the first settlers of Virginia—and that only intensified as white Americans, confronted with the increased presence of free blacks who were theoretically equal, developed new laws and practices to nullify this equality.

[*See also* American Colonization Society; Baptists and African Americans; Black Codes and Slave Codes, Colonial; Black Loyalists; Black Militia; Civil Rights; Crime and Punishment; Denmark Vesey Conspiracy; Free African Americans to 1828; Inheritance and Slave Status; Integration; Methodist Church and African Americans; Occupations; Race, Theories of; Religion; Segregation; Skin Color; Society of Friends (Quakers) and African Americans; Stereotypes of African Americans; Violence against African Americans; Urbanization; Voting Rights; *and* Work.]

BIBLIOGRAPHY

Berlin, Ira. *Slaves without Masters: The Free Negro in the Antebellum South.* New York: Pantheon, 1974.

Curry, Leonard P. *The Free Black in Urban America, 1800–1850: The Shadow of the Dream.* Chicago: University of Chicago Press, 1981.

Litwack, Leon F. *North of Slavery: The Negro in the Free States, 1790–1860.* Chicago: University of Chicago Press, 1961.

Schweninger, Loren. *Black Property Owners in the South, 1790–1915.* Urbana: University of Illinois Press, 1990.

Werner, John M. *Reaping the Bloody Harvest: Race Relations in the United States during the Age of Jackson, 1824–1849.* New York: Garland, 1986.

—WILLIAM PENCAK

African American Persistence against Discrimination

From 1830 to 1895 discrimination based on race permeated almost all aspects of American life. The institution of chattel slavery perpetuated the notion that African Americans were inferior to Americans of European descent, and the myth of their inferiority allowed for their unequal treatment under the law, which in turn supported their exclusion from the educational, governmental, business, and social structures open to white Americans. Whether blacks were enslaved or free, their lives were marred by the persistence of racial discrimination. In response, African Americans built parallel institutions through which to educate themselves, advocate the abolition of slavery, and challenge the laws that barred their access to education, the franchise, employment, and public spaces. Within private enclaves, African Americans armed themselves to combat discrimination in public arenas. Through leadership by example, they did much to displace the myth of black inferiority with the evident reality of black fortitude.

Discrimination in Education. Educational discrimination for most of the nineteenth century was supported by state laws and state constitutional provisions. From approximately 1830 until the legal end of slavery in 1865, laws in the southeastern United States prohibited the teaching of slaves, free blacks, and mulattoes to read and write. Those breaking the law were subject to fines as well as imprisonment.

In the northeastern United States during this time, the education of most African American schoolchildren in primary and secondary schools was segregated by race. *Roberts v. City of Boston* (1850) was the first case filed to challenge racial segregation in public schools. The plaintiff, Benjamin Roberts, brought suit on behalf of his daughter, Sarah Roberts, who was barred from attending the school closest to her home in Boston. The Massachusetts Supreme Court, led by Chief Justice Lemuel Shaw, upheld the local ordinance barring racial integration in Boston schools, with the court reasoning that the segregation provision did not violate the equality clause in the Massachusetts Constitution. However, owing to the efforts of African American Bostonians led by the abolitionist William Cooper Nell, the ordinance allowing racial segregation in public schools was abolished five years later, in 1855.

Throughout the nation, similar changes were equally slow in coming. Frederick Douglass felt the sting of segregation in his attempt to enroll his daughter Rosetta at Seward Seminary, in Rochester, New York. In 1848 Rosetta was admitted to the school, but she was placed in a room by herself and taught separately from the white schoolchildren. Although his daughter was later admitted to another white school, Douglass drew upon his experiences in calling for the end of segregated schooling.

Not all African Americans were as successful as Douglass in securing integrated education for their children. Thus, while working to end segregation in public schools, African Americans, often assisted by white philanthropists, founded their own primary, secondary, and postsecondary schools; blacks developed these institutions of learning out of necessity and a commitment to educating themselves. Mary Smith Kelsick Peake, previously employed by the American Missionary Association to teach freed slaves, created a primary, a secondary, and a postsecondary school all in a single year. She opened an elementary school for African American children in Hampton, Virginia, in 1861; the school later added a night program for adults and evolved into Hampton Institute, now Hampton University. From 1833 to 1881 an array of postsecondary schools were founded for the express purpose of educating African Americans, including Cheyney State College (Pennsylvania, 1839), Lincoln University (Pennsylvania, 1854), Wilberforce University (Ohio, 1854), Berea College (Kentucky, 1858), Edward Waters College (Florida, 1866), Rust College (formerly Shaw University; Mississippi, 1866), Fisk University (Tennessee, 1867), Howard University (formerly Howard Theological Seminary; Washington, D.C., 1867), Howard University Law School (Washington, D.C., 1868), Morehouse College (formerly Augusta Institute; Georgia, 1867), Talladega College (Alabama, 1869), Alcorn Agricultural and Mechanical College (Mississippi, 1871), Alabama State University (Alabama, 1874), Meharry Medical College (Tennessee, 1876), Fayetteville State University (North Carolina, 1877), Spelman College (formerly Atlanta Baptist Female Seminary; Georgia, 1881), and Tuskegee University (formerly Tuskegee Institute; Alabama, 1881). Historically black colleges and universities, that is, colleges founded specifically to educate blacks, have continued to graduate higher percentages of blacks than individually enroll nationwide.

African American men and women educated during the nineteenth century, in both integrated and segregated schools, went on to achieve extraordinary successes in the areas of law, medicine, and education. After completing her education at Oberlin College in 1865, Fannie Jackson Coppin became the first African American woman to serve as the principal of the Institute for Colored Youth in Philadelphia, in 1869. Her contemporary Edward Alexander Bouchet was the first African American to earn a doctorate in physics, from Yale in 1874. He went on to teach chemistry and physics at the same Institute for Colored Youth, which had supported his Yale education, for twenty-six years. Bouchet enjoyed the honor of election to Phi Beta Kappa, the most prominent honor society in the humanities, in 1884. In 1888 Aaron Albert Mossell became the first African American graduate of the University of Pennsylvania Law School. He later served as an attorney for the Frederick Douglass Memorial Hospital in Philadelphia. Five years after its founding, in 1886, Spelman Seminary (presently Spelman College) opened the first nursing school for African American women. In 1891 that school became connected to MacVicar Hospital and joined two other schools for black nurses connected to hospitals: Dixie Hospital, in Hampton, Virginia, and Provident Hospital Training School, in Chicago. Following in the medical tradition of her nursing foremothers, Georgia E. Patton Washington became the first black woman physician and surgeon to be licensed in Tennessee, in 1893, as well as the first black woman to open a practice in that state.

Segregation, Congress, and the Courts. Slavery was an ever-present thread woven deeply throughout the American legal tapestry. Free blacks in the United States lived under the constant threat of men who lurked about seeking to kidnap them and sell them into slavery. Black newspapers were replete with accounts of free blacks who were kidnapped, stripped of their freedom papers—papers signed by government officials as proof of freedom—and held in abominable conditions before appearing in slave auctions in the South. Despite the existence of personal liberty laws developed to protect free blacks from kidnapping, slavers continued to spirit away free blacks without retribution. By virtue of such negligence, kidnapping was practically sanctioned by law, and those who fell prey to kidnappers were given little or no legal redress. In efforts at self-defense, free blacks in the northern United States formed organizations to protect themselves, such as the Negro Vigilance Committee, founded in New York in 1835. That committee raised money to fund initiatives to prevent kidnapping, extract free blacks from the hands of slavers, and assist fugitive slaves who were escaping to freedom in the North.

With the passage of the Fugitive Slave Law of 1850, free blacks and abolitionists of all races risked their personal liberty in aiding fugitive slaves. Groups such as the New England Freedom Association (1845), organized for the sole purpose of assisting fugitives, became more fervent in pursuing their mission after the passage of the 1850 law, under which federal commissioners were appointed in each county in the United States to assist in its enforcement. The commissioners' actions were supported by federal marshals and ad hoc militias. Those attempting to rescue fugitive slaves and facilitate their escape were ordered to pay fines of up to one thousand dollars and suffered imprisonment. Several court cases concerning the enforcement of the law, such as *United States v. Hanway* (1851) and *Kentucky v. Dennison* (1861), offer evidence that African Americans were committed to protecting fugitive slaves' freedom, even at great personal expense. In the aforementioned cases, those who helped slaves escape recapture found themselves before criminal courts on charges of treason and escape.

In the same year that *Dennison* was decided, the nation split over the right of the southern states to be self-deter-

minative with regard to the ownership of slaves. This fissure between the northern and southern United States resulted in the bloody Civil War, which was waged from 1861 to 1865. The reunification of the United States brought about the passage of the Thirteenth, Fourteenth, and Fifteenth Amendments to the Constitution, collectively known as the Civil War Amendments. The Thirteenth Amendment, passed in 1865, declared slavery and involuntary servitude unconstitutional, excepting only their use as punishment for crimes. In response to this federal legislation, southern states enacted laws that prohibited African Americans from owning property, speaking publicly, assembling, making contracts, traveling freely, bearing arms, and testifying in court cases to which whites were party; these laws were collectively known as black codes. Congress responded in turn with the Fourteenth Amendment, ratified in 1868, which reversed the decision in *Dred Scott v. Sandford* (1857) denying citizenship rights to blacks. This amendment granted African Americans citizenship in the states where they resided and prohibited states from denying them due process or the equal protection of the law. African American males secured the vote in 1870 with the passage of the Fifteenth Amendment.

In an effort to give the Civil War Amendments more force, Congress passed three Civil Rights Acts, in 1866, 1871, and 1875. The Civil Rights Act of 1866 was enacted to enforce the Thirteenth Amendment and dealt mainly with acts of intentional discrimination by both governments and private persons. However, it did not prohibit practices that had incidentally discriminatory effects. The Civil Rights Act of 1871 was enacted mainly to enforce the Fourteenth Amendment. It prohibited discriminatory practices by state and local governments in violation of the amendment and intentional private discrimination that could be attributed to the acts of the government or officials acting at its direction. Under both acts, parties alleging a violation could petition a court for an order ending the prohibited activity and providing a monetary award for the violation of their rights. Both acts went virtually unenforced, however, until their revival in 1968. The Civil Rights Act of 1875, meanwhile, prohibited discrimination on the basis of race in public conveyances, such as railroads, and places of public amusement.

Even after the passage of the Civil Rights Acts, southern states continued to maneuver around the equal-protection guarantees of the Fourteenth Amendment by denying African Americans the right to serve as jurors. From 1879 to 1881 the Supreme Court decided four cases on this issue: *Strauder v. West Virginia* (1880), *Ex parte Virginia* (1880), *Neal v. Delaware* (1881), and *Virginia v. Rives* (1879). Although in *Strauder* the Court declared unconstitutional the statutory provision that excluded

African Americans from jury service, the lasting legacy of the remaining cases was not as positive. The Court decided in *Virginia v. Rives* that the mere lack of an African American presence on juries, regardless of how pervasive, was not a violation of the Fourteenth Amendment. This decision allowed southern states to continue excluding African Americans from juries and denying them further legal equality.

Despite such opposition to their status as free persons, African Americans remained steadfast in seeking the protection of the law and the courts. From the passage of the Civil Rights Act in 1875 to its repeal in 1883, African Americans drew upon its provisions to challenge racial segregation in public spaces. Their resistance to segregation placed them squarely before the courts in both criminal and civil cases. On railways, African American men and women were placed together in railcars separate from their white peers. White men and women were given the amenities of separate "Gentlemen" and "Ladies" cars, yet black women were denied entrance to ladies cars. Meanwhile, the African American, or "Colored," railcars doubled as smoking cars. These cars lacked heat in the winter and were dirty and in disrepair.

African Americans openly challenged these segregative practices. The black antislavery lecturer and abolitionist Charles Lenox Remond spoke out vehemently against segregation on the railroads. In his address to the Legislative Committee of the Massachusetts House of Representatives in 1842, he decried the distinctions made between blacks and whites and their unequal treatment on the railways. Remond also argued that treatment based on skin color was untenable, because lighter-skinned blacks could be mistaken for whites. This theme was revisited in 1892 by Homer Plessy, a man of one-eighth African blood who was arrested when he attempted to sit in a train car reserved for whites. He argued that his African blood was not distinguishable to him and that his denial of access to the seat reserved for whites was a violation of his Fourteenth Amendment rights. In the seminal case *Plessy v. Ferguson* (1896), the Supreme Court codified segregation by ruling that separate accommodations for whites and blacks were not in violation of the Fourteenth Amendment as long as they were "equal."

The abolitionist, journalist, and activist Ida B. Wells-Barnett had fared no better in her earlier fight against the railroad. While traveling to one of her teaching jobs in the 1880s, Wells was forcibly removed from a train for refusing to give up her seat in the ladies car. Outraged, she filed a lawsuit against the Chesapeake, Ohio, and Southwestern Railroad. One of the first cases of its kind to challenge segregation on railcars, Wells-Barnett's suit elicited much coverage from the black newspapers of the day, such as the *Christian Recorder*, established in 1846. In its

decision, the circuit court of Shelby County, Tennessee, ruled that Tennessee law provided for equal accommodations for blacks and whites alike on the railroad and that Wells-Barnett had been unlawfully removed. However, her victory was short-lived: the decision, made on the basis of state law, was reversed in 1883 as a result of the repeal of the public accommodation provisions of the federal Civil Rights Act of 1875. The repeal was accomplished through a series of Supreme Court cases known as the *Civil Rights Cases*, through which the provisions of the 1875 act were declared unconstitutional. In its reversal of the decision in favor of Wells-Barnett, the Tennessee court ruled that the railroad had met the requirements of equal accommodations and accused Wells-Barnett of hounding the court.

Wells-Barnett continued to fight against the injustices suffered by African Americans. She was best known in the latter half of the nineteenth century for her work as an antilynching crusader. In 1892 she wrote about the lynching of Thomas Moss, Calvin McDowell, and Henry Stewart in the newspaper she edited and partly owned, the *Memphis Free Speech and Headlight*. Moss, McDowell, and Stewart had been her close friends and the owners of the People's Grocery Store in Memphis. Their deaths spurred Wells to further research why lynching occurred. Her reporting on the subject revealed that allegations of black male rapes of white women, which were overwhelmingly false, were rarely the true impetus for lynching. Rather, the threat of black economic independence and prosperity to white business interests was a frequent motivating factor. Wells-Barnett's reporting eventually garnered death threats and the destruction of the office that housed the *Free Speech*. Undaunted, she continued to write widely on the subject, publishing *On Lynchings: Southern Horrors* (1892) and *A Red Record: Tabulated Statistics and Alleged Causes of Lynchings in the United States, 1892–1893–1894* (1895).

Economic Self-Determination. Because segregation denied African Americans access to white businesses and economic opportunities under threat of violence, African American men and women established their own means for economic self-determination. Most popularly known as the original "Aunt Jemima" of pancake fame, Nancy Green rose to prominence under the employ of the white Kentucky businessman Chris L. Rutt. The persona of Aunt Jemima remains a source of both consternation and celebration for African American women. In Green's time she was the first living and breathing African American woman to embody a brand name. However, she has been analyzed by scholars as the source of the asexual "Mammy" figure. The quintessential Mammy was a rotund African American woman, devoid of stereotypically female attributes, who was invariably ready and willing to serve her white employers. The image of Mammy has plagued African American women well into the twenty-first century, as they fight to be recognized—but not stereotyped—as both women and people of color who have been subjected to gender and racial oppression.

Green's contemporaries were no less dynamic in their impact. Blacks created two banks in 1888: the True Reformers' Bank in Richmond, Virginia, and the Capital Savings Bank in Washington, D.C. The Alabama Penny Savings Bank followed in 1890, as did the North Carolina Mutual Life Insurance Company in 1893; the latter was the first black insurance company to accrue $100 million in assets. It remains the largest black-owned insurance company in the United States.

The formation of these repositories of wealth was but one piece of evidence of the tremendous persistence and fortitude of African Americans. Within thirty years of the legal end of chattel slavery, blacks had achieved high levels of education and economic self-determination despite ubiquitous racial segregation and the threat of fatal violence. Yet, as the century came to a close, Timothy Thomas Fortune, the radical journalist and founder of the *New York Globe* (later known as the *New York Age*), cautioned against carrying excessive optimism into the twentieth century. In his book *Black and White: Land, Labor, and Politics in the South* (1884), Fortune described his experiences with racism and gave his assessment of the status of African Americans in the United States. His predictions regarding a new century of escalating violence toward blacks would become a reality, as the community that had emerged from slavery continued to negotiate the contested terrain of legal, economic, social and political equality.

[*See also* American Missionary Association; Black Capitalism and Economic Self-help; Black Church; Black Uplift; *Christian Recorder*; Civil Rights; Civil Rights Act of 1866; Civil Rights Act of 1875; Constitution, U.S.; *Dred Scott* Case; Douglass, Frederick; Education; Fifteenth Amendment; Fourteenth Amendment; Free African Americans before the Civil War (North); Fugitive Slave Law of 1850; Howard University; Integration; Laws and Legislation; Lynching and Mob Violence; Mulattoes; Nell, William Cooper; Progress; Race, Theories of; Racism; Remond, Charles Lenox; *Roberts v. City of Boston*; Rochester, New York; Segregation; Stereotypes of African Americans; Supreme Court; Thirteenth Amendment; Violence against African Americans; *and* Wells-Barnett, Ida.]

BIBLIOGRAPHY

Aptheker, Herbert, ed. *A Documentary History of the Negro People in the United States.* Vol. 1, *From Colonial Times through the Civil War.* New York: Citadel, 1990. Contains 179 primary-source documents that chronicle slavery, antislavery movements, resistance to segregation in education and public conveyances, the black fight for suffrage, and black soldiers in the Civil War.

Bolden, Tonya. *The Book of African-American Women: 150 Crusaders, Creators, and Uplifters.* Holbrook, MA: Adams Media, 1996. Offers biographical and anecdotal information on both famous and obscure African American women.

Cover, Robert M. *Justice Accused: Antislavery and the Judicial Process.* New Haven, CT: Yale University Press, 1975. Reviews U.S. courts' actions in antislavery cases and offers insight on judicial resistance to racial equality.

Hine, Darlene Clark, ed. *Black Women in America: An Historical Encyclopedia.* Brooklyn, NY: Carlson, 1993. The most comprehensive encyclopedia on the lives and struggles of African American women to date.

Hine, Darlene Clark. *Black Women in White: Racial Conflict and Co-operation in the Nursing Profession, 1890–1950.* Bloomington: Indiana University Press, 1989. Details the professionalization of black female nurses and their struggle to gain equal footing with white women.

Hyman, Harold M., and William M Wiecek. *Equal Justice under Law: Constitutional Development, 1835–1875.* New York: Harper and Row, 1982. Offers a thorough overview of the constitutional development of racial equality both before and after the Civil War.

Lane, Roger. *William Dorsey's Philadelphia and Ours: On the Past and Future of the Black City in America.* New York: Oxford University Press, 1991. Details the migration and settlement of southern blacks in Philadelphia after the Civil War and is particularly informative regarding the city's Institute for Colored Youth.

Morris, Thomas D. *Free Men All: The Personal Liberty Laws of the North, 1780–1861.* Baltimore: Johns Hopkins University Press, 1974. Argues that the personal liberty laws enacted in various states were the precursors to the Fourteenth Amendment.

Morton, Patricia. *Disfigured Images: The Historical Assault on Afro-American Women.* New York: Praeger, 1991. Provides a thorough overview of the historiography of the works that constructed collective perceptions of African American womanhood.

Read, Florence Matilda. *The Story of Spelman College.* Princeton, NJ: Princeton University Press, 1961. The first published history of Spelman College, one of two predominantly black colleges for women.

Smith, Jessie Carney, ed. *Black Firsts: 2,000 Years of Extraordinary Achievement.* Canton, MI: Visible Ink Press, 2003.

—TERI A. MCMURTRY-CHUBB

DISEASES AND EPIDEMICS. *See* Health and Medicine.

DISUNIONISM. The term *disunionism* refers to the concept of the peaceful secession of the free states of the North from the Union. William Lloyd Garrison began to agitate for that course in 1842 at antislavery meetings and especially in his abolitionist newspaper, the *Liberator*.

At face value, disunionism made slavery a sectional issue; it seemingly placed the burden of guilt solely on the region where chattel bondage existed. To be sure, repeal of the existence of the Union would have removed all vestiges of northern complicity with southern slavery and would have preserved the sanctity of abolitionists' souls as well. For Garrisonians the "peculiar institution" represented a national, as opposed to a purely southern, sin; free-state secession would have been tantamount to an act of atonement, not so much to assuage northern consciences but, as Garrisonian disunionists contended, to repent for an alliance with the crime of slavery. Thus, the Garrisonian battle cry of "No Union with Slaveholders" was a moral imperative similar to that of immediate emancipation, applying to all persons—northerners and southerners, slaveholders and nonslaveholders alike.

Disunionists specifically censured the document that created and sustained the federal government: the U.S. Constitution. They did so not because they deemed the Constitution to be an instrument of a coercive regime—as did the nonresistance movement—but because they considered the document a bulwark of slavery. Therein lay the essence of disunionism: a clarion call that rallied against a compact considered by Garrisonians to be egregiously proslavery.

Throughout the 1840s and 1850s Garrison advocated individual abjuration of the Union in the *Liberator*, prescribing the rejection of political parties (including the abolitionist-led Liberty Party) and the political process in general. Garrison urged all voters—not just nonresistants—to withdraw from the polls and to endorse what he considered a far more influential platform: disgust for a government and a constitution that supported human enslavement. Such acts of political abstinence would force upon legislators the ultimatum of either dissolving the Union or abolishing slavery. Should the former occur, reasoned the disunionists, emancipation would still be assured, because the slave states would be denied the economic and military sustenance provided by the federal government. The disunionists observed that without the North, the South would have to stand up to slave insurrections alone. Thus, disunionists confronted the issue of slavery by holding northerners responsible for the continuance of an evil institution and empowering them to end it.

Among the advocates of disunionism was Frederick Douglass. At the beginning of his abolitionist career in 1841, Douglass was, according to his second autobiography, *My Bondage and My Freedom* (1855), a faithful disciple of Garrison. Specifically, he adhered to Garrisonian doctrines concerning the proslavery nature of the Constitution and the potential efficacy of voting abstinence. Douglass broke from the Garrisonian abolitionists in 1847 when, against their advice, he decided to proceed with plans to establish an antislavery publication. Nevertheless, he remained an ardent proponent of disunionist

principles. Not until 1851, four years after he founded the *North Star* in Rochester, New York, did Douglass more formally retract his Garrisonian credentials.

As Douglass explained in his autobiography, his journalistic duties and the need to consider opposing viewpoints from non-Garrisonian abolitionists in western New York compelled him to study tactical issues more carefully. After reconsideration, and owing to his growing friendship with the New York philanthropist, abolitionist, and Liberty partisan Gerrit Smith, Douglass argued that political action was the most effective means to secure slavery's demise. He thought disunion unnecessary because he considered the Constitution maligned by Garrison to in fact be an antislavery document, designed, as the preamble reads, "to promote the general welfare, and secure the general blessings of liberty." Douglass's holding views so antithetical to Garrisonian convictions completed his estrangement from that circle of abolitionists.

With the onset of the Civil War, however, most Garrisonians modified their views toward the federal government's abolitionist capacities. For Garrisonians, disunion was meant to be an outlet available only to the free states; when slave states pursued secession Garrisonians pronounced them treasonous, arguing that such a course warranted nothing less than God's wrath and the Northern army's fury. Garrisonians embraced the Northern cause not because they wanted the nation restored but because they desired emancipation. Thus, Garrisonians spent the war years remaining opposed to a union with slaveholders. Along with abolitionists of all stripes, they dedicated their efforts to convincing President Abraham Lincoln, Republicans in Congress, and all Northerners, that the war was a struggle to end slavery—one that demanded support of the sectional conflict.

[*See also* Antislavery Press; Civil War; Constitution, U.S.; Douglass, Frederick; Emancipation; Garrison, William Lloyd; Garrisonian Abolitionists; Liberty Party; *My Bondage and My Freedom* (1855); Nonresistance; *North Star*; Political Participation; Slavery and the U.S. Constitution; *and* Smith, Gerrit.]

BIBLIOGRAPHY

Cain, William E., ed. *William Lloyd Garrison and the Fight against Slavery: Selections from the "Liberator."* Boston: Bedford Books, 1995.

Finkelman, Paul. "The Founders and Slavery: Little Ventured, Little Gained." *Yale Journal of Law and Humanities* 13 (2001): 413–449.

Kraditor, Aileen S. *Means and Ends in American Abolitionism: Garrison and His Critics on Strategy and Tactics, 1834–1850.* Reprint. Chicago: Ivan R. Dee, 1989.

Walters, Ronald G. *The Antislavery Appeal: American Abolitionism after 1830.* Baltimore, MD: Johns Hopkins University Press, 1976.

Wiecek, William M. *The Sources of Antislavery Constitutionalism in America, 1760–1848.* Ithaca, NY: Cornell University Press, 1977.

—RAYMOND JAMES KROHN

DOMINICAN REPUBLIC, ANNEXATION OF. The annexation of the Dominican Republic was a goal of President Ulysses S. Grant from 1869 to 1871. When the issue became controversial, Frederick Douglass's willingness to serve as a commissioner to that Caribbean country provided a kind of cover against the accusations of the Massachusetts senator Charles Sumner that the real issue was subjugation of a black nation to the United States. Sumner railed against the project in the Senate and eventually won enough support to kill the idea.

Grant imagined adding Dominica to the Union as an all-black state. He believed annexation of Dominica would spur commercial relations with the Caribbean and give Americans greater access to Hispaniola's mineral resources, while blacks who were discontented with their situation in America would have been invited to migrate there. Thus the racial concerns of both the blacks and their white neighbors would have received a kind of solution.

Lest one conclude that Grant somehow had departed from the latest racial thinking in making his proposal, it should be recalled that colonization of American blacks abroad had long exerted a fascination on some of the greatest American statesmen and intellectuals. For example, Thomas Jefferson repeatedly opined that because whites were so irredeemably prejudiced against blacks, and blacks were so understandably angry at whites, and since blacks had a natural right to self-government that they must and could never come to exercise in the United States, some overseas society should be established into which they could migrate.

This idea found its institutional embodiment in the American Colonization Society (ACS), one of the early Republic's most significant political organizations. Jefferson's successor as president, James Madison, served for years as ACS president and was followed in that post by the eminent Kentucky senator Henry Clay. Other ACS members included President John Tyler, Senators John Taylor and John Randolph of Virginia, and Chief Justice John Marshall.

When Abraham Lincoln eulogized Clay in 1852, the Illinoisan called for fulfillment of the ACS's aims as a "glorious consummation" of Clay's labors. During the Civil War Lincoln requested and Congress provided an appropriation to establish an American colony in Nicaragua, and Lincoln suggested that free, northern blacks go to that colony in anticipation of the wave of migration he expected to follow abolition.

Lincoln's secretary of state, William Henry Seward, endeavored during the administration of Lincoln's successor, Andrew Johnson, to purchase the Dominican Republic. Early in the Grant administration, the U.S. Navy intervened to prop up Grant's opposite number, the Dominican president Buenaventura Báez, who faced attack from Haiti and dissension within his own country.

Grant had high hopes for the prospective American territory (and his emissaries made clear that before becoming a state, Dominica would first have to go through a territorial stage). As he put it in his second State of the Union address, the Dominican Republic was a "weak power, numbering probably less than 120,000 souls, and yet possessing one of the richest territories under the sun, capable of supporting a population of 10,000,000 people in luxury." Annexation, Grant went on, would provide new employment to American workers, a greater market for American manufacturers and farmers, and a haven to which slaves from nearby Cuba and Puerto Rico could flee (which was an added incentive for Spain to abolish slavery in its island colonies and, somehow, for Brazil to abolish slavery within its domain).

If white Americans had believed Grant's projections, they might well have found them attractive. For example, because there were only 4 million former slaves in the United States, a refuge for 10 million people promised to solve the American racial problem in a way most Americans would have found highly satisfactory. Yet for Sumner, who in his advocacy of the cause of black Americans was decades ahead of his time, Dominican annexation would mean the tragic end of one of the world's two black republics—and, he said, it might ultimately entail the abolition of the other.

Grant requited Sumner's opposition by having Senate Republicans strip him of his Foreign Relations Committee chairmanship, but to no avail. The Dominican Republic remained independent.

[*See also* American Colonization Society; Civil War; Clay, Henry; Colonization; Douglass, Frederick; Grant, Ulysses S.; Haiti; Jefferson, Thomas; Johnson, Andrew; Lincoln, Abraham; Seward, William Henry; Sumner, Charles; *and* Tyler, John.]

BIBLIOGRAPHY

McFeely, William S. *Grant: A Biography*. New York: Norton, 1981.

Smith, Jean Edward. *Grant*. New York: Simon and Schuster, 2001.

—KEVIN R. C. GUTZMAN

DOUGLAS, STEPHEN A. (b. 23 April 1813; d. 3 June 1861), a U.S. Senator and presidential candidate. Stephen Arnold Douglas was born in Brandon, Vermont, the son of Stephen Arnold Douglass, a college-educated physician, and Sarah Fisk. (Douglas dropped the final "s" in his name in 1846.) In 1830 Douglas moved with his family to New York, where he began to study law, but three years later he headed west, where the training and qualifications for the legal profession were less formal. He eventually settled in Illinois, the state with which he is most associated, and was admitted to the bar a year later. He held a series of state positions, culminating in his serving as secretary of state and on the Illinois Supreme Court at the age of twenty-seven.

In 1843 the young Democrat was elected to the House of Representatives, where his first speech was a vigorous defense of Andrew Jackson. He quickly fashioned his political philosophy, which called for robust expansion westward to the Pacific, the annexation of Texas, and moving the border with British Canada farther north. In March 1847 Douglas married Martha Martin; the couple settled in Chicago and had two sons by 1850. Douglas invested heavily in large tracts of land around the city and used his political clout to help establish Chicago as a major rail hub. He was elected to the U.S. Senate, taking his seat in December 1847 and becoming chairman of the Senate Committee on Territories, which he fashioned into a post that oversaw virtually all aspects of westward expansion.

Careful to balance sectional hostilities and the evolving North-South debate on expansion, Douglas was instrumental in steering a center line in the Compromise of 1850. When the Compromise failed as a single bill, Douglas separated elements of the bill and steered them through Congress one at a time. In a national atmosphere that was becoming increasingly unreceptive to compromise as both pro- and antislavery arguments hardened, reaction to the Compromise was mixed. Douglas's underestimation of the moral dimensions of the slavery debate would later haunt him. He ran for the Democratic nomination for president in 1852 with the support of the nationalistic Young America movement, which advocated expansionism and the concept of "manifest destiny," but he came in third in the balloting. Soon after, in early 1853, Douglas's wife and newborn daughter both died, and from May to October of that year he traveled extensively across Europe. In England he declined a meeting with Queen Victoria after hearing that he would have to wear court dress and then moved on to Constantinople, the Crimea, and Russia, where he had an audience with Czar Nicolas I. His final stop on his journey was to meet with Napoleon III in Paris.

In 1854 Douglas introduced a bill to organize governments for territories west of Missouri, in what would become Kansas, Nebraska, and the Dakotas. In the Kansas-Nebraska Act, Douglas adopted the concept of popular sovereignty introduced by the Michigan senator Lewis Cass: the federal government would avoid the sensitive issue of whether new states would have slavery or free soil by having the citizens of the new state frame a constitution and vote on whether to allow or forbid slavery. To

Douglas, it was an exercise in people's democracy, an effort to geographically regionalize the slave debate and prevent further congressional acrimony over the issue. This position, however, violated the Missouri Compromise of 1820, which had banned all slavery west of Missouri. The Kansas-Nebraska Act was passed on 22 May 1854. However, Douglas's doctrine of popular sovereignty ignited intense controversy that engulfed the nation, with massive repercussions. Douglas was stunned by the chaos of "Bleeding Kansas," as proslavery and free-state factions fought to control the state's government; the caning of the Massachusetts senator Charles Sumner, a strong opponent of Douglas and the act, by a South Carolina congressman; and cries of treason from the North. The act negated the Missouri Compromise and the previous limitations of slavery's growth and led to the final collapse of the Whig Party. Abolitionists and Free-Soilers despised popular sovereignty, and Frederick Douglass spoke out in opposition to the bill.

Douglas again sought the Democratic nomination for president in 1856 but soon withdrew and supported the nomination and election of James Buchanan. The hornet's nest stirred up by popular sovereignty provoked a fierce confrontation between the new president and Douglas over how to deal with events in Kansas. Concurrently, Douglas fought to retain his Senate seat and faced the Republican candidate Abraham Lincoln. Their seven debates in 1858 became famous for articulating the opposing commentaries on the future of slavery and the Union. Douglas never tired of declaring that he did not "care if slavery is voted up or down," but he also stated that he thought that "this government of ours is founded on the white basis. It was made by the white man, for the benefit of the white man, to be administered by white men." He remained "opposed to taking any step that recognizes the Negro man or the Indian as the equal of the white man." Douglas was accused of being an architect of slave expansion while vigorously defending popular sovereignty as democratic and as a means of preventing federal intervention. Douglas won the election and returned to the Senate before launching a final bid to become president in 1860.

In 1860 Douglas was one of four presidential candidates. Deep rifts within the Democratic Party, with a southern faction breaking away under John C. Breckinridge, prompted Douglas to campaign personally across the country. The northern Democratic vote was solidly behind Douglas, and he won 29 percent of the popular vote, but the southern split helped his Republican rival, Abraham Lincoln, enter the White House.

For the last six months of his life Douglas campaigned to preserve the Union, believing that aim transcended all others. He met with Lincoln, defended the president and his actions in the Senate, and returned to Illinois to support the Union at a special meeting of the state legislature. In May 1861 in Chicago he fell ill, and he died a month later, on 3 June. Frederick Douglass wrote to Susan B. Anthony, "I rejoice not in the death of any man, but I cannot feel, that in the death of Stephen A. Douglass, a most dangerous man has been removed. No man of his time has done more than he to intensify hatred of the negro."

[*See also* Anthony, Susan B.; Antislavery Movement; Buchanan, James; Compromise of 1850; Democratic Party; Douglass, Frederick; Election of 1860; Free-Soil Party; Fugitive Slave Law of 1850; Kansas-Nebraska Act; Laws and Legislation; Lincoln, Abraham; Proslavery Thought; Republican Party; Slavery; Sumner, Charles; *and* Whig Party.]

BIBLIOGRAPHY

Douglas, Stephen Arnold. *Letters*. Edited by Robert Walter Johannsen. Urbana: University of Illinois Press, 1961.

Johannsen, Robert Walter. *Stephen A. Douglas*. New York: Oxford University Press, 1973.

—SAM HITCHMOUGH

DOUGLASS' MONTHLY.

Founded in 1859 by Frederick Douglass in Rochester, New York—on the same street and in the same room as his other newspapers—*Douglass' Monthly*, published under the motto "Avenge me of mine adversary," was Douglass's third newspaper. Similar in focus to his *North Star* (1847–1851) and *Frederick Douglass' Paper* (1851–1859), *Douglass' Monthly* (1859–1863) was a concise and appealingly produced version of Douglass's second newspaper. As he explained, his third paper was an antislavery broadsheet that never gave an uncertain sound to the trump of freedom and focused on imparting to its readers a basic understanding of American society.

Edited by Douglass and partially supported by the Rochester Ladies' Anti-Slavery Society, *Douglass' Monthly* printed political and antislavery news along with captivating editorials mostly written by Douglass himself. In these editorials Douglass asserted his deeply felt position that some individuals involved in the American abolitionist movement were relaxing their antislavery exertions and no longer making the case for justice and humanity to the heart and conscience of the nation on moral grounds.

Originally circulated in Britain, *Douglass' Monthly* was a rival to the *Anti-Slavery Advocate*, a highly radical Garrisonian monthly edited in Dublin, Ireland, and published in London. Part of the strength of *Douglass' Monthly*, whether in England or the United States, was that it provided an independent and influential black American voice that helped shape the antislavery movement before and during the Civil War. Douglass used *Douglass'*

Monthly as a sounding board for his argument that the liberation of the slave in America would mean peace, honor, and prosperity to the American nation. Thus, after secession Douglass was persistent in his demands that the United States government proclaim the war as primarily a battle to end slavery.

In support of Abraham Lincoln and black participation in the Civil War, *Douglass' Monthly* proclaimed that black men going into the U.S. Army and Navy were fighting a double battle: against slavery in the South and against prejudice and proscription in the North. Frederick Douglass made this call in *Douglass' Monthly* because he not only saw Lincoln as a man of unblemished private character but also understood that a war undertaken for the perpetual enslavement of black men, similar to what white men went through in the Revolutionary War, logically called for black men to help suppress it and to become familiar with the means of securing, protecting, and defending their own liberty.

During the first two years of the war, *Douglass' Monthly* repeatedly argued two points: that the war must be fought to end slavery and that black Americans must become a part of the military force that would be necessary to defeat slavery. *Douglass' Monthly* itself, however, would not survive the war; it ceased publication in 1863. Unfortunately, the only existing complete runs of Douglass's three newspapers, including *Douglass' Monthly*, were destroyed in a house fire in 1872. Frederick Douglass did not terminate *Douglass' Monthly* as a result of diminished support or because he thought that the need to speak out against slavery and prejudice against the black race ended with the Civil War. Rather, he ceased publication because he felt that he could better serve the abolitionist cause by accepting an expected army commission—which, however, never materialized. With genuine remorse, and not knowing that he would not get the commission, Douglass explained in August 1863 that publication of *Douglass' Monthly*, which had continued in one form (and name) or another during nearly sixteen years of editorial toil and covered a period remarkable for the intensity and fierceness of the moral struggle between slavery and freedom, would be discontinued.

[*See also* American Revolution; Antislavery Movement; Antislavery Press; Black Press; Civil War; Civil War, Participation and Recruitment of Black Troops in; Douglass, Frederick; *Frederick Douglass' Paper*; Garrisonian Abolitionists; Lincoln, Abraham; *North Star*; Rochester, New York; Rochester Ladies' Anti-Slavery Society; *and* Union Army, African Americans in.]

BIBLIOGRAPHY

Blassingame, John W., ed. *The Frederick Douglass Papers. Series 1, Speeches, Debates, and Interviews*. 5 vols. New Haven, CT: Yale University Press, 1979–1992.

Blight, David W. *Frederick Douglass' Civil War: Keeping Faith in Jubilee.* Baton Rouge: Louisiana State University Press, 1989.

Chesebrough, David B. *Frederick Douglass: Oratory from Slavery.* Westport, CT: Greenwood, 1998.

Douglass, Frederick. *The Life and Writings of Frederick Douglass.* Vol. 1, *Early Years, 1817–1849.* Edited by Philip S. Foner. New York: International Publishers, 1950.

McFeely, William S. *Frederick Douglass.* New York: Norton, 1991.

Ripley, C. Peter, ed. *The Black Abolitionist Papers.* Vol. 1, *The British Isles, 1830–1865.* Chapel Hill: University of North Carolina Press, 1985.

Sterling, Dorothy. *Ahead of Her Time: Abby Kelley and the Politics of Antislavery.* New York: Norton, 1991.

—GLEN ANTHONY HARRIS

DOUGLASS, ANNA MURRAY (b. c. 1813; d. 4 August 1882), the first wife of Frederick Douglass. The enigmatic first wife of Frederick Douglass, Anna Murray Douglass, has been misunderstood and misrepresented by historians as well as by her husband's associates since he first rose to fame in 1842. Her early life, including her birth and parentage, remain sparsely documented. Most historians agree that she was the daughter of Bambarra and Mary Murray, emancipated slaves from Denton in Caroline County, Maryland. As a young adult she lived in Baltimore, Maryland, working as a housekeeper and laundress in white homes. Despite refusing to demonstrate reading or writing skills throughout her life, she clearly had some interest in self-improvement in her youth because she first met Frederick Douglass, then known as Frederick Bailey, through mutual friends at the East Baltimore Mental Improvement Society, an organization of free blacks who promoted literacy.

The two had met by the late summer of 1838, when Anna sold many of her belongings to help Frederick purchase the train tickets for his escape. She also sewed the sailor uniform he wore as a disguise and accumulated the necessary items for starting a household. Once Frederick reached his destination in New York City, he wrote for her to join him. The Reverend James W. C. Pennington performed their marriage ceremony, and the young couple moved to New Bedford, Massachusetts, first using the last name of Johnson but soon changing it to Douglass.

The first years of the marriage appear to have been congenial. Anna bore four children—Rosetta, Lewis Henry, Charles Remond, and Frederick Douglass Jr.—during their residence in New Bedford. While Douglass searched for jobs on the city's docks, Anna kept house on a small budget. When the family moved to Lynn, Massachusetts, she also took in piecework from the local shoe factories and saved everything that her husband sent to her while he toured for the American Anti-Slavery Society.

Strain began to manifest in the Douglass marriage once Frederick became involved in the abolitionist movement. He spent a good deal of time away from home giving lectures, including two years in Europe. Most of his white associates expressed disdain for his wife, at their most generous referring to Anna as a poor intellectual match for her husband, and treated her like a servant in her own home. They, like historians, have focused on Anna's illiteracy and stoicism to bolster their arguments. Anna, however, had little time for intellectual pursuits while running a household and raising a family with little help from her husband.

By the late 1840s Anna lost much of her emotional support system. Her daughter, Rosetta, was away at school in Albany, New York; and her friend and household helper, Harriet Bailey, had married and moved to Springfield, Massachusetts. Meanwhile, her husband toured England, where rumors spread about the attention lavished on him by the English ladies. After his return in 1847 Douglass moved the family to Rochester, New York, taking Anna away from the small but active black community of which she had been a part in Lynn. Shortly thereafter she suffered the indignity of having the British reformer Julia Griffiths move into the Douglass home, which caused

Anna Murray Douglass, the first wife of Frederick Douglass, was misunderstood by his associates and has often been misrepresented by historians. This undated portrait is a print from a restored photograph. (Library of Congress.)

a storm of controversy alleging Frederick's infidelity with Griffiths. The departure of Griffiths was followed by the arrival of Ottilie Assing, who installed herself in the Douglass home for several months out of the year over the next twenty years. For much of her life Anna lived isolated from supportive African American companionship while hosting a string of white abolitionists who could barely conceal their disdain for her. Only the extended stays of Rosetta and her children and the companionship of Louisa Sprague, Rosetta's sister-in-law who lived in the Douglass home as a housekeeper, relieved Anna's loneliness.

Nevertheless, Anna understood her husband's role in fighting slavery and her role as his helpmate. She took pride in her husband's appearance and accomplishments and in keeping a well-ordered home. She continued to take an active part in operation of the household, even after Douglass had become wealthy enough to hire servants. After Anna's death her work was informally recognized by black women, who continued to refer to the home at Cedar Hill, Uniontown, D.C., as her home, and by Rosetta, who wrote a memoir of Anna's life and named her eldest daughter Annie. Even Douglass's second wife, Helen Pitts, did nothing to denigrate Anna's memory during her own marriage and life at Cedar Hill.

Rosetta's memoir, *My Mother as I Recall Her*, deserves particular attention as one of the only surviving documents about Anna Murray Douglass. Rosetta celebrated Anna's work, placing her mother squarely within the nineteenth-century "cult of domesticity." Rosetta used Anna as a symbol of the equality of black women within that sphere during an era in which black women were portrayed as either the sexually promiscuous "Jezebel" or the maternal caretaker "Mammy" of white families. On the other hand, not only did Anna actively support the end of slavery by aiding her husband's flight to freedom and allowing him to pursue antislavery work but also she maintained an impeccable home and preserved her own dignity and that of her marriage in the face of white assault. In Rosetta's narrative Anna emerges as a model of middle-class womanhood.

Douglass, for his part, recognized the role that Anna played in his life. During his first visit to England he maintained a cordial distance from his enthusiastic female admirers, and he defended his wife when anyone suggested that she was not a fit mate for him. After his return home in 1847 Anna conceived their last child, Annie, and Douglass risked his own arrest to reenter the United States to comfort Anna in the wake of that child's death ten years later. When Anna died in 1882, he fell into a depression that he described as being the darkest moment of his life. Nevertheless, he seemed less than concerned for Anna's feelings in bringing into their home two white women with whom he was rumored to be sexually involved. He

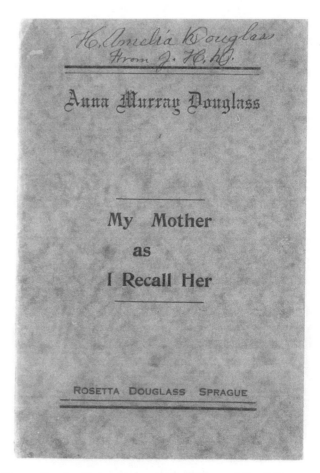

Rosetta Douglass Sprague's memoir, *My Mother as I Recall Her* (1900), is one of the few surviving documents about Anna Murray Douglass. Sprague says, near the beginning: "The story of Frederick Douglass's hopes and aspirations and longing desire for freedom has been told—you all know it. It was a story made possible through the unswerving loyalty of Anna Murray." (Library of Congress.)

also married a younger white woman within a year of Anna's death, much to the chagrin of his family and both the black and white communities.

For much of her life, Anna suffered from various ailments, particularly headaches that made her ill. In her later years she suffered from a stroke that confined her to a wheelchair and her bedroom. In August 1882 she died shortly after having a second stroke.

[*See also* American Anti-Slavery Society; Antislavery Movement; Bailey, Harriet; Baltimore, Maryland, Slavery in; Crofts, Julia Griffiths; Douglass, Annie; Douglass, Charles Remond; Douglass, Frederick; Douglass, Frederick, Jr.; Douglass, Lewis Henry; East Baltimore Mental Improvement Society; Free African Americans before the Civil War (North); Gender; Identity; Lynn, Massachusetts;

Marriage, Mixed; New York City; Pennington, James W. C.; Rochester, New York; *and* Women.]

BIBLIOGRAPHY

DeCosta-Willis, Miriam. "Smoothing the Tucks in Father's Linen: The Women of Cedar Hill." *Sage* 4.2 (Fall 1987): 30–33.

Render, Sylvia Lyons. "Afro-American Women: The Outstanding and the Obscure." *Quarterly Journal of the Library of Congress* 32.4 (October 1975): 306–321.

Sprague, Rosetta Douglass. "My Mother as I Recall Her." *Journal of Negro History* 8.1 (January 1923): 93–101.

Sterling, Dorothy, ed. *We Are Your Sisters: Black Women in the Nineteenth Century.* New York: Norton, 1984.

—LEIGH FOUGHT

Charles Remond Douglass, the third and youngest son of Frederick and Anna Murray Douglass, was named for a friend of his father's, the African American abolitionist Charles Lenox Remond. (National Park Service.)

DOUGLASS, CHARLES REMOND (b. 21 October 1844; d. 24 November 1920), soldier, journalist, and government clerk. Born in Lynn, Massachusetts, Charles Remond Douglass was the third and youngest son of Frederick and Anna Murray Douglass. Named for his father's friend and fellow black antislavery speaker Charles Lenox Remond, Charles attended the public schools in Rochester, New York, where the family moved in late 1847. As a boy, he delivered copies of his father's newspaper, *North Star*.

As a young man, Charles became the first black from New York to enlist for military service in the Civil War, volunteering for the Fifty-fourth Massachusetts Infantry Regiment. Unlike his brother Lewis, who also served in the Fifty-fourth and became a sergeant major in that regiment, Charles was unable to deploy with his fellow troops owing to illness. As late as November 1863 Charles remained at the training camp in Readville, Massachusetts. He ultimately joined another black regiment, the Fifth Massachusetts Cavalry, rising to the rank of first sergeant. After President Abraham Lincoln discharged Charles at the request of the elder Douglass in 1864 on the ground of poor health, Charles planned to go to Tennessee to invest in cotton lands. Instead, he tended the family farm and lived in his parents' house for two years, finding it difficult to secure an income-producing job. He married Mary Elizabeth Murphy, called Libbie, in 1866. Although this marriage was troubled by Libbie's accusations of infidelity and Charles's counter-accusations of jealousy, the couple had six children: Charles Frederick, Joseph Henry, Annie Elizabeth, Julia Ada, Mary Louise, and Edward.

After moving to Washington, D.C., Charles served as one of the first black clerks in the Freedmen's Bureau from 1867 to 1869 and in the Treasury Department from 1869 to 1875. When his father purchased the *New National Era* in 1870, Charles became one of the journal's correspondents, while his older brothers, Lewis Douglass and Frederick Douglass Jr., were in charge of editorials and business management, respectively. After serving as a clerk to the Santo Domingo Commission in 1871, Charles returned to the Caribbean when President Ulysses S. Grant appointed him consul to Puerto Plata, Santo Domingo. (The Santo Domingo Commission investigated the possibility of annexing the Dominican Republic to the United States. Grant saw the country as a potential home for southern blacks in the United States, to allow them to escape increasing oppression.)

In 1875 Charles became a clerk in the U.S. consulate in Santo Domingo but returned to the United States in 1879 after his wife died. At this time Charles's brothers and father divided Charles's surviving children among their households in order to care for them. Charles Frederick and Joseph Henry went to live with Frederick Douglass

Jr.; Julia Ada went to live with Frederick Douglass Sr.; and Mary Louise went to live with Lewis Douglass.

Charles then settled in Corona, New York, and entered the West India commission business. He married Laura Haley of Canandaigua, New York, on 30 December 1880, and the couple had one son, Haley George. Two years later he took a job in Washington, D.C., working as an examiner in the Pension Bureau. Ultimately becoming a real estate developer, Charles also held several commands in the District of Columbia National Guard and several high posts in the Grand Army of the Republic. He later served as the secretary and treasurer for the District of Columbia schools. In his capacity as school trustee, Charles was active in employing the first black teachers in the county schools and in assuring equal pay for these teachers as well. Along with his brother Lewis, Charles at times accompanied his father on his speaking engagements. He also served for many years as president of the Bethel Literary and Historical Association, a cultural and literary institution for blacks in Washington. Sponsoring weekly lectures during the winter season, the association engaged local black speakers, including Frederick Douglass. Charles himself also delivered several addresses to the association.

In 1892 Charles developed a summer resort in Maryland known as Highland Beach, a twenty-six-acre tract with fourteen hundred feet of beach frontage. Late in life he became a member of the National Association for the Advancement of Colored People, District of Columbia Branch. Although most of Charles's children did not live to adulthood, the famous violinist Joseph Henry Douglass, was among those who did—as did Haley George Douglass, who became a teacher at Dunbar High School in Washington, D.C., and later the mayor of Highland Beach. Charles Remond Douglass died in Washington, D.C.

[*See also* Antislavery Movement; Antislavery Press; Black Abolitionists; Black Press; Civil War; Civil War, Participation and Recruitment of Black Troops in; Dominican Republic, Annexation of; Douglass, Anna Murray; Douglass, Frederick; Douglass, Frederick, Jr.; Douglass, Lewis Henry; Fifty-fourth Massachusetts Infantry Regiment; Freedmen's Bureau; Grant, Ulysses S.; Haiti; Haitian Revolutions; Lincoln, Abraham; Lynn, Massachusetts; *New National Era*; *North Star*; Remond, Charles Lenox; Rochester, New York; Union Army, African Americans in; *and* Washington, D.C.]

BIBLIOGRAPHY

Cromwell, John Wesley. *History of the Bethel Literary Association.* Washington, DC: Press of R. L. Pendleton, 1896.

Douglass, Charles Remond. Letter to Frederick Douglass, 20 December 1863. The Frederick Douglass Papers. Library of Congress, Washington, D.C. http://memory.loc.gov/ammem/doughtml/doughome.html.

Gregory, James M. *Frederick Douglass, the Orator; Containing an Account of His Life, His Eminent Public Services, His Brilliant Career as Orator, Selections from His Speeches and Writings.* New York: Crowell, 1971.

McFeely, William S. *Frederick Douglass.* New York: Norton, 1991.

"Men of the Month." *Crisis* 3 (1921): 215.

Office of the Adjutant General, Commonwealth of Massachusetts. *Massachusetts Soldiers, Sailors, and Marines in the Civil War.* 8 vols. Norwood, MA: Norwood Press, 1931–1935.

—MARK G. EMERSON

DOUGLASS, FREDERICK (b. February 1818; d. 20 February 1895), the most important African American leader and intellectual of the nineteenth century. Frederick Douglass lived for twenty years as a slave and nearly nine years as a fugitive slave. From the 1840s to his death in 1895 he attained international fame as an abolitionist, editor, orator, statesman, and the author of three autobiographies that became classics of the slave narrative tradition. Douglass lived to see the Emancipation of the slaves during the Civil War and made a major contribution to interpreting the meaning of those epochal events. He labored for the establishment of black civil rights and witnessed their betrayal during Reconstruction and the Gilded Age. He advocated women's rights long before they were achieved.

It took nearly a century after his death for Douglass's work to receive widespread attention in school curriculums and in the scholarly fields of literature and history. With the flowering of African American history and culture in the 1960s, and a greatly increased attention to slavery, Douglass's autobiographies rose from obscurity and finally came back into print. By the early 2000s Douglass had become a common image in American history textbooks, and his speeches and other writings were more widely known. Along with Martin Luther King Jr. and W. E. B. Du Bois in the twentieth century and Harriet Tubman in his own time, Douglass attained an iconic position as a black person in America's pantheon of heroic figures. Reaching that lofty position was a long, hard journey through the thickets of racism and many changes in American history.

From Slave to Fugitive. Douglass was born on Holme Hill Farm along Tuckahoe Creek in Talbot County, on Maryland's Eastern Shore. Named Frederick Augustus Washington Bailey, he was the son of Harriet Bailey and, in all likelihood, her white master, and he came into the world in the cabin of his grandmother, Betsey Bailey. At age six Frederick was sent to live on Wye Plantation, owned by Colonel Edward Lloyd, the largest slaveholder in Maryland. During his two years at Wye Plantation, which he called the Great House Farm, Frederick saw his mother occasionally and for the last time in 1825; she died the following year. Douglass never knew the accurate identity of his father, although circumstantial evidence indicates that it was probably either his first owner, Aaron Anthony, or his second owner, Thomas Auld.

Because he was bequeathed to Auld on Anthony's death in 1826, Douglass was in the fullest sense an orphan from the age of eight. In 1827 Frederick was sent to live in Baltimore to be a companion for a white boy, Tommy Auld, Thomas Auld's nephew and the son of Hugh and Sophia Auld. During those formative years in a slaveholding city—yet one with a large free black population and many influences and opportunities a slave boy would never have encountered on Maryland's Eastern Shore—Frederick learned to read and write and to explore his remarkable gifts for curiosity and language. He also underwent a religious conversion and discovered a remarkable book, *The Columbian Orator*, a manual of oratory and a collection of speeches and dialogues from antiquity and the Enlightenment with an antislavery tone.

In 1833 Frederick was sent back to the town of Saint Michaels on the Eastern Shore to live in the home of his owner, Thomas Auld. By January 1834, finding the growing teenager to be more than he could handle, Auld hired

Frederick Douglass, in an engraved portrait that was the frontispiece for his *Narrative of the Life of Frederick Douglass*, 1845. (University of Rochester Library, Rare Books and Special Collections.)

him out to Edward Covey, a slave owner known for disciplining unruly young slaves. Under Covey's brutal regime, Frederick suffered many beatings, but in August 1834 the sixteen-year-old slave stood up to the hired master and fought him in a bloody brawl. Douglass would later immortalize the fight with Covey in his first autobiography, *Narrative of the Life of Frederick Douglass* (1845). Fashioning the story as his personal resurrection from psychological bondage, Douglass relates that Covey never laid a hand or a whip on him again after the fight.

In early 1835 Frederick was hired out as a field hand to yet another master, William Freeland, who did not subject him to physical punishment and allowed the brilliant young slave to conduct a Sabbath school among a band of "noble souls," his fellow teenage slaves, in which they practiced oratory and recited biblical passages. In April 1836 an escape plot that hatched among this band of brothers was betrayed and discovered. Frederick and his friends were jailed in Easton, Maryland, and the future abolitionist had every reason to think that he would be "sold south" to an obscure fate on a cotton plantation somewhere in Georgia or Alabama. However, for reasons that remain a mystery, his owner, Thomas Auld, sent Frederick back to Baltimore with the promise that after good behavior he would be freed on his twenty-first birthday.

The disgruntled young slave, inspired by language, Old Testament stories he had come to cherish, a rebellious spirit, and some good fortune, decided not to wait for the tenuous promise of his future freedom. Working as a caulker in the Baltimore shipyards from 1836 to 1838, Frederick met a young free black woman named Anna Murray who helped him plot his escape and would later become his wife. On 3 September 1838, at the age of twenty, Frederick fled slavery by train and by boat. Dressed in a sailor's clothing and with sailor's protection papers obtained from a friend, he fled across rivers and through great dangers to arrive first in Philadelphia and then in New York, where Anna joined him and where they were married on 15 September. The couple abruptly moved to New Bedford, Massachusetts, an enclave for fugitive slaves. Shortly after his arrival, Frederick adopted a new surname, Douglass, from the hero in Sir Walter Scott's novel *The Lady of the Lake*.

Several Lives in One. At the end of Douglass's third autobiography, *Life and Times of Frederick Douglass* (1881, 1892), he declares that he had lived several lives in one: "First, the life of slavery; secondly, the life of a fugitive from slavery; thirdly, the life of comparative freedom; fourthly, the life of conflict and battle; and fifthly, the life of victory, if not complete, at least assured." With an autobiographer's pride, Douglass wanted to demonstrate the struggle and achievement in his life. He had suffered and overcome, he insists. He had persevered through the potential hopelessness of a slave's early life, led his people ultimately through a great trial, and in the end reached at least a personal triumph. These are the images of an aging man summing up his life and attempting to control his historical reputation. Douglass's categories reveal his self-image as the fugitive slave who had risen to racial and national leader, the person and the nation regenerated in the crucible of the Civil War.

Like all great autobiographers, Douglass was trying to order the passage of time and thereby make sense of his own past. However, the stages through which Douglass envisioned his life are instructive. They represent many of the turning points that define his illustrious career. No chronology can convey the deeper meanings in such an eventful life. Douglass may have said this best himself in a speech titled "Life Pictures," first delivered in 1861. The final lines of that speech may have been unwittingly autobiographical. "We live in deeds, not years," said Douglass, "in thoughts, not breaths, in feeling, not fingers on a dial. We should count time by heartthrobs; he most lives who thinks the most, feels the noblest, acts the best."

These five stages of a seventy-seven-year life help clarify Douglass's changing place in the course of American history in the nineteenth century. Beyond his lifetime his significance can be comprehended in three additional ways. He is likely to always be remembered first for his heroic life, as the slave who willed his own freedom; fashioned a dramatic career as an activist and, later, a sagelike statesman; and emerged as a true "representative man" in a century that admired such figures. Second, he remains important as an artist—a writer and orator of uncommon skill and penetrating analysis of America's struggle over slavery and race—and as the narrator of his own story, the first two versions of which, *Narrative of the Life of Frederick Douglass* and *My Bondage and My Freedom*, are considered masterpieces of the literary American renaissance. Third, he endures as a thinker, important for his insights into both the alienation of blacks from and their embrace of America's ideals. No one ever exposed America's hypocrisy of sustaining slavery while celebrating freedom quite like Douglass. As activist, artist, and thinker, Douglass exemplifies the best and the worst in the American spirit, of slavery and freedom in a land of promise and contradiction.

Heroic Life. In his first two years living as a free man in New Bedford, Massachusetts, Douglass worked as a day laborer in the shipyard. He joined the African Methodist Episcopal Church, where he tried out his oratorical skills and became a class leader and local preacher. His first speech was an address condemning African colonization, the movement to persuade black Americans to immigrate to West Africa. Between 1839 and 1849 Douglass and his wife, Anna, had five children: Rosetta (b. 1839), Lewis (b. 1840), Frederick Jr. (b. 1842), Charles (b. 1844), and Annie (b. 1849). The growing family was close but placed a heavy burden on Anna because Douglass traveled frequently to lecture and participate in abolitionist activities across the American North and in Great Britain.

In August 1841 William Lloyd Garrison, the radical leader of the American Anti-Slavery Society, invited Douglass to deliver his first public abolitionist speech at a meeting on Nantucket Island, off the Massachusetts coast. At that gathering Douglass felt that he carried a "severe cross" as he spoke about his life to white people, but he made a powerful impression with both his story and his style. Garrison's organization hired him, and for the next three years Douglass launched his professional life as an orator and abolitionist. From 1841 to 1844, on countless antislavery platforms, the former slave told his stories of witnessing as a child the beating of his aunt Hester and the murder of a runaway slave by a cruel overseer, fighting with Covey until the slave breaker would harm him no more, discovering language and the fearful but liberating power of literacy, observing the damage that slavery did to the souls and psyches of slaveholders, and pursuing his overwhelming desire as a youth to gain his freedom. In these speeches Douglass told many of the episodes he would later connect in his *Narrative*. He spoke with such eloquence and knowledge that many members of his audiences did not believe that he had ever been a slave. Thus, after moving to Lynn, Massachusetts, Douglass wrote his first autobiography in late 1844, in part to declare just who he was in accurate terms but also to probe for himself and for his readers what freedom means when one understands its most brutal denials.

In February 1844 Nathaniel Rogers, the editor of the abolitionist paper *Herald of Freedom*, watched Douglass deliver two speeches in Concord, New Hampshire, and recorded his impressions. Rogers heard Douglass attack the hypocrisy of American churches that supported slavery. He listened as the black abolitionist described himself a "fugitive not *from* slavery—but *in* slavery" and called his New England hosts "enslavers," complicit with his former owners in the South. Douglass recited episodes that would soon appear in his *Narrative* but concluded, in Rogers's stunned observation, like "an insurgent slave taking hold on the right of speech, and charging on his tyrants the bondage of his race." Rogers found Douglass the orator both "fearful and magnificent." Douglass was an angry young man trying to use language to represent and to control his own pain. According to Rogers, Douglass "let out the outraged humanity that was laboring in him. . . . It was the volcanic outbreak of human nature long pent up in slavery and at last bursting its imprisonment." These descriptions of Douglass as a young orator capture some of the ways that language became the former slave's only real weapon of both self-revelation and advocacy against slavery on behalf of his people. Douglass mastered words, written and spoken, as had few other Americans in his generation from any background.

As the twenty-seven-year-old fugitive reimagines his "dark night of slavery" while in Covey's custody, he fashions in his *Narrative* an unforgettable metaphor of freedom. After months of beatings and unrelenting hard labor, Douglass relates that he considered himself "broken in body, soul, and spirit." Describing himself as a nearly suicidal teenager, Douglass the writer probes his memory for the contrast of beauty with wretchedness that allowed him to dream. "Our house stood within a few rods of the Chesapeake Bay," he remembers, "whose broad bosom was ever white with sails from every quarter of the habitable globe." Douglass then captures slavery and freedom with unparalleled artistry in the genre of slave narratives:

> Those beautiful vessels, robed in purest white, so delightful to the eye of freemen, were to me so many shrouded ghosts, to terrify and torment me with thoughts of my wretched condition. I have often, in the deep stillness of a summer's Sabbath, stood all alone upon the lofty banks of that noble bay, and traced, with saddened heart and tearful eye, the countless number of sails moving off to the mighty ocean. The sight of these always affected me powerfully. My thoughts would compel utterance; and there, with no audience but the Almighty, I would pour out my soul's complaint, in my rude way, with an apostrophe to the moving multitude of ships. (Blight, p. 83)

Douglass then shifts and speaks directly to the ships, trying to reenter a teenager's voice:

> You are loosed from your moorings and are free; I am fast in my chains, and am a slave! You move merrily before the gentle gale, and I sadly before the bloody whip! You are freedom's swift-winged angels, that fly around the world; I am confined in bands of iron! O that I were free! O that I were on one of your gallant decks and under your protecting wing! Alas, betwixt me and you, the turbid waters roll. (Blight, p. 84)

In such poetry Douglass wrote a psalm-like prayer of deliverance in his *Narrative*, rendering in the music of words the meaning of slavery's potential to destroy the human spirit but at the same time transcending his misery to declare at the end of his lament, in language reminiscent of the slave spirituals, that "there is a better day coming." Douglass's "heroism" was moral as much as physical, and it manifested in his ability to tell a story that was itself the best argument against slavery Americans had ever read. Douglass proved that language, in a society that valued it, could be a form of actual liberation. The slave who could tell his ascension story from bondage, and could wield words back at his former masters, could also achieve a certain degree of power and a new place for blacks in America.

After publishing his *Narrative* in 1845, Douglass sailed for the British Isles aboard the ship *Cambria*, where he was forced to accept second-class passage and where American passengers nearly mobbed him for delivering an abolitionist speech. Douglass arrived safely in Liverpool and then traveled to Ireland, where he spent three triumphant months lecturing in Cork, Dublin, and Belfast and where an Irish edition of his book was published and sold widely. Through 1846 and into early 1847 Douglass toured Scotland and England, speaking to large crowds in a celebrated lecture campaign that established him as the most sought-after American reformer. Douglass amazed his audiences in Britain and was treated more kindly and with far less racism there than he had been in the United States. He became the most prominent in a long line of African American reformers, speakers, and fugitives who found British society more open to their color, their plight, and their ideas.

As Douglass returned to America, a group of his British antislavery friends arranged for the purchase of his freedom from Thomas Auld for 150 pounds ($711). On his return to Massachusetts, Douglass decided to move his wife, Anna, and their burgeoning family west, to Rochester, New York. He hoped for a new beginning, a geographical and ideological break from the grip of William Lloyd Garrison and his antislavery network in New England. Douglass needed independence for his fertile mind and, he hoped, for his new career as he began what he called his "life of comparative freedom."

Douglass was on his own as he launched a newspaper, the *North Star*, first published on 3 December 1847. It would go through two more names, *Frederick Douglass' Paper* and *Douglass' Monthly*, and over the next sixteen years became the longest-lasting black abolitionist paper in the United States. Douglass became a tireless and innovative editor, although his paper always struggled to make ends meet. To keep it afloat, he received editorial assistance from Julia Griffiths, an Englishwoman Douglass had met during his British tour and who lived in Rochester between 1848 and 1851. He also received considerable sums of money to help underwrite the paper from the wealthy New York abolitionist Gerrit Smith. During these years Douglass shifted ideologically from the moral suasion of the Garrisonians to the political abolitionism of Smith's Upstate New York circle of activists. He came under the sway of colleagues and events that pushed him away from Garrison's tutelage. Garrison was deeply admired among northern free blacks and fugitive slaves for his genuine support of their civil rights. His radicalism against slavery gave hope to many blacks who wondered if they would ever have a future in America. However, Garrison's doctrinaire insistence on nonvoting (not participating in a political system that countenanced slavery), on nonresistance (pacifism), on the U.S. Constitution as a proslavery document and therefore altogether hostile to the antislavery cause, and on moral suasion (appealing to the heart and not the law of economic interest) as the only proper ways to attack the peculiar institution were no longer fulfilling to many black abolitionists.

Douglass was the leader of a new generation of black abolitionists, many of whom had been born in slavery, had escaped through some pathway of the legendary Underground Railroad, and had become pragmatic activists. The new generation included Harriet Tubman, Henry Highland Garnet, William Wells Brown, Ellen and William Craft, John Sella Martin, and many others. Wearing the experience of slavery on their backs and in their souls, they were less committed to philosophical abstractions like antipolitics and nonviolence than were white abolitionists. Some embraced almost any strategy against slavery and for free black rights that they thought might work. If the Constitution could be appropriated to the cause of abolition, even if largely in political and rhetorical ways, so be it. And if violent means could free people, then many black abolitionists accepted their necessity and looked for allies who might help them. By 1851 Douglass broke personally and philosophically with Garrison and became a full-blown political abolitionist who was willing to join political parties, harbor fugitive slaves and help them on the path to Canada, and forge alliances with violent radicals.

During the 1850s Douglass's political education took many significant turns. None was more important than his and other abolitionists' response to the passage of the Fugitive Slave Law of 1850. As part of the Compromise of 1850 the law established a much stricter judicial process by which escaped slaves in the North had to be returned to their former owners. The fleeing slave, desperate for safety and freedom, had become one of the most prominent images and realities evoked by abolitionists, and the new threat of capture radicalized many activists at the same time that it drove thousands of fugitives to move to Canada.

Numerous reports of fugitives rescued from slave catchers in the wake of the new law led many former nonresistants into acts of courage and violence. In 1851 Douglass harbored the three black fugitives who had killed one of their pursuers in Christiana, Pennsylvania. By rail the fugitives fled to Douglass's home in Rochester. He fed and sheltered them and then, with Julia Griffiths's assistance, drove them in his carriage to the Genessee River, where they boarded a steamer for Toronto. To Douglass the

Douglass, engraving by J. C. Buttre from a daguerreotype. This image was the frontispiece of Douglass's second autobiography, *My Bondage, My Freedom*, 1850–1855. (University of Rochester Library, Rare Books and Special Collections.)

Christiana fugitives were "heroic defenders of the just rights of man against manstealers and murderers." On the deck of the ship, just before departure to safety in Canada, one of the fugitives gave Douglass a revolver as a token of gratitude. He cherished the memento that had been taken from the hand of the dead slave catcher in Christiana.

Increasingly in the 1850s Douglass turned his attention to violent self-defense in the North and to the prospect of slave insurrection in the South. In a column published in 1854 titled "Is It Right and Wise to Kill a Kidnapper?" he not only justified violence in self-defense but also celebrated it. The "slaughter" of a slave catcher, wrote Douglass, "was as innocent in the sight of God, as would be the slaughter of a ravenous wolf in the act of throttling an infant." In the midst of the controversy over "bleeding Kansas" in 1856, he declared that the "slave's right to revolt is perfect." He shuddered at the horrors of slave insurrection, but "terrible as it will be," he admitted, "we accept and hope for it." In the despair following the *Dred Scott* decision in 1857, which declared that blacks had no social or legal future in America, Douglass saw slave rebellion as offering at least one path to black liberation. Fearfully, he predicted that "in an awful moment of depression and desperation, the bondman and bondwoman at the South may rush to one wild and deadly struggle for freedom." Ominously, he announced that he was in "no frame of mind" to see this prospect "long deferred."

This rhetorical and even personal espousal of violent means against slavery conditioned Douglass to support the plans of the radical and religiously inspired abolitionist John Brown. During his crusade to raise money and men for his ultimate raid on Harpers Ferry, Brown lived for three weeks in February 1858 in the attic apartment of Douglass's home in Rochester. Douglass gave Brown moral support, if not his own service. He knew just enough of Brown's vague plans for capturing the federal arsenal at Harpers Ferry and fomenting a slave revolution throughout Virginia to warn the old warrior that he was doomed. Douglass last met with Brown in August 1859 in Chambersburg, Pennsylvania. Although he refused to join the ill-fated raid, Douglass brought with him one new recruit, Shields Green, a twenty-five-year-old fugitive slave from Charleston, South Carolina, who, with relatives still trapped in slavery, was willing to give his life to the cause. Douglass seemed to know, however, that his own best work lay ahead of him and that Brown's raid would end, like most attempted slave insurrections, in death and failure. Douglass was willing to support violent means to weaken or destroy slavery, and though he admired Brown's moral fervor, he saw only doom in the old warrior's strategic planning.

In the wake of the October 1859 raid, Douglass fled north into Canada and boarded a steamer headed out the Saint Lawrence River to England. Because of a large cache of letters and other documents found in a trunk Brown had left behind at his hideout in Maryland, Douglass was prominent among the abolitionists implicated in the Harpers Ferry conspiracy. Hence, Douglass escaped from Rochester only a short time before federal marshals arrived to arrest him. As Brown's accomplice, Douglass would spend six months in Britain, returning to America because of the death of his beloved daughter Annie and because the federal government had decided not to make any prosecutions beyond Brown's martyrdom. By June 1860 Douglass had "little hope of the freedom of the slave by peaceful means," he wrote in a letter. "The only penetrable point of a tyrant," he said, "is the fear of death. The outcry that they make as to the danger of having their throats cut is because they deserve to have them cut." Others might lead insurrections, and Douglass would urge them on, but the great orator seemed to understand that his best role was as a leader of insurrectionary thought and political action.

Against the odds, Douglass hoped for a reformist rather than a revolutionary end to slavery. As he took heart at the rising sectional crises over the expansion of slavery into western territories, the turbulent decade of the 1850s saw Douglass embrace antislavery political parties. He attended party conventions and became an active campaigner, first for the Liberty and Free-Soil parties and eventually for the Republicans. With his roots in moral suasion, Douglass could still agonize between an ethical worldview and the realities of political power, between militancy and accommodation. His conversion to political action was part of a gradual ideological transformation to an antislavery interpretation of the Constitution.

Unlike some political abolitionists and Republicans, he was never convinced that the framers' intentions were actually antislavery. However, Douglass adopted the view that the Constitution could be an abolitionist instrument, especially regarding the extension of slavery into the West. He embraced the free-soil doctrine, which became the defining principle of the Republican Party after 1854, that slavery was a creature of local (state) law and freedom a creature of national (federal) law. Hence, Congress could, by its clear authority over the territories, stop the spread of slavery. As early as 1852, at the Free-Soil Party convention, Douglass spoke vehemently for repeal of the Fugitive Slave Law on constitutional grounds and argued that slavery was nothing more than a system of "piracy." However, Douglass had learned that politics and perfectionism did not always mix. He embraced a hard-earned pragmatism that made him admit in 1856, in an article ("Fremont and Dayton") in *Frederick Douglass' Paper*, that the

> time has passed for an honest man to attempt any defence of a right to change his opinion as to political methods of opposing Slavery. . . . Right Anti-Slavery action is that which deals the . . . deadliest blow upon slavery that can be given at that particular time. Such action is always consistent, however different may be the forms through which it expresses itself. (http://www.wlhn.org/dodgeco/histories/douglass/douglass_writings.htm)

During the presidential election years of 1856 and 1860, Douglass begrudgingly supported the Republican candidates, John C. Frémont and Abraham Lincoln, respectively. In the years between, he threw his allegiance to the Radical Abolitionist Party (and its leader, Gerrit Smith), the small successor of the old Liberty Party. In effect, Douglass had a party for his principles and a party for his hopes, two diverging "paths of duty," as he described his dilemma. Douglass was troubled by the racist underpinnings of the Republicans' nonextension argument about slavery; for too many white northerners nonextension meant exclusion of blacks from the western territories. Although the Republicans' lack of genuine abolitionism still angered the Rochester editor in the pivotal election of

1860, he sighed and worked for Lincoln's election in the state of New York. Douglass declared that he preferred the "brave and inspiring march of a storming party," but in its absence he would accept "the slow process of a cautious siege." To him the ultimate meaning of the Republican Party before secession was in its potential to cause southern reaction and disunion. Southern fears of Lincoln's potential victory, said Douglass, served as "tolerable endorsements of the antislavery tendencies of the Republican party."

Douglass welcomed the secession of the Deep South states in the wake of Lincoln's election in 1860. The secession winter was a confusing, fearful, and exhilarating time for abolitionists like Douglass. They were the targets of antiabolition mobs who blamed them for causing the disorder that led to disunion. Douglass was the victim of one such mob in Boston on 3 December 1860, when a gang led by hired thugs broke up a meeting at which he was to speak on the first anniversary of the execution of John Brown. Douglass was thrown down a staircase at Tremont Temple but, as a Boston newspaper reported, not before he "fought like a trained pugilist." In this charged atmosphere the black abolitionist expected that yet another form of compromise would probably still hold the Union together and delay what he most yearned for, a sanctioned war against the South and slavery. The firing on Fort Sumter in Charleston harbor, South Carolina, in April 1861 brought the first of these goals rapidly into reality. It would take nearly two more agonizing years for the second goal of a war for black freedom to materialize.

From the outset of the Civil War, Douglass saw the conflict in abolitionist terms. He urged the Lincoln administration to move aggressively to prosecute a war against slavery and slaveholders. Until well into 1862 the editor turned war propagandist found himself deeply frustrated with federal military policy (called "denial of asylum") toward fugitive slaves. Union troops were ordered to return those escaped slaves who fled within their lines. Moreover, for the first full year of the war, no black soldiers were admitted into Union forces, rejecting the wishes and overtures of many African American communities and leaders. From the beginning of the war Douglass wanted precisely what Lincoln did not want: a "remorseless revolutionary struggle," as the president put it, that would make black freedom indispensable to saving the Union. By late 1862, however, in the wake of the September battle of Antietam in Maryland, Lincoln concluded that to defeat the Confederacy, slavery would itself have to be destroyed. Thus, Douglass's views of Lincoln and his emancipation policies moved from cautious support in 1860, to outrage in 1861, and eventually to respect and admiration in 1863. Regarding the Emancipation Proclamation and the recruitment of black troops in late 1862, Douglass was the leading African American voice, urging and cheering on a war that transformed from an effort to save the Union into a struggle for black freedom and the reinvention of the American Republic.

These outcomes of the war, however, were by no means certain until the very end. In 1862 Douglass was offended by the Lincoln administration's plans for colonization of freed people. The administration attempted to recruit Douglass himself to lead the federal effort to relocate thousands of former slaves in foreign lands. The abolitionist vehemently rejected the government's offer, calling colonization, especially at this long-dreamed-of moment of emancipation, a "satanic spirit" and a "miserable philosophy." Douglass preferred instead to join the effort to recruit men for the Fifty-fourth Massachusetts Infantry Regiment, the first Northern unit of black infantry. The first two recruits were his sons, Lewis and Charles. The proud father was present on a balcony overlooking Beacon Street in Boston in May 1863 as the fated regiment marched toward glory in its send-off from the people of the state that sponsored it. Douglass even boarded the ship at the Boston wharf and accompanied his sons to the outer harbor, stepping off to a small boat and waving as they sailed to South Carolina. Both of Douglass's sons survived the war, and one, Lewis, participated in the famous charge on Fort Wagner outside Charleston, South Carolina, in July 1863. To Douglass the 200,000 black men in the Union ground and naval forces gave the war its most visible and poignant meaning.

Douglass met Lincoln three times. In August 1863, he visited Washington, D.C., for the first time and met with the president for a frank discussion of discriminations practiced against black troops. They hardly agreed on all issues, but Douglass left the meeting impressed with Lincoln's forthrightness and political skill. The second meeting took place in the capital city a year later. With the war in a bloody stalemate in Virginia, Lincoln's reelection was in jeopardy, and that summer Douglass flirted with supporting John C. Frémont's bid to replace the president on the Republican ticket. In August 1864 Lincoln invited the black leader to the White House for an extraordinary discussion. Worried that he might lose the fall election to the Democrat George B. McClellan, Lincoln sought Douglass's advice and help.

The president of the United States asked the most prominent black abolitionist to lead a scheme reminiscent of John Brown and Harpers Ferry. Concerned that if the Democrats won the election, they would pursue a negotiated, proslavery peace, Lincoln, according to Douglass, wanted "to get more of the slaves within our lines." Toward that end Douglass went north and organized some twenty-five agents willing to work at the front. In a letter

Douglass in a portrait photograph. Douglass was in his early twenties when the daguerreotype was invented, and he lived to see photography revolutionize portraiture and take its place as an important and popular technology and as a powerful tool for communication. (University of Rochester Library, Rare Books and Special Collections.)

to Lincoln dated 29 August 1864 Douglass outlined his plan for this "band of scouts," channeling slaves northward in an effort to liberate as many as possible before Election Day. Douglass was not convinced that this plan was fully "practicable," but he was ready to serve. Because military and political fortunes shifted dramatically with the fall of Atlanta to Union forces a week later, this government-sponsored underground railroad never emerged. Nevertheless, how remarkable this episode of cooperative planning must have been to both Douglass and Lincoln, as they worked together to accomplish the very "revolution" that had separated them ideologically in 1861.

The third encounter between Douglass and Lincoln occurred on 4 March 1865 at the president's second inauguration. Standing in the crowd, Douglass heard Lincoln declare slavery the "cause" and emancipation the "result" of the Civil War. He heard Lincoln's determination that to win the war, "every drop of blood drawn with the lash shall be paid by another drawn with the sword." Four years earlier and many times between, Douglass had dreamed of writing that speech for Lincoln. That evening the former slave attended the inaugural reception at the White House, an event that he recorded in *Life and Times of Frederick Douglass*. At first denied entrance by two policemen, Douglass was admitted only when the president was notified. Weary of a lifetime of such racial rejections, Douglass was immediately set at ease by Lincoln's cordial greeting, "Here comes my friend Douglass." Lincoln asked Douglass what he thought of the day's speech. Douglass demurred, urging the host to attend to his many visitors. Lincoln insisted, however, telling his black guest, "There is no man in the country whose opinion I value more than yours." Douglass replied, "Mr. Lincoln, that was a sacred effort." We can only guess at the thrill in Douglass's heart, knowing that the cause he had so long pleaded might finally come to fruition. He could honestly entertain the belief that he and Lincoln, the slaves and the nation, were walking that night into a new history.

Douglass remembered the immediate aftermath of the Civil War as a time of "vast changes" and personal ambivalence. "I felt that I had reached the end of the noblest and best part of my life," he lamented in 1881. "The antislavery platform had performed its work, and my voice was no longer needed. Othello's occupation was gone." Douglass's career was hardly over; he would play new roles in the postwar society as an orator; the editor for four years of the *New National Era*, a newspaper he took over in 1870 in Washington, D.C.; as the president of the Freedman's Savings and Trust Company in 1874, which folded under his management; and as a Republican Party functionary. During Reconstruction and beyond Douglass's leadership became more emblematic and less activist. President Rutherford B. Hayes appointed him to be the U.S. marshal for the District of Columbia in 1877, and in 1881 he accepted the appointment as the recorder of deeds in the District of Columbia from President James Garfield. In 1889 Douglass became a diplomat when President Benjamin Harrison made him the minister and consul general to Haiti, a post he held until 1891 when he resigned in protest against the United States' designs to seize Môle Saint-Nicolas, a Haitian island.

During the latter third of his life Douglass made a comfortable living, largely from his exhaustive lecture tours and his government positions. In 1872 his home in Rochester burned, under suspicion of arson. He lost many important papers in the fire, and amidst the chaos he decided to move his family to Washington, D.C., where he attempted with mixed results to obtain government jobs for two of his sons. Douglass's wife, Anna, never achieved literacy, despite the urgings of their daughter Rosetta and Douglass himself. Frederick and Anna shared an abiding love, and she was a skilled homemaker and a devoted mother. Nonetheless, their marriage was burdened by many strains. Douglass enjoyed the company of intellectuals, many of whom were women. One in particular, Ottilie Assing, a German woman of Jewish and radical political background, became Douglass's lover. Their relationship was one of friendship and passion. Assing came to America in the late 1850s in search of the author of *My Bondage and My Freedom* (1855), which she had just read. She lived in New Jersey but occasionally visited Rochester and stayed in the Douglass home. She also contributed money to Rosetta Douglass's education.

In 1878 Douglass purchased Cedar Hill, a large house and fifteen-acre estate on a hill in the Anacostia section of the District of Columbia. Four years later Anna, his wife of forty-four years, died after a long illness. Douglass was emotionally distraught for a time. However, in 1884 he married Helen Pitts, a graduate of Mount Holyoke College who had been his secretary and was white. The marriage caused considerable controversy in the black press and in Douglass's own family. The most famous black man in America had just married a white woman. To the sixty-six-year-old Douglass, however, the fuss was insignificant. In 1885 he and Helen went on a world tour that included England, France, Italy, Egypt, and Greece. Ottilie Assing moved back to Europe and in 1884 committed suicide in a park in Paris. She left much of her estate to Douglass's children. Very few letters survive from Douglass's side of his relationship with Assing; what is known has been derived mostly from her pen. He was a man of enormous pride in his accomplishments and devoted to the welfare of his children; and he loved Anna as his life companion all the way from his slave days in Baltimore to the great house at Cedar Hill. However, his was a complicated, passionate, intellectually expanding life, and Assing, as well as other friends, male and female, nurtured and challenged the nineteenth century's most conspicuous African American leader through his many trials and triumphs.

Orator and Writer. What constitutes the heroic? In Douglass's case, heroism emanated from the very nature of his life. He risked all and engaged in self-sacrifice to escape the bonds of chattel slavery; he was physical property become man. His heroism was of an even deeper kind, however—beyond physical courage. It was a form of moral heroism manifested in language. If America is an idea, no one in the nineteenth century, not even Abraham Lincoln, defined that idea better in the music of words than did Douglass. From an adolescent reading *The Columbian Orator* and the Bible and a young man lecturing on the abolitionist circuit, Douglass had become one of America's greatest public speakers by the 1850s, as well as the author of memoirs, enduring political analyses, at least one work of fiction, and probing social commentary.

Literacy was forbidden fruit for young slaves, and that is precisely why Douglass so desired to read and write while growing up in Baltimore and on the Eastern Shore. Words represented an unshackling of the spirit and an opening of the mind for the young Douglass. By watching his fellow slaves denied access to language and education, he perceived "the white man's power to enslave the black man," as he wrote in his *Narrative*. After his master, Hugh Auld, forbade his mistress, Sophia Auld, from continuing to teach Frederick to read, the twelve-year-old took inspiration from his dilemma. "I set out with high hope," he wrote in 1845, "and a fixed purpose, at whatever cost of trouble, to learn how to read. . . . What he [Auld] most dreaded, I most desired." Although he attended no formal school as a slave youth, from the day in 1830 that he purchased his copy of Caleb Bingham's *The Columbian Orator*, Douglass possessed the same schoolbook as his white playmates in the streets of Baltimore. That special book had a lasting effect on young Frederick's intellectual and spiritual growth. "Every opportunity I got, I used to read this book," Douglass recalls in the *Narrative*.

A best-seller as a school text for several decades after its publication in 1797, *The Columbian Orator* was both an elocution manual and a collection of some eighty-four selections, including prose, verse, plays, invented dialogues, and political speeches by famous orators from antiquity and the Age of Enlightenment. Most selections dealt with themes of nationalism, individual liberty, religious faith, or the democratic value of education. The book as a whole had an antislavery tone and served Douglass, he later said, as a "powerful denunciation of oppression." Moreover, from Bingham's introductory essay, "General Directions for Speaking," Douglass learned that orators and writers are not born of nature; they must practice and harness elements of nature's power and the beauty of words. *The Columbian Orator* was one of the few possessions Douglass carried with him during his escape from slavery in 1838.

A Voice like No Other. In his early years on the antislavery circuit, Douglass had to achieve a supremely dignified style of expression to gain recognition and respect. At the same time he became a master of the radical, moral, and political language of abolitionism. His speeches from countless platforms in the two decades before the Civil War were hardly polite discourse; they expressed both his own indictment of America's crime of slaveholding and appeals to America's founding creeds. He also became a master of mimicry, the speaker as political entertainer who was skilled at subversive theatrics during a golden age of oratory. He employed every tool in the orator's repertoire: wit, humor, pathos, ridicule, satire, anecdotes, illustrations, and intellectual and emotional appeals. The paradox in the early nineteenth century between democratic and aristocratic eloquence eventually produced no greater example than Douglass, the slave who mastered the master's language and spoke to America as no one else ever had about how the country could reinvent itself if it could imagine a way to destroy slavery.

Douglass's lecturing career spanned fifty-four years, from 1841 to 1895. He usually spoke as an advocate, but he also delivered historical and scientific addresses, and one of his fortes was the ceremonial or commemorative speech. Douglass believed an orator had to have moral force on his side. "Thus armed, a worm can thrash a mountain," he wrote. "Speech! Speech!" he declared, "the live, calm, grave, clear, pointed, warm, sweet, melodious and powerful human voice is the chosen instrumentality." His orations often lasted as long as two hours and were delivered without affectation. One observer remarked that Douglass spoke with "the dignity and grace of a courtier, and the bearing of a king." He was also extraordinarily adept at phrasing that produced lasting aphorisms:

> "There is a meaner thing than a slave, and that is a contented slave."
> "There is nothing slavery dislikes half as much as light."
> "Despotism is wakeful and always on watch."
> "The limits of tyrants are proscribed by those they oppress."

Indeed, one of his most famous statements, delivered in 1857 at the height of the political crisis over slavery, has stood the test of time and numerous protest strategies across the world. "Without struggle there is no progress," he said. "Power concedes nothing without a demand. It never did and it never will."

Douglass's address on 5 July 1852 is the rhetorical masterpiece of American abolitionism. He delivered "What to the Slave Is the Fourth of July?" at the invitation of the Rochester Ladies Anti-Slavery Society. Harriet Beecher Stowe's *Uncle Tom's Cabin* had just been published that spring and was taking the reading public by storm. For nearly two years at that point the nation had experienced great turmoil over the unresolved Compromise of 1850, especially the infamous Fugitive Slave Law. Several fugitive slave rescues had already occurred in northern communities, some abolitionists were embracing violent means of resistance, and American political parties were on the verge of tearing themselves apart over the expansion of slavery into the West. Douglass must have made his good abolitionist friends in Rochester squirm with discomfort.

In the magnificent speech he used three essential rhetorical moves. First, Douglass set his reformist-patriotic audience at ease, letting them relax amid accolades to the genius of the founding fathers. He called the Fourth of July an American "Passover" and spoke with hope about the nation's youth, that they were "still impressible" and open to change. He called the Declaration of Independence the "ringbolt" of the nation's destiny and urged his listeners to "cling to this day . . . and to its principles, with the grasp of a storm-tossed mariner to a spar at midnight."

In his second rhetorical move, his use of pronouns was a warning of what was to follow: the nation is *your* nation, the fathers *your* fathers, he declared. The nation's epic story is taught "in your common schools, narrated at your firesides, unfolded from your pulpits." Douglass began to remind his white audience of their national and personal declension. He reminded them of the biblical story of the children of Jacob boasting of Abraham's paternity but losing Abraham's faith. Then, as though slamming a hammer down on the lectern, Douglass said, "Pardon me . . . what have I . . . to do with your national independence?" What then followed was a bitter critique of American hypocrisy regarding slavery and racism. Douglass pulled no punches. As the painful analysis took hold, he issued a litany of accusative pronouns: "This Fourth of July is yours, not mine. You may rejoice, I must mourn." After this classic rhetorical device of reversal, Douglass took his anguished audience into the "sights and scenes" of slavery itself—punishments, sale by traders, denials of the humanity of bondpeople. He implicated the church and the state, and his subject was the evil done by Americans to other Americans. Douglass ended his rhetorical tirade with an apocalyptic warning that his well-churched, Bible-reading audience would have understood: "Oh! Be warned! Be warned! A horrible reptile is coiled up at your nation's bosom; the venomous creature is nursing at the tender breast of your youthful republic; for the love of God, tear away."

For twenty minutes, Douglass's six hundred listeners must have felt as though they were undergoing a hailstorm of humiliation. Then, in his conclusion—his third move—Douglass eased up on them, wiped their brows for them, and ended on a note of cautious hope. The principles of the Declaration of Independence were still available to be embraced; the founders' best wisdom could still be tapped. It was not yet too late. In an ending that appealed to America's geographic boundlessness, drew on

Psalm 68 to declare that blacks will rise on the world's historical stage, and then quoted William Lloyd Garrison's poem "God Speed the Year of Jubilee," Douglass transported his audience, the hall in which he stood, and almost history itself, into a realm inhabited only by great art. He had used language to move people; he had explained the nation's historical and political condition, and through the pain of his moral indictment, illuminated a path to a better day. In thought and feeling, Douglass the ironist had never been in better form, and the meaning of slavery and freedom in the United States had never been better expressed.

Douglass would deliver many more memorable and oft-quoted speeches—about the meaning of the Civil War, about Reconstruction and its constitutional transformations, about America's potential development of a "composite race," about the very American idea of the "self-made man," and about the nature of "race" as a social and biological concept. He would also speak on nearly every major political crisis the nation faced from 1850 to his death in 1895—slavery expansion, secession, black soldiers in the Civil War, major Supreme Court decisions, the relationship of economic to political rights, the exodus of blacks toward the West, the terror of lynching, America's role in the international community of the imperial age, and the majesty of the right to vote. Hardly an issue in American life escaped Douglass's eloquence, and audiences flocked to hear him.

During the final third of his life, from 1865 to the emergence of the leadership of Booker T. Washington, Douglass traveled extensively and spoke repeatedly about preserving a black abolitionist memory of Emancipation, the Civil War, and the achievements of Reconstruction. He found himself appalled at the way a culture of reconciliation between North and South helped erode and eventually crush the liberty and rights of African Americans. In 1871, at one of the early observances of Memorial Day at Arlington Cemetery outside Washington, D.C., Douglass declared ("Address at the Graves of the Unknown Dead") where he stood:

> We are sometimes asked in the name of patriotism to forget the merits of this fearful struggle, and to remember with equal admiration those who struck at the nation's life, and those who struck to save it—those who fought for slavery and those who fought for liberty and justice. I am no minister of malice . . . , but may my tongue cleave to the roof of my mouth if I forge the difference between the parties to that . . . bloody conflict. . . . I may say that if this war is to be forgotten, I ask in the name of all things sacred what shall men remember? (http://memory.loc.gov/ammem/doughtml/doughome.html.)

Douglass's voice was crucial in the late-nineteenth-century debate over the legacies of the Civil War. He tried to counter the influence of the "Confederate lost cause,"

which became not only a way of coping with defeat and a comforting narrative about noble sacrifice for white Southerners but also an aggressive racial ideology intended to control educational and political policy in the larger society. He also rejected much of the national, reconciliationist memory about the mutual valor of soldiers on both sides, fighting for equal glory. In a speech to a northern veterans' group in Madison Square in New York City in 1878, Douglass argued that "the war was not a fight between rapacious birds and ferocious beasts, a mere display of brute courage and endurance, but it was a war between men of thought, as well as of action, and in dead earnest for something beyond the battlefield." With pen and voice Douglass tried to keep alive a memory that placed Emancipation at the center of the nation's understanding of the meaning of the Civil War.

Literacy and Power. Douglass's writing can hardly be separated from his oratory. Much of his autobiographi-

Douglass, in a photograph that was the frontispiece for the *Life and Times of Frederick Douglass*, New Revised Edition of 1892, published in Boston. (University of Rochester Library, Rare Books and Special Collections.)

cal prose flows in sermonic tones and cadences. He became a first-rate political journalist in the sixteen years he edited his newspaper. He mastered the short, polemical editorial and the expository public letter. He could plead a case, write an exposé, or make moral abolitionist arguments aimed at the hearts and minds of his readers. In the 1850s he entered the political fray, supporting candidates and transforming his editorial page into a platform for political abolitionism. In his endorsement of John P. Hale, the Free-Soil Party candidate for president in 1852, Douglass announced a new political philosophy that would resonate with readers for decades to come: "Our rule of political action is this: the voter ought to see to it that his vote shall secure the highest good possible, at the same time that it does no harm." He could be a pragmatist and an ideologue, depending on the circumstances. In reaction to the Kansas-Nebraska Act of 1854, which opened vast western territory to the possibility of the expansion of slavery, Douglass likened compromises with the "Slave Power" to "thawing a deadly viper, instead of killing it." A radical directness characterized many of his editorials on the great crises over slavery's expansion. "The real issue to be made with the Slave Power is this," he declared. "Slavery, like rape, robbery, piracy, and murder, has no right to exist in any part of the world—that neither north or south of 36 deg. 30 min. shall it have a moment's repose, if we can help it." Such sentences fit well the orator's platform or the journalist's printed page.

By entering the debate over the Slave Power and party politics, Douglass found himself as a writer playing two divergent roles: the black representative and voice of the slaves and the political abolitionist concerned about national destiny and the welfare of the Union. His purpose was to capture the new national awareness about slavery and to convert it into an increased concern for black freedom. The two roles both conflicted with and served each other. If he could link white fears of a slaveholding conspiracy to black suffering, a common cause might yet be struck where only racism had reigned before. In that hope, Douglass found his own way to supporting the Republican Party in 1856 and beyond. He found it impossible to resist the appeal of a broad coalition that could discredit slavery, even if it fell short of calling for complete abolition and equal rights for blacks. On his editorial page Douglass demonstrated the skills of a realist, an opportunist, and a moralist all at once. Drawing on the pivotal crises of his time, he made himself into one of the great radical journalists of American history.

Like many journalists and memoirists, Douglass also tried his hand at fiction. In 1853 he published a novella, *The Heroic Slave*, in his newspaper and in *Autographs for Freedom*, a collection of antislavery testimonies edited by his close friend Julia Griffiths. The short work fictionalizes a real person, Madison Washington, a Virginia slave who escaped to Canada, returned to free his wife, and was recaptured in the effort. Washington was sold south to New Orleans on a slave ship, *Creole*, where he led a slave mutiny in 1841. In the novella, Douglass reimagines Washington as a courageous and brilliant leader, a man who is "intelligent and brave" and possesses "the head to conceive and the hand to execute." Douglass used the story in 1853, the very time when fugitive slave rescues and resistance peaked, to illustrate the virtues of violence. Washington's successful slave revolt thwarts stereotypes of blacks as passive drudges at the same time that it serves as a poignant story of regeneration through violence, an idea more abolitionists began to embrace. In whatever genre, as a writer Douglass experimented with the many elements of his own story at the same time that he tried to imagine a new future—for himself, for African Americans, and for the nation.

Thinker. Scholars long considered Douglass largely as a biographical subject, a "representative man," the ennobling example of the slave who became free. Only after more than a century was he treated as a true intellectual, a thinker of philosophical importance. Never a philosopher in the formal sense, the former slave nevertheless left a large body of thought worthy of interpretation for its enduring arguments and challenges. Douglass possessed what one scholar called a profound "commitment to argument," and he was particularly adept at reasoning. Although he was born a slave, he rose to greatness not only because he could stand as a symbol but also because he dedicated himself to endless curiosity, to homegrown learning and wide reading, and, finally, to investigating why his American world was the way it was. Douglass's great subject was America's essential contradiction: slavery and freedom in an expanding Republic, espousing creeds such as natural rights and equality, yet practicing inhumane violations of those very principles. America's faith in reason and its inheritance of liberty made this former slave a great student of paradox and irony.

Douglass was a unique voice of humanism, romantic individualism, political and reform ideology, and the jeremiadic tradition. He became one of America's greatest analysts of racism and human alienation. Despite a life full of anguish and struggle, and though many people influenced his career, Douglass embraced self-reliance as much as Ralph Waldo Emerson did, albeit for different reasons. Like Walt Whitman, he endlessly probed the meaning of the self in relation to society and history. Like Abraham Lincoln and many other contemporaries, Douglass believed in a providential view of history and in the

United States as a nation with a special destiny and unique obligations. In an age that mixed sacred and secular thought, he became a spiritual prophet for black aspirations in America.

By the late 1850s, and especially during the Civil War, Douglass employed the jeremiad as well as anyone. This was the tradition of rhetoric, at least as old as the Puritans in America, that levied chastisements and warnings against the fate of people who lose faith, violate their own principles, and fail to keep alive an inheritance. The black jeremiad characteristically issued warnings to white audiences about the judgment that was to come for the sin of slavery or racism. In 1859, in the midst of anxiety over the slavery crisis, Douglass bitterly attacked President James Buchanan for his handling of the Kansas question—the violence and fraudulent elections in the frontier conflict known as "Bleeding Kansas"—but, true to the jeremiadic tradition, turned his lament into a cry of hope: "Go on sir," he wrote, "let the nation go on sir. The end is at hand. The haughty Assyrians will yet be brought low—the ire of offended justice will yet flash upon your soul, and burn up your heart strings with unquenchable fire."

Douglass welcomed the Civil War when it came in 1861 and interpreted the process of disunion, total war, and Emancipation as a second American Revolution. He imagined himself as one of the new founders of a reinvented nation, rooted in the fact of black freedom and the promise of equality. In that philosophical vein, Douglass also made a major contribution to the broad biblical apocalypticism through which Americans, North and South, made sense of the war. In the crucible of such a bloody conflict, Douglass saw a cleansing and a regenerative power for American society. On the passage of the Emancipation Proclamation in 1863, he said in an editorial, "We are all liberated by this proclamation. . . . It is a mighty event for the bondman, but it is a still mightier event for the nation at large."

Douglass's personal religious outlook changed over time, moving from a Christian millennialism early in his career to a postwar religious liberalism and humanism. His millennialism was as much a conception of history as it was a belief in a genuine Second Coming of Christ, but it very much informed his activism and his concept of American nationalism. Regardless of the changes in his own religious journey, biblical imagery, metaphor, and traditions remained embedded in Douglass's rhetoric throughout his life, and he never ceased his attacks on religious hypocrisy.

During Reconstruction, Douglass's ideas aligned with the Radical Republicans' efforts to remake the South on the cornerstone of black suffrage and to guarantee that the Old South's leadership would never attain power again. However, framed by the classical ideology of liberal politics, Douglass's vision of Reconstruction lacked a thorough economic analysis. Political and moral phenomena dominated Douglass's mind and caused several unresolved contradictions in his postwar thought: he professed a strong belief in the sanctity of private property while demanding land for the powerless freedmen, he coupled laissez-faire individualism and black self-reliance with demands for federal aid to freedmen, and he implied that political liberty was both a sufficient and a necessary cause of economic independence and social equality. Although such inconsistencies might have limited his effectiveness, they were typical of the age and consistent with his own experience as a fugitive slave rising to fame.

Finally, Douglass's varied writings are significant for their searching analysis of the effects of racism. They offer a striking illustration of the concept of "double consciousness" famously described by W. E. B. Du Bois in *The Souls of Black Folk* in 1903. Had Douglass lived to read the passage about the African American dilemma of being "an American, a Negro; two souls, two thoughts, two unreconciled strivings, two warring ideals in one dark body," it might have struck him as an astute description of his own inner life. Douglass lived and analyzed what Du Bois would call the "double-aimed struggle" between national and racial identity. The reconciliation of such dualities was one of the central challenges of Douglass's personal and public life. In an 1853 editorial, Douglass described the black intellectual of the mid-nineteenth century as "isolated in the land of his birth—debarred by his color from congenial associations with whites . . . equally cast out by the ignorances of blacks."

Like virtually all black thinkers in the nineteenth century, Douglass never fully resolved his simultaneous beliefs in special racial gifts and the Enlightenment notion of a common human nature. Sometimes he asserted black cultural uniqueness, but he never relinquished his faith in human unity. In an 1884 interview Douglass declared that "there is no division of races. God almighty made but one race. I adopt the theory that in time the variety of races will be blended into one. . . . You may say that Frederick Douglass considers himself a member of the one race which exists." Douglass wanted to transcend race and all its insidious restrictions, although he knew as well as anyone that it was perhaps the defining feature of the America in which he grew old.

It was so defining that in 1893, the aging Douglass joined with the antilynching activist Ida B. Wells in publishing *The Reason Why the Colored American Is Not in the World's Columbian Exposition* (at Chicago), a bitter critique of racism and violence in the country. In January 1894 in Washington, D.C., Douglass delivered his last major speech, "The Lessons of the Hour," a bitter denunciation of lynching. The seventy-six-year-old lion rose to a full roar and spoke with his full descriptive and analytical powers. "Not a breeze comes to us from the late rebellious states that is not tainted and freighted with Negro blood," he charged. "In its thirst for blood and its rage for vengeance, the mob has blindly, boldly, and defiantly supplanted sheriffs, constables, and police."

Douglass examined the power of the Big Lie in public understanding. Three "excuses," he said, had been used over time to justify lynching: the fear of "insurrection," the claim of "Negro domination" in southern politics, and when those two were "worn out . . . the charge of assault upon defenseless women" by black men. Southern mobs were not spontaneous responses to preserve social order, as defenders of the Ku Klux Klan and lynching had claimed. Douglass ruthlessly exposed their "design, plan, purpose, and invention." Everything Douglass had fought and lived to attain in America's racial history seemed at risk as hundreds of blacks died each year at the hands of lynch mobs. In this stunning valedictory, however, the great orator threw lightning bolts of truth and reason at America's greatest problem. Characteristically, he even found ways to hope in the face of despair. "The picture is dark and terrible," he admitted. But "the lie" about lynching had to be met with "essential truth." And he called his audience to remember the better instincts of the nation's history. "Its voice," he pleaded, was once "the trump of an archangel, summoning . . . tyranny to judgment. . . . Toiling millions heard it and clapped their hands for joy. . . . Its mission was the redemption of the world from the bondage of ages." Still the dreamer, hoping that America's better angels could be marshaled against its ugliest inner hatreds, Douglass went out with a clarion call for justice.

Voice Falls Silent. Douglass suffered from heart trouble during his last years. On 20 February 1895 he died of a heart attack at Cedar Hill. He had just returned from a rally for women's suffrage. Funeral services were held in Washington at the Metropolitan African Methodist Episcopal Church, where Douglass had been a regular Sunday speaker for several years. On 26 February he was buried at Mount Hope Cemetery in Rochester, New York. The nation's most famed African American was dead, and the great voice went silent, but his writings, his symbol, and his legacies would endure and only grow with time in a nation that has yet to fully face the problems he so eloquently addressed.

In the twentieth century Douglass's image appeared repeatedly in African American poetry and prose. No one invoked the abolitionist's visage more subtly or effectively than Ralph Ellison in his great novel *Invisible Man*. One

Douglass, in an engraving by Augustus Robin, New York, after a photograph made by George K. Warren c. 1879. (University of Rochester Library, Rare Books and Special Collections.)

day at the offices of the protest organization for which Invisible has become an orator, an older member of the group, named Tarp, clambers onto a chair to hang a special picture on the wall. As Tarp steps down, the following exchange occurs with Invisible:

"Son, you know who that is?"
"Why yes," I said, "it's Frederick Douglass."
"Yessir, that's just who it is. You know much about him?"
"Not much. My grandfather used to tell me about him though."
"That's enough. He was a great man. You just take a look at him once in a while."
"Brother Tarp . . . thanks for the portrait of Douglass."
"Don't thank me, son," he said from the door. "He belongs to all of us." (pp. 328–329)

Invisible's grandfather (and Ellison's) had been a slave, and the narrator sometimes hears his grandfather's voice calling him to somehow be "more human." Ellison ends the scene with Invisible's looking up at the Douglass portrait, "feeling a sudden piety, remembering and refusing to hear the echoes of my grandfather's voice." Such is also the enduring condition of the nation's memory of Douglass. His voice is now more available than ever, but do we listen or refuse to hear the man in the picture on the wall?

[*See also* Abolitionism; African Americans and the West; African Methodist Episcopal Church; American Anti-Slavery Society; Anthony, Aaron; Antislavery Movement; Antislavery Press; Auld Family; Bailey Family; Bailey, Harriet; Baltimore, Maryland, Slavery in; Black Abolitionists; Black Militias; Black Politics; Black Press; Brown, John; Brown, William Wells; Buchanan, James; *Cambria* Incident; Canada; Caulker's Trade; Civil Rights; Civil War; Civil War, Participation and Recruitment of Black Troops in; Colonization; *Columbian Orator, The*; Compromise of 1850; Constitution, U.S.; Covey, Edward; Crime and Punishment; Crofts, Julia Griffiths; Discrimination; Disunionism; *Douglass' Monthly*; Douglass, Anna Murray; Douglass, Charles Remond; Douglass, Frederick, Jr.; Douglass, Lewis Henry; *Dred Scott* Case; Education; Election of 1860; Emancipation; Emancipation Proclamation; Emerson, Ralph Waldo; Emigration to Africa; Entrepreneurs; Fifty-fourth Massachusetts Infantry Regiment; *Frederick Douglass' Paper*; Free African Americans before the Civil War (North); Free-Soil Party; Freedman's Savings and Trust Company; Freedmen; Fugitive Slave Law of 1850; Garfield, James A.; Garnet, Henry Highland; Garrison, William Lloyd; Garrisonian Abolitionists; Green, Shields; Haiti; Harpers Ferry Raid; Harrison, Benjamin; Hayes, Rutherford B.; *Heroic Slave, The*; Johnson, Andrew; Kansas-Nebraska Act; Liberty Party; *Life and Times of Frederick Douglass*; Lincoln, Abraham; Literature; Lloyd, Edward, V; Lynching and Mob Violence; Lynn, Massachusetts; Marriage, Mixed; Môle Saint-Nicolas (Haiti) Annexation; Moral Suasion; *My Bondage and My Freedom*; Nantucket; *Narrative of the Life of Frederick Douglass*; *New National Era*; New York City; Nonresistance; *North Star*; Oratory and Verbal Arts; Political Participation; Race, Theories of; Racism; Radical Abolitionist Party; Reconstruction; Reform; Republican Party; Resistance; Riots and Rebellions; Rochester Ladies Anti-Slavery Society; Rochester, New York; Saint Michaels, Maryland; Slave Insurrections and Rebellions; Slave Narratives; Slave Resistance; Slavery; Slavery and the U.S. Constitution; Smith, Gerrit; Stowe, Harriet Beecher; Suffrage, Women's; Truth, Sojourner; Tubman, Harriet; *Uncle Tom's Cabin*; Underground Railroad; Union Army, African Americans in; Violence against African Americans; Voting Rights; Washington, Booker T.; Washington, D.C.; Wells-Barnett, Ida; *and* World's Columbian Exposition.]

BIBLIOGRAPHY

AUTOBIOGRAPHIES

Douglass, Frederick. "Fremont and Dayton." *Selected Address and Writings*. http://www.wlhn.org/dodgeco/histories/douglass/douglass_writings.htm.

Douglass, Frederick. *Life and Times of Frederick Douglass* (1881, 1892). New York: Collier, 1962.

Douglass, Frederick. *My Bondage and My Freedom* (1855). New York: Collier, 1969.

Douglass, Frederick. *Narrative of the Life of Frederick Douglass, an American Slave, Written by Himself* (1845). Edited by David W. Blight. Boston: Bedford, 2003.

COLLECTIONS OF DOUGLASS'S WRITINGS, EDITORIALS, AND SPEECHES

Blassingame, John W., ed. *The Frederick Douglass Papers*. 5 vols. New Haven, CT: Yale University Press, 1979.

Foner, Philip S., ed. *Frederick Douglass on Women's Rights*. Westport, CT: Greenwood, 1976.

Foner, Philip S., ed. *The Life and Writings of Frederick Douglass*. 5 vols. New York: International Publishers, 1950.

The Frederick Douglass Papers. Library of Congress, Manuscript Division. http://memory.loc.gov/ammem/doughtml/doughome.html.

COLLECTIONS OF ESSAYS ABOUT DOUGLASS

Andrews, William L., ed. *Critical Essays on Frederick Douglass*. Boston: G. K. Hall, 1991.

Lawson, Bill E., and Frank M. Kirkland, eds. *Frederick Douglass: A Critical Reader*. Malden, MA: Blackwell, 1999.

Rice, Alan J., and Martin Crawford, eds. *Liberating Sojourn: Frederick Douglass and Transatlantic Reform*. Athens: University of Georgia Press, 1999.

Sundquist, Eric J., ed. *Frederick Douglass: New Literary and Historical Essays*. Cambridge, MA: Cambridge University Press, 1990.

BIOGRAPHIES AND OTHER CRITICAL WORKS

Bingham, Caleb, ed. *The Columbian Orator* (1797). New York: New York University Press, 1997.

Blight, David W. *Frederick Douglass' Civil War: Keeping Faith in Jubilee*. Baton Rouge: Louisiana State University Press, 1989.

Fabian, Ann. *The Unvarnished Truth: Personal Narratives in Nineteenth-Century America*. Berkeley: University of California Press, 2000.

Foner, Philip S. *Frederick Douglass*. New York: Citadel, 1964.

Huggins, Nathan I. *Slave and Citizen: The Life of Frederick Douglass*. Boston: Little, Brown, 1980.

Lampe, Gregory P. *Frederick Douglass: Freedom's Voice, 1818–1845*. East Lansing: Michigan State University Press, 1999.

Martin, Waldo E. *The Mind of Frederick Douglass*. Chapel Hill: University of North Carolina Press, 1984.

McFeely, William S. *Frederick Douglass*. New York: Norton, 1991.

Preston, Dickson J. *Young Frederick Douglass: The Maryland Years*. Baltimore, MD: Johns Hopkins University Press, 1980.

Quarles, Benjamin. *Frederick Douglass* (1948). New York: Atheneum, 1968.

Stauffer, John. *The Black Hearts of Men: Radical Abolitionists and the Transformation of Race*. Cambridge, MA: Harvard University Press, 2002.

—DAVID W. BLIGHT

DOUGLAS, FREDERICK, JR. (b. 3 March 1842; d. 26 July 1892), journalist. As the second son and namesake of his father, Frederick Douglass Jr. was born in New Bedford, Massachusetts. He attended public schools in Rochester, New York, where he also helped his brothers, Lewis and Charles, to aid runaway slaves who were escaping to Canada on the Underground Railroad. While he did not serve in the Civil War as his brothers did, Frederick acted as a recruiting agent for the Fifty-fourth and Fifty-fifth Massachusetts Infantry regiments, as did his father. Fol-

Frederick Douglass Jr., Frederick Douglass's second son and third child, shown on a carte-de-visite of c. 1867–1870. The photographer was S. M. Fassett of Chicago. (National Park Service.)

lowing the war, Frederick attempted to enter the typographical workers' union. When that plan failed, he went with his brother Lewis in 1866 to Colorado, where Henry O. Wagoner, a longtime family friend, taught him the trade of typography. While he was in Colorado, Frederick worked with his brother Lewis in the printing office of the Red, White, and Blue Mining Company. In the fall of 1868 Frederick returned to Washington to work in a printing office but continued to encounter difficulties in securing a union card. When his father purchased the *New National Era* in 1870, Frederick became the newspaper's business manager, Lewis was in charge of editorials, and Charles worked as a correspondent. Frederick later served as a court bailiff under two District of Columbia marshals, as well as a clerk in the Office of the Recorder.

In 1871 Frederick Douglass Jr. married Virginia L. Hewlett of Cambridge, Massachusetts. Together they had seven children: Frederick Aaron, Jean Hewlett, Lewis Henry, Maud Ardelle, Charley Paul, Gertrude, and Robert

Small. Several of their children died young, however, including Frederick Aaron, at the age of fourteen. After the wife of his brother Charles Douglass died in 1879, Frederick and Virginia helped raise two of his sons, ten-year-old Charles Frederick and eight-year-old Joseph Henry. When Virginia died in 1890 in an influenza epidemic, Frederick never fully recovered; he died two years later at his home in Hillsdale, D.C. Lewis Douglass raised Frederick's son Charley Paul, who had been under the guardianship of E. M. Hewlett, Virginia's brother and a successful lawyer in Washington.

Always considered the most fragile and sensitive of Douglass's children, Frederick Douglass Jr. struggled not only in his career and with his health but also in finding a place in the political arena and the reform movement, where he was often in the shadow of his father. He campaigned unsuccessfully to be elected as a delegate to the Legislative Assembly of the District of Columbia in 1873. He was more effective, however, in writing editorials that described the struggles of southern blacks following the Civil War. He also kept scrapbooks of his father's activities in later years, providing researchers with valuable information.

[*See also* Antislavery Press; Black Family; Black Press; Canada; Civil War, Participation and Recruitment of Black Troops in; Douglass, Charles Remond; Douglass, Frederick; Douglass, Lewis Henry; Fifty-fifth Massachusetts Infantry Regiment; Fifty-fourth Massachusetts Infantry Regiment; *New National Era*; Reform; Rochester, New York; Underground Railroad; Wagoner, Henry O., Sr.; *and* Work.]

BIBLIOGRAPHY

"District Politics." *Evening Star* (Washington), 3 October 1873.

Gregory, James M. *Frederick Douglass, the Orator* (1893). New York: Crowell, 1971.

Holland, Frederic M. *Frederick Douglass: The Colored Orator*. Westport, CT: Negro Universities Press, 1969.

McFeely, William. *Frederick Douglass*. New York: Norton, 1991.

"A Solid South." *New York Times*, 25 September 1876.

U.S. Census Bureau. *Census of Population and Housing: 1880 Census*. http://www2.census.gov/prod2/decennial/1880.htm. Showing Charles Frederick and Joseph Henry, sons of Charles R. Douglass and nephews of Frederick Douglass Jr., living in the household of Frederick Douglass Jr.

"Young Frederick Douglass." *Plaindealer* (Detroit), 12 August 1892, 1.

—MARK G. EMERSON

DOUGLASS, LEWIS HENRY (b. 9 October 1840; d. 9 October 1908), a civil rights activist and a son of Frederick Douglass. Born in New Bedford, Massachusetts, Lewis Henry Douglass was the second child and eldest son of Frederick and Anna Murray Douglass. When Lewis was eight the family moved to Rochester, New York, where

Lewis Henry Douglass, the second child and eldest son of Frederick Douglass, was an activist for African Americans' civil rights. (National Park Service.)

the boy was educated in public schools. After finishing his education, Lewis helped his father with his newspaper *North Star*, learning the printer's trade. Considered the ablest of Douglass's children, Lewis was the person Frederick Douglass asked to secure his papers from John Brown after the Harpers Ferry raid to prevent federal marshals from discovering them.

During the Civil War, Lewis enlisted in the Fifty-fourth Massachusetts Infantry Regiment, attaining the rank of sergeant major and taking part in the attack on Fort Wagner, South Carolina, in July 1863. After the war Lewis and his brother Frederick Jr. went to Denver, Colorado, where Lewis worked as a secretary for the Red, White, and Blue Mining Company. While they were in Denver the brothers learned typography from a long-time family friend, Henry O. Wagoner Sr. In 1869 Lewis left Denver to work in the Government Printing Office in Washington, D.C., where he became embroiled in a controversy with the printers' union. The union labeled him a scab for working for lower wages, but it would not allow him to become a member and thereby earn a higher wage, claiming that he had not had proper training. Infuriated,

Frederick Douglass publicly denounced the union's practice as racist, emphasizing the transparent inaccuracy of the union's claim.

That same year Lewis married Helen Amelia Loguen, daughter of Jermain W. Loguen, a bishop of the African Methodist Episcopal Zion Church; a leader of the black community in Syracuse, New York; and a friend of Frederick Douglass's. Although the couple had no children of their own, they helped raise Mary Louise, the daughter of Lewis's youngest brother, Charles, after her mother's death. Lewis and Amelia also took custody of the son of Frederick Douglass Jr., Charley Paul, after both his parents died.

When his father purchased the *New National Era* in 1870, Lewis was in charge of editorials, Frederick Jr. handled business management, and Charles was one of the journal's correspondents. Under the administration of Ulysses S. Grant, Lewis served as a member of the council of legislation for two years and as a special agent for the post office for two years. Lewis held the office of assistant marshal for the District of Columbia under the administration of Rutherford B. Hayes. Thereafter he engaged in the real estate business.

Along with his brother Charles, Lewis accompanied his father on some speaking engagements. In fact, Lewis was himself active in agitating for equal rights for blacks. For example, with his father, Lewis was one of the delegates sent by the 1866 National Convention of Colored Men to confront President Andrew Johnson with their grievances against southern black codes, which deprived blacks of mobility and land ownership. Moreover, after the Supreme Court in 1883 declared the Civil Rights Act of 1875 null and void, Lewis called for state civil rights laws and for equal enforcement of those laws by both political parties. An activist until his death, Lewis delivered an address on Brown's Day at Harpers Ferry on 17 August 1906, as did W. E. B. Du Bois. Members of the Niagara Movement, an early civil rights organization, sponsored a pilgrimage to Harpers Ferry that year to pay homage to John Brown by touring the engine house where the abolitionist had staged his uprising.

[*See also* Antislavery Movement; Antislavery Press; Black Press; Brown, John; Civil Rights; Civil Rights Act of 1875; Civil War; Civil War, Participation and Recruitment of Black Troops in; Douglass, Anna Murray; Douglass, Charles Remond; Douglass, Frederick; Douglass, Frederick, Jr.; Fifty-fourth Massachusetts Infantry Regiment; Grant, Ulysses S.; Harpers Ferry Raid; Hayes, Rutherford B.; Johnson, Andrew; Laws and Legislation; Loguen, Jermain Wesley; National Conventions of Colored Men; *New National Era*; *North Star*; Rochester, New York; Supreme Court; Wagoner, Henry O., Sr.; *and* Washington, D.C.]

BIBLIOGRAPHY

Douglass, Frederick, and Robert G. Ingersoll. *Proceedings of the Civil Rights Mass-Meeting Held at Lincoln Hall, October 22, 1883. Speeches of Hon. Frederick Douglass and Robert G. Ingersoll*. Washington, DC: C. P. Farrell, 1883

Gregory, James M. *Frederick Douglass, the Orator* (1893). New York: Crowell, 1971.

McFeely, William S. *Frederick Douglass*. New York: Norton, 1991.

—MARK G. EMERSON

DOWNING, GEORGE THOMAS (b. 30 December 1819; d. 24 November 1903), African American civil rights leader. George Thomas Downing lived nearly eighty-four years, but the results of his struggles for civil rights persisted long past his death. He was born to Thomas and Rebecca West Downing in New York City and attended the Mulberry Street School, which educated many future leaders in the fight for black civil rights. When George turned fourteen, he and several schoolmates organized a literary society in which to read, write, and talk about various issues of the day—primarily slavery. The young men in the society adopted a resolution against celebrating the Fourth of July because they believed that the Declaration of Independence mocked black Americans.

Downing graduated from Hamilton College in Oneida County, New York, and began his fight for black civil rights by serving as an agent for the Underground Railroad. From 1857 to 1866 he led the fight against separate public schools for blacks and whites in Rhode Island. He helped repeal the 1821 New York state law stipulating that African Americans had to own property worth $250 before they could vote and a similar law in Rhode Island that targeted the Irish. He participated in campaigns to abolish segregated Jim Crow cars on the Baltimore and Ohio Railroad, to open the Senate gallery to blacks, and to end the nine o'clock curfew for blacks in Washington, D.C.

When the Civil War began in 1861, Downing joined Frederick Douglass to advocate the recruitment of African American soldiers into the Union army. Shortly after President Abraham Lincoln issued the Emancipation Proclamation on 1 January 1863, the Massachusetts governor John Albion Andrew called for volunteers for what became the Fifty-fourth Massachusetts Infantry Regiment. George Luther Stearns, a white abolitionist and backer of the revolutionary John Brown, went to Rochester, New York, in February 1863 to seek Douglass's help in recruiting blacks. A call for volunteers entitled "Men of Color to Arms" appeared in the March issue of *Douglass' Monthly*, and Douglass and other black leaders, including Downing, William Wells Brown, and Martin Robison Delany, traveled across Upstate New York persuading young black men to enlist in the Union army. Altogether, Douglass, Downing, and their fellow recruiters sent more than one hundred young men from Upstate New York into the Fifty-fourth Massachusetts.

In February 1866 Downing and Douglass paired up again as part of a delegation urging President Andrew Johnson to adopt a more stringent Reconstruction policy. Downing and the delegation also asked the Massachusetts senator Charles Sumner to support the Fourteenth Amendment, which would grant equal rights to blacks and whites. Downing also persuaded Douglass to begin publishing the *New National Era* in Washington, D.C.

Another civil rights battle fought by Downing involved the appointment of Douglass as minister to Haiti. In his inaugural address of 1871 President Ulysses S. Grant called for the ratification of the Fifteenth Amendment, which would grant African Americans the right to vote, and black leaders like Douglass and Downing were pleased at Grant's stance on black rights. They assumed that a black man would be appointed minister to the black Republic of Haiti, but over Downing's protests, President Grant appointed Ebenezer D. Bassett of New Haven, Connecticut, to the post. Downing urged Senator Sumner, the chairman of the Senate Foreign Relations Committee, to withdraw Bassett as nominee in favor of Douglass. President Grant refused on the grounds that he was having too much trouble getting appointments confirmed to withdraw one that appeared to be safe. The presidency of Rutherford B. Hayes did not improve conditions for Douglass, but his friends, including Downing, continued to agitate behind the scenes. Finally, on 25 June 1889 President Benjamin Harrison sent the secretary of state James G. Blaine to Douglass in order to offer him the post of minister to Haiti. Douglass served in that capacity from 1889 through 1891.

During his years as a trailblazing civil rights leader, Downing also established his career as a successful African American entrepreneur. He had learned the restaurant business from his father, a proprietor of a New York City restaurant and oyster house patronized by prominent people from all walks of life. In 1842 Downing became a caterer in New York City, and by 1846 he had built a summer catering business in Newport, Rhode Island. In 1850 he opened another such business in Providence while continuing the one in Newport. During the fall of 1854 Downing built the luxurious Sea Girt Hotel in Newport, and by 1888 he owned a large piece of real estate on Bellevue Avenue and a Newport street was named after him. He also donated funds to establish Newport's Touro Park and spent time and money in order to increase the city's architectural beauty and prosperity.

For twelve years after the Civil War, Downing operated the restaurant in the House of Representatives in Washington, D.C., which gave him the opportunity to influence and lobby policy makers. On 24 November 1841 Downing married Serena Leanora de Grasse, the daughter of George de Grasse, considered to be the protégé of Aaron Burr. They had three sons and three daughters.

Downing died after a long illness at his Bellevue Avenue residence. An editorial published in the *Boston Globe* on 23 July 1903 commented,

> Probably the foremost colored man in this country expired in the person of George T. Downing of Newport, Rhode Island. His skin fades almost out of sight when it is remembered that he fought not only for his own race but that his purse strings were always open in helping races who were oppressed.

[*See also* Andrew, John Albion; Bassett, Ebenezer D.; Blaine, James G.; Brown, John; Brown, William Wells; Civil War, Participation and Recruitment of Black Troops in; Delany, Martin Robison; *Douglass' Monthly*; Fifteenth Amendment; Fifty-fourth Massachusetts Infantry Regiment; Fourteenth Amendment; Grant, Ulysses S.; Haiti; Harrison, Benjamin; Jim Crow Car Laws; Johnson, Andrew; *New National Era*; Reconstruction; Rochester, New York; Stearns, George Luther; Sumner, Charles; Underground Railroad; *and* Washington, D.C.]

BIBLIOGRAPHY

Bayles, Richard H., ed. *History of Newport County, Rhode Island*. New York: L. E. Preston, 1888.

Editorial. *Boston Globe*, 23 July 1903.

Foner, Philip S., ed. *Frederick Douglass, Selected Speeches and Writings*. Rev. ed. Chicago: Lawrence Hill, 1999.

Obituary. *New York Times*, 22 July 1903.

Washington, S. A. M. *George Thomas Downing: Sketch of His Life and Times*. Newport, RI: Milne Printery, 1910.

—KATHY COVERT-WARNES

DREAMS. Centuries before Sigmund Freud synthesized Western knowledge about dreams and the unconscious, African Americans and whites interpreted dreams to express racial attitudes and to fashion their self-identity. Dreams were commonly used in the narratives written or told by African Americans to express feelings of love, rage, and sadness and to argue for better lives.

Much of this interpretive tradition came from African culture, where dreams foretold negative and positive events from births to deaths, or illnesses and cures. Dreams foreshadowed success or failure in love, economic efforts, or battle. Diviners or interpreters of dreams had widespread currency in West Africa. Every person understood that dreams were windows into the soul. Africans believed in a "little man inside me," who was often accompanied by a little white guide.

Blacks in early America sought expert readings of their dreams. In the Sea Islands of Georgia and South Carolina, among the Gullahs, people looked for spiritual guides to help seekers understand their dreams. Cunning women in the northern colonies were noted for their extraordinary talents with dreams. Chloe Russell of Massachusetts, also known as the "Old Witch" or "Black Interpreter," was reputed to possess powerful ability to foretell events based upon dream study. In 1800 she published a dream book purchased by whites as well as blacks.

Many African Americans used dreams to enable their self-identity. John Jea, an African-born slave in Brooklyn, New York, wanted desperately to read the Bible, an ability that he believed would help him gain his freedom. One night, in a dream, an angel appeared with an open Bible and taught Jea to read in Dutch and English. When he awoke, Jea was literate and used his new skill to demand his emancipation; after he received it, Jea became a preacher and retold his dream again and again.

Such spiritual awakenings were common. African American visionaries often told how "God struck me dead," sending them into a revelatory trance. George White, an early black itinerant minister, told the story of how he was struck dead at a camp meeting, a common venue for such events. White later dreamed of modish young people, who he understood were on their way to damnation. Another dream carried sexual connotations, when the devil, in the guise of a woman, had an enlarged mouth ready to receive the sinful. Dreams could have political implications. Murphy Stiel, a black Loyalist in Revolutionary New York City, recounted a dream in which he heard "a Voice like a Man's (but saw nobody)." The voice ordered Stiel to convey a message to Sir Henry Clinton, the British commander in chief in the city, that Clinton should tell General George Washington to surrender his troops or else God would make all the black people in America take up arms against the Patriots.

White people often borrowed dream inspiration from African Americans. The Quaker John Woolman, one of the first important white abolitionists, regularly used dreams as part of his evolving antislavery beliefs. His fellow Quaker Robert Pyle dreamed in the mid-eighteenth century of fears of ascending to heaven while carrying a black pot, which he believed symbolized a black slave. Benjamin Rush, a signer of the Declaration of Independence and a great post-Revolutionary abolitionist, dreamed himself to be in a paradise of negro slaves who judged applicants to heaven and allowed only the antislavery leader Anthony Benezet to enter. Post-Revolutionary Methodists and Baptists glorified enslaved peoples as the inheritors of the earth and peppered their dreams with appreciations of blacks. Black preachers regularly roused black and white churchgoers; whites adapted the ring shout trance methods learned from blacks.

Blacks in turn often associated whiteness with evil in their dreams. Rebecca Cox Jackson, a mixed-race woman and later founder of an interracial Shaker group in Philadelphia, had an early dream in which a white witch killed her siblings. In the dream Rebecca flew faster than the white witch and reached heaven safely. There her black grandmother sent her back to earth, saying that Rebecca had much work yet to do. African Americans used dreams to call for resistance to slavery.

Nat Turner, the leader of the largest slave rebellion in U.S. history, saw "white spirits and black spirits engaged in battle, and the sun was darkened." Turner claimed that God told him the time was coming when the first should be last, and the last should be first. Other blacks used dreams for petty anger. William Grimes, a fugitive slave, reported that friends would listen to the lottery numbers he dreamed and then almost always won a prize. Turner and Grimes were looking at life from different perspectives, but both used dreams to find manly purpose. In 1762 the black mathematician Benjamin Banneker dreamed of a heaven where "I look'd to see if I could Distinguish Men from Women but could not." Heaven was a place where earthly difference in gender fell away.

Black women used dreams in their search for purpose. One of the most contentious issues in American Protestantism focused on female preachers. Opposed by white and black male religious figures, African American women ministers were hampered by sex as well as race. Jarena Lee, a Philadelphia black woman, dreamed that God called her to minister: "I took a text, and preached in my sleep. I thought there stood before me a great multitude." Her emotional response to the call was so loud that she woke everyone in the house. Her quest to preach was rejected by Richard Allen, leader of the black church. She waited eight years and then dreamed of the sun, which burst forth with renewed splendor. Lee disregarded her male critics and went forth to preach. Similarly, Maria Stewart, who wrote one of the first books by a black woman, argued that black women needed a role change and urged them to "Possess the Spirit of Men." Such dreams abound in African American narratives. Dreams performed important roles in helping black men and women fashion new identities and realities.

[*See also* Allen, Richard; Banneker, Benjamin; Grimes, William; Identity; Jea, John; Lee, Jarena; Spirituality; *and* Woolman, John.]

BIBLIOGRAPHY

Sobel, Mechal. *Teach Me Dreams: The Search for Self in the Revolutionary Era*. Princeton, NJ: Princeton University Press, 2000.

—GRAHAM RUSSELL GAO HODGES

DRED SCOTT CASE. The *Dred Scott* case, referred to in case law as *Dred Scott v. Sandford*, 19 Howard (60 U.S.) 393 (1857), was the most important slavery-related decision in U.S. Supreme Court history. Speaking for a 7–2 majority, Chief Justice Roger B. Taney reached three major conclusions that fundamentally shook national politics and deeply affected the rights of free blacks, especially in the North. Taney held that 1) blacks, even free blacks in the North, could never be considered citizens of the United States and could not sue in federal court as citizens of the states in which they lived; 2) the ban on slavery in the western territories that was part of the Missouri Compromise was unconstitutional because Congress had no power to regulate the territories beyond the most minimal organization of a territorial government; and 3) neither Congress nor the territorial governments could ever prohibit slaveholding in the western territories, and thus neither a congressional ban on slavery in the territories

Dred Scott; his wife, Harriet Scott; and his children Eliza and Lizze, in wood engravings published by Frank Leslie, 1857. The images accompanied an article under the headline "Visit to Dred Scott—His Family—Incidents of His Life—Decision of the Supreme Court." (Library of Congress.)

nor a ban on slavery through popular sovereignty would be constitutional.

The case led to a hardening of views on race and politics in both the North and the South. The northern reaction helped the Republican Party. Abraham Lincoln's articulate critique of the case during his debates with Senator Stephen A. Douglas of Illinois thrust him into the national limelight and ultimately led to his nomination and election to the presidency in 1860. For African Americans the case was a disaster; the abolitionist orator—and escaped slave—Frederick Douglass called it "cold-blooded" and "devilish."

The case itself involved a slave named Dred Scott, whose late master was Captain John Emerson, an army surgeon. Emerson had taken Scott to a military post in Illinois, where slavery was illegal under state law, and to Fort Snelling in what would later become Minnesota, territory in which slavery had been prohibited by the Missouri Compromise. After Emerson's death, Scott asked Emerson's widow, Irene Sanford Emerson, to free him or to allow him to buy his freedom. She refused. Scott then sued. In 1850 a trial court in Saint Louis freed Scott on the basis of his residence—with his master's permission—in Illinois and in a territory made free by the Missouri Compromise. This decision followed Missouri precedents dating from 1824, which held that residence in a free jurisdiction led to the emancipation of a slave.

The Missouri Supreme Court reversed this result in *Scott v. Emerson* (1852), rejecting its precedents because of the "dark and fell spirit" of abolitionism, which the court claimed had taken over the North. In 1854 Scott began a new suit, in federal court, against his new owner, Irene Emerson's brother, John F. A. Sanford. (His name is misspelled as Sandford in the official report of the case.) Scott sued "in diversity," claiming that he was a "citizen of Missouri" while Sanford was a citizen of New York, and thus Scott asserted the right to sue Sanford in a federal court. Sanford denied that Scott could sue him, arguing that "Dred Scott is not a citizen of the State of Missouri, as alleged in his declaration, because he is a negro of African descent; his ancestors were of pure African blood, and were brought into this country and sold as negro slaves."

U.S. District Judge Robert W. Wells rejected Sanford's theory, concluding that *if* Dred Scott was free, then he could sue in federal court as a citizen of Missouri. However, after hearing all the evidence, Wells charged the jury to uphold Scott's slave status, based on the earlier Missouri decision that Scott was still a slave. Scott appealed to the U.S. Supreme Court, where he lost in a 7–2 decision. In his "Opinion of the Court," Chief Justice Taney held that Congress has no power to pass general laws to regulate the territories. He also held that the Missouri Compromise unconstitutionally deprived southerners of their property in slaves without due process of law or just compensation, in violation of the Fifth Amendment. By implication, this also meant that no territorial legislature could ever ban slavery in a federal territory, which in turn undermined the concept of "popular sovereignty" that the leading northern Democrat, Stephen A. Douglas, had developed during the debate over the Compromise of 1850 as a way of solving the problem of slavery in the western territories. Under *Dred Scott*, slavery would be legal in all the federal territories and could be prohibited only at statehood. This part of the decision shocked northerners who had long seen the Missouri Compromise as a central piece of legislation for organizing the settlement of the West and for accommodating differing sectional interests. It also shocked many northern Democrats who had supported opening up the Kansas and Nebraska territories to slavery under popular sovereignty.

Taney also denied that blacks could ever be citizens of the United States, rhetorically declaring:

> The question is simply this: Can a negro, whose ancestors were imported into this country, and sold as slaves, become a member of the political community formed and brought into existence by the Constitution of the United States, and as such become entitled to all the rights, and privileges, and immunities, guarantied [*sic*] by that instrument to the citizen? One of which rights is the privilege of suing in a court of the United States in the cases specified in the Constitution.

Ignoring that free black men in most of the northern states, as well as North Carolina, could vote at the time of the ratification of the Constitution, Taney declared that African Americans

> are not included, and were not intended to be included, under the word *citizens* in the Constitution, and can therefore claim none of the rights and privileges which the instrument provides and secures to citizens of the United States. On the contrary, they were at that time [1787–1788] considered as a subordinate and inferior class of beings who had been subjugated by the dominant race, and, whether emancipated or not, yet remained subject to their authority, and had no rights or privileges but such as those who held the power and Government might choose to grant them.

According to Taney blacks were "so far inferior, that they had no rights which the white man was bound to respect."

Taney's opinion outraged many northerners, especially members of the new Republican Party. Abraham Lincoln attacked the decision throughout his debates with Stephen A. Douglas in 1858. His articulate critique of the decision catapulted him to the presidential nomination in 1860. The decision led many Republicans to support black citizenship and fundamental rights for blacks and others to argue for black equality and suffrage.

For Frederick Douglass, the opinion was both an outrage and a call to increase efforts to end slavery. In an

1857 speech he argued that this "judicial incarnation of wolfishness" made his hopes "brighter" than ever before because the "open, glaring, and scandalous tissue of lies" found in the decision would serve the cause of liberty in the long run. He declared that

> we, the abolitionists and colored people, should meet this decision, unlooked for and monstrous as it appears, in a cheerful spirit. This very attempt to blot out forever the hopes of an enslaved people may be one necessary link in the chain of events preparatory to the downfall and complete overthrow of the whole slave system.

Douglass used the decision to denounce the followers of the abolitionist William Lloyd Garrison, who argued that the Constitution was proslavery and thus that abolitionists should reject political action. Garrisonians wanted northerners to secede from the Union. Douglass countered that the Constitution was not proslavery but that Taney's opinion was wrong and should be overturned by a combination of political action and appeals to God and conscience:

> Such a decision cannot stand. God will be true though every man be a liar. We can appeal from this hell-black judgment of the Supreme Court, to the court of common sense and common humanity. We can appeal from man to God. If there is no justice on earth, there is yet justice in heaven. You may close your Supreme Court against the black man's cry for justice, but you cannot, thank God, close against him the ear of a sympathising world, nor shut up the Court of Heaven. All that is merciful and just, on earth and in Heaven, will execrate and despise this edict of Taney.

While Douglass's rhetoric here seemed overblown at the time, his predictions proved to be remarkably accurate. In less than four years Lincoln was elected president on a platform that included a promise of rejecting Taney's conclusions and guaranteeing that slavery would be excluded from the territories. Southern secession and Civil War followed, and that in turn ended slavery.

Both the Lincoln administration and the Civil War Congress ignored the decision, banning slavery in all the western territories despite Taney's assertion that such an act was unconstitutional. In 1866 Congress sent the Fourteenth Amendment to the states, which declared that all persons born in the nation were citizens of the United States and of the state in which they lived. The ratification of this amendment, in 1868, made the civil rights aspects of *Dred Scott* a dead letter. The decision nevertheless remains a potent symbol of the denial of civil rights, and the constitutionalization of racism, under the Constitution of 1787.

[*See also* Abolitionism; Civil Rights; Civil Rights Act of 1866; Civil War; Compromise of 1850; Douglas, Stephen A.; Fourteenth Amendment; Free African Americans before the Civil War (North); Garrison, William Lloyd; Garrisonian Abolitionists; Lincoln, Abraham; Republican Party; Slavery; Supreme Court; Taney, Roger B., *and* Voting Rights.]

BIBLIOGRAPHY

Fehrenbacher, Don E. *The Dred Scott Case: Its Significance in American Law and Politics.* New York: Oxford University Press, 1978.

Finkelman, Paul. *Dred Scott v. Sandford: A Brief History with Documents.* Boston: Bedford, 1997.

—PAUL FINKELMAN

DUMAS, ALEXANDRE (b. 24 July 1802; d. 5 December 1870), French novelist and playwright. Alexandre Dumas was born Alexandre Dumas Davy de la Pailleterie in Villers-Cotteràts, northeast of Paris. His father was Thomas-Alexandre Dumas and his mother was Marie-Louise Elisabeth Labouret. Born in the French Caribbean, Thomas-Alexandre was the offspring of the Marquis Antoine Alexandre Davy de la Pailleterie and one of his black house slaves, Marie Céssette Dumas, who was from Jérémie, Saint Domingue. She died when Thomas-Alexandre was young; he was eventually brought to Paris at the age of fourteen. As Thomas-Alexandre's grandfather did not wish his mulatto grandson to officially use the name Davy de la Pailleterie, he enlisted in Napoleon's army as Thomas-Alexandre Dumas, at length attaining the rank of general.

The death of his father in 1806 left the young Alexandre Dumas and his mother in very bad financial circumstances. At the age of fourteen he apprenticed as a clerk with a local notary in Villers-Cotteràts. In 1822 he traveled to Paris, where he met François-Joseph Talma. Talma had attained influence and renown as an actor and inspired Dumas to seek success in the theater.

After writing several minor dramas, Dumas achieved fame in 1829 with the opening of his play *Henry III and His Court.* This production changed the course of French theater and was, in effect, the first French drama of the romantic movement. Although Dumas wrote several novels in the 1840s for which he became well-known to a broader audience, such as *The Count of Monte Cristo* and *The Three Musketeers,* it was as a playwright that he initially gained fame.

Dumas apparently did not see himself as a black man, but the ridicule directed toward him at an early age for his manner of dress may have been an indirect form of racism. His colonial African French ancestry made his works popular among many nineteenth-century African American abolitionists, including Frederick Douglass. This was especially true of his 1843 novel *Georges,* in which Dumas examines colonialism through the eyes of a half-French mulatto in Mauritius. Suffering rejection by the ruling white elite, Georges seeks revenge against those who have ostracized him from their society.

Douglass saw his own struggle for freedom and that of the black race in many of the characters of Dumas's stories. In *The Count of Monte Cristo*, the themes of emancipation and escape from captivity inspired African Americans in their struggle for freedom. Such themes, of course, were central to most of Douglass's speeches and editorials. Douglass had endured a struggle similar to that of Georges; rejection by the majority of American society pushed Douglass to travel in an effort to seek acceptance.

Dumas wrote numerous novels, plays, serialized stories, and travelogues as well as a culinary dictionary. After more than fifty years of writing, Dumas died in Puys, France, in 1870.

[*See also* Literature.]

BIBLIOGRAPHY
Blassingame, John W., John R. McKivigan, and Peter P. Hinks, eds. *The Frederick Douglass Papers*. Series 2, *Autobiographical Writings*. Volume 1, *Narrative*. New Haven, CT: Yale University Press, 1999.
Dumas, Alexandre. *The Works of Alexandre Dumas: Complete in Nine Volumes*. New York: Peter Fenelon Collier, 1893.

—PETER E. CARR

DUNBAR, PAUL LAURENCE (b. 27 June 1872; d. 9 February 1906), a poet and novelist. On hearing the news of Frederick Douglass's death on 20 February 1895, Paul Laurence Dunbar wrote a poetic tribute that began "A hush is over all the teeming lists." As a poet and Douglass's friend, Dunbar joined the nation in grieving the beloved abolitionist-orator, who had personally touched Dunbar's life with kind regard. Though years apart in age, Douglass and Dunbar were both devout servants of their people. Born in 1872 to Matilda and Joshua Dunbar in the home of his maternal grandmother in Dayton, Ohio, Dunbar later became a nationally recognized African American author of poems, stories, and novels that served to uplift his race. In similar ways Douglass and Dunbar used the oral and written word to promote racial pride.

In a letter to his mother dated 6 June 1893, Dunbar wrote about his first meeting with the great civil rights orator. To the young writer's surprise, Douglass was well aware of Dunbar's dialectic poetry when his nephew Douglas Douglass made the introductions. After dinner they all took turns reading Dunbar's poetry. Later, at Douglass's invitation, Dunbar paid a lengthier visit to Douglass at his home, Cedar Hill, in Uniontown, D.C. Following that visit Douglass declared Dunbar to be "the most promising young colored man in America."

Dunbar's mother, Matilda Glass Murphy Dunbar, is credited with her family's appreciation of literature, be-cause as a slave on a Kentucky plantation she often listened as her master read aloud to his wife. While married to Robert Murphy, she had two sons (Robert Travis and William Small). She then married Joshua Dunbar, a Canadian former slave with an impressive military record. On 29 October 1873, sixteen months after Paul's birth, his sister, Liza Florence, was born. Liza died at age two shortly after the Dunbars separated. Matilda worked hard as a domestic servant to support her family. Paul was the only black student at Dayton Central High School, and his scholarly endeavors as a member of the debating team, an editor of the school's newspaper, and the president of the Philomathean Literary Society greatly pleased his mother. Throughout his life he passionately desired to improve the image of his people by highlighting traditional song and stories. Many of the black experiences depicted in Dunbar's works were taken directly from stories recited by his mother.

Owing to racial prejudice and other circumstances, Dunbar was unable to attend college. He was working as an elevator operator when Frederick Douglass recognized that his poetic talent was being stifled by poverty. In conversation and readings, visitors to Douglass's Cedar Hill home were made aware of Dunbar's plight. Once, when the women's rights activist Mary Church Terrell visited, Douglass entertained her by reading Dunbar's works.

In 1893, at the age of seventy-one, Frederick Douglass and Charles A. Person (the son of the former U.S. delegate from Haiti) were appointed by the Haitian president Louis Modestin Florvil Hyppolite as commissioners to represent Haiti at the Chicago World's Fair, also known as the World's Columbian Exposition. It was in that capacity that Douglass offered employment to the talented young Dunbar, who served as his clerk. Dunbar wrote and recited his poetry on 25 August, Colored American Day, at the exposition. The audience was very impressed with his reading of "The Colored Soldiers," a poetic tribute to black soldiers.

A chain of letters prompted by a poem and a photograph to a fellow poet led to a courtship and, eventually, Dunbar's secret marriage on 6 March 1898 to Alice Ruth Moore of New Orleans. From a middle-class family, Moore was a teacher and already an accomplished writer of short stories and poems. The couple had marital problems and separated in 1902 when she moved to Delaware.

Dunbar suffered with respiratory illnesses long before his death. On 9 February 1906 in Dayton, at age thirty-three, his poetic voice was stilled. During his short life, Dunbar wrote thirteen books of poetry, four novels, and four books of short stories, as well as lyrics for musicals and operas. His first book of poetry, *Oak and Ivy*, was published in 1893, and his last, *Complete Poems*, was posthumously published in 1913. His four novels, published in quick succession, were *The Uncalled* (1898), *The*

Love of Landry (1900), *The Fanatics* (1901), and *The Sport of the Gods* (1902). An editorial tribute to Dunbar in the 10 February issue of the *Boston Evening Transcript* captured the sentiments of many admirers: "He won a place in American literature of which he can not be deprived by prejudice, because its history would be incomplete without the new and fine element which he supplied."

After the noted white nineteenth-century American novelist, critic, and editor William Dean Howells enthusiastically reviewed Dunbar's second book of verse, *Majors and Minors* (1895), in *Harper's Weekly*, he became the first African American writer to gain national and international recognition. Often compared to the style of Mark Twain, Dunbar's literary style appealed to many readers, and he was envied by white poets who longed for Howell's literary endorsement. With the backdrop of plantation life, a great deal of Dunbar's work focused on emancipation, reconstruction, and migration. There was a story to be told, and Dunbar skillfully captured the reader's attention. In 1925 Countée Cullen, one of the leading writers of the Harlem Renaissance, eulogized Dunbar in a poem that bore his name. Many African American literary notables, among them Langston Hughes, W. E. B. Du Bois, James Weldon Johnson, and Maya Angelou, applauded his contributions to African American literary expression.

[*See also* Black Uplift; Civil Rights; Discrimination; Douglass, Frederick; Emancipation; Haiti; Hyppolite, Louis Modestin Florvil; Identity; Literature; Racism; Reconstruction; *and* World's Columbian Exposition.]

BIBLIOGRAPHY

Brawley, Benjamin G. *Paul Laurence Dunbar, Poet of His People*. Port Washington, NY: Kennikat Press, 1967. Gives an overview of Dunbar's commitment to racial pride.

Dunbar, Paul Laurence. *Paul Laurence Dunbar Reader*. Edited by Jay Martin and Gossie H. Hudson. New York: Dodd, Mead, 1975. Contains photographs, letters, and poetry never before published in book form.

Honious, Ann. *What Dreams We Have: The Wright Brothers and Their Hometown of Dayton, Ohio*. Fort Washington, PA: Eastern National, 2003. A well-researched and well-written book with factual data on Dunbar's life, with an extensive bibliography.

—GLORIA GRANT ROBERSON

DU SABLE, JEAN BAPTISTE POINTE (b. c. 1745; d. 1818), African French pioneer. Jean Baptiste Pointe du Sable is reputed to be the founder of Chicago because he was the first non–Native American to build a home on the future site of the city. As an enterprising free black man on the Revolutionary frontier, Du Sable has become a symbolic figure of great importance to the modern-day African American community, especially in Chicago. The lack of much concrete evidence about his life seems only to enhance his mythic importance as a pioneering black settler and prominent frontiersman. Documents composed by English speakers spell his name variously as "Au Sable," "Point Sable," "Sabre," and "Pointe de Saible."

Du Sable's birth date is not known. It is thought that he was born in the town of Saint Marc on the island of Saint Domingue, in what later became the first free black republic in the Americas, Haiti. At the time of his birth, Saint Domingue was a French colony and the greatest producer of sugar in the Western Hemisphere. It was also one of its largest slave societies. His father was a Frenchman, apparently a mariner. His mother, like most inhabitants of Saint Domingue in the eighteenth century, had been born in Africa. It is not clear whether she was still a slave when she gave birth to Jean Baptiste. Other stories place his origins in French Canada.

Du Sable was an educated man, cultured enough to impress British officers. He allegedly went to school in France. If so, he apparently had arrived in North America by the 1760s and was determined to stay. One account maintains that he went to Canada and then worked his way west as a fur trapper and trader, like many other French Canadians. Another story asserts that he arrived in New Orleans and went north to Illinois. Somehow he made his way out to the Great Lakes region and became a skilled fur trader. In 1773 he purchased a trading post and farm near Peoria, Illinois. Soon thereafter, he built another trading post and home at the future site of Chicago, from where he traded as far away as Michilimackinac, Michigan.

Jean Baptiste Pointe Du Sable, undated portrait by Moss Engraving Company, New York City. Historians do not know of any likeness made during Du Sable's lifetime, so this image—like the one on the U.S. postage stamp—is conjectured. (Chicago Historical Society.)

In the 1770s the Great Lakes were claimed by the British Empire but inhabited primarily by Native Americans along with a few French fur traders and settlers. A black man was a rarity in the region at that time, but Du Sable had the skills, respect, and resources to maintain his status as a free man and merchant. To cement his relationship with the local inhabitants, he married a Pottawatomie woman known as Catherine. They had a son, Jean Baptiste Jr., and a daughter, Suzanne.

By 1779 he was living at his post at the mouth of the Chicago River. In that year British soldiers arrested him. Because he was French, and because France had just entered the Revolutionary War as an ally of the Americans, the British feared he might turn on them. As Du Sable was a Frenchman with influential ties to Native Americans and possibly American colonists, the British could not help suspecting him of being an enemy. Nevertheless, after a year the British released him. Du Sable's loyalties were local, to the fur trade of the Great Lakes and to those who supported it. Impressed by his skills and status within the fur trading society of the Great Lakes, the British hired him to supply one of their forts and to manage a trading post for them near Port Huron, Michigan, at the request of the local Indians. This kept Du Sable busy until the end of the American Revolution, when the British army pulled out of the region.

Du Sable returned to Chicago in 1784, where his estate was inventoried. He had a sizable trading post, a house full of French furniture, paintings, and other luxury items indicating how well off he was, two barns, a mill, a dairy, a bake house, a poultry house, a workshop, a stable, and many livestock. He and Catherine were formally married in a Catholic ceremony in 1788. Soon thereafter, their daughter married a Frenchman, probably a fur trader. In 1791 he received a grant for eight hundred acres from the U.S. government. A man who met him at Chicago in 1794 recalled that he was a large man, a fairly wealthy merchant, and a regular drinker of alcohol.

Du Sable left Chicago in 1800. He sold everything he owned there to a white trader, who soon sold it to white settlers, who for many years received the credit for founding Chicago. Du Sable's wife died at about this time, and he went to Saint Charles, Missouri, to live with his son, who died in 1814. He then went to live with his granddaughter, who does not seem to have been able to take care of him well, because he soon applied for social relief as a pauper. He died in Saint Charles the year Illinois became a state, in 1818.

Du Sable was virtually forgotten until the new interest in African American history of the mid-twentieth century turned him into a Chicago icon. He has become a figure of importance to African Americans and Haitian Americans, who see him as a distinguished early immigrant to America. His legacy has become a barometer of the growing influence of African Americans and Haitian Americans in Chicago's cultural life.

The first private nonprofit black museum in America, the DuSable Museum of African-American History, was opened in his name in 1961. In 1968 the state of Illinois recognized him as the man who founded Chicago, but Chicago city officials did not recognize him as Chicago's founder until 1999. A U.S. postage stamp with a conjectural portrait of Du Sable was created in 1987. Two streets, a high school, and a park in Chicago have been named after him. A movement is afoot to have him honored every 4 March as Chicago's founder, on the day when the city celebrates its birthday. A fascinating, if mysterious, historical figure, Jean Baptiste Pointe du Sable has become a fixture of Chicago's evolving self-image.

[*See also* American Revolution; Caribbean; Free African Americans to 1828; French Canada, Marriage, Mixed; Monuments, Museums, Public Markers; *and* Native Americans and African Americans.]

BIBLIOGRAPHY

Kaplan, Sidney, and Emma Nogrady Kaplan. *The Black Presence in the Era of the American Revolution*. Amherst: University of Massachusetts Press, 1989.

—EVAN HAEFELI

DUTCH REFORMED CHURCH AND AFRICAN AMERICANS.

The Dutch Reformed Church was the official church of the Netherlands and thus of its colonies, from Indonesia to South Africa to New Netherland in North America. A Calvinist Protestant faith, it shared much in common with Huguenots and Presbyterians in terms of ideas about, and policies toward, African Americans in America. A number of its members provided racist claims to justify the enslavement of Africans, but several ministers made notable efforts to convert Africans and spoke out boldly against slavery.

Dutch merchants began trading with Africa in the late sixteenth century. In 1596 one merchant was so bold as to bring a cargo of 130 Africans to the port city of Middelburg, Netherlands, in the hope of selling them off as slaves. The mayor objected, and the provincial assembly freed the Africans. In 1713, sixty years before the English did, the Dutch government declared slavery in the Netherlands illegal, codifying the long-accepted practice that any African slaves brought to the Netherlands automatically became free. Curiously, the Netherlands did not abolish slavery in its colonies until 1863, thirty years after the English had.

The Dutch Reformed Church offered its adherents contradictory ideas about the relationship between Christianity and slavery. The leading minister Godefridus Cornelisz Udemans published the first religious defense of slavery in 1638. In *'t Geestelijke roer van 't coopmans schip* (The spiritual rudder of the merchant's ship), Udemans justified the existence of slavery by pointing to the Old Testament. Citing the story of Noah, who cursed the descendants of Ham to eternal servitude because Ham had seen him lying asleep drunk and naked, and the story of the Israelites who condemned the defeated Gibeonites to perpetual servitude, Udemans claimed that both provided biblical sanction for the enslavement of a whole race. At the same time, Udemans was clearly uncomfortable with the idea of slavery. He much preferred servitude. He encouraged slave owners to treat their slaves well, to teach them about Christianity, and to reward conversion to Christianity and loyal service with manumission. He even suggested that slaves had a right to resist cruel masters, just as all men had a right to resist the rule of tyrants.

Udemans's hope that converted slaves would be freed touched on the widely held belief that slaves who converted to Christianity either automatically became free or at least became worthless as slaves because they believed they should be freed. Protestant theologians argued long and hard from the mid-seventeenth century onward that Christianity and slavery were not incompatible. Slaves could become Christians and still remain slaves—perhaps even better slaves than before. But few colonists accepted this before the American Revolutionary era. Members of the Dutch Reformed Church were especially reluctant to make their slaves Christians, and ministers suspected that many slaves who tried to become Christians only did so in the hope that it would make them free. For this reason, few African Americans in America were able to, or wanted to, join the Dutch Reformed Church.

Notwithstanding the opinions of many of their fellows, in the first half of the seventeenth century a handful of Dutch ministers in North America, the Caribbean, and Brazil made efforts to convert slaves. Several dozens of slaves were baptized into the Dutch Reformed Church in the period between the 1630s and 1650s. But Dutch ministers were wary about interfering with the authority of masters over their slaves. Most of the converts were slaves of the West India Company, under the command of Dutch officials but not the specific property of any particular individual. Some were probably slaves of the ministers themselves. In the mid-eighteenth century a few pietistic Dutch Americans, especially the minister Theodorus Frelinghuysen, made efforts to convert their slaves. But again, these were individual efforts within their own sphere of authority.

The racist possibilities of Dutch Reformed thinking about slavery manifested themselves in the writings of the minister Johan Picardt. In a history of the province of Drenthe (which had little connection to the slave trade) published in 1660, Picardt argued that not just the descendants of Ham (presumed to be Africans) but also those of his brother, Sem—Jews—were doomed to servile status by the Bible. The earth was destined to be ruled by the sons of Japheth, which he maintained were the Europeans. Arguing that slavery was normal in Africa, he implied that Africans were to blame for slavery. He also insisted that the only way to get African slaves to work properly was to beat them mercilessly. A popular preacher, an influential doctor, and a respected agriculturalist, Picardt's views carried much weight with many Dutchmen.

One Dutch Reformed minister came straight out and denounced slavery as a sin. Jacobus Hondius, a minister in the trading town of Hoorn, published in 1679 his *Swart register van duysend sonden* (Black list of a thousand sins). Because it was an alphabetical list, slavery appeared as sin number 810. Hondius expounded at length on the evils of slavery, for which he accepted no justification. Africans were humans as much as the Dutch and could not be enslaved by any right, natural or divine. The fact that Catholics, Jews, Turks, and heathens practiced slavery did not mean that good Dutch Protestants could as well. On the contrary, it provided further proof of how wrong slavery was. He denounced the leaders of the West and East India Companies for getting rich off the suffering of slaves and failing to spread the Dutch Reformed faith into their realms of influence in America, Africa, and Asia.

The great theological defender of slavery in the Dutch Reformed Church turned out to be an African who was born into slavery. Jacobus Capitein (1717–1747) was born a slave at the Dutch slave trading post of Elmina on the Gold Coast of Guinea. Capitein had the good fortune to be sold to a Dutchman, who took the eleven-year-old boy with him back to Middelburg. There, Capitein became free by law. However, he continued to enjoy the support of his former master. The Dutchman paid for his education into the ministry. After graduating from Leiden University in 1742, Capitein gave an oration on the question of whether Christianity was compatible with slavery. Published first in Latin and then in several Dutch editions, *Servitute, libertati christianae non contraria* (On slavery, which does not contradict Christian freedom) argued not only that Christianity was compatible with slavery but also that slavery did pagan Africans the great good of exposing them to the true Christian religion. That this was the opinion of a converted African only reinforced the power of the argument to justify slavery to the Dutch everywhere. It did not, however, persuade them to encourage more of their slaves to convert. Capitein was ordained a minister—a rare and notable achievement—and sent back to Elmina, where he failed to convert any Africans and died in poverty in 1747.

Other Dutchmen continued to speak out for and against slavery and the slave trade through the end of the eighteenth century. Those in America, however, acclimated themselves to the prevailing norms of Anglo-American slave society. Like the Huguenots, Dutch colonists, including many of the ministers, often relied on slave labor. It was easier for Dutch Reformed Church members to exploit their slaves if they stayed out of their church. This exclusion even led some rural Dutch farmers to speculate that African Americans had no souls.

The unwillingness of most Dutch Reformed to include African Americans within their church facilitated the development of a distinctive Dutch African American religion centered on Pinkster, the Dutch holiday of Pentecost. On this day Dutch masters gave their slaves the day off. Beginning at some point in the seventeenth century, slaves used the day to gather together and celebrate with drinking, dancing, and singing. Little is known about the exact content of the festivals, but they included much that was African under the rubric of celebrating a Christian holiday. Pinkster festivities became an increasingly public aspect of African American culture in the Hudson River valley as the eighteenth century wore on. By 1800 New York City and Albany, New York, were the sites of enormous gatherings of slaves and free blacks from the surrounding countryside. Pinkster remained a prominent fixture of regional culture through the 1830s, though celebrations gradually declined and finally disappeared around the time of the Civil War.

The Dutch Reformed Church did not play a role in the ending of slavery. In fact, Dutch Americans in New York and New Jersey proved to be some of the fiercest opponents of abolition. After both states voted for gradual abolition, Dutch Reformed ministers became outspoken advocates of colonization. Rather than provide for their freed slaves, many Dutch Americans preferred to let the local towns take care of them. Some efforts were made to provide schools and religious instruction for blacks, but they were sporadic and ill funded. The church gradually accepted the changing situation, even if not all its members did. When a New Brunswick Theological Seminary student in 1865 said that President Abraham Lincoln had deserved to be assassinated, he was promptly expelled.

[*See also* Capitein, Jacobus; Festivals; Huguenots and African Americans; New Jersey; New York City; Pinkster; Presbyterians and African Americans; Race, Theories of; *and* Religion.]

BIBLIOGRAPHY

De Jong, Gerald Francis. "The Dutch Reformed Church and Negro Slavery in Colonial America." *Church History* 40.4 (1971): 423–436.

Fabend, Firth Haring. *Zion on the Hudson: Dutch New York and New Jersey in the Age of Revivals*. New Brunswick, NJ: Rutgers University Press, 2000.

Hodges, Graham Russell. *Root and Branch: African Americans in New York and East Jersey, 1613–1863*. Chapel Hill: University of North Carolina Press, 1999.

—Evan Haefeli

E

EAST BALTIMORE MENTAL IMPROVEMENT SOCIETY.

During the nineteenth century, the landscape of early America flourished with service organizations committed to providing a myriad of social, economic, religious, and educational services to underprivileged and immigrant Americans. These beneficial organizations were autonomously controlled by fraternal, literary, and religious organizations; Americans knew them as mutual aid societies, literary societies, beneficial societies, and fraternal lodges. Armed with doctrines of self-reliance, reciprocal giving, and moral respectability they provided paying members with fellowship, a locus of community, and standards of living usually afforded only to upper-class Americans. Members of these organizations paid annual and monthly dues; in turn, they received educational services and opportunities, health care, financial assistance, low-interest loans, burial insurance, and family counseling. This was not charity but community uplift; such beneficial societies were controlled by members and were very popular among nineteenth-century African Americans. The federal government itself provided little federal assistance for citizens; moreover, available federal programs excluded African Americans.

In his second autobiography, *My Bondage and My Freedom* (1855), Frederick Douglass describes his membership in the East Baltimore Mental Improvement Society:

> I had, on the Eastern Shore, been only a teacher, when in the company of other slaves, but now there were colored persons who could instruct me. Many of the young calkers [*sic*] . . . had high notions about mental improvement . . . . The free ones . . . organized what they called the "East Baltimore Mental Improvement Society." . . . I was admitted, and was, several times, assigned a prominent part in its debates. (p. 319)

Douglass mentions the East Baltimore Mental Improvement Society again in his third autobiography, *Life and Times of Frederick Douglass* (1881, 1892), wherein he acknowledges a debt of gratitude owed to the members of the society. Following his expressions of gratitude Douglass provides a rhetorical defense of his freedom, which alludes to the training in classical rhetoric he received while a member of that society. In fact, Douglass's membership there provided his only opportunity for formal education among peers.

The East Baltimore Mental Improvement Society left few records. Douglass tells us its members were primarily free African Americans. Such organizations were alternately known as debating clubs, reading rooms, and literary societies. They attracted intellectual men and women by providing oratorical training, required reading lists, and educational lectures. Topics for research and debate generally included the literature of classic antiquity, science and astronomy, wisdom literature (specifically the moral, philosophical, and religious texts of the Bible), mathematics, and American history. Questions of liberty and freedom in the context of American slavery were passionately debated. In addition to engaging in research and debate, members wrote and analyzed literature and submitted exceptional pieces for publication in African American newspapers. Literary societies produced a number of African American intellectuals in addition to Frederick Douglass, notably, Maria W. Stewart and Francis Ellen Watkins Harper. The newspaper run by the antislavery movement leader William Lloyd Garrison, the *Liberator*, featured a listing of speakers who addressed African Americans at a New York literary society that was similar to the organization joined by Douglass. A sampling of speakers from 1836 included the lawyer and abolitionist Wendell Phillips; the mathematician and astronomer Nathaniel Bowditch; and the Harvard-educated antislavery leader and senator Charles Sumner.

Benefit societies were integral to African American uplift prior to the twentieth century. The existence of these societies demonstrates the rigorous intellectual discipline of nineteenth-century African Americans and discloses a crucial aspect of Frederick Douglass's early education.

[*See also* Black Uplift; Douglass, Frederick; Education; *Life and Times of Frederick Douglass*; *and My Bondage and My Freedom*.]

BIBLIOGRAPHY
Douglass, Frederick. *Life and Times of Frederick Douglass: His Early Life as a Slave, His Escape from Bondage, and His Complete History*. New York: Collier, 1962. Includes an introduction by Rayford W. Logan.

Douglass, Frederick. *My Bondage and My Freedom*. New York: Dover, 1969. Includes an introduction by Philip S. Foner.

Porter, Dorothy B. "The Organized Educational Activities of Negro Literary Societies, 1828–1846." *Journal of Negro Education* 5.4 (1936): 555–576.

—MISS HALE JOSEPH

ECONOMIC LIFE. Work has always characterized African American life in the Americas. From the first arrivals in the 1610s blacks came or were brought to the New World to labor. During the seventeenth century, Africans in North America, initially free but later largely enslaved, were important workers in subsistence economies. In the eighteenth century, as the American economy matured, enslaved blacks labored in staple crop agriculture, in seaboard trades, or as skilled assistants in small-scale industry. During the American Revolution a significant fraction toiled in the military services, while most continued in their former roles. After the Revolution, with the massive growth of the cotton industry, many blacks in the South became agricultural workers, with a few in urban areas turning to the arts, while in the upper South enslaved people worked in cereal agriculture. Blacks in the North faced a long-term crisis as rising immigration from northern Europe forced them out of traditional jobs as domestics and sailors, and crowded them from agricultural labor and work as artisans. By 1830 racism in the North had made African Americans peripheral laborers even as they remained the primary workers in the southern plantation economies.

The arrival of European settlers in North America made necessary large numbers of laborers to build and maintain the fledgling economies. During the first decades of these settlements, Africans or Creoles cleared forests and built fortifications, docks, roads, and housing for the tiny European depots along the Atlantic Coast. Because the English and Dutch did not have slavery at home, black Americans held a variety of statuses. Many, as in New Amsterdam, were enslaved as prisoners of war but later received emancipation and the plots of land they had occupied for generations. In the Chesapeake, blacks also were prisoners of war and indentured servants; they were also free, independent farmers, who paid taxes, voted, served in wars, and were often equal to their white neighbors. In New England blacks were servants and worked in the fisheries, on small farms as laborers, and occasionally as domestics. In the early decades of South Carolina black and white laborers toiled on small farms and in the pine tar industry. As the international slave trade largely bypassed North America in the seventeenth century, the act of forcing Africans into a state of perpetual servitude remained only a peripheral part of the coastal economy until the last quarter of the century. Before that time, blacks enjoyed decades of promised or actual freedom in societies that had slaves but did not fully depend upon them.

Enslavement became the dominant economic and legal status of black life in the late seventeenth century. Whether its origins lay in Peter Stuyvesant's decision in the 1640s to make New Amsterdam the principal slave depot in the American economy, or in the decision by the English Board of Trade following Bacon's Rebellion in 1676 to change the supply of laborers from white indentured servants to enslaved Africans, or in the general demand for tobacco workers in the Chesapeake and indigo laborers in South Carolina, an economic and legal revolution created slave societies and paved the way for the plantation economies of the next century.

By 1740 African Americans and newly arrived Africans had made South Carolina "like a negro country," with black majorities in the low country parishes working in huge gangs on the rice plantations. Many blacks labored but only a few whites joined them; in Charleston the prosperity built on black labor gave whites immense riches and created a demand for servants. In Charleston blacks could carve out semi-independent lives as artisans or by dominating the truck trade in food and fuel. Overwhelmingly, however, in South Carolina, Virginia, and Maryland, the economic function for African Americans was to work on staple crops that made the colonies profitable for the Crown and for the colonial gentry.

In the northern cities and countryside, blacks remained core laborers, albeit in smaller numbers and less concentration than in the South. Small farm slavery in which blacks, usually male, were general laborers for farmers characterized the cereal economies of rural Delaware, Pennsylvania, and New Jersey. In Philadelphia and New York enslaved blacks worked on docks and ships, as domestics, and as assistant artisans. In New England, though there were attempts to create sizable plantations in Connecticut, blacks, fewer in number than in the mid-Atlantic, worked in the seaport economies of the towns and cities and often as farm hands. New England's dominant system was family labor, but blacks frequently joined poor whites as temporary help.

The American Revolution set up the binary system of free and enslaved work in North America. The egalitarian messages of the Revolutionaries combined with growing religious discontent with the morality of slavery to doom the institution in New England and Pennsylvania. The process took longer in New York and New Jersey, home to most northern blacks, but by 1804 gradual emancipation was a fact in every state north of Delaware. The advent of gradual emancipation, which made all northern blacks at least legally free by 1830, did not insure a place in the burgeoning northern economy. Now free, blacks in large cities could create small niches in every artisan skill; however as the industrial revolution transformed most northern skilled labor into a proletariat by 1850, racism and job discrimination meant that blacks constituted only 2 percent of factory labor. Similar negative change occurred in domestic and seafaring work as Irish immigrants seized positions traditionally held by blacks. In rural areas blacks remained important laborers. Freedom took longer in New Jersey, New York's Hudson Valley, and Connecticut. Lacking financial help from their former masters, unable to gain credit, blacks could not purchase land and often served as cottagers, an early form of sharecropping, for their old masters. Many drifted into the cities in fruitless searches for work. The huge influx of immigrants meant that black percentages of northern populations, which had ranged from 5 to 20 percent of the total in the colonial eras, now dropped below 2 percent in the cities and were little higher in the countryside by 1850. Core laborers in the colonial period, blacks were shunted to the side in the profitable northern state economies of the early nineteenth century.

If there was no room for blacks in the northern states, the South, from Virginia to Georgia and west to New Orleans, built its economies around the labor of enslaved African Americans. After nearly being abolished in the 1780s, slavery boomed in the South with the invention of the cotton gin in 1793 and the expansion of white society into Native American territories above the Gulf of Mexico. Virginia became a cereal economy and found large profits in selling excess slaves to the surging economies across the southeast. Charleston, South Carolina, continued its colonial era dependence on rice but took advantage of the twenty-year extension of the international slave trade to import over 100,000 people before its expiration in 1807. While some enslaved Africans remained in South Carolina, many more were sold to would-be gentrified white farmers living in the interior. The Mississippi Valley economies, stagnant in the eighteenth century, boomed with the rise of King Cotton and quickly became dependent on the hard work of tens of thousands of enslaved African Americans. The few cities of the South also used slave labor to man the docks, work as artisans, serve as domestics, and do the work of the slavocracy. If in the northern states civil freedom translated into job discrimination and economic marginality, in the South slavery brought ample work but no freedom whatsoever.

There were vast changes in the economic status and lives of African Americans between 1830 and 1895, most obviously in the abolition of southern slavery in 1865. Despite these changes, there were also significant continuities in African American economic life over this eventful sixty-five-year period. Agriculture and personal service continued to be the principal means of earning a living for the vast majority of African Americans in 1895, as in 1830. And whether African Americans were enslaved or free, racism in all of its diverse forms, including discriminatory legal restrictions, hampered their efforts to make the most of their economic opportunities.

Antebellum Slavery. The 1830 federal census enumerated 2.3 million African Americans in the United States, of whom about 2 million were enslaved. By 1830 the abolition of slavery in almost every northern state had created the familiar antebellum dichotomy of the free North and the Slave South. Most slaves worked in agriculture. Although tobacco in the Chesapeake region, rice in the Georgia and South Carolina lowlands, and sugar in Louisiana were also important crops, by 1830 cotton had become the dominant agricultural product of the Slave South. The cultivation of cotton underwent tremendous expansion during the latter antebellum decades, with annual production rising from 178,000 bales in 1810 to over 4 million bales in 1860. Cotton requires two hundred frostless days a year, which largely confines its cultivation to the Deep South. By 1859 four states—Alabama, Mississippi, Louisiana, and Georgia—produced 79 percent of the nation's cotton output. The growth of the cotton economy bolstered that of the entire Slave South, in large part through raising the price and value of slaves. Between 1790 and 1860 as many as 1 million slaves were either sold or transferred from the Eastern Seaboard to western regions within the Slave South.

Cotton cultivation had relatively few economies of scale, and the crop was grown on both large plantations and relatively small farms. About one-quarter of the 8 million southern whites lived in slaveholding families. In 1860 roughly one-quarter of slaveholders owned from one to nine slaves, about half owned between ten and forty-nine slaves, and one-quarter owned more than fifty slaves. The average size of the slaveholding differed greatly from state to state. The median holding in Louisiana (a state that produced most of the sugar grown in the United States, a crop that required great economies of scale) was 49.3 slaves, and half of all slaves lived on plantations with 175 or more slaves. Slaveholdings in the Upper South were far smaller. In Delaware the median slaveholding per owner was 6.3 on the eve of the Civil War.

Slaves generally worked from dawn to dusk, six days a week. Men, women, and children (as soon as they were capable) all worked in agriculture. The nature and intensity of the work differed from crop to crop and from season to season. Rice cultivators in the Carolina Lowcountry often were given a daily task, upon successful completion of which they might have as much as half a day left for their own pursuits. Sugar and cotton cultivation was generally more regimented. Slaves worked in gangs and under the direct supervision of overseers. Harvests were the time of the most intense work on most plantations. Both field and house slaves, the young and the old, engaged in the time-critical tasks of gathering the crops. Between 50 percent and 75 percent of slaves on large plantations worked as field hands. The remainder worked as domestics or as carpenters, millwrights, or blacksmiths and at other artisanal occupations required on the largely self-sufficient plantations.

Slavery was not confined to agriculture. By the 1850s between 160,000 and 200,000 slaves, about 10 percent of the adult slave population, worked in industry—for example, in textile manufacturing, iron foundries, tobacco processing, and sawmills and gristmills. Some slaves worked in mines, on canals, and on railroads. Often the industrialists themselves directly owned the slaves employed in their operations. The Tredegar Iron Works in Richmond, Virginia, the largest rolling mill in the South, owned and used the labor of hundreds of slaves. In southern cities most slaves worked as domestics (black women outnumbered men in most cities), while others were dock workers, artisans, and day laborers. Most urban slaves enjoyed more autonomy than their rural counterparts. Frederick Douglass, who before escaping slavery spent much of his childhood in Baltimore, later wrote that "a city slave is almost a free citizen" compared with those in rural areas. But urban slavery was not thriving in the late antebellum period. Between 1840 and 1860 the proportion of slaves in the total population of the eight largest southern cities declined from 18 percent to 7 percent.

In many areas of the South, especially in the Carolina and Georgia lowlands, with their large black majorities, slaves directly participated in the market economy. They raised crops on their garden plots, and from the proceeds they sometimes accumulated property. At times slaves received cash bonuses or trading privileges from their owners. Some of the trading by slaves was known to their masters; other trading, involving the expropriation of property, was surreptitious. Some skilled slaves, especially in urban settings, were able to hire themselves out, paying their masters a percentage of their earnings. Within the oppressive environment of the slave system, the ingenuity of African Americans often found means of economic advancement as a means of asserting their autonomy.

Slavery on the eve of the Civil War was a profitable economic system and, except in some border states (like Delaware), showed little indication that it was in decline. There were almost 4 million slaves in 1860, with a market value to their owners commonly estimated at about $4 billion. Despite the abundant supply of enslaved persons, the result of the natural population increase of southern blacks, the price of a prime field hand had steadily increased over the late antebellum decades, rising from roughly four hundred to six hundred dollars in 1800 to almost three thousand dollars by 1860, an indication of slave owners' voting with their pocketbooks in the future of the slave system. If the North and South had been separate economies in 1860, the southern states would have been the fourth-largest economy in the world. The Civil War brought this system tumbling down, but slavery collapsed through its inhumanity, not because of its inefficiency.

Free Blacks. In 1830 there were roughly 300,000 free blacks in the United States, with about 60 percent of them living in slave states. Free blacks in the South were often concentrated in urban areas, and a large proportion were skilled artisans, such as carpenters and blacksmiths—one-quarter to one-third of free black men in the Upper South and as much as 75 percent in urban areas in the Deep South. Free black women worked as domestics, laundresses, weavers, and spinners. On the whole the economic status of free blacks in the South was somewhat higher than that of their counterparts in the North, in part because of less competition from immigrants. However, free blacks in the South suffered from a tight skein of restrictive legislation that greatly limited their ability to move freely, read or write, enter into certain professions, or meet without supervision. These restrictions prevented free blacks in the South from developing civic and political institutions akin to those in the North—although, as the historian Ira Berlin has suggested, without these outlets they often put their energies into economic advancement. In 1860 there were 16,172 free black property owners in the South, whose real estate holdings were worth over $20 million, or more than $1,250 per property owner, a remarkable achievement in the face of great obstacles.

Some free blacks achieved considerable wealth in certain areas, especially New Orleans and elsewhere in Louisiana. There was a separate mulatto caste in the state that included industrialists, real estate investors, physicians, and composers and constituted a "brown elite." One free black family in Louisiana owned five hundred slaves on the eve of the Civil War. Despite these extraordinary exceptions, most free blacks in the South, especially in rural areas, were extremely poor, scratching out a meager existence through hunting, foraging, and odd jobs, trying to keep the slave system at arm's length. The anomalous situation of free blacks in the South, especially the Deep South, grew increasingly precarious after Nat Turner's slave revolt in Virginia in 1831 and the rise of abolitionism in the same decade. The relative freedom of southern free blacks made them suspect, and their role was increasingly circumscribed.

In the North blacks tended to work as laborers or in forms of personal service, such as coachmen, teamsters, hod carriers, stevedores, porters, sailors, barbers, house servants, waiters, cooks, seamstresses, and dressmakers. Free blacks in the North were concentrated in urban areas, and by 1860 about 60 percent of northern blacks lived in cities, making them among the most urbanized ethnic and racial groups in the region. In rural areas farm labor and work as domestics were common occupations. Patterns of pervasive discrimination made it difficult for blacks to enter the skilled professions. Fugitive slaves often found it difficult to practice their accustomed trades in the North. Frederick Douglass, an experienced ship caulker, found that white caulkers in New Bedford, Massachusetts, would not let him work with them when he arrived from Maryland, and he survived for a year performing odd jobs before beginning his abolitionist career.

As Douglass's case shows, it was unusual for northern whites and blacks to work together in the same profession, and this resulted in separate labor markets for black and white men (and, to a lesser extent, for black and white women). If certain careers—for example, those of barbers, hairdressers, and waiters—were identified with African Americans, many vocational choices were not available, especially in burgeoning areas of industry such as textiles, iron and steel, and glassmaking. There were few state or municipal government jobs for blacks, with teachers in segregated black schools being one of the few exceptions. In New York City in 1860 only 10 percent of blacks worked in skilled professions, a much lower figure than for free blacks in southern cities.

One consequence of this pervasive discrimination was that many free blacks became self-employed entrepreneurs, such as dealers in secondhand clothing (this had been the militant abolitionist David Walker's occupation in Boston), hucksters of oysters, or purveyors of coal. Most self-employed blacks remained petty entrepreneurs, but some achieved great success, such as the hairdresser Pierre Toussaint in New York City, the sailmaker James Forten in Philadelphia, and Thomas Downing, the proprietor of a famous restaurant in Manhattan. Furthermore, despite discrimination, blacks in the North could enter professions closed to them in the South. By 1860 there were northern black printers, typesetters, doctors, pharmacists, lawyers, and even a few officeholders.

Post-Emancipation Agriculture. As the slave system crumbled in 1865, blacks in the South rejoiced at their freedom and worried about their future. In many ways their economic opportunities were bleak. In the immediate aftermath of Emancipation many southern states passed black codes that severely restricted the economic freedom of the former slaves. In Mississippi, for example, freedpersons were prohibited from owning farmland. They were also banned from leaving their employers for the duration of their labor contracts—and any black without a labor contract could be arrested and assigned to work. The black codes in their harshest forms were soon repealed, but some of their provisions lingered in the law codes for many decades, and others were reintroduced after the end of Reconstruction. Other economic problems abounded. With the failure of land reform, most slaves were now landless and without property. The economy of the South had been devastated by the Civil War. Between 1860 and 1870 the value of all real property (which excluded the loss in slave property) had declined by 30 percent, and in the latter year the output of all staple crops stood below their prewar levels.

A number of different systems of agricultural work developed after the Civil War. In many places in the South, the desire by former slaves for greater work autonomy, as well as the long-term insolvency of many planters, led to the development of a system of sharecropping, in which individual or small groups of blacks would work a parcel of land in return for a percentage of the crop. In the sharecropping system, tenant farmers were paid once a year, after the crops were harvested. The "settlin' time" had much potential for exploitation by landowners, who would determine the size of the payment and subtract from that whatever debts the sharecropper had accumulated in the course of the year. Many sharecroppers, unable to earn enough to cover their debts, found themselves in a condition of debt peonage, reinforced by laws that prohibited tenant farmers who owed debts from leaving the land. A tenure similar to sharecropping was land rental for an agreed-upon fee (such as several bales of cotton). Renters, unlike sharecroppers, owned their crops outright. In 1890 about three-quarters of black farmers in the South either rented or sharecropped.

There were other forms of agricultural land tenure. Some farm laborers, especially on large sugar plantations in Louisiana, worked for regular wages. In the decades after the Civil War a growing number of blacks owned their farms. In Georgia in 1900, for instance, 14 percent of all black farmers owned their own farms. However, much of the farmland purchased by black farmers was in small plots and on marginal land, and their holdings were often precarious, providing only the appearance of economic independence.

Whatever the form of land tenure, the vast majority of black agricultural laborers from 1865 to 1890 were dependent on white landowners and deeply impoverished. Black women living on farms often had two jobs—the care and feeding of their families and whatever farm work needed to be done. Rosina Hoard, born in 1859, told an interviewer late in her life, "I had my house work and de cookin' to do and to look after the chillum, but I'd go out and still pick my two hunnert pounds ob cotton a day."

Nonagricultural Labor. The 1890 census recorded occupations for about 3 million African Americans, representing most of the nation's adult black population. About 57 percent worked in agriculture and other extractive industries, compared with 40 percent for the population as a whole. African Americans were also overrepresented in domestic and personal service, which accounted for 31 percent of black workers, in contrast to 19 percent of all workers. The occupational patterns of African Americans reflected both the continuation of traditional forms of employment and pervasive patterns of discrimination. Domestic and personal service was by far the largest category of nonagricultural work. Women slightly outnumbered men in this category in the 1890 census. For black women, especially in urban settings, domestic service was the predominant form of work. For example, 98 percent of black female wage earners in Atlanta in 1880 were domestics.

Younger single women tended to work in the houses of their white employers as maids or nurses. Older women often worked as cooks or laundresses. Washerwomen generally worked from home, since laundry work could be interspersed with child care and other domestic duties. The wages of domestics in the South ranged from about four to eight dollars a month, and most domestics worked at least six days a week, from morning to night.

Outside the South, African Americans also continued to work in domestic and personal service in large numbers, but in some occupations they found themselves increasingly crowded out of the main categories by competition from immigrants on the one hand and a decline in white patronage on the other. New racial attitudes that discouraged relatively "intimate" personal contact between the races closed down some of the traditional avenues for black petty entrepreneurship, such as barbering and food service. For instance, in the mid-nineteenth century blacks ran a large percentage of the barbershops catering to whites in cities such as Philadelphia or New York. By the early twentieth century this was not the case. Shut out of the larger market, black businesses were increasingly limited to a black clientele.

Apart from agriculture and personal and domestic service, African Americans were substantially underrepresented. Most critically, in the 1890 census only 5 percent of blacks worked in manufacturing and mechanical industries, whereas 22 percent of all American workers had jobs in heavy industry. With only a few significant exceptions, African Americans were shut out of work opportunities in the industrializing America of the late nine-teenth century. Among the areas of industrial and semi-industrial employment open to African Americans were railroad construction in the South (folklorists still debate whether the famous legend of John Henry is based on actual events), lumber-mill and turpentine operations in the Deep South, and the nonfarm tobacco industry in the Upper South. But in the industrial North, African Americans were largely absent from industries as diverse as iron and steel manufacture, meatpacking, and the garment, chemical, and skilled construction industries. Their concentration in nonunionized and "unskilled" employment meant that as new waves of European immigrants arrived in urban areas, the relative position of African Americans declined, confined as they were largely to nonunion and low-paying work. What the historian Roger Lane has written of late-nineteenth-century Philadelphia can be extended to urban areas throughout the country, namely, that "most blacks were still doing the kind of jobs that had been done by the bottom layer of urban society in the Middle Ages."

Atop the vocational pyramid in black America in the late nineteenth century was a small group of entrepreneurs and professionals. A few rare individuals had considerable success as bankers, real estate investors, or owners of insurance companies. At the end of the period a few women were beginning to make considerable fortunes in the hair care industry. In the 1890 census almost thirty-four thousand African Americans were classified as professionals. Of those people, more than one-third were in the clergy, and an additional seven thousand were teachers, along with a scattering of lawyers, doctors, and dentists. Almost all African American professionals worked within the internal African American economy.

The economic situation of black America in 1895 was in many ways bleak. The efforts at progress made in many areas of economic life were increasingly limited by the tightening hand of Jim Crow and economic exclusion. Black leaders of the time expressed a range of views on how best to address the situation. By far the most influential was the position adopted by the educator Booker T. Washington, which received its most famous statement in September 1895 in his so-called Atlanta Compromise speech. At the core of Washington's view of race was his positive evaluation of the economic progress of southern blacks. Starting with nothing in the way of goods and property, Washington argued, they had fashioned their own economic progress and now numbered among their ranks entrepreneurs, publishers, editors, and bankers.

Whatever one thinks of Washington's broader views, he was surely correct to praise the tenacity and ingenuity of African Americans seeking economic self-advancement in the decades after the Civil War. His overall message was one of caution and conservatism. He urged blacks to keep in check their demands for equality under the law or extravagant dreams of economic advancement. He also urged blacks to remain in the South, where they would face less competition from new immigrants. Most blacks, Washington argued, were likely to be manual laborers for the foreseeable future and therefore needed to learn how to do those jobs in the most effective manner.

Washington's message that blacks make the best of a bad economic and disastrous political situation was subtler than many critics suppose, but in time many would come to question his view that economic advancement for blacks could be separated from their need for civic and political equality. In many ways Washington's sobering view of the political and economic realities that faced black southerners in 1895 was a cry of despair disguised in optimistic platitudes. Of all of Washington's exhortations in the Atlanta Compromise speech to his fellow blacks, it was no doubt the suggestion that "it is at the bottom of life we must begin, and not at the top" that they found the easiest to follow.

[*See also*; Discrimination; Douglass, Frederick; Downing, George Thomas; Entrepreneurs, Forten, James; Free African Americans before the Civil War (North); Free African Americans before the Civil War (South); Freedmen; Freedmen's Bureau; Gender; Jim Crow Car Laws; Laws and Legislation; Mulattoes; Racism; Reconstruction; Sharecropping; Slavery; Strikes; Urbanization; Washington, Booker T.; *and* Work.]

BIBLIOGRAPHY

Armstead, Myra B. Young. *"Lord, Please Don't Take Me in August": African Americans in Newport and Saratoga Springs, 1870–1930.* Urbana: University of Illinois Press, 1999.

Berlin, Ira. *Generations of Captivity: A History of African-American Slavery.* Cambridge, MA: Harvard University Press, 2003.

Bolster, W. Jeffrey. *Black Jacks: African American Seamen in the Age of Sail.* Cambridge, MA: Harvard University Press, 1997.

Dew, Charles B. *Bond of Iron: Master and Slave at Buffalo Forge.* New York: Norton, 1994.

Du Bois, W. E. B. *The Philadelphia Negro* (1899). New York: Schocken, 1967.

Foner, Eric. *Reconstruction: America's Unfinished Revolution, 1863–1877.* New York: Harper and Row, 1988.

Hudson, Larry E., Jr. *To Have and to Hold: Slave Work and Family Life in Antebellum South Carolina.* Athens: University of Georgia, 1997.

Hunter, Tera W. *To 'Joy My Freedom: Southern Black Women's Lives and Labors after the Civil War.* Cambridge, MA: Harvard University Press, 1997.

Jones, Jacqueline. *American Work: Four Centuries of Black and White Labor.* New York: Norton, 1998.

Kolchin, Peter. *American Slavery, 1619–1877.* New York: Hill and Wang, 1993.

Lane, Roger. *William Dorsey's Philadelphia and Ours: On the Past and Future of the Black City in America.* New York: Oxford University Press, 1991.

Litwack, Leon. *North of Slavery: The Negro in the Free States, 1790–1860.* Chicago: University of Chicago Press, 1961.

Litwack, Leon. *Trouble in Mind: Black Southerners in the Age of Jim Crow.* New York: Knopf, 1998.

Schweniger, Loren. *Black Property Owners in the South, 1790–1915.* Urbana: University of Illinois Press, 1990.

Starobin, Robert S. *Industrial Slavery in the Old South.* New York: Oxford University Press, 1970.

—PETER EISENSTADT
—GRAHAM RUSSELL GAO HODGES

EDUCATION. [*This entry contains two subentries dealing with the education of African Americans from 1619 through 1895. The first article provides a discussion of Christian education of slaves in early New England and contrasts Northern and Southern whites' attitudes towards the education of African Americans. The second article continues the discussion of education in the North and South through the establishment of black higher-education institutions after 1830.*]

The Rise of Hostility against African American Education through the 1830s

The hostility of whites toward African American education that characterized the early nineteenth century was never a foregone conclusion. In fact, during the seventeenth and eighteenth centuries, whites in both northern and southern communities generally tolerated if not encouraged the literary, religious, and vocational instruction of people of color. Especially in New England, where biblical literacy went to the core of Protestant theology, ministers often worked diligently to bring blacks into their spiritual fold. At the same time, colonial law mandated that all households provide their charges, free and enslaved, with sufficient literacy to read the Bible. Such legislation provided an additional incentive for New England slaveholders to tend to their bondpeople's spiritual and literary education.

Particularly in the South, this climate of educational permissiveness would largely disappear after the Revolution. Beginning in 1740, southern colonies and then states, including South Carolina, Georgia, and Virginia, banned the literary instruction of enslaved African Americans. Legislation also targeted free black education by the third decade of the nineteenth century. Further, while northern states never evinced the same desire to legislate against black education, the contemporaneous onset of school segregation complemented southerners' antieducation inclinations. As towns and cities throughout the region began to craft their first common school systems, they often elected to avoid integration through the creation of separate, often unequal, black institutions. In the end, early African Americans were largely responsible for their own literary improvement. Between 1619 and 1830 people of color throughout the nation opened and sustained countless private educational institutions. Withstanding systemic neglect and occasional violent opposition, African Americans crafted, funded, and managed their own schools, and with that responsibility came freedom and autonomy.

Colonization to Revolution. While antebellum whites, southern and northern, often considered black literacy to be incompatible with the "peculiar institution" of slavery, their colonial counterparts drew no such distinction. Cognizant of the English tradition precluding the enslavement of Christians, many early slaveholders were reluctant to provide bondpeople with religious and literary instruction. By the 1680s, however, colonial law largely allayed masters' concerns that conversion might necessitate manumission. In 1671, for example, Maryland legislators formally decreed that baptism in no way entitled slaves to freedom. By the close of the seventeenth century, Anglican clergymen like Morgan Godwyn began to press upon slaveholders to honor their Christian duty and tend to their slaves' spiritual salvation.

It is difficult to ascertain how many slaveholders heeded Godwyn's call, but the number of missionaries laboring to convert Africans to Christianity increased demonstrably during the early eighteenth century. In 1701, for example, the Church of England founded the Society for the Propagation of the Gospel in Foreign Parts (SPG), which dispatched the devoted to teach slaves and Native Americans to read the Holy Scriptures. As early as 1705 in Goose Creek Parish, South Carolina, the SPG instructor Samuel Thomas opened a small school for approximately twenty people of color, providing instruction in reading and writing. Despite these modest numbers, Thomas professed to know of one thousand additional slaves who desired a Christian education.

Also supported by the SPG, the French Protestant Elias Neau opened a similar institution in New York City. Neau invited whites, Native Americans, and blacks into his home for spiritual and literary instruction beginning in 1704, and by 1708 an estimated two hundred enslaved New Yorkers had attended Neau's institution. Four years later, however, accusations that Neau's pupils had plotted to murder their masters resulted in pressure to close the institution. After officials determined that none of Neau's students had, in fact, participated in the 1712 slave uprising, the city permitted the school to reopen despite strong opposition from white citizens.

In New England, where biblical literacy was central to Puritan theology, local ministers similarly sought to provide people of color with spiritual and literary instruction. As early as the 1670s, the Massachusetts missionary John

Eliot, often called the Apostle to the Indians, invited masters to surrender their slaves to his care for instruction in literacy and Christianity. He had planned to open a formal institution but died before he could realize his intentions. In 1693 the Boston minister Cotton Mather organized a Society of Negroes, ostensibly to expose local slaves to the catechism and the Bible. From seven to nine o'clock every Sunday evening, he bid bondpeople to listen to his sermons, to pray, and to study. Yet Mather's curriculum strayed well beyond literacy and theology. He explicitly sought to use education to influence slaves' behavior. He not only advised his attendants to avoid tardiness, intemperance, profanity, theft, and disobedience but also directed them to inform him of any bondpeople who failed to display similar restraint. The society disbanded after a brief existence. In 1717 Mather again invited blacks to study Scripture with him for two or three hours each evening, but this institution proved similarly short lived. As Mather's experience indicates, although colonial clergy assisted in efforts to expand black literacy, their schools were usually temporary, small-scale operations.

In contrast to the public activities of clergy like Eliot and Mather, the education of most enslaved New Englanders came, if at all, from their white masters and mistresses in the confines of their homes. White New Englanders considered all servants, black and white, both likely church members and part of their extended household. As a result, masters expected their servants and slaves to participate fully in the family's religious activities, including personally reading the Bible. As this practice suggests, most white New Englanders did not believe black education would undermine the slave system. Instead, slaveholders in the region traditionally held that spiritual instruction would both hasten African acculturation and instill bondpeople with those values—obedience, virtue, and temperance—that complemented their social position.

Consequently, no colony in the region formally proscribed black education, religious or literary. To the contrary, colonial law traditionally required heads of households to provide all their charges, black and white, with sufficient literacy to read the Bible. In 1642, for example, the Massachusetts General Court instructed town selectmen to keep a "vigilant eye" on all families to ensure that they were properly instructing their children and apprentices. The colony of Connecticut enacted a similar statute eight years later. New Haven followed suit in 1656. Collectively, laws mandating the education of apprentices, servants, and slaves confirm that a central objective of education for colonial New Englanders, black and white, was to create a literate clergy and laity. Universal literacy was necessary to ensure that every individual, regardless of race, gender, or social station, could read the Scriptures—an ability essential for both their own salvation and for that of the colony.

One of the most celebrated African Americans to capitalize on New England's early commitment to universal education was Phillis Wheatley. Born on the west coast of Africa, Wheatley was kidnapped at approximately eight years of age. After surviving forced transport across the Atlantic, she was purchased by the Bostonian John Wheatley in 1761. Expected to serve as a personal assistant to John's wife, Phillis was soon taught to read and write. In just sixteen months, John reported that Phillis was sufficiently literate to read classical Greek and Latin texts, astronomy, history, geography, and, most important, the Bible. As a teenager, Phillis Wheatley began to experiment with various forms of verse. She published her first poem in 1767 in the *Mercury*, a newspaper issued out of Newport, Rhode Island. Unable to find a Bostonian willing to distribute her poems, Wheatley eventually secured a publisher in London. In 1773 she released *Poems on Various Subjects, Religious and Moral*, a collection of thirty-nine of her writings.

Wheatley's poems became literary images of the contradictions inherent in her situation. Her verse embodied the spiritual and classical emphasis of her early education. Attracting comment within Boston and across the Atlantic, Wheatley's poetry belied the essentialist doctrine of black inferiority that underpinned much of the slave system. While this collection would be her only published volume, it eventually enabled her to gain her freedom. As the first volume of poetry published by an enslaved American, *Poems on Various Subjects* gave Wheatley sufficient notoriety to entice her master to manumit her in 1774, when she was twenty-one years old. Although she died just a decade later, early-nineteenth-century abolitionists revitalized popular interest in Wheatley's poetry, drawing explicitly on evidence of her literary acumen to attack proslavery ideology.

Southern Hostility, Northern Segregation. Beyond religious instruction, the apprenticeship system offered another source of literary training for seventeenth- and eighteenth-century African Americans. Indenture contracts often specified that, in addition to a trade, black men were to be taught to read, write, and cipher; black women were to be instructed in the "art" of reading and the "mystery" of housewifery. However, although apprenticeship provided people of color with much-needed access to vocational and literary education, the purpose of the institution, particularly in the South, began to transform from instruction to control during the early nineteenth century. Virginia in 1804 and Maryland in 1818 passed provisions empowering masters to decide whether or not to provide their black charges with literary in-

struction. If a master so desired, he could substitute a small amount of money in exchange for his apprentice's education. Thereafter, black girls were traditionally given the paltry sum of twenty dollars for their literacy, and black boys received a slightly larger payment of thirty dollars. In consequence of these legislative changes, apprenticeship became less and less an avenue to skilled trades and more often a vehicle for obtaining inexpensive and coerced labor. As the southern indenture system became increasingly black, the balance between education and service grew more disparate. By the second decade of the nineteenth century, the institution had evolved from one of mutual benefit with education at its center to another means for whites to obtain inexpensive and tractable black labor.

Such a trend mirrored the rising white hostility toward black education that intensified throughout the early nineteenth century. In the South white efforts to circumscribe black access to literacy began as early as 1740, when South Carolina became the first colony to officially enact antieducation legislation targeted at people of color. Passed in the wake of the Stono Rebellion, the legislation stated that anyone discovered teaching slaves to write or found employing bondpeople as scribes could be fined as much as one hundred pounds. In 1755 Georgia modeled its antieducation laws on the South Carolina precedent, extending them in 1770 to prohibit the teaching of reading as well as writing to slaves.

While eighteenth-century southerners curtailed slave education primarily through prohibitive legislation, their nineteenth-century counterparts also utilized extra-legal means. Violent attacks on black institutions became an increasingly common tactic among whites to suppress African American education during the nineteenth century. In 1811 whites in Richmond, Virginia, burned down the school founded by a free black, Christopher McPherson. Born into slavery, McPherson succeeded in securing two years of formal schooling with his master's consent. Obtaining sufficient knowledge to support himself as a clerk and an accountant, McPherson was emancipated in 1792, though he continued to serve his master in Norfolk for some time. He subsequently relocated to Richmond, where he opened a night school for free and enslaved black men in 1811. Shortly thereafter he reported that he was instructing twenty-five black pupils in arithmetic, geography, English grammar, religion, and astronomy. After McPherson published an advertisement for his institution in a local paper called the *Virginia Argus*, Richmond whites began to agitate to close the school, deeming McPherson's educational activities "impolitic" and "improper." He was soon charged with disturbing the peace and disorderly conduct. After these prosecutions proved un-

Colored schools in Philadelphia, listed in 1837, at a time when the climate for black education was particularly bad. Between 1831 and 1839, whites in a number of northern towns and cities were vehemently opposed to education for people of color. (Historical Society of Pennsylvania, Philadelphia Abolition Society Papers.)

successful, local whites took the matter into their own hands by setting the school ablaze and confining McPherson to a Williamsburg insane asylum. In the aftermath of the Richmond burning, it did not take white Virginians long to formally proscribe slave education, as Georgians and South Carolinians had done before them. In 1819 the state legislature outlawed instructing slaves to read or write. Less than one year later, local authorities put the statute to the test, raiding another black school in Richmond and closing it permanently.

Educational prospects for people of color in Charleston were little better than for those in Richmond. In 1821 local whites informed city ministers that they would no longer permit slaves to attend Sunday schools or night schools. Prior to this, colonial statutes restricting black literacy had been enforced laxly. Several schools existed in the city to instruct blacks from Charleston, Augusta, and other southern locales. But after Denmark Vesey's rumored rebellion the following year, educational opportunities for black Charlestonians plummeted. Charging that the existing antieducation statutes were insufficient and ineffective, a Charleston grand jury concluded that the number of schools operated by persons of color was intolerable. In response, they pressed for a city ordinance to prohibit free blacks from working as teachers.

Despite this patchwork of sporadically enforced statutes prohibiting slave education, at the close of the 1820s no state, southern or northern, had formally banned the literary instruction of free blacks. But in 1829, after the free black Bostonian David Walker released his inflammatory *Appeal to the Colored Citizens of the World*, which openly sanctioned violent rebellion, white southerners began to enlarge the scope of their antiliteracy legislation. Predictably, Georgia, the first state to formally ban slave literacy, was also the first to respond to Walker's *Appeal* by proscribing free black education. In December 1829 Georgia's general assembly enacted legislation with proposed penalties for teaching slaves or free blacks to read or to write that included a five hundred dollar fine, whipping, and, if necessary, prison. In addition, Georgia banned all free and enslaved people of color from working in print shops and presses.

North Carolina similarly moved to curtail the education of free and enslaved African Americans in the aftermath of Walker's *Appeal*. Beginning in 1818 local whites had pressed for antiliteracy legislation, but they met with no success. In 1830 the state legislature finally bowed to public pressure. In addition to banning the literary instruction of bondpeople, North Carolina also proscribed anyone from supplying slaves with written material. For such a violation whites could be charged up to two hundred dollars. Free people of color found guilty of this transgression could be imprisoned or whipped up to thirty-nine times. Additionally, if the content of publications supplied to slaves was deemed to be insurrectionary, jail time could extend for up to one year.

Virginia similarly responded to Walker's *Appeal* by ratcheting up their antiliteracy legislation. In 1830, by a vote of eighty-one to eighty, the state's House of Delegates passed a measure outlawing both Sabbath and private instruction for all African Americans, free and enslaved. The bill failed to pass the Virginia Senate, which rejected it by a vote of eleven to seven after some slaveholders voiced concerns that the state was infringing on their autonomy. But in less than four months' time, the two branches reached an agreement. In April 1831 Virginia enacted a measure barring slaves and free blacks from assembling for literary learning. Ironically, the act was slated to take effect in June 1831, just two months before Nat Turner's rebellion, the most important event inciting whites to suppress black access to literary education.

With the exception of Connecticut, northern states never enacted antieducation legislation, but communities throughout the region did begin to institute formal school segregation around the same time. While the early nineteenth century is commonly associated with a dramatic upsurge in access to public education, such a characterization wholly overlooks the simultaneous constriction of northern blacks' educational opportunities. Prior to the 1820s and early 1830s, African Americans in cities such as Boston, Philadelphia, and New York had limited access to local common schools. Nonetheless, the majority of blacks attended private religious or philanthropic institutions. In Philadelphia, for example, Quakers like Anthony Benezet had long championed the literary and religious education of people of color. In 1773 he opened a private school for free and enslaved blacks that offered rudimentary and advanced classical instruction. In 1789 another Quaker organization, the Association for the Free Instruction of Adult Colored Persons, provided night and Sabbath schooling in literacy and mathematics to men and women of color. By 1805 Philadelphians estimated that their city housed at least seven schools expressly for African Americans, with total enrollment exceeding five hundred students. Even as the city strengthened its commitment to public education, however, African Americans remained largely dependent on charity schools and private instruction. Local hostility toward school integration thrust most black children out of Philadelphia's common school system. By the late 1820s the city explicitly sanctioned segregation by supporting two separate schools for African Americans.

African American education in post-Revolutionary New York City followed a similar trajectory. In 1789, in the shadow of rising manumissions, white abolitionists founded the New York African Free School to monitor the morality of the budding free black population. From the beginning, white school supporters championed the importance of instructing black pupils, many new to freedom, in the virtues of deference, hard work, and sobriety. During the first decades of the nineteenth century, the school expanded exponentially. In 1815 it relocated to a larger facility, which was soon filled to capacity. Shortly thereafter trustees opened a second institution to serve the city's burgeoning free black community. By 1830 the New York African Free Schools instructed an estimated one thousand children annually. In 1834 the city assumed control of the private institutions, hoping to avert the integration of its public schools permanently.

Several New England communities adopted similar policies of formal school segregation during the early nineteenth century. Specifically, as towns and cities across the region began to draft their first formal school systems, many elected to eschew integration by supporting separate "African" schools with public funds. Nantucket, for example, opened its first black school in 1825, at the same time it constructed its first "public" school implicitly for the island's white residents. Portsmouth, New Hampshire, first funded its African School in 1827. One year later, Providence, Rhode Island, opened its first publicly funded black school just as the state was starting to build its formal school system.

In rare instances, pressure for separate schools came from members of the black community. Hartford, Connecticut, for example, segregated its school system in 1830, ostensibly in response to an appeal from the city's black residents. By this time, towns including Portland, Maine, and Salem, Massachusetts, sustained at least one segregated public school expressly for black children, and New Haven, New York City, and Philadelphia each supported multiple black institutions. Together the wave of southern antiliteracy laws and the emergence of northern school segregation signaled a growing white hostility toward black literary education that would explode in the early 1830s.

Black Activism, Self-Education. In light of the inclination of whites in the nineteenth century to neglect or circumscribe the educational opportunities of blacks, African Americans were often responsible for their own instruction. In the first three decades of the nineteenth century, free blacks in the urban Northeast increased their access to literary education considerably. In 1826, for example, the free black Baltimoreans Richard Greener and William Lively opened two private institutions for adults and children of color in their city. Congregants of the African Church in Rochester, New York, opened a Sabbath school for black children the same year. Free blacks in Philadelphia and New York City also launched private institutions around the same time. In 1827 black New Yorkers founded another evening school for black adults while their counterparts in Hartford opened a small Sabbath and day school in the basement of the African Church in the city. One year later, the African American schoolteacher Stephen Gloucester established the Academy for Colored Youth in Philadelphia, and New York's African Free School opened a separate institution for black women out of its Mulberry Street location.

Arguably, no free black community better exemplified the spirit of educational self-reliance than that of Boston. Following the Revolution local black children supposedly had equivalent access to the public schools of the city. However, in 1787 a contingent of free black Bostonians led by Prince Hall requested that the city provide their children with a separate publicly funded school because, they believed, free black children were ignored or treated cruelly in the city's integrated institutions. When the town denied their request, local blacks responded by opening a private school in Hall's residence. Shortly thereafter, sixty-six free blacks again petitioned the city to publicly fund a school expressly for black children. Again Boston's white officials refused their request. In response, black Bostonians intensified their commitment to independent education. In 1808 they relocated their school to a separate facility in Belknap Street Church, which they had helped to construct. For the next decade black Bostonians sustained the school largely by their own efforts. With that responsibility came autonomy. Over the next decade, the school's instructors—Cyrus Vassal (1808), Prince Saunders (1809–1812), and Peter Tracy (1813–1817)—were men of color.

In 1812 the city of Boston agreed to support the Belknap Street School, but the funds it offered, some two hundred dollars annually, were insufficient to keep the school afloat. Black Bostonians elected to personally supplement the city's inadequate contribution. In 1815 Abiel Smith, a local white merchant, willed a permanent endowment for black education in the city. As in Philadelphia and New York, however, white takeover of the black-run institution brought a host of difficulties. As the city assumed authority over the Belknap Street School, African Americans' tradition of educational autonomy vanished almost instantaneously. In 1817 white officials replaced the school's black instructor, Peter Tracy, with a white man, James Waldack, without notifying or discussing their decision with members of the black community. Where previously African Americans had hired teachers and set the school curriculum, the all-white school committee now had full authority over all such decisions. Further, black parents could do little to ensure that white instructors would treat their children respectfully.

Ultimately, black Bostonians found themselves back in the same situation that had propelled them out of the public schools in the first place. As voluntary separation morphed into rigid segregation, black Bostonians complained repeatedly of decrepit facilities and incompetent instructors. If such criticisms were commonplace among whites as well, they were at least free to enroll their children in an alternative institution if they so desired. Black children had no such liberty. The city's policy of formal school segregation mandated that they could attend only the Belknap Street School. Moreover, while white children, beginning in 1821, could advance from primary to grammar to high school if they chose, black children had no such opportunity. In the end, with Boston's decision to segregate all black children into a single institution, black educational opportunity in the city deteriorated precipitously.

By 1830 African Americans' educational prospects in both the North and the South were declining at a rapid clip. The onslaught of southern antiliteracy laws and northern school segregation had worked to control and constrict black access to literary instruction; and the climate for black schooling would grow worse, not better. Beginning in 1831 the nation experienced the greatest spike in violence against black schooling to that date. In the wake of Nat Turner's rebellion, southern states immediately expanded the boundaries of their educational policing. Further, between 1831 and 1839, whites in more than half a dozen northern towns and cities displayed vigorous, often violent resistance to the classical and vocational education of people of color. The climate for black education would, arguably, never be worse than in the tumultuous 1830s. African Americans would not see significant expansion in their educational opportunities until after the Civil War.

[*See also* American Revolution; Baptism; Benezet, Anthony; Black Codes and Slave Codes; Childhood; Class; Colleges and African Americans; David Walker's *Appeal*; Denmark Vesey Conspiracy; Discrimination; Free African Americans to 1828; Gender; Hall, Prince; Identity; Indentured Servitude; Integration; Language; Laws and Legislation; Literacy; Literature; Mather, Cotton, and African Americans; Missionary Movements; Native Americans and African Americans; Neau, Elias; New York African Free Schools; New York City; New York Slave Revolt of 1712; Race, Theories of; Resistance; Riots and Rebellions; Saunders, Prince; Segregation; Society for the Propagation of the Gospel in Foreign Parts; Society of Friends (Quakers) and African Americans; Stereotypes of African Americans; Stono Rebellion; Temperance; Violence against African Americans; Walker, David; Wheatley, Phillis; *and* Women.]

BIBLIOGRAPHY

Brown, Lois, ed. *Memoir of James Jackson, the Attentive and Obedient Scholar, Who Died in Boston, October 31, 1833, Aged Six Years and Eleven Months, by His Teacher, Miss Susan Paul.* Cambridge, MA: Harvard University Press, 2000.

Cornelius, Janet Duitsman. *"When I Can Read My Title Clear": Literacy, Slavery and Religion in the Antebellum South.* Columbia: University of South Carolina Press, 1991.

Cremin, Lawrence A. *American Education: The Colonial Experience, 1607–1783.* New York: Harper and Row, 1970.

Curry, Leonard P. *The Free Black in Urban America 1800–1850: The Shadow of the Dream.* Chicago: University of Chicago Press, 1981.

Mabee, Carleton. *Black Education in New York State: From Colonial to Modern Times.* Syracuse, NY: Syracuse University Press, 1979.

Morrow, Diane Batts. *Persons of Color and Religious at the Same Time: The Oblate Sisters of Providence, 1828–1860.* Chapel Hill: University of North Carolina Press, 2002.

Nash, Gary B. *Forging Freedom: The Formation of Philadelphia's Black Community, 1720–1840.* Cambridge, MA: Harvard University Press, 1988.

Schultz, Stanley K. *The Culture Factory: Boston Public Schools 1789–1860.* New York: Oxford University Press, 1973.

Woodson, Carter G. *The Education of the Negro prior to 1861: A History of the Education of the Colored People of the United States from the Beginning of Slavery to the Civil War* (1915). New York: Arno Press, 1968.

—HILARY MOSS

The Foundation of African American Education

Although Frederick Douglass credited his love of learning to his mother, it was only after her death that he learned that she had been able to read: "How she acquired this knowledge, I know not. . . . That a 'field hand' should learn to read, in any slave state, is remarkable; but the achievement of my mother, considering the place, was very extraordinary." After the Civil War most issues regarding black education were centered in the South, where the overwhelming majority of blacks lived. Before the war, on the other hand, most black education occurred in the North. There, although they were free, African Americans were generally excluded from white schools. In states where they were not excluded, they were sometimes taught separately from whites.

Educational practices varied throughout the North. For example, in Massachusetts in 1850 schools were integrated everywhere but in Boston, which maintained separate schools for blacks until the legislature prohibited the practice in 1855. Pennsylvania and Ohio established separate schools for black populations of twenty or more children, but in both states there were also areas, such as Oberlin and Cleveland, Ohio, where schools were integrated before the Civil War. New York authorized school commissioners to establish segregated schools, but, again, in some places, like Rochester and Syracuse, the schools were integrated. For states entering the Union, a segregated educational system was established by 1850. In the border states that had not constitutionally restricted blacks from schooling, de facto segregation accomplished similar results.

Northern Education. In response to segregation, blacks, in cooperation with abolitionists and white philanthropists, founded their own educational institutions. Antislavery societies and black self-help organizations were among the first to include educational programs, which ranged from formal to informal instruction in their offerings. Abolitionists established adult schools, Sabbath and evening schools, Bible classes, and lyceum lectures along with traditional schools for blacks. The schools' connections to the abolitionist movement provoked the ire of white citizens, however.

One of the most notable examples of conflict resulting from such associations was that encountered by Prudence Crandall, a Quaker schoolmistress who established a boarding school for girls in Canterbury, Connecticut, in 1831. Her admission of a black student caused white students to withdraw. On the advice of William Lloyd Garrison and other abolitionists, Crandall further announced the founding of a "High School for young colored Ladies and Misses" in 1833. Two months later the Connecticut legislature passed a law prohibiting the establishment of "any school, academy, or literary institution, for the instruction or education of colored persons who are not inhabitants of this state." Refusing to capitulate, Crandall and her students, some of whom indeed came from neighboring states, were subjected to continuous harassment.

Education TABLE 1. *Free Blacks Attending Schools – 1850*

Free States	Black Children In School	Black Children Ages 6–20	% Blacks Ages 6–20 In School
Maine	281	439	64.0
New Hampshire	73	149	49.0
Vermont	90	218	41.3
Massachusetts	1,439	3,594	40.0
Rhode Island	551	1,050	52.5
Connecticut	1,264	2,412	52.4
New York	5,447	15,178	35.9
New Jersey	2,326	11,755	19.8
Pennsylvania	6,499	18,096	35.9
Ohio	2,531	9,634	26.3
Indiana	927	4,622	20.0
Illinois	323	1,979	16.3
Michigan	207	809	25.6
Wisconsin	67	198	33.8
Minn. Territory	2	14	14.3
Iowa	17	129	13.2
Ks.-Not Organized	____	____	____
California	1	126	0.8
Oregon Territory	2	73	2.7

Slave States			
Delaware	187	7.134	2.6
Maryland	1,616	26,590	6.1
Kentucky	288	3,216	9.0
Missouri	40	704	5.7
Virginia	64	20,692	0.3
North Carolina	217	10,967	2.0
South Carolina	80	3,584	2.2
Georgia	1	1,124	0.1
Tennessee	70	2,595	3.0
Alabama	68	847	8.0
Mississippi	0	308	0.0
Florida	66	356	18.5
Louisiana	1,219	6,165	19.8
Arkansas	11	206	5.3
Texas	20	151	13.2

SOURCE: U.S. Bureau of the Census, *The Seventh Census of the United States: 1850* (Washington, DC: Robert Armstrong, 1853).

Education TABLE 2. *Whites Attending Schools – 1850*

Free States	White Children In School	White Children Ages 6–20	% Whites Ages 6–20 In School
Maine	185,941	212,782	87.4
New Hampshire	88,148	103,890	84.8
Vermont	92,152	108,429	85.0
Massachusetts	220,781	303,920	72.6
Rhode Island	28,359	44,943	63.1
Connecticut	82,433	114,264	72.2
New York	687,874	1,038,407	66.2
New Jersey	89,775	165,881	54.1
Pennsylvania	498,111	824,670	60.4
Ohio	512,278	757,633	67.6
Indiana	220,034	399,292	55.1
Illinois	181,969	335,463	54.2
Michigan	105,754	151,216	69.9
Wisconsin	56,354	104,882	53.7
Minn. Territory	207	1,737	11.9
Iowa	35,456	76,363	46.4
Ks.-Not Organized	____	____	____
California	992	9,484	10.5
Oregon Territory	1,875	4,452	42.1

Slave States			
Delaware	14,216	26,609	53.4
Maryland	60,447	147,717	40.9
Kentucky	130,917	302,901	43.2
Missouri	95,245	234,773	39.1
Virginia	109,711	345,265	31.8
North Carolina	100,591	214,454	46.7
South Carolina	40,293	107,813	37.4
Georgia	77,015	215,091	35.8
Tennessee	146,130	314,120	46.6
Alabama	62,778	176,657	35.5
Mississippi	48,803	121,089	40.3
Florida	4,764	18,097	26.3
Louisiana	32,838	84,256	39.0
Arkansas	23,350	67,545	34.6
Texas	19,369	59,335	32.6

SOURCE: U.S. Bureau of the Census, *The Seventh Census of the United States: 1850* (Washington, DC: Robert Armstrong, 1853).

Finally, in 1834, Crandall abandoned the school—although Connecticut did repeal the discriminatory law by the end of the decade.

By 1860 nearly every northern state provided public schools for blacks, but where education was segregated black schools were invariably inferior to white schools. Black students toiled in dilapidated facilities with overcrowded classrooms and overworked teachers. While black and white property owners alike paid taxes to support schools, black children were given little in return

Education TABLE 3. *Free Blacks Attending Schools – 1860*

Free States	Black Children In School	Black Children Ages 6–20	% Blacks Ages 6–20 In School
Maine	292	453	64.5
New Hampshire	80	147	54.4
Vermont	115	238	48.3
Massachusetts	1,615	2,959	54.6
Rhode Island	532	1,205	44.1
Connecticut	1,378	2,841	48.5
New York	5,964	21,717	26.2
New Jersey	2,741	8,961	30.6
Pennsylvania	7,573	19,675	38.5
Ohio	5,671	14,202	39.9
Indiana	1,122	4,529	24.8
Illinois	611	2,685	22.8
Michigan	1,105	2,414	45.8
Wisconsin	112	393	28.5
Minnesota	18	86	21.0
Iowa	138	382	36.1
Kansas	14	214	6.5
California	153	586	26.1
Oregon Territory	2	37	5.4
Slave States			
Delaware	250	8,617	2.9
Maryland	1,355	30,110	4.5
Kentucky	209	3,606	5.8
Missouri	155	1,010	15.3
Virginia	41	22,081	0.2
North Carolina	133	12,281	1.1
South Carolina	365	3,909	9.3
Georgia	7	1,296	0.5
Tennessee	52	2,891	1.8
Alabama	114	1.017	11.2
Mississippi	2	276	0.7
Florida	9	378	2.4
Louisiana	275	6,496	4.2
Arkansas	5	53	9.4
Texas	11	95	8.5

SOURCE: U.S. Bureau of the Census, *Statistics of the United States in 1860* (Washington, DC: G.P.O., 1866) 507; *Population of the United States in 1860* (Washington, DC: G.P.O., 1864).

Education TABLE 4. *Whites Attending Schools – 1860*

Free States	White Children In School	White Children Ages 6–20	% Whites Ages 6–20 In School
Maine	188,918	241,033	78.4
New Hampshire	82,854	99,020	83.7
Vermont	79,450	102,684	77.4
Massachusetts	247,678	360,708	66.7
Rhode Island	31,036	52,144	59.5
Connecticut	88,558	133,754	66.2
New York	799,856	1,240,126	64.5
New Jersey	116,475	215,095	54.2
Pennsylvania	662,388	1,013,468	65.4
Ohio	599,985	850,371	70.6
Indiana	336,969	516,409	65.3
Illinois	404,511	611,412	66.2
Michigan	187,499	258,286	72.6
Wisconsin	184,597	261,153	70.7
Minn. Territory	24,132	51,643	46.7
Iowa	167,470	247,044	67.8
Kansas	13,318	36,423	36.6
California	25,763	57,522	44.8
Oregon Territory	10,814	16,890	64.0
Slave States			
Delaware	18,422	32,609	56.5
Maryland	78,320	182,205	43.0
Kentucky	182,450	353,950	51.5
Missouri	203,333	396,183	51.3
Virginia	154,922	393,106	39.4
North Carolina	116,434	234,780	49.6
South Carolina	46,225	111,013	41.6
Georgia	94,680	236,454	40.0
Tennessee	162,970	415,077	39.3
Alabama	98,090	214,006	45.8
Mississippi	66,522	141,279	47.1
Florida	8,494	30,461	27.9
Louisiana	47,748	122,141	39.1
Arkansas	42,721	133,709	32.0
Texas	63,614	158,603	40.1

SOURCE: U.S. Bureau of the Census, Statistics of the United States in 1860 (Washington, DC: G.P.O., 1866) 507; Population of the United States in 1860 (Washington, DC: G.P.O., 1864).

for their parents' contributions. Another inadequacy was the shortage of well-trained black teachers. By the mid-nineteenth century a pattern of economic discrimination was already well established. Black teachers were paid less than whites to work in trying conditions, while white teachers were ostracized if they dared teach black children. While protesting the discriminatory conditions, blacks continued to send their children to school in the belief that some education was better than none. In fact, some blacks preferred segregation, since it protected black children from being persecuted by white school personnel and students. Black calls for integrated schools, however, increased after 1830.

Indeed, in the 1840s many black leaders, including Frederick Douglass, realized the need for an integrated public school system in order to properly prepare blacks for higher education. For Douglass, education was a higher priority than voting rights, since education—and fuller understanding of the workings of society—could empower black citizens to press for equal political and civil rights. In his hometown of Rochester, New York, Douglass demanded that the courts open all schools to blacks, insisting that segregated education was not worth the cost of black self-esteem. Elsewhere, blacks and white abolitionists took aim at school segregation in Boston.

Protests there were directed against the Boston Primary School Committee, which was responsible for assigning students to particular schools. The committee defended its segregative actions by citing failed school-integration experiments in other northern towns and warning the public of the potential for race mixing. The committee also resorted to postured paternalism, stating that it would be injurious to blacks to attend school with whites because blacks would learn of and internalize their inferiority. When blacks took the matter to court, the plaintiff was Sarah Roberts, a five-year-old African American child who was forced to attend Boston's Smith Grammar School, a black institution, despite the fact that there were five white elementary schools closer to her home. Her father, Benjamin Roberts, filed suit against the city of Boston in 1849.

To the dismay of the black community, the suit failed. In upholding school segregation, Chief Justice Lemuel Shaw stated that school segregation existed for the good of both races. Blacks then turned to legislative appeals for redress, and in 1855 the Massachusetts legislature passed a bill prohibiting racial or religious discrimination in determining the admission of students to any public school—an early victory in the protracted struggle against school segregation. But Shaw's defense of segregated schools on the basis of a "separate but equal" doctrine established a precedent that eventually led to the 1896 decision upholding that doctrine in *Plessy v. Ferguson*.

While the Boston victory encouraged blacks in other northern and midwestern states to follow similar strategies or appeal to court systems, progress was uneven. In addition, the act of desegregation by no means meant that black students were fully integrated into institutions or student bodies in meaningful, egalitarian manners. When Frederick Douglass's daughter Rosetta entered Seward Seminary, in Rochester, for example, she was assigned to a room separated from those of whites, and a teacher was appointed to instruct her alone. Douglass withdrew his daughter in protest. The principal of the seminary, espousing gradualism, suggested that the prejudice she faced might wane in time and that she could then be more meaningfully engaged in the school.

Two New England schools—Wesleyan University, in Connecticut, and Noyes Academy, in New Hampshire—provide early examples of racial segregation in higher education. In 1832 Charles B. Ray entered Wesleyan University amid student objections and, in time, harassment. Although the college president offered him protection, Ray eventually decided to leave. As a matter of policy Noyes Academy admitted qualified students regardless of race. In 1835, however, residents of the surrounding community objected to the interracial student body and destroyed the school.

Gradually, blacks—particularly light-skinned blacks—gained acceptance in white-dominated higher education. Two notable examples of colleges that admitted blacks are Oberlin College, in Ohio, and Berea College, in the border state of Kentucky. Founded in 1833, Oberlin had already been unique for its practice of admitting women; in 1835 the school decided to admit all students, "irrespective of color." Founded in 1855 by the Kentucky abolitionist John G. Fee, Berea College has been called "a child of Oberlin." Berea catered to two constituencies: recently emancipated blacks and whites from eastern Kentucky and other Appalachian states. Although it was originally assumed that Berea would not discriminate on the basis of race, not until after the issuance of the Emancipation Proclamation did Berea's catalog list the enrollment of ninety-six African Americans and ninety-one whites. After 1890 white racial attitudes hardened toward blacks in the region. In 1904 the passage of the Day law by the Kentucky legislature established de jure segregation in the state, and Berea was given an ultimatum: it could remain open, but only to whites.

The first black college graduate was John Brown Russwurm, who attended Bowdoin College, in Maine. By 1860 nearly thirty blacks had earned degrees at white institutions. That year, blacks constituted about 4 percent of the collective university student body; by then, other New England and midwestern colleges had also opened their doors to qualified blacks.

Informal Educational System of Slavery. Despite the insistence of white slaveholders that slaves remain illiterate, a system of informal learning developed prior to the issuance of the Emancipation Proclamation by President Abraham Lincoln in 1863. The slave codes established in every southern state mandated stiff punishment for slaves who attempted to learn to read or slaveholders who taught them. Yet African Americans effectively manipulated the slave system itself as a means of attaining education.

Douglass's autobiographical account of his acquisition of reading, writing, and numeracy skills demonstrates the resourcefulness of blacks who learned through this informal system.

Taught the letters of the alphabet by Sophia Auld, the wife of his master, Hugh Auld, Douglass soon realized the ramifications of literacy and its threat to the established order. When Auld learned that his wife's experiment to test whether or not a black was capable of learning had succeeded, he immediately forbade any further instruction. Auld's acknowledgment that education made a child "unfit" for slavery was a revelation to Douglass. Afterward, Douglass bribed young white playmates with biscuits in return for reading lessons from Webster's spelling book. Douglass learned to write as a laborer in the shipyard by observing the carpenters jotting letters on timber to indicate the part of the ship in which it would be used. He practiced writing by borrowing the young Tommy Auld's discarded copybooks. Douglass's initial opportunity for formal education, at a Sabbath school taught by a free black man, was eliminated when the school was attacked by a mob. In 1835, however, Douglass put his educational skills to use in starting a Sabbath school of his own.

A large southern plantation was a feudalistic, self-sustaining society where bondpersons manufactured or provided most needed goods and services. Apprenticeships and on-the-job training produced skilled craftspeople and artisans, such as carpenters, blacksmiths, weavers, and seamstresses, whose work required rudimentary literacy, numeracy, and knowledge of geography and science. Outside the plantation, rises in demand for skilled labor elicited higher prices for trained slaves on the auction block. Eventually, plantation owners who had more trained slaves than they needed hired them out to other plantations and retained a percentage of the profits, thereby increasing the return on their investment. In fact, the widespread practice of training slaves prompted Booker T. Washington to refer to the plantation as an "industrial school." Occasionally, skilled slaves were able to use their talents to purchase their freedom and ply their trade among free populations.

As the historian Henry Allen Bullock has shown, such professional permissiveness afforded slaves in personal service to slaveholders access to literacy sources like newspapers. Although slave codes strictly forbade the practice, even house slaves were sometimes given reading instruction to ensure the adequate performance of their duties. Young white and black children often associated and played together freely, with "play schools" serving as yet another source of literacy acquisition. When slaveholders provided religious instruction, it was most often for the purpose of making slaves docile and obedient rather than merely to save their souls; in this context, instruction for

the purpose of reading the Bible was actually encouraged. Other sources of information and knowledge were the oral and written narratives of fugitive slaves, which found their way into popular consumption through antislavery publications and public lectures. Further, these accounts would play an important role in the edifying aspects of the Underground Railroad.

Educative Function of the Underground Railroad. The Underground Railroad was a systematic effort by both blacks and whites to aid fugitive slaves in their escape from the South to the North and sometimes to Canada. The most well-traveled routes were a northeastern corridor, from Maryland's Eastern Shore through Delaware and Pennsylvania, and midwestern routes through border states such as Indiana and Ohio that terminated in Canada. Within the loosely connected network, Underground Railroad conductors and volunteers provided food, clothing, shelter, identity papers, and money to fugitive slaves. They identified safe houses and often used their own homes as stations. Many black mutual aid societies and fraternal organizations were actively—but clandestinely—involved in supporting all aspects of the Underground Railroad's operation, while the Religious Society of Friends, or Quakers, and other religious groups raised money, harbored fugitives, and guided them to successive stations. Along the way, schools established by free black communities in nonslave states provided temporary refuge as well as intermittent instruction.

Antebellum schools in the Midwest accommodated the children of free blacks as well as fugitives who had fled from southern states. In Indiana, for example, free blacks and antislavery Quakers founded the Union Literary Institute in 1846 in Randolph County. Operated as a manual-labor boarding school, pupils worked to pay off part of their expenses. Situated on property donated by free black farmers and white Quakers, the institution relied on income from the cultivation of land, monetary donations from a nearby black community, student tuition, and in-kind gifts. In 1847 tuition fees ranged from $2.67 to $5 per term, while board was $1 per week. Students were expected to supply an ax, a spade, and some of the furnishings for their rooms. In 1850, one hundred thirty-one students were enrolled, of whom ninety-seven were black. Although proportionately more boys than girls were enrolled, the institute was an early example of a coeducational as well as multiracial school.

There is some evidence, as presented in the Underground Railroad activist Levi Coffin's *Reminiscences* (1876), to suggest that the Union Literary Institute also served as a station on the Underground Railroad. At least two fugitives mentioned by Coffin attended the school for short periods as they waited for the opportunity to make

Sea Island School No. 1, St. Helena Island, South Carolina, established in April 1862. This illustration appeared in "Education among the Freedman," a broadside of the Pennsylvania Freedmen's Relief Commission, c. 1866–1870. In a caption, three teachers were named: Laura M. Towne, Ellen Murray, and Harriot W. Ruggles. (Library of Congress.)

their way to Canada. Manual labor was a prominent feature of this and other schools for blacks, prefiguring the educational philosophy of Booker T. Washington. Students who were fourteen years of age or older were required to perform four hours of manual labor each day. Their work consisted of performing chores related to the operation of the farm, as well as digging ditches, chopping wood, and building school facilities. Although studies were typically rudimentary, newspaper advertisements indicated that there were opportunities for exposure to more advanced subjects, such as physiology, chemistry, and natural philosophy. After the passage of the Fugitive Slave Law of 1850, however, free black communities in the Midwest and fleeing slaves were less likely to take advantage of such opportunities. The next advances in black educational history—and southern educational history in general—would occur as a result of the Emancipation Proclamation.

Freedmen's Bureau and Northern Missionaries. Anticipating the effects of the Emancipation Proclamation, General William T. Sherman called for assistance on the part of whites "to relieve the government of a burden that may hereafter become unsupportable. . . . A suitable system of cultivation and instruction must be combined with one providing for physical wants." Indeed, religious and other benevolent societies answered the call; convinced of the power of education to save souls, transform lives, and ensure freedom, such societies were committed to the need for a freedmen's school system. To meet this need, over thirty ecclesiastical freedmen's aid societies were formed.

Such efforts were led by the American Missionary Association, which had been organized in 1846 for the purpose of operating Christian missions and educational institutions at home and abroad. Other prominent groups contributing to black education included the Baptist Church (in the North), the Freedmen's Aid Society, and the General Conference of the Methodist Episcopal Church. While their primary efforts were concentrated on making freedpersons self-sufficient, education was instrumental to attaining that goal. Northern teachers joined the ranks of educators who had started schools for blacks during the war in response to calls for such by Union generals. The first of these schools opened at Fortress Monroe, in Virginia, in September 1861, under the leadership of Mary Peake, whose mother was black. Her school was the first black school in a slave state to have the legal authority and relative protection of the Union army. In 1862, under the auspices of the Port Royal Experiment, of South Carolina, the New England Freedmen's Society and the Union army collaborated on labor programs and organized schools in several southern states.

In 1865 the U.S. Congress passed an act creating the Bureau of Refugees, Freedmen, and Abandoned Lands—commonly known as the Freedmen's Bureau—which placed recently emancipated blacks under the special protection of the Union army. The Freedmen's Bureau supported the efforts of both aid societies and blacks in general that had been implemented before the war had begun. It gave schools an economic foundation and nominally protected newly arrived "Yankee schoolmarms" from physical harm; black as well as white northern women went south to preach the gospel of education, where they worked in the deplorable conditions of the devastated region and confronted the hatred of white southerners. The bureau also functioned as an organizing mechanism for the numerous aid societies operating throughout the South.

The curricula in freedmen's schools were rudimentary, typically including only reading, writing, arithmetic, and geography. The ultimate goal of the schools was to provide a full classical curriculum, like those found in New England schools. The middle-class values instilled in the commonly used *McGuffey's Readers* permeated lessons with warnings about cleanliness, godliness, the value of hard work, and the dignity and discipline of the manual arts. Charlotte Forten, perhaps the best known of black northern teachers, worked at Port Royal from 1862 to 1864. She was the granddaughter of James Forten, a radical abolitionist and free black who became wealthy as a sailmaker in Philadelphia. In addition to the teachers who were affiliated with aid societies, some former slaves taught in schools independent of the freedmen's societies. Eventually, black teachers graduated from freedmen's schools and took the places of northern teachers, most of whom returned home.

Black self-determination provoked a struggle for the control of their schools that would continue throughout the nineteenth century. The African Civilization Society, the African Methodist Episcopal Church, the Consolidated American Baptist Missionary Convention, and others had all taken up educational work in addition to their primary missions; other groups had been created specifically to aid freedmen's education. Operating between 1865 and 1870, the Freedmen's Bureau resented the tendency of freedmen to send their children to black-controlled private schools rather than to the less expensive northern, white-dominated schools. Eventually, white-controlled, public educational institutions in the South would exert control over black educational initiatives. Nevertheless, in every phase of the development of their educational system, the freedmen carried their share of the burden. They contributed $672,989 in taxes and tuition through the Freedmen's Bureau and donated approximately $500,000 through church organizations. By 1865 fourteen southern states had established 575 schools, employing 1,171 teachers for the 71,779 black and white children in regular attendance. Leading the effort were the states of Louisiana, Virginia, and North Carolina.

In addition to tuition and subscriptions, freedmen directly aided education-oriented societies by providing buildings and land, room and board, homes for teachers, fuel, books, and teachers' salaries, in part or in whole. Black teachers, school boards, and schools, after all, fostered race pride. As Frederick Douglass declared at the dedication of the Douglass Institute, an entirely black-owned and black-controlled school in Baltimore, "The mission of the Institution and that of the colored race are identical. . . . It is to teach the true idea of manly independence and self-respect." Through such institutions, blacks gained, in addition to the liberating aspects of education, practical knowledge and the skills necessary to protect themselves from victimization. The mid-nineteenth century would also mark the entrance of educational philanthropic foundations into the southern black educational system. As a result of this combination of factors, school attendance for blacks increased during the mid-nineteenth century but lagged considerably behind that of whites.

Beginnings of Educational Philanthropy. The first educational fund established through industrial philanthropy was created in 1867, when George Peabody entrusted a board of northern and southern white trustees with resources to be used "for the improvement of education among the poorer classes of the South without regard to race." The Peabody Fund granted scholarships to students who were studying to be teachers and promoted an educational philosophy that "sought to apply science to the industrial pursuits of man." While the fund's efforts on behalf of the common schools of the South contributed to the permanent system of education, black schools received disproportionately fewer resources than white schools.

The John F. Slater Fund was the first to be devoted exclusively to black education. Established in 1882, it benefited institutions of higher learning as well as public school systems. Of primary concern to Slater was the promotion of self-help among blacks. The fund's main objectives were to provide more normal work, that is, teacher preparation, and industrial work, such as training in carpentry, masonry, and agricultural pursuits, in black schools and colleges and to establish black training schools throughout the South. The Slater Fund initially provided support for extant black colleges in the rural South that best typified the Hampton-Tuskegee, or vocational-industrial, model.

By 1867 the Freedmen's Bureau stipulated that in order to obtain bureau aid, black communities had to acquire land to be held in trust and raise sufficient additional funds to construct schoolhouses and pay teachers' board. Only then would the bureau provide additional building supplies and arrange for teachers through the auspices of aid societies. Failure of communities to take part in the establishment of educational facilities meant that bureau aid would be withheld. Although the influence of northern educational philanthropic funds would not be fully realized until the turn of the century, the Freedmen's Bureau had established a precedent with its policy of demanding matching funds that would be followed by northern industrial foundations working in the South, such as the Julius Rosenwald Fund, which was chartered in 1917 but had begun functioning much earlier, and the General Education Board, which operated between 1902 and 1960.

Despite the financial burden placed upon blacks by such policies, the case of the state of Virginia illustrates the participation of freedmen with respect to meeting their educational needs. In Virginia freedmen had paid for 153 plots and schoolhouses by 1870; the costs for land, buildings, and subscriptions for the support of the schools exceeded $83,000 between 1866 and 1870. Freedmen also shouldered a substantial share of the costs in money, time, resources, and energy despite the fact that they were by and large living meager existences as sharecroppers and tenant farmers. Records from 1867 show that freedmen in Louisiana, Tennessee, and Virginia sustained forty-six schools entirely, contributed to the support of forty-two others, and had purchased thirty-three buildings—all through their own resources.

Black Higher Education. Although the educational progress of the southern states was uneven, a system of public education that was designed to meet the needs of freedpersons eventually emerged throughout the region by the late 1860s and 1870s. Already convinced of the need for common schools, black and white southerners alike began to turn their attention to the production of black leadership and a black professional class. Benevolent societies aided by the Freedmen's Bureau started to establish postsecondary institutions, often referred to as historically black colleges and universities or traditionally black institutions. The goal of missionary philanthropists was to produce, through a classical-liberal education, college-prepared leadership that could rise above the conditions of slavery and the de facto caste system. Missionary philanthropists blamed slavery, rather than innate inferiorities, for the incidental presence of undesirable moral and social values on the part of some blacks. They were joined by black religious denominations that agreed that the inculcation of New England values through a classical-liberal education was essential to the formation of a black professional class and black leadership.

Higher education manifested itself according to four different governance and organizational types. Among the first higher education institutions to be founded by northern whites, with the cooperation of churches, missionary organizations, and philanthropists, were some of the most well-known historically black institutions, such as Howard University, Fisk University, Spelman College, Tuskegee Normal and Industrial Institute (now Tuskegee University), and Hampton Normal and Agricultural Institute. Established in 1865 by the American Missionary Association and the Western Freedmen's Aid Commission of Cincinnati, Fisk University was named for General Clinton Bowen Fisk, of the Freedmen's Bureau. While the instructional programs of the Hampton and Tuskegee institutes were vocational in nature, universities such as Fisk and Howard offered liberal arts and professional curricula in medicine and law.

The second type among black institutions of higher education was privately supported colleges and universities founded under the ownership and control of northern white denomination boards, such as the Board of Education of the Methodist Episcopal Church, the American Baptist Home Mission Society, and the American Missionary Association. These institutions, which included Shaw University and the colleges of Bethune-Cookman, Rust, Morehouse, and Talladega, initially stressed instruction in the liberal arts and sciences, theological and religious training, and, eventually, teacher training.

The third type of black institutions was private colleges owned and governed by black denominational church organizations or conferences; a number of such colleges were founded between 1870 and 1890, which period marked the beginning of efforts by blacks themselves, whether independently or in conjunction with other groups, to establish and administer their own colleges. With the exception of Wilberforce, the colleges were owned, administered, and financed by blacks, and their teaching forces were composed entirely of blacks. Wilberforce, the nation's oldest private historically black college, was exceptional in being located in the North, in Ohio, and operated by whites. Founded in 1856 by the Methodist Episcopal Church, it was purchased in 1863 by the American Methodist Episcopal Church. Examples from this category also include Miles, Morris Brown, and Paul Quinn colleges. The last category of black institutions of higher education comprised state land-grant colleges as well as schools for teacher training.

The interest in black higher education on the part of the U.S. government was evidenced by the passage of the Morrill Acts. The original Morrill Act of 1862 charged land-grant colleges with the mission of serving the agricultural and industrial classes through the provision of scientific courses of study. That act set aside thirty thou-

Hampton Institute, a class in ancient history, photographed in the 1890s by Frances Benjamin Johnston. The topic is Egypt; the students—male and female—are African Americans and Native Americans. (Library of Congress.)

sand acres of public land per each state senator and representative and provided federal funding toward the establishment of those institutions. The second Morrill Act, passed in 1890, provided for "the more complete endowment and maintenance of colleges for the benefit of agriculture and the mechanic arts," with specific reference to those colleges established through the earlier act. While the Morrill Act of 1890 prohibited appropriations to any college where a distinction of race or color was made in the admissions policy, it was in accordance with the ruling in *Plessy v. Ferguson* (1896) in that it allowed for the establishment of separate colleges for white and black students "if the funds received in such state or territory be equitably divided." Examples of publicly controlled and supported black land-grant and normal institutions included North Carolina College for Negroes,

Winston-Salem Teachers College, Cheyney Training School for Teachers, and Florida Agricultural and Mechanical College. Despite the educational progress of the nineteenth century, white resistance took aim at education's greatest promises, namely, those of liberation and equal rights.

Retrenchment. After 1865 a new system of black codes replaced the elapsed slave codes of the South. Among other impositions, states placed taxes on blacks for the establishment and maintenance of black schools. Owing to Congressional Reconstruction, some blacks were able to write into state constitutions the basic educational ideals for which black delegates and their supporters had fought. By 1870 white southerners were permitting the education of blacks, but they rejected the idea that this should be done at public expense; those southerners who accepted the idea of public education for whites opposed the mixed-school policies that had been adopted by some states. Although the seed of education for blacks had taken root, another had also been planted that would have far-reaching educational and social consequences: the philosophy that blacks should be trained in a manner consistent with their collective social position. White southerners would find support for this idea in northern industrial philanthropists, who would become known as the architects of black education in the South during the post-Reconstruction era.

The Compromise of 1877 restored the South to parity with other regions and freed it from northern intervention in southern race relations. By that year each southern state had developed some form of school system through the work of benevolent societies and the Freedmen's Bureau. The South could boast of 2,677 schools, 3,300 teachers, and almost 150,000 students in regular attendance. During the end of the 1870s, however, standardized racial segregation arose and prompted the formulation of educational systems aimed at perpetuating the social order. The industrial philanthropists who began to focus their attention on black education in the 1880s emphasized the Hampton-Tuskegee model, whereby industrial education is offered at the college level, and opposed professional education, with the exception of training for health and social-service personnel to serve the black community. Comfortable with the ideology of the emerging dual system, industrial philanthropists were convinced that they could contribute to southern education irrespective of issues of racial inequality. As such, black institutions like Fisk University were forced to subvert the liberal-classical curriculum or risk the loss of funding.

The debate over a "special education" for blacks would continue into the twentieth century, as prominently fanned by the rhetoric of the black leaders Booker T. Washington and W. E. B. Du Bois. In a conversation with Harriet Beecher Stowe in 1853, after the publication of *Uncle Tom's Cabin* (1851–1852), Frederick Douglass expressed his opinion that economic self-determination necessarily preceded all other accomplishments. Opposed to both "purely educational institutions" and the "ordinary industrial school," Douglass posited institutions in which black youths would learn trades as well as literacy and numeracy:

> We must become mechanics; we must build as well as live in houses; we must make as well as use furniture; we must construct bridges as well as pass over them, before we can properly live or be respected by our fellow men. We need mechanics as well as ministers. We need workers in iron, clay, and leather. We have orators, authors, and other professional men, but these reach only a certain class, and get respect for our race

in certain select circles. To live here as we ought we must fasten ourselves to our countrymen through their everyday, cardinal wants. (Douglass, *Life and Times*, p. 288)

In 1870 less than 10 percent of black children in the South were attending school. By 1890 that number had risen to nearly 40 percent. In addition, by 1890 the percentage of literate blacks aged twenty-five years and older in southern states had increased to 41.8 percent, and almost half the South's black population aged ten years and older was literate. Finally, from 1868 to 1884 fewer than 500 blacks graduated from college, but the numbers increased dramatically. In 1876 alone 137 graduated, from 1885 to 1899 almost 1,000 would graduate, and by 1900 that number would rise to 1,883. The foundation that had been laid for black education resulted in a public elementary-school system serving southern black and white children alike—however unequally. In addition, historically black colleges and universities dotted the southern landscape, and their graduates would eventually use their education to challenge de jure segregation in both schools and society at large.

[*See also* American Missionary Association; Antislavery Press; Auld Family; Bible; Entrepreneurs; Black Church; Black Press; Black Uplift; Canada; Civil Rights; Discrimination; Douglass, Frederick; Economic Life; Emancipation Proclamation; Fisk, Clinton Bowen; Forten, James; Free African Americans before the Civil War (North); Free African Americans before the Civil War (South); Freedmen; Freedmen's Bureau; Fugitive Slave Law of 1850; Garrison, William Lloyd; Howard University; Integration; Literature; Methodist Episcopal Church; Oberlin College; Reconstruction; Religion and Slavery; *Roberts v. City of Boston*; Rochester, New York; Russwurm, John Brown; Segregation; Sharecropping; Society of Friends (Quakers); Stowe, Harriet Beecher; Supreme Court; *Uncle Tom's Cabin*; Underground Railroad; Voting Rights; *and* Washington, Booker T.]

BIBLIOGRAPHY

Anderson, James D. *The Education of Blacks in the South, 1860–1935*. Chapel Hill: University of North Carolina Press, 1988.

Bullock, Henry Allen. *A History of Negro Education in the South: From 1619 to the Present*. Cambridge, MA: Harvard University Press, 1967.

Butchart, Ronald E. *Northern Schools, Southern Blacks, and Reconstruction: Freedmen's Education, 1862–1875*. Westport, CT: Greenwood, 1980.

Coffin, Levi. *Reminiscences of Levi Coffin, the Reputed President of the Underground Railroad*. Richmond, IN: Friends United Press, 2001.

Douglass, Frederick. *Life and Times of Frederick Douglass: His Early Life as a Slave, His Escape from Bondage, and His Complete History* (1892). New York: Collier, 1962.

Douglass, Frederick. *My Bondage and My Freedom* (1855). New York: Penguin, 2003.

Litwack, Leon F. *North of Slavery: The Negro in the Free States, 1790–1860*. Chicago: University of Chicago Press, 1961.

Woodson, Carter G. *The Education of the Negro prior to 1861.* Salem, NH: Ayer, 1991.

—JAYNE R. BEILKE

ELAW, ZILPHA (b. ca. 1790; d. ?), itinerant evangelist. Born in a small community outside of Philadelphia, Zilpha Elaw was one of her parents' three surviving children. When her mother died in childbirth with her twenty-second child, Elaw was placed by her father with a Quaker family, where she remained between the ages of twelve and eighteen. She found herself disturbed by the silence of the Quaker mode of worship, having been raised in a family whose worship involved shouting and singing. She became increasingly drawn to the emotional appeal of evangelical Protestants and began proselytizing in the areas near Philadelphia after the death of her father around 1804. In particular, Elaw experienced conversion following a vision of being visited by Jesus while she was milking a cow. She described him standing in white with his arms stretched open to receive her. She experienced visions throughout her life; they became a source of her critiques of racism, sexism, and slavery.

In 1808 Elaw joined the Methodist Episcopal Society in Philadelphia. Two years later she married Joseph Elaw and moved to Burlington, New Jersey; they had one daughter. At one point, Joseph was expelled from the Methodist Episcopal Society, and he encouraged Zilpha to renounce her religion. She resisted, and their marriage was severely strained as a result.

In 1819 Elaw attended a weeklong revival and camp meeting at which she describes, in the memoir she would later write, receiving "sanctification" upon falling into a trance and seeing "by the light of the Holy Ghost, that my heart and soul were rendered completely spotless—and clean as a white sheet of paper." She was impressed at the lack of hierarchies at the revival: "both high and low, rich and poor, white and colored, all drank out of the living streams which flowed from the City of our God." At this meeting she gave her first public exhortation; with support and encouragement from the other women in attendance, she became an itinerant evangelist.

After her husband's death in 1823, both Elaw and her daughter were forced to find work as domestics in order to support themselves. Caring for the children of a white family, she became incensed that black children were barred from attending public schools. She opened a school for black children, which she ran for two years, until she felt that she was called by the Lord to the preach the Gospel. She traveled widely, preaching with a community of evangelists, including Jarena Lee. Despite being a member of the African Methodist Episcopal Society, she never preached under the auspices of a religious organization.

Elaw preached in the northeastern and mid-Atlantic states and also made trips in 1828 and 1839 to preach in the slaveholding states of Maryland and Virginia and in Washington, D.C., to both white and black converts. She claimed, "the pride of a white skin is a bauble of great value with many in some parts of the United States." Her message was a radical one of community and social equality in which the "high born [are removed] out of the midst of thee" and "the afflicted and poor people" are elevated. She counted herself as "one of the sons of God," and spoke of her "inner man." In 1840 she undertook travel to central England, as she believed that God had ordained her for more than what she had thus far undertaken in life. In England she recorded her *Memoirs of the Life, Religious Experience, and Ministerial Travels and Labours of Mrs. Zilpha Elaw, an American Female of Colour.* She returned to the United States in 1845, and her memoirs were published the following year. There is no record of her later years or death.

[*See also* African Methodist Episcopal Church; Autobiography; Education; Lee, Jarena; Religion; *and* Society of Friends (Quakers) and African Americans.]

BIBLIOGRAPHY

Andrews, William L., ed. *Sisters of the Spirit: Three Black Women's Autobiographies of the Nineteenth Century.* Bloomington: Indiana University Press, 1986.

Hine, Darlene, and Kathleen Thompson. *A Shining Thread of Hope: The History of Black Women in America.* New York: Broadway Books, 1998.

Moody, Joycelyn. *Sentimental Confessions: Spiritual Narratives of Nineteenth-Century African American Women.* Athens: University of Georgia Press, 2001.

—STACEY PAMELA PATTON

ELDRIDGE, ELLEANOR (b. 26 March 1785; d. c. 1845), pioneer businesswoman. Elleanor Eldridge was the last of seven daughters of Robin Eldridge, an African native, and Hannah Prophet, a Native American. The young Robin Eldridge was captured along with his entire family and brought to the United States to be sold as a slave. Later, in exchange for service in the American Revolution, he and his brothers were promised their freedom and two hundred acres of land. Though they were granted their freedom as promised, they were paid for their services in the worthless old continental currency and were therefore never able to claim any land. They did, however, eventually save enough money to purchase a small plot in Warwick, Rhode Island, where they built a house. Elleanor Eldridge was born free in Warwick.

When Eldridge was ten, her mother died, and against her father's wishes she went to work for her mother's employers, Joseph and Elleanor Baker. Eldridge was Mrs. Baker's namesake and a favorite of the Bakers, who paid her twenty-five cents a week to perform tasks such as spinning, weaving, and housework. She became a skilled weaver by the age of fourteen and was adept at arithmetic. At sixteen she hired out to work for the family of the captain Benjamin Greene as a spinner and later as a dairymaid, becoming an expert in the production of premium quality cheeses. She continued to work for Captain Greene until his death in 1812, leaving only briefly in 1803 after the death of her father to travel to Adams, Massachusetts; there, she sought the help of an aunt in acquiring the letters of administration necessary to allow her to settle her father's estate.

After Greene's death she returned to Adams, Massachusetts, to live with her sister Lettise. The two sisters began a business weaving, laundering, and soap making. They were so successful that after three years Eldridge had saved enough money to purchase a lot and build a house, which she rented out for forty dollars a year.

In 1815 Eldridge moved to Providence, Rhode Island, where another sister resided, and began a painting and wallpapering business. She supplemented this income during the winter by hiring out for domestic work to both private and business concerns. Within seven years she was able to purchase another lot and build a house large enough for her to live in one side and rent out the other. Within five years she had purchased two more lots and a house in Warwick, Rhode Island, by taking out a loan of $240 at 10 percent interest. She agreed to renew the note annually and with a $500 down payment purchased a $2,000 home.

In 1831 Eldridge contracted typhus for the second time in her life. Though she recovered, she relapsed during a visit to Massachusetts, and rumors began to circulate in Providence that she had died. Eldridge returned to Providence after several months of recovery to discover that her tenants had been evicted and her property auctioned off to pay the note.

In January 1837 Eldridge entered a lawsuit before the court of common pleas in Providence for trespass and ejectment because the auction had not been advertised and neither she nor her family had been notified of the impending sale of her properties. Though she lost the lawsuit, she was allowed to recover the property after a payment of $2,700, since there was no record of the advertisement of the sale. Supporters commented that no such action would have been taken against a white man or woman.

The antislavery author Frances H. Green wrote the *Memoirs of Elleanor Eldridge* in 1838. It is one of the few narratives of a free black woman.

[*See also* American Revolution; Entrepreneurs; Free African Americans to 1828; Military; *and* Women.]

BIBLIOGRAPHY

Green, Frances H. *Memoirs of Eleanor Eldridge*. Providence, RI: B.T. Albro, 1838. http://docsouth.unc.edu/neh/eldridge/eldridge.html.

Hine, Darlene Clark, and Kathleen Thompson. *A Shining Thread of Hope: The History of Black Women in America*. New York: Broadway Books, 1998.

Loewenberg, Bert James, and Ruth Bogin, eds. *Black Women in Nineteenth-Century American Life: Their Words, Their Thoughts, Their Feelings*. University Park: Pennsylvania State University Press, 1976.

—STACEY PAMELA PATTON

Elleanor Eldridge. *Memoirs of Elleanor Eldridge*, 1838, by the antislavery author Frances H. Green, is one of the few narratives of a free black woman. This picture of Eldridge was the frontispiece. (Duke University, Rare Books, Manuscripts, and Special Collections Library.)

ELECTION OF 1860. The election of 1860 was the most important in American history. It was perhaps even more important for blacks than for whites. The central issue of the campaign was the future of slavery in the federal territories and the nature of the Union itself. The outcome set the stage for secession, civil war, and, most important, an end to slavery. Four parties competed for the presidency. Frederick Douglass clearly understood that the fate of the nation was at stake. During a speech delivered in Geneva, New York, on 1 August 1860 he told the crowd:

> Slavery is the real issue—the single bone of contention between all parties and sections. It is the one disturbing force, and explains the confused and irregular motion of our political machine. Every thoughtful man who goes to the ballot box this fall will go there either to help or hinder slavery, or with the idea of neither helping nor hindering slavery. (Blassingame, p. 376)

Four Parties Competed. The Democrats nominated Stephen A. Douglas of Illinois. A classic northern Democrat, Douglas had almost always supported the interests of the South. In 1854 he had sponsored the Kansas-Nebraska Act, which had repealed most of the Missouri Compromise's ban on slavery in the territories. Under the act the settlers of a territory were allowed to decide whether they wanted slavery, under a theory known as popular sovereignty. In his famous debates with Lincoln in the 1858 senatorial race, Douglas had insisted that he did not care whether slavery was voted "up or down" in the territories. He consistently supported the Fugitive Slave Law of 1850 and defended the Supreme Court's 1857 decision to uphold slavery in the *Dred Scott* case. Despite this long record of supporting the South on most issues involving slavery, Douglas did not have the support of most of the southern wing of the party. In the two years before the election Douglas refused to endorse the idea of a federal slave code for the territories.

More important, he had refused to support the admission of Kansas to the Union under the fraudulently adopted Lecompton Constitution. Douglas may not have cared if the settlers of a territory voted slavery up or down, but he did think that the vote should be fair and that only bona fide settlers should cast ballots. A convention held in the Kansas town of Lecompton wrote a constitution allowing slavery in the new state. The constitutional convention was not even remotely representative of the people in the territory. Furthermore, the vote to ratify the constitution was tainted by bogus ballots and fraudulent voters who went to Kansas from Missouri solely to vote for slavery. Because of this, Douglas refused to support Kansas statehood.

In April 1860 the Democrats held their convention in Charleston, South Carolina. However, a number of delegates from the Deep South bolted the convention to prevent Douglas's nomination. The convention reconvened on 18 June in Baltimore, and Douglas was nominated along with his running mate, Hershel Johnson. Although he was from the Deep South state of Georgia, Johnson supported Douglas's position on popular sovereignty and

was representative of the significant support Douglas held in southern states, despite the departure of most of the southern delegates.

Delegates from the Deep South who had left the April convention also met in Baltimore in June and nominated John C. Breckinridge of Kentucky to run for president. The platform of this second Democratic Party called for a slave code for the territories and the annexation or purchase of Cuba, which would have provided more slaves and more land for slavery to expand. Breckinridge was from the Upper South and had some support outside that region. His running mate was Senator Joseph Lane of Oregon, who represented both the North and the West.

At a convention in Chicago the Republican Party nominated a dark horse, Abraham Lincoln of Illinois. Lincoln had limited political experience: a number of terms in the Illinois legislature and one term in the House of Representatives. However, he had ably debated Douglas in the 1858 senatorial race, and he was the party's most articulate critic of the *Dred Scott* decision. Lincoln's nomination came as a surprise on the third ballot, after Senator (and the former governor) William H. Seward of New York led for the first two convention ballots. Lincoln was the nominee of the new Republican Party, which had emerged six years earlier in opposition to the Kansas-Nebraska Act. Most Republicans had come out of the defunct Whig Party, although a significant number, including Salmon P. Chase of Ohio and Charles Sumner of Massachusetts, had been antislavery Democrats or Free-Soilers earlier in their careers. This was the first "sectional" party in the nation. Except for a few delegates from the Upper South and Texas, the Republican Party was entirely a northern organization. Lincoln, the westerner from Illinois, balanced his ticket not with a southerner but with Hannibal Hamlin, a former Democrat who, as a senator from Maine, gave the ticket eastern representation. The party's platform denounced the *Dred Scott* decision, opposed adding any new slave states to the Union, and demanded the admission of Kansas as a free state.

The fourth party in the race was even newer than the Republicans. Formed just for the 1860 election, the Constitutional Union Party nominated Senator John Bell of Tennessee and Edward Everett of Massachusetts. This party tried to ignore the entire issue of slavery in the territories and stood for the enforcement of existing federal laws.

Lincoln Succeeds; Southern States Secede. There were essentially two elections. In the North, Lincoln, Douglas, and Bell competed for votes. Lincoln carried all of the northern states, although New Jersey divided its electoral votes between Lincoln and Douglas. The greater population of the North meant that Lincoln did not need to carry

"The Rail Candidate," cartoon of 1860, probably by Louis Maurer, printed by Currier and Ives. Abraham Lincoln is straddling a rail symbolizing the Republicans' antislavery plank and his own backwoods origin. The white man holding one end of the rail is Horace Greeley, who carries in a pocket a copy of his newspaper, the New York *Tribune*. (Library of Congress.)

any electoral votes in the South to win. With 1,866,453 popular votes—almost all in the free states—Lincoln carried eighteen northern states and 180 electoral votes. This gave him a substantial electoral majority and a plurality of the popular vote. Douglas, Bell, and Breckinridge competed in the South. Breckinridge carried eleven southern states and won 72 electoral votes, but he had only 847,953 popular votes. Bell carried three states and won 39 electoral votes. His popular vote was the smallest of the three candidates, a mere 590,631. Douglas, on the other hand, had the fewest electoral votes (12) because he carried only one state (Missouri) and won three electors from New Jersey. However, he ran second in the popular vote, with 1,375,157 votes, the result of his vigorous campaigning across the nation.

Throughout the campaign southerners hinted that they would leave the Union if Lincoln was elected. Thus, Breckinridge billed himself as the candidate who could hold the Union together. His claim was true enough, but his campaign also implied that the Union would be secure only

if the South were in control of the government. Lincoln did not believe that the South would actually leave the Union as a result of his election. However, once the election was over, southerners began to act on their threats. By the end of December, South Carolina had called a secession convention and formally declared itself out of the Union. By the time Lincoln was inaugurated on 4 March 1861, six other states, all from the Deep South, had officially left the Union. These states seceded because they believed, or at least claimed to believe, that Lincoln and his administration would threaten slavery. In a desperate effort to preserve the Union the lame-duck Congress proposed a constitutional amendment—what would have been the Thirteenth Amendment—to guarantee that slavery could never be abolished by the national government. The states of the Deep South were not interested in this amendment, or any other compromises. They wanted to leave the Union and create their own southern nation.

In his inaugural address Lincoln reiterated what he had said throughout the campaign, declaring, "I have no purpose, directly or indirectly, to interfere with the institution of slavery in the States where it exists. I believe I have no lawful right to do so and I have no inclination to do so." This position dovetailed with accepted views of slavery and the Constitution. No serious legal scholars or politicians at the time believed that the national government could interfere with slavery in the states. However, Lincoln's position also made it clear that the Republicans were not going to back away from the pledge to prevent the spread of slavery into the territories. This meant that in the long run the South would steadily lose political power to an increasing number of free states. Lincoln pleaded for the seven wayward states to return to the Union, promising to take no actions against them if they did. He pointed out that they had taken "no oath registered in heaven to destroy the government," while Lincoln had taken "the most solemn one to 'preserve, protect, and defend'" the Union and the Constitution. Appealing to history and patriotism, to "the mystic chords of memory, stretching from every battle-field and patriot grave," he begged the South to return to the Union. But his plea fell on deaf ears.

While Lincoln had pledged "not to assail" the southern states, the new Confederate nation would not wait for Lincoln to act. Just over a month after his inauguration Confederate troops began shelling U.S. solders at Fort Sumter, in the harbor of Charleston, South Carolina. This led Lincoln to call for volunteers to defend the nation, which in turn led four Upper South states—Virginia, North Carolina, Tennessee, and Arkansas—to secede.

African Americans and the Election. For blacks the election of 1860 raised both hopes and anxieties. African Americans could vote in all the New England states except Connecticut, and those with a small amount of property could vote in New York. In the rest of the North blacks were political outsiders, observers of the electoral process but never part of it. Nevertheless, the 1860 election mattered to blacks, and in the North they followed it. From the perspective of African Americans there was almost no difference between the two Democratic candidates, Douglas and Breckinridge. Both supported slavery, the *Dred Scott* decision, and the complete subordination of free blacks. The same was true for the Constitutional Union Party. It was dedicated to supporting the political and constitutional status quo. That meant upholding *Dred Scott* and enforcing the Fugitive Slave Law. With a slaveholder at the head of the ticket and a northern conservative for vice president, the Constitutional Unionists had nothing to offer African Americans.

The Republicans, on the other hand, were far more complicated. As Lincoln said in his inaugural speech, the Republicans were not intent on touching slavery where it existed. The Republican Party was not an abolitionist party. In fact, some Republicans were unsympathetic to black civil rights in the North. On the other hand, the Republican Party was the first significant political organization in the nation's history to take an uncompromising stand against the spread of slavery. While the party at least officially did not oppose the Fugitive Slave Law, many of its leaders did. Salmon P. Chase, who had the third-highest number of convention votes when Lincoln gained the nomination, was known as the Attorney General for Fugitive Slaves. He was a stalwart friend of free blacks and fugitive slaves throughout the North. The man who ran second to Lincoln in the convention, William H. Seward, had also defended fugitive slaves and protected free blacks during his tenure as governor of New York. In an 1850 speech Seward had declared that there was "a higher law" than the Constitution that supported opponents of slavery. Chase, who became Lincoln's secretary of the treasury; Seward, who served as secretary of state; and Hamlin, Lincoln's running mate, were committed opponents of slavery, longtime critics of the fugitive slave laws, and well known as friends of African Americans. So, too, were other leading Republicans, like Senator Charles Sumner and Governor John Andrew in Massachusetts, Congressman Thaddeus Stevens of Pennsylvania, and most of the leaders of the Ohio party, including Senator Ben Wade and Congressman John Bingham. As Frederick Douglass observed in his third autobiography, *Life and Times of Frederick Douglass* (1881, 1892), "The lines between these parties and candidates were about as clearly drawn as political lines are capable of being drawn."

Lincoln was one of the Republican Party's most conservative leaders, but all who knew him understood his deep personal hatred for slavery. Moreover, even as a conservative within his party, Lincoln was the most antislavery candidate ever to run for the presidency on a major party ticket. In the summer of 1860 Senator Charles Sumner gave a four-hour Senate speech titled "The Barbarism of Slavery." Frederick Douglass printed the entire speech in his paper, praising it as the strongest antislavery speech ever given in the Senate. Whatever doubts many black leaders had about Lincoln, they understood that the core of the Republican Party in 1860 opposed slavery. Indeed, for the first time since the demise of the Federalist Party, blacks had a political party they could support and join. Not surprisingly, where they could vote, most blacks supported the Republican ticket. Frederick Douglass might have preferred Chase or Seward to lead the ticket, but he cast his ballot for Lincoln. He later wrote in *Life and Times*, "Into this contest I threw myself, with firmer faith and more ardent hope than ever before, and what I could by pen or voice was done with a will."

[*See also* Abolitionism; Andrew, John Albion; Black Politics; Chase, Salmon Portland; Confederate States of America; Constitution, U.S.; Democratic Party; Douglas, Stephen A.; *Dred Scott* Case; *Frederick Douglass' Paper*; Free African Americans before the Civil War (North); Free African Americans before the Civil War (South); Free-Soil Party; Fugitive Slave Law of 1793; Fugitive Slave Law of 1850; Kansas-Nebraska Act; *Life and Times of Frederick Douglass*; Lincoln, Abraham; Political Participation; Republican Party; Seward, William Henry; Slavery; Slavery and the U.S. Constitution; Stevens, Thaddeus; Sumner, Charles; *and* Whig Party.]

BIBLIOGRAPHY

Blassingame, John W., ed. *The Federick Douglass Papers*, Series 1, *Speeches, Debates, and Interviews*. Vol. 3. New Haven, CT: Yale University Press, 1985.

Douglass, Frederick. *The Life and Times of Frederick Douglass* (1892). New York: Collier, 1962.

Potter, David M. *The Impending Crisis: 1848–1861*. Completed and edited by Don E. Fehrenbacher. New York: Harper and Row, 1976.

—PAUL FINKELMAN

EMANCIPATION. [*This entry contains two subentries dealing with the emancipation of slaves from before the American Revolution through the ratification of the Emancipation Proclamation in 1865. The first article discusses the various means by which African Americans could gain freedom up to 1830, while the second article provides an overview of individual state abolitionist activity and the debate over emancipation through the Civil War.*]

Gaining Freedom from Slavery through 1830

The complex institution of slavery in North America varied greatly for the duration of its existence and throughout the continent. Most slaves yearned for freedom, but it was seldom handed to them; those who toiled throughout the development of the young American nation strove long and hard to be free.

Early New England settlers were primarily urban English families searching for religious freedom and financial prosperity. They settled on productive land that allowed them generous harvests. In addition, the sea provided an abundance of fish, and certain foodstuffs were traded to Caribbean islands. Simple economics indicated that the more labor working both land and sea, the larger the surplus. As a result, the demand for servants to assist family production grew. Workers were drawn from many sources; they included Native Americans, indentured servants from England, and slaves imported from the Caribbean or, rarely at first, from Africa.

Emancipation before the Revolution. Work was typically shared by the slaveholding family and slaves, all of whom worked together. In addition to field work, everyone cooperated in maintaining and caring for buildings, boats, equipment, and animals, producing workers with broad bases of marketable skills. A slave blacksmith, after performing labor at home, could service nearby farms for fees to be shared with his master. Many slave owners allotted plots of land on which slaves could grow their own food; their surplus was their property and could be sold or traded. This system applied to any labor done by slaves. Not all slaves were entitled to keep profits, but during the colonial and early national periods in the North, such arrangements were not uncommon. This autonomy alone gave black slaves the power to purchase freedom for themselves and others, as there was no other means to accomplish this goal.

As settlements moved south, the situation changed. Virginia was established as a single-crop agriculture colony; large farms, later plantations, were the rule. Outside of state capitals, very few cities arose, and even Annapolis and Richmond were more large towns than cities. Since most slaves lived in rural areas, there was less access to neighbors or potential customers, such that slaves had almost no way to earn money. Consequently, self-manumission was less common for slaves in these states, although it was not impossible. Those who achieved this goal tended to be skilled enough to set up their own businesses or plantations, amassing their own labor forces consisting primarily of slaves.

In Louisiana, self-purchase was possible and strictly regulated in order to protect the interests of slaves. Under Spain's rule a slave could approach his master and request self-purchase; if the owner refused to negotiate freedom, the slave had the right to petition the governor's court for a *carta de libertad*, which guaranteed freedom for the petitioner after the purchase price was paid. If the slave was sold after receiving his *carta*, it remained in effect for the next owner and was binding until the slave was free.

Another road to freedom was through the custom of freeing older slaves. If the freed slave was somewhat healthy, he might then accumulate wealth and succeed in purchasing his children. New England slaves tended to form family groups and belong to churches; family structure was strong, and this method of manumission was, if not common, certainly not unusual.

While these systems of emancipation did not prevail in all of the colonies, some accommodations were made prior to the Revolution in most of them. In New Amsterdam, where most slaves lived in the city, there was ample opportunity for slaves to earn and retain cash. The cosmopolitan atmosphere offered free blacks the opportunity to support families. Many found jobs as laborers, carters, and sailors, while others worked as merchants, cooks, or laundresses. As free black populations expanded in cities, African Americans gained employment as barbers, carpenters, dressmakers, and tailors; skills were often learned during slavery and adapted later in service occupations. Early American urban life tended to be physically integrated, with slaves, servants, and other service providers living in proximity to those they served; as such, there was very little racial or class segregation.

Sometimes slaves were manumitted for humane reasons; a slave owner might conclude that slavery was morally unsustainable and grant his or her slaves their freedom. In Virginia, manumission in this manner was under the jurisdiction of the legislature until 1782, such that individuals could not legally manumit slaves without receiving governmental permission. Other slave owners had religious principles, and as the antislavery movement grew, they acted upon them. As a result, urban Maryland and Pennsylvania, the home of many Quakers and Methodists, became the abode of many freedmen as well as slaves. Response to the labor market was also a factor affecting incidences of manumission; businessmen in 1800 were as responsive to the cost of labor as they are today.

Blacks were also simply turned out by their owners, particularly when they became unprofitable to feed and clothe; this custom was referred to as "going at large" or "half-freedom." This type of freedom was economically beneficial for the slaveholder, since the only freedom the slave had was temporary and contingent on his failure; if he proved successful in making a living, his slave status would be reactivated and his earnings confiscated. Not all owners, of course, were so self-serving; again, many willingly freed their slaves before legislation was enacted making emancipation mandatory.

Emancipation after the Revolution. The most significant releases of slaves prior to the Civil War resulted from legislative action taken by northern states following the Revolutionary War: Vermont prohibited slavery in 1777, Pennsylvania in 1780, Massachusetts in 1782, New York in 1799, and New Jersey in 1804. These legislative acts did not result in immediate freedom for all but, rather, staggered dismissal from bondage, as mitigated by such factors as age, health, and ability to earn a living and, more important, to prevent the chaos that would result from mass emancipation. By 1810 about three-quarters of all northern blacks were free; by 1830 virtually all would be. While this was the case in the North, southern slaves, of course, did not fare so well.

The American Revolution brought about several major shifts in labor relations. The supply of indentured servants dried up, leaving African slaves as the only option in terms of inexpensive labor. Concurrently, new ideas were circulating throughout the colonies, and words like *freedom* and *self-determination* became commonplace. During the colonial period, slavery laws had been enacted that governed relations between slaves and masters; when the Revolution began, British law no longer applied, and established legal protection for slaves effectively disappeared.

During the Revolution, the British promised freedom to any slaves who would bear arms against the rebels. Thousands of slaves elected to take this option; others fled their homes not to join the British but to resettle with their families in nonslave states. These two factors brought about reductions in the black populations in certain states; the reduction was estimated at about 30 percent in South Carolina, for example. In New York and Virginia slaves were permitted to serve in the Revolutionary army in their masters' stead. Maryland sanctioned armed service for slaves, and New York freed slave soldiers who served for three years. Virginia planters attempted to reenslave these substitute soldiers, but the Virginia General Assembly stepped in, ordering the immediate emancipation of veterans.

All of these changes caused major shifts in the northern labor force. Yet the loss of both indentured servants and soldier-slaves was not a major economic disaster in the North because industry, including fishing, trading, and textiles, had come to take precedence over farming; all required at least semiskilled labor. As such, it was more economically sound to pay wages to free men than to provide for slaves. Southern farmers, on the other hand, had no industries to fall back on and instead increased the size of their plantations, further institutionalizing slavery and imposing the master/subordinate philosophy into all facets of life. A wife was subordinate to her husband, a child to his parents—and the black labor force to everyone.

During the first decades following the Revolution many modifications were made relating to individual liberty. In 1808 federal legislation forbade the importation of slaves, causing the South to become entrenched in existing proslavery practices. In the North emancipation became the liberal response to the increased barbarity that arose on the cotton, tobacco, and rice plantations of the South. Since the law no longer protected slaves, extreme cruelty by owners and overseers passed for discipline, and even death was acceptable if a reasonable excuse was presented. Following the prohibition of the slave trade, the only way to legally increase the slave population was by natural increase; breeding was typically supervised, and family ties between slaves were effectively eliminated. The polarization of opinions regarding the institution of slavery festered for several decades, finally ending in the Civil War.

Before the Civil War began, slavery in the South was precariously balanced between plantation owners' total economic dependence on slave labor, the deep unrest brought about by increasingly oppressive treatment, and the awareness of these injustices by slaves. A growing white population was also becoming appalled by the cruelties of the system, as brought to their attention by vociferous abolitionists. It became more and more difficult for proslavery advocates to justify the system.

There were several private emancipation options available, particularly from Maryland northward. Before 1830, a common method of arranging emancipation for African American slaves was by will upon their owners' deaths. Although this was generally positive, it occasionally brought about hunger, if not starvation and death, to those freed. In time, legislation was passed compelling owners to retain responsibility for very young, very old, or infirm slaves, averting a burden on the general public. To the credit of many good men who saw the affront to dignity inherent in slavery, many healthy, able slaves were manumitted by will. George Washington's slaves were freed upon his death. Although it was against his most strongly avowed beliefs, Thomas Jefferson bequeathed freedom to the slave Sally Hemings's sons—who were, in fact, his own illegitimate children; in devising their freedom, he also requested that they be allowed to remain in the state of Virginia.

Ties of kinship among free blacks and slaves remained a source of private manumissions. If a free man married an enslaved wife, the man might earn money to purchase his wife as well as his children. Yet even these actions could not fully ensure freedom, as there were many kidnappers who captured freed slaves, taking them to nearby markets such as Richmond and selling them to dealers who quickly absconded with them. A free black man would be better off purchasing his family and keeping them as his own slaves in order to minimize that threat. Virginia eliminated this and other such problems by simply mandating that freed slaves had to leave the state or face reenslavement.

Colonization was also an option for African Americans from about 1817 through the late 1820s. The U.S. government established Liberia in West Africa to facilitate the deportation of blacks that might otherwise be societal burdens. Malcontents—proud men who did not take well to slavery—often found themselves on boats returning to Africa. For from Thomas Jefferson, who believed that the institution of slavery had adverse effects on free men, to the southern planters who were only too willing to be rid of troublemaking slaves, Liberia seemed the perfect answer. To some blacks, Africa, indeed, must have seemed the ultimate haven, offering a final escape from the threat of slavery.

If none of these roads to freedom was open, slaves often chose escape. This was relatively easy for a slave in Maryland, which was so close to the free states of the North. Frederick Douglass, born in Maryland and long a resident of Baltimore, traveled north by boat from the city. Since he had become literate early, he was able to forge papers that smoothed his passage; lawfully, however, he remained a slave. Only many years later did friends legally purchase his freedom. Initially, Douglass strenuously objected to this course of action because he did not wish to affirm the legal premise of slavery by doing so.

In contrast, slaves in the Deep South found reaching free territory more difficult. They had little opportunity to learn the geography of the land beyond their immediate surroundings, knowing only that by going north, they might find freedom. Certainly many more tried than succeeded. Encouragement was provided by abolitionists, as initiated by the ideals of the Quakers. The path to freedom, in time, came to be identified as the Underground Railroad, with the abolitionists who helped fugitive slaves known as conductors. With fleeing slaves passing from barn to barn, through tunnels and forests, the long road eventually ended, and they became free.

[*See also* Abolitionism; American Revolution; Black Family; Childhood; Emancipation, Gradual; Free African Americans to 1828; Hemings, Sally; Indentured Servitude; Jefferson, Thomas, on African Americans and Slavery; Kidnapping; Laws and Legislation; Manumission Societies; Murray, John (Lord Dunmore); Old Age; Religion; Segregation; Slave Trade; Slavery: Northeast; Society of Friends (Quakers) and African Americans; Urbanization; Washington, George, and African Americans; *and* Work.]

BIBLIOGRAPHY

Appleby, Joyce. *Thomas Jefferson*. New York: Times Books, 2003.

Berlin, Ira. *Many Thousands Gone: The First Two Centuries of Slavery in North America*. Cambridge, MA: Harvard University Press, 1998.

Fitzpatrick, John C., ed. *The Last Will and Testament of George Washington and Schedule of His Property* (1792). Mount Vernon, VA: Mount Vernon Ladies' Association of the Union, 1992.

Kolchin, Peter. *American Slavery, 1619–1877*. New York: Hill and Wang, 1993.

Whitman, T. Stephen. *The Price of Freedom: Slavery and Manumission in Baltimore and Early National Maryland*. Lexington: University Press of Kentucky, 1997.

—Toni Ahrens

Abolition through the Civil War

Emancipation, abolition, and manumission turned slaves into free persons. Although often used interchangeably, the three words have slightly different meanings. Emancipation came about when the state intervened to free a slave. Abolition took place when a state completely ended slavery. Manumission occurred when a master voluntarily freed a slave.

In 1776 the new United States was a slaveholding nation. Slavery was legal in every state, and slaves could be found throughout the nation. The American Revolution, particularly the ideology behind it, stimulated the end of slavery in the North. What has been called the "First Emancipation" began with the outbreak of the war, as a significant number of masters in New England allowed their male slaves to enlist in the Revolutionary army, thus not only gaining their own freedom but also fighting for the freedom of the new nation. In 1780 Pennsylvania passed a gradual abolition act, the first of its kind in history, which gradually ended slavery in that state. That same year Massachusetts abolished slavery outright in its new constitution. Both of those states, along with New York, New Hampshire, and the new state of Vermont, also allowed free black men to vote on the same basis as whites.

Over the next quarter century the rest of what became the North abolished slavery, usually through gradual abolition acts. Under the laws in question, all children of slaves were born free, though subject to an indenture, and new slaves could not be brought into the state. By 1830 the process of abolition was virtually complete. In 1790 there were over 40,000 slaves in the North; by 1830 there were only about 2,800 slaves in the region, with most— over 2,250—in New Jersey, which was the last state to pass a gradual abolition act. Except for Indiana (1816) and Illinois (1818), all of the northern states entering the Union after 1787 came in with no slaves. (Despite the Northwest Ordinance of 1787, which had banned slavery, a few slaves were held in Indiana until about 1830 and in Illinois until 1847.)

The huge drop in the number of northern slaves resulted in part from the deaths of aging slaves but also from private acts of manumission. Indeed, after the northern states passed gradual abolition statutes, support for the institution began to wane. In Pennsylvania, for example, the slave population went from 3,700 in 1790 to 1,700 in 1800 and to only 759 by 1810. New York passed a gradual abolition act in 1799, when the state had about 21,000 slaves. A decade later the state had only 15,000 slaves, and by 1820 there were only 10,000 in the state. Seven years later the state abolished the institution. Thus, when Frederick Douglass came to the North, he entered a region

"Emancipation," by Thomas Nast, engraved by King and Baird, 1865. Nast's optimistic vision of the future of free African Americans includes the vignettes at the right and center of a freedman's family gathered around a "Union" wood stove, with a picture of Lincoln on the wall. In contrast are, at the left, grim scenes of life under slavery. (Library of Congress.)

where slavery was almost nonexistent. Abolition—immediate and gradual—combined with private manumission had ended the institution there.

While abolition was taking place in the North, there was a brief, but important wave of private manumission in the South. Before the Revolution most of the southern colonies either prohibited private manumission or discouraged it. Restrictions on the mobility and opportunities available to free blacks also militated against private manumission. Nevertheless, some masters freed individual slaves for personal reasons. Those manumitted were usually the mistresses or lovers of male slave owners or the children produced by such relationships. During the Revolution a growing number of southern masters began to question the legitimacy of slave owning. Some southern masters manumitted slaves so they could serve in the Revolutionary army; they wondered what right they had to fight for their liberty while denying it to others. In 1782, responding to such sentiments, Virginia passed a law permitting private manumission, with former slaves being allowed to live in the state. In Maryland and Delaware similar sentiments and legislation led to manumission. In North Carolina and the new state of Tennessee free blacks were allowed to vote, indicating an evolving attitude toward slavery and free blacks.

In the aftermath of the Revolution the combination of ideology and religious sentiment led a few masters to take dramatic action to end their own involvement in slavery. John and Jonathan Pleasants, who together owned almost two hundred slaves, tried to manumit them in their wills. However, the men died before Virginia passed its 1782 law allowing masters to free their slaves. Robert Pleasants, the son of John and the brother of Jonathan, successfully sued all of his other relatives to enforce the wills after the 1782 law was passed. In the 1790s Robert "Councillor" Carter manumitted his more than five hundred slaves while also providing them with land and housing, which generosity Carter saw as his Christian duty. George Washington freed all his slaves in his will and provided land, and even pensions, for his former slaves. Washington hated slavery and declined to participate in its most seamy aspects, refusing "either to buy or sell slaves, 'as you would do cattle at a market.'" In 1785 Joseph Mayo, an obscure planter from Powhatan, bequeathed freedom to his 150 to 170 slaves. In 1814 Edward Coles, who had been James Madison's private secretary, took all of his slaves to Illinois, where he freed them. When he died in 1833, John Randolph of Roanoke manumitted all of his hundreds of slaves and provided money to purchase land for them in Ohio, since by that time Virginia had made it extremely difficult for freed blacks to remain in the state.

The most dramatic expansion of freedom came in Delaware and Maryland. In 1790 Maryland had only 8,043 free blacks and 103,036 slaves. The slave population grew slowly to 111,502 by 1810, when it began to decline. Part of this decline was due to the migration of masters and the interstate slave trade. Thousands of Maryland slaves ended their lives on cotton plantations in the Deep South, but thousands more lived out their lives as free people in their home state. The free black population more than doubled, to over 19,500, between 1790 and 1800. By 1830 there were over 50,000 free blacks in the state, and while the rate of growth declined, manumissions continued to increase the free population. By 1860 Maryland had 83,942 free blacks and just 87,189 slaves.

In Delaware the change was even more dramatic. There were 3,899 free blacks and 8,887 slaves in the state in 1790. Within a decade free blacks were in the majority, with 8,268 and only 6,153 slaves. By 1860 Delaware had 19,829 free blacks and just 1,798 slaves. The decreasing economic utility of slaves in the state undermined support for the institution. Thousands of slaves were sold off, but most were manumitted by masters who no longer had any strong economic interest in slavery and could not accept the idea of selling people.

As in Maryland and Delaware, the early national period saw a huge rise in the free black population in Virginia. In 1780 Virginia had an estimated free black population of 2,000. In 1782 the state allowed masters to free their slaves, and the free blacks were permitted to remain in the state. The free black population grew to 12,000 by 1790 and to 30,000 by 1810. Most of this growth was due to manumissions. In the next decade, however, the free black population grew by only 6,000, as the state made it almost impossible for freed slaves to remain in Virginia. In the 1820s the law was liberalized again, and the free black population grew by another 10,000, sitting at 46,000 in 1830. After that, growth was much slower, reflecting births among free African Americans rather than manumissions.

In the next thirty years the population grew by less than 9,000, as manumissions virtually ceased. In 1852 Virginia made it illegal for newly freed slaves to remain in the state; manumissions would also require expatriation. In 1860 there were 55,269 free blacks in the state, along with 472,494 slaves. The percentage of free blacks in the state is also illustrated in manumission rates. In 1700 free blacks were just 4.1 percent of the Virginia black population; this proportion grew to 9.3 percent by 1830. However, after 1830 the population grew much more slowly and was only 10.5 percent of the black population of the state. Kentucky, which broke off from Virginia, had a similar pattern, with less manumission over time. In 1852 the Kentucky legislature prohibited in-state manumission and required that any freed slaves be sent out of the United States altogether. By 1860 only 10,684 of the state's blacks were free, while 95.5 percent, or 225,483, were slaves.

As happened in the Chesapeake region, North Carolina witnessed a relatively rapid growth in the free black population after the Revolution. This occurred despite the fact that North Carolina prohibited private manumission, except in the case of "meritorious service." The County Courts had to approve all manumissions, although it was also possible for slaves to be freed by special acts of the legislature. After 1812 the state required the posting of a bond for every slave who was emancipated, to ensure that the former slave would not become a burden on the community. The county courts were apparently quite lenient in determining what constituted "meritorious service," and the free black population grew from 4,975 in 1790 to 19,543 by 1830. Quakers in the state created trust arrangements to acquire and free slaves or to have them held in trust in de facto freedom. Where courts had lenient notions of "meritorious service" Quakers helped numerous slaves gain their freedom. Between 1824 and 1826, for example, more than 2,000 slaves were manumitted in the state. After 1830 the growth was much less rapid, and by 1860 the free African American population had increased to only 30,463. This was in part a result of laws requiring that any manumitted slave leave the state; this growth of fewer than 11,000 people in thirty years could be accounted for mostly by natural increase. In 1861 the state prohibited manumission by will.

South Carolina had had a tradition of manumission, especially involving the mistresses of masters and their children. There were about 1,800 free blacks in the state in 1790 and over 6,800 by 1820. After that, manumission virtually ceased, and in the next forty years the free black population grew to just under 10,000, mostly from natural increase. Louisiana had a substantial free black population at statehood—7,585 free blacks constituted 18 percent of the state's black population—and a tradition of manumission inherited from its French and Spanish origins. By 1840 there were over 25,000 free blacks in the state. But after that time the free black population declined. Pressures on free blacks made life more difficult there, and the Americanization of French Louisiana led to a decline in manumissions. By 1860 the free black population had dropped to 18,647, which was only 5.3 percent of the total black population of the state. As slavery expanded in Louisiana, freedom declined.

In the rest of the lower South manumission was less common, and the free black populations were tiny. In the Deep South manumission was almost impossible. Blacks who performed extraordinary service—such as saving the life of a master or a member of the master's family—might become free, but only through acts of the legislature. In 1860 less than 1 percent of the African Americans in Alabama, Georgia, Mississippi, and Texas were free. Florida's 932 free blacks made up just 1.5 percent of the black population, while Tennessee's 7,300 free blacks were just 2.6 percent of the black population. Most of these states prohibited in-state manumission, and some prohibited manumission by will.

Free blacks had a significant impact on the manumission of slaves. Many free blacks were married to slaves. If a free man had a slave wife, then under the laws of the South his children were also slaves. Thus, many free blacks spent much of their lives trying to purchase loved ones, who they could then manumit. One tragic illustration of this comes from the slaves of Thomas Jefferson. In his will Jefferson emancipated five slaves, leaving about two hundred more in bondage. One of those freed was Joe Fossett, Jefferson's blacksmith. Jefferson's will provided that Fossett could live with his family in his cabin on the Monticello grounds and keep his blacksmith tools. However, revealing his inability to see slaves as people with human feelings—which was true of many masters—Jefferson did not free Fossett's wife and their eight children, who were subsequently purchased at auction by at least four masters and spread around the state. Fossett spent the rest of his life trying to buy back his family and manumit them; he was only partially successful.

Like Fossett, most slaves who were manumitted by their masters received their freedom at the time of their masters' deaths. Some masters granted freedom as a reward for a lifetime of loyal service. Others, facing the prospect of being denied their own rewards after death, feared that an angry God might not look kindly upon the soul of a slave owner. Some masters took their slaves north, especially their children and lovers. Cases such as these, however, were the exceptions. For the vast majority of the nation's slaves—3,953,760 in 1860—manumission was no more than a dream. It was illegal throughout the Deep South and rare everywhere else, except in Delaware and Maryland.

Even in Maryland manumission was never certain. The young Frederick Douglass may have been promised freedom by his owner, but if so, he was unprepared to wait or to accept the risk that his manumission might never occur. A promise of freedom could easily turn into a chain, a quick trip to the auction house, and a long journey to the cotton fields of the Deep South. At the time when Douglass ran away, there were about 50,000 free blacks in Maryland, including the woman who helped him escape and later married him, Anna Murray Douglass. Still, there were also over 100,000 slaves. Douglass eventually gained his legal freedom through the most atypical of methods: purchase. Friends in England raised enough money to purchase him from his owner, so that he could be legally manumitted and return to the United States.

Any master could, of course, take a slave to a free state and emancipate the slave there. Many did, although this placed a great hardship on the emancipated slave. Freedom in the North might mean never seeing relatives and friends. When the master was also the father of the slave, there were other complications. For example, in 1846 the Mississippi slave owner Edward Wells freed his slave Nancy, who was also his daughter, by taking her to Ohio, where he recorded a deed of manumission for her. When Wells later became ill, with a disease that proved fatal, Nancy returned to Mississippi to be with her father. She later tried to obtain the part of his estate that he had bequeathed to her in his will. The Mississippi court refused to let her receive the inheritance, however, holding that she was still a slave in Mississippi, even if she was free in Ohio. Indeed, she had returned to Mississippi to care for her dying father at the risk of losing her freedom.

For most slaves, however, the chance of someday losing freedom was remote, because they never could imagine being either manumitted or emancipated. In 1860 freedom was on the minds of millions of slaves but visibly on the horizon of none. The Civil War, of course, changed everything. Emancipation came to the federal territories and the District of Columbia early in the war, and after 1 January 1863, all slaves in the Confederacy were free—although they could not actually claim that freedom until the Continental army reached them and implemented the Emancipation Proclamation. In fact, the Proclamation was originally issued on questionable legal authority. Abraham Lincoln acted as commander in chief of the army to free the slaves of all those in rebellion against the United States, but he had no legal authority to touch those slaves in the loyal slave states or even in those parts of the Confederacy under U.S. control. On the other hand, some masters did free slaves in those regions, especially in Kentucky, so that they could enlist in the U.S. army. The masters gained the enlistment bounty, while the slaves gained their freedom. Eventually Congress declared that the wives and children of all black soldiers were also free. In December 1865 the Thirteenth Amendment completed the process, freeing those blacks in the loyal slave states and the recaptured parts of the Confederacy who could not be reached by the Emancipation Proclamation.

[See also Abolitionism; American Revolution; Antislavery Movement; Civil War; Civil War, Participation and Recruitment of Black Troops in; Confederate Policy toward African Americans and Slaves; Confederate States of America; Douglass, Anna Murray; Douglass, Frederick; Economic Life; Emancipation Proclamation; Free African Americans before the Civil War (North); Free African Americans before the Civil War (South); Freedmen; Lincoln, Abraham; Military; Religion and Slavery; Slavery; Slave Trade: Domestic; Society of Friends (Quakers); Thirteenth Amendment; Union Army, African Americans in; and Voting Rights.]

BIBLIOGRAPHY

Berlin, Ira. *Slaves without Masters: The Free Negro in the Antebellum South*. New York: Pantheon, 1975.

Franklin, John Hope. *The Emancipation Proclamation*. Garden City, NY: Doubleday, 1963.

Franklin, John Hope. *The Free Negro in North Carolina, 1790–1860*. Chapel Hill: University of North Carolina Press, 1943.

Zilversmit, Arthur. *First Emancipation*. Chicago: University of Chicago Press, 1967.

—PAUL FINKELMAN

EMANCIPATION PROCLAMATION. The Emancipation Proclamation was issued by President Abraham Lincoln on 1 January 1863. Although it did not immediately free any slaves, it redefined the Union's military goals, and a war that had been undertaken strictly to re-

"Proclamation of Emancipation" engraving by William Roberts, 1864; the portrait of Lincoln is after a photograph by Mathew Brady. The seven scenes contrast slavery and freedom. (National Portrait Gallery, Smithsonian Institution/Art Resource, N.Y.)

unite the country was transformed into a war of liberation. From 1863 onward, it was clear to both Northerners and Southerners that a Union victory would mean the permanent abolition of slavery.

The proclamation was months, if not years, in the making. Abolitionists had been pressuring the government to end slavery on moral grounds since the 1830s; they were joined in the 1850s by the Free-Soilers, who were concerned about the impact slavery was having on free laborers. The presidents of the 1850s—Millard Fillmore, Franklin Pierce, and James Buchanan—turned a deaf ear to antislavery protests, however, for all were southern sympathizers and had no interest in curtailing the institution.

When Abraham Lincoln was elected president on a Free-Soil platform in 1860, Southerners feared he would jeopardize slavery, and seven states seceded even before Lincoln took office. After Lincoln took office, some opponents of slavery hoped that he would respond to secession by attacking slavery, but this did not—and could not—happen right away. Although the president personally disliked slavery, he initially refused to take strong action against the "peculiar institution," fearing that the critical border states of Maryland, Missouri, and Kentucky would also leave the Union if he did so. He also felt that he could not risk the backlash that Emancipation might engender among Union Democrats—most of whom were willing to fight for reunion but not to end slavery.

Abolitionists continued to clamor for action throughout 1861 and the beginning of the Civil War, but Lincoln proved intransigent. As the war dragged on and entered its second year, the abolitionists' disappointment turned into fury. In an address delivered on 4 July 1862, Frederick Douglass condemned Lincoln in harsh terms, avowing that the people had "a right to hold Abraham Lincoln sternly responsible for any disaster or failure attending the suppression of this rebellion."

The great abolitionist would soon change his tune, however. Unbeknown to Douglass when he delivered his address, Lincoln was already at work drafting a proclamation of emancipation. He presented the document to his cabinet on 22 July 1862; the cabinet endorsed the measure but persuaded the president to wait for a Union military victory before issuing the proclamation, so that it did not appear to be an act of desperation.

That victory finally came on 17 September, in the battle of Antietam. The battle was actually more of a draw than a victory, but it was enough for Lincoln's needs; he issued a preliminary version of the Emancipation Proclamation five days later. The preliminary proclamation offered the Southern states a choice: they could save slavery by returning to the Union by 1 January 1863, or they could remain in rebellion and lose slavery forever. No

Southern states accepted the offer, and so the nation waited through the beginning of winter to see if the president would follow through on his threat when the New Year began.

On the evening of 1 January abolitionists across the nation gathered in various locations to await news of the president's decision. One of the largest gatherings was held in Boston, where the multitude of three thousand included Frederick Douglass. There was much tension in the crowd, Douglass later reported, as they waited and worried that the president might hold back, perhaps owing to his "kindly nature" or his wife's influence.

They need not have been concerned, for Lincoln was determined to make good on his promise. Although he had spent the day on 1 January shaking so many hands that his arm hurt, he took great care in signing the document. "If my name ever goes into history," he remarked, "it will be for this act, and my whole soul is in it. If my hand trembles when I sign the Proclamation, all who examine the document hereafter will say, 'He hesitated.'" After carefully inscribing his signature on the document, he judged it to be acceptable; the news was sent across the telegraph wires. When word arrived in Boston, Douglass and his fellow abolitionists erupted into an hours-long celebration that stretched late into the night.

Because the Emancipation Proclamation applied only to areas under Confederate control—areas that did not take orders from Abraham Lincoln—no slaves were immediately freed. This is not to say, however, that the document did not have an immediate impact. To begin with, a great number of Northern citizens and soldiers were further invigorated by the prospect of fighting a war not just of reunion but of liberation, with some regiments even adopting "Union and Liberty" as their motto. In addition, the proclamation ensured that important European powers, particularly France and England, would remain neutral with regard to the war and not throw their support behind the Confederacy. Perhaps most important, the proclamation also officially allowed African American troops to be enrolled in the Union army. The 178,975 black men who ultimately donned the blue played a key role in the war effort.

Of course, the impact of the proclamation was not entirely positive. Some Democrats withdrew their support of the war effort, and there were reports of soldiers deserting their units. At the other end of the political spectrum, a number of abolitionists criticized the document's limitations, particularly the provisions that preserved slavery in those areas already under Union control. Douglass later wrote that he did not share in these concerns, however: "For my own part, I took the proclamation, first and last, for a little more than it purported, and saw in its spirit a life and power far beyond its letter."

Ultimately, Douglass's faith in the proclamation was proven well founded. Although the Emancipation Proclamation did not by itself end slavery, it was the first and most important step in a chain of acts that culminated in the passage of the Thirteenth Amendment, which outlawed slavery forever. Speaking long after the war ended, Douglass described the document's impact succinctly: "This proclamation changed everything."

[*See also* Abolitionism; Civil War; Civil War, Participation and Recruitment of Black Troops in; Emancipation; Free African Americans before the Civil War (North); Free African Americans before the Civil War (South); Free-Soil Party; *Life and Times of Frederick Douglass*; Lincoln, Abraham; Lincoln, Mary Todd; Moral Suasion; Slavery; Thirteenth Amendment; *and* Union Army, African Americans in.]

BIBLIOGRAPHY

Cox, LaWanda. *Lincoln and Black Freedom: A Study in Presidential Leadership*. Columbia: University of South Carolina Press, 1981. The best extant study of Emancipation from the perspective of the White House.

Franklin, John Hope. *The Emancipation Proclamation*. Garden City, NY: Doubleday, 1963. Among the first studies to consider the consequences—both intended and unintended—of Lincoln's issuance of the Emancipation Proclamation.

Johnson, Michael P., ed. *Abraham Lincoln, Slavery, and the Civil War: Selected Writings and Speeches*. Boston: Bedford/St. Martin's, 2001. A well-chosen collection of documents that provides much insight into Lincoln's complex and constantly evolving views on the slavery question.

Litwack, Leon F. *Been in the Storm So Long: The Aftermath of Slavery*. New York: Knopf, 1979. This Pulitzer Prize–winning book explores the complex ways in which slaves responded to Emancipation.

—CHRISTOPHER BATES

EMERSON, RALPH WALDO (b. 25 May 1803; d. 27 April 1882), essayist, lecturer, and philosopher. Born in Boston and a resident of Concord, Massachusetts, for most of his life, Ralph Waldo Emerson was the ninth in a line of Congregational ministers. His father, William, died before Emerson's eighth birthday, and he and his siblings were raised by their mother, Ruth Haskins Emerson. Educated for the ministry at Harvard, Emerson ultimately quit his pastorate shortly after the death of his first wife in 1831. Dissatisfied with the structure and ritual of the church, Emerson sought a more expansive, democratic venue from which to preach. This he found on the lyceum lecture circuit. In the course of the following decades, he became one of the nation's most beloved and famed public lecturers. Many of his lecturers provided the material for his celebrated essays, which have not gone out of print since their initial publication.

Emerson ranks as the nineteenth century's greatest American liberal thinker. With Frederick Douglass, he was also the most important intellectual to engage the race issue. Friend of John Brown, the legendary abolitionist martyr who led the ill-fated raid on Harpers Ferry in 1859; associate of Theodore Parker and the other "Secret Six," who funded Brown's illicit raid; collaborator with the abolitionists William Lloyd Garrison and Wendell Phillips; and peripheral participant in the Underground Railroad, Emerson nevertheless remained conflicted about many issues relating to race and the character of the American nation. He simultaneously believed African American slavery to be an unmitigated evil and American greatness to be predicated on a set of traits that were probably unique to European Americans. For a person utterly nonconforming in almost every other way, Emerson proved rather typical when it came to race. Nagging doubts about African American inferiority inhibited his activism in the 1830s and 1840s and tempered his rhetoric in the 1850s and 1860s. Emerson never articulated a biracial vision of America.

Emerson's views offer unique and sometimes disturbing insights into the function of race in the culture of the antebellum North. Race prejudice profoundly influenced Emerson's actions and, more important, the lectures and essays that hugely shaped his times and still strongly resonate within American culture today. Emerson subscribed to a racialized conception of history throughout his life. Most clearly elaborated in his 1856 *English Traits*, Emerson's description of white America's unique promise relied on the prevalent "scientific" racism of the day. It was a decidedly romanticized view as well, as Emerson had only minimal contact with the African American community of New England. Even the formidable and famous Douglass failed to draw his interest. Emerson mused about Douglass's bloodlines in a draft of his 1844 address on slavery in the West Indies. Robert Lowell, Boston man of letters and abolitionist, claimed, probably erroneously, that Emerson dissented from making Douglass a member of the Concord Town and Country Club. Lowell resigned from the club when it refused to admit Douglass.

Limited by his romantic racialism, Emerson nevertheless evolved into an abolitionist. His early career is characterized by a basic indifference that lasted until 1837, when he presented his first lecture on slavery. His middle years, which date from the late 1830s through the 1840s, are the ones of the greatest evolution, incorporating the most dramatic shift in his thinking. Highlighted by his 1844 public celebration of emancipation in the West Indies and his sharp reaction to southern machinations surrounding the annexation of Texas and the Mexican-American War, this period features his most egalitarian statements, even as he largely remained on the periphery of the abolitionist movement. Gradually after 1844 he became more engaged in antislavery issues as he rethought many of his earlier assumptions about the intractable inferiority of the Africans in America and the Atlantic world. The Compromise of 1850 and the infamous Fugitive Slave Law it spawned sparked Emerson's full commitment to abolitionism. Even in the 1850s he altered his views about the stalwarts in the antislavery cause and the need to take up the fight himself more than he changed his notions about race.

Like other Transcendentalists—a group of ministers and other intellectuals that gathered at Emerson's home for intellectual discussions, particularly concerning the German idealist philosophy from which they gained their name—Emerson found himself drawn to John Brown, whom he had met in 1857 while Brown was in Massachusetts drumming up support for antislavery partisans in Kansas. Emerson donated twenty-five dollars to the cause after Brown's speech at the Concord Town Hall, where, according to Emerson, Brown "gave a good account of himself." In the fall of 1859, after Brown's infamous raid at Harpers Ferry, Emerson wrote to Virginia's governor Henry Alexander Wise seeking clemency for the condemned abolitionist. After Brown's execution, Emerson joined mourners in Boston in an effort to raise money for Brown's family. "John Brown was an idealist," he declared, "who believed in his ideas to that extent, that he existed to put them into action." In contrast to many Transcendentalist abolitionists, Brown "did not believe in moral suasion;—he believed in putting the thing through."

During the Civil War, even as he dissuaded his son from enlisting, Emerson supported the war effort, actively advocating the enlistment of black troops in the Union army. Emerson believed that free blacks and slaves had to prove both to themselves and to a white America steeped in racial prejudice the depth of their character as well as their ample moral fortitude. In his 1863 poem "Voluntaries," commemorating the black Fifty-fourth Massachusetts Infantry Regiment's heroic assault on Fort Wagner, Emerson advanced the same powerful sentiments about black agency that he had expressed in other contexts for decades. Whites might take credit for "freeing slaves," but genuine freedom had to be self-made. "The negro has saved himself," he noted, "and the white man very patronizingly says, I have saved you." Always as much a critic of the North as of the South, he hoped that African American heroism would compel "men of Northern brain," a reference to his own deeply held prejudices, to reconsider their prejudicial reservations concerning blacks' bravery and courage. "For freedom he will strike and strive," Emerson wrote, "And drain his heart till he be dead."

Emerson was especially energized by Lincoln's Preliminary Emancipation Proclamation, issued after the battle of Antietam. At last Emerson felt certain that the nation was headed in the right direction, even if at an all-too-deliberate pace. Emerson chose the occasion of Lincoln's proclamation of 22 September to deliver his last major antislavery address. "The President's Proclamation" articulated what Emerson believed to be the awesome importance of the act. Emancipation would remove the great impediment to genuine union of North and South. It would profit the nation in all ways, gain the respect and admiration of the high-minded both at home and abroad, and enable citizens to reclaim their honor; most important, the Proclamation would be irreversible: "We shall cease to be hypocrites and pretenders, but what we have styled our free institutions will be such."

Significantly, at this uniquely auspicious moment Emerson declined to reflect on the impact of the proclamation upon American blacks or offer any hopeful vision of the freed slaves' future. The lecturer seemed more concerned with his white neighbors and how "life in America had lost much of its attraction in the later years." The best Emerson could muster was a vague nod toward "a new audience [which] is found in the heart of the assembly," and a coda calling on Americans through their national government to protect "that ill-fated, much-injured race." As "a race naturally benevolent, joyous, docile, industrious, and whose very miseries sprung from their great talent for usefulness," African Americans would have "to find their way" under "the protection of American Law." His "Emancipation in the British West Indies" address, delivered almost twenty years earlier, went infinitely farther toward imagining equality. In the midst of a devestating war and on the verge of a second American revolution, Emerson's imagination largely failed him. Left out was any vision of a biracial American future and left unsaid entirely was a pronouncement on equality. Always assiduously careful to avoid hypocrisy, it seems altogether likely that Emerson still harbored great doubts about the intellectual, moral, and cultural abilities of African Americans. As he celebrated the coming denouement of slavery, Emerson failed to venture beyond the immediate great good of abolishing the nation's most heinous institution.

During Reconstruction, Emerson steadfastly supported the radicals. He readily grasped the new activist role of the national government necessitated by the exigencies of war and, like the Radical Republican senator Charles Sumner, championed the need for governmental action to protect the freedom critical to individual expression. With Sumner, Pennsylvania's Radical representative Thaddeus Stevens, and many other Republicans, Emerson endorsed the Freedmen's Bureau, the Fourteenth Amendment (which granted citizenship rights to freed slaves), and the expanded function of the central power in protecting the rights of all citizens of the nation. "We have seen slavery disappear like a painted scene in a theatre," he declared in "Resources," a lecture he gave frequently in the 1860s; "we have seen the most healthful revolution in the politics of the nation,—the Constitution not only amended, but construed in a new spirit." Consistent with his earlier inhibitions, however, Emerson turned silent on race after Emancipation; no sooner had the Union been restored and slavery abolished than Emerson, who once had seemed poised to slough off his racial assumptions, felt free to disown the issue of race in America.

The historiography of the relationship of Emerson and the Transcendentalists to reform in general and antislavery in particular underwent a striking turn in the last decade of the twentieth century. Few scholars any longer portray Emerson and other Transcendentalists as alienated outsiders who held themselves aloof from public affairs. All but dismissed is the one-dimensional portrait of the Transcendentalists as the historian Stanley Elkins's "intellectuals without responsibilities," whose philosophical idealism ensured at best a tangential relationship to antislavery. Scholars have unearthed an impressive array of evidence of the Concord sage's antislavery commitments. From his defense of abolitionists' freedom of speech in the 1830s to his genuine abolitionist credentials after 1850, Emerson emerges as highly engaged in the antislavery movement.

Even as Emerson is now understood to be an abolitionist, some nagging questions remain relating to race. Emerson remained silent on antislavery until 1837, virtually half of his life, and famously disparaged many abolitionists, whose eloquence he called "dog-cheap." Most important, Emerson recorded numerous observations in his journals and notebooks so disparaging of blacks as to make the modern reader cringe. In their full impact they seem to make it difficult to portray him even as "a mild North Atlantic racist," as the philosopher Cornel West has suggested. Even as the Concord sage remains a singularly deep and challenging thinker, who with the author Henry Thoreau, the women's rights activist Margaret Fuller, Theodore Parker, and others offered a profoundly important critique of American society, when it came to race, Emerson proved representative of his times.

[*See also* Brown, John; Caribbean; Compromise of 1850; Emancipation Proclamation; Fifty-fourth Massachusetts Infantry Regiment; Fourteenth Amendment; Freedmen's Bureau; Fugitive Slave Law of 1850; Garrison, William Lloyd; Harpers Ferry Raid; Mexican-American War; Parker, Theodore; Phillips, Wendell; Race, Theories of; Reconstruction; Secret Six; Stevens, Thaddeus; Sumner, Charles; Underground Railroad; *and* Union Army, African Americans.]

BIBLIOGRAPHY

Elkins, Stanley. *Slavery: A Problem in American Institutional and Intellectual Life*. Chicago: University of Chicago Press, 1959.

Emerson, Ralph Waldo. *Journals and Miscellaneous Notebooks*. 16 vols. Edited by William H. Gilman et al. Cambridge, MA: Belknap Press, 1960–1982.

Field, Peter S. *Ralph Waldo Emerson: The Making of a Democratic Intellectual*. Latham, MD: Rowman and Littlefield, 2002.

Gougeon, Leonard. *Virtue's Hero: Emerson, Antislavery, and Reform*. Athens: University of Georgia Press, 1990.

Gougeon, Leonard, and Joel Myerson. *Emerson's Antislavery Writings*. New Haven, CT: Yale University Press, 1995.

West, Cornel. *The American Evasion of Philosophy: A Genealogy of Pragmatism*. Madison: University of Wisconsin Press, 1989.

—PETER S. FIELD

EMIGRATION TO AFRICA. As early as 1780 Americans debated the return of African Americans to Africa. This action was supported by people on both sides of the color line, primarily because whites thought that this was the best course of action to improve black and white relations in the country, and some blacks agreed. By definition, however, when blacks developed such plans, they were called "emigrationists," and when whites created matching plans, they were called "colonizationists." Both groups were determined that blacks should leave the United States.

In many communities, black and white, there were discussions on the merits of colonization and emigration, which to many was the only viable scheme for ending slavery that was generally acceptable to whites. Against this backdrop of public debate over ending the slave trade and repatriating blacks, the American Colonization Society (ACS) was formed in Washington, D.C., in 1816. The ACS was to sponsor the settlement of "free persons of color" in Africa. Its membership included some of America's most notable citizens, among them the presidents James Madison and Andrew Jackson, statesmen such as Daniel Webster and Henry Clay, and Francis Scott Key, author of "The Star-Spangled Banner." They all argued that blacks should be returned to Africa because it was the "only natural home of black people." Central to the scheme was the belief that blacks would never be accepted in America. Motivated by a variety of concerns, some ACS members said they wanted to correct the injustices done to blacks by slavery, while other ACS members considered the existence of free blacks in America threatening to slavery. The overall belief was that blacks, who had been captives for nearly two hundred years, could best achieve their full potential in Africa.

With some early achievements, colonizationists tried to recruit well-known, successful blacks to support an exodus to Africa. The most common strategy was to lure influential black leaders with the prospect of power, wealth, and prestige. For example, James Forten, a wealthy black sailmaker, sensationalized the advantages of going to Africa. In 1815 Paul Cuffe, a black shipbuilder, began to repatriate blacks to Sierra Leone, while the Free African Union Society of Newport, Rhode Island, continued its appeal for a return-to-Africa movement. Established in 1780, the society was a benevolent and moral improvement organization, as well as an agency for black emigration. Its members believed that blacks should be productive members of society. They believed that blacks should have jobs, not drink alcohol, have legal marriages, and make an investment in land; but most important, they believed that blacks would be best served in their "native" land. On several occasions the Free African Union Society tried to establish its own settlement in Africa, but because of its lack of financing, from both white and black financiers, this early emigrationist movement was a failure. It was the ACS that founded the West African colony of Liberia, and between 1822 and 1861 it sent nearly fifteen thousand blacks back to Africa under its patronage.

The most consistent black advocates of emigration were Martin R. Delany, Henry Highland Garnet, Bishop Henry McNeal Turner, and Alexander Crummell. Many came to support emigration because of political events of the 1850s, notably the Compromise of the 1850, the Fugitive Slave Law of 1850, and the *Dred Scott* case, which gave cause for many black leaders to leave the country, fearing they would never have a future in the United States. All supporters of emigration insisted that blacks' greatest hope was the establishment of all-black settlements in Africa and the eventual creation of independent black states.

There are several historical accounts, including Bernard Boxill's, that allege that Frederick Douglass assailed the idea of shipping slaves to Africa. From the beginning of his lecturing career in 1841, Douglass gave his audiences a picture of what slavery was like and emphasized that slaves should be set free, "right here in America." Douglass heaped his greatest scorn on the idea of sending blacks to Africa:

All this native land talk is nonsense. The native land of the American Negro is America. His bones, his muscles, his sinews, are all American. His ancestors for two hundred and seventy years have lived, and labored and died on American soil, and millions of his posterity have inherited caucasian blood. (McFeely, p. 380)

Douglass tied the fate of all blacks together, the free and enslaved, those in the North and those in the South. "We are one," he proclaimed. "Our course is one, and we must help each other."

From his early speeches in New Bedford, Massachusetts, to his tumultuous debates with Delany, Douglass had always opposed blacks' leaving America to settle elsewhere. He joined William Lloyd Garrison in attacking the ACS, directing his hostility toward both black emigrationists and white colonizationists, and this animosity would be constant throughout his life. Douglass considered talk of leaving the United States destructive to African American communities.

It was not that Douglass doubted that blacks could not find a more comfortable and dignified life outside the United States: In the 1840s he had been tempted to accept the offer of English friends to establish himself and his family in England. It was rather that he believed that blacks should insist on the recognition of their legitimacy as Americans, and, more important, he believed that blacks who left the country would be denied their rightful birthright and would be abandoning slaves to their fate. He felt that free blacks were obliged to fight in their native land for the emancipation of their fellow black men and women in chains. It was unconscionable for blacks to leave America to serve their individual self-interests.

Douglass's single flirtation with emigration came in the spring of 1861, when he briefly considered endorsing emigration to Haiti. He planned a ten-week expedition to explore the island nation and the amenities it offered, even though he did not plan on moving there permanently himself. In his newspaper he noted that Haiti offered a refuge for African Americans "looking out into the world for a place to retreat, and asylum from the apprehended storm." Once the Civil War erupted, Douglass abandoned his planned trip to Haiti and his tepid support for emigration in favor of supporting the war effort.

With the exception of this short-lived episode in 1861, Douglass was an integrationist. He felt that blacks had a duty to remain in the United States and force it to live up to its ideals. He thought that emigration and colonization schemes would encourage the most enterprising and skilled black Americans to leave, and those were the people most needed for the struggle in the United States. Forever optimistic about the plight of black people in America, Douglass passionately opposed emigration, particularly in view of its stated ambition to solve the "Negro problem." His faith was rooted in the belief that "the country/people were to [*sic*] great to be small and to smart, just and to noble to oppress the weak." It bothered him a great deal that black men with "learning and ability" were among those advocating emigration.

[*See also* Africa, Idea of; American Colonization Society; Black Nationalism; Black Separatism; Civil Rights; Clay, Henry; Colonization; Compromise of 1850; Crummell, Alexander; Delany, Martin Robison; Douglass, Frederick; *Dred Scott* Case; Forten, James; Free African Americans before the Civil War (North); Free African American before the Civil War (South); Fugitive Slave Law of 1850; Garnet, Henry Highland; Garrison, William Lloyd; Haiti; Integration; Liberia; *and* Segregation.]

BIBLIOGRAPHY

Blight, David W. "The Bugbear of Colonization." In *Frederick Douglass' Civil War: Keeping Faith in Jubilee*. Baton Rouge: Louisiana State University Press, 1989: 145–147.

Blight, David W. *Frederick Douglass' Civil War: Keeping Faith in Jubilee*. Baton Rouge: Louisiana State University Press, 1989.

Boxill, Bernard R. "Douglass against the Emigrationists." In *Frederick Douglass: A Critical Reader*, edited by Bill E. Lawson and Frank M. Kirkland. Malden, MA: Blackwell, 1999: 22–47.

Brotz, Howard. "The Folly of Colonization." In *African American Social and Political Thought: 1850–1920*. New Brunswick, NJ: Transaction, 1992: 330.

Huggins, Nathan Irvin. *Slave and Citizen: The Life of Frederick Douglass*. Boston: Little, Brown: 1980.

McFeely, William S. *Frederick Douglass*. New York: Norton, 1991.

—FRED LINDSEY

ENTREPRENEURS. [*This entry contains two subentries dealing with African American entrepreneurs and their businesses from the Colonial period through 1895. The first article discusses the first African American entrepreneurs through 1830 and their long-term impact, while the second article discusses the successes, failures, and obstacles of African American entrepreneurs, including Frederick Douglass, after the Civil War.*]

African American Entrepreneurs in Early America

The term *entrepreneur* is defined as a person who organizes and promotes but, more precisely, as someone who manages and assumes the risk of a business. Black businessmen, shopkeepers, ship's captains, and financiers thus served as leaders of the African American entrepreneurial class in early America. Black entrepreneurs existed in African American communities throughout the colonial, Revolutionary, and early national periods. Perhaps the leading black entrepreneur was the Philadelphian James Forten. Born free, Forten was apprenticed to the white sailmaker Robert Bridges in 1786. After mastering both the craft and the business of sailmaking, he bought Bridges's shop in 1798. Until his death in 1842, Forten not only built his sailmaking business into one of the most prominent in the bustling city of Philadelphia but also secured real estate; made loans to both white and black citizens; and, according to the biographer Julie Winch, created a prosperous empire of investments. His estate was valued at more than sixty thousand dollars when he died.

Forten was not the only African American gentleman of property and economic standing in early national Philadelphia. The Reverend Richard Allen, who remains best known for establishing the Bethel African Methodist Episcopal Church in Philadelphia, held rental properties that provided a substantial income and started a chimney-sweeping business. Allen and another church leader, Absalom Jones, formed a benevolent and social reform organization called the Free African Society, but the two men also sought to become entrepreneurs in the early 1790s with their investment in a nail-producing business. In addition, several of Allen's parishioners at the Bethel Church were listed in Philadelphia directories of the 1810s and 1820s as masters of small businesses.

Black entrepreneurial activity stemmed from African American business ventures in both the colonies and the early Republic. Although most African-descended people were enslaved before the American Revolution, there were still black businessmen who established themselves as viable profit makers. In *Root and Branch*, a study of African American life in early New York and New Jersey, the historian Graham Russell Hodges reports that African-descended people established independent farms and small businesses in the 1640s, 1650s, and 1660s in colonial New York. African people arriving in Dutch New Amsterdam hailed from urban cultures with vibrant market systems. On the North American mainland free blacks established market stands that sold a variety of goods, including fish, corn, copper, and ivory.

Black entrepreneurial activity accelerated following the American Revolution. The growth of free black communities, primarily in urban locales, abetted the rise of black businessmen of various sorts. Prince Hall, who worked in the leather trade before the Revolution and was enslaved until the 1770s, established a leather-goods shop during the war. In 1777 he supplied the Continental army with leather goods, for which he received reimbursement. Free black businesses appeared increasingly between the 1780s and 1820s, in New York City; Boston; Newport and Providence, Rhode Island; Baltimore, Maryland; Philadelphia; Richmond, Virginia; and Charleston, South Carolina.

One pathway to economic independence for African Americans was working at jobs that white laborers and businessmen felt were beneath them and had abandoned. That is how black Philadelphians like Allen came to operate chimney-sweeping businesses. Allen's business was successful enough that he even hired out indentured servants. African American businesses also included barbershops, dry-cleaning operations, grog shops, brothels, and theaters.

The most famous early black theater company, the African Company, was started by a black businessman, William Brown, in New York City in 1821. As its first play, the troop of black actors staged William Shakespeare's

Richard III. Brown was the economic mover behind the company, which performed at another business enterprise of Brown's: the African Grove Theater, a tea garden and entertainment space for blacks. The African Company lasted only a few years before falling prey to prejudicial attitudes; the African Grove Theater met a similar fate when it closed in 1829.

Merchant activity provided black businessmen with the means to economic elevation. The celebrated ship captain Paul Cuffe, who owned several ships before his death in 1817, worked as a crewman in the whaling trade before becoming an independent ship owner. He bought his first ship with a business partner in 1787, working as a fisherman and whaler near Newfoundland, Canada. He secured a second vessel and then a third before 1800. By 1810–1811 Cuffe was an internationally known captain and reformer, with a crew on some voyages of nearly a dozen people of color. Absalom Boston, a freeborn black citizen of Massachusetts, though not as successful as Cuffe, nevertheless paralleled the great sea captain's rise. Starting as a mariner and general laborer at the outset of the nineteenth century, Boston was captaining the whaling ship *Industry* by the spring of 1822. He also operated a public inn and a general store.

Black business activity was not confined to free black communities in the North. Free blacks started a variety of establishments in Richmond, Charleston, and Baltimore as well. After the American Revolution in Richmond, African Americans started groceries, grog shops, saloons, and gaming houses. According to the historian Douglas R. Egerton, these black business owners, though small in number, testified to the entrepreneurial spirit in the African American community in the years after Virginia eased emancipation laws in 1782. Even after Richmond authorities closed down certain black businesses, black entrepreneurs created an underground presence.

By the 1810s and 1820s many black entrepreneurs used their prominent economic and social positions in the cause of social justice. Although a minor businessman by most standards, the free black activist David Walker utilized his used-clothing shop in Boston as an entrepôt of black reform. The author and publisher of *Appeal to the Coloured Citizens of the World*, a militant denunciation of American racial oppression that came out in 1829, Walker sewed copies of the pamphlet into clothing that was smuggled from his Boston shop onto southern plantations. Other reformers contributed to black schools, libraries, and charitable organizations.

In short, black entrepreneurial activity became an emblem of black abolitionism. It undercut white stereotypes about African American abilities while also providing an economic foundation for autonomous black reform movements.

[*See also* African Grove Theater; Allen, Richard; American Revolution; Black Press; Black Seafarers; Cuffe, Paul; David Walker's *Appeal*; Forten, James; Free African Americans to 1828; Free African Society; Hall, Prince; Indentured Servitude; Inventors; Jones, Absalom; Maritime Trades; New York City; Occupations; Political Participation; Walker, David; *and* Work.]

BIBLIOGRAPHY

Egerton, Douglas R. *Gabriel's Rebellion: The Virginia Slave Conspiracies of 1800 and 1802*. Chapel Hill: University of North Carolina Press, 1993.

Hodges, Graham Russell. *Root and Branch: African Americans in New York and East Jersey, 1613–1863*. Chapel Hill: University of North Carolina Press, 1999.

Horton, James Oliver, and Lois E. Horton. *In Hope of Liberty: Culture, Community, and Protest among Northern Free Blacks, 1700–1860*. New York: Oxford University Press, 1997.

White, Shane. *Stories of Freedom in Black New York*. Cambridge, MA: Harvard University Press, 2002.

Winch, Julie. *A Gentleman of Color: The Life of James Forten*. New York: Oxford University Press, 2002.

—RICHARD NEWMAN

African American Capitalism after the Civil War

Frederick Douglass's dream of going from rags to riches proved untenable for most blacks in the rural southern districts. During the Reconstruction era Douglass unsuccessfully advocated the formation of a national land and loan company to purchase large blocs of land for later sale to former enslaved blacks in the South. He believed that the absence of a public land policy was one of the failures of Reconstruction. Yet his moderate Republican views—coupled with his values of hard work, perseverance, and thrift—kept him from supporting the confiscation of lands to be redistributed to landless blacks. His promotion of hard work, perseverance, and thrift overlooked systemic racial barriers to economic progress, as evidenced by the tenant-farming system, unscrupulous white landowners, and southern white hostility to Reconstruction. Martin Robison Delany, a disillusioned black colleague and a former co-editor of the *North Star* who had advocated black emigration, made a futile attempt to engage Douglass in discourse about the systemic nature of racism and its adverse effect on black political, economic, and social progress.

A string of ventures from serving as president of the Freedman's Savings and Trust Company to his ownership of the black newspaper *New National Era* during the 1870s perhaps led the self-taught Douglass to maintain high aspirations. He probably found virtue in his visible leadership role as a former enslaved black and concluded that hard work, perseverance, and thrift were the means to black economic growth. Scholars, however, consider Douglass's postwar business ventures to be characterized by lackluster financial performances. His secure financial status and friendly white associations further distanced the self-made man from the bleak plight of the black landless masses as time passed. In 1886 Douglass, an internationally recognized figure who no longer required gainful employment and who had substantial savings, embarked on a leisurely tour of Europe with his wife, Helen Pitts Douglass.

Freedman's Savings and Trust Company. The roots of black capitalism were evident in loan and brokerage concerns before the Civil War. Stephen Smith, a black Underground Railroad operator in Columbia, Pennsylvania, had a reported net worth of $500,000 and made loans at a profit. The 1850 census for New Orleans, Louisiana, showed that eight mulattoes were involved in the brokerage business. It was also in New Orleans that General Nathaniel P. Banks established a bank for black soldiers and the free black community in 1864. Other military banking institutions in Beaufort, South Carolina, and Norfolk, Virginia, perhaps provided inspiration for the establishment of the Freedman's Savings and Trust Company in 1865.

Despite his lack of experience Douglass, always the consummate optimist, assumed the role of president of the savings and trust company in 1874, when the financially troubled banking institution showed a deficit of at least $200,000, unbeknownst to him. A naive Douglass initially considered his appointment an unimaginable dream, but within three months the bank was placed in bankruptcy, causing considerable personal damage to his reputation. To Douglass's credit, he was successful in promoting black self-help and thrifty practices through pamphlets circulated throughout the country. He perhaps found the greatest personal satisfaction in the increased number of black clerks and tellers employed at the savings and trust, who were being trained in proper banking methods.

In reality Douglass was unable to change the Freedman's Savings and Trust Company's plummeting course that began before his arrival because of a too-rapid increase in the number of branches, poor speculative investments, and exorbitant rates of return. The period of rapid expansion, which witnessed the establishment of thirty-four branches, was rumored to have the support of President Abraham Lincoln and the backing of the U.S. Congress. Even though these rumors were less than factual, former enslaved blacks believed the claims. The savings and trust company had opened ten branches within a year of its inception in 1865; by 1867 ten additional branches had opened. The bank operated in the black until 1870, when the trustees, through an amendment to the charter, received the authorization to invest one-half the funds in real estate investments in their own local com-

munities, which resulted in corruption. Finally, the embezzlement of funds and southern white hostility were obstacles too great to overcome. The Freedman's Savings and Trust Company closed in 1874. Some scholars argue that the closing of the savings and trust company left both whites and blacks with little confidence in the federal government for more than a decade. Others conclude that the company's failure later discouraged black commercial banking ventures, which meant black deposits were held in more secure thrifts.

Rise of Black Enterprise. In the mid-nineteenth century black enterprise accompanied by social responsibility was the norm. In 1878 Douglass purchased a fifteen-acre estate along with a twenty-room house in the District of Columbia, where he advocated for black causes and women's rights. His financial security was guaranteed with his appointment to prestigious government posts from 1877 to 1886 as well as with speaking engagements. Mary Pleasant, who passed for white at strategic moments, amassed a considerable fortune as the operator of a mulatto boardinghouse in San Francisco and used her influence in 1868 to finance a legal case to the California Supreme Court so that blacks might ride trolleys. John Jones, a Chicago black tailor who catered to a wealthy clientele, built a four-story office building and was appointed as county commissioner in 1874. The substantial material gains of Douglass, Pleasant, and Jones were atypical when many late nineteenth-century black tenant farmers lived in one- and two-room cabins in the South. Douglass's optimism about substantial black economic progress proved unfounded for the black masses. Even his own children struggled to attain financial independence and required his assistance.

Between 1865 and 1895 the rise of black banking institutions and increasing black thrift moved blacks one step closer to financial independence. However, between 1899 and 1905 one out of four black banks went out of business. In 1888 the Capitol Savings Bank opened with its headquarters in Washington, D.C., and its leadership comprising Henry Baker, Whitfield McKinley, W. S. Montgomery, John A. Pierre, Robert H. Terrell, and J. R. Wilder. At the same time a fraternal group, the Grand Fountain of the United Order of True Reformers, opened the Savings Bank in Richmond, Virginia, with William Washington Browne as president. The Mutual Bank and Trust Company in Chattanooga, Tennessee, was a short-lived bank established in 1889. A year later, B. H. Hudson, an educator and grocer, and W. R. Pettiford, a minister, helped establish the Alabama Penny Savings Bank in Birmingham. Thrifty black industrial workers loyally supported this bank. Yet expansion of three branches in Montgomery, Selma, and Anniston proved a financial miscalculation. These early black banking institutions failed because of poor commercial investments, speculation by officers, and mismanagement. Changing black leadership and overexpansion contributed to bank closures, but these early banks were significant developments in the progress toward black capitalism.

[*See also* Black Press; Civil War; Delany, Martin Robison; Douglass, Frederick; Freedman's Savings and Trust Company; Lincoln, Abraham; Mulattoes; *New National Era*; *North Star*; Progress; Racism; Reconstruction; Republican Party; Sharecropping; *and* Underground Railroad.]

BIBLIOGRAPHY

Du Bois, W. E. B. *The Souls of Black Folk* (1903). New York: New American Library, 1969.

Lindsay, Arnett G. "The Negro in Banking." *Journal of Negro History* 14.2 (April 1929): 156–201.

Miller, Douglas T. *Frederick Douglass and the Fight for Freedom*. New York: Facts on File, 1988.

—ROLAND BARKSDALE-HALL

EPISCOPALIANS (ANGLICANS) AND AFRICAN AMERICANS.

Black slaves were present in Virginia, England's first successful North American colony, since at least 1619. The Church of England was an active presence in England's North American colonies since the first settlement at Jamestown in 1607, when the Reverend Robert Hunt conducted services for the settlers there. With the arrival of the first African slaves, the Church of England began its efforts to educate and convert slaves to Christianity, and the first slaves were baptized in 1623. After 1789 these missionary duties were assumed by the newly formed American Protestant Episcopal Church. Whether these efforts were fostered by English or American religious organizations, the goal remained the same. Each was determined to gain black converts to Christianity and to better the condition of slaves, but neither the Church of England nor the American Episcopal Church openly advocated the emancipation of slaves.

Many African Americans sought instruction and were received into the Church of England. Government in the church was hierarchical, with authority flowing from God to the monarch to the archbishops to the bishops and then to the congregations. The Church of England, under the auspices of the Bishop of London, was the official state church only in Virginia, Maryland, and the four lower counties of New York. The policy of the church was to convert Africans, whether free or enslaved, in all English-held areas of North America and the West Indies. Slaves were found in all colonies but constituted a significant portion of the population in the Chesapeake and the lower South, where a large labor force was needed. There was less need for slavery in the New England and middle Atlantic colonies, where subsistence crop agriculture prevailed. Still, all northern colonies had a substantial slave population, particularly in New York City, where slaves made up about one-third of the population by the early eighteenth century.

Conversion and Education of Slaves. Problems faced by Anglican priests and missionaries who tried to convert slaves arose out of the rationale employed by Europeans to justify enslaving Africans. According to Christian belief, which had been in vogue since the fourteenth century, it was unjust for Christians to enslave other Christians but acceptable to enslave non-Christians. Since Africans were not Christians, they could be enslaved. Colonists feared that they would be forced to release converted slaves. The problem was partially resolved when all colonial legislatures by the end of the seventeenth century ruled that slavery was unaffected by conversion to Christianity, but whites feared that education and conversion would lead slaves to believe they were the social and spiritual equals of their owners. Consequently, some colonial legislatures banned all education of slaves.

Despite such legislative action, the Crown and church in England favored the education and conversion of slaves. To accomplish this end, Charles II in 1661 had urged the Council for Foreign Plantations to Christianize slaves. Further efforts to achieve conversions were made by the Crown in the 1680s, when colonial governors were instructed to encourage the proselytizing of slaves. To assist missionaries in the field, the Society for the Promotion of Christian Knowledge was founded in 1699 for the primary purpose of establishing libraries for the use of possible converts. The work of this society was enhanced after the Reverend Thomas Bray, an Anglican priest, returned from a 1696 visit to Maryland. Dr. Bray, who traveled at the behest of the Bishop of London, was appalled at the state of the Anglican Church in America and even more appalled by the halfhearted attempts being made to convert Indians, slaves, and members of other religious sects to the Church of England. On his return to England, Bray, on 16 June 1701, obtained a charter from William III to found the Society for the Propagation of the Gospel in Foreign Parts (SPG), to educate and instruct slaves and others in Christianity, a duty they saw as a moral responsibility.

The perceived duty to proselytize slaves was taken so seriously by the English church that from 1702 to 1776 more than three hundred missionaries were sent to America, all armed with Bibles, prayer books, and religious tracts. The hostile reception by colonists to Bishop William Fleetwood's denunciation of slavery in 1701 led the society to concentrate its efforts on saving the souls of slaves, rather than trying to eradicate slavery. One of the most difficult tasks the society faced was to convince slave owners that religion would not threaten slavery but could, in fact, reinforce the institution. Rather than stress the possibility of freedom or equality with whites, the missionaries strove to ease the suffering of slaves.

The first missionaries sent by the SPG were the Reverends George Keith and John Talbot, who successfully urged the establishment of Saint Mary's Church in Burlington, New Jersey, in 1702, the first Anglican missionary church in the world. Talbot urged the SPG to appoint a bishop for the American colonies. This idea was frequently considered but never acted upon by the home government, much to the relief of members of other Protestant sects. While schools were established in all the colonies, one of the most successful of the SPG-sponsored schools was the one in New York City. Founded in 1704 to instruct blacks, Indians, and white children, the school was under the supervision of the catechist Elias Neau, a New York merchant, who had long urged the establishment of such a school. The school was popular with New Yorkers of all races until the New York City slave rebellion of 1712, when townspeople came to the conclusion that teaching slaves to read had awakened discontent, which had led them to rebellion. Hostility against Neau eased when it became apparent that only one rebel slave had attended the school.

Neau's efforts to achieve conversions met with success, but William Vesey, minister of New York's Trinity Church, refused to admit qualified blacks to membership there. In this, Vesey and his congregation were following the custom of other colonies, where slaves were consigned either to a separate gallery or to a separate chapel. The stalemate in New York City was resolved when the city's governor, Robert Hunter, ordered John Sharpe, the chaplain of Fort Anne, to baptize qualified blacks in the fort's chapel. On Neau's death in 1722 his work was carried on by other missionaries, who admitted between forty and sixty New York City African Americans a year to church membership.

In South Carolina the first SPG missionary was the Reverend Samuel Thomas, who arrived in 1702. He began his missionary work in the Goose Creek parish of South Carolina, converting twenty slaves and teaching several others to read and write. By 1705 Thomas had more than a thousand slaves seeking instruction, despite opposition from some whites, who objected to worshipping with their slaves. The Reverend Francis Le Jau succeeded Thomas after the latter's death in 1706. Unlike his predecessor, Le Jau refused to educate any but well-behaved slaves whose owners had agreed to their seeking instruction. Saint Andrew's parish in South Carolina also witnessed some success in African American education and conversion when

the Reverend Ebenezer Taylor, assisted by two white women, successfully instructed several slaves in Christianity, with twenty-seven blacks seeking baptism. Countless others were kept from instruction by their masters, according to Taylor. In some cases, overly zealous priests were persecuted and occasionally driven from their parishes when they persisted in their efforts to educate and convert slaves. Even if priests were not ousted, they were impeded in their work when planters refused to have their children educated with African Americans.

The SPG's efforts in the South led to widespread interest in Christianity within the slave communities. While there was certainly a good deal of resistance on the part of some African Americans to accepting Christianity, others converted willingly. Most African Americans, for their part, were usually willing to accept Christianity but did so on their own terms. At the insistence of owners, missionaries stressed obedience to masters and downplayed spiritual equality, but slaves used religion not only to provide hope for salvation after death but also to offer solace and a form of escape from the realities of slavery. Religion and the singing of hymns that stressed freedom and equality even gave slaves a means of quietly resisting slavery.

Some slaves who converted became proselytizers themselves. Typical were two young slaves in South Carolina, Harry and Andrew, who were praised by the Archbishop of Canterbury in 1741 for their efforts to educate other slaves in an evening school. Both Harry and Andrew had themselves been trained as teachers by catechists in an SPG-sponsored school. The school remained in existence until 1763. Similar efforts by the SPG were seen in Georgia, North Carolina, and the Chesapeake colonies. In Williamsburg at mid-eighteenth century, missionaries baptized almost one thousand slaves in a twenty-year period. There were two successful schools in Philadelphia and others throughout Pennsylvania, all of which enjoyed a high rate of conversions.

Proselytizing efforts were successful in the South and middle Atlantic colonies, but missionaries were less successful in New England communities, where Anglicans were not welcomed. Despite the hostility, the SPG sent English missionaries, who established schools in all the New England colonies. They also employed American-born Anglican ministers, such as Timothy Cutler and Samuel Johnson. Many slaves joined Christian churches as a result of the religious revival that sparked the First Great Awakening in the early 1740s, but for the most part these converts were not attracted to the Church of England but to the evangelical religions, which stressed personal involvement and encouraged emotional responses from the congregation. The Society of Friends (Quakers) also drew African American converts in the latter part of the eighteenth century, since its members favored emancipation.

Anglican Church after the Revolution. Emancipation of many slaves accompanied and followed the American Revolution in the northern states. The war itself posed difficulties for both black and white religious leaders of the Church of England, who weathered the disintegration of the church that occurred during the Revolution. Most of the Anglican clergy refused to abandon their oaths of office to the king, the head of the Anglican Church, and were thus ostracized, imprisoned, or exiled from their parishes. After the war's conclusion, few Anglican ministers remained in America. Of those who stayed, William White, later bishop of Pennsylvania, led an effort in 1782 to form a general convention to gain recognition from the Church of England for an American national church. The Protestant Episcopal Church was formed in 1789, with Bishop William White presiding. The first general convention of the church established a House of Bishops and a House of Deputies and adopted a revised Book of Common Prayer that omitted the prayer to preserve the king and to give him victory over his enemies.

The Episcopal Church in the United States formed several black congregations and later ordained African American priests, mostly in the north. These priests largely served freed blacks. Among the most effective black religious leaders were Absalom Jones from Delaware and Richard Allen from Philadelphia, both slaves who had bought their own freedom. Deeply religious and committed to the Episcopal Church, Allen, who had experienced a religious conversion around 1777, traveled extensively to win converts. In 1787 he and Jones founded the Free African Religious Society, a mutual aid society for African Americans. Both served as lay ministers for the mostly free black members of Saint George's Methodist Episcopal Church in Philadelphia. Allen and Jones were so effective as lay ministers that the African American congregation of Saint George's grew dramatically, causing unease among white members.

Finally, in 1792, white members voted to segregate blacks in an upstairs gallery. Blacks left the church en masse when Jones and Allen, who had been kneeling in prayer, were pulled away from the sanctuary by whites. Indignant free blacks in Philadelphia decided that they preferred to be separate from whites and formed the Saint Thomas African Church, successfully applying in 1794 for membership in the Episcopal diocese of Pennsylvania, with Jones as pastor. Jones was ordained as a priest in 1802, becoming the first black Episcopal priest in America and a vocal critic of the institution of slavery. Allen was active in the African Church until he left Saint Thomas in 1816 for the Bethel African Church, which joined with other churches to form the African Methodist Episcopal Church. Allen served as the first bishop of the newly organized church and continued his protests against slavery and the slave trade.

Episcopalians after the Revolution neglected formal missionary work because they were most concerned with maintaining or rebuilding the membership of their church. A plan to expand the missionary effort among African Americans and Indians was offered in 1792 but abandoned in 1795 for lack of interest. Hence, the leadership did not again turn its attention to missionary work until the 1810s, perhaps inspired by the religious revival known as the Second Great Awakening of the early nineteenth century. John Henry Hobart, bishop of New York, and Alexander V. Griswold, bishop of the Eastern Diocese, which encompassed the New England states, both fostered missionary work in their diocese. During the same decade Richard Channing Moore, named bishop of Virginia in 1814, and Philander Chase, bishop of Ohio in 1819, encouraged missionary work with a more formal missionary society organized by the General Convention in 1735. Despite the best efforts of the missionaries, relatively few African Americans were attracted to the Episcopal Church in the nineteenth century.

Protestant Episcopal Church in the Nineteenth Century. African Americans may have been dissuaded from joining the Episcopal Church because the church did not take a strong stand against slavery. Achieving freedom for slaves was never the intent of the Church of England or its missionary arm, the SPG, or that of its American successor, the Protestant Episcopal Church. The major efforts of the Anglican, later Protestant Episcopal, Church in America were to achieve the conversions of African Americans to Anglicanism. While individual priests and catechists might have favored freedom upon conversion, prevailing fears among whites forced missionaries to focus their efforts on saving souls and ameliorating conditions for slaves.

Despite a general indifference to slavery on the part of Episcopalians, some efforts were made to persuade the church to take a stand against the institution and to attract African Americans to the church and the ministry. A few blacks reached high office, as did James Theodore Holly, born in Washington, D.C., who served as a deacon at Saint Matthew's Church in Detroit and as rector of Saint Luke's Church in New Haven Connecticut. There, with four other black clergymen, he established a society in 1856 to increase the number of black people in the Protestant Episcopal Church. Holly protested that blacks were not permitted to attend Episcopal seminaries and criticized the church for not openly opposing slavery. In 1874 James Theodore Holly was consecrated as the first black Episcopal Bishop in America.

While the prevailing opinion among Episcopal churchmen was that secular affairs were not their concern, the church tried to serve the spiritual needs of African Americans as settlement proceeded to the west. In 1853 the

Reverend Peter Williams Cassey, a young, free, black minister from Philadelphia, arrived in California to minister to the black communities in San Jose and San Francisco. Cassey stayed in California for twenty-nine years, founding Saint Philip's Mission School and a high school for black children in San Jose, the latter funded partially with his own money. He was ordained to the diaconate in 1866 and in 1881 was named the first black priest at Saint Cyprian's in New Bern, North Carolina.

The Protestant Episcopal Church also gave limited support, financial and otherwise, to the American Colonization Society and in 1847 sent Alexander Crummell, a New York-raised black man, to Liberia as a missionary for the church. Crummell returned to Washington, D.C., in 1873 and was appointed missionary to Saint Luke's Church, established for blacks in 1880, where he encouraged black Episcopal ministers in Washington to fight racism in the church.

While indifference to social problems was the rule, the church was affected by the Civil War when ten southern bishops broke from the northern church in 1860 to form the Protestant Episcopal Church in the Confederate States of America. In 1865 the dioceses were reunited and the Freedman's Commission was formed to found schools and churches to prepare black men to serve as ministers. The commission was disbanded in 1876 for lack of interest on the part of whites. That same year blacks in Baltimore founded a society to proselytize and educate blacks. Despite such efforts, from 1866 to 1877, there were only twenty black ordained ministers and only six of them became priests. Southern bishops in particular were reluctant to ordain blacks because of lingering prejudice.

Efforts were made to increase the number of black clergymen with the establishment of a black divinity school in Petersburg, Virginia, since blacks were not permitted in white schools. This school was founded at the behest of James Solomon Russell, a devout black man who wanted to become a church minister. In 1878 Russell approached Virginia Bishop Francis M. Whittle, who persuaded the Reverend Thomas Spencer and the Reverend Giles B. Cooke to work with black students. A seminary, Saint Stephen's Normal and Theological School, later known as the Bishop Payne Divinity School, opened to train black priests. While enrollment was low in the first few years, it increased to eighteen students by 1882.

Even with the establishment of this and other seminaries specifically geared to produce black priests, the Episcopal Church continued to have little appeal for African Americans, whose membership in the church by 1900 was only 15,000.

[*See also* African Methodist Episcopal Church; Allen, Richard; Education; Fraternal Organizations and Mutual Aid Societies; Great Awakening; Jones, Absalom; Laws and Legislation; Missionary Movements; Neau, Elias; New York Slave Revolt of 1712; Religion; Slavery: Lower South; Slavery: Northeast; Slavery: Upper South; Society for the Propagation of the Gospel in Foreign Parts; *and* Society of Friends (Quakers) and African Americans.]

BIBLIOGRAPHY

Davis, Brion David. *In the Image of God: Religion, Moral Values, and Our Heritage of Slavery*. New Haven, CT: Yale University Press, 2001.

Davis, Brion David. *Slavery and Human Progress*. New York: Oxford University Press, 1984.

Genovese, Eugene D. *Roll, Jordan, Roll: The World the Slaves Made*. New York: Pantheon Books, 1974.

Gilroy, Paul. *The Black Atlantic: Modernity and Double Consciousness*. Cambridge, MA: Harvard University Press, 1993.

Haynes, Stephen R. *Noah's Curse: The Biblical Justification of American Slavery*. New York: Oxford University Press, 2002.

Morgan, Kenneth. *Slavery and Servitude in Colonial North America: A Short History*. New York: New York University Press, 2001.

Morgan, Philip D. *Slave Counterpoint: Black Culture in the Eighteenth Century Chesapeake and Lowcountry*. Chapel Hill: University of North Carolina Press, 1998.

Nash, Gary B. *Red, White, and Black: The Peoples of Early North America*. 4th ed. Upper Saddle River, NJ: Prentice Hall, 2000.

Stark, Rodney. *For the Glory of God: How Monotheism Led to Reformations, Science, Witch-Hunts, and the End of Slavery*. Princeton, NJ: Princeton University Press, 2003.

—MARY LOU LUSTIG

EQUIANO, OLAUDAH (b. c. 1745; d. 1797), slave, freedman, mariner, author, abolitionist, and employee of the British government. Olaudah Equiano identified himself by this name only once in his life—on the title page of *The Interesting Narrative of the Life of Olaudah Equiano, or Gustavus Vassa, the African* (1789). In the *Narrative* itself Equiano wrote of his forename that it was an Ibo word meaning "change," "fortunate," or "loudly or well spoken," but this derivation has not been corroborated. Words similar to his surname have been identified in languages spoken both east and west of the Niger River, which flows south through Iboland, the southeastern region of present-day Nigeria, where Equiano claimed to have been born. He was accused almost immediately of fabrication, however, and he may have been born in North America. All other documentation of his life, including vital records and his own signatures, used the name Gustavus Vassa (sometimes Vasa, Vassan, and other variations). Both the *Narrative* and commercial and public records reveal that Equiano worked at sea as both a slave and a freedman beginning in the 1750s and continuing through much of his life. He purchased his own freedom in 1766 but worked within the slave system as a purchaser, conveyer, and overseer in the 1770s.

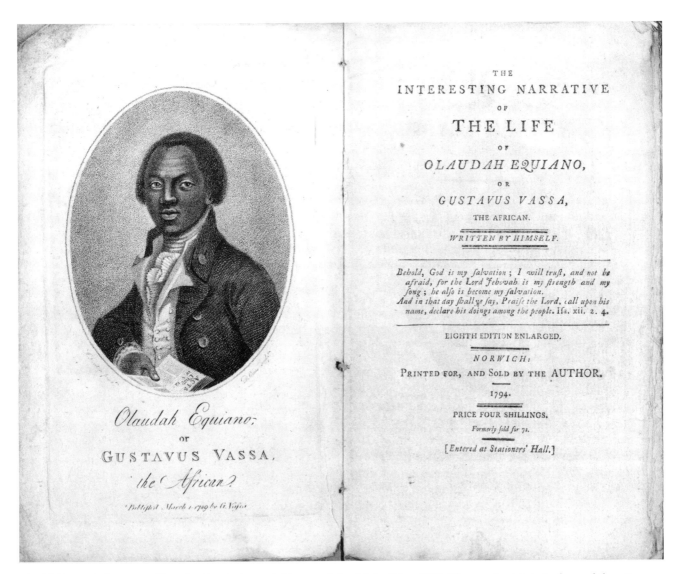

THE

INTERESTING NARRATIVE

OF

THE LIFE

OF

OLAUDAH EQUIANO,

OR

GUSTAVUS VASSA,

THE AFRICAN.

WRITTEN BY HIMSELF.

Behold, God is my salvation; I will trust, and not be afraid, for the Lord Jehovah is my strength and my song; he also is become my salvation. And in that day shall ye say, Praise the Lord, call upon his name, declare his doings among the people. Isa. xii. 2. 4.

EIGHTH EDITION ENLARGED.

NORWICH:

PRINTED FOR, AND SOLD BY THE AUTHOR.

1794.

PRICE FOUR SHILLINGS.

Formerly sold for 7s.

[*Entered at Stationers' Hall.*]

Olaudah Equiano;
or
GUSTAVUS VASSA,
the African?

Olaudah Equiano's *Interesting Narrative*, frontispiece and title page of the eighth edition, 1794. The narrative intertwined several thematic threads—abolitionist, religious, and entrepreneurial. (Library of Congress.)

Equiano began to identify himself as a Christian in the 1770s and then to associate with British abolitionists in the 1780s. He became an active member—indeed an employee of the British government—in the effort of the mid-1780s to establish a West African settlement of blacks then living in England. The settlement at Granville Town, later Freetown, in Sierra Leone was intended to offer opportunities for impoverished black Britons, usually called London's black poor, as well as to establish a commercial foundation and naval base to undermine the slave trade. In the language of the times, the goal was legitimate trade as a substitute for the illegitimate trade in slaves, although the slave trade had not yet been outlawed. Equiano lost his commission in 1787 because of conflict with other principals of the effort; nevertheless, black emigrants from England, Nova Scotia, and Jamaica did establish a settlement in Sierra Leone despite such difficulties as endemic malaria and inability to weaken the slave trade in the area.

Equiano went on to publish his *Narrative* and to promote it over the course of its nine editions as well as to answer critics who either defended the slave system or denounced him as a liar. He married and fathered two daughters, one of whom survived him and received a substantial inheritance upon his death on 31 March 1797. His influence on abolitionism was strong in the late eighteenth century but declined in the mid-nineteenth century. Twentieth-century interest in black literature and history reestablished him as a crucial figure in what has come to be known as the black Atlantic, the subculture created by eighteenth-century black people who traveled among points in West Africa, Great Britain, and the Americas or articulated ideas and values, uniformly antislavery, drawing from African, European, and American sources.

The *Narrative* intertwined several thematic threads—abolitionist, religious, and entrepreneurial. None was unique to Equiano—indeed, he identified many of his sources—but he was the first black man to unite these elements in an autobiography. As an abolitionist, Equiano wrote at a time when the slave trade and the institution of slavery came under concerted attack for the first time in Europe and the Americas. His strategy was to concede that slavery had seemed legitimate in earlier times and places but that both the horrors of the Atlantic slave system and the eighteenth-century understanding of Christianity had revealed unambiguously that slavery was indeed morally illegitimate.

In general, Equiano acknowledged that ancient slavery, particularly the Israelites' enslavement of conquered people as described in the Bible, had seemed acceptable before the period of the New Testament but should not be tolerated in the Christian world. Like many of his contemporaries, he considered sub-Saharan Africans to be descendants of the Israelites, and he attributed the ownership and sale of slaves in Ibo society to its supposedly Jewish roots. Thus slaves in Equiano's home society were in some ways protected by remnants of Old Testament laws mandating fair treatment of the enslaved, but in this biblical interpretation slavery itself was a feature of ancient times that should be erased from the modern world.

Moreover, in contrast to the relatively humane treatment of Ibo slaves, only obdurate defenders of the slave system claimed that New World slaves were treated fairly. Abolitionists like Equiano pointed to the abuses and cruelties of the Atlantic slave trade and New World slavery. Equiano himself had come to embody the abolitionism he promoted in the 1780s: his African family had owned slaves, and he himself had been both a victim of and an overseer within the slave system, but he finally converted to abolitionism. Whatever the accuracy of his historical argument, it was aimed at his contemporaries, who had often taken the enslavement of others for granted but lived in an era in which leading reformers envisioned the termination of both the slave trade and institutionalized slavery. In this regard Equiano shared the moral and historical understandings of eighteenth-century abolitionists, both black and white.

As a man of faith, Equiano claimed to recognize providence, a divine plan, at work in his life, even in the miseries of the Middle Passage, the westward ocean crossing to the Americas. He acknowledged that events did not happen at random in his life and that the divine plan involved his subjugation in slavery, his liberation, and his establishment as a spokesperson for black people. In this sense he conformed to such Old Testament models as Moses and Joseph. The *Narrative* contrasted belief in chance or fortune, which was a sign of an unconverted individual, to belief in providence, which was the mark of a Christian. Equiano's faith also prevented him from committing suicide in a time of despair.

The form of Christianity to which Equiano was most attracted was Calvinistic Methodism, represented by the Countess of Huntingdon, who supported several late-eighteenth-century black authors; the clergyman William Romaine, who preached in churches attended by Equiano and by London's black poor; and the revivalist George Whitefield, who preached in Britain and America—at least once with Equiano in the audience. While Wesleyan Methodism emphasized the individual's ability to earn grace and salvation through prayer, preparation, and good works, Calvinism, albeit demanding those acts, insisted that nothing the individual did was worthy of grace and salvation, which were God's free gifts. The appeal of Calvinistic Methodism derived from its vivid sense of divine providence and a social ethic that emphasized love and benevolence. The former assured black men and women that their sufferings were ultimately meaningful as part of a divine plan, while the latter suggested the means by which racism could be overcome and blacks and whites could coexist harmoniously. These religious convictions were shared by many Americans and Britons in the Calvinist tradition.

As an entrepreneur, Equiano exemplified one way in which blacks could gain and extend their freedom as well as improve their status in the world. Despite the horrors of the Middle Passage, as described in the *Narrative*, the young Equiano acquired an education in navigation and commerce during the voyage. He was curious about the functioning of the ship and found that some members of the crew were willing to answer his questions. As he matured, his commercial interests grew stronger, and he became a petty trader in glassware, produce, and livestock. Of course, employment in the slave trade and in plantation work was one of the impulses that he soon resisted.

Equiano's business sense and his honesty in bargaining formed one of the major themes of the *Narrative*, as when he noted that white men stole his goods, refused to pay him, or even threatened violence when he sought a fair exchange. These commercial interests led to his two major efforts of the 1780s and 1790s: the Sierra Leone venture and the publication and promotion of the *Narrative*. Although Equiano never sailed to Sierra Leone, the settlement project reflected one of the premises of eighteenth-century abolitionism—that commerce profitable to blacks and whites alike would be necessary to subdue the slave system, because trading in human beings would not cease without an advantageous replacement. Whatever the *Narrative*'s abolitionist and religious import, the book was meant to earn money for its author, thus gaining him some financial independence and security. Equiano registered his text in order to hold copyright, promoted the book, and saw it through nine editions in his lifetime; he left a legacy, probably derived largely from the book's proceeds, to his only surviving child.

As a leading figure of the black Atlantic, Equiano has appealed to modern readers for his written record of West African life as well as for his commercial ambition. Yet it is possible that he constructed the account of an Ibo boyhood out of materials available in eighteenth-century abolitionist texts and travelogues, supplemented by tales of African life he had heard from blacks he encountered in the Caribbean islands, North America, and England. Moreover, one cannot understand his entrepreneurship apart from his abolitionism and his religious beliefs, for all three were intertwined in his experience.

[*See also* Abolitionism; Autobiography; Black Seafarers; Entrepreneurs; Free African Americans to 1828; Literature; Maritime Trades; Methodist Church and African Americans; Slave Narratives; *and* Slave Trade.]

BIBLIOGRAPHY

Braidwood, Stephen J. *Black Poor and White Philanthropists: London's Blacks and the Foundation of the Sierra Leone Settlement, 1786–1791.* Liverpool, UK: Liverpool University Press, 1994.

Carretta, Vincent, ed. *Olaudah Equiano: The Interesting Narrative and Other Writings.* New York: Penguin Books, 2003.

Paget, Henry. *Caliban's Reason: Introducing Afro-Caribbean Philosophy.* New York: Routledge, 2000.

Walvin, James. *An African's Life: The Life and Times of Olaudah Equiano, 1745–1797.* New York: Continuum, 2000.

Zafar, Rafia. *We Wear the Mask: African Americans Write American Literature, 1760–1870.* New York: Columbia University Press, 1997.

—JOHN SAILLANT

ESTEBAN (b. c. 1500–1503; d. c. 1539), a Moroccan slave who participated in a Spanish expedition across the North American continent. Also known as Estevan, Estevanico, Stephen the Black, and the Black Moor, Esteban was born in Azamor (or Azemmour), Morocco, between 1500 and 1503. By 1527 he had been taken from Africa, most likely by Spanish or Portuguese slave traders, and brought to Spain, where he became the "personal servant" (that is, slave) of Andrés Dorantes de Carranza.

In 1527 Dorantes volunteered himself and Esteban for a Spanish expedition to the New World, commanded by Don Pánfilo de Narváez. The purpose of the journey was to conquer and claim land from the Isle of Florida (discovered and named fifteen years earlier by Juan Ponce de León) to northeastern Mexico. At its start the exploration included approximately six hundred men aboard five vessels; of those men only four were still alive when they reached what is today Galveston Island, Texas: Esteban, his master, Álvar Núñez Cabeza de Vaca, and Alonso Castillo Maldonado.

When they finally arrived in Mexico City in 1536, Carranza and Esteban chose to remain there, while Cabeza de Vaca and Maldonado returned to Spain. Before long Esteban was "bought" by the viceroy of Mexico City; he enjoyed several years of relative freedom within the city before returning to Spain in 1539. Esteban's time in Mexico gave him broad familiarity with the area and the customs of its people as well as fluency in several different native languages. Consequently, three years after returning from his first expedition Esteban was appointed as guide and translator for an exploration led by the Franciscan friar Marcos de Niza. This subsequent excursion would essentially follow the same route that Esteban and Cabeza de Vaca had taken previously and was intended to gather information for the Spanish conquistador Francisco Vásquez de Coronado, who planned to lead an expedition in 1540. Specifically, Marcos de Niza was instructed to bring back information about the Seven Cities of Cibola, where gold and precious stones were said to abound.

At some point in the journey Esteban and several others left the group to scout ahead—whether of Esteban's own volition or under orders from Marcos de Niza is unknown—and later sent runners bearing wooden crosses back to the friar to indicate that he and the others should follow. Historical accounts of what occurred from this point onward conflict greatly. Whatever the reason, Esteban and the few men he had brought with him continued walking until they reached Hawikuh, the Zuni pueblo believed to be the first of the "cities of gold." Upon entering Hawikuh that night, Esteban and his companions were taken to a large house on the outskirts of the village and were instructed to remain there. The following morning Esteban was dead.

Esteban is recognized as the first African to explore southwestern North America. Although several original documents from the 1500s contain references to the Black Moor, only two were written by men who actually traveled with him: *La relación* (The account), most likely the first indication of Esteban's existence, and a report from a subsequent journey undertaken in 1539. In the late 1990s a Texas photographer established the Estevanico Society, which is "dedicated to scholarly research into the life and journeys of Estevanico," including his origins in

Morocco and later enslavement by the Portuguese and Spanish. Members of the society are particularly concerned with learning the truth about Esteban's final journey.

[*See also* Europe; New Spain and Mexico; *and* Slave Trade.]

BIBLIOGRAPHY

Cabeza de Vaca, Álvar Núñez. *The Journey of Álvar Núñez Cabeza de Vaca and His Companions from Florida to the Pacific, 1528–1536.* Translated by Fanny Bandelier. Edited by A. F. Bandelier. New York: A. S. Barnes, 1905. http://www.pbs.org/weta/thewest/resources/archives/one/cabeza.htm.

Riley, Carroll L. "Blacks in the Early Southwest." *Ethnohistory* 19.3 (Summer 1972): 247–260.

—PENNY ANNE WELBOURNE

ETHNOLOGY. Proponents of ethnology, a pseudoscience popular in the mid-nineteenth century, claimed that races of people were, in fact, separate human species. Some southern proslavery advocates used the notion of ethnology to support the belief that as a separate species, individuals of African descent were an inferior race and perfectly suited for slavery, but only one major advocate of ethnology hailed from the southern states. Ethnology formed only a minor influence on racial thinking among the general populace, but it did gain support among the scientific community and some intellectuals.

The American school of ethnology, which was not an institution but more an informal movement, evolved from scientific principles set forth by Samuel George Morton, a Philadelphia physician. Having studied the internal cranial capacity of humans from various races and ethnic groups, Morton rejected prevailing theories, which held that environmental forces played the largest part in racial differentiation—for example, that Africans generally had dark skin because they lived in a climate with hot sun. Morton was convinced that the variations in cranial capacity he observed could not be related to environmental factors and therefore provided evidence of permanent racial distinctions. The implications of ethnology flew in the face of the prevailing fundamental biblical interpretation holding that all humans descended from a single pair, Adam and Eve, and raised the ire of many clerics and devoutly religious southerners.

Building on the belief that Africans formed a separate species, some proslavery scientists and physicians postulated that African Americans suffered from diseases and ailments peculiar to their species. Samuel L. Cartwright, a Louisiana physician otherwise respected for his treatment of cholera patients, wrote frequently of the "diseases and peculiarities of the negro race," in southern agricul-

tural and business journals, with his advice to slaveholders appearing frequently in *DeBow's Review*. In an 1851 article he described several "negro" diseases, including drapetomania, which caused slaves to run away. The cure for this ailment, according to Cartwright, included providing adequate clothing, food, and shelter and allowing nuclear families to live together. He advised slaveholders that slaves "have only to be kept in that state and treated like children, with care and kindness, attention and humanity, to prevent and cure them from running away."

Dysasthesia ethiopica, another "peculiar" disease, seemed most likely to affect free African Americans who had "not got some white person to direct and to take care of them." This mental affliction was accompanied by skin lesions readily identifiable by skilled physicians such as Cartwright. When slaves suffered from dysasthesia ethiopica, they exhibited a "stupidness of mind and insensibility of the nerves" which caused them to "break, waste and destroy" everything they handled. Common to the sufferer's behavior were abusing farm animals, breaking tools, and stealing. Cartwright also claimed that they tended to "wander about at night, and keep in a half nodding sleep during the day." The cure for this disease was simple, Cartwright maintained: simply bathe and oil the patient. "Slap the oil in with a broad leather strap; then put the patient to some hard kind of work in the open air and sunshine."

Josiah Nott, a southern physician and theorist molded a cultural adaptation of ethnology and applied it as a justification for enslaving men and women of African descent. As the most prominent southern member of the American school of ethnology, Nott earned notoriety following the publication of the article "The Mulatto a Hybrid—Probable Extermination of the Two Races If the Whites and Blacks Are Allowed to Intermarry." Appearing in the *American Journal of the Medical Sciences* in 1843, the article argued that as the offspring of separate species, mixed-race persons (mulattoes) were hybrids that would produce sterile children. Thus, miscegenation would eventually lead to the end of humanity. While Morton based his findings on careful statistics collected during scientific experiments, Nott never produced evidence to support his theories.

In the early 1850s Nott paired with the ethnologist George R. Gliddon, originally from Great Britain, to write a comprehensive book detailing the theories and variations of thought in the American school of ethnology. Appearing in 1854 as *Types of Mankind; or, Ethnological Researches, Based upon the Ancient Monuments, Paintings, Sculptures, and Crania of Races*, the work consolidated and condensed previous work in the field. *Types of Mankind* emphasized permanent differences between the races, argued that Caucasians had greater cranial capacity, and supported polygenesis: the notion that the various races were actually different species that originated from separate creations.

Frederick Douglass was one of the self-styled intellectuals who paid attention to ethnology, and it is quite likely that he read *Types of Mankind*. In his second autobiography, published in the year following Nott and Gliddon's book, Douglass admits to reading another work of natural science, James Cowles Prichard's *The Natural History of Man* (1848). Douglass remarked that a figure on page 157 closely resembled his mother, Harriet Bailey. The same image, incidentally an image of Egyptian pharaoh Ramses the Great, can be found in the first edition of *Types of Mankind*.

The American school of ethnology and *Types of Mankind* continued to be a topic of debate for the remainder of the 1850s. Clergymen attacked the book and ethnology in general for their contradiction of accepted religious doctrine and the denial of a single human creation. Ethnologists' attack on religion, more than their position on race, appalled many nineteenth-century Americans, North and South, but it took another controversial scientist to finally quell the voice of the American school. It was Charles Darwin and the 1859 publication of his *Origin of Species* that finally smothered the ethnologists. Using bona fide scientific method, Darwin demonstrated that the various species on Earth were not fixed by separate creations but instead were constantly changing and evolving.

[*See also* Black Family; Douglass, Frederick; Health; Marriage, Mixed; Mulattoes; Proslavery Thought; Race, Theories of; Racism; *and* Religion.]

BIBLIOGRAPHY

Cartwright, Samuel. "Diseases and Peculiarities of the Negro Race." *DeBow's Review* 11 (1851): 331–336.

Douglass, Frederick. *My Bondage and My Freedom.* Edited by John W. Blassingame, John R. McKivigan, and Peter P. Hinks. New Haven, CT: Yale University Press, 2003.

Finkelman, Paul. *Defending Slavery: Proslavery Thought in the Old South.* Boston: Bedford/St. Martin's, 2003.

Nott, J. C., and George R. Gliddon. *Types of Mankind; or, Ethnological Researches, Based upon the Ancient Monuments, Paintings, Sculptures, and Crania of the Races.* Philadelphia: J. B. Lippincott, Grambo, 1854.

Will, Thomas E. "The American School of Ethnology: Science and Scripture in the Proslavery Argument." *Southern Historian* 19 (1998): 14–34.

—L. DIANE BARNES

EUROPE. European visitors to the United States were keenly interested in slavery, African Americans, and race relations in America. Few blacks lived in Europe, as slavery had been abolished there, and almost no black Americans visited the Continent. European visitors held a spectrum of opinions about Americans and their customs: some praised qualities like ingenuity and democracy, while others criticized a lack of good manners. Europeans, though, were almost universal in their condemnation of slavery, even as they held a variety of opinions about African Americans.

Visitors traveling to northern states usually found their contact with African Americans to be agreeable. There were relatively few blacks in these areas; Europeans saw blacks working as both skilled and unskilled laborers. African Americans might carry luggage into an inn, serve meals in restaurants, or repair shoes. The Russian diplomat Pavel Svin'in visited the United States between 1811 and 1813. He went to a black Methodist service in Philadelphia, where he saw a bombastic preacher move the congregation to repentance. Svin'in was respectful of the church members but likened the minister to a Jacobin agitator stirring up a revolutionary crowd.

Most Europeans noticed that African Americans in the North suffered various types of discrimination. The French traveler Alexis de Tocqueville compiled a long list of difficulties encountered by free blacks: they were subject to physical intimidation if they tried to vote, could not marry whites, were barred from juries, attended inferior schools, and worshipped in different churches. James Boardman was present when blacks in New York City were not permitted to continue a Fifth of July celebration, held on that day to highlight the paradox of the existence of slavery in a "free" country. He noted that blacks were prohibited from being buried in the same cemeteries as white. The famed Frenchman Marquis de Lafayette, who fought for the Patriots during the American Revolution, returned to the United States in 1824 and noted the condition of northern blacks. At a banquet in New York City, Lafayette forcefully denounced recent legislation that effectively disenfranchised African Americans.

Europeans who traveled to slaveholding states were typically forthcoming in their observations of African Americans, with the clothing, work, living conditions, and punishment of slaves generating most of the comments. Europeans abhorred slavery and its inherent degradation and believed that it stained everything it touched. When the British tourist Isaac Candler passed from Pennsylvania to Maryland, he noted a significant change in the countryside. Neat farms and substantial houses gave way to slovenly pastures and ill-constructed huts. The roads became increasingly poor and the bridges more sporadic.

Many travelers believed slavery inhibited economic and social development because it held down wages and encouraged idleness. In 1822 the British tourist William Blane tartly noted that slavery did the least possible for people in terms of clothing, food, and wages; in return the slaves did the least work they could for their masters. The result was economic stagnation. When Lafayette visited Thomas Jefferson at Monticello, he concluded that the plantation would have been more profitable if Jefferson had run it with paid labor rather than slaves. Other Europeans agreed with Thomas Jefferson's famous remarks that slavery corrupted the morals of a society. Tocqueville, who thought slavery destroyed the character of the enslaver, was among them.

Even though Europeans were generally uncomfortable with slavery, they felt some sympathy for their white southern hosts. Travelers heard slaveholders complain about the problems of slavery while asserting in the next breath that they had no other choice but to maintain the peculiar institution. Such observations resonated with the many Europeans who believed in the necessity of a hierarchical society. Slave owners tried to put the best possible appearance on slavery, showing their guests only certain dimensions of southern life. Travelers usually noted that house servants were well dressed and appeared to be given preferential treatment; some found the physical conditions of most slaves to be relatively benign. Although he hated slavery, Lafayette thought Jefferson's slaves at least to be well treated.

Most Europeans, however, described horrid conditions for slaves on plantations. The rude huts of the typical slave quarter looked to one visitor like something fit only for monkeys. Others commented on the long work hours or poor labor conditions. A few witnessed or heard about whippings, beatings, and the consequential deaths of slaves. In 1807 the British traveler John Lambert related a story about a female slave owner who helped whip her slave's back until it was raw; she and her husband then applied pepper and salt to the wounds. The slave died in agony a few hours later. In 1820 the British tourist Adam Hodgson spoke with a twenty-two-year-old master who had recently shot one of his slaves for running away. Hodgson was stunned to hear that some of the men's neighbors had made sport of hunting down two runaway slaves. Another visitor learned that his host had whipped a female slave for not serving breakfast on time. Such incidents, though fairly unusual in early travel accounts, only served to strengthen the antislavery opinions of the authors.

Slave sales and the interstate slave trade were another source of macabre fascination for Europeans. Although they seldom witnessed the actual deportation of a slave from a plantation, travelers heard stories of slaves who committed suicide or mutilated themselves—perhaps cutting off a hand with an axe—rather than be sold away from friends and family. Travelers did attend slave auctions and were repulsed by the physical examination of the slaves and the heartrending scenes that accompanied the sundering of family ties. In Charleston, South Car-

olina, one English traveler saw African slaves march to a slave pen in the city's center, where whites used cash or horses to buy slaves. Other Europeans went inside slave pens, where slave traders housed bond servants before transporting them to the markets of the Deep South. The jail owned by the immensely successful slave traders Isaac Franklin and John Armfield in Alexandria, Virginia, attracted the most attention; Europeans could leisurely sip wine in the parlor and tour the facilities. One traveler was surprised by the cleanliness of the jail but also thought that his hosts had treated him kindly so that workers could have time to tidy up the building.

Although most Europeans disagreed with slavery, they did not agree on what to do about it and were divided about its future. Many, like Lafayette, wanted the institution terminated as quickly as possible; the Frenchman was a member of the American Colonization Society, which looked to send freed slaves back to Africa, and tried to persuade the statesmen James Monroe and James Madison to take up the cause of emancipation in Virginia. Lafayette's countryman Francois-Jean, Marquis de Chastellux, predicted that slavery, which created a crude system of aristocracy where poor whites could look down upon their slaves, would not soon wither away; racial solidarity created a powerful community in favor of slavery's preservation. Chastellux believed that the only way to end the institution was to allow it to fall beneath the weight of reason and humanity. The British traveler Charles Janson, who visited the United States in 1793, was even less optimistic. He hated slavery but advised against emancipation, as he predicted that abolition would destroy staple-crop production in the South and encourage slaves to take vengeance upon their owners. Thus, he believed, the best course of action was to invoke stringent regulations to ensure that owners provided enough food, clothing, and shelter for their bondpeople.

One of the few Europeans to defend slavery was Charles Sealsfield, born Karl Postl in Austria; Sealsfield purchased a plantation and slaves along the Red River in Louisiana. He understood the contradiction of slavery's denial of liberty in a democracy but saw no solution to the problem. His racism toward African Americans—he also wrote disparagingly about Native Americans—led him to argue that there was no feasible way to emancipate slaves. He concluded that the best course of action was to make slavery as humane as possible; judging from his writing, he believed that whites were doing their slaves a favor by owning them.

As might be expected, European contact with the United States declined during the Civil War. Europeans were deeply interested in the conflict but few visitors ventured across the Atlantic Ocean. The governments of Great Britain and France considered officially recognizing the Confederate States of America, but the politicians were too divided to take decisive action. Had either or both countries provided significant diplomatic, financial, or military assistance to the Confederacy, the Civil War might have had a different outcome. A longer war or a Confederate victory would have extended the life of American slavery.

Wartime European opinions of slavery and African Americans varied tremendously. Most working class Britons wanted to see the extinction of slavery, but unemployed textile workers in Lancashire, for instance, favored English intervention in the war to secure supplies of cotton. Although some British statesmen secretly hoped for a weakened, or even divided, America to emerge from the war, the English government had been committed for decades to destroying slavery. Once American president Abraham Lincoln signed the Emancipation Proclamation, which legally freed slaves in areas controlled by the Confederacy, the war unquestioningly became a referendum on the future of slavery in America. Great Britain could no longer consider aiding the South. France proved more sympathetic to the defense of slavery and assistance to the Confederacy—French ruler Napoleon III even created a puppet monarchy in Mexico—but would not act unilaterally. The defeat of the Confederacy proved agreeable to most Europeans.

The end of the Civil War might have brought peace but it did not revive European interest in the South or African Americans. Visitors were more interested in changes brought on by the industrial revolution or settlement of the American west. Native Americans, it seems, replaced slaves as the objects of curiosity for European travelers. And while racism remained a pressing problem in the United States, it did not attract the attention of Europeans that slavery did. Unless visitors had a special interest in Reconstruction or the racial problems of America, they usually bypassed the South and ignored northern African Americans altogether. Visitors took the political and social exclusion of African Americans for granted and rarely mentioned them in travel accounts. The few Europeans who wrote about African Americans reveal a range of opinions.

Charles Boissevain, a Dutch journalist, described steamboat workers as wild savages who sang merry songs. This depiction of the roustabouts who hoisted cotton bales onto the decks of riverboats reflected much of the prevailing European condescension towards blacks. Boissevain believed that African Americans did not have the intellectual capacity to govern whites, nor the good sense to vote responsibly. He predicted improved race relations in the United States, but only because more white immigrants would settle in the South and many blacks would move to Mexico.

H. G. Wells argued that there was no "Negro problem" in the United States. White Americans were the problem and needed to change their racial attitudes. Wells was one of the few Europeans to write candidly about racial prejudice. He understood that prejudice was not confined to the South and noted how three blacks were lynched in Springfield, Missouri. Wells, unlike most of his counterparts, noticed that blacks worked primarily in menial jobs. Still Wells, despite his advanced views in race, thought most of the African Americans were content with their inferiority. Instead of realizing that blacks were largely exploited, Wells though African Americans and immigrants weakened the power of organized labor and increased political corruption by working the worst jobs. In Boston Wells met with the African American activist Booker T. Washington and came away impressed. Wells described Washington as a statesman but disagreed with Washington's belief that black and white could live as separately as fingers. Wells argued that this intermingled distinctness could not endure because Americans—white and black—need to be educated on how the races were inseparable.

William Archer represented yet another viewpoint. Archer, whose book preface directly stated his disagreement with Wells, traveled the United States and made it a point to visit the South. Along the way he defended an African American man from a beating, denounced lynching, visited Tuskegee Institute, and decried the horrendous public health for blacks. Despite Archer's apparent sympathy for the plight of African Americans, he endorsed segregation, given the large proportion of blacks in the population. When riding in a train in Mississippi, Archer revealed, he did not want to sit next to the multitudes of African Americans. He described southern white reactions—segregation and Jim Crow laws, for instance—as a logical reaction and even endorsed the creation of a region or state within the United States for African Americans.

Archer also met with African American leaders Booker T. Washington and W. E. B. Du Bois. Like Wells before him, Archer made it a point to include the different philosophies of African American leaders in his book in order to educate literate Europeans. Both Wells and Archer, unlike most Europeans, understood how life in the American South forced whites and blacks to interact, sometimes on an almost equal level. The degree to which Europeans came to understand the racial travail of the United States is debatable, but there appears to be at least some familiarity with the black response to discrimination and segregation.

Booker T. Washington experienced this shallow understanding firsthand during his trip to Europe. Washington used the opportunity to recruit donors for his American activities, but found Europeans only dimly aware of conditions in the South and the plight of African Americans. He likened American racial problems to the attitudes of different European ethnic groups toward one another. Washington learned that widespread disfranchisement and discrimination were not unique to the United States. In Vienna, Austria, for instance, Washington was struck by the offhand remark of an Austrian who referred to some barefoot women as only Slovaks. He thought you might hear the same kind of cutting inflection in a white American's casual comment about an African American. Washington also noticed similarities between the poor European workers and American blacks. At least black women, he decided, had the opportunity for an education, and all African Americans were better off than the worst European peasants.

[*See also* American Colonization Society; Cemeteries and Burials; Crime and Punishment; Discrimination; Jefferson, Thomas, on African Americans and Slavery; Lafayette, Marquis de, and African Americans; Madison, James, and African Americans; Monroe, James, and African Americans; Slavery: Lower South; Slavery: Mid-Atlantic; Slavery: Northeast; Slavery: Upper South; Stereotypes of African Americans; Violence against African Americans; *and* Work.]

BIBLIOGRAPHY

Archer, William. *Through Afro-America: An English Reading of the Race Problem*. London: Chapman and Hall, 1910.

Berger, Max. *The British Traveller in America, 1836–1860*. Gloucester, MA: P. Smith, 1964.

Mathews, Basil. Booker T. Washington: *Educator and Interracial Interpreter*. College Park, MD: McGrath, 1969.

Mesick, Jane Louise. *The English Traveller in America, 1785–1835* (1920). Westport, CT: Greenwood, 1970.

Pachter, Marc, and Frances Wein, eds. *Abroad in America: Visitors to the New Nation, 1776–1914*. Reading, MA: Addison-Wesley, 1976.

Rapson, Richard L. *Britons View America: Travel Commentary, 1860–1935*. Seattle: University of Washington Press, 1971.

Tocqueville, Alexis de. *Democracy in America*. 2 vols. New York: Vintage, 1945.

Wells, H. G. *The Future in America: A Search after Realities*. New York: Harper and Brothers, 1906.

—ROBERT H. GUDMESTAD

EVOLUTION. When Charles Darwin published *The Origin of Species* in 1859, setting forth his theory of genetic evolution, he created an intense intellectual ferment that would ultimately rearrange popularly accepted fundamental concepts about life. Although earlier biologists had used the term *evolution* to describe changes in organisms, they had generally thought in terms of purposeful transformations, often directed by a higher intelligence. Darwin's theory was radically different in that it did not require any higher agency but instead relied on natural variations in populations of organisms. Some of the variations would be adaptive and lead to their holders successfully reproducing, while others would be destructive and lead to their holders dying out without leaving descendants.

Frederick Douglass rejected biological Darwinism, apparently out of revulsion at the possibility of nonhuman origins of humanity. His stance may have been related to many apologists for slavery having used the medieval concept of the "great chain of being" to posit the African as a link between the apes and "superior" Europeans. Even later scientists such as Charles Hamilton Smith justified racial bigotry by arguing for the theory of polygenesis, or "multiple Adams," by which blacks and whites were said to have separate origins instead of a common ancestor. Smith found fault with a long list of African and African American physical characteristics and claimed that these weaknesses were proof of African Americans' supposed inferiority and suitability only for a subordinate place in society.

Strongly interested in Lamarckian theories of evolution as driven by the inheritance of acquired characteristics, Douglass believed that human variability was a direct response to climactic pressures. People who moved to hotter lands would become darker, and their children would inherit their darker skin. However, there was a less enlightened side to Douglass's thoughts on the matter, particularly in his belief that the black man was better suited to the southern climate, which was more like that of Africa, and should not attempt to migrate north. Douglass used this argument in opposing the Exodusters, a post–Civil War group calling for migration to Kansas, where the abolitionist John Brown had fought fierce battles for the free-statehood movement. Douglass's theories reveal that he not only ignored the plain fact that whites had long succeeded in physical labor on southern farms, often alongside slaves but also sacrificed his belief in human adaptability to his cause.

Yet even as Douglass rejected biological Darwinism, he firmly embraced social Darwinism, loudly arguing that the African American must adapt to the changing society of postslavery America or perish. He opposed any suggestions that freed slaves should migrate to new homes—whether the Kansas of the Exodusters or the proposed African colonies of those who called for repatriation. Instead, Douglass strove to help equip freed slaves with the educational and economic opportunities they needed to better their lives in their current locations and avoid becoming a permanently dependent class.

[*See also* Black Nationalism; Brown, John; Douglass, Frederick; Emigration to Africa; *and* Exoduster Movement.]

BIBLIOGRAPHY

Martin, Waldo E. *The Mind of Frederick Douglass*. Chapel Hill: University of North Carolina Press, 1984. A topical study of the ideas held by Frederick Douglass.

McFeely, William S. *Frederick Douglass*. New York: Norton, 1991. A biography with extensive annotations and bibliography.

—LEIGH KIMMEL

EXODUSTER MOVEMENT.

With the return of the Democratic Party to power in the South following Reconstruction, African Americans watched their rights as citizens steadily disappear. Thousands of freed slaves dealt with the problem by leaving the South for a potentially better life in other regions of the country. One major destination of these emigrants was the new state of Kansas. In what is known as the Exoduster Movement, over twenty-five thousand African Americans migrated en masse during the 1870s and 1880s.

Southern blacks saw Kansas as an agricultural utopia. Rumors circulated that the state's land was more fertile and its climate more hospitable than in the South. Furthermore, since the Homestead Act of 1862 granted 160 acres of land to anyone, regardless of race, who agreed to pay a filing fee and farm the land for five years, African Americans believed Kansas offered them the chance to be landowners.

The idea of life in Kansas proved even more exciting to African Americans because of the state's political and racial history. The Republican Party, the party of Abraham Lincoln, dominated Kansas's politics. Without a strong Democratic influence, many black farmers felt their social and political rights would be protected. The belief that a fair chance at life existed in Kansas increased as rumors circulated that the state welcomed African Americans and promised treatment better than what they received in the South.

The rumors of a better life in the West expanded as a result of the abolitionist heritage of Kansas. Many African Americans pointed with hope to the fact that Kansas remained a part of the United States during the Civil War and openly supported the Emancipation Proclamation. The "Bleeding Kansas" heritage of the state, which involved fighting in the 1850s over slavery in the Kansas Territory, enticed black immigrants with the image of abolitionists standing up for African American rights. The fact that John Brown, who became a hero to many blacks and abolitionists following his raid on Harpers Ferry, Virginia, began his crusade against slavery by participating in the Kansas fighting added to the abolitionist image of the state.

These ideas provided hope to many black southerners. For those who made the move, life in Kansas indeed

Benjamin "Pap" Singleton (1808–1892) escaped from slavery and then sought to help other freed blacks. He led some 300 African Americans to Cherokee County, Kansas, in 1873, and by 1878 he had founded another colony at Dunlap in Morris County. These efforts paved the way for the exoduster movement. (Kansas State Historical Society.)

proved better than life in the South. One immigrant, George Washington Carver, who later became a leading black intellectual of the nineteenth century, farmed in Kansas for two years before leaving to pursue a formal education. The effort of the Exodusters showed that African Americans possessed the ability to participate in politics, support themselves financially, and contribute to the U.S. economy.

Most of the black immigrants settled in the western part of the state. While economic and social opportunities existed in greater numbers in Kansas, daily life still possessed its hardships. The land proved less fertile than expected.

African American farmers found that agricultural experiences in the South had left them unprepared for the hot summers, cold winters, and flat plains of the Midwest.

As African Americans moved into the state, several all-black communities developed, the most famous being Nicodemus. Founded by thirty colonists in 1877, Nicodemus grew quickly as more immigrants entered Kansas. By 1880 its population had reached over 250 African American residents. By the end of the 1880s, however, harsh winter blizzards and the fact that the major railroads bypassed the community caused Nicodemus to disappear.

Not every African American leader supported the migration to Kansas by black southerners. In his autobiography Frederick Douglass urged African Americans to remain in the South. He stated that the South was the longtime home of African Americans and that the region's racial attitudes were showing some improvement. Douglass felt that since the South needed labor, African Americans could bring about change by using their work as a bargaining tool for civil rights.

The Exoduster Movement ended during the late 1880s as word spread throughout the South that no more free land remained in Kansas. The lack of free land and the difficult life experienced by farmers in the region caused African Americans to look elsewhere for lives free from racial oppression. While the movement lasted only a short time, it demonstrated the desire of former slaves to exert their rights as citizens.

[*See also* African Americans and the West; Brown, John; Democratic Party; Douglass, Frederick; Entrepreneurs; *and* Harpers Ferry Raid.]

BIBLIOGRAPHY

Douglass, Frederick. *Life and Times of Frederick Douglass* (1881). London: Wordsworth, 1996.

Painter, Nell Irvin. *Exodusters: Black Migration to Kansas after Reconstruction*. New York: Knopf, 1976. The classic work on the Exoduster Movement and black migration.

Taylor, Quintard. *In Search of the Racial Frontier: African Americans in the American West, 1528–1990*. New York: Norton, 1998.

—ROB FINK